Alessandro Del Sole

Visual Basic® 2010

UNLEASHED

800 East 96th Street, Indianapolis, Indiana 46240 USA

Visual Basic® 2010 Unleashed

ISBN-10: 0-672-33100-4

ISBN-13: 978-0-672-33100-8

Library of Congress Cataloging-in-Publication Data

Del Sole, Alessandro.

Visual Basic 2010 unleashed / Alessandro Del Sole.

    p. cm.

Includes index.

ISBN 978-0-672-33100-8

1. BASIC (Computer program language) 2. Microsoft Visual BASIC. I. Title.

QA76.73.B3D467 2010

005.2'768–dc22

2010012721

Printed in the United States of America

First Printing: May 2010

Trademarks

Warning and Disclaimer

Bulk Sales

Pearson offers excellent discounts on this book when ordered in quantity for bulk purchases or special sales. For more information, please contact:

U.S. Corporate and Government Sales

1-800-382-3419

corpsales@pearsontechgroup.com

For sales outside of the U.S., please contact:

International Sales

+1-317-581-3793

international@pearsontechgroup.com

Editor-in-Chief
Karen Gettman

Executive Editor
Neil Rowe

Acquisitions Editor
Brook Farling

Development Editor
Mark Renfrow

Managing Editor
Patrick Kanouse

Project Editor
Mandie Frank

Copy Editor
Apostrophe Editing Services

Indexer
WordWise Publishing Services LLC

Proofreader
The Wordsmithery LLC

Technical Editor
Matt Kleinwaks

Publishing Coordinator
Cindy Teeters

Designer
Gary Adair

Compositor
Mark Shirar

Contents at a Glance

Table of Contents

Appendixes

Foreword

The first time I ever heard from Alessandro was through my blog contact form. A few years ago he reached out to me about his interest in donating an article to the Visual Basic Developer Center on MSDN. Reading his email, it was immediately apparent that Alessandro was passionate about programming and particularly the Visual Basic language. With a quick Internet search I was at his blog and learning about him and the Visual Basic Tips and Tricks community. Not long after we published his first article, Alessandro was awarded Microsoft Most Valuable Professional (MVP) for his exceptional community leadership and technical expertise.

I remember at the time how fun it was working with Alessandro and to see his excitement and passion for the developer community—something we both share. Today he continues to help me with the VB Dev Center to provide training content for developers. I always smile when I get an email from Alessandro, because I know he's going to reach out to help by sending me more articles or ideas on improving the site. When he told me he was writing this book, I was excited for the VB community, because I know how much his online content helps the community today. And the passion he has for Visual Basic comes through in everything he writes.

Visual Basic is an amazing language. I started picking it up around 2000 with the release of .NET and it really helped me navigate the vastness of the platform. Particularly things like background compilation and Intellisense gave me immediate cues about whether the code I was attempting to write was correct. Also, coming from a more dynamic language background, it was much easier to write the types of data-oriented systems I was building using a language that was both static and dynamic at the same time. With the release of Language Integrated Query (LINQ), data became much easier to work with and Visual Basic's support for LINQ is extremely full featured with its set of expanded query operators and easy to use language syntax. Coupled with the latest features in 2010 like implicit line continuation and multiline and statement lambdas makes Visual Basic one of the premiere modern programming languages of today. Millions of developers agree.

This book takes you on a journey through the .NET platform through the eyes of a Visual Basic developer. If you're just learning the platform this is a great place to start as Alessandro begins with the basics of the platform and the language, and then touches on a variety of different application development technologies and techniques. If you're already programming on the .NET platform, then this book will show you what's new, not only in the Visual Basic language, but also the .NET Framework 4.0 and Visual Studio 2010. I am personally very excited about this release.

Alessandro explains these concepts in a way that is very easy to understand with a language that's easy to use and his passion comes through in every paragraph. I know you will find this book filled with tips and tricks as well as development methodologies that you can apply to the modern applications you are building today. I really enjoyed reading this book and I'm sure you will too.

Beth Massi
Senior Program Manager, Microsoft Visual Studio

About the Author

Alessandro Del Sole, a Microsoft Most Valuable Professional (MVP) for Visual Basic, is well known throughout the global VB community. He is a community leader on the Italian "Visual Basic Tips and Tricks" website (http://www.visual-basic.it) that serves more than 41,000 VB developers, as well as a frequent contributor to the MSDN Visual Basic Developer Center. He enjoys writing articles on .NET development, writing blog posts on both his Italian and English blogs, and producing instructional videos. You can find him online in forums or newsgroups.

Dedication

To my parents, we live our lives many kilometers away from each other but I know you are always there for me. You are the best parents a son could ever desire. Thank you!

To my best friend Nadia, whose support during the writing of this book has been as fundamental as all my experience in the computer world, starting from my first article until becoming an MVP. I'm very glad to let the world know how special you are to me. Thanks for being always there.

Acknowledgments

First of all I would like to thank Brook Farling and all at Sams Publishing for giving me the great opportunity of writing the most important book of my life on Visual Basic. Behind the scenes a lot of people did hard work, so I would like to say "thanks!" to everyone, including the technical editor Matthew Kleinwaks and all the people involved in the review process.

Special thanks to all the Microsoft Visual Basic Team for doing a great job; particularly I would like to give my special thanks to Lisa Feigenbaum for helping me to contact the right people in the teams working on Visual Studio and the .NET Framework. She does her work with great passion and professionalism; her help has been so precious to me. Many thanks, Lisa.

Next I would like to thank Beth Massi from the VB Team for the opportunity of technical discussions on the Visual Basic language. She always creates great work producing content that helps others learn something new every day. If you are searching for information using VB against the most recent Microsoft technologies, take a look at her blog.

Great thanks also to some guys from the Italian subsidiary of Microsoft: Alessandro Teglia (my MVP Lead), who has a great passion for his work and for the MVP's community; he did a really great job when I had some important questions related to information required for this book, rapidly pointing me in the right direction, and Lorenzo Barbieri. His indications and suggestions on the Team System instrumentation were invaluable.

Thanks to my boss Giampiero Ianni for his cordiality.

I would like to thank my everyday friends; most of them aren't interested in application development but they're always happy when listening to me talk about computers, application development, and my books. Most of all, they are always ready to encourage me. Writing a large book like this is not easy, but they always have the right words when things are difficult. So my deep thanks to Roberto Bianchi, Alessandro Ardovini, Daniela Maggi, Maurizio Cagliero, Eugenio Ricci, Alessandra Gueragni, Francesca Bongiorni, Paolo Leoni, Meso, Luca Libretti, and Sara Gerevini. You guys really rock!

I'm a community leader and team member in the Italian "Visual Basic Tips & Tricks" community (www.visual-basic.it); therefore, I would like to thank all those guys who are the right stimulus for making things better every day; all those people who visited my blogs at least once or who read even one article of mine, and all those people who every day visit our website and follow us on forums, videos, articles, and blogs. Special thanks to my MVP colleagues Diego Cattaruzza, Antonio Catucci, and Raffaele Rialdi for their great support and precious suggestions. Thanks to Renato Marzaro and Marco Notari for their continuous support and encouragement.

We Want to Hear from You!

As the reader of this book, you are our most important critic and commentator. We value your opinion and want to know what we're doing right, what we could do better, what areas you'd like to see us publish in, and any other words of wisdom you're willing to pass our way.

As an executive editor for Sams Publishing, I welcome your comments. You can email or write me directly to let me know what you did or didn't like about this book—as well as what we can do to make our books better.

Please note that I cannot help you with technical problems related to the topic of this book. We do have a User Services group, however, where I will forward specific technical questions related to the book.

When you write, please be sure to include this book's title and author as well as your name, email address, and phone number. I will carefully review your comments and share them with the author and editors who worked on the book.

Email: feedback@samspublishing.com

Mail: Neil Rowe
         Associate Publisher
         Sams Publishing
         800 East 96th Street
         Indianapolis, IN 46240 USA

Reader Services

Visit our website and register this book at informit.com/register for convenient access to any updates, downloads, or errata that might be available for this book.

CHAPTER 1

Introducing the .NET Framework 4.0

As a Visual Basic 2010 developer, you need to understand the concepts and technology that empower your applications: the Microsoft .NET Framework. The .NET Framework (also simply known as .NET) is the technology that provides the infrastructure for building the next generation's applications that you will create. Although covering every aspect of the .NET Framework is not possible, in this chapter you learn the basis of the .NET Framework architecture, why it is not just a platform, and notions about the Base Class Library and tools. The chapter also introduces important concepts and terminology that will be of common use throughout the rest of the book.

What Is the .NET Framework?

Microsoft .NET Framework is a complex technology that provides the infrastructure for building, running, and managing next generation applications. In a layered representation, the .NET Framework is a layer positioned between the Microsoft Windows operating system and your applications. .NET is a platform but also is defined as a *technology* because it is composed of several parts such as libraries, executable tools, and relationships and integrates with the operating system. Microsoft Visual Studio 2010 relies on the new version of the .NET Framework 4.0. Visual Basic 2010, C# 4.0, and F# 2010 are .NET languages that rely on and can build applications for the .NET Framework 4.0. The new version of this technology introduces important new features that will be described later. In this chapter you get an overview of the most important features of the

.NET Framework so that you will know how applications built with Visual Basic 2010 can run and how they can be built.

Where Is the .NET Framework

When you install Microsoft Visual Studio 2010, the setup process installs the .NET Framework 4.0. .NET is installed to a folder named %windir%\Microsoft.NET\Framework\4.0. If you open this folder with Windows Explorer, you see a lot of subfolders, libraries, and executable tools. Most of the DLL libraries constitute the Base Class Library, whereas most of the executable tools are invoked by Visual Studio 2010 to perform different kinds of tasks, even if they can also be invoked from the command line. Later in this chapter we describe the Base Class Library and provide an overview of the tools; for now you need to notice the presence of a file named Vbc.exe, which is the Visual Basic Compiler and a command line tool. In most cases you do not need to manually invoke the Visual Basic compiler, because you will build your Visual Basic applications writing code inside Visual Studio 2010, and the IDE invokes the compiler for you. But it is worth mentioning that you could create the most complex application using Windows's Notepad and then run Vbc. Finally, it is also worth mentioning that users can get the .NET Framework 4.0 from Microsoft for free. This means that the Visual Basic compiler is also provided free with .NET, and this is the philosophy that characterizes the .NET development since the first version was released in 2002.

The .NET Framework Architecture

To better understand the structure of the .NET Framework, think about it as a layered architecture. Figure 1.1 shows a high-level representation of the .NET Framework 4.0 architecture.

The first level of the representation is the operating system; the .NET layer is located between the system and applications. The second level is the *Common Language Runtime (CLR)*, which provides the part of the .NET Framework doing the most work. We discuss the CLR later in this chapter. The next level is the *Base Class Library (BCL)*, which provides all .NET objects that can be used both in your code and by Visual Basic when creating applications. The BCL also provides the infrastructure of several .NET technologies that you use in building applications, such as WPF, Windows Forms, ASP.NET, WCF, and so on. The last level is represented by applications that rely on the previous layers.

DIFFERENCES WITH PREVIOUS VERSIONS

If you upgrade to Visual Basic 2010 from Visual Basic 2008, the main difference that you notice is that .NET 4.0 is a standalone infrastructure. You may remember that .NET Framework 3.5 was instead an incremental framework that needed the prior installation of .NET 2.0 and .NET 3.0. For example, LINQ was part of .NET 3.5 whereas WPF was part of .NET 3.0 and Windows Forms was part of .NET 2.0 (see Figure 1.2 for a graphical representation). With .NET 4.0 this incremental structure disappears, and all the frameworks, BCL, and tools are part of the new version.

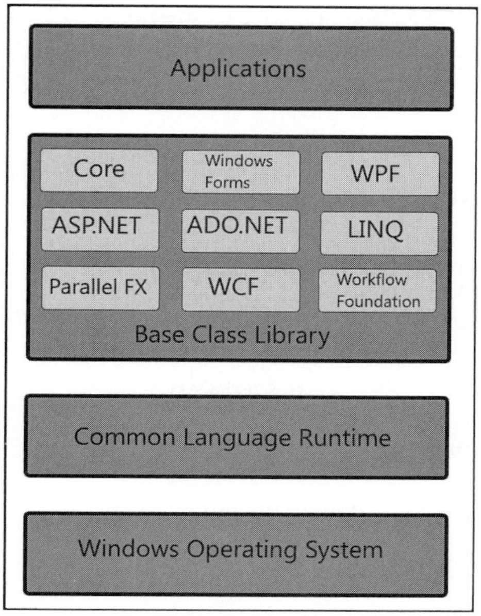

Applications
Core
Windows Forms
WPF
ASP.NET
ADO.NET
LINQ
Parallel FX
WCF
Workflow Foundation
Base Class Library
Common Language Runtime
Windows Operating System

FIGURE 1.1 The .NET Framework 4.0 architecture.

.NET 3.5 SP 1
LINQ
Entity Framework
AJAX
ASP.NET Dynamic Data
.NET 3.0
WPF
Workflow Foundation
WCF
Cardspace
.NET 2.0
CLR
Win Forms
ASP.NET
ADO.NET

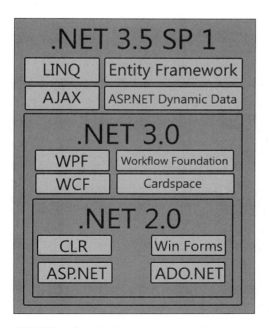

FIGURE 1.2 The incremental architecture of the .NET Framework 3.5 SP 1.

Although the various frameworks exposed by the BCL are discussed later in the book, in this chapter, now you get an overview of the library and can understand how it works and how you can use it. But before examining the BCL, consider the Common Language Runtime.

The Common Language Runtime

As its name implies, the *Common Language Runtime* provides an infrastructure that is common to all .NET languages. This infrastructure is responsible for taking control of the application's execution and manages tasks such as memory management, access to system resources, security services, and so on. This kind of common infrastructure bridges the gap that exists between different Win32 programming languages because all .NET languages have the same possibilities. Moreover, the Common Language Runtime enables applications to run inside a managed environment. The word *managed* is fundamental in the .NET development, as explained in next paragraph.

Writing Managed Code

When talking about Visual Basic 2010 development and, more generally, about .NET development, you often hear about writing *managed code*. Before the first version of .NET (or still with non-.NET development environments), the developer was the only responsible person for interacting with system resources and the operating system. For example, taking care of accessing parts of the operating system or managing memory allocation for objects were tasks that the developer had to consider. In other words, the applications could interact directly with the system, but as you can easily understand this approach has some big limitations both because of security issues and because damages could be dangerous. The .NET Framework provides instead a managed environment. This means that the application communicates with the .NET Framework instead of with the operating system, and the .NET runtime is responsible for managing the application execution, including memory management, resources management, and access to system resources. For example, the Common Language Runtime could prevent an application from accessing particular system resources if it is not considered *full-trusted* according to the Security Zones of .NET.

DIALING WITH THE SYSTEM

You can still interact directly with the operating system, for example invoking Windows APIs (also known as Platform Invoke or P/Invoke for short). This technique is known as writing unmanaged code that should be used only when strictly required. This topic is discussed in Chapter 49, "Platform Invokes and Interoperability with the COM Architecture."

Writing managed code and the existence of the Common Language Runtime also affect how applications are produced by compilers.

.NET Assemblies

In classic Win32 development environments, such as Visual Basic 6 or Visual C++, your source code is parsed by compilers that produce binary executable files that can be immediately interpreted and run by the operating system. This affects both standalone applications and dynamic/type libraries. Actually Win32 applications, built with Visual Basic 6 and C++, used a runtime, but if you had applications developed with different programming languages, you also had to install the appropriate runtimes. In .NET development things are quite different. Whatever .NET language you create applications with, compilers generate an *assembly*, which is a file containing .NET executable code and is composed essentially by two kinds of elements: MSIL code and metadata. MSIL stands for Microsoft Intermediate Language and is a high-level assembly programming language that is also object-oriented, providing a set of instructions that are CPU-independent (rather than building executables that implement CPU-dependent sets of instructions). MSIL is a common language in the sense that the same programming tasks written with different .NET languages produce the same IL code. Metadata is instead a set of information related to the types implemented in the code. Such information can contain signatures, functions and procedures, members in types, and members in externally referenced types. Basically metadata's purpose is describing the code to the .NET Framework. Obviously, although an assembly can have .exe extension, due to the described structure, it cannot be directly executed by the operating system. In fact, when you run a .NET application the operating system can recognize it as a .NET assembly (because between .NET and Windows there is a strict cooperation) and invoke the Just-In-Time compiler.

The Execution Process and the Just-In-Time (JIT) Compiler

.NET compilers produce assemblies that store IL code and metadata. When you launch an assembly for execution, the .NET Framework packages all the information and translates them into an executable that the operating system can understand and run. This task is the responsibility of the *Just-In-Time (JIT)* compiler. JIT compiles code on-the-fly just before its execution and keeps the compiled code ready for execution. It acts at the method level. This means that it first searches for the application's entry point (typically the Sub Main) and then compiles other procedures or functions (*methods* in .NET terminology) referenced and invoked by the entry point and so on, just before the code is executed. If you have some code defined inside external assemblies, just before the method is executed the JIT compiler loads the assembly in memory and then compiles the code. Of course loading an external assembly in memory could require some time and affect performance, but it can be a good idea to place seldom-used methods inside external assemblies, the same way as it could be a good idea to place seldom-used code inside separated methods.

The Base Class Library

The .NET Framework *Base Class Library (BCL)* provides thousands of reusable *types* that you can use in your code and that cover all the .NET technologies, such as Windows Presentation Foundation, ASP.NET, LINQ, and so on. Types defined in the Base Class Library enable developers to do millions of things without the need of calling unmanaged code and Windows APIs and, often, without recurring to external components. A *type* is something that states what an object must represent. For example, `String` and `Integer` are types, and you might have a variable of type `String` (that is, a text message) or a variable of type `Integer` (a number). Saying `Type` is not the same as saying `Class`. In fact, types can be of two kinds: *reference types* and *value types*. This topic is the specific subject of Chapter 4, "Data Types and Expressions"—a class is just a reference type. Types in the BCL are organized within *namespaces*, which act like a kind of types' containers, and their name is strictly related to the technology they refer to. For example, the `System.Windows.Forms` namespace implements types for working with Windows Forms applications, whereas `System.Web` implements types for working with Web applications, and so on. You will get a more detailed introduction to namespaces in Chapter 3, "The Anatomy of a Visual Basic Project," and Chapter 9, "Organizing Types Within Namespaces." Basically each namespace name beginning with `System` is part of the BCL. There are also some namespaces whose name begins with `Microsoft` that are still part of the BCL. These namespaces are typically used by the Visual Studio development environment and by the Visual Basic compiler, although you can also use them in your code in some particular scenarios (such as code generation).

The BCL is composed of several assemblies. One of the most important is MsCorlib.dll (Microsoft Core Library) that is part of the .NET Framework and that will always be required in your projects. Other assemblies can often be related to specific technologies; for example, the System.ServiceModel.dll assembly integrates the BCL with the Windows Communication Foundation main infrastructure. Also, some namespaces don't provide the infrastructure for other technologies and are used only in particular scenarios; therefore, they are defined in assemblies external from MsCorlib (Microsoft Core Library). All these assemblies and namespaces will be described in the appropriate chapters.

.NET Languages

Microsoft offers several programming languages for the .NET Framework 4.0. With Visual Studio 2010, you can develop applications with the following integrated programming languages:

▶ Visual Basic 2010

▶ Visual C# 4.0

▶ Visual F# 2010

▶ Visual C++ 2010

Visual J# is no longer part of the .NET Framework family. You can also integrate native languages with Microsoft implementations of Python and Ruby dynamic languages, respectively known as IronPython and IronRuby.

> **WHERE DO I FIND IRONPYTHON AND IRONRUBY?**
>
> IronPython and IronRuby are currently under development by Microsoft and are available as open source projects from the CodePlex community. You can download IronPython from http://ironpython.codeplex.com. You can find IronRuby at http://ironruby.codeplex.com.

There are also several third-party implementations of famous programming languages for .NET, such as Fortran, Forth, or Pascal, but discussing them is neither a purpose of this chapter nor of this book. It's instead important to know that all these languages can take advantage of the .NET Framework base class library and infrastructure the same as VB and C#. This is possible because of the Common Language Runtime that offers a common infrastructure for all .NET programming languages.

.NET Framework Tools

The .NET Framework also provides several command-line tools needed when creating applications. Among the tools are the compilers for the .NET languages, such as Vbc.exe (Visual Basic compiler), Csc.exe (Visual C# compiler), and MSBuild.exe (the build engine for Visual Studio). All these tools are stored in the C:\Windows\Microsoft.NET\ Framework\v4.0 folder. In most scenarios you will not need to manually invoke the .NET Framework tools, because you will work with the Microsoft Visual Studio 2010 Integrated Development Environment, which is responsible for invoking the appropriate tools when needed. Instead of listing all the tools now, because we have not talked about some topics yet, information on the .NET tools invoked by Visual Studio is provided when discussing a particular topic that involves the specific tools.

Windows Software Development Kit

Starting from Visual Studio 2008, with the .NET Framework and the development environment, the setup process will also install the Windows SDK on your machine. This software development kit provides additional tools and libraries useful for developing applications for the .NET Framework. In older versions of the .NET Framework and in the Microsoft Windows operating system, you had to install two different packages, formerly known as the .NET Framework SDK and the Microsoft Platform SDK. With the introduction of Windows Vista, the .NET Framework has become part of the core of the operating system; Microsoft released the Windows SDK that provides tools for building both managed and unmanaged applications. The Windows SDK is installed into the C:\Program Files\Microsoft SDKs\Windows\v7.0A folder, which includes several additional tools also used by Microsoft Visual Studio for tasks different from building assemblies, such as deployment and code analysis, or for generating proxy classes for Windows Communication Foundation projects. Also in this case you will not typically need to invoke these tools manually, because Visual Studio will do the work for you. You can find information on the Windows SDK's tools in the appropriate chapters.

What's New in .NET Framework 4.0

If you had development experiences with .NET Framework 3.5, you know that it has an *incremental* architecture. This means that .NET 3.5 (including technologies typical of this version such as LINQ) relies on .NET Framework 2.0 for most of the core .NET features and technologies such as Windows Forms, whereas it requires .NET Framework 3.0 for frameworks such as Windows Presentation Foundation, Windows Communication Foundation, Windows Workflow Foundation, and CardSpace. This means that .NET Framework 3.5 requires previous versions to be installed as a prerequisite. The .NET Framework 4.0 is instead a complete standalone technology that does not require other previous versions to be installed. Assuming you have some knowledge of .NET Framework 3.0 and 3.5, following are new technologies introduced by .NET 4.0 for your convenience:

▶ Windows Presentation Foundation

▶ Windows Communication Foundation

▶ ASP.NET (now including Ajax and MVC)

▶ ADO.NET Entity Framework

▶ Visual Studio Tools for Office

▶ Windows Workflow Foundation

The new version of these technologies is not just an addition of features, but the architecture has been revised and improved. The .NET Framework 4.0 also includes some frameworks that in the previous version had to be installed manually or as part of the .NET 3.5 Service Pack 1:

▶ ADO.NET Data Services

▶ Parallel Extensions for the Task Parallel Library, or *TPL* for short (related to the *parallel computing*)

▶ Code Contracts

The Windows Forms technology is still unchanged from .NET Framework 2.0. There are just a few additions regarding user controls, which is discussed in Chapter 30. "Creating Windows Forms 4.0 Applications."

Summary

Understanding the .NET Framework is of primary importance in developing applications with Visual Basic 2010 because you will build applications for the .NET Framework. This chapter presented a high-level overview of the .NET Framework 4.0 and key concepts such as the Common Language Runtime and the Base Class Library and how an application is compiled and executed. You also got an overview of the most important command-line tools and the .NET languages.

CHAPTER 2

Getting Started with the Visual Studio 2010 IDE

You develop Visual Basic applications using the Visual Studio 2010 Integrated Development Environment (*IDE*), which is the place where you will spend most of your developer life. Before diving deep into the Visual Basic language, you need to know what instruments you need to develop applications. Although the Visual Studio IDE is a complex environment, this chapter provides you with an overview of the most common tasks you will perform from within Visual Studio 2010 and the most important tools you will utilize so that you can feel at home within the IDE. You get an introduction to some of the new features introduced by the new version of the development environment, which can provide the basis for the rest of the book. You also learn about other advanced IDE features in Chapter 55, "Deployment Applications with ClickOnce."

What's New in Visual Studio 2010

The Visual Studio 2010 IDE relies on a new infrastructure that is quite different from its predecessors. Most of this infrastructure is now written in managed code, and several parts of the IDE are based on the *Windows Presentation Foundation* framework, such as the code editor, menus, and floating windows. Although behind the scenes this innovation is important (particularly if you develop Visual Studio extensions), being familiar with the WPF technology is not important when starting with the Visual Studio 2010 IDE because you will feel at home also with the new version. This is because the instrumentation is located and behaves the same as in the past. There are several benefits from having a managed infrastructure, such as new IDE features (the code editor zoom or the *IDE extensibility*, for example) and we discuss these topics later in the book. This chapter gives you an overview of the most common tools you need for developing your Visual Basic applications. (Deeper details on advanced IDE features are provided in Chapter 55.)

Start Page

When you first run Visual Studio 2010, you notice a new layout and a new Start Page, as shown in Figure 2.1.

FIGURE 2.1   The new Visual Studio 2010 Start Page.

The Start Page is one of the most important new features in the IDE. First, it offers a better organization of the most common tasks, based on *tabs*. Tabs are located on the right side of the screen and enable access to specific contents. On the left side of the screen you can instead find links for creating new projects and opening existing projects, as well as the list of recently opened projects. An important improvement to this list is that you can now easily remove recent projects by simply right-clicking the project name and then selecting the deletion command. The second new feature is that the Start Page now relies on the *Windows Presentation Foundation* technology and is completely written in *XAML* code. This means that it can be customized according to your needs. Customizing the

Start Page is beyond the scope of this chapter, whereas a deeper discussion on the default settings is absolutely necessary. The three default tabs are Get Started, Guidance and Resources and Latest News. The following paragraphs discuss them in detail.

Get Started Tab

The Get Started tab (see Figure 2.1) offers links to important resources, such as MSDN Walkthroughs (which are step-by-step tutorials on specific topics related to Visual Studio 2010), community and learning resources, and extensions for the IDE, such as custom add-ins or third-party components. (This is a topic that is discussed later in the book.) This tab is divided into subcategories, each related to a specific development area such as Windows, Web, Office, Cloud Computing, and SharePoint. When you click on each subcategory, you access a number of links to resources for learning about the selected area. Basically the Get Started tab's purpose is to offer links to useful resources about the development environment and to new and existing .NET technologies.

The Guidance and Resources Tab

The Guidance and Resources tab provides links useful for learning about designing and developing applications as well as about the application lifecycle management. Figure 2.2 shows how the tab appears in Visual Studio 2010.

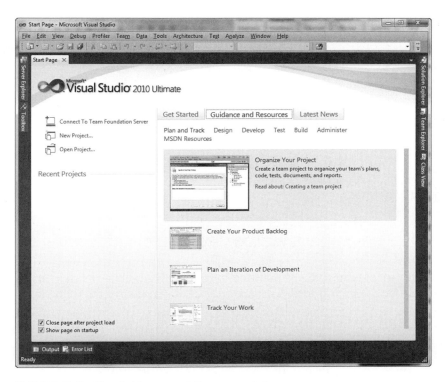

FIGURE 2.2   The Guidance and Resources tab.

This tab is divided into subcategories, each providing links to resources related to project planning, maintenance, and testing as well as application design and development. In some cases this documentation requires that Microsoft Visual Studio 2010 Team Foundation Server is installed on your machine.

The Latest News Tab

As in Visual Studio 2005 and Visual Studio 2008, Visual Studio 2010 can also show a list of news based on *RSS feeds* so that you can stay up-to-date with your favorite news channels. Now the list appears in the Latest News tab, as shown in Figure 2.3.

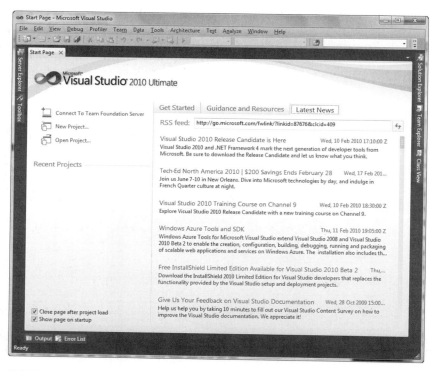

FIGURE 2.3   The Latest News tab shows updated news from the specified RSS channel.

By default, the news channel is an RSS feed pointing to the MSDN developer portal, but you can replace it with one of your favorites. To accomplish this, you have the following alternatives:

▶ Open the Latest News tab and replace the default link in the **RSS feed** field with a valid XML feed link (this is the easiest way).

▶ Open the Options window (for example by clicking the **Settings** link in the Visual Studio tab) and then select the Startup item. You find a text box named Start Page news channel (see Figure 2.4) where you can write your favorite link. Just ensure you are writing a valid XML feed link.

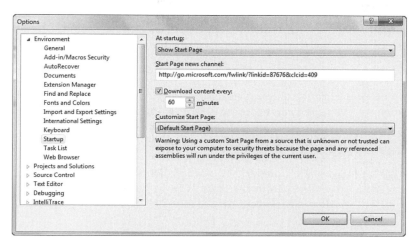

FIGURE 2.4   The Options window enables customizing the RSS Feeds news channel.

If you want to stay up-to-date with Visual Basic news, then you can consider replacing the default news channel with the Visual Basic Developer Center, which is at the following: http://services.social.microsoft.com/feeds/feed/VB_featured_resources. After this brief overview of the Start Page, we can begin discussing what's new in creating Visual Basic projects within Visual Studio 2010.

Working with Projects and Solutions

Each time you want to develop an application, you create a *project*. A project is a collection of files, such as code files, resources, data, and every kind of file you need to build your final assembly. A Visual Basic project is represented by a .Vbproj file, which is an Xml file containing all the information required by Visual Studio to manage files that constitute your project. Projects are organized in solutions. A *solution* is basically a container for projects. In fact, solutions can contain infinite projects of different kinds, such as Visual Basic projects, projects produced with programming languages different than Visual Basic, class libraries, projects for Windows client applications, *Windows Communication Foundation* services, and so on. In other words, a solution can include each kind of project you can create with Visual Studio 2010. Solutions also can contain external files, such as documents or help files, and are represented by a .Sln file that has Xml structure and that stores information required to manage all the projects contained in the solution. Visual Studio 2010 can also open solutions created with previous versions of the IDE.

> **TIP**
>
> You can upgrade previous versions of your solutions by simply opening them in Visual
> Studio 2010. The Upgrade Wizard can guide you through the upgrade process in a few
> steps. This converts the solution and project files to the new version but does not
> upgrade the target version of the .NET Framework to 4.0. Only older versions such as
> 1.0 and 1.1 are upgraded to 2.0, but all others retain their original version number.

Typically you manage your projects and solutions using the Solution Explorer window
discussed later in this chapter. We now focus on the creation of Visual Basic 2010 projects.

Creating Visual Basic Projects

Creating a new Visual Basic project is a simple task. You can either click the **File, New
Project** command or the **New Project** link from the Start Page. In both cases, Visual
Studio shows the New Project window, which you can see in Figure 2.5.

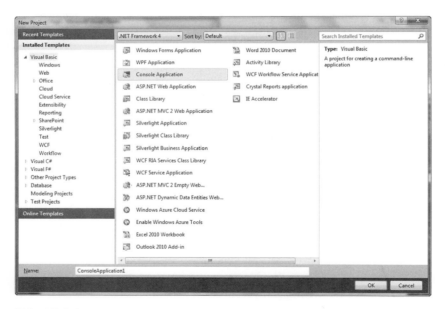

FIGURE 2.5   The New Project window for Visual Basic.

As you can see, the look of the New Project window is quite different from previous versions
of Visual Studio. To understand what kind of Visual Basic applications you can create, you
simply need to select the **Visual Basic** node on the left side of the window. After you click
the node, you see a lot of different kinds of applications you can create with Visual Basic
2010, such as Windows applications, Web applications, Office System customizations,
Silverlight applications, Windows Communication Foundation Services, and so on.

NOTE ABOUT AVAILABLE PROJECT TEMPLATES

The list of installed project templates can vary depending either on the Visual Studio 2010 edition or on additional items installed later (for example from the Visual Studio Gallery).

Each kind of application is represented by a specific project template, which provides a skeleton of a project for that particular kind of application, including all the references or the basic code files required. For example, the Windows Forms project template provides a skeleton of a project for creating a Windows application using the Windows Forms technology, therefore including references to the System.Windows.Forms.dll assembly, specific Imports directives, and Windows Forms objects represented by the appropriate code files. Moreover, Visual Studio will automatically enable the Windows Forms designer. Notice the detailed description for each template on the right side of the window every time you select a particular template.

NOTE

In the second part of this book you find in detail several kinds of applications you can build with Visual Basic 2010. For this reason a full description of each project template will be provided in the proper chapters. At the moment the description provided by Visual Studio for project templates is sufficient. Also consider that in this first part of the book the Console Application project template is used because it is the most appropriate for learning purposes.

Typically when you create a new project, Visual Studio also creates a solution containing that project. If you plan to add other projects to the solution, it can be a good idea to create a directory for the solution. This allows for a better organization of your projects, because one directory can contain the solution file and this directory can then contain subdirectories, each of them related to a specific project. To accomplish this, ensure that the Create Directory for Solution check box is selected (refer to Figure 2.5). The New Project window also offers some interesting features: the .NET Framework multitargeting, the ability of searching through templates, and the ability of managing templates. We now discuss each of these features.

Multitargeting

Like in Visual Studio 2008, in Visual Studio 2010 you can choose what version of the .NET Framework your application targets. This can be useful if you plan to develop applications with a high compatibility level and without new language features, but you still want to take the advantage of the new features of the IDE. You may choose one of the following:

- ▶ .NET Framework 4.0 (proposed by default)
- ▶ .NET Framework 3.5

► .NET Framework 3.0

► .NET Framework 2.0

To accomplish this choice, just select the appropriate version from the combo box at the top of the window, as shown in Figure 2.6.

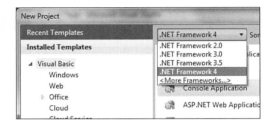

FIGURE 2.6   Choosing the .NET Framework version for your application.

NOTE

Please remember that, depending on what version of the .NET Framework you choose, you may not be able to use some libraries or technologies. For example, if you choose .NET Framework 3.0 as the target version, you cannot use LINQ, which is instead exposed by .NET Framework 3.5 and higher. So keep in mind these limitations when developing your applications.

Accessing Recent and Online Templates

Visual Studio 2010 provides the capability to access most recently used templates and to install additional templates from the Internet. About the first feature, you can easily access the most recently used project templates by clicking the **Recent Templates** item on the left side of the New Project window. In this way, you get a list of the recently used projects templates in case you still need them (see Figure 2.7).

You can also find additional online templates and install them to the local system. To accomplish this, simply click the **Online Templates** item in the New Project window. Visual Studio checks for the availability of online templates and shows a list of all the available templates, as shown in Figure 2.8.

As you can see, Visual Studio is listing all the online templates for both Visual Basic and Visual C#, showing a description of the template, information about the author, and a small picture with ratings when available. To download and install a template, simply double-click its name. After a few seconds you will be prompted to provide your agree-

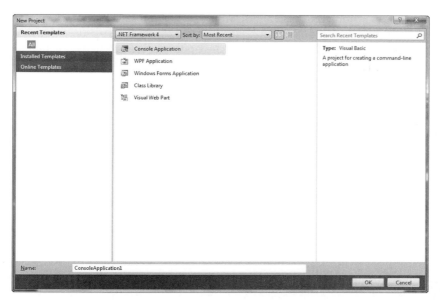

FIGURE 2.7   Accessing the most recently used projects templates.

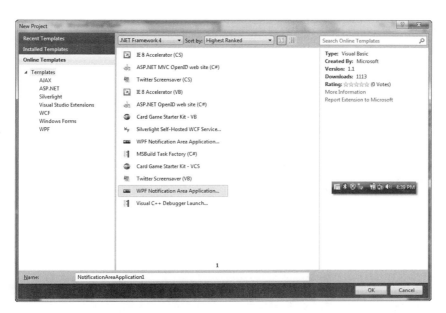

FIGURE 2.8   Additional online templates that you can add to Visual Studio 2010.

ment about the installation. You will be warned in the case that the new extension for Visual Studio does not contain a digital signature (see Figure 2.9). If you trust the publisher and want to go on, click **Install**. After a few seconds you see the newly installed project templates available among the other ones.

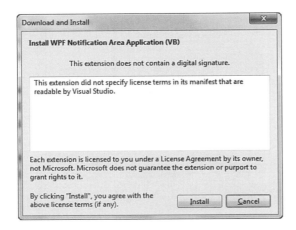

FIGURE 2.9   Visual Studio asks for confirmation before installing the additional template.

As in the previous versions of Visual Studio, you can still export projects as reusable project templates. We discuss this feature later in the book, when talking about the advanced IDE features.

Searching for Installed Templates

Visual Studio 2010 provides lots of default project templates, and as you saw before, you have the ability of adding your own custom ones, so sometimes it may be difficult to find the needed template in a certain moment. Because of this, the New Project window provides a search box that is located in the upper-right corner of the window (see Figure 2.10). Just begin typing the name of the project template you are looking for, and the New Project window shows all the projects templates that match your choice. Each time you type a character, the window updates showing the results matching your search string. As you can see in Figure 2.10, Visual Studio is showing all the project templates whose names match the *wor* search string.

> **NOTE**
>
> Remember that the search functionality can retrieve all projects templates related to your search string. This means that the search result can contain not only Visual Basic projects but every template name matching your criteria (for example, Visual C#, Visual F#, and so on).

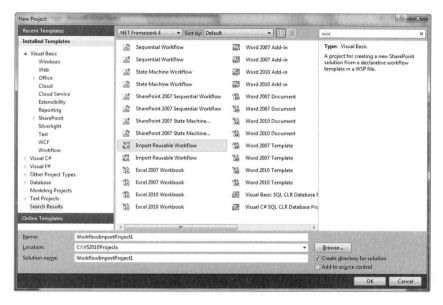

FIGURE 2.10   Searching for installed project templates using the new search feature.

Creating Reusable Projects and Items Templates

As in the previous versions, in Visual Studio 2010 you can create your custom projects and items templates, exporting them to disk and making them available within the IDE. (This topic is discussed in Chapter 55.) Now that you have seen the main new features for project creation, you are ready to create your first Visual Basic project.

Creating Your First Visual Basic 2010 Project

This section shows how easy it is to create a Visual Basic 2010 application and, if you have a long experience with Visual Studio, the differences between the new version and the previous ones of the development environment. You can create a new project for the Console by first opening the New Project window and then selecting the **Console Application** project template.

> **NOTE**
>
> Until Part 4, "Data Access with ADO.NET and LINQ," all code examples, listings, and code snippets are based on Console applications, so remember to create a Visual Basic project for the console when testing the code.

Name the new project as **MyFirst2010Program** and then click **OK** (see Figure 2.11 for details).

FIGURE 2.11   Creating your first VB 2010 application.

After a few seconds the new project is ready to be edited. Figure 2.12 shows the result of the project creation.

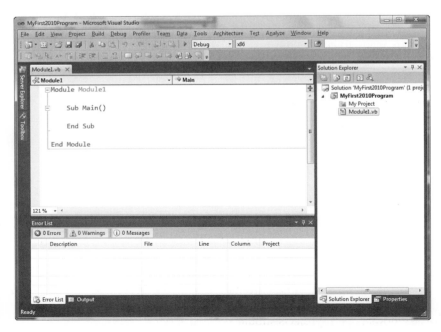

FIGURE 2.12   The creation of the first VB 2010 project.

As mentioned at the beginning of this chapter, the code editor and floating windows are now based on *Windows Presentation Foundation*. You see a new look for the tooling but this change in the infrastructure does not modify your development experience. You should feel at home with the new version of the environment because you can still find tools as in the previous versions. For example, you can access Solution Explorer, the Properties window, or the Error List exactly as you did before. The first difference you notice from the previous versions of Visual Basic is that now identifiers for custom objects have a light blue color. In this case, the identifier for the main module, which is Module1, is light blue and not black. Another interesting feature is that by pressing **Ctrl** and moving up and down the mouse wheel, you can zoom in and out with the code editor without the need to change the font settings each time the Visual Studio options changes. For our testing purposes, we could add a couple of lines of code to the Main method, which is the entry point for a Console application. Listing 2.1 shows the complete code for creating a VB 2010 application.

LISTING 2.1   Creating the First VB 2010 Application

```
Module Module1


    Sub Main()
        Console.WriteLine("Hello Visual Basic 2010!")
        Console.ReadLine()
    End Sub
End Module
```

WHAT IS A CONSOLE?

In a Console application, the System.Console class is the main object for working with the Windows console. Such a class provides methods for reading and writing from and to the Console and for performing operations versus the Console itself.

The code simply shows a message in the Console window and waits for the user to press a key. This is obviously a basic application, but you need it as the base for understanding other topics in this chapter.

Finding Visual Basic Projects

As in the previous versions, Visual Studio 2010 stores by default its information in a user-level folder called **Visual Studio 2010** and that resides inside the My Documents folder. Here you can find settings, add-ins, code snippets, and projects. For example, if you run Windows Vista or Windows 7, your projects should be located in C:\Users\UserName\Documents\Visual Studio 2010\Projects, in which UserName stands for the user that logged in Windows. Of course you can change the default projects directory by opening the Options window (Tools, Options command), selecting the Projects and Solutions item on the left side, and replacing the value for the Projects location text box.

Working with the Code Editor

The code editor in Visual Studio 2010 is now based on Windows Presentation Foundation. This innovation introduces new features to the Visual Basic code editor, too. Some of the new features are basically esthetical, whereas others are bound to enhance the coding experience. In this chapter we see just a few of the new IDE features, because the other ones are related to specific topics discussed later in the book. Particularly we now focus on the zoom functionality in the code editor, the gradient selection, and IntelliSense.

Zooming the Code

You can zoom the code editor in and out by simply pressing the **Ctrl** key and moving the mouse wheel up and down. This is a useful feature particularly if you are a presenter of technical speeches, because you can enlarge the code without modifying Visual Studio settings in the Options window. Figure 2.13 shows an example of this feature; notice how the font for the code is greater than the default settings and the right scrollbar is larger than normal.

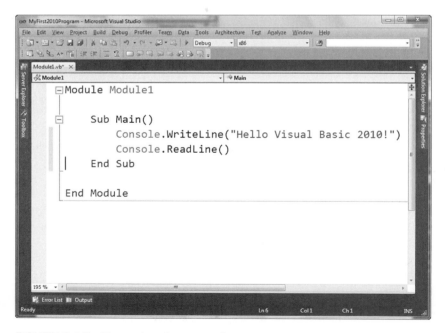

FIGURE 2.13   The code editor zoom feature enables real-time enlarging and reducing of the font size of the code without changing settings in Visual Studio.

IntelliSense Technology

IntelliSense is one of the most important technologies in the coding experience with Visual Studio. IntelliSense is represented by a pop-up window that appears in the code editor each time you begin typing a keyword or an identifier and shows options for auto-completing words. Figure 2.14 shows IntelliSense in action when adding a new instruction in code.

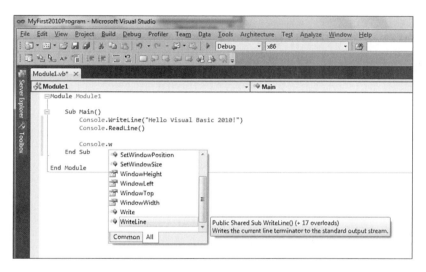

FIGURE 2.14   IntelliSense in action.

To auto-complete your code typing, you have the following alternatives:

▶ Press the **Tab** key. Auto-completes your words and enables you to write other code.

▶ Press the **Space** key. Auto-completes your words adding a blank space at the end of the added identifier and enables you to write other code.

▶ Press the **Enter** key. Auto-complete your words adding a couple of parentheses at the end of the completed identifier and positions the cursor on a new line. Use this technique when you need to invoke a method that does not require arguments.

▶ Press the left parenthesis. Auto-complete your words, adding a left parenthesis at the end of the completed identifier and waits for you to supply arguments.

▶ Press **Ctrl + Space** in order to bring up the full IntelliSense listing.

IntelliSense has been improved since Visual Studio 2008. In fact, it will be activated just when typing one character and is also active versus Visual Basic reserved words. Moreover, it remembers the last member you supplied to an object if you invoke that particular object more than once. For example, if you use IntelliSense to provide the `WriteLine` method to the `Console` object as follows:

```
Console.WriteLine()
```

and then if you try to invoke IntelliSense on the `Console` object again, it proposes as the first alternative of the `WriteLine` method you supplied the first time. IntelliSense is important because it lets you write code faster and provides suggestions on what member you add to your code.

Working with Tool Windows

As in the previous versions, lots of the Visual Studio tools are provided via *tool windows*. Tool windows are floating windows that can be docked to the IDE interface and are responsible for a particular task. As a general rule, in the View menu you can find the tool windows provided by Visual Studio 2010. Exceptions to this rule are the Test tool windows and the analysis tool windows that can be respectively invoked from the Test and Analyze menus. In this book we utilize several tool windows, and in this chapter you get an overview of the most used. In particular, we now focus on Solution Explorer, Error List, Properties, and Output windows. This is because these are the tool windows you will use in each of your projects. Other tool windows will be analyzed when applied to specific topics. To dock a tool window to the desired position in the IDE, just move the window onto the most appropriate arrow in the graphical cross that you see on the IDE and then release. Figure 2.15 represents this situation.

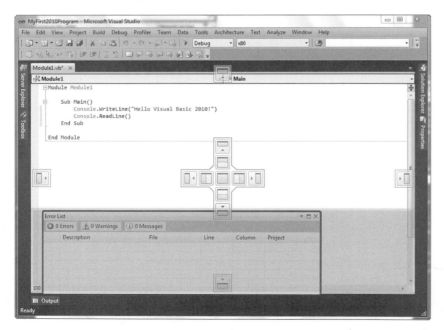

FIGURE 2.15   Docking a floating tool window to the IDE's interface.

Visual Studio 2010 automatically positions some tool windows in specific places of the IDE, but you can rearrange tool windows as much as you like. We can now discuss the previously mentioned tool windows.

The Solution Explorer Window

Solution Explorer is a special tool window that enables managing solutions, projects, and files in the projects or solution. It provides a complete view of what files compose your projects and enables adding or removing files and organizing files into subfolders. Figure 2.16 shows how a WPF project is represented inside Solution Explorer.

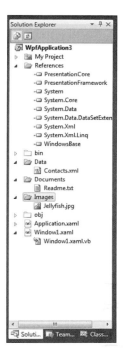

FIGURE 2.16   An example of the Solution Explorer tool window.

As you can see, at the root level there is the project. Nested are code files, subfolders containing pictures, data, and documents. You can also get a list of all the references in the project. You use Solution Explorer for adding and managing items in your projects other than getting a representation of which files constitute the project itself. By default, Solution Explorer shows only the items that compose the project. If you need a complete view of references and auto-generated code files, you need to click the **Show All Files** button located on the top-left portion of the window. To manage your project's items, you just need to right-click the project name and select the most appropriate command from the pop-up menu that appears. Figure 2.17 shows this pop-up menu.

	Build
	Rebuild
	Clean
	Publish...
	Run Code Analysis
	Calculate Code Metrics
	Add ▶
	Add Reference...
	Add Service Reference...
	View Class Diagram
	Debug ▶
	Add Project to Source Control...
	Cut
	Paste
	Rename
	Open Folder in Windows Explorer
	Properties

FIGURE 2.17   Solution items can be managed in Solution Explorer using the pop-up menu.

As you can see from Figure 2.17, the pop-up menu shows several tasks you can perform on your projects or solutions. You can easily add new items by selecting the **Add** command; you also can perform tasks against specific files if you right-click items in the solution instead of the project's name.

NOTE ABOUT ADDING ITEMS TO PROJECTS

In this book you will be asked lots of times to add new items to a project or to a solution, so you should keep in mind that this can be accomplished by right-clicking the project name in Solution Explorer and then clicking the **Add, New Item** command from the pop-up menu.

You can easily find Solution Explorer by pressing **Ctrl+Alt+L** if it is not available yet in the IDE.

Error List Window

The Error List tool window can show a list of all messages, including warnings and information, which are generated by Visual Studio during the development of your applications. Figure 2.18 shows the Error List tool window.

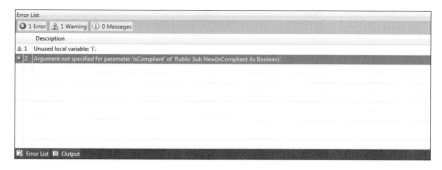

FIGURE 2.18   The Error List tool window.

Typically the Error List window can show three kinds of messages:

▶ Error messages

▶ Warning messages

▶ Information messages

Error messages are related to errors that prevent your application from running, for example, if your code cannot compile successfully. This can include any kind of problems that Visual Studio or the background compiler may encounter during the development process, for example, attempting to use an object that has not been declared, corrupted auto-generated Windows Forms files that must be edited in the Visual Studio designer, or corrupted Visual Studio files in situations that throw error messages that you can see in the Error List. Another kind of message is a warning. Basically warnings are related to situations that will not necessarily prevent your code from being successfully compiled or your application from running; in such cases warnings can be simply ignored. It's good practice to try to solve the problems that caused these messages to be shown. For example, running the Code Analysis tool will throw warnings on code that is not compliant with Microsoft guidelines for writing code. This means that the application will probably work, but something in your code should be improved. In both error and warning messages, you can be easily redirected to the code that caused the message simply by double-clicking the message itself. You can also get some help about the message by right-clicking it and then choosing the **Show Error Help** command from the pop-up menu.

Information messages are just to inform you about something. Usually information messages can be ignored with regard to the code; although they could be useful for understanding what the IDE wants to tell us. By default, the **Error List** shows the three kinds of messages together, but you could also choose to view only some of them, for example error messages excluded and so on. To filter the Error List results, simply click on the tab related to the kind of message you do not want to be shown. For example, click on the **Messages** tab if you want information messages to be excluded by the errors list. To include back information messages, click the same tab again. The Errors List can also be easily invoked by pressing **Ctrl+\\, Ctrl + E.**

The Properties Window

In the .NET development, everything has *properties*, which are peculiarities of a particular item. Classes can have properties; files can have properties; and so on. For example, the filename is a property of a file. You often need to set properties for your code, for .NET objects you use in your code, and for your files. To make things easier, Visual Studio provides a tool window named Properties window, which is a graphical tool for setting items' properties. Figure 2.19 represents the Properties window showing properties for a Windows Form object.

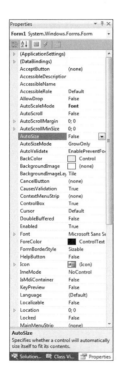

FIGURE 2.19   The Properties window.

Each time you select a property, you can see a description of that property at the bottom of the window. We could define the Properties window's structure as a two-column table, in which the left column specifies the property and the right column gets or sets the value for the property. Although you often need to set properties in code, the Properties window provides a graphical way to perform this assignment and can be particularly useful when designing the user interface or when you need to specify how a file must be packaged into the executable assembly. The Properties window can be easily invoked by pressing **F4**.

Output Window

Visual Studio often recurs to external tools for performing some actions. For example, when compiling your projects Visual Studio invokes the Visual Basic command-line compiler, so the IDE captures the output of the tools it utilizes and redirects the output to the Output window. Basically the Output window's purpose is to show results of actions that Visual Studio has to perform or that you require to be performed by Visual Studio. For example, when you compile your projects, the Output window shows the results of the build process. Figure 2.20 shows the Output window containing the results of the build process of a Visual Basic project.

FIGURE 2.20   The Output window showing results of a build process.

The Output window is also interactive. To continue with the example of compiling a process, if the compiler throws any errors, these are shown in the Output window. You can click the **Go to Next Message** or **Go to Previous Message** buttons to navigate error messages. After you do this, the current error message is highlighted. Each time you move to another error message, you will be redirected to the code that caused the error. The Output window can capture the output not only of the compiler but also of other tools that Visual Studio needs to use, such as the debugger. By the way, you can get a list of the available outputs by clicking the **Show Output From** combo box. After this first look to the main tool windows, we can begin examining another important feature of the Visual Studio IDE for Visual Basic: the My Project window.

My Project

My Project is a special tool that enables developers to set project properties. My Project is a window that can be invoked by double-clicking the same named item in Solution

Explorer or by clicking the **Project, Properties** command (the menu item text also includes the current project name). Figure 2.21 shows how My Project looks regarding the sample application we previously created.

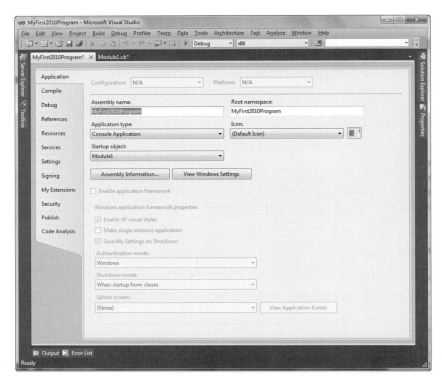

FIGURE 2.21   The My Project window.

My Project is organized in tabs; each tab represents a specific area of the project, such as application-level properties, external references, deployment options, compile options, debugging options, and many more. At the moment you don't need to learn each tab of My Project, because during the rest of the book we use it a lot of times, learning the meaning and purpose of each tab when appropriate. What you instead need now is to

▶ Understand what **My Project** is.

▶ Remember how you can open it.

▶ Learn the usage of the **Application** tab, which we will discuss first.

UNDERSTANDING MY PROJECT

Understanding My Project is also important for another reason: It provides most of the infrastructure for the My namespace that will be discussed in Chapter 20, "The 'My' Namespace." Most of settings that you can specify in My Project are then accessible invoking My. In Chapter 3, "The Anatomy of a Visual Basic Project," we describe the structure of My Project, so carefully read how it is composed.

Application Tab

Each application has some settings. Application settings can be the executable's name, icon, or metadata that will be grabbed by the operating system, such as the program version, copyright information, and so on. The purpose of the Application tab in My Project is to provide the ability to edit these kinds of settings. The Application tab is shown by default when you first open My Project. Figure 2.21 shows the Application tab. Some settings are common to every kind of Visual Basic projects, whereas other ones are related to specific project types. In this chapter you get an overview of the common settings, whereas specific ones will be treated when required in the next chapters.

Assembly Name

The Assembly name field sets the name of the compiled assembly, that is, your executable. By default, Visual Studio assigns this setting based on the project name, but you can replace it as needed.

Root Namespace

This particular field sets the *root level namespace* identifier. Namespaces will be discussed later in this book. You can think of the root namespace as the object that stores all that is implemented by your project. According to Microsoft specifications, the root namespace should be formed as follows: `CompanyName.ProductName.Version`. Basically this convention is optimal when developing class libraries or components but may not be necessary when developing standalone executables. By default, Visual Studio sets the root namespace based on the project name.

Application Type

This represents the application type (for example, Console application, Class Library, Windows Forms application) and is automatically set by Visual Studio on the appropriate choice. To ensure you will avoid any problems, you should not change the default setting.

Icon

This field allows setting an icon for the executable file. You can browse the disk and select an existing .ico file as the executable icon.

NOTE ABOUT ICONS

Assigning an icon to the executable file will not automatically assign icons to Windows Forms windows or WPF windows when developing client applications. In such scenarios you need to explicitly assign icons for each window, because the Icon item in the `Application` tab will just set the icon for the executable.

Startup Object

By setting the Startup Object field, you can specify what object will be executed first when running your application. For example, imagine you have a Windows Forms application with more than one window. You might want to decide what window must be the application's main window. With the Startup Object field, you can make this decision. Notice that the startup object changes based on the project type. For example, in a Windows Forms application the startup object is a Windows Form object whereas in a Console Application the default startup object is the `Sub Main` method. The name of the field also changes based on the project type. In a Windows Forms application it is called Startup Form, whereas in a Console Application it is called Startup Object.

CHANGING THE STARTUP OBJECT

Please be careful when changing the Startup object. A wrong choice could cause errors on your application and prevent it from running.

Assembly Information

By clicking the Assembly Information button, you get access to a new window called Assembly Information, as shown in Figure 2.22.

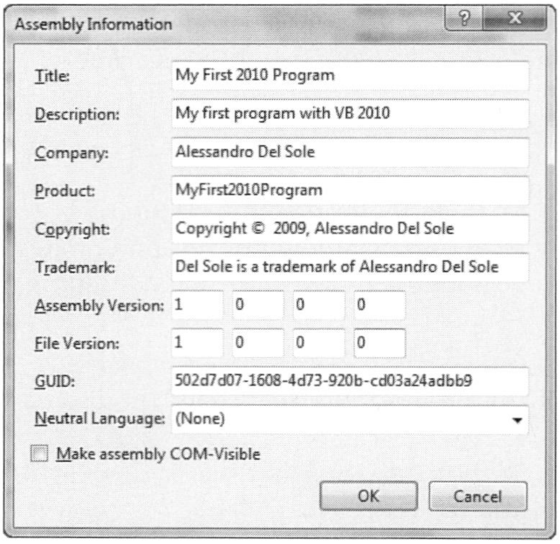

FIGURE 2.22   The Assembly Information window.

From this window you can specify several properties for your executable that will be visible both to the .NET Framework and to the Windows operating system. Table 2.1 explains each property.

TABLE 2.1   Assembly Information Explained

Property	Description
Title	The title for your application, for example, "My First 2010 Program."
Description	The description for your application, for example, "My first program with VB 2010."
Company	Your company name.
Product	The product name, for example, "My First 2010 Program."
Copyright	Copyright information on the author.
Trademark	Trademarks information.
Assembly version	Specifies the version number for the assembly in the style Major.Minor.Build.Revision. This information identifies the assembly for the .NET Framework.
File version	Specifies the version number for the executable in the style Major.Minor.Build.Revision. This information is visible to the Windows operating system.
GUID	A Globally Unique Identifier assigned to the assembly. You can replace with a new one or leave unchanged the GUID provided by the IDE.
Neutral language	Specifies what local culture is used as the neutral language.
Make assembly COM-Visible	.NET assemblies can be exposed to COM. By marking this flag you can accomplish this task later.

The Assembly Information tool is important because it enables you to specify settings that you want to be visible to your customers and other settings needed by the .NET Framework. Behind the scenes, all this information is translated into Visual Basic code, which is discussed more in Chapter 3.

View UAC Settings

With the introduction of Windows Vista, Microsoft introduced to the Windows operating system an important component, known as *User Access Control*. When enabled, this mechanism requires the user to explicitly grant elevated permissions to applications being run. Because of this and starting from Visual Studio 2008, you have the ability of specifying the permissions level your application will require for the UAC. For example, if your application needs to write to the Program Files folder (this is just an example and rarely a good idea), you need to ask for elevated permissions to the UAC. You can specify UAC settings for your application by clicking the **View Windows Settings** button. At this point Visual Studio generates a new XML manifest that will be packaged into your executable and that you can edit within the IDE. This file contains information for UAC settings and for specifying the operating systems that the application is designed to work for. Listing 2.2 shows an excerpt of the default content of the manifest, related to the UAC settings.

LISTING 2.2   The UAC Manifest Content

```xml
<?xml version="1.0" encoding="utf-8"?>
<asmv1:assembly manifestVersion="1.0" xmlns="urn:schemas-microsoft-com:asm.v1"
xmlns:asmv1="urn:schemas-microsoft-com:asm.v1" xmlns:asmv2="urn:schemas-microsoft-
com:asm.v2" xmlns:xsi="http://www.w3.org/2001/XMLSchema-instance">
  <assemblyIdentity version="1.0.0.0" name="MyApplication.app"/>
  <trustInfo xmlns="urn:schemas-microsoft-com:asm.v2">
    <security>
      <requestedPrivileges xmlns="urn:schemas-microsoft-com:asm.v3">
        <!— UAC Manifest Options
            If you want to change the Windows User Account Control level replace the
            requestedExecutionLevel node with one of the following.

            <requestedExecutionLevel  level="asInvoker" uiAccess="false" />
            <requestedExecutionLevel  level="requireAdministrator" uiAccess="false" />
            <requestedExecutionLevel  level="highestAvailable" uiAccess="false" />

            If you want to utilize File and Registry Virtualization for backward
            compatibility then delete the requestedExecutionLevel node.
        —>
        <requestedExecutionLevel level="asInvoker" uiAccess="false" />
      </requestedPrivileges>
    </security>
  </trustInfo>
</asmv1:assembly>
```

The requestedExecutionLevel element enables you to specify what permission level must be requested to the UAC. You have three possibilities, explained in Table 2.2.

TABLE 2.2   UAC Settings

Setting	Description
asInvoker	Runs the application with the privileges related to the current user. If the current user is a standard user, the application will be launched with standard privileges. If the current user is an administrator, the application will be launched with administrative privileges.
requireAdministrator	The application needs administrative privileges to be executed.
highestAvailable	Requires the highest privilege level possible for the current user.

To specify a privilege level, just uncomment the line of XML code corresponding to the desired level. You can also delete the `requestedExecutionLevel` node in case you want to use file and registry virtualization for backward compatibility with older versions of the Windows operating system.

PAY ATTENTION TO UAC REQUIREMENTS

Be careful of the combination of activities that you need to execute on the target machine and the user privileges, because bad UAC settings could cause big problems. A good practice is selecting the `asInvoker` level and architecting your application in a way that it will work on user-level folders and resources. Of course there can be situations in which you need deeper control of the target machine and administrator privileges, but these should be considered exceptions to the rule.

The Application Framework

In the lower part of the screen you can see the Enable Application Framework group, a feature that allows executing special tasks at the beginning and at the end of the application lifetime. For Console applications it is not available but it is relevant to other kinds of applications; for instance, in Windows Forms application it allows setting a splash screen or establishing what form is the main application form. The application framework is discussed in Chapter 20, "The 'My' Namespace."

Compiling Projects

Compiling a project (or *building* according to the Visual Studio terminology) is the process that produces a .NET assembly starting from your project and source code (according to the .NET architecture described in Chapter 1, "Introducing the .NET Framework 4.0"). An assembly can be a standalone application (.exe assembly) or a .NET class library (.dll assembly). To compile your project into an assembly you need to click the **Build** command in the Build menu. Notice that the Build command is followed by the name of your project. When invoking this command, Visual Studio launches, behind the scenes, the Visual Basic command-line compiler (Vbc.exe) and provides this tool all the necessary command-line options. For solutions containing different kinds of projects, Visual Studio launches the MSBuild.exe command-line utility that can compile entire solutions containing several projects written in different languages and of different types. MSBuild is discussed in Chapter 51, "Advanced Compilations with MSBuild." At the end of the build process, Visual Studio shows a log inside the Output window. Figure 2.23 shows the output log of the build process for the MyFirst2010Program sample application.

FIGURE 2.23   The **Output window** shows the compilation process results.

The compilation log shows useful messages that help you understand what happened. In this case there were no errors, but in situations in which the compilation process fails because of some errors in the code, you will be notified of what errors were found by the compiler. The Error List window shows a complete list of error messages and warnings and enables you to easily understand where the errors happened by simply double-clicking the error message. This operation redirects you to the code that generated the error. The executable (or the executables, in case of more than one project in the solution) will be put in a subfolder within the project's directory, called Bin\Debug or Bin\Release, depending on the output *configuration* you choose. Configurations are discussed next.

Debug and Release Configurations

Visual Studio provides two default possibilities for compiling your projects. The first one is related to the debugging phase in the development process and includes debug symbols that are necessary for debugging applications. The second one is related to the end of the development process and is the one you will use when releasing the application to your customers. Both ways are represented by *configurations*. By default, Visual Studio offers two built-in configurations: Debug and Release. When the Debug configuration is active, the Visual Basic compiler generates debug symbols that the Visual Studio debugger can process. Without these symbols, you cannot debug your applications with the Visual Studio debugger. The Release configuration basically excludes debug symbols from the build process, and it is the configuration you will use when building the final version of your application, that is, the executable that you will release to your customers. To set the current configuration you have two possibilities:

▶ Use the combo box located on the Visual Studio toolbar.

▶ Access the Compile options inside the My Project window.

Figure 2.24 shows the Compile tab in My Project.

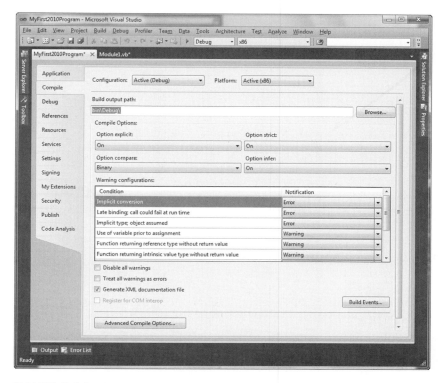

FIGURE 2.24   Compile options in the My Project window.

At the top of the window you can find a combo box called Configuration. There you can select the most appropriate configuration for you. By default, Visual Studio 2010 is set up on the Debug configuration. You could also consider building a custom configuration (although both Debug and Release can be customized instead of making new ones), which will be discussed next. Basically for our purposes it's suitable to leave unchanged the selection of the Debug configuration as the default, because we will study the Visual Studio debugging features in depth.

Creating Custom Configurations with Configuration Manager

There can be situations in which both the Debug and Release configurations are not enough for your needs. As we mentioned in the previous paragraph, with Visual Studio 2010 you can also create your custom configuration. To accomplish this you need to access the Configuration manager tool (see Figure 2.25), which is reachable using the Configuration manager command in the Build menu. There you can edit an existing configuration or create a new one.

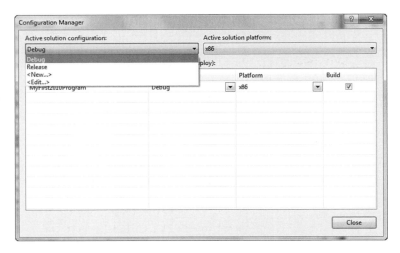

FIGURE 2.25   The Configuration Manager.

To create a new custom configuration, you can perform the following steps:

1. Click the **Active Solution Configuration** combo box and select the **New** option.

2. In the New Solution Configuration window, specify a name for the new configuration, and select an existing configuration (such as Debug) from which settings will be copied. Figure 2.26 shows an example.

3. When done, click **Close.**

4. Click the **Advanced Compiler Options** button in the Compile tab and specify what compile options must affect the new configuration. For example, you could decide to affect just compilations against 64-bit processors, so you just need to change the value in the Target CPU combo box. This is the point at which you can modify your real configuration settings and how your project should be built.

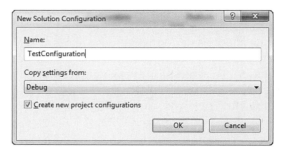

FIGURE 2.26   Creating a custom configuration that imports settings from an existing one.

Such modification influences just the new configuration. Moreover, if you decide to use the new configuration, you will have a new subfolder under the Bin subfolder in your project's main folder, which takes the name of your custom configuration and that contains the output of the build process made with that configuration. For our MyFirst2010Program sample, the project folder is named MyFirst2010Program and contains the Bin subfolder, which also contains the default Debug and Release subfolders. With your custom configuration, a new TestConfiguration subfolder will be available under Bin.

Background Compiler

Visual Basic 2010 offers a great feature: the *background compiler*. Basically, while you write your code the IDE invokes the Visual Basic compiler that will immediately compile the code and notify you about errors that occur, writing messages in the Error List window. This is possible because the Visual Basic compiler can compile your code on-the-fly while you type. As you can imagine, this feature is important because you will not necessarily need to build your project each time to understand if your code can be successfully compiled. Typical examples of the background compiler in action are error messages shown in the Error List window when typing code. Refer to Figure 2.19 to get an idea of this feature. You can just double-click the error message to be redirected to the line of code that caused the error. Also, the IDE underlines code containing errors with red squiggly lines so that it is easier to understand where the problem is.

Other Compile Options

Visual Studio 2010 enables developers to get deep control over the build process. With particular regard to Visual Basic, you can control other compile options that are specific to the language. Table 2.3 lists them in detail.

TABLE 2.3   Visual Basic Compile Options

Option	Meaning
Option Explicit	When set to On, the developer must declare an object before using it in code.
Option Strict	When set to On, the developer must specify the type when declaring objects. In other words, Object is not automatically assigned as the default type. Moreover, Option Strict On disallows late binding and conversions from one type to another where there is a loss of precision or data. You should always set Option Strict On unless strictly required.
Option Compare	Determines which method must be used when comparing strings (Binary or Text). The Binary option enables the compiler to compare strings based on a binary representation of the characters while the Text option enables string comparisons based on textual sorting, according to the local system international settings.
Option Infer	When set to On, enables local type inference (this feature will be discussed in Chapter 21, "Advanced Language Features").

OPTION STRICT ON

By default, Option Strict is Off. You can set it to On each time you create a new project but you can also change the default setting by clicking Tools, Options and then in the Options dialog expanding the Projects and Solutions node, finally selecting the VB Defaults element and changing the default setting.

Options shown in Table 2.3 are also considered by the background compiler, so you will be immediately notified when your code does not match these requirements. You can also specify how the Visual Basic compiler has to treat some kind of errors. This is what you see next.

Warning Configurations

Warning configurations state how the Visual Basic compiler should notify the developer of some particular errors, if just sending warning messages (which will not prevent from compiling the project) or error messages (which will instead prevent from completing the build process).

DO NOT IGNORE WARNING MESSAGES

Even if warning messages will not prevent the completion of the build process, they should never be blindly ignored. They could be suggestions of potential exceptions at runtime. You should always accurately check why a warning message is thrown and, possibly, solve the issue that caused the warning. A typical example of when warnings could be ignored is when running code analysis on code that does not need to be compliant with Microsoft specifications (for example, the user interface side of a Windows Forms application). In all other situations, you should be careful about warnings.

Depending on how you set the Visual Basic compile options discussed in the previous paragraph, Visual Studio will propose some default scenarios for sending notifications (and, consequently, influencing the build process). Table 2.4 lists the available warning conditions.

TABLE 2.4   Warning Conditions Details

Condition	Description

Implicit conversion	Checked when trying to assign an object of a type to an object of another type. For example the following code will cause the condition to be checked (implicit conversion from `Object` to `String`):
	 `Dim anObject As Object = "Hi!"`
	 `Dim aString As String = anObject`

TABLE 2.4   Continued

Condition	Description
Late binding	Checked when trying to assign at runtime a typed object to another one of type `Object`.
Implicit type	Checked when not specifying the type for an object declaration. If Option Infers is on, this condition is checked only for declarations at class level. For example, the following class level declaration would cause the condition to be checked: `Private Something` This condition is determined by `Option Strict On`.

Use of variable prior of assignment	Checked when attempting to use a variable that doesn't have a value yet. This is typical with instance variables. The following code causes this condition to be checked:
	
	`Dim p As Process`
	`Console.WriteLine`
	`(p.ProcessName.ToString)`
	
	In this case p must get an instance of the `Process` object before attempting to use it.

Function/operator without return value	Checked when a `Function` method or an operator definition performs actions without returning a value.
Unused local variable	Checked when a variable is declared but never used. It's a good practice to remove unused variables both for cleaner code and for memory allocation.
Instance variable accesses shared members	Checked when trying to invoke a member from an instance object that is instead a shared member.
Recursive operator or property access	Checked when trying to use a member (properties or operators) inside the code block that defines the member itself.

Duplicate or overlapping catch blocks	Checked when a `Catch` clause inside a `Try..Catch..End Try` code block is never reached because of inheritance. The following code causes the condition to be checked, because the `FileNotFoundException` inherits from `Exception` and therefore should be caught before the base class; otherwise `Exception` would be always caught before derived ones:
	
	`Try`
	
	`Catch ex As Exception`
	`Catch ex As FileNotFoundException`
	
	`End Try`

You also have the ability to change single notifications; just select the most appropriate notification mode for your needs. Based on the explanations provided in Table 2.4, be careful about the consequences that this operation could cause. If you are not sure about consequences, the best thing is leaving default options unchanged. There are also three other compile options, which are listed at the bottom of the Compile tab and that are described in Table 2.5.

TABLE 2.5   Additional Compile Options

Option	Description
Disable all warnings.	The Visual Basic compiler will not produce warning messages.
Treat all warnings as errors.	The Visual Basic compiler will treat all warning messages as if they were errors.
Generate XML documentation file.	When flagged, enables Visual Studio to generate an XML file for documenting the source code. If XML comments are included in the code, this file also contains description and detailed documentation for the code. This is useful when you need to automate the documentation process for your class libraries.

Advanced Compile Options

You can specify advanced settings for the build process. To accomplish this, you need to click the **Advanced Compile Options** button.

COMPILER SETTINGS AND CONFIGURATIONS

Advanced compiler settings are at the configuration level. This means that the Debug configuration has its own advanced settings and the Release configuration has its own settings, and your custom configurations will have their own settings. Please remember this when providing advanced settings.

Figure 2.27 shows the Advanced Compiler Settings window.

Here you can set compiler options to drive the build process. We now discuss options in details.

Optimizations

The Optimization tab offers options that would potentially lead to building a smaller and faster executable. This tab is composed of four options that we discuss.

Remove Integer Overflow Checks   When you make calculations in your code against Integer or Integer-style data types, the Visual Basic compiler checks that the result of the calculation falls within the range of that particular data type. By default, this option is turned off so that the compiler can do this kind of check. If you flag this check box, the

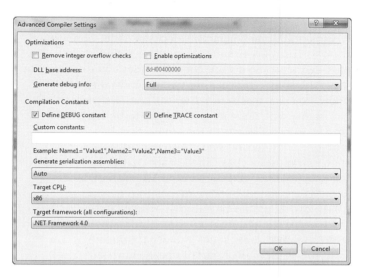

FIGURE 2.27   The Advanced Compiler Settings window.

compiler will not check for such overflows, and the application execution may result faster. Be careful about this choice, especially if your code implements calculations.

Enable Optimizations   When this check box is flagged, the compiler basically removes some *opcodes* that are required for interacting with the debugger. Moreover, the *Just-in-time* compilation is optimized because the runtime knows that a debugger will not be attached. On the other hand, this can result in major difficulties when debugging applications. For example, you might not use breakpoints at specific lines of code and, consequently, perform debugging tasks although the optimization process could produce a smaller and faster executable.

DLL Base Address   This option is available when developing class libraries and user controls and provides the ability to specify the *Base Address* for the assembly. As you may know, the base address is the location in memory where a Dll is loaded. By default, Visual Studio assigns a base address and represents it in hexadecimal format. If you need to provide a custom base address, this is the place where you can do it.

Generate Debug Information   Generating debug information when building your project allows you to use the debugger against your application. By default this option is set to Full, which means that full debug information is generated so that the debugger can be fully used to debug an application. (This is the case of the Debug configuration.) If you set this option to None, no debug information will be generated, whereas if you set this option to pdb-only, the compiler will produce just a .pdb file containing debug symbols and project state information.

Compilation Constants

You can use compilation constants to conditionally compile blocks of code. Conditional compilation relies on the evaluation to True of constants that will be included in the final assembly. The Visual Basic compiler defines some default constants that you can evaluate within your code, and you also have the ability of declaring custom constants. In the Advanced Compiler Settings window, you can specify whether the compiler needs to include the DEBUG and TRACE constants. The first one enables you to understand if the application is running in debug mode; in other words, if the application has been compiled using the Debug configuration. The second one is also related to debugging tasks; particularly, the .NET Framework exposes a class called `Trace` that is used in debugging and that can send the tracing output to the Output window when the TRACE constant is defined. If not, no output is generated, because invocations versus the `Trace` class are ignored. A full list of built-in constants can be found at MSDN Library at http://msdn.microsoft.com/en-us/library/dy7yth1w(VS.100).aspx. Evaluating constants in code is quite simple. You can use the `#If`, `#Else`, `#ElseIf`, and `#EndIf` directives. For example, if you want to evaluate whenever an application has been compiled with the Debug configuration, you could write the following code:

```
#If DEBUG Then
        Console.WriteLine("You are in Debug configuration")
#Else
        Console.WriteLine("You are not in Debug configuration")
#End If
```

which essentially verifies if the constant is defined and takes some action at that point. In our example, if the DEBUG constant is defined in the assembly, this means that it has been built via the Debug configuration.

Custom Constants   You can also define custom constants. This can be basically accomplished in two ways. The first is adding custom constants in the appropriate field of the Advanced compiler settings window. Each constant must have the form of `Name="Value"` and constants are separated by commas. The second way for providing custom constants is adding a `#Const` directive in your code. For example, the following line of code

```
#Const TestConstant = True
```

defines a constant named `TestConstant` whose value is set to `True`. The big difference in using a `#Const` directive is that it defines just private constants that have visibility within the code file that defines them.

Generate Serialization Assemblies

As we discuss in Chapter 43, "Serialization," serialization in .NET development is a technique that allows persisting the state of an object. Among several alternatives, this can be accomplished using a class called `XmlSerializer`. In such situations, the Visual Basic compiler can optimize applications that use the `XmlSerializer` class, generating additional assemblies for better performances. By default, this option is set to **Auto** so that

Visual Studio generates serialization assemblies only if you are effectively using Xml serialization in your code. Other options are On and Off.

Target CPU

You can specify what CPU architecture your applications will target. You can choose among 32-bit architectures (x86), 64-bit architectures (x64), Itanium processors, or simply target any architecture (AnyCPU).

Target Framework

From the Target Framework combo box, you can select the version of the .NET Framework that your application will target. The main difference with the same selection that you can do when creating a new project is that here you can target the .NET Framework Client Profile for versions 4.0, 3.5 Service Pack 1, and 3.5 Server Core. The .NET Framework Client Profile is a subset of the .NET Framework that provides the infrastructure for client applications and that can be included in your deployments instead of the full version. The Client Profile is discussed in Chapter 54, "Setup and Deployment Projects for Windows Installer."

Debugging Overview

In this section you get an overview of the debugging features in Visual Studio 2010 for Visual Basic applications. Although the debugger and debugging techniques are detailed in Chapter 5, "Debugging Visual Basic 2010 Applications," here we provide information on the most common debugging tasks, which is something that you need to know in this first part of your journey through the Visual Basic programming language.

Debugging an Application

To debug a Visual Basic application, you basically need to perform two steps:

- ▸ Enable the Debug configuration in the compile options.
- ▸ Press F5 to start debugging.

By pressing F5, Visual Studio runs your application and attaches an instance of the debugger to the application. Because the Visual Studio debugger needs the debug symbols to proceed, if you do not choose the Debug configuration, you cannot debug your applications. The instance of the debugger detaches when you shut down your application.

TIP

As an alternative to pressing F5, you can click the **Start Debugging** button on the Visual Studio standard toolbar.

The debugger monitors your application's execution and notifies for runtime errors; it allows you to take control over the execution flow as well. Figure 2.28 shows our sample

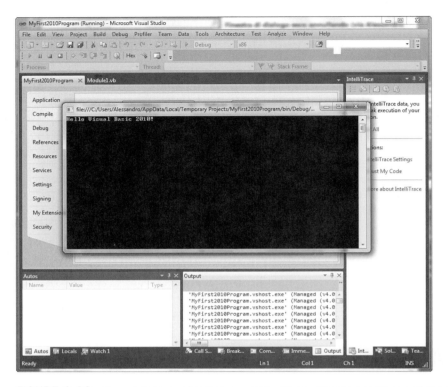

FIGURE 2.28   Our sample application running with an attached instance of the Visual Studio debugger.

application running with the Visual Studio debugger attached. In the bottom area of the IDE; you can notice the availability of some new windows, such as Locals, Watch 1, Watch 2, Call Stack, Breakpoints, Command Window, Immediate Window, and Output.

The Visual Studio debugger is a powerful tool; next you learn the most important tasks in debugging applications. Chapter 5 instead dives deeper into the debugger instrumentation for complex debugging tasks. Before explaining the tooling, it is a good idea to modify the source code of our test application so that we can cause some errors and see the debugger in action. We could rewrite the Sub Main method's code, as shown in Listing 2.3.

LISTING 2.3   Modifying the Sub Main for Debugging Purposes

```
Sub Main()

    'A text message
    Dim message As String = "Hello Visual Basic 2010!"
```

```
Console.WriteLine(message)

'Attempt to read a file that does not exist
Dim getSomeText As String =
             My.Computer.FileSystem.ReadAllText("FakeFile.txt")

Console.WriteLine(getSomeText)
Console.ReadLine()

End Sub
```

NEW TO VISUAL BASIC .NET?

If you are not an existing Visual Basic .NET developer, you may not know some of the objects and keywords shown in the code listings of this chapter. The code is the simplest possible, should be quite easy to understand, and is provided with comments. The next chapters guide you to the details of the programming language, so everything used here will be explained. At the moment, it is important for you to focus on the instrumentation more than on the code.

The code simply declares a message object of type String, containing a text message. This message is then shown in the Console window. This is useful for understanding breakpoints and other features in the code editor. The second part of the code will try to open a text file, which effectively does not exist, and store its content into a variable called getSomeText of type String. We need this to understand how the debugger catches errors at runtime, together with the edit and continue feature.

Breakpoints and Data Tips

Breakpoints enable you to control the execution flow of your application. Basically a breakpoint breaks the execution of the application at the point where the breakpoint itself is placed so that you can take required actions (situation known as *break mode*). You can then resume the application execution. To place a breakpoint on a specific line of code, just place the cursor on the line of code you want to debug and then press **F9**.

TIP

To add a breakpoint, you can also right-click the line of code you want to debug and select the **Breakpoint, Insert breakpoint** command from the pop-up menu or just click the leftmost column in the code window.

A breakpoint is easily recognizable, because it highlights in red the selected line of code (see Figure 2.29).

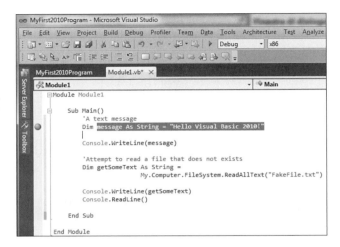

FIGURE 2.29   Placing a breakpoint in the code editor.

To see how breakpoints work, we can run the sample application by pressing **F5**. When the debugger encounters a breakpoint, it breaks the execution and highlights in yellow the line of code that is being debugged, as shown in Figure 2.30, before the code is executed.

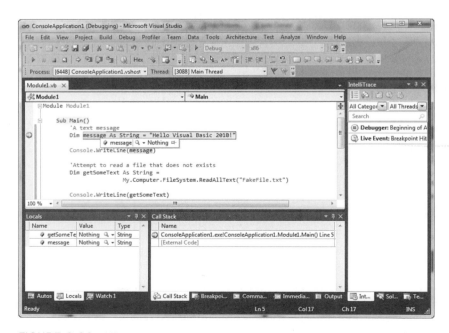

FIGURE 2.30   When encountering a breakpoint, Visual Studio highlights the line of code that is currently debugged.

If you take a look at Figure 2.31, you notice a couple of amazing things. First, if you pass with the mouse pointer over the message variable, IntelliSense shows the content of the variable itself, which at the moment contains no value (in fact is set to Nothing). This feature is known as Data Tips and is useful if you need to know the content of a variable or of another object in a particular moment of the application execution. Another interesting feature is that the Call Stack window shows that a breakpoint is currently available and encountered on the specified line of code. The Call Stack window is discussed in Chapter 5.

THE VISUAL STUDIO HISTORICAL DEBUGGER

If you run the Microsoft Visual Studio 2010 Ultimate edition, you notice also another window called Debug History that is a new feature of Visual Studio 2010. This window is known as the Visual Studio Historical Debugger and is specific to the Visual Studio Team System instrumentation and will be discussed in Chapter 57, "Introducing the Visual Studio Extensibility."

You can then execute just one line of code at a time, by pressing **F11**. For example, supposing we want to check if the message variable is correctly initialized at runtime, we could press F11 (which is a shortcut for the Step Into command in the Debug menu). The line of code where the breakpoint is placed will now be executed, and Visual Studio will highlight the next line of code. At that point you can still pass the mouse pointer over the variable to see the assignment result, as shown in Figure 2.31.

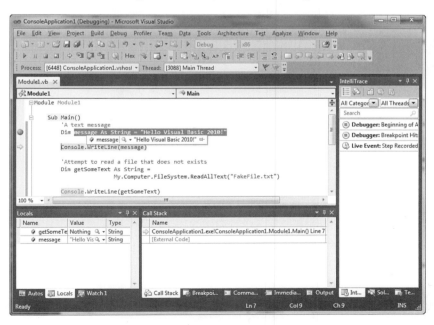

FIGURE 2.31   Using the Step Into command enables us to check if the variable has been assigned correctly.

When you finish checking the assignments, you can resume the execution by simply pressing **F5**. At this point the execution of the application continues until another breakpoint or a runtime error is encountered. We discuss this second scenario next.

About Runtime Errors

Runtime errors are particular situations in which an error occurs during the application execution but is not predictable by the developer or because of programming errors that are not visible at compile time. Typical examples of runtime errors are when you create an application and you give users the ability to specify a filename, but the file is not found on disk, or when you need to access a database and pass an incorrect SQL query string. Obviously in real-life applications you should predict such possibilities and implement the appropriate error handling routines (discussed in Chapter 6, "Handling Errors and Exceptions"), but for our learning purposes about the debugger, we need some code that voluntarily causes an error. Continuing the debugging we began in the previous paragraph, the application's execution resumption causes a runtime error, because our code is searching for a file that does not exist. When the error is raised, Visual Studio breaks the execution as shown in Figure 2.32.

As you can see, the line of code that caused the error appears highlighted. You also can see a pop-up window that shows some information about the error. In our example, the code searches for a file that does not exist, so a `FileNotFoundException` is thrown and was not

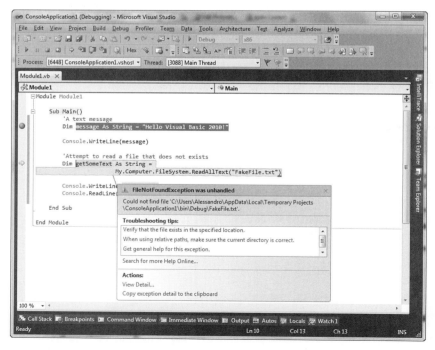

FIGURE 2.32   The Visual Studio debugger encounters a runtime error.

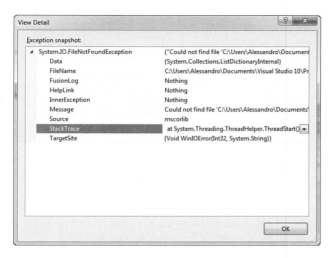

FIGURE 2.33   The View Detail window enables developers to examine deeply what caused an exception.

handled by error handling routines; therefore, the execution of the application is broken. Visual Studio also shows a description of the error message. (In our example it communicates that the code could not find the FakeFile.txt file.) Visual Studio also shows some suggestions. For example, the Troubleshooting tips suggest some tasks that you could do at this point, such as verifying that the file exists in the specified location, checking the path name or, last, getting general help about the error. Particularly, by clicking such a tip you are redirected to the MSDN documentation about the error. This can be useful when you don't exactly know what an error message means. There are other options within the Actions group. The most important is the one named View Detail. This enables you to open the View Detail window, which is represented in Figure 2.33.

Notice how the StackTrace item shows the hierarchy of calls to classes and methods that effectively produced the error. Another interesting item is the InnerException. In our example it is set to Nothing, but it's not unusual for this item to show a kind of exceptions tree that enables you to better understand what actually caused an error. For example, think of working with data. You might want to connect to SQL Server and fetch data from a database. You could not have sufficient rights to access the database, and the runtime might return a data access exception that does not allow you to immediately understand what the problem is. Browsing the InnerException can let you understand that the problem was caused by insufficient rights. Going back to the code, this is the point where you can fix it and where the Edit and Continue features comes in.

Edit and Continue

The Edit and Continue features enables you to fix bad code and resume the application execution from the point where it was broken, without the need of restarting the application. Basically you just need to run the application by pressing **F5**; then you can break its execution by pressing **Ctrl+Alt+Break** or selecting the **Break All** command in the Debug menu.

AVAILABILITY OF EDIT AND CONTINUE

Generally you can use the **Edit and Continue** features, but there are situations in which you will not. For example, if fixing your code may influence the general application behavior, you need to restart the application. Also, Edit and Continue is not available when running configurations that target 64-bits CPUs.

In our example we need to fix the code that searches for a not existing file. We can replace the line of code with this one:

```
Dim getSomeText As String = "Fixed code"
```

This simply replaces the search of a file with a text message. At this point we can press **F5** (or **F11** if we want to just execute the line of code and debug the next one) to resume the execution. Figure 2.34 shows how the application now runs correctly. The Edit and Continue feature completes the overview of the debugging features in Visual Studio. As we mentioned before, this topic is covered in detail in Chapter 6.

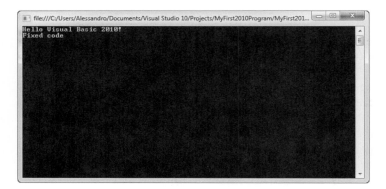

FIGURE 2.34   The sample application running correctly after fixing errors.

After this brief overview of the debugging features in Visual Studio 2010, it's time to talk about another important topic for letting you feel at home within the Visual Studio 2010 IDE when developing applications: getting help and documentation.

Browsing the Visual Basic and .NET Documentation

The *.NET Framework Base Class Library* is very large, and remembering all the objects that you can use in your applications (or the ones that .NET Framework relies on) is not possible. What is instead important is to know where to search for information. You have different tools available to browse the .NET Framework and its documentation, for Visual Basic, too. Because the goal of this chapter is to provide information on the primary tools you need for developing Visual Basic applications, getting help with the language and with the tooling is absolutely one of the primary necessities, as discussed next.

Online Help and the MSDN Library

Visual Studio 2010 ships with the MSDN Library, which is the place where you can find documentation for Visual Basic 2010 and the .NET Framework 4.0. There are basically two ways to access the MSDN Library: offline and online. To access the MSDN Library offline you have the following alternatives:

- ▶ Click the **View Help** command from the Help menu in Visual Studio.
- ▶ Press **F1** from wherever you are.
- ▶ Open the **Microsoft Visual Studio 2010 Documentation** shortcut that is available in Windows's Start, All Programs, Microsoft Visual Studio 2010 menu.
- ▶ Open the **MSDN Library** shortcut that is available in Windows's Start, All Programs, Microsoft Developer Network menu.

If you are writing code or performing a particular task on a tool within the IDE, pressing **F1** is the best choice because you will be redirected to the help page related to that instruction, code statement, or tool. If you are instead searching for information about a particular technology or framework, such as *WPF* or the *Visual Studio Tools for Office*, you could consider one of the other choices. To access the MSDN Library online, you just need an Internet connection. Then you can specify to always use the on-line help by selecting **Help, Manage Help Settings** and then click **Choose Online or Local Help**, or manually open one of the following websites, which are the main points of interest for a Visual Basic developer:

- ▶ The MSDN Library portal at http://msdn.microsoft.com/en-us/library/default.aspx
- ▶ The .NET Framework reference at http://msdn.microsoft.com/en-us/library/w0x726c2(VS.100).aspx
- ▶ The Visual Basic Developer Center at http://msdn.com/vbasic

You can also quickly find information on particular objects using built-in tools, such as the Object Browser.

Object Browser Window

The Object Browser is a special tool window that enables you to browse the .NET Framework class library. You can get a hierarchical view of the Base Class Library and of all the types defined in your solution, including types defined in referenced external assemblies. The Object Browser is useful because you can understand how a type is defined, what members it exposes, what interfaces it implements and what other classes it derives from. If the types are documented, you can get a description for each object or member.

TIP

You can activate the Object Browser by pressing **Ctrl+ALT+J**.

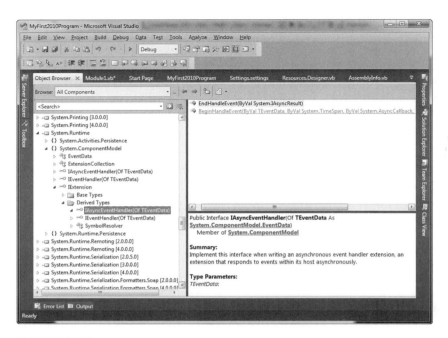

FIGURE 2.35   The Object Browser enables exploring .NET objects showing information.

Figure 2.35 represents, as an example, the Object Browser showing members of the `System.Windows.ContentElement` class.

The right side of the window lists methods and properties exposed by the selected object. When you click on a method or on a member of the object in the left side of the window, a short description of the object should appear in the bottom-right side of the Object Browser. If the description is not useful enough to understand the meaning of an object or of one of its members, you can just press F1, and Visual Studio shows the online help (if available) for the object or member. The Object Browser also provides links to objects used by the one you are exploring. Considering the example shown in Figure 2.35, you not only can see the description of a method, but you can also click on the parameters' identifiers to be redirected to the definition of the parameter. The Object Browser can also be invoked when writing code, as discussed next.

Invoking the Object Browser from the Code Editor

Often you need to know how particular .NET objects or members are structured or how they work. Visual Studio 2010 provides the ability of invoking the Object Browser directly from the code editor, by just right-clicking the object you want to browse and selecting the Go to Definition command from the pop-up menu. For example, imagine you want to know how the `Console` class is defined. To accomplish this, you can revisit the MyFirst2010Program example. When in the code editor, right-click the `Console` object. Figure 2.36 shows the pop-up menu.

By doing this, Visual Studio opens the Object Browser that automatically selects the `Console` class, showing also its methods on the right side of the screen (see Figure 2.37 for details).

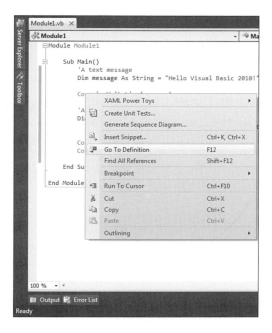

FIGURE 2.36   The Object Browser can be invoked from the code editor by clicking the Go to Type Definition command.

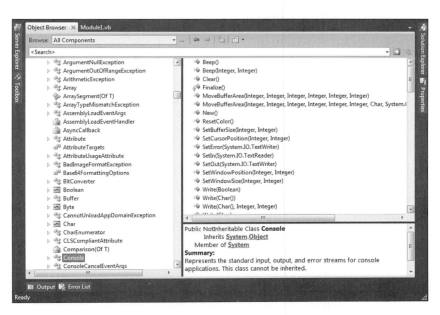

FIGURE 2.37   The **Object Browser** automatically shows the definition for the type you selected in the code editor.

This technique works with shared classes or, more generally, with declarations of noninstance classes, but there are situations in which you may want to learn about data types or instance members' definitions. For example, consider the following code:

```
Dim text As String
text = "Hi!"
```

If you try to run the Go to Definition command for the `text` identifier, you will be redirected to the first line of code, which effectively defines the text object. But what if you want to browse the `String` object? Fortunately there is another command that you can choose in such situations, which is named Go to Type Definition and that is still available in the pop-up menu. Invoking Go to Type Definition redirects to the definition of the type that characterizes the object you declared (in our example, `String`). The result will be the same as in Figure 2.37.

> **NOTE**
>
> Instance and shared members is discussed in detail in Chapter 7, "Class Fundamentals."

Although the Object Browser's purpose is not typically to provide help, definitely it is a good place for learning about .NET objects, both if you need information on their structure and if you need descriptions on their usage.

Summary

In this chapter we discussed basic things you need to know as a Visual Basic developer to feel at home within the Visual Studio 2010 Integrated Development Environment. Tasks such as creating projects, compiling projects, debugging applications, and searching for documentation are the most common in the developer life, and this chapter offers a fast way to understand all the primary tools you need for building applications with Visual Basic 2010. Now that you know how you can move inside the IDE, it's time to begin working with the Visual Basic programming language.

CHAPTER 3

The Anatomy of a Visual Basic Project

Although you can create lots of kinds of projects both for Windows and the Web with Visual Basic 2010, there is a common set of files for each project. In this chapter you learn which files give the structure to each project and how the files influence the building of an application. You also get an overview of references, namespaces, classes, modules, and Visual Basic keywords.

Brief Overview of Types and Members

In the second part of this book, we discuss important topics related to the object-oriented programming with Visual Basic 2010, and we explore features such as types, classes, modules, namespaces, interfaces, and class members. Before going into this, it would be a good idea to have at least an overview of classes, modules, namespaces, and class members because you will find these objects in code examples or in Visual Basic features that are shown prior to Chapter 7, "Class Fundamentals."

IF SOMETHING IS NOT CLEAR

The following is only a brief overview of some important topics. Don't be afraid if any of the following concepts are not clear or worry if things seem small. Starting in Chapter 4, "Data Types and Expressions," and continuing through Part 2, "Object-Oriented Programming with Visual Basic 2010," of this book, all concepts are discussed in detail.

Classes

Classes in .NET development represent objects whose declaration is enclosed within `Class..End Class` blocks. The following is an example of class declaration:

```
Class Person
End Class
```

Classes are *reference types* (explained more in Chapter 4) and can expose members that influence the object's behavior, such as *properties* and *methods*. Classes can implement interfaces and they can also be static (or `Shared` according to the VB terminology) and can provide support for inheritance.

Properties

Properties are characteristics of a type. For example, the previously shown class `Person` could have two properties, such as the first name and the last name:

```
Class Person
   Property FirstName As String
   Property LastName As String
End Class
```

PROPERTIES IN VISUAL BASIC 2010

Visual Basic 2010 introduces a new syntax for properties known as *auto-implemented properties*. To declare properties you need just the Property keyword without explicitly specifying getters and setters. This is discussed further in Chapter 7.

Methods

Methods are the .NET representation of what in other programming environments you define as functions and procedures. A method can be a member of classes, structures, and modules. Methods that return a value are represented by `Function..End Function` blocks, such as the following:

```
Function DoSomething() As String
     Return "A text message"
End Function
```

Methods that do not return a value are represented by `Sub..End Sub` blocks, such as the following:

```
Sub DoSomething()
'write your code here
End Sub
```

Methods can receive parameters that can be processed within code blocks. Such parameters are called, using .NET terminology, *arguments*. The following code block shows an example of an argument named `message`:

```
Sub DoSomething(ByVal message As String)
    Console.Writeline(message)
End Sub
```

Modules

Modules are defined within a `Module..End Module` code block. Modules are basically `Shared` classes but, unlike classes, they cannot implement interfaces. The following is an example of a module:

```
Module Module1


    Sub DoSomething()
        'Code goes here
    End Sub
End Module
```

Members defined inside modules don't require the name of the module when invoked.

Structures

Structures are .NET objects represented by a `Structure..End Structure` code block. Structures are value types, which are described more in Chapter 4, and for classes, can expose properties, methods, and so on. The following is an example of a structure declaration:

```
Structure SomeValues


    Property FirstValue As Boolean
    Property SecondValue As Integer

    Sub DoSomething()

    End Sub
End Structure
```

Inheritance

Inheritance is one of the most important features of the .NET Framework. A class can inherit or derive from another class, meaning that the new class can have all properties, methods, and members exposed by the first class, which is called base class, and can then define its own members. Inherited members can then be overridden to adapt their behavior to the new class' context. The .NET Framework provides one-level inheritance, meaning that a class can inherit from one other class per time. Each class derives implicitly from System.Object. The Inherits keyword is used to inherit classes. The following code provides an example of a base class named Person and of a derived class named Customer:

```
Public Class Person
    Public Property FirstName As String
    Public Property LastName As String

    'A new definition of System.Object.ToString
    Public Overrides Function ToString() As String
        Return String.Concat(FirstName, " ", LastName)
    End Function
End Class

Public Class Customer
    Inherits Person

    Public Property CompanyName As String

    Public Overrides Function ToString() As String
        Return CompanyName
    End Function

End Class
```

In the preceding example the Person class overrides (that is, provides a new definition of) the System.Object.ToString method. The Customer class exposes a new CompanyName property whereas, via inheritance, it exposes the FirstName and LastName properties. Finally, the class also overrides the Person.ToString method. Inheritance is discussed in Chapter 12. "Inheritance."

Namespaces

A *namespace* is basically a container of types. This means that one namespace can contain multiple classes, multiple modules, multiple interfaces, multiple structures, and so on. The following is an example of a namespace exposing two classes, one module, one structure, and one interface:

```
Namespace Test

    Class Person
        Property FirstName As String
        Property LastName As String
    End Class
```

```
Class Employee
    Inherits Person

    Property EmployeeID As Integer
End Class

Module Module1

    Sub DoSomething()

    End Sub
End Module

Interface ITest
    Sub TakeATest()
End Interface

Structure SomeValues
    Property FirstValue As Boolean
    Property SecondValue As Integer
End Structure
End Namespace
```

Namespaces are important for a better organization of types, but there is another reason. You could have two classes with the same name (for example, Employee) but with different properties. Namespaces enable you to avoid conflicts in such scenarios. You can access types exposed by a namespace by simply writing its identifier followed by a dot and then by the type name. For example, if you want to invoke the method DoSomething in Module1 you could write the following line of code:

```
Test.Module1.DoSomething()
```

Namespaces are described in detail in Chapter 9, "Organizing Types Within Namespaces."

Accessing Members

Unless you declare shared objects, you need to instantiate classes and structures before you can use members and store information within those objects. You instantiate a class declaring a variable and using the New keyword as in the following line of code:

```
Dim testPerson As New Person
```

Then you can set properties for the new instance or eventually invoke other members such as methods. For example, you could initialize testPerson's properties as follows:

```
testPerson.FirstName = "Alessandro"
testPerson.LastName = "Del Sole"
```

Basically when you need to invoke a member of a class, you type the name of the instance (in this example `testPerson`) followed by a dot and by the name of the member. For shared members, you just write the name of the class or structure followed by a dot and by the name of the member.

INITIALIZING MEMBERS

Visual Basic 2010 offers an alternative way for initializing members' valued when instantiating classes. This feature is known as Object Initializers and is discussed in Chapter 7.

Imports Directives

As we saw before, namespaces can expose objects that expose members. Moreover, namespaces can expose nested namespaces, exposing objects and so on. You often need to access members of objects exposed by nested namespaces. To avoid the need of typing the entire name of long (or nested) namespaces and writing long lines of code, the Visual Basic language offers the `Imports` directive. For example, consider the following lines of code that open a file on disk:

```
Dim myFile As New System.IO.FileStream("C:\test.bin",
                              IO.FileMode.Open)
```

```
myFile.Close()
```

The `FileStream` class is exposed by the `IO` namespace that is exposed by the `System` namespace. You could place the following directive at the beginning of the code:

```
Imports System.IO
```

At this point the first line of code could be rewritten as follows:

```
Dim myFile As New FileStream("C:\test.bin", FileMode.Open)
```

`Imports` directives are useful because they help to handle a much clearer code. Just remember that such directives must be the first lines of each code file. The only exception is constituted by the `Option` clause that must precede the `Imports` directives.

#Region..#End Region Directives

Visual Basic provides an efficient way for organizing your code within regions. A region represents a collapsible area of the code editor that can contain any code and that takes the advantage of the outlining feature of the Visual Studio 2010 code editor. Regions are defined with `#Region..#End Region` directives. The following code snippet shows how to define a region:

```
#Region "Private Members"
```

```
    Private firstItem As String
    Private secondItem As Integer
```

```
#End Region
```

The #Region directive requires the specification of a descriptive caption. When you declare regions, you can then collapse regions by clicking on the - (minus) symbol on the left of the #Region directive. When collapsed, the region shows just the descriptive caption and can then be expanded again by clicking on the + (plus) symbol. Also notice that the Visual Studio 2010 IDE allows collapsing a region by double-clicking anywhere on the #Region..#End Region connector line on the left side of the code window. Such directives will not be compiled and will not affect performances at all.

Attributes

Attributes are classes deriving from the System.Attribute class and provide declarative information to objects or members they are applied to, providing also the ability to change their behavior. As a convention, applying an attribute is also known as *decorating* or *marking* a member. Attributes are basically class instances; you can apply attributes enclosing their names within < > symbols; moreover they can receive arguments. The following are examples of decorating members with attributes:

```
<Serializable()> Class Test
```

```
End Class
```

```
<CLSCompliant(True)> Class Test
```

```
End Class
```

In the preceding snippets, the Serializable attribute creates a new instance of the System.SerializableAttribute class that indicates to the compiler that the decorated class can take advantage of the serialization process. The CLSCompliant attribute, whose value is True, means that the decorated class is compliant to Microsoft's Common Language Specifications. Attributes are discussed in Chapter 48, "Coding Attributes," and you often find examples in this book that require code to be decorated with attributes.

A New Feature: Implicit Line Continuation

Visual Basic 2010 introduces an important new feature when writing code (which is a historical change in the language) known as *implicit line continuation*. Back in older versions, if you needed to split a long line of code into more brief and readable lines of code in the editor, you needed to add an underscore (_) character. With Visual Basic 2010 this is no longer necessary, with a few exceptions. You can simply press Enter when you need to split a line of code, and the compiler will automatically recognize a line continuation, depending on what kind of code you are writing.

TIP

Implicit line continuation is not mandatory. If you prefer adding underscores for line continuation, of course you are still allowed to do it.

The following are situations in which the implicit line continuation is allowed:

▶ Within LINQ queries

▶ Within embedded expressions in LINQ to XML queries

▶ After dots

▶ After commas

▶ After brackets

▶ When decorating members with attributes

▶ Before an assignment

Let's see how implicit line continuation works. The first code snippet shows a LINQ query:

```
Dim query = From proc In Process.GetProcesses.AsEnumerable
            Where (proc.ProcessName.StartsWith("A"))
            Select proc
```

In Visual Basic 2008 you needed to add an underscore after the first and second line of code. Now this is no longer necessary. The second code snippet shows a LINQ to Xml query with embedded expressions without underscores:

```
Dim doc = <?xml version="1.0"?>
          <Processes>
            <%= From proc In query
              Select <Process>
                            <Name <%= proc.ProcessName %>/>
                     </Process>
            %>
          </Processes>
```

The third code snippet shows both commas and brackets without underscores:

```
Dim p As New List(Of Integer) From {
                               1,
                               2,
                               3,
                               4}
```

The fourth code snippet is about dots. In this case implicit line continuation can be useful when invoking methods or properties:

```
Dim appDataDir As String = My.Computer.FileSystem.
SpecialDirectories.AllUsersApplicationData()
```

The fifth code snippet shows implicit line continuation with attributes:

```
<CLSCompliant(True)>
Class Test

End Class
```

The sixth and last code snippet demonstrates how you can use implicit line continuation before an assignment:

```
Dim aValue As Integer
aValue =
        10
```

All the preceding code snippets are now perfectly legal. In all cases of the preceding examples, implicit line continuation is not allowed. For example, you still must add an underscore after the Handles clause when handling events:

```
Private Sub AnEventHandler(ByVal sender As Object, ByVal e As EventArgs) _
                        Handles anObject.Disposed

End Sub
```

Although you might expect such discussion in Chapter 2, "Getting Started with the Visual Studio 2010 IDE," about the code editor, you first need to get an overview of concepts that help you understand where implicit line continuation is allowed or disallowed.

Visual Basic 2010 Reserved Keywords

When writing code, you often define types or declare variables. Types and variables are recognizable via *identifiers*. An identifier is essentially the name of a type or of a variable and not necessarily a word that makes sense, although it is a good practice to assign human readable identifiers. For example, an identifier such as *DoSomething* is much better than *DoSmt*. For this, there are some words in the Visual Basic lexical grammar that you cannot use as identifiers for your variables because they are reserved for the language.

IDENTIFIERS NAMING CONVENTIONS

.NET programming principles establish that identifiers must match some rules when writing code, including identifiers. Such naming conventions are stated by the Common Language Specifications that are covered in Chapter 21, "Advanced Languages Features." For now keep in mind the best practice regarding human readable identifiers. Later in the book you learn how identifiers should be correctly written.

Table 3.1 shows a list of the Visual Basic 2010 reserved words.

TABLE 3.1   Visual Basic 2010 Reserved Keywords

AddHandler	AddressOf	Alias	And
AndAlso	As	Boolean	ByRef
Byte	ByVal	Call	Case
Catch	CBool	CByte	CChar
CDate	CDbl	CDec	Char
CInt	Class	CLng	CObj
Const	Continue	CSByte	CShort
CSng	CStr	CType	CUInt
CULng	CUShort	Date	Decimal
Declare	Default	Delegate	Dim
DirectCast	Do	Double	Each
Else	ElseIf	End	EndIf
Enum	Erase	Error	Event
Exit	False	Finally	For
Friend	Function	Get	GetType
GetXmlNamespace	Global	GoSub	GoTo
Handles	If	Implements	Imports
In	Inherits	Integer	Interface
Is	IsNot	Let	Lib
Like	Long	Loop	Me
Mod	Module	MustInherit	MustOverride
MyBase	MyClass	Namespace	Narrowing
New	Next	Not	Nothing

TABLE 3.1   Continued

NotInheritable	NotOverridable	Object	Of
On	Operator	Option	Optional
Or	OrElse	Overloads	Overridable
Overrides	ParamArray	Partial	Private
Property	Protected	Public	RaiseEvent
ReadOnly	ReDim	REM	RemoveHandler
Resume	Return	SByte	Select
Set	Shadows	Shared	Short
Single	Static	Step	Stop
String	Structure	Sub	SyncLock
Then	Throw	To	True
Try	TryCast	TypeOf	UInteger
ULong	UShort	Using	Variant
Wend	When	While	Widening
With	WithEvents	WriteOnly	Xor

USING RESERVED WORDS AS IDENTIFIERS

As an exception, you can use reserved words as identifiers enclosing them in a couple of square brackets. For example, New is a reserved word and cannot be used whereas [New] can be accepted. Although allowed, this practice should be used only in particular cases because it could lead to confusion, especially if you are not an experienced developer.

Although the code editor is powerful enough to advise when you are attempting to use a reserved keyword as an identifier, having a reference is practical.

VISUAL BASIC IS CASE-INSENSITIVE

When writing code remember that Visual Basic is a case-insensitive programming language. This means that, differently from C#, writing Hello is the same of writing HELLO or hello or heLLo. Take care with this feature when assigning identifiers.

Understanding Project Files

Each Visual Basic project is composed of several code files. Some of them are by default visible to the developer and are the ones that you need to edit to create your application. There are also some other files (which are hidden by default but that can be made visible manually) that we can consider as support files. To understand what kind of support these files offer, we have to think that most of the settings that we can provide to our applications via the My Project window are represented with Visual Basic code. Particularly, Visual Basic translates into code the content of the Application, Resources, Settings and My Extensions tabs. In this chapter you get a detailed description of files that represent the Application tab in My Project and then you get an overview of files that represent other tabs. Although you seldom edit these code files manually, because all of them have design time support from My Project (as detailed in Chapter 20, "The 'My' Namespace," when describing the My namespace), there could be some situations in which you need to manually edit them, so it's important to know something about them. Before going on, you need to click the **Show All Files** button in Solution Explorer. This gives visibility to several code files that are hidden by default and that provide the main infrastructure for each Visual Basic project.

Dissecting My Project

In Chapter 2 we introduced the My Project window and saw how it offers graphical tools for specifying some settings when developing applications, such as application information and compile options. Understanding My Project is important because it also provides the infrastructure of the My namespace, offering the ability for specifying important settings that are discussed in Chapter 20. For now, we need to know that My Project offers a graphical representation of information that is stored in some code files. In Solution Explorer you can notice an element named My Project. When you double-click this element, you are redirected to the My Project window. But when you enable the All Files view, you notice how the My Project element becomes a folder that can be expanded. Within this folder (which is physically stored inside the project's folder and contains all files described in this section), you can notice the presence of several files packaged into the assembly's metadata when you build the project. We now describe such files and how they work.

MY PROJECT IS VERSATILE

Depending on what kind of application you develop, My Project can implement additional tabs or remove some. For example, if you develop a Silverlight application you can find tabs in My Project that are specific for Silverlight and that will be discussed in the appropriate chapters.

Application.MyApp

The Application.myapp file is an XML representation of the project's main properties. Listing 3.1 shows the content of this file as it becomes available when you create a new Console application.

LISTING 3.1   The Content of Application.myapp

```
<?xml version="1.0" encoding="utf-8"?>
<MyApplicationData xmlns:xsi="http://www.w3.org/2001/XMLSchema-instance"
xmlns:xsd="http://www.w3.org/2001/XMLSchema">
  <MySubMain>false</MySubMain>
  <SingleInstance>false</SingleInstance>
  <ShutdownMode>0</ShutdownMode>
  <EnableVisualStyles>true</EnableVisualStyles>
  <AuthenticationMode>0</AuthenticationMode>
  <ApplicationType>2</ApplicationType>
  <SaveMySettingsOnExit>true</SaveMySettingsOnExit>
</MyApplicationData>
```

XML elements in this file are self-explanatory, and you may notice how each of them represents a particular item on the Application tab. The Application.myapp file is the brother of another file named Application.Designer.vb. Such a file basically stores information related to Windows Forms applications such as the authentication mode and the shutdown mode. It is the complement for those application options that you can see in the Windows Application Framework Properties group in the Application tab. Listing 3.2 shows the content of the Application.Designer.vb as it is generated for a Windows Forms application.

LISTING 3.2   The Content of Application.Designer.vb

```
Partial Friend Class MyApplication

        Public Sub New()
            MyBase.New(Global.Microsoft.VisualBasic.ApplicationServices.
    AuthenticationMode.Windows)
            Me.IsSingleInstance = false
            Me.EnableVisualStyles = true
            Me.SaveMySettingsOnExit = true
            Me.ShutDownStyle = Global.Microsoft.VisualBasic.ApplicationServices.
    ShutdownMode.AfterMainFormCloses
        End Sub

        Protected Overrides Sub OnCreateMainForm()
            Me.MainForm = Global.WindowsApplication1.Form1
        End Sub
End Class
```

For the sake of simplicity, in the preceding code some attributes are omitted that Visual Studio adds to class members and that are related to the debugger interaction. As you can see examining Listing 3.2, items in the Application tab of My Project have been mapped to Visual Basic properties. The Me identifier represents the instance of the current application. The OnCreateMainForm method establishes which window must be the startup one. In this case Form1 is the default name that Visual Studio assigns to the main window when a new project is created. If you also examine the code inside the IDE, you can notice how there are some comments in the code that advise that the code itself is auto-generated and that you should not edit it manually, because you can use the My Project designer that will automatically map changes to the Visual Basic code. You might need to set custom actions for application events (such as Startup or Shutdown, which are usually handled in the ApplicationEvents.vb file) and **Application.designer.vb** is the right place.

AssemblyInfo.vb

In Chapter 2 we discussed the **Assembly Information** dialog, describing how it is used for specifying information about applications. All the information is stored in a file named **AssemblyInfo.vb**. Listing 3.3 shows the content of this file as it is available when you create a new project.

LISTING 3.3   AssemblyInfo.vb Content

```
Imports System
Imports System.Reflection
Imports System.Runtime.InteropServices


' General Information about an assembly is controlled through the following
' set of attributes. Change these attribute values to modify the information
' associated with an assembly.


' Review the values of the assembly attributes

<Assembly: AssemblyTitle("WindowsApplication1")>
<Assembly: AssemblyDescription("")>
<Assembly: AssemblyCompany("")>
<Assembly: AssemblyProduct("WindowsApplication1")>
<Assembly: AssemblyCopyright("Copyright © 2009")>
<Assembly: AssemblyTrademark("")>

<Assembly: ComVisible(False)>

'The following GUID is for the ID of the typelib if this project is exposed to COM
<Assembly: Guid("5572d199-a7ca-48c3-98d3-56533cd6ba86")>
```

```
' Version information for an assembly consists of the following four values:
'
'       Major Version
'       Minor Version
'       Build Number
'       Revision
'
' You can specify all the values or you can default the Build and Revision Numbers
' by using the '*' as shown below:
' <Assembly: AssemblyVersion("1.0.*")>

<Assembly: AssemblyVersion("1.0.0.0")>
<Assembly: AssemblyFileVersion("1.0.0.0")>
```

As you can notice examining the Visual Basic code shown in Listing 3.3, there are several items whose identifier begins with the word Assembly, such as `AssemblyTitle`, `AssemblyCompany`, and so on. Each item is in relationship with fields of the Assembly Information dialog. Moreover such items are marked with an attribute named `Assembly`. Attributes are discussed in Chapter 48. The reason why it is useful knowing about the above file is that there are situations in which you need to edit this file manually. Examples are localization of WPF applications or marking an assembly as compliant to *Microsoft Common Language Specifications*.

Resources and the Resources.resx File

Visual Studio 2010 enables defining resources that you can embed in your assembly's metadata and use within your applications. Resources can include strings, icons, picture files, audio files, and so on. My Project offers a tab named Resources that provides a visual way for defining project level resources.

PRACTICAL USAGE OF RESOURCES

Although available in several kinds of projects, resources have to be used to fit particular scenarios. For example resources can be successfully used in Windows applications such as Console and Windows Forms, but they are not the best choice for Windows Presentation Foundation applications. So you need to pay attention when using resources according to the particular situations.

Figure 3.1 shows the Resources designer with the definition of a `String` resource named `TextMessage` that has a value and a description. We revisit the Resources tab in Chapter 20, where we discuss My namespace, but if you are curious, you can play with the designer to see what kind of resources you can add.

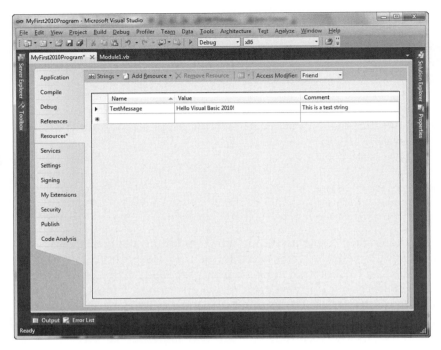

FIGURE 3.1   The My Resources designer.

Resources are supported by two files stored inside the My Project folder: Resources.resx and Resources.designer.vb. The first one is basically an XML schema used by Visual Studio for working with resources. Listing 3.4 shows the content of the schema.

LISTING 3.4   The Content of Resources.resx

```
<root>
  <xsd:schema id="root" xmlns="" xmlns:xsd="http://www.w3.org/2001/XMLSchema"
  xmlns:msdata="urn:schemas-microsoft-com:xml-msdata">
    <xsd:import namespace="http://www.w3.org/XML/1998/namespace" />
    <xsd:element name="root" msdata:IsDataSet="true">
      <xsd:complexType>
        <xsd:choice maxOccurs="unbounded">
          <xsd:element name="metadata">
            <xsd:complexType>
              <xsd:sequence>
                <xsd:element name="value" type="xsd:string" minOccurs="0" />
              </xsd:sequence>
              <xsd:attribute name="name" use="required" type="xsd:string" />
              <xsd:attribute name="type" type="xsd:string" />
              <xsd:attribute name="mimetype" type="xsd:string" />
```

```xml
                <xsd:attribute ref="xml:space" />
              </xsd:complexType>
            </xsd:element>
            <xsd:element name="assembly">
              <xsd:complexType>
                <xsd:attribute name="alias" type="xsd:string" />
                <xsd:attribute name="name" type="xsd:string" />
              </xsd:complexType>
            </xsd:element>
            <xsd:element name="data">
              <xsd:complexType>
                <xsd:sequence>
                  <xsd:element name="value" type="xsd:string" minOccurs="0"
msdata:Ordinal="1" />
                  <xsd:element name="comment" type="xsd:string" minOccurs="0"
msdata:Ordinal="2" />
                </xsd:sequence>
                <xsd:attribute name="name" type="xsd:string" use="required"
msdata:Ordinal="1" />
                <xsd:attribute name="type" type="xsd:string" msdata:Ordinal="3" />
                <xsd:attribute name="mimetype" type="xsd:string" msdata:Ordinal="4" />
                <xsd:attribute ref="xml:space" />
              </xsd:complexType>
            </xsd:element>
            <xsd:element name="resheader">
              <xsd:complexType>
                <xsd:sequence>
                  <xsd:element name="value" type="xsd:string" minOccurs="0"
msdata:Ordinal="1" />
                </xsd:sequence>
                <xsd:attribute name="name" type="xsd:string" use="required" />
              </xsd:complexType>
            </xsd:element>
          </xsd:choice>
        </xsd:complexType>
      </xsd:element>
    </xsd:schema>
    <resheader name="resmimetype">
      <value>text/microsoft-resx</value>
    </resheader>
    <resheader name="version">
      <value>2.0</value>
    </resheader>
    <resheader name="reader">
      <value>System.Resources.ResXResourceReader, System.Windows.Forms,
       Version=4.0.0.0, Culture=neutral, PublicKeyToken=b77a5c561934e089</value>
```

```
  </resheader>
  <resheader name="writer">
    <value>System.Resources.ResXResourceWriter, System.Windows.Forms, Ver-
sion=4.0.0.0, Culture=neutral, PublicKeyToken=b77a5c561934e089</value>
  </resheader>
  <data name="TextMessage" xml:space="preserve">
    <value>Hello Visual Basic 2010!</value>
    <comment>This is a test string</comment>
  </data>
</root>
```

This schema establishes how a resource is defined, with names, values, comments, and a *MIME* type that identifies the file type. At the end of the XML markup code, you can see how resources are stored. Continuing with our example, you can see the name of the resource (inside the data element), its value, and the description we provided via the designer. This schema is used by Visual Studio for design time purposes. To work with resources in our applications, Visual Studio also needs to provide Visual Basic code support for resources. Such support is provided by a code file named Resources.designer.vb. This file handles a reference to a .NET object called ResourceManager that is responsible for managing resources in code. Listing 3.5 shows the content of Resources.designer.vb. (For the sake of simplicity, auto-generated attributes are not covered here.)

LISTING 3.5   Content of Resources.designer.vb

```
Friend Module Resources


        Private resourceMan As Global.System.Resources.ResourceManager

        Private resourceCulture As Global.System.Globalization.CultureInfo

        Friend ReadOnly Property ResourceManager() As
        Global.System.Resources.ResourceManager
            Get
                If Object.ReferenceEquals(resourceMan, Nothing) Then
                    Dim temp As Global.System.Resources.ResourceManager =
        New Global.System.Resources.ResourceManager("MyFirst2010Program.Resources",
        GetType(Resources).Assembly)
                    resourceMan = temp
                End If
                Return resourceMan
            End Get
        End Property


        Friend Property Culture() As Global.System.Globalization.CultureInfo
            Get
```

```
            Return resourceCulture
        End Get
        Set(ByVal value As Global.System.Globalization.CultureInfo)
            resourceCulture = value
        End Set
    End Property

    Friend ReadOnly Property TextMessage() As String
        Get
            Return ResourceManager.GetString("TextMessage", resourceCulture)
        End Get
    End Property
End Module
```

At this point in the book you don't effectively need to know what each type used in code refers to, whereas it is useful to know the existence of the ResourceManager property that points to the project resources. (See the declaration of the temp variable.) This handles a reference to the application-level ResourceManager that enables access to resources. There is another property named Culture that is of type System.Globalization.CultureInfo. This property sets or returns the current localization for resources. The last property in the code is named TextMessage and is the Visual Basic representation of the string resource defined in My Project. This is a read-only property, because you cannot change it in code (you can change it only via designer) and returns a localized version of the resource invoking the GetString method of the ResourceManager class. GetString requires an object of type CultureInfo (in our code it's resourceCulture) that represents the culture that the resource must be localized to. The following line of code shows how you can access the preceding defined resource, which is discussed further in Chapter 20:

```
Dim myString As String = My.Resources.TextMessage
```

When you access resources, as shown in Chapter 20, you do not need to manually invoke this background code, but you need to know how it is structured to better understand what's happening behind the scenes. Resources are not the only feature in My Project that is supported by Visual Basic code for design time features. Settings are another one of these features.

Application Settings

Settings in Visual Basic development are particular objects that provide a managed way for manipulating applications and user level settings. For example, you could provide users with the ability of customizing options in the user interface of your application. To save and read such customizations to and from disk, you can use .NET Settings. My Project provides a tab named Settings that enables specifying information at the application or user level. Figure 3.2 shows an example.

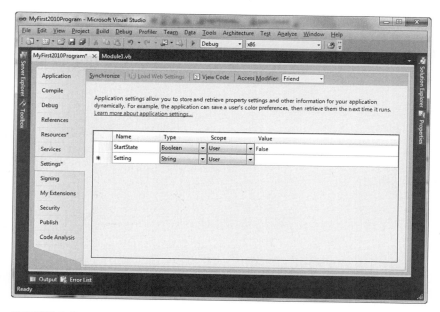

FIGURE 3.2   Settings Tab in My Project.

As you can see in Figure 3.2, you can specify an identifier for each setting, a type (which you can understand better by reading Chapter 4), the scope, and the value. For the scope, User means that only the user that runs the application can use that setting. Application means that the setting is available at the application level, independently from the user that logged into Windows (and therefore is available to all users). As with Resources, Settings will be also described in detail in Chapter 20. Settings are represented by a simple XML file, named Settings.settings. Listing 3.6 shows the content of Settings.settings after the addition of the sample setting.

VIEWING THE SETTINGS.SETTINGS FILE WITH THE XML EDITOR

In order to view the Xml content for the Settings.settings file, right-click the file name in Solution Explorer, select the **Open With** command and select **Xml (Text) Editor** in the Open With dialog.

LISTING 3.6   Settings.settings Content

```
<?xml version='1.0' encoding='utf-8'?>
<SettingsFile xmlns="http://schemas.microsoft.com/VisualStudio/2004/01/settings"
CurrentProfile="(Default)" GeneratedClassNamespace="My" GeneratedClass-
Name="MySettings" UseMySettingsClassName="true">
  <Profiles />
```

```
<Settings>
  <Setting Name="StartState" Type="System.Boolean" Scope="User">
    <Value Profile="(Default)">True</Value>
  </Setting>
</Settings>
</SettingsFile>
```

In the XML markup you can see the presence of a Settings node that stores as many Setting elements and as many settings that you specify in My Project. In our example there is just one Setting element that contains the name of the setting, the data type, the scope, and the default value (which means the value you specify in My Project). The Settings.settings file also has Visual Basic support, which is represented by another file named Settings.designer.vb. We do not need to examine all the content of this file when just a couple of parts of the code can be interesting for us. First, this file implements a property named Settings that is accessible via the My namespace, as detailed in Chapter 20. Listing 3.7 shows the definition of this property.

LISTING 3.7   Definition of the Settings Property

```
    Friend ReadOnly Property Settings() As
Global.MyFirst2010Program.My.MySettings
        Get
            Return Global.MyFirst2010Program.My.MySettings.Default
        End Get
    End Property
```

The Settings property represents the active instance of the Settings object that you can use in your applications. How the active instance is defined is beyond the scope of this chapter, but now you know that the Settings tab in My Project also has a counterpart in two support files. Just for your convenience, the following line of code shows how you can access settings and how we set them before:

```
Dim currentValue As Boolean = My.Settings.StartState
```

The value stored in the StartState setting will be assigned to a variable named currentValue. Examining My namespace in Chapter 20 can clarify the usage of Settings and Resources and of many other interesting features.

Understanding References

The Base Class Library exposes types through several assemblies that are part of the .NET Framework, and you will often need to invoke types from those assemblies. Moreover, although very rich, the BCL cannot define types covering every aspect of application development. This means that you will often need to use types exposed by other assemblies, such as other projects in the same solution or external compiled assemblies.

> **NOTE**
>
> Each time you create a new project, Visual Studio automatically adds references to some .NET assemblies that are necessary for each kind of application and that expose the BCL's core part, such as System.dll and System.Core.dll.

To use types defined in external assemblies, you need to *add a reference* in your project to the desired assembly. To accomplish this, right-click the project name in Solution Explorer and click the **Add Reference** command from the pop-up menu or select the **References** tab in My Project and click **Add**. This activates the Add reference dialog, as shown in Figure 3.3.

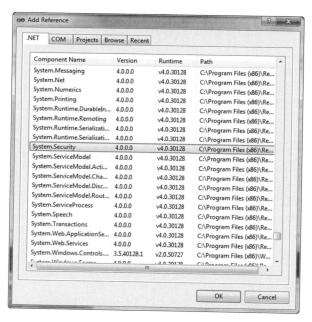

FIGURE 3.3   The Add Reference Dialog.

You need to select the assemblies you want to reference. More than one assembly can be selected by pressing **Ctrl** and then click on the name of the required assembly. The Add

Reference dialog is divided into several tabs. The default tab is named .NET and shows a list of all the available assemblies in the *Global Assembly Cache.*

WHAT IS THE GLOBAL ASSEMBLY CACHE?

The *Global Assembly Cache* (or *GAC*) can be described as a repository for information and locations on installed assemblies. The .NET Framework knows where assemblies can be found by browsing the GAC, which also can distinguish between different versions of an assembly. The GAC is discussed in detail in Chapter 53, "Understanding the Global Assembly Cache."

The Add Reference dialog shows the version number of assemblies; this is useful because you can have different versions of an assembly with the same name. It also shows the full path for the assembly. When you add a reference to an assembly, Solution Explorer updates the References node. For example, if you want to add security features to your applications, you need to add a reference to the System.Security.dll assembly (refer to Figure 3.3), which is part of the Base Class Library. When added, Solution Explorer looks like Figure 3.4.

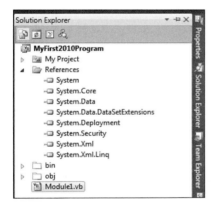

FIGURE 3.4   Solution Explorer is updated with the new reference.

You can use in your code types exposed by the specified assemblies that have *public visibility.* The Add Reference dialog provides other tabs. The Recent tab shows a list of all the most recently used assemblies for faster reuse. The Browse tab enables searching for assemblies that are not registered into the GAC. The Projects tab enables adding references to other projects in the solution. This is typically the case when you have a class library that exposes types that you want to use inside a client application. There is also another tab, named COM, which enables adding references to COM type libraries as we discuss next.

Adding References to COM Libraries

There could be situations in which you might be required to use COM type libraries in your .NET applications, scenario known also as COM Interop. This should be a spare scenario, because .NET and COM are such different architectures, and the second one was not born for working within the first one. Visual Studio 2010 enables you to add references to old type libraries. To accomplish this, you need to select the **COM** tab in the Add Reference dialog. All the registered COM type libraries will be shown within the dialog, and you can select needed components (see Figure 3.5).

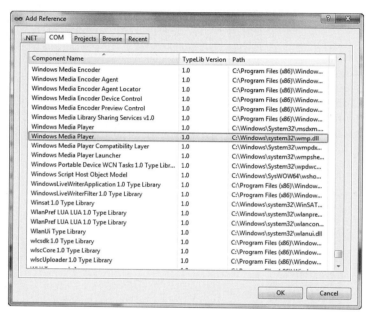

FIGURE 3.5   Adding a reference to a COM component.

For example, you might want to include the Windows Media Player functionalities in your application; for this purpose you can select the **Windows Media Player** component and then click **OK** (see Figure 3.5). Visual Studio will show a reference named WMPLib.dll in Solution Explorer and generate an assembly named Interop.WMPLib.dll. This assembly is a managed wrapper for the Windows Media Player component and will provide managed access to types exposed by the type library. More generally, Visual Studio generates an Interop.AssemblyName.dll assembly (where AssemblyName is the original name of the assembly) for each referenced type library, which is known as Primary Interoperability Assembly (also known as PIAs) and that allows interoperation between .NET and COM architectures. Different from previous versions of .NET Framework and Visual Studio, by default you no longer see the wrapper assemblies included in your build output because of a new feature called Deploy Without Primary Interoperability Assemblies.

Deploy Without PIAs

When deploying applications that reference a COM library, you also must include in your distribution the primary interoperability assemblies. In our example, the PIA is Interop.WMPLib.dll. In Visual Studio 2010 you can avoid including primary interoperability assemblies in your distributions, although you reference those assemblies. This is possible because Visual Studio can embed in your executable only the types that you effectively use from the referenced assembly. This avoids the need of including the assembly itself in the build output and, consequently, in the deployment process. For our sample scenario about including the Windows Media Player component, we could write a small application that has the name of a media file provided by the user and then launches WMP. Listing 3.8 accomplishes this.

LISTING 3.8   Using a COM Component in Code

```
Module Module1
    Sub Main()

        Console.WriteLine("Type the name of a media file:")
        Dim fileName As String = Console.ReadLine

        Dim wmp As New WMPLib.WindowsMediaPlayer
        wmp.openPlayer(fileName)
    End Sub
End Module
```

In the preceding code, you need to take a look at this simple line:

```
Dim wmp As New WMPLib.WindowsMediaPlayer
```

Declaring an instance of the `WMPLib.WindowsMediaPlayer` class is sufficient for Visual Studio to embed the definition of the `WindowsMediaPlayer` object inside our executable so that it will not need to include the entire Interop.WMPLib.dll assembly in the build output. As you may imagine, this is a great feature because if you have a large type library and you need to use only a few types, you can save space and preserve performances. The Deploy Without PIAs feature is enabled by default. If you instead prefer to avoid embedding types within your executable and including the primary interoperability assemblies in your build output, you simply need to right-click the referenced assembly in Solution Explorer and then click **Properties**. Continuing our example, we would need to select **WMPLib.dll** in Solution Explorer. The Properties window will show a property called Embed Interop Types that is set to True by default (see Figure 3.6).

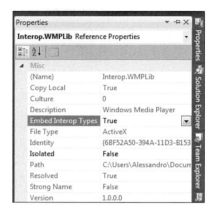

FIGURE 3.6   Enabling the Deploy Without PIAs feature setting
the Embed Interop Types property.

If you change the value to False, types will no longer be embedded in your executable, and the primary interoperability assemblies will be included in the build output.

VERIFYING TYPES EMBEDDING

If you are an experienced developer, you can easily verify if types have been embedded in your executable via the Deploy without PIAs feature by opening executables with tools such as Reflector or IL Disassembler.

Final Considerations

The first three chapters of this book provide a necessary overview of tools and features that you must understand before moving on. Now that you have completed the introductory steps, you are ready to get your hands dirty on the core of the Visual Basic 2010 programming language.

Summary

In this chapter you got an overview of some important language features. An overview was necessary because, before discussing a particular feature further, you need to know what that feature represents. You also got a complete list of the Visual Basic 2010 reserved words that you cannot use as identifiers for your variables. Another important topic we discussed is how a Visual Basic project is structured and what files compose a Visual Basic project. Finally, you got an overview of references and why they are important in developing applications. In this discussion you learned about a new feature of Visual Studio 2010 and .NET Framework 4.0: the deployment without the primary interoperability assemblies.

CHAPTER 4

Data Types and Expressions

Every programming task manipulates data. Data can be of different kinds; you will often work with strings, dates and time, numbers, files, and custom data. Each of them is represented by a data type. The .NET Framework 4.0 provides tons of built-in data types and enables developers to easily create their own custom data types. In this chapter you learn how the .NET Framework handles data types and how you can work with *value types* and *reference types*. When you gain knowledge of data types, you can learn how to use them with special Visual Basic language constraints such as loops, iterations, and special statements. This is a fundamental chapter, so you should pay particular attention to concepts that you need to understand before we discuss the object-oriented programming with Visual Basic 2010.

Common Type System

The .NET Framework provides a special way for manipulating data types, which is named *Common Type System*. The Common Type System is important, so you need to know something about it before reading discussions on data types. In its name, the word *Common* has two particular meanings. First, the Common Type System provides a unified model for exposing data types so that all the .NET languages, such as Visual Basic, Visual C#, and Visual F#, can consume the same data types. For example, a 32-bit integer is represented by the System.Int32 data type, and all the .NET languages can invoke the System.Int32 object for declaring integers because this type is provided by the

.NET Framework and is language-independent. Second, each data type is an object that inherits from the `System.Object` class as we discuss next.

Everything Is an Object

In the .NET development you may hear that everything is an object. This is because all the types in the .NET Framework, including built-in and custom types, inherit from the `System.Object` class. Inheritance is a concept that is part of the object-oriented programming topic and that will be discussed later in the book. We can define it as a way for reusing and extending data types so that developers can create their hierarchy of types. `System.Object` provides the primary infrastructure that all .NET types must have. The .NET Framework ships with thousands of built-in data types that all derive from `System.Object`. But why is this class so important in the Common Type System? The answer is simple: the Common Type System ensures that all .NET types inherit from `System.Object`; particularly both *value types* and *reference types* inherit from `System.Object`. At this point an overview of value types and reference types is required, before delving into both categories.

Introducing Value Types and Reference Types

Basically value types are those data types that store their data directly. Examples of value types are integers (`System.Int32`), Boolean (`System.Boolean`), and bytes (`System.Byte`). Value types are stored in a memory area called *Stack*. They are represented by (and defined via) structures that are enclosed in `Structure..End Structure` code blocks. The following is an example of a value type containing a value:

```
Dim anInteger As System.Int32 = 5
```

Reference types are instead data types that, as their name implies, are just a reference to the actual data. In other words, reference types store the address of their data in the Stack whereas the actual data is stored in the managed Heap. Reference types are represented by classes. The following is an example of reference type:

```
Class Person
    Property FirstName As String
    Property LastName As String
End Class
```

DON'T BE AFRAID OF MEMORY LOCATIONS

This paragraph is just an overview of value types and reference types. If you never heard about the Stack and the Managed Heap, don't worry. Details will be provided later in this chapter, when discussing value and reference types.

Reference types inherit directly from `System.Object` or from other classes that derive from `Object`. This is because `System.Object` is a reference type. So the question that you will probably ask now is, "If both value types and reference types have to inherit from System.Object, how can value types inherit from System.Object if it is a reference type?" The answer is that in the case of value types there is an intermediate type that is named System.ValueType that inherits from System.Object and ensures that all deriving objects are treated as value types. This is possible because the Common Language Runtime can distinguish how types are defined and consequently can distinguish between value types and reference types.

NAMING SYSTEM.OBJECT

Object is also a reserved word of the Visual Basic programming language and is the representation of System.Object. Because of this, we refer indistinctly to Object as System.Object.

System.Object and System.ValueType

At this point it is necessary to provide an overview of both System.Object and System.ValueType. Instead of showing a diagram of inheritance, it is a good idea to offer a Visual Studio-oriented view so that you can better understand what happens within the development environment. This can be accomplished via the Object Browser tool window that we introduced in Chapter 2, "Getting Started with the Visual Studio 2010 IDE." You can browse for both classes by just writing their name in the search box. Figure 4.1 shows how System.Object is defined, what members it exposes, and a full description.

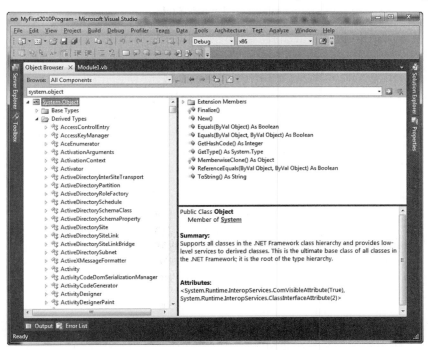

FIGURE 4.1   System.Object shown in detail in the Object Browser tool window.

Several things are worth mentioning. First, consider the class description. As you can see, System.Object is defined as the root of the type hierarchy, and all other classes within the .NET Framework derive from System.Object. This means that custom classes automatically inherit from Object. This class provides the infrastructure for all derived classes and exposes some methods. Because System.Object is important and because you will often invoke methods inherited from Object, it's convenient to get a simple reference for each method. Table 4.1 describes methods exposed by System.Object.

TABLE 4.1   Methods Exposed by System.Object

Method	Description
Equals	Compares two objects for equality
Finalize	Attempts to free up some resources during the object lifetime
New	Creates a new instance of the Object class
GetHashCode	Returns a hash code for the given object
GetType	Retrieves the qualified data type for the specified object
MemberwiseClone	Creates a shallow copy of the current Object instance
ReferenceEquals	Returns true if both the specified Object instances refer to the same instance
ToString	Provides a string representation of the Object

Methods listed in Table 4.1 are covered several times during the rest of the book, so don't be afraid if something is not clear at the moment. If you now refer back to Figure 4.1, you can see how the Object class has no base types. This is because, as we said before, Object is the root in the type hierarchy. Considering this last sentence, if you instead try to expand the Derived types node, you see a list of hundreds of .NET Framework built-in classes that derive from Object. One of these classes is System.ValueType. Figure 4.2 shows how this class is represented in the Object Browser.

You should focus on the description first. As you can see, System.ValueType is the base class for all value types. It is declared as MustInherit (a clause discussed in detail in Chapter 12, "Inheritance") that means it must necessarily be inherited and that it can't work as a standalone object, providing the base infrastructure for derived value types. If you expand the Base types node, you see that ValueType is a derived class from Object. If you then try to expand the Derived types node, you get a large list of types that inherit from ValueType, such as Boolean, Byte, and other primitive data types. As we mentioned before, the CLR can determine that a type deriving from System.ValueType must be treated as a value type and not as a reference type.

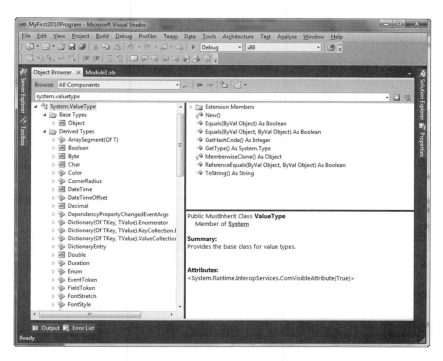

FIGURE 4.2   `System.ValueType` shown in detail in the Object Browser.

Understanding Value Types

Value types are data types that directly store data that they define. For example, a
`System.Int32` object represents a value type that can store an integer number as in the
following line of code:

```
Dim anInteger As System.Int32 = 5
```

Among value types, the most common are numeric types that enable, for example, performing math operations or implementing counters or just storing a numeric value. Value types
enable developers to choose the best data type according to the particular scenario. As we
mentioned at the beginning of this chapter, value types are basically `Structure` objects. The
.NET Framework provides several built-in value types that cover most needs in your development process, although you can create custom data types. In this section you learn about
most common built-in value types and about building your own structures, including how
value types are declared and used and how they are stored in memory.

.NET Framework Primitive Value Types

The .NET Framework Base Class Library provides lots of built-in value types that you can use according to your needs. Each value type is a structure exposed by the Base Class Library.

Visual Basic 2010 provides reserved words that are counterparts of the most common value type names. For example, the System.Int32 value type has an alias in the Integer reserved word. The following two lines of code are perfectly equivalent:

```
Dim anInteger As System.Int32 = 0
Dim anInteger As Integer = 0
```

You may use indistinctly both .NET names and the Visual Basic reserved words when referring to built-in value types.

NAMING CONVENTIONS

Although you are allowed to invoke value types with both .NET names and the Visual Basic counterparts' keywords, it's a best practice to choose the .NET names when developing reusable class libraries according to the Microsoft Common Language Specification. We discuss this topic later in this chapter. In such scenario it is a good practice because you should avoid language-dependent features and practices when developing assemblies bound to also work with other .NET languages. Basically this will not change the results, but your code will be cleaner, and you will use a .NET-oriented approach instead of a language-oriented one.

Table 4.2 lists the most common value types in the .NET Framework, showing a description and the Visual Basic-related keywords.

TABLE 4.2   Most Common Value Types in the .NET Framework 4.0

Value Type	Description	Visual Basic Reserved Keyword
System.Int16	Represents a numeric value with a range between −32768 and 32767.	Short
System.Int32	Represents a numeric value with a range between −2147483648 and 2147483647.	Integer
System.Int64	Represents a numeric value with a range between −9223372036854775808 and 9223372036854775807.	Long
System.Single	Represents a floating point number with a range from −3.4028235E+38 to 3.4028235E+38.	Single

TABLE 4.2   Continued

Value Type	Description	Visual Basic Reserved Keyword
System.Double	Represents a large floating number (double precision) with a range from −1.79769313486232e308 to 1.79769313486232e308.	Double
System.Boolean	Accepts True or False values.	Boolean
System.Char	Represents a single Unicode character.	Char
System.IntPtr	Represents a pointer to an address in memory.	–
System.DateTime	Represents dates, times, or both in different supported formats (see following paragraphs).	Date
System.Numerics.BigInteger	Represents an arbitrarily large integer with no maximum and minimum value.	–
System.Byte	Represents an unsigned byte, with a range from 0 to 255.	Byte
System.SByte	Represents a signed byte, with a range from −128 to 127.	SByte
System.UInt16	Represents a numeric positive value with range between 0 and 65535.	UShort
System.UInt32	Represents a numeric positive value with a range between 0 and 4294967295.	UInteger
System.UInt64	Represents a numeric positive value with a range between 0 and 18446744073709551615.	ULong
System.Decimal	Represents a decimal number in financial and scientific calculations with large numbers. A range between −79228162514264337593543950335 and 79228162514264337593543950335.	Decimal

TABLE 4.2   Continued

Value Type	Description	Visual Basic Reserved Keyword
System.TimeSpan	Represents an interval of time. The range is between -10675199.02:48:05.4775808 and 10675199.02:48:05.4775807 ticks.	
System.TimeZone	Represents time information according to the specific world's time zone.	
System.Guid	Allows generating *Globally Unique Identifiers*.	

UPGRADING FROM VISUAL BASIC 6

If you are upgrading from Visual Basic 6, you have to keep in mind that VB 6's Long is an Integer in .NET and that VB 6's Integer is now Short in .NET.

As you may notice in Table 4.2, most built-in value types are exposed by the System namespace except for the BigInteger type that is instead exposed by the System.Numerics namespace. BigInteger is a new type in the .NET Framework 4.0 and will be discussed later.

MEMORY REQUIREMENTS

You might wonder what should influence your choice when working with value types. The answer is that it depends. Of course you should take care of memory allocation. If you know that you need to work with a small number, you will probably do best if choosing a Byte instead of a Short. Regarding this, consider that Byte requires 8 bits, Short requires 16 bits, Integer and Single require 32 bits, Long and Double require 64 bits, and Decimal requires 128 bits. The Visual Basic compiler is optimized for 32-bit integers, so choosing Integer is of course a better choice than Short, but, in the case of very small numbers, choose Byte (1 byte) instead of Integer (4 bytes).

Using Value Types

In this paragraph you learn to use value types. The following demonstration assumes you have created a new Visual Basic project for the Console (see Chapter 2 for details). Listing 4.1 shows how you can declare variables storing value types. You can write the code inside the Main method for learning purposes.

LISTING 4.1   Using Value Types

```vb
Sub Main()
    'Declares an Integer
    Dim anInteger As Integer = 2

    'Declares a double and stores the result of a calculation
    Dim calculation As Double = 74.6 * 834.1

    'Declares one byte storing an hexadecimal value
    Dim oneByte As Byte = &H0

    'Declares a single character
    Dim oneCharacter As Char = "a"c

    'Declares a decimal number
    Dim sampleDecimal As Decimal = 8743341.353531135D

    'Declares a Boolean variable
    Dim isTrueOrFalse As Boolean = True

    'Declares a BigInteger
    Dim arbitraryInteger As New System.Numerics.BigInteger(800000)

    Console.WriteLine(anInteger)
    Console.WriteLine(calculation)
    Console.WriteLine(oneByte)
    Console.WriteLine(oneCharacter)
    Console.WriteLine(isTrueOrFalse)
    Console.WriteLine(arbitraryInteger)

    Console.ReadLine()
End Sub
```

You can declare variables of the desired value types using the `Dim` keyword followed by the identifier of the variable and by the `As` clause that then requires the type specification.

NOTES ABOUT DIM AND AS

`Dim` is the most important keyword for declaring variables and is commonly used in local code blocks. It is also worth mentioning that in .NET Framework you can declare different kinds of objects both with `Dim` and with other keywords according to the scope of the objects (such as fields, properties, classes). This is discussed in Chapter 7, "Class Fundamentals." Then in Chapter 21, "Advanced Language Features," you learn about another important feature in .NET Framework known as the Local Type Inference that avoids the need to add the `As` clause in particular scenarios such as data access with LINQ.

You can also declare more than one variable within the same `Dim` statement. You can write something like this:

```
Dim anInteger As Integer = 2, calculation As Double = 3.14,
    TrueOrFalse As Boolean = True
```

You can also declare more than one variable of the same type just by specifying such a type once, as in the following line of code:

```
'Three integers
Dim anInteger, secondInteger, thirdInteger As Integer
```

If you upgrade from Visual Basic 6, this is a great change because in a declaration like the preceding one VB 6 automatically assigns `Variant` instead of the appropriate data type. Generally you do not need to specify the constructor (the `New` keyword) when declaring value types. This is because in such situations the constructor addition is implicit and provided by the compiler behind the scenes. An exception to this general rule is the `BigInteger` type that instead allows the constructor to be explicit but it also allows in-line initialization. Listing 4.1 also shows how you can get the value stored in value types. In our example values are written to the Console window, but you can use values the most appropriate way for you. Figure 4.3 shows the result of the code in Listing 4.1.

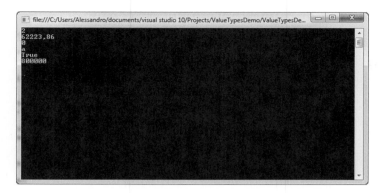

FIGURE 4.3   Using value types in our sample code produced this result.

Pay attention about using `Char` data types. `Char` represents a single character and differs from `String` because the latter one represents a set of characters. Because both types require their content to be enclosed within quotes, the value of a `Char` must be followed by the `C` letter that tells the compiler to treat that value as a single character. The `Decimal` data type also has a similar behavior. When you declare a decimal value (see Listing 4.1) you must ensure that the value is followed by the upper `D` character; otherwise the compiler treats the number as a `Double` raising an error. Identifiers like C and D are also known as *literal type characters* and are available for a number of primitive types, as summarized in Table 4.3.

TABLE 4.3   Literal type characters

Character	Type	Sample
C	Char	oneChar = "s"C
D	Decimal	oneDec = 87.2D
F	Single	oneSingle = 87.2F
I	Integer	anInt = 18I
L	Long	oneLong = 1324L
R	Double	oneDouble = 1234R
S	Short	oneShort = 18S
UI	UInteger	anInt = 18UI
UL	ULong	oneLong = 1324UL
US	UShort	oneShort = 18US

Literal type characters are not available for the following types:

▶ Boolean

▶ Byte

▶ Date

▶ Object

▶ SByte

▶ String

Assigning Value Types

At the beginning of the section we mentioned that value types directly store the data they refer to. This can be easily verified with assignments. Consider the following code:

```
Sub DoAssignments()

    Dim anInteger As Integer = 10
    Dim anotherInteger As Integer = anInteger

    Console.WriteLine(anInteger)
    Console.WriteLine(anotherInteger)

    Console.ReadLine()

End Sub
```

This code produces the following output:

```
10
10
```

This is because the value of anInteger has been assigned to another variable of type Integer, named anotherInteger. anotherInteger is basically a copy of the first variable and lives its own life, independent from anInteger. If you now write the following line of code after anotherInteger assignment

```
anotherInteger = 5
```

the code produces the following output:

```
10
5
```

So you have changed the value of anotherInteger while you left unchanged the value of anInteger, because they are two different objects with separate lives. Although this can appear obvious, it is important because it is the base for understanding later the different behavior in reference types. You may also use assignments in situations in which you need to get a result without knowing values that produce the result itself, such as in calculations that require an input from the user. With regard to this, consider the following code:

```
Dim firstNumber As Double = 567.43
Dim secondNumber As Double = 321.52

Dim result As Double = firstNumber * secondNumber

Console.WriteLine(result)
Console.ReadLine()
```

In the preceding code you get the result of a multiplication given two numbers. In real scenarios, the two numbers would be provided by the user and the result variable would store the result of the calculation. Such calculations are performed not on numbers but on the value of variables that store numbers. This means that you do not need to know in advance the numbers; you just work on variables and assignments.

> **NOTE**
>
> I could of course show a code example in which the input should be provided by the user. I have not yet discussed reference types, conversion operators, and parsing methods that will be discussed later, so my intent was to avoid confusion because user input is provided as String objects. There will be appropriate code examples when needed, as in the next paragraph.

Analyzing the Content of Value Types

In most cases you will require users to enter an input that you will then need to elaborate, or you could simply read the content of a text file and then convert such content into the appropriate .NET value type. Typically user input is provided as strings, and you will also get strings when reading text files. Although in business applications you need to implement validation rules on the user input, it is worth mentioning that value types offer common methods for analyzing the contents of a string and check if such content matches a particular value type. Even if we have not discussed yet the String object (which is a reference type), the following code samples are easy to understand. For example, consider the following code that declares some strings:

```
Dim firstValue As String = "1000"
Dim secondValue As String = "True"
Dim thirdValue As String = "123.456"
```

The content of each string is a representation of a particular value type: firstValue content represents an Integer, secondValue represents a Boolean, and thirdValue represents a Double. We could parse the content of each string and transform it into the appropriate value type as follows:

```
Dim anInteger As Integer = Integer.Parse(firstValue)
Dim aBoolean As Boolean = Boolean.Parse(secondValue)
Dim aDouble As Double = Double.Parse(thirdValue)
```

As you can see, value types expose a method called Parse that converts the string representation of a numeric or logical value into the correspondent value type. Integer.Parse converts the "1000" string into a 1000 integer and so on. If the compiler cannot perform the conversion, a FormatException error will be thrown, and the application execution will be broken. To avoid possible errors, you could use another method called TryParse that returns True if the conversion succeeds or False if it fails. For example, consider the following code:

```
Dim testInteger As Integer
Dim result = Integer.TryParse(secondValue, testInteger)
```

The code attempts to convert a string that contains the representation of a Boolean value into an Integer. Because this is not possible, TryParse returns False. Notice that in this particular case you don't perform an assignment to another variable (such as in the case of Parse) because TryParse requires the variable that will store the value as the second argument, passed by reference (a more detailed explanation on passing arguments by reference will be provided in Chapter 7).

VALUE TYPES METHODS

Because the purpose of this book is to examine the Visual Basic 2010 language features, whereas it cannot be possible to examine all the .NET Framework available types and members, only methods common to all value types are described. Methods and members specific to some value types are left to you for future studies. Always remember that when you do not know an object member, IntelliSense and the Object Browser together with the MSDN documentation can be your best friends, providing useful information.

Value types (including System.Char and System.DateTime) also expose two properties named MinValue and MaxValue that respectively contain the minimum accepted value and the maximum accepted value for each type. For example, the following line of code

```
Console.WriteLine(Integer.MinValue)
```

produces -2147483648 as the result. The following line of code

```
Console.WriteLine(Char.MaxValue)
```

produces the ? character as the result. Finally, the following line of code

```
Console.WriteLine(Date.MaxValue)
```

produces 31/12/9999 23:59:59 as the result.

MinValue and MaxValue can be useful for two purposes: The first purpose is for times you don't remember the minimum and maximum values accepted by a particular value type, whereas the second purppose is about comparisons; you might need to check if a value or a number is in the range of accepted values by a particular data type. Now we have completed a general overview of value types. Next studies focus on optimizations and on using special value types such as System.DateTime.

Optimization Considerations

When working with value types, you should always choose the best type fitting your needs. For example, if you need to work with a number that is composed in the Integer range, it would not be a good idea to use a Long type. Moreover, the Visual Basic compiler (and, behind the scenes, the CLR) provides optimizations for the System.Int32 and System.Double types, so you should always use these types when possible. For example, use an Int32 instead of an Int16 although the number you work with is composed in the range of the Int16. Other considerations about unsigned value types are related to compliance with *Microsoft Common Language Specification*, which is a topic discussed later in this chapter.

VALUE TYPES MEMORY ALLOCATION

You may wonder where value types are allocated in memory. The answer is that they are allocated in the area of memory called Stack. A full description will be provided after discussing reference types so that you can get a complete comparison.

NULLABLE TYPES

There are situations in which you need to assign null values to value types, for example when mapping SQL Server data types to .NET data types for fetching data. To accomplish this, the .NET Framework provides support for the Nullable types. Because nullable types have the syntax of Generics objects, and therefore you first need to know how Generics work, they will be discussed in Chapter 14, "Generics and Nullable Types."

Working with `BigInteger`

Because the `System.Numerics.BigInteger` is a new type in .NET 4.0, we spend a little time on it. `BigInteger` is a value type exposed by the System.Numerics namespace and requires a reference to the System.Numerics.dll assembly. Basically it represents a signed, arbitrarily large integer number. This means that it doesn't have minimum and maximum values, opposite of other value types such as `Integer` and `Long`. Instantiating a `BigInteger` is easy, as you can see from the following line of code:

```
Dim sampleBigInteger As New System.Numerics.BigInteger
```

You can assign any signed number to a `BigInteger`, because it has no minimum and maximum values, as demonstrated by the following code snippet:

```
'Neither minimum nor maximum values
sampleBigInteger = Byte.MinValue
sampleBigInteger = Long.MaxValue
```

`Byte` and `Long` are the smallest and the biggest acceptable signed integers. This special type directly supports integer types such as `SByte`, `Byte`, `UInteger`, `Integer`, `UShort`, `Short`, `ULong`, and `Long`. You can also assign to a `BigInteger` values of type `Double`, `Single`, and `Decimal`, but you do need to accomplish this passing the value as an argument to the constructor or performing an explicit conversion using `CType` (assuming that `Option Strict` is `On`). The following code demonstrates both situations:

```
'The constructor can receive arguments, Double is accepted
Dim sampleBigInteger2 As New _
                  System.Numerics.BigInteger(123456.789)

'Single is accepted but with explicit conversion
Dim singleValue As Single = CSng(1234.56)
Dim sampleBigInteger3 As New System.Numerics.BigInteger
sampleBigInteger3 = CType(singleValue, _
                  Numerics.BigInteger)
```

Notice that rounding will occur when converting floating types to `BigInteger`. Such structure also offers shared methods for performing arithmetic operations. You can add, subtract, divide, and multiply `BigIntegers` as in the following code:

```
'Assumes an Imports System.Numerics directive
'Sum
Dim sum As BigInteger =
    BigInteger.Add(sampleBigInteger, sampleBigInteger2)

'Subtract
Dim subtraction As BigInteger =
    BigInteger.Subtract(sampleBigInteger, sampleBigInteger2)
```

```
'Division
Dim division As BigInteger =
    BigInteger.Divide(sampleBigInteger, sampleBigInteger3)
```

```
'Multiplication
Dim multiplication As BigInteger =
    BigInteger.Multiply(sampleBigInteger2, sampleBigInteger3)
```

You can also perform complex operations, such as exponentiation and logarithm calculations as demonstrated here:

```
'Power
Dim powerBI As BigInteger = BigInteger.Pow(sampleBigInteger2, 2)
```

```
'10 base logarithm
Dim log10 As Double = BigInteger.Log10(sampleBigInteger3)
```

```
'natural base logarithm
Dim natLog As Double = BigInteger.Log(sampleBigInteger, 2)
```

As usual, IntelliSense can be your best friend when exploring methods from `BigInteger` and can help you understand what other math calculations you can perform.

Building Custom Value Types

Building custom value types is accomplished by creating *structures*. Because creating structures can also be a complex task and is part of the object-oriented programming topic, it is thoroughly discussed in Chapter 11, "Structures and Enumerations."

Understanding Reference Types

Reference types are represented by classes. Classes are probably the most important items in modern programming languages and are the basis of the object-oriented programming as we see later in the book. Reference types have one big difference versus value types: Variables that declare a reference type do not store the data of the type itself, whereas they just store an address to the data. In other words, they are just pointers to the data. To better explain (and understand) this fundamental concept, an example is necessary. Consider the following class `Person`, which exposes two simple properties:

```
Class Person


    Property FirstName As String
    Property LastName As String


End Class
```

You need to instantiate (that is, create an instance of) such a class so that you can then store data (in this case, setting properties) and then manipulate the same data. This can be accomplished by the following line of codes:

```
Dim onePerson As New Person
onePerson.FirstName = "Alessandro"
onePerson.LastName = "Del Sole"
```

STRONGLY TYPED OBJECTS

In .NET development, you often encounter the words *strongly typed*. This definition can be explained with an example. The onePerson object in the preceding code is strongly typed because it is of a certain type, Person. This means that onePerson can accept an assignment only from compliant objects, such as other Person objects. Such restriction is important because it avoids errors and problems. Moreover, the compiler knows how to treat such a specialized object. A variable of type Object is instead not strongly typed because it is just of the root type but is not specialized. Object can accept anything, but without restrictions the usage of nonstrongly typed objects could lead to significant problems. In Chapter 14 we discuss Generics; there you get a more thorough idea of strongly typed objects.

Now you have an *instance* of the Person class, named onePerson. Now consider the following line of code:

```
Dim secondPerson As Person = onePerson
```

A new object of type Person (secondPerson) is declared and is assigned with the onePerson object. Because of the equality operator, you would probably expect secondPerson to now be an exact copy of onePerson. We could consider at this point some edits to the secondPerson object, for example we could modify the first name:

```
secondPerson.FirstName = "Alex"
```

We can now try to check the result of the previous operations by simply writing the output to the Console window. Let's begin by writing the result of secondPerson:

```
Console.WriteLine(secondPerson.FirstName)
Console.WriteLine(secondPerson.LastName)
Console.ReadLine()
```

As you may correctly expect, the preceding code produces the following result:

```
Alex
Del Sole
```

Now let's simply write the result for onePerson to the Console window:

```
Console.WriteLine(onePerson.FirstName)
Console.WriteLine(onePerson.LastName)
Console.ReadLine()
```

This code produces the following result:

```
Alex
Del Sole
```

As you can see, editing the first name in secondPerson also affected onePerson. This means that secondPerson is not a copy of onePerson. It is instead *a copy of the reference* to the actual data. Now you should have a better understanding of reference types. We can say that, as their name implies, reference types have an address in memory where data is stored and variables declaring and instantiating reference types just hold a reference to that data. To get a real copy of data, you should write something like this:

```
Dim secondPerson As New Person
secondPerson.FirstName = onePerson.FirstName
secondPerson.LastName = onePerson.LastName
```

Then you could edit secondPerson's properties ensuring that this will not affect the onePerson object. As a clarification, notice that, in the .NET Framework, String is a reference type but it's actually treated as a value type as I will explain in a few paragraphs.

CLONING REFERENCE TYPES

Creating a clone for a reference type in the preceding way can be good with objects exposing only a few properties, so you might wonder how you can clone more complex reference types. There are more interesting techniques that are discussed in the "Deep Copy and Shallow Copy" section.

.NET Framework Primitive Reference Types

The .NET Framework 4.0 ships with tons of reference types exposed by the Base Class Library and that cover most needs. However, there is a bunch of reference types you will often use in the development process that lots of other reference types derive from. Table 4.4 shows a list of the most common reference types.

TABLE 4.4   Most Common Built-In Reference Types in .NET Framework

Type	Description
System.Object	The root class in the object hierarchy
System.String	Represents a string
System.Array	Represents an array of objects
System.Exception	Represents an error occurring during the application execution
System.IO.Stream	The base class for accessing other resources such as files or in-memory data.

Of course there are a lot of other reference types that you can use when developing real-life applications, and most of them are discussed in subsequent chapters of the book; however, the ones listed in Table 4.3 provide the basis for working with reference types. Most of them are the base infrastructure for other important derived classes. We previously discussed System.Object, so we will not do it again. It is instead worth mentioning how System.String is a reference type, although it seems natural to think about it as a value type. Basically System.String, or simply String, is used as a value type, so it will not be difficult to build strings. By the way, strings are immutable (that means "read-only"), so each time you edit a string, the runtime creates a new instance of the String class passing in the edited string. Because of this, editing strings using System.String can cause unnecessary usage of memory. In order to solve this problem, the .NET Framework provides more efficient ways, as you will see in the section "Working with Strings, Dates and Arrays."

Differences Between Value Types and Reference Types

Value types and reference types differ in several ways. In the previous sections we first saw how they differ in assignment and how a value type can directly store data, whereas a reference type stores only the address to the actual data. We now explain such implementation and we also provide information on the other differences between value and reference types.

Memory Allocation

Value types and reference types are differently allocated in memory. Value types are allocated in the *Stack*. The Stack is a memory area where methods are executed according to the *last-in, first-out* manner. The first method *pushed* to the Stack is the application entry point; that is, the Main method. When Main invokes other methods, the CLR creates a sort of restore point and pushes those methods to the Stack. When the method needs to be executed, data required by that method is also pushed to the Stack. When a method completes, the CLR removes (*popping*) it from the Stack together with its data, restoring the previous state. Because of this ordered behavior, the Stack is efficient, and the Common Language Runtime can easily handle it. Consider the following line of code, declaring a variable of type `Integer`, therefore a value type:

```
Dim anInteger As Integer = 5
```

Figure 4.4 shows how the `anInteger` variable is allocated in the Stack.

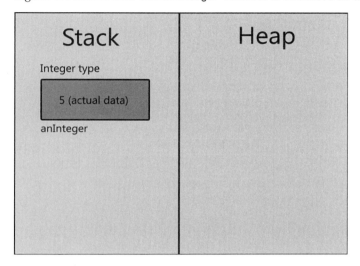

FIGURE 4.4   Value types are allocated in the Stack.

On the contrary, reference types are allocated in a memory area named *Managed Heap*. Different from the Stack, in the Managed Heap objects are allocated and deallocated randomly. This provides fast allocation but requires more work for the CLR. To keep things ordered, the CLR needs two instruments: *Garbage Collector* and *Memory Manager*. We provide details about this architecture in Chapter 8, "Managing an Object's Lifetime." At the moment we need to understand how reference types and their data are allocated. Consider the following lines of code, declaring a new version of the `Person` class and an instance of this class:

```
Class Person

    Property Name As String
    Property Age As Integer
End Class
Dim onePerson As New Person
onePerson.Name = "Alessandro Del Sole"
onePerson.Age = 32
```

As you can see, there is now a property in this class (Age) that is a value type. The instance of the class will be allocated in the Heap, whereas its reference (onePerson) will be allocated in the Stack. Figure 4.5 provides a visual representation of this scenario.

Because the Person class handles a value type in one of its properties, such value types stay in the Stack. Figure 4.6 completes this overview. In the second part of this book, we will have different opportunities to explore reference types and memory management when discussing the object's lifetime.

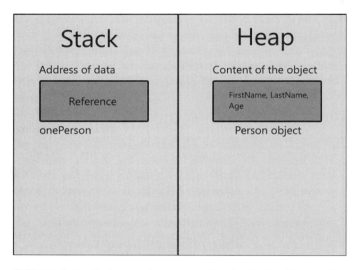

FIGURE 4.5 Reference types are allocated in the Heap, whereas their address resides in the Stack.

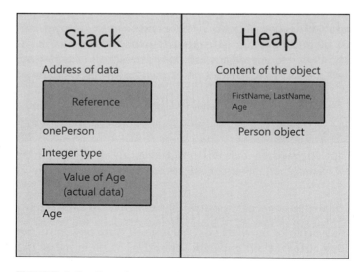

FIGURE 4.6 Complete overview of memory allocation for value and reference types.

Object-Oriented Differences

There are a couple of differences with regard to principles related to the object-oriented programming. Although these principles are discussed in detail in Part 2, "Object-Oriented Programming with Visual Basic 2010," it's convenient to have a small reference.

Inheritance

The first one is about inheritance, which is covered in Chapter 12. Classes (that is, reference types) support inheritance, whereas structures (value types) do not. Consider the following code:

```
Class Person


    Property FirstName As String
    Property LastName As String


End Class

Class Developer
    Inherits Person

    Property UsedProgrammingLanguage As String

    Public Overrides Function ToString() As String
        Return Me.LastName
    End Function
End Class
```

In this example, the `Person` class is the base class and provides the basic properties for representing a hypothetical person. The `Developer` class inherits from `Person` (see the `Inherits` keyword), and this means that the `Developer` class will expose both the `FirstName` and `LastName` properties plus the new one named `UsedProgrammingLanguage`. It also redefines the behavior of the default `ToString` method so that it can return a more significant name for the object. In Visual Basic 2010 you can inherit only from one object at a time. This means that `Developer` can inherit only from `Person` but not also from another object. If you need multiple-level inheritance, you should architect your objects framework so that a second class can inherit from the first one, the third one from the second one, and so on. Structures do not support inheritance at all, except for the fact that they inherit by nature from `System.ValueType`.

Interfaces Implementation

Both classes and structures provide support for interfaces implementation. For example, you could implement the `IComparable` interface in both cases:

```
Class Person
    Implements IComparable
```

```
    Property FirstName As String
    Property LastName As String

    Public Function CompareTo(ByVal obj As Object) As Integer Implements
        System.IComparable.CompareTo
        'Write your code here
    End Function
End Class

Structure Dimension
    Implements IComparable

    Public Function CompareTo(ByVal obj As Object) As Integer Implements
        System.IComparable.CompareTo
        'Write your code here
    End Function

    Property X As Integer
    Property Y As Integer
    Property Z As Integer
End Structure
```

Inheritance and interfaces are discussed in Part 2, so don't worry if something does not appear clear.

Constructors

When you declare a reference type, you need an instance before you can use it (with the exception of shared classes that are discussed in Chapter 7). Creating an instance is accomplished by invoking the *constructor* via the New keyword. When you instead declare a value type, the new variable is automatically initialized to a default value that is usually zero for numbers (or False for Boolean). Because of this, value types do not require invoking a default constructor. The Visual Basic compiler still accepts declaring a value type invoking the constructor, which will also initialize the type with the default value, but in this case you cannot initialize the value. The following code snippet demonstrates this:

```
'Declares an Integer and sets the value to zero
Dim anInt As New Integer
'Initialization not allowed with New
Dim anotherInt As New Integer = 1
'Allowed
Dim aThirdInt As Integer = 1
```

Finalizers

Finalizers are a topic related to the object's lifetime that we discuss in detail in Chapter 8. As for constructors, it's convenient having a small reference. We previously said that when methods using value types complete their execution, they are automatically removed from the Stack together with the data. This is managed by the CLR, and because of this ordered behavior, value types do not need to be finalized. On the contrary, reference types are allocated on the heap and have a different behavior. Deallocation from memory is handled by the Garbage Collector that needs instead finalizers on the reference types side to complete its work.

Performance Differences

We said a lot of times that value types store data directly whereas reference ones store only the address of the data. Although you can create and consume types according to your needs, there are some concerns with performances, particularly regarding methods. Methods can accept parameters, also known as arguments. Arguments can be value types or reference types. If you pass to a method a value type, you pass to that method all the data contained in the value type, which could be time-consuming and cause performance overhead. Passing a reference type will pass only the address to the data, so it could be faster and more efficient. There could be situations in which you do need to pass methods one or more value types. This depends only on your needs. Generally the performance difference in such a scenario could not be relevant, but it would depend on the size of the value type. If your method receives a large value type as an argument but is invoked only once, performance should not be affected. But if your method is invoked a lot of times, perhaps passing a reference type would be better. Just be aware of this when implementing your methods.

What Custom Type Should I Choose?

Answering this question is not simple. It depends. If you need to implement a custom type that will act similarly to a value type (for example, a type that works with numbers), you should choose a `Structure`. If you need to implement an object for storing a large amount of data, it could be a good idea to choose a class. Such considerations are not mandatory, and their purpose is letting you think a little bit more about what you are going to implement according to your needs.

Converting Between Value Types and Reference Types

In your developer life, you often need to convert one data type into another in different types of situations. For example, you might need to convert a value type into another one or just convert an instance of type Object into a strongly typed object. In this section you learn how to convert between data types and about conversion operators, beginning with basic but important concepts, such as implicit conversions, boxing, and unboxing.

Understanding Implicit Conversions

Previously we discussed the `System.Object` class. As you may remember, such a class is the root in the class hierarchy. That said, you can assign both reference types and value types to an `Object` instance because they both inherit from `System.Object`. Consider the following lines of code:

```
Dim anInt As Object = 10
Dim onePerson As Object = New Person
```

The first line assigns a value type (`Integer`) to an `Object` whereas the second one assigns an instance of the `Person` class to an `Object`. Visual Basic 2010 always enables such assignments because they are always safe. What is unsafe is trying to assign an `Object` to a strongly typed instance, such as assigning `Object` to an instance of the `Person` class. This is quite obvious, because `Object` can represent whatever type, and the compiler cannot be sure if that type is a `Person` and this might cause errors. Consider the following line of code:

```
Dim onePerson As Person = New Object
```

The code is trying to assign an instance of the `Object` class to an instance of `Person`. The Visual Basic compiler enables handling such situations in two different ways, depending on how `Option Strict` is set. We discussed `Option Strict` in Chapter 2, and now you can see the first usage. If `Option Strict` is set to `On`, the preceding line of code causes an error. The Visual Basic compiler does allow an implicit conversion from `Object` to a strongly typed object throwing an error message that you can see in the code editor. Figure 4.7 shows this error message.

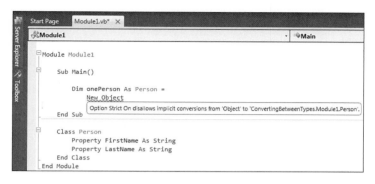

FIGURE 4.7   With `Option Strict On`, the Visual Basic compiler disallows implicit conversions.

This is useful because it prevents type conversion errors. If you want to perform an assignment of this kind, you need to explicitly convert `Object` into the appropriate data type. For example, this can be accomplished using the `CType` conversion operator, as in the following line of code:

```
Dim onePerson As Person = CType(New Object, Person)
```

A conversion operator offers another advantage: It communicates if the conversion is possible and, if not, you can handle the situation, particularly at runtime. By the way, the Visual Basic compiler provides a way to allow implicit conversions avoiding error messages. To accomplish this, you need to set `Option Strict` to `Off`. You can simply write the following line of code (preceding all the other code and `Imports` directives):

```
Option Strict Off
```

You could also adjust `Option Strict` settings in the Compiler tab of the My Project window as we saw in Chapter 2. Now assigning an `Object` to a `Person`, as we did before, is perfectly legal. But please be careful: If you do not need to perform such assignments, please avoid `Option Strict Off` and always prefer `Option Strict On`. This can ensure less runtime and compile time errors and enable you to write more efficient code.

OPTION STRICT OFF: **WHEN?**

You should never set `Option Strict` to `Off`. There is only one situation in which you should set `Option Strict` to `Off`, which is late binding. This topic will be discussed in Chapter 47, "Reflection." Outside this particular scenario, never set `Option Strict` to `Off` so that you can be sure that you work with strongly typed objects and that the compiler, debugger, and CLR enable you to find in a few seconds errors if occurring but also because of performance and other situations that you learn in the chapter on Generics. I suggest you set `Option Strict` to `On` as a default in the Visual Studio 2010 options.

Boxing and Unboxing

The Common Type System enables implicit conversions and conversions between reference types and value types and vice versa because both inherit from System.Object. Regarding this, there are two other particular techniques: *boxing* and *unboxing*. You often need to work with boxing and unboxing when you have methods that receive arguments of type Object. See the tip at the end of this section for details.

Boxing

Boxing occurs when converting a value type to a reference type. In other words, boxing is when you assign a value type to an Object. The following lines of code demonstrate boxing:

```
Dim calculation As Double = 14.4 + 32.12
Dim result As Object = calculation
```

The calculation variable, which stores a value deriving from the sum of two numbers, is a Double value type. The result variable, which is of type Object and therefore a reference type, is allocated in the heap and boxes the original value of calculation so that you now have two copies of the value, one in the Stack and one in the Heap. Figure 4.8 shows how boxing causes memory allocation.

Boxing requires performance overhead. This will be clearer when reading the next section.

Unboxing

Unboxing occurs when you convert a reference type to a value type. Basically you perform unboxing when converting an Object into a value type. Continuing with the previous example, the following line of code demonstrates unboxing:

```
Dim convertedResult As Double = CType(result, Double)
```

Unboxing can cause another copy of the original value (the same stored in the calculation variable) to be created and allocated in the Stack. Figure 4.9 shows a representation of what happens when unboxing a value.

Boxing and unboxing also cause performance overhead, and they should always be avoided if not truly needed. This is because value types store directly the data they refer to and therefore creating three copies of the data can consume more resources than necessary. If value types you box and unbox are small, performance might not be influenced (or, better, you might not see the difference). But if value types store a large amount of data, the loss of performance could be significant.

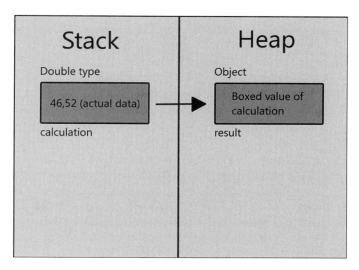

FIGURE 4.8   Boxing causes both Stack and Heap allocation.

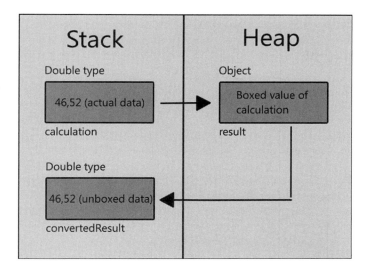

FIGURE 4.9   Unboxing causes a third copy of the original value to be created.

AVOIDING BOXING AND UNBOXING

Boxing and unboxing can be necessary if you have methods that receive arguments of type Object. There are a couple of best practices that you can take when implementing methods, such as using Generics or implementing overloads of methods that can accept multiple strongly typed arguments. Generics and overloads are discussed later in the book.

EARLY BINDING AND LATE BINDING

When talking about reference types, another important topic is early binding and late binding. Although this can be the right place to discuss them, I prefer to postpone such discussion until Chapter 47 about Reflection. In this way you first get a complete overview of reference types and then you get real examples of the late binding technique.

Deep Copy and Shallow Copy

In the "Understanding Reference Types" section, you saw how reference types assignments differ from value types assignments and how assignments are not enough to create a copy of a reference type. We also provided one basic solution to this problem, which was to create a new instance of a specified reference type and then assign each property of the target instance with values coming from the original one. But this is not enough, both because it is not complete and because it can be good only with small classes. To create a complete clone of a reference type, in the .NET development we can take advantage of two techniques: *deep copy* and *shallow copy*. Both techniques require the implementation of the ICloneable interface. Although we discuss interfaces later, concepts presented here are quite easy to understand. The ICloneable interface provides a unique method named Clone that enables developers to know that classes exposing such a method can easily be cloned. For example, consider the following implementation of the Person class that also implements the ICloneable interface:

```
Class Person
    Implements ICloneable

    Property FirstName As String
    Property LastName As String
    Property Work As Job

    Public Function Clone() As Object Implements System.ICloneable.Clone
        Return Me.MemberwiseClone
    End Function
End Class
```

The most interesting thing in the code is the Clone method required by the ICloneable interface. In the method body you should write code that performs the real copy of the reference type. Fortunately the Object class provides a method named MemberwiseClone that automatically returns a shallow copy of your reference type. The keyword Me indicates the current instance of the class. Because Clone must work with all possible types, it returns Object. (We see later how to convert this result.) The class exposes two String properties, FirstName and LastName. You may remember that, although String is a reference type behind the scenes, you will actually treat it as a value type. The class also exposes another property named Work of type Job. This is a new reference type representing a person's occupation. Job is implemented in the following way:

```
Class Job
    Property CompanyName As String
    Property Position As String
End Class
```

Given this implementation, we can simply create a *shallow copy*.

Shallow Copy

A shallow copy creates a new instance of the current object and copies values of members of the original to the new one but does not create copies of children (referenced) objects. Continuing the example of the preceding implementation, Clone creates a copy of the Person class into a new instance and copies members' values that are value types or Strings. Because Job is a pure reference type, the shallow copy provided by Clone will not also create a clone of Job. This is the explanation about what we said before, that a shallow copy creates a copy only of the specified instance but not of children objects. We can easily verify our assertions writing the following code:

```
Sub Main()


    'The original person
    Dim firstPerson As New Person
    firstPerson.FirstName = "Alessandro"
    firstPerson.LastName = "Del Sole"

    'Defines a work for the above person
    Dim randomJob As New Job
    randomJob.CompanyName = "Del Sole Ltd."
    randomJob.Position = "CEO"

    'Assignment of the new job
    firstPerson.Work = randomJob

    'Gets a shallow copy of the firstPerson object
    Dim secondPerson As Person = CType(firstPerson.Clone, Person)


    'Check if they are the same instances

    'returns False, 2 different instances:
    Console.WriteLine(firstPerson.FirstName Is secondPerson.FirstName)
```

```
    'returns True (still same instance of Job!):
    Console.WriteLine(firstPerson.Work Is secondPerson.Work)
    Console.ReadLine()
End Sub
```

The preceding code first gets a new instance of the Person class, setting some properties such as a new instance of the Job class, too. Notice how the result of the Clone method, which is of type Object, is converted into a Person instance using CType. At this point we can check what happened. The Is operator enables comparing two instances of reference types and returns True if they are related to the same instance. For the FirstName property, the comparison returns False because the shallow copy created a new, standalone instance of the Person class. But if we do the same check on the Work property, which is a child reference type of the Person class, the comparison returns True. This means that firstPerson.Work refers to the same instance of the Job class as in secondPerson.Work. And this also means that a shallow copy did not create a new copy of the Job class to be assigned to the secondPerson object. This is where the *deep copy* comes in.

Deep Copy

Deep copy is something complex that can create perfect copies of an entire object's graph. Basically, to perform a deep copy you have some alternatives. The easiest (and the one we can show at this point of the book) is to perform a shallow copy of the main object and then manually copy the other properties of children reference types. The best one instead recurs to Serialization, which is an advanced topic discussed in Chapter 43, "Serialization." At the moment we can focus on editing the previous implementation of the Clone method for performing a simple deep copy. We could also implement the ICloneable interface in the Job class, as follows:

```
Class Job
    Implements ICloneable

    Property CompanyName As String
    Property Position As String

    Public Function Clone() As Object Implements System.ICloneable.Clone
        Return Me.MemberwiseClone
    End Function
End Class
```

Now we can modify the Clone implementation inside the Person class, as follows:

```
Class Person
    Implements ICloneable

    Property FirstName As String
    Property LastName As String
    Property Work As Job
```

```
Public Function Clone() As Object Implements System.ICloneable.Clone

    Dim tempPerson As Person = CType(Me.MemberwiseClone, Person)

    tempPerson.Work = CType(Me.Work.Clone, Job)

    Return tempPerson

End Function
End Class
```

IMPLEMENTING ICLONEABLE

Of course implementing ICloneable in referenced classes is not the only way for providing deep copies. We could also generate a new instance of the Job class and manually assign values read from the original instance. But because we are discussing ICloneable and Clone, the example was completed this way.

Basically the code obtains first a shallow copy of the current instance of the Person class and then gets a shallow copy of the child instance of the Job class.

PAY ATTENTION TO RECURSIVE CLONE

Cloning objects with recursive calls to the Clone method could lead to a stack overflow if the hierarchy of your objects is particularly complex. Because of this, the previous implementation goes well with small classes and small objects graphs. If this is not the case, you should prefer serialization.

If we now try to run again the same check comparing the instances of firstPerson and secondPerson, the output will be the following:

```
False
False
```

This is because now the instances are different. We have two completely standalone instances of the Person class.

The `GetType` Keyword

Each time you create an instance of a class, the .NET runtime creates an instance behind the scenes of the `System.Type` class that represents your object. Because in the .NET development you have the ability to inspect at runtime instances of the `System.Type` class (known as Reflection) and to get a reference to that `System.Type`, the Visual Basic programming language offers the `GetType` keyword that enables accomplishing both tasks. The `GetType` keyword has two different behaviors: The first one is an operator whereas the second one is a method; typically `GetType` is used in comparing two instances of an object or in accessing metadata of a type at runtime. To understand `GetType`, here are a few examples. Consider this first code snippet:

```
'GetType here is related to the type
Dim testType As Type = GetType(Integer)

For Each method As System.Reflection.MethodInfo
              In testType.GetMethods
    Console.WriteLine(method.Name)
Next
Console.ReadLine()
```

In a few words the preceding code retrieves all the information and metadata related to the `System.Int32` type and then shows a list of all methods exposed by such type, using Reflection. (`MethodInfo` is an object representing the methods' information.) This is useful if you need to retrieve information on a particular data type. If you instead need to retrieve information about metadata of a specific instance of a data type, you can use the `GetType` method, as shown in the following code:

```
'GetType is here related to an instance
Dim testInt As Integer = 123456
Dim testType As Type = testInt.GetType

For Each method As System.Reflection.MethodInfo
              In testType.GetMethods
    Console.WriteLine(method.Name)
Next
Console.ReadLine()
```

In this particular situation you retrieve information of **an instance** of the `System.Int32` type and not of the type. You can also use `GetType` to compare two types for equality:

```
'Comparing two types
If testInt.GetType Is GetType(Integer) Then
    Console.WriteLine("TestInt is of type Integer")
End If
```

Conversion Operators

In the previous section we discussed converting between value types and reference types. Such kinds of conversions are not the only ones allowed by the .NET Framework because you often need to perform conversions between two value types or two reference types. For example, imagine that you want to represent a number as a text message. In such a case, you need to convert an Integer into a String; you could also have an Integer value that must be passed to a method that instead receives an argument of type Double. Another common scenario is when you work with user controls in the user interface. There are some controls such as ListBox and DataGridView on the Windows side or the DataGrid on the web side that can store any kind of object. If you show a list of Person objects inside a ListBox, the control stores a list of Object, so you need to perform an explicit conversion from Object to Person each time you need to retrieve information on a single Person. In this section we show how conversions between types can be performed.

Widening and Narrowing Conversions

With the exception of boxing and unboxing, basically conversions are of two kinds: *widening* conversions and *narrowing* conversions depending if the conversion is explicit or implicit. This is explained next.

Widening Conversions

Widening conversions occur when you try to convert a type into another one that can include all values of the original type. A typical example of a widening conversion is converting from an Integer into a Double, as in the following lines of code:

```
'Widening conversion
Dim i As Integer = 1
Dim d As Double = i
```

As you might remember from Table 4.2, Integer represents a numeric value whereas Double represents a large floating number. Therefore, Double is greater than Integer and therefore can accept conversions from Integer without loss of precision. Widening conversions do not need an explicit conversion operator, which instead happens for narrowing conversions.

Narrowing Conversions

As opposite of widening conversions, *narrowing conversions* occur when you attempt to convert a type into another that is smaller or with a loss of precision. For example, converting a Double into an Integer can cause a loss of precision because Double is a large floating number whereas Integer is just a numeric value, which is also smaller than Double. There are several ways to perform narrowing conversions, depending on how types you need to convert are implemented. Visual Basic 2010, continuing what was already available in previous versions of the language, provides an easy way to perform conversions between base types wrapped by Visual Basic keywords. For example, if we need to convert a `Double` into an `Integer`, we could write the following lines of code:

```
Dim d As Double = 12345.678
Dim i As Integer = CInt(d)
```

The `CInt` function converts the specified `Object` into an `Integer`. In this particular case the value of i becomes 12346, because the conversion caused a loss of precision and the Visual Basic compiler produced an integer number that is the most approximate possible to the original value. Another example is when you need to convert a number into a string representation of the number itself. This can be accomplished by the following line of code:

```
Dim s As String = CStr(i)
```

The `CStr` function converts the specified `Object` into a string. With particular regard to string conversions, all .NET objects expose a method named `ToString` that performs a conversion of the original data into a new `String`. The last line of code could be rewritten as follows:

```
Dim s As String = i.ToString()
```

`ToString` is also useful because you can format the output. For example, consider the following line of code:

```
Dim i As Integer = 123456
Dim s As String = i.ToString("##,##.00")
```

The `ToString` method enables specifying how the string should be formatted. On my machine the code produces the following output:

```
123,456.00
```

The output depends on regional settings for your system, with particular regard to separators.

USE TOSTRING **INSTEAD OF** CSTR

Because it enables you to format the result, `ToString` should be preferred to `CStr`. Moreover, you can override the standard implementation of `ToString` (provided by the `Object` class) so that you can provide your own conversion logic. This is discussed later, with regard to inheritance.

Table 4.5 shows the complete list of conversion functions provided by the Visual Basic grammar.

TABLE 4.5   Visual Basic Conversion Functions

Operator	Description
CInt	Converts an object into an Integer
CLng	Converts an object into a Long
CShort	Converts an object into a Short
CSng	Converts an object into a Single
CDbl	Converts an object into a Double
CBool	Converts an object into a Boolean
CByte	Converts an object into a Byte
CChar	Converts an object into a Char
CStr	Converts an object into a String
CObj	Converts an object into an instance of Object
CDate	Converts an object into a Date
CUInt	Converts an object into a UInteger
CULong	Converts an object into a ULong
CUShort	Converts an object into a UShort
CSByte	Converts an object into a SByte

REMEMBER THE LOSS OF PRECISION

Always take care when performing narrowing conversions because of the loss of precision, particularly with numeric values. Another particular case is when converting from String to Char. Such conversions retrieve only the first character of the specified string.

When narrowing conversions fail, an InvalidCastException will be thrown by the compiler. An example of this situation is when you attempt to convert a String into an Integer. Because String is a valid object expression, you do not get an error at compile time, but the conversion fails at runtime. Because of this, you should always enclose conversions within error handling code blocks (see Chapter 6, "Handling Errors and Exceptions" for details). There are also alternatives that are independent from the Visual Basic language and that are provided by the .NET Framework. The first way is using the

System.Convert class that is available on objects that implement the IConvertible inter-face. Convert exposes a lot of methods, each for converting into a particular data type. For example, the following line of code converts a string representation of a number into an integer:

```
Dim c As Integer = System.Convert.ToInt32("1234")
```

If the string contains an invalid number, a FormatException is thrown. Methods exposed by the Convert class are well implemented because they do not only accept Object expres-sions but also specific types, such as Integer, Boolean, String, and so on. IntelliSense can help you understand what types are supported. Table 4.6 provides an overview of the most common conversions methods exposed by System.Convert.

TABLE 4.6   System.Convert Most-Used Methods

Method	Description
ToBool	Converts the specified type into a Boolean.
ToByte	Converts the specified type into a Byte.
ToChar	Converts the specified type into a Char.
ToDateTime	Converts the specified type into a Date.
ToDecimal	Converts the specified type into a Decimal.
ToDouble	Converts the specified type into a Double.
ToInt16	Converts the specified type into a Short.
ToInt32	Converts the specified type into an Integer.
ToInt64	Converts the specified type into a Long.
ToSByte	Converts the specified type into a SByte.
ToSingle	Converts the specified type into a Single.
ToString	Converts the specified type into a String.
ToUInt16	Converts the specified type into an UShort.
ToUInt32	Converts the specified type into a UInteger.
ToUInt64	Converts the specified type into an ULong.

Notice that System.Convert also provides other methods that are not discussed here because they are related to particular situations that assume you have a deep knowledge of specific .NET topics and are out of the scope in a general discussion such as this one.

CType, DirectCast, TryCast

The Visual Basic programming language offers some other conversion operators that are probably the most commonly used because of their flexibility. The first one is CType. It converts from one type to another and, if the conversion fails, the Visual Basic compiler throws an exception. The good news is that the conversion is also performed by the background compiler, so if the target type's range exceeds the source one you are immediately notified of the problem. For example, the compiler knows that converting a Date into an Integer is not possible, so in such a scenario you will be immediately notified. If the conversion is legal (and therefore can compile) but types are populated at runtime with data that cannot be converted, an InvalidCastException is thrown. For example, the following code converts an Integer into a Short:

```
Dim i As Integer = 123456
Dim s As Short = CType(i, Short)
```

CType is also useful in unboxing. The following code converts from an Object that contains an Integer into a pure Integer:

```
Dim p As Object = 1
Dim result As Integer = CType(p, Integer)
```

Of course, it can also be used for converting between reference types:

```
Dim p As Object = New Person
Dim result As Person = CType(p, Person)
```

Basically CType is specific to the Visual Basic runtime and enables widening and narrowing conversions from one type into another type that accepts the first one. For example, a Double can be converted to an Integer, although with loss of precision. There are another couple of important operators, DirectCast and TryCast, which you can use the same way but which have different behavior. Both operators enable conversions when there is an inheritance or implementation relationship between the two types. For example, consider the following lines of code:

```
Dim d As Double = 123.456
Dim s As Short = CType(d, Short)
```

Converting from Double to Short using CType will succeed. Now consider the usage of DirectCast in the same scenario:

```
Dim d As Double = 123.456
Dim s As Short = DirectCast(d, Short)
```

This conversion will fail because neither Short inherits from Double nor is there an implementation relationship between the two types. A conversion failure is notified via an InvalidCastException. This means that you should use DirectCast only when you are sure that inheritance or implementation conditions between types are satisfied, although preferring DirectCast has some advantages in terms of performances because it directly relies on the .NET runtime. DirectCast conversions are also checked by the background compiler, so you will be immediately notified if conversions fail via the Error List window. DirectCast works with both value and reference types. If you work with reference types, it's a best practice to check if the two types are compliant so that you can reduce the risks of errors:

```
'In this example P is of type Object but stores a Person
If TypeOf (p) Is Person Then
    Dim result As Person = DirectCast(p, Person)
End If
```

The TypeOf operator compares an object reference variable to a data type and returns True if the object variable is compatible with the given type. As you may imagine, such checks can require performance overhead. There is also another particular operator that works only with reference types, known as TryCast. This one works exactly like DirectCast but instead of throwing an InvalidCastException, in case of conversion failure, it returns a null object (Nothing). This can be useful because you can avoid implementing an exceptions check, simplifying your code (that will only need to check for a null value) and reducing performance overhead. The last code snippet could be rewritten as follows:

```
'In this example P is of type Object but stores a Person
Dim result As Person = TryCast(p, Person)
```

If the conversion fails TryCast returns Nothing, so you will just need to check such a result.

Working with .NET Fundamental Types

There are special types that you will often work with, such as strings, date and time, and arrays. Although you will often work with collections, too (see Chapter 16, "Working with Collections"), understanding how such objects work is an important objective. The .NET Framework 4.0 simplifies your developer life because objects provide methods to perform the most common operations on the data.

NOTE ON EXTENSION METHODS

This section describes built-in methods from value and reference types. Because of the .NET infrastructure, all types provide the ability of invoking extension methods that could be potentially used for accomplishing some of the tasks proposed in this section. They will not be described because the scope of this chapter is to describe built-in members; you will need to understand extension methods, which are covered in Chapter 21.

Working with Strings

Working with strings is one of the most common developer activities. In the .NET Common Type System, `System.String` is a reference type. This might be surprising, because actually strings behave like value types. Regarding this, there are a couple of things to say. First, the `String` class cannot be inherited, so you can't create a custom class derived from it. Second, `String` objects are immutable like value types. What does this mean? It means that when you create a new `String` you cannot change it. Although you are allowed to edit a string's content, behind the scenes the CLR will not edit the existing string; it will instead create a new instance of the `String` object containing your edits. The CLR then stores such `String` objects in the Heap and returns a reference to them. We discuss later how to approach strings in a more efficient way; at the moment you need to understand how to work with them. The `System.String` class provides lots of methods for working with strings without the need to write custom code. Assuming you understand the previous section relating to reference types, you can learn how to manipulate strings using the most common `System.String` methods.

4

> ### SYSTEM.STRING **METHODS**
>
> `System.String` provides several methods for performing operations on strings. We discuss the most important of them. Each method comes with several overloads. Discussing every overload is not possible, so you learn how methods work and then you can use IntelliSense, the Object Browser, and the documentation for further information.

Comparing Strings

Comparing the content of two strings is an easy task. The most common way for comparing strings is taking advantage of the equality (=) operator, which checks if two strings have the same value. The following is an example that compares strings for equality:

```
Dim stringOne As String = "Hi guys"
Dim stringTwo As String = "How are you?"
Dim stringThree As String = "Hi guys"
'Returns False
Dim result1 As Boolean = (stringOne = stringTwo)
'Returns True
Dim result2 As Boolean = (stringOne = stringThree)
```

You can also use the equality operator inside conditional blocks, like in the following snippet:

```
If stringOne = stringTwo Then
    'Do something if the two strings are equal
End If
```

You instead check for strings inequality using the inequality operator (<>).

THE VISUAL BASIC COMPILER AND THE EQUALITY OPERATOR

When using the equality operator for strings comparisons, the Visual Basic compiler works differently from other managed languages. In fact, behind the scenes it makes a call to the `Microsoft.VisualBasic.CompilerServices.Operators.CompareString` method whereas other languages, such as C#, make an invocation to `System.String.Equals`.

The `String` class also exposes other interesting methods for comparing strings: `Equals`, `Compare`, `CompareTo` and `CompareOrdinal`. `Equals` checks for strings equality and returns a Boolean value of `True` if the strings are equal or `False` if they are not (which is exactly like the equality operator). The following code compares two strings and returns `False` because they are not equal:

```
Dim firstString As String = "Test string"
Dim secondString As String = "Comparison Test"

Dim areEqual As Boolean = String.Equals(firstString, secondString)
```

`Equals` has several signatures allowing deep control of the comparison. For example, you could check if two strings are equal according to the local system culture and without being case-sensitive:

```
Dim areCaseEqual As Boolean =
    String.Equals(firstString, secondString,

    StringComparison.CurrentCultureIgnoreCase)
```

The `StringComparison` object provides a way for specifying comparison settings and was introduced by .NET 2.0. IntelliSense provides descriptions for each available option. Then there is the `Compare` method. It checks if the first string is minor, equal, or greater than the second and returns an `Integer` value representing the result of the comparison. If the first string is minor, it returns -1; if it is equal to the second one, the method returns zero; last, if the first string is greater than the second, `Compare` returns 1. The following code snippet demonstrates this kind of comparison:

```
Dim firstString As String = "Test string"
Dim secondString As String = "Comparison Test"

Dim result As Integer = String.Compare(firstString, secondString)
```

In this case `Compare` returns 1, because the second string is greater than the first one. `Compare` enables specifying several comparing options. For example, you could perform the comparison based on case-sensitive strings. The following code demonstrates this:

```
Dim caseComparisonResult As Integer =
    String.Compare(firstString, secondString, True)
```

For Equals, Compare also enables a comparison based on other options, such as the culture information of your system. The next method is String.CompareTo whose return values are basically the same as String.Compare, but it is an instance method. You use it like in the following code:

```
Dim firstString As String = "Test string"
Dim secondString As String = "Comparison Test"

Dim result As Integer = firstString.CompareTo(secondString)
```

The last valuable method is String.CompareOrdinal, which checks for casing differences via ordinal comparison rules, which basically means comparing the numeric values of the corresponding Char objects that the string is composed of. The following is an example:

```
Dim firstString As String = "test"
Dim secondString As String = "TeSt"

'Returns:
'0 if the first string is equal to the second
'< 0 if the first string is less than the second
'> 0 if the first string is greater than the second
Dim result As Integer = String.CompareOrdinal(firstString, secondString)
```

Checking for Empty or Null Strings

The System.String class provides a method named IsNullOrEmpty that easily enables checking if a string is null or if it does not contain any characters. You can use such a method as follows:

```
If String.IsNullOrEmpty(stringToCheck) = False Then
    'The string is neither null nor empty
Else
    'The string is either null or empty
End If
```

Of course, you could also perform your check against True instead of False. In such situations both conditions (null or empty) are evaluated. This can be useful because you often need to validate strings to check if they are valid. There could be situations in which you need to just ensure that a string is null or not empty. In this case you should use the usual syntax:

```
If stringToCheck Is Nothing Then
    'String is null
End If
If stringToCheck = "" Then
```

```
    'String is empty
End If
```

Formatting Strings

Often you need to send output strings according to a particular format, such as currency, percentage, and decimal numbers. The `System.String` class offers a useful method named `Format` that enables you to easily format text. Consider the following code example, paying attention to comments:

```
'Returns "The cost for traveling to Europe is $1,000.00
Console.WriteLine(String.Format("The cost for traveling to Europe is {0:C}
                                dollars", 1000))
'Returns "You are eligible for a 15.50% discount"
Console.WriteLine(String.Format("You are eligible for a {0:P} discount",
                                15.55F))
'Returns "Hex counterpart for 10 is A"
Console.WriteLine(String.Format("Hex counterpart for 10 is {0:X}", 10))
```

The first thing to notice is how you present your strings; `Format` accepts a number of values to be formatted and then embedded in the main string, which are referenced with the number enclosed in brackets; for example {0} is the second argument of `Format`, {1} is the second one, and so on. Symbols enable the format; for example, `C` stands for currency, whereas `P` stands for percentage, and `X` stands for hexadecimal. Visual Basic 2010 offers the symbols listed in Table 4.7.

TABLE 4.7   Format Symbols Accepted

Symbol	Description
C or c	Currency
D or d	Decimal
E or e	Scientific
F or f	Fixed point
G or g	General
N or n	Number
P or p	Percentage
R or r	Roundtrip
X or x	Hexadecimal

> ### ROUNDTRIP
>
> Roundtrip ensures that conversions from floating point to `String` and that converting back is allowed.

Of course, you can format multiple strings in one line of code, as in the following example:

```
Console.Writeline(String.Format("The traveling cost is" &
                " {0:C}. Hex for {1} is '{1,5:X}'", 1000, 10))
```

The preceding code produces the following result:

```
The traveling cost is $1,000.00. Hex for 10 is '    A'
```

As you can see, you can specify a number of white spaces before the next value. This is accomplished typing the number of spaces you want to add followed by a : symbol and then by the desired format symbol. `String.Format` also enables the use of custom formats. Custom formats are based on the symbols shown in Table 4.8.

TABLE 4.8   Symbols You Can Use for Custom Formats

Symbol	Description
0	A numeric placeholder showing 0
#	A digit placeholder
%	Percentage symbol
.	Decimal dot
,	Thousands separator
;	Section separator
"ABC" or 'ABC'	String literals
\	Escape
E or e combined with + or −	Scientific

According to Table 4.7, we could write a custom percentage representation:

```
'Returns "Custom percentage %1,550"
Console.WriteLine(String.Format("Custom percentage {0:%##,###.##} ", 15.50))
```

Or you could also write a custom currency representation. For example, if you live in Great Britain, you could write the following line for representing the Sterling currency:

```
Console.WriteLine(String.Format("Custom currency {0:£#,###.00} ", 987654))
```

Another interesting feature in customizing output is the ability to provide different formats according to the input value. For example, you can decide to format a number depending if it is positive, negative, or zero. At this regard, consider the following code:

```
Dim number As Decimal = 1000
Console.WriteLine(String.
                Format("Custom currency formatting:
                {0:£#,##0.00;*£#,##0.00*;Zero}",
                number))
```

Here you specify three different formats, separated by semicolons. The first format affects positive numbers (such as the value of the number variable); the second one affects negative numbers, and the third one affects a zero value. The preceding example therefore produces the following output:

```
Custom currency formatting: £1,000.00
```

If you try to change the value of number to –1000, the code produces the following output:

```
Custom currency formatting: *£1,000.00*
```

Finally, if you assign number = 0, the code produces the following output:

```
Custom currency formatting: Zero
```

Creating Copies of Strings

Strings in .NET are reference types. Because of this, you cannot assign a string object to another string to perform a copy, because this action will just copy the reference to the actual string. Fortunately, the System.String class provides two useful methods for copying strings: Copy and CopyTo. The first one creates a copy of an entire string:

```
Dim sourceString As String = "Alessandro Del Sole"
Dim targetString As String = String.Copy(sourceString)
```

Copy is a shared method and can create a new instance of String and then put into the instance the content of the original string. If you instead need to create a copy of only a subset of the original string, you can invoke the instance method CopyTo. Such method works a little differently from Copy, because it returns an array of Char. The following code provides an example:

```
Dim sourceString As String = "Alessandro Del Sole"
Dim charArray(sourceString.Length) As Char
```

```
sourceString.CopyTo(11, charArray, 0, 3)
Console.WriteLine(charArray)
```

You first need to declare an array of char, in this case as long as the string length. The first argument of CopyTo is the start position in the original string. The second is the target array; the third one is the start position in the target array, and the fourth one is the number of characters to copy. In the end, such code produces Del as the output.

CLONE **METHOD**

The String class also offers a method named Clone. You should not confuse this method with Copy and CopyTo, because it will just return a reference to the original string and not a real copy.

Inspecting Strings

When working with strings you often need to inspect or evaluate their content. The System.String class provides both methods and properties for inspecting strings. Imagine you have the following string:

```
Dim testString As String = "This is a string to inspect"
```

You can retrieve the string's length via its Length property:

```
'Returns 27
Dim length As Integer = testString.Length
```

Another interesting method is Contains that enables knowing if a string contains the specified substring or array of Char. Contains returns a Boolean value, as you can see in the following code snippet:

```
'Returns True
Dim contains As Boolean = testString.Contains("inspect")
'Returns False

Dim contains1 As Boolean = testString.Contains("Inspect")
```

Just remember that evaluation is case-sensitive. There are also situations in which you might need to check if a string begins or ends with a specified substring. You can verify both situations using StartsWith and EndsWith methods:

```
'Returns False, the string starts with "T"
Dim startsWith As Boolean = testString.StartsWith("Uh")
'Returns True
Dim endsWith As Boolean = testString.EndsWith("pect")
```

Often you might also need to get the position of a specified substring within a string. To accomplish this, you can use the `IndexOf` method. For example you could retrieve the start position of the first "is" substring as follows:

```
'Returns 2
Dim index As Integer = testString.IndexOf("is")
```

The code returns 2 because the start index is zero-based and refers to the "is" substring of the "This" word. You do not need to start your search from the beginning of the string; you can specify a start index, or you can specify how the comparison must be performed via the `StringComparison` enumeration. Both situations are summarized in the following code:

```
'Returns 5
Dim index1 As Integer = testString.IndexOf("is", 3,
                    StringComparison.InvariantCultureIgnoreCase)
```

STRINGCOMPARISON ENUMERATION

You can refer to IntelliSense when typing code for further details on the `StringComparison` enumeration options. They are self-explanatory, and for the sake of brevity, all options cannot be shown here.

`IndexOf` performs a search on the exact substring. You might also need to search for the position of just one character of a set of characters. This can be accomplished using the `IndexOfAny` method as follows:

```
'Returns 1
Dim index2 As Integer = testString.
                    IndexOfAny(New Char() {"h"c, "s"c, "i"c})
```

The preceding code has an array of `Char` storing three characters, all available in the main string. Because the first character in the array is found first, `IndexOfAny` returns its position. Generally `IndexOfAny` returns the position of the character that is found first. There are counterparts of both `IndexOf` and `IndexOfAny`: `LastIndexOf` and `LastIndexOfAny`. The first two methods perform a search starting from the beginning of a string, whereas the last two perform a search starting from the end of a string. This is an example:

```
'Returns 5
Dim lastIndex As Integer = testString.LastIndexOf("is")
'Returns 22
Dim lastIndex1 As Integer = testString.LastIndexOfAny(New Char()
                    {"h"c, "s"c, "i"c})
```

Notice how `LastIndexOf` returns the second occurrence of the "is" substring if you consider the main string from the beginning. Indexing is useful, but this stores just the position of a substring. If you need to retrieve the text of a substring, you can use the SubString method that works as follows:

```
'Returns "is a string"
Dim subString As String = testString.Substring(5, 11)
```

You can also just specify the start index, if you need the entire substring starting from a particular point.

Editing Strings

The System.String class provides members for editing strings. The first method described is named Insert and enables adding a substring into a string at the specified index. Consider the following example:

```
Dim testString As String = "This is a test string"
'Returns
'"This is a test,for demo purposes only,string"
Dim result As String = testString.Insert(14, ",for demo purposes only,")
```

As you can see from the comment in the code, Insert adds the specified substring from the specified index but does not append or replace anything. Insert's counterpart is Remove, which enables removing a substring starting from the specified index or a piece of substring from the specified index and for the specified number of characters. This is an example:

```
'Returns "This is a test string"
Dim removedString As String = testString.Remove(14)
```

Another common task is replacing a substring within a string with another string. For example, imagine you want to replace the "test" substring with the "demo" substring within the testString instance. This can be accomplished using the Replace method as follows:

```
'Returns
'"This is a demo string"
Dim replacedString As String = testString.Replace("test", "demo")
```

The result of Replace must be assigned to another string to get the desired result. (See "Performance Tips" at the end of this section.) Editing strings also contain splitting techniques. You often need to split one string into multiple strings, especially when the string contains substrings separated by a symbol. For example, consider the following code in which a string contains substrings separated by commas, as in CSV files:

```
Dim stringToSplit As String = "Name,Last Name,Age"
```

You might want to extract the three substrings Name, Last Name, and Age and store them as unique strings. To accomplish this you can use the Split method, which can receive as an argument the separator character:

```
Dim result() As String = stringToSplit.Split(","c)
For Each item As String In result
    Console.WriteLine(item)
Next
```

The preceding code retrieves three strings that are stored into an array of String and produces the following output:

```
Name
Last Name
Age
```

Split has several overloads that you can inspect with IntelliSense. One of these enables you to specify the maximum number of substrings to extract and split options, such as normal splitting or splitting if substrings are not empty:

```
Dim result() As String = stringToSplit.Split(New Char() {","c}, 2,
                StringSplitOptions.RemoveEmptyEntries)
```

In this overload you have to explicitly specify an array of Char; in this case there is just a one-dimension array containing the split symbol. Such code produces the following output, considering that only two substrings are accepted:

```
Name
Last Name, Age
```

Opposite to Split, there is also a Join method that enables joining substrings into a unique string. Substrings are passed as an array of String and are separated by the specified character. The following code shows an example:

```
'Returns "Name, Last Name, Age"
Dim result As String = String.Join(",",
                New String() {"Name", "Last Name", "Age"})
```

Another way to edit strings is trimming. Imagine you have a string containing white spaces at the end of the string or at the beginning of the string or both. You might want to remove white spaces from the main string. The System.String class provides three methods: Trim, TrimStart, and TrimEnd that enable accomplishing this task, as shown in the following code (see comments):

```
Dim stringWithSpaces As String = "   Test with spaces   "
'Returns "Test with spaces"
Dim result1 As String = stringWithSpaces.Trim
'Returns "Test with spaces   "
```

```
Dim result2 As String = stringWithSpaces.TrimStart
'Returns "   Test with spaces"
Dim result3 As String = stringWithSpaces.TrimEnd
```

All three methods provide overloads for specifying characters different than white spaces. (Imagine you want to remove an asterisk.) Opposite to `TrimStart` and `TrimEnd`, `System.String` exposes `PadLeft` and `PadRight`. The best explanation for both methods is a practical example. Consider the following code:

```
Dim padResult As String = testString.PadLeft(30, "*"c)
```

It produces the following result:

```
*********This is a test string
```

Basically `PadLeft` creates a new string, whose length is the one specified as the first argument of the method and that includes the original string with the addition of a number of symbols that is equal to the difference from the length you specified and the length of the original string. In our case, the original string is 21 characters long whereas we specified 30 as the new length. So, there are 9 asterisks. `PadRight` does the same, but symbols are added on the right side, as in the following example:

```
Dim padResult As String = testString.PadRight(30, "*"c)
```

This code produces the following result:

```
This is a test string*********
```

Both methods are useful if you need to add symbols to the left or to the right of a string.

PERFORMANCE TIPS

Because of its particular nature, each time you edit a string you are not actually editing the string but you are instead creating a new instance of the `System.String` class. As you may imagine, this could lead to performance issues. That said, although it's fundamental to know how you can edit strings; you should always prefer the `StringBuilder` object especially when concatenating strings. `StringBuilder` is discussed later in this chapter.

Concatenating Strings

Concatenation is perhaps the most common task that developers need to perform on strings. In Visual Basic 2010 you have some alternatives. First, you can use the addition operator:

```
Dim firstString As String = "Hello! My name is "
Dim secondString As String = "Alessandro Del Sole"

Dim result As String = firstString + secondString
```

Another and better approach is the `String.Concat` method:

```
Dim concatResult As String =
                    String.Concat(firstString, secondString)
```

Both ways produce the same result, but both ways have a big limitation; because strings are immutable, and therefore the CLR needs to create a new instance of the `String` class each time you perform a concatenation. This scenario can lead to a significant loss of performance; if you need to concatenate 10 strings, the CLR creates 10 instances of the `String` class. Fortunately, the .NET Framework provides a more efficient way for concatenating strings: the `StringBuilder` object.

The StringBuilder Object

The `System.Text.StringBuilder` class provides an efficient way for concatenating strings. You should always use `StringBuilder` in such situations. The real difference is that `StringBuilder` can create a buffer that grows along with the real needs of storing text. (The default constructor creates a 16-byte buffer.) Using such the `StringBuilder` class is straightforward. Consider the following code example:

```
'Requires an Imports System.Text directive
Function ConcatenatingStringsWithStringBuilder() As String
        Dim result As New StringBuilder

        'Ensures that the StringBuilder instance
        'has the capacity of at least 100 characters
        result.EnsureCapacity(100)
        result.Append("Hello! My name is ")
        result.Append("Alessandro Del Sole")
        Return result.ToString
End Function
```

You simply instantiate the `StringBuilder` class using the `New` keyword and then invoke the `Append` method that receives as an argument the string that must be concatenated. In the end you need to explicitly convert the `StringBuilder` to a `String` invoking the `ToString` method. This class is powerful and provides several methods for working with strings, such as `AppendLine` (which appends an empty line with a carriage return), `AppendFormat` (which enables you to format the appended string), and `Replace` (which enables you to replace all occurrences of the specified string with another string). The `EnsureCapacity` method used in the code example ensures that the `StringBuilder` instance can contain at least the specified number of characters. Basically you can find in the `StringBuilder` class the same methods provided by the `String` class (`Replace`, `Insert`, `Remove`, and so on) so that working with `StringBuilder` will be familiar and straightforward.

Working with Dates

Together with strings, you often need to handle dates and moments in time. To accomplish this, the .NET Framework 4.0 provides the `System.DateTime` type, which is a value type.

MINVALUE AND MAXVALUE

Being a value type, `System.DateTime` has two shared fields, `MinValue` and `MaxValue`, which respectively store the minimum accepted date and the maximum one. Minimum date is 01/01/0001 00:00:00 a.m. whereas maximum date is 12/31/9999 11:59:59 p.m.

Creating Dates

The Visual Basic grammar offers also the `Date` keyword that is basically a lexical representation of the `System.DateTime` object, so you can use both definitions. For consistency, we use the `Date` reserved keyword but keep in mind that this keyword creates (or gets a reference to) an instance of the `System.DateTime` type. Basically working with dates is an easy task. You can create a new date creating an instance of the `DateTime` class:

```
Dim myBirthDate As New Date(1977, 5, 10)
```

The constructor has several overloads but the most common is the preceding one, where you can specify year, month, and day. For example, such values could be written by the user and then converted into a `DateTime` object. Another common situation in which you need to create a date is for storing the current system clock date and time. This can be easily accomplished using the `DateTime.Now` property as follows:

```
Dim currentDate As Date = Date.Now
```

Such code produces the following result, representing the moment when I'm writing this chapter:

```
8/4/2009 10:35:49 AM
```

When you get an instance of a `DateTime`, you can retrieve a lot of information about it. For example, consider the following code taking care of comments:

```
'Creates a new date; May 10th 1977, 8.30 pm
Dim myBirthDate As New Date(1977, 5, 10,
                            20, 30, 0)

'In 1977, May 10th was Tuesday
Console.WriteLine(myBirthDate.DayOfWeek.
                  ToString)
```

4

```
'8.30 pm
Console.WriteLine("Hour: {0}, Minutes: {1}",
                 myBirthDate.Hour,
                 myBirthDate.Minute)

'Is the date included within the Day Light Saving Time period?
Console.WriteLine("Is Day light saving time: {0}",
                 myBirthDate.IsDaylightSavingTime.
                 ToString)

'Is leap year
Console.WriteLine("Is leap: {0}",
                 Date.IsLeapYear(myBirthDate.Year).
                 ToString)
```

The code first creates the following date, representing my birth date: 5/10/1977 8:30:00
PM. Then it retrieves some information, such as the name of the day in the week (represented by the DayOfWeek enumeration), hours, and minutes (via the Hour and Minute integer properties) and the inclusion of the specified date within *Daylight Saving Time*.
The DateTime object also exposes a shared method named IsLeapYear that can establish if the specified year is a leap year. In our example, the year is not passed directly, but it is provided via the Year property of the myBirthDate instance. The following is the result of the code:

```
Tuesday
Hour: 20, Minutes: 30
Is Day light saving time: True
Is leap: False
```

Finally, you can declare dates with the so-called date literals. The following is an example of how you can customize the date format:

```
Dim customDate As Date = #2/25/2010 8:00:00 PM#
```

Converting Strings into Dates

It is not unusual to ask the user to provide a date within an application. Typically this is accomplished via the user interface and, if you do not provide a specific user control (such as the WPF DatePicker or the Win Forms DateTimePicker) for selecting dates in a graphical fashion, such input will be provided in the form of a string. Because of this, you need a way for converting the string into a date, unless the string is invalid (so you need validation) so that you can then manipulate the user input as an effective DateTime object. To accomplish this kind of conversion, the System.DateTime class provides two methods that you already saw when discussing value types: Parse and TryParse. For example, consider the following code that receives an input by the user and attempts to convert such input into a `DateTime` object:

```
Sub ParsingDates()
    Console.WriteLine("Please specify a date:")
    Dim inputDate As Date
    Dim result As Boolean = Date.TryParse(Console.ReadLine, inputDate)

    If result = False Then
        Console.WriteLine("You entered an invalid date")
    Else
        Console.WriteLine(inputDate.DayOfWeek.ToString)
    End If
End Sub
```

The `TryParse` method receives the string to convert as the first argument (which in this case is obtained by the Console window) and the output object passed by reference (`inputDate`); it returns `True` if the conversion succeeds or `False` if it fails. Basically the conversion succeeds if the input string format is accepted and recognized by the `DateTime` type. If you run this code and enter a string in the following format: 1977/05/10, the conversion succeeds because such format is accepted by `DateTime`. So you can then manipulate the new date as you like. (In the preceding example the code shows the day of the week for the specified date, which in my example is Tuesday.)

> **TIP**
>
> In many cases you work with data coming from a database. The ADO.NET engine and layered technologies, such as LINQ, map dates from databases directly into a `System.DateTime` object so that you will have the possibility of working and manipulating such objects from and to data sources.

Formatting Dates

You need to present dates for several scenarios, and you might be required to perform this task in different ways. Fortunately, the `System.DateTime` provides a lot of ways for formatting dates. The easiest way is invoking the `ToString` method, which accepts an argument that enables specifying how a date must be presented. For example, consider the following code snippet that writes the current date in both the extended (`D`) and the short (`d`) date formats:

```
Console.WriteLine(DateTime.Now.ToString("D"))
Console.WriteLine(DateTime.Now.ToString("d"))
```

Such code produces the following output:

```
Wednesday, August 05, 2009
8/5/2009
```

The result is based on the regional and culture settings of your system. Table 4.9 summarizes symbols that you can use with the ToString method.

TABLE 4.9   Date Formatting Symbols with ToString

Symbol	Preview
D	Wednesday, August 05, 2009
D	8/5/2009
T	3:11:26 PM
T	3:11 PM
F	Wednesday, August 05, 2009 3:11:26 PM
F	Wednesday, August 05, 2009 3:11 PM
G	8/5/2009 3:11:26 PM
G	8/5/2009 3:11 PM
S	2009-08-05T15:11:26
U	Wednesday, August 05, 2009 1:11:26 PM
U	2009-08-05 15:11:26Z

ToString also recognizes date literals. The following is an example of how you can customize and write a date:

```
Console.WriteLine(Date.Today.ToString("dd/MM/yyyy"))
```

The above code prints the current date in the Day/Month/Year format. System.DateTime provides a plethora of other useful methods that you can use for formatting dates. Such methods also return different data types, depending on the scenario in which they have to be used in. Table 4.10 summarizes the most important methods that you can always inspect with IntelliSense and the Object Browser.

TABLE 4.10   System.DateTime Useful Methods

Method	Description	Type Returned
ToLocalTime	Returns the full date representation according to regional settings	Date (System.DateTime)
ToLongDateString	Returns a long format date (without time)	String
ToShortDateString	Returns a short format date (without time)	String
ToLongTimeString	Returns a long format time (without date)	String

TABLE 4.10   Continued

Method	Description	Type Returned
ToShortTimeString	Returns a short format time (without date)	String
ToUniversalTime	Returns a full date representation according to the Coordinated Universal Time specifications.	Date (System.DateTime)
ToOADate	Returns an OLE Automation date format	Double
ToFileTime	Returns the Windows file time representation of a date	Long
ToFileTimeUtc	Returns the Windows file time representation of a date, according to the Coordinated Universal Time specifications.	Long

The following code snippet takes all the preceding methods to demonstrate how the output differs depending on the method:

```
Console.WriteLine("Local time: {0}", Date.Now.ToLocalTime)
Console.WriteLine("Long date: {0}", Date.Now.ToLongDateString)
Console.WriteLine("Short date: {0}", Date.Now.ToShortDateString)
Console.WriteLine("Long time: {0}", Date.Now.ToLongTimeString)
Console.WriteLine("Short time: {0}", Date.Now.ToShortTimeString)
Console.WriteLine("Universal time: {0}", Date.Now.
                ToUniversalTime.ToString)
Console.WriteLine("File time: {0}", Date.Now.
                ToFileTime.ToString)
Console.WriteLine("File time UTC: {0}", Date.Now.
                ToFileTimeUtc.ToString)
Console.WriteLine("OLE Automation date: {0}", Date.Now.
                ToOADate.ToString)
```

The preceding code produces the following result that you can compare with methods as described in Table 4.9:

```
Local time: 08/05/2009 14:57:22
Long date: Wednesday, August 05, 2009
Short date: 8/5/2009
Long time: 2:57:22 PM
Short time: 2:57 PM
Universal time: 8/5/2009 12:57:22 PM
File time: 128939506428847656
File time UTC: 128939506428886718
OLE Automation date: 40030.6231815741
```

Subtracting Dates and Adding Time to Time

It's not unusual to need to know the amount of time spent between two dates. The System.DateTime enables accomplishing this invoking a Subtract method, which returns a System.TimeSpan value. For example, consider the following code that subtracts a date from another one:

```
Dim birthDate As Date = New Date(1977, 5, 10, 20, 30, 0)
Dim secondDate As Date = New Date(1990, 5, 11, 20, 10, 0)

Dim result As System.TimeSpan = secondDate.Subtract(birthDate)

'In days
Console.WriteLine(result.Days)
'In "ticks"
Console.WriteLine(result.Ticks)
```

You can subtract two DateTime objects and get a result of type TimeSpan (discussed next). You can then get information on the result, such as the number of days that represent the difference between the two dates or the number of ticks. The above code produces the following result:

```
4748
4103124000000000
```

You can also add values to a date. For example you can edit a date adding days, hour, minutes, seconds, or ticks or incrementing the year. Consider the following code snippet:

```
Dim editedDate As Date = birthDate.AddDays(3)
editedDate = editedDate.AddHours(2)
editedDate = editedDate.AddYears(1)

Console.WriteLine(editedDate)
```

Such code adds three days and two hours to the date and increments the year by one unit. In the end it produces the following output:

```
5/13/1978 10:30:00 PM
```

Dates are important and although they allow working with time, too, the .NET Framework provides an important structure specific for representing pieces of time: System.TimeSpan.

NOTE ABOUT OPERATORS

You can use standard operators such as the addition and subtraction operators when working with both DateTime and TimeSpan objects. This is possible because both objects overload the standard operators. Overloading operators is discussed in Chapter 11, "Structures and Enumerations."

Working with Time

You often need to represent intervals of time in your applications, especially in conjunction with dates. The .NET Framework provides a structure, therefore a value type, named System.TimeSpan. Such structure can represent time from a minimum value (one tick) until a maximum value (one day). A tick is the smallest unit for time representations and is equal to 100 nanoseconds. Whereas TimeSpan represents a summed amount of time between two given time values, the time portion of a Date object represents a single specific moment in time.

MINIMUM AND MAXIMUM VALUES

As for other value types, System.TimeSpan also provides two shared properties named MinValue and MaxValue that return respectively the following ticks: -10675199.02:48:05.4775808 and 10675199.02:48:05.4775807. For the sake of clarity, both values are respectively equals to System.Int64.MinValue and System.Int64.MaxValue.

You can find several places in which using TimeSpan is needed other than simply working with dates. For example, you might want to create your performance benchmarks using the StopWatch object that returns a TimeSpan. Or you might need such structure when working with animations in WPF applications. The following code example simulates a performance test; a System.StopWatch object is started and an intensive loop is performed, and then the StopWatch gets stopped. The StopWatch class offers an Elapsed property that is of type TimeSpan and that can be useful to analyze the amount of elapsed time:

```
Dim watch As New Stopwatch

watch.Start()
For i = 0 To 10000
    'Simulates intensive processing
    System.Threading.Thread.SpinWait(800000)
Next
watch.Stop()

Console.WriteLine(watch.Elapsed.Seconds)
Console.WriteLine(watch.Elapsed.Milliseconds)
Console.WriteLine(watch.Elapsed.Ticks)
```

The preceding code produced the following result on my machine, but, of course, it will be different on yours, depending on your hardware:

```
49
374
493746173
```

Basically the TimeSpan structure is similar to the area of the DateTime type that is related to time. Notice that TimeSpan offers several similar properties, such as Days, Hours, Minutes, Seconds, Milliseconds, and methods such as AddDays, AddHours, AddMinute, and Subtract. TimeSpan is all about time; this means that although there are similarities, as mentioned before, with the time-related DateTime members, you cannot (obviously) work with dates. The following code provides an example about creating a TimeSpan instance starting from an existing date:

```
Sub TimeSpanInstance()
    Dim currentDate As Date = Date.Now
    'Because the System namespace is imported at project
    'level, we do not need an Imports directive
    Dim intervalOfTime As TimeSpan = currentDate.TimeOfDay

    Console.WriteLine("My friend, in the current date " &
                      "there are {0} days; time is {1}:{2}:{3}",
            intervalOfTime.Days,
            intervalOfTime.Hours,
            intervalOfTime.Minutes,
            intervalOfTime.Seconds)
End Sub
```

The preceding code produces the following result:

```
My friend, in the current date there are 0 days; time is 19:13
```

Because in the specified interval there is only the current day, the first argument returns zero. Take a look back at the section "Subtracting Dates and Adding Time to Time" to see an example of TimeSpan usage for an interval of time retrieved subtracting two dates.

Working with TimeZone and TimeZoneInfo

You might often ask what people are doing on the other side of world when in your country it's a particular time of the day. Working with time zones can also be important for your business if you need to contact people who live in different and far away countries. The .NET Framework provides two types, TimeZone and TimeZoneInfo, which enable retrieving information on time zones. Both types are exposed by the System namespace. For example, imagine you want to retrieve information on the time zone of your country. This can be accomplished as follows (assuming regional settings on your machine are effectively related to your country):

```
Dim zone As TimeZone = TimeZone.CurrentTimeZone
```

TimeZone is a reference type and through its CurrentTimeZone property it provides a lot of information such as the name of the time zone or the daylight-saving time period as demonstrated here:

```
Console.WriteLine(zone.DaylightName)
```

```
Console.WriteLine(zone.StandardName)
```

```
Console.WriteLine(zone.IsDaylightSavingTime(Date.Now))
```

This code produces the following result on my machine:

```
W. Europe Daylight Time
W. Europe Standard Time
```

```
True
```

The official MSDN documentation states that using the `TimeZoneInfo` class should be preferred instead of `TimeZone`. This is because `TimeZoneInfo` also provides the ability of creating custom time zones. The following code shows how you can retrieve current time zone information using `TimeZoneInfo`:

```
Dim tz As TimeZoneInfo = TimeZoneInfo.Local
'Shows the current time zone Identifier
Console.WriteLine(tz.Id)
```

Creating a custom time zone is also a simple task, which is accomplished by the following code:

```
Dim customZone As TimeZoneInfo = TimeZoneInfo.
    CreateCustomTimeZone("CustomTimeZone",
    Date.UtcNow.Subtract(Date.Now),
    "Custom Zone", "Custom Zone")
```

All you need is specifying a custom identifier, the difference between the UTC time span and the local time span, a daylight identifier, and a standard identifier. `TimeZoneInfo` also provides another useful method for enumerating time zones recognized by the system, named `GetSystemTimeZones` and that you can use like this:

```
For Each timez As TimeZoneInfo In TimeZoneInfo.GetSystemTimeZones
    Console.WriteLine(timez.DisplayName)
Next
```

An excerpt of the output provided by this simple iteration is the following:

```
(UTC-12:00) International Date Line West
(UTC-11:00) Midway Island, Samoa
(UTC-10:00) Hawaii
(UTC-09:00) Alaska
(UTC-08:00) Pacific Time (US & Canada)
(UTC-08:00) Tijuana, Baja California
(UTC-07:00) Arizona
(UTC-07:00) Chihuahua, La Paz, Mazatlan
(UTC-07:00) Mountain Time (US & Canada)
(UTC-06:00) Central America
(UTC-06:00) Central Time (US & Canada)
```

4

```
(UTC-05:00) Eastern Time (US & Canada)
(UTC-05:00) Indiana (East)
(UTC-04:30) Caracas
(UTC-04:00) Santiago
(UTC-03:30) Newfoundland
(UTC-01:00) Cape Verde Is.
(UTC) Casablanca
(UTC) Coordinated Universal Time
(UTC) Dublin, Edinburgh, Lisbon, London
(UTC) Monrovia, Reykjavik
(UTC+01:00) Amsterdam, Berlin, Bern, Rome, Stockholm, Vienna
(UTC+02:00) Windhoek
(UTC+03:00) Baghdad
(UTC+03:00) Kuwait, Riyadh
(UTC+03:00) Moscow, St. Petersburg, Volgograd
(UTC+03:00) Nairobi
(UTC+06:00) Almaty, Novosibirsk
(UTC+06:00) Astana, Dhaka
(UTC+06:30) Yangon (Rangoon)
(UTC+07:00) Krasnoyarsk
(UTC+08:00) Beijing, Chongqing, Hong Kong, Urumqi
(UTC+08:00) Perth
(UTC+08:00) Taipei
(UTC+09:00) Yakutsk
(UTC+09:30) Adelaide
(UTC+10:00) Vladivostok
(UTC+11:00) Magadan, Solomon Is., New Caledonia
(UTC+12:00) Auckland, Wellington
(UTC+12:00) Fiji, Kamchatka, Marshall Is.
(UTC+13:00) Nuku'alofa
```

Thanks to this information, you could use the `TimeZoneInfo` class for converting between time zones. The following code demonstrates how to calculate the hour difference between Italy and Redmond, WA:

```
'Redmond time; requires specifying the Time Zone ID
Dim RedmondTime As Date = TimeZoneInfo.
    ConvertTimeBySystemTimeZoneId(DateTime.Now, "Pacific Standard Time")

Console.WriteLine("In Italy now is {0} while in Redmond it is {1}",
                Date.Now.Hour,RedmondTime.Hour)
```

Invoking the `ConvertTimeBySystemZoneId` method, you can convert between your local system time and another time, based on the zone ID. If you don't know zone IDs, just replace the previous iterations for showing the content of the `timez.Id` property instead of `DisplayName`.

Working with GUIDs

How many times do you need to represent something with a unique identifier? Probably your answer is "very often." Examples are items with the same name but with different characteristics. The .NET Framework enables creating unique identifiers via the `System.Guid` structure (therefore a value type). Such type enables generating a unique, 128-bit string, identifier. To generate a unique identifier, invoke the `Guid.NewGuid` method that works as follows:

```
'Declaring a Guid
Dim uniqueIdentifier As Guid

'A unique identifier
uniqueIdentifier = Guid.NewGuid
Console.WriteLine(uniqueIdentifier.ToString)

'Another unique identifier,
'although to the same variable
uniqueIdentifier = Guid.NewGuid
Console.WriteLine(uniqueIdentifier.ToString)
```

If you run the preceding code, you notice that each time you invoke the `NewGuid` method a new GUID is generated, although you assign such value to the same variable. This makes sense, because you use the GUID each time you need a unique identifier. On my machine the preceding code produces the following result:

```
96664b7d-1c8a-42a5-830f-3548dfe3ff8e
4767a1ff-a7c8-4db0-b37e-5b22a387cf00
```

EXAMPLES OF GUIDS

The Windows operating system makes a huge usage of GUIDs. If you try to inspect the Windows Registry, you find lot of examples.

The `Guid.NewGuid` method provides auto-generated GUIDs. If you need to provide your own GUID, you can use the `New` constructor followed by the desired identifier:

```
'Specifying a Guid
uniqueIdentifier = New Guid("f578c96b-5918-4f79-b690-6c463ffb2c3e")
```

The constructor has several overloads, which enable generating GUIDs also based on bytes array and integers. Generally you use GUIDs each time you need to represent something as unique. Several .NET types accept GUIDs, so you need to know how you can create them in code, although this is not the only way.

Creating GUIDs with the Visual Studio Instrumentation

The Visual Studio IDE provides a graphical tool for generating GUIDs. You can run this tool by choosing the **Create Guid** command from the Tools menu. Figure 4.10 shows the Create Guid window.

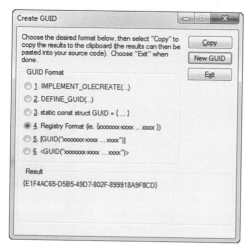

FIGURE 4.10   The Create GUID tool from Visual Studio.

You can choose what format you need for your GUID, such as Windows-like GUIDs. When you get your GUID, you can copy it to the clipboard and then reuse it in your code.

Working with Arrays

As a developer you of course know what arrays are. They are basically a place in which you can store a set of items, generally of the same type. In the .NET Framework 4.0 (as in older versions), arrays are reference types all deriving from the System.Array class and can be both one-dimensional and multidimensional.

ARRAYS VERSUS COLLECTIONS

Collections, especially generic ones, are generally more efficient than arrays. I always recommend working with collections instead of arrays, except when strictly needed. (For example, you might need jagged arrays.)

You can either declare an array and use it later in your code or declare it and assign it with objects. The following is an example of declaring an array of String objects, meaning that it can store only objects of type String:

```
Dim anArrayOfString() As String
```

In this line of code an array of String is declared. This array has no predefined bounds, so it is flexible and useful if you cannot predict how many items it needs to store. There is also an alternative syntax, which allows placing parentheses at the end of the type, as follows:

```
'Alternative syntax
Dim anArrayOfString As String()
```

You are free to use whichever syntax you like. For the sake of consistency the first one is used.

IS OPTION STRICT **ON?**

The preceding and the following code examples assume that Option Strict is set to On. If it is off, adding instances of System.Object is also allowed but might cause errors at runtime. It is recommended to set Option Strict to On to avoid implicit conversion, and this is one of those cases.

You can initialize arrays directly when declaring them, as in the following code that declares an array of strings and stores three instances of the System.String class:

```
'Inline initialization with implicit bounds
Dim anArrayOfThreeStrings() As String = New String() {"One", "Two", "Three"}
```

Notice how you assign an array using the New keyword followed by the type name and a couple of parentheses. Brackets contain the items to store. The declared array has no bounds limits, but actually after the assignment its upper bound is 2 so its bounds are determined by the number of values it is initialized with.

ARRAYS BASE

Arrays are zero-based. This means that an array with an upper bound of 2 can store three items (index of zero, index of one, and index of two).

This approach works with arrays of other .NET types, too, as in the following code in which Char and Byte are used:

```
Dim anArrayOfChar() As Char = New Char() {"a"c, "b"c, "c"c}
```

```
Dim anArrayOfByte() As Byte = New Byte() {1, 2, 3}
```

If you already know how many items the array can store, you can specify the bounds limits. For example, imagine you want to store three instances of System.Byte into an array of Byte. This can be accomplished via the following code:

```
Dim anExplicitBoundArrayOfByte(2) As Byte
anExplicitBoundArrayOfByte(0) = 1
anExplicitBoundArrayOfByte(1) = 2
anExplicitBoundArrayOfByte(2) = 3
```

INLINE INITIALIZATION WITH EXPLICIT BOUNDS

Inline initialization is not allowed against arrays declared with explicit bounds. In such situations the only allowed syntax is the one shown in the previous code snippet.

The upper limit is enclosed in parentheses. Storing items is accomplished through indices. (The first one is always zero.) As with assignment, you can retrieve the content of a particular item using indices:

```
'Outputs 2
Console.WriteLine(anExplicitBoundArrayOfByte(1).ToString)
```

You can also perform tasks on each element in the array using a For Each loop, as in the following code snippet, which works the same on an array of Byte and on array of String:

```
For Each value As Byte In anExplicitBoundArrayOfByte
    Console.WriteLine(value)
Next
For Each value As String In anArrayOfThreeStrings
    Console.WriteLine(value)
Next
```

Another important task that you should perform when working with not explicitly bound arrays is checking if they contain something. You can accomplish this checking if the array is Nothing:

```
If anArrayOfString Is Nothing Then
    'The array is not initialized
End If
```

This is because attempting to access a null array causes the runtime to throw an exception.

The ReDim Keyword

There are situations in which you need to increase the capacity of an array that you previously declared with explicit bounds. Let's retake one of the previous arrays:

```
Dim anExplicitBoundArrayOfByte(2) As Byte
anExplicitBoundArrayOfByte(0) = 1
```

```
anExplicitBoundArrayOfByte(1) = 2
anExplicitBoundArrayOfByte(2) = 3
```

At runtime you might need to store an additional Byte, so in this case you should first increase the array's size. To accomplish this, the Visual Basic grammar provides a special keyword named ReDim. ReDim basically redeclares an array of the same type with new bounds. But this keyword would also clean all the previously stored items; so what if you just need to add a new item to an existing list without clearing? Fortunately the Visual Basic grammar provides another keyword named Preserve that is the best friend of ReDim in such situations and enables maintaining the previously stored values, preventing cleaning. The following code redeclares the preceding array without cleaning previous values:

```
ReDim Preserve anExplicitBoundArrayOfByte(3)
```

At this point you can add a new item using the new available index:

```
anExplicitBoundArrayOfByte(3) = 4
```

Notice how you do not specify again the type of the array when using ReDim.

Multidimensional Arrays

Arrays can have multiple dimensions. Generally two-dimensional (also known as *rectangular*) and three-dimensional arrays are the most common situations. The following code declares a two-dimensional array with four values, but with no explicit dimensions specified:

```
Dim multiArray(,) As Integer = {{1, 2}, {3, 4}}
```

You can also specify dimensions as follows:

```
Dim multiArrayWithExplicitBounds(5, 1) As Integer
```

You cannot initialize arrays inline in the case of multidimensional arrays. You can then access indices as follows:

```
multiArrayWithExplicitBounds(1, 0) = 1
multiArrayWithExplicitBounds(2, 0) = 2
multiArrayWithExplicitBounds(1, 1) = 3
```

ARRAY LITERALS

Visual Basic 2010 offers a new feature for working with both multidimensional arrays and jagged arrays (discussed next), named Array Literals. Basically this feature enables the compiler to infer the appropriate type for arrays. Because it requires that you are familiar with the Local Type Inference, Array Literals are discussed in Chapter 21.

Jagged Arrays

Jagged arrays are basically arrays of arrays and are similar to multidimensional arrays. However, they differ because each item of a dimension is an array. Here you see examples of jagged arrays of `Integer`. To declare a jagged array, you can use the following syntax:

```
'A 9-entry array on the left and
'an unbound array on the right
Dim firstJaggedArray(8)() As Integer
```

As you can see, a jagged array declaration is characterized by a double couple of parentheses. You can also declare a jagged array that is not explicitly bound, as in the following code snippet:

```
Dim unboundJaggedArray()() As Integer
```

Although you can perform inline initializations, this coding technique could become difficult with complex arrays. Because of this, it could be more convenient declaring the array and then assigning its indices as follows:

```
Dim oneIntArray() As Integer = {1, 2, 3}
Dim twoIntArray() As Integer = {4, 5, 6}
unboundJaggedArray = {oneIntArray, twoIntArray}
```

By the way, the following initialization is perfectly legal:

```
Dim unboundJaggedArray()() As Integer _
    = {New Integer() {1, 2, 3}, New Integer() {4, 5, 6}}
```

As I explain in Chapter 21, the new *Array Literals* feature makes inline initialization easier. You can then normally access arrays (that is, items) in a jagged array, for example, performing a `For..Each` loop:

```
'Returns 1 2 3 4 5 6
        For Each arr As Integer() In unboundJaggedArray
            For Each item As Integer In arr
                Console.WriteLine(item.ToString)
            Next
        Next
```

Sorting, Creating, Copying and Inspecting Arrays with the `System.Array` Class

As I mentioned at the beginning of this section, all arrays derive from the `System.Array` class and therefore are reference types. This is an important consideration, because you have to know how to manipulate them. `System.Array` provides several static and instance members for performing tasks on arrays. Here we discuss the most important members and methods overloads, because all of them are self-explanatory, and IntelliSense will be your friend in showing the necessary information. First, here's an example of an array of byte:

```
Dim anArrayOfByte() As Byte = New Byte() {1, 2, 3}
```

In this array, bounds are not explicit. Particularly at runtime, you might need to access array indices but to avoid `IndexOutOfRange` exceptions you do need to know at least the upper bound. Just for clarification, imagine you want to perform a `For..Next` loop against an array. To accomplish this, you first need to know the bounds. The `GetLowerBound` and `GetUpperBound` methods enable retrieving lower and upper bounds of an array, as shown in the following code:

```
'Returns 0 and 2
Console.WriteLine("Lower bound {0}, upper bound {1}",
                anArrayOfByte.GetLowerBound(0).ToString,
                anArrayOfByte.GetUpperBound(0).ToString)
```

Both methods receive as an argument the dimension of the array. This is because they can work both on one-dimensional arrays and on multidimensional arrays. A zero dimension means that you are working with a one-dimensional array or with the first dimension of a multidimensional array. Another common task is about sorting arrays. There are two methods that you can use, `Sort` and `Reverse`. As you can easily understand, `Sort` performs ordering an array in an ascending way, whereas `Reverse` performs ordering in a descending way. Starting from the `anArrayOfByte` array, the following code reverses the order:

```
'Array now contains 3, 2, 1
Array.Reverse(anArrayOfByte)
```

To sort the array back, you can simply invoke the `Sort` method:

```
Array.Sort(anArrayOfByte)
```

Both methods perform ordering according to the `IComparable(Of T)` interface. You can also search for a particular item within an array. For this purpose you can use two methods: `IndexOf` and `BinarySearch`. Both return the index of the specified item, but the first one just stops searching when the first occurrence is found, whereas the second one searches through the entire array but only if the array is sorted according to the implementation of the `IComparable` interface. Their usage is very straightforward:

```
'A conversion to Byte is required
'Both return 1
Dim position As Integer = Array.IndexOf(anArrayOfByte, CByte(2))
Dim position2 As Integer = Array.BinarySearch(anArrayOfByte, CByte(2))
```

Both methods receive an `Object` as the second argument. But we have an array of `Byte`. Because writing just 2 tells the compiler to recognize such a number as an `Integer`, we need to explicitly convert it to `Byte`.

NOTE ON SYSTEM.ARRAY **METHODS**

System.Array also provides methods that take a lambda expression as arguments. Lambdas are discussed in Chapter 21, so this chapter does not apply them to arrays. A quick recap is done for your convenience in the appropriate place.

Another common task on arrays is copying. Because they are reference types, assigning an array to another just copies the reference. To create a real copy of an array, you can take advantage of the shared Copy method and of the instance CopyTo method. First, you need to declare a target array. Continuing the example about the anArrayOfByte array, you could declare the new one as follows:

```
'Declares an array to copy to,
'with bounds equals to the source array
Dim targetArray(anArrayOfByte.GetUpperBound(0)) As Byte
```

To ensure the upper bound is the same as in the original array, an invocation to the GetUpperBound method is made. Next you can copy the array:

```
'Copies the original array into the target,
'using the original length
Array.Copy(anArrayOfByte, targetArray, anArrayOfByte.Length)
```

Array.Copy needs you to pass the source array, the target array, and the total number of items you want to copy. Supposing you want to perform a complete copy of the source array, you can just pass its length. The alternative is to invoke the instance method CopyTo:

```
anArrayOfByte.CopyTo(targetArray, 0)
```

The method receives the target array as the first argument and the index where copying must begin as the second argument. A third way for copying an array is invoking the Clone method, which is inherited from System.Object. Note that Copy and CopyTo provide more granularity and control over the copy process. The last scenario creates arrays on-the-fly. You could need to perform such a task at runtime given a number of items of a specified type, for example when you receive several strings as the user input. The System.Array class provides a shared method named CreateInstance, which creates a new instance of the System.Array class. It receives two arguments: the System.Type that the array must be of and the upper bound. For example, the following code creates a new array of String that can store three elements:

```
Dim runTimeArray As Array = Array.CreateInstance(GetType(String), 2)
```

PAY ATTENTION TO CREATEINSTANCE

You should use CreateInstance with care, because you can write code that is correctly compiled but that can cause runtime errors (for example with regard to array bounds).

Because the first argument is the representation of the System.Type you want to assign to the array, you must use the GetType keyword to retrieve information about the type. You can assign items to each index invoking the SetValue method, which is an instance method. The following line of code assigns a string to the zero index of the previous array:

```
runTimeArray.SetValue(CStr("Test string"), 0)
```

If you want to retrieve your items, simply invoke the `GetValue` method specifying the index:

```
'Returns "Test string"
Console.WriteLine(runTimeArray.GetValue(0))
```

Common Operators

When working with data types, you often need to perform several tasks on them. Depending on what type you work with, the Visual Basic programming language offers different kinds of operators, such as arithmetic operators, logical and bitwise operators, and shift operators. In this section you learn about Visual Basic operators and how you can use them in your own code. Let's begin by discussing arithmetic operators that are probably the most frequent operators you will use.

Arithmetic Operators

Visual Basic 2010 provides some arithmetic operators, listed in Table 4.11.

TABLE 4.11   Arithmetic Operators

Operator	Description
+	Addition operator
-	Subtraction operator
*	Multiplication operator
/	Division operator
\	Integer division operator
^	Exponentiation operator
Mod	Integer division remainder

The first three operators are self-explanatory, so I would like to focus on the other ones. First, an important consideration should be done on the division operators. As shown in Table 4.11, Visual Basic offers two symbols, the slash (/) and backslash (\). The first one can be used in divisions between floating point numbers (such as `Double` and `Single` types), and the second can be used only in divisions between integer numbers. This baclslash is fast when working with integers and truncates the result in case it is a floating point number. Basically, the backslash accepts and returns just integers. To understand this concept, consider the following division between `Double`s:

```
'Division between double: returns 2.5
Dim dblResult As Double = 10 / 4
```

The result of such calculation is 2.5. Now consider the following one:

```
'Division between integers: returns 2
Dim intResult As Integer = 10 \ 4
```

The result of this calculation is 2. This is because the \ operator truncated the result, due to its integer nature. If you try to use such operators in a division involving floating point numbers, the Visual Basic compiler throws an exception which is useful for avoiding subtle errors. By the way, such an exception occurs only with Option Strict On, which you should always set as your default choice.

SUPPORTED TYPES

The integer division operator supports the following data types: SByte, Byte, Short, UShort, Integer, UInteger, Long, and ULong, that is, all numeric types that do not support a floating point.

For divisions between floating point numbers, it's worth mentioning that divisions between Single and Double are also allowed but this causes the compiler to perform some implicit conversions that should be avoided. In such situations, you should just perform an explicit conversion, as in the following code:

```
'Division between Single and Double
Dim singleValue As Single = 987.654
Dim doubleValue As Double = 654.321
Dim division As Single = singleValue / CSng(doubleValue)
```

The next interesting operator is the exponentiation operator. A simple example follows:

```
Dim result As Double = 2 ^ 4    'returns 16
```

The exponentiation operator returns a Double value. Because of this, even if operands are other types (such as Integer or Long), they will be always converted to Double. Behind the scenes, the ^ operator invokes the Pow method exposed by the System.Math class. So you could also rewrite the preceding line of code as follows:

```
Dim result As Double = System.Math.Pow(2,4)    'returns 16
```

The last built-in operator is Mod (which stands for *Modulus*) that returns the remainder of a division between numbers. The following lines of code show an example:

```
'Mod: returns 0
Dim remainder As Integer = 10 Mod 2
'Mod: returns 1
```

```
Dim remainder As Integer = 9 Mod 2
```

A typical usage of Mod is for determining if a number is an odd number. To accomplish this, you could create a function like the following:

```
Function IsOdd(ByVal number As Integer) As Boolean
  Return (number Mod 2) <> 0
End Function
```

If the remainder is different from zero, the number is odd and therefore returns True. Mod supports all numeric types, including unsigned types and floating point ones. The .NET Framework offers another way for retrieving the remainder of a division, which is the System.Math.IEEERemainnder method that works as follows:

```
'Double remainder
Dim dblRemainder As Double = System.Math.IEEERemainder(10.42, 5.12)
```

Although both Mod and IEEERemainder return the remainder of a division between numbers, they use different formulas behind the scenes and therefore the result may differ. According to the MSDN documentation, this is the formula for the IEEERemainder method:

```
IEEERemainder = dividend - (divisor * Math.Round(dividend / divisor))
```

This is instead the formula for the Modulus operator:

```
Modulus = (Math.Abs(dividend) - (Math.Abs(divisor) *
          (Math.Floor(Math.Abs(dividend) / Math.Abs(divisor))))) *
          Math.Sign(dividend)
```

You can see how calculations work differently, especially where Modulus gets the absolute value for dividend and divisor.

SYSTEM.MATH CLASS

This section provides an overview of the arithmetic operators built into the Visual Basic 2010 programming language. The System.Math class provides lots of additional methods for performing complex calculations but this is beyond the scope here.

Assignment Operators

You can use operators shown in the previous paragraph for incremental operations. Consider the following code:

```
Dim value As Double = 1


value += 1 'Same as value = value + 1
```

```
value -= 1 'Same as value = value - 1

value *= 2 'Same as value = value * 2

value /= 2 'Same as value = value / 2

value ^= 2 'Same as value = value ^ 2

Dim test As String = "This is"
test &= " a string" 'same as test = test & " a string"
```

You can therefore abbreviate your code using this particular form when performing operations or concatenations. Also notice that += assignment operator works on strings as well.

Logical, Bitwise and Shift Operators

Visual Basic 2010 offers logical, bitwise, and shift operators. Logical operators are special operators enabling comparisons between Boolean values and also returning Boolean values. Bitwise and shift operators enable performing operations bit by bit. Next let's discuss both logical and bitwise operators.

Logical Operators

In Visual Basic 2010, there are eight logical/bitwise operators: Not, And, Or, Xor, AndAlso,OrElse, IsFalse, IsTrue. In this subsection you learn about the first four, while the other ones will be covered in the next subsection. The first operator, Not, basically returns the opposite of the actual Boolean value. For example, the following lines of code return False because although the 43 number is greater than 10, Not returns the opposite:

```
'Returns False
Dim result As Boolean = (Not 43 > 10)
```

Logical operators can also be used with reference types. For example, you can return the opposite of the result of a comparison between objects (see section "Comparison Operators" for details):

```
Dim firstPerson As New Person
Dim secondPerson As New Person
'Returns True
result = (Not firstPerson Is secondPerson)
```

This code returns True; the comparison between firstPerson and secondPerson returns False because they point to two different instances of the Person class, but Not returns the opposite. Generally you use such operators for reverting the state of an object basing on a Boolean property. The next operator is And, which compares two Boolean values or expressions and returns True if both values or expressions are True; otherwise, if at least one value is False, And returns False. Here is an example of And:

```
'Returns False
result = 10 > 15 and 30 > 15
'Returns True
result = 20 > 15 and 30 > 15
'Returns True
result = 20 > 15 and 15 = 15
```

And is also useful for comparing Boolean properties of objects. For example, you might want to check if a text file exists on disk and that it is not zero-byte; you could write the following code:

```
If My.Computer.FileSystem.FileExists("C:\MyFile.txt") = True And
    My.Computer.FileSystem.ReadAllText("C:\MyFile.txt").Length > 0 Then
        'Valid file
End If
```

If both actions return True, And returns True. In our example this should mean that we encountered a valid text file. The next operator is Or. Such an operator works like this: if expressions or values are True, it returns True; if both are False, it returns False; and if one of the two expressions is True, it returns True. The following code demonstrates this scenario:

```
'Returns True
result = 10 > 15 or 30 > 15
'Returns True
result = 10 < 15 or 30 > 15
'Returns False
result = 10 > 15 or 30 < 15
```

The last operator is Xor (*eXclusive Or*). Such an operator compares two Boolean expressions (or values) and returns True only if one of the two expressions is True whereas in all other cases it returns False. Continuing the first example, Xor returns the values described inside comments:

```
'Returns True
result = 10 > 15 Xor 30 > 15
'Returns False
result = 20 > 15 Xor 30 > 15
'Returns False
result = 20 > 15 Xor 15 = 15
```

Short-Circuiting Operators

There are situations in which you do not need to perform the evaluation of the second expression in a Boolean comparison, because evaluating the first one provides the result you need. In such scenarios you can use two *short-circuiting operators*, AndAlso and OrElse. Short-circuiting means that code execution is shorter and performances are improved. Such operators are particularly useful when you need to invoke an external method from within an If..Then code block. For example, let's consider again the previous example for the And operator:

```
If My.Computer.FileSystem.FileExists("C:\MyFile.txt") = True And
    My.Computer.FileSystem.ReadAllText("C:\MyFile.txt").Length > 0 Then
        'Valid file
End If
```

The Visual Basic compiler performs both evaluations. What would it happen if the file does not exists? It throws a FileNotFoundException when the ReadAllText method is invoked, because the And operator requires both expressions to be evaluated. Of course, you should implement error handling routines for such code, but this example is just related to operators. You can simply prevent your code from encountering the previously described problem using AndAlso. You need to replace And with AndAlso, as in the following code:

```
    If My.Computer.FileSystem.FileExists("C:\MyFile.txt") = True AndAlso
My.Computer.FileSystem.ReadAllText("C:\MyFile.txt").Length > 0 Then
            'Valid file
    End If
```

AndAlso evaluates the first expression; if this returns False, the second expression is not evaluated at all. In this case, if the file does not exist, the code exits from the If block. AndAlso's counterpart is OrElse, which evaluates the second expression only when the first one is False. Finally, in Visual Basic there are two other operators named IsTrue and IsFalse. The first one works in conjunction with the OrElse operator while the second one with the AndAlso. You cannot explicitly invoke such operators in your code because it is the job of the Visual Basic compiler invoking them within an evaluation expression. This means that types that you want to be evaluated via OrElse or AndAlso must expose both of them. The following is a simple sample:

```
Public Structure myType
    Public Shared Operator IsFalse(ByVal value As myType) As Boolean
        Dim result As Boolean
        ' Insert code to calculate IsFalse of value.
        Return result
    End Operator
    Public Shared Operator IsTrue(ByVal value As myType) As Boolean
        Dim result As Boolean
        ' Insert code to calculate IsTrue of value.
        Return result
```

```
    End Operator
End Structure
```

Bitwise Operators

Performing bitwise operations basically means performing operations with two binary numbers, bit by bit. The problem here is that Visual Basic does not allow working directly with binary numbers, so you need to write code against decimal or hexadecimal numbers that the Visual Basic compiler will actually treat, behind the scenes, in their binary representation, but you still need to write them in a comprehensible way.

CONVERTING BETWEEN DECIMAL AND BINARY

You can use the Windows calculator to perform conversions between decimal/hexadecimal and binary numbers.

Bitwise operators in Visual Basic are still And, Or, Not, and Xor. But different from logical operations, in which such operators evaluate expressions, bitwise operations are related to bit manipulations. You might wonder why you would need to perform bitwise operations in the era of WPF, Silverlight, and other high-level technologies. You could get multiple answers to this question, but probably the most useful one is providing the example of applications that interact with hardware devices in which there is still the need of working in a bit-by-bit fashion. Another common situation in Visual Basic is the combination of Enum flags. Let's now see some examples. The And operator combines two operands into a result; inside such a result, it puts a 1 value where both operands have 1 in a particular position; otherwise it puts a zero. For a better explanation, consider the following code:

```
Dim result As Integer = 152 And 312
```

The binary counterpart for 152 is 10011000, whereas the binary counterpart for 312 is 100111000. The result variable's value is 24, whose binary counterpart is 11000. If you observe the following representation

```
 10011000
100111000
   11000
```

you can notice how the third line, which represents the result of the And operation, contains 1 only in positions in which both operands have 1. If you then convert the result back to a decimal number, you will get 24. The Or operator works similarly: It combines two operands into a result; inside such a result, it puts a 1 value if at least one of the operands has a 1 value in a particular position. Consider this code:

```
Dim result As Integer = 152 Or 312
```

Both 152 and 312 binary counterparts are the same as the previous example. The Or operator produces 110111000 as a binary output, whose decimal counterpart is 440. To understand this step, take a look at this comparison:

```
 10011000
100111000
110111000
```

It's easy to see that the result contains 1 where at least one of the operands contains 1 in a particular position. The Xor operator combines two operands into a result; inside such a result, it puts a 1 value if at least one of the operands has a 1 value in a particular position, but not if both have 1 in that position. (In such a case it places 0.) Consider this bitwise operation:

```
Dim result As Integer = 152 Xor 312
```

The 152 and 312 binary counterparts are the same as in the preceding example. But this line of code returns 416, whose binary counterpart is 110100000. So let's see what happened:

```
 10011000
100111000
110100000
```

As you can see, Xor placed 1 where at least one of the operands has 1 in a particular position, but where both operands have 1, it placed 0. The Not operator is probably the easiest to understand. It just reverses the bits of an operand into a result value. For example, consider this line of code:

```
Dim result As Integer = Not 312
```

In the following comparison, the second line is the result of the preceding negation:

```
100111000
011000111
```

This result has –313 as its decimal counterpart.

BINARY NUMBERS

This book does not teach binary numbers, so the code shown in this and in the following section assumes that you are already familiar with binary representations of decimal numbers.

Shift Operators

Shift operators are also something that makes more sense with binary numbers than with decimal or hexadecimal numbers, although you need to provide them via their decimal representations. Basically with shift operators you can move (that is, shift) a binary repre-

sentation left or right for the specified number of positions. The left-shift operator is <<
whereas the right-shift operator is >>. For example, consider the following Integer:

```
'Binary counterpart is
'101000100
Dim firstValue As Integer = 324
```

The binary representation for 324 is 101000100. At this point we want to left-shift such
binary for four positions. The following line accomplishes this:

```
'Returns 5184, which is
'1010001000000
Dim leftValue As Integer = firstValue << 4
```

With the left-shifting of four positions, the number 101000100 produces 1010001000000
as a result. Such binary representation is the equivalent of the 5184 decimal number,
which is the actual value of the leftValue variable. The right-shift operator works the
same but moves positions on the right:

```
'Returns 20, which is
'10100
Dim rightValue As Integer = firstValue >> 4
```

This code moves 101000100 for four positions to the right, so the binary result is 10100.
Its decimal equivalent is then 20, which is the actual value of the rightValue variable.

SUPPORTED TYPES

Shift operators support Byte, Short, Integer, Long, SByte, UShort, UInteger and
ULong data types. When using shift operators with unsigned types, there is no sign bit
to propagate and therefore the vacated positions are set to zero.

Concatenation Operators

As in the previous versions, Visual Basic 2010 still offers concatenation operators that are
the + and & symbols. The main difference is that the + symbol is intended for numeric
additions, although it can works also with strings; the & symbol is instead defined only
for strings, and it should be preferred when concatenating strings so that you can avoid
possible errors. Listing 4.2 shows an example of concatenation.

LISTING 4.2   Concatenation Operators

```
Module ConcatenationOperators
    Sub ConcatenationDemo()
```

```
        Dim firstString As String = "Alessandro"
        Dim secondString As String = "Del Sole"

        Dim completeString As String = firstString & secondString

        'The following still works but should be avoided
        'Dim completeString As String = firstString + secondString

    End Sub
End Module
```

Comparison Operators

As in its predecessors, Visual Basic 2010 still defines some comparison operators. Typically comparison operators are of three kinds: numeric operators, string operators, and object operators. Let's see such operators in details.

Numeric Comparison Operators

You can compare numeric values using the operators listed in Table 4.12.

TABLE 4.12   Numeric Comparison Operators

Operator	Description
=	Equality operator
<>	Inequality operator
<	Less than
>	Greater than
<=	Less than or equal to
>=	Greater than or equal to

Such operators return a Boolean value that is True or False. The following code snippet shows an example. (Comments within the code contain the Boolean value returned.)

```
Sub NumericOperators()

    Dim firstNumber As Double = 3
    Dim secondNumber As Double = 4
    Dim comparisonResult As Boolean = False

    'False
```

```
        comparisonResult = (firstNumber = secondNumber)
        'True
        comparisonResult = (secondNumber > firstNumber)
        'False
        comparisonResult = (secondNumber <= firstNumber)
        'True
        comparisonResult = (secondNumber <> firstNumber)
End Sub
```

String Comparison Operators

String comparison was discusses in the section "Working with Strings," so refer to that topic.

Objects Comparison Operators: Is, IsNot and TypeOf

You can compare two or more objects to basically understand if they are or point to the same instance or what type of object you are working with. Basically there are three operators for comparing objects: Is, IsNot, and TypeOf. Is and IsNot are intended to understand if two objects point to the same instance. Consider the following code:

```
Dim firstPerson As New Person
Dim secondPerson As New Person

'Returns True, not same instance
If firstPerson IsNot secondPerson Then

End If

'Returns False, not same instance
If firstPerson Is secondPerson Then

End If

'Returns True, same instance
Dim onePerson As Person = secondPerson
If secondPerson Is onePerson Then

End If
```

firstPerson and secondPerson are two different instances of the Person class. In the first comparison, IsNot returns True because they are two different instances. In the second comparison, Is returns False because they are still two different instances. In the third comparison, the result is True because you may remember that simply assigning a reference type just copies the reference to an object. In this case, both secondPerson and onePerson point to the same instance. The last example is related to the TypeOf operator.

Typically you use it to understand if a particular object has inheritance relationships with another one. Consider the following code snippet:

```
'Returns True
Dim anotherPerson As Object = New Person
If TypeOf anotherPerson Is Person Then

End If
```

We have here an `anotherPerson` object of type `Object`, assigned with a new instance of the `Person` class. (This is possible because `Object` can be assigned with any .NET type.) The `TypeOf` comparison returns `True` because `anotherPerson` is effectively an instance of `Person` (and not simply object). `TypeOf` is useful if you need to check for the data type of a Windows Forms or WPF control. For example, a `System.Windows.Controls.Button` control in WPF inherits from `System.Windows.Controls.FrameworkElement` and then `TypeOf x is FrameworkElement` returns `True`.

OPERATORS PRECEDENCE ORDER

Visual Basic operators have a precedence order. For further information, refer to the MSDN Library: http://msdn.microsoft.com/en-us/library/fw84t893(VS.100).aspx.

Iterations, Loops, and Conditional Code Blocks

Hundreds of programming techniques are based on loops and iterations. Both loops and iterations basically enable the repetition of some actions for a specific number of times or when a particular condition is `True` or `False`. All these cases are discussed next.

Iterations

Iterations in Visual Basic 2010 are performed via `For..Next` and `For Each` loops. Let's analyze them more in details.

For..Next

A `For..Next` loop enables repeating the same action (or group of actions) for a finite number of times. The following code shows an example in which the same action (writing to the Console window) is performed 10 times:

```
For i As Integer = 1 To 10
    Console.WriteLine("This action has been repeated {0} times", i)
Next
```

In such loops you need to define a variable of a numeric type (`i` in the preceding example) that acts as a counter.

You may also assign the variable with another variable of the same type instead of assigning a numeric value.

The above code produces the following result:

```
This action has been repeated 1 times
This action has been repeated 2 times
This action has been repeated 3 times
This action has been repeated 4 times
This action has been repeated 5 times
This action has been repeated 6 times
This action has been repeated 7 times
This action has been repeated 8 times
This action has been repeated 9 times
This action has been repeated 10 times
```

Notice that you can also initialize the counter with zero or with any other numeric value.

Use `Integer` or `UInteger` variables as counters in `For..Next` loops. This is because such data types are optimized for the Visual Basic compiler. Other numeric types are also supported but are not optimized, so you are encouraged to always use `Integer` or `UInteger`.

You can also decide how the counter must be incremented. For example, you could decide to increment the counter of two units instead of one (as in the previous example). This can be accomplished via the `Step` keyword:

```
For i As Integer = 1 To 10 Step 2
    Console.WriteLine("Current value is {0}", i)
Next
```

This code produces the following output:

```
Current value is 1
Current value is 3
Current value is 5
Current value is 7
Current value is 9
```

`Step` can also work with negative numbers and allows performing a going-back loop:

```
For i As Integer = 10 To 1 Step -2
```

```
    Console.WriteLine("Current value is {0}", i)
Next
```

You can also decide to break a For loop when a particular condition is satisfied, and you do not need to still perform the iteration. This can be accomplished with the Exit For statement, as shown in the following example:

```
For i As Integer = 1 To 10
    Console.WriteLine("Current value is {0}", i)
    If i = 4 Then Exit For
Next
```

In the preceding example, when the counter reaches the value of 4, the For loop is interrupted and control is returned to the code that immediately follows the Next keyword. There is also another way for controlling a For loop; there could be situations in which you need to pass the control directly to the next iteration of the loop when a particular condition is satisfied (which is the opposite of Exit For). This can be accomplished with the Continue For statement, as shown in the following code snippet:

```
For i As Integer = 1 To 10
    If i = 4 Then   'Ignore the 4 value
        i += 1 'Increments to 5
        Continue For   'Continues from next value, that is 6
    End If
    Console.WriteLine("Current value is  {0}", i)
Next
```

In the preceding example we are doing some edits on the counter. Notice that each time you invoke a Continue For, the counter itself is incremented one unit.

For Each

A For Each loop allows performing an action or a group of actions on each item from an array or a collection. Although collections are discussed in Chapter 16, it is a good idea to provide a code example with them, because this is the typical usage of a For Each loop. For example, consider the following code:

```
'A collection of Process objects
Dim procList As List(Of Process) = Process.GetProcesses.ToList

For Each proc As Process In procList
    Console.WriteLine(proc.ProcessName)
    Console.WriteLine("      " & proc.Id)
Next
```

In the preceding code snippet, there is a collection containing references to all the running processes on the machine. Each process is represented by an instance of the System.Diagnostics.Process class; therefore List(Of Process) is a collection of processes. Supposing we want to retrieve some information for each process, such as the name and the identification number, we can iterate the collection using a `For Each` statement. You need to specify a variable that is the same type of the item you are investigating. In the preceding code you are just performing reading operations, but you can also edit items' properties. For example, you might have a collection of `Person` objects, and you could retrieve and edit information for each `Person` in the collection, as in the following code:

```
'A collection of Person objects
Dim people As New List(Of Person)
'Populate the collection here..
'....
For Each p As Person In people
    p.LastName = "Dr. " & p.LastName
    Console.WriteLine(p.LastName)
Next
```

This code will add the `Dr.` prefix to the `LastName` property of each `Person` instance.

FOR..EACH AVAILABILITY

Behind the scenes, `For Each` can be used against objects that implement the `IEnumerable` or `IEnumerable(Of T)` interfaces. Such objects expose the enumerator that provides support about `For Each` iterations.

You can still use `Exit For` when you need to break out from a `For Each` statement. Basically a `For Each` loop has better performances with collections than with arrays, but you have to know that you can use it in both scenarios.

Loops

As in the previous versions of the language, Visual Basic 2010 offers two kinds of loops: `Do..Loop` and `While..End While`. In this section we take a look at both loops.

Do..Loop

The `Do..Loop` is the most used loop in Visual Basic and the most flexible. Basically such a loop can have two behaviors: repeating a set of actions until a condition is false and repeating a set of actions until a condition is true. The first scenario is accomplished using a `Do While` statement, as demonstrated in Listing 4.3.

LISTING 4.3   Performing a Do While Loop

```
Sub LoopWhileDemo()
    Dim max As Integer = 0
    Do While max < Integer.MaxValue
        max += 1
        'Do something else here
```

```
        If max = 7000000 Then Exit Do
    Loop
        Console.WriteLine("Done: " & max.ToString)
End Sub
```

The code is quite easy: Whereas the value of max is less than the maximum value of the Integer type, increment max itself is one unit. Do While evaluates a False condition. (The loop goes on because max is less than Integer.MaxValue.) The code also demonstrates how you can exit from a loop using an Exit Do statement. This passes the control to the next statement after the Loop keyword. The other scenario is when you need to evaluate a True condition. This can be accomplished via a Do Until loop. Listing 4.4 demonstrates this.

LISTING 4.4   Demonstrating a Do Until Loop

```
Sub LoopUntilDemo()
    Dim max As Integer = 0
    Do Until max = Integer.MaxValue
        max += 1

        If max = 7000000 Then Exit Do
    Loop
        Console.WriteLine("Done: " & max.ToString)
End Sub
```

The difference here is that the loop ends when the condition is True, that is, when the value of max equals the value of Integer.MaxValue. Same as before, Exit Do can end the loop. The interesting thing in both cases is that you can evaluate the condition on the Loop side instead of the Do one. Listing 4.5 shows how you could rewrite both examples.

LISTING 4.5   Evaluating Conditions on the Loop Line

```
'Loop is executed at least once
Sub LoopUntilBottomDemo()
    Dim max As Integer = 0
    Do
        max += 1
        If max = 7000000 Then Exit Do
    Loop Until max = Integer.MaxValue
        Console.WriteLine("Done: " & max.ToString)
End Sub

'Loop is executed at least once
Sub LoopWhileBottomDemo()
    Dim max As Integer = 0
    Do
```

```
        max += 1
        If max = 7000000 Then Exit Do
    Loop While max < Integer.MaxValue
    Console.WriteLine("Done: " & max.ToString)
End Sub
```

Both loops behave the same way as previous ones, with one important difference: Here the loop is executed at least once.

PERFORMANCE TIPS

Basically the For loops are faster than Do ones. Because of this you should prefer For loops particularly when you know that you will do a finite number of iterations.

While..End While

A While..End While loop performs actions when a condition is False. Listing 4.6 shows an example.

LISTING 4.6   **While..End While Loop**

```
Sub WhileEndWhileDemo()
    Dim max As Integer = 0
    While max < Integer.MaxValue
        max += 1

        If max = 7000000 Then Exit While
    End While
    Console.WriteLine("Done: " & max.ToString)
End Sub
```

Basically the loop behaves the same as Do While, because both evaluate the same condition.

NOTE

The While..End While loop is less efficient than a Do While and is deprecated, although it is still supported. You should then always prefer a Do While loop.

Conditional Code Blocks

If..Then..Else

The If..Then..Else is the most classical block for conditionally executing actions. An If evaluates an expression as True or False and according to this allows specifying actions to take. Listing 4.7 shows an example.

LISTING 4.7   Demonstrating the `If..Then..Else` Block

```vb
Sub IfThenElseDemo()
    Console.WriteLine("Type a number")
    'Assumes users type a valid number
    Dim number As Double = CDbl(Console.ReadLine)

    If number >= 100 Then
        Console.WriteLine("Your number is greater than 100")
    ElseIf number < 100 And number > 50 Then
        Console.WriteLine("Your number is less than 100 and greater than 50")
    Else
        'General action
        Console.WriteLine("Your number is: {0}", number)
    End If
End Sub
```

If checks if the condition is `True`; if so, it takes the specified action. Of course you can also specify to evaluate a condition for `False` (for example, `If something = False Then`). You can also use an `ElseIf` to delimit the condition evaluation. If no expression satisfies the condition, the `Else` statement provides an action that will be executed in such a situation.

CODING TIP

The Visual Studio 2010 IDE introduces a new important feature, which is known as *code blocks delimiters selection*. Because you can nest different `If..Then` blocks or you can have a long code file, when you place the cursor near either the If/Then keywords or near the `End If` statement, the IDE highlights the related delimiter (`End If`, if you place the cursor on an `If` and vice versa).

Notice how the code uses an `And` operator to evaluate the condition. You can, of course, use other operators such as logical and short-circuit operators as well. Another typical example is when you need to check if a condition is false using the `Not` operator. The following is an example:

```vb
If Not number >= 100 Then
    'Number is False
End If
```

Not also requires the same syntax when working with reference types but in this case you can also use the `IsNot` operator. The following example checks if the instance of the Person class is not null:

```vb
Dim p As Person  'p is actually null
```

```
'You can check with IsNot
If p IsNot Nothing Then
    'p is not null
Else
    'p is null
End If
```

IsNot is not available with value types.

Select Case

Select Case is a statement that allows evaluating an expression against a series of values. Generally Select Case is used to check if an expression matches a particular value in situations evaluated as True. Listing 4.8 provides an example.

LISTING 4.8   Using the Select Case Statement for Evaluating Expressions

```
Sub SelectCaseDemo()
    Console.WriteLine("Type a file extension (without dot):")
    Dim fileExtension As String = Console.ReadLine

    Select Case fileExtension.ToLower
        Case Is = "txt"
            Console.WriteLine("Is a text file")
        Case Is = "exe"
            Console.WriteLine("Is an executable")
        Case Is = "doc"
            Console.WriteLine("Is a Microsoft Word document")
        Case Else
            Console.WriteLine("Is something else")
    End Select
End Sub
```

The code in Listing 4.8 simply compares the string provided by the user with a series of values. If no value matches the string, a Case Else is used to provide a general result. Comparison is performed with the Is operator and the equality operator. The following syntax is also accepted:

```
Case "txt"
```

IntelliSense adds by default the Is = symbology that is definitely clearer. You can also break from a Select Case statement in any moment using an Exit Select statement. Select..Case also offers another syntax to apply when you want to check if a value falls within a particular range. To accomplish this you use the To keyword instead of the Is =

operators, like in the following code that waits for the user to enter a number and then checks what range the number falls in:

```vbnet
Console.WriteLine("Enter a number from 1 to 50:")
Dim result As Integer = CInt(Console.ReadLine)
Select Case result
    'The user entered a number in the range from 1 to 25
    Case 1 To 25
        Console.WriteLine("You entered {0} which is a small number",
                          result.ToString)
    'The user entered a number in the range from 26 to 50
    Case 26 To 50
        Console.WriteLine("You entered {0} which is a high number",
                          result.ToString)
    'The user entered a number < 1 or > 50
    Case Else
        Console.WriteLine("You entered a number which is out of range")
End Select
```

In other words, considering the preceding example, `Case 1 To 25` means: in case the value to check is in the range between the left value (1) and the right value (25), then take the nested action.

CODING TIP

For the `If..End If` block, the code blocks delimiters selection feature is also available for `Select..End Select` blocks.

PERFORMANCE TIPS

The Visual Basic compiler evaluates expressions as a sequence. Because of this, in `Select Case` statements it evaluates all conditions until the one matching the value is found. Consequently, the first `Case` instructions in the sequence should be related to values considered the most frequent.

Constants

Constants provide a way for representing an immutable value with an identifier. There could be situations in which your applications need to use the same value (which can be of any .NET type); therefore, it can be convenient to define an easy-to-remember identifier instead of a value. What would happen if such a value were a `Long` number? You declare constants as follows:

```vbnet
Const defaultIntegerValue As Integer = 123456789
Const aConstantString As String = "Same value along the application"
```

Constants are basically read-only fields that can be declared only at the module and class level or within a method and must be assigned with a value when declared. Constants within methods have *public* visibility by default, whereas constants at the module and class level can have one of the .NET scopes, as in the following lines:

```
Private Const defaultIntegerValue As Integer = 123456789
Public Const aConstantString As String= "Same value along the application"
```

The reason why constants must be assigned when declared is that the expression is evaluated at compile time. Starting from Visual Basic 2008, there are a couple of things to consider. Look at the following line of code:

```
Private Const Test = "Test message"
```

The type for the `Test` variable is not specified. Until Visual Basic 2005, with `Option Strict Off` such a declaration would assign `Object`. In Visual Basic 2008 and 2010, if `Option Infer` is `On`, the compiler assigns `String` whereas if it is `Off`, the compiler goes back assigning `Object`.

With..End With statement

Visual Basic provides an alternative way for invoking object members that is the `With..End With` statement. Consider the following code block, in which a new `Person` class is instantiated and then properties are assigned while methods are invoked:

```
Dim p As New People.Person
p.FirstName = "Alessandro"
p.LastName = "Del Sole"
Dim fullName As String = p.ToString
```

Using a `With..End With` statement you just need to specify the name of the class once and then simply type a dot so that IntelliSense shows up members that you can use, as follows:

```
Dim p As New People.Person
With p
    .FirstName = "Alessandro"
    .LastName = "Del Sole"
    Dim fullName As String = .ToString
End With
```

There is no difference between the two coding techniques, so feel free to use the one you like most. `With..End With` just offers the advantage of speeding the code writing up a little and can be useful if you have a lot of members to invoke or assign at one time.

WITH..END WITH **NOTE**

`With..End With` has no equivalent in other .NET languages, so if you have to interoperate it could be a good idea assigning members the normal way. Although the compiler translates the `With..End With` blocks as single members' invocations, in such scenarios the best approach is a .NET-oriented coding style more than a VB-oriented one.

Summary

Every development environment relies on data types. Basically the .NET Framework relies on two kinds of data types: value types and reference types. Both kinds of types are managed by the Common Type System, which provides a common infrastructure to .NET languages for working with types. In this chapter you learned the important basics of the .NET development and the Visual Basic language, which can be summarized as follows:

▶ Common Type System

▶ Value types and reference types

▶ System.Object and inheritance levels in value types and reference types

▶ Memory allocation of both value types and reference types

▶ Converting between types and conversion operators

▶ Most common value types and reference types

▶ Common operators

You often need to work with and analyze data types. Visual Basic 2010 provides several ways for performing work on types and data they store. To accomplish this you can use

▶ Iterations, such as For..Next and For..Each

▶ Loops, such as Do..Loop

▶ Conditional code blocks, such as If..End If and Select Case..End Select

It's important to understand all the preceding features because they often recur in your developer life; these features appear extensively in the rest of the book. But you also might encounter errors when working with types. The next two chapters discuss two fundamental topics in the .NET development with Visual Basic: debugging and handling errors.

CHAPTER 5

Debugging Visual Basic 2010 Applications

Debugging is one of the most important tasks in your developer life. Debugging enables you to investigate for errors and analyze the application execution flow over an object's state. Visual Studio 2010 offers powerful tools for making debugging an easier task. In this chapter you get details about the Visual Studio instrumentation, and you also learn how to make your code suitable to interact better with the debugger. Remember that some improvements introduced by Microsoft to the 2010 edition are specific to particular technologies (such as WPF or the Task Parallel Library) and therefore will eventually be described in the appropriate chapters. In this chapter you find information regarding the generality of Visual Basic applications. Chapter 2, "Getting Started with the Visual Studio 2010 IDE," provides an overview of the most common debugging tasks whereas in this chapter you learn about more advanced debugging tools and techniques available in the IDE. Be sure you read Chapter 2 before going on with this one.

Preparing an Example

Most debugging features illustrated in this chapter require some code before you can use them. At the moment we are more interested in the Visual Studio 2010 instrumentation than in complex code, so we start with a simple code example that is a good base for understanding how the debugger works. Therefore, you can create a new Visual Basic project for the Console and then type the code, as shown in Listing 5.1.

LISTING 5.1   Preparing the Base for the Debugger

```
Module Module1

    Sub Main()

        Console.WriteLine("Enter a valid string:")
        Dim lineRead As String = Console.ReadLine()

        Dim result As Boolean = Test(lineRead)

        Console.WriteLine("Is a valid string: " & result.ToString)
        Console.ReadLine()
    End Sub

    Function Test(ByVal name As String) As Boolean
        If String.IsNullOrEmpty(name) = False Then
            Return True
        Else
            Return False
        End If
    End Function
End Module
```

The code is quite simple. The application just asks the user to enter a string and then returns False if the string is null or is empty, whereas it returns True if the string is valid. With such simple code you can now begin learning the advanced debugging instrumentation available in Visual Studio 2010.

Debugging Instrumentation

The Visual Studio 2010 IDE offers several powerful tools for deeply debugging applications. Such tools are part of the development environment instrumentation and are discussed in this section.

Debugging in Steps

When the application execution breaks, for example when the debugger finds a breakpoint, you can usually continue to execute the application running just one line of code per time or a small set of lines of code per time. In Chapter 2, you learned about the Step Into command; in this section we discuss other similar commands that cause different debugger behaviors.

HOW CAN I EXECUTE SUCH TECHNIQUES?

Debugging techniques described in this section can be accomplished by invoking commands available in the Debug menu of Visual Studio 2010. In the meantime, shortcuts are available for invoking the same commands using the keyboard. These are provided when discussing each command.

Step Into

The Step Into command executes one instruction per time. It is similar to Step Over, but if the instruction to be executed is a method, the method is executed one instruction per time and, when finished, the execution goes back to the caller. You can invoke Step Into by pressing **F11**.

NOTE ON KEYBOARD SHORTCUTS

The keyboard shortcuts utilized in this chapter assume that you are using the Visual Studio default keyboard layout and can vary depending on the IDE configuration settings. The Debug menu shows the appropriate keyboard shortcuts for your active configuration.

Step Over

Similarly to Step Into, Step Over executes one instruction per time. The difference is that if the instruction to be executed is a method, the debugger does not enter the method and completes its execution before going back to the caller. You can invoke Step Over by pressing **F10**. This can be useful when you need to debug a portion of code that invokes several methods that you already tested and that you do not need to delve into each time.

Step Out

Step Out works only within methods and enables executing all lines of code next to the current one, until the method completes. If you consider the code shown in Listing 5.1 and place a breakpoint on the `If` statement inside the `Test` method definition, invoking Step Out can cause the debugger to execute all the lines of code next to the If, completing the execution of the method. In such an example, after Step Out completes, the control is returned to the second `Console.Writeline` statement in `Sub Main`. You can invoke Step Out by pressing **Shift+F11**.

Run to Cursor

You can place the cursor on a line of code, right-click the line of code, and tell the debugger to execute all the code until the selected line. This can be accomplished by selecting the **Run to Cursor** command on the pop-up menu.

Set Next Statement

Within a code block, you can set the next statement to be executed when resuming the application execution after a breakpoint or a stop. Continuing the previous code example, if you place a breakpoint on the first `Console.Writeline` statement, inside the `Main` method, the application stops the execution at that point. Now imagine you want the debugger to resume debugging from the second `Console.Writeline` statement (therefore skipping the debugging of the Test method invocation), executing the lines of code before. You can just right-click the Console.Writeline statement and select **Set Next Statement** from the pop-up menu, and this line will be the first that you can step through.

Show Next Statement

This command moves the cursor to the next executable statement. This can be useful if you have long code files, and breakpoints are not immediately visible. You can invoke it simply by right-clicking the code editor and choosing the **Show Next Statement** command from the pop-up menu.

Mixed Mode Debugging

You can debug Visual Basic applications built upon both managed and native code with the Mixed Mode feature. In the previous versions of the environment, this feature was only available for 32-bit applications while now it is available also for 64-bit applications. To enable mixed-mode debugging, follow these steps:

1. In Solution Explorer, select the project you want to debug.
2. Open My Project and select the **Debug** tab.
3. Select the **Enable Unmanaged Code Debugging** checkbox.

"Just My Code" Debugging

You may remember from Chapter 2 and Chapter 3, "The Anatomy of a Visual Basic Project," that every time you create a Visual Basic application the IDE generates some background code. Moreover, your code often invokes system code that you do not necessarily need to investigate. Starting from Visual Basic 2005, and then also in Visual Basic 2010, the IDE offers the capability of debugging just your own code, excluding system and auto-generated code. This feature is also known as Just My Code debugging. This is useful because you can focus on your code. Just My Code is enabled by default in Visual Studio 2010. To disable it or enable it, you simply need to open the Options window, select the **Debugging** node on the left, and then flag or unflag the **Enable Just My Code (Managed Only)** check box, as shown in Figure 5.1.

Behind the scenes, Just My Code adds (or removes) some .NET attributes to auto-generated code that can influence the debugger behavior. To see a simple example, open or create a project and then click the **Show All Files** button in Solution Explorer. After doing this, go to the Settings.designer.vb code file. Listing 5.2 shows the content of the My namespace definition inside the file.

LISTING 5.2   Understanding Just My Code Behind the Scenes

```
Namespace My

    <Global.Microsoft.VisualBasic.HideModuleNameAttribute(), _
     Global.System.Diagnostics.DebuggerNonUserCodeAttribute(), _
     Global.System.Runtime.CompilerServices.CompilerGeneratedAttribute()> _
```

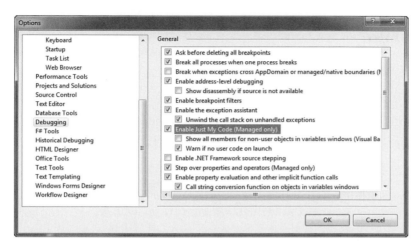

FIGURE 5.1   Enabling/disabling Just My Code debugging.

```
Friend Module MySettingsProperty

    <Global.System.ComponentModel.Design.HelpKeywordAttribute("My.Settings")> _
    Friend ReadOnly Property Settings() As
                    Global.DebuggingFeatures.My.MySettings
        Get
            Return Global.DebuggingFeatures.My.MySettings.Default
        End Get
    End Property
End Module
End Namespace
```

You can notice that the module `MySettingsProperty` is decorated with a particular attribute named `System.Diagnostics.DebuggerNonUserCodeAttribute`. This attribute indicates to the debugger that the code is not your code (user code) and it will not be debugged when Just My Code is on. Basically three attributes influence the debugger's behavior in this feature. Table 5.1 shows the complete list.

TABLE 5.1   Just My Code Attributes

Attribute	Description
DebuggerNonUserCode	Indicates to the debugger that the code is not user code and therefore is treated as system code
DebuggerHidden	Indicates to the debugger that code will not be visible at all to the debugger and therefore excluded from debugging
DebuggerStepThrough	Indicates to the debugger that the Step Into procedure is not allowed

Of course, you can use attributes of your own so that you can influence the behavior of the debugger when Just My Code is disabled.

Working with Breakpoints and Trace Points

In Chapter 2 we introduced breakpoints and saw how we can break the application execution before some statements are executed. In Visual Studio 2010, breakpoints are more powerful than in the previous versions of the IDE. We now discuss some interesting features of breakpoints when debugging Visual Basic applications.

The Breakpoints Window

Using the Breakpoints window you can manage all breakpoints in your solution. You can open such a window by pressing **Ctrl+Alt+B**. Supposing we placed three breakpoints in our sample application, Figure 5.2 shows how the Breakpoints window looks.

FIGURE 5.2   The Breakpoints window.

In the Breakpoints window you can easily manage your breakpoints. For example, you could delete, temporarily disable, or enable again the breakpoints. You can also specify the behavior for each breakpoint, such as Hit count, Filter, and other functionalities that we describe next. Also, you can easily switch to the source code in which the breakpoint is located or to the disassembly view. (See Figure 5.9 in the "Call Stack Window" section later in this chapter.) An important opportunity is exporting and importing breakpoints; Visual Studio 2010 can export to Xml files the list of breakpoints or import a list from an Xml file. If you have lots of breakpoints, you can search breakpoints according to specific criteria using the Label feature that we focus on next. Basically the Breakpoints window provides a graphical unified instrument for performing operations on breakpoints. We now discuss these operations.

Editing Breakpoints Labels

Visual Studio 2010 enables adding labels to breakpoints. Labels are a kind of identifier that can identify more than one breakpoint, and their purpose is categorizing breakpoints so that you can easily find and manage them within the Edit Breakpoint Label window. You can add a label to a breakpoint from the Edit Breakpoint Label window or by right-clicking the red ball on the left of the desired breakpoint in the code editor and then selecting the **Edit Labels** command from the pop-up menu. The Edit Breakpoint Labels window is shown in Figure 5.3.

FIGURE 5.3   The Edit Breakpoint Labels window enables categorizing breakpoints.

You simply need to specify labels and click **Add**. When you finish, select the label you want from the list and click **OK** so that the label is assigned to the breakpoint. You can assign the same label to multiple breakpoints performing the same steps or you can assign multiple labels to a single breakpoint. Assigning labels to breakpoints can be reflected into the **Breakpoints** window in which you can search for breakpoints specifying labels in the search box.

Location
You can change the position of a breakpoint by right-clicking the breakpoint and then selecting the **Location** command from the pop-up menu. In the appearing dialog you need to specify the line of code and character position in which you want the breakpoint to be moved to. This can be useful because you can move a breakpoint without losing breakpoint settings.

Hit Count
With the *hit* term we mean each time a breakpoint is encountered and therefore the application execution should stop. You can control the hit's behavior. For example, imagine you have a cyclic code that contains a breakpoint, but you need to break the execution only when the cycle arrives at a particular point. By using the Hit Count command, you can specify when the debugger must break the application. For example, consider the following code snippet:

```
For i As Integer = 0 To 3
    Console.WriteLine("Breakpoint test")
Next
```

Imagine you place a breakpoint on the `Console.WriteLine` statement and that you want the debugger to break only starting from the second iteration. You can specify this condition by right-clicking the breakpoint and then selecting the **Hit Count** command. In the Breakpoint Hit Count dialog you need to specify the condition. The default setting is always break, which means that the debugger breaks the execution each time a breakpoint is encountered. For our example, set the condition as **Break When the Hit Count Is Greater Than or Equal To** with value 2. Figure 5.4 shows the Hit Count window.

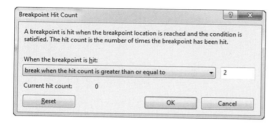

FIGURE 5.4　The Breakpoint Hit Count window enables customizing breakpoints' behavior.

With this setting, the above code would break on the second iteration. It can be convenient when you need to debug your code only from a certain point.

When Hit

When Hit enables specifying a tracepoint. The difference between a breakpoint and a tracepoint is that in this second case the debugger will not break the execution of the application and writes the information that you specify in the Output window. To set a hit condition, right-click a breakpoint and then select the **When Hit** command from the pop-up menu. This opens the When Breakpoint Is Hit window, which is shown in Figure 5.5.

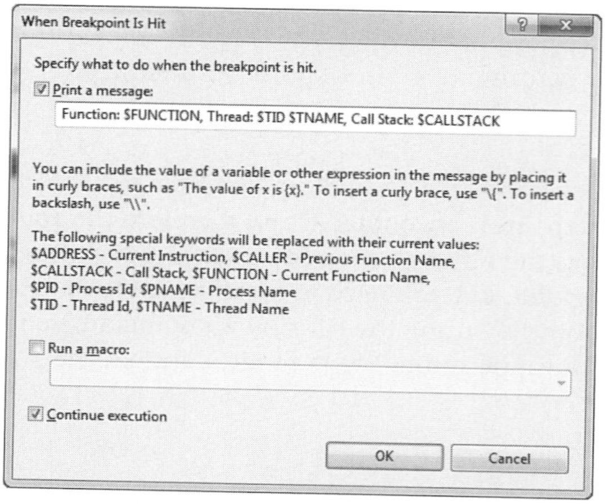

FIGURE 5.5　Specifying tracepoint conditions.

You can set one of the special expressions indicated in the window to build a kind of log message that will be written to the Output window. A tracepoint is highly customizable, so you can also specify a Visual Basic macro and decide whether the execution needs to continue. This feature is useful when you prefer getting a log message about the application state instead of breaking the execution.

Condition

Such a command enables specifying whether a breakpoint must be hit or not depending if the supplied expressions are evaluated to True or get changed. Information on conditions is provided by the following page of the MSDN Library: http://msdn.microsoft.com/en-us/library/za56x861(VS.100).aspx. When a condition is set, the debugger then steps into the Hit Count tool.

Locals Window

The Locals window shows the active local variables and their values. Considering the example in Listing 5.1, when stepping into the Main method the Local window shows information about lineRead and result variables, as shown in Figure 5.6.

FIGURE 5.6   The Locals window shows information on local variables.

As you can see, the window shows names of the local variables, their types (in our example Boolean and String), and their actual values. When a variable is not initialized yet, the window shows the default value (for example, Nothing for reference types and zero for Integers). Moreover, if a variable represents an object such as a class or a collection, the variable can be expanded to show members and their values. You can also change variables' values by double-clicking each one. Some variables cannot be viewed without executing code, such as in-memory queries (although they can be still viewed but the IDE will run the code in memory in order to be able to display the results).

Command Window

The Command window enables evaluating expressions or running functions without running the application or continuing the debug. Figure 5.7 shows the Command window evaluating an Integer.Parse statement and an invocation to our Test method.

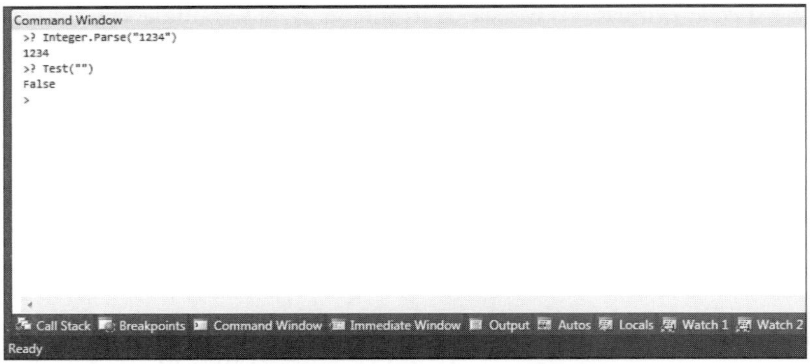

```
Command Window
>? Integer.Parse("1234")
1234
>? Test("")
False
>
```

🐾 Call Stack 🗷 Breakpoints 📟 Command Window 🔲 Immediate Window 🔲 Output 🗔 Autos 🗔 Locals 🗔 Watch 1 🗔 Watch 2
Ready

FIGURE 5.7   The Command window enables evaluating expressions and functions.

This can be useful, because we do not need to run our application to see if a method works, and we could also evaluate complex expressions before writing code. Just remember that only functions are allowed whereas procedures are not supported. Expressions can be constituted by several .NET objects and Visual Basic keywords, but not all of them are supported. You can get a complete list of supported keywords and expressions from the related MSDN web page available at this address: http://msdn.microsoft.com/en-us/library/099a40t6(VS.100).aspx. To evaluate an expression or test a function, you need to first write a question mark (?) symbol. Using a double question (??) mark causes the debugger to open a Quick Watch window, which is discussed later in this chapter. It is worth mentioning that the ? symbol works when either in debug mode or not, while the ?? symbol requires the IDE to be already in debug mode.

Call Stack Window

The Call Stack window shows the method calls stack frame. In other words, you can see how methods call run in the stack. The window can show the programming language that the method is written with and can also display calls to external code. By default, the Call Stack window shows information about Just My Code. To understand methods calls, press **F11** to step into the code. Figure 5.8 shows the Call Stack window related to Listing 5.1.

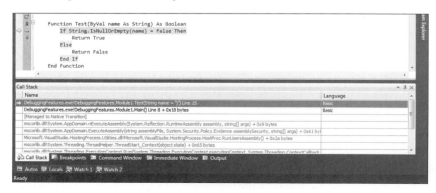

FIGURE 5.8   The Call Stack window shows methods calls in the Stack.

As you can see, the window shows the names of methods being executed and the programming language they were written with. Moreover, calls to .NET Framework system methods are shown. Another interesting feature is that you can see the assembly code for code execution. Right-click the window and select the **Go to Disassembly** command from the pop-up menu. As shown in Figure 5.9, you can see Visual Basic lines of code and the related underlying assembly code that you can step into by pressing **F11**.

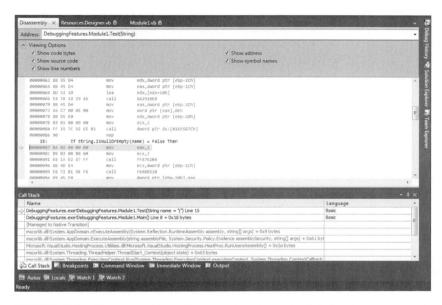

FIGURE 5.9   The assembly code execution shows in Call Stack.

You can also customize what kind of information you want to visualize by expanding the View Options control. This feature provides great granularity on what's happening behind the scenes and allows understandings if methods calls are executed correctly. You can invoke the Call Stack window also pressing **Ctrl+Alt+C**.

THREADS AND CALL STACK

The Call Stack window can show information only on the current thread. Therefore, methods calls on other threads are ignored by the window.

Watch Windows

Watch windows enable monitoring object variables or expressions so that you can track what a variable is doing. There are four Watch windows available so that you can track different objects or expressions. To add items to a Watch window, when in break mode right-click the object in the code editor and then select the **Add Watch** command from the pop-up menu. Continuing our example of Listing 5.1, imagine you want to keep track of the Test method state. Run the application in Step Into mode by pressing **F11**. When the debugger breaks the application execution, right-click the Test method definition and then click **Add Watch**. The method is considered as an expression. The first available Watch window is shown and contains the Test item but advertising that no argument has been supplied, as shown in Figure 5.10.

FIGURE 5.10   Adding an expression to a Watch window.

If you continue stepping into the code, you notice that when the debugger begins stepping into the Test method the expression will be first evaluated as False. (This is the default value for Boolean.) When the code completes the execution, the Watch window contains the actual evaluation of the expression; in our example, if the user writes a valid string in the Console window, the expression will be evaluated as True, as shown in Figure 5.11.

In this way you can control if your variables or methods are correctly executed.

Quick Watch Window

The Quick Watch window is an additional Watch window that enables quickly evaluating one expression or variable per time, choosing between items you previously added to Watch windows or right-clicking an object in the code editor and then selecting the Quick Watch command. In this scenario, the expression or variable is evaluated considering its state at the moment that you request the Quick Watch to appear. Figure 5.12 shows the Quick Watch window.

You can pick an expression from the Expression combo box. When you choose the expression, you can click **Reevaluate** to run the evaluation. Just remember that this dialog is a modal dialog and therefore you need to close it before you can go back to Visual Studio.

FIGURE 5.11 Evaluation of the expression is completed within the Watch window.

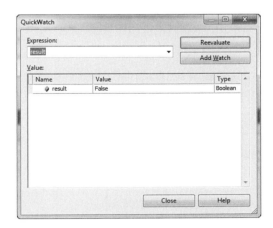

FIGURE 5.12 The Quick Watch window.

Threads Window

.NET applications can run multiple threads. This can happen also with your applications. You can get a view of the running threads and debugging threads within the Threads window, which you can enable by pressing **Ctrl+Alt+H**. Figure 5.13 shows the Threads window open when the sample application is in break mode.

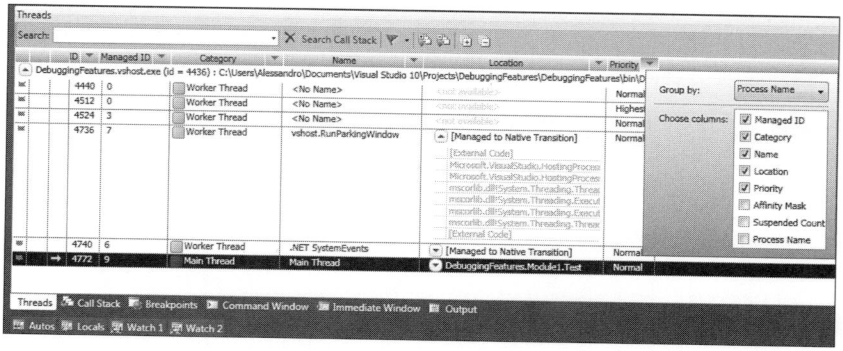

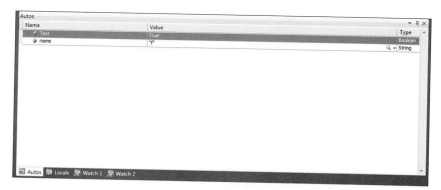

FIGURE 5.13   The Threads window.

The window shows a list of running threads and enables stepping into the call stack for the various threads. If the source code is available for threads different than the current one, you can step into this code. In our example the main thread is the Console application that is marked green. You can also organize and filter the view, search within the Call Stack, and get information on the thread's priority. The Threads window is particularly useful with multithreaded applications, whereas for Parallel applications the Visual Studio 2010 debugger provides other tools, which are described in Chapter 44, "Processes and Multithreading."

Autos Window

The Autos window shows the variables used by the current statement and by the previous three and next three statements. Figure 5.14 shows an example of the Autos window.

FIGURE 5.14   The Autos window.

For the Autos window, you can change variables' values by double-clicking each one.

64-BIT SUPPORT

One of the new features in the Visual Studio 2010 debugger is that now mixed mode with 64-bit applications debugging is supported.

Debugger Visualizers

Debugger visualizers are built-in tools that enable viewing information on objects, controls, members, and variables (generally complex data) in a particular format. For example, if you place a breakpoint on the following line of code of the sample project

```
Dim result As Boolean = Test(lineRead)
```

you can then open the Locals window and select the lineRead variable. In the Value column, notice the small magnifying glass that you can click. From there you can choose how you want to visualize information on the lineRead variable, such as Text format, XML format, and HTML format. Of course, trying to view the content of plain text as XML content dos not provide any benefits, but in the case you have a string representing XML data or HTML code, you could get an appropriate representation to understand what's happening. Visualizers are also useful when you have a large multiline string and you need to see how it is formatted. In our example, Figure 5.15 shows the Text visualizer for the lineRead variable.

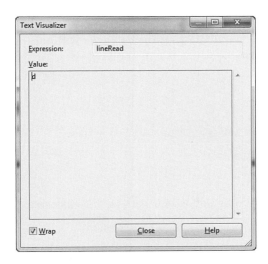

FIGURE 5.15   Viewing information with debugger visualizers.

Basically the visualizers' purpose is to provide a graphical tool for analyzing what's happening on expressions.

CUSTOM DEBUGGER VISUALIZERS

Visual Studio 2010 offers default debugger visualizers that are useful in common situations, but you might need custom visualizers. It is possible to build custom visualizers, but this is beyond the scope of this chapter. Information on creating custom visualizers is available in the MSDN documentation at the following address: http://msdn.microsoft.com/en-us/library/e2zc529c(VS.100).aspx

Debugging in Code

The .NET Framework offers the ability to interact with the debugger via managed code. You can use two classes, `System.Diagnostics.Debug` and `System.Diagnostics.Trace`, to verify conditions and evaluations that can be useful to provide feedback about your code if it is working correctly. Information generated by these classes can eventually be added to the application.

DEBUG AND TRACE ARE SINGLETON

Both `Debug` and `Trace` classes are single instance shared classes and therefore expose only shared members.

The Debug Class

The `Debug` class, exposed by the `System.Diagnostics` namespace, provides interaction with the Visual Studio debugger and enables understanding if your code is working correctly via instrumentation that evaluates conditions at a certain point of your code. Basically the `Debug` class exposes only shared methods and can display contents into the Output window so that you can programmatically interact with the debugger without the need to set breakpoints. Table 5.2 provides an overview of `Debug` methods.

TABLE 5.2   Debug Class Methods

Method	Description
Assert	Checks for a condition and shows a message if the condition is False
Close	Empties the buffer and releases trace listeners
Fail	Generates an error message
Flush	Empties the buffer and forces data to be written to underlying trace listeners
Indent	When writing to the Output window, increases the text indentation
Print	Writes the specified message to the listeners; supports text formatting
Unindent	When writing to the Output window, decreases the text indentation
Write	Writes the specified message to the listeners without line terminator; supports text formatting

TABLE 5.2   Continued

Method	Description
WriteIf	Writes the specified message to the listeners without a line terminator if the supplied condition is True; supports text formatting
WriteLine	Writes the specified message to the listeners with a line terminator; supports text formatting
WriteLineIf	Writes the specified message to the listeners with a line terminator if the supplied condition is True; supports text formatting

DEBUG OUTPUT

Saying that the Debug class can display contents to the Output window is true only in part. Developers can use other built-in outputs known as *trace listeners* to redirect the output. Later in this chapter we provide an overview of trace listeners.

Continuing the code example in Listing 5.1, try to add the following lines of code after the declaration and assignment of the result variable within the Main method:

```
Debug.WriteLine("Value of result is " & result.ToString)
Debug.WriteLineIf(result = True, "Result is valid because = True")
'If you type an empty or null string,
'then the condition "result=True" is False therefore
'shows an error message
Debug.Assert(result = True, "Needed a valid string")
```

Now run the application and type in a valid (nonempty) string. Figure 5.16 shows how the Output window appears when the runtime encounters the Debug methods.

FIGURE 5.16   Writing debug information to the Output window.

The first line shows the Boolean value of the result variable. The WriteLine method can be useful if you need to monitor objects' values without breaking the application. This method also adds a line terminator so that a new line can begin. The Write method does the same but does not add a line terminator. The WriteLineIf (and WriteIf) writes a message only if the specified condition is evaluated as True. If you enter a valid string, the WriteLineIf method writes a message. Notice that there is an invocation to the Assert method. This method causes the runtime to show a message box containing the specified message that is shown only if the specified expression is evaluated as False. According to this, if you enter a valid string in the sample application, the expression is evaluated as True therefore, no message is shown. If you instead enter an empty string (that is, press **Enter**), the runtime shows the dialog represented in Figure 5.17.

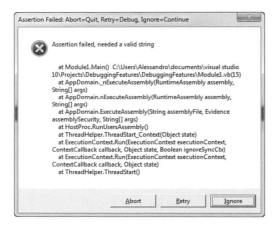

FIGURE 5.17   The Assertion dialog.

The Fail method, which is not shown in the example, shows a similar dialog but without evaluating any condition. In Table 5.2, methods descriptions mention trace listeners. We now provide an overview of the Trace class and then an overview of the particular objects.

The Trace Class

The Trace class, which is also exposed by the System.Diagnostics namespace, works exactly like the Debug class. One important difference influences the building process. The output of the Debug class is included in the build output only if the DEBUG constant is defined, whereas the Trace class' output is included in the build output only if the TRACE constant is defined. When you build your applications with the Debug configuration active, both constants are defined, so both outputs are included. The Release configuration defines instead only the TRACE constant, so it includes only this output.

Understanding Trace Listeners

In the preceding examples related to the Debug class (and consequently related to the Trace class too), we saw how to send the output of the debugger to the Output window. The .NET Framework enables sending the output to other targets, known as *trace listeners*. A trace listener is basically an object that "listens" to what is happening at debugging time and then collects information under various forms. For example, you could collect information as XML files or just send such information to the Output window. Both Debug and Trace classes expose a property named Listeners that represents a set of built-in listeners. Table 5.3 groups the .NET Framework built-in listeners.

TABLE 5.3   .NET Built-In Trace Listeners

Listener	Description
DefaultTraceListener	Redirects the output to the Output window.
TextWriterTraceListener	Redirects the output to a text file.
XmlWriterTraceListener	Redirects the output to an XML file.
EventLogTraceListener	Redirects the output to the operating system's events log.
DelimitedListTraceListener	Redirects the output to a text file. Information is separated by a symbol.
EventSchemaTraceListener	Redirects the output to an Xml schema that is formed on the supplied arguments.
ConsoleTraceListener	Redirects the output to the Console window.

SYSTEM.DIAGNOSTICS NAMESPACE REQUIRED

All listeners listed in Table 5.3 are exposed by the System.Diagnostics namespace, which is not mentioned for the sake of brevity. Usually this namespace is imported by default, according to the options set within My Project. If the background compiler advises that classes are not defined, you should add an Imports System.Diagnostics directive to your code.

When you invoke members from the Debug and Trace classes, by default the output is redirected to the output window. This is because the DefaultTraceListener is attached to the application by the debugger. Now suppose you want to redirect the output to a text file. This can be accomplished by writing the following lines of code:

```
Trace.Listeners.Clear()
```

```
Trace.Listeners.Add(New
    TextWriterTraceListener
    ("C:\users\alessandro\desktop\TraceOutput.txt"))

'This will ensure the file is closed when
'the debugger shuts down
Trace.AutoFlush = True
Trace.WriteLineIf(result = True, "You entered a valid string")
```

LISTENERS DO NOT OVERWRITE FILES

All built-in trace listeners that redirect output to a file do not overwrite the file itself if already existing. They just append information to an existing file. If you need to create a new file each time from scratch, remember to remove the previous version (for example, invoking the `File.Delete` method).

The `Trace.Listener.Clear` method ensures all previous information from other listeners gets cleared. You simply need to add a new instance of the `TextWriterTraceListener` class to listeners' collection. At this point you just need to supply the name of the output file as an argument. If you add the preceding code after the declaration and assignment of the `result` variable within the `Main` method of our main example, the output is redirected to a text file, as shown in Figure 5.18.

FIGURE 5.18   The debugging output has been redirected to a text file.

The `AutoFlush` property set as `True` ensures that the text file is correctly closed when the debugger shuts down. In the end, you write evaluations as you would do when sending output to the Output window (see `WriteLineIf` method). A class named `DelimitedListTraceListener` inherits from `TextWriterTraceListener` and enables writing information to a file using a delimitation symbol. By default, this symbol is a comma (basically output files are CSV files, Comma Separated Value, that can be opened with Microsoft Excel), but you can set the `Delimiter` property value with another symbol. The usage remains the same as its base class. You also might want to redirect output to an Xml file. This can be accomplished adding an instance of the `XmlWriterTraceListener` class, as shown in the following code:

```
Trace.Listeners.Clear()
Trace.Listeners.Add(New
    XmlWriterTraceListener
    ("C:\users\alessandro\desktop\TraceOutput.xml"))


'This will ensure the file is closed when
'the debugger shuts down
Trace.AutoFlush = True
Trace.WriteLineIf(result = True, "You entered a valid string")
```

The usage is the same as in the `TextWriterTraceListener` example. If you try to run the preceding code, you can obtain a well-formed Xml document, as shown in Figure 5.19.

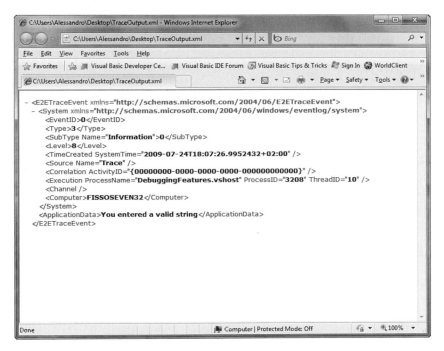

FIGURE 5.19   The output produced by the XmlWriterTraceListener class.

As you should understand, writing the output to an Xml document is a more powerful task because of the amount of information collected. All the information persisted to the Xml document is reflected by properties of the instance of the XmlWriterTraceListener class. Each property is named as the related information in the Xml document; for example, the Computer property represents the name of the computer running the debugger, the ProcessName property represents the name of the process that the debugger is attached to, and the ProcessID and ThreadID properties respectively represent the process identification number and thread identification number of the process. Another listener that you can use for producing Xml files is named EventSchemaTraceListener. This object will basically create an Xml schema starting from debugging information; the EventSchemaTraceListener constructor has several overloads that enable specifying how the schema will be formed. The following code shows an example:

```
Trace.Listeners.Add(New
        EventSchemaTraceListener("Test.xsd",
        "My listener",
        32768,
        TraceLogRetentionOption.LimitedCircularFiles,
        65536, 10))
```

Explaining this class in detail is beyond the scope of this book. If you would like to read further details on this class, you can read the official MSDN documentation at http://msdn.microsoft.com/en-us/library/system.diagnostics.eventschematracelistener(VS.100) .aspx. The EventLogTraceListener class works similar to the previous ones. The following lines of code attach a new instance of the class to the debugger, and the debug output is redirected to the Windows Event Log:

```
Trace.Listeners.Clear()
Trace.Listeners.Add(New EventLogTraceListener
                  ("Chapter 5 - Debugging applications"))

'This will ensure the log resources are released when
'the debugger shuts down
Trace.AutoFlush = True
Trace.WriteLineIf(result = True, "You entered a valid string")
```

APPLICATION LOG REQUIRES ADMINISTRATOR

Writing to the application log requires administrative privileges. If you run Windows Vista or Windows 7 and you have the User Account Control active on your system, you should also run Visual Studio 2010 as an administrator.

The preceding code creates a new entry in the application log of the operating system. Figure 5.20 shows the content of the application log, which is reachable via the Event viewer shortcut of the Administrative tools menu.

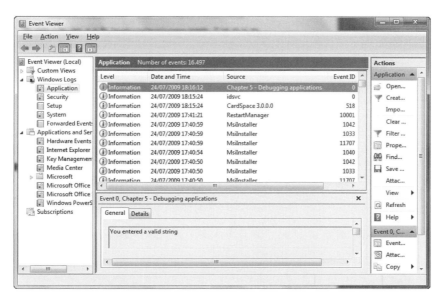

FIGURE 5.20   Windows's Event viewer shows the application log containing our debug output.

MY.APPLICATION.LOG

Visual Basic 2010 offers an alternative to the `EventLogTraceListener` that is provided by the My namespace. As we see in Chapter 20, "The 'My' Namespace," an object name `My.Application.Log` provides a simpler way for writing the trace output to the application log.

The last listener object is named `ConsoleTraceListener` and enables sending messages to the Console window. You use this object as the previous ones. At this point we should focus on an important feature of listeners: Hard coding listeners in Visual Basic code is not mandatory. The good news is that you can add listeners to a configuration file that can be manually edited externally from Visual Studio.

Setting Listeners in Configuration Files

To set listeners to a configuration file, first you need one. In Solution Explorer, right-click the project name and then select the **Add New Item** command from the pop-up menu. When the Add New Item dialog appears, you can search for the Application Configuration File template using the search box, as shown in Figure 5.21.

If you now double-click the configuration file in Solution Explorer, you notice a section that is named `System.Diagnostics`, as in the following snippet:

```
<system.diagnostics>
    <sources>
        <source name="DefaultSource" switchName="DefaultSwitch">
```

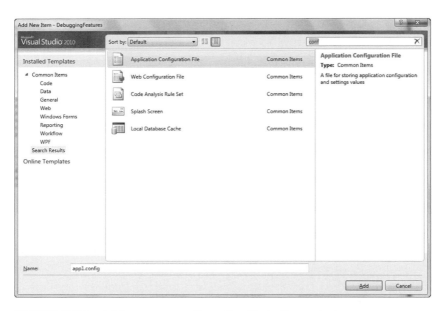

FIGURE 5.21   Adding a new configuration file to the project.

```
            <listeners>
                <add name="FileLog"/>
            </listeners>
        </source>
    </sources>
    <switches>
        <add name="DefaultSwitch" value="Information" />
    </switches>
</system.diagnostics>
```

Basically this section represents the same-named namespace and offers the capability to specify trace listeners. By default, a `DefaultTraceListener` is added. This can be understood examining the preceding code snippet. You might also add other listeners, such as a `TextWriterTraceListener` or an `XmlWriterTraceListener`. The following code snippet shows how you can add a `TextWriterTraceListener` to the App.config file, remembering that it must be nested into the `System.Diagnostics` node:

```
<trace autoflush="true">
  <listeners>
    <add name="DemoTestWriter"
        type="System.Diagnostics.TextWriterTraceListener"
        initializeData="output.txt"/>
    <!— If you want to disable the DefaultTraceListener—>
    <remove name="Default"/>
  </listeners>
</trace>
```

As you can see, you need to supply a name, the type (that is, the class name), and the output file. The following code snippet shows instead how you can add an `XmlWriterTraceListener`:

```
<trace autoflush="true">
  <listeners>
    <add name="DemoTestWriter"
         type="System.Diagnostics.XmlWriterTraceListener"
         initializeData="output.xml"/>
    <!-- If you want to disable the DefaultTraceListener-->
    <remove name="Default"/>
  </listeners>
</trace>
```

Of course, if you Visual Basic code you do not need also a configuration file. App.config could be a good choice if another person that cannot edit your source code should change how the debugger information is collected, because the configuration file can be edited externally from Visual Studio.

Using Debug Attributes in Your Code

In the section "'Just My Code' Debugging," I explained how some attributes can influence the debugger's behavior versus auto-generated code and that you can use versus your own code. The .NET Framework also provides other attributes that you can use to decorate your code for deciding how the debugger should behave versus such code. Table 5.4 lists other attributes that complete the list in Table 5.1.

TABLE 5.4   Debug Attributes

Attribute	Description
DebuggerVisualizer	Indicates the IDE that the code implements a custom debugger visualizer
DebuggerStepperBoundary	When a DebuggerNonUserCode attribute is also specified, causes the debugger to run the code instead of stepping through
DebuggerBrowsable	Establishes how data should be shown in the Data Tips windows
DebuggerDisplay	Allows customizing strings and messages in Data Tips
DebuggerTypeProxy	Allows overriding how data tips are shown for a particular type

As previously described in this chapter, discussing custom debugger visualizers is beyond the scope of this book, so the `DebuggerVisualizer` attribute is not discussed here.

NOTE ON DEBUG ATTRIBUTES

The above attributes are effectively used and useful when debugging the application from within Visual Studio. When you compile the application in Release mode, debug attributes are ignored and do not affect your code at runtime.

DebuggerStepperBoundary

This attribute is used only in multithreading scenarios and has effects only when a `DebuggerNonUserCode` is also specified. It is used to run code instead of stepping through it when you are stepping into user code that does not actually relate to the thread you were instead debugging. Due to its particular nature, this attribute is not discussed in detail. The MSDN Library provides additional information at this address: http://msdn.microsoft.com/en-us/library/system.diagnostics.debuggerstepperboundaryat-tribute(VS.100).aspx.

DebuggerBrowsable

The usage of the `DebuggerBrowsable` attribute in Visual Basic is quite new. Although supported because it's provided by the .NET Framework, decorating code with this attribute produced no effects until Visual Basic 2005. Now it is instead possible to use it to establish how an item should be visualized in Data Tips or variables windows specifying one of the following arguments exposed by the `System.Diagnostics.DebuggerBrowsableState` enumeration:

- `Collapsed`, which establishes that an item is collapsed and that you have to click the + symbol to expand it and see its children elements

- `Never`, which causes the specified item to never be visible in windows such as Autos and Locals

- `RootHidden`, which forces the debugger to show just the children elements of the specified item

For example, consider the following code snippet that retrieves an array of processes (each represented by an instance of the `System.Diagnostics.Process` class):

```
<DebuggerBrowsable(DebuggerBrowsableState.RootHidden)>
Private ProcessesList As Process()

Sub ShowProcesses()
    ProcessesList = Process.GetProcesses
End Sub
```

The preceding code causes the debugger to show only the children element of the array, excluding the root (`ProcessesList`), as shown in Figure 5.22.

DebuggerDisplay

The `DebuggerDisplay` attribute also enables establishing how an item should be shown inside Data Tips. With this attribute you can replace Visual Studio default strings and

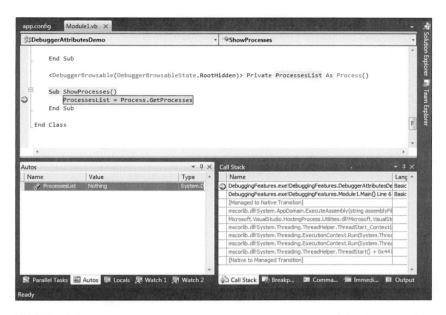

FIGURE 5.22 Using the `DebuggerBrowsable` you can establish how an object can be shown in debugger windows.

customize the description for an object within Data Tips. For example, imagine you have the code shown in Listing 5.2, in which a `Person` class and code creates a list of people.

LISTING 5.2   Using the DebuggerDisplay Attribute

```vb
Module Module1


    Sub Main()

        Dim p As New List(Of Person)
        p.Add(New Person With {.FirstName = "Alessandro", .LastName = "Del Sole"})
        p.Add(New Person With {.FirstName = "MyFantasyName",
                               .LastName = "MyFantasyLastName"})


        Console.ReadLine()
    End Sub
End Module

<DebuggerDisplay("This person is {FirstName} {LastName}")>
Class Person
    Property FirstName As String
    Property LastName As String
End Class
```

In this book it's not important to focus on how collections of objects are created, whereas it's interesting to understand what the `DebuggerDisplay` attribute does. Now place a breakpoint on the `Console.ReadLine` statement and then run the application. If you pass the mouse pointer over the p object, Data Tips for this object will be activated. The debugger then displays data that are formatted the way we described in the `DebuggerDisplay` attribute. Figure 5.23 shows the result of our customization.

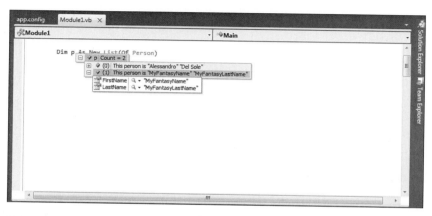

FIGURE 5.23   The `DebuggerDisplay` attribute enables customizing Data Tips messages.

DebuggerTypeProxy

As its name implies, the `DebuggerTypeProxy` enables overriding how debug information for a specific data type is shown within Data Tips. Listing 5.3 shows how you can implement such an attribute.

LISTING 5.3   Using the `DebuggerTypeProxy` Attribute

```vb
Module Module1

    Sub Main()

        Dim p As New List(Of Person)
        p.Add(New Person With {.FirstName = "Alessandro", .LastName = "Del Sole"})
        p.Add(New Person With {.FirstName = "MyFantasyName",
                             .LastName = "MyFantasyLastName"})

        Console.ReadLine()
    End Sub
End Module

<DebuggerTypeProxy(GetType(PersonProxy))>
Class Person
```

```
        Property FirstName As String
        Property LastName As String

End Class


Class PersonProxy
    Dim myProxy As Person

    Sub New(ByVal OnePerson As Person)
        myProxy = OnePerson
    End Sub

    ReadOnly Property Length As Integer
        Get
            Return String.Concat(myProxy.FirstName, " ", myProxy.LastName).Length
        End Get
    End Property
End Class
```

The `PersonProxy` class basically gets the instance of the `Person` class being debugged, reads the information from such instance, and returns via the `Length` property the length of the string composed by the `FirstName` and `LastName` properties. The `Length` property here is just a basic example, but it is useful to understand where the real proxy is. To activate the proxy, you need to decorate the `Person` class with the `DebuggerTypeProxy` attribute whose argument is the `Type` representation of what you need to debug. This type is retrieved using a `GetType` keyword. If you now try to run the application, you can see that the debugger can display the new `Length` information, as shown in Figure 5.24.

FIGURE 5.24 The `DebuggerTypeProxy` enables customizing the debug information.

So you have a powerful way to customize debug information.

Summary

Debugging is a primary task in developing applications. The Visual Studio 2010 IDE offers lots of useful tools that can enhance the debugging experience. In this chapter you learned what Just My Code is and then you learned how you can work with breakpoints and trace points, passing through debugging in steps. You also saw the debugger windows in action, enabling deep control over variables and objects. In the end you learned how to customize your own code to take advantages of the Visual Studio debugging tools decorating your code with debug attributes. But debugging is just one part in the development process that fights against errors. Exceptions are the other part that are discussed in Chapter 6, "Handling Errors and Exceptions."

Handling Errors and Exceptions

Every application might encounter errors during its execution, even when you spend several nights on testing the application and all the possible execution scenarios. Especially runtime errors are often unpredictable because the application execution is conditioned by user actions. Because of this, error handling is a fundamental practice that, as a developer, you need to know in depth. In this chapter you learn how the .NET Framework enables handling errors and how to get information to solve problems deriving such errors. In other words, you learn about .NET exceptions.

Introducing Exceptions

In development environments different than .NET, programming languages can handle errors occurring during the application execution in different ways. For example, the Windows native APIs return a 32-bit HRESULT number in case an error occurs. Visual Basic 6 uses the On Error statements, whereas other languages have their own error-handling infrastructure. As you can imagine, such differences cannot be allowed in the .NET Framework because all languages rely on the Common Language Runtime, so all of them must intercept and handle errors the same way. With that said, the .NET Framework identifies errors as *exceptions*. An exception is an instance of the System.Exception class (or of a class derived from it) and provides deep information on the error occurred. Such an approach provides a unified way for intercepting and handling errors. Exceptions are not only something occurring at runtime, during the application execution.

Exceptions can be *thrown* by the Visual Basic compiler also at compile time or by the background compiler when typing code. You can also notice that errors occurring when designing the user interface of an application or errors occurring when working within the Visual Studio 2010 IDE are mostly called exceptions. This is because such tasks (and most of the Visual Studio IDE) are powered by the .NET Framework. In Chapter 2, "Getting Started with the Visual Studio 2010 IDE," we introduced the Visual Studio debugger and saw how it can be used for analyzing error messages provided by exceptions (see the "About Runtime Errors" section in Chapter 2). In that case we did not implement any error handling routine because we just were introducing the debugging features of Visual Studio during the development process. But what if an error occurs at runtime when the application has been deployed to your customer without implementing appropriate error handling code? Imagine an application that attempts to read a file that does not exist and in which the developer did not implement errors checks. Figure 6.1 shows an example of what could happen and that should never happen in a real application.

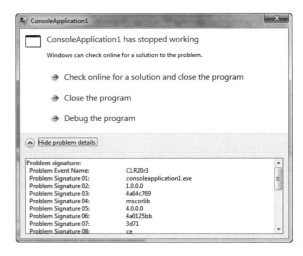

FIGURE 6.1   Without handling exceptions, solving errors is difficult.

As you can see from Figure 6.1, in case of an error the application stops its execution, and no resume is possible. Moreover, identifying what kind of error occurred can also be difficult. Because of this, as a developer it is your responsibility to implement code for intercepting exceptions and take the best actions possible to solve the problem, also based on users' choices. The best way to understand exceptions is to begin to write some code that causes an intercept errors, so this is what we are going to do in the next section.

Handling Exceptions

Visual Basic 2010 enables deep control over exceptions. With regard to this, an important concept is that you not only can check for occurring exceptions but you can also conditionally manage solutions to exceptions and raise exceptions when needed. In this section we discuss all these topics, providing information on how you can intercept and manage exceptions in your application.

Are You Upgrading from Visual Basic 6?

One of the (very few) commonalities between Visual Basic 6 and Visual Basic .NET and higher is the syntax approach. This should help a little more in migrating from Visual Basic 6 to 2010. Although Visual Basic 2010 (more precisely, VB.NET from 2002 to 2010) still enables the usage of the On Error Goto and On Error Resume statements, when developing .NET applications with Visual Basic, you should never use such statements for two reasons. First, exceptions are the only way that enables interoperation with other .NET languages such as Visual C# and Visual F#. This is fundamental when developing class libraries or components that could be potentially reused from other languages different than Visual Basic. The second reason is that the old-fashioned way for handling errors is not as efficient as handling .NET exceptions. If you decided to migrate, you should completely forget On Error and exclusively use exceptions.

System.Exception, Naming Conventions and Specialization

System.Exception is the most general exception and can represent all kinds of errors occurring in applications. It is also the base class for derived exceptions, which are specific to situations you may encounter. For example, the System.IOException derives from System.Exception, is thrown when the application encounters input/output errors when accessing the disk, and can be handled only for this particular situation. On the other hand, System.Exception can handle not only this situation but also any other occurring errors. You can think of System.Exception as of the root in the exceptions hierarchy. We explain later in code the hierarchy of exception handling. Classes representing exceptions always terminate with the word Exception. You encounter exceptions such as FileNotFoundException, IndexOutOfRangeException, FormatException, and so on. This is not mandatory, but a recommended naming convention. Generally .NET built-in exceptions inherit from System.Exception, but because they are reference types, you find several exceptions inheriting from a derived exception.

Try..Catch..Finally

You perform exception handling writing a Try..Catch..Finally code block. The logic is that you say to the compiler: "Try to execute the code; if you encounter an exception, take the specified actions; whenever the code execution succeeds or it fails due to an exception, execute the final code." The most basic code for controlling the execution flow regarding exceptions is the following:

```
Try
    'Code to be executed
Catch ex As Exception
    'Code to handle the exception
End Try
```

IntelliSense does a great job here. When you type the `Try` keyword and then press **Enter,** it automatically adds the `Catch` statement and the `End Try` terminator. The ex variable gets the instance of the `System.Exception` that is caught and that provides important information so that you can best handle the exception. To see what happens, consider the following code snippet:

```
Try
    Dim myArray() As String = {"1", "2", "3", "4"}

    Console.WriteLine(myArray(4))
Catch ex As Exception
    Console.WriteLine(ex.Message)
End Try
```

Here we have an array of strings in which the upper range of the array is 3. The `Try` block tries to execute code that attempts writing the content of the fourth index to the Console window. Unfortunately, such an index does not exist, but because the code is formally legal, it will be correctly compiled. When the application runs and the runtime encounters this situation, it throws an exception to communicate the error occurrence. So the `Catch` statement intercepts the exception and enables deciding what actions must be taken. In our example the action to handle the exception is to write the complete error message of the exception. If the code within `Try` succeeds, the execution passes to the first code after the `End Try` terminator. In our example the control transfers to the `Catch` block that contains code that writes to the Console window the actual error message that looks like the following:

```
Index was outside the bounds of the array
```

Basically the runtime never throws a generic `System.Exception` exception. There are specific exceptions for the most common scenarios (and it is worth mentioning that you can create custom exceptions as discussed in Chapter 12, "Inheritance") that are helpful to identify what happened instead of inspecting a generic exception. Continuing our example, the runtime throws an `IndexOutOfRangeException` that means the code attempted to access and index greater or smaller than allowed. Based on these considerations, the code could be rewritten as follows:

```
Try
    Dim myArray() As String = {"1", "2", "3", "4"}

    Console.WriteLine(myArray(4))

Catch ex As IndexOutOfRangeException
    Console.WriteLine("There is a problem: probably you are "
            & Environment.NewLine &
```

```
                " attempting to access an index that does not exists")
Catch ex As Exception
      Console.WriteLine(ex.Message)

End Try
```

As you can see, the most specific exception needs to be caught before the most generic one. This is quite obvious, because if you first catch the `System.Exception`, all other exceptions will be ignored. Intercepting specific exceptions can also be useful because you can both communicate the user detailed information, and you can decide what actions must be taken to solve the problem. Anyway, always adding a `Catch` block for a generic `System.Exception` is a best practice. This allows providing a general error handling code in case exceptions that you do not specifically intercept will occur. You could also need to perform some actions independently from the result of your code execution. The `Finally` statement enables executing some code either if the `Try` succeeds or if it fails, passing control to `Catch`. For example you might want to clean up resources used by the array:

```
Dim myArray() As String = {"1", "2", "3", "4"}


Try
      Console.WriteLine(myArray(4))

Catch ex As IndexOutOfRangeException
      Console.WriteLine("There is a problem: probably you are "
                  & Environment.NewLine &
                  " attempting to access an index that does not exists")
Catch ex As Exception
      Console.WriteLine(ex.Message)
Finally
      myArray = Nothing
End Try
```

Notice how objects referred within the `Finally` block must be declared outside the `Try..End Try` block because of visibility. The code within `Finally` will be executed whatever will be the result of the `Try` block. This is important; for example, think about files. You might open a file and then try to perform some actions on the file that for any reason can fail. In this situation you would need to close the file, and `Finally` ensures you can do that both if the file access is successful and if it fails (throwing an exception). An example of this scenario is represented in Listing 6.1.

LISTING 6.1   Use Finally to Ensure Resources Are Freed Up and Unlocked

```
Imports System.IO
```

```
Module Module1

    Sub Main()

        Console.WriteLine("Specify a file name:")
        Dim fileName As String = Console.ReadLine

        Dim myFile As FileStream = Nothing

        Try
            myFile = New FileStream(fileName, FileMode.Open)
            'Seek a specific position in the file.
            'Just for example
            myFile.Seek(5, SeekOrigin.Begin)
        Catch ex As FileNotFoundException
            Console.WriteLine("File not found.")
        Catch ex As Exception
            Console.WriteLine("An unidentified error occurred.")
        Finally
            If myFile IsNot Nothing Then
                myFile.Close()
            End If
        End Try

        Console.ReadLine()
    End Sub
End Module
```

The code in Listing 6.1 is quite simple. First, it asks the user to specify a filename to be accessed. Accessing files is accomplished with a `FileStream` object. Notice that the `myFile` object is declared outside the `Try..End Try` block so that it can be visible within `Finally`. Moreover, its value is set to `Nothing` so that it has a default value, although null. If we did not assign this default value, `myFile` would just be declared but not yet assigned so the Visual Basic compiler would throw a warning message. By the way, setting the default value to Nothing will not prevent a NullReferenceException at runtime unless the variable gets a value. The `Try` block attempts accessing the specified file. The `FileStream.Seek` method here is just used as an example needed to perform an operation on the file. When accessing files there could be different problems, resulting in different kinds of exceptions. In our example, if the specified file does not exist, a `FileNotFoundException` is thrown by the runtime, and the `Catch` block takes control over the execution. Within the block we just communicate that the specified file was not found. If instead the file exists, the code performs a seeking. In both cases, the `Finally` block ensures that the file gets closed, independently on what happened before. This is fundamental, because if you leave a file opened, other problems would occur.

Exceptions Hierarchy

In Listing 6.1 we saw how we can catch a specific exception, such as
FileNotFoundException, and then the general System.Exception. By the way,
FileNotFoundException does not directly derive from System.Exception; instead, it
derives from System.IO.IOException that is related to general input/output problems.
Although you are not obliged to also catch an IOException when working with files,
adding it could be a good practice because you can separate error handling for disk
input/output errors from other errors. In such situations the rule is that you have to catch
exceptions from the most specific to the most general. Continuing the previous example,
Listing 6.2 shows how you can implement exceptions hierarchy.

LISTING 6.2   Understanding Exceptions Hierarchy

```
Imports System.IO

Module Module1

    Sub Main()

        Console.WriteLine("Specify a file name:")
        Dim fileName As String = Console.ReadLine

        Dim myFile As FileStream = Nothing

        Try
            myFile = New FileStream(fileName, FileMode.Open)
            'Seek a specific position in the file.
            'Just for example
            myFile.Seek(5, SeekOrigin.Begin)
        Catch ex As FileNotFoundException
            Console.WriteLine("File not found.")
        Catch ex As IOException
            Console.WriteLine("A general input/output error occurred")
        Catch ex As Exception
            Console.WriteLine("An unidentified error occurred.")
        Finally
            If myFile IsNot Nothing Then
                myFile.Close()
            End If
        End Try

        Console.ReadLine()
    End Sub
End Module
```

FileNotFoundException is the most specific exception, so it must be caught first. It derives from IOException, which is intercepted as second. System.Exception is instead the base class for all exceptions and therefore must be caught last.

System.Exception Properties

The System.Exception class exposes some properties that are useful for investigating exceptions and then understanding what the real problem is. Particularly when you catch specialized exceptions, it could happen that such exception is just the last ring of a chain and that the problem causing the exception itself derives from other problems. System.Exception's properties enable a better navigation of exceptions. Table 6.1 lists available properties.

TABLE 6.1   System.Exception's Properties

Property	Description
Message	Gets the complete error message generated from the exception
Source	Represents the name of the application or the object that threw the exception
TargetSite	Retrieves the method that actually throws the exception
Data	Stores a sequence of key/value pairs containing additional information on the exception
Help	Allows specifying or retrieving the name of the help file associated with the exception
InnerException	Gets the instance of the exception object that actually caused the current exception
StackTrace	Retrieves the methods calls hierarchy in the Call Stack when the exception occurred

Listing 6.3 shows how you can retrieve deep information on the exception. In the example, information is retrieved for the System.IO.FileNotFoundException, but you can use such properties for each exception you like.

LISTING 6.3   Investigating Exceptions Properties

```
Imports System.IO
```

```vbnet
Module Module1

    Sub Main()
        Console.WriteLine("Specify a file name:")
        Dim fileName As String = Console.ReadLine

        Dim myFile As FileStream = Nothing

        Try
            myFile = New FileStream(fileName, FileMode.Open)
            'Seek a specific position in the file.
            'Just for example
            myFile.Seek(5, SeekOrigin.Begin)
        Catch ex As FileNotFoundException
            Console.WriteLine()
            Console.WriteLine("Error message: " & ex.Message & Environment.NewLine)
            Console.WriteLine("Object causing the exception: "
                            & ex.Source & Environment.NewLine)
            Console.WriteLine("Method where the exception is thrown; "
                            & ex.TargetSite.ToString & Environment.NewLine)
            Console.WriteLine("Call stack:" & ex.StackTrace & Environment.NewLine)

            Console.WriteLine("Other useful info:")
            For Each k As KeyValuePair(Of String, String) In ex.Data
                Console.WriteLine(k.Key & " " & k.Value)
            Next

        Catch ex As IOException
            Console.WriteLine("A general input/output error occurred")
        Catch ex As Exception
            Console.WriteLine(ex.Message)
        Finally
            If myFile IsNot Nothing Then
                myFile.Close()
            End If
        End Try

        Console.ReadLine()
    End Sub
End Module
```

If we run this code and specify a filename that does not exist, we can retrieve a lot of useful information. Figure 6.2 shows the result of the code.

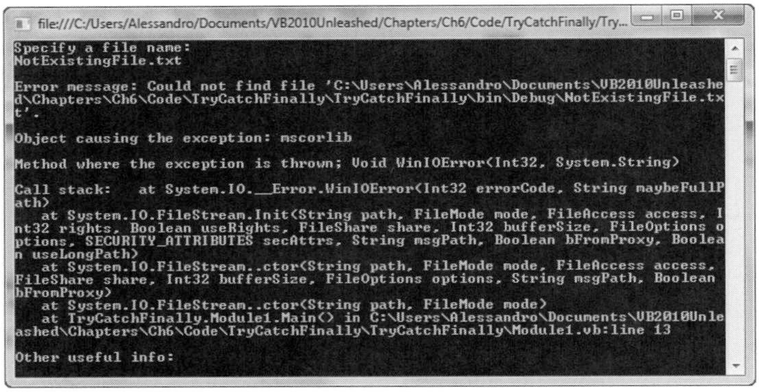

FIGURE 6.2   Getting information on the exception.

As you can see from Figure 6.2, the `Message` property contains the full error message. In production environments, this can be useful to provide customers a user-friendly error message. The `Source` property shows the application or object causing the exception. In our example it retrieves Mscorlib, meaning that the exception was thrown by the Common Language Runtime. The `Target` property retrieves the method in which the exception was thrown. It is worth mentioning that this property retrieves the native method that caused the error, meaning that the method was invoked by the Common Language Runtime. This is clearer if we take a look at the content of the `Stack` property. We can see the hierarchy of method calls in descending order: the `.ctor` method is the constructor of the `FileStream` class, invoked within the `Main` method; the next method, named `Init`, attempts to initialize a `FileStream` and is invoked behind the scenes by the CLR. `Init` and then invokes the native `WinIOError` function because accessing the file was unsuccessful. Analyzing such properties can be useful to understand what happened. Because there is no other useful information, iterating the `Data` property produced no result. By the way, if you just need to report a detailed message about the exception, you can collect most of the properties' content just invoking the `ToString` method of the `Exception` class. For example, you could replace the entire `Catch ex as FileNotFoundException` block as follows:

```
Catch ex As FileNotFoundException
    Console.WriteLine(ex.ToString)
```

This edit produces the result shown in Figure 6.3. As you can see, the result is a little different from the previous one. We can find a lot of useful information, such as the name of the exception, complete error message, filename, Call Stack hierarchy, and line of code that caused the exception.

Typically you use `ToString` just to show information, whereas you use properties to analyze exception information.

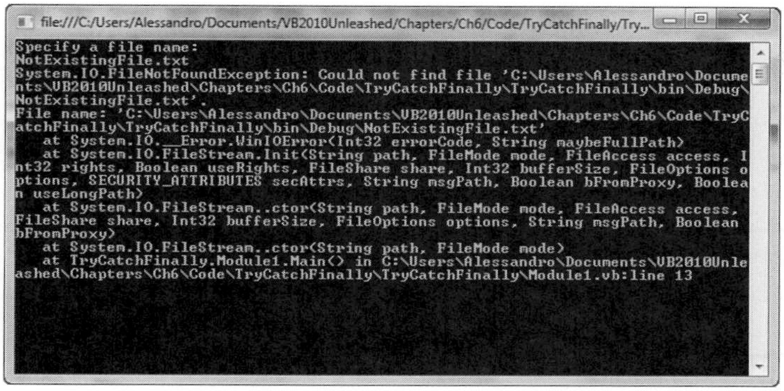

FIGURE 6.3   Invoking the `Exception.ToString` method offers detailed information.

CHECK VALUES INSTEAD OF CATCHING EXCEPTIONS

Catching exceptions is necessary but it is also performances consuming. There are situations in which you could simply check the value of an object instead of catching exceptions. For example, you could check with an `If..Then` statement if an object is null instead of catching a `NullReference` exception (when possible, of course). Exceptions are best left to handle "exceptional" situations that occur in code, so you should limit the over use of them when possible.

You can also ignore exceptions by simply not writing anything inside a `Catch` block. For example, the following code catches a `FileNotFoundException` and prevents an undesired stop in the application execution but takes no action:

```
Try
    testFile = New FileStream(FileName, FileMode.Open)

Catch ex As FileNotFoundException
End Try
```

Nested `Try..Catch..Finally` Blocks

You also have the ability to nest `Try..Catch..Finally` code blocks. Nested blocks are useful when you have to try the execution of code onto the result of another `Try..Catch` block. Consider the following code that has the purpose of showing the creation time of all files in a given directory:

```
Try
    Dim allFiles As String() =
```

```
        Directory.GetFiles("C:\TestDirectory")

    Try

        For Each f As String In allFiles
            Console.WriteLine(File.GetCreationTime(f).ToString())
        Next

    Catch ex As IOException

    Catch ex As Exception

    End Try

Catch ex As DirectoryNotFoundException

Catch ex As Exception
End Try
```

The first `Try..Catch` attempts reading the list of files from a specified directory. Because you may encounter directory errors, a `DirectoryNotFoundException` is caught. The result (being an array of `String`) is then iterated within a nested `Try..Catch` block. This is because the code is now working on files and then specific errors might be encountered.

Exit Try Statements

You can exit from within a `Try..Catch..Finally` block at any moment using an `Exit Try` statement. If there is a `Finally` block, `Exit Try` pulls the execution into `Finally` that otherwise resumes the execution at the first line of code after `End Try`. The following code snippet shows an example:

```
Try
    'Your code goes here
    Exit Try
    'The following line will not be considered
    Console.WriteLine("End of Try block")

Catch ex As Exception

End Try
'Resume the execution here
```

The Throw Keyword

There are situations in which you need to programmatically throw exceptions or in which you catch exceptions but you do not want to handle them in the `Catch` block that intercepted exceptions. Programmatically throwing exceptions can be accomplished via the

Throw keyword. For example, the following line of code throws an `ArgumentNullException` that typically occurs when a method receives a null argument:

```
Throw New ArgumentNullException
```

Typically you need to manually throw exceptions when they should be handled by another portion of code, also in another application. A typical example is when you develop class libraries. A class library must be the most abstract possible, so you cannot decide what actions to take when an exception is caught, because this is the responsibility of the developer who creates the application that references your class library. If both developers are the same person, this remains a best practice because you should always separate the logic of class implementations from the client logic (such as the user interface). To provide a clearer example, a class library cannot show a graphical message box or a text message into the Console window. It instead needs to send to the caller code the exception caught, and this is accomplished via the `Throw` keyword. We can provide a code example. Visual Studio 2010 creates a new blank solution and then adds a new Class Library project that you could name, for example, `TestThrow`. Listing 6.4 shows the content of the class.

LISTING 6.4   Throwing Back Exceptions to Caller Code

```
Imports System.IO


Public Class TestThrow

    Public Sub TestAccessFile(ByVal FileName As String)
        If String.IsNullOrEmpty(FileName) Then
            Throw New ArgumentNullException("FileName",
                    "You passed an invalid file name")
        End If
        Dim testFile As FileStream = Nothing

        Try
            testFile = New FileStream(FileName, FileMode.Open)

        Catch ex As FileNotFoundException
            Throw New FileNotFoundException("The supplied file name was not found")
        Catch ex As Exception
            Throw
        Finally
            If testFile IsNot Nothing Then
                testFile.Close()
            End If
        End Try
    End Function
End Class
```

The `TestThrow` class' purpose is just attempting to access a file. This is accomplished by invoking the `TestAccess` method that receives a `FileName` argument of type `String`. The first check is on the argument: If it is null, the code throws back to the caller an `ArgumentNullException` that provides the argument name and a description. In such a scenario the method catches but does not handle the exception. This is thrown back to the caller code, which is responsible to handle the exception (for example asking the user to specify a valid filename). The second check is on the file access. The `Try..Catch..Finally` block implements code that tries to access the specified file, and if the file is not found, it throws back the `FileNotFoundException` describing what happened. In this way the caller code is responsible for handling the exception, for example asking the user to specify another filename. Also notice how a generic `System.Exception` is caught and thrown back to the caller by simply invoking the `Throw` statement without arguments. This enables the method to throw back to the caller the complete exception information.

RETHROW TECHINQUE

Throwing back an exception to the caller code is also known as the rethrow technique.

Now we can create an application that can reference the `TestThrow` class library and handle exceptions on the client side. Add to the solution a new Visual Basic project for the Console and add a reference to the `TestThrow` class library by selecting **Project, Add Reference**. Adding a reference to another assembly enables using types exposed publicly from such an assembly. Finally, write the code shown in Listing 6.5.

LISTING 6.5   Handling Exceptions on the Client Side

```
Imports System.IO

Module Module1

    Sub Main()

        Console.WriteLine("Specify the file name:")
        Dim name As String = Console.ReadLine
        Dim throwTest As New TestThrow.TestThrow

        Try
            throwTest.TestAccessFile(name)
        Catch ex As ArgumentNullException
            Console.WriteLine("You passed an invalid argument")
        Catch ex As FileNotFoundException
            Console.WriteLine(ex.Message)
```

```
        Catch ex As Exception
            Console.WriteLine(ex.ToString)
        Finally
            Console.ReadLine()
        End Try
    End Sub
End Module
```

The code in Listing 6.5 first asks the user to specify a filename to access. If you press **Enter** without specifying any filename, the `TestAccessFile` method is invoked passing an empty string, so the method throws an `ArgumentNullException`, as shown in Figure 6.4.

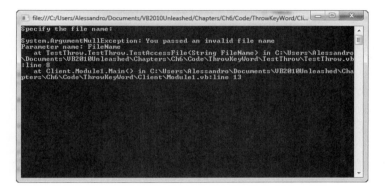

FIGURE 6.4   Passing an empty string as an argument causes an `ArgumentNullException`.

If this situation happened inside a Windows application, you could provide a `MessageBox` showing the error message. With this approach, you maintain logics separately. If you instead specify a filename that does not exist, the caller code needs to handle the `FileNotFoundException`, and the result is shown in Figure 6.5.

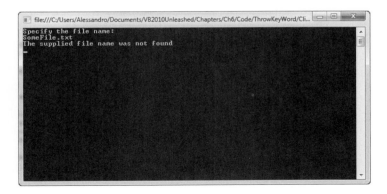

FIGURE 6.5   The caller code handles the `FileNotFoundException` and shows a user-friendly message.

The caller code writes the content of the `ex.Message` property to the Console window, which is populated with the error message provided by the `Thrown` statement from the class library. If any other kinds of exceptions occur, a generic `System.Exception` is handled, and its content is shown to the user.

CATCHING MOST EXCEPTIONS

Depending on what tasks you perform within a `Try..Catch` block, always catch exceptions specific for those tasks. For example, if your code works with files, don't limit to catch a `FileNotFoundException` but also consider file-related and disk-related exceptions. In order to get a listing of the exceptions that a class was designed to throw, you can read the MSDN documentation related to that class. The documentation in fact describes in detail what exceptions are related to the desired object.

Performance Overhead

Basically invoking the `Throw` keyword causes the runtime to search through all the code hierarchy until it finds the caller code that can handle the exception. Continuing our previous example, the Console application not necessarily could be the first caller code. There could be another class library that could rethrow the exception to another class that could then rethrow the exception to the main caller code. Obviously going through the callers' hierarchy is a task that could cause performance overhead, so you should take care about how many callers there are in your code to reduce the overhead. In the end, if the caller code is missing a `Catch` block, the result will be the same shown in Figure 6.1, which should always be avoided.

The When Keyword

Sometimes you may need to catch an exception only when a particular condition exists. You can conditionally control the exception handling using the `When` keyword, which enables taking specific actions when a particular condition is evaluated as `True`. Continuing the example of the previous paragraph, the `TestThrow` class throws an `ArgumentNullException` in two different situations (although similar). The first one is if the string passed to the `TestAccessFile` method is empty; the second one is if the string passed to the method is a null value (`Nothing`). So it could be useful to decide what actions to take depending on what is the actual matter that caused the exception. According to this, we could rewrite the code shown in Listing 6.5 as instead shown in Listing 6.6.

LISTING 6.6   Conditional Exception Handling With The `When` Keyword

```
Imports System.IO


Module Module1

    Sub Main()
```

```
        Console.WriteLine("Specify the file name:")
        Dim name As String = Console.ReadLine

        Dim throwTest As New TestThrow.TestThrow

        Try
            Dim result As Boolean = throwTest.TestAccessFile(name)

        Catch ex As ArgumentNullException When name Is Nothing
            Console.WriteLine("You provided a null parameter")
        Catch ex As ArgumentNullException When name Is String.Empty
            Console.WriteLine("You provided an empty string")
        Catch ex As FileNotFoundException
            Console.WriteLine(ex.Message)
        Catch ex As Exception
            Console.WriteLine(ex.ToString)
        Finally
            Console.ReadLine()
        End Try
    End Sub
End Module
```

As you can see from Listing 6.6, using the When keyword you can conditionally handle exceptions depending if the expression on the right is evaluated as True. In this case, when handling the ArgumentNullException, the condition is evaluating the name variable. If name is equal to Nothing, the exception is handled showing a message saying that the string is null. If name is instead an empty string (which is different from a null string), another kind of message is shown. When can be applied only to Catch statements and works only with expressions. Of course, you can use the When keyword also with value types; for example, you might have a counter that you increment during the execution of your code and, in case of exceptions, you may decide what actions to take based on the value of your counter. The following code gives an idea of such a scenario:

```
Dim oneValue As Integer = 0
Try
    'perform some operations
    'on oneValue
Catch ex As Exception When oneValue = 1

Catch ex As Exception When oneValue = 2

Catch ex As Exception When oneValue = 3

End Try
```

Catching Exceptions Without a Variable

You do not always need to specify a variable in the Catch block. This can be the case in which you want to take the same action independently from the exception that occurred. For example, consider the following code:

```
Try
    Dim result As String =
        My.Computer.FileSystem.ReadAllText("C:\MyFile.txt")

Catch ex As Exception
    Console.WriteLine("A general error occurred")
End Try
```

The ex variable is not being used and no specific exceptions are handled. So the preceding code can be rewritten as follows, without the ex variable:

```
Try
    Dim result As String =
        My.Computer.FileSystem.ReadAllText("C:\MyFile.txt")

Catch
    Console.WriteLine("A general error occurred")
End Try
```

Whichever exception occurs, the code shows the specified message. This also works with regard to the re-throw technique. The following code simply re-throws the proper exception to the caller:

```
Try
    Dim result As String =
        My.Computer.FileSystem.ReadAllText("C:\MyFile.txt")

Catch
    Throw
End Try
```

Summary

Managing errors is something that every developer needs to take into consideration. The .NET Framework provides a unified system for managing errors which is the exception handling. System.Exception is the root class in the exceptions hierarchy, and exceptions are handled using a Try..Catch..Finally block. You can create nested Try..Catch..Finally blocks and check exceptions conditionally using the When keyword. In the end you can programmatically generate exceptions using the Throw keyword that is particularly useful in class libraries development. This chapter provided a high-level overview of exceptions; now you can decide what kinds of exceptions you need to handle for your code and how to take actions to solve errors.

Class Fundamentals

In your everyday life, you perform all activities using objects. You use a fork to eat; you drive your car to reach your office; and you spend money to buy things. Each of these objects has its own characteristics. There are hundreds of car models; they have different colors, different engines, different accessories, but they all are cars. *Object-oriented programming (OOP)* is similar to this view of life. In fact, OOP relies on objects; for example, you can have an object that enables working on files or another object that enables managing pictures. In.NET development an object is typically represented by a class. Structures are also objects but their purpose is to represent a value more than to take actions. For car characteristics, objects have their own characteristics known as properties. But they also have some members that enable taking actions, known as methods. In this chapter you learn how classes in.NET development are structured and how to create your own classes, implementing all members that the .NET Framework enables in the context.

Declaring Classes

Classes in Visual Basic 2010 are declared with `Class..End Class` statements. Classes support the following visibility modifiers: `Public`, `Protected`, `Friend`, `Private` and `Protected Friend`. Classes with `Public` can be reached from other assemblies whereas classes with `Friend` visibility can be reached from within the assembly that defines them. Both modifiers are the only valid ones for non nested classes, as you will see later in this chapter.

CLASSES' SCOPE

For further information on types and members scope, see the section "Scope" in this chapter.

The following are the only acceptable class declarations:

```
Public Class Test

End Class
Friend Class Test

End Class
```

If you omit the qualifier (that is, `Public` or `Friend` keyword), the Visual Basic compiler assigns `Public` by default. Classes can define members, such as fields, properties, methods (all covered in this chapter) but also other classes and structures. The next section covers members that can be defined within classes so that you can have a complete overview about creating your custom classes.

CLASS LIBRARIES

You can define classes in whatever code file you like. Usually developers assign a single code file to one class. If you plan to develop a reusable assembly, exposing classes or types' definitions only, you can use the Class Library project template that enables building a .dll assembly that can be referenced by other projects and applications and that is particularly useful for the modular development.

Nested Classes

You can organize classes within other classes. The following code snippet shows how you can define a nested class:

```
Public Class Test

    Friend Class NestedClass

    End Class

End Class
```

Nested classes can also be marked as `Private`, and this is the only situation in which the qualifier is enabled. If you make a class private, you cannot use that class outside the class that defines it. Continuing with the preceding example, if the `NestedClass` class were marked as `Private`, you could use it only within the `Test` class. If a nested class is not private, you can invoke it the usual way; you need to write the full name of the class as follows:

```
Dim nc As New Test.NestedClass
```

Typically, classes are organized within namespaces (as described in Chapter 9, "Organizing Types Within Namespaces"), but there can be situations in which you need to organize small frameworks of classes, and then nested classes can be a good solution.

Fields

Fields are the places in which you store information to and read information from. They are declared in the form of class level variables and differ from local variables in that these are declared at the method or property level. The following code shows how simple it is to declare fields:

```
Class FieldsDemo

    'a private field
    Private counter As Integer

    'a public field
    Public publicCounter As Integer

    Public Sub DoSomething()

        'a local variable
        Dim localVariable As Integer = 0
    End Sub
End Class
```

Fields can be reachable from within the class and its members, and if you specify one of the appropriate qualifiers (such as `Public`), they can also be reached from the external world. Inside fields you store the actual information your custom objects need.

USING FIELDS

With the introduction of auto-implemented properties (see next section), fields are now typically used to store information at the class level. They lose part of their purpose regarding properties, although you can still use fields as a repository for property information when auto-implemented properties are not enough for your needs.

You can also provide inline initialization of fields, as in the following snippet:

```
Private counter As Integer = 2
```

```
'With reference types
Public inlineDemo As Person = New Person
```

Assigning a field inline or not is something that depends exclusively on your needs. Probably you will initialize fields at run-time when you receive an input from the user or with a value received from the constructor, whereas you might prefer inline initialization when you need to start from a certain value. Fields can also be read-only. When you need to provide a field with an immutable value, you can use read-only fields as follows:

```
'read-only fields
Private ReadOnly counter As Integer = 3
Private ReadOnly testReference As Person = New Person
```

A read-only value requires inline initialization. If not, zero will be assigned to value types and Nothing assigned to reference types. Read-only fields work similarly to constants with one big difference: Constants are evaluated at compile time whereas read-only fields are evaluated at runtime.

SCOPE

Fields, as much as properties, have scope. To understand how you can limit or grant access to fields and properties using the appropriate qualifiers, refer to the "Scope" section in this chapter.

Avoiding Ambiguities with Local Variables

As previously mentioned, fields are at class level contrary to local variables that are at the method/property level. There could be situations in which a local variable has the same name of a field. For example, consider the following code in which two items are named counter: a class level field and a local variable:

```
Public Class AvoidingAmbiguities

    Private counter As Integer

    Public Sub DoSomething()

        'a local variable
        Dim counter As Integer

        counter = CInt(Console.ReadLine)
    End Sub
End Class
```

The code will be correctly compiled; basically no conflict exists between the two counter members because the second one is enclosed within a method and has no external visibility. This also means that the assignment performed within the DoSomething method will not affect the counter private field. If you instead need to assign such a field, you need to use the Me keyword as follows:

```
Public Sub DoSomething()

    'a local variable
    Dim counter As Integer

    'Will assign the class level field
    Me.counter = CInt(Console.ReadLine)
End Sub
```

Properties

Properties are the public way that callers have to access data stored within fields. With properties you decide what kind of permissions users can have to read and write the actual information. Properties are typically used as fields but they act as methods. In Visual Basic 2010, properties have been completely revisited; in fact, until Visual Basic 2008, a typical property was implemented as follows:

```
Private _firstName As String

Public Property FirstName As String
    Get
        Return _firstName
    End Get
    Set(ByVal value As String)
        _firstName = value
    End Set
End Property
```

You had a private field in which you stored an incoming value and whose value you returned to the callers. Now in Visual Basic 2010, the same property can be defined as follows:

```
Public Property FirstName As String
```

This feature is known as *auto-implemented properties* and is something that was already available in Visual C# 3.0. Now you just need to specify the name and the type for the property. The Visual Basic compiler handles read-and-write operations for you. The resulting code is much cleaner, and you can avoid the need of writing several lines of code. If you had 10 properties, until Visual Basic 2008 you had to write 10 of the previously shown code blocks, whereas now you simply need to write 10 lines of code-defining properties. An interesting thing is that if you try to define a private field as in the old code and then an auto-implemented property, you receive this code:

```
'Error: field matching implicit
'auto-generated identifier
Private _firstName As String
Public Property FirstName As String
```

The Visual Basic compiler throws an exception because, behind the scenes, it creates a private field with the same name for handling read/write operations on the property. Of course, you can simply change the identifier if you need a private field for your purposes.

AUTO-IMPLEMENTED PROPERTIES IN THIS BOOK

Except when specifically needed, we always use auto-implemented properties when providing code examples that require properties. This is because they provide a much cleaner way for writing code; moreover, code samples seldom need customizations of the read/write actions.

Auto-implemented properties are straightforward if you need a default behavior for your properties that simply store and return a value., In some situations you need to perform manipulations over a value before you return it; you store a value provided by the user (property Setter) and then you return the value with some edits (property Getter). In this case you cannot use auto-implemented properties, but you can still write properties the old-fashioned way. The following code snippet shows an example:

```
Public Class Woman

    Private Const Prefix As String = "Mrs."

    Private _firstName As String
    Public Property FirstName As String
        Get
            Return Prefix & Me._firstName
        End Get
        Set(ByVal value As String)
            Me._firstName = value
        End Set
    End Property
End Class
```

In the preceding code, the value stored by the property is edited before it is returned by simply adding a prefix. Because the default Visual Studio's behavior is all about auto-implemented properties, you do not gain a great advantage from IntelliSense in this scenario. To write code faster, if you do not need auto-implemented properties, follow these steps:

1. Write an auto-implemented property;
2. On the following line of code, type the **End Property** delimiter.
3. The Visual Basic compiler throws an error and Visual Studio suggests adding the missing getter and setter as a solution. Click this action and you're done.

As an alternative you can simply type `Property` and then hit Tab so that Visual Studio will add a property stub using a predefined code-snippet.

There are also some situations in which you cannot use auto-implemented properties: read-only properties and write-only properties.

Read-Only Properties

It's not unusual to give a class the capability of exposing data but not of modifying such data. Continuing the example of the `Person` class, imagine you want to expose the `FirstName` and `LastName` properties plus a `FullName` property that returns the full name of the person. This property should be marked as read-only because only the `FirstName` and `LastName` properties should be editable, and `FullName` is the result of the concatenation of these two properties. You can therefore define a read-only property as follows:

```
Public Class Person

    Public Property FirstName As String
    Public Property LastName As String

    Public ReadOnly Property FullName As String
        Get
            Return Me.FirstName & " " & Me.LastName
        End Get
    End Property
End Class
```

The `ReadOnly` keyword marks properties as read-only. As you can easily understand, auto-implemented properties cannot work here because you need a space to write code for returning a value.

Write-Only Properties

Opposite to read-only properties, you can also implement write-only properties. In real-life applications, write-only properties are uncommon, so you will probably never implement such members. It makes much more sense providing read-only members than members that you can only write to but not read from. Anyway, you can implement write-only properties marking your properties with the WriteOnly keyword as demonstrated in the following code snippet:

```
Private _fictitiousCounter As Integer


Public WriteOnly Property FictitiousCounter As Integer
    Set(ByVal value As Integer)
        _fictitiousCounter = value
    End Set
End Property
```

You have different options here; one is storing the value received by the setter within a field that you can then eventually reutilize. Otherwise, you can perform some tasks directly within the setter.

Exposing Custom Types

Properties can expose both reference and value types, and they are not limited to built-in .NET types, meaning that you can expose your custom classes and structures through properties. The following code shows an Order class that exposes a property of type Customer; such type is another custom class representing a fictitious customer of your company:

```
Public Class Customer
    Public Property CompanyName As String
    Public Property ContactName As String
End Class


Public Class Order
    Public Property CustomerInstance As Customer
    Public Property OrderID As Integer
End Class
```

You can use the same technique for exposing custom structures. After all, you do nothing different than when you expose strings and integers. Remember that if you do not initialize properties with values, value types returned by properties will have a default value while reference types could result in null references causing runtime errors.

Accessing Properties

Accessing properties is a simple task. You access properties for both reading and writing information that a type needs. The following code demonstrates this:

```
Dim p As New Person


'Properties assignment (write)
p.FirstName = "Alessandro"
p.LastName = "Del Sole"
```

```
'Properties reading
If p.LastName.ToLower = "del sole" Then
    Console.WriteLine(p.LastName)
End If
```

Default Properties

Visual Basic language enables defining default properties. A *default property* is a property marked with the Default keyword that enables assignments to the objects defining the property without the need of invoking the property itself. Default properties are strictly related to data arrays and collections of objects, because they provide the ability of managing an index. For example, imagine you have an array of strings defined within a class as follows:

```
Private listOfNames() As String = _
    {"Alessandro", "Del Sole", "VB 2010 Unleashed"}
```

A default property enables easy access to such an array, both for reading and writing. The following code demonstrates how you can implement a default property:

```
Default Public Property GetName(ByVal index As Integer) As String
    Get
        Return listOfNames(index)
    End Get
    Set(ByVal value As String)
        listOfNames(index) = value
    End Set
End Property
```

PARAMETERS TYPES

The preceding example shows the most common use of default properties, where they accept a numeric index. By the way, default properties can accept any data type as the parameter, not only numeric types. The only rule is actually that the default property must have a parameter

Notice the Default keyword and how the property accesses the array taking advantage of the index argument to return the desired item in the array. Supposing the preceding definition was contained within a class named TestDataAccess, the following code demonstrates how you can access the default property:

```
Dim t As New TestDataAccess
t(2) = "Visual Basic 2010 Unleashed"
Console.WriteLine(t(1))
```

```
Console.WriteLine(t(2))
```

As you can see, you do not need to specify the property name when performing assignments or invocations. The preceding code would produce the following result:

```
Del Sole
Visual Basic 2010 Unleashed
```

INDEXERS

Visual Basic default properties can be compared to Visual C# *indexers*. It's important to know this terminology because you will often hear about indexers.

Scope

All .NET types and their members have *scope*, which represents the level of visibility and accessibility that a type or its members can have. For example, the *public* scope enables members of classes or structure within a class library to be reachable by other classes or assemblies. On the other hand, the *private* scope can prevent members of classes or structures to be reached from outside the class or structure in which they are defined. You assign scope to your objects or members via *qualifiers*, which are special keywords or combination of keywords that establish how an object or its members can be reached from outside the object. Table 7.1 summarizes scope levels in Visual Basic 2010.

TABLE 7.1   Scope Levels in Visual Basic 2010

Qualifier	Description
Public	Allow types and members to be accessed from anywhere, also from external assemblies. It assigns no access restrictions.
Private	Types and members are visible only within the object in which they are defined.
Friend	Types and members are visible within the assembly that contains declarations.
Protected	Types and members are visible within the objects they are defined in and from derived classes.
Protected Friend	Types and members are visible within the assembly, the objects they are defined in, and from derived classes.

The following code snippet gives you an alternative view of scope:

```
'The class is visible to other
'external assemblies.
Public Class ScopeDemo
```

```
'This field is visible only
'within the class
Private counter As Integer

'Visible within this assembly, this class,
'derived classes, other assemblies: no restrictions
Public Property FirstName As String
Public Property LastName As String

'Only within this class and derived classes
Protected Property Age As Integer

'Within this assembly
Friend Property ReservedInformation As String

'Within this assembly, this class and derived classes
Protected Friend Function ReturnSomeInformation()
    Return FirstName & " " & LastName
End Function
```

```
End Class
```

Public and Private qualifiers are self-explanatory, so you probably need some more information about the other ones. To make things easier, let's create a new class that derives from the preceding ScopeDemo, as in the following code snippet:

```
Public Class InheritedScopeDemo
    Inherits ScopeDemo
```

```
End Class
```

If you try to reach the base class' members, you notice that only the ones marked with Friend, Protected Friend, and Protected are visible to the new class (other than Public, of course). But this happens until you are working with one assembly, more precisely with the assembly that defines all the preceding members. What about another assembly referencing the first one? If you have created a Visual Basic solution for testing the preceding code, add a new Visual Basic project to the solution, and to the new project add a reference to the previous one. In the new project, write the following code:

```
Dim testScope As New Scope.InheritedScopeDemo
```

If you try to invoke members of the testScope object, you can see only the FirstName and LastName properties because they were marked as Public. This qualifier is the only one allowing members to be reached from external assemblies. As you may imagine, establishing the appropriate scope is fundamental. For example, you might need a field for storing some data that you do not want to share with the external world; marking a field as

Private prevents derived classes from reaching the field. So you should instead mark it as Protected or Protected Friend according to the access level you want to grant. Particularly when working with inheritance, scope is important.

Methods

In the .NET terminology, method is the word that represents procedures in other programming languages; basically a *method* is a member that performs an operation. Methods are of two kinds: Sub (which does not return values) and Function (which instead returns a value). The following are minimal examples of methods:

```
Sub DoSomething()
    If IO.File.Exists("C:\SomeFile.txt") = False Then
        Throw New IO.FileNotFoundException
    Else
        Console.WriteLine("The file exists")
    End If

End Sub


Function DoSomethingElse() As Boolean

    Dim result As Boolean = IO.File.Exists("C:\SomeFile.txt")
    Return result
End Function
```

This book makes intensive use of methods, so detailed descriptions on implementations are provided across chapters.

SCOPE

Methods' visibility within types can be assigned using one of the qualifiers listed in Table 7.1. If no qualifier is specified, Public is assigned by default.

Invoking Methods

To invoke a method you simply call its name. Continuing with the preceding example, you can invoke the DoSomething method by simply typing the following line:

```
DoSomething()
```

If the method is a Function, you should assign the invocation to a variable as follows:

```
Dim targetOfInvocation As Boolean = DoSomethingElse()
```

This is important if you need to evaluate the value returned by the method. If you do not need to evaluate the result, you can simply invoke Function as if it were Sub:

```
'Allowed
DoSomethingElse()
```

You can basically invoke functions anywhere you need a value. Continuing with the preceding example, the following code is acceptable:

```
Console.WriteLine(DoSomethingElse())
```

In the preceding examples, we act as if the method were defined within a module. If the method is exposed by a class, you need to add a dot symbol after the class name and then type the name of the method as follows:

```
Public Class Person


    Public Sub DoSomething()

    End Sub
End Class
...
Dim p As New Person
p.DoSomething()
```

The Visual Basic grammar also provides the Call keyword that enables invoking methods, but it's obsolete and deprecated. You can use it as follows:

```
Call DoSomething()
```

Methods Arguments: ByVal and ByRef

Methods can receive parameters and can then work with data provided by parameters. In the .NET terminology, parameters are also known as *arguments*. We mainly use the word *arguments* because it's the one that you typically find within the documentation and about topics related to.NET development. The following code shows a simple sample of a method definition receiving an argument and subsequent invocation of that method passing an argument:

```
Public Sub PrintString(ByVal stringToPrint As String)
    Console.WriteLine(stringToPrint)
End Sub

Sub RunTest()
```

```
    PrintString("Visual Basic 2010 Unleashed")
End Sub
```

Arguments can be passed by value and by reference. You pass arguments by value adding the `ByVal` keyword, whereas you pass them by reference specifying the `ByRef` keyword. If you do not specify either keyword, the Visual Basic code editor automatically adds a `ByVal` keyword and passes arguments by value as a default. There are differences between passing arguments by value and by reference; before providing code examples for a better understanding, these differences are all related to the variables you pass as arguments and can be summarized as follows:

▶ If you pass by value a value type, the compiler creates a copy of the original value so changes made to the argument are not reflected to the original data. If you pass a value type by reference, changes made to the argument are reflected to the original data, because in this case the argument is the memory address of the data;

▶ If you pass by reference a reference type, changes made to the argument are reflected to the original data because you are working on the reference pointer. If you pass a reference type by value, changes will not be reflected to the original data because the compiler creates a copy of the reference.

Listing 7.1 shows how value types can be passed by value and by reference.

LISTING 7.1   Passing Arguments by Value

```
Module ByValByRefDemo

    Dim testInt As Integer = 10

    'Creates a copy of the original value(testInt)
    'and does not change it. Returns 10
    Sub ByValTest(ByVal anInt As Integer)
        anInt = 20
        Console.WriteLine(testInt)
    End Sub

    'Gets the reference of the original value (testInt)
    'and changes it. Returns 20
    Sub ByRefTest(ByRef anInt As Integer)
        anInt = 20
        Console.WriteLine(testInt)
    End Sub

    Sub Main()
        ByValTest(testInt)
        ByRefTest(testInt)
        Console.ReadLine()
```

```
    End Sub

End Module
```

Both the ByValTest and ByRefTest methods receive an argument of type Integer. Such an argument is the testInt variable. In the ByValTest method, the argument is passed by value, so the compiler creates a copy of the original data and changes made to the argument variable are not reflected to the original one, in fact the code returns 10, which is the original value for the testInt variable. In the ByRefTest method, the argument is passed by reference. This means that the compiler gets the memory address of the original value and changes made to the argument variable are also reflected to the original data, in fact this code returns 20 which is the new value for the testInt variable. Now consider the following code that provides a similar demonstration for passing reference type both by value and by reference:

```
Dim testString As String = "Visual Basic 2010"
Sub ByValStringTest(ByVal aString As String)
    aString = "Visual Basic 2010 Unleashed"
    Console.WriteLine(testString)
End Sub

Sub ByRefStringTest(ByRef aString As String)
    aString = "Visual Basic 2010 Unleashed"
    Console.WriteLine(testString)
End Sub
```

Invoking the ByValStringTest method, passing the testString variable as an argument will not change the original value for the reasons previously explained. Invoking the ByRefStringTest method, still passing the testString variable as an argument, will also change the original value of the testString variable that becomes now Visual Basic 2010 Unleashed.

PASSING ARRAYS

When passing arrays as arguments, keep in mind that changes on the arguments' variables will be reflected to the original data if you pass the array by value or by reference. This is because arrays are reference types.

ParamArray Arguments

Another way for supplying arguments to a method is the ParamArray keyword. As its name implies, the keyword enables specifying an array of a given type to be accepted by the method. Each item in the array is then treated as a single argument. The following example shows how to implement ParamArray arguments:

```
Sub ParamArrayTest(ByVal ParamArray names() As String)
    'Each item in the array is an
```

```
    'argument that you can manipulate
    'as you need
    For Each name As String In names
        Console.WriteLine(name)
    Next
End Sub
```

You can then invoke the method as follows:

```
ParamArrayTest("Alessandro", "Del Sole", "Visual Basic 2010 Unleashed")
```

This method produces the following result, considering that each string is an argument:

```
Alessandro
Del Sole
Visual Basic 2010 Unleashed
```

ParamArray arguments are always passed by value, and because they are real arrays, they are reference types, so in reality arrays are passed by reference (and changes to the array values will persist). For example, you can first declare an array and then pass it to the method invocation:

```
Dim args() As String = {"Alessandro", "Del Sole",
                        "Visual Basic 2010 Unleashed"}
ParamArrayTest(args)
```

Because of being arrays, you can perform any other operations that these objects support. Basically you can pass to methods an array as an argument or an arbitrary number of single arguments that behind the scenes are turned into an array. Finally, remember that you cannot pass an array with empty fields. For example, the following code will not be compiled:

```
ParamArrayTest("Alessandro", , "Visual Basic 2010 Unleashed")
```

The Visual Basic background compiler shows an error message saying *Omitted Argument Cannot Match ParamArray Argument.*

Optional Arguments

Methods can receive optional arguments. This means that methods modify their behavior according to the number of arguments they received. Optional arguments are defined with the Optional keyword. The following code snippet shows how you can define optional arguments:

```
'Returns the full name of a person
Function FullName(ByVal FirstName As String,
                Optional ByVal LastName As String = "",
                Optional ByVal Title As String = "") As String
```

```
'Assumes that the optional Title parameter
'was not passed by comparing the default value
If Title = "" Then Title = "Mr. "

Dim result As New System.Text.StringBuilder
result.Append(Title)
result.Append(LastName)
result.Append(FirstName)

    Return result.ToString
End Function
```

The purpose of the preceding `FullName` method is simple (and simplified). It should return the full name of a person, but the `LastName` and `Title` arguments are optional, meaning that the caller must provide at least the `FirstName`. Optional arguments must be assigned with a default value; in the preceding code, the default value is an empty string.

DEFAULT VALUES

Default values for optional arguments must be constant expressions. This is the reason why I did not assign a `String.Empty` object but assigned a = "" value. The compiler provides the appropriate warnings if the default value is not good.

Default values are important for at least one reason: there are no other ways for understanding if an optional argument were passed, so a default value is needed for comparison. Moreover, there could be situations in which a default value would be necessary, for example for objects initializations. In the preceding code, to check if the optional `Title` parameter were passed, a comparison is performed against the `Title`'s value. If its value equals the default value, we can assume that the argument was not supplied. This example provides a custom value in case the argument was not passed. For example, if we write the following invocation

```
Console.WriteLine(FullName("Alessandro"))
```

we would get the following result: `Mr. Alessandro`. Behind the scenes, the Visual Basic compiler generates a new invocation that includes all optional parameters with a default value, as follows: `FullName("Alessandro","","")`. Although useful, optional arguments are not always the best choice, and we do not recommend their usage. This is because they are strictly related to the Visual Basic language and are not compliant with other .NET languages, so if you produce class libraries, you should be aware of this. Instead, the .NET Framework provides a cleaner way for handling methods with different arguments and signatures that is powerful, known as *overloading*, which is discussed next.

Optional Nullable Arguments   Visual Basic 2010, like F# and C# 4.0 as well, also introduces a new important feature related to optional arguments that has the capability to pass nullable types as optional arguments. For example, the following code is now allowed in VB 2010:

```
Sub NullableDemo(ByVal firstArgument As String, _
                 Optional ByVal secondArgument As _
                 Nullable(Of Integer) = Nothing)

    If secondArgument Is Nothing Then
        'We can assume that the
        'optional argument was not supplied
    End If
End Sub
```

As you can see, nullable arguments are now supported, but you are still required to provide a default value, which can also be null. Remember that optional nullable arguments can only go after non optional ones in the argument list. They are particularly useful when dealing with scenarios like Microsoft Office automation, where optional arguments are common.

Overloading Methods

One of the most powerful features in the object-oriented development with the .NET Framework is the capability of overloading methods. *Overloading* means providing multiple signatures of the same method, in which signature is the number and types of arguments a method can receive. The following code snippet shows an example of overloading:

```
Private Function ReturnFullName(ByVal firstName As String,
                                ByVal lastName As String)
    Return firstName & " " & lastName
End Function

Private Function ReturnFullName(ByVal firstName As String,
                                ByVal lastName As String,
                                ByVal Age As Integer)
    Return firstName & " " & lastName & " of age " & Age.ToString
End Function

Private Function ReturnFullName(ByVal title As String,
                                ByVal firstName As String,
                                ByVal lastName As String)
    Return title & " " & firstName & " " & lastName
End Function

Private Function ReturnFullName(ByVal title As String,
                                ByVal firstName As String,
                                ByVal lastName As String,
```

```
                                  ByVal Age As Integer)
      Return title & " " & firstName & " " & lastName & _
            " of age " & Age.ToString
End Function
```

As you can see, there are four different implementations of one method named
`ReturnFullName`. Each implementation differs from the others in that it receives a different
number of arguments. The preceding example is simple, and the arguments are self-
explanatory; each implementation returns the concatenation of the supplied arguments.
Probably you wonder why you need overloading and providing four different implementations of a single method when you would obtain the same result with optional arguments. The answer is that this approach is the only accepted method by the Microsoft
Common Language Specification and ensures that every .NET language can use the different implementations, whereas optional arguments are not supported from other .NET
languages. Another good reason for using overloads is that you can return strongly typed
results from methods. If you need to work with specific data types, you can use overloaded signatures instead of providing one signature that returns `Object`. The Visual Basic
grammar defines an `Overloads` keyword as one that can be used to define overloaded
signatures; the following example is an excerpt of the previous one, now using `Overloads`:

```
Private Overloads Function ReturnFullName(ByVal firstName As String,
                                ByVal lastName As String)
    Return firstName & " " & lastName
End Function

Private Overloads Function ReturnFullName(ByVal firstName As String,
                                ByVal lastName As String,
                                ByVal Age As Integer)
    Return firstName & " " & lastName & " of age " & Age.ToString
End Function
```

Basically there's no difference in using the `Overloads` keywords. If you decide to use it,
you must decorate it with all other definitions. To support overloading, signatures must
differ from each other in some points:

► Signatures cannot differ only in `ByVal` or `ByRef` arguments. If two signatures have
  two arguments of the same type, the arguments cannot differ only in `ByVal`/`ByRef`
  but they consist of different types.

► In the case of `Function`, overloaded implementations can return the same type or
  different types. If they return different types but have exactly the same arguments,
  the code cannot be compiled. This means that different implementations must have
  different arguments.

► If you decide to provide optional arguments, signatures cannot differ only on
  optional arguments. This is because there can be no ambiguity, in that the compiler
  has to know exactly what overloaded method it needs to invoke, based on the parameters you provide.

You invoke methods defined in this way as you would normally with other methods. Moreover, IntelliSense provides a great help on finding the most appropriate overload for your needs, as shown in Figure 7.1.

FIGURE 7.1   IntelliSense helps you choose among overloads.

Coercion

It can happen that an invocation to an overloaded method supplies a compliant type but not the same type established in the signature. For example, consider the following over-loaded method:

```
Private Sub CoercionDemo(ByVal anArgument As Double)
    Debug.WriteLine("Floating point")
End Sub

Private Sub CoercionDemo(ByVal anArgument As Integer)
    Debug.WriteLine("Integer")
End Sub
```

The Visual Basic compiler can decide what signature is the most appropriate according to the argument passed. This is particularly important when working with numeric types. Moreover, the compiler can also handle coercion, meaning that it can perform conversion when there's no loss of precision. Consider the following code:

```
Dim testValue As Byte = 123
CoercionDemo(testValue)
```

The `CoercionDemo` overloads do not support `Byte`, only `Double` and `Integer`. Because `Byte` is basically an integer type, the Visual Basic compiler converts the object into an `Integer` type because this expansion conversion will always be successful. The compiler can also decide what is the best overload fitting the scenario.

Overloading Properties

Now that you know what overloading is, you need to know that the technique is not limited to methods but can also be applied to properties. The following code snippet shows an example:

```
Property Test(ByVal age As Integer) As Integer
    Get

    End Get
    Set(ByVal value As Integer)
```

```
    End Set
End Property
Property Test(ByVal name As String) As String
    Get

    End Get
    Set(ByVal value As String)

    End Set
End Property
```

Because of their different implementations, in this scenario you cannot use auto-implemented properties, mainly because overloads cannot differ only because of their return type. To provide overloaded properties, you need to remember the same limitations listed for methods.

Exit from Methods

Methods execution typically completes when the `End Sub` or `End Function` statements are encountered. You often need to break methods execution before the execution completes. In the case of `Sub` methods, you can accomplish this using the `Exit Sub` statement. The following example checks the value of an integer and immediately breaks if the value is greater than 10. If not, it loops until the value is 10 and then breaks:

```
Sub TestingValues(ByVal anInteger As Integer)
    If anInteger > 10 Then
        Exit Sub
    ElseIf anInteger < 10 Then
        Do Until anInteger = 10
            anInteger += 1
        Loop
        Exit Sub
    End If
End Sub
```

You can also use the `Return` keyword without a value instead of `Exit Sub`. For `Function` methods, things are a little different because they return a value. When the method execution completes regularly, you return a value via the `Return` keyword. Until now you found several examples of methods returning values.

AVOID VISUAL BASIC 6 STYLE

If you migrate from Visual Basic 6, you probably return values from functions assigning the result to the name of the function itself. In .NET development this is depreciated, although it will be compiled. The `Return` keyword is optimized for returning values and all .NET languages have a specific keyword, so you should always prefer this approach.

When you instead need to break the method execution, you can use the `Exit Function` statement, as shown in the following code snippet:

```
Function TestingValue(ByVal anInteger As Integer) As Boolean

    Dim result As Boolean

    If anInteger < 10 Then
        Do Until anInteger = 10
            anInteger += 1
        Loop
        result = True
        'Returns False
    ElseIf anInteger = 10 Then
        Exit Function
    Else
        result = False
    End If
    Return result
End Function
```

Keep in mind that `Function` methods always have to return something. Because of this, `Exit Function` returns the default value of the return data type. In the preceding example, the method returns `Boolean`, so `Exit Function` returns `False`. If the method returned `Integer` or another numeric type, `Exit Function` would return zero. If the method returned a reference type, `Exit Function` would return `Nothing`. Another best practice in returning value is to assign the result of the evaluation to a variable (`result` in the preceding example) and then provide a single invocation to the `Return` instruction because this can optimize the compilation process, other than making coding easier.

Partial Classes

Starting from Visual Basic 2005, you can split the definition of a class across multiple parts using the *partial classes* feature. You do not actually create different classes; you simply create one class implemented within multiple parts, typically across multiple files. This feature was first introduced for separating Visual Studio's auto-generated code from developer's code but it is useful in different scenarios. To see a practical implementation of partial classes, simply create a new Windows Forms project. Then click the **Show All Files** button in Solution Explorer, expand the Form1.vb item, and double-click the **Form1.designer.vb** file. Inside this file you can find the definition of the Form1 class, as shown in Listing 7.2.

LISTING 7.2   Visual Studio Auto-Generated Partial Class

```
Partial Class Form1
```

```vb
    Inherits System.Windows.Forms.Form

    'Form overrides dispose to clean up the component list.
    <System.Diagnostics.DebuggerNonUserCode()> _
    Protected Overrides Sub Dispose(ByVal disposing As Boolean)
        Try
            If disposing AndAlso components IsNot Nothing Then
                components.Dispose()
            End If
        Finally
            MyBase.Dispose(disposing)
        End Try
    End Sub

    'Required by the Windows Form Designer
    Private components As System.ComponentModel.IContainer

    'NOTE: The following procedure is required by the Windows Form Designer
    'It can be modified using the Windows Form Designer.
    'Do not modify it using the code editor.
    <System.Diagnostics.DebuggerStepThrough()> _
    Private Sub InitializeComponent()
        components = New System.ComponentModel.Container()
        Me.AutoScaleMode = System.Windows.Forms.AutoScaleMode.Font
        Me.Text = "Form1"
    End Sub
End Class
```

As you can see, the class definition includes the Partial keyword. This indicates to the compiler that elsewhere in the project another piece of the class is defined within a different code file. In this case, the other piece is the Form1.vb file whose code is simple when you create a new project:

```vb
Public Class Form1


End Class
```

Both files implement one class. By the way, this approach makes your code much cleaner. In this example, partial classes help developers to concentrate on their own code ensuring that auto-generated code will not be confusing. The Visual Studio IDE makes a huge usage of partial classes; LINQ to SQL and ADO.NET Entity Framework are just a couple of examples. Following is a custom example of partial classes. Imagine you have this implementation of the Person class within a code file named Person.vb:

```vb
Public Class Person
```

```vb
Public Property FirstName As String
Public Property LastName As String
Public Property Age As Integer

Public Overrides Function ToString() As String
    Return String.Concat(FirstName, " ", LastName)
End Function

Public Sub New(ByVal Name As String, ByVal SurName As String,
              ByVal Age As Integer)
    Me.FirstName = Name
    Me.LastName = SurName
    Me.Age = Age
End Sub
End Class
```

Then you decide to implement the ICloneable interface to provide a custom implementation of the Clone method, but you want to separate the implementation from the rest of the class code. At this point you can add a new code file to the project and write the following:

```vb
Partial Public Class Person
    Implements ICloneable

    Public Function Clone() As Object Implements System.ICloneable.Clone
        Return Me.MemberwiseClone
    End Function
End Class
```

This last code will be still part of the Person class; simply it has been defined in another place.

PARTIAL CLASSES TIPS

You can split your classes within multiple files. Generally you create partial classes within just two files, but you have to know that you are allowed to create them within two or more files. Partial classes also take whatever scope you define in one of the partial class definitions.

Also notice how IntelliSense can improve your coding experience by showing a list of the partial classes that you can complete (see Figure 7.2).

FIGURE 7.2   IntelliSense helps choose the available partial classes.

A partial approach can also be applied to Structures as follows:

```
Partial Structure Test


End Structure
```

Partial classes indeed have a limitation: You cannot define them within other classes. For example, the following code will correctly be compiled, but it does not implement partial classes, while it creates two different classes:

```
Class TestPartial


    'Compiles, but creates a new partial class
    'instead of extending the previous Person
    Partial Class Person

    End Class
End Class
```

Another interesting feature first introduced by .NET Framework 3.5 is partial methods.

Partial Methods

Since Visual Basic 2008 and the .NET Framework 3.5, you can take advantage of another interesting feature that has been included in Visual Basic 2010: partial methods. Basically this feature has been mainly introduced in LINQ to ADO.NET, but it can be used in different scenarios for other language features. The concept behind partial methods is the same as partial classes: Methods implementations can be split across multiple parts. Partial methods have three particular characteristics: They must be `Private` methods, they cannot return values (that is, only `Sub` methods are allowed), and their bodies must be empty in the class in which methods are defined. Consider the following code, in which a class named `Contact` is split across partial classes and a partial method is defined:

```
Public Class Contact
```

```
Public Property FirstName As String
Public Property LastName As String
Public Property EmailAddress As String

Public Sub New(ByVal Name As String,
       ByVal LastName As String, ByVal Email As String)
    Me.FirstName = Name
    Me.LastName = LastName
    Me.EmailAddress = Email
End Sub

Partial Private Sub Validate(ByVal Email As String)
End Sub
```

End Class

A partial method is marked with the Partial keyword. It has a Private scope, returns no value, and its definition's body is empty. Suppose you want to implement the actual code for your method. For example, we could verify if the Email address provided by the user is a valid address; to accomplish this, we can use regular expressions.

ABOUT REGULAR EXPRESSIONS

Regular expressions are an advanced way to work with text. The .NET Framework provides the System.Text.RegularExpression namespace that exposes classes for managing regular expressions with .NET languages.

The following code shows how you can implement a partial class in which the actual code for a partial method is provided:

```
Partial Public Class Contact

    Private Sub Validate(ByVal Email As String)

        Dim validateMail As String = _
        "^([\w-\.]+)@((\[[0-9]{1,3}\." &
        "[0-9]{1,3}\.)|((\[\w-]+\.)+))" &
        "([a-zA-z]{2,4}|[0-9]{1,3})(\]?)$"

        If Text.RegularExpressions.
            Regex.IsMatch(Email, validateMail) _
            = False Then
            Throw New _
            InvalidOperationException _
```

```
            ("The specified mail address is not valid")
        End If
    End Sub
End Class
```

When you effectively implement the partial method, you do not need to mark it again as Partial. This qualifier must be added only in the empty method definition. The preceding code checks if the specified email address is valid; if it is not, it throws an InvalidOperationException.

To describe partial methods in another way, the concept is "to accomplish this particular task, you do need this particular method. But the implementation of the method is left to your choice."

Constructors

A constructor is a method you invoke to create a new instance of a class that is represented by the New keyword in Visual Basic. For example, if you have the following Contact class

```
Public Class Contact


    Public Property FirstName As String
    Public Property LastName As String
    Public Property Email As String
    Public Property Address As String


    Public Sub New()


    End Sub
End Class
```

you can then create a new instance of the Contact class as follows:

```
'First syntax
Dim aContact As Contact
aContact = New Contact

'Second syntax
Dim aContact As New Contact
```

```
'Third syntax
Dim aContact As Contact = New Contact
```

All the three preceding syntaxes are enabled, so you can use the one you prefer. (I use the second one for better readability.) In other words, creating an instance means giving life to a new copy of the object so that you can use it for your purposes, such as storing data or performing tasks. All classes must have a constructor. If you do not provide a constructor, Visual Basic provides one for you. The default constructor is hidden in the code editor, but it has public visibility and contains no code; it serves just for instantiating the object. If you want to make it visible, click the **Declaration** combo box in the code editor and select the **New** method, as shown in Figure 7.3.

FIGURE 7.3   Making the default constructor visible.

Constructors are useful for initializing objects' members. Because of this, and because constructors are basically methods, they can receive arguments. For example, you could implement the constructor in a way that receives appropriate arguments for initializing the Contact class' properties:

```
Public Sub New(ByVal name As String,
               ByVal surName As String,
               ByVal emailAddress As String,
               ByVal homeAddress As String)

    Me.FirstName = name
    Me.LastName = surName
    Me.Email = emailAddress
```

```
        Me.Address = homeAddress
End Sub
```

In this way you can easily assign members of the class. You invoke the parameterized constructor as follows:

```
Dim aContact As New Contact("Alessandro",
                            "Del Sole",
                            "alessandro.delsole@visual-basic.it",
                            "5Th street")
```

At this point your object is ready to be used and is populated with data. You might also want to add simple validations for arguments received by the constructor. This is important because if you need data initialization, you also need valid data. For example you can throw an ArgumentException if arguments are invalid:

```
Public Sub New(ByVal name As String,
               ByVal surName As String,
               ByVal emailAddress As String,
               ByVal homeAddress As String)

    If surName = "" Then _
        Throw New ArgumentException("surName")
    Me.FirstName = name
    Me.LastName = surName
    Me.Email = emailAddress
    Me.Address = homeAddress
End Sub
```

Continuing the discussion about members' initialization, you might have members (typically fields) with inline initialization. In this scenario, when you invoke the constructor, members' initialization is also performed even if the constructor contains no code about initialization. This is demonstrated by the following code snippet:

```
Public Class Contact

    Private ReadOnly InitializationDemo As Integer = 100

'Just for demo purposes!
    Public Sub New()
        Console.WriteLine(InitializationDemo.ToString)
        Console.ReadLine()
    End Sub
End Class
```

The constructor does not perform any initialization, but when the class gets instantiated, the value is assigned. The preceding code produces 100 as the output. Another interesting thing is that constructors are the only place in which you can initialize read-only fields. We can rewrite the preceding code as follows:

```
Public Class Contact

    Private ReadOnly InitializationDemo As Integer

    'Just for demo purposes!
    Public Sub New()
        InitializationDemo = 100
        Console.WriteLine(InitializationDemo.ToString)
        Console.ReadLine()
    End Sub
```

Notice that the code is correctly compiled and the produced output is 100. This technique is important if you plan to expose read-only members in your classes.

Overloading Constructors

Because constructors are effectively methods, they support the overloading feature. You can therefore provide multiple implementations of the New method, taking care of the limitations described for methods. You cannot use the Overloads keyword; the compiler does not need it. For example, continuing the example of the Contact class, we can provide different implementations of the constructor as follows:

```
Public Sub New()
    Me.FirstName = "Assigned later"
    Me.LastName = "Assigned later"
    Me.Email = "Assigned later"
    Me.Address = "Assigned later"
End Sub

Public Sub New(ByVal surName As String)
    If String.IsNullOrEmpty(surName) Then _
        Throw New ArgumentException("surName")

    Me.LastName = surName

    'Will be assigned later
    Me.FirstName = ""
    Me.Email = ""
    Me.Address = ""
End Sub

Public Sub New(ByVal name As String,
            ByVal surName As String,
```

```
                ByVal emailAddress As String,
                ByVal homeAddress As String)

    If surName = "" Then _
        Throw New ArgumentException("surName")
    Me.FirstName = name
    Me.LastName = surName
    Me.Email = emailAddress
    Me.Address = homeAddress
End Sub
```

The first overload receives no arguments and provides a default members' initialization. The second overload receives just an argument, initializing other members with empty strings. The last overload is the most complete and provides initialization features for all the properties exposed by the class.

Nested Invocations

Overloads are useful, but when working with constructors, you might want to consider a common place for initializing members. To accomplish this you can invoke constructors' overloads from another overload. For example, consider the following code snippet:

```
Public Sub New(ByVal LastName As String)
    Me.New(LastName, "")
End Sub

Public Sub New(ByVal LastName As String, ByVal Email As String)
    Me.LastName = LastName
    Me.Email = Email
End Sub
```

The first overload can invoke the second overload, passing required arguments. In the preceding example only an empty string is passed, but according to your scenario you could make a different elaboration before passing the argument. The good news in this technique is that you need to provide initialization code only once (in this case, in the second overload). By the way, take care about the hierarchical calls; the first overload can invoke the second one because this receives more arguments but not vice versa. This kind of approach can be used also because both overloads have an argument in common; for example, if you instead also had a ContactID property of type Integer that you wanted to initialize via the constructor and you had the following overloads:

```
Public Sub New(ByVal LastName As String)


End Sub

Public Sub New(ByVal ContactID As Integer)
```

```
End Sub
```

In this case the two overloads have no arguments in common; because of this, if you want to provide a common place for initializations, you need to implement a private constructor as follows:

```
Private Sub New()
    'Replace with your
    'initialization code
    Me.ContactID = 0
    Me.LastName = "Del Sole"
End Sub
```

Then you can redirect both preceding overloads to invoke a private constructor:

```
Public Sub New(ByVal LastName As String)
    Me.New()
    Me.LastName = LastName
End Sub

Public Sub New(ByVal ContactID As Integer)
    Me.New()
    Me.ContactID = ContactID
End Sub
```

PRIVATE CONSTRUCTORS

There is a little bit more to say about private constructors that is discussed later in this chapter about shared members. At the moment you need to remember that if you place a private constructor, you *must* remove the public one with the same signature. For example, if you have a `Private Sub New()`, you cannot also have a `Public Sub New()`.

Object Initializers

Since Visual Basic 2008 and .NET 3.5, the Visual Basic grammar offers another feature, named *object initializers,* that enables inline initialization of objects' members when creating an instance, without the need of providing specific constructors' overloads. For a better understanding, let's provide a practical example. We can implement the Contact class without implementing a constructor overloads that receives any arguments for initialization:

```
Public Class Contact


    Public Property FirstName As String
    Public Property LastName As String
    Public Property Email As String
```

```
    Public Property Address As String

End Class
```

To instantiate the class and initialize its members, according to the classical, old-fashioned syntax, we should write the following code:

```
Dim aContact As New Contact
With aContact
    .FirstName = "Alessandro"
    .LastName = "Del Sole"
    .Email = "alessandro.delsole@visual-basic.it"
    .Address = "5Th street"
End With
```

The Visual Basic 2008 and 2010 syntax enables instead the object initializers way, which works as in the following snippet:

```
Dim aContact As New Contact With {.LastName = "Del Sole",
    .FirstName = "Alessandro",
    .Email = "alessandro.delsole@visual-basic.it",
    .Address = "5Th street"}
```

You simply add the With keyword after the instance declaration. The keyword is followed by a couple of brackets. Within the brackets, you can easily assign members by writing members' names preceded by a dot symbol; members are separated by commas. This code demonstrates how you can provide inline initialization of members even if no constructor's overloads receive an appropriate number of arguments for the purpose of initialization. From now on I will often write code using object initializers; this feature is important with for advanced language features that are covered in the next part of the book.

WHY OBJECT INITIALIZERS?

You may wonder why this feature has been introduced to the .NET languages, considering that there were already several ways for providing initialization. The reason is LINQ. As you see later in the book, object initializers provide a way for initializing objects within queries; another important feature known as *anonymous types* takes advantage of object initializers. Chapter 21, "Advanced Languages Features," discusses anonymous types.

Shared Members

Classes can expose *instance* and *shared* members. Until now, all discussions used instance members for examples. It's important to understand what the difference between instance and shared members is, because you can successfully use both of them in your classes. Basically, when you create a new instance of a class, you create a copy of that class with its own life and its own data. On the other hand, with shared member you work with only one copy of a class and of its data. Classes can support different situations, such as all shared members or just a few shared members. For example, if you have a class exposing only shared members, you work with exactly one copy of the class. If you have only a few shared members within a class, all instances of that class access only one copy of the data marked as shared.

SHARED/STATIC

In Visual Basic we talk about shared members. This is because these members are marked with the Shared keyword. In other programming languages such behavior is represented by the "static" definition; shared and static mean the same thing. Typically the static definition is better when talking about interoperability with other .NET languages; both definitions refer to the same thing and we use the shared definition for consistency.

Generally you expose only shared members in two main circumstances: with mere methods libraries or with classes that can exist in only one copy (known as *singleton*), such as the Application class in Windows Forms applications. Now we cover how to implement shared members within classes.

Shared Classes

Visual Basic, differently from other .NET languages such as Visual C#, does not provide the capability of creating shared classes; to accomplish this you have two alternatives: create a class the usual way and mark all members as shared, or you can create a module. Modules are a specific Visual Basic feature that work almost as shared classes (see Chapter 10, "Modules").

Shared Fields

Shared fields are useful to store information that is common to all instances of a class. For example, imagine you have a class named Document and that represents a text document. You could implement a shared field acting as a counter of all the documents opened in your application:

```
Public Class Document


    Private Shared _documentCounter As Integer


    Public Sub New()
        _documentCounter += 1
    End Sub


End Class
```

The code in the example increments the counter each time a new instance is created. The documentCounter field is common to all instances of the Document class because it is marked with the Shared keyword.

Shared Properties

In an object-oriented approach, fields should be wrapped by properties that gain access to fields. This happens also with shared members. Continuing with the preceding example, a shared property would be implemented as follows:

```
Private Shared _documentCounter As Integer


Public Shared ReadOnly Property DocumentCounter As Integer
    Get
        Return _documentCounter
    End Get
End Property
```

In this case the property is also marked as read-only because its value is incremented only when a new instance of the class is created, passing through the related field, but of course shared properties support both Get and Set. Because the preceding code offers a read-only property, you cannot take advantage of the new auto-implemented properties feature. If you do not need a read-only property, you can declare a shared property as follows:

```
Public Shared Property DocumentCounter As Integer
```

By doing so, you can avoid the implementation of private shared fields.

Shared Methods

Shared methods can be invoked without the need of creating an instance of the class that defines them. As in the previous members, shared methods are decorated with the Shared keyword. A common use of shared methods is within class libraries that act as helper repositories of functions. For example, you can have a class that provides methods for compressing and decompressing files using the System.IO.Compression namespace. In such scenario, you do not need to create an instance of the class; in fact, shared methods just need to point to some files and not to instance data. The following code snippet provides an example of shared methods:

```
Public Class CompressionHelper


    Public Shared Sub Compress(ByVal fileName As String,
                               ByVal target As String)
        'Code for compressing files here
    End Sub

    Public Shared Sub Decompress(ByVal fileName As String,
```

```
                              ByVal uncompressed As String)
        'Code for decompressing files here
    End Sub
End Class
...
Sub Test()

    CompressionHelper.Compress("Sourcefile.txt", "Compressedfile.gz")

    CompressionHelper.Decompress("Compressedfile.gz", "Sourcefile.txt")

End Sub
```

As you can see, you invoke shared methods by writing the name of the class instead of creating an instance and invoking methods onto the instance. This approach is useful for organizing functions in libraries according to their purpose (established via the class name). If you try to invoke shared methods from an instance, the Visual Basic compiler throws a warning message advising that such invocation might be ambiguous. Of course, you can remove such warnings by editing the Instance Variable Accesses Shared Member option in the Compiler tab within My Project. By the way, I suggest you leave the default setting unchanged because it can help avoiding ambiguous code.

OVERLOADING

Shared methods, as with other methods, support overloading.

When implementing shared methods, you should be aware of some considerations. First, you cannot work with instance members from within shared methods. For example, the following code throws a compilation error:

```
'Instance field
Private instanceField As Integer

'Cannot refer to an instance member
Public Shared Function testSharedInstance() As Integer
    Return instanceField
End Function
```

To solve this error, you should mark as Shared the member you are working with (instanceField in the preceding example):

```
'Shared field
Private Shared sharedField As Integer

'Correct
Public Shared Function testSharedInstance() As Integer
```

```
      Return sharedField
End Function
```

The alternative is to change the method from shared to instance, removing the Shared keyword from the method definition. But this is not a game. You need to evaluate how your methods will behave and how they will use members exposed by your classes. According to this, you can decide if methods can be shared or must be instance ones. Another consideration is related to classes exposing only shared methods. Because in this scenario the class does not need to be instantiated, a private empty constructor must be supplied as follows:

```
Private Sub New()
    'No code
End Sub
```

This constructor contains no code (but it could for initialization purposes) and is just needed to prevent instance creation.

SHARED SUB MAIN

In all code examples shown until here, you saw how console applications provide a module containing the entry point for applications, which is the Sub Main. Because modules are basically shared classes, you can supply a class containing shared members also with a Shared Sub Main that works as in modules. Although modules are suggested instead of shared classes, because they cause less confusion and are a Visual Basic-specific feature, you need to know how to implement the Shared Sub Main within classes, because if you ever use conversion tools from Visual C# to VB (or if you get code examples translated into VB by Visual C# folks), you will typically find a class named Program containing the previously mentioned shared entry point.

Shared Constructors

Classes can implement shared constructors, as shown in the following code:

```
'Private visibility
Shared Sub New()
    'Initialization of shared
    'members
    instanceField = 10
End Sub
```

Shared constructors are particularly useful for initializing shared members or for loading data that is common to all instances of a class; a shared constructor is invoked immediately before the normal constructor that creates a new instance of the class. With that said, the following code is appropriate and accepted by the compiler:

```
Shared Sub New()
    'Initialization of shared
```

```
    'members
    instanceField = 10
End Sub

Sub New()

End Sub
```

Another important thing to take care of is that shared constructors have `Private` visibility and they are the only point in the class in which you can initialize a read-only field.

Common Language Specification

One of the most important features of the .NET Framework is the CLR, which offers a common infrastructure for different .NET languages. You may also remember from Chapter 1, "Introducing the .NET Framework 4.0," that all .NET compilers produce Intermediate Language (IL) code. Because of this, .NET languages can interoperate: An assembly produced with Visual Basic can be used by an application written in Visual C# and vice versa. But different languages have, of course, different characteristics; so if developers use specific features of a language, the risk is that another language cannot use that produced assembly or they might encounter several errors. This can occur when companies produce reusable components, such as class libraries or user controls that should be used from whatever .NET application written in whatever language you want without problems. To provide a common set of rules that developers should follow to ensure interoperability, Microsoft wrote the Common Language Specification (or CLS) that are a set of rules that every developer has to follow to produce reusable assemblies. This chapter provides an overview of the CLS and gives you information about applying such rules to the topics discussed in this chapter. Each time a new topic is covered, tips for making code CLS-compliant is provided.

COMMON LANGUAGE SPECIFICATION WEBSITE

Microsoft offers a dedicated page to CLS on the MSDN portal that you should look at: http://msdn.microsoft.com/en-us/library/12a7a7h3(VS.100).aspx

Where Do I Need to Apply?

CLS are important when producing reusable components, such as class libraries or user controls. Because only public classes and public members from public classes can be used from other applications also written in different languages, the Common Language Specification applies only to

▶ Public classes

▶ Public members exposed by public classes, such as methods or properties, and members that can be inherited

▶ Objects used by public members, such as types passed as arguments to methods

In all other cases, such as private members, applying CLS is ignored by the compiler. Another situation when you do not need to apply CLS is when you do not produce reusable components. For example, the UI side of a Windows application (Win Forms or WPF) is not required to be CLS-compliant because external applications will not invoke the UI.

Marking Assemblies and Types as CLS-Compliant

Chapter 2, "Getting Started with the Visual Studio 2010 IDE," and Chapter 3, "The Anatomy of a Visual Basic Project," offer an overview of assemblies. When you produce a reusable component such as a class library or a user control, such as a .dll assembly, you need to ensure that it is CLS-compliant. You can add the following attribute to the assembly definition:

```
<Assembly: CLSCompliant(True)>
```

This attribute tells the compiler to check if a type used in your code is CLS-compliant. If the compiler finds a CLS-incompliant type, it throws a warning message. Assembly members should also be marked as CLS-compliant, if you plan that they will be. For example, a class is defined CLS-compliant as follows:

```
<CLSCompliant(True)> Public Class Person
```

You might wonder why you should add this attribute at the class level if you specified one at the assembly level. The reason is that you might implement CLS-incompliant classes (therefore assigning False to the CLSCompliant attribute), and this is useful for communicating both the compiler and code analysis tools that a CLS-incompliant class should not be checked.

CODE ANALYSIS

There are different code analysis tools for checking if code is CLS-compliant. The first one is the well-known Microsoft FxCop, which can be installed by double-clicking the same-name shortcut in the Windows SDK subfolder of Windows's Start Menu. The second one is the code analysis instrumentation available in Visual Studio Team System, which is covered in Chapter 58, "Advanced Analysis Tools." Both tools are important for finding errors about CLS compliance of your code.

Naming Conventions

Assigning comprehensible identifiers to types and members is, of course, a best practice in every development environment. This becomes a rule in .NET development, especially if you want your code to be CLS-compliant. To understand this, you need to first know that the Common Language Specification enables only two notations, Pascal and Camel. If you are an old Visual Basic 6 developer or a Visual C++ one, you might be familiar with the Hungarian notation that is not supported by .NET rules. An identifier is Pascal-cased when the first letter of each word composing the identifier is uppercase. The following identifier is Pascal-case: FirstName. An identifier is instead defined as camel-case when the first character of the first word composing the identifier is lowercase. The following identifier is camel-cased: `firstName`. It's important to know this difference to understand where and when you should use one notation or the other one. You use the Pascal notation in the following situations:

▶ Namespaces' identifiers

▶ Identifiers of all public members within an assembly, such as classes, properties, methods, and custom types

Instead use the camel notation in the following situations:

▶ Identifiers of all private members within an assembly, such as fields, methods, and so on. This is not actually a requirement (because private members are not affected by CLS in terms of naming conventions) but a good programming practice.

▶ Arguments' names for methods, both public and private

No other naming notation is enabled in the Common Language Specification. Obviously, if you do not plan to write CLS-compliant code, you can use any notation you like, although, it's preferable to use a .NET-oriented notation. Another important rule about naming conventions is in methods' names. You should first place the name of the verb and then the target of the action. For example, `CompressFile` is correct whereas `FileCompress` is not. The following code shows an example of a well-formed class:

```
'Public members of an assembly
'are pascal cased
Public Class NamingConventionsDemo

    'private fields are camel-cased
    Private documentCounter As Integer = 0

    'public properties are pascal-cased
    Public Property FirstName As String

    'public methods are pascal-cased
    'arguments are camel-cased
    Public Function CompressFile(ByVal sourceFile As String,
                                 ByVal targetFile As String) As Boolean

    End Function

    'private methods are camel-cased
    'arguments are camel-cased
    Private Sub checkForFileExistance(ByVal fileName As String)

    End Sub

End Class
```

Because of their importance, this book follows the preceding naming conventions, even for CLS-incompliant code.

Rules About Classes

The Common Language Specification influences classes' implementation with basically a few rules. The most rules are related to inheritance as much as for methods. Because inheritance hasn't been covered yet, (discussed in Chapter 12, "Inheritance,"), the only rule mentioned here is that if a class exposes only shared members, it must have an empty private constructor and must be marked as NotInheritable, as follows:

```
<CLSCompliant(True)> Public NotInheritable Class GzipCompress
    'Empty private constructor
    Private Sub New()

    End Sub

    Public Shared Sub Compress(ByVal fileName As String,
                               ByVal target As String)

    End Sub

    Public Shared Sub Decompress(ByVal fileName As String,
                                 ByVal source As String)

    End Sub
End Class
```

The other rules about classes are described in Chapter 12.

Rules About Properties

The Common Language Specification provides a couple of rules about properties implementation:

- ▶ All properties exposed by a class must have the same access level, meaning that they must be all instance properties or all shared properties or all virtual properties. Virtual properties (that is, marked with the MustOverride keyword) are described in Chapter 12.

- ▶ Get, Set, and the property itself must return and receive the same type; the type must also be CLS-compliant. If the property returns String, both Get and Set must handle String, too. The type must be passed by value and not by reference.

Rules About Methods

CLS influence methods both for inheritance implementations and for declarations. You need to know that arguments with a nonfixed length must be specified only with the ParamArray keyword.

Rules About Arrays

For arrays, CLS rules are simple:

▶ Items within arrays must be CLS-compliant types.

▶ Arrays must have fixed length greater than zero.

▶ Arrays must be zero-based. (This is mostly a rule for compilers.)

Summary

In this chapter you learned several important concepts about object-oriented programming with Visual Basic 2010. You saw how classes are the most important item in the object-oriented programming; you learned how to declare classes and how to expose members from classes, such as methods, properties, and fields. Summarizing these features, you may remember how fields are the real state of objects and how properties are a way for ruling access to fields from the external world. You can also remember how methods are procedures that take actions. Methods are flexible also due to the overloading technique that enables implementing different signatures of the same method. There is a special method known as constructor, which creates an instance of a class and gives the class the real life. Each time you create an instance of a class, you create a new copy of an object with its own life and data. But there are situations in which you need only one copy of an object and data, and that is where shared members come in. You also took a tour of interesting features such as partial classes and partial methods that enable a better organization of your classes' infrastructure. But as in all fantastic worlds, the risk of doing something wrong is always there, especially if you consider the CLR infrastructure that enables .NET languages to interoperate among them. Because of this, a set of rules named Common Language Specification has been created to ensure that all classes and their members can be used from all .NET languages with the minimum risk of errors. After this overview of classes, it's time to understand how they live within memory.

CHAPTER 8

Managing an Object's Lifetime

Real life is often a great place to get programming examples. Think of life: Humans are born; they grow up; they live their lives; they do tons of things; and, at a certain point of life, they die. Managing objects in programming environments works similarly. You give life to an object by creating an instance; then you use it in your own application while it is effectively useful to the application. But there is a point at which you do not need an object anymore, so you need to destroy it to free up memory and other resources, bringing an object to "death." Understanding how object lifetime works in .NET programming is fundamental because it gives you the ability to write better code; code that can take advantage of system resources to consume resources the appropriate way or return unused resources to the system.

Understanding Memory Allocation

Chapter 4, "Data Types and Expressions," discusses value types and reference types, describing how both of them are allocated in memory: Value types reside in the stack whereas reference types are allocated on the managed heap. When you create a new instance of a reference type, via the New keyword, the .NET Framework reserves some memory in the managed heap for the new object instance. Understanding memory allocation is fundamental, but an important practice is to also release objects and resources when they are unused or unnecessary. This returns free memory and provides better performances. For value types the problem is of easy resolution: Being allocated on the stack, they are simply removed from memory when you assign the default zero value. The real problem is about reference types. Basically you need to destroy the instance of an object; to accomplish this you assign Nothing to the instance of a reference type.

When you perform this operation, the .NET Framework marks the object reference as no longer used and marks the memory used by the object as unavailable to the application, but it actually does not immediately free up the heap, and the runtime cannot immediately reuse such memory. Memory previously used by no-longer-referenced objects can be released by the .NET Framework after some time because the .NET Framework knows when it is the best moment for releasing resources. Such a mechanism is complex, but fortunately it is the job of the *garbage collector*.

Understanding Garbage Collection

In your applications you often create object instances or allocate memory for resources. When you perform these operations, .NET Framework checks for available memory in the heap. If available memory is not enough, .NET Framework launches a mechanism known as *garbage collection*, powered by an internal tool named *garbage collector*. The garbage collector can also be controlled by invoking members of the System.GC class, but the advantage is leaving .NET Framework the job of handling the process automatically for you. Basically the garbage collector first checks for all objects that have references from your applications, including objects referenced from other objects, enabling to keep alive object graphs. Objects having any references are considered as used and alive, so the garbage collector marks them as in use and therefore will not clean them up. With that said, any other objects in the heap are surely considered as unused and therefore the garbage collector removes the object and references to the object. After this, it compresses the heap and returns free memory space that can be reallocated for other new objects or resources. In all this sequence of operations, you do nothing. The garbage collector takes care of anything required. You can also decide to release objects when you do not need them any more setting their reference to Nothing so that you can free up some memory. The following snippet shows how you can logically destroy an instance of the Person class:

```
Dim p As New Person
p.FirstName = "Alessandro"
p.LastName = "Del Sole"

p = Nothing
```

When you assign an object reference with Nothing, the CLR automatically invokes the destructor (the Finalize method is covered in next section) that any class exposes because the most basic implementation is provided by System.Object. At this point there is a problem. The garbage collection behavior is known as *nondeterministic*, meaning that no one can predict the moment when the garbage collector is invoked. In other words, after you set an object reference to Nothing, you cannot know when the object will be effectively released. There can be a small delay, such as seconds, but also a long delay, such as minutes or hours. This can depend on several factors; for example, if no additional memory is required during your application's lifetime, an object could be released at the application shut down. This can be a problem of limited importance if you have only in-memory objects that do not access to external resources, such as files or the network. You do not have to worry about free memory because, when required, the garbage collector will kick in. Anyway, you can force a garbage collection process by invoking the `System.GC.Collect` method. The following is an example:

```
p = Nothing
'Forces the garbage collector
'so that the object is effectively
'cleaned up
System.GC.Collect()
```

Forcing the garbage collection process is not a good idea. As you can easily imagine, frequently invoking a mechanism of this type can cause performance overhead and significantly slow down your application performances. (Although .NET 4.0 introduces some improvements that are covered in last section of this chapter.) When you work with in-memory objects that do not access external resources, such as the `Person` class, leave the .NET Framework the job of performing a garbage collection only when required. The real problem is when you have objects accessing to external resources, such as files, databases, and network connections that you want to be free as soon as possible when you set your object to `Nothing` and therefore you cannot wait for the garbage collection process to kick in. In this particular scenario you can take advantage of two methods that have little different behaviors: `Finalize` and `Dispose`.

OUT OF SCOPE OBJECTS

Objects that go out of scope will also be marked for garbage collection if they have no external reference to them, even if you don't set them explicitly to `Nothing`.

Understanding the `Finalize` Method

The `Finalize` method can be considered as a destructor that executes code just before an object is effectively destroyed, that is when memory should be effectively released. This method is inherited from `System.Object`; therefore any class can implement the method taking care of declaring it as `Protected Overrides` as follows:

```
Protected Overrides Sub Finalize()
    'Write your code here for releasing
    'such as closing db connections,
    'closing network connections,
    'and other resources that VB cannot understand

    MyBase.Finalize() 'this is just the base implementation
End Sub
```

If you need to destroy an object that simply uses memory, do not invoke `Finalize`. You need instead to invoke it when your object has a reference to something that Visual Basic cannot understand because the garbage collector does not know how to release that reference, so you need to instruct it by providing code for explicitly releasing resources. Another situation is when you have references to something that is out of the scope of the object, such as unmanaged resources, network connections, and files references different than .NET streams. If an object explicitly provides a `Finalize` implementation, the CLR *automatically* invokes such a method just before removing the object from the heap. This means that you *do not* need to invoke it manually. Notice that `Finalize` is not invoked immediately when you assign `Nothing` to the object instance you want to remove. Although `Finalize` enables you to control how resources must be released, it does not enable you to control when they are effectively released. This is due to the nondeterministic behavior of the garbage collector that frees up resources in the most appropriate moment, meaning that minutes or hours can be spent between the `Finalize` invocations and when resources are effectively released, although invoking `Finalize` marks the object as no longer available. Of course you could force the garbage collection process and wait for all finalizers to be completed, if you want to ensure that objects are logically and physically destroyed. Although this is not a good practice, because manually forcing a garbage collection causes performance overhead and loss of .NET Framework optimizations, you can write the following code:

```
'Object here is just for demo purposes
Dim c As New Object
c = Nothing
GC.Collect()
GC.WaitForPendingFinalizers()
```

There are also a few considerations on what `Finalize` should contain within its body. Here is a simple list:

▶ Do not throw exceptions within `Finalize` because the application cannot handle them and therefore it would crash.

▶ Invoke only shared methods except when the application is closing; this will avoid invocations on instance members from objects that can be logically destroyed.

▶ Continuing the previous point, do not access external objects from within `Finalize`.

To complete the discussion, it is worth mentioning that destruction of objects that explicitly provide `Finalize` require more than one garbage collection process. The reason why destroyed objects are removed from the heap at least at the second garbage collection is that `Finalize` could contain code that assigns the current object to a variable, keeping a reference still alive during the first garbage collection. This is known as *object resurrection* and is discussed later in this chapter. As a consequence, implementing `Finalize` can negatively impact performances and should be used only when strictly required.

Understanding Dispose and the IDisposable Interface

One of the issues of the `Finalize` destructor is that you cannot determine whether resources will be freed up and when an object will be physically destroyed from memory. This is because of the nondeterministic nature of the garbage collector, meaning that unused references will still remain in memory until the GC kicks in, and generally this is not a good idea. It is instead a good approach providing clients the ability to immediately release resources (such as network connections, data connections, or system resources) just before the object is destroyed setting it to `Nothing`. The .NET Framework provides a way for releasing resources immediately and under your control, which is the `Dispose` method. Implementing `Dispose` avoids the need of waiting for the next garbage collection enabling cleaning up resources immediately, right before the object is destroyed. Differently from `Finalize`, `Dispose` must be invoked manually. To provide a `Dispose` implementation, your class must implement the `IDisposable` interface. Visual Studio 2010 provides a skeleton of `IDisposable` implementation when you add the `Implements` directive. The code in Listing 8.1 shows the implementation.

LISTING 8.1   Implementing the IDisposable Interface

```
Class DoSomething
    Implements IDisposable

#Region "IDisposable Support"
    Private disposedValue As Boolean ' To detect redundant calls

    ' IDisposable
    Protected Overridable Sub Dispose(ByVal disposing As Boolean)
        If Not Me.disposedValue Then
            If disposing Then
                ' TODO: dispose managed state (managed objects).
            End If

            ' TODO: free unmanaged resources (unmanaged objects) and
            ' override Finalize() below.
            ' TODO: set large fields to null.
        End If
        Me.disposedValue = True
    End Sub

    ' TODO: override Finalize() only if Dispose(ByVal disposing As Boolean) above
    'has code to free unmanaged resources.
    'Protected Overrides Sub Finalize()
```

```
'Do not change this code.  Put cleanup
'code in Dispose(ByVal disposing As Boolean) above.
'     Dispose(False)
'     MyBase.Finalize()
'End Sub

' This code added by Visual Basic to correctly implement the disposable pattern.
Public Sub Dispose() Implements IDisposable.Dispose
    ' Do not change this code.  Put cleanup
    'code in Dispose(ByVal disposing As Boolean) above.
    Dispose(True)
    GC.SuppressFinalize(Me)
End Sub
#End Region
End Class
```

Notice how Dispose is declared as Overridable so that you can provide different implementations in derived classes. Visual Studio is polite enough to provide comments showing you the right places for writing code that release managed or unmanaged resources. Also notice how there is an implementation of Finalize that is enclosed in comments and therefore is inactive. Such a destructor should be provided only if you have to release unmanaged resources. You invoke the Dispose method before setting your object reference to nothing, as demonstrated here:

```
Dim dp As New DoSomething
'Do your work here...

dp.Dispose()
dp = Nothing
```

As an alternative you can take advantage of the Using..End Using statement covered in next subsection. When implementing the Dispose pattern, in custom classes you need to remember to invoke the Dispose method of objects they use within their body so that they can correctly free up resources. Another important thing to take care of is checking if an object has already been disposed when Dispose is invoked but the auto-generated code for the Dispose method already keeps track of this for you.

DISPOSE AND INHERITANCE

When you define a class deriving from another class that implements IDisposable, you do not need to override Dispose unless you need to release additional resources in the derived class.

Using..End Using Statement

As an alternative to directly invoking Dispose, you can take advantage of the Using..End Using statement. This code block automatically releases and removes from memory the object that it points to, invoking Dispose behind the scenes for you. The following code example shows how you can open a stream for writing a file ensuring that the stream will be released even if you do not explicitly close it:

```
Using dp As New IO.StreamWriter("C:\TestFile.txt", False)
    dp.WriteLine("This is a demo text")
End Using
```

Notice how you simply create an instance of the object via the Using keyword. The End Using statement causes Dispose to be invoked on the previously mentioned instance. The advantage of Using..End Using is also that the resource is automatically released in cases of unhandled exceptions, and this can be useful.

Putting Dispose and Finalize Together

Implementing Dispose and Finalize cannot necessarily be required. It depends only on what kind of work your objects perform. Table 8.1 summarizes what and when you should implement.

TABLE 8.1   Implementing Destructors

What	When
No destructor	Objects that just work in memory and that reference other .NET in memory objects.
Finalize	Executing some code before the object gets finalized. The limitation is that you cannot predict when the GC comes in.
Dispose	Your objects access external resources that you need to free up as soon as possible when destroying the object.
Finalize and Dispose	Your objects access unmanaged resources that you need to free up as soon as possible when destroying the object.

You already have examples about Finalize and Dispose, so here you get an example of their combination. Before you see the code, you have to know that you will see invocations to Win32 unmanaged APIs that you do not need in real applications but these kinds of functions are useful to understand to know how to release unmanaged resources. Now take a look at Listing 8.2.

8

LISTING 8.2   Implementing Dispose and Finalize

```vb
Imports System.Runtime.InteropServices


Public Class ProperCleanup
    Implements IDisposable

    Private disposedValue As Boolean ' To detect redundant calls

    'A managed resource
    Private managedStream As IO.MemoryStream

    'Unmanaged resources
    <DllImport("winspool.drv")>
    Shared Function OpenPrinter(ByVal deviceName As String,
                                ByVal deviceHandle As Integer,
                                ByVal printerDefault As Object) _
                        As Integer
    End Function
    <DllImport("winspool.drv")>
    Shared Function _
    ClosePrinter(ByVal deviceHandle As Integer) _
                As Integer
    End Function

    Private printerHandle As Integer

    'Initializes managed and unmanaged resources
    Public Sub New()
        managedStream = New IO.MemoryStream
        OpenPrinter("MyDevice", printerHandle, &H0)
    End Sub

    'Just a sample method that does nothing
    'particular except for checking if the object
    'has been already disposed
    Public Function FormatString(ByVal myString As String) As String
        If disposedValue = True Then
            Throw New ObjectDisposedException("ProperCleanup")
        Else
            Return "You entered: " & myString
        End If
    End Function
```

```
    ' IDisposable
    Protected Overridable Sub Dispose(ByVal disposing As Boolean)
        If Not Me.disposedValue Then
            If disposing Then
                ' TODO: dispose managed state (managed objects).
                managedStream.Dispose()
            End If

            ' TODO: free unmanaged resources (unmanaged objects)
            ' and override Finalize() below.
            ' TODO: set large fields to null.
            ClosePrinter(printerHandle)
        End If
        Me.disposedValue = True
    End Sub

    ' TODO: override Finalize() only if Dispose(ByVal disposing As Boolean)
    ' above has code to free unmanaged resources.
    Protected Overrides Sub Finalize()
        ' Do not change this code.  Put cleanup code in
        ' Dispose(ByVal disposing As Boolean) above.
        Dispose(False)
        MyBase.Finalize()
    End Sub

    ' This code added by Visual Basic to correctly implement the disposable pattern.
    Public Sub Dispose() Implements IDisposable.Dispose
        ' Do not change this code.  Put cleanup code
        ' in Dispose(ByVal disposing As Boolean) above.
        Dispose(True)
        GC.SuppressFinalize(Me)
    End Sub
End Class
```

The code in Listing 8.2 has some interesting points. First, notice how both managed resources (a System.IO.MemoryStream) and unmanaged resources (OpenPrinter and ClosePrinter API functions) are declared. Second, notice how the constructor creates instances of the above resources. Because there are unmanaged resources, it is necessary to override the Finalize method. Visual Basic is polite enough to show you comments describing this necessity, so you simply uncomment the Finalize block definition. Such method invoke the Dispose one passing False as an argument; this can ensure that Dispose will clean up unmanaged resources as you can understand examining the conditional code block within the method overload that accepts a Boolean argument. Finally, notice how the other Dispose overload, the one accepting no arguments, invokes the other overload passing True (therefore requiring managed resources to be released), and then it invokes the GC.SuppressFinalize method to ensure that Finalize is not invoked. There are no unmanaged resources to release at this point because Finalize was previously invoked to clean unmanaged resources.

Object Resurrection

With the *object resurrection* phrase, we describe the scenario in which an object is restored after its reference was removed, although the object was not removed yet from memory. This is an advanced technique, but it is not very useful and Microsoft strongly discourages you from using it in your applications. It is helpful to understand something more about objects' lifetime. Basically an object being finalized can store a self-reference to a global variable, and this can keep the object alive. In simpler words, a reference to a "died" object is restored when within the Finalize method the current object is assigned (using the Me keyword) to a class level or module level variable. Here's a small code example for demonstrating object resurrection; keep in mind that the code is simple to focus on the concept more than on the code difficulty, but you can use this technique with more and more complex objects. You add this code to a module:

```
Public resurrected As ResurrectionDemo


Sub TestResurrection()
    Dim r As New ResurrectionDemo
    'This will invoke Finalize
    r = Nothing

End Sub
```

The resurrected variable is of type ResurrectionDemo, a class that will be implemented next. This variable holds the actual reference to the finalizing object so that it can keep it alive. The TestResurrection method creates an instance of the class and sets it to Nothing causing the CLR to invoke Finalize. Now notice the implementation of the ResurrectionDemo class and specifically the Finalize implementation:

```
Class ResurrectionDemo


    Protected Overrides Sub Finalize()
        'The object is resurrected here
        resurrected = Me
        GC.ReRegisterForFinalize(Me)
    End Sub
End Class
```

Notice how Finalize's body assigns the current object to the resurrected variable which holds the reference. When an object is resurrected, Finalize cannot be invoked a second time because the garbage collector removed the object from the finalization queue. This is the reason why the GC.ReRegisterForFinalize method is invoked. As a consequence, multiple garbage collections are required for a resurrected object to be cleaned up. At this point, just think of how many system resources this might require. Moreover, when an object is resurrected, previously referenced objects are also resurrected. This can result in application faults because you cannot know if objects' finalization already occurred. As mentioned at the beginning of this section, the object resurrection technique rarely takes place in real-life application because of its implications and generally can be successfully used only in scenarios in which you need to create pools of objects whose frequent creation and destruction could be time-consuming.

Advanced Garbage Collection

The garbage collection is a complex mechanism, and in most cases you do not need to interact with the garbage collector because, in such cases, you must be extremely sure that what you are doing is correct. The .NET Framework automatically takes care of what the CLR needs. Understanding advanced features of the garbage collector can provide a better view of objects' lifetime. The goal of this section is therefore to show such advanced features.

Interacting with the Garbage Collector

The System.GC class provides several methods for manually interacting with the garbage collector. In this chapter you already learned some of them. Remember Collect that enables forcing a garbage collection; WaitForPendingFinalizers enabling to wait for all Finalize methods to be completed before cleaning up resources; ReRegisterForFinalize that puts an object back to the finalization queue in object resurrection; and SuppressFinalize that is used in the Dispose pattern for avoiding unnecessary finalizations. There are other interesting members; for example, you can get an approximate amount of allocated memory as follows:

```
Dim bytes As Long = System.GC.GetTotalMemory(False)
```

You pass False if you do not want a garbage collection to be completed before returning the result. Another method is KeepAlive that adds a reference to the specified object preventing the garbage collector from destroying it:

```
GC.KeepAlive(anObject)
```

You can then tell the garbage collector that a huge amount of unmanaged memory should be considered within a garbage collection process; you accomplish this invoking the AddMemoryPressure method that requires the amount of memory as an argument. Next you can tell the garbage collection that an amount of unmanaged memory has been released invoking the RemoveMemoryPressure method. There are other interesting members enabling garbage collector interaction, covered in the next subsection for their relationship with the specific topic.

Understanding Generations and Operation Modes

The garbage collector is based on *generations* that are basically a counter representing how many times an object survived to the garbage collection. The .NET Framework supports three generations. The first one is named gen0 and is when the object is at its pure state. The second generation is named gen1 and is when the object survived to one garbage collection, whereas the last generation is named gen2 and is when the object survived to more than two garbage collections. This is a good mechanism for the garbage collector's performances because it first goes to remove objects at gen2 instead of searching for all live references. The garbage collection process is available in two modes: server and workstation. It is important to know this because in server mode the garbage collection runs on a single thread and therefore needs to block other threads while executing. In a workstation context, the garbage collection can be executed on multiple threads. This is known as concurrent GC. Until .NET Framework 3.5 SP 1, concurrent GC could perform garbage collections on both gen0 and gen1 concurrently or most of a gen2 without pausing managed code but never gen2 concurrently with the other ones. In .NET Framework 4.0 there is a new feature named *Background GC* that enables collecting all generations together, still limited to workstation mode, and that also enable allocating memory while collecting. The good news is that you can now take advantage of a feature introduced in .NET Framework 3.5, which enables registering from garbage collection events, for getting noticed about gen2 completion. The code in Listing 8.3 demonstrates this (read comments for explanations).

LISTING 8.3   Registering for garbage collection events

```vb
Sub Main()
    Try
        'Registers for notification about gen2 (1st arg) and
        'large objects on the heap (2nd arg)
        GC.RegisterForFullGCNotification(10, 10)

        'Notifications are handled via a separate thread
        Dim thWaitForFullGC As New Thread(New _
                            ThreadStart(AddressOf WaitForFullGCProc))
        thWaitForFullGC.Start()

    Catch ex As InvalidOperationException

        'Probably concurrent GC is enabled
        Console.WriteLine(ex.Message)
    End Try
End Sub

Public Shared Sub WaitForFullGCProc()
    While True
        'Notification status
```

```
    Dim s As GCNotificationStatus

    'Register for an event advising
    'that a GC is imminent
    s = GC.WaitForFullGCApproach()

    If s = GCNotificationStatus.Succeeded Then
        'A garbage collection is imminent

    End If

    'Register for an event advising
    'that a GC was completed
    s = GC.WaitForFullGCComplete()
    If s = GCNotificationStatus.Succeeded Then

        'A garbage collection is completed
    End If
    End While
End Sub
```

You can see how you can easily subscribe for garbage collection events invoking
`WaitForFullGCComplete` and `WaitForFullApproach`.

Summary

Understanding how memory and resources are released after objects usage is fundamental
in every development environment. In .NET this is accomplished by the garbage collector,
a complex mechanism that comes after you set an object reference to `Nothing` or when
you attempt to create new instances of objects but no more memory is available. You can
also implement explicit destructors, such as `Finalize` or `Dispose`, according to specific
scenarios in which you do need to release external or unmanaged resources before destroying an object. The garbage collection process has been improved in .NET Framework 4.0 so
that it can support a new operation mode, known as Background GC that enables executing the process across multiple threads in every generation step.

8

Organizing Types Within Namespaces

.NET Framework ships with tons of built-in types. Such an enormous quantity necessarily needs a hierarchical organization in which types must be divided into their areas of interest (data access, file manipulation, communications, and so on). Moreover, the .NET Framework provides an extensible platform, and companies can also build their own custom components exposing types that could have the same name of existing built-in types in.NET Framework. To avoid naming conflicts and to enable a hierarchical organization of the code, Visual Basic offer the *namespaces* feature discussed in this chapter.

Understanding What Namespaces Are

Namespaces provide a way for a better organization of the code and avoiding conflicts between types with the same name. Consider a complex hierarchical framework of objects (such as .NET Framework) in which you have the need to expose more than one type with a particular identifier. The typical example is when software companies produce class libraries; different companies could have the need to provide their own implementation of the Person class, or the same company could provide different implementations of the Person class within the same assembly, so there could be ambiguities for developers when invoking a particular implementation of the Person class. To solve this coding problem, programming languages in the .NET family offer the capability of organizing types within namespaces. For example, imagine using assemblies from two companies, Company1 and Company2 with both produced assemblies exposing their own implementation of the `Person` class. You need to use one of the two implementations, but you still need to reference both assemblies in your project. The following code

```
Dim p As New Person
```

can cause the Visual Basic compiler to throw an exception because it does not know which of the two implementations you want to invoke. By using namespaces, you can avoid this ambiguity as follows:

```
Dim p1 As New Company1.Person
Dim p2 As New Company2.Person
```

In this code example, `Company1` and `Company2` are namespaces that virtually encapsulate lots of types whereas both `Company1.Person` and `Company2.Person` represent the full name of the `Person` class. The .NET Framework Base Class Library highly relies on namespaces. The main namespace in the BCL is `System`, which is basically the root in the BCL hierarchy. `System` exposes dozens of other namespaces, such as `System.Xml`, `System.Data`, `System.Linq`, and so on. Each of these namespace expose types and other nested namespaces, and in this way a hierarchical framework is more maintainable. Namespaces solve a coding problem and an object implementation problem. This is because namespaces are all about coding, because the Common Language Runtime does not recognize namespaces, whereas it does recognize only full class names, such as `Company2.Person` in the previous example or `System.Object` or `System.Console`. Namespaces are just a logical feature that helps developers to write better organized and reusable code. Basically the CLR never encounters conflicts because it recognizes only full class names, but you learn later in this chapter that as a developer you may encounter such conflicts and a help in writing and organizing code is necessary, especially when working with long named classes (see the "Imports Directives" section).

Organizing Types Within Namespaces

Namespaces are defined within `Namespace..End Namespace` blocks. Every namespace can expose the following types and members:

- ▶ Classes
- ▶ Structures
- ▶ Enumerations
- ▶ Modules
- ▶ Interfaces
- ▶ Delegates
- ▶ Nested namespaces

Listing 9.1 shows an example of a namespaces exposing most of the preceding listed members.

LISTING 9.1   Organizing Types Within a Namespace

```vb
Namespace People

    Public Interface IContactable
        ReadOnly Property HasEmailAddress As Boolean
    End Interface

    Public MustInherit Class Person
        Public Property FirstName As String
        Public Property LastName As String

        Public Overrides Function ToString() As String
            Return FirstName & " " & LastName
        End Function
    End Class

    Public Enum PersonType
        Work = 0
        Personal = 1
    End Enum

    Public Class Contact
        Inherits Person
        Implements IContactable

        Public Property EmailAddress As String

        Public Overrides Function ToString() As String
            Return MyBase.ToString()
        End Function

        Public ReadOnly Property HasEmailAddress As Boolean _
                        Implements IContactable.HasEmailAddress
            Get
                If String.IsNullOrEmpty(Me.EmailAddress) Then
                    Return False
                Else
                    Return True
                End If
            End Get
        End Property
    End Class
```

```
    Public Class Employee
        Inherits Person

        Public Property Title As String

        Public Overrides Function ToString() As String
            Return Me.Title & " " & Me.FirstName & " " & Me.LastName
        End Function
    End Class

    Public Class Customer
        Inherits Person

        Public Property CompanyName As String
        Public Overrides Function ToString() As String
            Return Me.LastName & " from " & Me.CompanyName
        End Function

    End Class

    Module GlobalDeclarations
        Public Data As Object
    End Module

    Public Structure PersonInformation
        Public Property PersonCategory As PersonType
        Public Property HasEmailAddress As Boolean
    End Structure
End Namespace
```

As you can see from Listing 9.1, you can organize your custom objects within a namespace. The code implements an abstract class `Person`, three derived classes (`Contact`, `Employee`, and `Customer`), an interface (which is then implemented by the `Contact` class), an enumeration (`PersonType`), a structure (`PersonInformation`), and a module (`GlobalDeclarations`). The namespace becomes part of the full name of a type. For example, the full name for the `Contact` class is `People.Contact`. Therefore, if you need to access a type defined within a namespace, you need to refer to it writing the full name, as in the following line of code:

```
Dim firstContact As New People.Contact
```

ADDING IMPORTS

Later in this chapter we discuss the `Imports` directives that will prevent the need to add the namespace identifier to the full type name every time.

Namespaces can also expose partial classes. This is a common situation within .NET Framework built-in namespaces.

Why Are Namespaces So Useful?

The purpose of namespaces is to enable a better organization of types. Regarding this, there are situations in which an object's hierarchy could expose two different types with different behaviors but with the same name. For example, imagine you have two Person classes; the first one should represent a business contact, and the second one should represent your friends. Of course, you cannot create two classes with the same name within one namespace. Because of this, you can organize such types in different namespaces avoiding conflicts. The code in Listing 9.2 shows how you can define two Person classes within two different namespaces.

LISTING 9.2   Avoiding Conflicts with Different Namespaces

```
Namespace People

    Public Class Person
        Public Property FirstName As String
        Public Property LastName As String

        Public Overrides Function ToString() As String
            Return FirstName & " " & LastName
        End Function
    End Class
End Namespace

Namespace MyFriends
    'Will not conflict with People.Person
    Public Class Person
        Public Property FirstName As String
        Public Property LastName As String
        Public Property Sibling As String

        Public Overrides Function ToString() As String
            Return FirstName & " " & LastName & ": " & Sibling
        End Function
    End Class
End Namespace
```

This is the way how two classes with the same name can coexist within the same assembly. To access both of them you just need to invoke their full name as follows:

```
Dim aFriend As New MyFriends.Person
```

```
Dim aContact As New People.Person
```

> **NOTE**
>
> The `Person` class is here just an example. You can recur to inheritance as in Listing 9.1 instead of providing different namespaces, but the `Person` class is the simplest example possible for demonstrating topics, which is the reason to continue to use such a class.

Nested Namespaces

You can nest namespaces within namespaces to create a complex hierarchy of namespaces. However, you should be careful in creating complex hierarchies of namespaces because this can lead to particular complexity in your code that can cause difficulties in maintainability and reuse. You simply nest a namespace within another one by adding a new `Namespace..End Namespace` block. For example, in Listing 9.1 there are two different kinds of people: a personal contact and two business people (`Customer` and `Employee`). You could then consider defining a new namespace for your business objects and one for your personal objects. Listing 9.3 shows a shorter version of the first example, in which nested namespaces expose the two different kinds of classes.

LISTING 9.3   Implementing Nested Namespaces

```
Namespace People

    Public Interface IContactable
        ReadOnly Property HasEmailAddress As Boolean
    End Interface

    Public MustInherit Class Person
        Public Property FirstName As String
        Public Property LastName As String

        Public Overrides Function ToString() As String
            Return FirstName & " " & LastName
        End Function
    End Class
    Namespace Work
        Public Class Customer
            Inherits Person

            Public Property CompanyName As String
            Public Overrides Function ToString() As String
                Return Me.LastName & " from " & Me.CompanyName
            End Function
```

```
        End Class

        Public Class Employee
            Inherits Person

            Public Property Title As String

            Public Overrides Function ToString() As String
                Return Me.Title & " " & Me.FirstName & " " & Me.LastName
            End Function
        End Class
    End Namespace

    Namespace Personal
        Public Class Contact
            Inherits Person
            Implements IContactable

            Public Property EmailAddress As String

            Public Overrides Function ToString() As String
                Return MyBase.ToString()
            End Function

            Public ReadOnly Property HasEmailAddress As Boolean _
                        Implements IContactable.HasEmailAddress
                Get
                    If String.IsNullOrEmpty(Me.EmailAddress) Then
                        Return False
                    Else
                        Return True
                    End If
                End Get
            End Property
        End Class
    End Namespace
End Namespace
```

As you can see from Listing 9.3, nesting namespaces is an easy task. Creating complex hierarchies can lead to problems in code readability because of several possible indentations. Luckily Visual Basic enables an alternative syntax for defining nested namespaces without writing indented code. Listing 9.4 shows how you can create nested namespace with the alternative syntax.

LISTING 9.4   Nesting Namespace Without Indented Code

```
Namespace People

    Public Interface IContactable
        ReadOnly Property HasEmailAddress As Boolean
    End Interface

    Public MustInherit Class Person
        Public Property FirstName As String
        Public Property LastName As String

        Public Overrides Function ToString() As String
            Return FirstName & " " & LastName
        End Function
    End Class
End Namespace

Namespace People.Work
    Public Class Employee
        Inherits Person

        Public Property Title As String

        Public Overrides Function ToString() As String
            Return Me.Title & " " & Me.FirstName & " " & Me.LastName
        End Function
    End Class

    Public Class Customer
        Inherits Person

        Public Property CompanyName As String
        Public Overrides Function ToString() As String
            Return Me.LastName & " from " & Me.CompanyName
        End Function
    End Class
End Namespace

Namespace People.Personal
    Public Class Contact
        Inherits Person
        Implements IContactable

        Public Property EmailAddress As String
```

```
        Public Overrides Function ToString() As String
            Return MyBase.ToString()
        End Function

        Public ReadOnly Property HasEmailAddress As Boolean _
                        Implements IContactable.HasEmailAddress
            Get
                If String.IsNullOrEmpty(Me.EmailAddress) Then
                    Return False
                Else
                    Return True
                End If
            End Get
        End Property
    End Class
End Namespace
```

As you can see from Listing 9.4, you can nest namespaces by adding a dot after the parent namespace and then specifying the child namespace name without the need of nesting namespaces on the code side. This enables getting the same result, but your code will be more readable. By the way, you are free to use both methodologies.

Scope

Namespaces have scope of visibility. As a rule, namespaces have public visibility because they can be recognized within the project, from other projects that reference the project defining the namespace and from external assemblies. Because of this behavior, namespace declarations can be adorned neither with qualifiers nor with attributes. Members defined within namespaces can only be Friend or Public. If you do not want the external world to use some members defined within a namespace, you need to mark such members as Friend. By default, Visual Basic considers members within namespaces as Friend. If you want them to be of public access, you need to explicitly mark them as Public.

Root Namespace

Each application has a root namespace that contains all types defined in the application. When you create a new project, Visual Studio automatically assigns the root namespace (also known as first level namespace) with the name of the project. This is important to understand, for several reasons. First, if you develop class libraries or reusable components, the root namespace must follow the naming conventions of the Common Language Specification. Second, you must know how your types and auto-generated code are organized within your project. For example, the project containing the code of this chapter is named OrganizingTypesWithinNamespaces. By default, Visual Studio assigned the root namespace identifier with the OrganizingTypesWithinNamespaces identifier. Continuing the previous example, you access the `People` namespace in this way: `OrganizingTypesWithinNamespaces.People`. You then get access to `People`'s objects as follows:

```
OrganizingTypesWithinNamespaces.People.Person
```

To replace the identifier for your root namespace, you simply need to open the My Project window and open the Application tab. You find a text box named Root namespace, which is represented in Figure 9.1.

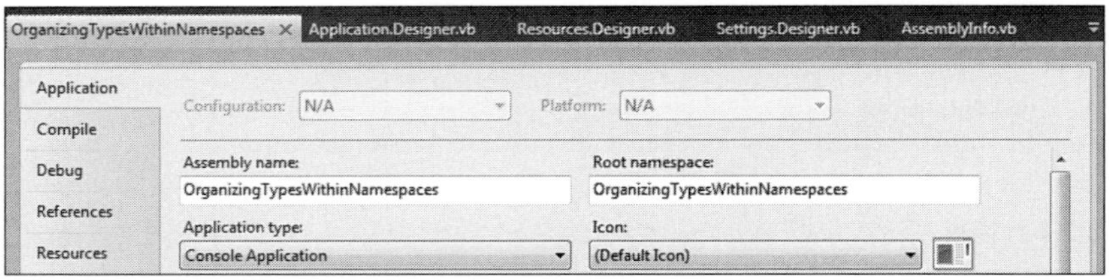

FIGURE 9.1   Checking and editing the root namespace.

Here you can change the root namespace; if you develop class libraries, the root namespace should have the following form: `CompanyName.ProductName`.

ROOT NAMESPACE

When invoking a member defined inside the root namespace, you do not need to include the name of the namespace. This is the only exception when invoking members. For example, if you need to access the `People` namespace we defined in the code example, simply type **People** and not `OrganizingTypesWithinNamespaces.People`.

Global Keyword

Namespaces are versatile and enable the creation of complex infrastructures of objects. There could be situations in which you need to define namespaces with names already defined in the .NET Framework, such as `System`. Although this should never be done, you might face some problems. Consider the following code:

```
Namespace System
    Public Class GlobalDemo
        Sub New()
            Throw New System.NotImplementedException
        End Sub
    End Class
End Namespace
```

Such code will not be compiled because the compiler looks for a `NotImplementedException` within our `System` namespace and not the one of the Base Class

Library. Although such a scenario is unusual, Microsoft's developers provided a way for avoiding such problems. You can use the `Global` keyword to ensure that the compiler invokes the specified member from the Base Class Library namespaces and not from custom ones. In our case, the `Throw` statement should be rewritten as follows:

```
Throw New Global.System.NotImplementedException
```

With this approach we can be sure that the appropriate objects from the Base Class Libraries namespaces will be invoked. This approach is always used behind the scenes by Visual Studio for auto-generated code. To get an example, you can simply inspect My Project's files.

Imports Directives

It often happens that you need to invoke types defined within long-named nested namespaces. To invoke types you need to write the full name of the type, which includes the identifier of the namespace that defines a particular type, as in the following code:

```
Dim aFile As New System.IO.FileStream("C:\test.txt",
                    System.IO.FileMode.Open)
Dim onePerson As New ImportsDirectives.People.Work.Customer
```

Although IntelliSense has been highly improved from previous versions and it helps in writing code, it can result quite annoyingly in typing long-named namespaces. To help developers in writing code faster, Visual Basic enables the usage of `Imports` directives. Such directives enable avoiding the need to write the full namespace identifier preceding the types' names. The preceding code can be rewritten as follows:

```
Imports System.IO
Imports ImportsDirectives.People.Work
...
        Dim aFile As New FileStream("C:\test.txt", FileMode.Open)
        Dim onePerson As New Customer
```

POSITION IN CODE OF IMPORTS **DIRECTIVES**

`Imports` directives can be added to each code file you need. They *must* be the first lines of code, preceding any other code except the `Option Strict`, `Option Compare`, `Option Explicit` and `Option Infer` directives that are the only lines of code always on the top.

Basically you can now invoke types exposed by the `System.IO` namespace without the need of writing the namespace identifier each time. In this particular code example we had just two invocations of members from the namespace, but in an application that manipulates files, you could have hundreds of invocations; with a single `Imports` directive. You do not need to write the namespace identifier before the types' names each time.

`System.IO` is a .NET built-in namespace, but the same applies to your own namespaces (in our example, the `ImportsDirectives.People.Work`). You can also take advantage of another technique that enables assigning an identifier to a long namespace so that invocations can be smarter (feature known as *namespace alias*):

```
Imports work = ImportsDirectives.People.Work
...
        Dim onePerson As New work.Customer
```

IMPORTING XML NAMESPACES

Starting from Visual Basic 2008, `Imports` directives also enable importing Xml namespaces. This feature is discussed in Chapter 28, "Manipulating Xml Documents with LINQ and Xml Literals," for LINQ to Xml.

`Imports` directives also enable importing class names. This enables invoking only shared members without the need of writing the full class name. Consider the following code, which deletes a file from disk:

```
System.IO.File.Delete("C:\text.txt")
```

`Delete` is a shared method exposed by the `System.IO.File` class. You can rewrite the above code as follows:

```
Imports System.IO.File
...
        Delete("C:\text.txt")
```

This can be useful if you need to invoke lots of shared members from a particular class.

Project Level Default Imports

By default, Visual Studio 2010 adds some auto-generated `Imports` directives each time you create a new Visual Basic project, so you do not need to manually add such statements. Default `Imports` are specific to the project type; this means that if you create a Console application, there will be `Imports` related to these kinds of application; if you create a Web application, there will be `Imports` related to the most common namespaces for Web applications and so on. You can easily add project level namespaces via the My Project window. In the References tab, you can find a group box named Imported namespaces, as shown in Figure 9.2.

You can simply click the check box corresponding to each available namespace to add project-level `Imports` directives. This avoids the need of manually typing such `Imports`.

FIGURE 9.2   Setting project-level namespaces.

Moreover, if a particular namespace is not available in the list, you can manually enter its name, and it will be added.

TIP

You can add a namespace alias also in the Imported namespaces list. For example, if you want to import the `System.Windows.Forms` namespace you can type something like `F = System.Windows.Forms` and then access namespace members as if you wrote the alias in the code (e.g. `F.TextBox`).

Avoiding Ambiguities

There might be situations in which you need to access objects with the same name, coming from different namespaces. For example, both Windows Forms and Windows Presentation Foundation technologies provides a `MessageBox` class. In interoperability scenarios, therefore where you have both references to Windows Forms and WPF assemblies, invoking such objects could result in ambiguities. For example, consider the following code:

```
Imports System.Windows.Forms
Imports System.Windows
Class Window1

    Public Sub MyMethod()
        MessageBox.Show("")
    End Sub
End Class
```

Both `System.Windows` and `System.Windows.Forms` namespaces expose a `MessageBox` class, but you need those `Imports` for working with other classes. In such situations, adding `Imports` directives can cause the background compiler to throw an exception. This is because the code is ambiguous in invoking the `MessageBox` class, because it is not clear which of the two classes the runtime should invoke. In this case you can avoid ambiguities by writing the full name of the class:

```
'Invokes the WPF MessageBox
System.Windows.MessageBox.Show("")
```

You could also solve this ambiguity by using namespace aliasing. Another example is the one provided by Listing 9.2. There we have two different implementations of the Person class, and therefore adding an Imports directive would lead to ambiguities. Because of this, in that case it is necessary to invoke members with their full name. Generally when you have multiple namespaces defining classes with the same name, you should write the full class name including the namespace. Probably this is one of the best examples for understanding why namespaces are so useful.

Namespaces and Common Language Specification

The Common Language Specification provides a couple of simple rules about namespaces. The first rule is about naming and establishes that namespaces identifiers must be Pascal-cased. For example, MyCustomTypes is a well-formed namespace identifier. The second rule establishes that to be CLS-compliant a namespace must expose at least five types (classes, structures, enumerations, delegates, and so on). If this is not your case, you should prefer single classes or modules or consider merging types within another namespace already containing other types.

Summary

.NET Framework Base Class Library ships with tons of built-in types that are organized within namespaces. As a developer you can build your custom types; therefore, you can organize them in namespaces. Namespaces are also a way to have different implementations of objects with the same name within a complex framework hierarchy. Because they are visible to other projects or assemblies, namespaces have a Public or Friend scope. Namespaces are also flexible; you can implement complex hierarchies nesting namespaces, and you can use whatever identifier you like. To avoid conflicts with .NET built-in namespaces, Visual Basic offers the Global keyword. You need have to face namespaces many times in object-oriented programming, so this chapter gives you the basis for feeling at home with this important feature of the .NET Framework.

Visual Basic programming language provides a simplified way for working with shared classes. In this brief chapter you learn about the module feature.

Modules Overview

Modules are a specific feature of Visual Basic programming language. You can think of modules as classes exposing only shared members; each module is defined within a `Module..End Module` code block. The following code provides an example of a module:

```
Module Module1


    Sub Main()
        'DoSomething is a method defined elsewhere
        DoSomething()
    End Sub


End Module
```

Differently from Visual C#, Visual Basic does not directly support shared classes, whereas it provides support for classes with only shared members. According to this, the preceding module is the Visual Basic representation of the following class:

```
Class Program
    Shared Sub Main()
        'DoSomething is a method defined elsewhere
        DoSomething()
```

```
        End Sub
      End Class
```

If you had any other member in this class, it should be marked as Shared. Modules are particularly useful when you want to implement objects and members that can be easily shared across your application and that do not need an instance.

Multiple modules can be defined in one code file, or multiple code files can define one or more modules as well. For example, the following module defines a field and a property that you can reach from anywhere in your project:

```
'From anywhere in your project you'll be able
'to reach the two objects
Module Declarations

    Friend myFirstField As String
    Friend Property myFirstProperty As Integer

End Module
```

Because you cannot create an instance of a module, you have just one copy in memory of both the field and the property. The following example defines instead a method that assigns variables defined inside a different module:

```
Module Methods
    Friend Sub DoSomething()
        myFirstField = "A string"
        myFirstProperty = 0
    End Sub
End Module
```

It is worth mentioning that, different from classes, you do not need to invoke methods writing first the name of the class that defines methods. For example, if the DoSomething method were defined within a class named Program, you should use the following syntax:

```
Program.DoSomething()
```

With modules this is not necessary, so you simply need to invoke the method name:

```
DoSomething()
```

This is true unless there is a conflict with the method name and a local method of the same name.

Scope

Typically modules are required within a project and are not usually exposed to the external world. Because of this, the default scope qualifier for modules is Friend. But because of their particular nature, modules are also allowed to be Public but neither Private nor

`Protected/Protected Friend`. Members defined within modules can instead be also marked as `Private`.

ABOUT PUBLIC MODULES

There is a particular exception to the previous discussion: creating a custom extension methods library. Because in Visual Basic you define extension methods within modules, if you want to export such methods, you need to mark them as `Public`. Extension methods are discussed in Chapter 21, "Advanced Language Features."

Differences Between Modules and Classes

There are some differences between modules and classes. In this brief section you take a look at the differences.

No Constructor

As previously mentioned, modules can be considered as shared classes, although Visual Basic provides support for classes with only shared members but not direct support for shared classes. Because of their shared nature, as a general rule modules do not support the constructor (`Sub New`). An exception is that you can declare a `Sub New` in a module that will be private and any code in the private constructor will be executed the first time any call to the module is made.

No Inheritance Support

Modules cannot inherit from other modules or classes or be inherited. Therefore, the `Inherits`, `NotInheritable`, and `MustInherit` keywords are not supported by modules.

INHERITANCE AND SHARED MEMBERS

Although it is not a good programming practice, it is legal to create a `NotInheritable` `Class` that exposes only shared members.

No Interface Implementation

Modules cannot implement interfaces. If you need to implement interfaces, you should consider developing a class with shared members instead of a module.

Summary

Modules are an alternative for working with shared members and data. Although with some limitations if compared to classes, they are useful for exchanging information across the project. In this chapter you got an overview of modules, and you saw what the differences between modules and classes are.

10

CHAPTER 11

Structures and Enumerations

Until now, we discussed a lot of important concepts about.NET development with Visual Basic. Just to mention some key topics, we covered class fundamentals, objects' lifetime, types' organization, and exceptions' handling. We applied all these concepts to reference types (classes). But in your developer life, you will often work with value types, both built-in and custom ones. In Chapter 4, "Data Types and Expressions," you started with the most important built-in value types in the .NET Framework, but to complete your skills you now need to know how to implement your own value types. In this chapter you get this information. You first understand structures and how to create them. Then you learn how to extend structures with custom versions of operators. Finally, you learn about enumerations, another kind of value types in.NET Framework. This is not just a simple illustration, because you also gain information on memory allocation to get a complete overview of this development area.

Structures in .NET development are the way to create custom value types. You find a lot of similarities between classes and structures, although this section explains some important differences. You create structures using a Structure..End Structure block. The following code provides an example of a structure representing a fictitious order received by your company:

```
Public Structure Order

    Public Property OrderID As Integer
    Public Property OrderDate As Date
    Public Property ShippedDate As Date
    Public Property CustomerID As Integer
```

```
    Public Property EmployeeID As Integer
    End Sub
End Structure
```

Structure can expose several members, such as fields, properties, and methods, as it happens for classes. The first important difference is about constructors. First, to create an instance of a structure, it is not mandatory to use the New keyword as for classes. The following code shows how you can instantiate a structure:

```
Dim o As Order
Dim o1 As New Order
```

Both syntaxes are legal. The only difference is that if you don't use the New keyword the variable will be marked as unused until you assign a value and the VB compiler will show a warning message about this. Then you can simply assign (or invoke) members of the structure typing the name followed by a dot:

```
o.OrderDate = Date.Now
o.OrderID = 1
'Other assignments..
```

Notice that, when you declare a structure without assigning its members, the compiler assigns the structure members a default value (which is usually zero for value types and Nothing for reference types). You can also utilize the object initializers feature discussed in Chapter 7, "Class Fundamentals," to initialize members of a structure. The following syntax is allowed but requires the specification of the New keyword:

```
Dim o As New Order With {.OrderID = 1, .OrderDate = Date.Now,
    .ShippedDate = Date.Now.AddDays(1), .CustomerID = 1,
    .EmployeeID = 1}
```

The second difference is that Visual Basic automatically provides an implicit constructor with no parameters, and you are not enabled to explicitly provide a constructor that receives no parameters; if you try, the Visual Basic compiler throws an error. You are instead enabled to provide a constructor that receives arguments, as follows:

```
Public Sub New(ByVal Id As Integer,
               ByVal OrderDate As Date,
               ByVal ShippedDate As Date,
               ByVal CustomerId As Integer,
               ByVal EmployeeId As Integer)

    Me.OrderID = Id
    Me.OrderDate = OrderDate
    Me.ShippedDate = ShippedDate
    Me.CustomerID = CustomerId
```

```
    Me.EmployeeID = EmployeeId
End Sub
```

As previously stated, structures can expose methods and fields but also shared members. Consider the following new implementation of the structure:

```
Public Structure Order

    Private Shared orderCount As Integer

    Public Property OrderID As Integer
    Public Property OrderDate As Date
    Public Property ShippedDate As Date
    Public Property CustomerID As Integer
    Public Property EmployeeID As Integer

    Public Sub New(ByVal Id As Integer,
                ByVal OrderDate As Date,
                ByVal ShippedDate As Date,
                ByVal CustomerId As Integer,
                ByVal EmployeeId As Integer)

        Me.OrderID = Id
        Me.OrderDate = OrderDate
        Me.ShippedDate = ShippedDate
        Me.CustomerID = CustomerId
        Me.EmployeeID = EmployeeId

        orderCount += 1
    End Sub

    Public Shared Function Count() As Integer
        Return orderCount
    End Function
End Structure
```

As you can see, now there is a private shared field that provides a counter for the instances of the type. Moreover, a shared method named `Count` returns the number of instances of the structure. The following code snippet demonstrates how the method works:

```
Dim firstOrder As New Order(1, Date.Now, Date.Now, 1, 1)
Dim secondOrder As New Order(2, Date.Now, Date.Now, 1, 1)
'Returns 2
Console.WriteLine(Order.Count)
```

The preceding code returns 2, because there are two active instances of the structure. Notice that the code would not work if you initialize the structure using object initializers, because the orderCount field is incremented in the parameterized constructor.

Assignments

Because structures are value types, assigning an instance of a structure to a variable declared as of that type creates a full copy of the data. The following brief code demonstrates this:

```
'Creates a real copy of firstOrder
Dim thirdOrder As Order
thirdOrder = firstOrder
```

In the preceding code, thirdOrder is a full copy of firstOrder. You can easily check this by using the data tips feature of the Visual Studio Debugger or adding the variable to a Watch window.

Passing Structures to Methods

Structures can be passed to methods as arguments. For example, consider the following method that simulates an order processing taking an instance of the previously shown Order structure:

```
Private Sub ShowOrderInfo(ByVal orderInstance As Order)
    Console.WriteLine("Order info:")
    Console.WriteLine("ID: {0}, Date received: {1}",
                       orderInstance.OrderID,
                       orderInstance.OrderDate)
    Console.ReadLine()
End Sub
```

You can then simply invoke the method passing the desired instance as follows:

```
Dim firstOrder As New Order(1, Date.Now, Date.Now, 1, 1)
ShowOrderInfo(firstOrder)
```

The preceding code produces an output that looks like this:

```
ID: 1, Date received: 08/19/2009 23:41:37
```

Members' Visibility

Structures' members require you to specify a scope qualifier. Structures accept only Private, Public, and Friend qualifiers. If no qualifier is specified, Public is provided by default. Only fields can also be declared using the Dim keyword and are equivalent to Public. The following line demonstrates this:

```
Public Structure Order
'Means Public:
    Dim orderCount As Integer
```

Inheritance Limitations and Interfaces Implementation

As for other built-in value types, structures implicitly inherit from the System.ValueType type that inherits from System.Object. This is the only inheritance level allowed for structures. This means that, different from reference types (classes), structures can neither inherit nor derive from other structures; therefore, the Inherits keyword is not allowed within structures. Because structures derive from System.Object, they inherit only from such class as the Equals, GetHashCode, and ToString methods that can also be overridden within structures. Chapter 12, "Inheritance," provides detailed information on inheritance and overriding. Structures can instead implement interfaces; therefore, the Implements keyword is enabled. Chapter 13, "Interfaces" discusses interfaces.

Memory Allocation

Structures are value types. This means that they are allocated in the stack. Such behavior provides great efficiency to structures, because when they are no longer necessary, the CLR simply removes them from the stack and avoids the need of invoking the garbage collector as happens for reference types. But this is just a general rule. Structures' members can expose any kind of .NET type and therefore reference types, too. The following revisited implementation of the Order structure provides an example, exposing an OrderDescription property of type String that is a reference type:

```
Public Structure Order


    Public Property OrderID As Integer
    Public Property OrderDate As Date
    Public Property ShippedDate As Date
```

```
    Public Property CustomerID As Integer
    Public Property EmployeeID As Integer

    Public Property OrderDescription As String
End Structure
```

In this scenario, the garbage collection process is invoked to free up memory space when the `OrderDescription` is released and therefore causes some performance overhead. With that said, value types are faster and more efficient than reference types only if they do not expose members that are reference types. Another important consideration is that when you pass or assign a structure to a method or to a variable, the actual value and data of the structure is passed (or copied in assignments) unless you pass the structure to a method by reference. If the data you want to represent is large, you should consider reference types.

Organizing Structures

You can optimize structures' efficiency with a little bit of work. This work is related to the order that you implement members within a structure. For example, consider the following code:

```
Public Structure VariousMembers
    Public Property anInteger As Integer
    Public Property aByte As Byte
    Public Property aShort As Short
End Structure
```

Notice the order how members are exposed. Because of their memory allocation in bytes, it's preferable to expose members in the order of bytes they require. With that said, this is a revisited, more efficient version of the structure:

```
Public Structure VariousMembers
    Public Property aByte As Byte
    Public Property aShort As Short
    Public Property anInteger As Integer
End Structure
```

If you are in doubt, don't worry. The .NET Framework offers an interesting attribute named `StructLayout`, exposed by the `System.Runtime.InteropServices` namespaces, which tells the compiler to organize a structure in the most appropriate way and that you can use as follows:

```
'Requires
'Imports System.Runtime.InteropServices
<StructLayout(LayoutKind.Auto)>
Public Structure VariousMembers
    Public Property aByte As Byte
    Public Property aShort As Short
```

```
    Public Property anInteger As Integer
End Structure
```

> **IMPORTANT NOTE**
>
> Remember that if you use the StructLayout attribute, you cannot pass your structure to unmanaged code such as Windows APIs. If you try, the compiler throws an exception. This is because the Windows APIs expect members to be presented in a predefined order and not reorganized at compile time.

Overloading Operators

In Chapter 4 you learned about operators offered by the Visual Basic grammar. Although Visual Basic does not enable creating new custom operators, it offers the possibility of *overloading* existing operators. In other words, you have the ability to extend existing operators with custom versions. You might wonder when and why this could be necessary. You get an answer to this question with the following code. Consider the simple structure that represents a three-dimensional coordinate:

```
Public Structure ThreePoint


    Public Property X As Integer
    Public Property Y As Integer
    Public Property Z As Integer


    Public Sub New(ByVal valueX As Integer, ByVal valueY As Integer,
                ByVal valueZ As Integer)
        Me.X = valueX
        Me.Y = valueY
        Me.Z = valueZ
    End Sub
End Structure
```

Now imagine that, for any reason, you want to sum two instances of the structure using the + operator. If you try and write the following code

```
'Won't compile, throws an error
Dim result As ThreePoint = t1 + t2
```

the Visual Basic compiler throws an error saying that the + operator is not defined for the ThreePoint structure. You should begin understanding why operator overloading can be a good friend. The same situation is for other operators. In Visual Basic you overload operators using a Public Shared Operator statement within your type definition. For example, the following code overloads the + and - operators:

```
Public Shared Operator +(ByVal firstValue As ThreePoint,
                        ByVal secondValue As ThreePoint) As ThreePoint
    Return New ThreePoint With {.X = firstValue.X + secondValue.X,
                                .Y = firstValue.Y + secondValue.Y,
                                .Z = firstValue.Z + secondValue.Z}
End Operator

Public Shared Operator -(ByVal firstValue As ThreePoint,
                        ByVal secondValue As ThreePoint) As ThreePoint
    Return New ThreePoint With {.X = firstValue.X - secondValue.X,
                                .Y = firstValue.Y - secondValue.Y,
                                .Z = firstValue.Z - secondValue.Z}
End Operator
```

Of course this is just an example, and you might want to perform different calculations. Both overloads return a ThreePoint structure whose members have been populated with the sum and the difference between the X, Y, and Z properties, respectively, from both initial instances. When overloading operators, you need to remember that some of them require you to also overload the negation counterpart. For example, the equality = operator cannot be overloaded alone but requires the overloading of the inequality <> operator. You will be informed by the Visual Basic background compiler when an operator can't be overloaded alone. The following code shows an overloading example of equality and inequality operators for the ThreePoint structure:

```
Public Shared Operator =(ByVal firstValue As ThreePoint,
                        ByVal secondValue As ThreePoint) As Boolean
    Return (firstValue.X = secondValue.X) _
            AndAlso (firstValue.Y = secondValue.Y) _
            AndAlso (firstValue.Z = secondValue.Z)
End Operator

Public Shared Operator <>(ByVal firstValue As ThreePoint,
                        ByVal secondValue As ThreePoint) As Boolean
    Return (firstValue.X <> secondValue.X) _
            OrElse (firstValue.Y <> secondValue.Y) _
            OrElse (firstValue.Z <> secondValue.Z)
End Operator
```

IntelliSense can help you understand what operators can be overloaded. For your convenience a list of operators that can be overloaded is summarized in Table 11.1.

TABLE 11.1 Operators That Can Be Overloaded

Operator	Type
+	Unary/Binary
-	Unary/Binary
Not	Unary
IsTrue	Unary
IsFalse	Unary
*	Binary
/	Binary
\	Binary
&	Binary
^	Binary
Mod	Binary
Like	Binary
CType	Unary
=	Logical
<>	Logical
>, >=	Logical
<, =<	Logical
And/Or/Xor	Logical
<<	Shift
>>	Shift

OPERATORS CONTEXT

Overloading operators is discussed in this chapter because operators such as sum or subtraction make more sense with value types, but obviously this technique is also allowed with classes, for example for comparison operators. You can certainly overload operators within reference types, too.

Overloading CType

The CType operator also can be overloaded to provide appropriate mechanisms for converting to and from a custom type. The interesting thing in overloading CType is that you have to consider both situations studied in Chapter 4, known as widening and narrowing conversions (see that topic for further details). Continuing the previous example of the ThreePoint structure, the following code snippet offers a special implementation of CType enabling conversions to and from an array of integers:

```
'From ThreePoint to Array of Integer
Public Shared Narrowing Operator CType(ByVal instance As ThreePoint) _
                                    As Integer()
    Return New Integer() {instance.X,
                          instance.Y,
                          instance.Z}
End Operator


'From Integer() to ThreePoint
Public Shared Widening Operator CType(ByVal instance As Integer()) _
                                    As ThreePoint
    If instance.Count < 3 Then
        Throw New ArgumentException("Array is out of bounds",
                                "instance")
    Else
        Return New ThreePoint With {.X = instance(0),
                                    .Y = instance(1),
                                    .Z = instance(2)}
    End If
End Operator
```

The code is quite simple. Notice how you must specify a keyword corresponding to the effective kind of conversion (Widening and Narrowing) and how, within the Widening definition, the code performs a basic validation ensuring that the array of integers contains at least three items.

CTYPE CONVENTIONS

As a convention, your type should implement an overload of CType that converts from a String into the custom type. Such conversion should also be offered implementing two methods conventionally named as Parse and TryParse that you saw in action in Chapter 4 with several primitive types.

Structures and Common Language Specification

The Common Language Specification has established specific rules for structures. If you want your structure to be CLS-compliant, you need to overload the equality and inequality operators and redefine the behavior of the Equals and GetHashCode methods inherited from Object. Listing 11.1 shows an example of a CLS-Compliant structure.

LISTING 11.1   Building a CLS-Compliant Structure

```
<CLSCompliant(True)>
Public Structure ClsCompliantStructure

    Public Shared Operator =(ByVal obj1 As CLSCompliantStructure,
                             ByVal obj2 As CLSCompliantStructure) As Boolean
        Return obj1.Equals(obj2)
    End Operator

    Public Shared Operator <>(ByVal obj1 As CLSCompliantStructure,
                              ByVal obj2 As CLSCompliantStructure) As Boolean
        Return Not obj1.Equals(obj2)
    End Operator

    Public Overrides Function Equals(ByVal obj As Object) As Boolean
        Return Object.Equals(Me, obj)
    End Function

    Public Overrides Function GetHashCode() As Integer
        Return Me.GetHashCode
    End Function
End Structure
```

If you are not already familiar with overriding, you can read the next chapter and then take a look back at the preceding code.

Enumerations

Enumerations are another kind of value types available in the .NET Framework. They represent a group of constants enclosed within an Enum..End Enum code block. An enumeration derives from System.Enum, which derives from System.ValueType. The following is an example of enumeration:

```
'These are all Integers
Public Enum Sports
    Biking      '0
    Climbing    '1
    Swimming    '2
    Running     '3
    Skiing      '4
End Enum
```

By default, enumerations are sets of integer values. The preceding code defines a Sports enumeration of type Integer, which stores a set of integer constants. The Visual Basic compiler can also automatically assign an integer value to each member within an enumeration, starting from zero as indicated in comments. You can eventually manually assign custom values, but you should avoid this when possible, because the standard behavior ensures that other types can use your enumeration with no errors. The following code shows instead how you can change the result type of an enumeration:

```
Public Enum LongSports As Long
    Biking
    Climbing
    'and so on...
End Enum
```

IntelliSense can help you understand that enumerations support only numeric types, such as Byte, Short, Integer, Long, UShort, UInteger, ULong, and SByte. Notice that enumerations can be made of mixed numeric data types if assigned with values of different numeric types.

WRITING ENUMERATIONS

Enumerations are easy to use and fast to implement. They are essentially read-only groups of read-only constants. Because of this, use them when you are sure that those values need no modifications; otherwise, consider implementing a structure instead.

Using Enumerations

You use enumerations as any other .NET type. For example, consider the following method that receives the Sports enumeration as an argument and returns a response depending on what value has been passed:

```
Private Sub AnalyzeSports(ByVal sportsList As Sports)
    Select Case sportsList
        Case Is = Sports.Biking
            Console.WriteLine("So, do you really like biking my friend?")
        Case Is = Sports.Climbing
            Console.WriteLine("I do not like climbing like you!")
        Case Else
            Console.WriteLine("Every sport is good!")
    End Select
End Sub
```

The following code snippet then declares a variable of type Sports, assigns a value, and then invoke the method passing the variable:

```
Dim mySport As Sports = Sports.Climbing
AnalyzeSports(mySport)
```

Notice how IntelliSense comes in when you need to specify a value whose type is an enumeration. Figure 11.1 shows the IntelliSense's pop-up window related to our custom enumeration.

FIGURE 11.1   IntelliSense provides flexibility in choosing and assigning enumerations.

Useful Methods from `System.Enum`

As mentioned at the beginning of this section, all enumerations derive from the `System.Enum` class. Such a type exposes some shared methods that enable performing operations on enumerations. This subsection explains how you can take advantage of methods for working on enumerations.

GetValues and GetNames

The first two methods described are `GetValues` and `GetNames`. Both enable retrieving an array of items stored within an enumeration, but `GetValues` gets an array of integers corresponding to the numeric values of enumerations' items whereas `GetNames` retrieves an array of strings storing the names of enumerations' items. Continuing the example of the `Sports` enumeration, consider the following code:

```
For Each item As Integer In System.Enum.GetValues(GetType(Sports))
    Console.WriteLine(item)
Next
```

This code's output is the following list:

```
0
1
2
3
4
```

GetNames works similarly except that it returns an array of strings:

```
For Each item As String In System.Enum.GetNames(GetType(Sports))
    Console.WriteLine(item)
Next
```

And this code produces the following output:

```
Biking
Climbing
Swimming
Running
Skiing
```

Notice how both methods require a System.Type argument instead of a System.Enum; therefore, it's necessary to invoke the GetType operator. Another interesting thing is about syntax. The System.Enum class full name for invoking its methods is used here because the Enum class is exposed by the System namespace that is always imported at project level. Technically you could just write invocations as follows: Enum.GetNames. But this is not allowed in Visual Basic because of conflicts with the Enum reserved keyword. To use the simplified syntax, you can enclose the Enum work within square brackets as follows:

```
[Enum].GetNames(GetType(Sports))
```

The Visual Basic compiler enables this syntax perfectly equivalent to the previous one. Notice that the IDE will add the square brackets for you when typing Enum. Now, let's discover other useful methods.

GetName

GetName works similarly to GetNames, except that it returns just a single name for a constant. Consider the following code:

```
'Returns Climbing
Console.WriteLine(System.Enum.GetName(GetType(Sports), 1))
```

You just need to pass the type instance and the value in that enumeration that you want to retrieve the name of.

IsDefined

IsDefined checks if the specified constant exists within an enumeration and returns a Boolean value. The following code looks first for an existing value and then for a non existing one:

```
'Returns True
Console.WriteLine(System.Enum.IsDefined(GetType(Sports), "Climbing"))
'Returns False
Console.WriteLine(System.Enum.IsDefined(GetType(Sports), "Soccer"))
```

ToString and Parse

System.Enum also provides two methods for converting to and from string. The ToString method is inherited from System.Object and is redefined so that it can provide a string representation of the specified value. Consider the following code snippet:

```
'Sports.Climbing
Dim mySport As Sports = CType(1, Sports)
Console.WriteLine(mySport.ToString)
```

Such code returns Climbing, which is the string representation of the specified constant value. Also notice how, if Option Strict is On, you must explicitly convert the value into a Sports enumeration using CType. Parse is basically the opposite of ToString and gets the corresponding numeric value within an enumeration depending on the specified string. The following code provides an example:

```
Console.WriteLine("Enter your favorite sport:")
Dim sport As String = Console.ReadLine
Dim result As Sports = CType(System.Enum.Parse(GetType(Sports),
                       sport, True), Sports)
'Returns 2
Console.WriteLine("The constant in the enumeration for {0} is {1}",
                  sport.ToString, CInt(result))
Console.ReadLine()
```

The above code requires the input from the user, who has to enter a sport name. Using Parse, the code obtains the element in the enumeration corresponding to the entered string. For example, if you enter Swimming, the code produces the following output:

```
The constant in the enumeration for Swimming is 2
```

Notice how Parse can receive a third argument of type Boolean that enables specifying if the string comparison must ignore casing.

ASSIGNING ENUMS TO INTEGERS

You can assign an enumeration variable to an Integer type without a conversion operator.

Using Enums As Return Values From Methods

A common usage of enumerations is representing different results from methods that return a numeric value, as it often happens for Windows API functions or for methods that return a number for communicating the result of the code. For example, consider the following code which defines an enumeration that a method uses in order to communicate the result of a simple elaboration on a file:

```
Public Enum Result
    Success = 0
    Failed = 1
    FileNotFound = 2
End Enum

Public Function ElaborateFile(ByVal fileName As String) As Result
    Try
        Dim text As String = My.Computer.FileSystem.ReadAllText(fileName)

        'Do some work here on your string

        Return Result.Success

    Catch ex As IO.FileNotFoundException
        Return Result.FileNotFound
    Catch ex As Exception
        Return Result.Failed
    End Try
End Function
```

Actually each `Return` statement returns an Integer value from 0 to 2 depending on the method result, but using an enumeration provides a more convenient way for understanding the result, as demonstrated in the following code:

```
Sub OpenFile()
    Dim res As Result = ElaborateFile("myfile.txt")
    'Success = 0
    If res = Result.Success Then
        Console.WriteLine("Success")
        'FileNotFound = 2
    ElseIf res = Result.FileNotFound Then
        Console.WriteLine("File not found")
        'Failed = 1
    ElseIf res = Result.Failed Then
        Console.WriteLine("The elaboration failed")
    End If
End Sub
```

Enum Values As Bit Flags

Enumerations can be designed for supporting bitwise operations by marking them with the Flags attribute. This allows combining enumeration values with bitwise operators such as OR. Consider the following implementation of the Sports enumeration that was described previously:

```
<Flags>
Public Enum Sports
    Biking
    Climbing
    Swimming
    Running
    Skiing
End Enum
```

By applying the Flags attribute, the values for each enumeration value now become bitflag patterns that have a binary representation such as the following:

```
00000000
00000001
00000010
00000100
00001000
```

Basically combining all values with the OR operator will result in a 11111111 binary value. For example, you could perform an evaluation like the following:

```
'sportsTest is 0000010
Dim sportsTest As Sports =
    Sports.Biking And Sports.Climbing Or Sports.Swimming
```

This kind of approach is really useful when you want to be able to perform bitwise operations and comparisons.

Enumerations and Common Language Specification

When introducing enumerations, you learned that they support only numeric types. There is another limitation if you plan to implement CLS-compliant enumerations. Only CLS-compliant types can characterize CLS-compliant enumerations; therefore, the SByte, UShort, UInteger, and ULong types cannot be used within CLS-compliant enumerations. Another important consideration is that CLS-compliant enumerations must be decorated with the Flag attribute. The following is an example of a CLS-compliant enumeration:

```
<Flags()> Public Enum ClsCompliantEnum As Byte
    FirstValue = 0
    SecondValue = 1
    ThirdValue = 2
End Enum
```

NOTE

The `Flag` attribute indicates the compiler that an enumeration has to be considered as a bit field.

Summary

In this chapter you saw in action another important part of the .NET development with Visual Basic, which is related to creating custom value types. Structures are the .NET way for building custom value types and can expose methods, properties, and fields. There are several similarities with classes, but structures are value types allocated in the stack and cannot inherit or derive from other structures but can implement interfaces. Because of their nature, structures are susceptible of operations. This requires, in certain situations, the need for specific operators. The .NET Framework enables overloading operators to provide custom implementations of unary, binary, and logical operators, a technique that is allowed also for classes. Another kind of value types is enumerations, which represent a group of read-only constants and that are optimized for `Integer` values, offering several shared methods for performing operations on constants composing the enumeration. An overview of how Common Language Specification rules the implementation of structures and enumerations completes the chapter.

CHAPTER 12

Inheritance

Inheritance is the feature that enables designing classes that *derive* from simpler classes, known as *base classes*. Derived classes implement members defined within the base class and have the possibility of defining new members or of redefining inherited members. Members that a derived class inherits from the base one can be methods, properties, and fields, but such members must have Public, Protected, Friend or Protected Friend scope (see Chapter 7, "Class Fundamentals," for details about scopes). In .NET development inheritance represents a typical *"is-a"* relationship. For a better understanding, a good example is real life. When you say "person," you identify a general individual. Every one of us is a person, with a name and a last name. But a person also has a gender, either man or woman. In such a situation, a single person is the base class and a woman is a derived class, because it inherits the name and last name attributes from the person but also offers a gender attribute. But this is only the first layer. Each man or each woman can have a job and jobs are made of roles. So a woman can be employed by a company; therefore, as an employee she will have an identification number, a phone number, and an office room number. In this representation there is a deeper inheritance; because a person can be compared to a base class, a woman can be compared to an intermediate base class (also deriving from the person), and the employee is the highest level in the inheritance hierarchy. If we want to go on, we could still define other roles, such as secretary, program manager, receptionist, phone operator, and so on. Each of these roles could be represented by a class that derives from the employee role. As you can see, this articulate representation is something that in a development environment such as.NET Framework enables defining a complex but powerful framework of objects. In this chapter you get a complete overview of the inheritance features in.NET Framework with Visual Basic 2010, and you will understand how you can take advantage of inheritance for both building hierarchical frameworks of custom objects and more easily reusing your code.

Applying Inheritance

Before explaining how inheritance is applied in code, a graphical representation can be useful. Figure 12.1 shows how you can create robust hierarchies of custom objects with inheritance.

FIGURE 12.1   A graphical representation of a custom framework of objects using inheritance.

You derive a class from a base class using the `Inherits` keyword. For example, consider the following implementation of the `Person` class that exposes some basic properties:

```
Public Class Person

    Public Property FirstName As String
    Public Property LastName As String

    'A simplified implementation
    Public Function FullName() As String
        If FirstName = "" And LastName = "" Then
          Throw New _
          InvalidOperationException("Both FirstName and LastName are empty")
        Else
            Return String.Concat(FirstName, " ", LastName)
        End If
    End Function
End Class
```

INHERITS SYSTEM.OBJECT

In the .NET Framework development, every class inherits from System.Object. Because of this, there is no need to add an inherits directive each time you implement a custom type, because the Visual Basic compiler will do this for you behind the scenes.

The class also offers a FullName method that returns the concatenation of the two FirstName and LastName properties, providing a simplified and basic validation that here is for demonstration purposes. Now we can design a new class that inherits from Person, and in this scenario Person is the *base class*. The new class is named Contact and represents a personal contact in our everyday life:

```
Public Class Contact
    Inherits Person

    Public Property Email As String
    Public Property Phone As String
    Public Property BirthDate As Date
    Public Property Address As String

End Class
```

Contact is the *derived class*. It receives all public members from Person (in this example both the FirstName and LastName properties and the FullName method) and provides implementation of custom members. This is a typical application of .NET inheritance, in which one derived class inherits from the base class. The .NET Framework does not enable inheriting from multiple classes. You can create a derived class from only a base class. But there are situations in which multiple levels of inheritance would be required; continuing the example of the Person class, there are several kinds of people that you will meet in your life, such as customers, employees of your company, and personal contacts. All these people will have common properties, such as the first name and the last name; therefore, the Person class can be the base class for each of them, providing a common infrastructure that can then be inherited and customized. But over a person representation, if you consider a customer and an employee, both people will have other common properties, such as a title, a business phone number, and an email address. They will differ in the end because of proper characteristics of their role. For this purpose you can implement intermediate classes that are derived classes from a first base class and base classes for other and more specific ones. For example, you could implement an intermediate infrastructure for both customers and employees. The following code snippet provides a class named BusinessPerson that inherits from Person:

```
Public Class BusinessPerson
    Inherits Person

    Public Property Email As String
    Public Property Title As String
```

```
    Public Property BusinessPhone As String

End Class
```

This class inherits the `FirstName` and `LastName` properties from `Person` (other than methods such as `ToString` and other public methods exposed by `System.Object`) and exposes other common properties for classes with a different scope. For example, both a customer and an employee would need the preceding properties but each of them needs its own properties. Because of this, the `BusinessPerson` class is the intermediate derived class in the hierarchic framework of inheritance. Now consider the following classes, `Customer` and `Employee`:

```
Public Class Customer
    Inherits BusinessPerson

    Public Property CustomerID As Integer
    Public Property CompanyName As String
    Public Property Address As String
    Public Property ContactPerson As String

End Class

Public Class Employee
    Inherits BusinessPerson

    Public Property EmployeeID As Integer
    Public Property HomePhone As String
    Public Property MobilePhone As String
    Public Property HireDate As Date

End Class
```

Both classes receive the public properties from `BusinessPerson` and both implement their custom properties according to the particular person they intend to represent. We can summarize the situation as follows:

Customer exposes the following properties:

- ▶ `FirstName` and `LastName`, provided at a higher level by `Person`
- ▶ `Email`, `Title`, and `BusinessPhone` provided by `BusinessPerson`
- ▶ `CustomerID`, `CompanyName`, `Address`, and `ContactPerson` provided by its implementation

Employee exposes the following properties:

- ▶ `FirstName` and `LastName`, provided at a higher level by `Person`
- ▶ `Email`, `Title`, and `BusinessPhone` provided by `BusinessPerson`

- ► EmployeeID, HomePhone, MobilePhone, and HireDate provided by its implementation

Because at a higher level we also exposed a method named FullName, which has public visibility, such a method is also visible from derived classes.

MEMBERS' SCOPE AND INHERITANCE

Remember that only Public, Protected, Friend, and Protected Friend members can be inherited within derived classes.

When available, you can use derived classes the same way as you would do with any other class, even if you do not know at all that a class derives from another one. The following, simple code demonstrates this:

```
'Employee inherits from BusinessPerson
'which inherits from Person
Dim emp As New Employee With {.EmployeeID = 1,
    .Title = "Dr.",
    .LastName = "Del Sole",
    .FirstName = "Alessandro",
    .Email = "alessandro.delsole@visual-basic.it",
    .BusinessPhone = "000-000-000000",
    .HomePhone = "000-000-000000",
    .MobilePhone = "000-000-000000",
    .HireDate = New Date(6 / 24 / 2009)}
```

Until now we saw only properties in an inheritance demonstration. Methods are also influenced by inheritance and by interesting features that make them powerful.

INHERITANCE AND COMMON LANGUAGE SPECIFICATION

The Common Language Specification establishes that a CLS-compliant class must inherit only from another CLS-compliant class; otherwise, it will not be CLS-compliant.

Illustrating `System.Object` in Detail

As you remember from Chapter 4, "Data Types and Expressions," in.NET development all types implicitly derive from System.Object, considering both reference and value types. Because of the inheritance relationship, custom types also inherit some methods, and therefore you have to know them. Table 12.1 summarizes inherited methods.

TABLE 12.1   System.Object Methods

Member	Description
Finalize	Performs cleanup operations; already described in Chapter 8, "Managing an Object's Lifetime"
GetType	Returns the System.Type object related to the instance of the class
GetHashCode	Returns the hash code for the current instance
New	Creates an instance of the class
Equals	Checks for equality between instances of the class
MemberwiseClone	Provides a shallow copy of a class instance
ReferenceEquals	Checks if the two specified instances are the same instance
ToString	Provides a string representation of the current object

You need to understand what members are exposed by System.Object because they will be all inherited by your custom classes and by all built-in classes in.NET Framework. I already discussed Finalize and GetType methods, respectively, in Chapter 8 and Chapter 4. Such methods are inherited by all .NET types. The GetHashCode method returns the hash that is assigned at runtime by the CLR to a class instance. The following code provides an example:

```
Dim p As New Object


Dim hashCode As Integer = p.GetHashCode
Console.WriteLine(hashCode.ToString)
```

On my machine the code produces the following result: 33156464. This is useful to uniquely identify a class' instance. New is the constructor, as described in Chapter 7. When creating custom classes, a constructor is inherited and implicitly defined within classes and constitutes the default constructor. Object also exposes two shared members, Equals and ReferenceEquals that return a Boolean value. It's worth mentioning that shared methods are also inherited by derived classes, but they cannot be overridden (as better described in next section). For example, the following code establishes if both specified objects are considered the same instance:

```
'Two different instances
Dim firstObject As New Object
Dim secondObject As New Object

'Returns False
Dim test As Boolean = Object.ReferenceEquals(firstObject, secondObject)
```

Next, code instead checks if two instances are considered equal by the compiler:

```
'Returns False
Dim test As Boolean = Object.Equals(firstObject, secondObject)
```

There is also an overload of the Equals method that is instead an instance method. The following code shows an example of instances comparisons using Equals:

```
'Returns False
Console.WriteLine(firstObject.Equals(secondObject))
'Copies the reference to the instance
Dim testObject As Object = firstObject
'Returns True
Console.WriteLine(testObject.Equals(firstObject))
```

For assignments, it is always possible to assign any type to an Object instance as demonstrated here:

```
Dim aPerson As New Person
Dim anObject As Object = aPerson
```

Because Object is the mother of all classes, it can receive any assignment. The last method in System.Object (that you will often use) is ToString. This method provides a string representation of the object. Because System.Object is the root in the class hierarchy, this method just returns the pure name of the class. Therefore, the following line of code returns System.Object:

```
Console.WriteLine(firstObject.ToString)
```

But this is not appropriate for value types, in which you need a string representation of a number, or for custom classes, in which you need a custom representation. Taking the example of the famous Person class, it would be more useful to get a string composed by the last name and the first name instead of the name of the class. Fortunately, the .NET Framework inheritance mechanism provides the ability to change the behavior of inherited members as it is exposed by base classes, known as *overriding*.

Introducing Polymorphism

Polymorphism is another key concept in the object-oriented programming. As its name implies, polymorphism enables an object to assume different forms. In .NET development, it basically means that you can treat an object as another one, due to the implementation of common members. A first form of polymorphism is when you assign base classes with derived classes. For example, both `Contact` and `Customer` classes are derived of the `Person` class. Now consider the following code:

```
Dim c As New Contact
Dim cs As New Customer

'C is of type Contact
Dim p As Person = c
```

The new instance of the `Person` class receives an assignment from an instance of the `Contact` class. This is always possible because `Person` is the parent of `Contact` (in which base is the parent of derived). Therefore you might also have the following assignment:

```
'Cs is of type Customer
Dim p As Person = cs
```

In this scenario, `Person` is polymorphic in that it can "impersonate" multiple classes that derive from itself.

RETRIEVING THE ACTUAL TYPE

Use the `TypeOf` operator, discussed in Chapter 4, to check if the polymorphic base class is representing a derived one.

Basically polymorphism is useful when you need to work with different kinds of objects using one common infrastructure that works the same way with all of them. Now let's continue with the preceding example. The `Person` class exposes the usual `FirstName` and `LastName` properties also common to `Contact` and `Customer`. At this point you can remember how our previous implementations of the `Person` class offered a method named `FullName` that returns the concatenation of both the `LastName` and `FirstName` properties. For the current discussion, consider the following simplified version of the `FullName` method, as part of the `Person` class:

```
Public Function FullName() As String
    Return String.Concat(FirstName, " ", LastName)
End Function
```

All classes deriving from `Person` inherit this method. All deriving classes do need a method of this kind for representing the full name of a person, but they would need different implementations. For example, the full name for a customer should include the company name, whereas the full name for a personal contact should include the title. This means that all classes deriving from `Person` will still need the `FullName` method (which is part of the commonalities mentioned at the beginning of this section) but with a custom implementation fitting the particular need. For this, the .NET Framework enables realizing polymorphism by *overriding* members, as the next section describes.

> **NOTE ON POLYMORPHISM**
>
> Overriding is the most important part of polymorphism in.NET development, but also interfaces play a role. Chapter 13, "Interfaces," explain how interfaces complete polymorphism.

Overriding Members

When a class derives from another one, it inherits members, and the members behave as they are defined in the base class. (For this purpose remember the scope). As for other .NET languages, Visual Basic enables redefining inherited methods and properties so that you can change their behavior. This technique is known as overriding and requires a little work on both the base class and the derived class. If you want to provide the ability of overriding a member, in the base class you have to mark such member as `Overridable`. Let's continue the example of the `Person` class, defined as follows:

```
Public Class Person


    Public Property FirstName As String
    Public Property LastName As String

    'Simplified version, with no validation
    Public Function FullName() As String
        Return String.Concat(LastName, " ",
                             FirstName)
    End Function

End Class
```

The goal is providing derived classes the ability of overriding the `FullName` method so that they can provide a custom and more appropriate version. So the method definition must be rewritten as follows:

```
Public Overridable Function FullName() As String
```

At this point we could provide a simplified version of the `Contact` class, inheriting from `Person`. Such implementation will override the `FullName` method to provide a custom result. Let's begin with the following code:

```
Public Class Contact
    Inherits Person

    Public Property Email As String
```

```
Public Overrides Function FullName() As String
    'By default returns the base class'
    'implementation
    Return MyBase.FullName()
End Function
End Class
```

Two things are important here. First, the Overrides keyword enables redefining the behavior of a member that has been marked as Overridable in the base class. Second, Visual Studio automatically provides an implementation that is the behavior established in the base class, due to the MyBase keyword that is discussed later. IntelliSense is powerful in this situation, too, because when you type the Overrides keyword, it will show all overridable members, as shown in Figure 12.2, making it easier to choose what you have to override.

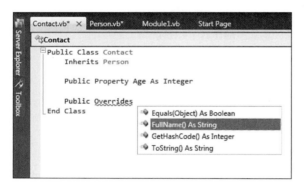

FIGURE 12.2   IntelliSense helps you choose overridable members.

Figure 12.2 is also useful to understand what members from System.Object are overridable. The instance overload of Equals, GetHashCode, and ToString are methods that you can redefine. You cannot instead override (neither mark as Overridable) shared members, and this is demonstrated by the fact that the shared overload of Equals and ReferenceEquals are not available in the IntelliSense pop-up window. At this point we could provide a new implementation of the FullName method specific for the Contact class:

```
Public Overrides Function FullName() As String
    'A simplified implementation
    'with no validation
    Dim result As New Text.StringBuilder
    result.Append(Me.FirstName)
    result.Append(" ")
    result.Append(Me.LastName)
    result.Append(", Email:")
    result.Append(Me.Email)
```

```
      Return result.ToString
End Function
```

Now you can create a new instance of the `Contact` class and invoke the `FullName` method to understand how overriding changed its behavior:

```
Dim testContact As New Contact With _
    {.FirstName = "Alessandro",
     .LastName = "Del Sole",
     .Email = "Alessandro.delsole@visual-basic.it"}
Console.WriteLine(testContact.FullName)
```

The preceding code produces the following result:

```
Alessandro Del Sole, Email:Alessandro.delsole@visual-basic.it
```

Such a result is, of course, more meaningful if related to the specific kind of class. Another common situation is redefining the behavior of the `ToString` method that is inherited from `Object` and that is marked as `Overridable`. For example, in the `Contact` class we could override `ToString` as follows:

```
Public Overrides Function ToString() As String
    Dim result As New Text.StringBuilder
    result.Append(Me.FirstName)
    result.Append(" ")
    result.Append(Me.LastName)
    result.Append(", Email:")
    result.Append(Me.Email)

    Return result.ToString

End Function
```

We can then invoke this method as follows:

```
Console.WriteLine(testContact.ToString)
```

Typically overriding `ToString` is more appropriate if you need to return a string representation of a class, as in the preceding example. The `FullName` method is just an example of how you can override a custom method that is defined in a base class of yours and that is not inherited from `System.Object`.

OVERRIDDEN IS OVERRIDABLE

When a member is overridden using the `Overrides` keyword, the member is also implicitly `Overridable`. Because of this, you cannot use the `Overridable` keyword on a member marked with `Overrides`; the compiler would throw an error message, requiring you to remove the `Overridable` keyword.

328 CHAPTER 12 Inheritance

NotOverridable Keyword

You can mark an overridden method or property as NotOverridable so that derived classes cannot override them again. The NotOverridable keyword cannot be used versus methods or properties that do not override a base member. Continuing the example of the Contact class previously defined, the NotOverridable keyword can be used as follows:

```
Public NotOverridable Overrides Function FullName() As String
    Return String.Concat(MyBase.FullName(), ": ", Email)
End Function
```

In this way the FullName method within the Contact class overrides the base class, but derived classes cannot override it again. Basically NotOverridable is used only within derived classes that override base class's members, because in a base class the default behavior for members is that they cannot be overridden unless you explicitly mark them as Overridable.

Overloading Derived Members

You can use the overloading technique described in Chapter 7 also within derived classes, with a few differences. You saw in Chapter 7 how overloaded members must not be marked with the Overloads keyword within a class. Instead in a derived class using the Overloads keyword is mandatory if you implement a new overload of a member with different signature. The following code provides an example of overloading the FullName method within the Contact class that you previously saw:

```
Public Overloads Function FullName(ByVal Age As Integer)
    Return MyBase.FullName & " of age: " & Age.ToString
End Function
```

If another signature of the member is available within the derived class, the Overloads keyword is required; otherwise, the compiler throws a warning message saying that another signature is declared as Overrides or Overloads. If instead no other signatures are available within the derived class, the Overloads keyword is required to prevent from *shadowing* the base class's member. Shadowing will be discussed at the end of this chapter.

Conditioning Inheritance

Inheritance is an important feature in OOP with .NET. There could be situations in which inheritance is not good, for example to prevent others from accessing members in the base class. Or there could be custom frameworks implementations in which a high-level class should not be used directly, and therefore it should be always inherited. The Visual Basic language enables accomplishing both scenarios via special keywords, as discussed in the next section.

NotInheritable Keyword

There are situations in which you might want to prevent inheritance from your classes. This can be useful if you do not want a client to modify in any way the base object's behavior and its members. To accomplish this, you simply need to mark a class with the NotInheritable keyword. The following code shows an example of a class that cannot be derived:

```
Public NotInheritable Class BusinessPerson
    Inherits Person

    Public Property Email As String
    Public Property Title As String
    Public Property BusinessPhone As String
End Class
```

As you can see, the BusinessPerson class is marked as NotInheritable and cannot be derived by other classes. It can still inherit from other classes but, obviously, members cannot be marked as Overridable, being not inheritable. Another typical example of not inheritable classes is when you have a class exposing only shared members, as shown in the following code:

```
<CLSCompliant(True)>
Public NotInheritable Class CompressionHelper

    Private Sub New()

    End Sub

    Public Shared Sub CompressFile(ByVal source As String,
                                   ByVal target As String)
        'Your code goes here
    End Sub

    Public Shared Sub DecompressFile(ByVal compressed As String,
                                     ByVal original As String)
        'Your code goes here
    End Sub
End Class
```

The class is also decorated with the CLSCompliant attribute because such a situation is explicitly established by the Common Language Specification. NotInheritable is the Visual Basic counterpart of the sealed keyword in Visual C#. It's important to know also the C# representation, because in .NET terminology not inheritable classes are defined as sealed and many analysis tools use this last word. NotInheritable classes provide better performance; the compiler can optimize the usage of this kind of classes, but obviously you cannot blindly use classes that cannot be inherited only to avoid a small overhead. You should always design classes that fit your needs.

> **NOTE**
>
> As a better programming practice, developers should always mark classes with NotInheritable unless they explicitly plan for the class to be inheritable by a consuming class.

MustInherit and MustOverride Keywords

Inheritance is straightforward because it enables building custom objects' frameworks. In this context, an object can represent the base infrastructure for different kinds of classes. We saw how the Person class is the base infrastructure for the Customer, Employee, and Contact derived classes. Because of its implementation, the Person class does nothing special. It has a generic behavior, and you will probably never create instances of that class, whereas it is more likely that you will create instances of its derived classes. In this scenario, therefore, when you have a general purpose base class that acts just as a basic infrastructure for derived classes, you can force a class to be inherited so that it cannot be used directly. To accomplish this, the Visual Basic language provides the MustInherit keyword that states that a class will work only as a base class and cannot be used directly unless you create a derived class.

> **ABSTRACT CLASSES**
>
> In .NET terminology, classes marked as MustInherit are also known as *abstract classes*. This is important to remember because you will often encounter this term within the documentation and in several analysis tools.

The following code shows a new implementation of the Person class:

```
Public MustInherit Class Person


    Public Property FirstName As String
    Public Property LastName As String
End Class
```

Now you can only derive classes from Person. Another interesting feature is the capability to force members to be overridden. This can be accomplished using the MustOverride keyword on methods and properties. Continuing with the example of the person class, we can rewrite the FullName method definition as follows:

```
Public MustOverride Function FullName() As String
```

When you mark a method with MustOverride, the method has no body. This makes sense because if it must be redefined within a derived class, it would be totally unhelpful providing a base implementation. The same thing happens with properties, meaning that you will have only a declaration.

Inheriting from an Abstract Class

When you create a class that inherits from an abstract class (that is, marked as MustInherit), the only thing you need to pay particular attention to is overriding members. To help developers in such a scenario, the Visual Studio IDE automatically generates members' stubs for methods and properties marked as MustOverride in the base abstract class. For example, if you create a new implementation of the Contact class, when you press **Enter** after typing the Inherits line of code, Visual Studio generates an empty stub for the FullName method as follows:

```
Public Class Contacts
    Inherits Person

    Public Overrides Function FullName() As String

    End Function
End Class
```

At this point you can be sure that all MustOverride members have an implementation. In our example you might want to complete the code adding the implementation shown in the "Overriding Members" section in this chapter.

Abstract Classes and Common Language Specification

The Common Language Specification contains a small rule regarding abstract classes. This rule establishes that to be CLS-compliant, members in abstract classes must explicitly be marked as CLSCompliant. The following code provides an example:

```
<CLSCompliant(True)>
Public MustInherit Class Person

    <CLSCompliant(True)> Public Property FirstName As String
    <CLSCompliant(True)> Public Property LastName As String

    <CLSCompliant(True)> Public MustOverride Function FullName() As String

End Class
```

Accessing Base Classes Members

Sometimes you need to access base classes' members from derived classes. There are several reasons for accomplishing this and therefore you need to know how. Visual Basic provides two special keywords for invoking base members, MyBase and MyClass. Both are discussed in this section.

MyBase Keyword

When you need to get a reference to the base class of the derived class you are working on, you can invoke the MyBase keyword. This keyword represents an instance of the base class and enables working on members as they are exposed by the base class, instead of the ones exposed by the derived class. Consider the following implementation of the Person class, in which a FullInformation method provides a representation of all the info supplied to the class:

```
Public Class Person

    Public Property FirstName As String
    Public Property LastName As String
    Public Property Age As Integer

    Public Overridable Function FullInformation() As String
        Dim info As New Text.StringBuilder

        info.Append("Name: ")
        info.Append(Me.FirstName)
        info.Append(" Last name: ")
        info.Append(Me.LastName)
        info.Append(" Age: ")
        info.Append(Me.Age.ToString)
        Return info.ToString
    End Function
End Class
```

Now we can create a new implementation of the Contact class, inheriting from Person. A new class needs to override the FullInformation method from the base class. When you type the Overrides keyword, Visual Studio generates a default implementation that looks like the following:

```
Public Overrides Function FullInformation() As String
    Return MyBase.FullInformation
End Function
```

Basically the code returns the result offered by the FullInformation method as it is implemented in the base class, which is accomplished via the MyBase keyword. We can now rewrite the complete code for the Contact class as follows:

```
Public Class Contact
    Inherits Person

    Public Property Title As String
```

```
    Public Overrides Function FullInformation() As String
        Dim firstInfo As String = MyBase.FullInformation

        Dim newInfo As New Text.StringBuilder
        newInfo.Append(firstInfo)
        newInfo.Append(" Title: ")
        newInfo.Append(Me.Title)
        Return newInfo.ToString
    End Function
End Class
```

Notice that the overridden method does not perform a complete string concatenation while it invokes first the `MyBase.FullInformation` method. This is a best practice, because one of inheritance purposes is favoring code reusability; therefore, this invocation is better than rewriting the code from scratch. The following code snippet shows how you can interact with both base class and with derived class properties, assuming that `FirstName` and `LastName` have been declared as `Overridable` in the base class and overridden within the derived class:

```
Public Sub New(ByVal name As String,
               ByVal surName As String,
               ByVal age As Integer,
               ByVal title As String)

    'Goes to the base class properties
    MyBase.FirstName = name
    MyBase.LastName = surName

    'Current instance properties
    Me.Age = age
    Me.Title = title
End Sub
```

ME AND MYBASE

The Me keyword refers to the instance of the current class, whereas MyBase refers to the base class that the current class derives from. This difference is evident when a member is overridden, but if members are not redefined, both keywords refer to the same code.

There are a few things to know about constructors within derived classes; the next section provides this information.

MyClass Keyword

Another way for accessing base classes' members is the MyClass keyword. Imagine you have a base class exposing some overridable members, such as properties or methods; then you have a derived class that overrides those members. The MyClass keyword avoids the application of overriding and invokes members on the derived class as if they were NotOverridable on the base class. In other words, MyClass enables executing members of a base class in the context of a derived class, ensuring that the member version is the one in the base class. Listing 12.1 shows an example.

LISTING 12.1   Demonstrating the **MyClass** Keyword

```
Public Class BaseClassDemo


    Public Overridable ReadOnly Property Test As String
        Get
            Return "This is a test in the base class"
        End Get
    End Property

    Public Function DoSomething() As String
        Return MyClass.Test
    End Function
End Class

Public Class DerivedClassDemo
    Inherits BaseClassDemo

    Public Overrides ReadOnly Property Test As String
        Get
            Return "This is a test in the derived class"
        End Get
    End Property
End Class
Module Module1
    Sub Main()

        Dim derived As New DerivedClassDemo

        'Invokes the member within the derived
        'class but as if it was not overridden
        Dim result As String = derived.DoSomething
    End Sub
End Module
```

The `BaseClassDemo` base class exposes an overridable property that returns a text message, for demo purposes. It also exposes a public method that just shows the text stored within the `Test` property. Within the derived `DerivedClassDemo`, the `Test` property is overridden whereas the `DoSomething` method is not. This method is still available when you create an instance of the `DerivedClassDemo` class. Because the method is defined within the base class and then it is executed within the derived class's context, if you implemented the method as follows:

```
Public Function DoSomething() As String
    Return Me.Test
End Function
```

it would return the content of the derived `Test` property. There are instead situations in which you want to ensure that only base class members are used within other members that are not overridden; this can be accomplished using the `MyClass` keyword. If you run the code shown in Listing 12.1, the `result` variable contains the following string: `"This is a test in the base class"` although the `DoSomething` method has been invoked on an instance of the derived class. Of course, you can still use the overridden `Test` property for other purposes in your derived class. `MyClass` is similar to `Me` in that both get a reference to the instance of the current class, but `MyClass` behaves as if members in the base class were marked as `NotOverridable` and therefore as if they were not overridden in the derived class.

Constructors' Inheritance

The previous section discussed the `MyBase` keyword and how it can be used to access members from a base class. The keyword also has another important purpose, which is about constructors. Consider the following constructor that is implemented within the `Person` class (that is, the base class) shown in the previous section:

```
Public Sub New(ByVal firstName As String,
               ByVal lastName As String,
               ByVal age As Integer)

    Me.FirstName = firstName
    Me.LastName = lastName
    Me.Age = age
End Sub
```

The problem now is in derived classes. The rule is that if you have a constructor receiving arguments in the base class, you do need to provide a constructor receiving arguments also within a derived class, and the constructor needs to invoke the base class. The following code shows how a constructor needs to be implemented within the `Contact` class:

```
Public Sub New(ByVal name As String,
```

```
                ByVal surName As String,
                ByVal age As Integer,
                ByVal title As String)

        MyBase.New(name, surName, age)
        Me.Title = title
End Sub
```

As you can see from the preceding code snippet, the first line of code is an invocation to the constructor of the base class and *this is a rule that you must follow*. After that line of code, you can provide any other initialization code. This particular requirement is necessary if you plan to provide a constructor that receives arguments within the base class, whereas it's not necessary if you implement a constructor that does not receive arguments or if you do not provide any constructor (which is implicitly provided by the Visual Basic compiler).

Shadowing

The beginning of this chapter explained that classes can inherit from base classes exposed by class libraries such as .dll assemblies and that you do not necessarily need the source code. It can happen that you create a class deriving from another class exposed by a compiled assembly and implement a new member. It can also happen that the publisher of the compiled base class releases a new version of the class, providing a member with the same name of your custom member, but you cannot edit the base class, because you don't have the source code. Visual Basic 2010 provides an interesting way for facing such a situation, known as *shadowing*. Although the Visual Basic compiler still enables compiling (it throws warning messages), basically your class needs to "shadow" the member with the same name of your custom one. This is accomplished using the Shadows keyword. For example, consider this particular implementation of the Person class, exposing also a Title property, of type String:

```
Public Class Person


    Public Property FirstName As String
    Public Property LastName As String
    Public Property Title As String


End Class
```

Now consider the following implementation of the Contact class, which requires a value defined within the Titles enumeration:

```
Public Class Contact
    Inherits Person

    Public Property Title As Titles
```

```
End Class

Public Enum Titles
    Dr
    Mr
    Mrs
End Enum
```

The `Contact` class exposes a `Title` property, but its base class already has a `Title` property; therefore, the Visual Basic compiler shows a warning message related to this situation. If you want your code to use the derived `Title` property, you need to mark your member with `Shadows` as follows:

```
Public Class Contact
    Inherits Person

    Public Shadows Property Title As Titles
End Class
```

You can accomplish the same result by marking the property within the derived class as `Overloads`:

```
Public Overloads Property Title As Titles
```

In this particular example we can use auto-implemented properties. If the property within the derived class returned the same type of the one within the base class, it would make more sense using old-fashioned properties so that you have the ability to customize the behavior.

Overriding Shared Members

Shared members cannot be overridden. This means that you can only use them as they have been inherited from the base class or provide a shadowing implementation for creating a new definition from scratch. For example, consider this simplified implementation of the `Person` class, which exposes a shared `Counter` property:

```
Public Class Person

    Public Shared Property Counter As Integer
End Class
```

If you now create a `Contact` class that inherits from `Person`, you can use the `Counter` property as previously implemented, or you can shadow the base definition as follows:

```
Public Class Contact
    Inherits Person
```

```
    Public Shared Shadows Property Counter As Integer
End Class
```

If you intend to provide an overloaded member with a different signature, you can use overloading as follows:

```
Public Shared Shadows Property Counter As Integer
Public Shared Shadows Property Counter(ByVal maximum As Integer) As Integer
    Get

    End Get
    Set(ByVal value As Integer)

    End Set
End Property
```

Another limitation of shared members is that you cannot invoke `MyBase` and `MyClass` keywords within them. Moreover, you cannot invoke shared members using the `MyBase` keyword. For example, if you assign the `Counter` shared property defined in the person class, you must write `Person.Counter = 0` instead of `MyBase.Counter = 0`.

Practical Inheritance: Building Custom Exceptions

In Chapter 6, "Error Handling and Exceptions," you learned about exceptions in .NET development; you saw what exceptions are and how you can intercept exceptions at runtime to create well-formed applications that can handle errors. The .NET Framework ships with hundreds of exceptions related to many aspects of .NET development. There could be situations in which you need to implement custom exceptions. Building custom exceptions is possible due to inheritance. A custom exception can inherit from the root `System.Exception` class or from another exception (such as `System.IO.IOException`) that necessarily inherits from `System.Exception`. Custom exceptions should always be CLS-compliant. Let's retake the `Person` class implementation, adding a method that returns the full name of the person and that requires at least the last name:

```
Public Class Person

    Public Property FirstName As String
    Public Property LastName As String

    Public Function FullName() As String

        If String.IsNullOrEmpty(Me.LastName) Then
            Throw New MissingLastNameException("Last name not specified")
        Else
            Return String.Concat(LastName, " ", FirstName)
        End If
```

```
    End Function
End Class
```

As you can see, if the LastName property contains an empty or null string the code throws a MissingLastNameException. This exception is custom and must be implemented.

NAMING CONVENTIONS

Remember that every exception class's identifier *must* terminate with the Exception word. Microsoft naming convention rules require this.

The MissingLastNameException is implemented as follows:

```
<Serializable()>
Public Class MissingLastNameException
    Inherits Exception

    Public Sub New()
        MyBase.New()
    End Sub

    Public Sub New(ByVal message As String)
        MyBase.New(message)
    End Sub

    Public Sub New(ByVal message As String, ByVal inner As Exception)
        MyBase.New(message, inner)
    End Sub

    Protected Sub New(ByVal info As Runtime.Serialization.SerializationInfo, _
                      ByVal context As _
                      Runtime.Serialization.StreamingContext)
        MyBase.New(info, context)
    End Sub
End Class
```

There is a series of considerations:

▶ As a custom exception, it inherits from System.Exception.

▶ The class is decorated with the Serializable attribute; this is one of the Common Language Specification establishments and enables developers to persist the state of the exception to disk (see Chapter 43, "Serialization").

▶ Custom exceptions expose three overloads of the base constructors plus one overload marked as Protected that is therefore available to eventually derived classes and that receives information on serialization.

▶ Custom exceptions are caught exactly as any other built-in exception.

When you have your custom exception, you can treat it as other ones:

```
Try
    Dim p As New Person
    'Will cause an error, because
    'the LastName was not specified
    Console.WriteLine(p.FullName)
Catch ex As MissingLastNameException
    Console.WriteLine("ERROR: please specify at least the last name")
Catch ex As Exception
    Console.WriteLine("Generic error")
    Console.WriteLine(ex.ToString)
Finally
    Console.ReadLine()
End Try
```

The preceding code intentionally causes an exception to demonstrate how the `MissingLastNameException` works, by missing to assign the `LastName` property in the `Person` class instance.

AVOID COMPLEX INHERITANCE CHAINS

Building a complex inheritance chain is something that should be carefully considered, because as the chain grows, the child classes will be tied and rely on the base classes not changing, at risk of disrupting the inheritance chain.

Summary

Inheritance is a key topic in the object-oriented programming with Visual Basic and .NET Framework. In this chapter you learned lots of important concepts. First you learned what inheritance is and how you can take advantage of inheritance for creating frameworks of custom objects. Then you saw how to derive classes from base classes using the `Inherits` keyword and how your derived classes automatically inherit some members from `System.Object`, which is the root in the class hierarchy. When deriving classes you need to consider how constructors and shared members behave, and the chapter provided an overview. But inheritance would be of less use without polymorphism. You saw how polymorphism requires implementing one common infrastructure for multiple objects taking advantage of the ability to redefine inherited members' behavior. For this purpose, the .NET Framework enables the overriding technique that you can use to modify the behavior of derived members. You often want to condition inheritance, establishing when classes should be sealed (`NotInheritable`) or abstract (`MustInherit`). In inheritance scenarios you also often need to have access to base class members; therefore, you need the `MyBase` and `MyClass` keywords. But you seldom work with theories; because of this, the chapter closes with a practical demonstration of inheritance, showing how you can build custom exceptions to use in your applications.

Most people have a car. Cars have an engine, four wheels, gear, and other instrumentations. There are lots of different companies that produce cars, and each company produces different models. All companies have to build car models adhering to some particular specifications established by the law, and such specifications provide information on what minimal components will compose cars, including a list of those components that therefore are common to every car. In.NET development we can compare interfaces to the previously described law specifications. Interfaces provide a list of members that an object must implement to accomplish particular tasks in a standardized way. They are also known as *contracts*, because they rule how an object must behave to reach some objectives. You saw an example in Chapter 8, "Managing an Object's Lifetime," for the `IDisposable` interface that must be implemented if an object wants to provide the capability to release resources that are not only in-memory objects, according to a standardized way, meaning that.NET Framework knows that the `Dispose` method from `IDisposable` is required to free up resources. In this chapter you first learn how to define and implement custom interfaces; then you get an overview of the most common interfaces in.NET Framework. You learn why interfaces are important because you will surely wonder why you should use them.

Defining Interfaces

An interface is a reference type which is defined within an `Interface..End Interface` block. Interfaces define only signatures for members that classes will then expose and are basically a set of the members' definitions. Imagine you want to create an interface that defines members for working with documents. This is accomplished with the following code:

```
Public Interface IDocument

    Property Content As String
    Sub Load(ByVal fileName As String)
    Sub Save(ByVal fileName As String)

End Interface
```

The interface is marked as `Public` because the default scope for interfaces is `Friend`. Assigning public visibility ensures external assemblies use the interface (which is a common scenario).

INTERFACES SCOPE

Interfaces can be declared `Private`, `Protected`, or `Protected Friend` only if they are defined within a type such as a class.

As a convention, interface identifiers begin with a capital `I`. This is not mandatory (except when creating CLS-compliant interfaces), but I strongly recommend you follow the convention. The most important consideration is that the interface definition contains only members' definitions with no body. For both `Load` and `Save` methods' definition, there is only a signature but not the method body and implementation, which are left to classes that implement the interface. Another important thing is that members defined within interfaces cannot be marked with one of the scope qualifiers, such as `Public`, `Friend`, and so on. By default, members defined by interfaces are `Public`. Finally, being reference types, interfaces need to be treated as such. See Chapter 4, "Data Types and Expressions", for further information on reference types.

NESTED CLASSES

Interfaces can surprisingly define classes. A class defined within an interface is a typical `Class..End Class` block as you would normally define one. This is certainly an uncommon scenario and can be useful to avoid naming conflicts with other classes, but you have to know that it is possible.

Implementing and Accessing Interfaces

Implementing interfaces means telling a class that it needs to expose all members defined within the interface. This task is accomplished by using the Implements keyword followed by the name of the interface. The following code snippet shows how to implement the IDocument interface within a Document class:

```
Public Class Document
    Implements IDocument

    Public Property Content As String Implements IDocument.Content

    Public Sub Load(ByVal fileName As String) Implements IDocument.Load
    End Sub

    Public Sub Save(ByVal fileName As String) Implements IDocument.Save
    End Sub

End Class
```

You immediately notice that, when pressing Enter, the Visual Studio IDE automatically generate members' templates for you. This is useful: You do not need to waste your time in writing members' signatures. You also notice that when a member is defined within a class because of the interface implementation, the Implements keyword is also added at the end of the member followed by the related element in the interface.

MULTIPLE IMPLEMENTATIONS

Different from inheritance, classes and structures can implement more than one interface. You see an example later in the chapter when discussing IEnumerable and IEnumerator.

The Document class is basic and is for demo purposes only. To complete the implementation example, we can write code to populate methods for performing operations established in the interface, as shown in Listing 13.1.

LISTING 13.1   Implementing Interfaces

```
Public Class Document
    Implements IDocument

    Public Property Content As String Implements IDocument.Content

    'Gets the content of a text document
    Public Sub Load(ByVal fileName As String) Implements IDocument.Load
```

```
        Try
            Content = My.Computer.FileSystem.ReadAllText(fileName)
        Catch ex As Exception
            Throw
        End Try
    End Sub

    'Saves a text document to file
    Public Sub Save(ByVal fileName As String) Implements IDocument.Save
        Try
            My.Computer.FileSystem.WriteAllText(fileName,
                                            Content, False)
        Catch ex As Exception
            Throw
        End Try
    End Sub

End Class
```

Basically when you implement interfaces, you need to populate members' templates with
your own code. This can ensure that your object is respecting the contract established by
the interface. When a class implements an interface, it also needs to access members that
it defines. You have two alternatives for this purpose. The first one is simple and intuitive
and consists of creating an instance of the class that implements the interface. Continuing
with the example of the Document class shown in Listing 13.1, the following code shows
how you can accomplish this:

```
Dim myDocument As New Document
myDocument.Load("SomeDocument.txt")

Console.WriteLine(myDocument.Content)
```

The code basically invokes instance members of the class with no differences for normal
classes' implementations. The second alternative is declaring an *interface variable*. You
declare a variable whose type is the interface; the variable receives the result of an explicit
conversion from the class that implements the interface to the interface itself. More than
words, code can provide a good explanation:

```
Dim myDocument As IDocument = CType(New Document, IDocument)
myDocument.Load("SomeDocument.txt")

Console.WriteLine(myDocument.Content)
```

The result is the same. You often find code that makes use of interface variables, so spend
a little time to become familiar with this approach. After this discussion you will probably

wonder why you need to define and implement interfaces because you just need to write code as you would do without them. The answer is *polymorphism.*

Passing Interfaces As Method Arguments

One of the most powerful features when working with interfaces is that methods can receive interfaces as parameters. This means that you can pass in any object as these parameters so long as it implements the given interface. The following example shows a method that accepts an argument of type IList, meaning that any object implementing the IList interface can be accepted:

```
'Interfaces as parameters
Public Class WorkWithLists
    Public Function Elaborate(ByVal items As IList) As Integer
        'Just for demo, returns 0 if the list contains something
        If items.Count > 0 Then
            Return 0
        Else
            'if not, adds a new object to the list
            Dim item As New Object
            items.Add(item)
            Return -1
        End If
    End Function

End Class
```

This is with no doubt one of the most important features in programming by contracts with interfaces.

Interfaces and Polymorphism

Chapter 12, "Inheritance," discusses polymorphism with a basic purpose to offer a common infrastructure to different kinds of objects. In the discussion, interfaces find their natural habitat. They provide a common set of members that classes need to implement if they need to perform a particular series of tasks. A typical example is the IDisposable interface that you met in Chapter 8. All classes that need to provide a mechanism for releasing resources implement that interface, which exposes a set of common members. Another example is the ICloneable interface that defines a Clone method that classes can implement to provide the ability to copy a class instance. You can easily understand that interfaces are generic; they are not specific to any class, but instead they are the most generic as possible so that the generality of classes can implement them. To provide a code example, let's retake the IDocument interface proposed in the previous section. This inter-face was implemented by a Document class. But the same interface can be implemented in other kinds of classes. For example, we can define an Invoice class that can implement the same IDocument interface because it exposes a common set of members that can be easily used within the Invoice class. Then the new class can provide new members specific to its particular needs and behavior. The following code demonstrates this:

```
Public Class Invoice
    Implements IDocument

    Public Property Content As String Implements IDocument.Content

    Public Sub Load(ByVal fileName As String) Implements IDocument.Load

    End Sub

    Public Sub Save(ByVal fileName As String) Implements IDocument.Save

    End Sub

    Public Property InvoiceNumber As Integer

    Public Function CalculateDiscount(ByVal price As Decimal,
                                      ByVal percent As Single) As Decimal

    End Function

End Class
```

As you can see, the IDocument interface can serve the Invoice class with its members; then the class defines new members (InvoiceNumber and CalculateDiscount) strictly related to its behavior. By the way, the IDocument interface provides polymorphic code that can be used in different situations and objects with a common infrastructure.

Interfaces Inheritance

Two situations are related to both inheritance and interfaces. The first scenario is when you create a class that derives from another one that implements an interface. In such a scenario the derived class also inherits members implemented through an interface and does not need to implement the interface again. Moreover, if the base class is marked as overridable members implemented via an interface, the derived class can override such members if not private. The second scenario is a pure interface inheritance, in which an interface can inherit from another one. Continuing the previous examples, we can consider creating an `IInvoice` interface that inherits from `IDocument` providing some more specific members to represent an invoice. The following code demonstrates this:

```
Public Interface IInvoice
    Inherits IDocument

    'New members
    Property InvoiceNumber As Integer
    Function CalculateDiscount(ByVal price As Decimal,
                              ByVal percent As Single) As Decimal

End Interface
```

As you can see, the `Inherits` keyword is used also for interface inheritance. In this example the new interface inherits all members' definitions from the `IDocument` interface plus adds two new members, the `InvoiceNumber` property and the `CalculateDiscount` method.

Defining CLS-Compliant Interfaces

The Common Language Specification also provides rules for interfaces. The first rule is that if you mark an interface as CLS-compliant, you cannot use CLS-incompliant types within signatures. The following interface is not correct because it is marked as `CLSCompliant` but uses a noncompliant type:

```
'Incorrect: UInteger is not CLS compliant
<CLSCompliant(True)> Public Interface ITest

    Property Counter As UInteger

End Interface
```

The second rule is that a CLS-compliant interface cannot define shared members. The last rule is that all members must be explicitly marked with the `CLSCompliant` attribute. The following is an example of CLS-compliant interface:

```
<CLSCompliant(True)> Public Interface IClsCompliant

    <CLSCompliant(True)> Property Counter As Integer
    <CLSCompliant(True)> Function DoSomething() As Boolean

End Interface
```

NAMING CONVENTIONS

It is an implicit rule that identifiers for all CLS-compliant interfaces *must* begin with a capital I letter. IDocument is a correct identifier whereas MyDocumentInterface is not. Also identifiers cannot contain the underscore character (_) and are written according to the Pascal-casing conventions.

Most Common .NET Interfaces

Because of their importance in polymorphism, the .NET Framework defines a large quantity of interfaces implemented by the most types within the Framework. You need to understand the most common built-in interfaces because they provide great flexibility in your code, too, and in several situations you need to implement such interfaces in your objects that need to perform particular tasks. Table 13.1 summarizes the most common .NET interfaces.

TABLE 13.1   Most Common Interfaces

Interface	Description
ICloneable	Its purpose is to provide methods for cloning objects.
IDisposable	Implemented when a class needs to provide methods for releasing resources.
IEnumerable	Implemented to provide the Enumerator, which enables objects to be iterated.
IComparable	When an object wants to provide the capability of sorting, it must implement this interface.
IConvertible	To be implemented if an object enables conversion.
IFormattable	Provides support for formatting data.

The ICloneable interface is discussed in Chapter 4, and the IDisposable interface is discussed in Chapter 8; therefore, this chapter does not revisit these interfaces. Instead learn how you can implement the other ones in your code.

The IEnumerable Interface

You implement the IEnumerable interface each time you want your class to support For..Each loops. Each time you iterate an object (typically a collection) using For Each, it is because that object implements IEnumerable. The .NET Framework offers lots of collections (including generic ones) and enables creating custom collections inheriting from built-in ones; therefore, implementing IEnumerable will probably be spared for you. It's important to understand how the interface works, especially for its intensive usage when working with LINQ. IEnumerable provides one method, named GetEnumerator, which generally is implemented as follows:

```
Public Function GetEnumerator() As System.Collections.IEnumerator _
    Implements System.Collections.IEnumerable.GetEnumerator
    Return CType(Me, IEnumerator)

End Function
```

As you can see, the method returns the result of the conversion of the class instance to an IEnumerator object; this means that IEnumerable must be implemented together with another interface, named IEnumerator that offers methods and properties for moving between items in a collection and for providing information on the current item. To provide an example, imagine you have a class named Contacts that acts as a repository of items of type Contact and that implements IEnumerable to provide iterations' capabilities. Listing 13.2 shows how this is accomplished in code, including a sample loop performed invoking For..Each.

LISTING 13.2   Implementing IEnumerable and IEnumerator

```
Public Class Contacts
    Implements IEnumerable, IEnumerator

    Public Function GetEnumerator() As System.Collections.IEnumerator _
        Implements System.Collections.IEnumerable.GetEnumerator
        Return CType(Me, IEnumerator)
    End Function

    Private position As Integer = -1

    Public ReadOnly Property Current As Object _
        Implements System.Collections.IEnumerator.Current
        Get
            Return Items(position)
        End Get
    End Property

    Public Function MoveNext() As Boolean _
        Implements System.Collections.IEnumerator.MoveNext
        position += 1
        Return (position < Items.Length)
    End Function

    Public Sub Reset() Implements System.Collections.IEnumerator.Reset
        position = -1
    End Sub
```

```
        Private Items() As Contact = New Contact() {New Contact With _
                                        {.FirstName = "Alessandro",
                                        .LastName = "Del Sole",
                                        .Email = "alessandro.delsole" & _
                                                "@visual-basic.it",
                                        .PhoneNumber = "000-0000-00"},
                                        New Contact With _
                                        {.FirstName = "Robert",
                                        .LastName = "Green",
                                        .Email = "email@something.com",
                                        .PhoneNumber = "000-0000-00"} _
                                        }

End Class

Public Class Contact

    Public Property FirstName As String
    Public Property LastName As String
    Public Property Email As String
    Public Property PhoneNumber As String

End Class
Module Module1

    Sub Main()

        Dim c As New Contacts
        'Returns "Del Sole", "Green"
        For Each Cont As Contact In c
            Console.WriteLine(Cont.LastName)
        Next

        Console.ReadLine()
    End Sub
End Module
```

The Contacts class stores an array of Contact objects and provides a private field, position, which is used for returning information. The Current property returns the item in the array corresponding to the current position, whereas the MoveNext method increments the position variable and returns True if the position number is still less than the upper bound in the array. In the end, Reset just restores the initial value for position. You also notice how, within the Sub Main in Module1, a simple For..Each loop is given for demonstration purposes. If you run the code, you see that it correctly returns last names for both actual contacts within the `Contacts` class.

IENUMERABLE(OF T)

As for other interfaces a generic version of `IEnumerable` supports specific types. Because Chapter 15, "Delegates and Events," discusses generics, this chapter shows the nongeneric version that basically works the same except that it is related to `Object`.

The `IComparable` Interface

You implement the `IComparable` interface when you want to offer custom comparison instrumentation to your objects. `IComparable` requires you to implement a `CompareTo` method that returns an `Integer` value which is less than zero if the instance is less than the compared object, zero if the instance equals the compared object and greater than zero if the instance is greater than the compared object. For example, imagine you want to provide a comparison to the `Person` class based on the length of the `LastName` property. Listing 13.3 shows how you can accomplish this.

LISTING 13.3   Implementing the `IComparable` Interface

```
Public Class Person
    Implements IComparable

    Public Property FirstName As String
    Public Property LastName As String
    Public Property Email As String


    Public Function CompareTo(ByVal obj As Object) As Integer Implements
System.IComparable.CompareTo
        If Not TypeOf (obj) Is Person Then
            Throw New ArgumentException
        Else

            Dim tempPerson As Person = DirectCast(obj, Person)

            If Me.LastName.Length < tempPerson.LastName.Length Then
                Return -1
            ElseIf Me.LastName.Length = tempPerson.LastName.Length Then
                Return 0
            Else
                Return 1
```

```
            End If

        End If
    End Function
End Class
Module Module1

    Sub Main()
        Dim p1 As New Person With {.LastName = "Del Sole",
                                   .FirstName = "Alessandro"}
        Dim p2 As New Person With {.LastName = "AnotherLastName",
                                   .FirstName = "AnotherFirstName"}

        Dim c As New ComparableHelper(p1)
        Console.WriteLine(c.CompareTo(p2))
        Console.ReadLine()
    End Sub

End Module
```

You may notice how a first check is performed on the object type, which must be `Person`. If not, the code throws an `ArgumentException` (meaning that the argument is not valid). The comparison is accomplished in a simple way using unary operators. Next, to perform the comparison you just need to create an instance of the `Person` class and then invoke its `CompareTo` method, passing the `Person` you want to compare to the current instance.

ICOMPARER **INTERFACE**

If you want to provide custom sorting for arrays, you need to implement the `IComparer` interface. The following article in the Microsoft Knowledge Base provides a good example that is extensible to Visual Basic 2010.

Utilizing the Generic `IComparable(Of T)`

Although Chapter 15 discusses generics, this is a good point for showing something interesting about them. Lots of interfaces within the .NET Framework have a generic counterpart. For example, there is an `IEnumerable(Of T)` or `IComparable(Of T)`, in which `T` is a specific .NET type instead of `Object`, which would require conversions and, therefore, performance overhead. We could rewrite the `Person` class shown in Listing 13.3 using the `IComparable(Of T)` interface to provide support for `Person` objects. This is accomplished by the following code:

```
Public Class Person
    Implements IComparable(Of Person)

    Public Property FirstName As String
```

```
    Public Property LastName As String
    Public Property Email As String

    Public Function CompareTo(ByVal other As Person) As Integer _
          Implements System.IComparable(Of Person).CompareTo
        If Me.LastName.Length < other.LastName.Length Then
            Return -1
        ElseIf Me.LastName.Length = other.LastName.Length Then
            Return 0
        Else
            Return 1
        End If
    End Function

End Class
```

You soon notice how DirectCast conversions disappear and how the CompareTo method receives an argument of type Person instead of Object. This means less code and more precision. In Chapter 15 and Chapter 16, "Working with Collections," you gain detailed information about generics and generic collections.

The IConvertible Interface

Objects implementing the IConvertible interface expose a series of ToXXX methods exactly as the Convert class does so that such objects can easily be converted into another type. This example uses a structure instead of a class, for the sake of simplicity. Listing 13.4 shows how the IConvertible interface can be implemented.

LISTING 13.4 Implementing the IConvertible Interface

```
Public Structure ThreePoint
    Implements IConvertible

    Public Function GetTypeCode() As System.TypeCode Implements _
        System.IConvertible.GetTypeCode

        Return TypeCode.Object
    End Function

    'Just a custom return value
    Public Function ToBoolean(ByVal provider As System.IFormatProvider) _
        As Boolean Implements System.IConvertible.ToBoolean
        Return X > Y
    End Function

    Public Function ToByte(ByVal provider As System.IFormatProvider) _
        As Byte Implements System.IConvertible.ToByte
```

```vbnet
        Return Convert.ToByte(SumPoints)
    End Function

    Public Function ToChar(ByVal provider As System.IFormatProvider) _
        As Char Implements System.IConvertible.ToChar
        Return Convert.ToChar(SumPoints)
    End Function

    Public Function ToDateTime(ByVal provider As System.IFormatProvider) _
        As Date Implements System.IConvertible.ToDateTime
        Return Convert.ToDateTime(SumPoints)
    End Function

    Public Function ToDecimal(ByVal provider As System.IFormatProvider) _
        As Decimal Implements System.IConvertible.ToDecimal
        Return Convert.ToDecimal(SumPoints)
    End Function

    Public Function ToDouble(ByVal provider As System.IFormatProvider) _
        As Double Implements System.IConvertible.ToDouble
        Return Convert.ToDouble(SumPoints)
    End Function

    Public Function ToInt16(ByVal provider As System.IFormatProvider) _
        As Short Implements System.IConvertible.ToInt16
        Return Convert.ToInt16(SumPoints)
    End Function

    Public Function ToInt32(ByVal provider As System.IFormatProvider) _
        As Integer Implements System.IConvertible.ToInt32
        Return SumPoints()
    End Function

    Public Function ToInt64(ByVal provider As System.IFormatProvider) _
        As Long Implements System.IConvertible.ToInt64
        Return Convert.ToInt64(SumPoints)
    End Function

    Public Function ToSByte(ByVal provider As System.IFormatProvider) _
        As SByte Implements System.IConvertible.ToSByte
        Return Convert.ToSByte(SumPoints)
    End Function

    Public Function ToSingle(ByVal provider As System.IFormatProvider) _
        As Single Implements System.IConvertible.ToSingle
        Return Convert.ToSingle(SumPoints)
```

```vbnet
    End Function

    'Required "Overloads"
    Public Overloads Function ToString(ByVal provider As System.IFormatProvider) _
        As String Implements System.IConvertible.ToString
        Return String.Format("{0}, {1}, {2}", Me.X, Me.Y, Me.Z)
    End Function

    Public Function ToType(ByVal conversionType As System.Type,
                           ByVal provider As System.IFormatProvider) _
                           As Object Implements System.IConvertible.ToType
        Return Convert.ChangeType(SumPoints, conversionType)
    End Function

    Public Function ToUInt16(ByVal provider As System.IFormatProvider) _
        As UShort Implements System.IConvertible.ToUInt16

        Return Convert.ToUInt16(SumPoints)
    End Function

    Public Function ToUInt32(ByVal provider As System.IFormatProvider) _
        As UInteger Implements System.IConvertible.ToUInt32
        Return Convert.ToUInt32(SumPoints)
    End Function

    Public Function ToUInt64(ByVal provider As System.IFormatProvider) _
        As ULong Implements System.IConvertible.ToUInt64
        Return Convert.ToUInt64(SumPoints)
    End Function

    Public Property X As Integer
    Public Property Y As Integer
    Public Property Z As Integer

    Public Sub New(ByVal valueX As Integer,
                   ByVal valueY As Integer,
                   ByVal valueZ As Integer)
        Me.X = valueX
        Me.Y = valueY
        Me.Z = valueZ
    End Sub

    Public Function SumPoints() As Integer
        Return (Me.X + Me.Y + Me.Z)
    End Function
End Structure
```

13

The ThreePoint structure is simple; it just exposes three integer properties (x, y and z) whose sum is returned via a SumPoints method. The goal of the IConvertible implementation is therefore enabling returning the result of the method converted into different types. Basically each conversion method invokes the corresponding one of the Convert class, with some exceptions. The first one is the ToBoolean method, which returns a customized result depending on the value of x and y, but this is just for demonstration purposes. (You can invoke the Convert.ToBoolean as well.) The second exception is the ToString method. When you implement an interface that provides a method already existing in the class (even because of inheritance), Visual Studio renames the interface's method adding a 1 in the end. For example, every class exposes ToString because it is inherited from System.Object; therefore the ToString version provided by the interface is automatically renamed to ToString1. But this is not elegant. A better technique is overloading because the method is marked with Overloads and named correctly.

IMPORTANT NOTICE

IConvertible does not adhere to the Common Language Specification, because it makes use of CLS-incompliant types, such as UInt16, UInt32, and so on. You should be aware of this if you plan to develop objects that need instead to be CLS-compliant.

The IFormattable Interface

The IFormattable interface enables implementing a new overload of the ToString method to provide customized string formatting with deep control over the process, also defining custom qualifiers. Listing 13.5 shows how you can implement the IFormattable interface.

LISTING 13.5   Implementing the IFormattable Interface

```
Imports System.Globalization


Public Class Person
    Implements IFormattable

    Public Property FirstName As String
    Public Property LastName As String
    Public Property Email As String

    Public Overloads Function ToString(ByVal format As String,
                        ByVal formatProvider As System.IFormatProvider) _
                        As String Implements System.IFormattable.ToString

        If String.IsNullOrEmpty(format) Then format = "G"
        If formatProvider Is Nothing Then formatProvider = _
```

```
                          CultureInfo.CurrentCulture

        Select Case format
            'General specifier. Must be implemented
            Case Is = "G"
                Return String.Format("{0} {1}, {2}",
                       Me.FirstName, Me.LastName, Me.Email)
            Case Is = "F"
                Return FirstName
            Case Is = "L"
                Return LastName
            Case Is = "LF"
                Return String.Format("{0} {1}", Me.LastName, Me.FirstName)
            Case Else
                Throw New FormatException
        End Select
    End Function
End Class

Module Module1
    Sub Main()
        Dim p As New Person With {.FirstName = "Alessandro",
            .LastName = "Del Sole",
            .Email = "alessandro.delsole@visual-basic.it"}

        Console.WriteLine("{0:G}", p)
        Console.WriteLine("{0:L}", p)
        Console.WriteLine("{0:F}", p)
        Console.WriteLine("{0:LF}", p)
        Console.ReadLine()
    End Sub
End Module
```

Listing 13.5 shows a particular implementation of the Person class, which exposes the FirstName, LastName, and Email properties. It implements the IFormattable interface that offers a new overload of the ToString method. This method receives two arguments; the first one, format, represents the qualifier. For example, in standard formatting the c letter represents currency. Here you can specify your own qualifiers. Because of this, the first check is if format is null or empty. In such case, a G qualifier is assigned by default. G stands for General and is the only qualifier that *must* be implemented. When you provide G, you can create your own qualifiers. The next check is on formatProvider that basically represents the culture for string formatting. If null, the code assigns the local system culture. The subsequent Select..End Select block takes into consideration some identifiers as custom qualifiers. L stands for LastName, F stands for FirstName, and LF stands for LastName + FirstName. You can change or extend this code simply by intercepting your custom identifiers within this block. Running the code shown in Listing 13.5 produces the following result:

```
Alessandro Del Sole, alessandro.delsole@visual-basic.it
Del Sole
Alessandro

Del Sole Alessandro
```

You can easily compare the output result with the code and understand how custom formatting works.

Summary

In this chapter you learned about interfaces, another key topic in the object-oriented programming. Interfaces, which are defined within `Interface..End Interface` blocks, provide signatures of sets of members that an object must implement to accomplish specific tasks. You may remember the example of the `IDisposable` interface that must be implemented by objects that need to provide methods for freeing up resources. You saw how to create and implement custom interfaces in your code via the `Implements` keyword and then how to invoke objects that implement interfaces both creating class instances and via interface variables. You understood why interfaces are important and why the .NET Framework makes an intensive usage of interfaces, talking about polymorphism and how interfaces can contribute to provide standardized infrastructures for multiple objects. It's important to define interfaces adhering to the Common Language Specification, so you got information about this. Finally, code examples have been provided for the most common .NET built-in interfaces, to provide a deeper understanding of how things happen behind the scenes and to reuse those interfaces in your code.

CHAPTER 14

Generics and Nullable Types

When you organize your home things, you probably place things according to their kind. For example, you have a place for food that is different from the place where you put clothes. But also foods are different. You will not treat fish like meat or pizza and so on. So you need safe places for each kind of food, avoiding the risks deriving from considering all foods the same way; the same is for clothes and any other home item. The .NET development would be similar without Generics. Consider groups of .NET objects of different types, all grouped into a collection of `Object`. How can you be sure to treat an item in the collection as you should if the collection stores different types that you identify as Object? What if you want to create just a collection of strings? Generics solve this problem. In this chapter you learn what Generics are, getting the basics about them. In Chapter 16, "Working with Collections," you then learn about generic collections and see why Generics are so useful. This chapter also introduces nullable types, which are generic on their own.

Introducing Generics

Generic types are .NET types that can adapt their behavior to different kind of objects without the need of defining a separate version of the type. In other words, you can implement an only generic type to work with integers, strings, custom reference types, and any other .NET type with a single implementation. Generics offer several advantages:

▶ **Strongly typed programming techniques:** Generic objects can hold only the specified type and avoid accidents of handling objects of different types within the same group.

▶ **Better performances:** Because Generics enable handling only the specified type, they avoid the need of boxing and unboxing from and to `System.Object`, and this retains for performance overhead.

▶ **Code reuse:** As you will better see in a few moments, Generics enable creating objects that behave the same way and that have the same infrastructure whatever kind of .NET type you pass them.

▶ **The ability of writing better code:** Avoiding working with nongeneric `System.Object`, you not only get all IntelliSense features for the specified type, but you also take advantages from not using late-binding techniques.

Generally the use of Generics is related to the creation of strongly typed collections for storing groups of items of the same type. Because of this, there are two considerations: the first one is that you should check if the .NET Framework provides a built-in generic collection suiting your needs before creating custom ones (read Chapter 16); the second consideration is that code examples shown in this chapter will be related to creating a generic collection so that you know how to create one if .NET built-in generics are not sufficient for you.

Creating and Consuming Generics

Creating a generic type is accomplished by providing a parameterized type definition. The following is an example:

```
Class CustomType(Of T)


End Class
```

The `Of` keyword is followed by the type that the new object can handle. `T` is the *type parameter* and represents the .NET type that you want to be held by your generic type. The type parameter's name is left to your own choosing, but you often find `T` as a common name in the .NET Framework base class library. At this point you must write code to manipulate the `T` type in a way that will be convenient for possibly every .NET type. Now imagine you want to build a custom collection that you want to reuse with any .NET type. Listing 14.1 shows how to accomplish this.

LISTING 14.1   Building a Custom Generic Type

```
Public Class CustomType(Of T)
```

```
    Private items() As T

    Public Sub New(ByVal upperBound As Integer)
        ReDim items(upperBound - 1)
    End Sub

    Private _count As Integer = 0
    'Cannot provide auto-implemented properties when read-only
    Public ReadOnly Property Count As Integer
        Get
            Return _count
        End Get
    End Property

    Public Sub Add(ByVal newItem As T)
        If newItem IsNot Nothing Then
            Me.items(Me._count) = newItem
            Me._count += 1
        End If
    End Sub

    Default Public ReadOnly Property Item(ByVal index As Integer) As T
        Get
            If index < 0 OrElse index >= Me.
                Count Then Throw New IndexOutOfRangeException
            Return items(index)
        End Get
    End Property
End Class
```

> **TIP**
>
> You notice that the code in Listing 14.1 uses arrays to store objects. Arrays do not
> support removing objects or, at least, this cannot be accomplished easily, and this is
> the reason why you only find an Add method. By the way, in this particular case you do
> not need to focus on how to add and remove items (Chapter 16 is about this) whereas
> you instead need to understand how to handle the generic type parameter.

The code shows how simple it is to manage the type parameter. It can represent any .NET
type but, as in the previous example, an array can be of that type and store objects of that
type. Because arrays cannot be empty, the constructor receives the upper bound that is
then used by ReDim. The Add method equally receives an argument of type T whose value
is pushed into the array. This introduces another important concept: generic methods,

that is, where methods can accept generic parameters (named *type argument*). Notice how a Count property returns the number of items in the array. In this particular scenario, auto-implemented properties cannot be used because a read-only property needs a Get block. Finally, the Item property enables retrieving the specified object in the array at the given index. The new class therefore can handle different types with the same infrastructure.

WHAT CAN BE GENERICS?

You can define as generic the following types: classes, interfaces, delegates, structures, and methods.

Consuming Generic Types

To instantiate and consume generic types, you pass to the constructor the type you want to be handled. For example, the following code creates a new instance of the CustomType class enabling it to handle only integers or types that are converted to Integer via a widening conversion:

```
Dim integerCollection As New CustomType(Of Integer)(2)
integerCollection.Add(0)
integerCollection.Add(1)
'Writes 1
Console.WriteLine(integerCollection(1).ToString)
```

Basically you pass the desired type to the constructor after the Of keyword. When invoking the Add method, you can notice how IntelliSense tells you that the method can receive only Integer. If you pass a different type, you get an error message. But this does not work only with .NET common types. You can use this technique with custom types, too. For example, you can create a generic collection of Person objects (supposing you have defined a Person class in your code) as follows:

```
Dim onePerson As New Person
onePerson.FirstName = "Alessandro"
onePerson.LastName = "Del Sole"

Dim secondPerson As New Person
secondPerson.FirstName = "Robert"
secondPerson.LastName = "White"

Dim personCollection As New CustomType(Of Person)(2)
personCollection.Add(onePerson)
personCollection.Add(secondPerson)
'Returns 2

Console.WriteLine(personCollection.Count)
```

Hopefully Generics' purpose is now clearer. Their purpose is to provide reusable infrastructures for different types avoiding mixed groups of objects in favor of strongly typed objects.

Implementing Generic Methods

In Listing 14.1 you saw how to implement a method that receives a generic type parameter. By the way, generic methods are something more. You can add the Of keyword to a generic method to parameterize the method, other than getting generic-type parameters. The following code provides an example, where two arrays of integers are swapped:

```
'Array are passed by reference in this case
Public Sub Swap(Of T1)(ByRef array1() As T1, ByRef array2() As T1)
    Dim temp() As T1
    temp = array1
    array1 = array2
    array2 = temp

End Sub
```

Continuing the executive code shown in the "Consuming Generic Types" section, the following snippet shows how you can invoke the generic method above to swap the content of two arrays of integers:

```
Dim arr1() As Integer = {1, 2, 3}
Dim arr2() As Integer = {4, 5, 6}
integerCollection.Swap(Of Integer)(arr1, arr2)

'Demonstrates that arr2 now
'contains values previously
'stored in arr1
For Each item In arr2
    Console.WriteLine(item)
Next
```

Understanding Constraints

With constraints you can control Generics' behavior, and both provide additional functionalities and limit the implementation to specific data types. Let's begin by understanding constraints on methods.

Methods Constraints

Imagine you want the ability to compare two items within an array. To accomplish this you need to take advantage of the IComparable interface, and because of this, you want to require that the type argument implements the IComparable interface. The following code demonstrates this:

```
Public Function CompareItems(Of T As IComparable)(ByVal sourceArray() As T,
                                       ByVal index1 As Integer,
                                       ByVal index2 As Integer)
                              As Integer

    Dim result As Integer = _
                sourceArray(index1).CompareTo(sourceArray(index2))

    Return result
End Function
```

Notice how the As clause in the method argument requires the type to implement the IComparable interface. If the type does not implement the interface, the generic method cannot be used. This simplifies how objects can be compared, in that you can directly invoke the CompareTo method on the first item in the array. This approach is useful for another reason: If you did not specify the IComparable constraint, you could attempt a conversion from T to IComparable at runtime, but this would throw an InvalidCastException if the object does not implement the interface. Therefore using constraints you can ensure that your objects suit your needs.

Type Constraints

At a higher level, you can apply constraints to generic objects' definitions. For example you can require the type parameter to implement the IComparable interface as follows:

```
Public Class CustomType(Of T As IComparable)

End Class
```

You can specify what interfaces the object must implement or what class it has to inherit from. This is an example that accepts types deriving from System.IO.Stream:

```
Public Class CustomType(Of T As System.IO.Stream)

End Class
```

In this example, acceptable types would be StreamWriter, StreamReader, BinaryWriter, and BinaryReader objects.

New Constraints

You can combine the As New keywords to require the type argument to expose an explicit parameterless constructor. This is accomplished by the following definition:

```
Public Class CustomType(Of T As New)
    Public Sub TestInstance()
```

```
        Dim instance As New T
    End Sub
End Class
```

The `TestInstance` method is an example of how you can instantiate the `T` type. This approach gives you the ability to create new instances of the type and prevents the type from being an interface or an abstract (`MustInherit`) class.

Providing Multiple Constraints

You can combine multiple constraints to provide a series of requirements in your generic types. Multiple constraints are enclosed in curly braces and separated by commas. The following code defines a generic type accepting only reference types that implement the `ICloneable` interface and an explicit parameterless constructor:

```
Public Class CustomType(Of T As {Class, ICloneable, New})

End Class
```

INHERITANCE CONSTRAINT

You can also provide inheritance constraints other than interfaces constraint, as described at the beginning of this section. Simply provide the name of the abstract or base class you require to be inherited in the type parameter.

The `Class` keyword in the constraint indicates that only reference types are accepted. You use the `Structure` keyword if you want to accept only value types, keeping in mind that in such a scenario you cannot combine it with the `New` keyword. The following code demonstrates how you can directly access the `Clone` method because of the `ICloneable` implementation constraint:

```
Public Sub TestConstraint()
    Dim newObj As New T
    Dim clonedObj As Object = newObj.Clone()
End Sub
```

NESTED TYPES

The type parameter can be used only within the body of the generic type. Nested types can still take advantage of the type parameter as well so that you can create complex infrastructures in your generic types.

Overloading Type Parameters

You can overload generic definitions providing different signatures for the type parameter, similar to what happens in methods overloads. The following code provides an example:

```
Public Class CustomType


End Class


Public Class CustomType(Of T1, T2)


End Class


Public Class CustomType(Of T As {Class, ICloneable, New})


End Class
```

It is worth mentioning that providing a nongeneric version of your class is not necessary. In this way you can provide different implementations for your generic types. Now consider the following overloading attempt:

```
Class CustomType(Of T1, T2)


End Class


'Fails at compile time


Class CustomType(Of T1 As IComparable, T2 As ICloneable)


End Class
```

This code is not compiled because although in the second definition some constraints are defined, the type implementation is considered by the compiler with the same identical signature. Similarly you can provide overloaded methods using techniques learned in Chapter 7, "Class Fundamentals," but against generic methods as demonstrated in the following code:

```
Sub DoSomething(Of T1, T2)(ByVal argument1 As T1, ByVal argument2 As T2)


End Sub


Sub DoSomething(Of T)(ByVal argument As T)


End Sub
```

Overloading provides great granularity over Generics implementation, and you will often see examples in built-in generic collections.

Introducing Nullable Types

As we mentioned talking about value types and reference types, value types have a default value that is typically zero whereas reference types have a default value that is Nothing. This is because a reference type can store null values, whereas value types cannot. Attempting to assign a null value to a value type would result in resetting to the default value for that type. This is a limitation, because there are situations in which you need to also store null values in value types, for example when fetching data from a SQL Server database. You can have a hypothetical Orders table where the Ship date column enables null values. SQL Server has its own data types, and one of these is the DBNull that enables null values. Because Visual Basic 2010 enables mapping SQL Server data types to .NET data types, as you see in Part 4, "Data Access with ADO.NET and LINQ," it could be a problem trying to map a NULL type in SQL Server into a DateTime type in VB. To avoid such problems, starting from .NET Framework 2.0, Microsoft introduced the *Nullable types*.

14

WHY NULLABLE TYPES IN THIS CHAPTER?

I'm covering nullable types in this chapter because they are generic types and are required in the next chapters.

Nullable types were first introduced with Visual Basic 2005 and differ from other types because they can both have a value but can also have a null value. Nullable types are generic types, and variables are declared as Nullable(Of T) or adding a question mark just after the type name. You declare a nullable value type as follows:

```
Dim nullInt As Nullable(Of Integer)
```

You can also add inline initialization:

```
Dim nullInt As Nullable(Of Integer) = Nothing
```

Nullable types expose two properties, HasValue and Value. The first one is of type Boolean and allows understanding if a variable stores a value so that you can avoid using it if it is null. The second one returns the actual value of the type. For example, the following code checks if the preceding declared nullInt variable has a value and shows its value if it has one:

```
'Has no value, so WriteLine is not executed
If nullInt.HasValue Then
```

```
    Console.WriteLine(nullInt.Value)
End If
```

Because we assigned `Nothing`, `HasValue` is `False`. The next example declares a `Boolean` nullable and demonstrates how you can use the value. Moreover, the code shows the alternative syntax for declaring nullable types, writing the question mark:

```
Dim nullBool As Boolean? = False
If nullBool.HasValue Then
    Console.WriteLine(nullBool.Value)
End If
```

Nullable types also expose a method called `GetValueOrDefault` which returns the current value for the type instance if the `HasValue` property is `True`. If `HasValue` is `False`, the method returns the default value for the type or the specified default value. The following code describes how you use `GetValueOrDefault`:

```
Dim anInt As Integer? = 10
'HasValue is True, so returns 10
Dim anotherInt As Integer = anInt.GetValueOrDefault

Dim anInt As Integer?
'HasValue is False, so returns 0
'which is the default Value for Integer
Dim anotherInt As Integer = anInt.GetValueOrDefault

Dim anInt As Integer?
'HasValue is False, so returns the default value
'specified as the method argument
Dim anotherInt As Integer = anInt.GetValueOrDefault(10)

Dim anInt As Integer? = 5
'HasValue is True, so returns the current value
'while the method argument is ignored
Dim anotherInt As Integer = anInt.GetValueOrDefault(10)
```

Using nullables is straightforward, and you will understand why they are so useful in Part 5, "Building Windows Applications."

Summary

Generics are a great benefit in the .NET development with Visual Basic 2010. Generics are .NET types that can adapt their behavior to different kinds of objects without the need of defining a separate version of the type. In other words, you can implement an only generic type being able to work with integers, strings, custom reference types and any other .NET type with a single implementation. They provide several benefits, including strongly typed programming, IntelliSense support and better performance. Basically

Generics require the Of keyword to specify the type parameter that you can manipulate in your object body.

Brief Reminder

Remember that you should first check if one of the built-in generic types satisfies your needs before you create a new custom one. This will avoid additional work and error possibilities.

Within Generics definition you can implement your own custom methods both in the usual fashion and as generic methods, which basically still require the Of keyword followed by the type specification. Generics are also very flexible thanks to the constraints feature. It allows accepting only types that accord to the specified requirements, such as interfaces implementation, inheritance, presence of an explicit constructor. Nullable types are special generic types that allow null values for value types. They basically work like other types but expose a HasValue property for checking if the object is null or populated. During the rest of the book you will find hundreds of Generics usages, especially after Chapter 16 where I will cover collections and generic collections.

14

Delegates and Events

Until now you saw how to create and manipulate your objects, working with the result of operations performed onto object instances or shared members. All the work we made until now does not provide a way for understanding the moment when a particular thing happens or for being notified of a happening. In.NET development, as for many other programming environments, getting notifications for happenings and knowing the moment when something happens is accomplished handling *events*, which are information that an object sends to the caller, such as the user interface or a thread, about its state so that the caller can make decisions according to the occurred event. Events in .NET programming are powerful and provide great granularity about controlling each happening. This granularity can take place because of another feature named *delegates*, which provide the real infrastructure for event-based programming and, because of this, we first discuss delegates before going into the events discussion.

Understanding Delegates

Delegates are *type safe* function pointers. The main difference between classic function pointers (such as C++ pointers) and delegates is that function pointers can point anywhere, and this can be dangerous, whereas delegates can point only to those methods that respect delegates' signatures. Delegates hold a reference to a procedure (its address) and enable applications to invoke different methods at runtime, but such methods must adhere to the delegate signature; moreover, delegates enable invoking a method from another object. This is important according to the main purpose of delegates, which is offering an infrastructure for handling events.

WHERE ARE DELEGATES USED?

Generally delegates are used in event handling architectures, but they are powerful and can be used in other advanced techniques. You find examples of delegates usage in multithreading or in LINQ expressions. In Chapter 21, "Advanced Language Features," you learn about lambda expressions that enable implementing delegates on-the-fly.

Delegates are reference types deriving from `System.Delegate`. Because of this they can also be defined at namespace level, as you might recall from Chapter 9, "Organizing Types Within Namespaces," or at the class and module level as well. In the next section you learn to define delegates. Pay attention to this topic, because delegates have their particular syntax for being defined and that can be a little bit confusing.

Declaring Delegates

A delegate is defined via the `Delegate` keyword followed by the method signature it needs to implement. Such a signature can be referred to as a `Sub` or as a `Function` and may or may not receive arguments. The following code defines a delegate that can handle reference to methods able to check an email address, providing the same signature of the delegate:

```
Public Delegate Function IsValidMailAddress(ByVal emailAddress _
                                 As String) As Boolean
```

DELEGATES SUPPORT GENERICS

Delegates support generics, meaning that you can define a `Delegate Function (Of T)` or `Delegate Sub(Of T)`.

Notice that `IsValidMailAddress` is a type and not a method as the syntax might imply. `emailAddress` is a variable containing the email address to check while any methods respecting the signature return a Boolean value depending on the check result. To use a delegate, you need to create an instance of it. The delegate's constructor requires you to specify an `AddressOf` clause pointing to the actual method that accomplishes the required job. After you get the instance, the delegate points to the desired method that you can call using the `Invoke` method. The following code demonstrates the described steps:

```
'The method's signature is the same of the delegate: correct
Function CheckMailAddress(ByVal emailAddress As String) As Boolean

    'Validates emails via regular expressions, according to the
```

```
    'following pattern
    Dim validateMail As String = "^([\w-\.]+)@((\[[0-9]{1,3}\." & _
        "[0-9]{1,3}\.)¦(([\w-]+\.)+))([a-zA-z]{2,4}¦[0-9]{1,3})(\]?)$"

    Return Text.RegularExpressions.Regex.IsMatch(emailAddress,
                                                 validateMail)
End Function

Sub Main()
    'Creates an instance of the delegate and points to
    'the specified method
    Dim mailCheck As New IsValidMailAddress(AddressOf CheckMailAddress)

    'You invoke a delegate via the Invoke method
    Dim result As Boolean = mailCheck.
                            Invoke("alessandro.delsole@visual-basic.it")
    Console.WriteLine("Is valid: {0}", result)
End Sub
```

At this point you might wonder why delegates are so interesting if they require so much code just for a simple invocation. The first reason is that you can provide how many methods you like that respect the delegate signature and decide which of the available methods to invoke. For example, the following code provides an alternative (and much simplified) version of the CheckMailAddress method, named CheckMailAddressBasic:

```
Function CheckMailAddressBasic(ByVal emailAddress As String) As Boolean
    Return emailAddress.Contains("@")

End Function
```

Although different, the method still respects the delegate signature. Now you can invoke the new method simply by changing the AddressOf clause, without changing code that calls Invoke for calling the method:

```
    'Alternative syntax: if you already declared
    'an instance, you can simply do this assignment
    mailCheck = AddressOf CheckMailAddressBasic

    'No changes here!
    Dim result As Boolean = mailCheck.
                            Invoke("alessandro.delsole@visual-basic.it")
    Console.WriteLine("Is valid: {0}", result)
```

If you still wonder why all this can be useful, consider a scenario in which you have hundreds of invocations to the same method. Instead of replacing all invocations, you simply change what the delegate is pointing to. `Invoke` is also the default member for the `Delegate` class, so you can simply rewrite the above invocation as follows:

```
Dim result As Boolean = mailCheck("alessandro.delsole@visual-basic.it")
```

This also works against methods that do not require arguments.

ADVANCED DELEGATES TECHNIQUES

Starting with Visual Basic 2008, the .NET Framework introduced new language features such as lambda expressions and relaxed delegates. Both are intended to work with delegates (and in the case of lambda expressions to replace them in some circumstances), but because of their strict relationship with LINQ, they are discussed in Chapter 21, which is preparatory for the famous data access technology.

Combining Delegates: Multicast Delegates

A delegate can hold a reference (that is, the address) to a method. It is possible to create delegates holding references to more than one method by creating multicast delegates. A multicast delegate is the combination of two or more delegates into a single delegate, providing the delegate the ability to make multiple invocations. The following code demonstrates how to create a multicast delegate, having two instances of the same delegate pointing to two different methods:

```
'The delegate is defined at namespace level
Public Delegate Sub WriteTextMessage(ByVal textMessage As String)


'....
Private textWriter As New WriteTextMessage(AddressOf WriteSomething)
Private complexWriter As New WriteTextMessage(AddressOf _
                                    WriteSomethingMoreComplex)

Private Sub WriteSomething(ByVal text As String)
    Console.WriteLine("Simply report your text: {0}", text)
End Sub

Private Sub WriteSomethingMoreComplex(ByVal text As String)
    Console.WriteLine("Today is {0} and you wrote {1}",
                Date.Today.ToShortDateString, text)
End Sub

'Because Combine returns System.Delegate, with Option Strict On
'an explicit conversion is required.
Private CombinedDelegate As WriteTextMessage = CType(System.Delegate.
                                Combine(textWriter,
                                complexWriter),
                                WriteTextMessage)
```

```
'....
CombinedDelegate.Invoke("Test message")
```

In this scenario you have two methods that behave differently, but both respect the delegate signature. A new delegate (`CombinedDelegate`) is created invoking the `System.Delegate.Combine` method that receives the series of delegates to be combined as arguments. It is worth mentioning that `Combine` returns a `System.Delegate`; therefore, an explicit conversion via `CType` is required with `Option Strict On`. With a single call to `CombinedDelegate.Invoke`, you can call both `WriteSomething` and `WriteSomethingMoreComplex`. The preceding code produces the following output:

```
Simply report your text: Test message
Today is 24/09/2009 and you wrote Test message
```

DELEGATE KEYWORD AND SYSTEM.DELEGATE

`Delegate` is a reserved keyword in Visual Basic. Because of this, to invoke the `System.Delegate.Combine` shared method the full name of the class has been utilized. You can still take advantage of the shortened syntax including `Delegate` within square brackets. In other words, you can write something like this: `[Delegate].Combine(params())`. This works because the `System` namespace is imported by default, and square parentheses make the compiler consider the enclosed word as the identifier of a class exposed by one of the imported namespaces, instead of a reserved keyword.

Handling Events

Events are members that enable objects to send information on their state to the caller. When something occurs, an event tells the caller that that things occurred so that the caller can make decisions on what actions to take. Generally you handle events in UI-based applications, although not always. The .NET Framework takes a huge advantage from delegates to create event infrastructures, and this is what you can do in creating your custom events. In this section you first learn how to catch existing events, and then you get information on creating your own events. This approach is good because it provides a way to understand how delegates are used in event handling.

Registering for events: AddHandler and RemoveHandler

To provide your applications the capability of intercepting events raised from any object, you need to register for events. Registering means giving your code a chance to receive notifications and to take actions when it is notified that an event was raised from an object. To register for an event notification, you use the `AddHandler` keyword that requires two arguments: The first one is the event exposed by the desired object, and the second one is a delegate pointing to a method executed when your code is notified of an event occurring. The code in Listing 15.1 shows an example using a System.Timers.Timer object.

LISTING 15.1   Registering and Catching Events

```
Public Class EventsDemo
    'Declares a Timer
    Private myTimer As Timers.Timer

    'A simple counter
    Private counter As Integer

    'Interval is the amount of time in ticks
    Public Sub New(ByVal interval As Double)
        'Register for notifications about the Elapsed event
        AddHandler myTimer.Elapsed, AddressOf increaseCounter
        'Assigns the Timer.Interval property
        Me.myTimer.Interval = interval
        Me.myTimer.Enabled = True
    End Sub

    'Method that adheres to the delegate signature and that is
    'executed each time our class get notifications about
    'the Elapsed event occurring
    Private Sub increaseCounter(ByVal sender As Object,
                                ByVal e As Timers.ElapsedEventArgs)
        counter += 1
    End Sub
End Class
```

Comments within Listing 15.1 should clarify the code. Notice how the AddHandler instruction tells the runtime what event from the Timer object must be intercepted (Elapsed). Also notice how, via the AddressOf keyword, you specify a method that performs some action when the event is intercepted. AddHandler at this particular point requires the method to respect the ElapsedEventHandler delegate signature. With this approach, the increaseCounter method is executed every time the System.Timers.Timer.Elapsed event is intercepted. AddHandler provides great granularity on controlling events, because it enables controlling shared events and works within a member body, too. The AddHandler counterpart is RemoveHandler, which enables deregistering from getting notifications. For example, you might want to deregister before a method completes its execution. Continuing with the example shown in Listing 15.1, you can deregister before you stop the timer:

```
RemoveHandler myTimer.Elapsed, AddressOf increaseCounter
Me.myTimer.Enabled = False
```

As you see in the next section, this is not the only way to catch events in Visual Basic.

Declaring Objects with the `WithEvents` Keyword

By default, when you declare a variable for an object that exposes events, Visual Basic cannot see those events. This is also the case of the previous section's example, where you declare a `Timer` and then need to explicitly register for event handling. A solution to this scenario is to declare an object with the `WithEvents` keyword that makes events visible to Visual Basic. Thanks to `WithEvents`, you do not need to register for events, and you can take advantage of the `Handles` clause to specify what event a method is going to handle. The code in Listing 15.2 demonstrates this, providing a revisited version of the `EventsDemo` class.

LISTING 15.2   Catching Events with `WithEvents` and `Handles`

```
Public Class WithEventsDemo

    Private WithEvents myTimer As Timers.Timer

    Private counter As Integer

    Public Sub New(ByVal interval As Double)
        Me.myTimer.Interval = interval
        Me.myTimer.Enabled = True
    End Sub

    Private Sub increaseCounter(ByVal sender As Object,
                        ByVal e As Timers.ElapsedEventArgs) _
                        Handles myTimer.Elapsed

        counter += 1
    End Sub
End Class
```

Notice that if you do not specify a `Handle` clause, the code cannot handle the event, although it respects the appropriate delegate's signature.

WPF EXCEPTION

An exception to the last sentence is Windows Presentation Foundation (WPF). Because of the particular events' infrastructure (routed events), the code can catch events even if you do not explicitly provide a `Handles` clause. Of course, take care of this situation.

Offering Events to the External World

In the previous section you learned how to handle existing events. Now it's time to get your hands dirty on implementing and raising custom events within your own objects. Basically Visual Basic provides two ways for implementing events: the `Event` keyword and custom events, an addition still alive from VB 2005. Let's discover both of them.

Raising Events

You declare your own events utilizing the `Event` keyword. This keyword requires you to specify the event name and eventually a delegate signature. Although not mandatory (`Event` allows specifying no arguments), specifying a delegate signature is useful so that you can take advantage of `AddHandler` for subsequently intercepting events. The code in Listing 15.3 shows an alternative implementation of the `Person` class in which an event is raised each time the `LastName` property is modified.

LISTING 15.3   Implementing and Raising Events

```
Public Class Person
    Public Event LastNameChanged(ByVal sender As Object,
                                 ByVal e As EventArgs)

    Public Property FirstName As String

    Private _lastName As String
    Public Property LastName As String

        Get
            Return _lastName
        End Get
        Set(ByVal value As String)
            If value <> _lastName Then
                _lastName = value
                RaiseEvent LastNameChanged(Me, EventArgs.Empty)
            End If
        End Set
    End Property

End Class
```

Notice that in this particular case you need to implement the `LastName` property the old-fashioned way, so that you can perform subsequent manipulations. The code checks that the property value changes; then the `LastNameChanged` event is raised, and this is accomplished via the `RaiseEvent` keyword. Also notice how the `LastNameChanged` event definition adheres to the `EventHandler` delegate signature. This can be considered as the most general delegate for the events infrastructure. The delegate defines two arguments: The

first one, which is generally named `sender`, is of type `Object` and represents the object
that raised the event and a second argument, generally named e, of type
`System.EventArgs` that is the base type for classes containing events information. You get
a deeper example in next section. At this point intercepting the event is simple. You just
need to register for event notifications or create an instance of the `Person` class with
`WithEvents`. The following code demonstrates this:

```
Sub TestEvent()
    Dim p As New Person
    AddHandler p.LastNameChanged,
            AddressOf personEventHandler
    p.LastName = "Del Sole"
    Console.ReadLine()
End Sub

Private Sub personEventHandler(ByVal sender As Object,
                        ByVal e As EventArgs)
    Console.WriteLine("LastName property was changed")
End Sub
```

Now every time you change the value of the `LastName` property you can intercept the edit.

Passing Event Information

In the previous code example you got a basic idea about passing event information via the
base `System.EventArgs` class. In the .NET Framework you can find hundreds of classes that
inherit from `System.EventArgs` and that enable passing custom event information to
callers. This is useful whenever you need additional information on what happened
during the event handling. Continuing with the previous example, imagine you want to
check if the `LastName` property value contains blank spaces while you raise the
`LastNameChanged` event, sending to callers this information. This can be accomplished
creating a new class that inherits from `System.EventArgs`. Listing 15.4 shows how you can
implement the class and how you can take advantage of it in the `Person` class.

LISTING 15.4   Providing Custom Event Information

```
Public Class LastNameChangedEventArgs
    Inherits EventArgs

    Private _lastName As String
    Public ReadOnly Property LastName As String
        Get
            Return _lastName
        End Get
    End Property

    Public ReadOnly Property ContainsBlank As Boolean
```

```
            Get
                Return Me.LastName.Contains(" ")
            End Get
        End Property

        Public Sub New(ByVal lastName As String)
            Me._lastName = lastName
        End Sub
    End Class

Public Class Person
    Private _lastName As String
    Public Property LastName As String

        Get
            Return _lastName
        End Get
        Set(ByVal value As String)
            If value <> _lastName Then
                _lastName = value
                Dim e As New LastNameChangedEventArgs(value)
                RaiseEvent LastNameChanged(Me, e)
            End If
        End Set
    End Property

    Public Event LastNameChanged(ByVal sender As Object,
                        ByVal e As LastNameChangedEventArgs)

End Class
```

Notice how the LastNameChangedEventArgs class exposes public properties representing information you want to return to the caller. When raising the event in the Person class, you create a new instance of the LastNameChangedEventArgs and pass the required information elaborated by the instance. Now you can change the event handler described in the previous section as follows:

```
    Private Sub personEventHandler(ByVal sender As Object,
                        ByVal e As LastNameChangedEventArgs)
        Console.WriteLine("LastName property was changed")
        Console.WriteLine("Last name contains blank spaces: " &
                        e.ContainsBlank)
    End Sub
```

In this way you can easily handle additional event information. Finally, it is important to understand how you can get the instance of the object that raised the event, because it is something that you will often use in your applications. You accomplish this by simply converting the sender into the appropriate type. The following code shows how to get the instance of the Person class that raised the above LastNameChanged event:

```
Dim raisingPerson As Person = DirectCast(sender, Person)
```

Creating Custom Events

Starting from Visual Basic 2005, you have the ability to define your own events implementing the *custom events*. They are useful because they provide a kind of relationship with a delegate. Generally custom events are also useful in multithreaded applications. You declare a custom event via the Custom Event keywords combination, supplying the event name and signature as follows:

```
Public Custom Event AnEvent As EventHandler
    AddHandler(ByVal value As EventHandler)

    End AddHandler

    RemoveHandler(ByVal value As EventHandler)

    End RemoveHandler

    RaiseEvent(ByVal sender As Object, ByVal e As System.EventArgs)

    End RaiseEvent
End Event
```

IntelliSense is very cool here, because when you type the event declaration and press **Enter**, it adds a skeleton for the custom event that is constituted by three members: AddHandler is triggered when the caller subscribes for an event with the AddHandler instruction; RemoveHandler is triggered when the caller removes an event registration; and RaiseEvent is triggered when the event is raised. In this basic example the new event is of the type EventHandler, which is a delegate that represents an event storing no information and that is the most general delegate. Now take a look at the following example that demonstrates how to implement a custom event that can affect all instances of the Person class:

```
Public Delegate Sub FirstNameChangedHandler(ByVal info As String)


Dim handlersList As New List(Of FirstNameChangedHandler)

Public Custom Event FirstNameChanged As FirstNameChangedHandler
    AddHandler(ByVal value As FirstNameChangedHandler)
        handlersList.Add(value)
        Debug.WriteLine("AddHandler invoked")
```

15

```
        End AddHandler

        RemoveHandler(ByVal value As FirstNameChangedHandler)
            If handlersList.Contains(value) Then
                handlersList.Remove(value)
                Debug.WriteLine("RemoveHandler invoked")
            End If
        End RemoveHandler

        RaiseEvent(ByVal info As String)
            'Performs the same action on all instances
            'of the Person class
            For Each del As FirstNameChangedHandler In handlersList
                'del.Invoke(info ......
            Next
        End RaiseEvent
    End Event
```

This code provides an infrastructure for handling changes on the FirstName property in the Person class. In this case we build a list of delegates that is populated when the caller registers with AddHandler. When the caller invokes RemoveHandler, the delegate is popped from the list. The essence of this resides in the RaiseEvent stuff, which implements a loop for performing the same operation on all instances of the delegate and therefore of the Person class. To raise custom events you use the RaiseEvent keyword. For this, you need to edit the FirstName property implementation in the Person class as follows:

```
    Private _firstName As String
    Public Property FirstName As String

        Get
            Return _firstName
        End Get
        Set(ByVal value As String)
            If value <> _firstName Then
                _firstName = value
                RaiseEvent FirstNameChanged(FirstName)
            End If
        End Set
    End Property
```

You raise the event the same way for noncustom events, with the difference that custom events provide deep control over what is happening when the caller registers, deregisters, or raises the event.

Summary

Delegates are type-safe function pointers that store the address of a Sub or Function, enabling the invoking of different methods at runtime. Delegates are reference types declared via the Delegate keyword and that enable invoking methods via the Invoke method. They can be used in different programming techniques, but the most important scenario where you use delegates is within event-based programming. Events take advantage of delegates in that the objects require their signature to be respected. Coding events is something that can be divided into main areas, such as catching events and exposing events from your objects. To catch events you can register and deregister via the AddHandler and RemoveHandler keywords, or you simply declare objects exposing events via the WithEvents reserved word, and then you provide event handlers respecting the appropriate delegate signature and adding the Handles clause. You instead define your own events in two ways: via the Event keyword or with custom events. The advantage of providing custom events is that you can have deep control over the event phases, such as registering and deregistering. In this discussion, it is important to remember that you can provide custom event information creating classes that inherit from System.EventArgs where you can store information useful to the caller.

15

CHAPTER 16

Working with Collections

Applications often require working with data. Until now you got information on how to store data within classes and structures, but it is common for you to need to create groups of data. In .NET development this is accomplished using special classes known as *collections*, which enable storing a set of objects within one class. The .NET Framework provides lots of collections, each of them specific to a particular need or scenario. The main distinction is between nongeneric collections and generic collections, but all of them can store a set of objects. Collections are not merely groups of data. They are the backend infrastructure for engines such as the ADO.NET Entity Framework and LINQ, so understanding collections is an important task. At a higher level collections infrastructure is offered by the System.Collections namespace and by some interfaces that bring polymorphism to collections. In this chapter you learn about the .NET Framework's collections, both nongeneric and generic ones. You also learn how to create and consume custom collections, and you get an overview of concurrent collections.

Understanding Collections Architecture

Collections are special classes that can store sets of objects; the .NET Framework offers both nongeneric and generic collections. Whatever kind of collection you work on, collections implement some interfaces. The first one is ICollection that derives from IEnumerable and provides both the enumerator (which enables For..Each iterations) and special members, such as Count (which returns the number of items within a collection) and CopyTo (which copies a collection to an array). Collections also implement IList or IDictionary; both inherit from ICollection and expose members that enable adding, editing, and removing items from a collection. The difference is that IDictionary works with key/value pairs instead of single objects as IList.

The previously mentioned interfaces are about nongeneric collections. If you work with generic collections, the collections implement the generic counterpart of those interfaces such as ICollection(Of T), IList(Of T), and IDictionary(Of TKey, TValue). It's important to understand this implementation because this provides similarities between collections so that you can learn members from one collection and be able to reuse them against other kinds of collections.

USE THE OBJECT BROWSER

Remember that the Object Browser tool can provide thorough information on objects' architecture meaning that if you don't remember what members are exposed by a collection, this tool can be your best friend.

Working with Nongeneric Collections

The System.Collections namespace defines several nongeneric collections. The namespace also defines interfaces mentioned in the previous section. Here you learn to work with nongeneric collections so that in the next section you can easily understand why generic ones are more efficient.

The ArrayList Collection

System.Collections.ArrayList is the most common nongeneric collection in the .NET Framework and represents an ordered set of items. With the word *ordered* we mean that you add items to the collection one after the other, which is different from sorting. ArrayList collections can store any .NET type because, at a higher level, it accepts items of type Object. The following code shows how you can create a new ArrayList and how you can set how many items it can contain by setting the Capacity property:

```
Dim mixedCollection As New ArrayList
mixedCollection.Capacity = 10
```

Adding new items to an ArrayList is a simple task. To accomplish this you invoke the Add method that receives as an argument the object you want to add, as demonstrated by the following snippet:

```
mixedCollection.Add(32)
mixedCollection.Add("32")
mixedCollection.Add("Alessandro")
mixedCollection.Add(Date.Today)
```

The preceding code adds an Integer, two Strings, and a Date. Of course, you can also add composite custom types. Always be careful with ArrayLists. The first two items' value is

32, but the first one is an `Integer` whereas the second is a `String`. If you would like to compare such items or iterate them, you should explicitly convert from `String` to `Integer` or vice versa, and this would require boxing/unboxing operations. Generally you work with collections of a single type; therefore, I suggest you avoid nongeneric collections in favor of generic ones. For example, if you have to work with a set of strings, you should use the `List(Of String)`. The second part of this chapter discusses generic collections.

WHY YOU SHOULD PREFER GENERICS

The second part of this chapter is about generic collections. You should prefer this kind of collections for two reasons; the first is that they are strongly typed and avoid the possibility of errors that can be caused when working with items of type `Object`. The second reason is that each time you add a value type to a nongeneric collection, the type is first subject to boxing (that was discussed in Chapter 4, "Data Types and Expressions") that can cause performance overhead and does not provide the best object management.

You can also add a block of items in a single invocation using the `AddRange` method. The following code shows how you can add an array of strings to the existing collection:

```
Dim anArray() As String = {"First", "Second", "Third"}
mixedCollection.AddRange(anArray)
```

Add and AddRange add items after the last existing item. You might want to add items at a specified position. This can be accomplished via the `Insert` and `InsertRange` methods whose first argument is the position and the second one is the object. The following code demonstrates this:

```
mixedCollection.Insert(3, "New item")
mixedCollection.InsertRange(3, anArray)
```

To remove items from the collection you have two methods, `Remove` that enables removing a specific object and `RemoveAt` that enables removing the object at the specified position:

```
'Removes the string "32"
mixedCollection.RemoveAt(1)
'Removes 32

mixedCollection.Remove(32)
```

An interesting method is also `TrimToSize` that enables resizing the collection based on the number of items effectively stored. For example, consider the following code:

```
Dim mixedCollection As New ArrayList
mixedCollection.Capacity = 10
```

16

```
mixedCollection.Add(32)
mixedCollection.Add("32")
mixedCollection.Add("Alessandro")
mixedCollection.Add(Date.Today)

mixedCollection.TrimToSize()
```

When created, the ArrayList can store up to 10 items. After the TrimToSize invocation, Capacity's value is 4, which is the number of items effectively stored. If you have a large collection, the ArrayList provides a BinarySearch method that enables searching the collection for a specified item, returning the index of the item itself:

```
'Returns 2
Dim index As Integer = mixedCollection.BinarySearch("Alessandro")
```

If the item is not found within the collection, the return value is a negative number. If the collection contains more than one item matching the search criteria, BinarySearch returns only one item which is not necessarily the first one. This collection also exposes other interesting members that are summarized in Table 16.1.

TABLE 16.1   ArrayList Members

Member	Description
Count	A property that returns the number of items within the collection.
CopyTo	A method that copies the ArrayList instance into an array.
Contains	A method that returns True if the specified item exists within the collection.
ToArray	Copies the content of the ArrayList into an array of Object.
IndexOf	Returns the zero base index of the specified item.
GetRange	Creates a new ArrayList that is just a subset of the initial one, based on the specified criteria.
Sort	Performs a sorting operation over the collection.
Reverse	Performs a descending sorting operation over the collection.
Item	Property that gets or sets an item at the specified index. This is the default property of the ArrayList class.
Clear	Removes all items from the collection.

You can access an item from the ArrayList using the index as follows:

```
Dim anItem As Object = mixedCollection(0)
```

Of course, you need to perform a conversion into the appropriate type, which is something that you can accomplish in line if you already know the type:

```
Dim anItem As Integer = CInt(mixedCollection(0))
```

If the conversion fails, an `InvalidCastException` is thrown. The `ArrayList` implements the `IList` interface and thus can take advantage of the enumerator; therefore, you can iterate it via a `For..Each` loop as follows:

```
For Each item As Object In mixedCollection
    Console.WriteLine(item.ToString)

Next
```

You just need to pay attention to the fact that each item is treated as an `Object`; therefore, you must be aware of conversions. The `ArrayList` collection provides members that you find in other kinds of collections, so this is the reason why the most common members are discussed here.

The Queue Collection

The `System.Collections.Queue` collection works according to the FIFO (First-In, First-Out) paradigm, meaning that the first item you add to the collection is the first pulled out from the collection. `Queue` exposes two methods, `Enqueue` that adds a new item to the collection and `Dequeue` that removes an item from the collection. Both methods receive an argument of type `Object`. The following code provides an example:

```
Sub QueueDemo()

    Dim q As New Queue
    q.Enqueue(1)
    q.Enqueue(2)

    'Returns
    '1
    '2
    Console.WriteLine(q.Dequeue)
    Console.WriteLine(q.Dequeue)

End Sub
```

You just need to invoke the `Dequeue` method to consume and automatically remove an item from the collection. You can also invoke the `Peek` method which just returns the first item from the collection without removing it. Always be careful when adding items to a

16

queue because you are working in a fashion that is not strongly typed. If you plan to work with objects of a specified type (for example, you need a collection of `Integer`), consider using a `Queue(Of T)` that behaves the same way except that it is strongly typed. The collection also exposes a `Count` property that returns the number of items in the collection. The constructor provides an overload that enables specifying the capacity for the collection.

The Stack Collection

The `System.Collections.Stack` collection mimics the same-named memory area and works according to the LIFO (Last-In, First-Out) paradigm meaning that the last item you add to the collection is the first that is pulled out from the collection. `Stack` exposes three important methods: `Push` that adds an item to the collection, `Pop` that allows consuming and removing an item from the collection, and `Peek` that returns the top item in the collection without removing it. The following is an example:

```
Dim s As New Stack


s.Push(1)
s.Push(2)


'Returns 2 and leaves it in the collection
Console.WriteLine(s.Peek)
'Returns 2 and removes it
Console.WriteLine(s.Pop)
'Returns 1 and removes it
Console.WriteLine(s.Pop)
```

As for `Queue`, here you work with `Object` items. Although this enables pushing different kinds of objects to the collection, it is not a good idea. You should prefer the generic counterpart (`Stack(Of T)`) that enables working with a single type in a strongly typed fashion. The `Stack` collection also exposes the `Count` property which returns the number of objects that it stores.

The HashTable Collection

The `System.Collections.HashTable` collection can store items according to a key/value pair, where both key and value are of type `Object`. The `HashTable` peculiarity is that its items are organized based on the hash code of the key. The following code provides an example:

```
Dim ht As New Hashtable
ht.Add("Alessandro", "Del Sole")
ht.Add("A string", 32)
ht.Add(3.14, New Person)


'Number of items
Console.WriteLine(ht.Count)
```

```
'Removes an item based on the key
ht.Remove("Alessandro")
```

Items within a `HashTable` can be accessed by the key, as shown in the last line of code in the preceding example. It also offers two methods named `ContainsKey` and `ContainsValue` that enable checking if a key or a value exists within the collection, as demonstrated here:

```
'Checks if a key/value exists
Dim checkKey As Boolean = ht.ContainsKey("A string")
Dim checkValue As Boolean = ht.ContainsValue(32)
```

Note that if you do not check if a key already exist, as in the preceding example, and attempt to add a key that already exists, then an `ArgumentException` is thrown. This is because keys must be unique. A single item within the collection is of type `DictionaryEntry` that exposed two properties, `Key` and `Value`. For example, you can iterate a `HashTable` as follows:

```
'iterate items
For Each item As DictionaryEntry In ht
    Console.WriteLine("{0} {1}", item.Key, item.Value)
Next
```

`HashTable` also offers two other properties named `Keys` and `Values` that return an `ICollection` containing respectively keys in the key/value pair and values in the same pair, as demonstrated here:

```
'iterate keys
For Each key As Object In ht.Keys
    Console.WriteLine(key)
Next
```

It is recommend that you use a strongly typed `Dictionary(Of T, T)` that provides more efficiency. (And this suggestion is appropriate when discussing other dictionaries.)

The `ListDictionary` Collection

The `System.Collections.Specialized.ListDictionary` collection works exactly like `HashTable` but it differs in that it is more efficient until it stores up to 10 items. It is not preferred once the items count exceeds 10.

The `OrderedDictionary` Collection

The `System.Collections.Specialized.OrderedDictionary` collection works like `HashTable` but it differs in that items can be accessed via either the key or the index, as demonstrated by the following code:

```
Dim od As New OrderedDictionary
od.Add("a", 1)
```

```
'Access via index
Dim item As DictionaryEntry = CType(od(0), DictionaryEntry)
Console.WriteLine(item.Value)
```

The SortedList Collection

The System.Collections.SortedList collection works like HashTable but it differs in that items can be accessed either via the key, or the index items are automatically sorted based on the key, for example, look at the following code:

```
Dim sl As New SortedList
sl.Add("Del Sole", 2)
sl.Add("Alessandro", 1)

For Each item As String In sl.Keys
    Console.WriteLine(item)
Next
```

It sorts items based on the key; therefore, it produces the following result:

```
Alessandro
Del Sole
```

The HybridDictionary Collection

The System.Collections.Specialized.HybridDictionary collection is a dynamic class in that it implements a ListDictionary until the number of items is small and then switches to HashTable if the number of items grows large. Technically it works like HashTable.

The StringCollection Collection

The System.Collections.Specialized.StringCollection is similar to the ArrayList collection except that it is limited to accepting only strings. The following code provides an example:

```
Dim stringDemo As New StringCollection


stringDemo.Add("Alessandro")
stringDemo.Add("Del Sole")

'Returns True
Dim containsString As Boolean = stringDemo.Contains("Del Sole")

stringDemo.Remove("Alessandro")
```

Basically you can use the same members of ArrayList and perform the same operations.

The `StringDictionary` Collection

The `System.Collections.Specialized.StringDictionary` collection works like the `HashTable` collection but differs in that it accepts only key/value pairs of type `String`, meaning that both keys and values must be `String`. The following is a small example:

```
Dim stringDemo As New StringDictionary


stringDemo.Add("Key1", "Value1")
stringDemo.Add("Alessandro", "Del Sole")

'Simple iteration
For Each value As String In stringDemo.Values
    Console.WriteLine(value)
Next
```

You can recall the `HashTable` collection for a full member listing.

The `NameValueCollection` Collection

The `NameValueCollection` behaves similarly to the `StringDictionary` collection, but it differs in that `NameValueCollection` enables accessing items via either the key or the index. The following code snippet provides a brief demonstration:

```
Dim nv As New NameValueCollection


nv.Add("First string", "Second string")

Dim item As String = nv(0)
```

The `Add` method also provides an overload accepting another `NameValueCollection` as an argument.

The `BitArray` Collection

The `System.Collections.BitArray` collection enables storing bit values represented by Boolean values. A `True` value indicates that a bit is on (1) whereas a `False` value indicates that a bit is off (0). You can pass to the `BitArray` arrays of `Integer` numbers or Boolean values, as demonstrated by the following code:

```
Dim byteArray() As Byte = New Byte() {1, 2, 3}
'Length in zero base
Dim ba As New BitArray(byteArray)

For Each item As Object In ba
    Console.WriteLine(item.ToString)
Next
```

16

This code produces the following output, which is a human-readable representation of the bits in the collection:

```
True
False
False
False
False
False
False
False
False
True
False
False
False
False
False
False
True
True
False
False
False
False
False
False
```

The constructor also accepts a `length` argument that enables specifying how large the collection must be.

The `BitVector32` Collection

`System.Collections.Specialized.BitVector32` has basically the same purpose of `BitArray` but it differs in two important elements; the first one is that `BitVector32` is a structure that is a value type and therefore can take advantage of a faster memory allocation. On the other hand, the collection manages only 32-bit integers. All data is stored as 32-bit integers that are effectively affected by changes when you edit the collection. The most important (shared) method is `CreateMask` that enables creating a mask of bits. The method can create an empty mask (which is typically for the first bit) or create subsequent masks pointing to the previous bit. When done, you can set the bit on or off passing a Boolean value. The following code provides an example:

```
'Passing zero to the constructor
'ensures that all bits are clear
Dim bv As New BitVector32(0)
```

```
Dim bitOne As Integer = BitVector32.CreateMask
Dim bitTwo As Integer = BitVector32.CreateMask(bitOne)
Dim bitThree As Integer = BitVector32.CreateMask(bitTwo)

bv(bitOne) = True
bv(bitTwo) = False
bv(bitThree) = True
```

The Data property stores the actual value of the collection, as demonstrated here:

```
'Returns 5 (the first bit + the second bit = the third bit)
Console.WriteLine(bv.Data)
```

If you instead want to get the binary representation of the data, you can simply use the name of the instance. The following code demonstrates this:

```
Console.WriteLine(bv)
```

This code produces the following result:

```
BitVector32{00000000000000000000000000000101}
```

MEMBERS AND EXTENSION METHODS

Collections provide special members, such as properties and methods, and are extended by most of the built-in extension methods. Providing a thorough discussion on each member is not possible; IntelliSense can put you in the right direction to provide explanations for each member. Moreover each member has a self-explanatory identifier; therefore, it is difficult to understand what a member does when you understand the high-level logic. In this chapter you are introduced to the most important members from collections so that you can perform the most common operations.

Working with Generic Collections

The .NET Framework offers generic counterparts of the collections described in the previous section. Moreover, it offers new generic collections that are specific to particular technologies such as WPF. In this section you learn to work with generic built-in collections and how you can take advantage of a strongly typed fashion. Generic collections are exposed by the System.Collections.Generic namespace except a different namespace is explained.

The List(Of T) Collection

The System.Collections.Generic.List(Of T) collection is a generic ordered list of items. It is a strongly typed collection, meaning that it can accept only members of the specified type. It is useful because it provides support for adding, editing, and removing items

16

within the collection. For example, imagine you need to store a series of `Person` objects to a collection. This can be accomplished as follows:

```
Dim person1 As New Person With {.FirstName = "Alessandro",
                                .LastName = "Del Sole",
                                .Age = 32}
Dim person2 As New Person With {.FirstName = "XXXXX",
                                .LastName = "ZZZZZZZZ",
                                .Age = 44}
Dim person3 As New Person With {.FirstName = "YYYYY",
                                .LastName = "DDDDDDDD",
                                .Age = 18}

Dim personList As New List(Of Person)
personList.Add(person1)
personList.Add(person2)
personList.Add(person3)
```

You notice that the `List(Of T)` has lots of members in common with its nongeneric counterpart that is the `ArrayList`. This is because the first one implements the `IList(Of T)` interface, whereas the second one implements `IList` but both provide the same members with the generics difference. The following code shows how you can access an item within the collection using the `IndexOf` method and how you can remove an item invoking the `Remove` method, passing the desired instance of the `Person` class:

```
'Returns the index for Person2
Dim specificPersonIndex As Integer = personList.IndexOf(person2)

'Removes person3
personList.Remove(person3)
```

The `List(Of T)` still provides members such as `Capacity`, `AddRange`, `Insert`, and `InsertRange` whereas it exposes a method named `TrimExcess` that works like the `ArrayList.TrimToSize`. Because the `List(Of T)` implements the `IEnumerable(Of T)` interface, you can then iterate the collection using a classic `For..Each` loop but each item is strongly typed, as demonstrated here:

```
For Each p As Person In personList
    Console.WriteLine(p.LastName)
Next
```

If you need to remove all items from a collection, you can invoke the `Clear` method, and when you do not need the collection anymore, you simply assign it to `Nothing`:

```
personList.Clear()
personList = Nothing
```

There are also other interesting ways to interact with a collection, such as special extension methods. Extension methods are discussed in Chapter 21, "Advanced Language Features." For now, you simply need to know that they are special methods provided by the IEnumerable(Of T) interface that enables performing particular operations against a collection. For example, the Single method enables retrieving the unique instance of a type that matches the specified criteria:

```
'Returns a unique Person whose LastName
'property is Del Sole
Dim specificPerson As Person = personList.Single(Function(p) _
                               p.LastName = "Del Sole")
```

This method receives a lambda expression as an argument that specifies the criteria. Lambda expressions are also discussed in Chapter 21. Another interesting method is FindAll, which enables generating a new List(Of T) containing all the type instances that match a particular criteria. The following snippet retrieves all the Person instances whose LastName property starts with the letter "D":

```
'Returns a new List(Of Person) storing
'all Person instances whose LastName starts
'with "D"
Dim specificPeople = personList.FindAll(Function(p) _

                       p.LastName.StartsWith("D"))
```

As usual IntelliSense can be your best friend in situations such as this. Because all members from each collection cannot be described here, that technology can help you understand the meaning and the usage of previously mentioned members whose names are always self-explanatory.

INVESTIGATING COLLECTIONS AT DEBUG TIME

You may remember from Chapter 5, "Debugging Visual Basic 2010 Applications," the Data Tips features of the Visual Studio debugger. They are useful if you need to investigate the content of collections while debugging, especially if you need to get information on how collections and their items are populated.

Working with Collection Initializers

Visual Basic 2010 introduces a new language feature known as *collection initializers*. Basically this feature works like the object initializers, except that it is specific for instantiating and populating collections inline. To take advantage of collection initializers, you need to use the From reserved keyword enclosing items within brackets, as demonstrated in the following code:

```
'With primitive types
Dim listOfIntegers As New List(Of Integer) From {1, 2, 3, 4}
```

16

The preceding code produces the same result as the following:

```
Dim listOfIntegers As New List(Of Integer)


listOfIntegers.Add(1)
listOfIntegers.Add(2)
listOfIntegers.Add(3)
listOfIntegers.Add(4)
```

You can easily understand how collection initializers enable writing less code that's more clear. This feature can also be used with any other .NET type. The following code snippet shows how you can instantiate inline a `List(Of Person)`:

```
'With custom types
Dim person1 As New Person With {.FirstName = "Alessandro",
                                .LastName = "Del Sole",
                                .Age = 32}
Dim person2 As New Person With {.FirstName = "XXXXX",
                                .LastName = "ZZZZZZZZ",
                                .Age = 44}
Dim person3 As New Person With {.FirstName = "YYYYY",
                                .LastName = "DDDDDDDD",
                                .Age = 18}

Dim people As New List(Of Person) From {person1,
                                        person2,
                                        person3}
```

The code also shows how you can take advantage of implicit line continuation if you have long lines for initializations. When you have an instance of the new collection, you can normally manipulate it. Of course, this feature works with any other collection type.

NON GENERIC COLLECTIONS

Collection initializers are also supported by nongeneric collections using the same syntax.

The ReadOnlyCollection(Of T) Collection

The `System.Collections.ObjectModel.ReadOnlyCollection(Of T)` is the read-only counterpart of the `List(Of T)` class. Being read-only, you can add items to the collection only when you create an instance, but then you cannot change it. The constructor requires an argument of type `IList(Of T)` so that the new collection will be generated starting from an existing one. The following code demonstrates how you can instantiate a new `ReadonlyCollection`:

```
Dim person1 As New Person With {.FirstName = "Alessandro",
                                .LastName = "Del Sole",
                                .Age = 32}
Dim person2 As New Person With {.FirstName = "XXXXX",
                                .LastName = "ZZZZZZZZ",
                                .Age = 44}
Dim person3 As New Person With {.FirstName = "YYYYY",
                                .LastName = "DDDDDDDD",
                                .Age = 18}

Dim people As New List(Of Person) From {person1, person2, person3}

Dim readonlyPeople As New ReadOnlyCollection(Of Person)(people)
```

As an alternative, you can create a `ReadonlyCollection` invoking the `List(Of T).AsReadOnly` method, as shown in the following code:

```
'Same as above
Dim readonly As ReadOnlyCollection(Of Person) = people.AsReadOnly
```

Invoking `AsReadOnly` produces the same result of creating an explicit instance.

The `Dictionary(Of TKey, TValue)` Collection

The `System.Collections.Generic.Dictionary(Of TKey, TValue)` collection is the generic counterpart for the `HashTable`. Each item within a `Dictionary` is a key/value pair; therefore, the constructor requires two arguments (`TKey` and `TValue`) where the first one is the key and the second one is the value. The following code shows instantiating a `Dictionary(Of String, Integer)` in which the `String` argument contains a person's name and the `Integer` argument contains the person's age:

```
Dim peopleDictionary As New Dictionary(Of String, Integer)
peopleDictionary.Add("Alessandro", 32)
peopleDictionary.Add("Stephen", 27)

peopleDictionary.Add("Rod", 44)
```

A single item in the collection is of type `KeyValuePair(Of TKey, TValue)` and both arguments reflect the collection's ones. For a better explanation, take a look at the following iteration that performs an action on each `KeyValuePair`:

```
For Each item As KeyValuePair(Of String, Integer) In peopleDictionary
    Console.WriteLine(item.Key & " of age " & item.Value.ToString)
```

Next

The above code will produce the following output:

```
Alessandro of age 32
Stephen of age 27
Rod of age 44
```

Each `KeyValuePair` object has two properties, `Key` and `Value`, which enable separated access to parts composing the object. You can then manipulate the `Dictionary` like you would other collections.

The `SortedDictionary(Of TKey, TValue)` Collection

The `System.Collections.Generic.SortedDictionary(Of TKey, TValue)` works exactly like the `Dictionary` collection except that items are automatically sorted each time you perform a modification. We can rewrite the code shown in the section about the `Dictionary(Of TKey, TValue)` collection as follows:

```
Dim peopleDictionary As New SortedDictionary(Of String, Integer)

peopleDictionary.Add("Alessandro", 32)
peopleDictionary.Add("Stephen", 27)
peopleDictionary.Add("Rod", 44)

For Each item As KeyValuePair(Of String, Integer) In peopleDictionary
    Console.WriteLine(item.Key & " of age " & item.Value.ToString)

Next
```

This code will produce the following result:

```
Alessandro of age 32
Rod of age 44
Stephen of age 27
```

Notice how the result has a different order than the one we added items to the collection with. In fact, items are sorted alphabetically. This collection performs sorting based on the `Key` part.

The `ObservableCollection(Of T)` Collection

The `System.Collections.ObjectModel.ObservableCollection(Of T)` is a special collection that is typically used in WPF applications. Its main feature is that it implements the `INotifyPropertyChanged` interface, and therefore it can raise an event each time its items are affected by any changes, such as adding, replacing, or removing. Thanks to this mechanism, the `ObservableCollection` is the most appropriate collection for the WPF data-binding because it provides support for two-way data-binding in which the user interface gets notification of changes on the collection and is automatically refreshed to reflect those changes. Although a practical example of this scenario is offered in the chapters about WPF, this section shows you how the collection works. The first consideration is that such an object is defined by the WindowsBase.dll assembly that is added by default to WPF applications' references, whereas you need to manually add one in other kinds of applications. (This example uses the Console application template; therefore, you need to manually add a reference to the assembly to reproduce the code.) Second, the ObservableCollection is exposed by the System.Collections.ObjectModel namespace, meaning that you need to add an Imports directive for this namespace. Now consider the following code snippet:

```
Dim people As New ObservableCollection(Of Person)
AddHandler people.CollectionChanged,

        AddressOf CollectionChangedEventHandler
```

The people variable represents an instance of the collection, and its purpose is to store a set of Person class instances. Because the collection exposes a CollectionChanged event, which enables intercepting changes to items in the collection, we need an event handler to understand what is happening. The following code shows an example of event handler implementation:

```
Private Sub CollectionChangedEventHandler(ByVal sender As Object,
                    ByVal e As Specialized.
                    NotifyCollectionChangedEventArgs)

    Select Case e.Action
        Case Is = Specialized.NotifyCollectionChangedAction.Add
            Console.WriteLine("Added the following items:")
            For Each item As Person In e.NewItems
                Console.WriteLine(item.LastName)
            Next
        Case Is = Specialized.NotifyCollectionChangedAction.Remove
            Console.WriteLine("Removed or moved the following items:")
            For Each item As Person In e.OldItems
                Console.WriteLine(item.LastName)
            Next
    End Select
End Sub
```

The System.Collections.Specialized.NotifyCollectionChangedEventArgs type exposes some interesting properties for investigating changes on the collection. For example, the Action property enables you to understand if an item was added, moved, replaced, or removed by the collection via the NotifyCollectionChangedAction enumeration. Next, the collection exposes other interesting properties such as NewItems, which returns an IList object containing the list of items that were added, and OldItems, which returns an IList object containing the list of items that were removed/moved/replaced. The

16

NewStartingIndex and the OldStartingIndex provide information on the position where changes (respectively adding and removing/replacing/moving) occurred. Now consider the following code, which declares three new instances of the Person class and then adds them to the collection and finally removes one:

```
Dim person1 As New Person With {.FirstName = "Alessandro",
                                .LastName = "Del Sole",
                                .Age = 32}
Dim person2 As New Person With {.FirstName = "XXXXX",
                                .LastName = "ZZZZZZZZ",
                                .Age = 44}
Dim person3 As New Person With {.FirstName = "YYYYY",
                                .LastName = "DDDDDDDD",
                                .Age = 18}


people.Add(person1)
people.Add(person2)
people.Add(person3)
people.Remove(person1)
```

The ObservableCollection basically works like the List one; therefore, it exposes methods such as Add, Remove, RemoveAt, and so on, and it also supports extension methods. The good news is that each time a new item is added or an item is removed, the CollectionChanged event is raised and subsequently handled. Because of our previous implementation, if you run the code, you get the following output:

```
Added the following items:
Del Sole
Added the following items:
ZZZZZZZZ
Added the following items:
DDDDDDDD
Removed or moved the following items:
Del Sole
```

Because of its particularity, the ObservableCollection(Of T) can also be useful in scenarios different from WPF that remain the best place where you can use it.

The ReadonlyObservableCollection(Of T) Collection

As for the List(Of T) and also for the ObservableCollection(Of T), there is a read-only counterpart named ReadonlyObservableCollection(Of T) which works like the ReadonlyCollection(Of T) plus the implementation of the CollectionChanged event. The collection is also exposed by the System.Collections.ObjectModel namespace.

The LinkedList(Of T) Collection

Think of the System.Collections.Generic.LinkedList(Of T) collection as a chain in which each ring is an item in the collection that is linked to the others. In other words, an item is linked to the previous one and the next one and points to them. Each item in the collection is considered as a LinkedListNode(Of T), so if you decide to create a LinkedList(Of Person), each Person instance will be represented by a LinkedListNode(Of Person). Table 16.2 summarizes the most common methods and properties for the collection over the ones that you already know (derived from IList(Of T)).

TABLE 16.2   LinkedList Members

Member	Type	Description
AddFirst	Method	Adds a new item as the first in the collection
AddLast	Method	Adds a new item as the last in the collection
AddBefore	Method	Adds a new item before the specified node
AddAfter	Method	Adds a new item after the specified node
Clear	Method	Clears all items in the collection
Contains	Method	Checks if the specified item exists in the collection
CopyTo	Method	Copies the collection into an array
Count	Property	Returns the number of items in the collection
First	Property	Returns the first node in the collection
Last	Property	Returns the last node in the collection
Remove	Method	Removes the specified item from the collection
RemoveFirst	Method	Removes the first item from the collection
RemoveLast	Method	Removes the last item from the collection

The following code provides an example of creating and consuming a LinkedList(Of Person) collection (see comments for explanations):

```
Dim person1 As New Person With {.FirstName = "Alessandro",
                                .LastName = "Del Sole",
                                .Age = 32}
Dim person2 As New Person With {.FirstName = "XXXXX",
```

```
                                .LastName = "ZZZZZZZZ",
                                .Age = 44}
Dim person3 As New Person With {.FirstName = "YYYYY",
                                .LastName = "DDDDDDDD",
                                .Age = 18}

'Creates a new LinkedList
Dim linkedPeople As New LinkedList(Of Person)

'Creates a series of nodes
Dim node1 As New LinkedListNode(Of Person)(person1)
Dim node2 As New LinkedListNode(Of Person)(person2)
Dim node3 As New LinkedListNode(Of Person)(person3)

'The first item in the collection
linkedPeople.AddFirst(node1)

'The last one
linkedPeople.AddLast(node3)

'Add a new item before the last one and after
'the first one
linkedPeople.AddBefore(node3, node2)

'Removes the last item
linkedPeople.RemoveLast()
'Gets the instance of the last item
'(person2 in this case)
Dim lastPerson As Person = linkedPeople.Last.Value

'Determines if person1 is within the collection
Dim isPerson1Available As Boolean = linkedPeople.Contains(person1)
```

The most important difference between this collection and the other ones is that items are linked. This is demonstrated by an `Enumerator` structure exposed by every instance of the collection that enables moving between items, as demonstrated in the following code snippet:

```
Dim peopleEnumerator As LinkedList(Of Person).
    Enumerator = linkedPeople.GetEnumerator

Do While peopleEnumerator.MoveNext
    'Current is a property that is of type T
    '(Person in this example)
    Console.WriteLine(peopleEnumerator.Current.LastName)
Loop
```

This code basically demonstrates that items in the collections are linked and that each one points to the next one.

The `Queue(Of T)` and `Stack(Of T)` Collections

The .NET Framework offers generic versions of the `Queue` and `Stack` collections, known as `System.Collections.Generic.Queue(Of T)` and `System.Collections.Generic.Stack(Of T)`. Their behavior is the same as nongeneric version, except that they are strongly typed. Because of this, you already know how to work with generic versions so they are not discussed here.

Building Custom Collections

Generally built-in collections are good for most scenarios. There could be situations in which you need to implement custom collections. You have basically two alternatives: creating a collection from scratch or recur to inheritance. The first choice can be hard; typically you create a class implementing the `ICollection(Of T)` and `IList(Of T)` (or `IDictionary`) interfaces but you need to manually write code for performing the most basic actions onto items. The other choice is inheriting from an existing collection. This is also a good choice for another reason: You can create your custom base class for other collections. Imagine you want to create a custom collection that stores sets of `FileInfo` objects, each one representing a file on disk. It would not be useful to reinvent the wheel, so inheriting from `List(Of T)` is a good idea. The following code inherits from `List(Of FileInfo)` and extends the collection implementing a new `ToObservableCollection` method, which converts the current instance into an `ObservableCollection(Of FileInfo)` and overrides `ToString` to return a customized version of the method:

```
Public Class FileInfoCollection
    Inherits List(Of FileInfo)


    Public Overridable Function ToObservableCollection() As _
            ObservableCollection(Of FileInfo)
        Return New ObservableCollection(Of FileInfo)(Me)
    End Function

    Public Overrides Function ToString() As String
        Dim content As New StringBuilder

        For Each item As FileInfo In Me
            content.Append(item.Name)
        Next
        Return content.ToString
    End Function
End Class
```

Now you have a strongly typed collection working with `FileInfo` objects; moreover you extended the collection with custom members.

Concurrent Collections

The .NET Framework 4.0 introduces the Task Parallel Library (TPL), which offers support for multicore CPU architectures. The library exposes new generic collections, via the `System.Collections.Concurrent` namespace that is new in .NET 4.0. Table 16.3 gives you a list of the new classes.

TABLE 16.3   Concurrent Collections

Name	Description
ConcurrentStack(Of T)	A thread-safe stack collection
ConcurrentQueue(Of T)	A thread-safe queue collection
ConcurrentDictionary(Of TKey, TValue)	A thread-safe strongly typed dictionary of key/value pairs
ConcurrentBag(Of T)	A thread-safe list of objects
ConcurredLinkedList(Of T)	A thread-safe collection in which items are linked to one another

You get an overview of these collections in the appropriate chapters, but for completeness, you now have a full list of available collections.

Summary

Applications often require data access. You store data within classes and structures, but often you need to group a set of data and collections to help you in this task. The .NET Framework offers both nongeneric collections (such as `ArrayList`, `Queue`, `Stack`, and `HashTable`) and generic ones (such as `List(Of T)`, `ObservableCollection(Of T)`, `Dictionary(Of TKey, TValue)`, `Queue(Of T)` and `Stack(Of T)`). In both cases you have the ability of adding, removing, and editing items within collections using generally the same members (due to the interfaces implementations). Moreover, Visual Basic 2010 introduces the *collection initializers* feature that enables instantiating and populating collections inline. Although you typically use collections for manipulating data, the .NET Framework provides some special read-only collections, such as `ReadonlyCollection(Of T)`. Finally, you learned to create custom collections, which is not an uncommon scenario.

CHAPTER 17

Visually Designing Objects

Visual Studio 2010 is a great place for writing code. It offers a powerful code editor with the presence of IntelliSense that dramatically simplifies your coding experience. Writing code is only one aspect of application development. Architecting objects before writing code is as important as writing the code itself. Visual Studio is powerful enough to let you reach both objectives at one time: graphically designing objects for your applications and contextually writing code related to such objects. The built-in tool that allows performing this task is known as *Class Designer*, and in this chapter you get a high-level overview of it.

Visual Studio Class Designer

Visual Studio 2010 offers an instrument known as *Visual Studio Class Designer* that has been a part of the IDE since the previous versions. You can design objects in a visual way by taking advantage of a graphical tool. You design objects; Visual Studio generates code. In this chapter you learn how to design objects according to object-oriented principles using the Class Designer to create a new implementation of the Person class and of a couple of derived classes. Before continuing to read, simply create a new, empty VB project for the Console. This is the base for your subsequent work.

> **NOTE ON VISUAL BASIC EXPRESS**
>
> The Visual Studio Class Designer is available only on Visual Studio 2010 Standard Edition or higher; therefore, if you have only Visual Basic 2010 Express, you can skip this chapter.

Enabling the Class Designer

To enable the Visual Studio Class Designer, you need to click the **View Class Diagram** button in Solution Explorer. When ready, the Class Designer appears as a new window within the IDE and shows a graphical representation of the main application module, including the definition of the `Main` method. Basically all tasks you can perform on the Class Designer can be accomplished by invoking commands exposed by the context menu that you get when right-clicking the designer's surface. Figure 17.1 shows the previously mentioned representation of `Module1` and the available commands.

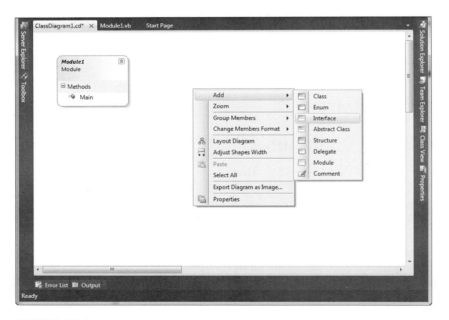

FIGURE 17.1   The Visual Studio Class Designer when launched plus available commands for design operations.

Figure 17.1 also shows the Add command expanded; it provides a list of available objects that you can add to the diagram. Such objects include classes, enumerations, interfaces, structures, delegates, and modules. You can also select the **Comment** command to add sticky notes on the designer's surface. Table 17.1 summarizes the goal of other commands in the context menu.

TABLE 17.1   Commands List for the Class Designer

Command	Description
Add	Provides subcommands for adding objects to the designer's surface.
Zoom	Allows zooming the designer surface for a better visualization.
Group Members	Establishes how objects' members must be grouped. *By Kind* means that members are divided in types groups (for example, properties, methods, and so on). *By Access* means that members are grouped according to their scope (for example, all public members, all private members, and so on). *Sorted Alphabetically* means that objects' members are listed in alphabetical order with no grouping options.
Change Members Format	Sets how members' names appear.
Layout Diagram	Rearranges items on the designer's surface for a better view.
Adjust Shapes Width	Automatically adapts objects' width so that their members' names are more readable.
Export Diagram as Image	Allows exporting the generated diagram as an image, in different formats such as .Bmp, .Jpg, .Png, and .Tiff.

CLASS DIAGRAMS FILES

Class diagrams generated with the Visual Studio Class Designer are stored within a **.cd** file that becomes part of the solution. By default, the file is named ClassDiagram1.cd, but you can rename it as you like via Solution Explorer.

At this point it's time to use the Class Designer. Your goal is to design an IPerson interface that an abstract class named Person can implement and that will also is the base class for two other derived classes, Customer and Contact, both created with this interesting graphical tool.

Adding and Designing Objects

The first step to perform is creating an interface. To accomplish this, follow these steps:

1. Right-click the designer surface (see Figure 17.1) and select the **Add, Interface** command.

2. When the New Interface dialog appears, specify the IPerson name and leave all other options unchanged, which are self-explanatory. Figure 17.2 shows the dialog. This adds a new item on the designer, representing an interface.

FIGURE 17.2   The New Interface dialog allows specifying the name of the new interface and other settings as the access level and the filename.

3. Right-click the new interface and select the **Add, |Property** command. For each object type the context menu provides specific commands related to members that the particular object can contain. Figure 17.3 shows how you can accomplish this. When the new property is added to the interface, it is focused and highlighted for renaming, so rename it to FirstName. Notice that the default type for members is Integer; therefore, you need to open the Properties window (by pressing **F4**) and write the appropriate type in the Type field.

4. Repeat the previous step to add a new LastName property and a FullName method, both of type String. About methods, the Class Designer implements Sub methods by default that are switched to Function when you specify a return type via the Properties window. This step is shown in Figure 17.4.

If you now double-click the new interface, Visual Studio 2010 shows the code that it generated behind the scenes, as shown in Listing 17.1.

LISTING 17.1   **IPerson** Interface with Code Generated by Visual Studio

```
Public Interface IPerson
    Property LastName As String
    Property FirstName As String
    Function FullName() As String
End Interface
```

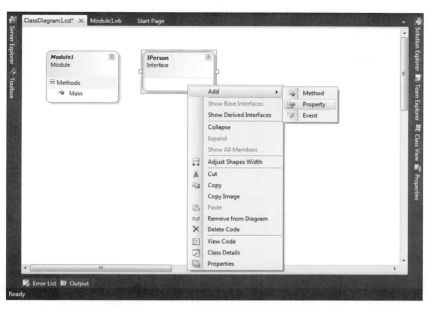

FIGURE 17.3   Adding members to the new interface.

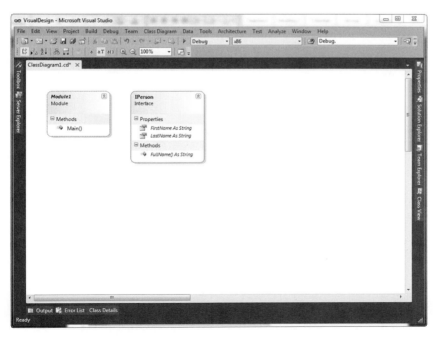

FIGURE 17.4   Specifying a return type for methods and the new completed interface.

The next step is to add an abstract class named `Person`, which serves as the base class for subsequent classes. To accomplish this, right-click the designer and select the **Add, Abstract Class** command. Name the new class `Person` and, when ready, you notice within the designer that is marked as `MustInherit`. Next, double-click the new class and add an `Implements IPerson` statement below the class declaration. This ensures that the new class is going to implement the `IPerson` interface. This is reflected in the class diagram and confirmed by the appearance of properties and methods defined within the interface inside the new class and by a rounded symbol that identifies an interface relationship. Figure 17.5 shows the result of the preceding operations.

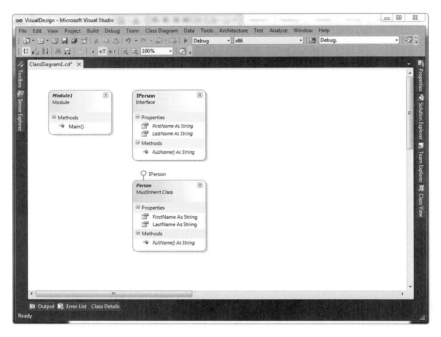

FIGURE 17.5   A new abstract class that implements an interface, all in design way.

Listing 17.2 shows the full code for the `Person` class.

LISTING 17.2   Code for an Abstract Class

```
Public MustInherit Class Person
    Implements IPerson

    Public Property FirstName As String Implements IPerson.FirstName
    Public MustOverride Function FullName() As String Implements IPerson.FullName
```

```
    Public Property LastName As String Implements IPerson.LastName
End Class
```

Notice how the `FullName` method is declared as `MustOverride`. The Properties window offers deep control to classes. Table 17.2 summarizes the most important properties except those related to filenames and locations.

TABLE 17.2   Class Control Properties

Property	Description
Access	Use to set class's scope.
Name	The class name.
Custom attributes	Use to decorate the class with attributes.
Inheritance modifiers	Set to `MustInherit` for an abstract class, to `NotInheritable` for a sealed class, or to `None` for a general implementation.

The Properties window also offers the Remarks and Summary fields that allow specifying descriptions under the form of XML comments, and this feature is available for all members, not just classes. Also, the Properties window shows the Generic, Implements, and Inherits fields which are disabled by design.

Implementing Derived Classes

The Class Designer is powerful enough to provide support for class inheritance. Suppose you want to create two classes deriving from `Person`, for example `Contact` and `Customer`. To create a `Contact` class that inherits from `Person`, follow these steps:

1. Right-click the designer surface and select the **Add, Class** command. When the New Class dialog appears, specify the class name and leave the other properties unchanged.

2. When the new class is added to the designer's surface, double-click it and in the code editor add an `Inherits Person` statement below the class declaration, then switch back to the class diagram. This establishes an inheritance relationship between the two classes. You notice that the designer does not show inherited properties while it is limited to show overridden methods (`FullName` in our example).

3. Add two new properties, `Age` of type `Integer` and `Email` of type `String`, using skills gained in the Previews subsection. The result of this implementation is shown in Figure 17.6.

17

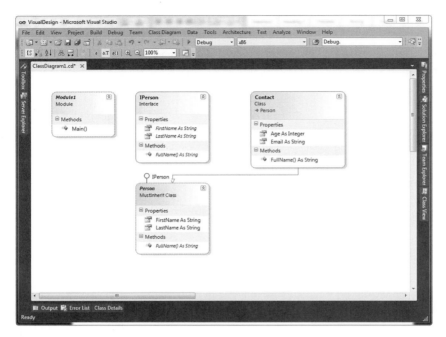

FIGURE 17.6   The implementation of a derived class.

Now create a new `Customer` class that still inherits from `Person` following the previous listed steps, adding two new properties: `CompanyName` of type `String` and `CustomerID` of type `Integer`. The result of this new implementation is shown in Figure 17.7.

To understand how Visual Studio interpreted your operations, click both the `Customer` and `Contact` class. For your convenience, the code of both classes is shown in Listing 17.3.

LISTING 17.3   Code for Derived Classes Generated by the IDE

```
Public Class Contact
    Inherits Person

    Public Property Age As Integer
    Public Property Email As String

    Public Overrides Function FullName() As String
    End Function
End Class
Public Class Customer
    Inherits Person

    Public Property CustomerID As Integer
    Public Property CompanyName As String
```

```
      Public Overrides Function FullName() As String
      End Function
End Class
```

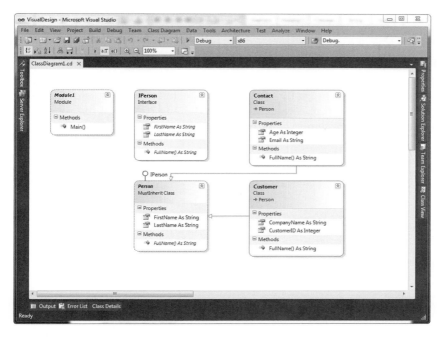

FIGURE 17.7   The implementation of a second derived class.

It's worth noticing how the IDE correctly wrote inheritance code and marked as `Overrides` the `FullName` method in both classes. Obviously the generated code can be considered as a mere template; therefore, you have to populate it your own way. To complete your work, you need to write the methods body for `FullName` in both classes. The following is an example related to the `Contact` class:

```
Public Overrides Function FullName() As String
    Return String.Format("{0} {1}, of age: {2}",
                        Me.LastName,
                        Me.FirstName,
                        Me.Age.ToString)
End Function
```

While the following is the implementation for the `Customer` class:

```
    Public Overrides Function FullName() As String
        Return String.Format("Customer {0} is {1}",
                        Me.CustomerID,
```

```
                    Me.CompanyName)
    End Function
```

In this section you have seen an alternative way for designing classes in Visual Basic 2010 that is important, particularly to get a hierarchical representation. Most of all, such work has been completed with a few mouse clicks.

Creating Multiple Diagrams

You are not limited to creating one diagram. You can add multiple class diagrams to your project so that you can have a graphical representation of a complex hierarchical object's structure. To add diagrams to your project, simply right-click the project name in Solution Explorer and select the **Add New Item** command. When the Add New Item dialog appears, select the **Class Diagram** item in the Common Items list. (See Figure 17.8).

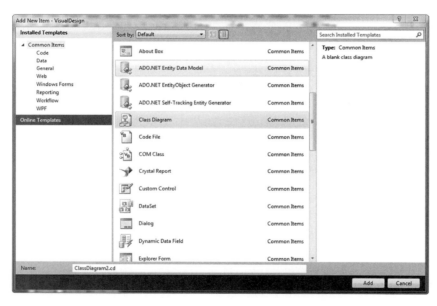

FIGURE 17.8   Adding a new class diagram to the project.

This can be useful if you have to graphically represent complex frameworks, and if you need large design surfaces.

Exporting the Diagram

As a respectable graphical tool, the Class Designer can export diagrams as images. The tool supports the following image formats:

▶ Windows Bitmap (24 Bit)

▶ Portable Network Graphics (.Png)

- Jpeg

- Tag Image File Format (.Tiff)

- Graphics Interchange Format (.Gif)

To export diagrams to images, simply right-click the designer's surface and select the **Export Diagram as Image** command. Figure 17.9 shows the Export Diagram as Image dialog.

FIGURE 17.9   Exporting diagrams to images.

You can select multiple diagrams if available. You need to select the location, which by default points to the project's folder. The combo box at the bottom of the dialog allows you to choose the image format.

Class View Window

Since the previous versions of Visual Studio, the IDE offers another graphical tool for managing objects, known as the Class View window. To enable this tool you can press **Ctrl+Shift+C** if it's not already available as a floating window. Basically it's a browsing tool that shows a graphical representation of the objects' hierarchy in your solution and that allows searching for specific members or getting information about types being part of your project, including base types. Figure 17.10 shows this tool window in action, pointing to the same project used in the previous section.

17

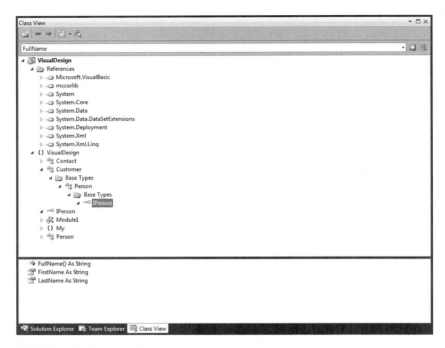

FIGURE 17.10   The Class View tool window.

As you can see in Figure 17.10, the Class View allows browsing custom objects in your projects (including base types such as interfaces) and built-in objects invoked by your project. Moreover, you can browse references to assemblies and expand them so that you can still get information on members for your custom objects. The Class View window also provides a Settings command that allows specifying what kind of objects will be shown. (For example, you can decide if the view must include base types.)

Class Details Window

Another interesting tool that allows designing objects by taking advantage of the visual instrumentation of the IDE is the Class Details Window that you enable by selecting **View, Other Windows, Class Details**. This tool displays members from the selected object in the Class Diagram designer and allows adding, editing, or removing members from the object, such as methods, properties, events and so on. It is worth mentioning that the tool supports IntelliSense, for example when you provide the data type. Figure 17.11 shows an example.

You supply the member name according to the member type, then you specify the data type and the modifier. With regard to the modifier, a list of modifiers is available from a combo box. You can also select the **Hide** checkbox if you want a member to be removed from the visual diagram.

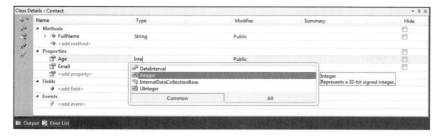

FIGURE 17.11   The Class Details tool window.

Summary

In this chapter you saw how to design objects for your application using the built-in Visual Studio tool known as Visual Studio Class Designer. This tool allows designing objects via a specific designer that offers support for adding all kinds of .NET objects, such as classes, structures, interfaces, delegates, enumerations, and modules. Behind the scenes, this tool generates code related to design operations. You saw how easily you can implement interfaces, abstract classes, and derive classes learning steps that you will be required to perform for other objects. Completing the topic, the chapter provided information on creating multiple diagrams and exporting diagrams to images. The last topic in this chapter is an overview of the Class View tool window that is basically an object browser limited to the current solution.

17

"Generate From Usage" Coding Techniques

Writing the code of your application is one of the tasks that you will spend a lot of time on. During the years, the Visual Studio IDE evolved with several functionalities for helping developers in writing code faster and easier: syntax highlighting, more and more advanced IntelliSense capabilities, and specific code editors for different kinds of files taking advantage of the previously mentioned features. Although the availability of such deep functionalities existed, the previous versions of the IDE lacked the capability to help developers in implementing new objects on-the-fly—objects that you did not previously consider but that later become necessary or existing objects that must be extended. You might perhaps consider this tooling as old-fashioned, but it is instead useful for at least a couple of reasons: You are writing code and you understand that you need a new object that was not part of the architecture; you can implement the object according to the needs that you gradually discover while writing code. Second, such an approach is also used in advanced techniques such as the test-driven development. In this chapter you learn how to use this instrumentation and get the most out of its capabilities.

Coding New Types

One of the most important new features in the Visual Studio 2010 IDE is the ability to generate on-the-fly objects that do not exist yet. This feature is known as Generate From Usage. To understand how it works, simply create a new Console application named `GenerateFromUsage` and within the `Main` method type the following code:

```
Sub Main()
    Dim p As New Person

End Sub
```

Because the `Person` class has not been implemented, the Visual Basic compiler throws an exception, offering the usual pop-up button that suggests solutions. But with Visual Basic 2010 things change; now you have additional solutions, as shown in Figure 18.1.

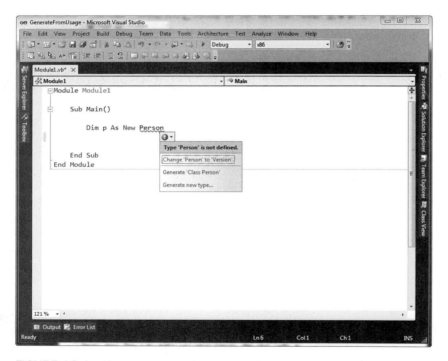

FIGURE 18.1   New error correction options for Visual Studio 2010.

As you can see in Figure 18.1, the IDE provides the ability of generating a new `Person` class directly when writing code offering a Generate 'Class Person' object. There is also another choice named Generate, which is discussed later in this chapter. Now focus on the first choice and click the **Generate 'Class Person'** command. At this point Visual Studio creates a new code file named Person.vb that you can find in Solution Explorer as part of the project. This code file contains a basic definition for the `Person` class that is simply declared as follows:

```
Class Person
End Class
```

DEFAULT ACCESSIBILITY

When generating objects on-the-fly, Visual Studio assigns the default visibility to both objects and members. If you want to provide a different scope, you need to do it by writing qualifiers manually or by selecting the **Generate Other** command.

Now go back to the Main method; you notice that the error message disappeared. Type the following assignment:

```
p.LastName = "Del Sole"
```

Because the LastName property is not exposed by the Person class, the Visual Basic compiler throws a new error still offering solutions, as shown in Figure 18.2.

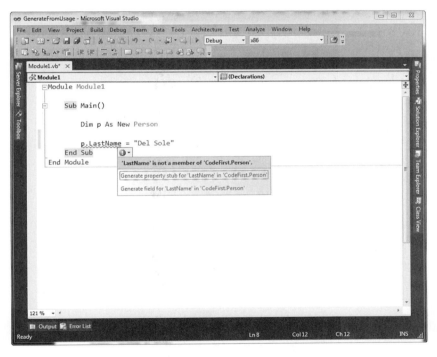

FIGURE 18.2   Generating members on-the-fly.

The IDE correctly recognizes the assignment and proposes adding a new property or a new field in the Person class. Click the **Generate property stub** to add a new property that is implemented in the Person class as follows:

```
Class Person
    Property LastName As String
```

18

The IDE also correctly specifies the data type to the property (String in the preceding example) based on the assignment content. Repeat this last step to add a second property named FirstName of type String using your first name for convenience. My code looks like the following:

```
p.LastName = "Del Sole"
p.FirstName = "Alessandro"
```

Now we should provide a method that returns the full name for the person. Generating a method stub is also an easy task. Simply write the following:

```
Dim fullName As String = p.FullName
```

Now the IDE offers three different solutions, as shown in Figure 18.3.

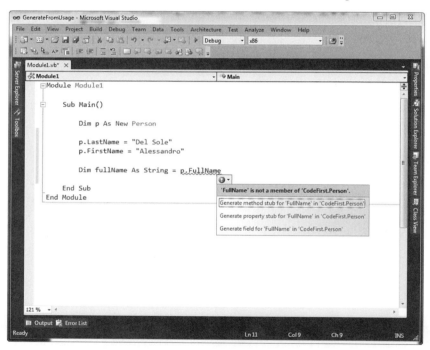

FIGURE 18.3   Generating a new method stub.

You can choose to generate a method, property, or field. The IDE can distinguish what kind of solutions it can propose in that particular coding scenario. Click the **Generate method stub** command, and Visual Studio implements the FullName method as follows:

```
Function FullName() As String
    Throw New NotImplementedException
End Function
```

The new method simply throws a `NotImplementedException`; therefore, you need to replace it with your code. All examples shown until now in this book provide the following implementation:

```
Function FullName() As String
    Return String.Concat(LastName, " ", FirstName)
End Function
```

At this point you have generated your definitely working `Person` class without exiting from the code editor. This is the most basic approach to the new feature, but such tooling is powerful and allows defining different kinds of objects according to the context that you are writing code in. This is what the next sections discuss.

Generating Shared Members

Visual Studio is intelligent enough to understand whenever you try to define a shared member. For example, imagine you want to implement a method that returns the number of active instances of the `Person` class. If you type the following code:

```
Person.ReturnInstanceCount()
```

and then select the **Generate method stub** correction option, Visual Studio generates the following code:

```
Shared Sub ReturnInstanceCount()
    Throw New NotImplementedException
End Sub
```

On-the-Fly Code and Object Initializers

You might often use object initializers to create objects instances in line; generating code on-the-fly is powerful. Consider the following declaration:

```
Dim p As New Person With {.FirstName = "Alessandro",
                          .LastName = "Del Sole"}
```

When you write this code, the `Person` class and its `FirstName` and `LastName` properties do not exist. At this point you can open the correction options and choose the **Generate Class** command. Visual Studio automatically associates the previous assignments to the class that is initialized in line and generates the appropriate members. Code generation for the previous code snippet produces the following result:

```
Class Person
    Property LastName As String
    Property FirstName As String

End Class
```

18

With a single mouse click you have accomplished a task that would normally require a couple more steps, as described in the previous section.

Generating Complex Objects

You can now generate new objects on-the-fly taking advantage of default solutions proposed by Visual Studio. You are not limited to generating previously described classes and members. Visual Studio enables you to generate the following types:

- ▶ Classes
- ▶ Structures
- ▶ Interfaces
- ▶ Delegates
- ▶ Enumerations

The following is instead the list of members that you can generate for the preceding types:

- ▶ Methods
- ▶ Properties
- ▶ Fields

You can generate objects on-the-fly by running the New Type dialog that you can activate choosing **Generate Other** solution instead of **Generate Class**. For example, imagine you want to generate a new structure on-the-fly. First, type the following line of code:

```
Dim threeDim As New ThreePoint
```

Because the `ThreePoint` type does not exist, Visual Studio 2010 throws an error proposing fixes. At this point, click the **Generate New Type** solution, as shown in Figure 18.4.

The Generate New Type window displays, which allows getting deeper control over the type generation, as shown in Figure 18.5.

As you can see there are several options for generating a new type. First, the Access combo box allows specifying the accessibility level that can be Public, Friend, or the default level for the selected type. The Kind combo box allows specifying what type you intend to generate. Figure 18.5 also shows a list of available types. For our example, leave the default settings unchanged. In the lower part of the dialog, you can establish where the type must be declared and in what file. You can select what project (if the solution contains more than one project) defines the new type and what code file declares the new type. Here it's worth mentioning that you can decide to create a new file (default choice) or to add the

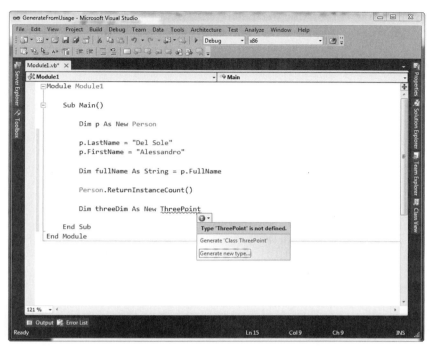

FIGURE 18.4   Selecting the Generate Other command for constructing different types.

FIGURE 18.5   The Generate New Type dialog.

code to an existing one using the Add to Existing File control box. When you click **OK**, the new type is created. Visual Studio generates the following structure declaration:

```
Public Structure ThreePoint

End Structure
```

Now you can repeat the steps when you added members to the Person class in the first section of this chapter. For example, first write the following code:

```
ThreePoint.X = 10
ThreePoint.Y = 20
ThreePoint.Z = 30
```

None of the X, Y, and Z properties has been implemented yet within the `ThreePoint` structure; therefore, you can add them via the correction options. (Refer to Figure 18.2 for a recap.)

Interfaces Additions

The Visual Studio 2010 IDE offers default solutions according to naming conventions it finds in your code. This is particularly true if you want to generate interfaces instead of other types. For example, if you type

```
Dim interfaceVariable as ITestInterface
```

The IDE notices that `ITestInterface`'s identifier begins with the `I` letter; therefore, it assumes you want to generate an interface. Because of this, the default solution in the correction options will not be Generate Class but Generate Interface. The stub for the new interface is simply the following:

```
Interface ITestInterface
End Interface
```

If you want to change the accessibility level for the new interface, you need to generate it invoking the Generate New Type window or writing the appropriate qualifier manually.

Summary

An overview about one of the most important new IDE features in Visual Studio 2010 that also applies to Visual Basic 2010, known as Generate From Usage was presented. You saw how you can generate objects on-the-fly, writing first code and then generating objects that you invoke with just a couple of mouse clicks. You also saw how you can generate customized objects running the Generate New Type dialog that provides deep control over types to be generated on-the-fly.

CHAPTER 19

Manipulating Files and Streams

Manipulating files, directories, drives, and pathnames has always been one of the most common requirements for every role in IT for home users. Since MS-DOS you have probably had this necessity tons of times. In application development for the .NET Framework with Visual Basic 2010, manipulating files is even more straightforward because you have two opportunities: accessing system resources with the usual ease due to self-explanatory classes and members and because of the Common Language Runtime as a supervisor. In this chapter you learn how to manipulate files, directories, and drives by taking advantage of specific .NET classes. Moreover, you learn about transporting such simplicity into more general data exchange objects, known as streams.

Manipulating Directories and Pathnames

The .NET Framework makes it easier to work with directories and pathnames, providing the System.IO.Directory and System.IO.Path classes. Such classes offer shared methods for accessing directories and directory names, allowing deep manipulation of folders and names. To be honest, System.IO.Path also provides members for working against filenames, and due to its nature it is included in this section. There are also situations in which you need to work against single directories as instances of .NET objects, and this is where the System.IO.DirectoryInfo class comes in. In this section you learn to get the most from such classes for directory manipulation.

> **TIP**
>
> All code examples provided in this chapter require an `Imports System.IO` directive to shorten lines of code.

The `System.IO.Path` Class

Often you need to work with pathnames, directory names, and filenames. The .NET Framework provides the `System.IO.Path` class, offering shared members that allow manipulating pathnames. For example, you might want to extract the filename from a pathname. This is accomplished invoking the `GetFileName` method as follows:

```
'Returns "TextFile.txt"
Dim fileName As String = Path.GetFileName("C:\TextFile.txt")
```

The `GetExtension` method returns instead only the file extension and is used as follows:

```
'Returns ".txt"
Dim extension As String = Path.GetExtension("C:\TextFile.txt")
```

To ensure that a filename has an extension, you can also invoke the `HasExtension` method that returns `True` if the filename has one. There are situations in which you need to extract the filename without considering its extension. The `GetFileNameWithoutExtension` accomplishes this:

```
'Returns "TextFile"
Dim noExtension As String = Path.
                            GetFileNameWithoutExtension("C:\TextFile.txt")
```

Another common situation is retrieving the directory name from a full pathname that includes a filename, too. The `GetDirectoryName` method allows performing this:

```
'Returns "C:\Users\Alessandro\My Documents"
Dim dirName As String =

    Path. GetDirectoryName("C:\Users\Alessandro\My Documents\Document.txt")
```

When working with filenames, you might want to replace the extension. This is accomplished by invoking the `ChangeExtension` method as follows:

```
'Returns "MyFile.Doc"
Dim extReplaced As String = Path.ChangeExtension("MyFile.Txt", ".doc")
```

Notice that such a method simply returns a string that contains the required modification but does not rename the file on disk (which is covered later). Path is also useful when you need to create temporary files or to store files in the Windows's temporary folder. You invoke the `GetTempFileName` method to get a unique temporary file:

```
Dim temporaryFile As String = Path.GetTempFileName
```

The method returns the filename of the temporary file so that you can easily access it and treat it like any other file, being sure that its name is unique. If you instead need to access Windows's temporary folder, you can invoke the `GetTempPath` method as follows:

```
Dim temporaryWinFolder As String = Path.GetTempPath
```

You could combine both temporary folder name and temporary filename to create a temporary file in the temporary folder. Combining pathnames is accomplished invoking the `Combine` method, which just takes two arguments such as the first pathname and the second one. You can also generate a random filename invoking the `GetRandomFileName` method:

```
Dim randomFile As String = Path.GetRandomFileName
```

The difference with `GetTempFileName` is that this one also creates a physical file on disk, returning the full path. `System.IO.Path` offers two other interesting methods: `GetInvalidFileNameChars` and `GetInvalidPathChars` that both return an array of `Char` storing, respectively, with unaccepted characters within filenames and within directory names. They are useful if you generate a string that will be then used as a file or folder name.

The `System.IO.Directory` Class

To access directories you take advantage of the `System.IO.Directory` class that offers shared members that allow performing common operations on folders. All members are self-explanatory. For example, you can check if a directory already exists and, if not, create a new one as follows:

```
If Not Directory.Exists("C:\Test") Then
    Directory.CreateDirectory("C:\Test")
End If
```

The `Move` method allows moving a directory from one location to another; it takes two arguments, the source directory name and the target name:

```
Directory.Move("C:\Test", "C:\Demo")
```

If the target directory already exists, an `IOException` is thrown. You can easily get or set attribute information for directories invoking special methods. For example you can get the directory creation time invoking the `GetCreationTime` method that returns a `Date` type or the `SetCreationTime` that requires a date specification, to modify the creation time:

```
Dim createdDate As Date = Directory.GetCreationTime("C:\Demo")
Directory.SetCreationTime("C:\Demo", New Date(2009, 5, 10))
```

19

TABLE 19.1   Members for Getting/Setting Attributes

Method	Description
GetAccessControl/SetAccessControl	Gets/Sets the ACL entries for the specified directory via a System.Security.AccessControl .DirectorySecurity object
GetCreationTime/SetCreationTime	Gets/Sets the creation time for the directory
GetCreationTimeUtc/ SetCreationTimeUtc	Gets/Sets the directory creation time in the Coordinated Universal Time format
GetLastAccessTime/SetLastAccessTime	Gets/Sets the directory last access time
GetLastAccessTimeUtc/ SetLastAccessTimeUtc	Gets/Sets the directory last access time in the Coordinated Universal Time format
GetLastWriteTime/SetLastWriteTime	Gets/Sets the directory last write time
GetLastWriteTimeUtc/ SetLastWriteTimeUtc	Gets/Sets the directory last write time in the Coordinated Universal Time format

Table 19.1 summarizes members for getting/setting attributes.

You can easily get other information, such as the list of files available within the desired directory. Until .NET Framework 3.5 SP 1 you were limited in invoking the GetFiles method, returning an array of string (each one is a filename), which works like this:

```
'Second argument is optional, specifies a pattern for search
Dim filesArray() As String = Directory.GetFiles("C:\", "*.exe")
```

Now in .NET 4.0 you can invoke the EnumerateFiles that returns an IEnumerable(Of String) and that works like this:

```
'get files
Dim filesEnumerable As IEnumerable(Of String) = _
                    Directory.EnumerateFiles("C:\", "*.exe")

For Each item In filesEnumerable
    Console.WriteLine("File name: {0}", item)
Next
```

Probably this difference does not make much sense at this particular point of the book, but you learn later that IEnumerable objects are LINQ-enabled; therefore, you can write LINQ queries against sequences of this type. Similarly to GetFiles and EnumerateFiles, you invoke GetDirectories and EnumerateDirectories to retrieve a list of all subdirectories' names within the specified directory. Next, the GetFilesEntries and

EnumerateFilesEntries return a list of all filenames and subdirectories names within the specified directory.

To delete a directory you simply invoke the Delete method. Notice that it works only if a directory is empty and simply requires the directory name:

```
'Must be empty
Directory.Delete("C:\Demo")
```

If the folder is not empty, an IOException is thrown. Delete has an overload that accepts a Boolean value if you want to delete empty subdirectories, too. The Directory class also provides the ability of retrieving a list of available drives on your machine. This is accomplished by invoking the GetLogicalDrives method that returns an array of String that you can then iterate:

```
Dim drivesOnMyMachine() As String = Directory.
                            GetLogicalDrives
For Each drive In drivesOnMyMachine
    Console.WriteLine(drive)

Next
```

On my machine the preceding code produces the following output:

```
A:\
C:\
D:\
E:\
```

The last example is about retrieving the current directory, which is accomplished by invoking the GetCurrentDirectory method:

```
Dim currentFolder As String = Directory.GetCurrentDirectory
```

You can also easily set the current folder by invoking the shared SetCurrentDirectory method, passing the folder name as an argument. Accessing directories via the Directory class is straightforward, but in some circumstances you have no access to specific information. For this, there is a more flexible class that allows working on specific directories: DirectoryInfo.

19

The `System.IO.DirectoryInfo` Class

The `System.IO.DirectoryInfo` class represents a single directory. More precisely, an instance of the `DirectoryInfo` class handles information about the specified directory. It inherits from `System.IO.FileSystemInfo`, which is a base class that provides the basic infrastructure for representing directories or files. You create an instance of the `DirectoryInfo` class passing the desired directory name as an argument to the constructor:

```
Dim di As New DirectoryInfo("C:\Demo")
```

Basically you have the same members that you already learned about for the `Directory` class, with some differences. First, now members are instance members and not shared. Second, methods summarized in Table 19.1 are now properties. Third, members are invoked directly on the instance that represents the directory; therefore, you do not need to pass the directory name as an argument. For example, you remove an empty directory invoking the instance method `Delete` as follows:

```
di.Delete()
```

An interesting property is `DirectoryInfo.Attributes`, which allows specifying values from the `System.IO.FileAttributes` enumeration and that determine directory behavior. For example, you can make a directory hidden and read-only as follows:

```
di.Attributes = FileAttributes.Hidden Or FileAttributes.ReadOnly
```

When you specify values from such enumeration, IntelliSense can help you understand what the value is about; it's worth mentioning that such values are self-explanatory. There are situations in which you do not programmatically create instances of `DirectoryInfo`, whereas instead you receive an instance from some other objects. For example, the `Directory.CreateDirectory` shared method returns a `DirectoryInfo` object. In such cases you can get further information as the directory name invoking the `FullName` property, which returns the full pathname of the folder, or the `Name` property that just returns the name without path. Both work like this:

```
Dim directoryFullName As String = di.FullName
Dim directoryName As String = di.Name
```

Use the `DirectoryInfo` class each time you need to store information for specific directories, for example within collections.

The `System.IO.DriveInfo` Class

Similarly to `System.IO.DirectoryInfo`, `System.IO.DriveInfo` provides access to drives information. Using this class is straightforward; it provides information on the disk type, disk space (free and total), volume label, and other self-explanatory properties that you can discover with IntelliSense. The following example shows how you can create an instance of the class and retrieve information on the specified drive:

```
Sub DriveInfoDemo()
    Dim dr As New DriveInfo("C:\")

    Console.WriteLine("Drive type: {0}", dr.DriveType.ToString)
    Console.WriteLine("Volume label: {0}", dr.VolumeLabel)
    Console.WriteLine("Total disk space: {0}", dr.TotalSize.ToString)
    Console.WriteLine("Available space: {0}",
                    dr.AvailableFreeSpace.ToString)
    dr = Nothing
End Sub
```

Handling Exceptions for Directories and Pathnames

When working with directories and pathnames, encountering exceptions is not so uncommon. Table 19.2 summarizes directory-related exceptions.

TABLE 19.2   Directory-Related Exceptions

Exception	Description
IOException	General exception that happens when operations on directories fail (such as creating existing directories, deleting nonempty directories, and so on.)
DirectoryNotFoundException	Thrown when the directory is not found
PathTooLongException	Thrown when the pathname exceeds the size of 248 characters for folders and 260 for filenames
UnauthorizedAccessException	Thrown if the caller code doesn't have sufficient rights to access the directory
ArgumentNullException	Thrown when the supplied argument is Nothing
ArgumentException	Thrown when the supplied argument is invalid

19

It is important to implement Try..Catch blocks for handling the previously described exceptions and provide the user the ability to escape from such situations.

Manipulating Files

Manipulating files is a daily task for every developer. Luckily the .NET Framework provides an easy infrastructure for working with files. In this section you learn about the `System.IO.File` and `System.IO.FileInfo` classes that also represent some important concepts before you go into streams.

The `System.IO.File` Class

The `System.IO.File` class provides access to files on disk exposing special shared members. For example, you can easily create a text file invoking two methods: `WriteAllText` and `WriteAllLines`. Both create a new text file, put into the file the given text, and then close the file; however, the second one allows writing the content of an array of strings into multiple lines. The following code provides an example:

```
File.WriteAllText("C:\Temp\OneFile.txt", "Test message")


Dim lines() As String = {"First", "Second", "Third"}
File.WriteAllLines("C:\Temp\OneFile.txt", lines)
```

Such methods are useful because they avoid the need to manually close files on disk when you perform the writing operation. You can also easily create binary files invoking the `WriteAllBytes` method that works like the previous ones but requires the specification of an array of byte instead of text. The following is a small example:

```
File.WriteAllBytes("C:\Temp\OneFile.bin", New Byte() {1, 2, 3, 4})
```

Reading files' content is also straightforward. There are reading counterparts of the previously described method. `ReadAllText` and `ReadAllLines` allow retrieving content from a text file; the first one returns all content as a `String`, whereas the second one returns the content line by line by putting in an array of `String`. This is an example:

```
Dim text As String = File.ReadAllText("C:\Temp\OneFile.txt")
Dim fileLines() As String = File.ReadAllLines("C:\Temp\OneFile.txt")
```

Similarly you can read data from binary files invoking `ReadAllBytes`, which returns an array of `Byte`, as follows:

```
Dim bytes() As Byte = File.ReadAllBytes("C:\Temp\OneFile.bin")
```

For text files, you can also append text to an existing file. You accomplish this invoking `AppendAllText` if you want to put an entire string or `AppendAllLines` if you have a sequence of strings. This is an example:

```
Dim lines As IEnumerable(Of String) = _
            New String() {"First", "Second", "Third"}.AsEnumerable
```

```
File.AppendAllLines("C:\Temporary\Test.txt", lines)
File.AppendAllText("C:\Temporary\Text.txt",
                   "All text is stored within a string")
```

Notice how an array of strings is converted into an IEnumerable(Of String) invoking the AsEnumerable extension method, which is discussed in Chapters 21, "Advanced Languages Feature," and 24, "LINQ to Objects." AppendAllLines takes an IEnumerable(Of String) as a parameter but you can also pass an array of strings because arrays are actually enumerable. After reading and writing, copying is also important. The Copy method allows creating copies of files, accepting two arguments: the source file and the target file. This is an example:

```
File.Copy("C:\OneFolder\Source.txt", "C:\AnotherFolder\Target.txt")
```

You can also move a file from a location to another, invoking Move. Such a method is also used to rename a file and can be used as follows:

```
File.Move("C:\OneFolder\Source.txt", "C:\AnotherFolder\Target.txt")
```

Another useful method is Replace. It allows replacing the content of a file with the content of another file, making a backup of the first file. You use it as follows:

```
File.Replace("C:\Source.Txt", "C:\Target.txt", "C:\Backup.txt")
```

Of course you are not limited to text files. The File class offers two important methods that provide a basic encryption service, Encrypt and Decrypt. Basically Encrypt makes a file accessible only by the user that is currently logged into Windows. You invoke it as follows:

```
File.Encrypt("C:\Temp\OneFile.txt")
```

If you try to log off from the system and then log on with another user profile, the encrypted file will not be accessible. You need to log on again with the user profile that encrypted the file. To reverse the result, simply invoke Decrypt:

```
File.Decrypt("C:\Temp\OneFile.txt")
```

Finally you can easily delete a file from disk. This is accomplished with the simple Delete method:

```
File.Delete("C:\Temp\OneFile.txt")
```

The File class also has members similar to the Directory class. Consider the summarization made in Table 19.1 about the Directory class's members. The File class exposes the same members with the same meaning; the only difference is that such members now affect files. Those members are not covered again because they behave the same on files.

19

MEMBERS RETURNING STREAMS

The `System.IO.File` class exposes methods that return or require streams, such as `Create` and `Open`. Such members are not covered here for two reasons: The first one is that the streams discussion will be offered later in this chapter, whereas the second one is that streams provide their own members for working against files that do the same as file members and therefore a more appropriate discussion is related to streams.

The `System.IO.FileInfo` Class

Similarly to what I explained about the `System.IO.DirectoryInfo` class, there is also a `System.IO.FileInfo` counterpart for the `System.IO.File` class. An instance of the `FileInfo` class is therefore a representation of a single file, providing members that allow performing operations on that particular file or getting/setting information. Because `FileInfo` inherits from `System.IO.FileSystemInfo` like `DirectoryInfo`, you can basically find the same members. You create an instance of the `FileInfo` class passing the filename to the constructor, as demonstrated here:

```
Dim fi As New FileInfo("C:\MyFile.txt")
```

You can set attributes for the specified file assigning the `Attributes` property, which receives a value from the `System.IO.FileAttributes` enumeration:

```
fi.Attributes = FileAttributes.System Or FileAttributes.Hidden
```

You can still perform operations invoking instance members that do not require the file-name specification, such as `CopyTo`, `Delete`, `Encrypt`, `Decrypt`, or `MoveTo`. The `FileInfo`, such as `Length` (of type `Long`) that returns the file size in bytes; `Name` (of type `String`) that returns the filename and that is useful when you receive a `FileInfo` instance from somewhere else; `FullName` that is the same as `Name` but also includes the full path; `Exists` that determines if the file exists; and `IsReadOnly` that determines if the file is read-only. Using `FileInfo` can be useful if you need to create collections of objects, each representing a file on disk. Consider the following custom collections that stores series of `FileInfo` objects:

```
Class MyFileList
    Inherits List(Of FileInfo)

End Class
```

Now consider the following code that retrieves the list of executable filenames in the specified folder and creates an instance of the `FileInfo` class for each file, pushing it into the collection:

```
Module FileInfoDemo


    Sub FileInfoDemo()
```

```vb
        'An instance of the collection
        Dim customList As New MyFileList

        'Create a FileInfo for each .exe file
        'in the specified directory
        For Each itemName As String In _
            Directory.EnumerateFiles("C:\", "*.exe")

            Dim fileReference As New FileInfo(itemName)
            customList.Add(fileReference)
        Next

        'Iterate the collection
        For Each item In customList
            Console.WriteLine("File: {0}, length: {1}, created on: {2}", _
                            item.Name, item.Length, item.CreationTime)
        Next
    End Sub
End Module
```

In this particular case enclosing the code within a module is just for demonstration purposes. Notice how you can access properties for each file that you could not know in advance. As for `DirectoryInfo`, `FileInfo` also exposes properties that are counterparts for methods summarized in Table 19.1 and that this time are related to files. Refer to that table for further information.

Handling File Exceptions

Refer to Table 19.2 for exceptions that can occur when working with files. Other than those exceptions, you may encounter a `FileNotFoundException` if the specified file does not exist.

Understanding Permissions

The .NET Framework provides a high-level security mechanism over system resources, so it can happen that you attempt to access, in both reading or writing, directories or files but you do not have the required rights. To prevent your code from failing at runtime, you can check if you have permissions. When working with files and directories, you need to check the availability of the `System.Security.FileIOPermission` object. For example, the following code asks the system (`Demand` method) if it has permissions to read local files:

```vb
Dim fp As New FileIOPermission(PermissionState.None)
fp.AllLocalFiles = FileIOPermissionAccess.Read
Try
    fp.Demand()
Catch ex As Security.SecurityException
    Console.WriteLine("You have no permission for local files")
Catch ex As Exception
End Try
```

19

If your code has no sufficient permissions, a `SecurityException` is thrown. Checking for permission is absolutely a best practice and should be applied where possible. In Chapter 46, "Working with Assemblies," you get some more information about the security model in the .NET Framework.

Introducing Streams

Streams are sequences of bytes exchanged with some kind of sources, such as files, memory, and network. A stream is represented by the abstract `System.IO.Stream` class that is the base class for different kinds of streams and that implements the `IDisposable` interface. The `Stream` class exposes some common members that you find in all other streams. Table 19.3 summarizes the most important common members.

TABLE 19.3   Streams Common Members

Member	Description
Close	Closes the stream and releases associated resources
Write	Writes the specified sequence of bytes to the stream
WriteByte	Writes the specified byte to the stream
Read	Reads the specified number of bytes from the stream
ReadByte	Reads a byte from the stream
Length	Returns the stream's dimension (property)
Seek	Moves to the specified position in the stream
Position	Returns the current position (property)
CanRead	Determines if the stream supports reading (property)
CanWrite	Determines if the stream supports writing (property)
CanSeek	Determines if the stream supports seeking (property)
BeginRead	Starts an asynchronous reading operation
BeginWrite	Starts an asynchronous writing operation
EndRead	Waits for an asynchronous operation to be completed

Now that you have a summarization of common members, you are ready to discover specific kinds of streams that inherit from `Stream`.

Reading and Writing Text Files

You create text files instantiating the `StreamWriter` class, which is a specific stream implementation for writing to text files. The following code, that will be explained, provides an example:

```
Dim ts As New StreamWriter("C:\Temporary\OneFile.txt",
                           False, System.Text.Encoding.UTF8)

ts.WriteLine("This is a text file")
ts.WriteLine("with multi-line example")
ts.Close()
```

The constructor provides several overloads; the one used in the code receives the file name to be created—a Boolean value indicated whether the text must be appended if the file already exists and how the text is encoded. `WriteLine` is a method that writes a string and then puts a line terminator character. When you are done you must close the stream invoking `Close`. You can also invoke `Write` to put in just one character. The reading counterpart is the `StreamReader` that works in a similar way, as demonstrated here:

```
Dim rf As New StreamReader("C:\Temporary\OneFile.txt",
                           System.Text.Encoding.UTF8)
Dim readALine As String = rf.ReadLine
Dim allContent As String = rf.ReadToEnd

rf.Close()
```

`StreamReader` provides the ability to read one line (`ReadLine` method), one character per time (`Read` method), or all the content of the stream (`ReadToEnd` method) putting such content into a variable of type `String`. In both `StreamWriter` and `StreamReader` the constructor can receive an existing stream instead of a string. This is exemplified by the following code:

```
Dim fs As New FileStream("C:\Temporary\OneFile.txt", FileMode.Create)
Dim ts As New StreamWriter(fs)

'Work on your file here..
ts.Close()

fs.Close()
```

First you need an instance of the `FileStream` class, which basically allows opening a communication with the specified file and with the mode specified by a value of the `FileMode` enumeration (such as `Create`, `Append`, `CreateNew`, `Open`, and `OpenOrTruncate`). This class provides support for both synchronous and asynchronous operations. Then you point to the `FileStream` instance in the constructor of the `StreamWriter`/`StreamReader` class. Remember to close both streams when you are done.

19

Reading and Writing Binary Files

You can read and write data to binary files using the `BinaryReader` and `BinaryWriter` classes. Both require a `FileStream` instance and allow reading and writing arrays of bytes. The following is an example of creating a binary stream:

```
Dim fs As New FileStream("C:\Temporary\OneFile.bin", FileMode.CreateNew)
Dim bs As New BinaryWriter(fs)

Dim bytesToWrite() As Byte = New Byte() {128, 64, 32, 16}

bs.Write(bytesToWrite)
bs.Close()
fs.Close()
```

The `Write` method allows writing information as binary but it also accepts base .NET types such as integers and strings, all written as binary. It provides several overloads so that you can also specify the offset and the number of bytes to be written. To read a binary file you instantiate the `BinaryReader` class. The following example retrieves information from a file utilizing a `Using..End Using` block to ensure that resources are correctly freed up when no longer necessary:

```
fs = New FileStream("C:\Temporary\OneFile.bin", FileMode.Open)
Using br As New BinaryReader(fs)
    If fs IsNot Nothing AndAlso fs.Length > 0 Then
        Dim buffer() As Byte = br.ReadBytes(CInt(fs.Length))
    End If
End Using
fs.Close()
```

In this case the `ReadBytes` method, which is used to retrieve data, reads a number of bytes corresponding to the file length. Because binary data can have different forms, `ReadBytes` is just one of a series of methods for reading .NET types such as `ReadChar`, `ReadInt32`, `ReadString`, `ReadDouble`, and so on.

Using Memory Streams

Memory streams are special objects that act like file streams but that work in memory, providing the ability to manipulate binary data. The following code creates a `MemoryStream` with 2 Kbytes capacity and puts in a string:

```
Dim ms As New MemoryStream(2048)


Dim bs As New BinaryWriter(ms)
```

```
bs.Write("Some text written as binary")
bs.Close()
ms.Close()
```

To retrieve data you use a `BinaryReader` pointing to the `MemoryStream` as you saw in the paragraph for binary files. So, in this example, you can simply invoke `ReadString` as follows:

```
'The stream must be still open
Using br As New BinaryReader(ms)
    If ms IsNot Nothing AndAlso ms.Length > 0 Then
        Dim data As String = br.ReadString

    End If
End Using
ms.Close()
```

Using Streams with Strings

Although not often utilized, you can take advantage of `StringReader` and `StringWriter` for manipulating strings. The following example generates a new `StringBuilder` and associates it to a new `StringWriter`. Then it retrieves the list of filenames in the C:\ directory and puts each string into the writer. You notice that, because of the association between the two objects, changes are reflected to the `StringBuilder`. Try this:

```
Dim sBuilder As New Text.StringBuilder
Dim sWriter As New StringWriter(sBuilder)

For Each name As String In Directory.GetFiles("C:\")
    sWriter.WriteLine(name)
Next
sWriter.Close()


Console.WriteLine(sBuilder.ToString)
```

To read strings you can use the `StringReader` object, whose constructor requires a string to be read. To continue with the example, we can read the previously created `StringBuilder` line by line:

```
Dim sReader As New StringReader(sBuilder.ToString)
Do Until sReader.Peek = -1
    Console.WriteLine(sReader.ReadLine)

Loop
```

19

You notice lots of similarities between string streams and `StreamWriter/StreamReader`, because basically both work with text.

Compressing Data with Streams

One of the most interesting features of streams starting from .NET Framework 2.0 is the ability to compress and decompress data utilizing the `GZipStream` and `DeflateStream` objects. Both are exposed by the `System.IO.Compression` namespace, and basically they both compress data using the *GZip* algorithm. The only difference is that the `GZipStream` writes a small header to compressed data. The interesting thing is that they work similarly to other streams, and when you write or read data into the stream, data is automatically compressed or decompressed by the runtime. The good news is that you are not limited to compressing files, but any other kind of stream. Basically compressing and decompressing data is quite a simple task. There are situations in which you need more attention according to the kind of data you need to access for files. To make comprehension easier, take a look at the code example provided in Listing 19.1 that contains comments that explain how such streams work. The purpose of the example is to provide the ability to compress and decompress files that is a common requirement in applications. You are encouraged to read comments within the code that can help you get started with the `GZipStream`.

.NET 4.0 IMPROVEMENTS

The .NET Framework 4.0 introduces a couple new improvements to the `System.IO.Compression` namespace. First, the limit of 4 Gigabytes for compressed data has been removed. Second, the compression algorithm has been improved to not compress again already affected data.

LISTING 19.1   Compressing and Decompressing Streams

```
Imports System.IO
Imports System.IO.Compression

Module Compression

    Sub TestCompress()
        Try
            Compress("C:\Temp\Source.Txt",
                     "C:\Temp\Compressed.gzp")
        Catch ex As FileNotFoundException
            Console.WriteLine("File not found!")
        Catch ex As IOException
            Console.WriteLine("An input/output error has occurred:")
            Console.WriteLine(ex.Message)
        Catch ex As Exception
            Console.WriteLine(ex.Message)
```

```vbnet
        End Try
    End Sub

    Sub TestDecompress()
        Try
            Decompress("C:\Temp\Compressed.gzp",
                        "C:\Temp\Original.txt")

        Catch ex As FileNotFoundException
            Console.WriteLine("File not found!")
        Catch ex As IOException
            Console.WriteLine("An input/output error has occurred:")
            Console.WriteLine(ex.Message)
        Catch ex As Exception
            Console.WriteLine(ex.Message)
        End Try
    End Sub

    Public Sub Compress(ByVal inputName As String, ByVal outputName As String)

        'Instantiates a new FileStream
        Dim infile As FileStream

        Try
            'The Stream points to the specified input file
            infile = New FileStream(inputName, FileMode.Open, FileAccess.Read,
                                    FileShare.Read)

            'Stores the file length in a buffer
            Dim buffer(CInt(infile.Length - 1)) As Byte

            'Checks if the file can be read and assigns to the "count"
            'variable the result of reading the file
            Dim count As Integer = infile.Read(buffer, 0, buffer.Length)

            'If the number of read byte is different from the file length
            'throws an exception
            If count <> buffer.Length Then
                infile.Close()
                Throw New IOException
            End If
            'closes the stream
            infile.Close()
            infile = Nothing

            'Creates a new stream pointing to the output file
            Dim ms As New FileStream(outputName, FileMode.CreateNew,
```

```vb
                              FileAccess.Write)

        'Creates a new GZipStream for compressing, pointing to
        'the output stream above leaving it open
        Dim compressedzipStream As New GZipStream(ms,
                                         CompressionMode.Compress,
                                         True)
        'Puts the buffer into the new stream, which is
        'automatically compressed
        compressedzipStream.Write(buffer, 0, buffer.Length)

        compressedzipStream.Close()
        ms.Close()
        Exit Sub
    Catch ex As IO.FileNotFoundException
        Throw
    Catch ex As IOException
        Throw
    Catch ex As Exception
        Throw
    End Try
End Sub

Public Sub Decompress(ByVal fileName As String, ByVal originalName As String)

    Dim inputFile As FileStream

    'Defining the stream for decompression
    Dim compressedZipStream As GZipStream

    'Defining a variable for storing compressed file size
    Dim compressedFileSize As Integer

    Try

        'Reads the input file
        inputFile = New FileStream(fileName,
                              FileMode.Open,
                              FileAccess.Read,
                              FileShare.Read)

        'Reads input file's size
        compressedFileSize = CInt(inputFile.Length)

        'Creates a new GZipStream in Decompress mode
        compressedZipStream = New GZipStream(inputFile,
```

```vb
                                    CompressionMode.Decompress)

'In compressed data the first 100 bytes store the original
'data size, so let's get it
Dim offset As Integer = 0
Dim totalBytes As Integer = 0

Dim SmallBuffer(100) As Byte

'Reads until there are available bytes in the first 100
'and increments variables that we'll need for sizing
'the buffer that will store the decompressed file
Do While True

    Dim bytesRead As Integer = compressedZipStream.
                              Read(SmallBuffer, 0, 100)

    If bytesRead = 0 Then
        Exit Do
    End If

    offset += bytesRead
    totalBytes += bytesRead
Loop

compressedZipStream.Close()
compressedZipStream = Nothing

'Creates a new FileStream for reading the input file
inputFile = New FileStream(fileName,
                           FileMode.Open,
                           FileAccess.Read,
                           FileShare.Read)

'and decompress its content
compressedZipStream = New GZipStream(inputFile,
                                CompressionMode.Decompress)

'Declares the buffer that will store uncompressed data
Dim buffer(totalBytes) As Byte

'Reads from the source file the number of bytes
'representing the buffer length, taking advantage
'of the original size
compressedZipStream.Read(buffer, 0, totalBytes)

compressedZipStream.Close()
```

19

```
          compressedZipStream = Nothing

          'Creates a new file for putting uncompressed
          'data
          Dim ms As New FileStream(originalName,
                                  FileMode.Create,
                                  FileAccess.Write)

          'Writes uncompressed data to file
          ms.Write(buffer, 0, buffer.Length)
          ms.Close()
          ms = Nothing
          Exit Sub

          'General IO error
      Catch ex As IOException
          Throw
      Catch ex As Exception
          Throw
          Exit Try
      End Try
   End Sub
End Module
```

TIP

You use `GZipStream` and `DeflateStream` the identical way. The only difference is about the header in the compressed stream. If you need further information on the difference, here is the official MSDN page: http://msdn.microsoft.com/en-us/library/system.io.compression.deflatestream(VS.100).aspx.

Notice how, at a higher level, you just instantiate the stream the same way in both compression and decompression tasks. The difference is the `CompressionMode` enumeration value that determines if a stream is for compression or decompression. With this technique you can invoke just the two custom methods for compressing and decompressing files, meaning that you could apply it to other kinds of data, too.

Networking with Streams

The .NET Framework provides functionalities for data exchange through networks taking advantage of streams; in particular, it exposes the `System.Net.Sockets.NetworkStream` class. Basically reading and writing data via a `NetworkStream` instance passes through a `System.Net.Sockets.TcpClient` class's instance. Code in Listing 19.2 shows how you can both write and read data in such a scenario. See comments in code for explanations.

LISTING 19.2   Networking with NetworkStream

```vbnet
Imports System.Net.Sockets
Imports System.Text

Module Network

    Sub NetStreamDemo()
        'Instantiating TcpClient and NetworkStream
        Dim customTcpClient As New TcpClient()
        Dim customNetworkStream As NetworkStream

        Try
            'Attempt to connect to socket
            '127.0.0.1 is the local machine address
            customTcpClient.Connect("127.0.0.1", 587) 'Port
            'Gets the instance of the stream for
            'data exchange
            customNetworkStream = customTcpClient.GetStream()

            'The port is not available
        Catch ex As ArgumentOutOfRangeException
            Console.WriteLine(ex.Message)
            'Connection problem
        Catch ex As SocketException
            Console.WriteLine(ex.Message)
        End Try

        'Gets an array of byte from a value, which is
        'encoded via System.Text.Encoding.Ascii.GetBytes
        Dim bytesToWrite() As Byte = _
            Encoding.ASCII.GetBytes("Something to exchange via TCP")

        'Gets the stream instance
        customNetworkStream = customTcpClient.GetStream()
        'Writes the bytes to the stream; this
        'means sending data to the network
        customNetworkStream.Write(bytesToWrite, 0,
                                    bytesToWrite.Length)

        'Establishes the buffer size for receiving data
        Dim bufferSize As Integer = customTcpClient.
                                    ReceiveBufferSize
        Dim bufferForReceivedBytes(bufferSize) As Byte

        'Gets data from the stream, meaning by the network
```

```
customNetworkStream.Read(bufferForReceivedBytes, 0,
                         bufferSize)

        Dim result As String = Encoding.ASCII.GetString(bufferForReceivedBytes,
                             0, bufferSize)
    End Sub
End Module
```

There are obviously several ways for data exchange, and this is probably one of the most basic ones in the era of Windows Communication Foundation. This topic is related to streams, so an overview was necessary.

Summary

Working with files, directories, and drives is a common requirement for each application. The .NET Framework provides two main classes for working with directories: System.IO.Directory and System.IO.Path. The first one allows performing operations such as creating, moving, renaming, and investigating for filenames. The second one is about directory and filename manipulation other than gaining access to Windows's temporary folder. Similar to Directory, the System.IO.DirectoryInfo class provides access to directory operations and information, but the difference is that an instance of such a class represents a single directory. If you instead need to get information on physical drives on your machine, simply create an instance of the System.IO.DriveInfo class. Similar to Directory and DirectoryInfo, the System.IO.File and System.IO.FileInfo classes provide access to files on disk, and their members are the same as for directory classes except that they allow working with files. The last part of the chapter is about streams. Streams are sequences of bytes that allow exchanging different kinds of data. All stream classes inherit from System.IO.Stream. StreamReader, and StreamWriter allow reading and writing text files. BinaryReader and BinaryWriter allow reading and writing binary files. MemoryStream allows reading and writing in-memory binary data. StringReader and StringWriter allow managing in-memory strings. GZipStream and DeflateStream allow compressing data according to the GZip algorithm. NetworkStream allows exchanging data through a network. Writing and reading data can often require several lines of code. Luckily the Visual Basic language offers an important alternative known as the My namespace that is covered in next chapter.

CHAPTER 20

The My Namespace

The great debate is always the same: better Visual Basic or Visual C#? Because of the .NET Framework, the Common Language Runtime, and the IL language, the languages' evolution brought both VB and C# to do basically the same things. Of course, there are some differences, and one language has some features that the other one does not have, as with the case of void lambdas in C#, which have been introduced in VB only with this last version, or the case of VB's XML literals that C# does not have. Differences are obvious. One of the Visual Basic features that does not have commonalities with other managed languages is the My namespace, belonging to VB starting from Visual Basic 2005. In this chapter you consider the My namespace that can write productive code, according to the philosophy of "less code, more productivity."

Introducing My

The My namespace provides shortcuts for accessing several common objects in .NET development. Basically My exposes classes that wrap existing built-in objects and reoffers them under an easier to use fashion. By using My, you can access lots of development areas generally writing less code than you would if you used usual techniques. At a higher level My exposes the following members:

▶ My.Application, a property exposing members that allows access to other properties of the current application

▶ `My.Computer`, a property exposing members that provides shortcuts to common operations with your machine, such as the file system or the Registry

▶ `My.Settings`, a property that provides code support for the Settings tab in My Project and that also allows using settings from your application

▶ `My.Resources`, a namespace that defines several objects providing support for the Resources tab in My Project and allowing handling resources in code

▶ `My.User`, a property providing members for getting or setting information about the current user that logged into the operating system

▶ `My.WebServices`, a property allowing retrieving information on web services consumed by your application

The preceding listed `My` members are the most general, and you can find them in every kind of Visual Basic application. There are also specific extensions for the `My` namespace related to specific applications, such as WPF. (A description is at the end of this chapter.) `My` is interesting because it can be also be extended with custom members providing great flexibility to your applications. If something within `My` does not satisfy you, you can change it. After all, `My` is a namespace, meaning that it is implemented in code.

"MY" IS A RESERVED KEYWORD

Due to its particular role within the Visual Basic programming language, although it just refers to a namespace, My is also a reserved word in Visual Basic.

My.Application

The `My.Application` properties expose members allowing getting information on the running instance of the application. This information can be divided into three major groups: application information at assembly level, culture for localization and deployment, and environment information. Let's discover all these features.

APPLICATION FRAMEWORK

In specific kinds of applications, such as Windows Forms and WPF applications, My.Application also provides support for the *application framework* and *application events*. This is discussed in the last section of this chapter.

Retrieving Assembly Information

Basically `My.Application` maps the same-named tab within My Project. Because of this, it provides the ability of investigating in code assemblies' information. This can be accomplished via the `My.Application.Info` property (of type `Microsoft.VisualBasic.ApplicationServices.AssemblyInfo`) that retrieves information about the current assembly, such as the name, version, company name, copyright, and so on. The following code shows how you can accomplish this:

```
'Assembly information
Console.WriteLine("Assembly name: {0}",
                  My.Application.Info.AssemblyName)
Console.WriteLine("Assembly version: {0}",
                  My.Application.Info.Version)
Console.WriteLine("Company name: {0}",
                  My.Application.Info.CompanyName)
'Returns the directory where the application is running from
Console.WriteLine("Running from: {0}",
                  My.Application.Info.DirectoryPath)
```

Another interesting feature is that you can get information on all referenced assemblies, as shown in the following iteration:

```
Console.WriteLine("References:")
For Each item In My.Application.Info.LoadedAssemblies
    Console.WriteLine(item)
Next
```

The `LoadedAssemblies` property is of type `ReadonlyCollection(Of System.Reflection.AssemblyInfo)`, so you become more skilled after reading Chapter 47, "Reflection."

Working with Cultures

In Chapter 36, "Localizing Applications," you get more information about localizing applications, but at this particular point of the book, you can get an interesting taste using `My`. Basically two cultures are settable for your application: the thread's culture, which is about string manipulation and formatting, and the user interface culture, which is about adapting resources to the desired culture. You can get information on both by invoking the `Culture` and `UICulture` properties from `My.Application`; then you can set different cultures for both the main culture and UI culture by invoking the `ChangeCulture` and `ChangeUICulture` methods. The following code accomplishes this:

```
Dim culture As CultureInfo = My.Application.Culture
Console.WriteLine("Current culture: {0}", culture.Name)

Dim UICulture As CultureInfo = My.Application.UICulture
Console.WriteLine("Current UI culture: {0}", UICulture.Name)

My.Application.ChangeCulture("it-IT")
My.Application.ChangeUICulture("it-IT")

Console.WriteLine("New settings: {0}, {1}",
```

```
My.Application.Culture.Name,
My.Application.UICulture.Name)
```

First, the code retrieves information about cultures. Such information is of type
`System.Globalization.CultureInfo`. This object provides lots of information on
cultures, but in this case we use `Name` that returns the culture name. Notice how you can
change cultures by invoking `ChangeCulture` and `ChangeUICulture` just by passing a string
representing the culture's name. On my machine the preceding code produces the
following result:

```
Current culture: en-US
Current UI culture: en-US
New settings: it-IT, it-IT
```

If you need to pass a custom culture, you should create a new `CultureInfo` object and
then pass the name of the new culture. Typically you will not remember each culture
name, so if you want to investigate available cultures, you can write a simple iteration
taking advantage of the shared `GetCultureInfo` method:

```
For Each c In CultureInfo.GetCultures(CultureTypes.AllCultures)
    Console.WriteLine(c.Name)
Next
```

Deployment and Environment Information

The `My.Application` property basically allows managing the following environment
information:

- ▶ Getting information on the ClickOnce deployment for the current application

- ▶ Retrieving environment variables

- ▶ Writing entries to the Windows Applications log

- ▶ Retrieving command line arguments

Next you see in detail how you can get/set such information using `My.Application`.

Deployment Information

It can be useful to get information on the state of the deployment if your application has
been installed via the ClickOnce technology (discussed in detail in Chapter 55,
"Deploying Applications with ClickOnce"). You might want to provide the ability of
downloading files on-demand or to implement additional behaviors according to the
updates status. You can use the `IsNetworkDeployed` property to know if an application has

been deployed to a network via ClickOnce and the `My.Application.Deployment` property (which wraps `System.Deployment.Application.ApplicationDeployment`) to make other decisions. The following code shows information on the deployment status only if the application has been deployed to a network:

```
'Deployment and environment information
If My.Application.IsNetworkDeployed = True Then
    Console.
    WriteLine("Application deployed to a network via ClickOnce")

    Console.WriteLine("Current deployment version: {0}",
            My.Application.Deployment.CurrentVersion)
    Console.WriteLine("The application runs from: {0}",
            My.Application.Deployment.ActivationUri)
    Console.WriteLine("Is first time run: {0}",
            My.Application.Deployment.IsFirstRun)
End If
```

The `CurrentVersion` property is useful to understand the current *deployment* version, while `ActivationUri` is the address where the application manifest is invoked from. You can also programmatically check for updates invoking specific methods, such as `CheckForUpdate`, `CheckForUpdateAsync`, and `CheckForUpdateAsyncCancel`. The following is an example:

```
My.Application.Deployment.CheckForUpdate()
```

Luckily, `My.Application.Deployment` members' names are self-explanatory, and with the help of IntelliSense and a little bit of curiosity, you have in your hands all the power of such an object.

Retrieving Environment Variables

There are situations where you need to retrieve the content of the operating system's environment variables. This can be accomplished by invoking the `GetEnvironmentVariable` that receives the name of the variable as an argument. The following code shows how to retrieve the content of the PATH environment variable:

```
Dim PathEnvironmentVariable As String = My.Application.
                                GetEnvironmentVariable("PATH")
```

Writing Entries to the Windows' Applications Log

The .NET Framework provides several ways for interacting with the operating system logs, but the My namespace offers an easy way to write information to the Windows application log. My.Application offers a Log property, of type `Microsoft.VisualBasic.Logging.Log`,

20

which exposes members for writing information. The following code snippet shows how you can write a message to the application log invoking the `WriteEntry` method:

```
My.Application.Log.WriteEntry("Demonstrating My.Application.Log",
                              TraceEventType.Information)
```

The first argument is the message, and the second one is a member of the `TraceEventType` enumeration whose members are self-explanatory, thanks to IntelliSense, and allow specifying the level of your message. Alternatively, you can write the content of an entire exception invoking the `WriteException` method:

```
Try

Catch ex As Exception
    My.Application.Log.WriteException(ex)
End Try
```

You can also get control over the listeners and the file used by the .NET Framework by utilizing the `TraceSource` and `DefaultFileLogWriter`.

Retrieving Command-Line Arguments

If you need to retrieve command-line arguments for your application, `My.Application` offers a convenient way. To complete the following demonstration, go to the Debug tab of My Project and set whatever command-line arguments you like in the Command Line Arguments text box. `My.Application` offers a `CommandLineArgs` property, which is a `ReadOnlyCollection(Of String)` that stores such arguments. Each item in the collection represents a command-line argument. The following code shows how you can iterate such collection and check for available command-line arguments:

```
For Each argument As String In My.Application.CommandLineArgs
    Console.WriteLine(argument)
Next
```

My.Computer

`My.Computer` provides lots of shortcuts for accessing features on the local system, starting from the clipboard arriving at the Registry, passing through audio capabilities. This is basically a class exposing several properties, each one related to a computer area. This is a list of `My.Computer` properties:

- ▶ `FileSystem`: Provides members for accessing files, directories, and other objects on disk
- ▶ `Clipboard`: Provides members for setting data to and getting data from the system clipboard
- ▶ `Audio`: Allows playing audio files
- ▶ `Mouse`: Allows retrieving information on the installed mouse

▶ Keyboard: Provides members for getting information on the state of keys in the keyboard

▶ Registry: Provides members for getting and setting information to Windows Registry

▶ Network: Offers members for performing operations within the network that the computer is connected to

▶ Ports: Allows retrieving information on the computer's serial ports

▶ Screen: Allows retrieving information on the screen properties (Windows Forms only)

▶ Info: Provides a series of information about the running machine

As usual, IntelliSense provides detailed information on each member from the preceding properties. In the next section you learn to access your machine information with My.Computer, but providing examples for each member is not possible. Because of this, members for the biggest areas are summarized and code examples for the most important members are provided.

Working with the File System

My.Computer provides lots of shortcuts for performing most-common operations on files and directories via the FileSystem property. Members are self-explanatory and easy to understand, so you can always take advantage of IntelliSense. To demonstrate how easy it is to work with the file system, let's go through some examples. The following code copies a directory into another one, then it creates a new directory, and finally it retrieves the current directory:

```
My.Computer.FileSystem.CopyDirectory("C:\Source", "C:\Target")
My.Computer.FileSystem.CreateDirectory("C:\Temp")

Dim currentDir As String = My.Computer.FileSystem.CurrentDirectory
```

You can also get information on Windows's special directories via the SpecialDirectories property as follows:

```
'Gets My Pictures path
Dim picturesFolder As String =
    My.Computer.FileSystem.SpecialDirectories.MyPictures
```

Working with files is also straightforward. For example, you can read or create a text file in one line of code:

```
'Read the content of a text file
Dim content As String =
    My.Computer.FileSystem.ReadAllText("C:\ADocument.txt")

'Creates a new text file
My.Computer.FileSystem.WriteAllText("C:\ADocument.txt", "File content",
                            append:=False)
```

20

This can be useful if you do not need to create a text file dynamically, for example line by line. For files, you can simply iterate a directory to get an array of strings storing all file-names as follows:

```
For Each item As String In My.Computer.FileSystem.GetFiles("C:\")
    'Do something here
Next
```

This last example allows extracting the filename of a full path name:

```
'Returns MyFile.txt
Dim parsedString As String =
    My.Computer.FileSystem.GetName("C:\Temp\MyFile.txt")
```

`My.Computer.FileSystem` is straightforward and simplifies access to the file system resources avoiding the need to write lots of lines of code.

Working with the Clipboard

The `My.Computer.Clipboard` property provides members for working with the system clipboard. Table 20.1 summarizes the members.

TABLE 20.1   `My.Computer.Clipboard` Members

Member	Description
Clear	Clears the clipboard content
ContainsAudio	Checks if the clipboard contains an audio file
ContainsData	Checks if the clipboard contains data according to the specified format
ContainsFileDropList	Checks if the clipboard contains a file drop-down list
ContainsImage	Checks if the clipboard contains an image
ContainsText	Checks if the clipboard contains some text
GetAudioStream	Gets an audio file from the clipboard as a stream
GetData	Gets data from the clipboard according to the specified format
GetDataObject	Gets data from the clipboard as `IDataObject`
GetImage	Retrieves an image from the clipboard
GetFileDropDownList	Retrieves a file drop-down list from the clipboard
GetText	Retrieves text from the clipboard
SetAudio	Copies the specified audio to the clipboard
SetData	Copies the specified custom data to the clipboard

TABLE 20.1 Continued

Member	Description
SetDataObject	Copies the specified `System.Windows.Forms.DataObject` to the clipboard
SetImage	Copies the specified image to the clipboard
SetText	Copies the specified text to the clipboard

The following code shows how you can clear the clipboard and then copy some text; in the end the code checks if some text is available and, if so, returns the text:

```
My.Computer.Clipboard.Clear()
My.Computer.Clipboard.SetText("This is some text")

If My.Computer.Clipboard.ContainsText Then
    Console.WriteLine(My.Computer.Clipboard.GetText)
End If
```

Playing Audio Files

`My.Computer.Audio` provides three methods for audio files reproduction. The first one is Play, which can play a .Wav file. The following is an example:

```
My.Computer.Audio.Play("C:\MySound.Wav", AudioPlayMode.WaitToComplete)
```

You need to pass at least the filename as the first argument; as an alternative, you can pass the .wav file as a byte array or a FileStream. The AudioPlayMode enumeration allows specifying how the audio file needs to be played. WaitToComplete means that no other code will be executed until the reproduction ends; Background, which is the default setting, means that the audio is reproduced asynchronously; last, BackgroundLoop means that the audio file is reproduced in the loop until you explicitly invoke the Stop method as follows:

```
My.Computer.Audio.Play("C:\MySound.Wav",
                    AudioPlayMode.BackgroundLoop)
'Other code...
My.Computer.Audio.Stop()
```

The last method is PlaySystemSound, whose first argument is the system sound to reproduce, which works like this:

```
My.Computer.Audio.PlaySystemSound(Media.SystemSounds.Exclamation)
```

Sounds examples other than Exclamation are Asterisk, Beep, Hand, and Question.

Managing the Keyboard

You can check for the state of some keyboard keys. My.Computer.Keyboard allows accomplishing this via six properties. Three are about the Caps-lock, Num-lock, and Scroll-lock keys, whereas the other three allow getting the state (pressed or not) of Alt, Shift, and Ctrl. The following code provides a complete example:

```
'All Boolean values
Console.WriteLine(My.Computer.Keyboard.AltKeyDown)
Console.WriteLine(My.Computer.Keyboard.CtrlKeyDown)
Console.WriteLine(My.Computer.Keyboard.ShiftKeyDown)
Console.WriteLine(My.Computer.Keyboard.CapsLock)
Console.WriteLine(My.Computer.Keyboard.NumLock)

Console.WriteLine(My.Computer.Keyboard.ScrollLock)
```

Working with the Registry

My.Computer provides fast access to Windows Registry. It exposes a Registry property wrapping lots of functionalities of Microsoft.Win32.Registry class for faster work. My.Computer.Registry offers some properties, of type Microsoft.Win32.RegistryKey, representing the most important areas of the Registry, such as HKEY_LOCAL_MACHINE (wrapped by the LocalMachine property), HKEY_ALL_USER (wrapped by Users), HKEY_CURRENT_USER (wrapped by CurrentUser), and HKEY_CLASSES_ROOT (wrapped by ClassesRoot). All of them provide methods for creating subkeys, querying, deleting, and setting values within subkeys. For example, the following code (which requires an Imports Microsoft.Win32 directive) creates a subkey in the HKEY_CURRENT_USER\Software key, providing a company name and the application name. The code also sets permissions for writing/reading the key and its eventual subkeys:

```
Dim regKey As RegistryKey = My.Computer.Registry.
              CurrentUser.CreateSubKey("Software\DelSole\MyApplication",
              RegistryKeyPermissionCheck.ReadWriteSubTree,
              RegistryOptions.None)
```

Because the CreateSubKey returns a RegistryKey object, you can invoke instance members from this type. For example, you can add values to the new key by invoking the SetValue method as follows:

```
'Value-name, actual value
regKey.SetValue("MyValue", 1)
```

You get the value of the desired subkey by invoking the GetValue method as follows:

```
'Returns "1"
Dim value As String = CStr(My.Computer.Registry.
    GetValue("HKEY_CURRENT_USER\Software\DelSole\MyApplication",
                                        "MyValue",
                                        Nothing))
```

Remember that `GetValue` returns `Object`, so you need to perform an explicit conversion according to the value type you expect. You also have the ability to determine what kind of value is associated to a value name. This can be accomplished by getting a `RegistryValueKind` value, such as `DWord`, `Binary`, `String`, and `QWord`, (which is an enumeration from `Microsoft.Win32`) via the `GetValueKind` method so that you can also be more precise when requiring values:

```
'Returns DWORD
Dim valueKind As RegistryValueKind = regKey.GetValueKind("MyValue")

If valueKind = RegistryValueKind.DWord Then
        Dim value2 As Integer = _
            CInt(My.Computer.
            Registry.
            GetValue("HKEY_CURRENT_USER\Software\DelSole\MyApplication",
                "MyValue", Nothing))
End If
```

There is also a `GetNames` method that returns an array of strings, each representing a value in the specified subkey if more than one value is stored within the subkey. The following code instead removes the previously created value:

```
regKey.DeleteValue("MyValue")
```

Remember to close the Registry key when you do not use it anymore:

```
regKey.Close()
```

Finally, you can delete a subkey by invoking the `DeleteSubKey` as follows:

```
My.Computer.Registry.
    CurrentUser.DeleteSubKey("Software\DelSole\MyApplication",
    True)
```

Other than the mentioned properties about Registry areas, `My.Computer.Registry` exposes just two interesting methods, `SetValue` and `GetValue`, which basically require you to specify long strings and that usually can be replaced by the same-named methods of the instance of `RegistryKey`. By the way, with `My.Computer.Registry` you can perform lots of tasks onto the system Registry writing code easier and faster.

Accessing the Network

If your machine is connected to a network, you can use the `My.Computer.Network` property that wraps some functionalities of the `System.Net` namespace. The most interesting members are the `IsNetworkAvailable` property that returns `True` if the machine is connected, the `DownloadFile` method that allows downloading a file from the network, `UploadFile` that allows uploading a file to the specified target on the network, and `Ping` that sends a ping to the specified address. The following code checks first for network availability, then sends a ping to my English language blog, and in the end attempts to download a file from the Italian VB Tips & Tricks community (where I'm a team member) passing credentials as strings:

```
If My.Computer.Network.IsAvailable Then
    Try

        '2000 is the timeout
        Dim available As Boolean = My.Computer.
                                    Network.
                                    Ping("http://community.visual-
basic.it/AlessandroEnglish",

                                    2000)


        My.Computer.Network.DownloadFile("http://www.visual-
basic.it/scarica.asp?ID=1016",

                                    "C:\WpfDemo.zip",
                                    "MyUserName",
                                    "MyPassword")
    Catch ex As System.Net.WebException

    Catch ex As Exception

    End Try
End If
```

Notice how a `System.Net.WebException` is caught in case there are any network problems especially with the `DownloadFile` method. The `DownloadFile` requires you to specify the source as the first argument and the target file as the second one. You can also specify the source as a `System.Uri`; moreover the method can also download html contents. `UploadFile` works similarly, in that it requires the name of the file to be uploaded and the address, also allowing credentials specifications. Both methods offer several overloads that IntelliSense explains in details. About `Ping`, the methods returns `True` if the website is reachable.

Getting Computer Information

`My.Computer` provides the ability of retrieving information on the current machine. The first information is the machine name, which is available from `My.Computer.Name`, a property of type `String`. Second is the `My.Computer.Info` property of type `Microsoft.VisualBasic.Devices.ComputerInfo`, which collects information such as the total and available memory, both physical and virtual or the name, platform, and version of the operating system. The following code shows how you can get some information on the system:

```
Console.WriteLine("Computer name {0}: ", My.Computer.Name)
Console.WriteLine("Total physical memory {0}: ",
                  My.Computer.Info.TotalPhysicalMemory)
Console.WriteLine("Available physical memory {0}: ",
                  My.Computer.Info.AvailablePhysicalMemory)
Console.WriteLine("Operating system full name {0}: ",
                  My.Computer.Info.OSFullName)
Console.WriteLine("Operating system version: {0}",
                  My.Computer.Info.OSVersion)
Console.WriteLine("Installed User Interface culture: {0}",
                  My.Computer.Info.InstalledUICulture.Name)
```

My.Computer also exposes a Clock property that offers three subproperties: GmtTime that returns the local date and time expressed as GMT, LocalTime that returns the local date and time, and TickCount that returns the number of ticks considering the machine timer. This is how you can use it:

```
Console.WriteLine("GMT Time for local machine: {0}",
                  My.Computer.Clock.GmtTime.ToString)
```

You can interact with system hardware with two other properties, Mouse and Screen. The first one allows knowing if your mouse has a wheel, if buttons' functionalities are swapped, or how many lines the scroll will be each time you move the wheel. This is an example:

```
Console.WriteLine("Mouse buttons are swapped: {0}",
                  My.Computer.Mouse.ButtonsSwapped.ToString)
Console.WriteLine("Mouse has wheel: {0}",
                  My.Computer.Mouse.WheelExists.ToString)
```

Screen is also interesting because it allows retrieving information on your display, such as the resolution, the device name, or the actual working area. The following is an example:

```
Console.WriteLine("Screen resolution: {0} x {1}",
                      My.Computer.Screen.Bounds.Width,
                      My.Computer.Screen.Bounds.Height)
Console.WriteLine("Bits per pixel: {0}",
                      My.Computer.Screen.BitsPerPixel)
Console.WriteLine("Working area: {0} x {1}",
                      My.Computer.Screen.WorkingArea.Width,
                      My.Computer.Screen.WorkingArea.Height)
```

20

Figure 20.1 shows the global result of the preceding code running on my machine.

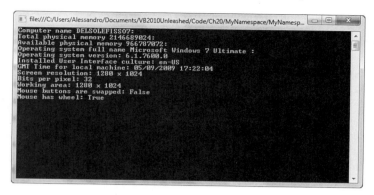

FIGURE 20.1   Information on the local machine using My.Computer.

As you can see you can obtain detailed information about both the computer and the operating system, including localization properties. My.Computer members for retrieving information are always self-explanatory, but you can always take advantage of IntelliSense and the Object Browser tool.

My.Settings

One of the most common requirements for applications is providing the ability of storing user preferences, such as the graphic theme, personal folders, options, and so on. Generally there are two kinds of settings that the .NET Framework allows saving within the application configuration file: application-level settings and user-level settings. Application-level settings are related to the general behavior of the application, and users will not have the ability of providing modifications. User-level settings are related to each user profile that runs the applications and allows storing and editing preferences. Starting from Visual Basic 2005, My namespace provides a class named My.Settings, which offers members that easily allow working with settings at both levels, but only user-level settings can be written. At a higher level My.Settings is the code representation of the Settings tab in My Project. Because of this we start discussing My.Settings by talking about the Settings designer and then explaining how you can work with settings in code. With that said, create a new Console project (if not yet) and open My Project; then click the **Settings** tab. Figure 20.2 shows the Settings Designer.

Basically each setting is represented by a variable that can be of any .NET type (as long as it is marked as serializable) storing the desired value. This variable can be provided at both application level and user level, with the condition that only user-level variables can be also written. You now learn how to design settings and then how to use them in code. Imagine you want to provide a simple way for checking if the application is running for the first time. In the Name column replace the default Settings identifier with IsFirstTimeRun. In the Type column choose the Boolean type from the combo box, and in the Scope column ensure that User is selected. In the Value column choose True from the combo box. Notice that Visual Studio can provide appropriate values depending on

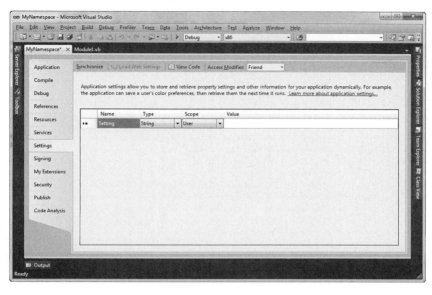

FIGURE 20.2   Settings designer.

the setting type; for Boolean values, it offers `True` and `False`. After this sequence, your Settings Designer looks like Figure 20.3.

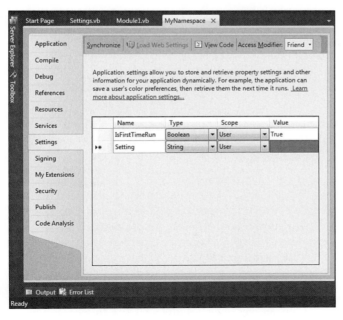

FIGURE 20.3   Providing a Boolean user-level setting.

You can now write some code to check if the application is running for the first time and, if so, set the IsFirstTimeRun setting to False as follows:

```
Sub UserSettingsDemo()

    If My.Settings.IsFirstTimeRun = True Then
        Console.WriteLine("The application is running for the first time")
            My.Settings.IsFirstTimeRun = False
            My.Settings.Save()
    Else
        Console.
        WriteLine("The application is already familiar with your system!")
    End If

End Sub
```

When you first launch the application, you get the following result:

```
The application is running for the first time
```

The code also changed the IsFirstTimeRun setting from True to False; this is possible because it is a user-level setting. If it were an application-level setting, it would be offered as a read-only property.

APPLICATION-LEVEL ONLY SETTINGS

With the Settings Designer you can define different kinds of settings, both at application level and user level. Among these settings, Connection Strings and Web Services URL are only available at application level to avoid modifications in code. In this way, only the appropriate personnel can make the right modifications if needed.

Notice also that you have to invoke the Save method; otherwise changes will not be saved. To check that everything works, simply rerun the application; you should now get the following message:

```
The application is already familiar with your system!
```

With the same technique you can easily define other settings of different type. You are not limited to types shown in the default combo box. You can choose any other .NET type that supports serialization by clicking the **Browse** command at the bottom of the combo box. This displays the Select a Type window (see Figure 20.4) where you can make your choice.

Settings definitions and default values are stored within the application configuration (app.config) file as XML definition. If your project does not already contain a configuration file, Visual Studio 2010 adds one. User-level settings are defined within a section

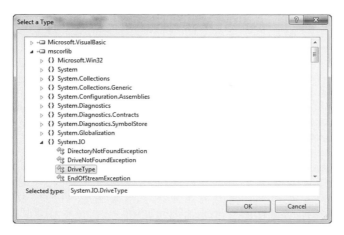

FIGURE 20.4   Selecting a nondefault .NET type for designing settings.

named userSettings. The following is an excerpt from the app.config file for the demo project showing the definition of the previously described IsFirstTimeRun setting:

```
<userSettings>
    <MyNamespace.My.MySettings>
        <setting name="IsFirstTimeRun" serializeAs="String">
            <value>True</value>
        </setting>
    </MyNamespace.My.MySettings>
</userSettings>
```

Notice how each setting is defined by a setting node that also defines the setting's name and way of serialization. (Although serialized as a string, based on its value, the .NET Framework can recognize the setting as Boolean.) Each setting node has a child node named value that stores the default value for the setting.

CONFIGURATION FILE NAMING

Your application configuration file is named app.config as long as it is included in your project folder. When the application is built into the target folder (such as the default Debug and Release subfolders), the configuration file takes the complete name of the executable (for example, MyApplication.exe) plus the .config extension (for example, MyApplication.exe.config).

Similarly, application-level settings are stored within a section named applicationSettings. The following is the excerpt related to the test setting previously shown:

```
<applicationSettings>
    <MyNamespace.My.MySettings>
```

20

```
    <setting name="Setting" serializeAs="String">
        <value>test</value>
    </setting>
  </MyNamespace.My.MySettings>
</applicationSettings>
```

Settings also have a Visual Basic code counterpart. Each setting is mapped to a Visual Basic property. To understand this, click the **Show All Files** button in Solution Explorer and then expand the My Project folder; double-click the **Settings.designer.vb** file under Settings.Settings. Among the code that defines My.Settings, you can also find the definition for your custom settings. The IsFirstTimeRun setting defined in the previous example is mapped to a VB property as follows:

```
<Global.System.Configuration.UserScopedSettingAttribute(), _
 Global.System.Diagnostics.DebuggerNonUserCodeAttribute(), _
 Global.System.Configuration.DefaultSettingValueAttribute("True")> _
Public Property IsFirstTimeRun() As Boolean
    Get
        Return CType(Me("IsFirstTimeRun"), Boolean)
    End Get
    Set(ByVal value As Boolean)
        Me("IsFirstTimeRun") = Value
    End Set
End Property
```

The System.Configuration.UserScopedSettingAttribute tells the compiler that the setting has user-level scope, whereas the System.Configuration.DefaultSettingValueAttribute tells the compiler that the default value for the property is True. Notice how an explicit conversion with CType is performed to avoid any problems when deserializing. Now you know how and where settings are defined, but you still probably do not know where they are actually stored when you run the application outside Visual Studio (for example in production environments). The .NET Framework creates a folder for the application within the AppData\Local folder in Windows, which has user-level scope. If you consider the current example, named MyNamespace on my machine, the .NET Framework created the following folders structure (on Windows 7 but it is the same on Windows Vista): C:\Users\Alessandro\AppData\Local\MyNamespace\MyNamespace.vshost.exe_Url_wizb0y pr4ultyjhh1g1o352espg4ehdd\1.0.0.0. This auto-generated folder contains a file named user.config that contains the simple, following markup:

```
<?xml version="1.0" encoding="utf-8"?>
<configuration>
    <userSettings>
        <MyNamespace.My.MySettings>
            <setting name="IsFirstTimeRun" serializeAs="String">
                <value>False</value>
            </setting>
```

```
        </MyNamespace.My.MySettings>
    </userSettings>
</configuration>
```

As you can see it is the same piece of XML code that was originally defined within the application configuration file, but now it stays as a single file within a user-level folder. This file is the place where changes to an application's settings are effectively saved. Visual Studio provides a convenient way for restoring such files to the default settings' value by just clicking the **Synchronize** button in the Settings Designer.

My.Settings Events

My.Settings provides some interesting events that allow understanding of what is happening behind the scenes. Here are the following four events:

▶ SettingChanging, which is raised just before a setting value is changed

▶ PropertyChanged, which is raised just after a setting value has been changed

▶ SettingsLoaded, which is raised just after settings values are loaded

▶ SettingsSaving, which is raised just before settings values are persisted to disk

To handle such events you simply need to double-click the **Settings.vb** file that is automatically added by Visual Studio when you define a custom setting. The file just contains a partial class definition for My.Settings so that it makes it easier to write custom code without putting your hands on the auto-generated one. Creating event handlers is straightforward. When the Settings.vb file is open, select the **MySettings events** item in the upper-left combo box and select the event you want to handle in the upper right, as shown in Figure 20.5. When selected, Visual Studio 2010 automatically generates an event handler stub.

For example, imagine you want to validate a setting before changes are saved. To accomplish this, add a new String setting in the Settings Designer and name the setting as ValidationTest. The goal is to avoid saving the string value if it is null. The following code accomplishes this:

```
Private Sub MySettings_SettingsSaving(ByVal sender As Object,
                                ByVal e As
                    System.ComponentModel.CancelEventArgs) _
                                Handles Me.SettingsSaving

    If My.Settings.ValidationTest Is Nothing Then
        Throw New NullReferenceException("Cannot save a null string")
        e.Cancel = True
    End If

End Sub
```

The SettingsSaving event allows performing some checks before values are saved. The e variable of type System.ComponentModel.CancelEventArgs provides a Cancel property that

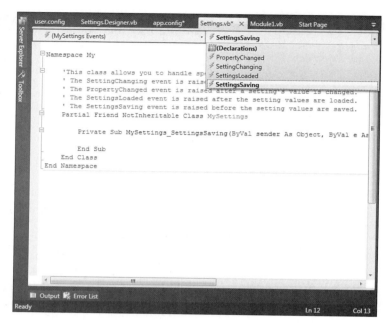

FIGURE 20.5   Handling **My.Settings** events.

cancels saving when set to True. The following example shows instead how you can handle the SettingChanging event that is raised before a setting value gets changed:

```vb
Private Sub MySettings_SettingChanging(ByVal sender As Object,
                                       ByVal e As _
                                       System.Configuration.
                                       SettingChangingEventArgs) _
                                       Handles Me.SettingChanging
    Console.WriteLine("About to change the settings values")
    'Waits for one second
    System.Threading.Thread.Sleep(1000)
End Sub
```

My.Settings provides a convenient way for managing user settings in a strongly typed way offering a modern infrastructure that is more efficient than older .ini files.

My.Resources

Visual Studio and the .NET Framework allow including resources within your application. Basically resources are different kinds of information that would be usually available from external files, such as sounds, images, and text. You can embed in your application all resources you want using My.Resources and the Resources Designer.

WPF RESOURCES

Things behave little differently in WPF and Silverlight applications. Because of their particular infrastructure, embedding resources using the Resources Designer is a practice that you must avoid. To understand how WPF resources work, take a look at the official page in the MSDN Library: http://msdn.microsoft.com/en-us/library/ms750613(VS.100).aspx.

Differently from other My members, My.Resources is a namespace defining subsequent members that can wrap in code resources that you define in the designer. At this point you need to open **My Project** and then select the **Resources** tab. Figure 20.6 shows the Resources Designer.

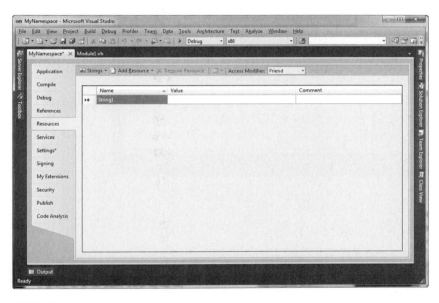

FIGURE 20.6   The Resources Designer.

Each time you add a new resource, Visual Studio generates a .NET property that provides managed access to the resource itself. For example, in the Name column replace the String1 default identifier with TestString and type **Resources demonstration** in the Value column. If you like, you can also provide a comment. Visual Studio generates a TestString property of type String and Friend visibility that you can access like any other property, as in the following code:

```
Console.WriteLine(My.Resources.TestString)
```

The interesting thing is that the Visual Basic compiler will try to format the string according to the current culture settings. Clicking the **Add Resource** button you will be prompted with a series of kinds of files to add as resources. If you add a text file, the file will be represented by a String property. Particularly, you can both add existing or new files. For example, click the **Add Resource** button and select the **New Image, JPEG Image...** command. After you specify the new image name, Visual Studio 2010 shows the image editor where you can leverage your drawing ability. Figure 20.7 shows an editor in action.

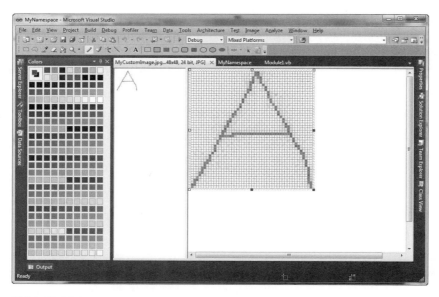

FIGURE 20.7   The Visual Studio 2010's built-in image editor.

After you create your image, or even if you add an existing one from disk, the IDE generates a property of type System.Drawing.Bitmap pointing to the image. If you have a Windows Forms application, you could simply recall your image as follows:

```
'PictureBox1 is a Windows Forms "PictureBox" control
'MyCustomImage is the name of the new custom image
Me.PictureBox1.Image = My.Resources.MyCustomImage
```

You can then pick images from resources if you need to populate a PictureBox control at design time by clicking the **Browse** button from the Properties window to set the Image property. Figure 20.8 shows how you can select an image directly from resources.

The same is for icons; you can create and draw a new icon with the Visual Studio Designer and then assign it to a Windows Forms Icon property. For audio files, you can add only .Wav files to ensure that they are automatically recognized as audio files. Such files are then mapped as System.IO.UnmanagedMemoryStream objects and can be played via My.Computer as follows:

FIGURE 20.8   Assigning an image to a PictureBox picking from resources.

```
My.Computer.Audio.Play(My.Resources.
                       AnAudioFile,
                       AudioPlayMode.WaitToComplete)
```

You can also add files different than text, pictures, icons, and audio. When Visual Studio cannot recognize a file type, it returns it from resources as byte array (System.Byte()), so you should implement code to analyze the particular resource. Visual Studio also creates a project-level folder named Resources where it stores resource files. Another interesting thing is to understand how resources are defined in code. Each time you add a resource via the designer, the IDE generates a Visual Basic property for it. For example, the following code shows how the new jpeg image is mapped in code:

```
Friend ReadOnly Property MyCustomImage() As System.Drawing.Bitmap
    Get
        Dim obj As Object = ResourceManager.
                            GetObject("MyCustomImage", resourceCulture)
        Return CType(obj, System.Drawing.Bitmap)
    End Get
End Property
```

And this is how the first string resource is mapped:

```
Friend ReadOnly Property TestString() As String
    Get
        Return ResourceManager.
            GetString("TestString", resourceCulture)
    End Get

End Property
```

The ResourceManager class provides methods for retrieving resources according to the specified culture that by default is the system one. Such properties are available in the Resources.designer.vb file that should never be edited manually.

Getting Resources by Name in Code

There are situations in which you need to access resources by name in code. This can be accomplished via the Reflection, which is a topic discussed in Chapter 47. The following code provides an example:

```
'Returns the specified resource of type String
'usage:
'Dim myRes As String = GetResourceByName("TestString")
Function GetResourceByName(ByVal resourceName As String) As String
    'An example for [Application Name].[Resource File]
    'is the current app:
    'MyNamespace.Resources.resx
    Dim rm As New ResourceManager("[Application Name].[Resource File]",
                              Assembly.GetExecutingAssembly)

    Return rm.GetString(resourceName)
End Function
```

In this case the method returns resources of type String but you can implement methods that return a different type.

My.User

My.User is a property that allows getting information on the user that logged into the Windows operating system and that is running the application. Such a property is of type Microsoft.VisualBasic.ApplicationServices.User and is a wrapper of this last mentioned one, meaning that you can invoke both and obtain the same results. Utilizing My.User is straightforward because it offers just a few but easy-to-understand members, as summarized in Table 20.2.

TABLE 20.2   My.User Members

Member	Type	Description
CurrentPrincipal	Property	Retrieves information on the current user based on the System.Security.Principal implementation for a role-based security
InitializeWithWindowsUser	Method	Associates the application with the current principal that logged into Windows
Name	Property	A string that stores the name of the currently logged user
IsAuthenticated	Property	A Boolean value representing if the current user is authenticated

TABLE 20.2   Continued

Member	Type	Description
IsInRole	Method	Returns True if the current user belongs to the specified role

Listing 20.1 shows how you can get information on the current user that runs the application. Notice how an invocation to `InitializeWithWindowsUser` is required to associate the current user to the application.

LISTING 20.1   Using `My.User` to Get Information on the Current User

```
Module Module1

    Sub Main()
        MyUserInformation()
        Console.ReadLine()
    End Sub

    Sub MyUserInformation()
        My.User.InitializeWithWindowsUser()
        Console.WriteLine("Current user is: {0}", My.User.Name)
        Console.WriteLine("User is authenticated: {0}", My.User.IsAuthenticated)
        Console.WriteLine("Application is running as Administrator: {0}",
                          My.User.IsInRole("BUILTIN\Administrators"))
        Console.WriteLine(My.User.CurrentPrincipal.
                          Identity.AuthenticationType.ToString)
    End Sub

End Module
```

The code shown in Listing 20.1 produces, on my machine, the following output:

```
Current user is: DELSOLEFISSO7\Alessandro
User is authenticated: True
Application is running as Administrator: False
NTLM
```

Notice how the username is provided as "Computer name\user name" and also how the role for the `IsInRole` method requires the name of the machine. (`BUILTIN` is a default value for all machines.) The authentication type is determined via the `CurrentPrincipal.Identity.AuthenticationType` property. Here, `Identity` is a `System.Security.Principal.IIdentity` object that provides information about a user, considering the role-based security system in the .NET Framework (for more information check the MSDN documentation). With a few lines of code you can get information about the current user without the need of dealing with classes and members from the `Microsoft.VisualBasic.ApplicationServices.User` object.

My.WebServices

When you have in your application references to web services, you can easily reach members provided by the proxy classes using `My.WebServices`. For example, if you have a proxy class named `DataAccess` exposing a `GetCustomers` method, you can simply write the following line:

```
My.WebServices.DataAccess.GetCustomers()
```

This is a rapid way for invoking members from referenced web services (as long as they are in the same solution of your application).

Extending My

One of the most interesting features of the `My` namespace is that it is extensible with custom members. You can both extend `My` at the root level or extend existing members such as `Application` and `Computer`. The first goal of this section is to show how you can extend `My` at the higher level, implementing functionalities for working with collections, such as a property that allows converting from a generic collection into an `ObservableCollection(Of T)`. We need to mimic how Visual Basic 2010 handles the `My` namespace, so first add a new module to the project and name it **MyCollectionsUtils**. Each member you want to be added to `My` must start with the **My** letters; this is the reason for using the `MyCollectionsUtils` identifier. The compiler can then distinguish that this member belongs to `My` if you enclose it within such a namespace. Add a reference to the WindowsBase.dll assembly (not required in WPF applications) and then write the code shown in Listing 20.2.

LISTING 20.2   Extending My at Root Level

```
Imports System.Collections.ObjectModel

Namespace My

    <Global.Microsoft.VisualBasic.HideModuleName(),
     Global.System.Diagnostics.DebuggerNonUserCode()>
    Module MyCollectionsUtils

        Private helper As New _
                ThreadSafeObjectProvider(Of ObservableCollectionHelper)

        Friend ReadOnly Property CollectionsUtils _
```

```
                As ObservableCollectionHelper
            Get
                Return helper.GetInstance
                helper = Nothing
            End Get
        End Property
    End Module

End Namespace

Class ObservableCollectionHelper

    Public Function ConvertToObservableCollection(Of T) _
                    (ByVal collection As ICollection(Of T)) _
                    As ObservableCollection(Of T)
        Return New ObservableCollection(Of T)(collection)
    End Function

End Class
```

FRIEND VISIBILITY

Module's members are marked as `Friend` to reproduce the default Visual Basic behavior.

There are some tasks to perform after examining Listing 20.2. First, notice how the `ObservableCollectionHelper` class exposes a public method that effectively converts an `ICollection(Of T)` into a new `ObservableCollection`. Also notice how there is the need to explicitly provide a `Namespace My..End Namespace` declaration, which encloses custom members for `My`. The `MyCollectionsUtils` module exposes members that are effectively accessible via `My`. To replicate the VB default behavior, the module is marked as `System.Diagnostics.NonUserCode` so that the debugger does not step into such code (if you instead need debugger support, simply remove this attribute) and as `Microsoft.VisualBasic.HideModuleName` that prevents the module name to be shown by IntelliSense when invoking your custom members. Then notice how the helper field is of type `ThreadSafeObjectProvider(Of T)`. According to the Microsoft documentation, this is a best practice because it ensures that each thread invoking `My.CollectionsUtils` has access to a separate instance. The read-only property `CollectionsUtils` then wraps the `ObservableCollectionHelper.ConvertToObservableCollection` method exposing through the `GetInstance` invocation. When you have created your extension, you can use it in a simple way. The following code shows how you can convert a `List(Of Integer)` into an `ObservableCollection` using your custom `My.CollectionsUtils` member:

```
Dim someInts As New List(Of Integer) From {1, 2, 3}
```

```
Dim obs As ObservableCollection(Of Integer) =

        My.CollectionsUtils.ConvertToObservableCollection(someInts)

For Each number As Integer In obs
    Console.WriteLine(number)
Next
```

After seeing how you can extend My at the root level, let's now see how you can customize existing members.

Extending My.Application and My.Computer

Extending existing members such as Application and Computer is straightforward, because both are implemented as partial classes, so you can simply add your own partial classes without the need of editing auto-generated code. Previous considerations remain unchanged, meaning that your partial classes' names need to start with My (such as MyApplication and MyComputer) and that both must be enclosed within an explicit declaration of a Namespace My..End Namespace code block. For example, imagine you want to extend My.Application with a method that associates a file extension with your application so that each time you double-click a file with that particular extension it will be opened by your application. Listing 20.3 accomplishes this (notice that if you run Windows Vista or Windows 7 you need to start Visual Studio with administrative rights).

LISTING 20.3   Extending My.Application

```
Imports Microsoft.Win32


Namespace My

    Partial Friend Class MyApplication

        Public Function AssociateExtension(ByVal extension As String,
                                           ByVal mimeType As String) As Boolean
            Try
                'Creates a registry entry for the extension
                My.Computer.Registry.ClassesRoot.
                CreateSubKey(extension).SetValue("",
                mimeType, RegistryValueKind.String)

                'Creates a registry entry for the Mime type
                'Environment.GetCommandLineArgs(0) returns
                'the executable name for Console applications
                My.Computer.Registry.ClassesRoot.
                CreateSubKey(mimeType & "\shell\open\command").
                SetValue("", Environment.GetCommandLineArgs(0) & " ""%1"" ",
```

```
            RegistryValueKind.String)

            Return True
        Catch ex As Exception
            Return False
        End Try
    End Function
End Class

End Namespace
```

Notice how the `MyApplication` class is marked as `Partial Friend`. This is required to match the definition provided by Visual Basic to `My.Application`. Now you can use the extension as you would normally do with `My.Application`. The following is an example:

```
Dim succeeded As Boolean =
    My.Application.AssociateExtension(".ale",
    "AlessandroDelSole/document")
```

Extending `My.Computer` works similarly. For example, we could implement a property that returns the MIME type for the specified filename. Code in Listing 20.4 accomplishes this.

LISTING 20.4 Extending `My.Computer`

```
Imports Microsoft.Win32


Namespace My
    Partial Friend Class MyComputer

        Public ReadOnly Property MimeType(ByVal fileName As String) As String
            Get
                Return getMimeType(fileName)
            End Get
        End Property

        Private Function getMimeType(ByVal fileName As String) As String

            Dim mimeType As String = String.Empty

            Dim fileExtension = System.IO.Path.
                            GetExtension(fileName).ToLower()
            Dim registryKey = Registry.ClassesRoot.
                        OpenSubKey(fileExtension)

            If registryKey IsNot Nothing And _
                        registryKey.GetValue("Content Type") _
```

```
                    IsNot Nothing Then

        mimeType = registryKey.
                    GetValue("Content Type").ToString
    Else
        mimeType = ""
    End If
    Return mimeType
End Function


End Class

End Namespace
```

You still need to mark the class as `Partial Friend` enclosing it within the `My` namespace declaration. At this point you can use your extension as usual, for example to retrieve the MIME type of a text file:

```
Dim mimeType As String = My.Computer.MimeType("Testfile.txt")
```

Of course, you are not limited to extending `Application` and `Computer` but you can also extend `Settings` and `Resources`.

Extending My.Resources and My.Settings

Extending `My.Resources` and `My.Settings` is also possible although with a few differences. `Resources` is a namespace, so you need to declare it as follows:

```
Namespace My.Resources
    Friend Module MyResources
        'Your code here
    End Module

End Namespace
```

Generally you do not need custom extensions to `Resources`; you could decide to offer alternative localized versions of some contents. Extending `My.Settings` works more similarly to `Application` and `Computer`, but generally you do not need to provide custom extensions here because the Visual Studio 2010 Designer provides a graphical environment for performing all operations you need and selecting all available .NET types.

My in Different Applications

Now that you know how `My` can be customized, you can easily understand why different kinds of Visual Basic applications have their own customizations, provided by the IDE. For example, Windows Forms applications provide a `My.Forms` property that allows access to forms instances, as follows:

```
Dim oneForm As Form1 = My.Forms.Form1
```

This is mainly due to the support offered in code by the My namespace to the Application Framework feature. This feature allows executing special tasks at the beginning and at the end of the application lifetime, such as showing splash screens or establishing what form is the main application form. In Windows Forms applications the application framework is enabled by default, and you can get in touch with it by opening My Project and selecting the **Application** tab, as shown in Figure 20.9.

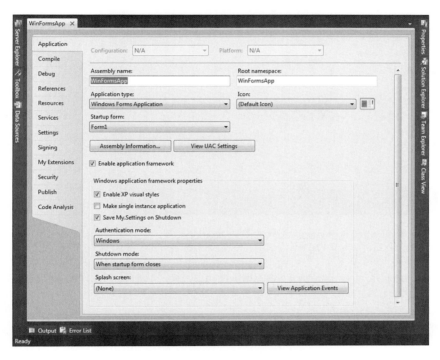

FIGURE 20.9   The application framework designer for Windows Forms applications.

Enabling the application framework allows visually managing features with no lines of code, although you are allowed to customize the related auto-generated code. For example, the following line manually establishes that My.Settings has to be saved when the application shuts down:

```
My.Application.SaveMySettingsOnExit = True
```

The following line shows instead how you can set the minimum number of milliseconds for a splash screen to be shown:

```
My.Application.MinimumSplashScreenDisplayTime = 1000
```

For WPF applications the application framework is slightly different, as shown in Figure 20.10.

20

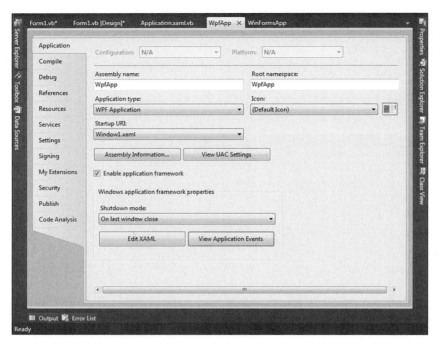

FIGURE 20.10   The application framework for WPF applications.

The following lines show how you can take advantage of My.Application in WPF to retrieve some information:

```
'The main Window XAML's uri
Dim startup As String = My.Application.StartupUri.ToString

'Main Window
Dim mainWindow As Window = My.Application.MainWindow

'Application resources
Dim appResources As ResourceDictionary = My.Application.Resources
```

Generally all members are self-explanatory, so IntelliSense can be a great friend to you in this situation, too. In both Windows Forms and WPF applications, the **View Application Events** button redirects you to the appropriate file for defining application events (Application.xaml.vb in WPF and Application.Designer.vb in Win Forms). For web applications, Silverlight applications do not support the My namespace whereas ASP.NET applications do not offer the My.Application and My.WebServices members; they instead expose the My.Response and My.Request properties that respectively wrap members from System.Web.HttpResponse and System.Web.HttpRequest.

Understanding Application Events

Applications that provide support for the application framework can be also managed with application events. This is the typical case of client applications such as Windows Forms and WPF applications. Windows Forms applications provide the following events:

- NetworkAvailabilityChanged, which is raised when the network becomes available or the connection is no longer available

- ShutDown, which is raised when the application shuts down

- Startup, which is raised when the application starts

- StartupNextInstance, which is raised when another instance of the application starts up

- UnhandledException which is raised when the application encounters an unhandled exception during tasks that involve the application framework

Applications events are handled within the code file that implements My.Application customizations, which by default is Application.designer.vb. The following example shows how you can intercept the network state change:

```
Private Sub MyApplication_NetworkAvailabilityChanged(ByVal sender As Object,
                                    ByVal e As Microsoft.VisualBasic.
                                    Devices.
                                    NetworkAvailableEventArgs) _
                                    Handles
                                    Me.NetworkAvailabilityChanged

    If e.IsNetworkAvailable = False Then
        'Network no longer available
    Else
        'Network available
    End If

End Sub
```

In WPF applications you have more events that you can handle. First, application events in WPF are handled in the Application.xaml.vb file. You have the following events available:

- Activated, which is raised when the application gets the foreground focus

- Deactivated, which is raised when the application loses the foreground focus

- DispatcherUnhandledException, which is raised when the Dispatcher object encounters an unhandled exception

- Exit, which is raised when the application shuts down

- ▶ `LoadCompleted, Navigated, Navigating, NavigationFailed, NavigationProgress,` and `NavigationStopped`, which are raised in case of navigation applications, which is self-explanatory if you think of navigation between pages

- ▶ `Startup`, which is raised when the application starts up and specifies the main UI object

- ▶ `FragmentNavigation`, which is raised when navigating to a specific XAML Uri

- ▶ `SessionEnding`, which is raised when the user logs off from Windows or is shutting down the system

The following example shows how you can intercept the `SessionEnding` event and decide to back up your work if the `e.ReasonSessionEnding` property has value `ReasonSessionEnding.Shutdown`:

```
Private Sub Application_SessionEnding(ByVal sender As Object,
                           ByVal e As _
                           SessionEndingCancelEventArgs) _
                           Handles Me.SessionEnding

    If e.ReasonSessionEnding = ReasonSessionEnding.Shutdown Then
        'Backup your files here
    End If

End Sub
```

Application events provide a great way for getting information on what happens behind the scenes of the application lifetime.

Summary

The `My` namespace is a unique feature of Visual Basic language starting from VB 2005, offering lots of shortcuts to most common operations. In this chapter you saw how you can interact with your application with `My.Application` and how you can perform operations on your system with `My.Computer`, including file operations, Registry operations and clipboard operations. You then got information about an important feature provided by `My.Settings`, which has the capability to save and load user preferences using the Visual Studio Designer and managed code, which is a convenient way if compared to old initialization files. Next you saw about `My.Resources`, a special place for embedding files in your executable, typically for Console and Windows Forms applications. Finally, you got in touch with one of the most important features in `My`: the ability to extend the namespace with custom members, both at root level and existing members.

CHAPTER 21

Advanced Language Features

The previous version of the .NET Framework, numbered 3.5, introduced revolutionary technologies such as LINQ. Because of its complex infrastructure, all .NET languages (especially VB and C#) required new keywords, syntaxes, and constructs to interact with LINQ but that could be successfully used in lots of other scenarios. Visual Basic 2010 continues to support those language features and introduces new ones to make your coding experience even better. Most of language features discussed in this chapter are important for the comprehension of the next chapters, so I recommend you to pay particular attention to topics presented here.

Local Type Inference

Local type inference is a language feature that allows you to omit specifying the data type of a local variable even if Option Strict is set to On. The Visual Basic compiler can deduce (*infer*) the most appropriate data type depending on the variable's usage. The easiest way to understand and hopefully appreciate local type inference is to provide a code example. Consider the following code and pay attention to the comments:

```
Sub Main()
    'The compiler infers String
    Dim oneString = "Hello Visual Basic 2010!"

    'The compiler infers Integer
    Dim oneInt = 324
```

```
    'The compiler infers Double
    Dim oneDbl = 123.456

    'The compiler infers Boolean
    Dim oneBool = True
End Sub
```

As you can see, the code doesn't specify the type for all variables because the compiler can infer the most appropriate data type according to the usage of a variable. To ensure that the VB compiler inferred the right type, simply pass the mouse pointer over the variable declaration to retrieve information via a useful tooltip, as shown in Figure 21.1.

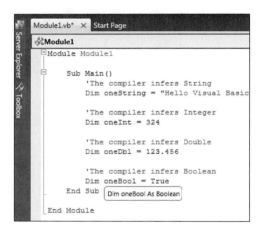

FIGURE 21.1   A tooltip indicates what type the Visual Basic compiler inferred to local variables.

BEHIND THE SCENES OF LOCAL TYPE INFERENCE

Types' inference is determined via the *dominant type* algorithm. You can get further information in the Visual Basic 9.0 language specifications document available at http://www.microsoft.com/downloads/details.aspx?FamilyID=39DE1DD0-F775-40BF-A191-09F5A95EF500&displaylang=en.

Obviously the local type inference works also with custom types, as demonstrated by the following example:

```
Dim p As New Person With {.FirstName = "Alessandro",
                          .LastName = "Del Sole"}
'The compiler infers Person
Dim onePerson = p
```

You can also use local type inference within loops or in any other circumstance you like:

```
'The compiler infers System.Diagnostic.Process
For Each proc In Process.GetProcesses
    Console.WriteLine(proc.ProcessName)
Next
```

Option Infer Directive

To enable or disable local type inference, the Visual Basic grammar provides the Option Infer directive. Option Infer On enables inference whereas Option Infer Off disables it. Generally you do not need to explicitly provide an Option Infer directive because it is offered at the project level by Visual Studio. By default, Option Infer is On. If you want to change default settings for the current project, simply open My Project and then switch to the **Compile** tab. There you can find the Visual Basic compiler options including Option Infer. If you instead want to change settings for each new project, simply choose the **Options** command from the Tools menu. When the Options dialog appears, move to the **Projects and Solutions** tab and select the **VB defaults** item, as shown in Figure 21.2.

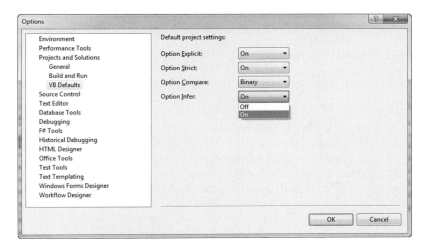

FIGURE 21.2   Changing the default behavior for Option Infer.

You then need to add an Option Infer On directive if you want to switch back to local type inference.

Local Type Inference Scope

The word *local* in the Local Type Inference definition has a special meaning. Local type inference works only with local variables defined within code blocks, whereas it does not work with class-level declarations. For example, consider the following code:

```
Class Person

    Property LastName As String
    Property FirstName As String

    Function FullName() As String
        'Local variable: local type inference works
        Dim completeName = Me.LastName & " " & Me.FirstName
        Return completeName
    End Function
End Class
```

Local type inference affects the `completeName` local variable, which is enclosed within a method. Now consider the following code:

```
'Both Option Strict and Option Infer are On
Class Person
    'Local type inference does not work with
    'class level variables. An error will be
    'thrown.
    Private completeName
```

The preceding code will not be compiled because local type inference does not affect class-level declarations; therefore, the Visual Basic compiler throws an error if `Option Strict` is On. If `Option Strict` is `Off`, the `completeName` class-level variable will be considered of type `Object` but still it is not affected by local type inference, so be aware of this possible situation. The conclusion is that you always need to explicitly provide a type for class-level variables, whereas you can omit the specification with local variables.

WHY LOCAL TYPE INFERENCE?

If you are an old-school developer you probably will be surprised and perhaps unhappy by local type inference because you always wrote your code the most strongly typed possible. Generally you will not be obliged to declare types taking advantage of local type inference except when you need to generate *anonymous types*, which are discussed later in this chapter. I always use (and suggest) the local type inference because it's straightforward and avoids the need of worrying about types, especially with different kinds of query result when working with LINQ. I often use this feature in the rest of the book.

Array Literals

Visual Basic 2010 introduces a new feature known as array literals. Basically it works like the local type inference but it is specific to arrays. For example, consider this array of strings declaration as you would write it in Visual Basic 2008:

```
Dim anArrayOfStrings() As String = {"One", "Two", "Three"}
```

Now in Visual Basic 2010 you can simply write it as follows:

```
'The compiler infers String()
Dim anArrayOfStrings = {"One", "Two", "Three"}
```

According to the preceding code, you are still required to only place a couple of parentheses, but you can omit the type that is correctly inferred by the compiler as you can easily verify by passing the mouse pointer over the variable declaration. Of course, array literals work also with value types, as shown here:

```
'The compiler infers Double
Dim anArrayOfDouble = {1.23, 2.34, 3.45}
'The compiler infers Integer
Dim anArrayOfInteger = {4, 3, 2, 1}
```

Array literals also support mixed arrays. For example, the following array is inferred as an array of Object:

```
'Does not work with Option Strict On
Dim mixedArray = {1.23, "One point Twentythree"}
```

The preceding code will not be compiled if Option Strict is On and the compiler will show a message saying that the type cannot be inferred, which is a situation that can be resolved explicitly by assigning the type to the array. You could therefore explicitly declare the array as Dim mixedArray() As Object but you need to be careful in this because mixed arrays could lead to errors.

Multidimensional and Jagged Arrays

Array literals also affect multidimensional and jagged arrays. The following line of code shows how you can declare a multidimensional array of integers taking advantage of array literals:

```
Dim multiIntArray = {{4, 3}, {2, 1}}
```

In this case you do not need to add parentheses. The Visual Basic compiler infers the type as follows:

```
Dim multiIntArray(,) As Integer = {{4, 3}, {2, 1}}
```

Figure 21.3 shows how you can check the inferred type by passing the mouse pointer over the declaration, getting a descriptive tooltip.

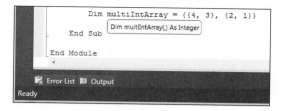

FIGURE 21.3   Type inference for a multidimensional array.

Array literals work similarly on a jagged array. For example, you can write a jagged array of strings as follows:

```
Dim jaggedStringArray = {({"One", "Two"}),
                         ({"Three", "Four"})}
```

This is the same as writing:

```
Dim jaggedStringArray()() As String = {({"One", "Two"}),
                                       ({"Three", "Four"})}
```

And the same as for multidimensional arrays in which the code editor can provide help on type inference, as shown in Figure 21.4.

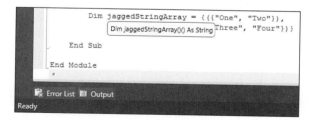

FIGURE 21.4   Type inference for a jagged array.

Array literals can help in writing more elegant and shorter code.

Extension Methods

Extension methods are a feature that Visual Basic 2010 inherits from its predecessor. As for other features discussed in this chapter, their main purpose is being used with LINQ, although they can also be useful in hundreds of different scenarios. Basically extension methods are special methods that can extend the data type they are applied to. The most important thing is that you can extend existing types even if you do not have the source code and without the need to rebuild class libraries that expose types you go to extend—and this is important. For example, you can extend .NET built-in types, as you see in this section, although you do not have .NET source code. We now discuss extension methods in two different perspectives: learning to use existing extension methods exposed by .NET built-in types and implementing and exporting custom extension methods. The first code example retrieves the list of processes running on the system and makes use of an extension method named ToList:

```
Dim processList = Process.GetProcesses.ToList
```

ToList converts an array or an IEnumerable collection into a strongly typed List(Of T), in this case into a List(Of Process) (notice how the assignment works with local type inference) Extension methods are easily recognizable within IntelliSense because they are characterized by the usual method icon plus a blue down arrow, as shown in Figure 21.5.

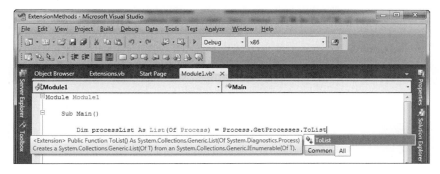

FIGURE 21.5   Recognizing extension methods within IntelliSense.

They are also recognizable because the method definition is marked as <Extension> as you can see from the descriptive tooltip shown in Figure 21.5, but this will also be discussed in creating custom methods. The next example uses the AsEnumerable method for converting an array of Process into an IEnumerable(Of Process):

```
Dim processEnumerable As IEnumerable(Of Process) =
                    Process.GetProcesses.AsEnumerable
```

Extension methods can execute hundreds of tasks, so it is not easy to provide a general summarization, especially because they can be customized according to your needs. At a higher level, .NET built-in extension methods accomplish three main objectives: converting types into other types, data filtering, and parsing. The most common built-in .NET extension methods are provided by the System.Linq.Enumerable class and are summarized in Table 21.1.

TABLE 21.1   Built-in Extension Methods

Method	Description
Aggregate	Accumulates items of a sequence
All	Checks whether elements within a sequence satisfy a condition
Any	Checks whether any elements within a sequence satisfy a condition
AsEnumerable	Converts a sequence of elements into an IEnumerable(Of T)
Average	Retrieves the result of the average calculation from the members of a sequence
Cast	Performs the conversion from an IEnumerable(Of T) into the specified type. It is generally used explicitly when the compiler cannot infer the appropriate type
Concat	Returns the concatenation of two sequences
Contains	Checks if a sequence contains the specified item
Count	Returns the number of items in a sequence
DefaultIfEmpty	Returns the elements of the specified sequence or the type parameter's default value in a singleton collection if the sequence is empty
Distinct	Ensures that no duplicates are retrieved from a sequence or removes duplicates from a sequence
ElementAt	Obtains the object in the sequence at the specified index
ElementAtOrDefault	Like ElementAt but returns a default value if the index is wrong
Except	Given two sequences, creates a new sequence with elements from the first sequence that are not also in the second one
First	Gets the first element of a sequence
FirstOrDefault	Like First but returns a default value if the first element is not what you are searching for
GroupBy	Given a criteria, groups elements of a sequence into another sequence
GroupJoin	Given a criteria, joins elements from two sequences into one sequence
Intersect	Creates a sequence with common elements from two sequences
Join	Join elements from two sequences based on specific criteria, such as equality
Last	Retrieves the last item in a sequence
LastOrDefault	Like Last but returns a default value if the specified instance is not found

TABLE 21.1   Continued

Method	Description
LongCount	Returns the number of items in a sequence under the form of `Long` (`System.Int64`) type
Max	Retrieves the highest value in a sequence
Min	Retrieves the minimum value in a sequence
OfType	Filters an `IEnumerable` collection according to the specified type
OrderBy	Orders elements in a sequence using the specified criteria
OrderByDescending	Orders elements in a sequence using the specified criteria in a descending order
Reverse	Reverses the order of items in a sequence
Select	Puts an item into a sequence for queries
SelectMany	Puts more than one item into a sequence for queries
SequenceEquals	Determines whether two sequences are equal by comparing the elements by using the default equality comparer for their type or using a specified comparer
Single	Returns the only item from a sequence that matches the specified criteria
SingleOrDefault	Like `Single` but returns a default value if the specified item could not be found
Skip	When creating a new sequence, skips the specified number of items and returns the remaining items from the starting sequence
SkipWhile	Like `Skip` but only while the specified condition is satisfied
Sum	In a sequence of numeric values, returns the sum of numbers
Take	Returns the specified number of items starting from the beginning of a sequence
TakeWhile	Like `Take` but only while the specified condition is satisfied
ThenBy	After invoking `OrderBy`, provides the ability of a subsequent ordering operation
ThenByDescending	After invoking `OrderBy`, provides the ability of a subsequent ordering operation in a descending way
ToArray	Converts an `IEnumerable(Of T)` into an array
ToDictionary	Converts an `IEnumerable(Of T)` into a `Dictionary(Of T, T)`
ToList	Converts an `IEnumerable(Of T)` into a `List(Of T)`

TABLE 21.1   Continued

Method	Description
ToLookup	Converts an IEnumerable(Of T) into a LookUp(Of TSource, TKey)
Union	Creates a new sequence with unique elements from two sequences
Where	Filters a sequence according to the specified criteria

ARGUMENTS AS LAMBDAS

In most cases you use lambda expressions as arguments for extension methods. Lambda expressions are discussed later in this book; therefore, examples where lambdas are not used are provided.

In next part of this book, which is dedicated to data access with LINQ, you see how extension methods are used for filtering, ordering, and parsing data. The following code snippet shows an example of filtering data using the Where extension method:

```
'A real app example would use
'a lambda expression instead of a delegate
Dim filteredProcessList = Process.GetProcesses.
    Where(AddressOf EvaluateProcess).ToList

Private Function EvaluateProcess(ByVal p As Process) As Boolean
    If p.ProcessName.ToLowerInvariant.StartsWith("e") Then Return True
End Function
```

The preceding code simply adds Process objects to a list only if the process name starts with the e letter. The evaluation is performed through a delegate; although in this chapter you learn how to accomplish this using the lambda expression. Table 21.1 cannot be exhaustive because the .NET Framework offers other extension methods specific to some development areas that are eventually discussed in the appropriate chapters. IntelliSense provides help about extension methods not covered here. By reading Table 21.1 you can also understand that extension methods from System.Linq.Enumerable work on or return results from a *sequence of elements*. This notion is important because you use such methods against a great number of different collections (that is, sequences of elements of a particular type), especially when working with LINQ.

EXTENSION METHODS BEHAVIOR

Although extension methods behave as instance methods, the Visual Basic compiler translates them into static methods. This is because extension methods are defined within modules (or static classes if created in Visual C#).

Coding Custom Extension Methods

One of the most interesting things when talking about extension methods is that you can create your custom extensions. This provides great power and flexibility to development because you can extend existing types with new functionalities, even if you do not have the source code for the type you want to extend. There are a set of rules and best practices to follow in coding custom extension methods; the first considerations are the following:

▶ In Visual Basic, extension methods can be defined only within modules, because they are considered as shared methods by the compiler.

▶ Only Function and Sub methods can be coded as extensions. Properties and other members cannot work as extensions.

▶ Methods must be decorated with the System.Runtime.CompilerServices.Extension attribute. Decorating modules with the same attribute is also legal but not required.

▶ Extension methods can be overloaded.

▶ Extension methods can extend reference types, value types, delegates, arrays, interfaces, and generic parameters but cannot extend System.Object to avoid late binding problems.

▶ They must receive at least an argument. The first argument is always the type that the extension method goes to extend.

For example, imagine you want to provide a custom extension method that converts an IEnumerable(Of T) into an ObservableCollection(Of T). The ObservableCollection is a special collection exposed by the System.Collections.ObjectModel namespace from the WindowsBase.dll assembly, which is usually used in WPF applications. (You need to add a reference to WindowsBase.dll.) The code in Listing 21.1 shows how this can be implemented.

LISTING 21.1 Implementing Custom Extension Methods

```
Imports System.Runtime.CompilerServices
Imports System.Collections.ObjectModel

<Extension()> Module Extensions
    <Extension()> Function ToObservableCollection(Of T) _
                        (ByVal List As IEnumerable(Of T)) _
                        As ObservableCollection(Of T)
        Try
            Return New ObservableCollection(Of T)(List)
        Catch ex As Exception
            Throw
        End Try
```

```
        End Function

End Module
```

The code in Listing 21.1 is quite simple. Because the `ObservableCollection` is generic, the `ToObservableCollection` extension method is also generic and goes to extend the generic `IEnumerable` type, which is the method argument. The constructor of `ObservableCollection` provides an overload that accepts an `IEnumerable` to populate the new collection and then returns an instance of the collection starting from the `IEnumerable` data. Using the new method is straightforward:

```
Dim processCollection = Process.GetProcesses.ToObservableCollection
```

Now suppose you want to extend the `String` type to provide an extension method that can check whether a string is a valid email address. In such a situation the best check can be performed using regular expressions. The following code shows how you can implement this extension method:

```
'Requires an Imports System.Text.RegularExpressions statement
<Extension()> Function IsValidEMail(ByVal EMailAddress As String) _
            As Boolean
    Dim validateMail As String = _
    "^([\w-\.]+)@((\[[0-9]{1,3}\.[0-9]{1,3}\.)" & _
    "¦(([\w-]+\.)+))([a-zA-z]{2,4}¦[0-9]{1,3})(\]?)$"

    Return Regex.IsMatch(EMailAddress, _
                    validateMail)

End Function
```

The goal is not to focus on the comparison pattern via regular expressions, which is complex. Just notice how the result of the comparison (`Regex.IsMatch`) is returned by the method that extends `Strings` because such type is the first (and only) argument in the method. You can then simply use the method as follows:

```
Dim email As String = "Alessandro.delsole@visual-basic.it"
If email.IsValidEMail Then
    Console.WriteLine("Valid address")
Else
    Console.WriteLine("Invalid address")
End If
```

You may remember that extension methods are basically shared methods but behave as instance members; this is the reason why the new method is available on the `email` instance and not on the `String` type.

Overloading Extension Methods

Extension methods support the overloading technique and follow general rules already described in Chapter 7, "Class Fundamentals," especially that overloads cannot differ only because of their return type but must differ in their signature.

Exporting Extension Methods

You can create libraries of custom extension methods and make them reusable also from other languages. This could be useful if you need to offer your extension methods to other applications written in different programming languages. To accomplish this, you need to be aware of a couple of things. First, the module defining extensions must be explicitly marked as `Public`, and the same is true for methods. Second, you need to write a public sealed class with an empty private constructor, because the CLR provides access to extension methods through this class, to grant interoperability between languages. Listing 21.2 shows a complete example.

LISTING 21.2   Building an Extension Methods Library

```
Imports System.Runtime.CompilerServices
Imports System.Collections.ObjectModel
Imports System.Text.RegularExpressions

<Extension()> Public Module Extensions
    <Extension()> Public Function ToObservableCollection(Of T) _
                        (ByVal List As IEnumerable(Of T)) _
                        As ObservableCollection(Of T)
        Try
            Return New ObservableCollection(Of T)(List)
        Catch ex As Exception
            Throw
        End Try
    End Function

    <Extension()> Public Function IsValidEMail(ByVal EMailAddress As String) _
                As Boolean
        Dim validateMail As String = _
        "^([\w-\.]+)@((\[[0-9]{1,3}\.[0-9]{1,3}\.)" & _
        "¦(([\w-]+\.)+))([a-zA-z]{2,4}¦[0-9]{1,3})(\]?)$"

        Return Regex.IsMatch(EMailAddress, _
                        validateMail)

    End Function
```

```
End Module

Public NotInheritable Class MyCustomExtensions

    Private Sub New()

    End Sub
End Class
```

Basically creating a public sealed class is necessary because modules are a specific feature of Visual Basic; therefore, such a class is the bridge between our code and other languages. By compiling the code shown in Listing 21.2 as a class library, .NET languages can take advantage of your extension methods.

TESTING CUSTOM EXTENSION LIBRARIES

If you want to be sure that class libraries exposing custom extension methods work correctly, simply create a new Visual C# project (a VB one is good as well) and add a reference to the new assembly. Then write code that invokes extended types and check via IntelliSense if your custom methods are effectively available.

EXPORTING EXTENSION METHODS TIPS

Exporting extension methods requires a little bit of attention. For example, extending types in which you do not own the source code can be dangerous because it may lead to conflicts if in the future the original author adds extensions with the same name. It can be instead a good idea to encapsulate extensions within specific namespaces. Microsoft created a document containing a series of best practices that can be found at the following address: http://msdn.microsoft.com/en-us/library/bb384936(VS.100).aspx

Anonymous Types

As their name implies, *anonymous types* are .NET objects that have no name and can be generated on-the-fly. They were first introduced with .NET Framework 3.5, and their main purpose is collecting data from LINQ queries. Generally you prefer named types to anonymous types outside particular LINQ scenarios; however, it's important to understand how anonymous types work. Declaring an anonymous type is straightforward, as shown in the following code snippet:

```
Dim anonymous = New With {.FirstName = "Alessandro",
                          .LastName = "Del Sole",
                          .Email = "",
                          .Age = 32}
```

As you can see, no name for the new type is specified, and a new instance is created just invoking the New With statement. Creating an anonymous type takes advantage of two previously described features, object initializers and local type inference. Object initializers are necessary because anonymous types must be generated in one line, so they do need such a particular feature; local type inteference is fundamental, because you have no other way for declaring a new type as an anonymous type, meaning that only the compiler can do it via local type inference. This is the reason why declaring an anonymous type cannot be accomplished using the As clause. For example, the following code throws an error and will not be compiled:

```
'Throws an error: "the keyword does not name a type"
Dim anonymous As New With {.FirstName = "Alessandro",
                          .LastName = "Del Sole",
                          .Age = 32}
```

Local type inference is also necessary for another reason. As you can see, you can assign *but not declare* properties when declaring an anonymous type. (FirstName, LastName, Age, and Email are all properties for the new anonymous type that are both implemented and assigned.) Therefore, the compiler needs a way to understand the type of a property and then implement one for you, and this is only possible due to the local type inference. In the preceding example, for the FirstName, LastName, and Email properties, the compiler infers the String type, whereas for the Age property it infers the Integer type. When you have an anonymous type, you can just use it like any other .NET type. The following code provides an example:

```
'Property assignment
anonymous.Email = "alessandro.delsole@visual-basic.it"
'Property reading
Console.WriteLine("{0} {1}, of age: {2}",
                  anonymous.FirstName,
                  anonymous.LastName,
                  anonymous.Age.ToString)
```

As previously mentioned, you can work with an anonymous type like with any other .NET type. The difference is that anonymous types do not h1ave names. Such types can also implement read-only properties. This can be accomplished using the Key keyword with a property name, as demonstrated here:

```
'The Age property is read-only and can
'be assigned only when creating an instance
Dim anonymousWithReadOnly = New With {.FirstName = "Alessandro",
                                      .LastName = "Del Sole",
                                      Key .Age = 32}
```

In this example the Age property is treated as read-only and therefore can be assigned only when creating an instance of the anonymous type. You probably wonder why anonymous types can be useful. You get more practical examples in Part 4, "Data Access with ADO.NET and LINQ."

Relaxed Delegates

When you code methods that are pointed to by delegates, your methods must respect the delegate's signature. An exception to this rule is when your method receives arguments that are not effectively used and therefore can be omitted. Such a feature is known as *relaxed delegates*. The simplest example to help you understand relaxed delegates is to create a Windows Forms application. After you've created your application, drag a **Button** control from the toolbox onto the form's surface. Double-click the new button to activate the code editor so that Visual Studio generates an event handler stub for you and type the following code:

```
Private Sub Button1_Click(ByVal sender As System.Object,
                          ByVal e As System.EventArgs) _
                          Handles Button1.Click
    MessageBox.Show("It works!")
End Sub
```

As you can see, the method body simply shows a text message but does not make use of both sender and e arguments received by the event handler (which is a method pointed by a delegate). Because of this, Visual Basic allows an exception to the method signature rule, and therefore the preceding method can be rewritten as follows:

```
'Relaxed delegate
Private Sub Button1_Click() Handles Button1.Click
    MessageBox.Show("It works! - relaxed version")
End Sub
```

The code still works correctly because the compiler can identify the preceding method as a relaxed delegate. This feature can be useful especially in enhancing code readability.

Lambda Expressions

Lambda expressions exist in the .NET development from the previous version, and therefore they have been available since Visual Basic 2008. Because of their flexibility, they are one of the most important additions to .NET programming languages in the past years. The main purpose of lambda expressions, as for other language features, is related to LINQ, as you see in the next chapters. They can also be successfully used in lots of programming scenarios. Lambdas in Visual Basic 2010 have been improved in several aspects: To provide a logical approach we discuss lambda expressions by first talking about the VB 2008 syntax and then diving into the new characteristics. Basically lambda expressions in Visual Basic are anonymous methods that can be generated on-the-fly within a line of code and can replace the use of delegates. The easiest explanation of lambdas is that you can use a lambda wherever you need a delegate.

UNDERSTANDING LAMBDA EXPRESSIONS

Lambda expressions are powerful, but they are not probably easy to understand at first. Because of this, several steps of explanations are provided before describing their common usage, although this might be annoying.

You create lambda expressions using the `Function` keyword. When used for lambda expressions, such keyword returns a `System.Func(Of T, TResult)` (with overloads) delegate that encapsulates a method that receives one or more arguments of type `T` and returns a result of type `TResult`. `System.Func` is defined within the `System.Core.dll` assembly and can accept as many `T` arguments for as many parameters that are required by the anonymous method. The last argument of a `System.Func` type is always the return type of a lambda. For example, the following line of code creates a lambda expression that accepts two `Double` values and returns another `Double` constituted by the multiplication of the first two numbers:

```
Dim f As Func(Of Double, Double, Double) = Function(x, y) x * y
```

As you can see, the `Function` keyword does not take any method name. It just receives two arguments, and the result is implemented after the last parenthesis. Such a lambda expression returns a `System.Func(Of Double, Double, Double)` in which the first two doubles correspond to the lambda's arguments, whereas the third one correspond to the lambda's result type. You can then invoke the obtained delegate to perform a calculation, as in the following line:

```
'Returns 12
Console.WriteLine(f(3, 4))
```

Of course, this is not the only way to invoke the result of a lambda expression, but it is an important starting point. Basically the code provides a lambda instead of declaring an explicit delegate. Now consider the following code that rewrites the previously shown lambda expression:

```
Function Multiply(ByVal x As Double, ByVal y As Double) As Double
    Return x * y
End Function
Dim f As New Func(Of Double, Double, Double)(AddressOf Multiply)

'Returns 12
Console.WriteLine(f(3, 4))
```

As you can see, this second code explicitly creates a method that performs the required calculation that is then passed to the constructor of the `System.Func`. Invoking the delegate can then produce the same result. The difference is that using a lambda expression brought major elegance and dynamicity to our code. `System.Func` can receive up to 16 arguments; independently from how many arguments you need, remember that the last one is always the return value. Another common scenario is a lambda expression that evaluates an expression and returns a Boolean value. To demonstrate this, we can recall the `IsValidEMail` extension method that was described in the "Extension Methods" section to construct complex code. Listing 21.3 shows how you can invoke extension methods for a lambda expression to evaluate if a string is a valid email address, getting back `True` or `False` as a result.

LISTING 21.3   Complex Coding with Lambda Expressions

```
Module TestLambda

    Sub ComplexEvaluation()
        Dim checkString As Func(Of String, Boolean) = Function(s) s.IsValidEMail
        Console.WriteLine(checkString("alessandro.delsole@visual-basic.it"))
    End Sub
End Module

<Extension()> Module Extensions
    <Extension()> Public Function IsValidEMail(ByVal EMailAddress As String) _
            As Boolean
        Dim validateMail As String = _
        "^([\w-\.]+)@((\[[0-9]{1,3}\.[0-9]{1,3}\.)" & _
        "|(([\w-]+\.)+))([a-zA-z]{2,4}|[0-9]{1,3})(\]?)$"

        Return Regex.IsMatch(EMailAddress, _
                        validateMail)
    End Function
End Module
```

If you look at Listing 21.3 you notice that the `checkString` delegate takes a `String` to evaluate and returns `Boolean`. Such an evaluation is performed invoking the `IsValidEMail` extension method.

OK, BUT WHY LAMBDAS?

Probably you wonder why you should need lambda expressions instead of simply invoking methods. The reason is code robustness offered by delegates, as you will remember from Chapter 15, "Delegates and Events." Therefore if you decide to use delegates, using lambda expressions is a good idea while it becomes a necessity if you access data with LINQ.

You often use lambda expressions as arguments for extension methods. The following code shows how you can order the names of running processes on your machine, including only names starting with the "e" letter:

```
Dim processes = Process.GetProcesses.
```

```
       OrderBy(Function(p) p.ProcessName).
       Where(Function(p) p.ProcessName.ToLowerInvariant.
       StartsWith("e"))
```

The `OrderBy` extension method receives a lambda expression as an argument that takes an object of type `System.Diagnostics.Process` and orders the collection by the process name, whereas the `Where` extension method still receives a lambda as an argument pointing to the same `Process` instance and that returns `True` if the process name starts with the "e" letter. To get a complete idea of how the lambda works, the best way is rewriting code without using the lambda. The following code demonstrates this concept; and the first lambda remains to provide an idea of how code can be improved using such a feature:

```
'An explicit method that evaluates the expression
Private Function EvaluateProcess(ByVal p As Process) As Boolean
    If p.ProcessName.ToLowerInvariant.StartsWith("e") Then
        Return True
    Else
        Return False
    End If
End Function
    Dim processes = Process.GetProcesses.
                    OrderBy(Function(p) p.ProcessName).
                    Where(AddressOf EvaluateProcess)
```

As you can see, avoiding the usage of lambda expressions requires you to implement a method that respects the signature of the `System.Func` delegate and that performs the required evaluations. Such a method is then pointed via the `AddressOf` keyword. You can easily understand how lambda expressions facilitate writing code and make code clearer, especially if you compare the `OrderBy` method that still gets a lambda expression. For the sake of completeness, it's important to understand that lambda expressions improve the coding experience, but the Visual Basic compiler still translates them the old-fashioned way, as explained later in the "Lexical Closures" section. All the examples provided until now take advantage of the local type inference feature and leave to the VB compiler the work of inferring the appropriate types. The next section discusses this characteristic.

Type Inference and Lambda Expressions

At a higher level, lambda expressions fully support local type inference so that the Visual Basic compiler can decide for you the appropriate data type. For lambdas, there is something more to say. Basically type inference is determined on how you write your code. For example, let's recall the first lambda expression at the beginning of this section:

```
Dim f As Func(Of Double, Double, Double) = Function(x, y) x * y
```

In the preceding code, local type inference affects both arguments and the result of the `Function` statement; the compiler can infer `Double` to the x and y parameters and therefore can determine `Double` as the result type; this is possible only because we explicitly provided types in the delegate declaration, that is, `Func(Of Double, Double, Double)`.

Because a local type inference is determined by the compiler using the *dominant algorithm*, there must be something explicitly typed. For a better understanding, rewrite the preceding code as follows:

```
'The compiler infers Object
Dim f = Function(x, y) x * y
```

In this case because no type is specified anywhere, the compiler infers Object for the f variable, but in this special case it also throws an exception because operands are not supported by an Object, and therefore the code will not be compiled if Option Strict is On. If you set Option Strict Off, you can take advantage of late binding. In such a scenario both the result and the arguments will be treated as Object at compile time, but at runtime the CLR can infer the appropriate type depending on the argument received by the expression. The other scenario is when the type result is omitted but arguments' types are provided. The following code demonstrates this:

```
Dim f = Function(x As Double, y As Double) x * y
```

In this case the result type for the f variable is not specified, but arguments have been explicitly typed so that the compiler can infer the correct result type.

Multiline Lambdas

Visual Basic 2010 now provides support for multiline lambda expressions, a feature that was already available in Visual C#. Basically there is now the ability to write complete anonymous delegates within a line of code, as demonstrated in the following snippet:

```
Console.WriteLine("Enter a number:")
Dim number = CDbl(Console.ReadLine)

Dim result = Function(n As Double)
                If n < 0 Then
                    Return 0
                Else
                    Return n + 1
                End If
            End Function

Console.WriteLine(result(number))
```

In this particular case the compiler can infer the System.Func(Of Double, Double) result type because the n argument is of type Double. Within the method body you can perform required evaluations, and you can also explicitly specify the return type (take a look at the first lambda example) to get control over the System.Func result. Another example is for multiline lambdas without variable declarations, as in the following code:

```
Dim processes = Process.GetProcesses.
                Where(Function(p)
```

```
            Try
                'Returns True
                p.ProcessName.ToLowerInvariant.
                StartsWith("e")
            Catch ex As Exception
                Return False
            End Try
        End Function)
```

Basically this code performs the same operations described in the "Lambda Expressions" section, but now you have the ability to write more complex code, for example if you need to provide error handling infrastructures as previously shown.

Sub Lambdas

Back in Visual Basic 2008, lambda expressions were represented only by functions that could return a value and that were realized via the `Function` keyword, as shown at the beginning of this section. Visual Basic 2010 also introduces a new feature, known as *Sub lambdas* that C# developers know as *anonymous methods*. This new feature allows using the `Sub` keyword instead of the `Function` one so that you can write lambda expressions that do not return a value. The following code demonstrates this:

```
Dim collection As New List(Of String) From {"Alessandro",
                                "Del Sole",
                                alessandro.delsole@visual-basic.it"}


collection.ForEach(Sub(element) Console.WriteLine(element))
```

The preceding code iterates a `List(Of String)` collection and sends to the console window the result of the iteration. A `Sub` lambda is used because here no return value is required.

ARRAY.FOREACH AND LIST(OF T).FOREACH

The `System.Array` and the `System.Collections.Generic.List(Of T)` classes offer a `ForEach` method that allows performing loops similarly to the `For..Each` statement described in Chapter 4, "Data Types and Expressions." The difference is that you can take advantage of lambda expressions and eventually of delegates to iterate elements.

Consider that trying to replace `Sub` with `Function` causes an error. (That makes sense, because `Console.WriteLine` does not return values while `Function` does.) Like `Function`, arguments' types within `Sub` can be inferred by the compiler. In this case the element is of type `String`, because it represents a single element in a `List(Of String)` collection. Generally you can use `Sub` lambdas each time a `System.Action(Of T)` is required, opposite to the `System.Func(Of T, T)` required by `Function`. `System.Action(Of T)` is a delegate that represents a method accepting just one argument and that returns no value. `Sub` lambdas can also be implemented as multiline lambdas. The following code shows a multiline implementation of the previous code, where a simple validation is performed onto every string in the collection:

```
' "collection" has the same previous implementation
collection.ForEach(Sub(element)
                    Try
                        If String.IsNullOrEmpty(element) = False Then
                            Console.WriteLine(element)
                        Else
                            Console.
                            WriteLine("Cannot print empty strings")
                        End If
                    Catch ex As Exception

                    End Try
                End Sub)
```

In this way you can also implement complex expressions, although they do not return a value.

LAMBDA EXPRESSIONS AND OBJECT LIFETIME

When methods end their job, local variables get out of scope and therefore are subject to garbage collection. By the way, lambda expressions within methods hold references to local variables unless you explicitly release resources related to the lambda. Consider this when planning objects' lifetime management.

Lexical Closures

To provide support for lambda expressions, the Visual Basic compiler implements a background feature known as *lexical closures*. Before going into the explanation, remember that you will not generally use closures in your code because they are typically generated for compiler use only, but it's important to know what they are and what they do. Basically lexical closures allow access to the same class-level variable to multiple functions and procedures. A code example provides a better explanation. Consider the following code, in which the `Divide` method takes advantage of a lambda expression to calculate the division between two numbers:

```
Class ClosureDemo


    Sub Divide(ByVal value As Double)
        Dim x = value
        Dim calculate = Function(y As Double) x / y
        Dim result = calculate(10)
    End Sub
End Class
```

Because both the `Divide` method and its lambda expression have access to the x local variable, the compiler internally rewrites the preceding code in a more logical way that looks like the following:

```
Class _Closure$__1


    Public x As Double

    Function _Lambda$__1(ByVal y As Double) As Double
        Return x * y
    End Function
End Class

Class ClosureDemo

    Sub Divide(ByVal value As Double)
       Dim closureVariable_A_8 As New _
           _Closure$__1
       _Closure$__1.closureVariable_A_8 = value

       Dim calculate As Func(Of Double, Double) _
       = AddressOf _Closure$__1._Lambda$__1
       Dim result = calculate(10)

    End Sub
End Class
```

Identifiers are not easy to understand, but they are generated by the compiler that is the only one responsible for their handling. The lexical closure feature creates a new public class with a public field related to the variable having common access; moreover it generated a separated method for performing the division that is explicitly accessed as a delegate (and here you will remember that lambdas can be used every time you need a delegate) from the `Divide` method. In conclusion, lexical closures provide a way for a logical organization of the code that provides behind-the-scenes support for lambda expressions but, as stated at the beginning of this section, they are exclusively the responsibility of the Visual Basic compiler.

Ternary If Operator

The ternary `If` operator is generally used with lambda expressions and allows evaluating conditions on-the-fly. With this operator you can evaluate a condition and return the desired value either in case the condition is `True` or it is `False`. Imagine you have a `Person` class exposing both `FirstName` and `LastName` string properties and that you want to first verify that an instance of the `Person` class is not `Nothing` and, subsequently, that its

LastName properties are initialized. The following code shows how you can accomplish the first task (see comments):

```
Sub EvaluatePerson(ByVal p As Person)
    'Check if p (a Person instance) is Nothing
    'If it is Nothing, returns False else True
    'The result is returned as a delegate
    Dim checkIfNull = If(p Is Nothing, False, True)

    'If False, p is Nothing, therefore
    'throws an exception
    If checkIfNull = False Then
        Throw New ArgumentNullException("testPerson")
    End If

End Sub
```

As you can see, the If operator receives three arguments: The first one is the condition to evaluate; the second is the result to return if the condition is True; whereas the third one is the result to return if the condition is False. In this specific example, if the Person instance is null the code returns False; otherwise it returns True. The result of this code is assigned to a Boolean variable (checkIfNull) that contains the result of the evaluation. If the result is False, the code throws an ArgumentNullException. Basically you could write the preceding code in a simpler way, as follows:

```
If p Is Nothing Then
    'do something
Else
    Throw New ArgumentNullException
End If
```

The difference is that with the ternary operator you can perform inline evaluations also with lambda expressions, and this scenario is particularly useful when working with LINQ queries. Now it's time to check if the LastName property was initialized. The following code snippet shows an example that returns a String instead of a Boolean value:

```
Dim executeTest = If(String.IsNullOrEmpty(p.LastName) = True,
                "LastName property is empty",
                "LastName property is initialized")
```

The explanation is simple: If the LastName property is an empty string or a null string, the code returns a message saying that the property is empty; otherwise it returns a message saying that the property has been correctly initialized. Basically you could rewrite the code in the classic fashion as follows:

```
If String.IsNullOrEmpty(p.LastName) = True Then
    'LastName property is empty
```

```
Else
    'LastName property is initialized
End If
```

The following lines show how you can test the preceding code:

```
'Throws an ArgumentNullException
EvaluatePerson(Nothing)
'A message says that the LastName property is initialized
EvaluatePerson(New Person With {.LastName = "Del Sole"})
```

Generic Variance

Visual Basic 2010 introduces the concept of generic variance, divided into two areas: covariance and contra variance. This concept is basically related to inheritance versus generics and generic collections; a couple of examples are provided next for a better explanation.

Covariance

Basically *covariance* allows assigning strongly typed collections (such as List) of derived classes to IEnumerable collections of abstract classes. The code in Listing 21.3 shows how covariance works.

LISTING 21.3   Covariance in Visual Basic 2010

```
Module Covariance

    Sub Main()

        'Using collection initializers
        Dim stringsCollection As New List(Of String) _
                        From {"Understanding ", "covariance ", "in VB 2010"}

        'This code is now legal
        Dim variance As IEnumerable(Of Object) = stringsCollection

        For Each s In variance
            Console.WriteLine(s)
        Next

        Console.ReadLine()
    End Sub
End Module
```

If you examine Listing 21.3 you notice that the variance variable is generic of type `IEnumerable(Of Object)` and receives the assignment of a generic `List(Of String)` content, in which `Object` is the base class of `String`. Until Visual Basic 2008 this code was illegal, and therefore it would throw a compile exception. In Visual Basic 2010 this code is legal but it works only with `IEnumerable(Of T)` collections. If you try to replace `IEnumerable(Of Object)` with `List(Of Object)`, the compiler still throws an error suggesting that you use an `IEnumerable`. By the way, you assigned a collection of `String` to a collection of `Object`, and this is how covariance works. The `For..Each` loop correctly recognizes items in the `IEnumerable` as `String`, and therefore it produces the simple, following output:

```
Understanding
covariance
in VB 2010
```

Contra Variance

Contra variance basically works the opposite of covariance: From a derived class we can take advantage of an abstract class or of a base class. To understand how contra variance works, the best example is to create a client application in which two events of the same control are handled by the same event handler. For this, create a new Windows Presentation Foundation application and write the following XAML code to define a simple `Button` control:

```
<Button Content="Button" Height="50" Name="Button1" Width="150" />
```

CREATING WPF APPLICATIONS

If you are not familiar with WPF applications, you notice one important thing when creating such projects: The designer provides a graphical editor and the code editor for the XAML code (which is XML-styled). You can write the previous snippet within the XAML code editor or drag a `Button` control from the toolbox onto the Window, which is not a problem. You can also notice, in Solution Explorer, the presence of the code-behind file that has an .xaml.vb extension. There you can write the code shown next. Chapter 31, "Creating WPF Applications," discusses WPF applications in detail.

Like other controls, the `Button` control exposes several events. For example, let's consider the `MouseDoubleClick` event and the `KeyUp` event and decide that it would be a good idea to handle both events writing a unique event handler. To accomplish this, we can take advantage of contra variance. Consider the following code, which explicitly declares handlers for events:

```
Public Sub New()
```

```
' This call is required by the Windows Form Designer.
InitializeComponent()

' Explicitly specify handlers for events
AddHandler Button1.KeyUp, AddressOf CommonHandler
AddHandler Button1.MouseDoubleClick, AddressOf CommonHandler
End Sub
```

Both events point to the same delegate, which is implemented as follows:

```
Private Sub CommonHandler(ByVal sender As Object,
                          ByVal e As EventArgs)
    MessageBox.Show("You did it!")
End Sub
```

The `KeyUp` event should be handled by a delegate that receives a `System.Windows.Input.KeyEventArgs` argument, whereas the `MouseDoubleClick` by a delegate receives a `System.Windows.Input.MouseButtonEventArgs` argument. Because both objects inherit from `System.EventArgs`, we can provide a unique delegate that receives an argument of such type and that can handle both events. If you now try to run the application, you see that the message box is correctly shown if you either double-click the button or press a key when the button has the focus. The advantage of contra variance is that we can take advantage of abstract classes to handle the behavior of derived classes.

Summary

In this chapter you got the most out of some advanced language features that provide both special support for the LINQ technology and improvements to your coding experience. Local Type Inference enables developers to avoid specifying types in local variables assignment because the Visual Basic compiler automatically provides the most appropriate one. Array Literals, a new VB 2010 feature, extend local type inference to arrays. Extension methods allow extending existing objects, even if you do not own the source code (such as in case of the .NET Framework) with custom methods. Anonymous types allow generating no-name types on-the-fly that you often use within LINQ queries. Relaxed delegates allow writing code smarter and faster because you are authorized to not respect delegates' signatures if you do not use arguments. Lambda expressions strengthen your code by introducing anonymous delegates that can be generated on-the-fly, improving your code quality and efficiency; multiline lambdas, and sublambdas introduced by VB 2010 that make VB even nearer to C#. Generic covariance and contra variance provide further control over generic `IEnumerable` collections when you work with inheritance.

CHAPTER 22

Introducing ADO.NET and DataSets

For many years .NET developers have written data-centric applications in only two ways: connected or disconnected modes. For the disconnected fashion, DataSets played an important role, and still today lots of developers build or maintain applications based on DataSets, and probably you are one of them. But times change and technology goes on. Different data platforms, such as the ADO.NET Entity Framework and LINQ to SQL, have been introduced to the .NET world, and the classic approach is becoming obsolete. If you think of Silverlight applications, you cannot use DataSets. You instead use LINQ. Of course, there can be situations in which you can still take advantage of the old approach (such as the connected mode), and this is left to your strategy. Because of these considerations, the purpose of this chapter to provide a quick recap on connected mode and disconnected mode with DataSets. We instead focus deeper on what is new in data access with LINQ in next chapters. Basically, you get information that can put you on the right track for comparing and appreciating the power of LINQ.

Introducing ADO.NET

SYSTEM REQUIREMENTS

To proceed with the code examples shown in this chapter, you need to have Microsoft SQL Server 2008 Express installed on your system. You also need to install the sample Northwind database, available for free from the MSDN Code Gallery at http://code.msdn.microsoft.com/northwind.

ADO.NET is the .NET Framework area that provides you with the ability to access data from databases. ADO.NET can be observed from two perspectives, known as connected and disconnected modes, and can access data from different data sources thanks to data providers. In the next sections you learn about providers and connection modes and how you can access data in a connected environment.

After completing these procedures, a recap on DataSets is offered before starting to learn LINQ in the next chapter.

Data Providers

Data providers are .NET objects that allow the .NET Framework to speak with data sources. Data sources are generally databases, such as SQL Server, Oracle, and Access, but also Microsoft Excel's spreadsheets. The .NET Framework includes several built-in data providers exposed by the System.Data namespace. Table 22.1 summarizes built-in data providers.

TABLE 22.1   .NET Data Providers

Provider	Namespace
SQL Server	System.Data.SqlClient
OleDb	System.Data.OleDb
ODBC	System.Data.Odbc
Oracle	System.Data.Oracle (requires reference to the System.Data.Oracle.dll assembly). Notice that you cannot reference the Oracle client if you are using the .NET Framework 4.0 Client Profile.

These are the most common providers, but several companies provided their own, such as MySQL or PostgreSQL. Notice also how the OleDb provider is available to provide support for data sources such as Microsoft Access databases or Excel spreadsheets. In this book, for this chapter and to the ones dedicated to LINQ, Visual Basic topics utilizing the SQL Server provider are covered. There are obviously some differences when writing code for each provider; however, you also find several similarities in connecting to data sources and manipulating data. Such operations are discussed in next sections.

Connection Modes

ADO.NET provides support for both connected and disconnected modes. The big difference between the two modes is that in a connected fashion you explicitly open and close connections against a data source so that you can work with data. This is something that you accomplish with `Connection`, `DataReader` and `Command` objects. In a disconnected environment you basically work against in-memory data that is later persisted to the underlying data source. Generally this is achieved with DataSets, although you see starting from Chapter 25, "LINQ to SQL," how such an approach is the same in LINQ to ADO.NET. I'm sure that you already worked with both modes in your developer experience, so here's just a quick recap so that you appreciate the difference between what you learn in this chapter and what you learn studying LINQ.

Understanding Connections and Data Readers

To establish a connection to a database, you need to create an instance of the `SqlConnection` class passing the connection string as an argument. Then you invoke the `Open` method to open the connection so that you can perform your data operations. Finally, you invoke `Close` to close the connection. The following code, which requires an `Imports System.Data.SqlClient` directive, demonstrates how you establish a connection to the Northwind database:

```
Using myConnection As New _
      SqlConnection("Data Source=.\SQLEXPRESS;Initial Catalog=Northwind;" & 
                 "Integrated Security=True;MultipleActiveResultSets=True")
      myConnection.Open()


End Using
```

Utilizing a `Using..End Using` block ensures that the connection will be correctly released without the need of invoking `Close`.

Inserting Data

To perform an insert operation, you create an instance of the `SqlCommand` class passing the SQL instructions that perform the actual insertion. The constructor also requires the connection to be specified. The following code demonstrates this:

```
Using myConnection As New _
      SqlConnection("Data Source=.\SQLEXPRESS;Initial Catalog=Northwind;" & 
                 "Integrated Security=True;MultipleActiveResultSets=True")

      myConnection.Open()

   Using addCustomer As New SqlCommand("INSERT INTO CUSTOMERS(CompanyName, "& 
                               "CustomerID) VALUES (@COMPANYNAME, 
                               @CUSTOMERID)",
```

22

```
                                        myConnection)
        addCustomer.Parameters.AddWithValue("@COMPANYNAME", "Del Sole")
        addCustomer.Parameters.AddWithValue("@CUSTOMERID", "DELSO")
        addCustomer.ExecuteNonQuery()
    End Using
End Using
```

Notice how you can provide parameterized query strings specifying values with the
`SqlCommand.Parameters.AddWithValue` method. The code adds a new customer to the
`Customers` table in the database, specifying to fields, `CompanyName`, and `CustomerID`. The
`ExecuteNonQuery` method allows executing a Transact-SQL operation instead of a simple
query.

Updating Data

Updating data works similarly to inserting, in that you write the same code, changing the
SQL instructions in the query string. The following code provides an example affecting
the previously added customer:

```
Using updateCustomer As New SqlCommand("UPDATE CUSTOMERS SET " &
                                "COMPANYNAME=@NAME WHERE
                                 CUSTOMERID=@ID",
                                myConnection)
        updateCustomer.Parameters.AddWithValue("@NAME", "Alessandro Del Sole")
        updateCustomer.Parameters.AddWithValue("@ID", "DELSO")
        updateCustomer.ExecuteNonQuery()
End Using
```

So, you simply use an `Update` SQL instruction.

Deleting Data

Deletion works the same as other operations, differing only about the SQL code that uses
a `Delete` statement. The following code demonstrates this:

```
Using deleteCustomer As New SqlCommand("DELETE FROM WHERE CUSTOMERID=@ID",
                                myConnection)
        deleteCustomer.Parameters.AddWithValue("@ID", "DELSO")
        deleteCustomer.ExecuteNonQuery()
End Using
```

Querying Data

Querying data is the last operation; it is important because it demonstrates a fundamental object: the `SqlDataReader`. The object allows retrieving a series of rows from the

specified database object. The following code demonstrates how you can retrieve a series of customers:

```
Using myConnection As New _
      SqlConnection("Data Source=.\SQLEXPRESS;Initial Catalog=Northwind;" &
                       "Integrated Security=True;MultipleActiveResultSets=True")

    myConnection.Open()

    Using queryCustomers As New SqlCommand("SELECT * FROM CUSTOMERS",
                                   myConnection)

        Dim reader As SqlDataReader = queryCustomers.ExecuteReader()

        While reader.Read
           Console.WriteLine("Customer: {0}", reader("CompanyName"))
        End While

    End Using
End Using
```

The query string contains a projection statement that allows querying data. The ExecuteReader method sends the reading query string to the data source and retrieves the desired information. Now that you have recalled the ways for working with data in a connected mode, it is time to recall the disconnected mode and DataSets.

Introducing DataSets

A DataSet is basically an in-memory database that allows working in a disconnected mode. Being disconnected means that first a connection is open, data is read from the data source and pushed to the DataSet, and finally the connection is closed and you will work against in-memory data stored by the DataSet. DataSets introduced a first attempt of typed programming against in-memory data, a concept that has been unleashed in the modern data access layers such as LINQ to SQL and ADO.NET Entity Framework. Now you get a quick recap on DataSets with Visual Basic before facing LINQ.

Creating DataSets

You create DataSets starting from a database adding a new data source to your project. This is accomplished by clicking the **Add New Data Source** command from the Data menu in Visual Studio 2010. This launches the Data Source Configuration Wizard where you choose the Database source, as shown in Figure 22.1.

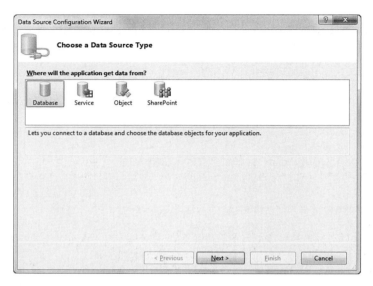

FIGURE 22.1   The first step of the Data Source Configuration Wizard.

When you proceed, you are prompted for specifying if you want to create a DataSet or an Entity Data Model. Select DataSet and click Next. At this point you are prompted to specify the database connection. For example, with the Northwind database available on SQL Server, your connection looks similar to the one shown in Figure 22.2 which represents what I have on my machine.

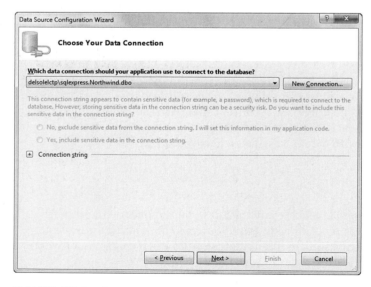

FIGURE 22.2   Specifying the database connection.

Next you are prompted to specify database objects you want to be represented by the new DataSet. Choose how many tables you like but ensure that the Products table is also selected, to complete the next code examples. When the wizard completes, Visual Studio generates a DataSet that you can manage via the designer, represented in Figure 22.3.

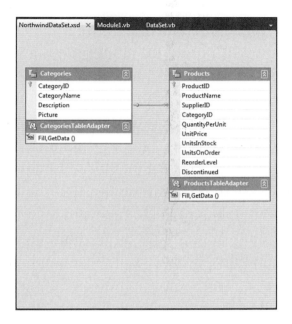

FIGURE 22.3   The DataSet designer.

The designer shows how database objects have been mapped into the DataSet. Each table is represented by a DataTable object. Each record in a table is represented by a DataRow object while each field is a property having its own data type. DataSets use Data Adapters to read and write data. A Data Adapter is actually a bridge between the data source and the DataSet. Basically each DataTable works with a specific adapter; with more than one adapter, there is the need of an object taking care of all of them, which is the job of the TableAdapterManager. If you work with Windows Forms and WPF (new in VS 2010) applications, Visual Studio generates all adapters for you. For Console applications, like in the following example, a few steps must be performed manually. When you have your DataSet, you need an instance of the DataSet and of table adapters:

```
'DataSet here is also the project name
Imports DataSet.NorthwindDataSetTableAdapters
...
    Dim WithEvents NWindDataSet As New NorthwindDataSet
    Dim WithEvents ProductsTblAdapter As New ProductsTableAdapter
    Dim WithEvents TblAdapterManager As New TableAdapterManager
```

Then you populate the DataSet's object invoking the adapter `Fill` method. In the meantime you also assign a `TableAdapterManager` if you have more than one adapter:

```
ProductsTblAdapter.Fill(NWindDataSet.Products)
TblAdapterManager.ProductsTableAdapter = ProductsTblAdapter
```

The next paragraphs recap insert/update/delete operations. At the moment remember that you can save back changes to your data source invoking the adapter's `Update` method as follows:

```
ProductsTblAdapter.Update(NWindDataSet.Products)
```

Inserting Data

Each `DataTable` exposes a `NewTableRow` method, where `Table` is the name of the `DataTable`. In the example of the `Products` table, the method is named `NewProductsRow`. This method returns a new instance of the `ProductRow` object that you can fill with your information. Finally you invoke the `AddProductsRow` method to send your data to the DataSet. Of course, each table has a corresponding `Add` method. The following code demonstrates how you can insert a new product:

```
'Insert
Dim row As NorthwindDataSet.ProductsRow = NWindDataSet.
                                          Products.NewProductsRow
row.ProductName = "Italian spaghetti"
row.Discontinued = False

NWindDataSet.Products.AddProductsRow(row)
ProductsTblAdapter.Update(NWindDataSet.Products)
```

Generally when performing CRUD (Create/Read/Update/Delete) operations you work against rows.

Updating Data

To update a row, you first retrieve the instance of the corresponding `DataRow` so that you can perform manipulations. Then you can update your data. The following snippet demonstrates this:

```
'Update
Dim getRow As NorthwindDataSet.ProductsRow
getRow = NWindDataSet.Products.FindByProductID(1)

getRow.Discontinued = True
ProductsTblAdapter.Update(NWindDataSet.Products)
```

Notice how the instance has been retrieved via the `FindByProductID` method. When you create a DataSet, Visual Studio generates a `FindByXXX` method that allows you to retrieve the instance of the specified row.

Deleting Data

Deleting a row is even simple. You get the instance of the row and then invoke the `DataRow.Delete` method. The following code demonstrates this:

```
'Delete
Dim delRow As NorthwindDataSet.ProductsRow
delRow = NWindDataSet.Products.FindByProductID(1)
delRow.Delete()

ProductsTblAdapter.Update(NWindDataSet.Products)
```

To delete an object you could also invoke the `TableAdapter.Delete` method but this would require the complete specification of the row's properties.

Querying Data

You query data from DataSets basically by writing query strings. But this was the old approach; now in Visual Basic 2010 you can take advantage of LINQ to DataSets, which is covered in Chapter 26, "LINQ to DataSets."

Summary

ADO.NET is the .NET Framework area providing the data access infrastructure for data access. With ADO.NET you access data in two modes: connected and disconnected. For the connected mode, you create `Connection` objects to establish a connection, `Command` objects to send SQL query strings to the data source, and `DataReader` for fetching data; finally you close the `Connection` object. In a disconnected environment, you take advantage of DataSets that are in-memory representations of databases and where each table is a `DataTable` object, each record is a `DataRow` object, and where `TableAdapter` objects act like a bridge between the database and the `DataSet`. You perform CRUD operations invoking the `Add`, `Delete`, `Update`, and `New` methods of `DataTable` objects, whereas a better technique for querying data is offered by LINQ to DataSets in Chapter 26. After this brief recap on the old-fashioned data access techniques, you are ready to start a new journey through the LINQ technology.

CHAPTER 23

Introducing LINQ

Developers create applications that in most cases need to access data sources and manipulate data. During the years hundreds of different data sources and file formats saw the light, and each of them has its own specifications, requirements, and language syntaxes. Whenever an application requires accessing data from a database or parsing a structured file, in most cases manipulation commands are supplied as strings, making it difficult to reveal bugs at compile time. LINQ solves all these problems in one solution, changing how developers write code and improving productivity. This chapter provides an overview of this revolutionary technology that is reprised and discussed in detail in the next chapters.

What Is LINQ?

The LINQ project has been the most important new feature in.NET Framework 3.5, affecting both Visual Basic 2008 and Visual C# 3.0. LINQ stands for *Language INtegrated Query* and is a project that Microsoft began developing in 2003. The first beta versions saw the light starting from 2005 until it became part of the CLR with .NET 3.5, and due to its importance, it is still part of .NET Framework 4.0. As its name implies, LINQ is a technology that allows querying data directly from the programming language. To understand why LINQ is so important and why it is so revolutionary, we have to first start a brief discussion. Most real-world applications need to access data, by querying, filtering, and manipulating data as well. The word "data" has several meanings. In the modern computer world there are hundreds of different data sources, such as databases,

XML documents, Microsoft Excel spreadsheets, web services, in-memory collections, and so on. Moreover, each of these kinds of data sources can be further differentiated. For example, there is not just one kind of database, but there are lots of databases, such Microsoft SQL Server, Microsoft Access, Oracle, MySQL, and so on. Each of these databases has its own infrastructure, its own administrative tools, and its own syntax. As you can easily imagine, developers need to adopt different programming techniques and syntaxes according to the specific data source they are working on, and this can be complex. Obviously accessing an XML document is completely different from accessing a SQL Server database; therefore, there is the need for specific types and members for accessing such data sources, and one is different from the other one. So, the first thing that Microsoft considered is related to the plethora of programming techniques to adopt depending on the data source. The next part of this discussion is related to practical limitations of the programming techniques before LINQ came in. For example, consider accessing a SQL Server database with DataSets. Although powerful, this technique has several limitations that can be summarized as follows:

▶ You need to know both the SQL Server syntax and the Visual Basic/Visual C# syntax. Although preferable, this is not always possible, and in some cases it is it can lead to confusion.

▶ SQL queries are passed to the compiler as strings. This means that if you write a bad query (for example because of a typo), this will not be visible at compile time but only when your application runs. IntelliSense support is not provided when writing SQL syntax; therefore typos can easily happen. The same occurs for possibly bad query logical implementations. Both scenarios are certainly to be avoided, but often they can be subtle bugs to identify.

▶ In most cases the developer will not also deeply know the database structure if she is not also an administrator. This means that she cannot necessarily know what data types are exposed by the database, although it is always a preferable situation.

Now consider querying in-memory collections of .NET objects. Before LINQ, you could only write long and complex For and For..Each loops or conditional code blocks (such as If..Then or Select..Case) to access collections. The last example is related to XML documents: Before LINQ, you had two ways for manipulating XML files. The first one was treating them as text files, which is one of the worst things in the world, The second method was to recur to the System.Xml namespace that makes things difficult when you need to simply read and write a document. All these considerations caused Microsoft to develop LINQ; so again we ask the question, "What is LINQ?" The answer is the following: LINQ provides a unified programming model that allows accessing, querying, filtering, and manipulating different kinds of data sources, such as databases, Xml documents, and in-memory collections, using the same programming techniques independently from the data source. This is accomplished via special keywords of typical SQL derivation that are now integrated into.NET languages and that allow working in a completely object-oriented way. Developers can take advantage of a new syntax that offers the following returns:

▶ The same techniques can be applied to different kinds of data sources.

▶ Because querying data is performed via new keywords integrated in the language, this allows working in a strongly typed way, meaning that eventual errors can be found at compile time instead of spending a large amount of time investigating problems at runtime.

▶ Full IntelliSense support.

LINQ syntax is straightforward, as you see in this chapter and in the following ones and can deeply change how you write your code.

> ### LINQ IN THIS BOOK
>
> LINQ is a big technology and has lots of features so that discussing the technology in deep detail would require a dedicated book. What you find in this book is first the Visual Basic syntax for LINQ. Second, you learn how to use LINQ for querying and manipulating data, which is the real purpose of LINQ. You will not find dedicated scenarios such as LINQ in WPF, LINQ in Silverlight, and so on. Just keep in mind that you can bind LINQ queries to every user control that supports the IEnumerable interface or just convert LINQ queries into writable collections (which is shown here) to both present and edit data via the UI. For example, you can directly assign (or first convert to a collection) a LINQ query to a Windows Forms BindingSource control or to a WPF CollectionViewSource one or to an ASP.NET DataGrid as well.

LINQ Examples

To understand why LINQ is revolutionary, the best way is beginning with some code examples. In the next chapters you get a huge quantity of code snippets, but this chapter offers basic queries to provide a high-level comprehension. Imagine you have a Person class exposing the FirstName, LastName, and Age properties. Then, imagine you have a collection of Person objects, of type List(Of Person). Last, imagine you want to extract from the collection all Person instances whose LastName property begins with the D letter. This scenario is accomplished via the following code snippet that uses a LINQ query:

```
' "people" is of type List(Of Person)
Dim peopleQuery = From pers In people
                  Where pers.LastName.StartsWith("D")
                  Order By pers.Age Descending
                  Select pers
```

This form of code is known as *query expression* because it allows extracting from a data source only a subset of data according to specific criteria. Notice how query expressions are performed using some keywords that recall the SQL syntax, such as From, Where, Order By, and Select. Such keywords are also known as clauses, and the Visual Basic grammar offers a large set of clauses that is examined in detail in the next chapters. The first consideration is that while typing code IntelliSense speeds up your coding experience, providing the usual appropriate suggestions. This is due to the integration of clauses with the language. Second, because clauses are part of the language, you can take advantage of the background compiler that determines if a query expression fails before running the application. Now let's examine what the query does. The `From` clause specifies the data source to be queried, in this case a collection of `Person` objects, which allows specifying a condition that is considered if evaluated to `True`; in the above example, each `Person` instance is taken in consideration only if its `LastName` property begins with the `D` letter. The `Order By` clause allows sorting the result of the query depending on the specified criteria that here is the value of the `Age` property in descending order. The `Select` clause extracts objects and pulls them into a new `IEnumerable(Of Person)` collection that is the type for the `peopleQuery` variable. Although this type has not been explicitly assigned, local type inference is used, and the Visual Basic compiler automatically infers the appropriate type as the query result. Another interesting consideration is that queries are now strongly typed. You are not writing queries as strings because you work with reserved keywords and .NET objects, and therefore your code can take advantage of the Common Language Runtime control, allowing better results at both compile time and at runtime. Working in a strongly typed way is one of the greatest LINQ features thanks to its integration with the CLR.

IMPLICIT LINE CONTINUATION

Differently from Visual Basic 2008, in Visual Basic 2010 you can omit the underscore (_) character within LINQ queries as demonstrated by the previous code.

The same result can be obtained by querying a data source with extension methods. The following code demonstrates this:

```
Dim peopleQuery2 = people.Where(Function(pers) pers.LastName.
                    StartsWith("D")).OrderBy(Function(pers) pers.Age).
                    Select(Function(pers) pers)
```

The .NET Framework offers extension methods that replicate Visual Basic and Visual C# reserved keywords and that receives lambda expressions as arguments pointing to the data source.

Language Support

In Chapter 21, "Advanced Language Features," you got an overview of some advanced language features in the Visual Basic 2010 language. Some of those features were already introduced with Visual Basic 2008 and have the purpose of providing support for LINQ. Particularly, the language support to LINQ is realized via the following features:

- ▶ Local type inference
- ▶ Anonymous types
- ▶ Lambda expressions

▶ Extension methods

▶ If ternary operator

▶ Nullable types

▶ Xml literals

▶ Object initializers

The addition of keywords such as `From`, `Where`, and `Select` complete the language support for this revolutionary technology. In the next chapters you see LINQ in action and you learn how to use all the language features and the dedicated keywords.

Understanding Providers

The .NET Framework 4.0 provides the ability of using LINQ against six built-in kinds of data sources, which are summarized in Table 23.1.

TABLE 23.1   LINQ Standard Providers

Provider name	Description
LINQ to Objects	Allows querying in-memory collections of .NET objects
LINQ to DataSets	Allows querying data stored within DataSets
LINQ to SQL	Allows querying and manipulating data from an SQL Server database via a specific object relational mapping engine
LINQ to XML	Allows querying and manipulating Xml documents
LINQ to Entities	Allows querying data exposed by an Entity Data Model (see ADO.NET Entity Framework for details)
Parallel LINQ	A new implementation that allows querying data using the Task Parallel Library

Therefore there is a specific LINQ implementation according to the data source (objects, datasets, SQL databases, and Xml documents). Such implementations are known as standard providers. Due to their importance, each provider is covered in a specific chapter. LINQ implementation is also referred to as providers or standard providers. There could be situations in which you need to use a custom data source and you would like to take the advantage of the LINQ syntax. Luckily LINQ is also extensible with custom providers that can allow access to any kind of data source, and this is possible due to its particular infrastructure. (A deep discussion on LINQ infrastructure is out of the scope here, and you might want to consider a specific publication, while the focus is on the Visual Basic language for LINQ.) Custom implementations such as LINQ to CSV, LINQ to Windows Desktop Search, and LINQ to NHibernate give a good idea about the power of this technology.

EXTENDING LINQ

The following document in the MSDN Library can help you get started with extending LINQ with a custom provider: http://msdn.microsoft.com/en-us/library/bb546158.aspx.

Overview of LINQ Architecture

Providing deep information on the LINQ architecture is out of the scope of this book Getting a high-level overview can help you understanding how LINQ works. Basically LINQ is the last layer of a series, as shown in Figure 23.1.

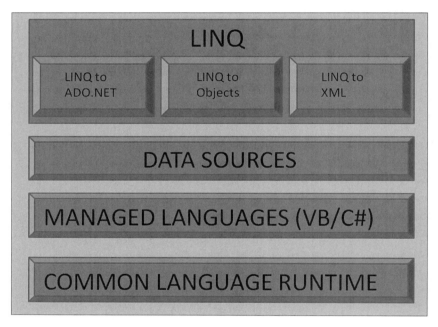

FIGURE 23.1   LINQ is at the top of a layers infrastructure.

At the bottom there is the Common Language Runtime that provides the runtime infrastructure for LINQ. The next layer is constituted by the managed languages that offer support to LINQ with special reserved keywords and features. The next layer is all about data and is represented by data sources that LINQ allows querying. The last layer is LINQ itself with its standard providers. You may or may not love architectures built on several layers, but LINQ has one big advantage: particularly when working with databases: It will do all the work behind the scenes for sending the SQL commands to the data source avoiding the need for you to perform it manually, offering also several high-level classes and members for accessing data in a completely object-oriented way. You see practical demonstrations of this discussion in the appropriate chapters.

Summary

In this chapter you got a brief overview of Language INtegrated Query that will be better discussed in the next chapters. You learned what LINQ is and how it can improve querying data sources thanks to integrated reserved keywords and taking advantage of a strongly typed approach. You got an overview of the built-in LINQ providers, and you got information on the specific language support for LINQ. Now you are ready to delve into LINQ in next chapters.

CHAPTER 24

LINQ to Objects

Linq changes the way you write code. This is something that you will often hear when talking about LINQ. It provides the ability of querying different data sources taking advantage of the same syntax, background compiler, IntelliSense, and CLR control with its intuitive programming model. LINQ's syntax is so straightforward that you become familiar with the technology quickly. In this chapter you learn about LINQ to Objects, which is the starting point of every LINQ discussion. You see how easy querying .NET objects is, such as in-memory collections, and you see in the next chapters how basically you can use the same approach against different data sources and LINQ providers. Take your time to read this chapter; it's important—especially the second part, which is about standard query operators, which explains concepts that pervade every LINQ provider and that will not be explained again in other chapters, except where expressly required.

Introducing LINQ to Objects

In the previous chapter I provided an overview of the LINQ technology and told you that it provides a unified programming model for querying different types of data sources using generally the same syntax constructs. You got a few examples of LINQ syntax, but from now on you see LINQ in action in different scenarios, therefore with more examples. This chapter is about LINQ to Objects, which is the standard provider for querying in-memory objects. This definition considers collections, arrays, and any other object that implements the IEnumerable or IEnumerable(Of T) interface (or interfaces deriving from them). LINQ to

Objects can be basically considered as the root of LINQ providers, and it's important to understand how it works because the approach is essentially the same in accessing databases and Xml documents. We focus on code more than on introducing the provider with annoying discussions, so let's start.

Querying in Memory Objects

LINQ to Object's purpose is querying in-memory collections in a strongly typed fashion using recently added keywords that recall SQL instructions syntax and that are now integrated in the Visual Basic language, allowing the compiler to manage your actions at compile time. Before querying data, you need a data source. For example, imagine you have the following `Product` class that represents some food products of your company:

```
Class Product
    Property ProductID As Integer
    Property ProductName As String
    Property UnitPrice As Decimal
    Property UnitsInStock As Integer
    Property Discontinued As Boolean
End Class
```

CODING TIP: USING OBJECT INITIALIZERS

In this chapter and the next ones dedicated to LINQ, you notice that in most cases classes do not implement an explicit constructor. You see the advantages of object initializers in both normal code and in LINQ query expressions, which is the reason why custom classes have no explicit constructors. This is not a mandatory rule whereas it is instead an approach specific to LINQ that you need to be familiar with.

At this point consider the following products, as a demonstration:

```
Dim prod1 As New Product With {.ProductID = 0,
                               .ProductName = "Pasta",
                               .UnitPrice = 0.5D,
                               .UnitsInStock = 10,
                               .Discontinued = False}

Dim prod2 As New Product With {.ProductID = 1,
                               .ProductName = "Mozzarella",
                               .UnitPrice = 1D,
                               .UnitsInStock = 50,
                               .Discontinued = False}

Dim prod3 As New Product With {.ProductID = 2,
```

```
                            .ProductName = "Crabs",
                            .UnitPrice = 7D,
                            .UnitsInStock = 20,
                            .Discontinued = True}

Dim prod4 As New Product With {.ProductID = 3,
                               .ProductName = "Tofu",
                               .UnitPrice = 3.5D,
                               .UnitsInStock = 40,
                               .Discontinued = False}
```

The code is simple; it just creates several instances of the `Product` class populating its properties with some food names and characteristics. Usually you collect instances of your products in a typed collection. The following code accomplishes this, taking advantage of collection initializers:

```
Dim products As New List(Of Product) From {prod1,
                                           prod2,
                                           prod3,
                                           prod4}
```

Because the `List(Of T)` collection implements `IEnumerable(Of T)`, it can be queried with LINQ. The following query shows how you can retrieve all nondiscontinued products in which the `UnitsInStock` property value is greater than 10:

```
Dim query = From prod In products
            Where prod.UnitsInStock > 10 _
            And prod.Discontinued = False
            Order By prod.UnitPrice
            Select prod
```

CODING TIP: IMPLICIT LINE CONTINUATION

In LINQ queries you can take advantage of the new Visual Basic 2010 feature known as *implicit line continuation* that avoids the need of writing the underscore character at the end of a line. An exception in LINQ queries is when you use logical operators, as in the preceding code snippet, in which the underscore is required. The code provides an easy view of this necessity. As an alternative, you can place the logical operator (And, in the example) on the preceding line in order to avoid the underscore.

Such kind of LINQ query is also known as *query expression*. The `From` keyword points to the data source; the prod identifier represents one product in the products list. The `Where` keyword allows filtering data in which the specified condition is evaluated to `True`. The `Order By` keywords allow sorting data according to the specified property. `Select` pushes each item that matches the specified `Where` conditions into an `IEnumerable(Of T)` result.

Notice how local type inference avoids the need of specifying the query result type that is inferred by the compiler as IEnumerable(Of Product). Later in this chapter you will better understand why type inference is important in LINQ queries for anonymous types' collections. At this point you can work with the result of your query; for example, you can iterate the preceding query variable to get information on the retrieved products:

```
For Each prod In query
    Console.WriteLine("Product name: {0}, Unit price: {1}",
                    prod.ProductName, prod.UnitPrice)
Next
```

This code produces on your screen a list of products that are not discontinued and where there is a minimum of 11 units in stock. For your convenience, Listing 24.1 shows the complete code for this example, providing a function that returns the query result via the Return instruction. Iteration is executed later within the caller.

LISTING 24.1   Querying In-Memory Collections with LINQ

```
Module Module1


    Sub Main()

        Dim result = QueryingObjectsDemo1()

        For Each prod In result
            Console.WriteLine("Product name: {0}, Unit price: {1}",
                            prod.ProductName, prod.UnitPrice)
        Next
        Console.Readline()
    End Sub



    Function QueryingObjectsDemo1() As IEnumerable(Of Product)

        Dim prod1 As New Product With {.ProductID = 0,
                                       .ProductName = "Pasta",
                                       .UnitPrice = 0.5D,
                                       .UnitsInStock = 10,
                                       .Discontinued = False}

        Dim prod2 As New Product With {.ProductID = 1,
                                       .ProductName = "Mozzarella",
                                       .UnitPrice = 1D,
                                       .UnitsInStock = 50,
                                       .Discontinued = False}
```

```
        Dim prod3 As New Product With {.ProductID = 2,
                                       .ProductName = "Crabs",
                                       .UnitPrice = 7D,
                                       .UnitsInStock = 20,
                                       .Discontinued = True}

        Dim prod4 As New Product With {.ProductID = 3,
                                       .ProductName = "Tofu",
                                       .UnitPrice = 3.5D,
                                       .UnitsInStock = 40,
                                       .Discontinued = False}

        Dim products As New List(Of Product) From {prod1,
                                                   prod2,
                                                   prod3,
                                                   prod4}

        Dim query = From prod In products
                    Where prod.UnitsInStock > 10 _
                    And prod.Discontinued = False
                    Order By prod.UnitPrice
                    Select prod

        Return query
    End Function
End Module



Class Product
    Property ProductID As Integer
    Property ProductName As String
    Property UnitPrice As Decimal
    Property UnitsInStock As Integer
    Property Discontinued As Boolean
End Class
```

If you run the code in Listing 24.1, you get the following result:

```
Product name: Mozzarella, Unit price: 1
Product name: Tofu, Unit price: 3.5
```

Such a result contains only those products that are not discontinued and that are available in more than 11 units. You can perform complex queries with LINQ to Objects. The following example provides a LINQ to Objects representation of what you get with relational databases and LINQ to SQL or LINQ to Entities. Consider the following class that must be added to the project:

```
Class ShippingPlan
    Property ProductID As Integer
    Property ShipDate As Date
End Class
```

The purpose of the `ShippingPlan` is storing the ship date for each product, represented by an ID. Both the `ShippingPlan` and Product classes expose a `ProductID` property that provides a basic relationship. Now consider the following code that creates four instances of the `ShippingPlan` class, one for each product and a collection of items:

```
Dim shipPlan1 As New ShippingPlan With {.ProductID = 0,
                                        .ShipDate = New Date(2010, 1, 1)}
Dim shipPlan2 As New ShippingPlan With {.ProductID = 1,
                                        .ShipDate = New Date(2010, 2, 1)}
Dim shipPlan3 As New ShippingPlan With {.ProductID = 2,
                                        .ShipDate = New Date(2010, 3, 1)}
Dim shipPlan4 As New ShippingPlan With {.ProductID = 3,
                                        .ShipDate = New Date(2010, 4, 1)}

Dim shipPlans As New List(Of ShippingPlan) From {
                                        shipPlan1,
                                        shipPlan2,
                                        shipPlan3,
                                        shipPlan4}
```

At this point the goal is to retrieve a list of product names and the related ship date. This can be accomplished as follows:

```
Dim queryPlans = From prod In products
    Join plan In shipPlans On plan.ProductID Equals prod.ProductID
    Select New With {.ProductName = prod.ProductName,
                    .ShipDate = plan.ShipDate}
```

As you can see the `Join` clause allows joining data from two different data sources having in common one property. This works similarly to the `JOIN` Sql instruction. Notice how you can take advantage of anonymous types to generate a new type on-the-fly that stores only the necessary information, without the need of creating a custom class for handling that information. The problem is now another one. If you need to use such a query result within a method body, no problem. The compiler can distinguish what and how many members an anonymous type exposes so that you can use such members in a strongly typed way. The problem is when you need to return a query result like that as the result of a function. You cannot declare a function as an `IEnumerable(Of anonymous type)`, so you should return a nongeneric `IEnumerable` which, in other words, returns an `IEnumerable(Of`

Object); therefore, you cannot invoke members from anonymous types except if you recur to late binding. This makes sense, because anonymous types' members have visibility only within the parent member that defines them. To solve this problem, you need to define a custom class holding query results. For example, consider the following class:

```
Class CustomProduct
    Property ProductName As String
    Property ShipDate As Date
End Class
```

It stores information from both `Product` and `ShippingPlan` classes. Now consider the following query:

```
Dim queryPlans = From prod In products
    Join plan In shipPlans On plan.ProductID Equals prod.ProductID
    Select New CustomProduct With {.ProductName = prod.ProductName,
                        .ShipDate = plan.ShipDate}
```

It creates an instance of the `CustomProduct` class each time an object matching the condition is encountered. In this way you can return the query result as the result of a function returning `IEnumerable(Of CustomProduct)`. This scenario is represented for your convenience in Listing 24.2.

LISTING 24.2   Complex LINQ to Objects Queries

```
Function QueryObjectsDemo2() As IEnumerable(Of CustomProduct)
    Dim prod1 As New Product With {.ProductID = 0,
                        .ProductName = "Pasta",
                        .UnitPrice = 0.5D,
                        .UnitsInStock = 10,
                        .Discontinued = False}

    Dim prod2 As New Product With {.ProductID = 1,
                        .ProductName = "Mozzarella",
                        .UnitPrice = 1D,
                        .UnitsInStock = 50,
                        .Discontinued = False}

    Dim prod3 As New Product With {.ProductID = 2,
                        .ProductName = "Crabs",
                        .UnitPrice = 7D,
                        .UnitsInStock = 20,
                        .Discontinued = True}

    Dim prod4 As New Product With {.ProductID = 3,
                        .ProductName = "Tofu",
                        .UnitPrice = 3.5D,
```

```vb
                                .UnitsInStock = 40,
                                .Discontinued = False}

        Dim products As New List(Of Product) From {prod1,
                                                   prod2,
                                                   prod3,
                                                   prod4}

        Dim shipPlan1 As New ShippingPlan With {.ProductID = 0,
                                                .ShipDate = New Date(2010, 1, 1)}
        Dim shipPlan2 As New ShippingPlan With {.ProductID = 1,
                                                .ShipDate = New Date(2010, 2, 1)}
        Dim shipPlan3 As New ShippingPlan With {.ProductID = 2,
                                                .ShipDate = New Date(2010, 3, 1)}
        Dim shipPlan4 As New ShippingPlan With {.ProductID = 3,
                                                .ShipDate = New Date(2010, 4, 1)}

        Dim shipPlans As New List(Of ShippingPlan) From {
                                                    shipPlan1,
                                                    shipPlan2,
                                                    shipPlan3,
                                                    shipPlan4}

        Dim queryPlans = From prod In products
                         Join plan In shipPlans On _
                         plan.ProductID Equals prod.ProductID
                         Select New CustomProduct _
                         With {.ProductName = prod.ProductName,
                               .ShipDate = plan.ShipDate}

        Return queryPlans
    End Function
    Sub QueryPlans()
        Dim plans = QueryObjectsDemo2()
        For Each plan In plans
            Console.WriteLine("Product name: {0} will be shipped on {1}",
                          plan.ProductName, plan.ShipDate)
        Next
        Console.ReadLine()
    End Sub
```

If you invoke the QueryPlans method, you get the following output:

```
Product name: Pasta will be shipped on 01/01/2010
Product name: Mozzarella will be shipped on 02/01/2010
Product name: Crabs will be shipped on 03/01/2010
Product name: Tofu will be shipped on 04/01/2010
```

You would obtain the same result with anonymous types if the iteration were performed within the method body and not outside the method itself. This approach is always useful and becomes necessary in scenarios such as LINQ to Xml on Silverlight applications. LINQ to Objects offers a large number of operators, known as *standard query operators* that are discussed in this chapter. An important thing you need to consider is that you can also perform LINQ queries via extension methods. Language keywords for LINQ have extension methods counterparts that can be used with lambda expressions for performing queries. The following snippet provides an example of how the previous query expression can be rewritten invoking extension methods:

```
Dim query = products.Where(Function(p) p.UnitsInStock > 10 And _
            p.Discontinued = False).
            OrderBy(Function(p) p.UnitPrice).
            Select(Function(p) p)
```

Notice how extension methods are instance methods of the data source you are querying. Each method requires a lambda expression that returns instances of the Product class, allowing performing the required tasks. Before studying operators, there is an important concept that you must understand that is related to the actual moment when queries are executed.

Understanding Deferred Execution

When the CLR encounters a LINQ query, the query is not executed immediately. LINQ queries are executed only when they are effectively used. This concept is known as *deferred execution* and is part of all LINQ providers that you encounter, both standard and custom ones. For example, consider the query that is an example in the previous discussion:

```
Dim query = From prod In products
            Where prod.UnitsInStock > 10 _
            And prod.Discontinued = False
            Order By prod.UnitPrice
            Select prod
```

This query is not executed until you effectively use its result. If the query is defined within a function and is the result of the method, the Return instruction causes the query to be executed:

```
Dim query = From prod In products
            Where prod.UnitsInStock > 10 _
            And prod.Discontinued = False
            Order By prod.UnitPrice
            Select prod
'The query is executed here:
Return query
```

24

Iterating the result also causes the query to be executed:

```
Dim query = From prod In products
            Where prod.UnitsInStock > 10 _
            And prod.Discontinued = False
            Order By prod.UnitPrice
            Select prod
'The query is executed here, the Enumerator is invoked
For Each prod In query
    Console.WriteLine("Product name: {0}, Unit price: {1}",
                      prod.ProductName, prod.UnitPrice)
Next
```

Another example of query execution is when you just invoke a member of the result as in the following example:

```
Console.WriteLine(query.Count)
```

You can also force queries to be executed when declared, invoking methods on the query itself. For example, converting a query result into a collection causes the query to be executed as demonstrated here:

```
Dim query = (From prod In products
             Where prod.UnitsInStock > 10 _
             And prod.Discontinued = False
             Order By prod.UnitPrice
             Select prod).ToList 'the query is executed here
```

This is also important at debugging time. For example, consider the case where you have a query and you want to examine its result while debugging, taking advantage of Visual Studio's data tips. If you place a breakpoint on the line of code immediately after the query and then pass the mouse pointer over the variable that receives the query result, the data tips feature pops up a message saying that the variable is an in-memory query and that clicking to expand the result processes the collection. This is shown in Figure 24.1.

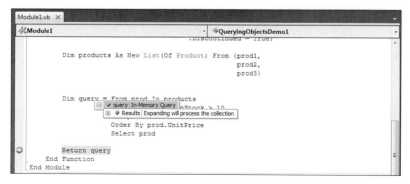

FIGURE 24.1   Visual Studio data tips show how the query has not been executed yet.

At this point the debugger executes the query in memory. When executed, you can inspect the query result before it is passed to the next code. Data tips enable you to examine every single item in the collection. Figure 24.2 demonstrates this.

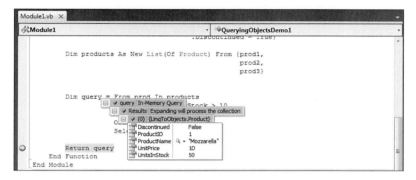

FIGURE 24.2   The debugger executes the query so that you can inspect its result.

TIP

The preceding discussion is also valid if adding query result variables to the Watch window.

Deferred execution is a key topic in LINQ development, and you always need to keep in mind how it works to avoid problems in architecting your code.

Introducing Standard Query Operators

Querying objects with LINQ (as much as Xml documents and ADO.NET models) is accomplished via the standard query operators that are a set of Visual Basic keywords allowing performing both simple and complex tasks within LINQ queries. This chapter covers standard query operators illustrating their purpose. For this, remember that this topic is important because you need operators in other LINQ providers as well. You can also notice that standard query operator generally have extension methods counterparts that you can use as well.

CODING TIPS

The following examples consistently use local type inference and array literals. They dramatically speed up writing LINQ queries, and therefore using such a feature is something that you should try in practical examples. Of course nothing prevents you from using old-fashioned coding techniques, but showing the power of Visual Basic 2010 is one of this book's purposes.

Projection Operators

LINQ query expressions extract values from data sources and then push results into a sequence of elements. This operation of pushing items into a sequence is known as *projection*. `Select` is the projection operator for LINQ queries. Continuing the example of products shown in the previous section, the following query creates a new sequence containing all products names:

```
Dim productNames = From prod In products
                   Select prod.ProductName
```

The query result is now an `IEnumerable(Of String)`. If you need to create a sequence of objects, you can simply select each single item as follows:

```
Dim productSequence = From prod In products
                      Select prod
```

This returns an `IEnumerable(Of Product)`. You can also pick more than one member for an item:

```
Dim productSequence = From prod In products
                      Select prod.ProductID, prod.ProductName
```

This returns an `IEnumerable(Of Anonymous type)`. Of course, for an anonymous type, you can use the extended syntax that also allows specifying custom properties names:

```
Dim productSequence = From prod In products
                      Select ID = prod.ProductID,
                      Name = prod.ProductName
```

This is basically the equivalent of the following:

```
Dim productSequence = From prod In products
                      Select New With {.ID = prod.ProductID,
                      .Name = prod.ProductName}
```

There is an extension counterpart for `Select`, which is the `Select` extension method that receives a lambda expression as an argument that allows specifying the object or member that must be projected into the sequence and that works like this:

```
'IEnumerable(Of String)
Dim prodSequence = products.Select(Function(p) p.ProductName)
```

Of course query expressions may require more complex projections, especially if you work on different sources. There is another projection operator known as `SelectMany` that is an extension method but that can be performed in expressions, too. To continue with the next examples, refer to the "Querying In-Memory Objects" section and retake the

ShippingPlan and Product classes and code that populates new collections of such objects. After you've done this, consider the following query:

```
Dim query = From prod In products
            From ship In shipPlans
            Where prod.ProductID = ship.ProductID
            Select prod.ProductName, ship.ShipDate
```

With nested From clauses we can query different data sources, and the Select clause picks data from both collections, acting as SelectMany that has an extension method counterpart that accepts lambda expressions as arguments pointing to the desired data sources.

Restriction Operators

LINQ offers an operator named Where that allows filtering query results according to the specified condition. For example, continuing with the previous examples of a collection of products, the following code returns only nondiscontinued products:

```
Dim query = From prod In products
            Where prod.Discontinued = False
            Select prod
```

The same result can be accomplished by invoking a same-named extension method that works as follows:

```
Dim result = products.Where(Function(p) p.Discontinued = False).
            Select(Function(p) p)
```

Where supports lots of operators on the line that are summarized in Table 24.1.

TABLE 24.1   Operators Supported by Where

Operator	Description
<, >	Major and minor operators that return True if the value is respectively smaller or greater than the other one
=, <>	Equality and inequality operators for value types comparisons
Is	Returns True if the comparison between two objects succeeds
IsNot	Returns True if the comparison between two objects does not succeed
And	Allows specifying two conditions and returns True if both conditions are true
AndAlso	Allows specifying two conditions and returns True if both conditions are true but if the first one is False, the second one is skipped
Or	Allows specifying two conditions and returns True if at least one of the conditions is evaluated to True

24

TABLE 24.1   Continued

Operator	Description
OrElse	Allows specifying two conditions and returns True if both conditions are True
Like	Compares a string to a pattern and returns True if the string matches the pattern
Mod	Returns the remainder of a division between numbers

The following code provides a more complex example of filtering using Where and logical operators to retrieve the list of executable files that have been accessed within two dates:

```
Dim fileList = From item In My.Computer.FileSystem.
                        GetDirectoryInfo("C:\").GetFiles
                Where item.LastAccessTime < Date.Today _
                AndAlso item.LastAccessTime > New Date(2009, 9, 10) _
                AndAlso item.FullName Like "*.exe"
                Select item
```

The preceding code uses AndAlso to ensure that the three conditions are True. Using AndAlso short circuiting offers the benefit of making evaluations more efficient in one line. Notice how Like is used to provide a pattern comparison with the filename. You find a lot of examples about Where in this book, so let's discuss other operators.

Aggregation Operators

Aggregation operators allow performing simple mathematic calculations on a sequence's items using the Aggregate and Into clauses. The combination of such clauses can affect the following methods:

- ▶ Sum, which returns the sum of values of the specified property for each item in the collection

- ▶ Average, which returns the average calculation of values of the specified property for each item in the collection

- ▶ Count and LongCount, which return the number of items within a collection, respectively as Integer and Long types

- ▶ Min, which returns the lowest value for the specified sequence

- ▶ Max, which returns the highest value for the specified sequence

For example, you can get the sum of unit prices for your products as follows:

```
'Returns the sum of product unit prices
Dim totalAmount = Aggregate prod In products
                Into Sum(prod.UnitPrice)
```

Generally you need to specify the object property that must be affected by the calculation (UnitPrice in this example) and that also works the same way in other aggregation operators. The following code shows instead how you can retrieve the average price:

```
'Returns the average price
Dim averagePrice = Aggregate prod In products
                Into Average(prod.UnitPrice)
```

The following snippet shows how you can retrieve the number of products in both Integer and Long formats:

```
'Returns the number of products
Dim numberOfItems = Aggregate prod In products
                Into Count()
```

```
'Returns the number of products as Long
Dim longNumberOfItems = Aggregate prod In products
                    Into LongCount()
```

The following code shows instead how you can retrieve the lowest and highest prices for your products:

```
'Returns the lowest value for the specified
'sequence
Dim minimumPrice = Aggregate prod In products
                Into Min(prod.UnitPrice)
```

```
'Returns the highest value for the specified
'sequence
Dim maximumPrice = Aggregate prod In products
                Into Max(prod.UnitPrice)
```

All of the preceding aggregation operators have extension methods counterparts that work similarly. For example, you can compute the minimum unit price as follows:

```
Dim minimum = products.Min(Function(p) p.UnitPrice)
```

Such extension methods require you to specify a lambda expression pointing to the member you want to be part of the calculation. Other extension methods work the same way.

> **NOTE**
>
> When using aggregation operators, you do not get back an IEnumerable type. You instead get a single value type.

Understanding the Let Keyword

The Visual Basic syntax offers a keyword named Let that can be used for defining temporary identifiers within query expressions. The following code shows how you can query Windows Forms controls to get a sequence of text boxes:

```
Dim query = From ctrl In Me.Controls _
            Where TypeOf (ctrl) Is TextBox _
            Let txtBox = DirectCast(ctrl, TextBox) _
            Select txtBox.Name
```

The Let keyword allows defining a temporary identifier so that you can perform multiple operations on each item of the sequence and then invoke the item by its temporary identifier.

Conversion Operators

LINQ query results are returned as IEnumerable(Of T) (or IQueryable(Of T) as you see in next chapters), but you often need to convert this type into a most appropriate one. For example, query results cannot be edited unless you convert them into a typed collection. To accomplish this LINQ offers some extension methods whose job is converting query results into other .NET types such as arrays or collections. For example let's consider the Products collection of the previous section's examples and first perform a query expression that retrieves all products that are not discontinued:

```
Dim query = From prod In products
            Where prod.Discontinued = False
            Select prod
```

The result of this query is IEnumerable(Of Product). The result can easily be converted into other .NET types. First, you can convert it into an array of Product invoking the ToArray extension method:

```
'Returns Product()
Dim productArray = query.ToArray
```

Similarly you can convert the query result into a List(Of T) invoking ToList. The following code returns a List(Of Product) collection:

```
'Returns List(Of Product)
Dim productList = query.ToList
```

You can perform a more complex conversion with ToDictionary and ToLookup. ToDictionary generates a Dictionary(Of TKey, TValue) and receives only an argument that via a lambda expression specifies the key for the dictionary. The value part of the key/value pair is always the type of the query (`Product` in this example). This is an example:

```
'Returns Dictionary(Of Integer, Product)
Dim productDictionary = query.ToDictionary(Function(p) _
                                            p.ProductID)
```

Because the value is a typed object, the `Value` property of each `KeyValuePair` in the `Dictionary` is an instance of your type; therefore, you can access members from `Value`. The following snippet demonstrates this:

```
For Each prod In productDictionary
    Console.WriteLine("Product ID: {0}, name: {1}", prod.Key,
                      prod.Value.ProductName)
Next
```

The next operator is `ToLookup` that returns an `ILookup(Of TKey, TElement)` where `TKey` indicates a key similarly to a `Dictionary` whereas `TElement` represents a sequence of elements. Typically such a type can be used in mapping one-to-many relationships between an object. Continuing the example of the `Product` class we can provide an elegant way for getting the product name based on the ID. Consider the following code snippet that returns an `ILookup(Of Integer, String)`:

```
Dim productLookup = query.ToLookup(Function(p) p.ProductID, _
                                   Function(p) p.ProductName & " has " & _
                                   p.UnitsInStock & " units in stock")
```

We can now query the products sequence based on the `ProductID` property and extract data such as product name and units in stock. Because of the particular structure of `ILookup`, a nested `For..Each` loop is required and works like the following:

```
For Each prod In productLookup
    Console.WriteLine("Product ID: {0}", prod.Key)

    For Each item In prod
        Console.WriteLine("    {0}", item)
    Next
Next
```

Prod is of type `IGrouping(Of Integer, String)`, a type that characterizes a single item in an `ILookup`. If you run this code you get the following result:

```
Product ID: 0
    Pasta has 10 units in stock
Product ID: 1
```

```
    Mozzarella has 50 units in stock
Product ID: 3
    Tofu has 40 units in stock
```

Opposite from operators that convert into typed collections or arrays, two methods convert from typed collections into `IEnumerable` or `IQueryable`. They are named `AsEnumerable` and `AsQueryable` and their usage is straightforward:

```
Dim newList As New List(Of Product)
'Populate your collection here..

Dim anEnumerable = newList.AsEnumerable
Dim aQueryable = newList.AsQueryable
```

There is another operator that filters a sequence retrieving only items of the specified type, generating a new sequence of that type. Such an operator is named `OfType` and is considered a conversion operator. The following code provides an example, where from an array of mixed types only `Integer` types are extracted and pushed into an `IEnumerable(Of Integer)`:

```
Dim mixed() As Object = {"String1", 1, "String2", 2}
Dim onlyInt = mixed.OfType(Of Integer)()
```

This is the equivalent of using the `TypeOf` operator in a query expression. The following query returns the same result:

```
Dim onlyInt = From item In mixed
              Where TypeOf item Is Integer
              Select item
```

It is not uncommon to need to immediately convert a query result into a collection, so you can invoke conversion operators directly in the expression as follows:

```
Dim query = (From prod In products
             Where prod.Discontinued = False
             Select prod).ToList
```

Remember that invoking conversion operators causes the query to be executed.

Generation Operators

Most of LINQ members are offered by the `System.Enumerable` class. This also exposes two shared methods, `Range` and `Repeat`, which provide the ability to generate sequences of elements. `Range` allows generating a sequence of integer numbers, as shown in the following code:

```
'The sequence will contain 100 numbers
'The first number is 40
```

```
Dim numbers = Enumerable.Range(40, 100)
```

It returns IEnumerable(Of Integer); therefore you can then query the generated sequence using LINQ. Repeat allows instead generating a sequence where the specified item repeats the given number of times. Repeat is generic in that you need to specify the item's type first. For example, the following code generates a sequence of 10 Boolean values and True is repeated 10 times:

```
Dim stringSequence = Enumerable.Repeat(Of Boolean)(True, 10)
```

Repeat returns IEnumerable(Of T), where T is the type specified for the method itself.

Ordering Operators

Ordering operators allow sorting query results according to the given condition. Within LINQ queries this is accomplished via the Order By clause. This clause allows ordering query results in both ascending and descending fashions, where ascending is the default way. The following example sorts the query result so that products are ordered from the one that has the lowest unit price to the one having the highest unit price:

```
Dim query = From prod In products
            Order By prod.UnitPrice
            Select prod
```

To get a result ordered from the highest value to the lowest, you use the Descending keyword as follows:

```
Dim queryDescending = From prod In products
                      Order By prod.UnitPrice Descending
                      Select prod
```

This can shape the query result opposite of the first example. You can also provide more than one Order By clause to get subsequent ordering options. Using extension methods provides a little bit more granularity in ordering results. For example you can use the OrderBy and ThenBy extension methods for providing multiple ordering options as demonstrated in the following code:

```
Dim query = products.OrderBy(Function(p) p.UnitPrice).
ThenBy(Function(p) p.ProductName)
```

As usual, both methods take lambdas as arguments. There are also OrderByDescending and ThenByDescending extension methods that order the result from the highest value to the lowest. The last ordering method is Reverse that reverses the query result and that you can simply use as follows:

```
Dim revertedQuery = query.Reverse()
```

Set Operators

Set operators allow removing duplicates and merge sequences and exclude specified elements. For example you could have duplicate items within a sequence or collection; you can remove duplicates using the `Distinct` operator. The following provides an example on a simple array of integers:

```
Dim someInt = {1, 2, 3, 3, 2, 4}
'Returns {1, 2, 3, 4}
Dim result = From number In someInt Distinct
             Select number
```

The result is a new IEnumberable(Of Integer). In real scenarios you could find this operator useful in LINQ to SQL or the Entity Framework for searching duplicate records in a database table. The next operator is `Union`, which is an extension method and merges two sequences into a new one. The following is an example:

```
Dim someInt = {1, 2, 3, 4}
Dim otherInt = {4, 3, 2, 1}

Dim result = someInt.Union(otherInt)
```

The preceding code returns an IEnumerable(Of Integer) containing 1, 2, 3, 4, 4, 3, 2, 1. The first items in the new sequences are those from the collection that you invoke `Union` on. Next operator is `Intersect`, which is another extension method. This method creates a new sequence with elements that two other sequences have in common. The following code demonstrates this:

```
Dim someInt = {1, 2, 3, 4}
Dim otherInt = {1, 2, 5, 6}

Dim result = someInt.Intersect(otherInt)
```

The new sequence is an IEnumerable(Of Integer) containing only 1 and 2, because they are the only values that both original sequences have in common. The last set operator is `Except` that generates a new sequence taking only those values that two sequences do not have in common. The following code is an example, which then requires a further explanation:

```
Dim someInt = {1, 2, 3, 4}
Dim otherInt = {1, 2, 5, 6}
Dim result = someInt.Except(otherInt)
```

Surprisingly, this code returns a new IEnumerable(Of Integer) containing only 3 and 4, although 5 and 6 also are values that the two sequences do not have in common. This is because the comparison is executed only on the sequence that you invoke `Except` on, and therefore all other values are excluded.

Grouping Operators

The grouping concept is something that you of course already know if you ever worked with data. Given a products collection, it would be useful dividing products into categories to provide a better organization of information. For example, consider the following Category class:

```
Class Category
    Property CategoryID As Integer
    Property CategoryName As String
End Class
```

Now consider the following review of the Product class, with a new CategoryID property:

```
Class Product
    Property ProductID As Integer
    Property ProductName As String
    Property UnitPrice As Decimal
    Property UnitsInStock As Integer
    Property Discontinued As Boolean
    Property CategoryID As Integer
End Class
```

At this point we can write code that creates instances of both classes and populates appropriate collections, as in the following snippet:

```
Sub GroupByDemo()

    Dim cat1 As New Category With {.CategoryID = 1,
                                   .CategoryName = "Food"}

    Dim cat2 As New Category With {.CategoryID = 2,
                                   .CategoryName = "Beverages"}

    Dim categories As New List(Of Category) From {cat1,
                                                  cat2}

    Dim prod1 As New Product With {.ProductID = 0,
                                   .ProductName = "Pasta",
                                   .UnitPrice = 0.5D,
                                   .UnitsInStock = 10,
                                   .Discontinued = False,
                                   .CategoryID = 1}

    Dim prod2 As New Product With {.ProductID = 1,
```

24

```
                                        .ProductName = "Wine",
                                        .UnitPrice = 1D,
                                        .UnitsInStock = 50,
                                        .Discontinued = False,
                                        .CategoryID = 2}

    Dim prod3 As New Product With {.ProductID = 2,
                                        .ProductName = "Water",
                                        .UnitPrice = 0.5D,
                                        .UnitsInStock = 20,
                                        .Discontinued = False,
                                        .CategoryID = 2}

    Dim prod4 As New Product With {.ProductID = 3,
                                        .ProductName = "Tofu",
                                        .UnitPrice = 3.5D,
                                        .UnitsInStock = 40,
                                        .Discontinued = True,
                                        .CategoryID = 1}

    Dim products As New List(Of Product) From {prod1,
                                                prod2,
                                                prod3,
                                                prod4}
```

To make things easier to understand, only two categories have been created. Notice also how each product now belongs to a specific category. To group foods into the Food category and beverages into the Beverages category, you use the Group By operator. This is the closing code of the preceding method, which is explained just after you write it:

```
    Dim query = From prod In products
                Group prod By ID = prod.CategoryID
                Into Group
                Select CategoryID = ID,
                        ProductsList = Group

    ' "prod" is inferred as anonymous type
    For Each prod In query
        Console.WriteLine("Category {0}", prod.CategoryID)

        ' "p" is inferred as Product
        For Each p In prod.ProductsList
            Console.WriteLine("    Product {0}, Discontinued: {1}",
                            p.ProductName, p.Discontinued)
        Next
    Next
```

```
End Sub
```

The code produces the following result:

```
Category 1
     Product Pasta, Discontinued: False
     Product Tofu, Discontinued: True
Category 2
     Product Wine, Discontinued: False
     Product Water, Discontinued: False
```

Basically Group By requires you to specify a key for grouping. This key is a property of the type composing the collection you are querying. The result of the grouping is sent to a new IEnumerable(Of T) sequence represented by the Into Group statement. Finally you invoke Select to pick up the key and items grouped according to the key; the projection generates an IEnumerable(Of anonymous type). Notice how you need a nested For..Each loop; this is because each item in the query result is composed of two objects: the key and a sequence of object (in this case sequence of Product) grouped based on the key. The same result can be accomplished using extension methods' counterpart that work like this:

```
Dim query = products.GroupBy(Function(prod) prod.CategoryID,
                             Function(prod) prod.ProductName)
```

Union Operators

You often need to create sequences or collections with items taken from different data sources. If you consider the example in the previous "Grouping Operators" section, it would be interesting to create a collection of objects in which the category name is also available so that the result can be more human-readable. This is possible in LINQ using union operators (not to be confused with the union Set operator keyword), which perform operations that you know as joining. To complete the following steps, simply recall the previously provided implementation of the Product and Category classes and the code that populates new collections of products and categories. The goal of the first example is to create a new sequence of products in which the category name is also available. This can be accomplished as follows:

```
Dim query = From prod In products
            Join cat In categories On _
            prod.CategoryID Equals cat.CategoryID
            Select CategoryName = cat.CategoryName,
                   ProductName = prod.ProductName
```

The code is quite simple to understand. Both products and categories collections are queried, and a new sequence is generated to keep products and categories whose CategoryID is equal. This is accomplished via the Join keyword in which the On operator requires the condition to be evaluated as True. Notice that Join does not accept the equality operator (=), whereas it requires the Equals keyword. In this case the query result is an

IEnumerable(Of Anonymous type), but of course you could create a helper class exposing properties to store the result. You can then iterate the result to get information on your products, as in the following snippet:

```
For Each obj In query
    Console.WriteLine("Category: {0}, Product name: {1}",
                      obj.CategoryName, obj.ProductName)
Next
```

The code produces the following output:

```
Category: Food, Product name: Pasta
Category: Beverages, Product name: Wine
Category: Beverages, Product name: Water
Category: Food, Product name: Tofu
```

This is the simplest joining example and is known as *Cross Join*, but you are not limited to this. For example you might want to group items based on the specified key, which is known as *Group Join*. This allows you to rewrite the same example of the previous paragraph but taking advantage of joining can get the category name. This is accomplished as follows:

```
Dim query = From cat In categories
            Group Join prod In products On _
            prod.CategoryID Equals cat.CategoryID
            Into Group
            Select NewCategory = cat,
                   NewProducts = Group
```

Notice that now the main data source is Categories. The result of this query is generating a new sequence in which groups of categories store groups of products. This is notable if you take a look at the Select clause, which picks sequences instead of single objects or properties. The following iteration provides a deeper idea on how you access information from the query result:

```
For Each obj In query
    Console.WriteLine("Category: {0}", obj.NewCategory.CategoryName)

    For Each prod In obj.NewProducts
        Console.WriteLine("   Product name: {0}, Discontinued: {1}",
                          prod.ProductName, prod.Discontinued)
    Next
Next
```

Such nested iteration produces the following output:

```
Category: Food
   Product name: Pasta, Discontinued: False
```

```
        Product name: Tofu, Discontinued: True
Category: Beverages
        Product name: Wine, Discontinued: False
        Product name: Water, Discontinued: False
```

The *Cross Join with Group Join* technique is similar. The following code shows how you can perform a cross group join to provide a simplified version of the previous query result:

```
Dim query = From cat In categories
            Group Join prod In products On _
            prod.CategoryID Equals cat.CategoryID
            Into Group
            From p In Group
            Select CategoryName = cat.CategoryName,
                   ProductName = p.ProductName
```

Notice that by simply providing a nested `From` clause pointing to the group you can easily select what effectively you need from both sequences, for example the category name and the product name. The result, which is still a sequence of anonymous types, can be simply iterated as follows:

```
For Each item In query
    Console.WriteLine("Product {0} belongs to {1}",
                      item.ProductName,
                      item.CategoryName)
Next
```

It produces the following output:

```
Product Pasta belongs to Food
Product Tofu belongs to Food
Product Wine belongs to Beverages
Product Water belongs to Beverages
```

The last union operator is known as *Left Outer Join*. It is similar to the cross group join, but it differs in that you can provide a default value in case no item is available for the specified key. Consider the following code:

```
Dim query = From cat In categories
            Group Join prod In products On _
            prod.CategoryID Equals cat.CategoryID
            Into Group
            From p In Group.DefaultIfEmpty
            Select CategoryName = cat.CategoryName,
                   ProductName = If(p IsNot Nothing,
                   p.ProductName, "No available product")
```

Notice the invocation of the `Group.DefaultIfEmpty` extension method that is used with the `If` ternary operator to provide a default value. You can then retrieve information from the query result as in the cross group join sample.

Equality Operators

You might want to compare two sequences to check if they are perfectly equal. The `SequenceEqual` extension method allows performing this kind of comparison. It compares if a sequence is equal considering both items and the items order within a sequence, returning a Boolean value. The following code returns `True` because both sequences contains the same items in the same order:

```
Dim first = {"Visual", "Basic", "2010"}
Dim second = {"Visual", "Basic", "2010"}
'Returns True
Dim comparison = first.SequenceEqual(second)
```

The following code returns instead `False`, because although both sequences contain the same items, they are ordered differently:

```
Dim first = {"Visual", "Basic", "2010"}
Dim second = {"Visual", "2010", "Basic"}
'Returns False
Dim comparison = first.SequenceEqual(second)
```

Quantifiers

LINQ offers two interesting extension methods for sequences, Any and All. Any allows checking if at least one item in the sequence satisfies the specified condition. For example, the following code checks if at least one product name contains the letters "of":

```
Dim result = products.Any(Function(p) p.ProductName.Contains("of"))
```

The method receives a lambda as an argument that specifies the condition and returns `True` if the condition is matched. `All` instead allows checking if all members in a sequence match the specified condition. For example, the following code checks if all products are discontinued:

```
Dim result = products.All(Function(p) p.Discontinued = True)
```

Same as above, the lambda argument specifies the condition to be matched.

Concatenation Operators

Sequences (that is, IEnumerable(Of T) objects) expose a method named Concat that allows creating a new sequence containing items from two sequences. The following code shows an example in which a new sequence of strings is created from two existing arrays of strings:

```
Dim firstSequence = {"One", "Two", "Three"}
Dim secondSequence = {"Four", "Five", "Six"}

Dim concatSequence = firstSequence.Concat(secondSequence)
```

The result produced by this code is that the concatSequence variable contains the following items: "One", "Two", "Three", "Four", "Five", and "Six". The first items in the new sequence are taken from the one you invoke the Concat method on.

Elements Operators

There are some extension methods that allow getting the instance of a specified item in a sequence. The first one is Single that gets the instance of only the item that matches the specified condition. For example, the following code gets the instance of the only product whose product name is Mozzarella:

```
Try
    Dim uniqueElement = products.Single(Function(p) p.
                                   ProductName = "Mozzarella")


Catch ex As InvalidOperationException
    'The item does not exist
End Try
```

Single takes a lambda expression as an argument in which you can specify the condition that the item must match. It returns an InvalidOperationException if the item does not exist in the sequence (or if more than one element matches the condition). As an alternative you can invoke SingleOrDefault, which returns a default value if the item does not exist instead of throwing an exception. The following code returns Nothing because the product name does not exist:

```
Dim uniqueElement = products.SingleOrDefault(Function(p) p.
                        ProductName = "Mozzarell")
```

The next method is First. It can return either the first item in a sequence or the first item that matches a condition. You can use it as follows:

```
'Gets the first product in the list
```

24

```
Dim firstAbsolute = products.First

Try
    'Gets the first product where product name starts with P
    Dim firstElement = products.First(Function(p) p.ProductName.
                                                StartsWith("P"))
Catch ex As InvalidOperationException
    'No item available
End Try
```

The previous example is self-explanatory: If multiple products have their name starting with the P letter, `First` returns just the first one in the sequence or throws an `InvalidOperationException` if no item is available. There is also a `FirstOrDefault` method that returns a default value, such as `Nothing`, if no item is available. Finally there are `Last` and `LastOrDefault` that simply return the last item in a sequence and that work like the preceding illustrated ones.

Partitioning Operators

Partitioning operators allow accomplishing a technique known as paging, which is common in data access scenarios. There are two main operators in LINQ: `Skip` and `Take`, in which `Skip` avoids selecting the specified number of elements, and `Take` puts the specified number of elements into a sequence. Code in Listing 24.3 shows an example of paging implementation using the two operators.

LISTING 24.3   Implementing a Basic Paging Technique

```
Module Partitioning

    Private pageCount As Integer
    Private Products As List(Of Product)

    Sub PopulateProducts()
        Dim prod1 As New Product With {.ProductID = 0,
                                       .ProductName = "Pasta",
                                       .UnitPrice = 0.5D,
                                       .UnitsInStock = 10,
                                       .Discontinued = False}

        Dim prod2 As New Product With {.ProductID = 1,
                                       .ProductName = "Mozzarella",
                                       .UnitPrice = 1D,
                                       .UnitsInStock = 50,
                                       .Discontinued = False}

        Dim prod3 As New Product With {.ProductID = 2,
```

```
                                          .ProductName = "Crabs",
                                          .UnitPrice = 7D,
                                          .UnitsInStock = 20,
                                          .Discontinued = True}

        Dim prod4 As New Product With {.ProductID = 3,
                                          .ProductName = "Tofu",
                                          .UnitPrice = 3.5D,
                                          .UnitsInStock = 40,
                                          .Discontinued = False}

        Products = New List(Of Product) From {prod1,
                                                 prod2,
                                                 prod3,
                                                 prod4}
    End Sub

    Function QueryProducts() As IEnumerable(Of Product)

        Dim query As IEnumerable(Of Product)
        'If pageCount = 0 we need to retrieve the first 10 products
        If pageCount = 0 Then
            query = From prod In Products _
                    Order By Prod.ProductID _
                    Take 10

        Else
            'Skips the already shown products
            'and takes next 10
            query = From prod In Products _
                    Order By Prod.ProductID _
                    Skip pageCount Take 10

        End If

        'In real applications ensure that query is not null
        Return query
    End Function
End Module
```

The private field pageCount acts as a counter. According to its value, the query skips the number of elements already visited represented by the value of pageCount. If no elements were visited, the query skips nothing. The code invoking QueryProducts increase or decrease by 10 units the pageCount value depending if you want to move forward or backward to the collection items.

Summary

In this chapter you got a high-level overview of LINQ key concepts. In this particular discussion you learned about LINQ to Objects as the built-in provider for querying in-memory collections seeing LINQ in action via specific Visual Basic keywords that recall the SQL syntax, such as `From`, `Select`, `Where`, and `Join`. You can build LINQ queries while writing Visual Basic code, taking advantage of the background compiler, IntelliSense, and CLR control. Such queries written in the code editor are known as *query expressions*. Query expressions generally return an `IEnumerable(Of T)`, but they are not executed immediately. According to the key concept of deferred execution, LINQ queries are executed only when effectively utilized, and this is something that you find in subsequent LINQ providers. With LINQ you can build complex query expressions to query your data sources; this is accomplished via the standard query operators, which are covered in the last part of the chapter. LINQ to Objects is the basis of LINQ, and most of the concepts shown in this chapter will be revisited in next ones.

CHAPTER 25

LINQ to SQL

How many times did you face runtime errors when sending SQL instructions to your databases for querying or manipulating data? Your answer is probably "several times." Sending SQL instructions in the form of strings has been, for years, the real way for accessing data in the .NET development, but one of the main disadvantages was the lack of compile time control over your actions. Experienced developers can also remember when they had to work against databases in a connected environment taking care of everything that happened. LINQ to SQL solves several of these issues, providing both a disconnected way for working with data, where data is mapped into an object model that you work with until you decide to save back data, and a strongly typed programming fashion that improves your productivity by checking queries and CRUD operations at compile time. In this chapter you explore the most important LINQ to SQL functionalities, learning the basics of data access with such technology.

Introducing LINQ to SQL

LINQ to SQL is an object relational mapping engine for Microsoft SQL Server relational databases. In the previous version of the .NET Framework it was the first built-in LINQ provider for SQL Server offering not only the capability of querying data (as instead it is for LINQ to DataSets) but also a complete infrastructure for manipulating data, including connections, queries, and *CRUD* (Create/Read/Update/Delete) operations. LINQ to SQL is effectively another layer in the data access architecture, but it is responsible for everything starting from opening the connection until closing. One of the advantages from LINQ to SQL is that you will basi-cally query your data using the usual LINQ syntax thanks to the unified programming model offered by the technology. But this is not the only advantage. Being an object rela-tional mapping engine makes LINQ to SQL mapping databases' tables and relationships into .NET objects. This allows working in a disconnected way and in a totally strongly typed fashion so that you can get all the advantages of the CLR management. Each table from the database is mapped into a .NET class whereas relationships are mapped into .NET properties, providing something known as *abstraction*. This allows working against a conceptual model instead of against the database, and you will work with objects until you finish your edits that will be persisted to the underlying data source only when effec-tively required. This provides several advantages: First, you work with strongly typed objects, and everything is managed by the Common Language Runtime. Second, you do not work connected to the database, so your original data will be secure until you send changes after validations. According to the LINQ terminology, classes mapping tables are called *entities*. A group of entity is referred to as an *entity set*. Relationships are instead called *associations*. You access LINQ to SQL features by creating specific classes that are described in next section.

LINQ INTERNALS

This is a language-focused book, so discussing LINQ to SQL internals and architecture is not possible. A discussion of this kind would probably require a specific book. Here you will instead learn of manipulating and querying data with LINQ to SQL and the Visual Basic language, getting also the fundamental information about architecture when necessary.

Prerequisites

This chapter assumes that you have installed Microsoft SQL Server 2008, at least the Express Edition, possibly with the Advanced Services version that also includes SQL Server Management Studio Basic. If you did not install it yet, you can download it from here: http://www.microsoft.com/express/sql/default.aspx.

Next, the code examples require the SQL Server version of the Northwind sample database from Microsoft, which is downloadable from here: http://code.msdn.microsoft.com/ northwind. If you installed SQL Server Management Studio (Basic or higher) it is a good idea to attach the Northwind database to the SQL Server instance so that you can simulate a production environment.

Understanding LINQ to SQL Classes

To access SQL Server databases with LINQ to SQL, you need a LINQ to SQL class. This kind of class is generated by Visual Studio when you select members for the new object model and contains all the Visual Basic code that represents tables, columns, and relationships. Adding a LINQ to SQL class is also necessary to enable the Visual Studio OR/M Designer for LINQ to SQL. To understand what these sentences mean, follow these preliminary steps:

▶ Create a new project for the Console and name it **LinqToSql**.

▶ Establish a connection to the Northwind database via the Server Explorer tool window (or the Database Explorer if you work with Visual Basic Express).

▶ In Solution Explorer, right-click the project name and select **Add, New Item**. When the Add New Item dialog appears move to the Data folder and select the **LINQ to SQL Classes** item, replacing the default name with **Northwind.dbml**. Figure 25.1 shows this scenario.

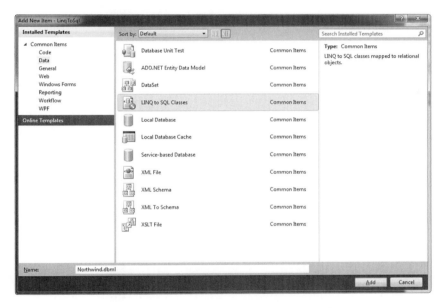

FIGURE 25.1   Adding a new LINQ to SQL class to the project.

When you click **Add**, after a few seconds the Visual Studio 2010 IDE shows the LINQ to SQL Object Relational Designer that appears empty, as shown in Figure 25.2.

The designer provides a brief description of its job, requiring you to pick items from either the Server Explorer window or from the toolbox. You need to pick tables from the Northwind database, passing them to Visual Studio to start the mapping process. Look at Figure 25.3 and then expand Server Explorer to show the Northwind database structure; then expand the Tables folder.

Now keep the Ctrl key pressed and click on both the **Categories** and **Products** tables. Our goal is to provide an example of a master-details relationship. When selected, drag the tables onto the designer surface until you get the result shown in Figure 25.4.

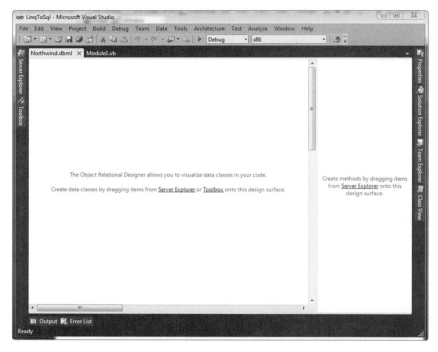

FIGURE 25.2   The LINQ to SQL designer popping up for the first time.

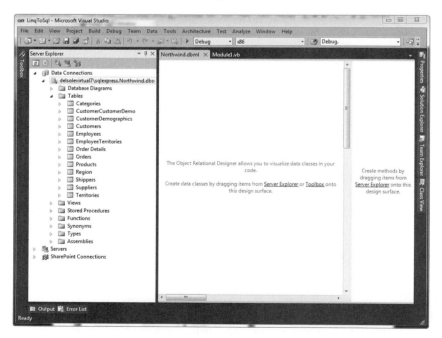

FIGURE 25.3   Preparing to pick tables from the Northwind database.

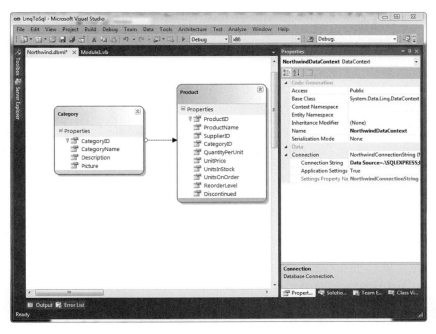

FIGURE 25.4   The LINQ to SQL designer is now populated.

At this point we can begin making some considerations. Visual Studio generated a diagram that is the representation of Visual Basic code. This diagram contains the definition of two entities, `Category` and `Product`. Each of them is mapped to Visual Basic classes with the same name. If you inspect the diagram, you notice that both classes expose properties. Each property maps a column within the table in the database. Figure 25.4 also shows the Properties window opened to show you a new, important concept, the `System.Data.Linq.DataContext` class. Every LINQ to SQL object model defines a class that inherits from `DataContext` and which is basically the main entry point of a LINQ to SQL class. It is, in other words, an object-oriented reference to the database. It is responsible for

- Opening and closing connections
- Handling relationships between entities
- Keeping track, with a single instance, of all changes applied to entities during all the object model lifetime
- Translating Visual Basic code into the appropriate SQL instructions
- Managing entities' lifetime, no matter how long

Visual Studio generates a new `DataContext` class forming its name concatenating the database name with the `DataContext` phrase, so in our example the class is named `NorthwindDataContext`. This class, as you can see in Figure 25.4, exposes some properties including the connection string, base class, and access modifier.

INHERITANCE AND SERIALIZATION

Although this chapter also covers advanced LINQ to SQL features, some things are out of the scope in this language-focused book, such as inheritance and serialization of data contexts. Such features are better described in the MSDN documentation at the following address: http://msdn.microsoft.com/en-us/library/bb386976(VS.100).aspx

Now click the Category item in the designer that represents an entity described in Figure 25.5 within the Properties window.

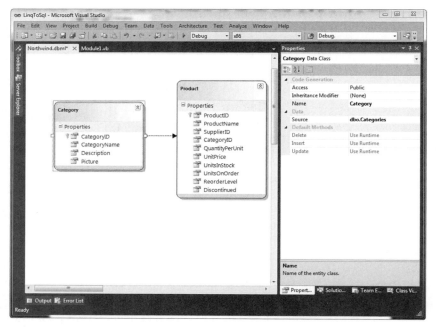

FIGURE 25.5   Examining the Category class.

It is interesting to understand that such a class has public access that requires code (Use Runtime definition) to support Insert/Update/Delete operations. The Source property also tells us what the source table in the database is. Now click on the arrow that establishes the relationship. Figure 25.6 shows how the Properties window describes such an object.

Notice how a one-to-many relationship is represented. The Child Property property shows the "many" part of the one-to-many relationship, whereas Parent Property shows the "one" part of the relationship.

RELATIONSHIPS

LINQ to SQL supports only one-to-many relationships, which is different from the ADO.NET Entity Framework that also supports many-to-many relationships.

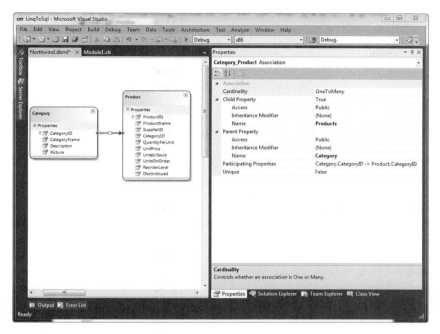

FIGURE 25.6   Examining associations.

Now that you have a clearer idea about LINQ to SQL classes in a graphical way, it's time to understand the architecture. This kind of a class is referred via a .dbml file that groups nested files. To see nested files you need to activate the **View All Files** view in Solution Explorer. The first nested file has a .dbml.diagram extension and is the class diagram that we just saw in the Visual Studio Designer. All edits, including Visual Studio-generated items that are performed onto the designer and then reflected into a .designer.vb file (in our example, Northwind.designer.vb). This file is fundamental because it stores code definitions for the `DataContext`, entities, and associations classes. Understanding how this file is defined is important, although you should never edit it manually. Listing 25.1 shows the definition of the `NorthwindDataContext` class:

LISTING 25.1   The NorthwindDataContext Class Definition

```
<Global.System.Data.Linq.Mapping.DatabaseAttribute(Name:="Northwind")> _
Partial Public Class NorthwindDataContext
    Inherits System.Data.Linq.DataContext

    Private Shared mappingSource As System.Data.Linq.Mapping.MappingSource = _
                          New AttributeMappingSource()

    Partial Private Sub OnCreated()
    End Sub
    Partial Private Sub InsertCategory(instance As Category)
```

```vb
    End Sub
    Partial Private Sub UpdateCategory(instance As Category)
    End Sub
    Partial Private Sub DeleteCategory(instance As Category)
    End Sub
    Partial Private Sub InsertProduct(instance As Product)
    End Sub
    Partial Private Sub UpdateProduct(instance As Product)
    End Sub
    Partial Private Sub DeleteProduct(instance As Product)
    End Sub

    Public Sub New()
        MyBase.New(Global.LinqToSql.My.MySettings.Default.
                   NorthwindConnectionString, mappingSource)
        OnCreated
    End Sub

    Public Sub New(ByVal connection As String)
        MyBase.New(connection, mappingSource)
        OnCreated
    End Sub

    Public Sub New(ByVal connection As System.Data.IDbConnection)
        MyBase.New(connection, mappingSource)
        OnCreated
    End Sub

    Public Sub New(ByVal connection As String,
                   ByVal mappingSource As System.Data.Linq.
                   Mapping.MappingSource)
        MyBase.New(connection, mappingSource)
        OnCreated()
    End Sub

    Public Sub New(ByVal connection As System.Data.IDbConnection,
                   ByVal mappingSource As System.Data.Linq.
                   Mapping.MappingSource)
        MyBase.New(connection, mappingSource)
        OnCreated()
    End Sub

    Public ReadOnly Property Categories() As System.Data.Linq.Table(Of Category)
        Get
            Return Me.GetTable(Of Category)
        End Get
    End Property
```

```
    Public ReadOnly Property Products() As System.Data.Linq.Table(Of Product)
        Get
            Return Me.GetTable(Of Product)
        End Get
    End Property
End Class
```

The class is marked with the `DataBase` attribute and inherits from `DataContext`, meaning that it has to be a managed reference to the database. The constructor provides several overloads, most of them accepting a connection string if you do not want it to be stored in the configuration file (which is the default generation). Two properties are important, `Categories` and `Products` of type `System.Data.Linq.Table(Of T)`. This type offers a .NET representation of a database table. The `GetTable` method invoked within properties creates `Table(Of T)` objects based on entities. Notice how several partial methods for Insert/Update/Delete operations are defined and can be extended later. Similar to the `DataContext` class, both `Product` and `Category` classes have a Visual Basic definition within the same file. As a unified example, Listing 25.2 shows the definition of the Category class.

LISTING 25.2   The Category Class Definition

```
<Global.System.Data.Linq.Mapping.TableAttribute(Name:="dbo.Categories")> _
Partial Public Class Category
    Implements System.ComponentModel.INotifyPropertyChanging,
               System.ComponentModel.INotifyPropertyChanged

    Private Shared emptyChangingEventArgs As PropertyChangingEventArgs = _
               New PropertyChangingEventArgs(String.Empty)

    Private _CategoryID As Integer

    Private _CategoryName As String

    Private _Description As String

    Private _Picture As System.Data.Linq.Binary

    Private _Products As EntitySet(Of Product)

    Partial Private Sub OnLoaded()
    End Sub
    Partial Private Sub OnValidate(action As System.Data.Linq.ChangeAction)
    End Sub
```

25

```vb
   Partial Private Sub OnCreated()
   End Sub
   Partial Private Sub OnCategoryIDChanging(value As Integer)
   End Sub
   Partial Private Sub OnCategoryIDChanged()
   End Sub
   Partial Private Sub OnCategoryNameChanging(value As String)
   End Sub
   Partial Private Sub OnCategoryNameChanged()
   End Sub
   Partial Private Sub OnDescriptionChanging(value As String)
   End Sub
   Partial Private Sub OnDescriptionChanged()
   End Sub
   Partial Private Sub OnPictureChanging(value As System.Data.Linq.Binary)
   End Sub
   Partial Private Sub OnPictureChanged()
   End Sub

   Public Sub New()
       MyBase.New
       Me._Products = New EntitySet(Of Product)(AddressOf Me.attach_Products,
                                    AddressOf Me.detach_Products)
       OnCreated
   End Sub

   <Global.System.Data.Linq.Mapping.ColumnAttribute(Storage:="_CategoryID",
           AutoSync:=AutoSync.OnInsert, DbType:="Int NOT NULL IDENTITY",
           IsPrimaryKey:=True, IsDbGenerated:=True)> _
   Public Property CategoryID() As Integer
       Get
           Return Me._CategoryID
       End Get
       Set(ByVal value As Integer)
           If ((Me._CategoryID = Value) _
             = False) Then
               Me.OnCategoryIDChanging(Value)
               Me.SendPropertyChanging()
               Me._CategoryID = Value
               Me.SendPropertyChanged("CategoryID")
               Me.OnCategoryIDChanged()
           End If
       End Set
   End Property
```

```vb
<Global.System.Data.Linq.Mapping.ColumnAttribute(Storage:="_CategoryName",
        DbType:="NVarChar(15) NOT NULL", CanBeNull:=False)> _
Public Property CategoryName() As String
    Get
        Return Me._CategoryName
    End Get
    Set(ByVal value As String)
        If (String.Equals(Me._CategoryName, Value) = False) Then
            Me.OnCategoryNameChanging(Value)
            Me.SendPropertyChanging()
            Me._CategoryName = Value
            Me.SendPropertyChanged("CategoryName")
            Me.OnCategoryNameChanged()
        End If
    End Set
End Property


<Global.System.Data.Linq.Mapping.ColumnAttribute(Storage:="_Description",
        DbType:="NText", UpdateCheck:=UpdateCheck.Never)> _
Public Property Description() As String
    Get
        Return Me._Description
    End Get
    Set(ByVal value As String)
        If (String.Equals(Me._Description, Value) = False) Then
            Me.OnDescriptionChanging(Value)
            Me.SendPropertyChanging()
            Me._Description = Value
            Me.SendPropertyChanged("Description")
            Me.OnDescriptionChanged()
        End If
    End Set
End Property


<Global.System.Data.Linq.Mapping.ColumnAttribute(Storage:="_Picture",
        DbType:="Image", UpdateCheck:=UpdateCheck.Never)> _
Public Property Picture() As System.Data.Linq.Binary
    Get
        Return Me._Picture
    End Get
    Set(ByVal value As System.Data.Linq.Binary)
        If (Object.Equals(Me._Picture, Value) = False) Then
            Me.OnPictureChanging(Value)
            Me.SendPropertyChanging()
            Me._Picture = Value
```

25

```vbnet
                Me.SendPropertyChanged("Picture")
                Me.OnPictureChanged()
            End If
        End Set
    End Property


    <Global.System.Data.Linq.Mapping.AssociationAttribute(Name:="Category_Product", _
            Storage:="_Products", ThisKey:="CategoryID", OtherKey:="CategoryID")> _
    Public Property Products() As EntitySet(Of Product)
        Get
            Return Me._Products
        End Get
        Set(ByVal value As EntitySet(Of Product))
            Me._Products.Assign(Value)
        End Set
    End Property


    Public Event PropertyChanging As PropertyChangingEventHandler Implements _
            System.ComponentModel.INotifyPropertyChanging.PropertyChanging


    Public Event PropertyChanged As PropertyChangedEventHandler Implements _
            System.ComponentModel.INotifyPropertyChanged.PropertyChanged


    Protected Overridable Sub SendPropertyChanging()
        If ((Me.PropertyChangingEvent Is Nothing) _
                = false) Then
            RaiseEvent PropertyChanging(Me, emptyChangingEventArgs)
        End If
    End Sub


    Protected Overridable Sub SendPropertyChanged(ByVal propertyName As [String])
        If ((Me.PropertyChangedEvent Is Nothing) _
                = false) Then
            RaiseEvent PropertyChanged(Me, _
                                New PropertyChangedEventArgs(propertyName))
        End If
    End Sub


    Private Sub attach_Products(ByVal entity As Product)
        Me.SendPropertyChanging
        entity.Category = Me
    End Sub


    Private Sub detach_Products(ByVal entity As Product)
        Me.SendPropertyChanging
        entity.Category = Nothing
```

```
      End Sub
End Class
```

The class is marked with the System.Data.Linq.TableAttribute attribute, meaning that it has to represent a database table. It implements both the INotifyPropertyChanging and INotifyPropertyChanged interfaces to provide the ability of notifying the user interface of changes about entities. It then defines partial methods that you can extend and customize when a particular event occurs. (This is covered when discussing data validation.) Each property is decorated with the System.Data.Linq.Mapping.ColumnAttribute that represents a column within a database table. This attribute takes some arguments that are self-explanatory. The most important of them are Storage that points to a private field used as a data repository and DbType that contains the original SQL Server data type for the column. It is worth mentioning that Visual Basic provides an appropriate type mapping according to the related SQL data type. A primary key requires two other attributes, IsPrimaryKey = True and AutoSync. The second one establishes that it has to be auto-incremented and synchronized when a new item is added. In the end, notice how Set properties members perform a series of actions, such as raising events related to the beginning of property editing, storing the new value, and finally raising events related to the property set completion. This is auto-generated code from Visual Studio, and you should never change it manually. You are instead encouraged to use the LINQ to SQL designer that reflects changes in code. The last file for a LINQ to SQL class has a .dbml.layout extension and is just related to the diagram layout. Now that you are a little bit more familiar with LINQ to SQL classes, you can begin querying data with LINQ to SQL.

Behind the Scenes of LINQ to SQL Classes

The Visual Studio 2010 IDE generates LINQ to SQL classes invoking a command-line tool named SQLMetal.exe that is part of the Windows SDK for .NET Framework. The following is an example of the command line for performing a manual generation of LINQ to SQL classes for the Northwind database and Visual Basic:

```
SQLMetal.exe /Server:.\SQLExpress /DataBase:Northwind /dbml:Northwind.dbml
/language:VisualBasic
```

Of course, SQLMetal.exe offers other command-line options for generating LINQ to SQL classes, but in most cases you do not need such manual generation, because the IDE will do all the appropriate work for you. There is only one scenario when you need to manually create a LINQ to SQL class, which is when mapping SQL Server Compact Edition databases and that is discussed at the end of this chapter. For further information on SQLMetal, visit the official page on MSDN: http://msdn.microsoft.com/en-us/library/bb386987(VS.100).aspx.

Querying Data with LINQ to SQL

Before you begin querying data with LINQ to SQL, you need to instantiate the `DataContext` class. Continuing with the console application example started in the previous section, you can declare such an instance at the module level as follows:

```
Private northwind As New NorthwindDataContext
```

CLASS LEVEL DECLARATION

In this example the instance is declared at the module level because a console application is covered. In most cases you work with client applications such as WPF or Windows Forms; therefore, the instance will be generated at the class level.

Declaring a single instance at the module or class level allows one `DataContext` to manage entities for all the object model lifetime.

REAL-WORLD LINQ

In my client applications I used to follow this approach: I provide a class level declaration of the `DataContext` but I instantiate the object within the constructor. This allows handling exceptions that could occur at runtime while attempting to connect to the database, other than performing other initialization actions.

When you create such an instance, the `DataContext` connects to the database and provides required abstraction so that you can work against the object model instead of working against the database. The `DataContext` class' constructor also accepts a connection string if you want it to be hard-coded instead of storing it within a configuration file. You have different alternatives for querying data. For example, you might want to retrieve the complete list of products that is accomplished as follows:

```
'Returns Table(Of Product)
Dim allProduct = northwind.Products
```

Such code returns a `System.Data.Linq.Table(Of Product)` that is an object inheriting from `IQueryable(Of T)` and that represents a database table. `IQueryable(Of T)` is the general type returned by LINQ to SQL queries and inherits from `IEnumerable(Of T)` but also offers some more members specific for data manipulation. Although this type can be directly bound to user interface controls for presenting data as much as `IEnumerable`, it does not support data editing. A `Table(Of T)` instead supports adding, removing, and saving objects.

LINQ TO SQL AND WINDOWS FORMS

Chapter 30, "Building Windows Forms Applications," provides an example about binding LINQ to SQL models to Windows Forms controls so that you get a complete overview of the technology.

To perform LINQ queries using filtering, ordering, and projection operators, you simply use the LINQ keywords and the same programming techniques provided by the unified programming model of this technology. A little difference from LINQ to Objects is that LINQ to SQL queries return an `IQueryable(Of T)` instead of `IEnumerable(Of T)`. For example, the following LINQ query returns the list of products in which the unit price is greater than 10:

```
'Returns IQueryable(Of Product)
Dim queryByPrice = From prod In northwind.Products
                   Where prod.UnitPrice > 10
                   Select prod
```

You can also convert a query into an ordered collection such as the `List(Of T)` using extension methods:

```
'Returns List(Of Product)
Dim queryByPrice = (From prod In northwind.Products
                    Where prod.UnitPrice > 10
                    Select prod).ToList
```

Remember that *LINQ queries are effectively executed only when used*; therefore, the first example does not run the query until you invoke something on it. The second query is instead executed immediately because of the `ToList` invocation. For example, the following iteration would cause the first query to be executed when the enumerator is invoked:

```
'Returns IQueryable(Of Product)
Dim queryByPrice = From prod In northwind.Products
                   Where prod.UnitPrice > 10
                   Select prod

'Query is executed now
For Each prod In queryByPrice
    Console.WriteLine(prod.ProductName)
Next
```

This iteration shows the list of product names. You can also perform more complex queries that are probably what you will do in your real applications. The following method queries products for the specified category, given the category name taking only

25

products that are not discontinued, finally ordering the result by the number of units in stock for product:

```
Function QueryByCategoryName(ByVal categoryName As String) _
        As List(Of Product)

    Dim query = From categories In northwind.Categories
                Where categories.CategoryName = categoryName
                Join prod In northwind.Products
                On prod.CategoryID Equals categories.CategoryID
                Where prod.Discontinued = False
                Order By prod.UnitsInStock
                Select prod


    Return query.ToList
End Function
```

You can invoke the method and iterate the result as follows:

```
Dim productsList = QueryByCategoryName("Seafood")


For Each prod In productsList
    Console.WriteLine("Product name: {0}, unit price: {1}",
                      prod.ProductName,
                      prod.UnitPrice)
Next
```

The preceding code produces the following result:

```
Product name: Rogede sild, unit price: 9.5000
Product name: Nord-Ost Matjeshering, unit price: 25.8900
Product name: Gravad lax, unit price: 26.0000
Product name: Konbu, unit price: 6.0000
Product name: Ikura, unit price: 31.0000
Product name: Carnarvon Tigers, unit price: 62.5000
Product name: Escargots de Bourgogne, unit price: 13.2500
Product name: Jack's New England Clam Chowder, unit price: 9.6500
Product name: Spegesild, unit price: 12.0000
Product name: Röd Kaviar, unit price: 15.0000
Product name: Inlagd Sill, unit price: 19.0000
Product name: Boston Crab Meat, unit price: 18.4000
```

In other cases you need to data-bind your result to user interface controls. If you work with Windows Forms applications, a good idea is returning a

`System.ComponentModel.BindingList(Of T)` that is a collection specific for data-binding. So the preceding method could be rewritten as follows:

```
Function QueryByCategoryName(ByVal categoryName As String) _
        As System.ComponentModel.BindingList(Of Product)

    Dim query = From categories In northwind.Categories
                Where categories.CategoryName = categoryName
                Join prod In northwind.Products
                On prod.CategoryID Equals categories.CategoryID
                Where prod.Discontinued = False
                Order By prod.UnitsInStock
                Select prod

    Return New System.ComponentModel.
                BindingList(Of Product)(query.ToList)
End Function
```

Similarly, for WPF applications you would return an `ObservableCollection(Of T)`:

```
Function QueryByCategoryName(ByVal categoryName As String) _
        As System.ObjectModel.ObservableCollection(Of Product)

    Dim query = From categories In northwind.Categories
                Where categories.CategoryName = categoryName
                Join prod In northwind.Products
                On prod.CategoryID Equals categories.CategoryID
                Where prod.Discontinued = False
                Order By prod.UnitsInStock
                Select prod

    Return New System.ObjectModel.ObservableCollection(query)
End Function
```

25

IMPORTANT NOTE ON LINQ TO SQL QUERIES

An important consideration must be done when performing LINQ to SQL queries (and LINQ to Entities queries in the next chapter). LINQ to SQL queries can execute only members that have a corresponding type or function in SQL Server and the SQL syntax; otherwise an exception will be thrown. For example, try to invoke the ToLowerInvariant method on the categories.CategoryName statement within the Where clause in the previous method. The Visual Basic compiler correctly compiles the code, because the .NET Framework correctly recognizes all members. But SQL Server does not have a function that does the same, so a NotSupportedException will be thrown at runtime. Therefore, always ensure that .NET members you invoke have a counterpart in SQL Server. Keep in mind this rule also for the next chapter.

You could also take advantage of anonymous types for collecting data from different tables into a unique collection. The following code obtains a list of products for the given category name, picking up some information:

```
Dim customQuery = From prod In northwind.Products
                  Join cat In northwind.Categories On
                  prod.CategoryID Equals cat.CategoryID
                  Order By cat.CategoryID
                  Select New With {.CategoryName = cat.CategoryName,
                                   .ProductName = _
                                   prod.ProductName,
                                   .UnitPrice = prod.UnitPrice,
                                   .Discontinued = _
                                   prod.Discontinued}
```

This query, when executed, returns an IQueryable(Of Anonymous type). As you already know, lists of anonymous types can be iterated or also bound to user interface controls for presenting data but cannot be edited. If you need to create custom objects from query results, such as collecting data from different tables, you first need to implement a class that groups all required data as properties. Consider the following class:

```
Class CustomObject
    Property CategoryName As String
    Property ProductName As String
    Property UnitPrice As Decimal?
    Property Discontinued As Boolean?
End Class
```

Now you can rewrite the preceding query as follows, simply changing the Select clause allowing generating a new CustomObject instance:

```
Dim customQuery = From prod In northwind.Products
```

```
              Join cat In northwind.Categories On
              prod.CategoryID Equals cat.CategoryID
              Order By cat.CategoryID
              Select New CustomObject _
                      With {.CategoryName = cat.CategoryName,
                            .ProductName = prod.ProductName,
                            .UnitPrice = prod.UnitPrice,
                            .Discontinued = prod.Discontinued}
```

Now the query returns an `IQueryable(Of CustomObject)`. You can convert it into a typed collection according to your needs or simply iterate it as in the following example:

```
For Each obj In customQuery
    Console.WriteLine("Category name: {0}, Product name: {1},
                    Unit price: {2}, Discontinued: {3}",
                    obj.CategoryName, obj.ProductName,
                    obj.UnitPrice, obj.Discontinued)
Next
```

Providing this approach instead of working against anonymous types can allow you to bind your collections to user interface controls and provide two-way data binding, or simpler, can provide the ability of programmatically coding Insert/Update/Delete operations as explained in the next section.

Insert/Update/Delete Operations with LINQ

LINQ to SQL is not just querying data but is also a complete infrastructure for data manipulation. This means that you can perform Insert/Update/Delete operations against your object model using LINQ. Let's discuss first how a new entity can be added to an entity set.

Inserting Entities

You instantiate a new entity as any other .NET class and then set its properties. The following code shows how you can add a new `Product` to the `Products` entity set. Notice how the method receives the belonging category as an argument, which is required for setting the one-to-many relationship:

```
Sub AddProduct(ByVal categoryReference As Category)
    Dim aProduct As New Product

    aProduct.ProductName = "Italian spaghetti"
    aProduct.Discontinued = False
    aProduct.QuantityPerUnit = "10"
    aProduct.UnitPrice = 0.4D
```

```
      'Setting the relationship
      aProduct.Category = categoryReference

      'Adding the new product to the object model
      northwind.Products.InsertOnSubmit(aProduct)
End Sub
```

You simply set property values as you would in any other .NET class. Here you have to pay attention to add a non-null value to non-nullable members. In the previous example, QuantityPerUnit is a non-nullable and therefore must be assigned with a valid string. You can then omit assigning nullable members. LINQ to SQL can provide auto-increment functionalities on primary keys that in the original SQL Server database implement such a feature. In this example, ProductID is not assigned because it is an auto-incrementable primary key. You set a one-to-many relationship simply assigning the property referring to the other part of the relationship (Category in the preceding example) with the instance of the entity that completes the relationship. When this is performed, you invoke the InsertOnSubmit method on the instance of the entity set that receives the new entity (respectively Products and Product in our example). This method saves the new data into the object model, but it does not send data to the underlying database until you invoke the SubmitChanges method as follows:

```
Sub SaveChanges()
    Try
        northwind.SubmitChanges()

    Catch ex As SqlClient.SqlException

    Catch ex As Exception

    End Try
End Sub
```

This effectively saves data to the database. If something fails, you need to handle a SqlClient.SqlException exception. Now add an invocation to the custom SaveChanges method after the InsertOnSubmit one. At this point you can invoke the custom AddProduct method for programmatically adding a new product that must be bound to a specific category because of the one-to-many relationship. Working with a Console application you can add such an invocation within the Main module. The following code accomplishes this:

```
Dim cerealsCategory As Category = _
    northwind.Categories.Single(Function(cat) _
    cat.CategoryName = "Grains/Cereals")

AddProduct(cerealsCategory)
```

You need the instance of the category you want to pass to the method. To accomplish this you can invoke the `Single` extension method on the categories' collection to get the unique category with the specified name, taking advantage of a lambda expression. As an alternative, you can directly pass a lambda as an argument as follows:

```
AddProduct(northwind.Categories.
           Single(Function(cat) cat.CategoryName = "Grains/Cereals"))
```

Both solutions accomplish the same result.

GETTING INSTANCES IN CLIENT APPLICATIONS

In client applications such as Windows Forms, WPF, or Silverlight, getting an instance of an entity is even simpler. You just need to retrieve the current element of the data control (for example, `ComboBox`, `DataGrid`, or `DataGridView`) or better, the current selected item in the data source bridge control, such as `BindingSource` or `CollectionViewSource`.

If you run this code and everything works fine, your new product is added to the `Products` table of the `Northwind` database when the `DataContext.SubmitChanges` method is invoked and a relationship with the `Grains/Cereals` category will also be set. You can easily verify this by opening Server Explorer and then expanding the Northwind Tables folder; finally right-click the **Products** table and select **Show Table Data**. (If you have instead a local copy of the Northwind database, you need to double-click the database copy available in the Bin\Debug or Bin\Release folder to open it in Server Explorer.) Figure 25.7 reproduces the scenario, showing also the new product.

One thing that you need to remember is to check if an entity already exists to prevent malicious runtime exceptions. To accomplish this, you can take advantage of the Single extension method that throws an exception if the specified entity does not exist; therefore, it can be added. With that said, the `AddProduct` method can be rewritten as follows (see comments in code):

```
Sub AddProduct(ByVal categoryReference As Category)
    Try
        Dim productCheck = northwind.Products.
                            Single(Function(prod) _
                            prod.ProductName = "Italian spaghetti")
        productCheck = Nothing

        'the Product does not exists, so add it
    Catch ex As InvalidOperationException
        Dim aProduct As New Product

        aProduct.ProductName = "Italian spaghetti"
        aProduct.Discontinued = False
        aProduct.QuantityPerUnit = "10"
```

FIGURE 25.7   Checking that the new product has been correctly saved to the database.

```
        aProduct.UnitPrice = 0.4D
        aProduct.CategoryID = categoryReference.CategoryID

        'Setting the relationship
        aProduct.Category = categoryReference

        'Adding the new product to the object model
        northwind.Products.InsertOnSubmit(aProduct)
        SaveChanges()

    End Try
End Sub
```

Now that you know how to create and save data, it's also important to understand how updates can be performed.

ADDING MULTIPLE ENTITIES

Because the `DataContext` can handle all CRUD operations during an application's lifetime, you can add all entities you need and send them to the underlying database with a unique `DataContext.SubmitChanges` invocation. Alternatively, instead of making an `InsertOnSubmit` invocation for each new entity, you can also send a unique insertion invoking the `InsertAllOnSubmit` method.

Updating Entities

Updating existing entities is even easier than adding new ones. First, you need to catch the instance of the entity you want to update. When you get the instance, you simply edit its properties and then invoke the `DataContext.SubmitChanges` method. The following code provides an example:

```
Sub UpdateProduct(ByVal productInstance As Product)


    'Throws an exception if a null value is passed
    If productInstance Is Nothing Then
        Throw New NullReferenceException
    Else
        With productInstance
            .ProductName = "Italian Linguine"
            .UnitsInStock = 100
        End With
    End If

    SaveChanges()
End Sub
```

This method requires an instance of the `Product` entity to be updated. To get an instance of the desired product, you can still take advantage of a lambda, but this time exception handling is reverted, as you can see from the following snippet:

```
Try
    UpdateProduct(northwind.Products.
                    Single(Function(prod) prod.
                    ProductName = "Italian spaghetti"))

    'The specified product does not exists
Catch ex As InvalidOperationException

End Try
```

When the `NorthwindDataContext.SubmitChanges` method is invoked, data is updated also to the underlying database. Notice that you can update multiple entities and the `SubmitChanges` method sends changes all at once. You can easily check for correct updates following the steps shown in the previous paragraph and summarized in Figure 25.7.

Deleting Entities

Deleting an entity works similarly to update, at least for retrieving the entity instance. Deletion is performed by invoking the `DeleteOnSubmit` method, which works opposite to the `InsertOnSubmit`. The following is an example, which also checks if the entity exists:

```
Sub DeleteProduct(ByVal productInstance As Product)


    If productInstance Is Nothing Then
        Throw New NullReferenceException
    Else
        northwind.Products.DeleteOnSubmit(productInstance)
        SaveChanges()
    End If
End Sub
```

Remember how the custom `SaveChanges` method invokes the `NorthwindDataContext.SubmitChanges` one. The following code shows invoking the previous method for performing a product deletion:

```
Try
    DeleteProduct(northwind.Products.
                Single(Function(prod) prod.
                ProductName = "Italian spaghetti"))

    'The specified product does not exists
Catch ex As InvalidOperationException

End Try
```

Similarly to `InsertAllOnSubmit`, you can also invoke `DeleteAllOnSubmit` to remove multiple entities from the object model.

Mapping Stored Procedures

LINQ to SQL allows mapping stored procedures from the SQL Server database into a .NET method that you can use within your object model and that is managed by the running instance of the `DataContext`. In this way you do not lose advantage of stored procedures when working with LINQ. To map a stored procedure, go back to the Visual Studio Designer for LINQ to SQL and ensure that the Methods pane is opened on the right side of the designer; then open Server Explorer, expand the database structure, and expand the Stored Procedures folder. After you've done this, drag the stored procedure you need onto the Methods pane. Figure 25.8 shows how to accomplish this against the Northwind database of the current example.

Notice also how the Properties window shows method properties, such as access qualifier and signature. The Return type property is set as auto-generated because the result is determined according to the stored procedure type. Some procedures return a single result

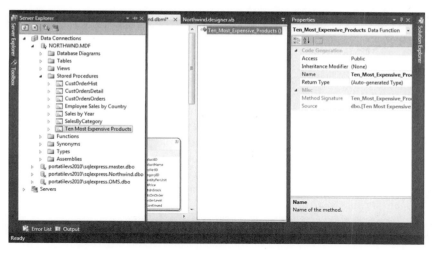

FIGURE 25.8   Mapping a stored procedure to a .NET method in LINQ to SQL.

value, and therefore the returned type is ISingleResult(Of T) whereas other ones can return multiple result values, and therefore the returned type is IMultipleResult(Of T). Behind the scenes, a stored procedure is mapped into a method but such a method also requires a support class mapping types used by the stored procedure. The following code is excerpted from the Northwind.designer.vb file and shows the class definition:

```
Partial Public Class Ten_Most_Expensive_ProductsResult

    Private _TenMostExpensiveProducts As String

    Private _UnitPrice As System.Nullable(Of Decimal)

    Public Sub New()
        MyBase.New
    End Sub

    <Global.System.Data.Linq.Mapping.
          ColumnAttribute(Storage:="_TenMostExpensiveProducts",
          DbType:="NVarChar(40) NOT NULL", CanBeNull:=False)> _
    Public Property TenMostExpensiveProducts() As String
        Get
            Return Me._TenMostExpensiveProducts
        End Get
        Set(ByVal value As String)
            If (String.Equals(Me._TenMostExpensiveProducts, value) = False)
            Then
                Me._TenMostExpensiveProducts = value
```

```
                End If
            End Set
        End Property


        <Global.System.Data.Linq.Mapping.ColumnAttribute(Storage:="_UnitPrice",
                DbType:="Money")> _
        Public Property UnitPrice() As System.Nullable(Of Decimal)
            Get
                Return Me._UnitPrice
            End Get
            Set(ByVal value As System.Nullable(Of Decimal))
                If (Me._UnitPrice.Equals(Value) = False) Then
                    Me._UnitPrice = Value
                End If
            End Set
        End Property
End Class
```

The class basically works like other auto generated classes in that it sets or returns values taken from the data source. The method that actually performs the action is mapped as follows within the NorthwindDataContext class definition:

```
<Global.System.Data.Linq.Mapping.
        FunctionAttribute(Name:="dbo.[Ten Most Expensive Products]")> _
Public Function Ten_Most_Expensive_Products() As   _
        ISingleResult(Of Ten_Most_Expensive_ProductsResult)
    Dim result As IExecuteResult = Me.ExecuteMethodCall(Me,
                                    CType(MethodInfo.GetCurrentMethod,
                                    MethodInfo))
    Return CType(result.ReturnValue,
                    ISingleResult(Of Ten_Most_Expensive_ProductsResult))
End Function
```

The System.Data.Linq.Mapping.FunctionAttribute attribute decorates the method signature with the original stored procedure name. As you can see, this particular method returns an ISingleResult(Of T), and invocation to the stored procedure is performed via reflection. Invoking in code, a stored procedure is as simple as in other methods usage. The following code takes an ISingleResult(Of T):

```
'Gets the list of the ten most expensive
'products from the Products table
Dim result = northwind.Ten_Most_Expensive_Products
```

You can then iterate the result to get a list of the products as in the following example:

```
For Each r In result
    Console.WriteLine(r.UnitPrice)
Next
```

This simple iteration produces the following result:

```
263,5000
123,7900
97,0000
81,0000
62,5000
55,0000
53,0000
49,3000
46,0000
45,6000
```

Notice that an `ISingleResult` can be iterated only once; otherwise you get an `InvalidOperationException`. If you plan to access this result multiple times, the only way is to convert the result into a generic collection such as the `List(Of T)`. The following code converts the stored procedure result into a `List`, making possible iterations more than once:

```
'Gets the list of the ten most expensive
'products from the Products table into
'a List(Of T)
Dim result = northwind.Ten_Most_Expensive_Products.ToList
```

Also notice that converting to `IQueryable(Of T)` will not allow the result to be accessed more than once.

Using the Log

LINQ to SQL sends SQL instructions each time it has to perform an operation on our demand. This is accomplished via its complex infrastructure that relies on the .NET Framework. By the way, as a developer you may be interested in understanding what really happens behind the scenes and in getting information about the real SQL instructions sent to SQL Server. Luckily you can use a SQL log that allows showing SQL instructions. You simply need to set the `DataContext.Log` property as follows, before taking actions you want to inspect:

```
northwind.Log = Console.Out
```

If you want to monitor everything happening, simply add the preceding code after the creation of the `DataContext` instance. If you apply this code before running the first example shown in the "Insert/Update/Delete operations with LINQ" section, you get the result shown in Figure 25.9.

FIGURE 25.9   Showing the LINQ to SQL log result.

As you can see, this is useful because you get an idea about the actual SQL instructions sent by LINQ to SQL to SQL Server. The `DataContext.Log` property is of type `System.IO.TextWriter`; therefore, you can assign it with a stream pointing to a file on disk if you want the SQL output to be redirected to a file instead of the Console window.

Advanced LINQ to SQL

While you become familiar with LINQ to SQL, you understand how it allows performing usual data operations in a strongly typed way. Because of this, you also see the need to perform other operations that you are used to making in classical data development, such as data validation and handling optimistic concurrency. The next section describes this but also something more.

Custom Validations

Validating data is one of the most important activities in every data access system, so LINQ to SQL provides its own methodologies, too. To accomplish data validation, you can take advantage of partial methods. You may remember that in Chapter 21, "Advanced Language Features," you got a practical example of partial methods when discussing LINQ to SQL. Validation rules are useful in LINQ to SQL for two main reasons: The first one is that they enable you to understand if supplied data is compliant to your requirements; the second one is that they allow checking if supplied data has a SQL Server type counterpart. The following code example demonstrates both examples. Imagine you want to add a new product to the object model and then save changes to the database, as you already did following the steps in the first part of the previous section. If you take a look at the `QuantityPerUnit` property, for example, recurring to the Visual Studio Designer, you notice that it is mapped to a `String` .NET type, but its SQL Server counterpart type is `NVarChar(20)`, meaning that the content of the property is a string that must not be longer than 20 characters; otherwise, saving changes to SQL Server will be unsuccessful. To provide validation rules, the first step is to add a partial class. With that said, right-click the project name in Solution Explorer, then select **Add New Class**, and, when requested, supply the new class name, for example **Product.vb**. When the new class is added to the project, add the `Partial` keyword as follows:

```
Partial Public Class Product

End Class
```

At this point we can implement a partial method that performs validation. Because partial methods' signatures are defined within the Northwind.designer.vb code file, here we can implement the full method body as follows:

```
Private Sub OnQuantityPerUnitChanging(ByVal value As String)
    If value.Length > 20 Then Throw New _
        ArgumentException _
        ("Quantity per unit must be no longer than 20 characters")
End Sub
```

Notice that you have to handle methods whose names finish with `Changing`, which map an event that is raised before changes are sent to the object model. The code checks for the length of the supplied value, and if it does not match the NVarChar(20) type of SQL Server throws an `ArgumentException`. To understand how it works, consider the following code that creates a new product and then attempts to write changes:

```
Sub AddProduct(ByVal categoryReference As Category)
    Try
        Dim productCheck = northwind.Products.
                            Single(Function(prod) _
                            prod.ProductName = "Italian spaghetti")
        productCheck = Nothing

        'the Product does not exists, so add it
    Catch ex As InvalidOperationException

        Try
            Dim aProduct As New Product

            aProduct.ProductName = "Italian spaghetti"
            aProduct.Discontinued = False

            'The string is 22 characters long
            aProduct.QuantityPerUnit = "1000000000000000000000"
            aProduct.UnitPrice = 0.4D
            aProduct.CategoryID = categoryReference.CategoryID

            'Setting the relationship
            aProduct.Category = categoryReference
```

25

```
            'Adding the new product to the object model
            northwind.Products.InsertOnSubmit(aProduct)
            SaveChanges()

        Catch e As ArgumentException
            Console.WriteLine(e.Message.ToString)
            Exit Try
        Catch e As Exception

        End Try
    End Try
End Sub
```

Notice how a nested `Try..End Try` block has been provided to handle eventual `ArgumentNullException` errors coming from validation. You can still invoke the `AddProduct` method in the previous section as follows:

```
AddProduct(northwind.Categories.
        Single(Function(cat) cat.CategoryName = "Grains/Cereals"))
```

If you now try to run the code, you get an error message advising that the `QuantityPerUnit` content cannot be longer than 20 characters. In this way you can control the content of your data but also ensure that data matches the related SQL Server type. By using this technique you can perform validation on each data you want.

DATA VALIDATION AND THE UI

One common scenario is implementing the `IDataErrorInfo` interface in partial classes so that its members can send notifications to the user interface. Windows Forms and WPF applications can take advantage of notifications for presenting error messages in ways different than a simple messages box. The official documentation for the interface is available here: http://msdn.microsoft.com/en-us/library/system.componentmodel.idataerrorinfo(VS.100).aspx.

Handling Optimistic Concurrency

Optimistic concurrency is a scenario in which multiple clients send changes to the database simultaneously. LINQ to SQL allows resolving optimistic concurrency with the `DataContext.ChangeConflicts.ResolveAll` method. Such method receives an argument that is an enumeration of type `System.Data.Linq.RefreshMode` and allows resolving the exception with one of the enumeration members summarized in Table 25.1.

TABLE 25.1   RefreshMode Enumeration Members

Member	Description
KeepCurrentValues	If any changes, keeps original values in the database

TABLE 25.1   Continued

Member	Description
KeepChanges	If any changes, keeps changes but other values are updated with original database values
OverwriteCurrentValues	Overrides all current values with original values from database

The following is an example of handling optimistic concurrency, providing a revisited version of the previously utilized SaveChanges custom method:

```
Sub SaveChanges()
    Try
        northwind.SubmitChanges()

    Catch ex As System.Data.Linq.ChangeConflictException

        northwind.ChangeConflicts.ResolveAll(Data.Linq.RefreshMode.
                                       KeepCurrentValues)
        northwind.SubmitChanges()
    Catch ex As SqlClient.SqlException

    Catch ex As Exception

    End Try
End Sub
```

Notice first how a ChangeConflictException is handled. Here the ChangeConflicts.ResolveAll method is required to resolve concurrency. The KeepCurrentValues argument allows keeping original values in the database. Also notice how a subsequent invocation to SubmitChanges is made. This is necessary because the first invocation caused the exception; therefore, another execution must be attempted.

Using SQL Syntax Against Entities

LINQ to SQL also allows writing SQL code against entities so that you can still take advantage of the object model if you prefer the old-fashioned way of manipulating data. The DataContext class offers an instance method named ExecuteQuery(Of T) that allows sending SQL instructions in string form. For example, the following code retrieves a list of products for the Grain/Cereals category, ordered by product name:

```
Sub DirectSqlDemo()

    Dim products = northwind.
        ExecuteQuery(Of Product)("SELECT * FROM PRODUCTS WHERE " & _
                            "CATEGORYID='5' ORDER BY PRODUCTNAME")
```

```
    For Each prod In products
        Console.WriteLine(prod.ProductName)
    Next
End Sub
```

ExecuteQuery(Of T) returns an IEnumerable(Of T) that you can then treat as you like, according to LINQ specifications. You can also send SQL instructions directly to the database invoking the ExecuteCommand method. This method returns no value and allows performing Insert/Update/Delete operations against the data. For example, the following code updates the product name of a product:

```
northwind.ExecuteCommand("UPDATE PRODUCTS SET " & _
        "PRODUCTNAME='Italian mozzarella' WHERE PRODUCTID='72'")
```

If you then want to check that everything work correctly, simply get the instance of the product and get information:

```
Dim updatedProduct = _
    northwind.Products.First(Function(prod) prod.ProductID = 72)

'Returns "Italian mozzarella"
Console.WriteLine(updatedProduct.ProductName)
```

Remember: Sending SQL instructions can prevent you from taking advantage of compile-time checking offered by the LINQ syntax and exposes your code to possible runtime errors. Be aware of this.

LINQ to SQL with SQL Server Compact Edition

LINQ to SQL is not limited to querying and manipulating data from SQL Server databases, but you can also perform the same operations against SQL Server Compact Edition databases (with .sdf extensions). The only big difference is that generating LINQ to SQL classes for this engine is not supported by the Visual Studio IDE (as it already was in Visual Studio 2008), so you have to perform a couple of steps manually. First, run the Visual Studio command prompt which you can find in **Start, All Programs, Microsoft Visual Studio 2010, Visual Studio Tools**. When you get the command line, move to the folder where the SQL Compact database is available. For example, you can play with the Northwind database in the compact edition version. With that said, type the following command line:

```
CD C:\Program Files\Microsoft SQL Server Compact Edition\v3.5\Samples
```

Next, type the following command line:

```
SQLMetal /dbml:Northwind.dbml /language:VisualBasic Northwind.sdf
```

This step generates a `.dbml` file, which is a complete LINQ to SQL class. To create a LINQ to SQL project supporting your .sdf database, you simply create a Visual Basic project, right-click the project name in Solution Explorer and then select the **Add Existing Item** command. When the dialog appears, select the newly created LINQ to SQL class and you're done. Remember that you can use all LINQ to SQL possibilities with SQL Server Compact Edition databases as well, so everything you learned in this chapter is also applicable to SQL Compact files. Of course, there are limitations due to the database's structure (for example SQL Compact databases do not support stored procedures), but this is something that is related more to SQL Server than Visual Basic. By the way, LINQ to SQL is the same in both SQL Server and SQL Compact.

Writing the Connection String

Different from classic LINQ to SQL, when you work with SQL Compact databases, you need to manually pass the connection string to the database; this is because the class generation could not take advantage of the IDE automation. This means that when you declare an instance of the `DataContext` class, you need to pass the connection string. For example, instantiating the `DataContext` for Northwind would be something like this:

```
Private NorthwindContext As New _
        Northwind("Data Source=E:\My Folder\ Northwind.sdf")
```

Summary

LINQ to SQL is a built-in object relational mapping engine for Microsoft SQL Server databases. The engine maps database information such as tables and columns into .NET objects such as classes and properties, allowing working in a disconnected fashion against an object model rather than against the database. Mapped classes are known as entities. Adding LINQ to SQL classes to your projects can provide the ability of using LINQ for both querying entities and performing CRUD operations via specific methods offered by the `DataContext` class, which is responsible for managing the connection and entities during an application's lifetime, including keeping track of changes that can be submitted to the database in one shot. LINQ to SQL also offers a trace log to understand what SQL instructions were sent to the database and provides the ability of handling optimistic concurrency as much as validating data taking advantage of partial methods. Finally, you can still write your queries the old-fashioned way sending SQL instructions directly to the data source. LINQ to SQL is useful if you need to work with a light weight or/m and if you are limited to SQL Server databases. If you instead need something more flexible and powerful, you should consider the ADO.NET Entity Framework discussed in next chapter.

CHAPTER 26

LINQ to DataSets

For many years datasets have been the main data access technology for .NET developers, including Visual Basic programmers. Although the .NET Framework 3.5 introduced new object relational mapping technologies such as LINQ to SQL and ADO.NET Entity Framework, Datasets are still much diffused especially in older applications. Because of this, Microsoft produced a LINQ standard provider that is specific for querying datasets: *LINQ to DataSets*. In this chapter you do not find information on manipulating datasets (see Chapter 22, "Introducing ADO.NET and DataSets"); instead you learn to query existing datasets using LINQ, and you become familiar with some peculiarities of this provider that are not available in the previous ones.

Querying Datasets with LINQ

LINQ to DataSets is the standard LINQ provider for querying datasets and is offered by the `System.DataSet.DataSet Extensions` namespace. Querying means that LINQ can only get information for datasets but not for manipulating them. If you need to add, remove, replace, or persist data versus datasets, you need to use old-fashioned techniques. Instead you can improve getting information using LINQ. Generally you use datasets in Windows or Web applications. This chapter shows you code within a Console application. This is because we need a high level of abstraction so that all the code you see here can be used in both

Windows and Web applications (except for Silverlight applications that do not support datasets). To complete the proposed examples, follow these steps:

▶ Create a new console application and name the project **LinqToDataSets**.

▶ Establish a connection to the Northwind database via the **Server Explorer** window.

▶ Add a new dataset including the Customers, Orders, and Order Details tables.

When done, you need to manually write some code that populates the dataset. Usually such tasks are performed by Visual Studio if you generate a dataset within Windows Forms or WPF applications; however, in this case you need to do it. With that said write the following code that declares three TableAdapter objects and populates them with data coming from tables:

```
Imports LinqToDataSets.NorthwindDataSetTableAdapters


Module Module1

    Dim NwindDataSet As New NorthwindDataSet

    Dim NorthwindDataSetCustomersTableAdapter As CustomersTableAdapter _
        = New CustomersTableAdapter()
    Dim NorthwindDataSetOrdersTableAdapter As OrdersTableAdapter _
        = New OrdersTableAdapter()
    Dim NorthwindDataSetOrderDetailsTableAdapter As _
        Order_DetailsTableAdapter _
        = New Order_DetailsTableAdapter


    Sub Main()
        NorthwindDataSetCustomersTableAdapter.Fill(NwindDataSet.Customers)
        NorthwindDataSetOrdersTableAdapter.Fill(NwindDataSet.Orders)
        NorthwindDataSetOrderDetailsTableAdapter.
                    Fill(NwindDataSet.Order_Details)
    End Sub
End Module
```

Now you are ready to query your dataset with LINQ. Basically LINQ syntax is the same as for other providers but with a few exceptions:

▶ LINQ queries DataTable objects, each representing a table in the database.

▶ LINQ to DataSets queries return EnumerableRowCollection(Of DataRow) instead of IEnumerable(Of T) (or IQueryable(Of T)), in which DataRow is the base class for strongly typed rows. The only exception is when you create anonymous types within queries. In such situations, queries return IEnumerable(Of Anonymous type).

You can use LINQ to simply retrieve a list of objects. For example, consider the following code that retrieves the list of orders for the specified customer:

```
Private Sub QueryOrders(ByVal CustomerID As String)


    Dim query = From ord In NwindDataSet.Orders
            Where ord.CustomerID = CustomerID
            Select ord
End Sub
```

As you can see, the syntax is the same as other providers. The query variable type is inferred by the compiler as `EnumerableRowCollection(Of OrdersRow)`. There is a particular difference: The query result is not directly usable if you want to provide the ability of editing data. As it is, the query can only be presented; you need first to convert it into a `DataView` using the `AsDataView` extension method. The following code rewrites the preceding query, providing the ability of binding data to a control:

```
Dim query = (From ord In NwindDataSet.Orders
        Where ord.CustomerID = CustomerID
        Select ord).AsDataView
```

When you invoke `AsDataView` you can bind a LINQ query to any user control that supports data binding, such as the Windows Forms `BindingSource`. Don't invoke instead `AsDataView` if you simply need to get information without the need of manipulating data (for example, with a `For..Each` loop). You can use other query operators to get different information; the following code shows, as an example, how you can get the number of orders made by the specified customer using the `Aggregate` clause:

```
Private Function QueryOrders(ByVal CustomerID As String) As Integer


    Dim ordersByCustomer = Aggregate ord In NwindDataSet.Orders
                        Where ord.CustomerID = CustomerID
                        Into Count()


    Return ordersByCustomer
End Function
```

26

STANDARD QUERY OPERATORS

LINQ to DataSets allows querying datasets using standard query operators offered by LINQ to Objects; because of this the chapter does not explore standard operators. It also provides some additions discussed in next section.

Building Complex Queries with Anonymous Types

Same as you would do with other LINQ providers, you can build complex queries taking advantage of anonymous types in LINQ to DataSets. The following code shows how you can join information from the Orders and Order_Details tables retrieving information on order details for each order made by the given customer. Projection is accomplished generating anonymous types:

```
Private Sub QueryOrderDetails(ByVal CustomerID As String)


    Dim query = From ord In NwindDataSet.Orders
                Where ord.CustomerID = CustomerID
                Join det In NwindDataSet.Order_Details
                On det.OrderID Equals ord.OrderID
                Select New With {.OrderID = ord.OrderID,
                                 .OrderDate = ord.OrderDate,
                                 .ShippedDate = ord.ShippedDate,
                                 .ShipCity = ord.ShipCity,
                                 .ProductID = det.ProductID,
                                 .Quantity = det.Quantity,
                                 .UnitPrice = det.UnitPrice}
End Sub
```

The query variable is of type `IEnumerable(Of Anonymous type)`, which is different from normal queries. Remember that `IEnumerable` results cannot be edited; therefore, you are limited to presenting data through specific controls such as `BindingSource`. In LINQ to DataSets `IEnumerable(Of Anonymous type)`, queries do not support `AsDataView`; therefore, you should consider creating a new `DataTable`, which is shown in the first example of the next section.

LINQ to DataSets' Extension Methods

As a specific provider for datasets, LINQ to DataSets exposes some special extension methods generally required when converting from data rows collections into other objects. In this section you get an overview of methods and their usage.

Understanding `CopyToDataTable`

Tables from databases are represented within datasets via `DataTable` objects. You can create custom tables in code using a special extension method named `CopyToDataTable` which can convert from `EnumerableRowCollection (Of T)` into a new `DataTable`. For example, imagine you want to create a subset of orders from the `Orders` table and that you want to create a new table with this subset of information. The following code accomplishes this:

```
Dim query = (From ord In NwindDataSet.Orders
             Where String.IsNullOrEmpty(ord.ShipCountry) = False
```

```
        Select ord).CopyToDataTable
query.TableName = "FilteredOrders"
NwindDataSet.Tables.Add(query)
```

The query retrieves only the orders where the `ShipCountry` property contains something and creates a new `DataTable` with this piece of information. The query variable's type is `DataTable`; therefore, you can treat this new object as you would versus a classical table as demonstrated by assigning the `TableName` property and by the addition of the new table to the dataset. You can also create custom tables with more granularities taking advantage of anonymous types. For example, imagine you want to create a table that wraps information from both the `Orders` and `Order_Details` tables. You need to manually create a new table, add columns, perform the query, and then add rows. The following code demonstrates this:

```
Private Function CreateCustomTable() As DataTable

    'Create a new table
    Dim customTable As New DataTable("Custom_orders")

    'Add columns
    With customTable
        With .Columns
            .Add("OrderID", GetType(Integer))
            .Add("Quantity", GetType(Short))
            .Add("UnitPrice", GetType(Decimal))
        End With
    End With

    'Retrieve data from different sources
    Dim query2 = From ord In NwindDataSet.Orders,
                    det In NwindDataSet.Order_Details
               Where det.Quantity > 50
               Select New With {.OrderID = ord.OrderID,
                                .Quantity = det.Quantity,
                                .UnitPrice = det.UnitPrice}

    'Add rows
    For Each item In query2
        customTable.Rows.Add(New Object() {item.OrderID,
                                           item.Quantity,
                                           item.UnitPrice})
    Next

    Return customTable
End Function
```

26

Notice how the new table is created in code and how columns are added. The
`Columns.Add` method allows specifying the type (via the `GetType` keyword) for each
column. We just want to retrieve the `OrderID`, `Quantity`, and `UnitPrice` information only
for those products whose quantity is greater than 50. The LINQ query returns an
`IEnumerable(Of Anonymous types)`. Because of this, you need to iterate the collection and
instantiate a new array of `Object` for each row, containing the specified information.
When you have the new table populated, you can add it to the dataset and use it as any
other table.

Understanding `Field(Of T)` and `SetField(Of T)`

The `Field` generic extension method allows retrieving a strongly typed form for all values
from a given column within a table. Basically `Field` receives as an argument the column
name or the column index and then tries to convert values in a column into the specified
type. Because of this, when using `Field` you should also predict some exceptions, such as
`InvalidCastException` that can occur if the conversion fails, `NullReferenceException` if
`Field` attempts to access a non-Nullable null value, and `IndexOutOfRangeException` if
you pass an invalid index for the column. For example, the following code retrieves all
strongly typed versions of orders' data:

```
Private Sub FieldDemo()


    Try
        Dim query = From ord In NwindDataSet.Orders
                    Where ord.Field(Of Date)("ShippedDate") < Date.Today
                    Select New With {
                            .OrderID = ord.
                                    Field(Of Integer)("OrderID"),
                            .OrderDate = ord.
                                    Field(Of Date)("OrderDate"),
                            .ShipCountry = ord.
                                    Field(Of String) _
                                    ("ShipCountry")
                            }
    Catch ex As InvalidCastException
        'Conversion failed

    Catch ex As NullReferenceException
        'Attempt to access to a non nullable
        'null object

    Catch ex As IndexOutOfRangeException
        'Wrong index

    Catch ex As Exception
```

```
    End Try
End Sub
```

There is also a `SetField` method that allows putting a strongly typed value into the specified field, and that works like this:

```
ord.SetField(Of Date)("OrderDate",Date.Today)
```

Summary

Although Microsoft is making lots of investments in much more modern technologies such as ADO.NET Entity Framework, datasets are a data source that you can find in tons of applications. Because of this, the .NET Framework provides the LINQ to DataSets provider that allows querying datasets via the LINQ syntax. Datasets are particular; therefore, there are specific extension methods that you can use versus datasets, such as `CopyToDataTable` that generates a new `DataTable` from a LINQ query and `Field` that allows getting strongly typed information from columns. In this chapter you got an overview of how LINQ works over datasets, and you can use retrieved information in your applications.

CHAPTER 27

Introducing ADO.NET Entity Framework

Most applications require accessing data. This is a sentence that you already read in this book and probably in many other places, but it is so important. During the past years .NET developers had to access data using DataSets or they were required to work directly against the database. A new way for working with data was introduced in .NET 3.5 with LINQ to SQL, which is revolutionary because it proposes a conceptual object model that allows working with managed objects, being responsible for whatever is necessary in managing also the underlying database. But it has some limitations. It supports only SQL Server databases; it does not support many-to-many relationships; and it does not provide support for modeling data before creating a database. To provide a modern data platform based on the idea of the conceptual object model, Microsoft created the ADO.NET Entity Framework that was first introduced in .NET Framework 3.5 SP 1 and that now is part of .NET Framework 4.0 in the second version. In this chapter you get started with the Entity Framework by learning to perform the most common operations on data and understanding the basics of such a platform.

Introducing Entity Framework

ADO.NET Entity Framework is a modern data platform included in .NET Framework 4.0 as the second version, also known as EF 4. It is basically an object relational mapping engine but it is powerful, absolutely more flexible and powerful than LINQ to SQL. It allows creating conceptual object models, known as Entity Data Models that provide a high level of abstraction from the underlying data source.

Abstraction means that tables and tables' columns within a database are mapped into .NET classes and properties, meaning that you do not work against the database but with .NET objects that represent the database so that you can take advantage of manipulating .NET objects under the CLR control, with IntelliSense support and the background compiler check. You do not need to have knowledge of the database infrastructure, although this is always suggested, because the Entity Framework is responsible for communications between the object model and the data source. It provides the entire necessary infrastructure so that you can focus only on writing code for manipulating and querying data. Working with an abstractive object model means taking advantage of all the .NET Framework's power and all available Visual Studio instrumentation. In the next section you start with the EF by understanding Entity Data Models.

Understanding Entity Data Models

The best way to understand Entity Data Models (from here on just EDMs for brevity) is to create one. First, create a new Visual Basic project for the Console and name it **EntityFramework**. The next steps require the Northwind database that you installed in Chapter 25, "LINQ to SQL." Right-click on the project name in Solution Explorer and select **Add New Item**. When the Add New Item dialog appears, move to the Data Node, select the **ADO.NET Entity Data Model** item template, and name it **Northwind.edmx**, as shown in Figure 27.1.

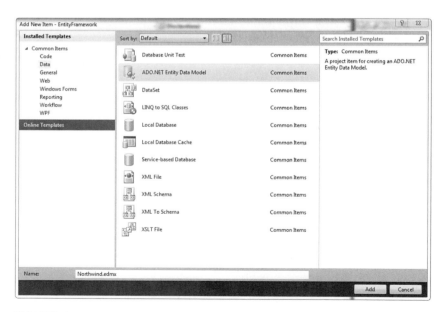

FIGURE 27.1   Adding a new Entity Data Model.

When you click **Add**, the Entity Data Model Wizard starts. In the first screen you need to specify the source for the EDM. With EF 4 you can create EDMs starting from an existing database or modeling custom EDMs from scratch. Select the existing database options, as shown in Figure 27.2.

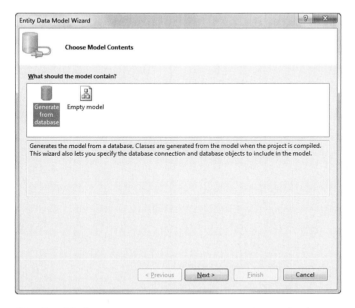

FIGURE 27.2   Creating an EDM from an existing database.

The next screen is important because it requires the specification of the database. You can click **New Connection** or select one of the favorite connections from the appropriate combo box. Figure 27.3 shows how on my machine the connection points to Northwind as it is available on SQL Server.

Notice how the connection string is represented in the dialog box. Also notice that this is not the usual connection string, because it contains metadata information that will be clearer when the EDMs' infrastructure is explained. You decide whether to save the string in the configuration file. The next step is crucial, because you have to select what database objects you want to be mapped into the EDM. Figure 27.4 shows the dialog box.

FOREIGN KEY COLUMNS SUPPORT

The ADO.NET Entity Framework 4 supports mapping foreign keys from the database into the model. This is the reason why you find a new checkbox in the Entity Data Model wizard, as shown in Figure 27.4. Simply select the checkbox in order to add the foreign key's support.

Also notice how you are required to specify a model namespace. This is important because the namespace stores Visual Basic definitions for objects that are mapped to database objects, which are explained later. You can write your own or leave the default identifier unchanged. At the moment, just choose the Categories and Products tables and then

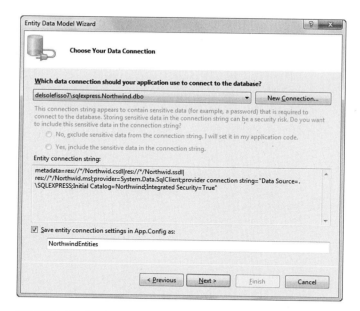

FIGURE 27.3   Choosing the database and connection settings.

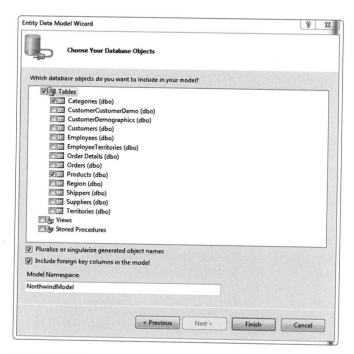

FIGURE 27.4   Selecting objects for the new EDM.

click `Finish`. After a few moments, when Visual Studio generates the code for the object model, the EDM Designer opens as shown in Figure 27.5.

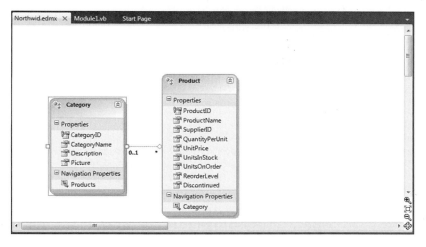

FIGURE 27.5   The EDM Designer for Visual Studio.

The object model available in the Visual Studio designer is, behind the scenes, defined by a new Xml document that is the schema for the Entity Data Model. This Xml file is the one with the .edmx extension, in our case Northwind.edmx. The schema is divided into three sections that are summarized in Table 27.1.

TABLE 27.1   Sections of the Entity Data Model

Section name	Description
Conceptual Schema Definition Language	Defines entities, relationships, and inheritance. .NET classes are generated based on this section.
Store Schema Definition Language	Provides a representation of the original database.
Mapping Specification Language	Maps entities as they are defined in the CSDL against db objects as they are defined in the SSDL.

Much work is accomplished behind the scenes by a command-line tool named EdmGen.exe that is invoked by Visual Studio. To understand how an EDM is composed, in Solution Explorer right-click the Northwind.edmx file; select **Open With**, and when the

Open With dialog appears, double-click the **Xml editor** option. At this point Visual Studio shows the content of the EDM as an Xml file instead of the designer. The file contains three sections as described in Table 27.1. Listing 27.1 shows the CDSL definition (which is actually the second section in the XML file).

LISTING 27.1   Conceptual Schema Definition Language

```
<!-- CSDL content -->
<edmx:ConceptualModels>
    <Schema Namespace="NorthwindModel" Alias="Self"
xmlns:store="http://schemas.microsoft.com/ado/2007/12/edm/EntityStoreSchemaGenerator
" xmlns="http://schemas.microsoft.com/ado/2008/09/edm">
        <EntityContainer Name="NorthwindEntities">
          <EntitySet Name="Categories" EntityType="NorthwindModel.Category" />
          <EntitySet Name="Products" EntityType="NorthwindModel.Product" />
          <AssociationSet Name="FK_Products_Categories"
                          Association="NorthwindModel.FK_Products_Categories">
            <End Role="Categories" EntitySet="Categories" />
            <End Role="Products" EntitySet="Products" />
          </AssociationSet>
        </EntityContainer>
        <EntityType Name="Category">
          <Key>
            <PropertyRef Name="CategoryID" />
          </Key>
          <Property Name="CategoryID" Type="Int32" Nullable="false"
                    store:StoreGeneratedPattern="Identity" />
          <Property Name="CategoryName" Type="String" Nullable="false" Max
                    Length="15" Unicode="true" FixedLength="false" />
          <Property Name="Description" Type="String" MaxLength="Max" Unicode="true"
                    FixedLength="false" />
         <Property Name="Picture" Type="Binary" MaxLength="Max" FixedLength="false"/>
          <NavigationProperty Name="Products"
                          Relationship="NorthwindModel.FK_Products_Categories"
                          FromRole="Categories" ToRole="Products" />
        </EntityType>
        <EntityType Name="Product">
          <Key>
            <PropertyRef Name="ProductID" />
          </Key>
          <Property Name="ProductID" Type="Int32" Nullable="false"
                    store:StoreGeneratedPattern="Identity" />
          <Property Name="ProductName" Type="String" Nullable="false" MaxLength="40"
```

```
                           Unicode="true" FixedLength="false" />
        <Property Name="SupplierID" Type="Int32" />
        <Property Name="QuantityPerUnit" Type="String" MaxLength="20"
                           Unicode="true" FixedLength="false" />
        <Property Name="UnitPrice" Type="Decimal" Precision="19" Scale="4" />
        <Property Name="UnitsInStock" Type="Int16" />
        <Property Name="UnitsOnOrder" Type="Int16" />
        <Property Name="ReorderLevel" Type="Int16" />
        <Property Name="Discontinued" Type="Boolean" Nullable="false" />
        <NavigationProperty Name="Category"
                            Relationship="NorthwindModel.FK_Products_Categories"
                            FromRole="Products" ToRole="Categories" />
      </EntityType>
      <Association Name="FK_Products_Categories">
        <End Role="Categories" Type="NorthwindModel.Category" Multiplicity="0..1"/>
        <End Role="Products" Type="NorthwindModel.Product" Multiplicity="*" />
      </Association>
    </Schema>
  </edmx:ConceptualModels>
```

You can notice how entities (EntityType) are defined along with scalar properties (Property), relationships (Association), entity sets (EntitySet), and a container named NorthwindEntities. The next section that we consider is the SSDL, which is constituted by the Xml markup code shown in Listing 27.2 and which is actually the first section in the XML file.

LISTING 27.2   The Store Schema Definition Language

```
  <edmx:StorageModels>
  <Schema Namespace="NorthwindModel.Store" Alias="Self"
          Provider="System.Data.SqlClient" ProviderManifestToken="2008"
xmlns:store="http://schemas.microsoft.com/ado/2007/12/edm/EntityStoreSchemaGenerator
"

            xmlns="http://schemas.microsoft.com/ado/2009/02/edm/ssdl">
      <EntityContainer Name="NorthwindModelStoreContainer">
        <EntitySet Name="Categories" EntityType="NorthwindModel.Store.Categories"
                   store:Type="Tables" Schema="dbo" />

        <EntitySet Name="Products" EntityType="NorthwindModel.Store.Products"
                   store:Type="Tables" Schema="dbo" />
        <AssociationSet Name="FK_Products_Categories"
                        Association="NorthwindModel.Store.FK_Products_Categories">
          <End Role="Categories" EntitySet="Categories" />
          <End Role="Products" EntitySet="Products" />
```

```
            </AssociationSet>
          </EntityContainer>
          <EntityType Name="Categories">
            <Key>
              <PropertyRef Name="CategoryID" />
            </Key>
            <Property Name="CategoryID" Type="int" Nullable="false"
                      StoreGeneratedPattern="Identity" />
            <Property Name="CategoryName" Type="nvarchar" Nullable="false"
                      MaxLength="15" />
            <Property Name="Description" Type="ntext" />
            <Property Name="Picture" Type="image" />
          </EntityType>
          <EntityType Name="Products">
            <Key>
              <PropertyRef Name="ProductID" />
            </Key>
            <Property Name="ProductID" Type="int" Nullable="false"
                      StoreGeneratedPattern="Identity" />
            <Property Name="ProductName" Type="nvarchar" Nullable="false"
                      MaxLength="40" />
            <Property Name="SupplierID" Type="int" />
            <Property Name="CategoryID" Type="int" />
            <Property Name="QuantityPerUnit" Type="nvarchar" MaxLength="20" />
            <Property Name="UnitPrice" Type="money" />
            <Property Name="UnitsInStock" Type="smallint" />
            <Property Name="UnitsOnOrder" Type="smallint" />
            <Property Name="ReorderLevel" Type="smallint" />
            <Property Name="Discontinued" Type="bit" Nullable="false" />
          </EntityType>
          <Association Name="FK_Products_Categories">
            <End Role="Categories" Type="NorthwindModel.Store.Categories"
                Multiplicity="0..1" />
            <End Role="Products" Type="NorthwindModel.Store.Products"
                Multiplicity="*" />
            <ReferentialConstraint>
              <Principal Role="Categories">
                <PropertyRef Name="CategoryID" />
              </Principal>
              <Dependent Role="Products">
                <PropertyRef Name="CategoryID" />
              </Dependent>
            </ReferentialConstraint>
          </Association>
        </Schema>
      </edmx:StorageModels>
```

Basically this schema is similar to the previous schema, except that it represents the database structure as you can see from type definition within `Property` elements. The last schema is the Mapping Definition Language that is illustrated in Listing 27.3.

LISTING 27.3   Mapping Definition Language

```xml
<edmx:Mappings>
  <Mapping Space="C-S"
          xmlns="http://schemas.microsoft.com/ado/2008/09/mapping/cs">
    <EntityContainerMapping
     StorageEntityContainer="NorthwindModelStoreContainer"
     CdmEntityContainer="NorthwindEntities">
      <EntitySetMapping Name="Categories"><EntityTypeMapping Type
                      Name="NorthwindModel.Category">
                      <MappingFragment StoreEntitySet="Categories">
        <ScalarProperty Name="CategoryID" ColumnName="CategoryID" />
        <ScalarProperty Name="CategoryName" ColumnName="CategoryName" />
        <ScalarProperty Name="Description" ColumnName="Description" />
        <ScalarProperty Name="Picture" ColumnName="Picture" />
      </MappingFragment></EntityTypeMapping></EntitySetMapping>
      <EntitySetMapping Name="Products"><EntityTypeMapping Type
                      Name="NorthwindModel.Product">
                      <MappingFragment StoreEntitySet="Products">
        <ScalarProperty Name="ProductID" ColumnName="ProductID" />
        <ScalarProperty Name="ProductName" ColumnName="ProductName" />
        <ScalarProperty Name="SupplierID" ColumnName="SupplierID" />
        <ScalarProperty Name="QuantityPerUnit" ColumnName="QuantityPerUnit" />
        <ScalarProperty Name="UnitPrice" ColumnName="UnitPrice" />
        <ScalarProperty Name="UnitsInStock" ColumnName="UnitsInStock" />
        <ScalarProperty Name="UnitsOnOrder" ColumnName="UnitsOnOrder" />
        <ScalarProperty Name="ReorderLevel" ColumnName="ReorderLevel" />
        <ScalarProperty Name="Discontinued" ColumnName="Discontinued" />
      </MappingFragment></EntityTypeMapping></EntitySetMapping>
      <AssociationSetMapping Name="FK_Products_Categories" Type
                          Name="NorthwindModel.FK_Products_Categories"
                          StoreEntitySet="Products">
        <EndProperty Name="Categories">
          <ScalarProperty Name="CategoryID" ColumnName="CategoryID" />
        </EndProperty>
        <EndProperty Name="Products">
          <ScalarProperty Name="ProductID" ColumnName="ProductID" />
        </EndProperty>
        <Condition ColumnName="CategoryID" IsNull="false" />
      </AssociationSetMapping>
    </EntityContainerMapping>
```

27

```
    </Mapping>
</edmx:Mappings>
```

The content of the MDL is quite simple, in that each `ScalarProperty` represents an entity's property and establishes mapping between the property and the related column name in the database table.

Understanding the `ObjectContext` class: The Visual Basic Mapping

Schemas in the Entity Data Model have a Visual Basic counterpart that effectively allows you to write code to work against entities. To understand this, enable the **View All Files** view in Solution Explorer and expand the **Northwind.edmx** file. Finally, open the **Northwind.designer.vb** code file. Similar to the `DataContext` class in LINQ to SQL, the ADO.NET Entity Framework provides a class named `System.Data.Objects.ObjectContext`. This class, also referred to as the object context, acts as a reference to the Entity Data Model and encapsulates the entities' definition so that you can work with entities. It is also responsible for opening and closing connections, persisting data, keeping track of changes, and persisting data back to the database. `ObjectContext` is just the base class (as the `DataContext` is in LINQ to SQL) that every entity data model inherits from. Listing 27.4 shows how the object context is defined in our specific scenario.

LISTING 27.4   ObjectContext definition

```
Public Partial Class NorthwindEntities
    Inherits ObjectContext

    Public Sub New()
        MyBase.New("name=NorthwindEntities", "NorthwindEntities")
        OnContextCreated()
    End Sub

    Public Sub New(ByVal connectionString As String)
        MyBase.New(connectionString, "NorthwindEntities")
        OnContextCreated()
    End Sub

    Public Sub New(ByVal connection As EntityConnection)
        MyBase.New(connection, "NorthwindEntities")
        OnContextCreated()
    End Sub
    Partial Private Sub OnContextCreated()
    End Sub
    Public ReadOnly Property Categories() As ObjectSet(Of Category)
        Get
            If (_Categories Is Nothing) Then
                _Categories = MyBase.CreateObjectSet(Of Category)("Categories")
```

```
            End If
            Return _Categories
        End Get
    End Property

    Private _Categories As ObjectSet(Of Category)
    Public ReadOnly Property Products() As ObjectSet(Of Product)
        Get
            If (_Products Is Nothing) Then
                _Products = MyBase.CreateObjectSet(Of Product)("Products")
            End If
            Return _Products
        End Get
    End Property

    Private _Products As ObjectSet(Of Product)
    Public Sub AddToCategories(ByVal category As Category)
        MyBase.AddObject("Categories", category)
    End Sub

    Public Sub AddToProducts(ByVal product As Product)
        MyBase.AddObject("Products", product)
    End Sub
End Class
```

First, notice how several constructors' overloads give the ability to instantiate the object context passing also a connection string if you want this to be supplied in code. Next notice the `Categories` and `Products` properties, respectively `ObjectSet(Of Category)` and `ObjectSet(Of Product)`. An `ObjectSet(Of T)` represents an entity set and provides several methods and members for manipulating entities, such as the `AddObject` or `DeleteObject` methods. In the end notice the presence of two methods, `AddToCategories` and `AddToProducts`. For compatibility with the previous version of the Entity Framework, Visual Studio still generates as many `AddTo` methods as many entities are included in the EDM. Anyway, such methods are considered as deprecated, and you are encouraged to invoke `ObjectSet(Of T).Add` and `ObjectSet(Of T).DeleteObject` methods for manipulating entities. Basically properties of type `ObjectSet` handle references to a series of objects. Such objects are defined in the same code file, one for each entity. For the sake of simplicity, Listing 27.5 shows only the definition of the `Category` class whereas the `Product` class is left out, being substantially defined using the same concepts.

LISTING 27.5   The Category Entity Definition

```
<EdmEntityTypeAttribute(NamespaceName:="NorthwindModel", Name:="Category")>
<Serializable()>
<DataContractAttribute(IsReference:=True)>
```

```vb
Partial Public Class Category
    Inherits EntityObject

    Public Shared Function CreateCategory(ByVal categoryID As Global.System.Int32,
                        ByVal categoryName As Global.System.String) _
                        As Category
        Dim category As Category = New Category
        category.CategoryID = categoryID
        category.CategoryName = categoryName
        Return category
    End Function


    <EdmScalarPropertyAttribute(EntityKeyProperty:=True,
                            IsNullable:=False)>
    <DataMemberAttribute()>
    Public Property CategoryID() As Global.System.Int32
        Get
            Return _CategoryID
        End Get
        Set(ByVal value As Global.System.Int32)
            If (_CategoryID <> value) Then
                OnCategoryIDChanging(value)
                ReportPropertyChanging("CategoryID")
                _CategoryID = StructuralObject.
                            SetValidValue(value)
                ReportPropertyChanged("CategoryID")
                OnCategoryIDChanged()
            End If
        End Set
    End Property


    Private _CategoryID As Global.System.Int32
    Partial Private Sub OnCategoryIDChanging _
                        (ByVal value As Global.System.Int32)
    End Sub


    Partial Private Sub OnCategoryIDChanged()
    End Sub


    <EdmScalarPropertyAttribute(EntityKeyProperty:=False,
                            IsNullable:=False)>
    <DataMemberAttribute()>
    Public Property CategoryName() As Global.System.String
        Get
            Return _CategoryName
        End Get
```

```
    Set(ByVal value As Global.System.String)
        OnCategoryNameChanging(value)
        ReportPropertyChanging("CategoryName")
        _CategoryName = StructuralObject.
                        SetValidValue(value, False)
        ReportPropertyChanged("CategoryName")
        OnCategoryNameChanged()
    End Set
End Property


Private _CategoryName As Global.System.String
Partial Private Sub OnCategoryNameChanging(ByVal value As Global.System.String)
End Sub


Partial Private Sub OnCategoryNameChanged()
End Sub


<EdmScalarPropertyAttribute(EntityKeyProperty:=False, IsNullable:=True)>
<DataMemberAttribute()>
Public Property Description() As Global.System.String
    Get
        Return _Description
    End Get
    Set(ByVal value As Global.System.String)
        OnDescriptionChanging(value)
        ReportPropertyChanging("Description")
        _Description = StructuralObject.SetValidValue(value, True)
        ReportPropertyChanged("Description")
        OnDescriptionChanged()
    End Set
End Property


Private _Description As Global.System.String
Partial Private Sub OnDescriptionChanging(ByVal value As Global.System.String)
End Sub


Partial Private Sub OnDescriptionChanged()
End Sub


<EdmScalarPropertyAttribute(EntityKeyProperty:=False, IsNullable:=True)>
<DataMemberAttribute()>
Public Property Picture() As Global.System.Byte()
    Get
        Return StructuralObject.GetValidValue(_Picture)
    End Get
    Set(ByVal value As Global.System.Byte())
```

27

```
            OnPictureChanging(value)
            ReportPropertyChanging("Picture")
            _Picture = StructuralObject.SetValidValue(value, True)
            ReportPropertyChanged("Picture")
            OnPictureChanged()
        End Set
    End Property


    Private _Picture As Global.System.Byte()
    Partial Private Sub OnPictureChanging(ByVal value As Global.System.Byte())
    End Sub


    Partial Private Sub OnPictureChanged()
    End Sub


    <XmlIgnoreAttribute()>
    <SoapIgnoreAttribute()>
    <DataMemberAttribute()>
    <EdmRelationshipNavigationPropertyAttribute("NorthwindModel",
                                        "FK_Products_Categories",
                                        "Products")>
    Public Property Products() As EntityCollection(Of Product)
        Get
            Return CType(Me, IEntityWithRelationships).RelationshipManager.
                GetRelatedCollection(Of Product) _
                ("NorthwindModel.FK_Products_Categories", "Products")
        End Get
        Set(ByVal value As EntityCollection(Of Product))
            If (Not value Is Nothing) Then
                CType(Me, IEntityWithRelationships).
                    RelationshipManager.InitializeRelatedCollection(Of Product) _
                    ("NorthwindModel.FK_Products_Categories", "Products", value)
            End If
        End Set
    End Property
End Class
```

Each entity class derives from `System.Data.Object.EntityObject` and is decorated with the `EdmEntityTypeAttribute` attribute, which defines the object context and the entity name. Notice how the class is also marked as `DataContract`, which means serializable by the Windows Communication Foundation technology for data exchange over networks. Then you can find as many properties as many columns in the database table, marked with the `EdmScalarPropertyAttribute` attribute, establishing that each property is a *scalar property* in the EDM (therefore mapping to a column) and with the `DataMemberAttribute` attribute that establishes that the member can be exchanged via WCF. Entity classes also declare partial methods that are related to specific events; for example, `OnPictureChanging` is invoked when the caller code sends a request for editing a new or existing picture, whereas the `OnPictureChanged` is invoked when editing is completed.

Navigation Properties in Code

Finally notice how those things named *Navigation Properties* in the EDM are also defined within entity classes. Basically a navigation property is a .NET property of type `EntityCollection(Of T)` or `EntityReference(Of T)`, depending on what side of the relationship they are mapped to. An `EntityCollection(Of T)`, as in the case of the `Category` class, represents the "many" part of the relationship whereas an `EntityReference(Of T)`, as in the case of the `Product` class, represents the "one" part of the relationship. Navigation properties are decorated with the `EdmRelationShipNavigationPropertyAttribute` that basically maps a foreign key in the database, requiring specifying the namespace name, the foreign key name, and the entity set. Such properties return (or receive) an `IEntityWithRelationships` type that can (via the `RelationshipManager.` `GetRelatedCollection(Of T)` method for returning or via the `RelationshipManager.` `InitializeRelatedCollection(Of T)` method for setting) handle associations. Now that you have a clearer idea of what Visual Basic requires behind the scenes, you are ready to understand the usage of some interesting design-time tools.

Entity Designer Tool Windows

When the EDM designer is active, you notice that some new tool windows appear in the IDE. The first one is the Mapping Details tool window, which shows how database objects are mapped to .NET types. Figure 27.6 shows the Mapping Details window.

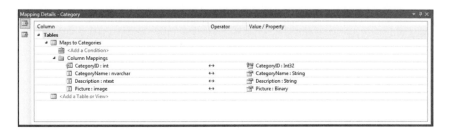

FIGURE 27.6   The Mapping Details tool window.

As you can see in Figure 27.6, on the left side of the Window, you can find the original SQL definition whereas on the right side of the window, you can find the .NET type utilized to map SQL types into the EDM. You can manually edit such mapping, but the suggestion is you leave unchanged what the IDE proposes by default unless you understand that a bad mapping from SQL to .NET has been performed. The second tool is the Model Browser, which provides a hierarchical graphical view of the object model so that you can easily browse both the conceptual model and the store model. Figure 27.7 shows the tool window.

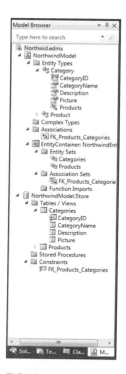

FIGURE 27.7   The Model Browser tool window.

In this new version of Visual Studio, the tool window also simplifies performing opera-tions on the entity data model, such as updating the model itself, as explained later in this chapter with regard to stored procedures. Other than these tool windows, you can take advantage of the Properties window for getting information on the objects that compose the entity data model. For example, if you click the blank space in the designer, the Properties window shows high-level information on the EDM, such as the database schema name, the entity container name (that is, the object context), or the model name-space. Figure 27.8 provides an overview.

Similarly you can get information on the entities' definition by clicking the desired entity name in the designer. Figure 27.9 represents the Properties window showing information about the Category entity.

Basically the window shows information about the class implementation, such as the class name, the inheritance level, or the access level other than the related entity set container name. If you instead try to click a navigation property, the Properties window provides information on how relationships are handled. For example, the name of the foreign key, the return type, and multiplicity type is shown in a human-readable fashion, as demon-strated in Figure 27.10.

Useful information can also be retrieved on relationships. If you click the association line that conjuncts entities in the designer, the Properties window not only shows how the

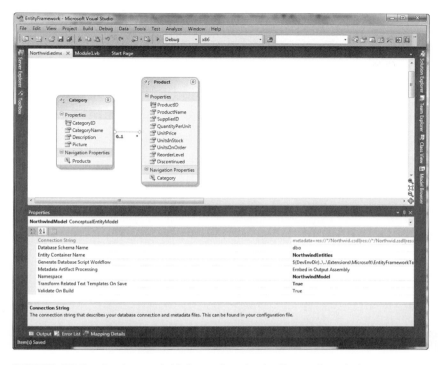

FIGURE 27.8   Getting model information via the Properties window.

relationship is defined but also enables you to choose custom behavior when deleting entities (for example, Cascade). Of course, this must be supported (or just enabled) in the underlying database. In the case of SQL Server databases, you can modify associations' behaviors using SQL Server Management Studio. Figure 27.11 shows such a scenario.

The last use of the Properties window is getting and setting values for scalar properties. For example, click the **QuantityPerUnit** property in the Product entity. Figure 27.12 shows how the Properties window displays.

Properties are self-explanatory, and you can get more information simply by clicking the property you are interested in, and the tool window will be updated with information. Consider two properties: Entity Key, which establishes if the scalar property represents a primary key, and StoreGeneratedPattern, which provides the ability to auto-generate the column in the database during insert and update operations. This tooling is particularly useful because here you can manually change the entities' behavior without the need to edit the auto-generated Visual Basic code; this job belongs to Visual Studio and you should always let it do this for you.

27

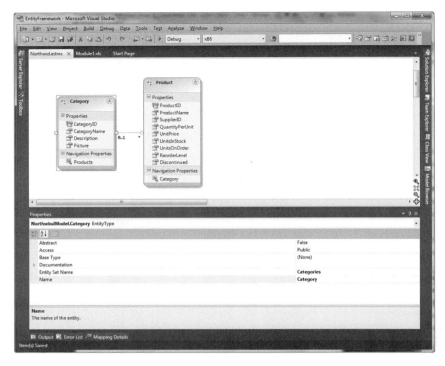

FIGURE 27.9   Getting entity information with the Properties window.

Insert/Update/Delete Operations for Entities

The ADO.NET Entity Framework offers a complete infrastructure for manipulating data, meaning that it offers the ability to add, update and remove data to and from the object model and subsequently from the database. Let's discover these features.

Instantiating the `ObjectContext`

The first task you need to accomplish when working with the ADO.NET Entity Framework in code to get an instance of the `ObjectContext` class. At the beginning of this chapter I told you to create a new Visual Basic project for the Console, so let's continue on this path. At module level (or class level, in most common scenarios) declare a variable of type `NorthwindEntities` that represents our object context as follows:

```
Private northwindContext As NorthwindEntities
```

Within the `Sub Main` (or in the constructor if you work with classes), create the actual instance:

```
Sub Main()
    Try
        northwindContext = New NorthwindEntities
```

FIGURE 27.10   Getting information on navigation properties with the Properties window.

```
Catch ex As SqlClient.SqlException
Catch ex As Exception

End Try

End Sub
```

Notice how a `System.Data.SqlClient.SqlException` general exception is handled in case of problems.

CODING TIPS ON THE OBJECT CONTEXT

The `ObjectContext` class's constructor provides two overloads that accept the connection string if you want it to be hard-coded instead of storing within the configuration file. You just need to pass the string as an argument to the constructor. The second tip is about declaring a variable and creating the instance. I usually prefer to provide a class-level declaration so that the variable can be reached by all code in my class (or classes if the variable is Friend) but also for another reason: I can handle exceptions when creating the actual instance within the code block that performs this action. I do not like code examples in which the instance is generated at the class level, but this is obviously just a suggestion.

27

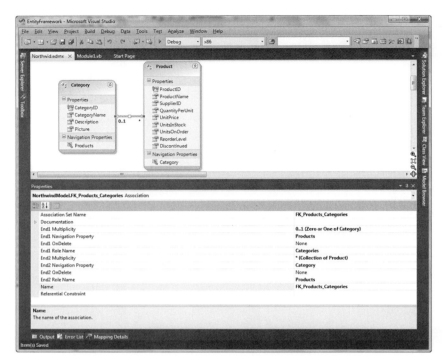

FIGURE 27.11   Getting associations information via the Properties window.

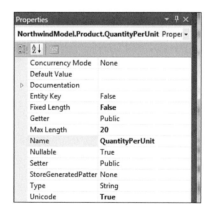

FIGURE 27.12   Getting information on scalar properties.

When you have the object context instance, you can read and write data on your object model.

Adding Entities

Adding entities against an entity data model requires you to pass the instance of the entity to the Add method exposed by the entity set. For example, in our demonstration scenario we have a Products entity set exposing an Add method. The following code shows how you can programmatically create a new product and add it to the object model:

```vb
Sub AddProduct(ByVal categoryReference As Category)
    Try

        Dim check = northwindContext.Products.
                    Single(Function(p) p.
                    ProductName = "Italian spaghetti")

    Catch ex As InvalidOperationException

        Try
            Dim prod As New Product
            With prod
                .ProductName = "Italian spaghetti"
                .QuantityPerUnit = "10 packs"
                .Discontinued = True
                .SupplierID = 4
                .UnitPrice = 0.5D
                .UnitsInStock = 100
                .UnitsOnOrder = 50

                .Category = categoryReference
            End With

            northwindContext.Products.AddObject(prod)
            northwindContext.SaveChanges()

        Catch e As Exception
    'Exception handling when saving changes
        End Try

    Catch ex As Exception
        'Handle general exceptions here
    End Try
End Sub
```

First, the code checks if the product already exists based on the specified condition. This is accomplished invoking the `Single` extension method, whose support is new in .NET Framework 4.0. It is something that you already saw in LINQ to SQL and not discussed thoroughly here. Notice how you simply set properties for the new product. The custom method receives a `Category` instance as an argument. This is necessary for setting a one-to-many relationship between the new product and the desired category. Setting the relationship just requires you to assign the `.Category` property with the category instance. When done, you simply invoke the `northwindContext.Products.AddObject` method passing the new product and then invoke the `SaveChanges` method for sending changes to the database.

TRACKING CHANGES

Remember that the `ObjectContext` instance can keep track of changes during the application lifetime, so you might invoke its `SaveChanges` method just once to persist all changes. The object context takes advantage of the `System.Data.Objects.ObjectManager` class that is responsible for handling the entity state which is how an entity lives within the object model: attached or detached. Generally entities are attached by default unless you detach them explicitly. Remember that detaching an entity prevents the object context from keeping track of changes onto such an entity.

In Chapter 25 I explained how you can use Visual Studio to inspect the database for checking if changes were correctly submitted to the database. The good news is that the same technique can be also used when working with EDMs.

Deleting Entities

Deleting entities is also a simple task. You first need to get the instance of the entity you want to remove and then invoke the `ObjectSet(Of T).DeleteObject` method. The following code shows how to get the instance of the specified product and then to remove it first from the model and then from the database:

```
Sub DeleteProduct()

    Try
        Dim check = northwindContext.Products.
                    Single(Function(p) p.
                    ProductName = "Italian spaghetti")

        northwindContext.Products.DeleteObject(check)
        northwindContext.SaveChanges()

        'Does not exist
```

```
Catch ex As InvalidOperationException

    End Try
End Sub
```

Same as in previous code, we take advantage of the `Single` method that throws an `InvalidOperationException` if the object does not exist.

DELETING ENTITIES WITH RELATIONSHIPS

In this chapter you see simplified examples focusing on the technology. In some situations you need to delete entities with relationships; for example, imagine you have an `Order` class with associated `OrderDetails`. When you delete the order, probably you want to remove associated details. To accomplish this, you need to work at the database level and enable it to cascade the deletion. For SQL Server databases you can accomplish this within SQL Server Management Studio, changing properties for the foreign key related to the relationship.

Updating Entities

Updating entities is a little bit different from adding and deleting in that there is no Update method in the `ObjectContext`. You simply get the instance of the object you want to update, change its properties, and then invoke `SaveChanges`. The following code demonstrates this:

```
Sub UpdateProduct()


    Try
        Dim check = northwindContext.Products.
                    Single(Function(p) p.
                    ProductName = "Italian spaghetti")

        check.Discontinued = True
        check.UnitsInStock = 30
        northwindContext.SaveChanges()

        'Product does not exist
    Catch ex As InvalidOperationException

    Catch ex As UpdateException
    End Try
End Sub
```

Just remember to check if the product exists before trying an update. Notice also how an `UpdateException` is caught; this is thrown when there is some problem in sending updates to the data source.

Handling Optimistic Concurrency

Of course, the ADO.NET Entity Framework provides the ability to handle optimistic concurrency exceptions. Basically you need to intercept eventual `System.Data.OptimisticConcurrencyException` instances. When intercepted, you need to invoke the `ObjectContext.Refresh` method that allows solving the concurrency problem. The following code revisits the `AddProduct` custom method described in the "Adding Entities" subsection:

```vb
Sub AddProduct(ByVal categoryReference As Category)


    Try

        Dim check = northwindContext.Products.
                    Single(Function(p) p.
                    ProductName = "Italian spaghetti")

    Catch ex As InvalidOperationException

        Dim prod As New Product
        With prod
            .ProductName = "Italian spaghetti"
            .QuantityPerUnit = "10 packs"
            .SupplierID = 4
            .UnitPrice = 0.5D
            .UnitsInStock = 100
            .UnitsOnOrder = 50
        End With

        northwindContext.AddToProducts(prod)

        Try
            northwindContext.SaveChanges()
        Catch e As OptimisticConcurrencyException
            northwindContext.Refresh(Objects.RefreshMode.ClientWins,
                                     northwindContext.Products)
            northwindContext.SaveChanges()
        Catch e As Exception

        End Try

    Catch ex As Exception
        'Handle general exceptions here
    End Try
End Sub
```

If an `OptmisticConcurrencyException` is thrown, first you need to invoke the `ObjectContext.Refresh` mode that is responsible for solving concurrency problems. It receives two arguments: The first one is one value from the `System.Data.Objects.RefreshMode` enumeration: `ClientWins` that establishes that changes made to the object model are not replaced with original values from the database, and `StoreWins` that establishes that changes made to the object model are replaced with original values from the database. These establishments make sense only when you invoke `ObjectContext.SaveChanges` again. Of course, in this book it is not possible to reproduce a real concurrency scenario, but now you know what the main objects are for handling this situation.

Validating Data

As in LINQ to SQL, you can take advantage of partial methods to accomplish custom data validations; however, there is an important difference. Entity Data Model generation takes care of providing a better mapping between SQL Server types and .NET types. Chapter 25 provides an example of the custom validation rule for ensuring that a string is not greater than 20 characters. In the Entity Framework this is not necessary. For example, take a look at the Properties window showing properties for the `Product.QuantityPerUnit` property as previously shown in Figure 27.12.

Notice how there is a Max Length property that limits the size of the string to 20 characters. To understand what happens, try to run the `AddProduct` method previously described to set the `QuantityPerUnit` property with a value longer than 20 characters. When you run the code and encounter `ObjectContext.SaveChanges`, an `UpdateException` will be thrown. So, if bad values are entered, intercepting these exceptions is a good idea. You can still implement your custom validation rules. To accomplish this, add a new class to your project and name it **Product** (just note that the Product class generated from the IDE is partial).

Inside the class definition you can implement a partial method that performs validations. For example, you might want to prevent users from adding discontinued products. This can be accomplished as follows:

```
Partial Public Class Product
    Private Sub OnDiscontinuedChanging(ByVal value As Boolean)
        If value = True Then
            Throw New ArgumentException _
            ("Although supported, please avoid adding " & _
             "discontinued products if they are new additions")
        End If
    End Sub
End Class
```

27

Similar to LINQ to SQL, there are methods related to each property in the entity and whose names finish with `Changing` and `Changed`. You provide validation rules on `Changing` methods, which map to an event occurring just before changes are sent to the model. If a `Product` with the `Discontinued` property set to `True` is added to the EDM, an `ArgumentException` is thrown.

Querying EDMs with LINQ to Entities

LINQ to Entities is the standard LINQ provider for querying entities within an Entity Data Model. Generally you use the same LINQ syntax for querying Entities, too, so you will not encounter particular difficulties.

> **USING STANDARD QUERY OPERATORS**
>
> LINQ to Entities supports standard query operators described in Chapter 24, "LINQ to Objects," to perform complex query expressions.

The one big difference is about eager loading that is explained after showing the code. As in LINQ to SQL, LINQ to Entities queries return an `IQueryable(Of T)`, unless you convert the result into a different type using extension methods at the end of the query. The following code returns the list of products for the specified category, taking only those products that are not discontinued and sorting the result by unit price:

```
Sub LINQtoEntitiesDemo(ByVal CategoryName As String)


    Dim query = From prod In northwindContext.Products.
                Include("Category")
                Where prod.Category.CategoryName = CategoryName _
                And prod.Discontinued = False
                Order By prod.UnitPrice
                Select prod

    Console.WriteLine("Category: {0}",
                CategoryName)

    For Each prod In query
        Console.WriteLine("Product name: {0}, Unit price: {1:c}",
                    prod.ProductName, prod.UnitPrice)
    Next
End Sub
```

As you can see, the LINQ syntax works similarly to other LINQ providers except that here the `Include` method has been invoked on the entity set instance. This method requires an argument of type `String`, which is the name of the navigation property mapped to the entity being queried; that is, the name of the entity set that the queried entity has a relationship with. `Include` performs that technique known as eager loading that allows loading related entities. This is necessary if you want to perform comparisons as in the preceding example, where an evaluation must be done on the category name that the current product belongs to. In other words, if you do not invoke `Include`, you will only have available `Products` information but not `Categories` information while you need this to perform the comparison. You can take advantage of standard query operators described in Chapter 24 to accomplish complex LINQ queries against entities as well.

Querying EDMs with Entity SQL

LINQ to Entities is not the only way to query data exposed by EDMs. An important alternative named Entity SQL allows querying entity data models providing both the ability to send SQL instructions to the data source and to treat query results as managed entities. To accomplish this, the `ObjectContext` class exposes a method named `CreateQuery(Of T)` that queries the EDM via the specified set of SQL instructions. The following example shows how you can retrieve a list of products for the `Grains/Cereals` category in Northwind, sorting the result by the product name:

```
Sub EntitySQLDemo()
    Try
        Dim grainProducts = northwindContext.
            CreateQuery(Of Product)("SELECT * FROM PRODUCTS WHERE " & _
            "CATEGORYID='5' ORDER BY PRODUCTNAME").
            Execute(Objects.MergeOption.AppendOnly)
    Catch ex As EntitySqlException
        Console.WriteLine("An error occurred in column: {0}",
                          ex.Column.ToString)
    Catch ex As Exception
        Console.WriteLine(ex.ToString)
    End Try
End Sub
```

`CreateQuery(Of T)` returns an `ObjectQuery(Of T)` that represents a strongly typed query against entities. As with any other LINQ query, Entity SQL queries are executed when they are effectively used, for example in `For..Each` loops, when converting to collections, or when explicitly invoking the `Execute` method as previously done. The method receives an argument of type `System.Data.Objects.MergeOption` that allows specifying how data retrieved from the database must be merged into the object model with existing data. Table 27.2 summarizes available values.

TABLE 27.2   `System.Data.Object.MergeOption` Enumeration Values

Value	Description
AppendOnly	Objects existing in the object context are also not loaded from the data source
NoTracking	Entity Framework does not keep track of changes on entities.
OverwriteChanges	Data is always loaded from the data source and changes to the object model are replaced.
PreserveChanges	Data is always loaded from the data source but changes to the object model are preserved.

The .NET Framework 4.0 also introduces new features to Entity SQL, such as the ability of querying the database directly. This can be accomplished invoking the `ObjectContext.ExecuteStoreQuery(Of T)` method, which still returns an `ObjectResult(Of T)`, but it differs from `CreateQuery(Of T)` in that this last mentioned method queries the model, whereas `ExecuteStoreQuery` queries the database. You can invoke it as follows:

```
Dim grainProducts = northwindContext.
    ExecuteStoreQuery(Of Product)("SELECT * FROM PRODUCTS WHERE " & _
    "CATEGORYID='5' ORDER BY PRODUCTNAME")
```

This method is basically the EF equivalent of the `DbCommand.ExecuteReader` class that you should already know from previous data access programming models. It works in the current transaction context within an opened connection. The last example is about executing arbitrary SQL instructions against the database. For example, imagine you want to delete products. This is not a query but a simple invocation of SQL instructions. For this purpose you can take advantage of the `ObjectContext.ExecuteStoreCommand`, which can be used as follows:

```
Dim numberOfRows As Integer = _
    northwindContext.ExecuteStoreCommand("DELETE FROM PRODUCTS")
```

The method does not return a type result because it does not actually execute a query, just an arbitrary command, and returns the number of rows affected by the command you passed as an argument. Entity SQL is a complex query engine and there is much more to say than what is presented in this introductory chapter. The best place for finding more information on such a query possibility in Entity Framework is the official page on the MSDN library, which is available at http://msdn.microsoft.com/en-us/library/bb399560(VS.100).aspx.

Mapping Stored Procedures

The Entity Framework 4 makes importing stored procedures into the object model easier, as opposed to the first version of the technology that required a manual operation on the model files. In this section you learn to add stored procedure mappings to the entity data model. To accomplish this, first open the Visual Studio designer by double-clicking the Northwind.edmx file in Solution Explorer. When ready, right-click the designer and select the **Update Model from Database** command. This launches again the wizard that allows selecting database objects not included yet in the entity data model. At this point expand the Stored Procedures item and select the **Ten Most Expensive Products** stored procedure, as shown in Figure 27.13.

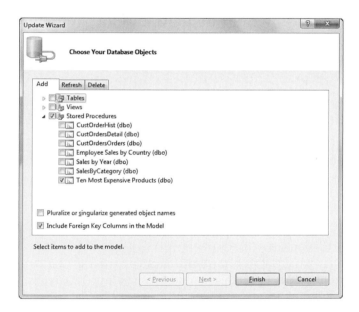

FIGURE 27.13   Adding a stored procedure to the EDM.

Generally you can follow these steps to add database objects to the EDM if you did not do it before. This operation provides mappings for the stored procedure. Basically the mapping lets the stored procedure to be mapped into a .NET method that returns a value; therefore, you need to know what kind of value such methods must return. To accomplish this, open the Server Explorer tool window, expand the Northwind database structure, and then expand the Stored Procedures folder; finally double-click the **Ten Most Expensive Products** stored procedure. Now the Visual Studio 2010 IDE shows the SQL instructions for the previously selected stored procedure, as shown in Figure 27.14.

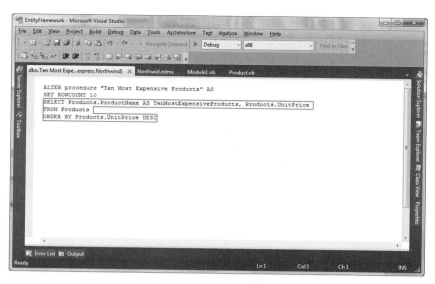

FIGURE 27.14   Examining SQL instructions for the stored procedure.

Examining the SQL code, it is quite simple to understand that the stored procedure returns a list of product names. Now switch back to the EDM designer so that the Model Browser tool window becomes active. Inside the window expand the EntityContainer: NorthwindEntities item and then right-click the **Function Import** command, as shown in Figure 27.15, or simply right-click the designer and then select **Add, Function Import**. This finalizes importing the stored procedure as a .NET method.

After a few seconds the Add Function Import dialog appears. In the Function Import Name field you need to specify the identifier for the new .NET method; type **TenMostExpensiveProducts**. Now click the **Get Column Information** button so that Visual Studio can retrieve information on database objects and corresponding .NET types used by the stored procedure. This is useful because the TenMostExpensiveProducts choice in the grid shows a String mapping in the EDM. Therefore it confirms what we saw when examining the SQL instructions, which is returning a series of strings. Because of this, select the String type in the Scalars combo box. In the Returns a Collection Of group box, specify what the new method must return. Figure 27.16 shows how the dialog should look after you've completed the preceding operations.

You can specify entities, complex types, or scalar properties as well. When you've done this, you are ready to invoke your stored procedure as a .NET method being part of the entity data model, exposed by the NorthwindEntities class. For example, if you want to retrieve the list of the ten most-expensive products, you can write something like this:

```
For Each prod In northwindContext.TenMostExpensiveProducts
    Console.WriteLine(prod)
Next
```

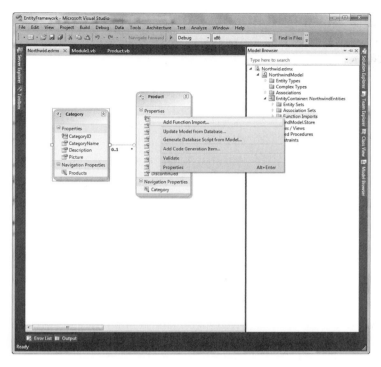

FIGURE 27.15   Adding a Function Import for mapping the stored procedure.

Behind the scenes, mapping a stored procedure is something that Visual Basic accomplishes by adding the following invocation to the ExecuteFunction(Of T) method to the NorthwindEntities class definition:

```
Function TenMostExpensiveProducts() As ObjectResult(Of Global.System.String)
  Return MyBase.ExecuteFunction(Of Global.System.String) _
      ("TenMostExpensiveProducts")
End Function
```

By completing this, you have the basic knowledge for working with the ADO.NET Entity Framework; you can learn more from the MSDN documentation.

Summary

In this chapter you got a high-level overview of ADO.NET Entity Framework 2.0, also known as EF 4. Entity Framework is a modern data platform providing a high abstraction layer from the database that allows working with a conceptual model instead of working directly with the data source. Database objects are mapped to the .NET equivalent into an Entity Data Model object model. Entities are a key concept in the EF and are classes representing database tables, as much as scalar properties represent tables' columns and

27

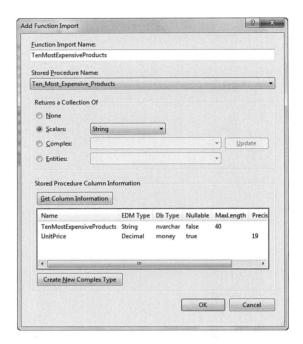

FIGURE 27.16   The Add Function Import dialog box allows mapping stored procedures.

navigation properties represent relationship. The ObjectContext class is responsible for managing the EDM lifetime, including the execution of Insert/Update/Delete operations that can be performed by invoking specific methods from entities. Querying data is instead accomplished via LINQ to Entities, a specific LINQ provider for the EF, and Entity SQL. Finally, you saw how mapping stored procedures to the object model takes advantage of features that are new in Visual Studio 2010.

CHAPTER 28

Manipulating Xml Documents with LINQ and Xml Literals

With the growing diffusion of the Internet during the years, one of the most common needs has been establishing standards for information exchange across computers in different parts of the world. For such an exchange, the Xml file format was introduced to provide a unified standard that was specific to structured data. Because of its flexibility, the Xml file format became popular among developers, and the .NET Framework has always offered a built-in way for manipulating Xml documents: the System.Xml namespace. With the advent of LINQ in Visual Basic 2008, things have been improved. Although the System.Xml namespace still exists for several reasons, a more efficient way for manipulating Xml documents is now available in Visual Basic due to important features such as LINQ to Xml and Xml literals that are also integrated into the language syntax. In this chapter you learn about manipulating Xml documents using LINQ to Xml and Xml literals, and you discover how much more powerful this opportunity is when compared to the System.Xml namespace.

KNOWLEDGE OF XML

The goal of this chapter is not explaining Xml syntax and documents structure, so you are required to be familiar with Xml syntax and implementation.

Introducing LINQ to Xml

LINQ to Xml is the standard LINQ provider for reading, creating, and manipulating Xml documents with the .NET languages starting from Visual Basic 2008 and Visual C# 3.0. Such a provider is implemented in the System.Xml.Linq.dll assembly and generally supports all operators available in LINQ to Objects with a few differences due to the Xml document structure and to other specific language features. The good news is that you can take advantage of the unified programming model offered by LINQ to perform Xml manipulations via the classical LINQ syntax that you already know. Visual Basic 2010, like its predecessor, offers particular syntax paradigms for LINQ to Xml that is also described in this chapter. You first learn how to create and manipulate Xml documents using managed objects, whereas in the second part of this chapter, you become skillful with Xml literals that can allow you to write code more quickly and cleanly.

The `System.Xml.Linq` Namespace

The System.Xml.Linq namespace exposes objects for creating, reading, and manipulating Xml documents. All objects inherit from System.Xml.Linq.XObject. Table 28.1 summarizes and describes available objects.

TABLE 28.1   Objects Available in the **System.Xml.Linq** Namespace

Object	Description
XDocument	Represents an entire Xml document
XElement	Represents an Xml element with attributes
XAttribute	Represents an Xml attribute
XComment	Represents a comment within an Xml document
XDeclaration	Represents the Xml declaration, including version number and encoding
XNode	Represents an Xml node which is made of an Xml element and children elements
XName	Provides a name to an Xml element or attribute
XCData	Represents a CData section
XText	Represents a text node
XContainer	Represents a container for nodes
XNamespace	Declares an Xml namespace
XDocumentType	Represents a Document Type Definition (DTD) typically for Xml schemas

You create an Xml document declaring an instance of the XDocument class:

```
Dim myDocument As New XDocument
```

When you have the instance you can add all acceptable objects mentioned in Table 28.1. The first required element is the Xml declaration that can be added as follows and that is mandatory:

```
myDocument.Declaration = New XDeclaration("1.0", "utf-8", "no")
```

If you want to add comments to your Xml documents, you can create as many instances of the XComment class for as many comments as you need to add:

```
myDocument.Add(New XComment("My first Xml document with LINQ"))
```

The next step is creating a first-level XElement that stores nested XElement objects:

```
Dim mainElement As New XElement("Contacts")
```

Now you can create nested elements and specify some attributes, as demonstrated in the following code:

```
'An Xml element with attributes
Dim firstNestedElement As New XElement("Contact")
Dim attribute1 As New XAttribute("LastName", "Del Sole")
Dim attribute2 As New XAttribute("FirstName", "Alessandro")
Dim attribute3 As New XAttribute("Age", "32")
firstNestedElement.Add(attribute1)
firstNestedElement.Add(attribute2)
firstNestedElement.Add(attribute3)

Dim secondNestedElement As New XElement("Contact")
Dim attribute4 As New XAttribute("LastName", "White")
Dim attribute5 As New XAttribute("FirstName", "Robert")
Dim attribute6 As New XAttribute("Age", "40")
secondNestedElement.Add(attribute4)
secondNestedElement.Add(attribute5)
secondNestedElement.Add(attribute6)

'In-line initialization with an array of XAttribute
Dim thirdNestedElement As New XElement("Contact", New XAttribute() {
                                       New XAttribute("LastName", "Red"),
                                       New XAttribute("FirstName", "Stephen"),
                                       New XAttribute("Age", "41")})
```

When you create an XAttribute you then need to invoke the XElement.Add instance method to assign the new attribute. Basically creating elements and assigning attributes is a simple task because classes are self-explanatory, and IntelliSense helps you understand what arguments the constructors need. But if you take a look at the last instance, you can see that things may become difficult, especially if you think that you could create an array of XElement with nested XElement definitions, with nested XAttribute definitions. We see later in this chapter how Xml literals make things easier; for now let's focus on fundamentals. The next step is to add all nested `XElement` objects to the main `XElement` as follows:

```
With mainElement
    .Add(firstNestedElement)
    .Add(secondNestedElement)
    .Add(thirdNestedElement)
End With
```

`mainElement` now stores a sequence of Xml elements that must be added to the document as follows:

```
myDocument.Add(mainElement)
```

In the end you can simply save your Xml document to disk by invoking the Save method:

```
myDocument.Save("C:\Contacts.xml")
```

This method has several overloads that also allow specifying a stream instead of a string of file options for controlling formatting. If you just want to check your result, simply invoke `XDocument.ToString` as follows:

```
Console.WriteLine(myDocument.ToString)
```

This line of code allows you to see how your document is formed. The output follows:

```
<!—My first Xml document with LINQ—>
<Contacts>
  <Contact LastName="Del Sole" FirstName="Alessandro" Age="32" />
  <Contact LastName="White" FirstName="Robert" Age="40" />
  <Contact LastName="Red" FirstName="Stephen" Age="41" />
</Contacts>
```

Creating an Xml document with the `System.Xml.Linq` namespace is more intuitive than the older `System.Xml` namespace, but things can go better as you see later. At the moment you need to know how to load and parse existing documents.

Loading and Parsing Existing Xml Documents

To load an existing Xml document you simply invoke the shared `XDocument.Load` method as follows:

```
Dim myDocument = XDocument.Load("C:\Contacts.xml")
```

You can get a new instance of `XDocument` and get access to its members via numerous methods and properties that the class offers. Table 28.2 summarizes the most important members.

TABLE 28.2   Most Important Members of the XDocument Class

Member	Type	Description
AddAfterSelf	Method	Adds the specified content just after the node whose instance is invoking the method itself
AddBeforeSelf	Method	Adds the specified content just before the node whose instance is invoking the method itself
AddFirst	Method	Adds the specified content as the first node in the document
ReplaceWith	Method	Replace the node whose instance is invoking the method with the specified content
Root	Property	Returns the root XElement
Remove	Method	Removes the node from its parents
RemoveNodes	Method	Removes children nodes from the object instance that is invoking the method
Element	Method	Retrieves an XElement instance of the specified Xml element
Descendants	Method	Returns an IEnumerable(Of XElement) collection of descendant XElement objects
FirstNode/LastNode/NextNode/PreviousNode	Properties	Return the instance of the node which position is indicated by the property name

28

Notice that both XDocument and XElement classes expose methods in Table 28.2, and XElement can also load and save Xml content as much as XDocument. Both XDocument and XElement classes also allow parsing strings containing Xml representation to get an appropriate object. This is accomplished invoking the Parse method as in the following example:

```
Dim document As String = "<?xml version=""1.0""?>" & Environment.NewLine & _
                    "    <Contacts>" & Environment.NewLine & _
                    "        <Contact FirstName=""Alessandro"" Last
                        Name=""Del Sole"" Age=""32""/>" & _
                    Environment.NewLine & _
```

```
         "           <Contact FirstName=""Robert"" Last
                     Name=""White"" Age=""40""/>" & _
         Environment.NewLine & _
         "   </Contacts>"
```

```
Dim resultingDocument As XDocument = XDocument.Parse(document)
resultingDocument.Save("C:\Contacts.xml")
```

This can be useful if you need to get a real Xml document from a simple string.

Querying Xml Documents with LINQ

You can take advantage of the LINQ syntax for querying Xml documents. Consider the following Xml file:

```
<Contacts>
  <Contact LastName="Del Sole" FirstName="Alessandro" Age="32" />
  <Contact LastName="White" FirstName="Robert" Age="40" />
  <Contact LastName="Red" FirstName="Stephen" Age="41" />
</Contacts>
```

Now imagine you want to get a list of last names for people with an age greater than 40. This can be accomplished by the following query:

```
Dim query = From element In myDocument.Descendants("Contact")
            Where Integer.Parse(element.Attribute("Age").Value) >= 40
            Select element.Attribute("LastName").Value
```

The Descendants method returns an IEnumerable(Of XElement) storing all XElement objects whose XName is the one specified as the argument. To get the value of an attribute, for example about comparisons as in our situation, you invoke the XElement.Attribute().Value property that contains the actual value of the XAttribute instance whose name is specified within Attribute(""). Notice how an explicit conversion is required from String to Integer to perform an evaluation on numbers. The preceding query returns an IEnumerable(Of String). If you need to generate custom results, you can take advantage of anonymous types as in the following query that get only the LastName and Age values:

```
Dim query = From element In myDocument.Descendants("Contact")
            Let age = Integer.Parse(element.Attribute("Age").Value)
            Where age >= 40
            Select New With {.LastName = element.
                                        Attribute("LastName").Value,
                        .Age = age}
```

The preceding query returns IEnumerable(Of anonymous type). Notice how the Let keyword is used to provide a temporary identifier that can be both used for performing a comparison and for assignment to the anonymous type's Age property. With the exception of anonymous types, as you remember from the LINQ to Objects discussion, generally

LINQ to Xml query results are directly bindable to user interface controls, such as the `BindingSource` in Windows Forms or the `CollectionViewSource` in WPF. By the way, remember that, if you do not select just one attribute per element (which would return an `IEnumerable(Of String)`), this would work as collections of `XElement`, and therefore it is not the best approach because you need to work against your business objects and not against `XElement` instances. Just to provide a simple example, if you need an iteration over your query, iterating an `IEnumerable(Of XElement)` would not probably make much sense while it instead would with a `List(Of Contact)`. The appropriate approach is creating a class that maps each element within the Xml document. For example, consider the following simplified implementation of the `Contact` class:

```
Class Contact
    Property FirstName As String
    Property LastName As String
    Property Age As Integer
End Class
```

At this point you can write a LINQ query that generates a collection of `Contact` and that can be both mapped to a user interface control and that can be edited:

```
'Returns a List(Of Contact)
Dim contactCollection = (From element In myDocument.Descendants("Contact")
                         Let age = Integer.Parse(element.
                                                 Attribute("Age").Value)
                         Select New Contact With {.FirstName = element.

                                      Attribute("FirstName").Value,
                                      .LastName = element.

                                      Attribute("LastName").Value,
                                      .Age = age}).ToList
```

Now you have a `List(Of Contact)` that can be both used for presenting data or for editing. On the contrary, you could create an Xml document starting from a collection of objects, but this is something you see in a more efficient way in the discussion of Xml literals in next section.

Xml Literals

The `System.Xml.Linq` namespace is powerful. By the way, manipulating complex Xml documents that store lots of data can lead to writing less elegant and more complex code. Luckily the Visual Basic language provides a powerful feature for manipulating Xml documents, known as *Xml literals*. In other words, you can write Xml markup together with the Visual Basic code. The following code provides an example:

```
'The compiler infers XDocument
```

```
Dim Contacts = <?xml version="1.0"?>
                   <Contacts>
                       <Contact LastName="Del Sole"
                           FirstName="Alessandro"
                           Age="32"
                           email="alessandro.delsole@visual-basic.it"/>
                       <!— Fantasy name—>
                       <Contact LastName="White"
                           FirstName="Robert"
                           Age="45"
                           email="address1@something.com"/>
                   </Contacts>
```

This means that you can write entire Xml documents integrating Xml markup and Visual Basic code. Here IntelliSense features are less powerful than in the classic Visual Studio Xml editor, but they are good enough to provide syntax colorization and code indentation. Figure 28.1 shows what the preceding code looks like in the Visual Basic code editor.

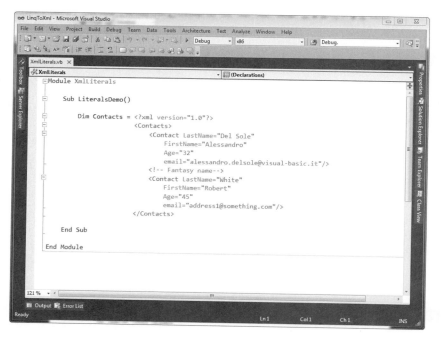

FIGURE 28.1   Xml literals in the Visual Basic code editor.

Just think that you can paste from the clipboard the content of long and complex Xml documents, such as Microsoft Excel workbooks or Open Xml documents, and take advantage of Xml literals. The Visual Basic compiler can then map Xml nodes to the appropriate .NET type. In the previous example, Contacts and Contact are mapped to XElement objects, whereas properties of each `Contact` element are mapped to `XAttribute` objects. The previous example also takes advantage of local type inference. In such a scenario the Visual Basic compiler infers the `XDocument` type for the `Contacts` variable. This is because the Xml markup contains the Xml declaration. If you do not specify such a declaration, the Xml markup is mapped to an `XElement`, as in the following code:

```
'The compiler infers XElement
Dim Contacts = <Contacts>
                    <Contact LastName="Del Sole"
                        FirstName="Alessandro"
                        Age="32"
                        email="alessandro.delsole@visual-basic.it"/>
            </Contacts>
```

If you do not want to take advantage of local type inference, you need to pay attention to what type the Xml markup is mapped to. For example, both the following code snippets throw an `InvalidCastException`:

```
'Throws an InvalidCastException
'Cannot assign to XElement markup that
'ships with the Xml declaration
Dim Contacts As XElement = <?xml version="1.0"?>
                            <Contacts>
                                <Contact LastName="Del Sole"
                                    FirstName="Alessandro"
                                    Age="32"
                                    email="alessandro.delsole@visual-basic.it"/>
                                        <!-- Fantasy name-->
                                <Contact LastName="White"
                                    FirstName="Robert"
                                    Age="45"
                                    email="address1@something.com"/>
                            </Contacts>
'Throws an InvalidCastException
'Cannot assign to XDocument markup that
'does not have the Xml declaration
Dim Contacts As XDocument = <Contacts>
                                <Contact LastName="Del Sole"
                                    FirstName="Alessandro"
                                    Age="32"
                                    email="alessandro.delsole@visual-basic.it"/>
                                <!-- Fantasy name-->
                                <Contact LastName="White"
                                    FirstName="Robert"
                                    Age="45"
                                    email="address1@something.com"/>
                            </Contacts>
```

Xml literals are powerful because they allow you to write more elegant code and provide a view of your Xml documents as you would within an Xml editor that is better than generating nodes, elements, and attributes the old-fashioned way. The preceding code has one limitation: It is hard-coded, meaning that values have been added manually. This would be a big limitation because you often need to dynamically generate Xml documents (for example generating elements for each member within a data source). Luckily Xml literals makes this easier, providing the ability to embed local variables' values and LINQ queries within the Xml markup, as shown in next section.

BEHIND THE SCENES

The Visual Basic compiler parses Xml documents, elements, and attributes written with Xml literals into the appropriate .NET types, such as XDocument, XElement, and XAttribute. Comments are included in such a mapping and converted into XComment objects and so on. Please refer to Table 28.1 to recall available objects.

LINQ Queries with Xml Literals

Xml literals provide an alternative syntax for LINQ to Xml queries in Visual Basic code. Let's retake the first Xml document used in the "System.Xml.Linq Namespace" section, which looks like the following but with a slight modification:

```
<?xml version="1.0" encoding="utf-8"?>
<Contacts>
  <Contact FirstName="Alessandro"
           LastName="Del Sole"
           Age="32"
           Email="alessandro.delsole@visual-basic.it">
  </Contact>
  <!--The following are fantasy names-->
  <Contact FirstName="Stephen"
           LastName="Red"
           Age="40"
           Email="address1@something.com">
  </Contact>
  <Contact FirstName="Robert"
           LastName="White"
           Age="41"
           Email="address2@something.com">
  </Contact>
  <Contact FirstName="Luke"
           LastName="Green"
           Age="42"
           Email="address3@something.com">
  </Contact>
  <Person FirstName="Alessandro"
```

```
        LastName="Del Sole">
  </Person>
</Contacts>
```

There is a `Person` element that we want to be excluded. The goal is querying all `Contact` elements whose age is greater than 40. Instead of recurring to the classical syntax, you can write the following code:

```
Dim doc = XDocument.Load("Contacts.xml")


Dim query = From cont In doc.<Contacts>.<Contact>
            Where Integer.Parse(cont.@Age) >= 40
            Select cont
```

The preceding code uses new symbols for querying documents known as Xml Axis Properties. Table 28.3 summarizes Xml axis.

TABLE 28.3   Xml Axis

Symbol	Description
...<>	Xml Axis Descendants Property. Returns all descendant elements of the Xml document named as the identifier enclosed within the symbols.
.<>	Xml Axis Child Property. Returns children of an `XElement` or `XDocument`.
.@	Xml Axis Attribute Property. Returns the value of an attribute within an Xml element.

In other words, the preceding query can be described by this sentence: "Process all Contacts' children Contact elements." The difference with the Xml Axis Descendants Properties can be explained with another example. Consider the following document that is just a revalidation of the previous one:

```
<?xml version="1.0" encoding="utf-8"?>
<Contacts>
  <Contact>
    <FirstName>Alessandro</FirstName>
    <LastName>Del Sole</LastName>
    <Age>32</Age>
    <Email>alessandro.delsole@visual-basic.it</Email>
  </Contact>
  <Contact>
    <FirstName>Stephen</FirstName>
    <LastName>Red</LastName>
    <Age>40</Age>
    <Email>address1@something.com</Email>
```

```
  </Contact>
  <Person>
    <FirstName>Robert</FirstName>
    <LastName>White</LastName>
  </Person>
</Contacts>
```

Now each `Contact` element has subelements. If you wanted to get a collection of all `LastName` elements for all elements, you could use the Xml Axis Descendants property as follows:

```
'Returns a collection of all <LastName></LastName>
'elements within the document
Dim onlyLastNames = From cont In doc...<LastName>
```

It's worth mentioning that such a query also includes results from the `Person` element, because it exposes a `LastName` attribute. So if you need to filter results depending on the root element, you should invoke the Axis Descendants property. Notice also how in both the previous code examples an explicit conversion is required when you need a comparison against non-String data. In this particular case the comparison is done against an integer number (40); therefore, you can invoke the `Integer.Parse` method—because you expect that the `Age` attribute contains the string representation of a number. Xml Axis properties provide therefore a simplified and cleaner way for querying Xml documents. Just remember that, as discussed in the previous section, *you will need helper classes for mapping each XElement content into a .NET type* to provide data-binding features to your code.

WHY OPTION STRICT ON **IS IMPORTANT**

One of the last code snippets had an explicit conversion using `Integer.Parse`. If you set `Option Strict On` and you forget to perform such a conversion, the compiler throws an exception requiring you to perform an appropriate conversion, which is always good. If you instead set `Option Strict Off`, no conversion is required at compile time, but in all cases you encounter errors at runtime except if you assign the value of an attribute to a String variable. You should always keep `Option Strict On`.

Understanding Embedded Expressions

With embedded expressions you can include local variables or perform dynamic queries within Xml literals. For example, let's look again at the first example about Xml literals, where an Xml document contains a couple of contacts. Imagine you want to generate a contact starting from some variables (that you could populate at runtime with different values) instead of hard-coding the last name, first name, and age. This can be accomplished as follows:

```
'All with type inference
Dim FirstName = "Alessandro"
Dim LastName = "Del Sole"
```

```
Dim Age = 32

Dim Contacts = <?xml version="1.0"?>
                <Contacts>
                    <Contact LastName=<%= LastName %>
                        FirstName=<%= FirstName %>
                        Age=<%= Age %>
                        email="alessandro.delsole@visual-basic.it"/>
                    <!-- Fantasy name-->
                    <Contact LastName="White"
                        FirstName="Robert"
                        Age="45"
                        email="address1@something.com"/>
                </Contacts>
```

Although the second contact in the list is equal to the first example, the first contact is generated with embedded expressions. You create an embedded expression including an expression within <%= and => symbols. While you write the expression after the opening tag, IntelliSense works as usual to improve your coding experience. In this way you can create elements dynamically. But this code works just for one element. What if you need to dynamically generate as many elements for as many items stored within a collection or within a database table? Imagine you have a Contact class that is implemented as follows:

```
Class Contact
    Property FirstName As String
    Property LastName As String
    Property Age As Integer
    Property EmailAddress As String
End Class
```

Now imagine that within a method body you create a collection of Contact. For demo purposes, four instances of the Contact class are created and then pushed into a new collection:

```
Dim firstContact As New Contact With {.FirstName = "Alessandro",
                    .LastName = "Del Sole",
                    .EmailAddress = "alessandro.delsole@visual-basic.it",
                    .Age = 32}


'Now fantasy names
Dim secondContact As New Contact With {.FirstName = "Stephen",
                    .LastName = "Red",
                    .EmailAddress = "address1@something.com",
                    .Age = 40}
Dim thirdContact As New Contact With {.FirstName = "Robert",
                    .LastName = "White",
                    .EmailAddress = "address2@something.com",
```

28

```
                        .Age = 41}
Dim fourthContact As New Contact With {.FirstName = "Luke",
                        .LastName = "Green",
                        .EmailAddress = "address3@something.com",
                        .Age = 42}


Dim people As New List(Of Contact) From {
                    firstContact,
                    secondContact,
                    thirdContact,
                    fourthContact}
```

Our goal is to generate an Xml document that contains all the preceding created contacts as Xml nodes. This is accomplished by the following code:

```
Dim newDocument = <?xml version="1.0"?>
                    <Contacts>
                        <%= From cont In people
                            Where cont.Age > 32
                            Select <Contact
                                    FirstName=<%= cont.FirstName %>
                                    LastName=<%= cont.LastName %>
                                    Age=<%= cont.Age %>
                                    Email=<%= cont.EmailAddress %>>
                                </Contact>
                            %>
                    </Contacts>
```

```
newDocument.Save("C:\Contacts.xml")
```

Embedding an expression means that you can also embed a LINQ query. Notice how the query is part of the first embedded expression and how the Select clause allows the creation of a new XElement object using Xml literals where nested embedded expressions can provide advantage of local variables. The previous code can produce the following result (remember that only people with an age greater than 32 have been included):

```
<Contacts>
  <Contact FirstName="Stephen" LastName="Red" Age="40"
        Email="address1@something.com"></Contact>
  <Contact FirstName="Robert" LastName="White" Age="41"
        Email="address2@something.com"></Contact>
  <Contact FirstName="Luke" LastName="Green" Age="42"
        Email="address3@something.com"></Contact>
</Contacts>
```

Taking advantage of Xml literals and embedded expressions, you dynamically created an Xml document that can contain an infinite number of elements. This example was related to a simple generic collection, but you can easily understand what kinds of results you can reach if you need to generate Xml documents from database tables. If you work with LINQ to SQL or with ADO.NET Entity Framework, the code remains the same; the only exception is that the data source in the `From` clause is the `DataContext` instance or the `ObjectContext` one.

> **NOTE**
>
> Xml literals can map any kind of Xml markup. For example, you can dynamically generate WPF controls writing XAML code that Visual Basic recognizes as Xml and that can be assigned to `XElement` objects. Another useful example is a Microsoft Excel workbook saved as Xml format that can be entirely pasted into the Visual Basic editor. Other than writing cleaner code, the ability to wrap any Xml content is probably the best feature of Xml literals.

Xml Schema Inference

LINQ to Xml and Xml literals are both powerful features but they have a limitation: Within embedded expressions or when using the literals symbols in queries, IntelliSense support is not as good as usual, especially when you need to invoke Xml attributes. This means that in most situations you need to remember and manually write code that maps attributes with no IntelliSense support. This can lead to errors, because elements and attributes within Xml documents are case-sensitive, so typing age instead of `Age` results in a runtime error. To solve this issue, Visual Basic offers a nice feature known as the Xml Schema Inference Wizard that is a tool integrated in the IDE and that is specific for Visual Basic. The tool allows generating an Xml schema from the Xml document you query and allows enabling IntelliSense support. First, you need an Xml document. The following is a simplified list of customers that is the base document:

```
<?xml version="1.0" encoding="utf-8" ?>
<Customers xmlns="DelSole.Customers">
  <Customer CustomerID="DELSO" CompanyName="Del Sole Ltd."
            Country="Italy" Address="Unspecified"
            Email="alessandro.delsole@visual-basic.it"/>

  <!— Not real names —>
  <Customer CustomerID="GREEN" CompanyName="Green Corp."
            Country="Italy" Address="Unspecified"
            Email="address1@something.com"/>

  <Customer CustomerID="WHITE" CompanyName="White Corp."
```

28

```
                 Country="Italy" Address="Unspecified"
                 Email="address2@something.com"/>
</Customers>
```

Notice how an Xml namespace declaration has been added to the `Customers` node. This is important and is explained later. Save the file as **Customers.xml**. When you get the document, right-click the project name in Solution Explorer and select **Add New Item**. When the Add New Item dialog box appears, select the **XML to Schema** template and name it **CustomersSchema.xsd**, as shown in Figure 28.2.

FIGURE 28.2   The XML to Schema item template.

After you click **Add**, a dialog named Infer Xml Schema Set from Xml Documents appears, requiring you to specify the Xml document as the base. You are not limited to specifying existing Xml documents; you can manually write the document (or paste it from the clipboard) or specify an Xml document that is available on a network. This can be useful if you want to generate schemas for RSS feeds. Click the **Add from File** button and select the **Customers.xml** document. (You can notice that Visual Studio automatically points to the project folder making the selection easier.) Figure 28.3 shows how the dialog looks.

The good news is that you are not limited to just one document; you can add multiple documents to generate multiple schemas at one time. When you finish and click **OK**, Visual Studio generates an .Xsd document whose content is the following:

```
<?xml version="1.0" encoding="utf-8"?>
<xs:schema attributeFormDefault="unqualified"
           elementFormDefault="qualified"
```

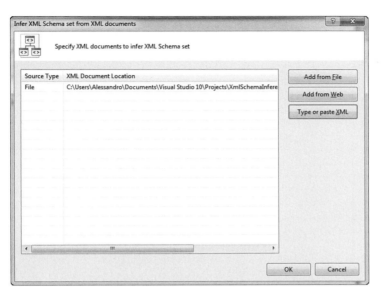

FIGURE 28.3   Selecting the Xml document for generating Xml schemas from.

```
        targetNamespace="DelSole.Customers"
        xmlns:xs="http://www.w3.org/2001/XMLSchema">
  <xs:element name="Customers">
    <xs:complexType>
      <xs:sequence>
        <xs:element maxOccurs="unbounded" name="Customer">
          <xs:complexType>
            <xs:attribute name="CustomerID" type="xs:string"
                          use="required" />
            <xs:attribute name="CompanyName" type="xs:string"
                          use="required" />
            <xs:attribute name="Country" type="xs:string"
                          use="required" />
            <xs:attribute name="Address" type="xs:string"
                          use="required" />
            <xs:attribute name="Email" type="xs:string"
                          use="required" />
          </xs:complexType>
        </xs:element>
      </xs:sequence>
    </xs:complexType>
  </xs:element>
</xs:schema>
```

The schema is simple because the structure of our starting document is simple. Notice how the schema declaration contains a targetNamespace attribute that maps the Xml namespace we provided within the original document. You can also get a visual representation of the new schema via the Xml Schema Explorer tool window that is available by clicking **View, Xml Schema Explorer**. The tool window is shown in Figure 28.4.

FIGURE 28.4   The Xml Schema Explorer tool window.

This window is helpful to understand the hierarchical structure of an Xml schema. For the newly created schema, notice the custom namespace at the root level and then the root document node, named Customers. Within the child node, Customer, you can see nested attributes and mappings to data types. Also notice how Visual Studio tell us that Customer is part of a one-to-many relationship (1..*).

XML SCHEMA DESIGNER

Visual Studio 2010 introduces a new designer for Xml schemas that is also enabled each time you work with such documents. The editor is now based on WPF and allows generating or editing schema with a powerful designer. This tool is not described here but you can easily understand how to take advantage of its instrumentation to edit schemas at the first time you see it.

At this point you are ready to write Visual Basic code. The first thing to do is to add an Imports directive pointing to the Xml namespace. Starting from Visual Basic 2008, the Imports keyword can import Xml namespaces, too, as follows:

```
Imports <xmlns:ds="DelSole.Customers">
```

IMPORTING XML NAMESPACES

Each time you need to work with Xml documents or schemas that define an Xml name-space, you need to import that namespace. This is because otherwise you should rewrite the Xml namespace declaration every time you write an Xml element within your document. By importing the namespace, you do not need to worry anymore about Xml namespaces. Microsoft Excel's workbooks or XAML markup code are good exam-ples of this.

This is the point where IntelliSense can provide support for your schemas. Now you can understand why the addition of an Xml namespace within the original document was necessary. At this point you could write whatever query you need. The following query is simple but its purpose is not to show how you can query data; instead its purpose is to demonstrate IntelliSense capabilities in Xml literals after the addition of an Xml schema:

```
Dim custDoc = XDocument.Load("Customers.xml")


Dim customers = From cust In custDoc...<ds:Customer>
            Select cust.@CompanyName
```

At the point at which you type the ...< symbols, IntelliSense shows all the available options for the schema allowing the selection of available nodes. Figure 28.5 shows IntelliSense in action.

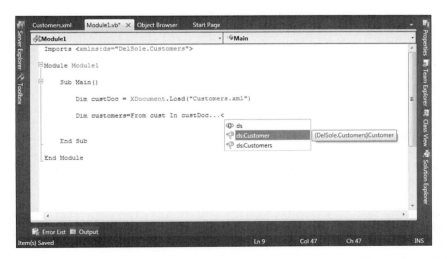

FIGURE 28.5   Xml Schema Inference enables IntelliSense in LINQ queries with Xml literals.

As you can imagine, this is helpful because now you are not required to remember every element in the Xml document and to type it manually. And of course this works not only with Xml elements but also with Xml attributes, which is what you get when beginning to write the .@ symbols. Figure 28.6 represents such a situation.

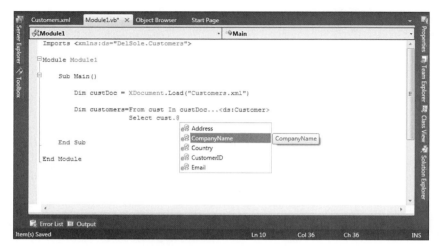

FIGURE 28.6   IntelliSense also allows you to select attributes.

If you have multiple schemas or multiple namespaces, IntelliSense can provide support for all of them making your coding experience straightforward.

Summary

The .NET Framework offers a special LINQ provider named LINQ to Xml that enables working with Xml documents. Via the System.Xml.Linq namespace, this provider allows creating and manipulating Xml documents in an efficient way. Classes such as XDocument, XElement, XAttribute, XComment, and XDeclaration are self-explanatory and allow easy generation of Xml documents. To query Xml documents you just write LINQ queries using the unified syntax that you already know, with a few additions such as the Descendants or Attribute properties. Although efficient, System.Xml.Linq can be confusing when Xml documents become larger. Luckily Visual Basic provides the Xml literals feature that allows writing Xml markup code directly into the VB code editor. To make things real, with embedded expressions you can generate documents putting local variables, expressions, and LINQ queries within Xml literals so that you can generate Xml documents dynamically. Visual Basic also takes care of your coding experience and provides the Xml Schema Inference Wizard that generates an Xml schema starting from the Xml document you want to query with LINQ to Xml and allows enabling IntelliSense for that particular document, avoiding the risk of typos.

CHAPTER 29

Overview of Parallel LINQ

Modern computers have multiple processors or multicore processors. The benefit of having such hardware is that it provides, among other things, the ability for scaling data processing over all the available processors via multiple threads, instead of using one processor and possibly one thread. Until .NET Framework 3.5, no native library was offered to take advantage of multicore architectures, so you could only unleash your processors as if they were one. Luckily, .NET Framework 4.0 introduces a new fundamental framework known as *Task Parallel Library* that is all about parallel computing and multicore architectures. The framework is discussed in detail in Chapter 45, "Parallel Programming," but now you learn how to take advantage of parallelism in performing LINQ queries using Parallel LINQ to improve your code performances.

Introducing PLINQ

Parallel LINQ, also known as *PLINQ*, is a new LINQ implementation provided by .NET Framework 4.0 that enables developers to query data using the LINQ syntax but takes advantage of multicore and multiprocessor architectures that have support by the Task Parallel Library (discussed in Chapter 45). Creating "parallel" queries is an easy task, although there are some architectural differences with classic LINQ (or more generally with classic programming) that is discussed during this chapter. Basically to create a parallel query you just need to invoke the AsParallel extension method onto the data source you are querying. The following code provides an example:

```
Dim range = Enumerable.Range(0, 1000)


'Just add "AsParallel"
Dim query = From num In range.AsParallel
            Where (IsOdd(num))
            Select num
```

Generally you can take advantage of Parallel LINQ and the Task Parallel Library only in particular scenarios, such as intensive calculations or large amounts of data. Because of this, to give you an idea of how PLINQ can improve performance, the code presented in this chapter simulates intensive work on easier code so that you can focus on PLINQ instead of other code.

Simulating an Intensive Work

Parallel LINQ provides benefits when you work in extreme situations such as intensive works or large amounts of data. In different situations PLINQ is not necessarily better than classic LINQ. To understand how PLINQ works, first we need to write code that simulates an intensive work. After creating a new Console project, write the following method that simply determines if a number is odd but suspending the current thread for a big number of milliseconds invoking the System.Threading.Thread.SpinWait shared method:

```
'Checks if a number is odd
Private Function IsOdd(ByVal number As Integer) As Boolean
    'Simulate an intensive work
    System.Threading.Thread.SpinWait(1000000)
    Return (number Mod 2) <> 0
End Function
```

Now that we have an intensive work, we can compare both classic and parallel LINQ queries.

Measuring Performances of a Classic LINQ Query

The goal of this paragraph is to explain how you can execute a classic LINQ query over intensive processing and measure its performance in milliseconds. Consider the following code:

```
Private Sub ClassicLinqQuery()
    Dim range = Enumerable.Range(0, 1000)

    Dim query = From num In range
                Where (IsOdd(num))
                Select num

    'Measuring performance
```

```
    Dim sw As Stopwatch = Stopwatch.StartNew

    'Linq query is executed when invoking Count
    Console.WriteLine("Total odd numbers: " + query.Count.ToString)
    sw.Stop()
    Console.WriteLine(sw.ElapsedMilliseconds.ToString)
    Console.ReadLine()
End Sub
```

Given a range of predefined numbers (`Enumerable.Range`), the code looks for odd numbers and collects them into an `IEnumerable(Of Integer)`. To measure performance, we can take advantage of the `Stopwatch` class that basically starts a counter (`Stopwatch.StartNew`). Because, as you already know, LINQ queries are effectively executed when you use them, such a query is executed when the code invokes the `Count` property to show how many odd numbers are stored within the `query` variable. When done, the counter is stopped so that we can get the number of milliseconds needed to perform the query itself. By the way, measuring time is not enough. The real goal is to understand how CPU is used and how a LINQ query impacts performance. To accomplish this, right-click the **Windows Task Bar** and start the **Task Manager**. Then click the **Performance** tab, and in the end click the **Always on Top** command in the **Options** menu. This provides a way for looking at the CPU usage while running your code. The previous code, which can be run by invoking the `ClassicLinqQuery` from the `Main` method, produces the following result on my dual-core machine:

```
Total odd numbers: 500
7664
```

This means that executing a query versus the intensive processing took about 7 1/2 seconds. The other interesting thing is about the CPU usage. Figure 29.1 shows that during the processing the CPU was used for a medium percentage of resources. Obviously this percentage can vary depending on the machine and on the running processes and applications.

That CPU usage was not full is not necessarily good, because it means that all the work relies on a single thread and is considered as running on a single processor. Therefore there is an overload of work only for such resources while other resources are free. To scale the work over multiple threads and multiple processors, a Parallel LINQ query is, of course, more efficient.

Measuring Performances of a PLINQ Query

To create a parallel query, you simply need to invoke the `AsParallel` extension method for the data source you want to query. Copy the method shown in the previous paragraph and rename it as `PLinqQuery`; then simply change the first line of the query as follows:

```
Dim query = From num In range.AsParallel
```

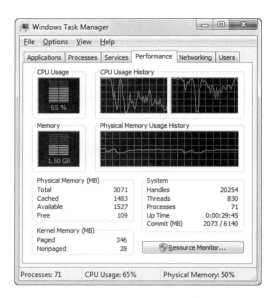

FIGURE 29.1   CPU usage during a classic LINQ query.

Different from a LINQ query, AsParallel returns a ParallelQuery(Of T) that is exposed by the System.Linq namespace and that is specific for PLINQ, although it works as an IEnumerable(Of T) but it allows scaling data over multicore processors. Now edit Sub Main so that it invokes the PLinqQuery method and runs the code again. Figure 29.2 shows what you should see when the application is processing data.

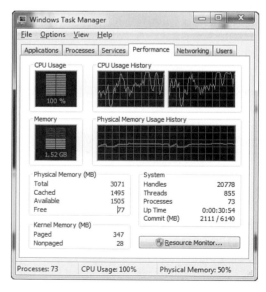

FIGURE 29.2   CPU usage during a Parallel LINQ query.

It is worth noticing that now all processors are being used, and this is demonstrated by the 100% percent CPU usage. Processing was scaled along all available processors. On my dual core machine, the previous code produces the following result:

```
Total odd numbers: 500
3451
```

The PLINQ query took only 3 1/2 seconds, which is less than half of the classic LINQ query result. So you can understand how PLINQ can dramatically improve your code performance, although there are some other considerations to do as discussed in the next paragraphs.

CONVERTING TO SEQUENTIAL QUERIES

PLINQ queries are evaluated in parallel, meaning that they take advantage of multi-core architectures, also thanks to the `ParallelQuery(Of T)` class. If you want to convert such a result into an `IEnumerable(Of T)` and provide sequential evaluation of the query, you can invoke the `AsSequential` extension method from the query result variable.

Ordering Sequences

One of the most important consequences of Parallel LINQ (and, more generally, of parallel computing) is that processing is not done sequentially as it would happen on single-threaded code. This is because multiple threads run concurrently. To understand this, the following is an excerpt from the iteration on the result of the parallel query:

```
295
315
297
317
299
319
```

You would probably instead expect something like the following, which is produced by the classic LINQ query:

```
295
296
297
298
299
300
```

29

If you need to work in sequential order but you do not want to lose the capabilities of PLINQ query, you can invoke the AsOrdered extension method that preserves the sequential order of the result, as demonstrated by the following code snippet:

```
Dim query = From num In range.AsParallel.AsOrdered
```

If you now run the code again, you get an ordered set of odd numbers.

AsParallel and Binary Operators

There are situations in which you use operators that take two data sources; among such operators, there are the following binary operators: Join, GroupJoin, Except, Concat, Intersect, Union, Zip, and SequenceEqual. To take advantage of parallelism with binary operators on two data sources, you need to invoke AsParallel on both collections, as demonstrated by the following code:

```
Dim result = firstSource.AsParallel.Except(secondSource.AsParallel)
```

The following code still works but it won't take advantage of parallelism:

```
Dim result = firstSource.AsParallel.Except(secondSource)
```

Using ParallelEnumerable

The System.Linq namespace for .NET 4.0 introduces a new ParallelEnumerable class, which is the parallel counterpart of Enumerable and provides extension methods specific to parallelism, such as AsParallel. You can use ParallelEnumerable members instead of invoking AsParallel because both return a ParallelQuery(Of T). For example the PLINQ query in the first example could be rewritten as follows:

```
Dim range = ParallelEnumerable.Range(0, 1000)


'Just add "AsParallel"
Dim query = From num In range
            Where (IsOdd(num))
            Select num
```

In this case the range variable is of type ParallelEnumerable(Of Integer), and therefore you do not need to invoke AsParallel. By the way, there are some differences in how data is handled, and this may often lead AsParallel to be faster. Explaining in detail the ParallelEnumerable architecture is out of the scope in this introductory chapter, but if you are curious you can take a look at this blog post from the Task Parallel Library Team: http://blogs.msdn.com/pfxteam/archive/2007/12/02/6558579.aspx.

Controlling PLINQ Queries

PLINQ offers additional extension methods and features to provide more control over tasks that effectively run queries, all exposed by the `System.Linq.ParallelEnumerable` class. In this section you get an overview of extension methods and learn how you can control your PLINQ queries.

Setting the Maximum Tasks Number

As explained in Chapter 45, the Task Parallel Library relies on tasks instead of threads, although working with tasks basically means scaling processing over multiple threads. You can specify the maximum number of tasks that can execute a thread invoking the `WithDegreeOfParallelism` extension method, passing the number as an argument. The following code demonstrates how you can get the list of running processes with a PLINQ query that runs a maximum of three concurrent tasks:

```
Dim processes = Process.GetProcesses.
                AsParallel.WithDegreeOfParallelism(3)
```

Forcing Parallelism in Every Query

Not all code can benefit from parallelism and PLINQ. Such technology is intelligent enough to determine if a query can benefit from PLINQ according to its *shape*. The shape of a query consists of the operator it requires and algorithm or delegates that are involved. PLINQ analyzes the shape and can determine where to apply a parallel algorithm. You can force a query to be completely parallelized, regardless of its shape, by simply invoking the `WithExecutionMode` extension methods that receive an argument of type `ParallelExecutionMode` that is an enumeration exposing two self-explanatory members: `ForceParallelism` and `Default`. The following code demonstrates how you can force a query to be completely parallelized:

```
Dim processes = Process.GetProcesses.
                AsParallel.WithExecutionMode( _
                ParallelExecutionMode.ForceParallelism)
```

Merge Options

PLINQ automatically partitions query sources so that it can take advantage of multiple threads that can work on each part concurrently. You can control how parts are handled by invoking the `WithMergeOptions` method that receives an argument of type `ParallelMergeOptions`. Such enumeration provides the following specifications:

- ▶ `NotBuffered`, which returns elements composing the result as soon as they are available

29

▶ FullyBuffered, which returns the complete result, meaning that query operations are buffered until every one has been completed

▶ AutoBuffered, which leaves to the compiler to choose the best buffering method in that particular situation

You invoke WithMergeOptions as follows:

```
Dim processes = Process.GetProcesses.
                AsParallel.WithMergeOptions( _
                ParallelMergeOptions.FullyBuffered)
```

With the exception of the ForAll method that is always NotBuffered and OrderBy that is always FullyBuffered, generally other extension methods/operators can support all merge options. The full list of operators is described in the following page of the MSDN Library: http://msdn.microsoft.com/en-us/library/dd547137(VS.100).aspx.

Canceling PLINQ Queries

If you need to provide a way for canceling a PLINQ query, you can invoke the WithCancellation method. You first need to implement a method to be invoked when you need to cancel the query. The method receives a CancellationTokenSource argument (which sends notices that a query must be canceled) and can be implemented as follows:

```
Dim cs As New CancellationTokenSource


Private Sub DoCancel(ByVal cs As CancellationTokenSource)
    'Ensures that query is cancelled when executing
    Thread.Sleep(500)
    cs.Cancel()
End Sub
```

When you have a method of this kind, you need to start a new task by pointing to this method as follows:

```
Tasks.Task.Factory.StartNew(Sub()
                                DoCancel(cs)
                            End Sub)
```

When a PLINQ query is canceled, an OperationCanceledException is thrown so that you can handle cancellation, as demonstrated in the following code snippet:

```
Private Sub CancellationDemo()
    Try

        Dim processes = Process.GetProcesses.
                        AsParallel.WithCancellation(cs.Token)

    Catch ex As OperationCanceledException
```

```
            Console.WriteLine(ex.Message)
        Catch ex As Exception

        End Try
    End Sub
```

To cancel a query, simply invoke the `DoCancel` method.

Handling Exceptions

In single-core scenarios, LINQ queries are executed sequentially. This means that if your code encounters an exception, the exception is at a specific point, and the code can handle it normally. In multicore scenarios multiple exceptions could occur, because more threads are running on multiple processors concurrently. Because of this, PLINQ provides a special way for intercepting and handling exceptions. Such a way is constituted by the `AggregateException` class that is specific for exceptions within parallelism. Such a class exposes a couple of interesting members, such as `Flatten` that is a method that turns it into a single exception and `InnerExceptions` that is a property storing a collection of `InnerException` objects, each representing one of the occurred exceptions.

DISABLE JUST MY CODE

In order to correctly catch an `AggregateException` you need to disable the Just My Code debugging in the debug options, otherwise the code execution will break on the query and will not allow you to investigate the exception.

Consider the following code, in which an array of strings stores some null values and that causes `NullReferenceException` at runtime:

```
Private Sub HandlingExceptions()
    Dim strings() As String = New String() {"Test",
                                             Nothing,
                                             Nothing,
                                             "Test"}

    'Just add "AsParallel"
    Try
        Dim query = strings.AsParallel.
                    Where(Function(s) s.StartsWith("T")).
                    Select(Function(s) s)
        For Each item In query
            Console.WriteLine(item)
        Next

    Catch ex As AggregateException
```

```
      For Each problem In ex.InnerExceptions
          Console.WriteLine(problem.ToString)
      Next

    Catch ex As Exception

    Finally
        Console.ReadLine()
    End Try
End Sub
```

In a single-core scenario a single `NullReferenceException` is caught and handled the first time the code encounters the error. In multicore scenarios an `AggregateException` could happen due to multiple threads running on multiple processors; therefore, you cannot control where and how many exceptions can be thrown. Consequently, the `AggregateException` stores information on such exceptions. The previous code shows how you can iterate the `InnerExceptions` property.

Summary

Multicore and multiprocessor architectures are part of the real world today. Because of this, .NET Framework 4.0 provides a specific LINQ implementation known as Parallel LINQ that allows scaling query executions over multiple threads and processors so that you can get benefits in improving performances of your code. In this chapter you learned how to invoke the `AsParallel` method for creating parallelized queries and comparing them to classic LINQ queries. You also saw how to control queries forcing parallelism, implementing cancellation, setting the maximum number of tasks, and handling the `AggregateException` exception. In Chapter 45 you get more granular information on the Task Parallel Library so that you can have a complete overview of parallel computing with .NET Framework 4.0 and Visual Basic 2010.

CHAPTER 30

Creating Windows Forms 4.0 Applications

Client applications need to offer a graphical user interface to make applications easier to use and more intuitive. For the past years Windows Forms has been the unique way to provide user interfaces in client .NET applications. It is a straightforward infrastructure that is popular among developers. But technology goes on and new additions have been introduced to the .NET Framework since version 3.0. This chapter provides an overview about what Win Forms is today and about what's new in Win Forms 4.0, providing a sample application that shows how you can take advantage of the few additions. Windows Forms is considered obsolete. Being part of the .NET Framework, this book must provide an overview. But you see something more interesting in Chapter 31, "Creating WPF Applications," and subsequent chapters. For now, enjoy what's new in Win Forms 4.0.

What Windows Forms Is Today

The goal of this chapter is to provide an overview of the Windows Forms technology summarizing how Windows Forms works and how you can take advantage of recent .NET features. This is because Windows Forms has been for many years the one and only user interface platform, whereas with the growth of Windows Presentation Foundation, it becomes necessary to provide information on this quite new technology. Windows Forms is quite obsolete when compared to the power and flexibility of WPF, but.NET Framework necessarily needs to provide support for Windows Forms because it is settled in application development, but you have to know that Microsoft will no longer invest in Win Forms. This means that you can, of course, use it in your applications, but the strong suggestion is that you begin taking a serious look at WPF because tomorrow's user interfaces will be based on it. This chapter assumes that you have at least one year of experience in developing Windows applications with Windows Forms. If not, or if you are not interested in getting information on what's new, you can skip this chapter and get friendly with WPF in Chapter 31.

Creating Windows Forms Applications

Visual Studio 2010 allows creating Windows Forms applications the same way as in previous versions, so you should be familiar with the steps described in this section. To create a Windows Forms application, follow these steps:

1. Click the **New Project** command in the File menu.

2. In the New project dialog select the Windows Forms Application template in the Windows folder. Figure 30.1 shows how you can accomplish this.

3. Click **OK** to create the new project and then design your application with user controls.

FIGURE 30.1   Creating a Windows Forms application.

When Visual Studio completes creating the new project, you notice that nothing changes from the previous versions of the IDE. You still see the designer and the Toolbox on the left showing available controls. Figure 30.2 shows what you get at this point.

There are no particular new features in this area, so let's discover what is new.

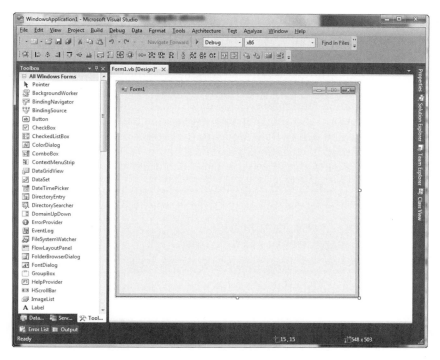

FIGURE 30.2   The Windows Forms designer is ready.

What's New in Windows Forms 4.0

As mentioned at the beginning of this chapter, Microsoft no longer invests in Windows Forms. Because of this, only one new feature is constituted by the Microsoft Chart control that allows adding chart graphics capabilities to your applications. This user control is available in the Data tab in the Toolbox. Later in this chapter you see an example about this addition.

THE TRUE STORY OF CHART

Chart control was originally provided as a separate download for Microsoft .NET Framework 3.5 with Service Pack 1. That was the first time that this control appeared. In .NET Framework 4.0 the Chart control is part of the platform as a new addition. This is the reason why we consider the control as one new thing in Win Forms 4.0.

You still find the WPF Interoperability tab containing the ElementHost control that allows utilizing WPF contents and the Visual Basic PowerPacks 3.0 controls.

Available Windows Forms Controls

Windows Forms offer lots of user controls, but they will not be summarized here. You can find a full list on the official MSDN portal, which is available at the following address: http://msdn.microsoft.com/en-us/library/3xdhey7w(VS.100).aspx.

30

Building Windows Forms Applications with ADO.NET Entity Framework and Chart Control

The goal of this chapter is to show how you can take advantage of the new features in.NET Framework 4.0 with Windows Forms. In this section you learn how to create an application that queries and manipulates master-detail data from the Northwind database via the ADO.NET Entity Framework, also showing data results as a chart. When you create a new Win Form project, add a new Entity Data Model to the project pointing to the Northwind database as you learned in Chapter 27, "Introducing the ADO.NET Entity Framework." The EDM needs to get the Customers, Orders, and Order_Details tables. Ensure that your result looks like Figure 30.3.

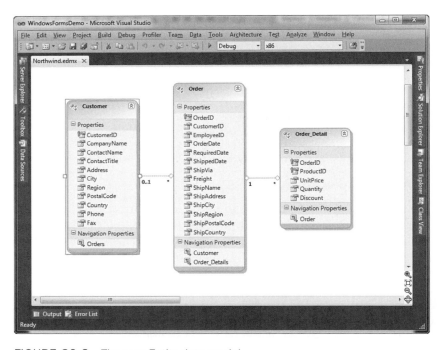

FIGURE 30.3   The new Entity data model.

We want to provide a detailed view for customers, a data grid for associated orders, and a chart representation for order details. To keep in mind what you accomplish, Figure 30.4 shows the final application running.

Now you need to add data sources so that you can drag them from the Data Sources window. Opposite to WPF applications, in Windows Forms you need to manually add entities at this point. Follow these steps:

1. Select the **Add New Data Source** command from the Data menu.

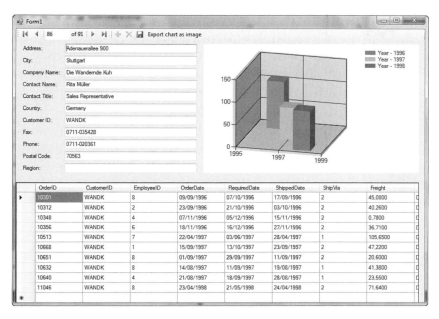

FIGURE 30.4   The sample application of this chapter while running.

2. In the first dialog, choose **Object** and then click **Next**. This allows you to choose entities as data sources.

3. Flag the **Customer**, **Order**, and **Order_Detail** object, as shown in Figure 30.5.

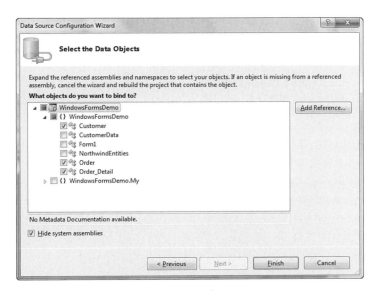

FIGURE 30.5   Choosing objects as data sources.

When you click **Finish**, your data sources will be available in the **Data Sources** window, as shown in Figure 30.6, which is enabled when you are back on the form. Notice that Visual Studio previously added the `NorthwindEntities` object, but you cannot directly drag its children onto the form, opposite to WPF.

FIGURE 30.6   The Data Sources window shows entities.

Now you are ready to drag your controls. In Data Sources, select the **Details** view for the `Customer` object using the combo box that appears when you click `Customer`. Now drag `Customer` onto the form's surface and wait until the appropriate `BindingNavigator` and `BindingSource` controls are generated. Right-click the **Save** button and click **Enable** so that you can use it to save changes. When ready, drag the `Orders` object (nested in `Customer`) onto the form and wait until Visual Studio creates a `BindingSource` for orders and a `DataGridView`. When ready, select the **Chart** control from the Data tab in the Toolbox and drag it onto the form. Because the `Chart` control can also export graphics to images, add a `SaveFileDialog` control. Finally, add a new button on the `CustomersBindingNavigator` toolbar and name it **ExportChartToolStripButton**, ensuring that the `DisplayStyle` property is set to **Text** and that the `Text` property is assigned with **Export Chart as Image**. Figure 30.7 shows how the designer looks after this sequence of operations, but of course you can change the controls' position as you like.

Now it is time to write Visual Basic code, so switch to the code editor. The first step is to declare the object context and populate data sources. At class level, write the following code:

```
Private northwind As NorthwindEntities
```

```
Private Sub PopulateDataSources()
    'Populates the CustomersBindingSource
    'with Customers from the model using
```

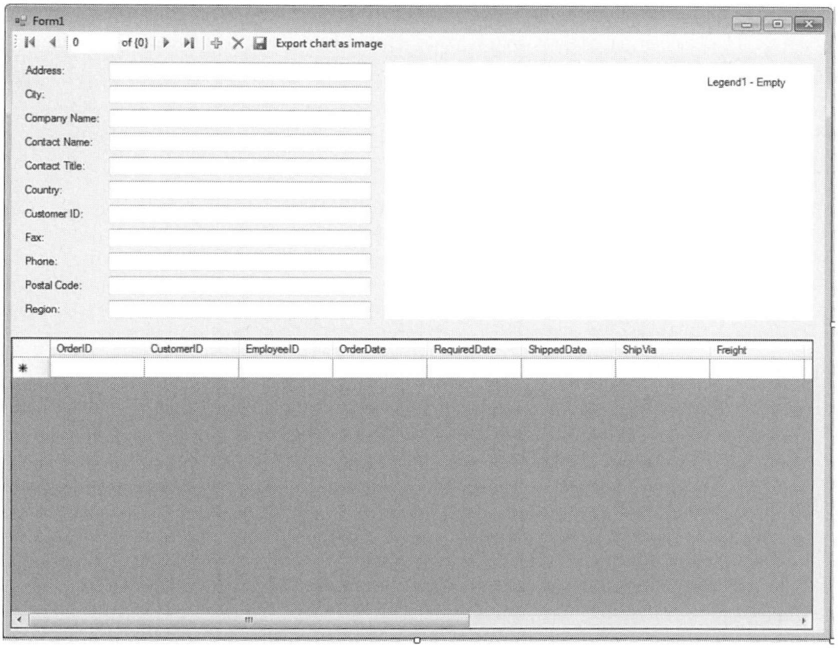

FIGURE 30.7   The form after the design operations.

```
    'eager loading
    Me.CustomerBindingSource.DataSource = northwind.
                                        Customers.Include("Orders")

    'Populates the OrderBindingSource
    'establishing a relationships with Customers
    Me.OrdersBindingSource.DataSource = CustomerBindingSource
    Me.OrdersBindingSource.DataMember = "Orders"

    'To be set explicitly in EF
    Me.OrdersBindingSource.AllowNew = True
End Sub
```

ADDING LINQ QUERIES

In the preceding example the full lists of customers and orders are retrieved, but you could also replace the code with a LINQ query getting only the needed information. For example, you could filter only customers living outside the United States.

Notice how the OrdersBindingSource is populated assigning the CustomersBindingSource and then assigning the DataMember property with only the effectively needed collection. This establishes a relationship between the two entity sets. Also notice how you need to explicitly set the AllowNew property to True if you want to provide the ability of adding data. This is specific to Entity Framework where the operation is not automated. Now provide a constructor whose body will instantiate the object context and a Form.Load event handler that will populate the data sources:

```
Public Sub New()


    ' This call is required by the designer.
    InitializeComponent()

    ' Add any initialization after the InitializeComponent() call.
    Me.northwind = New NorthwindEntities
End Sub

Private Sub Form1_Load(ByVal sender As System.Object,
                        ByVal e As System.EventArgs) Handles MyBase.Load
    PopulateDataSources()
End Sub
```

HANDLING EVENTS

In Windows Forms you do not need to explicitly set event handlers via the AddHandler keyword because this is accomplished behind the scenes by Visual Studio. When you add a control, the IDE provides a WithEvents declaration so that providing event handlers is reduced to writing a Sub that respects the appropriate delegate signature and that refers to a particular event via the Handles keyword. It is also important to mention that you do not need to manually write the event handler stub. You can simply select from the Visual Studio Class Name and Method Name combo boxes both the object and the event you need to handle, as shown in Figure 30.8. Selecting an event generates the event handler stub for you.

Now let's write an event handler for saving changes. You can still use the Visual Studio Class Name and Method Name combo boxes, or if in design mode, double-click the **Save** button to let Visual Studio generate an event handler stub. The code for the event handler can take advantage of techniques discussed in Chapter 27 about updates and optimistic concurrency, so it will be the following:

```
Private Sub CustomerBindingNavigatorSaveItem_Click(ByVal sender As Object,
                                ByVal e As EventArgs) _
```

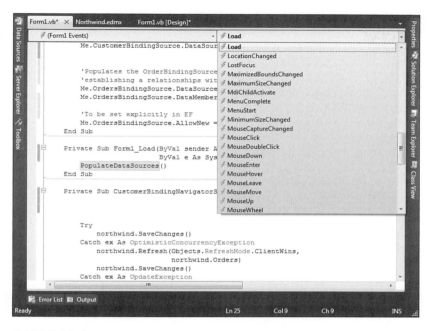

FIGURE 30.8   Using Visual Studio's Class Name and Method Name combo boxes to automate event handler stubs generation.

```
                                                       Handles _
                                  CustomerBindingNavigatorSaveItem.Click

        Try
            northwind.SaveChanges()
        Catch ex As OptimisticConcurrencyException
            northwind.Refresh(Objects.RefreshMode.ClientWins,
                            northwind.Orders)
            northwind.SaveChanges()
        Catch ex As UpdateException
            MessageBox.Show(ex.Message)
        Catch ex As Exception
            MessageBox.Show(ex.ToString)
        End Try
    End Sub
```

At the moment you have all the code necessary for manipulating data. Remember from Chapter 27 that the object context in the Entity Framework can keep track of changes during the application lifetime. According to this, the instance of the NorthwindEntities class can manage insert/update/delete operations and changes as well.

WHAT ABOUT LINQ TO SQL?

There are situations where you might want to use a LINQ to SQL object model instead of an Entity Data Model. To accomplish this, you first establish the database connection and add a LINQ to SQL class to your project, dragging database objects to the designer's surface. Next you simply need to add new data sources as you did previously for EDMs, choosing object data sources and then selecting the desired entities from the available one. When done, you can practice what you learned in Chapter 25, "LINQ to SQL," including validation.

Providing Custom Validation

Following what you learned in Chapter 27, you can provide custom data validation on entities. For example, imagine you want to validate the user input on the `ShippedDate` order's property ensuring that its value is not greater than today's date. To accomplish this, add a new partial class named `Order` and manage the `OnShippedDateChanging` partial method as follows:

```
Partial Public Class Order
    Private Sub OnShippedDateChanging(ByVal value As Date?)
        If value > Date.Today Then
        Throw New _
        ArgumentException("The shipped date cannot be greater than today",
                          "value")
        End If
    End Sub
End Class
```

Now switch back to the code for the main form and add the following event handler associated to the `OrdersBindingSourceControl` that allows handling exceptions in a user interface-oriented fashion:

```
Private Sub OrdersBindingSource_DataError(ByVal sender As Object,
                                  ByVal e As System.Windows.Forms.
                                  BindingManagerDataErrorEventArgs)_
                                  Handles OrdersBindingSource.
                                  DataError
    MessageBox.Show(e.Exception.Message, "", MessageBoxButtons.OK,
                MessageBoxIcon.Error)
End Sub
```

You can then eventually add custom validation for any other entity you need following the same steps. When running the application, if the user tries to enter an invalid date, an `ArgumentException` is thrown providing the specified error message.

Understanding Chart Control

The Microsoft Chart Control is defined within the System.Windows.Forms.DataVisualization.dll assembly and is exposed by the System.Windows.Forms.DataVisualization.Charting namespace. It allows creating chart graphics from different data sources that can be bound manually or take advantage of automated data-binding features. In this section you learn about the most important features of the chart control so that you can easily get started.

FINDING DOCUMENTATION

Microsoft offers extensive documentation on the Chart control. The first document is the MSDN official page that is available at the following address: http://msdn.microsoft.com/en-us/library/system.windows.forms. datavisualization.charting.chart(VS.100).aspx. Next check out Alex Gorev's blog that contains a lot of practical examples and that is reachable at http://blogs.msdn.com/ alexgor/.

The good news is that you can take advantage of the Visual Studio Designer to completely manage the Chart control with the mouse. Now refer to Figure 30.4 and watch how the graphic is drawn. When you create a new chart, the chart offers a drawing area. This area is represented by a collection named ChartAreas. Each item in the collection, therefore a single ChartArea, represents the place where the chart will be drawn. Generally a single ChartArea is required for simple charts but you can edit the behavior of each item. Chart areas support 3D graphics. For example, select the Chart control in the designer and open the Properties window. Click the **Browse** button for the ChartAreas property, which brings up the ChartArea Collection Editor dialog. Here you can add new areas or edit existing ones. By default a single area is provided. Expand the **Area3DStyle** item and set the following properties to enable 3D charts:

▶ Enable3D as True

▶ Rotation as 15; this provides better visibility in our scenario

▶ LightStyle as Realistic; this improves lightening on the chart

Figure 30.9 shows the result of these operations.

You notice that changes are automatically reflected to the control at design time. The second most important property is another collection, named Series. The collection stores Series objects, representing items in the chart. You access single Series via the indexer. To edit the series at design time, open the Series Collection Editor dialog by clicking the **Browse** button related to the Series property in the Properties window. By default, every time you create a Chart control a default Series named Series1 is added. Figure 30.10 shows the dialog pointing to the default Series, which provides a lot of properties, but now you see the most important.

Series are divided into points. X points represent each item on the X-axis, while Y points represent each item on the Y-axis. Each series is bound to a specific ChartArea via the

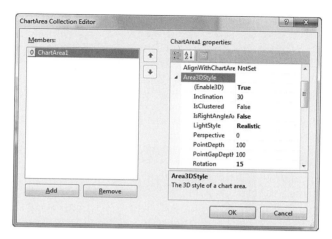

FIGURE 30.9   Designing chart areas.

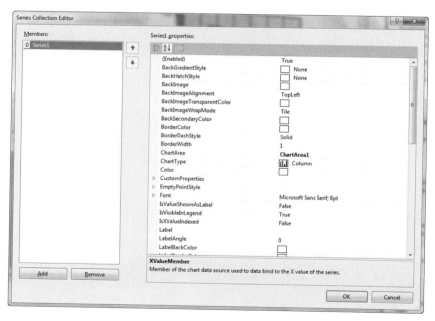

FIGURE 30.10   Designing chart series.

ChartArea property. You can change the appearance of style by setting the ChartType property that is set to Column by default. For example, you might want a pie chart or other kinds of graphics. Pyramid, Pie, or Funnel are just examples of available layouts that you can examine by simply expanding the combo box. Series can be data bound, either manually or in code, for example assigning LINQ queries results or DataSets. The DataSource property allows assigning data sources, and you can also specify what objects must be bound to the X-axis (XValueMember) and to the Y-axis (YValueMembers). You can pick up existing objects by simply opening the combo boxes. (Later in this chapter you see how to data bind in code.) The X-axis and Y-axis can show only primitive types; generally you leave the job of binding the most appropriate type to the .NET Framework, but you can change the setting of the XValueType and YValueType property that are set to Auto by default. Chart supports data binding from different data sources, summarized in the following list:

▶ IEnumerable, IList and IListSource objects; this means also LINQ query results

▶ DataSets, DataView, and DataReader objects

▶ Arrays

▶ OleDbDataAdapter, OleDbCommand, SqlDataAdapter, and SqlCommand objects

You can perform data binding in code invoking several different methods. DataBindTable automatically creates series starting from a table-like object (such as entity sets from Entity Framework or DataTables) and performs simple binding for X and Y values where X has the same name and no multiple Y values are allowed. DataBindCrossTable works similarly but provides grouping functionalities allowing multiple Y values (as used in the code example). The DataSource property and the DataBind method provide support for multiple Y values and perform simple bindings, being also used by the Visual Studio Designer. You can also perform data binding on specific points, invoking the Points.DataBind method that provides the ability to provide different data sources for X and Y values and multiple Y values. It is powerful and flexible but requires more work. For each series you can specify a Label that contains text to be shown onto each item in the chart, a Tooltip that contains text to be shown just when you pass with the mouse pointer over items in the chart, and Legend that provides a description about the series. Another interesting property for the Chart control is the Palette that provides different colors for the graphics. At this point it is time to write code to populate your chart. You can also discover some other interesting features while writing code.

Populating the Chart Control

Now we have to write code to show data in the Chart control. Imagine you want to get the total cost that customers paid to your company for orders, divided by year. To accomplish this, we first need a custom class for storing the year and the total amount per year. Add a new class to the project and name it CustomerData. The code for the new class is the following:

```
Public Class CustomerData
    Public Property TotalAmount As Decimal
    Public Property Year As Integer
End Class
```

Then we can write the following LINQ query, which creates an IEnumerable(Of CustomerData) (the custom class that was defined at the beginning of this section) and that can be bound to the chart:

```
Function Query(ByVal CustomerID As String) As  _
```

```
        IEnumerable(Of CustomerData)

    Dim result = From cust In northwind.Customers.Include("Orders")
                 Where cust.CustomerID = CustomerID
                 Join ordr In northwind.Orders.Include("Order_Details")
                 On ordr.CustomerID Equals cust.CustomerID
                 Let totalAmount =
                 Aggregate ord_det In ordr.Order_Details
                 Into Sum(ord_det.UnitPrice)
                 Select New CustomerData With {.TotalAmount = totalAmount,
                                               .Year =
                                    ordr.OrderDate.Value.Year}


    Return result.AsEnumerable
End Function
```

Notice how the Let keyword allows declaring a temporary variable that is assigned with another LINQ query, which returns the amount of price. The method receives a CustomerID argument that filters orders depending on the specified customer. This method needs to be invoked each time you select a different customer. To accomplish this, you can handle the CurrentChanged event from the CustomersBindingSource object that is raised every time you move between customers. In the event handler you need to get the instance of the current customer that is provided by the CurrentItem property and then invoke the Query method passing the CustomerID. The following code demonstrates this:

```
Private Sub CustomersBindingSource_CurrentChanged(ByVal sender As Object,
                                            ByVal e As EventArgs) _
                        Handles CustomerBindingSource.
                        CurrentChanged


  'Get the instance of the current customer
  Dim currentItem As Customer = CType(Me.CustomerBindingSource.Current,
                              Customer)


  Dim source = Query(currentItem.CustomerID)
  Try
      'Required to refresh the chart
      Chart1.Series.Clear()
      'Groups by Year, shows the year on the X axis,
      'shows the total price on the Y axis, formats
      'the tooltip as currency
      Chart1.DataBindCrossTable(source, "Year",
                                "Year",
                                "TotalAmount",
```

```
                                    "Tooltip=TotalAmount{C2}")

    Catch ex As Exception
    End Try
End Sub
```

Notice how you need to clear the series before binding again; otherwise the chart will not be correctly updated. The `DataBindCrossTable` method takes different arguments. The first one is the data source, which is the query result. The second one is the member that the result must be grouped by (`Year`). The third argument is the member that provides text for items on the X-axis. In this case, each value of the `Year` property will be the X-axis text for items in the chart. The fourth argument gives values to the Y-axis while the last argument allows specifying additional properties at runtime. In this particular case the `Tooltip` property for each series shows the total amount formatted as currency. You specify formatting options between brackets. Basically with just this line of code you can provide full data binding from your query result (or another data source) to the Chart control. To complete the sample application, let's provide code for exporting the graphic to an image file. This is another great capability of the Chart control. Just add the following event handler:

```
Imports System.Windows.Forms.DataVisualization.Charting
....
Private Sub ExportChartToolStripButton_Click(ByVal sender As System.Object,
                                    ByVal e As System.EventArgs) _
        Handles ExportChartToolStripButton.Click
    With SaveFileDialog1
        .Filter = "Jpeg files¦*.jpg¦Png files¦*.png¦" & _
                "Bmp files¦*.bmp¦Tiff files¦*.tiff¦Gif files¦*.gif"
        .ShowDialog()
        If String.IsNullOrEmpty(.FileName) = False Then
            Me.Chart1.SaveImage(.FileName,
            CType(.FilterIndex - 1, ChartImageFormat))
        End If
    End With
End Sub
```

The Chart control provides a `SaveImage` method that takes the target filename as the first argument and a `ChartImageFormat` as the second argument. This is an enumeration that summarizes available file formats and that are .NET supported formats. To simplify the code, in this case the `SaveFileDialog1.Filter` string has been structured so that the related `FilterIndex` corresponds to the appropriate value in the `ChartImageFormat`. In this way you can simply work on the `FilterIndex` instead to provide a conditional block to understand what file format the user selected.

30

Running the Sample Application

You are ready to run the application. When you run it, you get a result similar to Figure 30.4. You can try to move between customers to see how the chart graphic will be updated. You can also try to add and edit orders to complete CRUD operations. Finally you can test exporting graphic to images.

Summary

This chapter presented information on Windows Forms in Visual Basic 2010 and .NET Framework 4.0. Basically you saw how there are no differences in the Win Forms architecture compared to the previous .NET versions, but you got an overview of how to implement Entity Data Models and the new Chart control. For this component you also got a high-level overview. The sample application allows creating a master-details form that can access data from the Northwind database and that shows a chart with data results. Although still very used, Windows Forms is an obsolete technology for creating user interfaces. Subsequently you learn about the new fashion: Windows Presentation Foundation.

CHAPTER 31

Creating WPF Applications

Over the years, the requirement for high-quality applications dramatically increased. Modern technologies enable users to perform even more complex tasks; technology and computers are a significant part of users' lives. Computer applications need to respond to such requests. The user experience is something that cannot be disregarded anymore, even if an application works perfectly on data access. The more complex the task an application can perform, the more important is the need of an interactive user interface that enables the user to easily perform tasks through the application. And this is something that is strictly related to different kinds of applications: business applications, home applications, and multimedia and entertainment applications. For many years developers could build user interfaces based on the Windows Forms, which has been a good and important framework for creating user experiences with the .NET technology. Windows Forms has big limitations, especially if you need to create dynamic interfaces or complex data-bindings. With the purpose of providing a unified programming model for building advanced user interfaces, being suitable for combining data access, dynamic interfaces, multimedia, and documents capabilities, Microsoft created the Windows Presentation Foundation technology (WPF), which dramatically increases developer productivity and also offers a great environment for styling the application layout by a professional designer. WPF combines in one framework all you need to build new generation applications. If you are an experienced WPF developer, maybe this chapter is just a quick recap for you. If you are new to WPF, this and the following chapters give you the basics for beginning to build modern applications with Visual Basic 2010.

What Is WPF?

Windows Presentation Foundation, also referred to as WPF, is the most recent framework from Microsoft for building user interfaces in desktop applications. WPF is not intended to be a replacement for Windows Forms, whereas it can be considered as a revolutionary alternative for building rich client applications. As explained in Chapter 30, "Creating Windows Forms 4.0 Applications," Windows Forms' development will no longer be continued in favor of WPF. Windows Presentation Foundation offers several advantages that make user interface development straightforward. First, it is built on the top of the Microsoft DirectX® graphic libraries, meaning that WPF applications can embed audio, videos, pictures, animations, and 3D graphics, all in a .NET-oriented fashion, with few lines of code. You can create rich client applications continuing to write Visual Basic code as you are already used to doing. WPF takes advantage of the GPU support of a graphics card, but it is also fully compatible with software rendering and can fall back on that when a GPU is not available (although it is actually expensive in terms of performance). Second, WPF has a powerful data-binding engine that makes it easier to build data-oriented applications. Third, it provides a separation layer between the developer and the designer so that professional designers can completely restyle the application's layout with specific tools, improving what the developer built. In my personal experience, many developers are afraid of WPF because it completely changes the way developers built the presentation layer of their applications. WPF completely changes the way you think of your user interfaces but does not change the way you write Visual Basic code. Of course, WPF has some big differences with Windows Forms in its architecture; therefore, you necessarily need a different approach to some problems. As an example, WPF handles events via the routed events that are completely different from the event infrastructure in Windows Forms. You can handle events in WPF the same way you do in Windows Forms. The way you write code is basically the same, on the top of different technologies. This is the most important feature of the .NET Framework. WPF was first introduced in 2006 with .NET Framework 3.0 and special extensions for Visual Studio 2005 extensions.

Improvements in WPF 4

Several improvements were introduced to WPF with .NET Framework 3.5 and Visual Studio 2008; but with .NET Framework 4.0 and Visual Studio 2010, WPF reaches a high level of productivity. You can now build applications with full Windows 7 support and with multitouch features. The Visual Studio 2010 designer has been highly improved to make your WPF experience even more straightforward (including the visual data-binding new user controls such as the DataGrid). If you played with previous editions of WPF, you may remember how the designer lacked some important features that were instead available in the Windows Forms Designer. Now lots of things have been fixed and improved so that existing Windows Forms developers can move to WPF with more simplicity.

PERSONAL SUGGESTIONS ON APPROACHING WPF

I delivered several technical speeches on Windows Presentation Foundation, and one thing I noticed is that lots of developers do not approach WPF correctly. This is because the Internet is full of impressive demo applications with enhanced user interfaces and graphical experience and there are lots of presentation demos that are built to show advanced WPF topics. Seeing a 3D application with animations is surely impressive but can be quite frustrating if you try to reproduce it after a few days' experience with WPF. Because of this, often developers do not continue studying WPF. The best approach is instead to understand what one needs to work with WPF even if the UI is not so impressive. When you know how user controls work and how they are built, you can easily search within the MSDN library to make them nicer.

In the next sections you learn the foundations of WPF and learn about specific features of this interesting technology.

NOTE

You may have noticed that this book dedicates just one chapter to Windows Forms whereas five chapters are about WPF. This is not strange; this is why WPF is becoming very popular among .NET developers and Microsoft is heavily investing in WPF for their own applications. The same Visual Studio 2010's code editor is built with WPF, and most of the new IDE extensibility features take advantage of WPF. You need to learn how WPF works so that you can be ready to move your existing WinForms applications to WPF if your customer requires this or so that you can present innovative applications to customers. This is a language-oriented book; therefore, covering every aspect of the WPF technology is not possible. If you wish to learn more about the WPF technology, consider *windows Presentation Foundation Unleashed* from Sams Publishing.

WPF Architecture

WPF relies on a layered architecture that is represented in Figure 31.1. The first layer is the Windows operating system. The second layer is constituted by the combination of two communicating layers: User32, which is the part of the operating system responsible for exchanging messages with applications, and the DirectX libraries, which are the real power of WPF. The next layer is named Milcore and is written in unmanaged code. It is responsible for integrating the unmanaged area of the architecture with the managed architecture that starts from the next layer, the Common Language Runtime, which is basically the root of every managed activity or layer. The PresentationCore is the first WPF layer that is responsible for implementing several important features such as the XAML language (covered later) or the integration with media contents. The next layer is the PresentationFramework, which is fundamental because it exposes all namespaces and classes that developers can take advantage of for building applications (and that are also utilized by Visual Studio when generating new projects).

FIGURE 31.1   Windows Presentation Foundation architecture.

PresentationFramework exposes namespaces and classes through a complex hierarchy of inheritance, in which the root class is `System.Object`. The hierarchy provides the infrastructure for the user interface elements. This hierarchy is composed of the following list of classes, where each class inherits from the previous one:

▶ `System.Object`

▶ `System.Threading.DispatcherObject`

▶ `System.Windows.DependencyObject`

▶ `System.Windows.Media.Visual`

▶ `System.Windows.UIElement`

▶ `System.Windows.FrameworkElement`

▶ `System.Windows.Controls.Control`

The `System.Threading.DispatcherObject` is responsible for threading and messages that WPF relies on. The dispatcher takes advantage of the User32 messages for performing cross thread calls. The WPF architecture is also based on a complex properties infrastructure that in most cases replaces methods and events. This is because a property-based architecture is preferable for showing contents of UI controls and because they better integrate with other development models. To provide this infrastructure, the WPF architecture exposes the `System.Windows.DependencyObject` class that implements a common set of properties for derived objects. The main capability of this class is keeping track of properties changes so that bound objects can automatically update their status according to those changes. `System.Windows.Media.Visual` is responsible for the graphic rendering of all elements belonging to the user interface, under the form of a tree (known as Visual Tree that is covered later). `System.Windows.UIElement` adds other functionalities to the infrastructure, such as the ability to receive input from the user and other overridable members. `System.Windows.FrameworkElement` is important, exposing special features of WPF such as objects lifetime, styles, animations, and the data-binding engine. The last class is `System.Windows.Controls.Control` that is basically the base class for WPF user controls and that adds further functionalities that empower base controls and custom user controls. Now that you have a basic knowledge of the WPF architecture, it is time to create the first application.

Building WPF Applications with Visual Studio 2010

You create WPF applications in Visual Studio 2010 by selecting one of the available project templates. WPF project templates are available in the Windows section of the New Project window, as shown in Figure 31.2, and are summarized in Table 31.1.

FIGURE 31.2   Available project templates for WPF applications.

TABLE 31.1   WPF Project Templates

Template	Description
WPF application	Allows creating a WPF desktop application for Windows
WPF browser application	Allows creating a WPF application that can be run within a Web browser
WPF User Control Library	Allows creating WPF user controls
WPF Custom Control Library	Allows redefining WPF controls at code level

This chapter shows you WPF in action with a desktop Windows application. Select the **WPF application** template and name the new project **WPFDemo_Chapter31**. After a few seconds, the IDE displays, as shown in Figure 31.3.

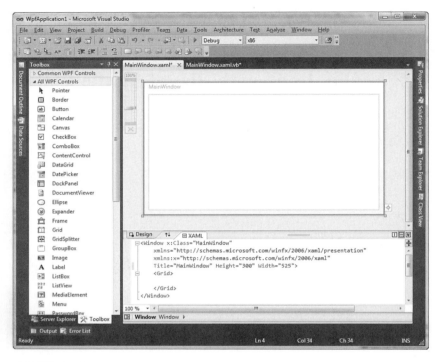

FIGURE 31.3   The IDE is ready on a new WPF project.

As you can see, things are a little different from a Windows Forms project. In the upper side of the IDE you can see the designer showing the main window of the new application. On the left side there is the Toolbox; this is a tool that you already understand and that contains specific WPF controls. In the lower side of the IDE, there is a special code editor for the eXtensible Application Markup Code (simply known as XAML, pronounced as *ZAMEL*) that you must know as a WPF developer. The next section describes XAML and explains how it works. In Solution Explorer you can see a new kind of files, with the .xaml extension. Each .Xaml file can represent a window, control (or set of controls), or set of resources. For each .Xaml file there is a Visual Basic code-behind file (with a .xaml.vb extension) that you can access by simply expanding the filename. The reason for this separation between the .Xaml file and the .Xaml.vb file is part of a key concept in the WPF development, which is the separation of roles between developers and designers that is described better in the next section.

WPF applications enable you to take advantage of the My Project designer similarly to other kinds of client applications. If you examine the window, you see these similarities, and you also see how different options are self-explanatory.

Understanding the eXtensible Application Markup Language (XAML)

In Windows Presentation Foundation applications, the user interface is defined via the *eXtensible Application Markup Language*, also referred to as *XAML*, which is a markup language that allows defining the interface in a declarative mode and that derives from the XML language. This markup language is revolutionary because it allows separating the roles of designers and developers. Professional designers can style the application's layout by using specific tools that allow generating and editing XAML without the need of knowing the programming fundamentals, leaving unchanged the code that empowers the application.

NOTE ON DESIGNER TOOLS

Designers typically use professional tools such as Microsoft Expression Blend for styling WPF and Silverlight applications. Because this book's focus is developer-oriented, the usage of Expression Blend for manipulating XAML is covered, whereas the focus is on what you do need to know as a developer from within Visual Studio 2010.

This discussion provides an explanation that for each .Xaml file there is a VB code-behind file. The .Xaml file contains XAML code that defines the user interface, whereas the .Xaml.vb code-behind file contains Visual Basic code that makes the user interface alive with the rest of the application. XAML logic is simple: Each Xml element represents a user control, whereas each Xml attribute represents a property to a control. Because of the special Xml syntax, XAML refers to a specific Xml schema for WPF controls.

XAML AND SILVERLIGHT

You need to learn how XAML works if you are also interested in developing rich Internet applications with Microsoft Silverlight. As explained in Chapter 39, "Building Rich Internet Applications with Silverlight," Silverlight is also based on XAML for the UI side.

Now take a look at Listing 31.1 that simply contains the code generated by Visual Studio 2010 when a new project is created.

LISTING 31.1   XAML Default Code for a WPF project

```
<Window x:Class="MainWindow"
    xmlns="http://schemas.microsoft.com/winfx/2006/xaml/presentation"
    xmlns:x="http://schemas.microsoft.com/winfx/2006/xaml"
    Title="MainWindow" Height="240" Width="500">
    <Grid>

    </Grid>
</Window>
```

In WPF applications every window is wrapped by a `System.Windows.Window` control. The root element in the XAML code is a `Window` element. The `x:Class` attribute (which is actually a property) points to the Visual Basic class that handles the Window on the runtime side. The `Title` property simply contains text shown on the window's title bar. `Width` and `Height` are self-explanatory properties that define the window's size. Also notice how Xml schemas are imported via `xmlns` tags; such schemas have two purposes: enabling IntelliSense in the XAML code editor and ensuring that only valid elements are used in the XAML code. `Grid` is one of the WPF *panels*. Different from Windows Forms, user controls in WPF are arranged within panels; the last part of this introduces them better. By the way, now you understand better what was explained at the beginning of this section: In XAML every element (except for resources) represents a control with properties (attributes). XAML offers a hierarchical organization of controls. For example a `Window` can contain one or more panel that can contain other panels that can contain controls, and so on. This hierarchical logic is straightforward because it enables great customizations of the interface, as you see in this chapter and subsequent ones. As previously stated, the XAML editor fully supports IntelliSense. You can check this out by simply writing code, as demonstrated in Figure 31.4.

FIGURE 31.4   The XAML code editor fully supports IntelliSense.

You are not obliged to manually type XAML code to design your user interface. Every time you drag a control from the Toolbox onto the designer, Visual Studio generates the related XAML code for you. In some circumstances manually editing the XAML code is a good task to fix a controls' position. Moreover, although initially writing XAML can seem annoying, when you understand its hierarchical logic, it becomes straightforward, also due to IntelliSense. Generally what you perform manually writing XAML can be accomplished with the design tools.

Declaring and Using Controls with the Designer and XAML

To add controls to the user interface, you have two possibilities: dragging controls from the Toolbox onto the designer surface and manually writing XAML. For a better under-standing, we first show how to drag from the Toolbox. With the Toolbox open, click the **Button** control and drag it onto the designer. When you release it, the IDE should look like Figure 31.5.

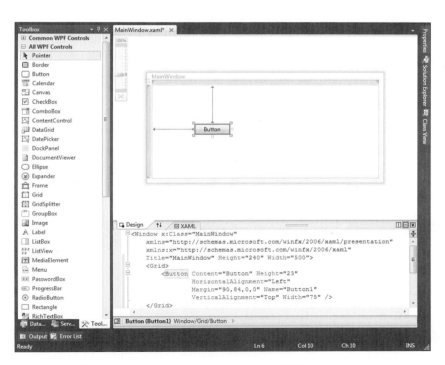

FIGURE 31.5   Dragging controls and generating XAML.

As you can see from Figure 31.5, Visual Studio also generates the XAML code for the controls you add to the UI. For the new button, this is the XAML code generated:

```
<Button Content="Button" Height="23"
        HorizontalAlignment="Left"
```

```
Margin="90,84,0,0" Name="Button1"
VerticalAlignment="Top" Width="75" />
```

Confirming that each control is represented as an Xml element, the most interesting properties here are Name, which assigns an identifier to the control, and Content, which stores the control's content. To manage your controls you now have two choices: editing its XAML code or using the Properties window, which is represented in Figure 31.6.

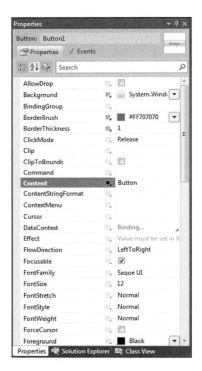

FIGURE 31.6   Managing controls with the Properties window.

If you are not familiar with WPF, probably you can find lots of properties that you do not know yet. You can learn most of these properties in this book and in your further studies; what it is important here is to understand how the designer allows taking control of the UI members. The Properties window for WPF controls also offers a special tab that you can enable by clicking the **Events** button (in the upper side of the tool window) and that enables associating event handlers to each event exposed by that specific control (see Figure 31.7). Obviously event handlers are written in Visual Basic code; the next section explains how you handle events.

Declarative and Imperative Modes

Writing (or letting Visual Studio to generate) XAML code is known as *declarative mode*. This is because XAML simply allows declaring elements required by the user interface but does not allow them taking actions. By the way, an important statement is that with

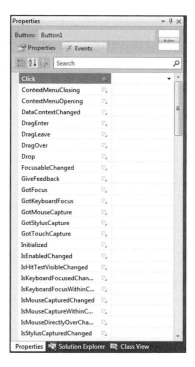

FIGURE 31.7   The Properties window allows selecting event handlers. Simply click on the combo near the desired event and pick an event handler.

Visual Basic (or Visual C# as well) you can do anything you do in XAML, meaning that you can declare user interface elements in Visual Basic code and add them to the user interface at runtime. Moreover, managing controls with Visual Basic allows them taking actions. This is the *imperative mode*. For a better explanation, consider the following XAML code that declares a simple button:

```
<Button Content="Button" Height="30"
        Name="Button1"
        Width="100"/>
```

The same thing can be also accomplished in Visual Basic. The following code demonstrates this:

```
Dim Button1 As New Button
With Button1
    .Width = 100
    .Height = 30
    .Content = "Button1"
End With
Me.Grid1.Children.Add(Button1)
```

The difference is that in Visual Basic you need to explicitly add your control to a panel in the user interface.

Understanding Visual Tree and Logical Tree

When talking about WPF applications, you will often hear about the Logical Tree and the Visual Tree. The Logical Tree is basically a tree representation of the .NET classes for user interface controls. Consider the following XAML code:

```
<Window>
    <StackPanel Orientation="Horizontal" Margin="5">
        <TextBlock Text="Sample controls" Margin="5"/>
        <Button Content="Test button" Margin="5"/>
    </StackPanel>
</Window>
```

This code makes use of .NET objects within a hierarchical structure that can be refigured in a Logical Tree, as shown in Figure 31.8.

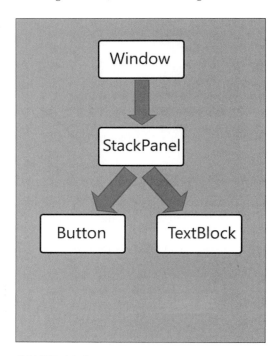

FIGURE 31.8   The Logical Tree provides a hierarchical view of the UI elements.

Starting from Visual Studio 2008 SP 1, you can investigate the Logical Tree in a more convenient way, with the Document Outline tool window (you find it in **View, Other Windows**) that provides a hierarchical view of the interface with previews (see Figure 31.9).

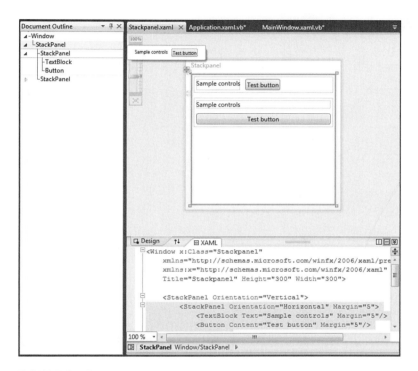

FIGURE 31.9   Investigating the Logical Tree with the Document Outline tool.

The Visual Tree is a little bit more complex concept that is important. As explained in the next chapters, WPF controls are the result of the aggregation of primitive elements, and they can be completely redefined with control templates. For example, a default Button is made of Chrome, ContentPresenter, and TextBlock controls. The combination of these elements creates a Visual, which represents a visual element in the user interface. The Visual Tree is thus the representation of all the visual elements in the UI that are rendered to the screen, plus their components. Consider the following simple XAML:

```
<StackPanel Orientation="Horizontal" Margin="5">
    <Button Content="Test button" Margin="5"/>
</StackPanel>
```

The visual tree representation is reported in Figure 31.10.

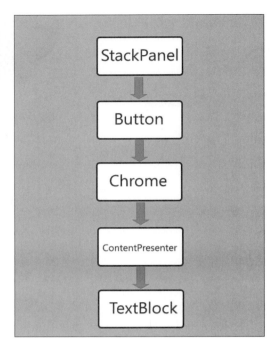

FIGURE 31.10   The Visual Tree representation for UI elements.

Understanding the Visual Tree is important for understanding another key concept in the WPF development, routed events, which are described just after introducing how you handle events in WPF.

Handling Events in WPF

You handle events in WPF the same way you do in other kinds of applications: You code a Visual Basic event handler and associate the handler to a control event. What actually changes is the way you assign the handler to the event. For example you can assign an event handler to a control event directly within the XAML code editor. To accomplish this you simply type the name of the event you want to handle (events are recognizable within IntelliSense with the Lightning icon) and then press Tab when IntelliSense shows the <New Event Handler> pop-up command (see Figure 31.11 for details).

This generates an event handler stub in your code-behind file. Continuing the example of the previous button, Visual Studio first assigns a new identifier to the Click event in XAML, which looks like this:

```
Click="Button1_Click"
```

As you can see, the IDE generates the event handler's identifier considering the control's name. Now right-click the event handler's name and select the **Navigate to Event**

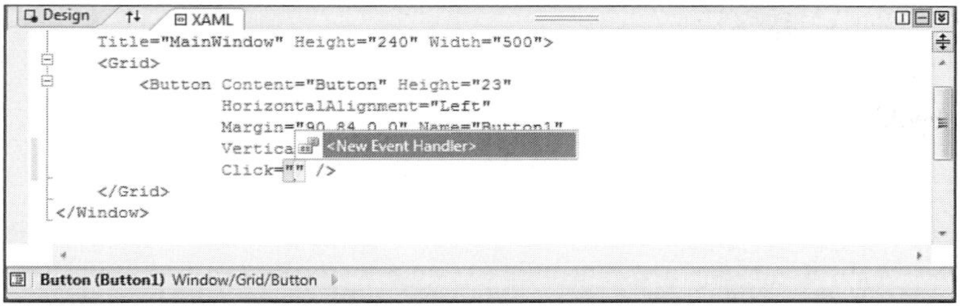

FIGURE 31.11   Generating a new event handler with IntelliSense.

Handler command from the pop-up menu. This redirects to the Visual Basic event handler generated for you, which looks like this:

```
Private Sub Button1_Click(ByVal sender As System.Object,
                         ByVal e As System.Windows.RoutedEventArgs)

End Sub
```

It is worth mentioning two aspects. The first one is that the event handler signature requires an e argument of type RoutedEventArgs. WPF introduces the concept of routed events that is covered in the next section. The second one is that in this case there is no Handles clause. This is because the IDE added an AddHandler instruction behind the scenes in the Window1.g.vb file (which is generated at compile time). Notice that such a file name depends on the current Window name, in this case Window1. As an alternative you can specify the Handles clause the same way you would do in other kinds of applications, but in this case you must not specify the event handler in XAML, to avoid an event being caught twice. You can also double-click a control in the designer to generate an event handler for the default event. For example, a button's default event is Click, so double-clicking a button in the designer generates an event handler stub for handling the Click event. The default event for a TextBox control is TextChanged, so double-clicking a text box generates an event handler stub for the TextChanged event, and so on. When you add event handlers by double-clicking controls, such handlers use the Handles clause on the method name. As previously mentioned, the last alternative is to assign an existing event handler to a control's event with the Properties window.

A More Thorough Discussion: Introducing the Routed Events

WPF introduces a revolutionary way to generate and handle events, known as *routed events*. When a user's interface element generates an event, the event passes along through the entire Visual Tree, rethrowing the event for each element in the tree. The WPF runtime can then understand what element first generated the event that is the actual handled event. Event handlers whose job is managing a routed event must include an object of type System.Windows.RoutedEventArgs in their signature. For a better understanding, consider the following basic XAML code that simply implements three buttons:

```
<StackPanel Button.Click="OnClick">
    <Button Width="100" Height="30"
            Content="Button One" Name="Button1" />
```

```
<Button Width="100" Height="30"
        Content="Button Two" Name="Button2" />
<Button Width="100" Height="30"
        Content="Button Three" Name="Button3" />
</StackPanel>
```

Notice how no event handler is specified for buttons, whereas a unique handler is specified within the `StackPanel` definition taking advantage of the `Button.Click` attached event. This allows establishing one event handler for each button in the `StackPanel`'s children. In the code-behind file, write the following handler:

```
Private Sub OnClick(ByVal sender As Object, ByVal e As RoutedEventArgs)

    Dim element As FrameworkElement = CType(e.Source, _
                                            FrameworkElement)

    Select Case element.Name
        Case Is = "Button1"
            MessageBox.Show("You clicked Button1")
        Case Is = "Button2"
            MessageBox.Show("You clicked Button2")
        Case Is = "Button3"
            MessageBox.Show("You clicked Button3")
    End Select
End Sub
```

Thanks to routed events, we can write just one common handler. To get the instance of the element that actually generated the event, you need to convert the `e.Source` property (which is of type `Object`) into the appropriate type. In this case the conversion could be with a `Button` type, but `FrameworkElement` is utilized to include different kinds of elements or controls. This is because with routed events you can intercept events from each element in the Visual Tree (such as the `ContentPresenter` for buttons), thus not only user controls.

Introducing Routing Strategies: Direct, Tunneling, and Bubbling

Routed events are implemented according to three modes, known as *routing strategies*. Strategies are implemented by the `System.Windows.RoutingStrategy` enumeration and can be summarized as follows:

- ▶ *Direct:* The event is generated directly against the target object. This is what usually happens in other kinds of .NET applications, such as Windows Forms, and is the most uncommon strategy in WPF.

- ▶ *Tunnel:* In the tunneling strategy, an event is generated from the root object and passes through the entire Visual Tree until getting to the target object.

- ▶ *Bubble:* The bubbling strategy is opposite to the tunneling one, meaning that an event starts from the target object and passes back through the Visual Tree.

In most cases, such as the preceding code example, you face tunneling routed events or bubbling ones. Offering a thorough discussion on routed events is beyond the scope of this chapter; you can refer to the MSDN official page that you can find at http://msdn.microsoft.com/en-us/library/ms742806(VS.100).aspx.

Arranging Controls with Panels

WPF changes the way you arrange controls on the user interface. This is because one goal of WPF is to provide the ability to create dynamic interfaces that can be rearranged according to the user's preferences or when the user resizes the interface. Because of this, WPF controls are arranged within special containers, known as panels. WPF provides several panels, each allowing different arrangement possibilities. This is different from Windows Forms where you simply place controls on the user interface, but the controls are not flexible. Although there is the availability of some kinds of panels, Windows Forms panels are not as versatile as WPF panels. In this section you learn about WPF panels and how you use them to arrange controls. The most important thing that you have to keep in mind is that WPF controls have a hierarchical logic; therefore, you can nest multiple panels to create complex user experiences. Panels are all exposed by the System.Windows.Controls namespace from the PresentationFramework.dll assembly.

The Grid Panel

The Grid is one of the easiest panels to understand in WPF. It basically allows creating tables, with rows and columns. In this way you can define cells and each cell can contain a control or another panel storing nested controls. The Grid is versatile in that you can just divide it into rows or into columns or both. The following code defines a Grid that is divided into two rows and two columns:

```
<Grid>
    <Grid.RowDefinitions>
        <RowDefinition />
        <RowDefinition />
    </Grid.RowDefinitions>
    <Grid.ColumnDefinitions>
        <ColumnDefinition />
        <ColumnDefinition />
    </Grid.ColumnDefinitions>

</Grid>
```

RowDefinitions is basically a collection of RowDefinition objects, and the same is for ColumnDefinitions and ColumnDefinition. Each item respectively represents a row or a column within the Grid. You can also specify a Width or a Height property to delimit row and column dimensions; if you do not specify anything, both rows and columns are dimensioned at the maximum size available, and when resizing the parent container, rows and columns are automatically rearranged. The preceding code simply creates a table with four cells. The Visual Studio 2010 Designer offers a convenient way for designing rows and columns. When the cursor is within the `Grid` definition in the XAML code editor or when the `Grid` has the focus in the designer, you simply use the `Rows` and `Columns` properties in the Properties window. Figure 31.12 shows how you add columns to the `Grid` and how you can set properties for each column. Adding rows works exactly the same.

FIGURE 31.12   Adding columns with design tools.

To place controls in the `Grid`, you specify the row and column position. The following code places two buttons, the first one in the upper-left cell and the second one in the upper-right cell:

```
<Button Width="100" Height="50" Grid.Column="0"
        Grid.Row="0" Name="Button1" Content="First button"/>
<Button Width="100" Height="50" Grid.Column="1"
        Grid.Row="0" Name="Button2" Content="Second button"/>
```

To place controls, you select the column via the `Grid.Column` property, whose index is zero-based, meaning that 0 is the first column from the left. This kind of property is known as *attached property* and allows setting a property of a parent container from within the current object. Specifying the row works similarly, in that you assign the row via the `Grid.Row` attached property. The property's index is also zero-based, meaning that 0 represents the first row from the top. You can also place nested containers within a cell or a single row or column. The following code shows how to nest a grid with children control into a single cell:

```
<Grid Grid.Row="1" Grid.Column="0">
    <Grid.ColumnDefinitions>
        <ColumnDefinition />
```

```
        <ColumnDefinition />
    </Grid.ColumnDefinitions>
    <Grid.RowDefinitions>
        <RowDefinition />
        <RowDefinition />
    </Grid.RowDefinitions>

    <Button Width="50" Height="50" Grid.Column="0"
        Grid.Row="0" Name="Button3" Content="Button3"/>
    <Button Width="50" Height="50" Grid.Column="1"
        Grid.Row="0" Name="Button4" Content="Button4"/>
</Grid>
```

If you run the code shown in this section, you get the result shown in Figure 31.13 that gives you an idea on how controls are can be placed within a Grid.

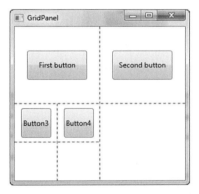

FIGURE 31.13   Arranging controls within a Grid.

SHOWING GRID LINES

Grid lines are not shown by default. To make them visible, add a ShowGridLines property to the Grid element and set its value to True.

PERSONAL SUGGESTION

Each time you study a WPF container, try to resize the application windows or controls so that you can get a good idea of how panels work.

The `StackPanel` Panel

The `StackPanel` panel allows placing controls near each other, as in a stack that can be arranged both horizontally and vertically. As with other containers, the `StackPanel` can contain nested panels. The following code shows how you can arrange controls horizontally and vertically. The root `StackPanel` contains two nested panels:

```
<StackPanel Orientation="Vertical">
    <StackPanel Orientation="Horizontal" Margin="5">
        <TextBlock Text="Sample controls" Margin="5"/>
        <Button Content="Test button" Margin="5"/>
    </StackPanel>

    <StackPanel Orientation="Vertical" Margin="5">
        <TextBlock Text="Sample controls" Margin="5"/>
        <Button Content="Test button" Margin="5"/>
    </StackPanel>
</StackPanel>
```

The `Orientation` property can be set as `Horizontal` or `Vertical`, and this influences the final layout. One of the main benefits of XAML code is that element names and properties are self-explanatory, and this is the case of `StackPanel`'s properties, too. Remember that controls within a `StackPanel` are automatically resized according to the orientation. If you do not like this behavior, you need to specify `Width` and `Height` properties. If you run this code, you get the result shown in Figure 31.14.

FIGURE 31.14   Arranging controls within `StackPanels`.

If you want to provide a dynamic user interface, you need to take care of some considerations. If you do not provide static `Width` and `Height` values, your controls will be resized along with the `StackPanel`, which also automatically adapts to its parent container. Alternatively, controls arranged within a `StackPanel` are not resized, but they have the limitation of being hidden when decreasing the parent's container size, as better represented in Figure 31.15.

FIGURE 31.15   Resizing fixed controls within a `StackPanel` causes them to be hidden.

If you predict that your application may encounter such a situation, you should implement a `WrapPanel` panel, which is covered in the next subsection.

The `WrapPanel` Panel

The `WrapPanel` container basically works like `StackPanel`, but it differs in that it can rearrange controls on multiple lines in the interface so that they are never hidden. Figures 31.16 and 31.17 show how the `WrapPanel` allows rearranging controls when resizing the parent container (a `Window`, in our examples).

FIGURE 31.16   `WrapPanel` arranges controls similarly to the `StackPanel`.

FIGURE 31.17   `WrapPanel` rearranges controls dynamically making them always visible, as if they were implemented line by line.

In code terms, the panel is represented by a `WrapPanel` element in XAML. The following code reproduces what you saw in the previous figures:

```
<WrapPanel>
    <TextBlock Text="WrapPanel test" Margin="5"/>
    <Button Width="140" Height="30" Content="Test Button"
            Margin="5"/>
    <TextBlock Text="Second test" Margin="5"/>
</WrapPanel>
```

The `VirtualizingStackPanel` Control

There are situations in which you need to show a big number of elements in your user interface. This is the case of the `DataGrid` or `ListBox` controls, which can display hundreds of elements within a single control. This would of course heavily affect the application performances if you were using a classic `StackPanel`, which would simply show all the available items. The `VirtualizingStackPanel` control offers a valid alternative that can calculate how many items can appear in a particular moment and then arranges controls according to the calculation result. Generally you do not need to implement the `VirtualizingStackPanel` manually (it is the default item template of data controls) but, if you need to, you simply write the following definition:

```
<VirtualizingStackPanel>
    <!—Nest controls here...—>
</VirtualizingStackPanel>
```

This kind of panel works like the `StackPanel`, with the previously described difference.

The Canvas Panel

Most WPF containers allow the dynamic rearrangement of controls within the user interface. This is useful when you want your user to adjust interface settings, but it can complicate things when you need to place controls in a fixed, unchangeable place (as basically happens in Windows Forms). To accomplish this you use the Canvas container, which allows absolute placement, meaning that it allows specifying the position of nested controls. When you place controls into a Canvas container, you specify the absolute position with some attached properties: `Canvas.Left`, `Canvas.Top`, `Canvas.Right`, and `Canvas.Bottom`. The following code shows how you place a button that never changes its position in the user interface, thanks to the `Canvas.Left` and `Canvas.Top` attached properties:

```
<Canvas>
    <Button Width="100" Height="50" Content="Test Button"
            Canvas.Left="30" Canvas.Top="50"/>
</Canvas>
```

The DockPanel Panel

The `DockPanel` container has some similarities with the `StackPanel` in that it allows arranging child controls near each other. The main difference in `DockPanel` is that child controls are docked to the panel sides according to the direction you specify, and also they are docked to each other and you can establish the position and size for each child control. The most common usage of the `DockPanel` panel is creating interfaces for placing menus and toolbars. The following example shows how you can dock multiple toolbars and their buttons within a `DockPanel`:

```
<DockPanel VerticalAlignment="Top"
           LastChildFill="True">
    <ToolBar DockPanel.Dock="Top"
             Name="MainToolbar" >
        <Button Content="First Button"/>
        <Button Content="Second Button"/>
    </ToolBar>

    <ToolBar DockPanel.Dock="Top"
             Name="NextToolbar" >
        <Button Content="First Button"/>
        <Button Content="Second Button"/>
    </ToolBar>
</DockPanel>
```

You set the DockPanel orientation by specifying either the VerticalAlignment property or HorizontalAlignment. The LastChildFill is a property that indicates whether child controls must completely fill the available blank space in the container. Notice how within child controls (such as the Toolbars) you specify the docking position by taking advantage of an attached property named DockPanel.Dock, whose value indicates where the control must be docked within the DockPanel. This is because child controls are not limited to being docked into one side of the panel but can be docked into any of the four sides. The preceding code produces the result shown in Figure 31.18.

FIGURE 31.18   Docking controls within a DockPanel.

The ViewBox Panel

The ViewBox panel allows adapting nested controls to its size, including the content of controls. For example, consider the following code:

```
<Viewbox>
    <Button Width="150" Height="75">
        ViewBoxed button
    </Button>
</Viewbox>
```

You immediately notice how the button's text is expanded to best fit the button size. This also happens if you decrease or increase the window size, as demonstrated in Figure 31.19.

In a few words, the ViewBox allows resizing controls and their content.

Managing Windows

WPF allows managing windows similarly to Windows Forms, although there are some obvious differences, such as the fact that WPF windows can be considered as the root container for all other child panels when arranging UI elements. Whatever way you

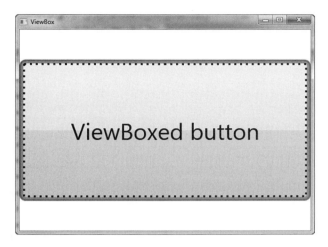

FIGURE 31.19   The ViewBox panel in action.

decide to apply windows properties, at design time such properties are addressed in XAML code, but you are also allowed to set them at runtime in Visual Basic code. Available properties allow establishing the window startup position, its resize mode, its appearance on the task bar, and so on. Table 31.2 summarizes the most important available properties.

TABLE 31.2   Window's Properties

Name	Description
Title	Specifies text for the window title bar
WindowStartupLocation	Specifies the position for the window when it is first loaded (can be Manual, CenterScreen, or CenterOwner)
WindowState	Specifies the window state when loaded (can be Normal, Maximized, or Minimized)
WindowStyle	Specifies the window layout style (None, SingleBorderWindow, ThreeDBorderWindow, or ToolWindow)
TopMost	Makes the window always visible on top
ShowInTaskBar	Makes the window title visible in the operating system task bar
Background	Allows specifying a brush for the background color (see Chapter 33., "Brushes, Styles, Templates, and Animations in WPF")
BorderBrush	Specifies a color or brush for the Window border
BorderThickness	Specifies how huge the border is

You can take advantage of the Properties tool window for setting the previously mentioned properties at design time. The following XAML code snippet shows how you can set some window properties:

```
<!— The following code sets the Window as Maximized,
    its startup position at the center of the screen,
    its style as a Window with 3D borders and keeps it
    always on top. It also replaces the default title—>
<Window x:Class="MainWindow"
    xmlns="http://schemas.microsoft.com/winfx/2006/xaml/presentation"
    xmlns:x="http://schemas.microsoft.com/winfx/2006/xaml"
    Title="Chapter 31 demonstration" Height="240" Width="500"
    WindowStartupLocation="CenterScreen"
    WindowState="Maximized" WindowStyle="ThreeDBorderWindow"
    Topmost="True">
</Window>
```

This is what you do at design time. The same result can be accomplished in managed code as follows:

```
'Me is the current Window
With Me
    .Title = "Chapter 31 demonstration"
    .WindowStartupLocation = Windows.WindowStartupLocation.
                             CenterScreen
    .WindowState = Windows.WindowState.
                   Maximized
    .WindowStyle = Windows.WindowStyle.
                   ThreeDBorderWindow
    .Topmost = True
End With
```

To add additional Window objects to your project you simply select the **Project, Add Window** command and assign the filename in the New Item dialog. Remember that every Window in the project inherits from System.Windows.Window. When you have multiple windows in your project, you can also establish which of them must be the startup object. To accomplish this, go to My Project and select the new window in the Startup URI combo box. Figure 31.20 shows how to accomplish this.

The window is specified via the related XAML file address (Uri).

Instantiating Windows at Runtime

Creating and displaying windows at runtime is a common task in every client application. To accomplish this you simply create an instance of a System.Windows.Window and then invoke the Show or ShowDialog methods, depending if the Window must be considered a

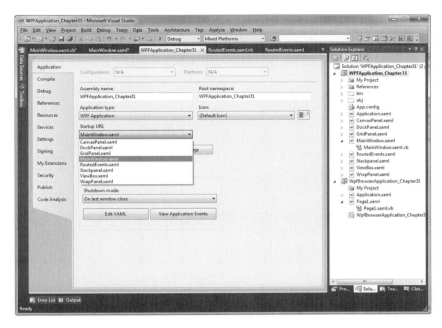

FIGURE 31.20   Selecting a different `Window` as the startup object.

modal dialog or not. The following Visual Basic code demonstrates how you create and show a new `Window`:

```vbnet
Dim aWindow As New Window
'Set your Window properties here...
aWindow.ShowDialog()
'....
aWindow.Close()
```

In the preceding code a new `Window` is generated from scratch, so this requires specifying all properties. In most cases you can instead create and show instances of existing windows that you implemented at design time; for this, in the above code you just replace `Window` with the name of your custom window. Basically this works the same as Windows Forms, although all the backend technology is completely different. This approach helps you when moving your Windows Forms applications to WPF.

Introducing the Application Object

As for Windows Forms, WPF also provides an `Application` class that allows interacting with your application instance. The class exposes several methods and properties that generally allow getting or assigning settings available within My Project. First, you need to get the instance of the running application. You accomplish this by assigning the `Application.Current` property to a variable as follows:

```
Dim myApp As Application = CType(Application.Current, Application)
```

When you get the instance of the application, you can get or set required information. The following code shows how you can retrieve the startup Uri (which corresponds to the startup object referred to a XAML file), the main application window, and assembly information:

```
'Gets the startup object under the form of a XAML file
Dim startupObject As Uri = myApp.StartupUri

'Gets (but also allows setting) the application main window
Dim mainWindow As Window = myApp.MainWindow

'Get assembly information
With myApp.Info
    Dim companyName As String = .CompanyName
    Dim appName As String = .ProductName

    'get other info here...
End With
```

The `Application` class does not directly expose a `Close` method as instead happens in Windows Forms. If you want to programmatically shut down your application, you invoke the `Current.Close` shared method as follows:

```
Application.Current.Shutdown()
```

Table 31.3 summarizes the most important members of the `Application` class.

TABLE 31.3   Application Class's Most Important Members

Member	Type	Description
Current	Property	Returns the instance of the running application.
Dispatcher	Property	Returns the instance of the Dispacther for the current application. The Dispatcher is responsible for managing threads.
FindResource	Method	Searches for the specified resource (which is generally at XAML level).
Info	Property	Returns a collection of assembly information.
LoadComponent	Method	Loads a XAML file from the specified Uri and then converts the resulting object into an instance that is added to the application.
Main	Method	The application entry point.

TABLE 31.3 Continued

Member	Type	Description
MainWindow	Property	Returns the instance of the Window object that is first run at startup.
Resources	Property	Returns a collection of resources.
Run	Method	Runs a WPF application.
Shutdown	Method	Shuts down the application.
ShutdownMode	Property	Gets or sets how an application must shut down.
StartupUri	Property	Returns the Uri of the XAML file that is loaded at startup.
Windows	Property	Returns a collection of Window objects that have been instantiated in the application.

> **TIP**
>
> Chapter 20, "The My Namespace," discussed the My namespace. WPF applications provide a special extension of My that allows interacting with the application simply by invoking the My.Application property.

The Application class is also important for another reason: It contains the entry point (that is, the Sub Main) that effectively runs your application and is the place where you control application events, such as the startup or the shutdown. This class is implemented as a partial class. In Solution Explorer you can find the Application.Xaml file that can store application-level resources; the file has a code-behind counterpart named Application.Xaml.vb where you can write code that influences the entire application instead of single elements of the user interface. The following code shows how you can handle the Startup and Exit events that represent the initial and final moments of the application lifetime:

```
Class Application


    ' Application-level events, such as Startup, Exit,
    ' and DispatcherUnhandledException
    ' can be handled in this file.

    Private Sub Application_Startup(ByVal sender As Object,
                                    ByVal e As System.Windows.
                                                    StartupEventArgs) _
                                    Handles Me.Startup
        MessageBox.Show("Application is starting up")
    End Sub
```

```
    Private Sub Application_Exit(ByVal sender As Object,
                                ByVal e As System.Windows.ExitEventArgs) _
                                Handles Me.Exit
        MessageBox.Show("Application is closing")
    End Sub
End Class
```

Generally you use the `Application` class for controlling specific moments in the lifetime; when you instead need to set application properties, the best choice is opening the My Project designer.

Brief Overview of WPF Browser Applications

Since the first version of WPF, developers have been allowed to build applications that can run within a web browser, such as Microsoft Internet Explorer or Mozilla Firefox. This kind of applications is named WPF Browser Applications (formerly known as Xaml Browser Applications) or simply XBAP. There are several differences between a client application and an XBAP; first, Browser Applications can be only executed online (from the Internet or an intranet). Second, they are executed with the limitations of the Internet Zone of the .NET Framework's Code Access Security rules. Because of this, Browser Applications cannot perform several tasks. The main advantage is instead that, keeping in mind the previously mentioned limitations), you can use the same programming model.

CHOOSE SILVERLIGHT

WPF Browser Applications were first introduced when the real Web counterpart of WPF, Silverlight, was not at today's levels. Silverlight is the real .NET offering for creating rich Internet applications, with both multimedia and business capabilities. You should absolutely prefer Silverlight applications to Browser Applications. Browser Applications are kept for compatibility reasons, but situations where you should use them are limited. If your company needs an online application with WPF capabilities but with a small number of functionalities, Browser Applications could do well, but Silverlight provides a full-featured environment for each kind of rich web application.

You create an application of this kind by selecting the **WPF Browser Application** project template from the New Project window. Then, create a new Browser Application naming the project **WpfBrowserApplication_Chapter31**. When the project is ready, you soon notice another difference from classic WPF applications. In the XAML code editor, you can see how the root object is now a `Page` instead of a `Window`. This is required for applications to work within a web browser. The second difference you can notice is the presence of a strong name file (with .pfx extension) in Solution Explorer. This is required because of the CAS rules. At this point we can implement some features to see the application in action. The goal of the example is to create an application that can validate an email address showing the validation result. Listing 31.2 shows the user interface implementation, which is simple.

LISTING 31.2   Defining the XBAP's Interface

```
<Page x:Class="Page1"
      xmlns="http://schemas.microsoft.com/winfx/2006/xaml/presentation"
      xmlns:x="http://schemas.microsoft.com/winfx/2006/xaml"
      xmlns:mc="http://schemas.openxmlformats.org/markup-compatibility/2006"
      xmlns:d="http://schemas.microsoft.com/expression/blend/2008"
      mc:Ignorable="d"
      d:DesignHeight="300" d:DesignWidth="300"
      Title="Page1">
    <StackPanel>
        <Label Content="Enter the e-mail address to validate:" Margin="5"/>
        <TextBox Name="MailTextBox" Margin="5"/>
        <Button Width="100" Height="30" Content="Validate" Margin="5"
                Name="Button1" />
    </StackPanel>
</Page>
```

On the Visual Basic side, we need to implement a method that validates the user input and an event handler for the button's Click event. Code in Listing 31.3 shows how to accomplish this.

LISTING 31.3   Providing Actions for the XAML Browser Application

```
Imports System.Text.RegularExpressions


Class Page1

    Private Sub Button1_Click(ByVal sender As System.Object,
                              ByVal e As System.Windows.RoutedEventArgs) _
                              Handles Button1.Click

        If String.IsNullOrEmpty(Me.MailTextBox.Text) = True Then Exit Sub

        MessageBox.Show("Is a valid address: " & IsValidEMail(Me.MailTextBox.Text))

    End Sub

    Function IsValidEMail(ByVal EMailAddress As String) _
                As Boolean
        Dim validateMail As String = _
        "^([\w-\.]+)@((\[[0-9]{1,3}\.[0-9]{1,3}\.)" & _
        "|(([\w-]+\.)+))([a-zA-z]{2,4}|[0-9]{1,3})(\]?)$"

        Return Regex.IsMatch(EMailAddress, _
```

```
                              validateMail)

      End Function
End Class
```

Simply notice how you handle a routed event the same way you would in a Windows application. The `IsValidEmail` method is something already explained in this book that makes use of regular expressions for validation. If you run the application, you get the result shown in Figure 31.21.

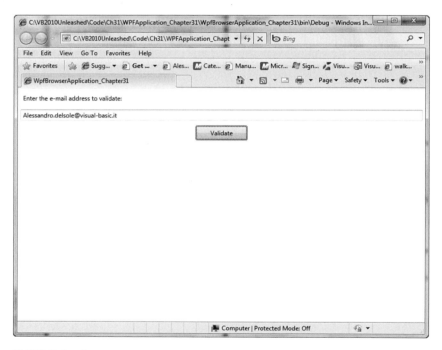

FIGURE 31.21   The WPF Browser Application running in the default web browser.

When the application is launched from the Visual Studio debugger, the default web browser is launched pointing to the application.

XBAP DEPLOYMENT

Deploying an XBAP is a task that you should perform through ClickOnce. This technology, that will be covered in Chapter 55, "Deploying Applications with ClickOnce," is perfect for this purpose for some reasons: It can deploy the application to a Web server; it can manage CAS settings; and it can deploy an application as "online," a required scenario for XBAPs. Finally, ClickOnce cannot install assemblies to the GAC, and thus you can be sure that the target machine will not be affected.

Summary

In this chapter you took a first look at the Windows Presentation Foundation technology. You saw what WPF is and how it is architected. You then saw how to create your first WPF application with Visual Studio 2010, getting a high-level introduction of the XAML markup language and the interaction with managed code. For the architecture, you learned about some concepts such as the Logical Tree and the Visual Tree. For the Visual Tree, understanding this led you to another key concept: routed events, which allow generating cascade events through the hierarchic structure of the user interface. After this you made a contact with WPF, understanding how you arrange controls within panels, getting also a first overview of all available panels. Last, you saw in action another kind of client application with WPF: Browser Applications, seeing how this kind of applications can run within a Web browser, although with some limitations due to their nature. With these basics, you are now ready to take some more control over WPF. This is the goal of next chapters.

31

WPF Common Controls

Being a technology for Windows client applications, Windows Presentation Foundations offers built-in controls that you can immediately use in your applications to build rich user interfaces. Obviously you can also build your own custom controls. WPF 4 offers a good standard toolbox ready to be consumed, provided by the System.Windows.Controls namespace. If you are new to WPF and you come from the Windows Forms experience, you can certainly find differences in controls implementation between the two technologies, but, fortunately, you will feel at home because of names; look for WPF controls that are counterparts of Windows Forms interface elements. In this chapter you first learn some important features in WPF controls; next you take a tour through the most common user controls so that you can start building your user interface.

Introducing WPF Controls Features

Before using WPF controls, you need to understand some behaviors. In Chapter 31, "Creating WPF Applications," you learned that UI elements, including controls, are generally declared in XAML code. You also saw how to assign a name to controls to interact with them in Visual Basic code. XAML allows declaring and implementing controls even if you do not assign a name. For example, the following Button declaration is legal:

```
<Button Width="100" Height="50" Click="OnClick"/>
```

The control declared in this way works normally as you would expect, also raising click events that you can handle in managed code. This is possible because of the particular WPF architecture part that implements routed events discussed in Chapter 31. When an unnamed control raises an event, the event passes through the entire Visual Tree, and the WPF runtime can intercept the event independently from the control name. Providing a name therefore is useful when you need to assign properties in managed code or when you want to assign an event handler to a specific visual element. Another interesting feature is that WPF controls are generally defined as *lookless*. This means that WPF controls are classes that expose a series of properties defining the behavior of controls while the look is assigned via a *template*. Basically when you drag a WPF control from the toolbox to the designer, the control takes advantage of a standard template that defines its layout, but templates can be completely customized or overridden with the so called *control templates*. Chapter 33, "Brushes, Styles, Templates, and Animations in WPF," provides more examples and explanations, but you need to understand the concept before examining common controls. Basing controls' layout on templates allows roles separation between developers and designers and is the reason why Microsoft created a tool such as Expression Blend. Another fundamental feature in WPF control is that it can contain almost any visual elements. This is possible with the `ContentControl` item that is the subject of next section.

WPF CONTROLS AND SILVERLIGHT CONTROLS

Understanding WPF controls is useful for Silverlight development, too. In most cases you notice that controls described here have a counterpart in Silverlight, and this is the reason why a similar discussion is not done for Silverlight.

Understanding the `ContentControl`

One of the biggest presentation benefits in WPF is the capability for controls to show more than simple text. Particularly, all controls exposing a `Content` property can nest complex visual elements to offer special effects with or without text. For example, consider the following button whose content is just text:

```
<Button Name="Button1" Width="100" Height="100" Content="Click me!"/>
```

The `Content` property can be declared in a hierarchical fashion so that you can take advantage of the XAML logic for nesting complex elements. The following example shows how you can replace the button text with a movie:

```
<Button Name="Button1" Width="100" Height="100">
    <Button.Content>
        <MediaElement Source="MyVideo.wmv" LoadedBehavior="Play"/>
    </Button.Content>
</Button>
```

At this point your button plays a video instead of showing the `Click me!` text. This is possible because of a special element named `ContentControl` that provides the ability to embed complex visual elements within controls offering the `Content` property. Basically it is an invisible element, but its presence is noticeable when you can get these results. Another example is nesting multiple elements within a panel as the child element of the `ContentControl`. The following example shows how you can embed text and video together:

```
<Button Name="Button1" Width="100" Height="100">
    <Button.Content>
    <StackPanel>
        <MediaElement LoadedBehavior="Play"
                      Source="MyVideo.wmv"/>
        <TextBlock Text="Click me!"/>
    </StackPanel>
    </Button.Content>
</Button>
```

It is fundamental to understand the existence of the `ContentControl` because even the most classic controls can be enriched with complex visual elements with a couple lines of code.

Understanding Common Controls

In this section you learn about the most common controls in Windows Presentation Foundation. In most cases we provide XAML implementation, because this is the place where you define your user interface; remember that everything you do in XAML is reproducible in Visual Basic code for runtime handling (see Chapter 31).

Border

Consider the `Border` control as a special container that draws a border around the child control, with the specified color, thickness, and corner radius. The following XAML code draws a red border with a depth of 3 around a rectangle:

```
<Border BorderBrush="Red" BorderThickness="3"
        CornerRadius="8">
    <Rectangle Height="100"/>
</Border>
```

Changes are immediately visible in the Visual Studio designer. Notice that the `Border` can nest just one child element, so if you want to add multiple visual elements, you need to encapsulate them within a container such the `Grid` or `StackPanel`. Figure 32.1 shows the result of the preceding code.

FIGURE 32.1   Drawing a border.

SPECIFYING DIFFERENT BRUSHES

In the preceding code the BorderBrush is assigned with a SolidColorBrush (Red), but according to the hierarchical logic of XAML, you could set it with a different brush such as LinearGradientBrush.

Button

In Chapter 31 you saw some Button examples in action, so we do not cover this again here.

Calendar

The Calendar control is new in .NET 4 and shows a calendar where you can select a particular day in the specified month and year. The following XAML code defines a calendar with a custom border and a TextBox that contains the selected date to be assigned programmatically:

```
<StackPanel Orientation="Horizontal">
    <Calendar Name="Calendar1" Margin="5"
        BorderBrush="Blue" BorderThickness="3"
        SelectedDatesChanged="Calendar1_SelectedDatesChanged">
    </Calendar>
    <TextBox Name="TextBox1" Margin="5" Height="30" Width="200"/>
</StackPanel>
```

The SelectedDatesChanged event is raised when the user clicks a different date. The following is instead the event handler that gets the instance of the calendar and sends the selected date to the text box:

```
Private Sub Calendar1_SelectedDatesChanged(ByVal sender As Object,
                                ByVal e As Windows.Controls.
                                SelectionChangedEventArgs)

    Dim currentCalendar = CType(sender, Calendar)
    Me.TextBox1.Text = currentCalendar.SelectedDate.Value.ToString

End Sub
```

Figure 32.2 shows the result of our work.

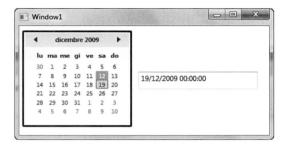

FIGURE 32.2   Implementing a `Calendar` control.

You can also programmatically assign the `SelectedDate` property with an object of type `Date` to change the date shown in the `Calendar` control with a different one.

CheckBox

The WPF `CheckBox` controls works like any other same-named controls in other technologies. Take a look at the following XAML code:

```
<CheckBox Name="Check1" Content="I will do this"
          Margin="5" Checked="Check1_Checked"
          Unchecked="Check1_Unchecked"/>
```

The `CheckBox`'s text is set via the `Content` property. Setting `Content` also means that you can fill the control with visual elements other than text. It exposes two events, `Checked` and `Unchecked`, that are raised when you place or remove the flag from the control and that can be handled as follows:

```
Private Sub Check1_Checked(ByVal sender As System.Object,
                           ByVal e As System.Windows.RoutedEventArgs)
    MessageBox.Show("Checked")
End Sub

Private Sub Check1_Unchecked(ByVal sender As Object,
                             ByVal e As System.Windows.RoutedEventArgs)
    MessageBox.Show("Unchecked")
End Sub
```

Finally you invoke the IsChecked Boolean property for verifying whether the control is checked. Figure 32.3 shows how the control appears.

FIGURE 32.3   Implementing a CheckBox.

ComboBox

The WPF ComboBox also works the same as in other technologies. The following XAML snippet shows how you implement a sample ComboBox showing a list of hypothetical customers:

```
<ComboBox Name="CustomerNamesCombo"
          Width="200" Height="30"
          SelectionChanged="CustomerNamesCombo_SelectionChanged">
    <ComboBox.Items>
        <ComboBoxItem Content="Alessandro"/>
        <ComboBoxItem Content="Brook"/>
    </ComboBox.Items>
</ComboBox>
```

Each item in the control is represented by a ComboBoxItem object whose Content property sets the item's content that can be also something different from text. (For example, you might embed a video through a MediaElement control). The SelectionChanged event is raised when the user selects an item.

DESIGNER TOOLS FOR ADDING ITEMS

You can add items to a ComboBox by clicking the button on the Items property in the Properties window. This shows a dialog where you can take advantage of the Visual Studio designer tools.

This control is powerful because it also supports data-binding. The next example renames the ComboBox into ProcessNamesCombo, setting the ItemsSource property as follows:

```
<ComboBox Name="ProcessNamesCombo"
          Width="200" Height="30" ItemsSource="{Binding}"
          SelectionChanged="CustomerNamesCombo_SelectionChanged">
```

This ensures that items will be populated at runtime via data-binding. The following Visual Basic code shows how you populate the `ComboBox` via a LINQ query with the list of running processes' names:

```
Private Sub MainWindow_Loaded(ByVal sender As Object,
                              ByVal e As RoutedEventArgs) _
                              Handles Me.Loaded
    Dim procList = From proc In Process.GetProcesses.
                   AsEnumerable
                   Select proc.ProcessName

    'Assuming the Combo's name is now ProcessNamesCombo
    Me.ProcessNamesCombo.ItemsSource = procList
End Sub
```

If you want to handle items selection, you write an event handler such as the following:

```
Private Sub CustomerNamesCombo_SelectionChanged(ByVal sender As Object,
                              ByVal e As SelectionChangedEventArgs)

    Dim selectedProcess = CType(CType(sender, ComboBox).SelectedItem, _
                          String)

    MessageBox.Show("You selected " & selectedProcess)
End Sub
```

Basically you need to get the instance of the selected item (`ComboBox.SelectedItem`) and then convert it into the appropriate type, which in this case is `String`. If you bounded a list of `Process` objects, instead of their name, conversion would return `Process`, and you need to add a `DisplayMemberPath` attribute on the XAML side pointing to the property you want to show (for example, `ProcessName`). Figure 32.4 shows the result of the data-bound `ComboBox`.

DataGrid

The `DataGrid` control is new in the .NET Framework 4.0 and enables presenting and editing tabular data. A complete example is available in Chapter 35, "Introducing Data-binding."

DatePicker

The `DatePicker` control is also new in the .NET Framework 4.0 and shows a pop-up calendar where you can pick a date; the date is then bound to a text box placed near the control. The `DatePicker` is used in data-binding techniques (see Chapter 35). The following XAML code shows how you can implement a `DatePicker`; the selection, which is mapped by the `SelectedDate` property of type `Date`, is then bound to a second, external text box to demonstrate how the value can be consumed by other user controls:

```
<StackPanel Orientation="Horizontal">
```

FIGURE 32.4   Binding a ComboBox to a list of objects.

```
<DatePicker Name="DatePicker1" Margin="5"
        SelectedDateChanged="DatePicker1_SelectedDateChanged" />
<TextBox Name="TextBox2" Margin="5"
        Text="{Binding ElementName=DatePicker1,
                        Path=SelectedDate}"
        Height="30" Width="200"/>

</StackPanel>
```

Figure 32.5 shows how the DatePicker appears.

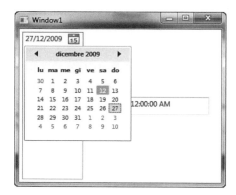

FIGURE 32.5   Implementing a DatePicker.

The `DatePicker` exposes an event called `SelectedDateChanged` that is raised when the user selects another date. The following event handler shows an example of handling the event:

```
Private Sub DatePicker1_SelectedDateChanged(ByVal sender As Object,
                                  ByVal e As _
                                  SelectionChangedEventArgs)

    'Use the "e" object to access the DatePicker control
    '(Source represents
    'the instance)
    MessageBox.Show("The new date is " & CType(e.Source,
                DatePicker).SelectedDate.
                Value.ToLongDateString)
End Sub
```

DocumentViewer

The `DocumentViewer` control enables viewing flow documents. A complete example is available in Chapter 34, "Manipulating Documents and Media."

Ellipse

The `Ellipse` element is not properly a user control because it is actually a geometric shape. It is useful to understand how the element works because you can use it when creating your custom control templates. The following XAML code declares an `Ellipse`:

```
<Ellipse Width="150" Height="80" Stroke="Red"
        StrokeThickness="3" Fill="Orange"/>
```

The most important properties are `Width` and `Height` that define dimensions. `Stroke` defines the color that surrounds the ellipse, and `StrokeThickness` is a value indicating the stroke depth. As with other geometric shapes, `Ellipse` background can be assigned via the `Fill` property. Figure 32.6 shows the drawn ellipse.

Expander

The `Expander` control is a special kind of control container that can be expanded or collapsed and that is useful for organizing your controls. The following is an example of `Expander` with nested controls:

```
<Expander Name="Expander1" Header="Expand to view controls"
        Background="LightBlue">
    <StackPanel>
        <ComboBox Name="Combo1" Margin="10">
            <!— Add your items here...—>
        </ComboBox>
        <ListBox Name="List1" Margin="10">
```

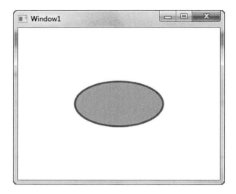

FIGURE 32.6   Drawing and filling an ellipse.

```
                <!— Add your items here...—>
            </ListBox>
        </StackPanel>
    </Expander>
```

You must use a panel, as in the preceding example, if you want to add multiple visual elements because the Expander's Content property supports just one element. You access members by simply invoking their names as if they were not nested inside the Expander. Figure 32.7 shows the Expander in action.

FIGURE 32.7   Implementing the Expander and nesting controls.

Frame

The Frame control enables showing Html contents, including web pages. The most basic usage is assigning its Source property with an Uri, as in the following example:

```
<Frame Source="http://www.visual-basic.it" />
```

Figure 32.8 shows how the website appears in the Frame control.

FIGURE 32.8   Opening a website with a Frame control.

This control exposes a `Navigate` method that enables programmatically browsing html contents and/or web pages as in the following snippet:

```
Frame1.Navigate(New Uri("Http://www.visual-basic.it"))
```

You can also point to an html file on disk; just remember that each content name must be converted into `Uri`.

USING WEBBROWSER

Later this chapter discusses the `WebBrowser` control that provides better functionalities for browsing web pages. Frame should be considered as an Html document viewer more than a real browsing control.

GroupBox

The WPF `GroupBox` control has the same purpose for same named controls in other technologies, offering a container with a header and a border for grouping nested controls. The following code shows how you can implement a `GroupBox`, assigning its headers and nesting controls:

```
<GroupBox Name="Group1" Margin="5">
    <GroupBox.Header>
        <TextBlock Text="Set your options"/>
    </GroupBox.Header>
```

```
<StackPanel Margin="10">
    <CheckBox Name="Check3" Content="Set a single option"/>
    <RadioButton Name="Radio3" Content="Use this"/>
    <RadioButton Name="Radio4" Content="Use that"/>
</StackPanel>
</GroupBox>
```

Figure 32.9 shows the output of this code.

FIGURE 32.9   Grouping controls with a GroupBox.

Notice that in this example the Header property is defined in the hierarchical fashion, meaning that you can add to the header complex visual elements other than simple text. For example you can add a StackPanel nesting an image with text.

Image

The Image control enables presenting images. A complete example is available in Chapter 34.

Label

The Label control shows a text message, as in the following code example:

```
<Label Name="Label1" Content="A sample value"/>
```

WPF offers the TextBlock control that provides deeper customizations features for text, so you should prefer the one covered in more detail later in this chapter.

ListBox

The `ListBox` control enables listing a series of items. The good news is that you are not limited to text items but you can also add complex items. Each item is represented by a `ListBoxItem` object, nested in the `ListBox`. The following example shows how you can declare a `ListBox` in XAML code:

```
<ListBox Name="ListBox1">
    <ListBoxItem Content="Item 1"/>
    <ListBoxItem Content="Item 2"/>
    <!— Creating a complex item,
        with text and picture —>
    <ListBoxItem>
        <ListBoxItem.Content>
            <StackPanel>
                <TextBlock Text="Item 3 with image"/>
                <Image Source="MyImage.jpg" />
            </StackPanel>
        </ListBoxItem.Content>
    </ListBoxItem>
</ListBox>
```

Typically a `ListBox` is populated at runtime via data-binding. Basically concepts are the same as illustrated for the `ComboBox` control, so take a look there for a recap. To accomplish data-binding, simply specify the `ItemsSource` markup extension as follows:

```
<ListBox Name="ListBox1" ItemsSource="{Binding}"/>
```

Then in Visual Basic code you assign the `ItemsSource` property with a data-source as demonstrated in the following LINQ query that returns a list of names about running processes:

```
Dim procList = From proc In Process.GetProcesses.
                AsEnumerable
                Select proc.ProcessName


Me.ListBox1.ItemsSource = procList
```

You access items in the `ListBox` via some properties such as the following:

- `SelectedItem`, of type `Object`, which returns the instance of the selected item in the `ListBox`. The returned object must be converted into the appropriate type.

- `Items`, which returns a read-only collection of items in the control.

In Chapter 35 you see a more extensive example of data-binding using the `ListBox`. Figure 32.10 shows the result for the data-bound implementation.

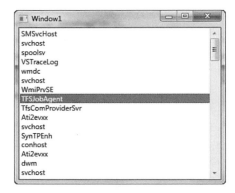

FIGURE 32.10   A data-bound `ListBox`.

DATA-BINDING

The `ListBox` control is generally intended for presenting data, even if you can customize items' template with `TextBox` controls. For two-way data-binding, prefer the `DataGrid` control described in Chapter 35.

ListView

The `ListView` control offers a higher customization level if compared to the `ListBox` and can also be used for receiving the user input other than just presenting data. Same as for the `ListBox`, you might want to consider the `DataGrid` control for advanced data-binding techniques. To present a series of items, the ListView can be declared the same way as the `ListBox`. Things are better when you instead want to use such control with columns, such as in a grid. Consider the following XAML code that declares a `ListView` data-bound to the list of running processes:

```
<ListView Name="ListView1" ItemsSource="{Binding}">
    <ListView.View>
        <GridView>
            <GridViewColumn Header="Process ID">
                <GridViewColumn.CellTemplate>
                    <DataTemplate>
                        <TextBlock Text="{Binding Path=Id}"/>
                    </DataTemplate>
                </GridViewColumn.CellTemplate>
            </GridViewColumn>
            <GridViewColumn Header="Process name">
                <GridViewColumn.CellTemplate>
                    <DataTemplate>
                        <TextBlock
                          Text="{Binding Path=ProcessName}"/>
```

```
            </DataTemplate>
          </GridViewColumn.CellTemplate>
        </GridViewColumn>

      </GridView>
    </ListView.View>
</ListView>
```

The `View` property establishes how the control will look. The `GridView` creates a nested grid with column definitions. Each `GridViewColumn` represents a single column where you can customize cells by defining the `CellTemplate` item. A `DataTemplate` item is nested that actually stores one or more visual elements that show how each object in the `ListView` appears. See Chapter 35 for more details on data-binding; at the moment consider that the `Binding Path` extension points to the specified property of the associated data source. Then you simply assign the `ItemsSource` property, as in the following Visual Basic code that retrieves the list of running processes:

```
Me.ListView1.ItemsSource = Process.GetProcesses.AsEnumerable
```

This populates the `ListView` that just shows two properties from the data source. Figure 32.11 shows the result of the code.

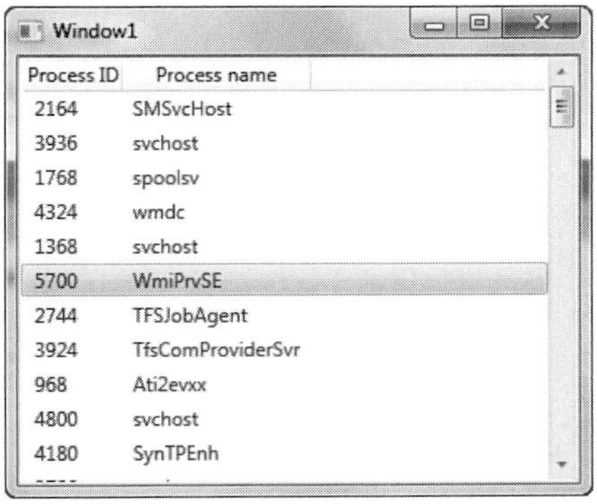

FIGURE 32.11   The result for the data-bound `ListView`.

MediaElement

The `MediaElement` control enables playing multimedia files. A complete example is available in Chapter 34.

Menu

WPF still enables creating user interfaces based on menus via the `Menu` control. You nest inside the `Menu` control many `MenuItem` objects and as many commands as you need; you can also nest `MenuItem` objects into other `MenuItem` to create submenus. Menus in WPF are highly customizable, because you can specify background and foreground colors, add images and other visual elements, and set different fonts for specific menu items. The following example shows how to accomplish this:

```
<DockPanel LastChildFill="True" VerticalAlignment="Top">
    <Menu DockPanel.Dock="Top">

        <MenuItem Header="First menu" IsEnabled="True"
                DockPanel.Dock="Top">

            <MenuItem Header="_TestMenu"/>
            <Separator/>
            <MenuItem IsEnabled="True" Name="Copy"
                    Click="Copy_Click">
                <MenuItem.Header>_Copy</MenuItem.Header>
            </MenuItem>
            <MenuItem IsEnabled="True" Name="Paste"
                    Click="Paste_Click"
                    ToolTip="Paste your text">
                <MenuItem.Header>_Paste</MenuItem.Header>
            </MenuItem>
            <Separator />

            <MenuItem Name="FontMenuItem" Header="Item with another font"
                FontFamily="Tahoma" FontSize="16" FontStyle="Italic"
                FontWeight="Bold"
                />
        </MenuItem>

        <MenuItem Header="Second menu" DockPanel.Dock="Top"
                Background="Blue" Foreground="White">

            <!—<MenuItem Header="Item with bitmap image">
                <MenuItem.Icon>

                    <Image Source="Immages/MyImage.png" />
                </MenuItem.Icon>
            </MenuItem>—>

            <MenuItem Header="Checkable item" IsCheckable="True"
                    IsChecked="True" />
            <MenuItem Header="Disabled item" IsEnabled="False"
                    Name="DisabledMenuItem"/>

        </MenuItem>
    </Menu>
</DockPanel>
```

There are a lot of properties that you can set within menus. Table 32.1 summarizes the most important ones that were used in the preceding code.

TABLE 32.1 Most common properties in `Menu` and `MenuItems`

Property	Description
`Header`	Sets the content of the item
`IsEnabled`	Sets the item enabled or disabled (True or False)
`Name`	Assigns an identifier so that you can interact in VB code
`Tooltip`	Provides a description over the item when the mouse passes over
`IsCheckable`	Sets the item to be flagged via a check box
`Icon`	Sets the menu item's icon

By assigning the `Click` property for each `MenuItem`, you can handle the click event, as in the following code snippet:

```
Private Sub Copy_Click(ByVal sender As System.Object,
                        ByVal e As System.Windows.RoutedEventArgs)
    MessageBox.Show("You clicked Copy")
End Sub

Private Sub Paste_Click(ByVal sender As System.Object,
                        ByVal e As System.Windows.RoutedEventArgs)
    MessageBox.Show("You clicked Paste")
End Sub
```

Notice that the main `Menu` item is placed inside a `DockPanel` container that provides better arrangement for this kind of control. Figure 32.12 shows the result of the menu implementation.

FIGURE 32.12 Implementing menus and submenus.

PasswordBox

The `PasswordBox` control is a special text box intended for entering passwords and that automatically hides characters. The following code snippet shows an example:

```
<StackPanel Orientation="Horizontal">
    <PasswordBox Name="PasswordBox1" Margin="5"
                 Width="150" MaxLength="20"
                 PasswordChar="*"/>
    <Button Name="PasswordButton" Width="100" Height="30"
            Margin="5" Content="Check password"
            Click="PasswordButton_Click"/>
</StackPanel>
```

By default characters are hidden with a dot, but you can replace it via the `PasswordChar` property (optional). The `MaxLength` property limits the password length (optional). Such control exposes the `Password` property of type `String` that is the entered password, as demonstrated by the following code:

```
Private Sub PasswordButton_Click(ByVal sender As Object,
                                 ByVal e As RoutedEventArgs)
    Dim myPassword = "TestPassword"
    If PasswordBox1.Password = myPassword Then
        MessageBox.Show("Password matches")
    Else
        MessageBox.Show("Password does not match")
    End If
End Sub
```

Figure 32.13 shows the result of the code.

FIGURE 32.13   Implementing a `PasswordBox`.

The main event in the `PasswordBox` is `PasswordChanged` that is raised when the control's content changes.

ProgressBar

The `ProgressBar` control requires you to set some start properties, such as `Minimum`, `Maximum`, and `Value`. Then you can increase the value at runtime. The following XAML code declares a `ProgressBar`:

```
<ProgressBar Name="ProgressBar1" Height="30"
```

```
Value="0"
Minimum="0" Maximum="10000"/>
```

To update the progress value, a good approach is making this asynchronously. This can be accomplished by invoking the `Dispatcher`, which is the WPF object responsible for managing threads. This points to the `ProgressBar.SetValue` to update the progress value. So the first step is to create a custom delegate that matches `SetValue`'s signature:

```
Private Delegate Sub updateDelegate(ByVal depProperty As _
                System.Windows.DependencyProperty, _
                ByVal value As Object)
```

The next step is to provide code that updates the progress value. This is just a demonstration loop that invokes the dispatcher while increasing the progress value:

```
Private Sub HandleProgressBar()
    Dim value As Double = ProgressBar1.Value

    Dim updateProgressBar As New _
        updateDelegate(AddressOf _
                            ProgressBar1.SetValue)

    Do Until ProgressBar1.Value = ProgressBar1.Maximum
        value += 1

        Dispatcher.Invoke(updateProgressBar, _
            System.Windows.Threading.DispatcherPriority.Background, _
            New Object() {ProgressBar.ValueProperty, value})
    Loop
End Sub
```

The `Dispatcher.Invoke` method invokes the delegate, which does nothing but invoking `ProgressBar.SetValue`. The other interesting argument is an array of `Object` storing the dependency property to be updated (`ProgressBar.ValueProperty`), which will be reflected onto `Value`, and its value. Figure 32.14 shows the result of the code.

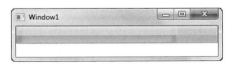

FIGURE 32.14   The `ProgressBar` value increasing.

RadioButton

The RadioButton control works similarly to the CheckBox, differing in that this enables one choice among several alternatives, but basically it exposes the same properties. The following XAML code declares two RadioButton controls:

```
<StackPanel>
    <RadioButton Name="Radio1" Content="First option"/>
    <RadioButton Name="Radio2" Content="Second option"/>
</StackPanel>
```

Each instance exposes the IsChecked property and the Checked and Unchecked events. For this, take a look back at the CheckBox discussion. Figure 32.15 shows how the controls look.

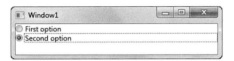

FIGURE 32.15   Adding RadioButton selection.

Rectangle

The Rectangle element is another common geometric shape that you can utilize in custom control templates. Drawing a rectangle is easy, as demonstrated in the following code example:

```
<Rectangle Width="150" Height="50"
           Fill="Orange" Stroke="Red"
           StrokeThickness="3"/>
```

You simply define its dimensions, specifying Stroke and StrokeThickness as for the ellipse (optional). Figure 32.16 shows how the object is drawn.

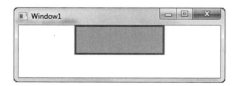

FIGURE 32.16   Drawing a rectangle.

Rectangle also has the RadiusX and RadiusY properties that you can assign to round corners.

RichTextBox

WPF 4 offers a RichTextBox control that works differently from Windows Forms and requires you to understand flow documents. This topic will be discussed in Chapter 34.

ScrollBar

You can implement scrollbars with the `ScrollBar` control. The following code provides an example:

```
<ScrollBar Name="Scroll1" Maximum="100" Minimum="0"
           Value="50" Scroll="Scroll1_Scroll"/>
```

The implementation is simple, because you just have to provide the `Minimum`, `Maximum`, and current `Value`. The `Scroll` event is instead raised when the selector position changes. The event handler is then implemented as follows:

```
Private Sub Scroll1_Scroll(ByVal sender As System.Object,
                          ByVal e As Primitives.
                          ScrollEventArgs)

End Sub
```

WPF offers a more versatile control, named `ScrollViewer`, as described in the next section.

ScrollViewer

The `ScrollViewer` element enables scrolling its entire content with both horizontal and vertical scrollbars. This can be easily understood directly at design time. Type the following XAML code:

```
<ScrollViewer VerticalScrollBarVisibility="Auto"
              HorizontalScrollBarVisibility="Auto">
    <StackPanel>
        <TextBlock Width="1000"/>
        <TextBlock Height="2000"/>
    </StackPanel>
</ScrollViewer>
```

You notice that, because of the big width and height values, the `ScrollViewer` provides both scrollbars, as demonstrated in Figure 32.17.

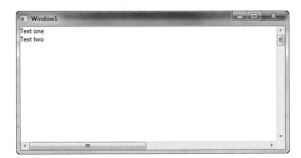

FIGURE 32.17   Implementing a `ScrollViewer`.

This control is useful when you need to arrange multiple elements in a fixed fashion, but you still want to provide the ability of scrolling them within the window.

Separator

The Separator `control` is used for drawing a separation line between visual elements. I provided an example above when discussing the `Menu` control.

Slider

The `Slider` control provides a selector that you can use to set a particular value that is generally bound to another control. Chapter 34 provides an example binding a `Slider` to a `MediaElement` for controlling the volume; however, at the moment consider the following code:

```
<Slider Name="Slider1"
        Maximum="10" Minimum="0" Value="5"
        AutoToolTipPlacement="BottomRight"
        TickPlacement="TopLeft" TickFrequency="1"
        />
<TextBlock Text="{Binding ElementName=Slider1,
           Path=Value}"/>
```

A `Slider` requires a `Minimum` and `Maximum` value, whereas `Value` is the current selected value. You can place tool tips reporting the value (`AutoToolTipPlacement`) specifying the position (`TopLeft` or `BottomRight`). Moreover you can place ticks so that visualization is clearer and decide how many ticks to place (`TickFrequency`). For example, the preceding code can produce 10 ticks (one per possible value). The `TextBlock` simply shows the value of the slider via data-binding, which is generally the preferred way for binding a `Slider` value to another control. This object raises a `ValueChanged` event when the user moves the selector to another value. Figure 32.18 shows the result of the preceding code.

FIGURE 32.18   Setting values with a `Slider`.

StatusBar

WPF enables placing status bars at the bottom of a Window. This is accomplished by declaring a StatusBar object that nests StatusBarItems elements. The good news is that you are not limited to adding text to a StatusBar, because you can add several kinds of visual elements. The following example shows adding text and a ProgressBar into a StatusBar:

```
<StatusBar>
    <StatusBarItem Name="Item1" Content="Ready"/>
    <StatusBarItem Name="Item2">
        <ProgressBar Name="Progress1"
            Minimum="0" Maximum="200" Value="50"
            Width="50" Height="15" />
    </StatusBarItem>
</StatusBar>
```

Figure 32.19 shows the result of the preceding code. You access members in the bar at the Visual Basic level via their identifiers.

FIGURE 32.19   A StatusBar with nested controls.

TabControl

The TabControl enables splitting an area into tabs. Each tab is represented by a TabItem object, and tabs are enclosed within a TabControl.TabItems collection. The following code demonstrates how you can implement a TabControl with both standard and customized tabs:

```
<TabControl>
    <TabControl.Items>
        <TabItem Header="Tab1">
            <!— Nest your controls here.. —>
```

```
        </TabItem>
        <TabItem Foreground="Blue"
                 Background="Orange">
            <TabItem.Header>
                <StackPanel Orientation="Horizontal">
                    <TextBlock Text="Tab2"/>
                    <!— Replace with a valid image
                    <Image Source="MyImage.jpg"/>—>
                </StackPanel>
            </TabItem.Header>
        </TabItem>
    </TabControl.Items>
</TabControl>
```

You set the tab header content assigning the Header property for each TabItem and then nest controls within the element. Notice how you can customize tabs by setting Foreground and Background and declaring the Header in a hierarchical fashion to place multiple elements. Figure 32.20 shows the TabControl implementation.

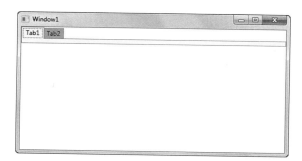

FIGURE 32.20   Implementing a TabControl.

You can also customize the header with text and an image, as you can check in the comment placed in the code. Then you access nested controls simply via their name as you would do in any other situation.

TextBlock

The TextBlock control enables showing text messages. Its purpose is similar to the Label's purpose, but it differs in that TextBlock offers deeper control over text customization. The following example demonstrates how you can present customized text using the TextBlock:

```
<TextBlock Name="TextBlock1" FontFamily="Tahoma"
           FontSize="20" FontStyle="Italic"
           FontWeight="Bold"
           Text="Sample text with TextBlock">
```

```
    <TextBlock.Foreground>
        <LinearGradientBrush>
            <GradientStop Offset="0" Color="Blue"/>
            <GradientStop Offset="0.5" Color="Violet"/>
            <GradientStop Offset="1" Color="Green"/>
        </LinearGradientBrush>
    </TextBlock.Foreground>
</TextBlock>
```

Font properties are of particular interest. `FontFamily` indicates the font name, `FontStyle` indicates if the font is normal or oblique, whereas `FontWeight` sets the font depth. IntelliSense enhancements in WPF 4 enable easy selections for available members on each of the previously mentioned properties. Figure 32.21 shows the result of the preceding code.

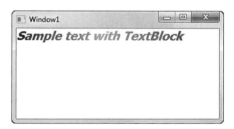

FIGURE 32.21   Drawing a `TextBlock`.

Because of its flexibility, the `TextBlock` control is often used in custom control templates that require customizing text. You can also set the `TextBlock` text at runtime by assigning the `Text` property.

TextBox

Another typical control that is also provided by WPF is the `TextBox`. You declare one as follows:

```
<TextBox Name="TextBox1"
        TextChanged="TextBox1_TextChanged"/>
```

The most common event is `TextChanged` that is raised when the text is modified and that can be handled as follows:

```
Private Sub TextBox1_TextChanged(ByVal sender As System.Object,
                                 ByVal e As System.Windows.Controls.
                                 TextChangedEventArgs)
```

End Sub

The e object of type TextChangedEventArgs offers a Changes collection property that can be iterated to get a list of changes that affect the control's content. The TextBox control provides support for undo actions (that is, Ctrl+Z) and a SelectedText property that enables you to easily retrieve in VB code the currently selected text in the control.

ToolBar

The ToolBar control enables creating toolbars for your WPF applications. You can add multiple ToolBar objects within a ToolBarTray object. The following XAML code shows how you can define a simple toolbar; you have to replace image files with valid ones:

```
<ToolBarTray>
    <ToolBar>
        <Button Name="NewButton"
                Click="NewButton_Click">
          <Image Source=NewDocument.png" />
        </Button>
        <Button Name="OpenButton"
                Click="OpenButton_Click">
          <Image Source="OpenFolder.png" />
        </Button>
        <Button Name="SaveButton"
                Click="SaveButton_Click">
          <Image Source="Save.png" />
        </Button>
    </ToolBar>
</ToolBarTray>
```

Notice how the code implements primitive Button controls that you can manage in Visual Basic code with classic event handlers for the Click event. Following this logic you can place additional ToolBar objects inside the ToolBarTray. Figure 32.22 shows how the ToolBar looks.

FIGURE 32.22   Implementing a ToolBar.

TreeView

The TreeView is another important control, and WPF provides its own implementation that exposes a TreeView.Items collection where you nest nodes. Each node is represented by a TreeViewItem object. You can build complex items as in the following example:

```
<TreeView Name="TreeView1">
    <TreeView.Items>
        <TreeViewItem Header="Root Node" Name="RootNode"
                      Tag="Information for this node">
            <TreeViewItem Header="Node0" Name="Node0"/>
            <TreeViewItem Header="Node1" Name="Node1">
                <TreeViewItem Header="SubNode"
                              Name="SubNode"/>
            </TreeViewItem>
        </TreeViewItem>
    </TreeView.Items>
</TreeView>
```

The text in the node is specified with the Header property while additional information can be assigned with the Tag property. Assigning the Name property is also useful because you can interact with nodes in managed code. To add nodes at runtime you simply create an instance of the TreeViewItem class and then add it to the specified node as demonstrated here:

```
Dim nt As New TreeViewItem
With nt
    .Header = "New sub node"
    .Tag = "Runtime added"
End With

Node0.Items.Add(nt)
```

Figure 32.23 shows the result for all the preceding code.

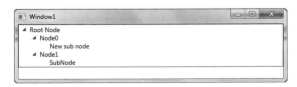

FIGURE 32.23   Implementing and populating a TreeView.

The TreeView can also be populated via data-binding with the ItemsSource property and exposes the SelectedItem property, exactly as it happens for the ComboBox and ListBox controls, so you can apply the same techniques.

WebBrowser

Because the .NET Framework 3.5 SP 1 `WebBrowser` control is available for WPF developers, the control provides specific functionalities for browsing websites. You add it to the user interface by simply declaring a `WebBrowser` element as follows:

```
<WebBrowser Name="Browser1"/>
```

Then you can control the `WebBrowser` behavior from Visual Basic code; the following are methods exposed by the `WebBrowser` allowing navigation:

```
'Open the specified web-site
Browser1.Navigate(New Uri("Http://www.visual-basic.it"))
'Back to the previous page
Browser1.GoBack()
'Forward to the next page
Browser1.GoForward()
'Refresh the page
Browser1.Refresh()
```

The `WebBrowser` also exposes some events, and the most important is `LoadCompleted` that is raised when the control completes loading a web page. This can be handled to get useful information on the visited website, as in the following code snippet:

```
Private Sub Browser1_LoadCompleted(ByVal sender As Object,
                          ByVal e As NavigationEventArgs) _
                          Handles Browser1.Navigated
    MessageBox.Show(e.Uri.ToString)
End Sub
```

The e object of type `NavigationEventArgs` provides properties that retrieve information such as the website `Uri` or the `WebResponse` instance.

WindowsFormsHost

The `WindowsFormsHost` control enables interoperability with the Windows Forms technology and provides a way for hosting Win Forms user controls within a WPF application.

INTEROPERABILITY TIPS

I often answer questions in online forums about WPF, and one of the most common questions is about interoperability between Windows Forms and WPF, especially for developers that are moving their applications to WPF. There are so many architectural differences between the two technologies that interoperability is not a task that I suggest. You should recur to interoperability only when there is no other way of rewriting a WPF version of a Windows Form control, which is improbable.

To host a Windows Forms control, you drag the `WindowsFormsHost` element from the Toolbox onto the Window surface. The next step is adding a reference to the System.Windows.Forms.dll assembly. If you want to host Windows Forms controls built-in the .NET Framework, you need to add an Xml namespace declaration at the Window level; the following line of XAML code demonstrates this:

```
xmlns:wf="clr-namespace:System.Windows.Forms;assembly=System.Windows.Forms"
```

At this point you can simply nest the desired control inside the `WindowsFormsHost` declaration, as in the following example that adds a `System.Windows.Forms.PictureBox`:

```
<WindowsFormsHost Height="100"
                  Name="WindowsFormsHost1"
                  Width="200">
    <wf:PictureBox x:Name="Picture1"/>
</WindowsFormsHost>
```

Notice that you need to provide the `x:Name` attribute to make the control reachable from the Visual Basic code. At this point you can interact with the `PictureBox` like you would in any other Windows Forms application by simply invoking its identifier, as demonstrated in the following code snippets where the code loads an image file and assigns it to the `PictureBox`; this particular example also requires a reference to the System.Drawing.dll assembly:

```
'This is Windows Forms code inside a WPF application
Me.Picture1.Image = System.Drawing.Image.
                    FromFile("C:\Picture.jpg")
```

Of course this technique works with custom user controls as well; you just need to add an Xml namespace reference pointing to the appropriate assembly exposing the custom user control (including the current project), and then you can consume the control itself.

Using Common Dialogs

In WPF 4 common dialogs are wrappers of Win32 dialogs. They are exposed by the Microsoft.Win32 namespace and are `OpenFileDialog` and `SaveFileDialog`. (WPF also provides a `PrintDialog` control exposed by the System.Windows.Controls namespace.) The following code demonstrates how you instantiate both dialogs:

```
'Instantiating an OpenFileDialog
Dim od As New Microsoft.Win32.OpenFileDialog
With od
    .Title = "Your title here..."
    .Filter = "All files¦*.*"
```

```
        .ShowReadOnly = True

    If .ShowDialog = True Then
        Dim fileName As String = .FileName
    End If
End With

'Instantiating a SaveFileDialog
Dim sd As New Microsoft.Win32.SaveFileDialog
With sd
    .Title = "Your title here..."
    .InitialDirectory = "."
    .Filter = "All files¦*.*"
    If .ShowDialog = True Then
        Dim fileName As String = .FileName
    End If
End With
```

Notice that the ShowDialog method returns a Nullable(Of Boolean) where True means that the user clicks **OK**, False when she clicks **Cancel**, and Nothing when she closes the dialog.

Summary

In this chapter you took an overview of WPF's most common used controls that you can use in your client applications, understanding how they can be both implemented in XAML or VB code. Also we covered some particular aspects about them, such as their so-called *lookless* implementation, understanding why they can also be nameless because of routed events.

CHAPTER 33

Brushes, Styles, Templates, and Animations in WPF

Building rich user experiences has become an important business. Functionalities are no more the only requirement, even in business applications, because an attractive user interface also plays a fundamental role. WPF offers the ideal platform for enriching the user interface with interactive content, such as animations, media files, dynamic documents, and graphical effects. WPF is also the ideal platform for building graphics manipulation applications, where geometry or 3D graphic have a great place for running. Before you learn such important features, it is important for you to get knowledge about some graphics fundamentals so that you can enrich visual elements. It is worth mentioning that one of the biggest benefits of WPF is that you can take complete control over UI elements' customization. You can fill them with impressive gradients, you can completely rewrite their layout while keeping their behavior safe, and you can animate them along the user interface ensuring that they will still work as you effectively expect. The goal of this chapter is to illustrate customization so that you can make your user interface more and more attractive.

Introducing Brushes

Probably lots of times you wanted to fill your UI controls with interesting background textures or with gradients or simply set a particular color, maybe as the background or the foreground. In Windows Presentation Foundation you fill visual elements with brushes. WPF defines several kinds of brushes, all deriving from `System.Windows.Media.Brush`. The following list summarizes available brushes:

- `SolidColorBrush`, which allows filling a graphical object with a single color. Colors are exposed as static properties from the `System.Windows.Media.Colors` class.

- `LinearGradientBrush`, which enables filling a graphical object with a linear gradient composed of multiple colors.

- `RadialGradientBrush`, which is similar to the previous one, but the gradient is circular.

- `ImageBrush`, which enables filling a graphical object with a picture.

- `DrawingBrush`, which enables filling a graphical object with geometrical shapes or pen drawings.

- `SelectionBrush`, which enables defining the highlighting color when selecting text in specific controls.

- `CaretBrush`, which enables defining the mouse pointer color in particular controls. Actually `CaretBrush` is a property exposed by controls such as `TextBox` and `RichTextBox`, which accept Brush objects.

- `VisualBrush`, which enables filling a graphical object with the content of another element in the user interface.

- `BitmapCacheBrush`, which provides the ability of caching a visual element instead of rendering it again and is useful when you need to recall the same visual elements multiple times.

You can apply brushes to properties in visual elements exposing a `Background`, `Foreground`, or `Fill` property, such as user controls and geometrical shapes. In the next sections you learn to fill your UI elements with the previously listed brushes. Before providing examples, create a new WPF project with Visual Basic 2010. Divide the default `Grid` into eight rows and adjust `Window`'s size as follows:

```
<Window x:Class="MainWindow"
    xmlns="http://schemas.microsoft.com/winfx/2006/xaml/presentation"
    xmlns:x="http://schemas.microsoft.com/winfx/2006/xaml"
    Title="MainWindow" Height="550" Width="550">
    <Grid>
        <Grid.RowDefinitions>
            <RowDefinition />
            <RowDefinition />
            <RowDefinition />
            <RowDefinition />
            <RowDefinition />
            <RowDefinition />
            <RowDefinition />
```

```
            <RowDefinition />
        </Grid.RowDefinitions>
    </Grid>
</Window>
```

ABBREVIATING LINES OF CODE

To make lines of code shorter, add an `Imports System.Windows.Media` directive in the Visual Basic code behind the file.

Applying a `SolidColorBrush`

The `System.Windows.Media.SolidColorBrush` object enables filling an object with a single color. Generally the color is applied to the `Fill` property of geometric shapes and to the Background or Foreground properties in UI controls. The following code demonstrates how to apply a `SolidColorBrush`:

```
<Rectangle Grid.Row="0" Width="200" Margin="5">
    <Rectangle.Fill>
        <SolidColorBrush Color="Red"/>
    </Rectangle.Fill>
</Rectangle>
```

The Color property receives a value of type `System.Windows.Media.Color`. Colors are exposed by the `System.Windows.Media.Colors` class as shared properties. The result of this color brush is shown in Figure 33.1.

FIGURE 33.1   Applying a `SolidColorBrush`.

Applying a color at runtime in Visual Basic code is also a simple task. The following snippet shows how you can set it within the code-behind file:

```
Dim rect As New Rectangle


Dim scb As New SolidColorBrush(Colors.Red)
rect.Fill = scb
```

Applying a `LinearGradientBrush`

A `LinearGradientBrush` enables applying a gradient color to fill a visual element. Valid targets are the `Fill` property for geometric shapes—`Background` and `Foreground` properties for user controls. The following code draws a `Rectangle` and demonstrates that the gradient is applied both as background color (`Fill` property) and as foreground (`Stroke`):

```
<Rectangle Grid.Row="1" Width="200" Margin="5" Name="GradientRectangle"
                StrokeThickness="3">
  <Rectangle.Fill>
    <LinearGradientBrush StartPoint="0,0" EndPoint="0,1">
        <GradientStop Offset="0" Color="Orange"/>
        <GradientStop Offset="0.5" Color="Red"/>
        <GradientStop Offset="0.9" Color="Yellow"/>
    </LinearGradientBrush>
  </Rectangle.Fill>
  <Rectangle.Stroke>
      <LinearGradientBrush StartPoint="0,0" EndPoint="0,1">
          <GradientStop Offset="0" Color="Blue"/>
          <GradientStop Offset="0.5" Color="Green"/>
          <GradientStop Offset="0.9" Color="Violet"/>
      </LinearGradientBrush>
    </Rectangle.Stroke>
</Rectangle>
```

First, it is worth mentioning that the `StrokeThickness` property of `Rectangle` specifies the shape's border size. Each color in the gradient is represented by a `GradientStop` element. Its `Offset` property requires a value from 0 to 1 and specifies the color position in the gradient, whereas the color property accepts the color name or the color hexadecimal representation. Also notice how `StartPoint` and `EndPoint` properties in the `LinearGradientBrush` enable influencing the gradient direction. Figure 33.2 shows the result of the preceding code.

You can define a `LinearGradientBrush` in Visual Basic code for runtime appliance. This is accomplished by the following code:

```
Dim lgb As New LinearGradientBrush
```

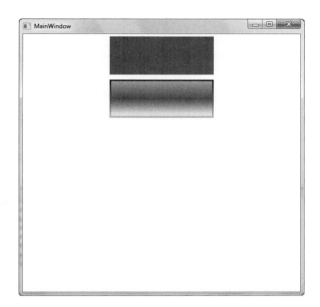

FIGURE 33.2   Applying a `LinearGradientBrush`.

```
lgb.GradientStops.Add(New GradientStop With {.Offset = 0,
                                             .Color = Colors.Red})
lgb.GradientStops.Add(New GradientStop With {.Offset = 0,
                                             .Color = Colors.Yellow})
lgb.GradientStops.Add(New GradientStop With {.Offset = 0,
                                             .Color = Colors.Orange})
'rect is a Rectangle instance
rect.Fill = lgb
```

Notice how you add instances of the `GradientStop` class to the `GradientStops` collection.
Each `GradientStop` requires both `Offset` (of type `Double`) and `Color` (of type
`System.Windows.Media.Color`) properties to be set. Colors are exposed by the
`System.Windows.Media.Colors` class as shared properties.

Applying a `RadialGradientBrush`

The `RadialGradientBrush` brush works exactly like the `LinearGradientBrush`, except that
it creates a circular gradient. The following code shows how it is possible to apply such a
brush to an `Ellipse`:

```
<Ellipse Width="100" Margin="5" Grid.Row="2" Stroke="Black"
         StrokeThickness="2" >
    <Ellipse.Fill>
```

```
    <RadialGradientBrush>
            <GradientStop Offset="0" Color="Blue"/>
            <GradientStop Offset="0.5" Color="Green"/>
            <GradientStop Offset="0.9" Color="Violet"/>
    </RadialGradientBrush>
  </Ellipse.Fill>
</Ellipse>
```

You are not limited to the Ellipse shape, but for demo purposes it is the one that best fits the example. Figure 33.3 shows the result of the brush applied.

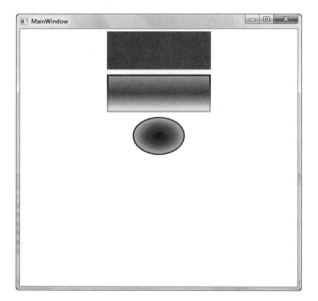

FIGURE 33.3   The result of the RadialGradientBrush.

The Visual Basic code for applying the brush at runtime is similar to the one for the linear gradient. The following code snippet provides an example:

```
Dim ragb As New RadialGradientBrush
ragb.GradientStops.Add(New GradientStop With {.Offset = 0,
                                              .Color = Colors.Red})
ragb.GradientStops.Add(New GradientStop With {.Offset = 0,
                                              .Color = Colors.Yellow})
ragb.GradientStops.Add(New GradientStop With {.Offset = 0,
                                              .Color = Colors.Orange})
rect.Fill = ragb
```

Applying an `ImageBrush`

You can fill a visual element with an image file taking advantage of the `ImageBrush` brush. This object is useful even if you want to fill text with image textures. The following code snippet shows how to apply an `ImageBrush` as a button background and as the text foreground color:

```
<StackPanel Grid.Row="3" Orientation="Horizontal">
    <Button Width="100" Margin="5" Content="Hello!"
        Foreground="Yellow">
        <Button.Background>
            <ImageBrush Opacity="0.5"
                ImageSource=
            "/StylesBrushesTemplatesAnimations;component/Images/Avatar.jpg" />
        </Button.Background>
    </Button>

    <TextBlock Margin="5"
                FontFamily="Segoe UI" FontSize="40" Text="Hello!"
                FontWeight="Bold" >
        <TextBlock.Foreground>
          <ImageBrush ImageSource=
            "/StylesBrushesTemplatesAnimations;component/Images/Avatar.jpg"/>
        </TextBlock.Foreground>
    </TextBlock>
</StackPanel>
```

> **NOTE**
>
> In the previous code, the Avatar.jpg file is just a sample picture of me. I suppose you might prefer to replace my face with one of your favorite pictures!

The image is specified by assigning the `ImageSource` property with the image's Uri. The previous code produces the result shown in Figure 33.4 (see the last row).

If you want to add your images to the application resources so that you can easily refer to them when applying the `ImageBrush`, follow these steps:

1. Write the `ImageBrush` element in the XAML code editor.
2. Open the **Properties** window pointing to the brush.
3. Select the `ImageSource` property and click the available button. The **Choose Image** dialog displays, as shown in Figure 33.5, where you can browse for your image. When added, its address will be assigned to the `ImageProperty` in the XAML code under the form of a packed Uri.

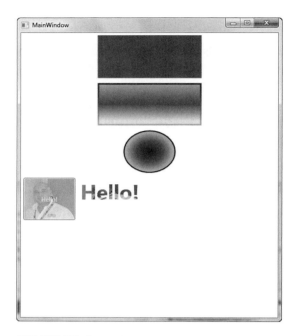

FIGURE 33.4   Applying an `ImageBrush` as background and foreground color.

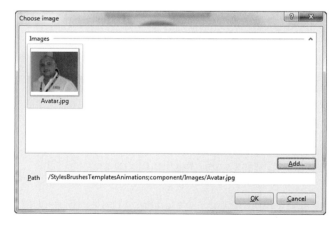

FIGURE 33.5   Selecting an image with the designer tools.

Applying an `ImageBrush` in Visual Basic code is also a simple task, demonstrated by the following code snippet:

```
Dim myButton As New Button
Dim imgb As New ImageBrush
```

```
imgb.ImageSource = New BitmapImage _
    (New _
    Uri("/StylesBrushesTemplatesAnimations;component/Images/Avatar.jpg",
    UriKind.Relative))
myButton.Background = imgb
```

Notice how, in Visual Basic code, you specify the image by creating first an instance of the BitmapImage class whose constructor receives an argument of type Uri pointing to the actual image file.

Applying SelectionBrush and CaretBrush

WPF 4 introduces two new objects, SelectionBrush and CaretBrush, which are properties of type System.Windows.Media.Brush and that accept brushes to be assigned to them. The first one enables you to apply a brush to the highlighting color when selecting text, whereas the second one applies a brush to the mouse caret within the control. Controls that can receive application of these brushes are TextBox and PasswordBox. SelectionBrush can be also applied to FlowDocumentPageViewer, FlowDocumentReader, and FlowDocumentScrollViewer. You apply both brushes as child nodes of the desired control. The following code demonstrates how to apply a linear gradient color for both the highlighting selection color and the caret color:

```
<TextBox Grid.Row="4" Margin="5"
        FontSize="20" FontWeight="Bold"
        Name="TextBox1">
    <TextBox.SelectionBrush>
        <LinearGradientBrush>
            <GradientStop Offset="0" Color="Chartreuse"/>
            <GradientStop Offset="0.5" Color="Violet"/>
            <GradientStop Offset="1" Color="Blue"/>
        </LinearGradientBrush>
    </TextBox.SelectionBrush>

    <TextBox.CaretBrush>
        <LinearGradientBrush>
            <GradientStop Offset="0" Color="Red"/>
            <GradientStop Offset="0.5" Color="Yellow"/>
            <GradientStop Offset="1" Color="Orange"/>
        </LinearGradientBrush>
    </TextBox.CaretBrush>
</TextBox>
```

Figure 33.6 shows the result of this code, although the caret gradient is not visible at this point, but you will see there are no problems on your screen.

FIGURE 33.6   Applying `SelectionBrush` and `CaretBrush`.

You can apply different kinds of brushes, such as `ImageBrush` or `VisualBrush`, as described in the next section.

Applying a `VisualBrush`

The `VisualBrush` enables filling an object with the content of another visual element in the user interface. For example, you could set a button's background with the content of a `MediaElement` that is playing a video. Applying a `VisualBrush` is simple, in that you just need to assign its `Visual` property with the name of the visual element you want to bind. The following code example shows how you can assign another visual element currently in the user interface as the background of a button:

```
<Button Width="100" Margin="5" Grid.Row="5">
    <Button.Background>
        <VisualBrush Visual="{Binding ElementName=GradientRectangle}"/>
    </Button.Background>
</Button>
```

The requirement is that the source visual element has a `Name` property set. You assign the visual element with the `Binding` markup extension, whose `ElementName` property points to the actual visual element. You learn more about the `Binding` extension in Chapter 35, "Introducing Data-Binding." The previous example produces the result shown in Figure 33.7.

Basically the button's background is not a color but is a rectangle with all its properties. It is worth mentioning that if you make modifications to the binding source, the changes

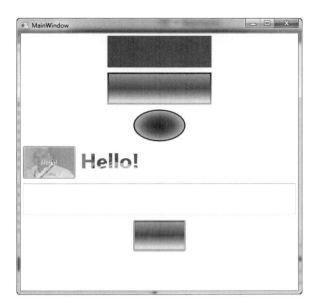

FIGURE 33.7   Applying a `VisualBrush`.

will be reflected into the `VisualBrush`. This is the real power of this brush. For example, try to use a `TextBox` as the source element; when you write in the `TextBox`, your text will be reflected into the `VisualBrush`.

Applying a DrawingBrush

The `DrawingBrush` brush enables painting an area with a so called *drawing*. A drawing, according to the MSDN documentation, can be a shape, an image, a video, text, or other and is an instance of the `System.Windows.Media.Drawing` class. The following code sample fills a rectangle with a `DrawingBrush` defining a drawing where two ellipses intersect each other:

```
<Rectangle Width="100"
           Grid.Row="6">
    <Rectangle.Fill>
        <DrawingBrush>
            <DrawingBrush.Drawing>
                <GeometryDrawing>
                    <GeometryDrawing.Brush>
                        <LinearGradientBrush>
                            <GradientStop Offset="0" Color="Blue"/>
                            <GradientStop Offset="0.7" Color="LightBlue"/>
                        </LinearGradientBrush>
                    </GeometryDrawing.Brush>
                    <GeometryDrawing.Geometry>
```

```
                          <GeometryGroup>
                            <EllipseGeometry RadiusX="0.1" RadiusY="0.5"
                                             Center="0.5,0.5" />
                            <EllipseGeometry RadiusX="0.5" RadiusY="0.1"
                                             Center="0.5,0.5" />
                          </GeometryGroup>
                        </GeometryDrawing.Geometry>
                    </GeometryDrawing>
                </DrawingBrush.Drawing>
            </DrawingBrush>
        </Rectangle.Fill>
</Rectangle>
```

Other than the brush, it is interesting here how ellipses are declared via `EllipseGeometry`
objects that are the geometric representation of ellipses and are enclosed within a
`GeometryGroup` that basically can group different kinds of geometric representations, such
as `LineGeometry` or `RectangleGeometry`. (These classes derive from
`System.Windows.Media.Geometry`, for your further studies.) Figure 33.8 shows the result of
the above snippet.

Now that you know about WPF brushes, you are ready to get an overview of another great
feature: styles.

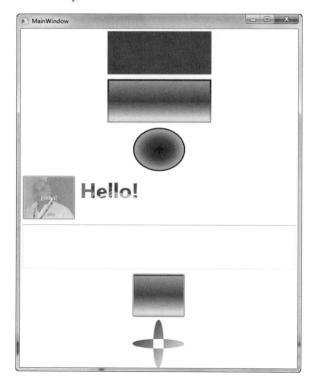

FIGURE 33.8   Applying a `DrawingBrush`.

Applying a `BitmapCacheBrush`

WPF 4 introduces the concept of *cached composition*, which provides the ability of storing a visual element to a cache so that redrawing an element is faster and provides better performance instead of rendering the graphic element each time it needs to be used. Among the others, with cached composition you can cache images to apply as a brush. This is accomplished by first declaring a `BitmapCache` object that establishes the rules for caching the desired object and then by applying a `BitmapCacheBrush` to the visual element. The following code demonstrates how to apply a `BitmapCacheBrush` as the background of two `TextBlock` controls, by using cached composition (comments in the code will help you understand better):

```
<StackPanel Grid.Row="7">
    <StackPanel.Resources>
        <!— an image pointing to the previously added
            resource —>
        <Image x:Key="cachedImage"
Source="/StylesBrushesTemplatesAnimations;component/Images/Avatar.jpg">
            <!— supposing we'll use the same image multiple
                times, we can cache it instead of
                rendering each time —>
            <Image.CacheMode>
                <!— RenderAtScale = 1 means that it is cached
                    at its actual size (no zoom) —>
                <BitmapCache RenderAtScale="1"
                            EnableClearType="False"
                            SnapsToDevicePixels="False"/>
            </Image.CacheMode>
        </Image>
        <!— Applying the cached image as a brush —>
        <BitmapCacheBrush x:Key="cachedBrush"
            Target="{StaticResource cachedImage}"/>
    </StackPanel.Resources>

    <TextBlock Text="Text one..." FontSize="24"
                Height="60" Foreground="Blue"
                FontWeight="Bold"
                Background="{StaticResource cachedBrush}"/>
    <TextBlock Text="Text two..." FontSize="24"
                Height="60" Foreground="Green"
                FontWeight="Bold"
                Background="{StaticResource cachedBrush}"/>
</StackPanel>
```

The `BitmapCache.RenderAtScale` property establishes when the visual element has to be cached. If assigned with 1, as in the preceding example, the visual element is cached at its natural size. For example, you could assign such a property with 2 in case you want to

cache the visual element only when it is zoomed at the double of its size. The
`BitmapCache.EnableClearType` property lets you decide if you want to apply Clear Type
precision to the visual elements but it is useful only with text. The
`BitmapCache.SnapsToDevicePixels` property should be assigned with True when you need
precise pixel-alignment and generally takes the same value of the `EnableClearType` property. Finally notice how the `BitmapCacheBrush` object points to the image via the Target
property and how it is applied to `TextBlock` controls via the `Background` property pointing
to the new resource. The preceding code produces the result shown in Figure 33.9.

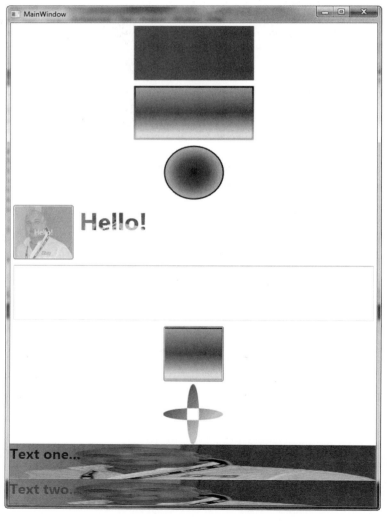

FIGURE 33.9   Applying `BitmapCachedBrush` objects.

Introducing Styles

One of the biggest benefits of WPF user controls is that their layout is completely customizable. As explained further in the "Introducing Control Templates" section, you can completely redefine their layout and behavior using templates. There are situations in which you have multiple controls of the same type and you want them to have the same properties. For example, you might want to implement three buttons and each button should have the same width, height, and font as the other ones. To avoid the need of applying the same properties for each control, which can be annoying if you have dozens of controls, you can define a Style. A style is an instance of the System.Windows.Style class and enables you to define a set of common properties for the specified type of control. Styles are defined within the Resources section of a Window, of panels, or at application level (Application.xaml file). Each style must have an identifier assigned via the x:Key attribute and is applied to controls assigning their Style property. Code in Listing 33.1 defines a style for buttons and applies the style to three buttons in the interface.

LISTING 33.1   Defining and Assigning a Style for Buttons

```
<Window x:Class="Styles"
    xmlns="http://schemas.microsoft.com/winfx/2006/xaml/presentation"
    xmlns:x="http://schemas.microsoft.com/winfx/2006/xaml"
    Title="Styles" Height="300" Width="300">
    <StackPanel>
        <StackPanel.Resources>
            <Style x:Key="ButtonStyle" TargetType="Button">
                <Setter Property="Width" Value="100"/>
                <Setter Property="Height" Value="40"/>
                <Setter Property="Foreground" Value="Blue"/>
                <Setter Property="FontFamily" Value="Verdana"/>
                <Setter Property="Margin" Value="5"/>
                <Setter Property="Background">
                    <Setter.Value>
                        <LinearGradientBrush>
                            <GradientStop Offset="0.2" Color="Orange"/>
                            <GradientStop Offset="0.8" Color="Red"/>
                        </LinearGradientBrush>
                    </Setter.Value>
                </Setter>
            </Style>
        </StackPanel.Resources>

        <Button Style="{StaticResource ButtonStyle}" Content="Hello!"/>
        <Button Style="{StaticResource ButtonStyle}" Content="Another styled"/>
        <Button Style="{StaticResource ButtonStyle}" Content="Button three"/>
    </StackPanel>
</Window>
```

33

Understanding the scope of styles is important. In the code example the style is defined at the panel level, meaning that buttons outside the panel cannot get the style applied. Notice how the `TargetType` property enables specifying the target control type. If not specified, WPF assumes `FrameworkElement` as the target. Properties are specified via `Setter` elements. Each setter requires the target `Property` specification and its value. You can also define a complex value splitting its definition creating a `Setter.Value` node, which can store multiple lines of XAML code, as in Listing 33.1 where the technique is used to define a `LinearGradientBrush` gradient. Finally notice how the new style is assigned to buttons setting the `Style` property, pointing to the style identifier via a XAML markup extension named `StaticResource`.

STATICRESOURCE AND DYNAMICRESOURCE

In different situations you can often find controls pointing to resources via `StaticResource` or `DynamicResource` markup extensions. The difference is that a `StaticResource` is something defined in the XAML that will not change during the application lifetime. It will be assigned only once even before its actual point of use. A `DynamicResource` instead is assigned when its value is effectively required and if its content changes during the application lifetime, its changes are reflected to the caller.

Running the code can produce the interesting result shown in Figure 33.10.

FIGURE 33.10 Styling multiple controls of the same type with Styles.

On the Visual Basic side, you create and apply a style as in the following code snippet:

```
Dim buttonStyle As New Style
'Need to specify the System.Type
buttonStyle.TargetType = GetType(Button)
'The Setter.Property member is assigned with a dependency property exposed
'by the System.Type
buttonStyle.Setters.Add(New Setter With {.Property = Button.WidthProperty,
                                          .Value = "100"})
Button1.Style = buttonStyle
```

This can be particularly useful if you need to generate a style at runtime, although you generally define styles at design time; therefore, declaring and applying them via XAML is the most preferable way (so that designers can eventually take advantage of XAML for their work).

Styles Inheritance

You can define a style that inherits from another one to extend it with new settings. This is accomplished by specifying the BasedOn property as follows:

```
<Style x:Key="InheritedStyle" TargetType="Button"
       BasedOn="{StaticResource ButtonStyle}">
    <Setter Property="FontWeight" Value="ExtraBold"/>
</Style>
```

If you now assign this new style to a button, it can take all the style properties of the base style plus the FontWeight value.

Understanding Triggers

Until now you saw how styles can be applied to controls without condition. This is useful, but it is more useful for deciding when to apply a style. The easiest example is to consider a button; you apply a background color that you might want to change when the mouse pointer passes over the button, and this behavior should be replicated for each button in the UI via styles. To conditionally apply styles, you use *triggers*. A trigger essentially represents a condition that enables applying a particular style when the condition is evaluated as True. Triggers are defined within a Style.Triggers collection, and each of them requires specifying the property affected by the condition and a Boolean value (True or False) that determines when the trigger has to be executed. Code in Listing 33.2 retakes the first style example, adding a trigger condition in the final part of the code.

LISTING 33.2   Applying a Single Trigger Condition

```
<Style x:Key="ButtonStyle" TargetType="Button">
    <Setter Property="Width" Value="100"/>
    <Setter Property="Height" Value="40"/>
    <Setter Property="Foreground" Value="Blue"/>
    <Setter Property="FontFamily" Value="Verdana"/>
    <Setter Property="Margin" Value="5"/>
    <Setter Property="Background">
        <Setter.Value>
            <LinearGradientBrush>
                <GradientStop Offset="0.2" Color="Orange"/>
                <GradientStop Offset="0.8" Color="Red"/>
            </LinearGradientBrush>
```

```
            </Setter.Value>
        </Setter>

        <Style.Triggers>
            <Trigger Property="IsMouseOver" Value="True">
                <Setter Property="Background">
                    <Setter.Value>
                        <LinearGradientBrush>
                            <GradientStop Offset="0.2" Color="Red"/>
                            <GradientStop Offset="0.8" Color="Yellow"/>
                        </LinearGradientBrush>
                    </Setter.Value>
                </Setter>
            </Trigger>
        </Style.Triggers>
</Style>
```

Applying the trigger described in code can cause buttons to have a different background color when the mouse pointer passes over them. In this way we applied a style according to just one condition, but there are situations in which multiple conditions have to be evaluated. For example, continuing the Button control discussion, we could decide to apply a style when the mouse pointer passes over the control and also if the button is enabled. This can be accomplished using a `MultiTrigger` object. A `MultiTrigger` can contain multiple condition specifications and as many setters for as many properties aswe want to apply in the style. The following code snippet demonstrates how to declare a `MultiTrigger` for the preceding implemented style:

```
<Style.Triggers>
    <MultiTrigger>
        <MultiTrigger.Conditions>
            <Condition Property="IsMouseOver" Value="True"/>
            <Condition Property="IsEnabled" Value="True"/>
        </MultiTrigger.Conditions>
        <Setter Property="Background">
            <Setter.Value>
                <LinearGradientBrush>
                    <GradientStop Offset="0.2" Color="Red"/>
                    <GradientStop Offset="0.8" Color="Yellow"/>
                </LinearGradientBrush>
            </Setter.Value>
        </Setter>
    </MultiTrigger>
</Style.Triggers>
```

In this case the new background is applied only when both conditions are evaluated as `True`.

Introducing Control Templates

WPF controls have a particular structure, in which the layout system is separated from the behavior. When searching resources about WPF controls, you often find a definition stating that they are *lookless*. This means that WPF controls simply have no default aspect, whereas they expose a common set of properties that can be assigned for defining the layout and the behavior. This common set is referred to as `control template`. The WPF system provides a default control template for each available control in the Base Class Library. You can then override the existing template or create a custom one. Control templates are so versatile because you can completely redesign the control look while keeping its original behavior, but you can also improve the behavior. For example, you can use an `Ellipse` as a control template for a `Button`. The new `Button` will look like an `Ellipse`, but your user can still click it and you can still handle button events.

USE EXPRESSION BLEND

Creating custom control templates can be a hard task to accomplish with Visual Studio. This is a developer tool and therefore cannot offer advanced design features as Expression Blend does. If you plan to make intensive use of custom control templates, use Blend. Use just Visual Studio if your custom templates are basic implementations. In the next examples you see something easy to implement with Visual Studio, although the logic of control templates is fully implemented.

Basically control templates are implemented as styles, but actually they are not simple styles. The difference between styles and templates is that styles affect existing properties within an existing template, whereas a control template can completely override or replace properties and layout of a control. Talking in code terms, a control template is defined within a `Style` definition, setting the `Template` property and assigning the Value of this property. Code in Listing 33.3 shows how to utilize an `Ellipse` as the control template for buttons, where the background gradient color changes when the button is pressed or when the mouse pointer flies over it.

LISTING 33.3   Building a Control Template

```
<Window.Resources>
    <Style x:Key="ButtonStyle1" TargetType="{x:Type Button}">
        <Setter Property="Template">
            <Setter.Value>
                <ControlTemplate TargetType="{x:Type Button}">
                    <Grid>
                        <Ellipse x:Name="ellipse" Stroke="Black">
                            <Ellipse.Fill>
                                <LinearGradientBrush EndPoint="0.5,1"
                                                     StartPoint="0.5,0">
                                    <GradientStop Color="Black" Offset="0"/>
                                    <GradientStop Color="White" Offset="1"/>
```

```
                                </LinearGradientBrush>
                            </Ellipse.Fill>
                        </Ellipse>
                        <ContentPresenter HorizontalAlignment=
                         "{TemplateBinding HorizontalContentAlignment}"
                         VerticalAlignment=
                         "{TemplateBinding VerticalContentAlignment}"
                         SnapsToDevicePixels=
                         "{TemplateBinding SnapsToDevicePixels}"
                         RecognizesAccessKey="True"/>
                    </Grid>
                    <ControlTemplate.Triggers>
                        <Trigger Property="IsFocused" Value="True"/>
                        <Trigger Property="IsDefaulted" Value="True"/>
                        <Trigger Property="IsMouseOver" Value="True">
                            <Setter Property="Fill" TargetName="ellipse">
                                <Setter.Value>
                                    <LinearGradientBrush EndPoint="0.5,1"
                                                         StartPoint="0.5,0">
                                        <GradientStop Color="White" Offset="0"/>
                                        <GradientStop Color="Black" Offset="1"/>
                                    </LinearGradientBrush>
                                </Setter.Value>
                            </Setter>
                        </Trigger>
                        <Trigger Property="IsPressed" Value="True">
                            <Setter Property="Fill" TargetName="ellipse">
                                <Setter.Value>
                                    <LinearGradientBrush EndPoint="0.5,1"
                                                         StartPoint="0.5,0">
                                        <GradientStop Color="#FF4F4F4F"
                                                      Offset="0"/>
                                        <GradientStop Color="#FF515050"
                                                      Offset="1"/>
                                        <GradientStop Color="White"
                                                      Offset="0.483"/>
                                    </LinearGradientBrush>
                                </Setter.Value>
                            </Setter>
                        </Trigger>
                        <Trigger Property="IsEnabled" Value="False"/>
                    </ControlTemplate.Triggers>
                </ControlTemplate>
            </Setter.Value>
        </Setter>
    </Style>
</Window.Resources>
```

TIP: RESTYLING WINDOWS

Control templates are not limited to user controls but they can be successfully implemented for completely restyling Window objects layout so that you can create custom windows while still taking advantage of their behavior. The template's `TargetType` is therefore `Window`.

If you look at the code, you can notice how the button default aspect is replaced by an `Ellipse` within the `ControlTemplate` value of the `Template` property. Probably some concepts you learned about styles help you understand what is happening. Triggers enable changing the background color according to specific mouse actions. Don't forget to add the `ContentPresenter` element in your custom templates because it enables showing text or other UI elements within your control. Generally control templates are assigned to controls using the `DynamicResource` markup extension. The following XAML line assigns the above custom control template to a button:

```
<Button Click="Button_Click" Name="Button1"
        Style="{DynamicResource ButtonStyle1}"
        Width="100" Height="80" Content="Button"/>
```

Changes will be also automatically reflected at design time. You can also assign an event handler for the `Click` event to ensure that everything is working fine:

```
Private Sub Button_Click(ByVal sender As System.Object,
                         ByVal e As System.Windows.RoutedEventArgs)
    MessageBox.Show("You clicked!")
End Sub
```

Figure 33.11 shows how the button looks within the running application when the mouse pointer passes over it.

FIGURE 33.11   The custom control template designs a button as an ellipse.

RECOMMENDATION

Control templates enable creating amazing control layouts but this is not necessarily a good choice. Remember that users prefer to easily associate a simple control shape to a particular action more than having colored and funny controls that they cannot easily recognize.

Introducing Transformations

Transformations are special objects that modify the appearance of visual elements of type `FrameworkElement`, applying interesting effects such as rotation or translation, keeping unchanged the visual element's functional behavior. For example, with transformations you can rotate a `ListBox` 180 degrees, but it will still work as usual; only the layout changes. Transformations are important to understand if you intend to apply animations to visual elements. I cover animations in the next section. Keep in mind that when you apply animations, basically you animate transformation objects that affect visual elements. You apply transformations by adding a `RenderTransform` node for your visual element at the XAML level. I explain this by dividing a `Grid` into four cells where each cell must contain a `ListBox`. To accomplish this, write the following XAML code that divides the grid and provides a common set of properties for `ListBox` instances via a style:

```
<Grid Name="Grid1">
    <Grid.RowDefinitions>
        <RowDefinition/>
        <RowDefinition/>
    </Grid.RowDefinitions>
    <Grid.ColumnDefinitions>
        <ColumnDefinition/>
        <ColumnDefinition/>
    </Grid.ColumnDefinitions>
    <Grid.Resources>
        <Style x:Key="ListStyle" TargetType="ListBox">
            <Setter Property="Margin" Value="5"/>
            <Setter Property="Width" Value="160"/>
            <Setter Property="Height" Value="160"/>
            <Setter Property="ItemsSource" Value="{Binding}"/>
        </Style>
    </Grid.Resources>
</Grid>
```

At this point, each cell contains a `ListBox`, as in the next sections. Before going into that, switch to the code behind file and handle the `Window.Loaded` event as follows:

```
Private Sub Transforms_Loaded(ByVal sender As Object,
                         ByVal e As System.Windows.RoutedEventArgs) _
                         Handles Me.Loaded
```

```
'Gets a list of names for running processes
'and populates the Grid.DataContext so that children
'elements will pick up data from it
Me.Grid1.DataContext = From proc In Process.GetProcesses
                       Select proc.ProcessName
End Sub
```

The `DataContext` property is basically the data-source for a given container, and all children controls pick up data from it. In this case, assigning the `Grid1.DataContext` property populates all children `ListBoxes`.

CHECKING THE SAMPLES RESULT

For the sake of simplicity, and because the design actions are reflected to the designer, only one figure will be provided about the transformations result. Figure 33.11 shows the complete results. The interesting thing is that `ListBox` controls continue working independently of their skew or position on the screen.

Applying `RotateTransform`

`RotateTransform` is a transformation that enables rotating a visual element for the specified number of degrees and at the specified position. The following code adds a `ListBox` in the upper-left cell, and it is rotated 180 degrees:

```
<ListBox Name="RotateListBox" Grid.Row="0" Grid.Column="0"
       Style="{StaticResource ListStyle}">
  <ListBox.RenderTransform>
     <RotateTransform Angle="180" CenterX="80" CenterY="80"/>
  </ListBox.RenderTransform>
</ListBox>
```

Notice how the `Angle` property specifies the degrees, whereas `CenterX` and `CenterY` represent the position of rotation. In the preceding example the rotation comes in at the center of the `ListBox` (both values are the half of `Width` and `Height`). Generally transformations are automatically reflected to the designer, so you should see the result of what you are doing. Figure 33.11 shows the result of this transformation (see the upper-left cell). Notice also how the control is working normally even if it is in an unusual position.

Applying `ScaleTransform`

`ScaleTransform` enables dynamically resizing a control. The following code demonstrates how a `ListBox` can be scaled to different dimensions:

```
<ListBox Name="ScaleListBox" Grid.Row="0" Grid.Column="1"
       Style="{StaticResource ListStyle}">
  <ListBox.RenderTransform>
```

```
        <ScaleTransform CenterX="0" CenterY="0" ScaleX="0.6" ScaleY="0.6"/>
    </ListBox.RenderTransform>
</ListBox>
```

Notice how scaling is expressed in percentage with the ScaleX and ScaleY properties. A value of 0.6 means that the control is scaled to 60% of its original dimensions. A value of 1 means 100% (that is, the original size), whereas a value bigger than 1 enlarges the visual element. Take a look at the upper-right cell in Figure 33.11 to get an idea about the result. With animations, ScaleTransform enables animating visual elements by making them larger or smaller.

Applying SkewTransform

SkewTransform enables skewing a visual element for the specified angles on both the X-axis and Y-axis, simulating 3D depth for 2D objects. The following code demonstrates how to apply to a ListBox a horizontal skew of 15 degrees and a vertical skew of 30 degrees, where the center point is established by CenterX and CenterY properties:

```
<ListBox Name="SkewListBox" Grid.Row="1" Grid.Column="0"
        Style="{StaticResource ListStyle}">
    <ListBox.RenderTransform>
        <SkewTransform AngleX="15" AngleY="30" CenterX="50" CenterY="50" />
    </ListBox.RenderTransform>
</ListBox>
```

Skewing is probably the most impressive transform if you then try to use visual elements and controls, discovering that they work exactly as if they were not transformed. Figure 33.11 shows the result of skewing (see the bottom-left cell).

Applying TranslateTransform

TranslateTransform simply enables moving a visual element from a position to another one in the layout system. This is useful if you want to build animations capable of moving visual elements. The following example shows how you can translate a ListBox of 50 points on the X-axis and of 100 points on the Y-axis:

```
<ListBox Name="TranslateListBox" Grid.Row="1" Grid.Column="1"
        Style="{StaticResource ListStyle}">
    <ListBox.RenderTransform>
        <TranslateTransform X="50" Y="100" />
    </ListBox.RenderTransform>
</ListBox>
```

The result of this translation is shown in Figure 33.12 (see the bottom-right cell).

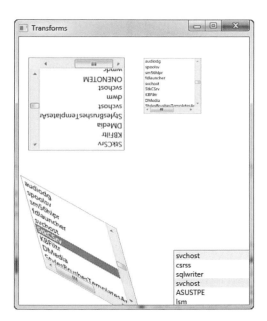

FIGURE 33.12   The result of applying transformations.

Applying Multiple Transforms

You can apply multiple transformations by contextually implementing a `TransformGroup` as a nested node of `RenderTransform`. The following code demonstrates how you can both rotate and skew a visual element:

```
<ListBox Name="SkewListBox" Grid.Row="1" Grid.Column="0"
        Style="{StaticResource ListStyle}">
    <ListBox.RenderTransform>
        <TransformGroup>
            <SkewTransform AngleX="15" AngleY="30" CenterX="50"
                            CenterY="50" />
            <RotateTransform Angle="180" CenterX="80" CenterY="80"/>
        </TransformGroup>
    </ListBox.RenderTransform>
</ListBox>
```

A COUPLE OF IMPORTANT NOTES

Another transformation named `MatrixTransform` is also available and enables building custom transformations. This is quite a complex object and is beyond of the scope of this book. Visit the official MSDN page at http://msdn.microsoft.com/en-us/library/system.windows.media.matrixtransform(VS.100).aspx.

Next, RenderTransform is not the only place for putting transformations. There is another node named LayoutTransform that requires a transformation to be applied before the WPF layout system comes in. This can be useful only when you effectively need the parent of the affected element to adjust the transformed size, but in all other cases use RenderTransform that offers better performance, especially with animations.

Introducing Animations

WPF offers lots of interesting features about graphics and multimedia to provide a great user experience with rich client applications; animations are one of these features. They enable visual elements (or just some portions of them) to move along the UI or to dynamically change their aspect during the specified interval. Subsequent sections explain how you can apply animations to WPF visual elements. There are different kinds of animations in WPF; and we cover the most common of them, DoubleAnimation and ColorAnimation.

> **NOTE**
>
> There is a special type of animation based on timelines that is not easy to implement with Visual Studio, whereas it is the easiest animation that you can realize with Expression Blend. With that said, from a developer perspective, this chapter covers animations based on storyboards.

Animations are cool in that they can also be eventually controlled by pausing, removing, stopping, and manually playing and are represented by System.Windows.Media.Animation.Storyboard objects. Each Storyboard can define one or more DoubleAnimation or ColorAnimation that applies to transformations (see previous section for details). To decide the time when animations need to come in, you define them within the control's triggers specifying an EventTrigger that basically requires you to specify the event representing the moment for the animation to run, For example, if you want an animation to start when a window is loaded, the EventTrigger points to Window.Loaded. Before providing any code example, add a new window to your current WPF project or create a new project from scratch. When the new window is ready, divide the default Grid into four cells by typing the following XAML:

```
<Grid Name="Grid1">
        <Grid.RowDefinitions>
            <RowDefinition/>
            <RowDefinition/>
        </Grid.RowDefinitions>

        <Grid.ColumnDefinitions>
            <ColumnDefinition/>
            <ColumnDefinition/>
        </Grid.ColumnDefinitions>
    </Grid>
</Grid>
```

Applying `DoubleAnimation`

A `DoubleAnimation` object enables animating the specified transform property; it allows reverting the motion and specifying the duration and if the animation needs to be repeated unlimitedly. The first example animates an image, applying the animation to a `SkewTransform` and to a `ScaleTransform` contextually. Code in Listing 33.4 shows how to accomplish this.

LISTING 33.4   Applying a `DoubleAnimation` to an Image

```
        <Image Grid.Row="0" Grid.Column="0" Name="Image1"
Source="/StylesBrushesTemplatesAnimations;component/Images/Avatar.jpg">

            <Image.RenderTransform>
                <TransformGroup>
                    <SkewTransform x:Name="SkewImage"/>
                    <ScaleTransform x:Name="ScaleImage"/>
                </TransformGroup>
            </Image.RenderTransform>

            <Image.Triggers>
                <EventTrigger RoutedEvent="Image.Loaded">
                    <EventTrigger.Actions>
                        <BeginStoryboard>
                            <Storyboard>
                                <DoubleAnimation Storyboard.TargetName="SkewImage"
                                                 Storyboard.TargetProperty="AngleY"
                                                 From="0" To="15" Duration="0:0:3"
                                                 AutoReverse="True"
                                                 RepeatBehavior="Forever" />
                                <DoubleAnimation Storyboard.TargetName="ScaleImage"
                                                 Storyboard.TargetProperty="ScaleX"
                                                 From="1" To="0.3" Duration="0:0:3"
                                                 AutoReverse="True"
                                                 RepeatBehavior="Forever" />
                                <DoubleAnimation Storyboard.TargetName="ScaleImage"
                                                 Storyboard.TargetProperty="ScaleY"
                                                 From="1" To="0.3" Duration="0:0:3"
                                                 AutoReverse="True"
                                                 RepeatBehavior="Forever" />
                            </Storyboard>
                        </BeginStoryboard>
                    </EventTrigger.Actions>
                </EventTrigger>

            </Image.Triggers>
        </Image>
```

33

The code first applies to transformations. They are empty, with no properties set, therefore with no changes to the `Image`. But they have a name so that they can be referred to from the storyboard. The `EventTrigger` within triggers specifies the `Image.Loaded` routed event, which establishes that the animation will run when the image is loaded. The `BeginStoryboard` object is basically a container for children `Storyboard` objects. In the code example there is just one `Storyboard` that contains multiple `DoubleAnimation` objects. Notice how each `DoubleAnimation` refers to a transformation via the `Storyboard.TargetName` attached property and to the particular transformation's property via the `Storyboard.TargetProperty` attached property. `From` and `To` respectively specify the starting and finish points of the animation. In the case of the `SkewTransform`, they specify the angle degrees, whereas in the case of the `ScaleTransform` they specify the scaling percentage. `Duration` is a property for specifying how many hours:minutes:seconds the animation will last; `AutoReverse` specifies if the animation has to be repeated back, and `RepeatBehavior` specifies how long the animation will last (`Forever` is self-explanatory). At this point run the application to have your image skewed and scaled via the animation. Refer to Figure 33.12 to see an approximate result. (Figures cannot show animations running!) Next, the code example about `DoubleAnimation` is applied to a `TextBlock` object for animating text. In this case you see the conjunction of a `RotateTransform` and `SkewTransform`. Code in Listing 33.5 provides the previously mentioned example.

LISTING 33.5   Applying `DoubleAnimation` to a `TextBlock`

```
<TextBlock Grid.Row="0" Grid.Column="1" Text="Animated Text" FontSize="24"
           FontFamily="Verdana" FontWeight="Bold"
           HorizontalAlignment="Center"
           VerticalAlignment="Center" RenderTransformOrigin="0.5 0.5">

<TextBlock.Foreground>
  <LinearGradientBrush>
    <GradientStop Offset="0" Color="Red" />
    <GradientStop Offset="0.5" Color="Yellow" />
    <GradientStop Offset="1" Color="Orange"/>
  </LinearGradientBrush>
</TextBlock.Foreground>

<TextBlock.RenderTransform>
    <TransformGroup>
        <RotateTransform x:Name="RotateText" />
        <SkewTransform x:Name="SkewText"/>
    </TransformGroup>
</TextBlock.RenderTransform>

<TextBlock.Triggers>
  <EventTrigger RoutedEvent="TextBlock.Loaded">
    <BeginStoryboard>
```

```
        <Storyboard Name="TextAnimation">
          <DoubleAnimation Storyboard.TargetName="RotateText"
                           Storyboard.TargetProperty="Angle"
                           From="0" To="360" Duration="0:0:5"
                           RepeatBehavior="Forever" />

          <DoubleAnimation Storyboard.TargetName="SkewText"
                           AutoReverse="True"
                           Storyboard.TargetProperty="AngleX"
                           From="0" To="45" Duration="0:0:5"
                           RepeatBehavior="Forever" />

        </Storyboard>
      </BeginStoryboard>
    </EventTrigger>
  </TextBlock.Triggers>
</TextBlock>
```

The logic is the same, with the `EventTrigger` and transformations. The first `DoubleAnimation` is applied to a `RotateTransform` that affects rotation degrees. Run the code to get an idea of the result and refer to Figure 33.12 for a graphical representation.

Applying `ColorAnimation`

A `ColorAnimation` enables animating colors within a brush, such as `LinearGradientBrush` and `RadialGradientBrush`. Basically a color is replaced with another one passing through a gradient. The next example is a little bit particular because it will be applied to a `DataGrid` control to demonstrate that also business controls can receive animations. The `DataGrid` exposes an `AlternatingRowBackground` property that enables specifying a different color for alternating rows. The goal of the example is animating colors in the background of such rows. For this, code in Listing 33.6 shows how to apply the described color animation.

LISTING 33.6   Applying a ColorAnimation

```
<DataGrid Name="CustomerDataGrid" AutoGenerateColumns="True"
          Grid.Row="1" Grid.Column="1" Margin="5">
    <DataGrid.AlternatingRowBackground>
        <LinearGradientBrush EndPoint="0.5,1" StartPoint="0.5,0">
            <GradientStop Color="Black" Offset="0" />
            <GradientStop Color="Black" Offset="1" />
            <GradientStop Color="White" Offset="0.4" />
            <GradientStop Color="White" Offset="0.6" />
        </LinearGradientBrush>
    </DataGrid.AlternatingRowBackground>
    <DataGrid.Triggers>
```

```
                <EventTrigger RoutedEvent="DataGrid.Loaded">
                    <EventTrigger.Actions>
                        <BeginStoryboard>
                            <Storyboard>
                                <ColorAnimation From="Black" To="Violet"
                                                Duration="0:0:2"
                                                Storyboard.TargetProperty=
                                    "AlternatingRowBackground.GradientStops[0].Color"
                                                AutoReverse="True"
                                                RepeatBehavior="Forever"/>
                                <ColorAnimation From="Black" To="Chartreuse"
                                                Duration="0:0:2"
                                                AutoReverse="True"
                                                RepeatBehavior="Forever"
                                                Storyboard.TargetProperty=
                                    "AlternatingRowBackground.GradientStops[3].Color"/>
                            </Storyboard>
                        </BeginStoryboard>
                    </EventTrigger.Actions>
                </EventTrigger>
            </DataGrid.Triggers>
        </DataGrid>
```

As you can see, this kind of animation basically works like DoubleAnimation except that
From and To require you to specify the source and target colors. When referring to a
GradientStop, you enclose its index within square parentheses. (Remember that the index
is zero-based). To complete the example, it is necessary to populate the DataGrid with
some data. Switch to the code behind file and write the code in Listing 33.7, which
defines a Customer class, creates some instances of the class, and a List(Of Customer)
collection that is the data source.

LISTING 33.7   Populating the DataGrid

```vb
Public Class Animations

    Private Sub Animations_Loaded(ByVal sender As Object,
                            ByVal e As System.Windows.RoutedEventArgs) _
                            Handles Me.Loaded

        Dim cust1 As New Customer With {.Address = "7Th street",
                .CompanyName = "Del Sole", .ContactName = "Alessandro Del Sole"}
        Dim cust2 As New Customer With {.Address = "5Th street",
                .CompanyName = "Fictitious Red & White",
                .ContactName = "Robert White"}
```

```
        Dim custList As New List(Of Customer) From {cust1, cust2}
        Me.CustomerDataGrid.ItemsSource = custList
    End Sub
End Class

Public Class Customer
    Public Property CompanyName As String
    Public Property Address As String
    Public Property ContactName As String
End Class
```

Run the application. You get the result represented in Figure 33.13.

FIGURE 33.13   The result of applied animations.

Working with Animation Events

Storyboard objects expose events that can help you get control over the animations. The first step is assigning a name to the desired storyboard, as in the following example:

```
<Storyboard Name="ImageStoryBoard">
```

After you assign a name to the `Storyboard`, you can handle events summarized in Table 33.1.

TABLE 33.1   Storyboard Events

Event	Occurs When
Completed	The animation completes.
Changed	An object is modified.
CurrentGlobalSpeedInvalidated	The time progress rate changes.
CurrentStateInvalidated	The CurrentState property of the animation clock changes.
CurrentTimeInvalidated	The CurrentTime property of the animation clock changes.
RemoveRequested	The animation clock is removed.

Generally you handle the `Completed` event to make an action when an animation completes, as in the following code snippet:

```
Private Sub ImageStoryBoard_Completed(ByVal sender As Object,
                            ByVal e As System.EventArgs) _
                            Handles ImageStoryBoard.Completed
    'Write code for the animation completion
End Sub
```

Notice how animations do not throw routed events, whereas they raise standard events. `Storyboard` objects also expose some methods that enable controlling the animation in code, such as `Begin`, `Stop`, `Pause`, `Seek`, and `Resume`, which are all self-explanatory. Moreover, you can set in Visual Basic code also some animation properties that I explained through XAML code, as in the following code snippet:

```
With ImageStoryBoard
    .AutoReverse = True
    .RepeatBehavior = System.Windows.Media.Animation.
                    RepeatBehavior.Forever
    .Duration = New TimeSpan(0, 0, 5)
End With
```

Animations can be also applied to 3D graphics that are beyond the scope of this book but that you can explore through the MSDN documentation.

Creating Animations with Visual Basic

Maybe you understood that XAML is the best way for creating, customizing, and managing visual elements. Generally writing VB code is something that you should practice only when there is an effective need of applying effects at runtime. This can also be the case of animations. Code in Listing 33.8 shows how to create at runtime a new button and how to apply an animation that increases and decreases the button's height. The code is not difficult to understand when you have a clear idea of the sequence of elements required within an animation.

LISTING 33.8   Creating an Animation in VB code

```vb
Public Class Animations
    Private myAnimation As Animation.DoubleAnimation
    Private WithEvents aButton As Button
    Private heightAnimationStoryboard As Animation.Storyboard

    Private Sub CreateRuntimeAnimation()

        'An instance of a new Button
        aButton = New Button With {.Width = 150, .Height = 50,
                                .Content = "Runtime button",
                                .Name = "RuntimeButton"}

        'Associates the button's name to the Window names collection
        '(required at runtime)
        Me.RegisterName(aButton.Name, aButton)

        'Adds the Button to the Grid at the given row/column
        Grid.SetColumn(aButton, 0)
        Grid.SetRow(aButton, 1)
        Grid1.Children.Add(aButton)

        'Creates a new DoubleAnimation, with properties
        myAnimation = New Animation.DoubleAnimation
        With myAnimation
            .AutoReverse = True
            'From and To are Nullable(Of Double)
            .From = 50
            .To = 15
            .RepeatBehavior = Animation.RepeatBehavior.Forever
            .Duration = New TimeSpan(0, 0, 3)
        End With

        'Sets the target control via its name
        Animation.Storyboard.SetTargetName(myAnimation, aButton.Name)
        'Sets the target property
        Animation.Storyboard.SetTargetProperty(myAnimation,
                                    New PropertyPath(Button.
                                    HeightProperty))
```

33

```
        'Create a new storyboard instance and adds the animation
        'to the storyboard's collection of animations
        heightAnimationStoryboard = New Animation.Storyboard
        heightAnimationStoryboard.Children.Add(myAnimation)
    End Sub

    'Starts the animation when the button is loaded
    Private Sub aButton_Loaded(ByVal sender As Object, ByVal e As RoutedEventArgs) _
                            Handles aButton.Loaded
        heightAnimationStoryboard.Begin(aButton)
    End Sub
End Class
```

The one thing you have to pay attention to is registering the button name because otherwise it will not be accessible at runtime by the animation. Another thing that is worth
mentioning regards how you set the storyboard target property. This is accomplished via
the StoryBoard.SetTargetProperty shared method that requires the animation instance
and a PropertyPath instance that receives a dependency property as an argument. Figure
33.14 represents a particular moment of the animation running.

FIGURE 33.14   The application runs the Visual Basic-generated animation.

Summary

Windows Presentation Foundation offers great benefits about customizing user interface elements. In this chapter you got a high-level overview of modes allowed for customizing elements and for making them more interesting to the final user. First, you got information about brushes; you saw how many brushes are offered by WPF and how you can apply them for coloring or filling visual elements. Next you learned about styles, understanding how you can take advantage of them for setting a common set of properties for the specified control type. Subsequently, you got an overview of control templates, learning how you can completely redefine the graphical aspect of a user control while keeping safe its behavior. Next you got information on transformations, understanding how they can dynamically change controls' appearance. Finally you took a tour of animations, seeing how you can enrich your user interface with cool animations that take advantage of transformations. In the next chapter I discuss other important features of WPF, such as the ability to create dynamic documents and manage media contents.

CHAPTER 34

Manipulating Documents and Media

W indows Presentation Foundation offers native controls for working with media contents and for manipulating documents. This last topic is also important because documents are one of the most common requirements in modern applications, and WPF provides a way for creating and managing documents that can be dynamically arranged to offer a better user experience. In this chapter you learn how to take advantage of media contents to enrich your applications and to manipulate dynamic documents through built-in controls exposed by the .NET Framework.

Viewing Images

You use the `System.Windows.Controls.Image` control to show images. The Visual Studio 2010 designer provides some improvements to help you manage more images than in the past editions. To see how the control works, create a new WPF project that will be used for all examples in this chapter and name it as **DocumentsAndMedia**. When ready, drag an `Image` control from the toolbox onto the new `Window`; then set its dimensions as you like. To view an image, you need to set the `Source` property that basically points to an `Uri`. Open the Properties window by pressing **F4** and then click the button for the Source property. At this point you can select one or more images to add as resources to your project, as shown in Figure 34.1. When you add your images at this point, simply select the one you want to be shown inside the `Image` control. When you click **OK**, Visual Studio generates a subfolder in the project main folder, naming the new folder as Images and setting the build action for added images as Resource.

FIGURE 34.1   Adding images to the project.

Visual Studio also automatically sets the Source property for you, taking advantage of the packed Uri, as demonstrated by the following line of XAML code:

```
<Image Source="/DocumentsAndMedia;component/Images/IMG006.jpg"
       Stretch="Fill" Name="Image1" />
```

The Stretch property enables establishing how pictures will be tiled inside the Image control. Fill, which is the default value, dynamically adapts the picture to fill the entire Image control, but when you resize the control you may lose the original aspect ratio. If you instead use Uniform you can keep the aspect ratio and dynamically adapt the picture; while setting UniformToFill the picture will work like Uniform except that it will clip the source image so that the layout will be based on the Image control size. If you instead assign the Stretch property with None, the source image will be shown in its original size. Figure34.2 shows how the image looks with Stretch set as Fill.

You can also assign the Source property at runtime from Visual Basic code so that you can provide users the ability of selecting different pictures. Differently from the XAML code, in VB you need to create first an instance of the BitmapImage class and assign some of its properties as follows:

```
Private Sub LoadPicture(ByVal fileName As String)


    Dim img As New BitmapImage
    With img
        .BeginInit()
        .BaseUri = New Uri("MyPicture.jpg")
        .EndInit()
    End With

    Image1.Source = img
End Sub
```

FIGURE 34.2   Showing images with the `Image` control.

Basically you invoke `BeginInit` to start editing; then you set `BaseUri` pointing to the desired file and finally invoke `EndInit` to finish editing. When you perform these steps, you can assign the new instance to the `Image.Source` property.

Playing Media

Windows Presentation Foundation enables easily reproducing media files, such as audio and videos, through the `System.Windows.Controls.MediaElement` control. This basically enables reproducing, among others, all media contents supported by the Windows Media Player application, thus .Wmv, .Wma, .Avi, and .Mp3 files. This section shows you how to build a simple media player using `MediaElement` and Visual Basic 2010. Now add a new `Window` to an existing project setting this as the main window. The goal of the next example is to implement a media player and buttons for controlling media reproduction. Code in Listing 34.1 declares the user interface.

LISTING 34.1   Defining the User Interface for a Simple Media Player

```
<Window x:Class="PlayingMedia"
    xmlns="http://schemas.microsoft.com/winfx/2006/xaml/presentation"
    xmlns:x="http://schemas.microsoft.com/winfx/2006/xaml"
    Title="PlayingMedia" Height="300" Width="600">
    <Grid>
```

```
    <Grid.RowDefinitions>
        <RowDefinition />
        <RowDefinition Height="50" />
    </Grid.RowDefinitions>
    <MediaElement Name="Media1" Grid.Row="0" LoadedBehavior="Manual"
                  Volume="{Binding ElementName=VolumeSlider, Path=Value}"
                  MediaFailed="Media1_MediaFailed"
                  MediaEnded="Media1_MediaEnded"/>

    <StackPanel Orientation="Horizontal" Grid.Row="1">
        <Button Name="PlayButton" Width="70" Height="40"
                Margin="5" Click="PlayButton_Click"
                Content="Play"/>

        <Button Name="PauseButton" Width="70" Height="40"
                Margin="5" Click="PauseButton_Click"
                Content="Pause"/>

        <Button Name="StopButton" Width="70" Height="40"
                Margin="5" Click="StopButton_Click"
                Content="Stop"/>

        <Button Name="BrowseButton" Width="40" Height="40"
                Margin="5" Content="..."
                Click="BrowseButton_Click"/>

        <Slider Name="VolumeSlider" Width="80" Margin="5"
                Minimum="0" Maximum="1" Value="0.5"
                TickFrequency="0.1"
                AutoToolTipPlacement="TopLeft"
                TickPlacement="BottomRight"
                ToolTip="Adjust volume"/>
    </StackPanel>
    </Grid>
</Window>
```

The MediaElement control has basically no look, so when you place it onto the user interface, it has a transparent background and border, although you can replace this with your
custom background and border. The LoadedBehavior property enables establishing how
the media file needs to be reproduced; for example, Play means that the associated video
will be automatically played when the control is loaded, whereas Manual means that
playing will be started via Visual Basic code at the specified moment. (IntelliSense can
help you to choose the most appropriate self-explanatory option.) You associate a media
file to the MediaElement assigning the Source property, but this is not mandatory because
you can accomplish this later in code. The Volume property enables adjusting reproduction

volume, and its range is between 0 and 1. In this example the `Volume` value is bound to the `VolumeSlider.Value` property. The control also offers some events such as `MediaFailed` and `MediaEnded` that respectively are raised when an error occurs when attempting to open the media file and when the reproduction completes. The `MediaElement` control also provides some methods for controlling reproduction in code, such as `Play`, `Pause`, and `Stop`. Code in Listing 34.2 shows how to implement the features and how to allow media selection from disk.

LISTING 34.2   Controlling the `MediaElement` in Code

```
Public Class PlayingMedia

    Dim sourceMedia As String = String.Empty

    Private Sub Media1_MediaEnded(ByVal sender As System.Object,
                                  ByVal e As System.Windows.
                                  RoutedEventArgs)
        'Playing completed
    End Sub

    Private Sub Media1_MediaFailed(ByVal sender As System.Object,
                                   ByVal e As System.Windows.
                                   ExceptionRoutedEventArgs)
        MessageBox.Show(e.ErrorException.Message)
    End Sub

    Private Sub PlayButton_Click(ByVal sender As System.Object,
                                 ByVal e As System.Windows.RoutedEventArgs)
        If String.IsNullOrEmpty(Me.sourceMedia) = False Then
            Me.Media1.Play()
        End If
    End Sub

    Private Sub PauseButton_Click(ByVal sender As System.Object,
                                  ByVal e As System.Windows.RoutedEventArgs)
        If String.IsNullOrEmpty(Me.sourceMedia) = False Then
            Me.Media1.Pause()
        End If
    End Sub

    Private Sub StopButton_Click(ByVal sender As System.Object,
                                 ByVal e As System.Windows.RoutedEventArgs)
        If String.IsNullOrEmpty(Me.sourceMedia) = False Then
            Me.Media1.Stop()
```

```
        End If
    End Sub

    Private Sub BrowseButton_Click(ByVal sender As System.Object,
                            ByVal e As System.Windows.RoutedEventArgs)
        Dim dialog As New Microsoft.Win32.OpenFileDialog

        With dialog
            .Title = "Select a media file"
            .Filter = "Avi & Wmv¦*.avi;*.wmv¦Audio¦*.wma;*.mp3¦All files¦*.*"
            If .ShowDialog = True Then
                Me.sourceMedia = .FileName
                Me.Media1.Source = New Uri(sourceMedia,
                                    UriKind.RelativeOrAbsolute)
            End If
        End With
    End Sub
End Class
```

Notice how the MediaFailed event handler shows an error message in case an exception is thrown and how the media file is assigned under the form of an Uri to the MediaElement.Source property. This also means that you can assign an Uri such as a Web address to play a media content stored on a website. At this point you can run the application, click the Browse button to select your media content and click Play. Figure 34.3 shows the application playing a video.

The MediaElement control also offers a Position property (of type TimeSpan) that provides the ability to seek the desired position within the media content.

Manipulating Documents

One of the most important requirements in modern applications is the ability to manage documents. WPF offers the System.Windows.Documents namespace that exposes objects that enable creating flexible and dynamic documents that can adapt their layout dynamically to the user interface. These kinds of documents take advantage of the Clear Type™ technology and are hosted inside FlowDocument objects. A FlowDocument is composed of Paragraph objects where you can place and format your text. Paragraphs are powerful because they enable adding figures, bulleted lists, fully functional hyperlinks, and text formatting. To present and browse a flow document, you need to add a FlowDocumentReader control to the user interface. Flexibility and dynamicity are just two benefits of a larger number. Another cool feature in flow documents is that users can interact with documents as if they were reading a book, so they can add annotations and highlights that can be stored to disk for later reuse. Annotations are provided by the System.Windows.Annotations namespace that needs to be imported at the XAML level. The goals of next code example are

- ▶ Illustrating how you can create flow documents
- ▶ Illustrating how you can add and format text within flow documents
- ▶ Implementing features for adding annotations to documents and saving them to disk

FIGURE 34.3   The sample application playing a video.

Add a new Window to the current one, setting it as the startup page. When ready, write the XAML code shown in Listing 34.3 that implements the UI side of the application. The code is explained at the end of the listing.

NOTE

The content of the sample flow document is just an excerpt of the content of Chapter 31, "Creating WPF Applications," which is provided as an example, but that you can replace with a more complete text of yours.

LISTING 34.3   Implementing Flow Documents

```
<Window x:Class="ManipulatingDocuments"
    xmlns="http://schemas.microsoft.com/winfx/2006/xaml/presentation"
    xmlns:x="http://schemas.microsoft.com/winfx/2006/xaml"
    xmlns:ann="clr-namespace:System.Windows.Annotations;assembly=PresentationFrame-
work"
    Title="ManipulatingDocuments" Height="480" Width="600">
    <Grid>
```

```
<Grid.RowDefinitions>
    <RowDefinition />
    <RowDefinition Height="40"/>
</Grid.RowDefinitions>

    <StackPanel Grid.Row="1" Orientation="Horizontal">
    <StackPanel.Resources>
        <Style x:Key="ButtonStyle" TargetType="Button">
            <Setter Property="Width" Value="100"/>
            <Setter Property="Height" Value="30"/>
            <Setter Property="Margin" Value="5"/>
        </Style>
    </StackPanel.Resources>

        <Button Command="ann:AnnotationService.CreateTextStickyNoteCommand"
                CommandTarget="{Binding ElementName=FlowReader1}"
                Style="{StaticResource ButtonStyle}">
                Add note</Button>
        <Separator/>
        <Button Command="ann:AnnotationService.CreateInkStickyNoteCommand"
                CommandTarget="{Binding ElementName=FlowReader1}"
                Style="{StaticResource ButtonStyle}">
            Add Ink
        </Button>
        <Separator/>
        <Button Command="ann:AnnotationService.DeleteStickyNotesCommand"
                CommandTarget="{Binding ElementName=FlowReader1}"
                Style="{StaticResource ButtonStyle}">
                Remove note
        </Button>
        <Separator/>
        <Button Command="ann:AnnotationService.CreateHighlightCommand"
                CommandTarget="{Binding ElementName=FlowReader1}"
                Style="{StaticResource ButtonStyle}">
                Highlight
        </Button>
        <Separator/>
        <Button Command="ann:AnnotationService.ClearHighlightsCommand"
                CommandTarget="{Binding ElementName=FlowReader1}"
                Style="{StaticResource ButtonStyle}">
                Remove highlight
        </Button>
    </StackPanel>

<FlowDocumentReader Grid.Row="0"  BorderThickness="2" Name="FlowReader1">
    <FlowDocument Name="myDocument"
```

```
TextAlignment="Justify"
IsOptimalParagraphEnabled="True"
IsHyphenationEnabled="True"
IsColumnWidthFlexible="True"
ColumnWidth="300"
ColumnGap="20">
<Paragraph FontSize="36" FontWeight="Bold"
        FontStyle="Oblique">Chapter 31</Paragraph>
<Paragraph FontSize="24" FontWeight="Bold">Introducing
        WPF</Paragraph>
<Paragraph>
    Windows Presentation Foundation relies on a layered architecture
    that is represented in Figure 31.1. The first layer is the
    Windows operating system. The second layer is constituted by the
    combination of two communicating layers:
    User32, which is the part of the operating system responsible
    for exchanging messages with applications, and the DirectX
    libraries which are the real power of WPF.
    <!— Add other text here.... —>
    <Figure Width="300">
        <BlockUIContainer>
            <StackPanel>
                <!—Replace the image file with a valid one—>
                <Image
            Source="/DocumentsAndMedia;component/Images/31fig01.tif"
                    Width="200"
                    Height="300"
                    Stretch="Fill" />
                <Separator></Separator>
                <TextBlock VerticalAlignment="Center"
                        Width="220" TextWrapping="Wrap"
                        FontSize="10" FontStyle="Italic">
                    Figure 31.1 - WPF architecture
                </TextBlock>
            </StackPanel>
        </BlockUIContainer>
    </Figure>
    <Bold>PresentationFramework</Bold> exposes namespaces
    and classes
    through a complex hierarchy of inheritance,
    where the root class is of course System.Object.
    Such hierarchy provides the infrastructure for the user
    interface elements.
    This hierarchy is composed by the following list of classes,
```

```
                        where each class inherits from the previous one:
                    </Paragraph>
                    <List>
                        <ListItem>
                            <Paragraph
                             FontFamily="Courier New">System.Object</Paragraph>
                        </ListItem>
                        <ListItem>
                            <Paragraph
                             FontFamily="Courier New">
                             System.Threading.DispatcherObject</Paragraph>
                        </ListItem>
                        <ListItem>
                            <Paragraph FontFamily="Courier New">
                             System.Windows.DependencyObject</Paragraph>
                        </ListItem>
                        <ListItem>
                            <Paragraph
                             FontFamily="Courier New">
                             System.Windows.Media.Visual</Paragraph>
                        </ListItem>
                    </List>
                    <Paragraph>
                        The
                        <Hyperlink
                            NavigateUri="http://msdn.microsoft.com/en-
                            us/library/ms750441(VS.100).aspx
                            #System_Threading_DispatcherObject">
                            System.Threading.DispatcherObject</Hyperlink>
                        is responsible for threading and messages which
                        WPF relies on. The dispatcher takes advantage
                        of the User32 messages for performing
                        cross thread calls.
                    </Paragraph>
                </FlowDocument>
            </FlowDocumentReader>
        </Grid>
</Window>
```

Let's begin by illustrating the FlowDocumentReader control. It basically provides a container for flow documents and automatically implements buttons for browsing multiple page documents and controlling documents' layout, as you see later in Figure 34.4. The FlowDocument object instead contains the document and exposes some interesting properties. The previous code uses the most important ones. TextAlignment enables specifying how the text must be aligned within the document and can have one of the following values: `Center`, `Right`, `Left`, or `Justify`. `IsOptimalParagraph` set as `True` enables paragraph layout optimization. `IsHyphenationEnable` set as `True` enables word hyphenation in the document. `IsColumnWidthFlexible` set as `True` means that the value of the `ColumnWidth` property is not fixed. This last property takes place when you enable the document view by columns. The `ColumnGap` property indicates the spacing between columns. A complete list of properties is available in the MSDN Library: http://msdn.microsoft.com/en-us/library/system.windows.documents.flowdocument_members(VS.100).aspx. For the document content, notice the following techniques:

▶ You divide the content into multiple `Paragraph` objects to provide different paragraph formatting.

▶ You can add inline formatting. For example, the following line contains bold formatting within a paragraph:

```
<Bold>PresentationFramework</Bold> exposes namespaces and classes
```

▶ You can also add fully functional hyperlinks as in the following sample line:

```
<Hyperlink
 NavigateUri="http://msdn.microsoft.com/en-

us/library/ms750441(VS.100).aspx#System_Threading_DispatcherObject">
        System.Threading.DispatcherObject</Hyperlink>
```

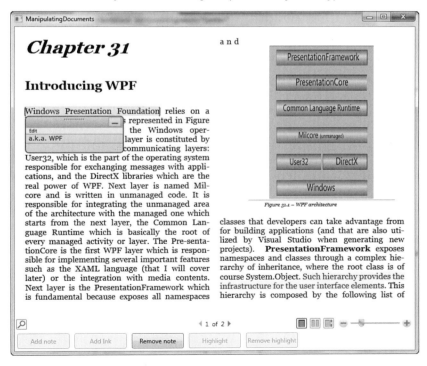

FIGURE 34.4   Viewing and annotating a flow document.

The sample document also shows how to implement bulleted lists via a List object that contains ListItem elements. It is interesting how flow documents also support figures insertion via a Figure element that contains a BlockUIContainer object nesting an Image control storing the figure and a TextBlock control describing the figure. Notice how each paragraph and subparagraph can be customized by setting font properties different from other paragraphs. Switching the discussion to buttons implementation, instead of handling Click events the code makes use of a technique known as *commanding* that takes advantage of built-in commands associated to specific actions; basically each button is associated to one of the built-in actions for the annotation service via the Command property and points to the flow document as the target of the action (CommandTarget). At this point there is the need of writing code that enables the annotation service at the application startup so that the user can annotate or highlight text and then save annotations to disk for later reuse. The annotation service relies on the System.Windows.Annotations namespace that provides an AnnotationService class whose instance allows editing the document. Next, the System.Windows.Annotations.Storage namespace provides objects for storing annotations to Xml files for later reuse. Code in Listing 34.4 shows how to implement the annotation service with Visual Basic. The code must be written to the code-behind file for the current window and contains comments for better reading.

LISTING 34.4   Implementing the Annotation Service

```vb
Imports System.Windows.Annotations
Imports System.Windows.Annotations.Storage
Imports System.IO

Public Class ManipulatingDocuments

    Dim annotationStream As FileStream

    Private Sub ManipulatingDocuments_Initialized(ByVal sender As Object,
                                    ByVal e As System.EventArgs) _
                                    Handles Me.Initialized

        'Gets the instance of the AnnotationService pointing to the FlowDocument
        Dim annotationServ As AnnotationService = _
            AnnotationService.GetService(FlowReader1)

        'Declares a store for annotations
        Dim annotationArchive As AnnotationStore

        'If no annotation service already exists for
        'the current flow document...
        If annotationServ Is Nothing Then
```

```
        '...creates a new service
        ' and a new store to an Xml file
        annotationStream = New FileStream("annotations.xml",
                                    FileMode.OpenOrCreate)
        annotationServ = New AnnotationService(FlowReader1)

        'Gets the instance of the stream
        annotationArchive = New XmlStreamStore(annotationStream)

        'Enables the document
        annotationServ.Enable(annotationArchive)
    End If
End Sub

Private Sub ManipulatingDocuments_Closed(ByVal sender As Object,
                                ByVal e As System.EventArgs) _
                                Handles Me.Closed
    Dim annotationServ As AnnotationService = _
        AnnotationService.GetService(FlowReader1)

    'If an instance of the annotation
    'service is available
    If annotationServ IsNot Nothing And _
        annotationServ.IsEnabled Then

        'shuts down the service
        'and releases resources
        annotationServ.Store.Flush()
        annotationServ.Disable()
        annotationStream.Close()
    End If
End Sub
End Class
```

Notice how the annotation service startup is placed inside the Window.Initialized event handler, whereas the annotation service shutdown is placed inside the Windows.Closed event handler. Now run the demo application by pressing **F5**. As you can see on the screen, if you resize the window, the flow document content is automatically and dynamically adapted to the window's layout. Moreover you can decide, using the appropriate controls on the FlowDocumentReader, how the document has to be viewed (for example if one or two pages appear on the window or with zoom enabled). The best way for getting a feeling about how this works is to resize the window. Figure 34.4 shows how the application looks, showing also an example of annotation.

APPLYING ANNOTATIONS AND HIGHLIGHT

You apply annotations or highlights by just selecting the desired text and then pressing one of the related buttons. You write the annotation text just after clicking the green box. Annotations are editable also when reloaded.

You can also add ink annotations to your documents. Figure 34.5 shows how ink annotations look and how text is exposed with fonts different than the standard one. Also notice how the hyperlink is correctly highlighted and functional so that if you click it you will be redirected to the related web page associated via the NavigateUri property in the XAML code.

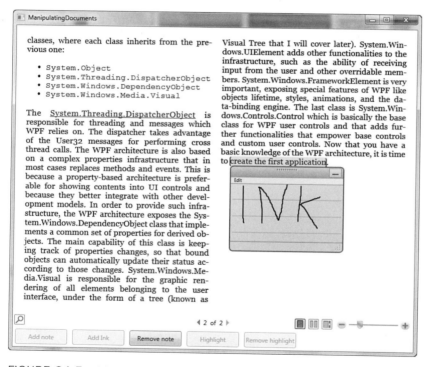

FIGURE 34.5   Adding ink notes and viewing formatted text.

Annotations are automatically stored into an Xml file, as implemented in code. Remember to resize the window to understand the flexibility of flow documents and of the FlowDocumentReader control.

Understanding the `RichTextBox` Control

WPF offers a `RichTextBox` control that works as you would expect for some aspects, thus allowing advance formatting and image support, but it differs from other technologies in that such control stores its content as a flow document. This is the reason for discussing this control in the current chapter. In XAML code the control definition looks like this:

```
<RichTextBox Name="RichTextBox1">
    <!— add your flow document here —>
</RichTextBox>
```

You could nest within the control the flow document shown in the previous section to get a fully editable document or simply write your text into the control, where such text takes standard formatting settings. You can also load an existing file into the `RichTextBox`, which requires some lines of code. The following method shows how to load a document as text:

```
Private Sub LoadDocument(ByVal fileName As String)

    Dim range As TextRange

    If File.Exists(fileName) Then
        range = New TextRange(RichTextBox1.Document.ContentStart,
                        RichTextBox1.Document.ContentEnd)

        Using documentStream As New FileStream(fileName,
                                    FileMode.
                                    OpenOrCreate)
            range.Load(documentStream,
                    System.Windows.DataFormats.Text)
        End Using
    End If
End Sub
```

The `TextRange` class basically represents the text area, and the code takes the entire area from start to end. Then the code invokes the `TextRange.Load` method to open the specified stream and converts the file content into a `System.Windows.DataFormats.Text` format that is acceptable for the `RichTextBox`. Notice that the previous example loads a text document that is then converted into XAML by the runtime. You can also load contents from XAML files using the `DataFormats.Xaml` option. To save the document content you need to invoke the `TextRange.Save` method. The following method shows an example:

```
Private Sub SaveDocument(ByVal fileName As String)
    Dim range As New TextRange(Me.RichTextBox1.Document.ContentStart,
```

```
                          Me.RichTextBox1.Document.ContentEnd)

    Using documentStream As New FileStream(fileName,
                                    FileMode.Create)
        range.Save(documentStream, DataFormats.Xaml)
    End Using

End Sub
```

In this case the document content is saved under the form of XAML content but you can still use the `Text` option to save such content as text, although this can cause a loss of formatting settings due to the restrictive conversion.

Implementing Spell Check

The `RichTextBox` control provides built-in spell check support. This can be enabled by setting the `SpellCheck.IsEnabled` property as follows:

```
<RichTextBox Name="RichTextBox1" SpellCheck.IsEnabled="True">
```

When enabled, when the user types unrecognized words in the English grammar the words are highlighted in red, and by right-clicking the highlighted word a list of valid alternatives is suggested, similar to what happens in applications such as Microsoft Word. Figure 34.6 shows how the spell check feature can help users to fix typos in their documents.

FIGURE 34.6   The built-in spell check feature helps users fix typos.

Viewing XPS Documents

Starting from Windows Vista, Microsoft introduced a new file format known as XPS that is a portable file format for documents and is useful because you can share documents without the of having installed the application that generated that kind of document because you simply need a viewer. WPF offers full support for XPS documents, also offering a `DocumentViewer` control that enables developers to embed XPS viewing functionalities in their applications. Support for XPS documents is provided by the

ReachFramework.dll assembly (so you need to add a reference) that exposes the
System.Windows.Xps.Packaging namespace. For code, you simply drag the
DocumentViewer control from the toolbox onto the Window surface so that the generated
XAML looks like the following:

```
<DocumentViewer Name="DocumentViewer1" />
```

At design time you can notice how such control offers a number of buttons for adjusting
the document layout, for zooming and printing. XPS documents are fixed documents
differently from flow documents, so you need to create an instance of the XpsDocument
class and get a fixed sequence of sheets to be assigned to the Document property of the
viewer, as demonstrated in the following code snippet that enables loading and presenting
an XPS document:

```
Dim documentName As String = "C:\MyDoc.xps"
Dim xpsDoc As XpsDocument

xpsDoc = New XpsDocument(documentName, IO.FileAccess.ReadWrite)
DocumentViewer1.Document = xpsDoc.GetFixedDocumentSequence
```

Figure 34.7 shows a sample XPS document opened in the DocumentViewer control.

FIGURE 34.7   Viewing XPS documents through the DocumentViewer control.

So with a few steps you can embed XPS functionalities in your applications.

Summary

This chapter was an overview about manipulating media and documents in WPF 4. You saw how you can present pictures with the `Image` control and how to reproduce media contents, such as videos and audio, through the `MediaElement` control, which also exposes events that you can intercept to understand the state of reproduction. Then flow documents and the `FlowDocumentReader` and `RichTextBox` controls were covered, understanding how documents can be produced for dynamic arrangement within the user interface. Finally we discussed about WPF support for XPS documents through the `DocumentViewer` control and the `XpsDocument` class.

CHAPTER 35

Introducing Data-Binding

Many developers erroneously think of WPF as just a multimedia platform. WPF is instead a complete framework for rich client applications development, including data-centric applications. This technology offers a powerful data-binding engine, and the new version included in .NET Framework 4.0 also provides some improvements that make the data-binding experience easier, especially if you are new to WPF. This chapter provides a high-level introduction to the data-binding in WPF 4 with Visual Basic 2010, discussing the most important .NET objects that you can explore in further studies by applying WPF-specific patterns such as Model-View-ViewModel.

SYSTEM REQUIREMENTS

Code examples are provided that require the Northwind database to be installed and made available on SQL Server 2008 Express or higher. You should already have done this if you read the chapters about LINQ.

In this case, this note is just a quick reminder.

Introducing the Data-Binding

Windows Presentation Foundation offers a powerful data-binding engine, held by the `System.Windows.Data` namespace, which makes even simpler binding data to the user interface and receiving input from the user as well. At a higher level you perform data-binding between a user control and a data source making use of the `Binding` markup extension, that lots of controls enable. It is worth mentioning that in WPF a data source can be a collection of .NET objects but also a property from another user control. The following examples show you both scenarios. Particularly you receive an explanation of the new `DataGrid` control for tabular data representations and the `ObservableCollection(Of T)` in action for binding to a collection. Before going on, create a new WPF project with Visual Basic and name it `IntroducingDataBinding`. When the code editor is ready, write the following XAML code that divides the root `Grid` into two columns and adds some controls that will be necessary for next examples:

```xaml
<Grid Name="Grid1">
    <Grid.ColumnDefinitions>
        <ColumnDefinition Width="200" />
        <ColumnDefinition />
    </Grid.ColumnDefinitions>

    <StackPanel Grid.Column="0">
        <TextBox Name="ValueTextBox"
                 Margin="5"/>

        <Slider Name="ValueSlider" Margin="5"
                Minimum="0" Maximum="10"/>
    </StackPanel>
    <StackPanel Grid.Column="1">
        <DataGrid Name="DataGrid1"
                  Height="150"/>
        <TextBox Margin="5" Foreground="Red"
                 Name="LogBox"
                 Height="100"/>
    </StackPanel>
</Grid>
```

Utilized user controls now have no other properties than the one necessary for defining their layout, which are set in code in the next sections.

Binding UI Elements with the Binding Markup Extension

You perform data-binding between a user control and a data source via the `Binding` XAML markup extension. Such an extension requires specifying two properties: `ElementName`, which is the source item name and `Path` that is the property containing the actual data to bind, whose name must be exposed by the object assigned to `ElementName`. The following example, in which you have to substitute to the first `TextBox` in the earlier example, shows how to bind the context of a `TextBox` to the value of a `Slider` control so that when the user moves the selector, the slider value is reflected into the `TextBox`:

```xaml
<TextBox Text="{Binding ElementName=ValueSlider,
```

```
                        Path=Value}"
        Name="ValueTextBox"
        Margin="5"/>
```

`Binding` has to be applied to the property that will present bound data, in this case `Text`. If you now run the application and move the selector on the slider, you see how its value is reflected as the `TextBox.Text` content, as demonstrated in Figure 35.1.

FIGURE 35.1   Binding a control's property to another control's content.

This is the most basic data-binding example and can be considered as the one-way mode, because the binding is performed only from the data-source (the `Slider.Value` property) to the UI control (the `TextBox`). In fact, the data-binding does not return a value from the `TextBox` to the `Slider`. To accomplish this, which means updating the `Slider` value according to the `TextBox` content, we need the two-way data-binding that enables binding from and to the data source. You apply for two-way data-binding by adding the `Mode=TwoWay` assignment within the `Binding` markup extension. The following code demonstrates this:

```
<TextBox Text="{Binding ElementName=ValueSlider,
                        Path=Value, Mode=TwoWay}"
        Name="ValueTextBox"
        Margin="5"/>

<Slider Name="ValueSlider" Margin="5"
        Minimum="0" Maximum="10"
        Value="{Binding ElementName=ValueTextBox,
        Path=Text, Mode=TwoWay}"/>
```

Notice how both controls need to set binding on the two-way mode so that they can reflect each other's value. If you run the application you can see how the slider's selector value is updated according to the text box content. One-way and two-way are not the

35

only allowed modes. Table 35.1 summarizes available data-binding modes in WPF, exposed by the `System.Windows.Data.BindingMode` enumeration.

TABLE 35.1   Available Data-Binding Modes

Mode	Description
OneWay	The data-binding is performed only from the data source to the UI. Changes on the data source are reflected to the UI but not vice versa.
TwoWay	The data-binding is performed from the data source to the UI and vice versa. Changes on the data source are reflected to the UI and changes via the UI are reflected to the data source.
OneWayToSource	Changes on the UI are reflected to the data source but not vice versa. This is basically the opposite of OneWay.
OneTime	The data-binding is performed from the data source to the UI only once. When performed, changes are ignored and the UI is not updated. This is useful for presenting data, where you are sure that you will not update the data source.
Default	Applies the most convenient mode according to the user control. For example, the TextBox supports the two-way mode and thus this is the default mode. When you do not specify a different mode, this is the default.

Creating Bindings with Visual Basic

In case you need to create data-binding expressions at runtime, you need to write some Visual Basic code. Basically you need an instance of the `System.Windows.Data.Binding` class setting some of its property and then pass such instance to the target control. The following snippet reproduces the data-binding expression described in the previous section, this time utilizing Visual Basic code:

```
Dim bind As New Binding
'Instead of ElementName, use Source assigning the control
bind.Source = ValueSlider
bind.Path = New PropertyPath("Value")
bind.Mode = BindingMode.TwoWay
'You set the binding considering a dependency property
Me.ValueTextBox.SetBinding(TextBox.TextProperty, bind)
```

Until now you saw the most basic data-binding technique that can be useful when you need to make controls depend on other controls' properties. In the next section you will see data-binding techniques against data sources based on .NET collections.

Understanding the `DataGrid` and the `ObservableCollection`

In most cases you perform data-binding operations against .NET collections, even when fetching data from databases. WPF offers a different binding mechanism, such as user controls like the new `DataGrid`, the `ListView`, or the `ListBox`; moreover you can bind specific data to single controls like TextBox (for example when building master-details representations). In this book, which targets Visual Basic 2010 and .NET 4.0, you get an example of how to take advantage of the new DataGrid control, which offers a convenient and fast way for tabular data. The goal of next example is binding a collection of objects to a DataGrid allowing insert/update/delete operations onto the collection. First, add a new implementation of the Person class to the project as follows:

```
Public Class Person


    Public Property FirstName As String
    Public Property LastName As String
    Public Property Age As Integer


End Class
```

Now add a new People class, which inherits from ObservableCollection(Of Person) as follows:

```
Imports System.Collections.ObjectModel


Public Class People
    Inherits ObservableCollection(Of Person)


End Class
```

This new collection is the data source for binding to the DataGrid. Now go the VB code behind the file for the main window. Basically we need to declare a variable of type People and handle the Window_Loaded event to instantiate some Person objects to populate the collection. The following code accomplishes this:

```
Private WithEvents source As People


Private Sub MainWindow_Loaded(ByVal sender As Object,
                        ByVal e As System.Windows.
                        RoutedEventArgs) Handles Me.Loaded

    Dim personA As New Person With {.FirstName = "Alessandro",
                                .LastName = "Del Sole",
                                .Age = 32}
    'fantasy name
    Dim personB As New Person With {.FirstName = "Robert",
                                .LastName = "White",
                                .Age = 35}

    source = New People From {personA, personB}
```

```
    Me.Grid1.DataContext = source

    'If you plan to data-bind only the DataGrid:
    'Me.DataGrid1.ItemsSource = source
End Sub
```

Notice how easy it is to create an instance of the `People` collection with collection initial-izers. The most important thing here is the assignment of the `Grid.DataContext` property. As a general rule, `DataContext` is a property that points to a data source, and all children controls within the panel that exposes the `DataContext` property will populate picking up data from this property. This also means that `DataContext` has scope; for example, the `Window.DataContext` property can share data to all controls in the user interface, whereas the `DataContext` from a particular panel can share data only with controls nested in that particular panel, as in the previous code example where only controls nested in the `Grid` (including thus the `DataGrid`) can populate picking data from the `DataContext`. This is not mandatory. If you have a single control that you want to bind, you do not need to assign the `DataContext`, whereas you can simply assign the specific control data property. For instance, the `DataGrid` control exposes an `ItemsSource` property (like `ListView` and `ListBox`) that populates the control. Data-binding to user interface controls in WPF is generally possible thanks to the implementation of the `INotifyPropertyChanged` interface. Substantially controls can reflect changes from data sources that implement that interface. The `ObservableCollection(Of T)` generic collection also implements behind the scenes and therefore can notify the user interface of changes so that it can be refreshed automati-cally. This is the reason why we use such a collection in the example. This specialized collection is also interesting because it enables getting information on what changed on data. It exposes a `CollectionChanged` event that offers an e argument of type `NotifyCollectionEventArgs` that offers some useful information. For example it enables intercepting when an item is added or removed or retrieving a collection of added items. Continuing with the example, suppose you want to create a sort of log to write a message each time an item is added or removed from the `source` collection. This is useful for demonstrating that the collection is effectively updated with changes performed through the user interface. The second `TextBox` in the user interface of the sample application is the place where log messages will be put. According to this consideration, consider the following code snippet that provides an event handler for the `CollectionChanged` event:

```
'Requires an Imports System.Collections.Specialized directive    Private Sub
source_CollectionChanged(ByVal sender As Object,
                                ByVal e As _
                                NotifyCollectionChangedEventArgs) _
                                Handles source.CollectionChanged

        Me.LogBox.Text += e.Action.ToString & Environment.NewLine
    End Sub
```

The code simply sends to the text box the current value of the `System.Collection.Specialized.NotifyCollectionChangedAction` enumeration, which can be one of the following: Add, Remove, Move, Replace, or Reset. If you perform multiple CRUD operations on an ObservableCollection instance, you might also be interested in the NewItems and OldItems properties in e. They respectively represent a collection of items added to the data source and a collection of items affected by a remove, replace, or move operation. Before running the application, it is necessary to perform a couple of operations on the DataGrid at the XAML level; therefore switch back to the XAML code editor. Extend the DataGrid declaration as follows:

```
<DataGrid Name="DataGrid1"
          AutoGenerateColumns="True"
          AlternatingRowBackground="LightGreen"
          ItemsSource="{Binding}"
          Height="150"/>
```

First, the DataGrid automatically generates columns for you according to each property exposed by a single item (Person) in the bound collection (People). Second, the ItemsSource, which populates the control, is set to Binding with no arguments meaning that the data-binding will be performed at runtime. Notice how the AlternatingRowBackground property enables specifying a color (which you can eventually replace with a brush) for the background in alternating rows. Now run the application. You get the result shown in Figure 35.2.

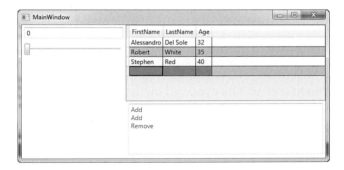

FIGURE 35.2   The data-bound DataGrid allows presenting and manipulating data.

DATAGRID BINDING TIPS

Different from controls such as the ListView and the ListBox, the DataGrid allows binding any collection implementing IList or IBindingList. This is because such control requires a place for editing, other than presenting. So remember this requirement when you try to bind to a DataGrid the result of LINQ queries, which requires conversion into a generic collection. For LINQ, if you try to bind LINQ to Xml, query results also remember to create a class for holding objects, just like the Person class and People collection instead of directly binding the query result.

If you play with the DataGrid you can easily understand how it enables adding, removing, and editing items. The log text box stores messages each time you perform an operation, confirming that the underlying collection is actually affected by changes performed through the user interface. You can then plan to implement some code for saving your data. The DataGrid exposes other interesting properties:

▶ SelectedItem, which returns the instance of the selected object in the control

▶ CurrentCell, which returns the content of the selected cell

▶ CanUserAddRows and CanUserRemoveRows, which respectively provide (or not) the user the ability of adding and deleting rows

▶ CanUserReorderColumns, CanUserResizeColumns, CanUserSortColumns which respectively provide (or not) the ability of changing the order of resizing and sorting columns

▶ CanUserResizeRows, which provides (or not) the ability of resizing rows

▶ RowStyle, which allows overriding the style for rows

Until now you saw simple data-binding tasks, although the last code example provides a good way for understanding the mechanism. WPF data-binding is even more complex and the .NET Framework offers specific objects that are important in more articulate scenarios. The next section describes such objects taking advantage of new Visual Studio features.

Discussing the New Drag'n'Drop Data-Binding

Visual Studio 2010 introduces to the WPF development a new interesting feature at the IDE level. The feature is known as drag'n'drop data-binding and is something that was already available in Windows Forms for many years. Now you can simply build data forms in WPF too with such new tooling. The base idea is that you can build a data form by simply dragging items from the Data Sources window, and Visual Studio will generate all the code for you, including master-details scenarios. There is also other good news in Visual Studio 2010, which is the Data Sources window support for entities from an Entity Data Model based on the ADO.NET Entity Framework. This section explains how you can take advantage of the new WPF drag'n'drop data-binding to easily build data forms, explaining the meaning and behavior of the auto-generated code.

TIP

The drag'n'drop data-binding has obviously some limitations, and in many cases you need to put your hands over the auto-generated code or, differently, write your own data-binding code from scratch. This new technique offers several advantages: The result is completely customizable, as in the style of WPF applications; second, if you are new to data-binding in WPF, it allows you to simply understand how things work against a more complex data-source (such as an EDM or a DataSet). Finally, it also provides the ability of separating the data-source from the user interface, although this is something that you will probably need to edit according to your application logic.

To complete the next code examples, follow these steps after creating a new WPF project in Visual Basic:

1. Create a new WPF project for Visual Basic.

2. Add a new Entity Data Model based on the Northwind sample database, ensuring that you include the Customers and Orders tables. If you need a recap, take a look at Chapter 27, "Introducing the ADO.NET Entity Framework."

After this brief introduction, it is time to understand how easy building data forms is with WPF 4.

Creating Tabular Data Forms

The goal of the next example is to show how simple it is to create tabular data representations, also taking a look at necessary objects for performing data-binding in code. To accomplish this, first divide the default Grid into two columns as follows:

```
<Grid>
    <Grid.ColumnDefinitions>
        <ColumnDefinition Width="200"/>
        <ColumnDefinition/>
    </Grid.ColumnDefinitions>
</Grid>
```

Next, add a ListBox control either by dragging it from the Toolbox or by writing the following code (for better layout purposes, ensure that you place it in the left column):

```
<ListBox Name="CustomersListBox"
        Grid.Column="0"/>
```

This ListBox stores a list of customers' names that will be added shortly. Now open the Data Sources window by clicking **Shift+Alt+D**. The result looks similar to Figure 35.3, depending on how many entities you added to the Entity Data Model.

As you can see, the Data Sources window now also lists entities coming from Entity Data Models, and this is a new feature in Visual Studio 2010. The default icon near each entity name indicates that data will be represented as tabular, but you can replace this representation with a list view or with a details view simply by selecting the appropriate value from the combo box on the right side of each entity name. (At the moment leave unchanged the default selection.) Now, expand the Customers entity (as shown in Figure 35.3) and select the CompanyName item; then drag it onto the ListBox and release the mouse. When you release the mouse, you will not notice anything new on the designer surface, but look at what happened in the XAML code editor:

```
<Window.Resources>
    <CollectionViewSource x:Key="CustomersViewSource"
                          d:DesignSource=
                          "{d:DesignInstance my:Customer,
                                            CreateList=True}" />
```

35

FIGURE 35.3 The Data Sources window now lists entities from EDMs, too.

```
</Window.Resources>
<Grid DataContext="{StaticResource CustomersViewSource}">
    <Grid.ColumnDefinitions>
        <ColumnDefinition Width="200"/>
        <ColumnDefinition/>
    </Grid.ColumnDefinitions>
    <ListBox Name="CustomersListBox"
            Grid.Column="0" DisplayMemberPath="CompanyName"
            ItemsSource="{Binding}" />
</Grid>
```

Visual Studio generates some code, both XAML and Visual Basic, each time you perform some drag'n'drop action. For now it generated a CollectionViewSource object within the window's resources. You may compare the WPF CollectionViewSource to the Windows Forms' BindingSource control, which basically acts like a bridge between the underlying data collection and the user interface. The code states that such CollectionViewSource is populated via a list (CreateList=True) of Customer instances. This statement is accomplished via the d:DesignInstance custom markup extension, exposed by the d Xml namespace that points to Microsoft Expression Blend schema for WPF. This is useful because it provides resources for design-time data-binding. Notice also how Visual Studio added a DataContext property for the default Grid, whose source is the above described CollectionViewSource. In this way, all child controls will populate picking data from the CollectionViewSource. You can get an example of this by taking a look at the ListBox overridden definition: It is populated with data-binding (`ItemsSource` property) and shows just the value of the `CompanyName` property (`DisplayMemberPath`) for each item in the bound collection. Now drag onto the form the `Orders` item from the Data Sources window, ensuring that you drag the one nested within `Customers`. When dragged and dropped, the result should look like in Figure 35.4.

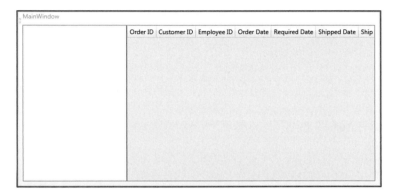

FIGURE 35.4   The result of the drag'n'drop operations in the Visual Studio designer.

First, notice how the new `DataGrid` control simply enables building tabular data representations. By simply dragging the data source, Visual Studio generated all the necessary items for you. If you now take a look at the XAML code editor, you will first notice a second `CollectionViewSource` referring to the `Orders` data:

```
<CollectionViewSource x:Key="CustomersOrdersViewSource"
                      Source="{Binding Path=Orders,
                      Source={StaticResource CustomersViewSource}}" />
```

Notice how the source for the data-binding is the `Orders` collection from the previously generated `CustomersViewSource` object of type `CollectionViewSource`. Next, Visual Studio also generated markup code for the `DataGrid`. For this, it did not take advantage of columns auto-generation, whereas it instead created specific columns for each property in the bound collection. This enables the IDE to also generate custom cell templates that can show data with the appropriate control. The following is the XAML code for the `DataGrid`:

```
<DataGrid AutoGenerateColumns="False"
          EnableRowVirtualization="True"
          Grid.Column="1"
          ItemsSource="{Binding
          Source={StaticResource CustomersOrdersViewSource}}"
          Name="OrdersDataGrid"
          RowDetailsVisibilityMode="VisibleWhenSelected">
    <DataGrid.Columns>
        <DataGridTextColumn x:Name="OrderIDColumn"
```

35

```
                         Binding="{Binding Path=OrderID}"
                         Header="Order ID"
                         Width="SizeToHeader" />
<DataGridTextColumn x:Name="CustomerIDColumn"
                         Binding="{Binding Path=CustomerID}"
                         Header="Customer ID"
                         Width="SizeToHeader" />
<DataGridTextColumn x:Name="EmployeeIDColumn"
                         Binding="{Binding Path=EmployeeID}"
                         Header="Employee ID"
                         Width="SizeToHeader" />
<DataGridTemplateColumn x:Name="OrderDateColumn"
                             Header="Order Date"
                             Width="SizeToHeader">
    <DataGridTemplateColumn.CellTemplate>
        <DataTemplate>
            <DatePicker
             SelectedDate="{Binding Path=OrderDate}" />
        </DataTemplate>
    </DataGridTemplateColumn.CellTemplate>
</DataGridTemplateColumn>
<DataGridTemplateColumn x:Name="RequiredDateColumn"
                             Header="Required Date"
                             Width="SizeToHeader">
    <DataGridTemplateColumn.CellTemplate>
        <DataTemplate>
            <DatePicker
             SelectedDate="{Binding Path=RequiredDate}" />
        </DataTemplate>
    </DataGridTemplateColumn.CellTemplate>
</DataGridTemplateColumn>
<DataGridTemplateColumn x:Name="ShippedDateColumn"
                             Header="Shipped Date"
                             Width="SizeToHeader">
    <DataGridTemplateColumn.CellTemplate>
        <DataTemplate>
            <DatePicker
             SelectedDate="{Binding Path=ShippedDate}" />
        </DataTemplate>
    </DataGridTemplateColumn.CellTemplate>
</DataGridTemplateColumn>
<DataGridTextColumn x:Name="ShipViaColumn"
                         Binding="{Binding Path=ShipVia}"
                         Header="Ship Via"
```

```
                              Width="SizeToHeader" />
          <DataGridTextColumn x:Name="FreightColumn"
                              Binding="{Binding Path=Freight}"
                              Header="Freight"
                              Width="SizeToHeader" />
          <DataGridTextColumn x:Name="ShipNameColumn"
                              Binding="{Binding Path=ShipName}"
                              Header="Ship Name"
                              Width="SizeToHeader" />
          <DataGridTextColumn x:Name="ShipAddressColumn"
                              Binding="{Binding Path=ShipAddress}"
                              Header="Ship Address"
                              Width="SizeToHeader" />
          <DataGridTextColumn x:Name="ShipCityColumn"
                              Binding="{Binding Path=ShipCity}"
                              Header="Ship  City"
                              Width="SizeToHeader" />
          <DataGridTextColumn x:Name="ShipRegionColumn"
                              Binding="{Binding Path=ShipRegion}"
                              Header="Ship Region"
                              Width="SizeToHeader" />
          <DataGridTextColumn x:Name="ShipPostalCodeColumn"
                              Binding="{Binding Path=ShipPostalCode}"
                              Header="Ship Postal Code"
                              Width="SizeToHeader" />
          <DataGridTextColumn x:Name="ShipCountryColumn"
                              Binding="{Binding Path=ShipCountry}"
                              Header="Ship Country"
                              Width="SizeToHeader" />
      </DataGrid.Columns>
  </DataGrid>
```

The DataGrid data source is set via the ItemsSource property pointing to the
CustomersOrdersViewSource object, which includes information from both Customers and
related Orders. The rest of the code is quite simple to understand. Each column has a cell
template, which is of type DataGridTextColumn for text fields. Other built-in types are
DataGridHyperLinkColumn for displaying hyperlinks, DataGridCheckBoxColumn for displaying Boolean values with a check box control, and DataGridComboBoxColumn that allows
selecting items from within a combo box. It is worth mentioning that for data types that
the DataGrid has no default counterpart for, Visual Studio generates a custom cell
template with DataGridTemplateColumn objects. In this case the custom template has been
generated for embedding DatePicker controls for setting and displaying dates within cells.

35

DESIGNING COLUMNS

The IDE provides a convenient way for designing columns with the designer instrumentation. Simply select the DataGrid and in the Properties window, click **Columns**. Figure 35.5 shows how you can edit existing columns or add new ones, also setting data-binding at design time.

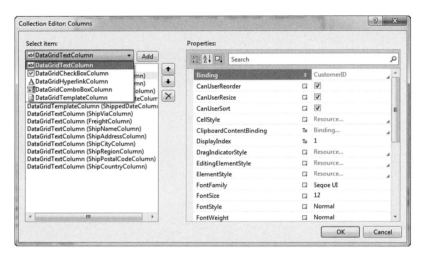

FIGURE 35.5   Designing columns with Visual Studio.

This is not enough, of course, in that some Visual Basic code is also required for fetching data and assigning such data to the user interface for presenting. If you now open the Visual Basic code behind the file for the current Window, you get the result shown in Listing 35.1.

LISTING 35.1   The VB Auto-Generated Code for the Drag'n'Drop Data-Binding

```
'Add an Imports directive followed by the project namespace
Imports IntroducingDataBinding
Class MainWindow

    Private Function GetCustomersQuery(ByVal NorthwindEntities As NorthwindEntities)_
                    As System.Data.Objects.ObjectQuery(Of Customer)

        Dim CustomersQuery As System.Data.Objects.ObjectQuery(Of Customer) = _
                        NorthwindEntities.Customers
        'Update the query to include Orders data in Customers.
        'You can modify this code as needed.
        CustomersQuery = CustomersQuery.Include("Orders")
        'Returns an ObjectQuery.
```

```
        Return CustomersQuery
    End Function

    Private Sub Window_Loaded(ByVal sender As System.Object,
                             ByVal e As System.Windows.RoutedEventArgs) _
                             Handles MyBase.Loaded

        Dim NorthwindEntities As NorthwindEntities = New NorthwindEntities()
        'Load data into Customers. You can modify this code as needed.
        Dim CustomersViewSource As System.Windows.Data.CollectionViewSource = _
            CType(Me.FindResource("CustomersViewSource"),
            System.Windows.Data.CollectionViewSource)
        Dim CustomersQuery As System.Data.Objects.ObjectQuery(Of Customer) = _
            Me.GetCustomersQuery(NorthwindEntities)
        CustomersViewSource.Source = CustomersQuery.Execute(System.Data.Objects.
                                                        MergeOption.AppendOnly)
    End Sub
End Class
```

The GetCustomersQuery method returns the full list of customers and related orders, returning a new Entity Framework object, ObjectQuery(Of T). Such an object type represents a typed query and is also capable of receiving data back. Of course such a query is a default one; therefore, you may customize it according to your needs. When the window is loaded, other than the ObjectContext instance, notice how the code retrieves the instance of the CustomersViewSource (of type CollectionViewSource) via the FindResource method, which enables searching for a resource declared in XAML. This instance will finally receive the executed query so that its result will be reflected to the user interface. Basically the process is the following: The query fetches data; data is assigned to a CollectionViewSource instance; because this instance is bound to a UI control (such as the DataGrid), fetched data is reflected to the UI and vice versa. This is also because the DataGrid control provides support for the two-way data-binding, and this is also allowed by the ObjectQuery(Of T) class. At this point you can run the application to see the result shown in Figure 35.6.

With a few mouse clicks you can build an application that can present tabular data. You can click inside the DataGrid for editing existing data or for adding new rows. If you want to save data to the underlying database, you should simply implement a control, such as a Button, whose Click event handler invokes the ObjectContext.SaveChanges method, and you are done. But you see this example in the next section, which is interesting but that requires a little bit of manual work.

Creating Master-Details Forms

Similarly to what already happened in Windows Forms, creating master-details forms in WPF 4 is also straightforward. This also enables you to understand other important concepts for the data-binding. Add a new window to the current project and name it

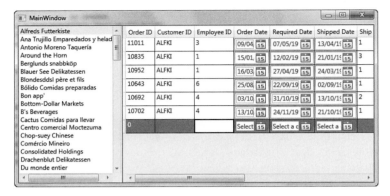

FIGURE 35.6   The tabular data application running.

MasterDetails. Divide the default Grid into four cells, so that you can also add special buttons, as follows:

```
<Grid>
    <Grid.ColumnDefinitions>
        <ColumnDefinition Width="200"/>
        <ColumnDefinition/>
    </Grid.ColumnDefinitions>
    <Grid.RowDefinitions>
        <RowDefinition/>
        <RowDefinition Height="50"/>
    </Grid.RowDefinitions>
</Grid>
```

Repeat the step of adding a ListBox and binding the customer's CompanyName property, same as in the first part of the previous subsection, ensuring that the ListBox is placed in the upper-left column. Visual Studio 2010 generates for you exactly the same XAML code of the previous example. Now go to the Data Sources window, select the **Orders** item nested within Customers, and from the combo box, select **Details**. At this point drag **Orders** onto the upper-right cell of the window. Figure 35.7 shows the result of this operation.

Notice how Visual Studio generated a series of controls, basically couples of Label/TextBlock. Also notice how the IDE can recognize the bound data type and of adding the appropriate controls. For example, for dates, it adds to the form some DatePicker controls. Instead of a DataGrid, the auto-generated XAML code contains a new Grid with a series of children controls. Listing 35.2 shows an excerpt of the content of the new Grid.

LISTING 35.2   Excerpt of the Auto-Generated XAML Code for Details

```
<Grid DataContext="{StaticResource CustomersOrdersViewSource}"
      Grid.Column="1"
      Grid.Row="0" Name="Grid1" >
```

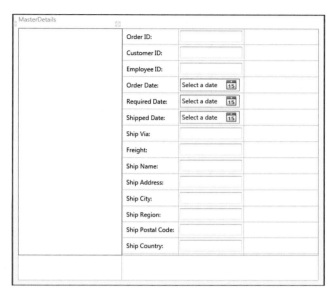

FIGURE 35.7   The result of the master-details drag'n'drop.

```xml
<Grid.ColumnDefinitions>
    <ColumnDefinition Width="Auto" />
    <ColumnDefinition Width="Auto" />
</Grid.ColumnDefinitions>
<Grid.RowDefinitions>
    <RowDefinition Height="Auto" />
    <RowDefinition Height="Auto" />
    <RowDefinition Height="Auto" />
    <RowDefinition Height="Auto" />
    <RowDefinition Height="Auto" />
    <RowDefinition Height="Auto" />
    <RowDefinition Height="Auto" />
    <RowDefinition Height="Auto" />
    <RowDefinition Height="Auto" />
    <RowDefinition Height="Auto" />
    <RowDefinition Height="Auto" />
    <RowDefinition Height="Auto" />
    <RowDefinition Height="Auto" />
    <RowDefinition Height="Auto" />
</Grid.RowDefinitions>
<Label Content="Order ID:" Grid.Column="0" Grid.Row="0"
        HorizontalAlignment="Left" Margin="3"
        VerticalAlignment="Center" />
<TextBox Grid.Column="1" Grid.Row="0" Height="23"
        HorizontalAlignment="Left" Margin="3" Name="OrderIDTextBox"
```

```
                Text="{Binding Path=OrderID}"
                VerticalAlignment="Center" Width="120" />
        <Label Content="Customer ID:" Grid.Column="0" Grid.Row="1"
               HorizontalAlignment="Left" Margin="3"
               VerticalAlignment="Center" />
        <TextBox Grid.Column="1" Grid.Row="1" Height="23"
                 HorizontalAlignment="Left" Margin="3" Name="CustomerIDTextBox"
                 Text="{Binding Path=CustomerID}"
                 VerticalAlignment="Center" Width="120" />
        <Label Content="Employee ID:" Grid.Column="0" Grid.Row="2"
               HorizontalAlignment="Left" Margin="3"
               VerticalAlignment="Center" />
        <TextBox Grid.Column="1" Grid.Row="2" Height="23"
                 HorizontalAlignment="Left"
                 Margin="3" Name="EmployeeIDTextBox"
                 Text="{Binding Path=EmployeeID}"
                 VerticalAlignment="Center" Width="120" />
        <Label Content="Order Date:" Grid.Column="0" Grid.Row="3"
               HorizontalAlignment="Left" Margin="3"
               VerticalAlignment="Center" />
        <DatePicker Grid.Column="1" Grid.Row="3" Height="25"
                    HorizontalAlignment="Left" Margin="3"
                    Name="OrderDateDatePicker"
                    SelectedDate="{Binding Path=OrderDate}"
                    VerticalAlignment="Center" Width="115" />
        <!--Following other controls... -->
</Grid>
```

Basically the code implements pairs of labels/text. For dates, you can notice the presence of DatePicker controls whose SelectedDate property is bound to the date property from the data source. If you take a look at the Visual Basic auto-generated code, you see no differences with the one shown in the first example. Now there is some other work to do. Building a master-details form requires providing controls for navigating, adding, deleting, and saving items. At this point add the following XAML code, which implements some buttons whose meaning is self explanatory:

```
<StackPanel Grid.Row="1" Grid.Column="1" Orientation="Horizontal">
    <StackPanel.Resources>
        <Style TargetType="Button" x:Key="ButtonStyle">
            <Setter Property="Width" Value="80"/>
            <Setter Property="Height" Value="40"/>
            <Setter Property="Margin" Value="5"/>
        </Style>
    </StackPanel.Resources>
    <Button Style="{StaticResource ButtonStyle}" Content="Save"
```

```
                Name="SaveButton" Click="SaveButton_Click"/>
        <Button Style="{StaticResource ButtonStyle}" Content="Add"
                Name="AddButton" Click="AddButton_Click"/>
        <Button Style="{StaticResource ButtonStyle}" Content="Delete"
                Name="DeleteButton" Click="DeleteButton_Click"/>
        <Button Style="{StaticResource ButtonStyle}" Content="Next"
                Name="NextButton" Click="NextButton_Click"/>
        <Button Style="{StaticResource ButtonStyle}" Content="Back"
                Name="BackButton" Click="BackButton_Click"/>
</StackPanel>
```

Now switch to the Visual Basic code. The first task is moving the `ObjectContext` declaration at class level, to make it reachable from within other methods. Replace the `NorthwindEntities` variable declaration with the `northwindContext` name to avoid conflicts, move it to class level, and edit the first line of the `Window_Loaded` event as follows:

```
Private northwindContext As NorthwindEntities


Private Sub Window_Loaded(ByVal sender As System.Object,
                          ByVal e As System.Windows.RoutedEventArgs) _
                          Handles MyBase.Loaded

    Me.northwindContext = New NorthwindEntities
```

The first button that can be handled is the `SaveButton`. The `Click` event handler is the following:

```
Private Sub SaveButton_Click(ByVal sender As System.Object,
                             ByVal e As System.Windows.
                             RoutedEventArgs)
    'Handle your logic here, such as exceptions
    'and optmistic concurrency
    Try
        Me.northwindContext.SaveChanges()
    Catch ex As Exception

    End Try
End Sub
```

The second task is moving to class level the `CollectionViewSource` objects declarations so that we can invoke them within event handlers. They actually are enclosed in the `Window_Loaded` event handler and thus have no external visibility. Moreover, we also need to manually declare and get the instance of the `CustomersOrdersCollectionViewSource` object because the application needs to provide the ability of adding and removing items only to the `Orders` collection. (Performing this on `CustomersViewSource` would affect `Customers`, too.) Code in Listing 35.3 summarizes the edits that you need to do manually at this point.

LISTING 35.3   Moving CollectionViewSource Declarations at Class Level

```
Private CustomersViewSource As CollectionViewSource
Private CustomersOrdersViewSource As CollectionViewSource

Private Sub Window_Loaded(ByVal sender As System.Object,
                          ByVal e As System.Windows.RoutedEventArgs) _
                          Handles MyBase.Loaded

    Me.northwindContext = New NorthwindEntities
    'Load data into Customers. You can modify this code as needed.
    Me.CustomersViewSource = CType(Me.FindResource("CustomersViewSource"),
                             CollectionViewSource)
    Me.CustomersOrdersViewSource =
                        CType(Me.FindResource("CustomersOrdersViewSource"),
                        CollectionViewSource)

    Dim CustomersQuery As System.Data.Objects.
                        ObjectQuery(Of IntroducingDataBinding.Customer) = _
                        Me.GetCustomersQuery(northwindContext)
    CustomersViewSource.Source = CustomersQuery.
                             Execute(System.Data.Objects.
                                 MergeOption.AppendOnly)
End Sub
```

The next buttons require explaining other concepts, which the next sections cover.

Understanding Views and Binding Lists

CollectionViewSource objects expose an interesting property named View. It basically provides the ability of filtering, sorting, and navigating through a bound collection of items. To understand how a view works, the best example in our scenario is handling the Next and Back buttons. The following code snippet shows how easy it is to navigate back and forward through items:

```
Private Sub NextButton_Click(ByVal sender As System.Object,
                             ByVal e As System.Windows.RoutedEventArgs)
    If Me.CustomersOrdersViewSource.View.CurrentPosition < _
        CType(Me.CustomersOrdersViewSource.View, CollectionView).
        Count - 1 Then
        Me.CustomersOrdersViewSource.View.MoveCurrentToNext()
    End If
End Sub


Private Sub BackButton_Click(ByVal sender As System.Object,
                             ByVal e As System.Windows.RoutedEventArgs)
```

```
    If Me.CustomersOrdersViewSource.View.CurrentPosition > 0 Then
        Me.CustomersOrdersViewSource.View.MoveCurrentToPrevious()
    End If
End Sub
```

The code simply calculates the position and enables moving back or forward only if there are any other items that can be navigated. Notice how the CustomersOrdersViewSource.View property exposes the Count property, representing the current position being examined in the collection. Also notice methods such as MoveCurrentToNext and MoveCurrentToPrevious that enable moving back and forward to another item. Other interesting members from views are self-explanatory and are summarized in Table 35.2.

TABLE 35.2   Views' Most Common Members

Member	Type	Description
CanSort	Property	Returns a Boolean value indicating whether the collection can be sorted.
CanFilter	Property	Returns a Boolean value indicating whether the collection can be filtered.
CanGroup	Property	Returns a Boolean value indicating whether the collection can be grouped.
MoveCurrentTo	Method	Sets the specified item as the current item in the collection.
MoveCurrentToFirst	Method	Sets the first item in the collection as the current item.
MoveCurrentToLast	Method	Sets the last item in the collection as the current item.
MoveCurrentToNext	Method	Sets next item in the collection as the current item.
MoveCurrentToPrevious	Method	Sets the previous item in the collection as the current item.
CurrentItem	Property	Returns the instance of the current item in the collection. Because it is of type Object, it must be converted into the appropriate type.
CurrentPosition	Property	Returns an index corresponding to the current item in the collection.

Also notice how, to retrieve the items count, a CType operator converts from CollectionViewSource.View into a CollectionView object. This last one represents a single view, and the conversion is required because Option Strict is On and the View property is of type ICollectionView. Views from CollectionViewSource objects are straightforward, because they also support data-binding but they have several limitations.

As you can recap from Table 35.2, no member is exposed for adding, editing, or removing items in the underlying data collection. To provide the ability of CRUD operations, the best approach is utilizing a System.Window.Data.Binding ListCollectionView, which also offers a reference to data collections but provides more capabilities. With that said, at class level, declare the following variables:

```
Private WithEvents CustomerView As BindingListCollectionView
Private CustomersOrdersView As BindingListCollectionView
```

Now, in the Window_Loaded event handler, add the following lines as the last lines of code in the method:

```
Me.CustomerView = CType(Me.CustomersViewSource.View, _
                        BindingListCollectionView)
Me.CustomersOrdersView = CType(Me.CustomersOrdersViewSource.View, _
                        BindingListCollectionView)
```

This converts views references to two BindingListCollectionView objects. Now with these you can perform insert/update/delete operations to the underlying collection, which is picked up from the CollectionViewSource associations and that is data-bound to the BindingListCollectionView, too. To understand how this works, write the following handler for the Click event about the Add button so that we can provide the ability of adding a new order:

```
Private Sub AddButton_Click(ByVal sender As System.Object, _
                            ByVal e As System.Windows.RoutedEventArgs)
    'A new order
    Dim newOrder As Order

    'Adds a new order to the view and assigns the instance
    'to the newly declared order
    newOrder = CType(Me.CustomersOrdersView.AddNew(), Order)

    'If I need to assign properties to newOrder before
    'it is sent to the collection, then this is the place

    'Sends the new order to the view
    Me.CustomersOrdersView.CommitNew()
End Sub
```

The AddNew method adds an instance of the specified object type to the view, and the addition is automatically reflected to the bound user interface controls. The CType conversion is required because the method returns Object; therefore, converting to the appropriate type returns the effective instance of the order. This is not actually required, but it is useful if you want to set some default properties before the object is sent to the underlying collection. Notice that this code submits the new item to the underlying collection, but the new object will not persist to the underlying database until you invoke the `ObjectContext.SaveChanges` method. Removing items works similarly, in that you simply retrieve the current object instance and invoke one of the allowed methods. The following event handler for the `Delete` button demonstrates this:

```
Private Sub DeleteButton_Click(ByVal sender As System.Object,
                        ByVal e As System.Windows.
                        RoutedEventArgs)
   If Me.CustomersOrdersView.CurrentPosition > -1 Then

       Dim result = MessageBox.Show("Are you sure?",
                           "", MessageBoxButton.YesNo)
       If result = MessageBoxResult.Yes Then
          Me.CustomersOrdersView.
             RemoveAt(Me.CustomersOrdersView.CurrentPosition)
       Else
          Exit Sub
       End If
   End If
End Sub
```

In this case I'm using `RemoveAt` to remove the item at the current position, but you can also invoke `Remove` that requires the instance of the current object. Basically `RemoveAt` requires fewer lines of code. Before running the application, there is one thing that you need to take care of and that is the fact that the a `BindingListCollectionView` content needs to be refreshed each time you move to another item in the master part of the master-details relationships. Considering our code example, you need to remember the `BindingListCollectionView` referred to orders each time you select a different customer. To accomplish this you handle the `CurrentChanged` event in the master part of the relationship, as demonstrated by the following code:

```
Private Sub CustomerView_CurrentChanged(ByVal sender As Object,
                        ByVal e As System.EventArgs) _
                        Handles CustomerView.CurrentChanged
   Me.CustomersOrdersView = CType(Me.CustomersOrdersViewSource.View,
                        BindingListCollectionView)
End Sub
```

The preceding event handler is invoked when you click a different customer in the user interface and refreshes the `CustomersOrdersView` (of type `BindingListCollectionView`) object pointing to the actual orders collection referred by the underlying `CollectionViewSource`, which effectively keeps the data-binding alive. At this point you can run the application and get the result summarized in Figure 35.8.

FIGURE 35.8   The master-details application running.

BINDING TO DATASETS

The drag'n'drop data-binding works the same with DataSets and you can still take advantage of `CollectionViewSource` and `BindingListCollectionView` objects. The code remains the same as the previously shown examples, whereas the difference is where you need to persist data to the database or fetch data, where you can respectively use DataSet methods and LINQ to DataSets.

You can now play with additional controls such as Add, Delete, Next, and Back. When you are done, try and save changes to ensure that new or edited data is correctly persisted to the database. This sample application can be enhanced in several other ways. For example you can implement entities validation or showing details for a single order using LINQ. These topics are beyond the scope of an introductory chapter about data-binding, but you can further explore them with the help of the MSDN documentation. Particularly I suggest you read this blog post by Beth Massi from Microsoft, where she discusses WPF validation on entities: http://blogs.msdn.com/bethmassi/archive/2009/07/07/implementing-validation-in-wpf-on-entity-framework-entities.aspx. Although the blog post targets the .NET Framework 3.5 SP 1, this technique is convenient on .NET 4.0, too.

Implementing String Formatters and Value Converters

The need to represent strings in a more appropriate format when binding data to the user interface is not uncommon. For example, you might want to present money values or percentages. In WPF you can accomplish this in two modes: string formatters and the

IValueConverter interface. This section describes both, showing how they can be used for better presentation purposes.

Implementing String Formatters

Starting from .NET 3.5 SP 1, you can apply string formats directly in the XAML `Binding` markup extension that performs data-binding. This allows expressing a particular value type in a more convenient string format. For a better understanding, consider Figure 35.8 Notice now the `Freight` field is shown as a decimal number but probably you might want to display it with your currency symbol. Locate the XAML code that implements the `Freight` textbox and apply the `StringFormat` property as shown in the following code snippet:

```
<TextBox Grid.Column="1" Grid.Row="7" Height="23"
         HorizontalAlignment="Left" Margin="3"
         Name="FreightTextBox"
         Text="{Binding Path=Freight, StringFormat=c}"
         VerticalAlignment="Center" Width="120" />
```

The `BindingBase.StringFormat` property is applied within the `Binding` markup extension and requires the specification of the formatter. Figure 35.9 shows how the `Freight` field is now represented with a currency symbol.

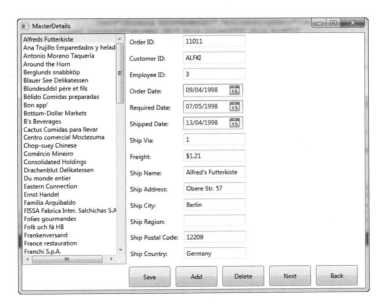

FIGURE 35.9   Representing strings with `StringFormat`.

Table 35.3 summarizes the most common `StringFormat` values.

TABLE 35.3   Most Common Formatters Values

Value	Description
c or C	Represents a value as a string with currency symbol.
p or P	Formats a value as a string with percentage representation.
D	Formats a date value as an extended string representation (for example, Monday, 21 October 2009).
D	Formats a date value as a short string representation (for example, 10/21/2009).
F	Provides a string representation of a decimal number with floating point. It is followed by a number that establishes how many numbers follow the floating point (for example, 3.14 can be represented by F2).
E	Scientific formatting.
X	Hexadecimal formatting.
G	General.

The good news is that string formatters also provide converting back the user input. For the `Freight` example, if you type a value into the field, it is represented as a currency in the user interface, but it is correctly saved to the data source according to the required type. `StringFormat` also enables string formatting as it happens in Visual Basic code. Consider the following code:

```
<TextBox Name="FreightTextBox"
         Text="{Binding Path=Freight, StringFormat=Amount: {0:c}}"/>
```

In the preceding code the `Amount` word takes the place of 0 at runtime. So the result will be `Amount: $ 1.21`. There is another useful technique known as `MultiBinding`. The following code demonstrates how it is possible to apply multiple formatters with `MultiBinding`:

```
<!—Applies date and currency formatting—>
<TextBlock>
  <TextBlock.Text>
    <MultiBinding StringFormat="Order date: {0:D}, Cost: {1:C}">
      <Binding Path="OrderDate"/>
      <Binding Path="OrderPrice"/>
    </MultiBinding>
  </TextBlock.Text>
</TextBlock>
```

Several user controls, such as `Button` and `Label`, also offer a `ContentStringFormat` property that enables applying formatting to the control's content the same way as `StringFormat` works. The following is an example:

```
<Label ContentStringFormat="C" Content="200"/>
```

Similarly, controls such as `ListView`, `ListBox`, and `DataGrid` offer the `HeaderStringFormat` and `ItemStringFormat` properties that enable, respectively, formatting the header content for columns and items in the list. String formatters are straightforward, but there are situations in which you need more extensive control over value representation, especially when you need to actually convert from one data type to another. This is where `IValueConverter` comes in.

Implementing the `IValueConverter` Interface

There are situations in which default conversions provided by string formatters are not enough, especially if you have to implement your custom logic when converting from the user input into another type. With `IValueConverter` you can implement your custom logic getting control over the conversion process from and to the data source. To follow the next steps, create a new class and name it `CustomConverter`. When the new class is ready, implement the `IValueConverter` interface. The resulting code will be the following:

```vb
Public Class CustomConverter
    Implements IValueConverter


    Public Function Convert(ByVal value As Object,
                    ByVal targetType As System.Type,
                    ByVal parameter As Object,
                    ByVal culture As
                    System.Globalization.CultureInfo) _
                    As Object Implements _
                    System.Windows.Data.IValueConverter.Convert


    End Function

    Public Function ConvertBack(ByVal value As Object,
                    ByVal targetType As System.Type,
                    ByVal parameter As Object,
                    ByVal culture As System.Globalization.
                    CultureInfo) As Object _
                    Implements _
                    System.Windows.Data.IValueConverter.
                    ConvertBack
```

35

```
      End Function
End Class
```

The interface implementation requires two methods, `Convert` and `ConvertBack`. The first one manages data when applying from the data source to the user interface, whereas the second one manages the conversion when getting back from the user interface to the data source. The most important argument in the `Convert` method is parameter, which represents how data must be converted. Such data is stored by the value argument. Implementing `Convert` is quite easy, in that generally you simply need to format value as a string according to parameter's establishment, and this can be accomplished taking advantage of the current culture. The following is the standard `Convert` implementation:

```
Public Function Convert(ByVal value As Object,
                        ByVal targetType As System.Type,
                        ByVal parameter As Object,
                        ByVal culture As _
                        System.Globalization.CultureInfo) _
                        As Object Implements System.Windows.Data.
                        IValueConverter.Convert

    If parameter IsNot Nothing Then
        Return String.Format(culture, parameter.ToString, value)
    End If

    Return value
End Function
```

Basically it ensures that on the XAML side a valid converter property (reflected by parameter), which is described later, has been provided and that it is not null. In this case the method returns the string representation of the value according to the system culture. If no converter is specified, the method simply returns the value. `ConvertBack` is a little bit more complex, because it has to convert strings (that is, the user input) into a more appropriate type. The goal of this example is providing conversion from `String` to `Decimal`, for money fields. The following code snippet implements the method (see comments for explanations):

```
Public Function ConvertBack(ByVal value As Object,
                            ByVal targetType As System.Type,
                            ByVal parameter As Object,
                            ByVal culture As System.Globalization.
                            CultureInfo) As Object _
                            Implements System.Windows.Data.
                            IValueConverter.ConvertBack

    'If the type to send back to the source is Decimal or Decimal?
    If targetType Is GetType(Decimal) OrElse targetType _
```

```
                 Is GetType(Nullable(Of Decimal)) Then

        Dim resultMoney As Decimal = Nothing

        'Checks if the input is not null
        If Decimal.TryParse(CStr(value), resultMoney) = True Then
            'in such case, it is returned
            Return CDec(value)
            'if it is empty, returns Nothing
        ElseIf value.ToString = String.Empty Then
            Return Nothing
        Else
            'If it is not empty but invalid,
            'returns a default value
            Return 0D
        End If
    End If

    Return value
End Function
```

It is worth mentioning that you need to provide conversion for nullable types, as in the preceding code, if you work against an Entity Data Model. If your user interface simply presents data, but does not receive input from the user, you can implement ConvertBack by simply putting a Throw New NotImplementedException as the method body. The MSDN official documentation suggests an interesting best practice when implementing custom converters. This requires applying the ValueConversion attributes to the class; this attribute enables specifying data types involved in the conversion, as in the following line that has to be applied to the CustomConverter class:

```
<ValueConversion(GetType(String), GetType(Decimal))>
```

The first attribute's argument is the type that you need to convert from, whereas the second one is the type that you need to convert to. Custom converters must be applied at XAML level. This requires first adding an xml namespace pointing to the current assembly that defines the class. For the previous example, add the following namespace declaration within the Window element definition, taking care to replace the IntroducingDataBinding name with the name of your assembly (IntelliSense will help you choose):

```
xmlns:local="clr-namespace:IntroducingDataBinding"
```

When you have a reference to the assembly, which can be useful for utilizing other classes at the XAML level, you need to declare a new resource that points to the custom converter. Within the Window.Resources element, add the following line:

```
<local:CustomConverter x:Key="customConverter"/>
```

Now that the converter has an identifier and can be used at the XAML level, you simply pass it to the bound property you want to convert. For example, suppose you want to format and convert the `Freight` property from the `Order` class. The following code demonstrates how to apply the converter:

```
<TextBox Grid.Column="1" Grid.Row="7" Height="23"
        HorizontalAlignment="Left" Margin="3"
        Name="FreightTextBox"
        Text="{Binding Path=Freight,
            Converter={StaticResource customConverter},
            ConverterParameter='\{0:c\}'}"
        VerticalAlignment="Center" Width="120" />
```

You pass the converter identifier to the `Converter` property of the Binding markup extension. The `ConverterParameter` receives the conversion value, which are the same in Table 35.3. If you run the application you get the result shown in Figure 35.9, the difference is that with custom converters you can control how the conversion and formatting processes behave.

Summary

The data-binding is a key concept in every kind of application, and this is true for WPF, too. In the first part of this chapter, you learned how you apply data-binding to simple controls with the `Binding` markup extension in XAML code, to bind some properties to the value of other controls or to a .NET data source. For this, you got an overview of the new `DataGrid` control and of the `ObservableCollection(Of T)` generic class (which you already studied) this time applied to WPF. You saw how the `DataGrid` supports the two-way data-binding also due to the underlying support for the technique offered by the `ObservableCollection`. In the second part of the chapter we covered a new feature in Visual Studio 2010, the drag'n'drop data-binding that is now available in WPF like it was in Windows Forms. After this discussion the `StringFormat` and `IValueConverter` objects were presented for formatting and converting objects to and from `String`. There is much more to say about data access in WPF, but it is beyond the scope here. An interesting resource that you should keep within your bookmarks is the Visual Studio Data Team Blog, where you can find blog posts about data access and data-binding in WPF and that is managed by the guys that created the drag'n'drop data-binding. You can find it here: http://blogs.msdn.com/vsdata. The next chapter is the last one on WPF and is related to another important topic: localization.

CHAPTER 36

Localizing Applications

Limiting applications' user interfaces to just one language means limiting your business. If you want to increase the possibilities of your applications being sold worldwide, you need to consider creating user interfaces that support multiple languages and culture specifications of your users. Of course, you can give users the option to select the desired language or provide localized interfaces for a particular country, but the main concept is that localization is a common requirement in modern applications. The .NET Framework helps developers in localizing applications with several kinds of resources. In this chapter you consider how to localize smart client applications and explore Windows Forms and WPF applications to understand the fundamentals of localization in both technologies.

AVAILABLE TECHNIQUES

Localizing applications is something that you can accomplish in several ways in both Windows Forms and WPF. This chapter discusses the most commonly used techniques—just remember that they are not the only ones.

Introducing .NET Localization

The .NET Framework provides the infrastructure for application localization via the `System.Globalization` namespace. The most important class in this namespace is the `CultureInfo` class that allows getting or setting information on the current application culture or on new custom settings. Generally this class works with the `System.Threading.Thread.CurrentThread` class that provides access to the thread representing your executable and that exposes the `CurrentCulture` and `CurrentUICulture` properties that you can assign with a `CultureInfo` object. The following code demonstrates how to get information on the current thread culture and how to set a new `CultureInfo`:

```
'Requires an Imports System.Globalization directive


'Gets the current culture and shows information
Dim culture As CultureInfo = System.Threading.Thread.
                            CurrentThread.CurrentCulture
Console.WriteLine(culture.DisplayName)


'Creates an instance of the CUltureInfo class
'based on the Italian culture and sets it as
'the current culture
Dim customCulture As New CultureInfo("it-IT")
System.Threading.Thread.CurrentThread.
        CurrentCulture = customCulture
```

The `CultureInfo` class provides lots of properties that enable applications to adhere to the required culture specifications. For example, `DisplayName` shows the name of the culture as it appears on the system, `DateTimeFormat` specifies the appropriate format for date and time in the specified culture, and `NumberFormat` provides specifications on how numbers and percentage need to be formatted in the specified culture. In this chapter you learn how to localize smart client applications, thus Windows Forms and WPF.

Windows Forms Localization

If you are an experienced Windows Forms developer, maybe you already faced the localization problem with this technology. There are different ways for localizing a Windows Forms application, but basically all of them rely on managed resources. The easiest way for localizing a Windows Forms application is to take advantage of the Visual Studio Designer so that the IDE generates the appropriate resources files for you. An example is of course the best way for providing explanations; the goal of this an example is to localize a Windows Forms application in both English and Italian. Run Visual Studio 2010, create a new Windows Forms project with Visual Basic 2010, and name it **WindowsFormsLocalization**. Follow these steps:

1. Drag a `Button` from the toolbox onto the new form surface, and set its `Text` property as `Localized button`.

2. Drag a `Label` from the toolbox onto the new form surface, and set its `Text` property as `Localized label`.

3. Select the form, and in the Properties window set its `Localizable` property as `True`; then set its `Language` property as `Italian`.

4. Select the `Button` and set its `Text` property as `Pulsante localizzato` (in Italian).

5. Select the `Label` and set its `Text` property as `Etichetta localizzata`.

6. Build the project and enable the **Show All Files** view in Solution Explorer.

You notice that Visual Studio has generated a new it-IT subfolder under Bin\Debug (or Bin\Release) containing a satellite assembly where localized resources are stored. Moreover, Visual Studio generated a new localized resources file for the current form named Form1.it-IT.resx storing the localized information for design time. If you try to run the application, you notice that it is still localized in English. This is because you need to explicitly assign in code the new localized culture. This can be accomplished by adding the following code (which requires an `Imports System.Globalization` directive) at the beginning of the application startup, which is typically the constructor, before the `InitializeMethod` is invoked:

```
Public Sub New()


    With Threading.Thread.CurrentThread
        .CurrentUICulture = New CultureInfo("it-IT")
        .CurrentCulture = New CultureInfo("it-IT")
    End With
    ' This call is required by the designer.
    InitializeComponent()

    ' Add any initialization after the InitializeComponent() call.


End Sub
```

The code simply assigns to the current thread the new culture information that will be retrieved from the related subfolder and satellite assembly. Figure 36.1 shows how the application looks with localized controls.

FIGURE 36.1   The localized Windows Forms application in action.

Windows Forms localization is straightforward because you can take advantage of the Visual Studio Designer. Unfortunately this is not the same in WPF applications, where a number of manual steps are required, as explained in the next section.

WPF Localization

In WPF the localization process is also based on resources but with different steps. Also, there are some alternative techniques for accomplishing localization but we cover the most common.

NOTE ON INSTALLED CULTURE

Code examples shown in this section assume that your system's regional settings are based on the en-US (English-United States) culture. If your system is based on different regional settings, replace en-US with the culture information that suits your system.

When you compile a WPF project, the XAML code is parsed into a more efficient file format known as BAML (Binary Application Markup Language). Generally each Baml file represents a resource that is then linked into the executable storing all resources. To localize a WPF application you need to localize Baml objects and put the result into a satellite assembly. This is accomplished using a command-line tool named LocBaml.exe, which is available for free from the MSDN. It is distributed as C# source code so you need to open it inside Visual Studio and compile it. At the moment this chapter is being written, LocBaml source code is available for .NET Framework versions prior than 4.0 so in order to make it work with next examples you need to perform some steps that are described in the next subsection.

LOCBAML FOR .NET 4.0

You can check for the availability of a new version of LocBaml targeting .NET 4.0 at the following address: http://msdn.microsoft.com/en-us/library/ms771568(VS.100).aspx. When Microsoft makes it available, you can skip the next section and go to the "Localizing a WPF Application" section.

Preparing the LocBaml tool

Until a new version of LocBaml is available for .NET 4.0, you can download the previous version and upgrade it manually. To accomplish this follow these steps:

1. If not installed, install Visual C# on your machine (the Express Edition is also supported).

2. Download the LocBaml source code from this address: http://download.microsoft.com/download/f/6/e/f6e32974-726e-4054-96af-9c747bf89a6e/LocBaml.exe.

3. Uncompress the downloaded archive into any folder you like.

4. Start Visual Studio 2010 and create a new Console Application with Visual C#, naming the project as LocBaml.

5. Save the new project into a different folder than the downloaded source code.

6. Remove the Program.cs and AssemblyInfo.cs code file from the project. Notice that the second file is just a duplicate of the one generated by the IDE and so can be safely removed.

7. Using the **Project, Add Existing Item** command, add all the code files (with .cs extension) from the downloaded source code folder to the current project folder.

8. Add a reference to the following assemblies: WindowsBase.dll, PresentationCore.dll, PresentationFramework.dll

9. In the new project, add a folder named Resources and add to this new folder the StringTable.resText file which you can pick from the same-named folder of the original LocBaml code.

10. After you've added the file, open the Properties window and set the Build Action property as **Embedded Resource**.

11. Open the LocBaml.csproj project file with the Windows Notepad and add the following lines (if not already available) within an `ItemGroup` node:

```
<EmbeddedResource Include="Resources\StringTable.resText">
  <LogicalName>Resources.StringTable.resources</LogicalName>

</EmbeddedResource>
```

12. In Solution Explorer click Properties and ensure that the BamlLocalizaion.LocBaml is set as the startup object in the Application tab.

Now build the project. At this point you have a new version of LocBaml.exe which targets the .NET Framework 4.0.

Localizing a WPF Application

When you have completed the steps required to prepare LocBaml, imagine you want to create a localized version for the Italian culture of a WPF application based on English as the primary culture. Create a new WPF project with Visual Basic and name it as **WpfLocalization**, and simply add the code shown in Listing 36.1 on the XAML side. The goal is to provide a WPF counterpart of the Windows Forms example shown in the previous section.

LISTING 36.1   Preparing the User Interface Before Localization

```
<Window x:Class="MainWindow"
    xmlns="http://schemas.microsoft.com/winfx/2006/xaml/presentation"
    xmlns:x="http://schemas.microsoft.com/winfx/2006/xaml"
    Title="MainWindow" Height="350" Width="525">
    <StackPanel>
        <Button Name="Button1" Width="100" Margin="5"
                Height="40" Content="Localized button"/>
```

36

```
        <TextBlock Text="Localized text"
                   Margin="5"
                   Name="TextBlock1"/>
    </StackPanel>
</Window>
```

The first step required to localize a WPF application is to specify the neutral-language specification at assembly level. Click the **Show All Files** button in Solution Explorer, expand **My Project**, and double-click **AssemblyInfo.vb**; finally uncomment the following line of code:

```
<Assembly: NeutralResourcesLanguage("en-US",
         UltimateResourceFallbackLocation.Satellite)>
```

This is required because the application looks for localization resources inside external satellite assemblies, and at least one culture must be provided as neutral. This is simply the culture you are writing code with. The next step is to open the project file, thus click the **File, Open, File** command and browse the project folder; then open the **WpfLocalization.vbproj** file. At this point you need to add the following line of Xml markup inside one of the `PropertyGroup` items:

```
<UICulture>en-US</UICulture>
```

This works with the neutral language specification and ensures that a satellite assembly for current culture resources will be generated. The successive step is marking UI elements in XAML as localizable. This is accomplished by adding an `x:Uid` attribute to each localizable member, assigning an identifier equal or similar to the element name. This task can be accomplished manually but can be difficult if you have a lot of elements to mark as localizable, so the most common option is running the MSBuild compiler that automates this for you. Save the project, and then open a command prompt pointing to the project folder. At this point write the following command lines following the exact sequence shown:

```
msbuild /t:updateuid WpfLocalization.vbproj
msbuild /t:checkuid WpfLocalization.vbproj
```

The first command line adds an `x:Uid` attribute to each UI element possible (updateuid), whereas the second one performs a check to verify that all localizable members have an `x:Uid`. When MSBuild completes, you notice how visual elements have been marked as localizable, as shown in Listing 36.2.

LISTING 36.2   The XAML Code Marked as Localizable by MsBuild

```
<Window x:Uid="Window_1" x:Class="MainWindow"
    xmlns="http://schemas.microsoft.com/winfx/2006/xaml/presentation"
    xmlns:x="http://schemas.microsoft.com/winfx/2006/xaml"
    Title="MainWindow" Height="350" Width="525">
    <StackPanel x:Uid="StackPanel_1">
```

```
        <Button x:Uid="LocalizedButton" Name="LocalizedButton" Margin="5"
                Width="140" Height="40"
                Content="Localized button"/>
        <TextBlock x:Uid="LocalizedTextBlock" Name="LocalizedTextBlock" Margin="5"
                Text="Localized text"/>
    </StackPanel>
</Window>
```

Now build the project again in Visual Studio. You now notice that in the project output folder (Bin\Debug or Bin\Release) there is a new subfolder named en-US, which contains a WpfLocalization.Resources.dll satellite assembly containing localized resources for the en-US culture. So the goal now is to create a similar folder/assembly structure per culture. In this case you see how to create a localized satellite assembly for the Italian culture, but you can replace it with a different one. A subsequent step requires invoking LocBaml. The need is to extract resources information and edit the information with localized ones. The following command line parses the neutral language resources and creates an editable .CSV file where you can place custom information:

```
LocBaml.exe /parse en-US\WpfLocalization.resources.dll
/out:WpfLocalization.csv
```

When ready, open the generated WpfLocalization.csv file with an appropriate editor, such as Microsoft Excel or Visual Studio. Figure 36.2 shows how the content of the file appears in Microsoft Excel.

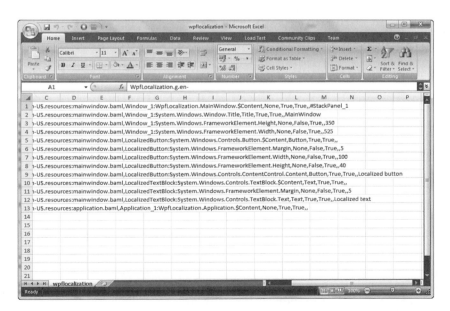

FIGURE 36.2   The extracted resources information opened in Excel.

If you inspect the content of the file, among other things you notice the content of UI elements. For example, row 2 contains the Window title, row 9 contains the Button text as the last word, whereas row 12 contains the TextBlock text. At this point you simply need to replace original values with new ones. Continuing the example of the Italian localization, perform the following replacements:

▶ In row 2 replace MainWindow with Finestra principale.

▶ In row 9 replace Localized button with Pulsante localizzato.

▶ In row 12 replace Localized text with Testo localizzato.

Figure 36.3 represents how the file will look like after edits.

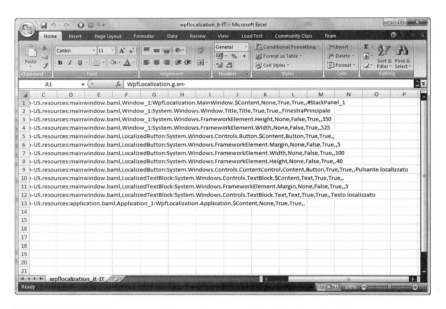

FIGURE 36.3   Resources information are edited for localization.

Now save the file with a different name, for example **WpfLocalization_it-IT.csv**. When done, you need to manually create a new directory where the new localized resources will be published; create a folder named **it-IT** inside the same folder of en-US. At this point you still need to invoke LocBaml to build the localized satellite assembly; write the following command line:

```
LocBaml.exe /generate en-US\WpfLocalization.resources.dll /trans: WpfLocalization
_it-IT.csv /out:c:\ /cul:it-IT
```

The /generate option tells LocBaml to generate a new satellite assembly, translating (/trans) the specified .csv file into the desired culture (/cul). The /out option allows specifying the target directory that in this example is the hard drive root folder. When ready, move the newly generated WpfLocalization.resources.dll assembly from C:\ into the it-IT subfolder you created before. The last step is to initialize the desired culture information at the application startup. In Application.xaml.vb provide a constructor as follows:

```
Imports System.Globalization
Imports System.Threading

Class Application

    Public Sub New()
        Thread.CurrentThread.CurrentUICulture = _
            New CultureInfo("it-IT")
        Thread.CurrentThread.CurrentCulture = _
            New CultureInfo("it-IT")
    End Sub
End Class
```

This is different from Windows Forms, because in WPF the Application class is the actual application entry point. If you now run the application, you get the result shown in Figure 36.4 where you can see how UI elements have been localized.

FIGURE 36.4   Localized UI elements in the WPF sample application.

Summary

In this chapter we covered localization; first we discussed information on how the .NET Framework provides objects for application localization at a general level. Next the discussion focused on Windows Forms applications localization, taking advantage of the Visual Studio Designer and of managed resources files. Finally you saw how localization works in WPF applications, understanding how a number of manual steps are required, such as adding the neutral language resource and culture information to the project file, running MsBuild to mark visual elements as localizable, and running LocBaml to generate satellite resources assemblies.

36

Building ASP.NET Web Applications

Many of the most common activities in everyday life are often performed via the Internet and websites. You book a flight via air companies' websites; you book tickets for the theater via the Internet; and you can make payments via the Internet. Also, most companies (and probably yours, too) have local networks running internal Web applications for several kinds of purposes, such as office automation, storing data, and so on. Being a complete technology, the .NET Framework offers its own Web platform for developing websites based on .NET, which is named ASP.NET. This is an engine for websites running on the server side, which enables building robust Web applications taking advantage of managed code. In this chapter you start with the ASP.NET programming model and with building Web applications with Visual Basic 2010, also leveraging some of the new features typical of ASP.NET 4.0.

Introducing the ASP.NET Model

Until now different kinds of client applications, such as Console, Windows Forms, and WPF were discussed. For this last technology, the discussion was deeper because of the innovations brought into the desktop applications development. Developing Web applications for ASP.NET with Visual Basic 2010 is different. If you are an existing Web developer, this chapter will probably just be an overview of some new features introduced by .NET 4.0. However, if you are new to ASP.NET, although you can find lots of similarities with the client world in writing managed code and in creating applications, the code in the Web environment runs differently. So you need to understand where the code is running and why scaling applications is fundamental therefore, you also need to understand the concept of the stateless nature of the Web so that you can handle it in your applications, which is discussed next.

Understanding Page Requests

When you create a Web application, the application will be hosted on a web server. This is the place where your Visual Basic compiled code actually resides. When the code is executed, the ASP.NET engine renders it as HTML so that it can be consumed on the client side by a web browser such as Internet Explorer and Fireox, which can interpret HTML and display web pages. When you type a website address into your browser, it sends a web page request. This is then translated into an address that searches for the server hosting the requested page. When the server receives the request, the installed web server software catches the request and, if this is about an ASP.NET web page, passes the request to the ASP.NET engine so that this can render the result as HTML and return it to the calling browser. Samples of web server software are Internet Information Services (IIS) and the Cassini Web Server. Visual Studio 2010 ships with its own web server, named ASP.NET Development Server, which enables simulating a web server environment on the development machine for testing applications. But you do not write HTML, whereas you write Visual Basic code that is compiled into an assembly residing on the server; so the ASP.NET engine sends requests to your code for processing and then it returns the processing result as HTML that can be consumed by client browsers. All these operations are fine, but there is a problem: In a desktop environment you have one user running one instance of the application that works against its set of data and information; even if you have hundreds of database records to load, the application will be responsive in most cases. The same is not true for web applications if you think that one Web application hosted on a server could potentially receive hundreds of concurrent requests; therefore, elaborating hundreds of data requests concurrently can cause a bottleneck with hard performances problems. Fortunately ASP.NET provides a mechanism for scalability that lets the application solve performance problems the best way possible.

Scalability and Performances

Scalability is basically the capability of an application to well serve requests without getting too slow or crashing when the amount of work increases. As described before, in a single user environment such as desktop applications, scalability is a plus but not a requirement whereas it is in a web environment, where multiple requests can come to a web page. Because you do not want your application to get too slow or to crash when a big number of simultaneous requests come, whereas you instead want requests to be served in a small amount of time, you need to be aware of scalability and performances. Luckily ASP.NET has its own mechanism that serves for applications scalability and that we now describe. Think of desktop applications for a moment; in such environment all the work is in memory, when you load data into variables; variables are instances of managed objects that you release when no more are needed so that the garbage collection process frees up unused resources. In a web environment this is not possible because the application resides on one server and serving a big number of requests would lead soon to out-of-memory errors, so the mechanism of state management must be necessarily different. The following is the list of operations that occur against the code when ASP.NET receives a request:

1. ASP.NET creates an instance of the `Page` object, which is the Web counterpart of `Form` and `Window`.

2. Because `Page` is a managed object, when ASP.NET processes the request it releases the reference of the page instance.

3. The Garbage Collection process clears from the managed heap all objects that no longer have any reference, including released `Page` objects.

This is cool because when an object completes its work, it is soon removed from memory, and this improves scalability. The problem is that if the object is no longer available, also data exposed by that object is no longer available; this means that if the same user sends another request to the same page (that is, creating a new instance of the `Page` object), such page will result empty. This is frequent, if you think of web pages that require filling some fields before making available other controls that require the page to be reloaded. So this is the reason why ASP.NET needs a different state management, which is provided by the `Application` and `Session` state objects that will be discussed later. Another problem that travels hand in hand with scalability is performance. Each time you send a page request, you have to wait a few seconds. This is normal because sending the request takes time and waiting for the server to respond takes other time. Also, elaborating complex data requires additional time because the number of bytes to transfer is increased. With complex web applications, performance can become a problem, so a better approach is designing pages differently. ASP.NET Ajax and Silverlight (discussed in Chapter 39, "Building Rich Internet Applications with Silverlight") are better choices, but first you need to get some skills on ASP.NET before trying those technologies. The first step for acquiring such skills is starting to create your first Web project with VB 2010.

Available Project Templates

Basically there are two kinds of project templates for building ASP.NET web applications with VB 2010: *Web Site and Web Application*. There are several differences between the two templates, but the major differences follow:

▶ The website template has no project file, whereas Web Application has one. Choosing this second template brings more familiarity for other Visual Studio projects.

▶ The website template produces no compiled assemblies and requires the source code to be deployed, whereas the Web Application template allows building a compiled assembly and no source code is required.

▶ A website is simpler in its structure than the Web Application project template.

Due to their natures, this chapter shows examples based on the Web Application template. There are multiple Web Application templates, specific to particular scenarios. They are all reachable in the Web folder of the New Project dialog, as shown in Figure 37.1.

FIGURE 37.1   Web Application project templates available with VB 2010.

The most basic project template is the ASP.NET Web Application one. There are project templates dedicated to ASP.NET MVC and ASP.NET Dynamic Data applications, other than templates for building user controls. When building a complete working example later in this chapter, we use the ASP.NET Web Application template that provides a skeleton of a Web application with preconfigured pages. For the first experiments, create a new project based on the ASP.NET Empty Web Application. This generates a new empty project, where the first thing you have to do is add some pages. Pages in ASP.NET are represented by Web forms.

Web Forms and Master Pages

ASP.NET Web applications are made of pages. These can be standalone pages or ones providing common elements for each page. Standalone pages are generally known as Web forms, while the other kind is known as master page.

Web Forms

A Web form represents a page in ASP.NET (a file with an .Aspx extension) and is composed of markup code known as XHTML and of a code-behind part made of Visual Basic code. The concept is similar to the WPF development where the XAML code is for the user interface and the Visual Basic code makes the UI alive. The same is for Web forms, but the difference is that the UI is provided via XHTML code. This acronym stands for *Extensible Hypertext Markup Language* and is intended as an enhancement of classic HTML. The XHTML code in a Web form contains markup for page layout, user controls, and eventually scripts. Each Web application needs at least a Default.aspx page, so right-click the project name in Solution Explorer and select **Add New Item**. In the Add New Item dialog, select the Web Form template, name it **Default.Aspx** and then click **OK**. When ready, the new page is made of some XHTML code. The following is the basic code of a Web form, including a Label control for demonstrating some concepts:

```
<%@ Page Language="vb" AutoEventWireup="false"
        CodeBehind="Default.aspx.vb"
        Inherits="WebApplication1.WebForm1" %>

<!DOCTYPE html PUBLIC "-//W3C//DTD XHTML 1.0 Transitional//EN"
            "http://www.w3.org/TR/xhtml1/DTD/xhtml1-transitional.dtd">

<html xmlns="http://www.w3.org/1999/xhtml">
<head runat="server">
    <title></title>
</head>
<body>
    <form id="form1" runat="server">
    <div>
        <asp:Label ID="Label1" runat="server" Text="Label"></asp:Label>
    </div>
    </form>
</body>
</html>
```

The most important thing you need to remember is that code is executed on the server, so it is fundamentally adding a runat="server" attribute for each control; otherwise, it will not be correctly consumed by client browsers.

37

STYLING TIPS

ASP.NET enables styling and applying themes to Web forms via Cascade Style Sheets (Css) files. A simpler way for styling controls is choosing the AutoFormat option that's available when you click the smart tag.

Notice how the markup code contains classic HTML items that will be correctly rendered to client browsers. Each Web form has a code behind a file, which you can find in Solution Explorer by enabling the **Show All Files** view and then expanding the desired web page file. When you double-click the Visual Basic code-behind file on a new Web form, you can notice that it is nothing but a class providing an event handler for the Page.Load event. As explained in next subsection, a Web form has a lifetime that is established by events.

Page Lifetime and Page Events
Each page has a lifetime that you need to understand so that you can ensure changes you made through a postback are not ignored or overwritten. Page lifetime is articulated in

events, each of them representing a particular moment. Although starting from ASP.NET 2.0 the Page class offers a bigger number of events, the most important are the following:

▶ Init, which is where the page initializes controls

▶ Load, which is when the page is loaded and you can play with controls

▶ PreRender, which occurs just before the page is rendered as HTML

Cached and Postback Events

Earlier in this chapter you learned that the biggest difference between the ASP.NET programming model and the client one is that in the ASP.NET development you cannot keep objects in memory and that, for scalability purposes, a page is reloaded each time you need to process some data. Reloading a page happens when you interact with controls on the page. Such controls raise events depending on the action you took onto them, which are divided into two categories: cached events and postback events. Cached events occur on controls that do not require an immediate page reload. The typical example is the TextBox control where a TextChanged event is raised every time you edit the text, but the page is not reloaded at each edit. Postback events instead occur on controls that will cause an immediate page reload, such as Button and ComboBox. This is convenient because you expect immediate data processing when you click the Button or select a combo box item. At this point cached events will also be elaborated at the page reload. Reloading a page means destroying the instance of the current page and then creating a new instance of the current page. This is good because you avoid overhead when working with big amounts of data, but the problem is that all objects and values held by the previous instance are lost, so you need a mechanism for restoring the original object values. Such mechanism is typically the ViewState object that is covered later in more details; at the moment look at how you store an object value (such as the text stored in a TextBox) inside the ViewState before the page is reloaded at the Button click:

```
Protected Sub Page_Load(ByVal sender As Object,
                        ByVal e As System.EventArgs) _
                        Handles Me.Load
    If Not Page.IsPostBack Then
        Me.TextBox1.Text = CStr(Me.ViewState("MyText"))
    End If
End Sub


Protected Sub Button1_Click(ByVal sender As Object,
                            ByVal e As EventArgs) _
                            Handles Button1.Click
    Me.ViewState("MyText") = Me.TextBox1.Text
End Sub
```

Basically the only situation when a postback event does not occur is when you open the website, meaning that the page is loaded for the first time. You can check if the page is being loaded for the first time in the Page_Load event handler, where you read the value of the `Page.IsPostBack` property. If true, you can retrieve the content of the `ViewState` property to restore the original values.

TIP

If you use the `ComboBox` control, remember to set its `AutoPostBack` property as `True` so that it will cause a postback each time you select an item, when such behavior is desired

---

Considering cached and postback events, the following is the updated list for the page lifetime:

1. `Init`
2. `Load`
3. Cached events
4. Postback events
5. `PreRender`

ASP.NET Controls

ASP.NET offers both server and HTML controls. Server controls run on the server side and emulate or are built upon existing HTML tags, but provide more advanced features and usability. They also are object-oriented controls and support events, whereas HTML controls don't. Generally, HTML controls are more and more limited if compared to ASP.NET controls; although, they can be still processed on the server by adding the usual `runat="server"` tag. The next sections list the most common controls from both types.

Server Controls

Server controls are typically user interface objects that users can take advantage of when running a Web application on clients. You can notice that in most cases ASP.NET server controls are counterparts of HTML controls, but provide a fully object-oriented development environment and full support for managed code. Table 37.1 summarizes the most common server controls.

TABLE 37.1   Most Common Server Controls

Control	Description
`AdRotator`	Shows a series of advertisements
`BulletedList`	Shows a bulleted list of items
`Button`	A button that can be clicked
`Calendar`	Provides a monthly calendar
`CheckBox`	A check box control for Boolean check state

TABLE 37.1   Continued

Control	Description
CheckBoxList	A group of multiselection check boxes
DataList	A drop-down list with database data
DetailsView	Can show a single record of data
DropDownList	A drop-down list enabling single selection
FileUpload	Provides the capability of uploading files
GridView	Enables tabular data representations
HiddenField	Keeps data that will be hidden in the UI
HyperLink	A hyperlink to open other websites
Image	Shows a picture
ImageButton	A button containing a picture instead of text
ImageMap	Enables creating image regions that can be clicked
Label	Enables presenting static text
LinkButton	A button with hyperlink functionalities
ListBox	Enables scrolling a list of items
MultiView	Provides the capability of creating tabbed user interfaces
Panel	A container for other controls
RadioButton	A button with single option choice
RadioButtonList	A group of radio button controls
RangeValidator	Checks if the specified entry is between upper and lower bounds
RequiredFieldValidator	Checks for the existence of an entry
Substitution	A control that does not enable storing its content in cache
Table	Enables presenting data within tables
TextBox	A control that accepts text
View	One item in a Multiview control
Wizard	Enables creating wizards
Xml	Provides combination between Xml and XSLT objects

All controls in Table 37.1 are then rendered as their HTML equivalent so that they can be consumed by Web browsers.

HTML Controls

HTML controls in ASP.NET are representations of their classic HTML. Table 37.2 summarizes the most common among available HTML controls.

TABLE 37.2   HTML Controls

Control	Description
HtmlAnchor	Allows accessing the <a> HTML element on the server
HtmlButton	A button that can be clicked
HtmlForm	A form control
HtmlGenericControl	An element that cannot be mapped to any specific HTML control
Image	A control showing a picture
HtmlInputButton	Expects input via a button
HtmlInputCheckBox	Expects input via a Checkbox
HtmlInputFile	Expects input from a file
HtmlInputHidden	Hides its content
HtmlInputImage	Expects an image as the input
HtmlInputRadioButton	Expects input via a RadioButton
HtmlInputText	Expects input via some text
HtmlTable	Represents a table
HtmlTableCell	Represents a cell within a table
HtmlTableRow	Represents a row within a table
HtmlTextArea	Represents an area of text

The main difference between HTML controls and their ASP.NET counterparts is that ASP.NET versions can be accessed on the server side with managed code by adding an ID attribute and the runat="server" attribute, although HTML controls actually work on the server side.

Handling Events

Due to the code-behind logic, handling events in ASP.NET applications looks similar to what you saw about WPF. This means that you have a user control implemented on the XHTML side and an event handler in the Visual Basic side.

> **HANDLING EVENTS TIP**
>
> If you need to catch events from objects that are not user controls, such as business objects or collections, you just write the event handler in Visual Basic code the usual way.

For example, consider the following XHTML code that provides a Button and a Label:

```
<form id="form1" runat="server">
<div>
    <asp:Button ID="Button1" runat="server" Text="Button"/>
    <asp:Label ID="Label1" runat="server"></asp:Label>
</div>
</form>
```

You can handle the `Button.Click` as usual, for example with the following code that writes a message to the `Label`:

```
Protected Sub Button1_Click(ByVal sender As Object,
                            ByVal e As EventArgs) Handles Button1.Click
    Me.Label1.Text = "You clicked!"
End Sub
```

Notice that you can also specify the event handler in the XHTML code, avoiding the Handles clause on the VB side, exactly as in WPF. The `Click` event handler is specified with the `OnClick` attribute:

```
<asp:Button ID="Button1" runat="server" Text="Button"
OnClick="Button1_Click" />
```

And then you write the event handler without `Handles`:

```
Protected Sub Button1_Click(ByVal sender As Object,
                            ByVal e As EventArgs)
    Me.Label1.Text = "You clicked!"
End Sub
```

Understanding State Management

As I told you at the beginning of this chapter, ASP.NET applications have to manage their state in a different way than client applications. State is managed via some special objects: `Application`, `Cache`, `Context`, `Session`, and `ViewState`. All of them work with the `Object` type, and you use them like dictionaries, so they accept key/value pairs. The next subsections give you explanation and examples.

The Application State

One of the most common situations with websites is that you have many people using the website concurrently. If you want to hold shared information across all the application instances, you use the `Application` state. The following is an example:

```
Application("SharedKey") = "Shared value"
```

```
Dim sharedString As String = CStr(Application("SharedKey"))
```

Notice the key/value semantics and how you need to perform an explicit conversion from `Object` to `String`. You will not use `Application` often because each application instance runs on a separate thread that could modify the information and therefore could corrupt the values, too.

The Cache State

The ASP.NET `Cache` has the same scope of `Application`, meaning that both can be accessed by all page requests. The primary difference is that `Cache` enables holding information in memory, which avoids the need of re-creating and retrieving objects. This is good if you want to maintain updatable objects but could cause overhead (always considering that the bigger the amount of data to transfer is, the lower is the performance) because it requires memory, so it should be used when actually needed or when you ensure that performance is acceptable. The following is an example of storing and retrieving information with `Cache`:

```
Cache("MyUpdatableDataKey") = "My updatable data"
Dim myUpdatableData As String = CStr(Cache("MyUpdatableDataKey"))
```

There is also an alternative way for adding objects to the cache, which is the `Cache.Add` method that provides the ability of setting advanced settings for the object, as demonstrated in this code:

```
Protected Sub Page_Load(ByVal sender As Object,
                        ByVal e As System.EventArgs) _
                        Handles Me.Load

    Dim callBack As New CacheItemRemovedCallback( _
        AddressOf Cache_ItemRemoved)

    'Sets the key, adds the data, sets the CacheDependency,
    'sets the expiration mode, expiration time, priority
    'and delegate to invoke when the item is removed
    Cache.Add("MyUpdatableDataKey", "My updatable data", Nothing,
```

37

```
            Cache.NoAbsoluteExpiration, New TimeSpan(0, 0, 45), _
            CacheItemPriority.High, callBack)

    'Removes the item
    Cache.Remove("MyUpdatableDataKey")
End Sub

Private Sub Cache_ItemRemoved(ByVal key As String, _
                             ByVal item As Object, _
                             ByVal reason As CacheItemRemovedReason)
    'The item has been removed
End Sub
```

The most interesting settings are the expiration mode and the priority. The first one can be `Cache.NoAbsoluteExpiration` (like in the preceding code), which means that the data will always be available during the page lifetime, whereas `Cache.SlidingExpiration` means that the data will be removed after it is not accessed for the specified amount of time. Priority is also important in case you have lots of objects in memory and ASP.NET is about to encounter out-of-memory problems. At this point ASP.NET begins evicting items according to its priority. (An object with lower priority is evicted before another one with high priority.)

The Context State

You use the `Context` state when you want to hold state only for the lifetime of a single request. This is useful when you need to have information in memory for a long period of time, and you do need to ensure that keeping such information does not affect scalability. This is an example:

```
Context.Items("MyStringKey") = "My string value"
Dim contextString As String = CStr(Context.Items("MyStringKey"))
```

The context information is accessed at the page level and will not be available again on the next request.

Using Cookies for Saving Information

Cookies are pieces of information that user's browser can hold and that can have a max size of 4 Kbytes. Each time the browser opens your web application, it recalls all cookies provided by the website. The following are examples of writing and reading cookies:

```
'Write a cookie
Dim aCookie As New HttpCookie("MyCookie")
aCookie.Value = "Information to store"
aCookie.Expires = New DateTime(10, 10, 2010)
Response.Cookies.Add(aCookie)

'Read a cookie
```

```
Dim getCookie As HttpCookie = Request.Cookies("MyCookie")
Dim cookieVale As String = getCookie.Value
```

Notice that the Expires property of type Date is required to specify that the cookie information will no longer be valid after that date, whereas the Value property is of type String so that you can store information without conversions.

The Session State

ASP.NET provides the ability of holding per-user information via the Session object. When a user opens the website, ASP.NET creates a cookie with a session identifier and then manages the session for that user based on the ID. The only issue is that you have no way for understanding when the user leaves the website, so a Session state expires after 20 minutes as a default. The following is an example:

```
Session("MyKey") = "User level information"
Dim userInfo As String = CStr(Session("MyKey"))
```

The ViewState State

To provide support for the work that a page needs to do in its lifetime, ASP.NET provides a mechanism known as ViewState. Basically it provides the infrastructure that serializes values for each control in the page. For example, when a page is rendered, a control has a particular value. When this value changes, and such change raises an event, ASP.NET makes a comparison between the ViewState and form variables so that it can update the control value. (The TextBox control with its TextChanged event is the most common examples.) Such a mechanism is available behind the scenes, but you can also use the ViewState by yourself. The following is an example that makes an object available at page level:

```
ViewState("MyPageDataKey") = "Page-level information"
Dim myPageData As String = CStr(ViewState("MyPageDataKey"))
```

Making this information at the page level means making it available also when the page is posted back, but that decreases performance because the size of bytes to transfer is bigger. Excluding the user controls necessary to your Web form, you should use ViewState for your needs with care.

Creating a Web Application with VB 2010 with Navigation and Data-Binding

Visual Basic 2010 makes it easier to create Web applications with navigation capabilities, because the Web Application project template provides a master page implementation with default pages and designer tools for adding further elements. If you want to create a data-centric Web application, the .NET Framework 4.0 offers specific controls (some of them new in .NET 4.0) that enable supplying a data source and data-binding capabilities with a few mouse clicks. This section shows you how to reach this objective. Select **File, New Project** and from the Web projects folder, select the **ASP.NET Web Application** template; name the new project as **NorthwindOrders**, and then click **OK**. When the project is available in Solution Explorer, notice the presence of some web pages (Default.aspx and About.aspx) and of the master page (the Site.Master file). Now click on the **Site.Master** file. At this point you see the simplest example of a master page, as shown in Figure 37.2.

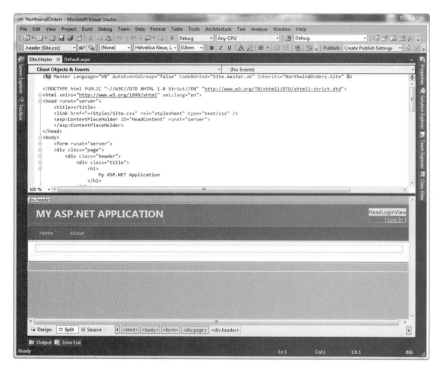

FIGURE 37.2   The default master page for the new web application.

Master Pages

A master page is a special page with .master extension, which provides a template containing a set of common elements for each page in the application. A master page typically contains elements such as headers, footers, and navigation elements so that you can implement one time a number of elements that each page can contain. Visual Studio provides a specific item template for creating a master page, but the simplest way for understanding how it works is examining a basic one. When you create a new project using the ASP.NET Web Application template, such as in the current example, the IDE adds a master page for you. As you can see Visual Studio implements by default a couple of links for navigating between pages, such as Home and About. Both links have related Web pages in the project, which are Default.aspx and About.aspx. Also notice how there is a Login link that points to a Login.aspx page stored in the Account folder, which also contains other auto-generated pages for registering to the Web application and for password management. The most basic code for designing a master page is the following:

```
<%@ Master Language="VB" AutoEventWireup="false"
    CodeBehind="Site1.master.vb"
    Inherits="WebApplication3.Site1" %>

<!DOCTYPE html PUBLIC "-//W3C//DTD XHTML 1.0 Transitional//EN"
        "http://www.w3.org/TR/xhtml1/DTD/xhtml1-transitional.dtd">

<html xmlns="http://www.w3.org/1999/xhtml">
<head runat="server">
    <title></title>
    <asp:ContentPlaceHolder ID="head" runat="server">
    </asp:ContentPlaceHolder>
</head>
<body>
    <form id="form1" runat="server">
    <div>
        <asp:ContentPlaceHolder ID="ContentPlaceHolder1" runat="server">

        </asp:ContentPlaceHolder>
    </div>
    </form>
</body>
</html>
```

The most important element is the ContentPlaceHolder that defines a region for contents in the seb page. You can simply compare this basic code with one of the auto-generated master page, where you notice the presence of a navigation menu and the login view:

```
<%@ Master Language="VB" AutoEventWireup="false" CodeBehind="Site.master.vb"
    Inherits="NorthwindOrders.Site" %>

<!DOCTYPE html PUBLIC "-//W3C//DTD XHTML 1.0 Strict//EN"
"http://www.w3.org/TR/xhtml1/DTD/xhtml1-strict.dtd">
<html xmlns="http://www.w3.org/1999/xhtml" xml:lang="en">
<head runat="server">
```

37

```
    <title></title>
    <link href="~/Styles/Site.css" rel="stylesheet" type="text/css" />
    <asp:ContentPlaceHolder ID="HeadContent" runat="server">
    </asp:ContentPlaceHolder>
</head>
<body>
    <form runat="server">
    <div class="page">
        <div class="header">
            <div class="title">
                <h1>
                    My ASP.NET Application
                </h1>
            </div>
            <div class="loginDisplay">
                <asp:LoginView ID="HeadLoginView" runat="server"
                    EnableViewState="false">
                    <AnonymousTemplate>
                        [ <a href="~/Account/Login.aspx"
                            ID="HeadLoginStatus"
                            runat="server">Log In</a> ]
                    </AnonymousTemplate>
                    <LoggedInTemplate>
                        Welcome <span class="bold"><asp:LoginName
                                ID="HeadLoginName"
                                runat="server" /></span>!
                        [ <asp:LoginStatus ID="HeadLoginStatus"
                            runat="server"
                            LogoutAction="Redirect" LogoutText="Log Out"
                            LogoutPageUrl="~/"/> ]
                    </LoggedInTemplate>
                </asp:LoginView>
            </div>
            <div class="clear hideSkiplink">
                <asp:Menu ID="NavigationMenu" runat="server" CssClass="menu"
                        EnableViewState="false" IncludeStyleBlock="false"
                        Orientation="Horizontal">
                    <Items>
                        <asp:MenuItem NavigateUrl="~/Default.aspx"
                         Text="Home"/>
                        <asp:MenuItem NavigateUrl="~/About.aspx"
                         Text="About"/>
                        <asp:MenuItem NavigateUrl="~/Orders.aspx"
                         Text="Orders" Value="Orders">
```

```
                    </asp:MenuItem>
                </Items>
            </asp:Menu>
        </div>
    </div>
    <div class="main">
        <asp:ContentPlaceHolder ID="MainContent" runat="server"/>
    </div>
    <div class="clear">
    </div>
</div>
<div class="footer">

</div>
</form>
</body>
</html>
```

The goal of the sample application is fetching the list of orders from the Northwind database, showing the list in a `GridView` control (with editing capabilities) and adding navigation features to the master page, so in next section you see how to add the data source and how to add data-bound controls.

Adding the Data Model

The first thing to add in the Web project is the data source. This can be of different kinds, for example both LINQ to SQL classes and Entity Data Models are supported. The example will be based on the Entity Framework so you also see a new control in ASP.NET 4.0, thus add a new entity data model named **Northwind.edmx** and add to the model the `Orders` table from the database. Such steps have been described a lot of times in this book, (see Chapter 27, "Introducing the ADO.NET Entity Framework" for a full discussion) so we will not show them again in detail. When you have the data, you need a place for presenting and editing the data, so you need a new Web Form.

Adding a New Web Form

To add a new Web Form to the project, right-click the project name in Solution Explorer and select **Add New Item**. When the same-named dialog appears, click the **Web** folder. Among all available items, you see how you can add a Web Form (which is just a Web page) or a Web Form Using Master Page. This second template is useful if you want to show the new page within a master page, differently from the first template which is instead for free pages. Select the second template so that we can link the new page to the master page, and name the new page as **Orders.aspx** (see Figure 37.3); then click **OK**.

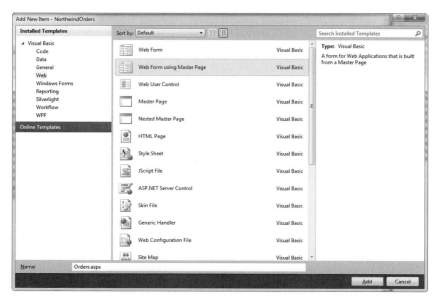

FIGURE 37.3   Adding a new Web Form using a master page.

At this point Visual Studio asks you to indicate a master page from the project to link the new Web Form. In our case only one master page is available, so select it on the right side of the dialog, as shown in Figure 37.4.

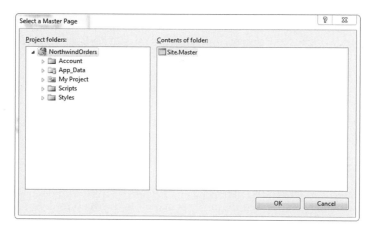

FIGURE 37.4   Specifying the master page to be associated to the new Web Form.

If you now double-click the **Orders.Aspx** page, you get a new empty page linked to the master page, thus having navigation features. Now that we have a page, we can bind it to the data source.

Adding Data Controls

ASP.NET 4.0 offers a number of data controls that can be used to bind a data source to user controls and that act like a bridge. One of the controls new in ASP.NET 4.0 is the `EntityDataSource`, which enables binding an entity data model to a graphic control.

ENABLING THE DESIGNER

By default Visual Studio shows the HTML code for the pages. In order to enable the Visual Studio designer, click the Design button for switching to the full designer view or the Split button in order to get both the designer and the html code on the same view.

In the toolbox expand the Data tab and drag the EntityDataSource control onto the Orders page until you get the result shown in Figure 37.5.

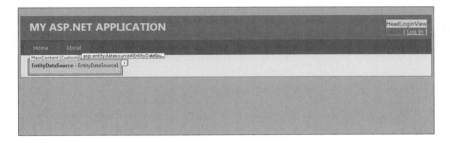

FIGURE 37.5   Adding an `EntityDataSource` control to the page.

The good news is that you can configure the control and bind it to a data source without writing a single line of code. Build the project so that all data references are updated and then click the right arrow on the `EntityDataSource` and then click the **Configure data-source** item. This launches the Configure Data Source Wizard, whose first dialog is shown in Figure 37.6. Basically you simply need to specify the source entity data model in the first combo box and then the container name you want to associate to the data control in the lower combo box; then click **Next** to access the second dialog of the wizard.

In the second dialog you have the opportunity of choosing the entity you want to be mapped into the `EntityDataSource`. There you can select only a desired number of columns or all columns, as represented in Figure 37.7.

This is all you need to configure the data source. Now a control for viewing and editing data is necessary. In the toolbox double-click a `GridView` control so that it will be added to the page under the `EntityDataSource`. When ready, click the right arrow to access configuration properties. This shows up the `GridView` Tasks pop-up window; here you specify the `EntityDataSource1` control in the Choose Data Source field to enable data-binding. Also select the **Enable Paging**, **Enable Sorting**, and **Enable Selection** check boxes. Figure 37.8 provides a graphical representation of this series of operations.

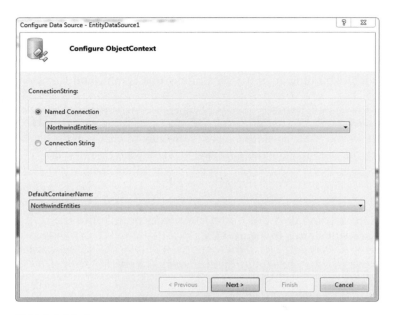

FIGURE 37.6   Associating the entity data model to the EntityDataSource control.

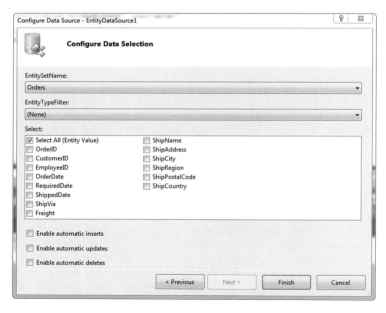

FIGURE 37.7   Choosing entity and entity columns for mapping into the EntityDataSource.

FIGURE 37.8   Applying data-binding and data options in the GridView Tasks pop-up.

With a few mouse clicks you configured your new Web Form to present and edit data without writing a single line of Visual Basic code. There is only a bunch of XHTML code required to set properties for each added control, which in our case is the following:

```
<asp:EntityDataSource ID="EntityDataSource1" runat="server"
    ConnectionString="name=NorthwindEntities"
    DefaultContainerName="NorthwindEntities" EnableFlattening="False"
    EntitySetName="Orders">
</asp:EntityDataSource>
<asp:GridView ID="GridView1" runat="server" AllowPaging="True"
    AllowSorting="True" DataSourceID="EntityDataSource1">
    <Columns>
        <asp:CommandField ShowSelectButton="True" />
    </Columns>
</asp:GridView>
```

This is possible because the ASP.NET data controls implement all functionalities required to access and edit data by simply assigning some properties. Our page is absolutely ready for showing and editing orders from the database. I want to show you another couple of features for filtering data that can also let you understand how powerful ASP.NET is.

RUNTIME DATA-BINDING TIP

Most of ASP.NET data controls expose a `DataSource` property that can be assigned at runtime with a custom data source, such as a `List(Of T)`. When assigned this property, you invoke the control's `DataBind` method to perform the binding.

37

Adding Filtering Capabilities

It would be interesting having filtering capabilities; for example we could implement a filter that enables fetching all orders with the ShipCity property value that starts with the specified text. Thus in the toolbox double-click a TextBox and a Button. These controls will be automatically placed onto the page (they will be placed at the top if that is where the cursor is in the designer). Now replace the Name property value of the TextBox with FilterTextBox; while in the Button properties change the Name value with FilterButton and the Text property with Filter. To provide filtering capabilities over the data source, ASP.NET offers the QueryExtender control that you can find within data controls in the toolbox. Add it to the page and then simply assign its TargetControlID property with EntityDataSource1, which is the name of the data control to be queried or filtered. Now you need to specify an expression for filtering; these kind of expressions are known as *search expressions*. ASP.NET offers more than one search expression, but the simplest and appropriate for our purposes is SearchExpression. This object requires the specification of the search type and of the columns to be interrogated but this is not sufficient; a ControlParameter element needs to be nested so that you can specify the control where the search criteria are inserted (in our case the textbox) and the .NET type involved in the expression. Talking in code terms, you need to manually write the following code inside the QueryExtender:

```
<asp:QueryExtender ID="QueryExtender1" runat="server"
    TargetControlID="EntityDataSource1">
    <asp:SearchExpression DataFields="ShipCity" SearchType="StartsWith">
        <asp:ControlParameter ControlID="FilterTextBox" Type="String" />
    </asp:SearchExpression>
</asp:QueryExtender>
```

The only Visual Basic code we need to write is the event handler for the Page.Loaded event to check the PostBack state. This is accomplished by writing the following code in the Orders.aspx.vb code file:

```
Protected Sub Page_Load(ByVal sender As Object,
                        ByVal e As System.EventArgs) _
                        Handles Me.Load
    If Not Page.IsPostBack Then
        FilterTextBox.Text = ""
    End If
End Sub
```

This is all we need, no other code. Before running the sample Web application, let's make the new Web Form reachable from the master page.

Adding Navigation Controls

Open the master page in the designer. You see the availability of two buttons named Home and About. These are menu items inside a Menu control that simply point to the associated Web Form. You can add menu items to the menu by first clicking the smart tag (that is, the right arrow) and then clicking the **Edit Menu Items** link in the Menu Tasks pop-up dialog. This launches the Menu Item Editor, where you can add new menu items. Click the **Add a Root Item** button that is the first on the left. When the new item is added, set the Text property as Orders. (This also automatically sets the Value property.) Then click the NavigateUrl property and click the available button to associate a Web page. In the Select URL dialog, choose the **Orders.aspx** web page, as shown in Figure 37.9.

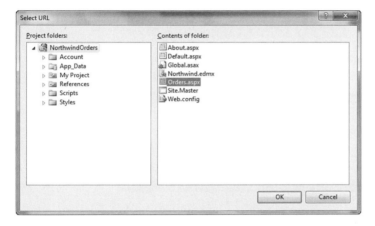

FIGURE 37.9   Associating a web page to the new menu item.

At this point the Menu Item Editor dialog looks like Figure 37.10, which you can take as a reference when setting properties.

Now you can see a new Orders button associated to the same-named Web page.

Running the Application

At this point you can run the demo application by pressing **F5**. Figure 37.11 shows the Orders page, showing a list of orders filtered according to the given search criteria.

Also notice how paging features have been correctly implemented. Finally try clicking the page buttons that provide navigation capabilities.

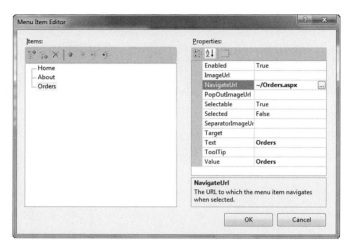

FIGURE 37.10   The Menu Item Editor dialog enables adding menu items to the master page.

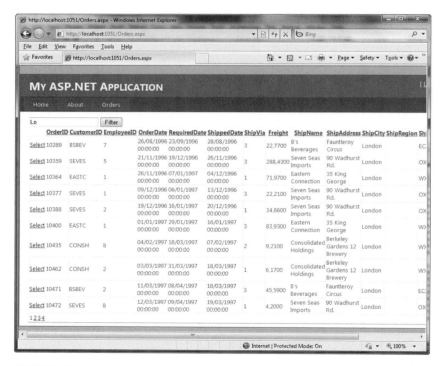

FIGURE 37.11   The sample web application running.

Configuring a Web Application for Security

The sample web application that was illustrated in the previous section has one important limitation: It can be accessed by anonymous users that can access important data. If your application just presents information, in most cases anonymous access is a good idea. But if instead your application has the purpose of managing data or restricted information, you want to force users to login with their own credentials, such as username and password. ASP.NET provides a convenient and easy way for configuring web applications to require login credentials (by storing user information inside a SQL Server database) but also roles and registration; another interesting new feature is that in the past you had to implement your own login page while in Visual Studio 2010; this is generated for you when creating the project. To start configuring security for your Web application, click the **ASP.NET Configuration** button in Solution Explorer (the one with the icon representing a hammer). This runs the ASP.NET Web Site Administration Tool, a web application executed in your web browser. Such tool allows configuring different parts in the web application, but for the current example just click the Security tab. When you click this tab, you can access different security options, including setting users and roles. There is also a guided procedure that you can utilize to configure the application security; thus click the **Use the Security Setup Wizard to Configure Security Step by Step** hyperlink. There are seven steps to complete, but the first one is just a welcome message, so you can click **Next**. Starting from the second step, execute the following tasks:

1. Specify the access method by selecting between **From the Internet** and **From a Local Area Network**. The first option is more restrictive and requires users to register with their credentials, such as username and password. This is particularly useful when you do not know who will access the website and you want a user to log in with credentials. Moreover, if a website is available on the Internet it can be reached by non-Windows environments and therefore Windows authentication is not appropriate. Instead the local intranet option should be used only when the web application runs only inside of your company, because it relies on Windows and domain authentication only, although this simplifies your work because you will not have to configure users. For the current example, where user administration is also covered, select the Internet security and then click **Next**.

2. Simply click **Next** at step 3, because we do not need to change storage information (such as the database provider);

3. Click the **Enable Roles for This Website** check box and then click **Next**. This is important because securing the web application requires at least one role. Typically a website includes at least an administration role, so in the **New Role Name** textbox, type **Administrator** and then click **Add Role**. The new role will be added to the roles list, so click **Next**.

4. Sign up for a new account by providing required information. This is important because the web application requires at least one user that later will be associated to

37

the role. When ready, click **Create User**. You will be told that adding the new user was successful, so click **Next**.

5. Specify access rules to the web application by allowing or denying access permissions to specific roles or users. The default rule is that all registered users and roles can access the application, but you can delete the existing rule and create new rules granting permissions to selected users/roles. For example you can select a folder of the application, by first expanding the root folder on the left and then selecting the permission (Allow or Deny) for the users or roles in the **Rules Applies To** item. When set this, click **Next**.

6. In the last step simply click **Finish**.

SQL SERVER DATABASE

When you configure users or when users register to claim access to the Web application, the user information is stored inside a default SQL Server database that Visual Studio generates for you. If you want to use a SQL Server database different from the default one, use the Aspnet_regsql.exe command-line tool that creates the appropriate tables.

With a few steps you quickly configured your application for requesting registration and login. The last step before running the application is associating the main user to the Administrator role. To accomplish this, click **Manage Users** and then **Edit User**. When the user administration page appears, click the check box for **Administrator**. Finally, click **Save**. Now close the configuration tool, run the application, and try to open the Orders page. As you see, you cannot view the requested page until you do not log in with the previously created user's credentials. When you log in you can browse the application. The really cool thing is that the Login page generated for you by Visual Studio 2010 is bound to the SQL Server database where user information is stored, so you do not need to write code to check if a user has permissions to access. This is performed for you behind the scenes by the application that takes advantage of auto-generated elements.

Summary

In this chapter we made an overview of the ASP.NET technology and of how you can build websites based on the technology. You read about important concepts on the ASP.NET model and how it maintains the application state; then you learned how to create a seb application with Visual Basic 2010. For this, you first saw what Web Forms are and how the logic is divided into XHTML code for the user interface side and into Visual Basic code for performing executive tasks. You took a look at available user controls, both server and HTML controls; then you put your hands on a sample web application to manage data exposed from an Entity Data Model. Finally, you saw the steps necessary to configure security for websites implementing login credentials.

CHAPTER 38

Publishing ASP.NET Web Applications

To make your Web application reachable by other users, you need to deploy it to a host Web server, either on the Internet or on a local area network, such as your company's network. ASP.NET 4.0 and Visual Studio 2010 enhance the deployment experience for Web applications introducing a new tool named MSDeploy. In this chapter you both recap how to publish a Web application using the old-fashioned ways and how to publish an application using the new MSDeploy.

Deployment Overview

Deploying a Web application is something that can be accomplished directly from within Visual Studio 2010, as it was for its predecessors. You can publish a Web application to the following destinations:

▶ A Web server with Internet Information Services installed

▶ A website with the FrontPage extensions installed

▶ An FTP site

▶ The local file system

▶ The local Internet Information Services

What actually changes from previous versions of Visual Studio is how you deploy Web applications.

The 1-Click Deployment

Visual Studio 2010 introduces the logic of deployment simplification with *1-Click deployment*. What does it mean?

It simply means that you supply the required information such as Web address and credentials, and then you make just click once on the button that will do the rest of the work for you, independently from the destination type. The reason for this important new way to deploy Web applications is the introduction of a new tool named MSDeploy, which is described later and that can deploy articulated Web applications. For now let's begin to see how you can deploy Web applications to FTP sites and IIS servers with the 1-Click deployment.

Classic Publishing

Visual Studio 2010 still provides the ability of publishing Web applications the usual way, so it supports direct deployment to FTP sites, websites with FrontPage extensions enabled, the file system, and the local Internet Information Services, although you notice some innovations in the graphical user interface of the deployment window. For example, you might want to deploy the NorthwindOrders Web application, created in Chapter 37, "Building ASP.NET Web Applications," to an FTP site. In Solution Explorer right-click the project name and then click Publish. This launches the Publish Web dialog; here expand the Publish Method combo box and then select FTP. At this point the dialog looks like Figure 38.1.

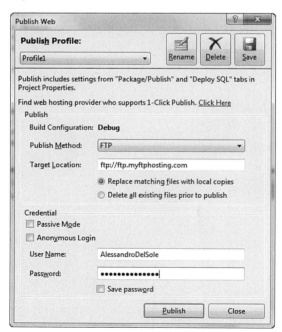

FIGURE 38.1   Publishing a Web application to an FTP site.

CREATING PROFILES

You can create a reusable profile for maintaining the specified deployment settings. When provided the specified deployment information, click the **Publish Profile** combo box and select **New**. Then simply type the name of the new profile, enter the required information for the specified Web destination, and then click **Save**.

Simply click **Publish** so that Visual Studio 2010 publishes your Web application to the specified FTP.

PROVIDERS' FIREWALL

Several Internet service providers or hosts enable firewalls to avoid unrecognized incoming connections. If you want to publish web applications to a Web or FTP site, you need to ensure that the host's firewall accepts connections from Visual Studio 2010.

Another example is publishing the application to IIS, which can be also particularly useful for testing purposes. You accomplish this by setting the File System option in the Publish Method combo box; then type the IIS instance address as demonstrated in Figure 38.2. Notice that publishing to the local IIS requires Visual Studio 2010 to be launched with administrative privileges.

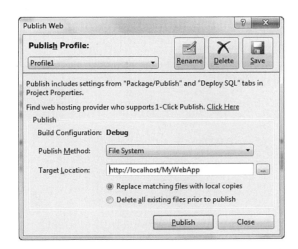

FIGURE 38.2   Publishing the Web application to Internet Information Services.

You can eventually click the **Browse** button to select an existing Web folder or create a new one inside IIS.

MSDeploy Publish

One of the new features in deploying Web applications is the Microsoft Web Deployment Tool, also known as MSDeploy that is a command-line tool included in the .NET Framework 4 and which can build advanced deployment scripts. MSDeploy is an advanced tool in that it can

▶ Publish Web applications and their settings.

▶ Deploy SQL Server databases.

▶ Direct advanced deployment to Internet Information Services web servers.

▶ Publish GAC, COM, and Registry settings.

MSDeploy is a complex tool, and writing the appropriate command lines can be annoying. Fortunately Visual Studio 2010 allows publishing Web applications via MSDeploy through the Publish Web dialog as demonstrated later. Before getting into that, you need to know how Web applications are packaged before deployment.

Understanding Packages

When you deploy a Web application via MSDeploy, the application is first packaged into one archive that makes deployment easier. The package contains all the required information about the host Web server and files and settings required by the application. You set package information in the Package/Publish Web tab of My Project, as shown in Figure 38.3.

Here you can find default settings for the local IIS, but you can place settings provided by the system administrator of the target machine. To build the package, simply right-click the project name in Solution Explorer and click **Build Deployment Package**. Basically the package contains the following elements:

▶ The package containing the application and settings

▶ The destination manifest, which contains information on how to reach the target server

▶ The command line script that will be passed to MSDeploy

When you have your package, you are ready to deploy it with MSDeploy.

Deploy with MSDeploy

Visual Studio 2010 provides the opportunity to deploy Web applications with MSDeploy through its instrumentation. Simply right-click the project name in Solution Explorer and then click **Publish**. When the Publish Web dialog appears, select the **MSDeploy Publish** option from the Publish Method combo box. Figure 38.4 shows how the dialog appears.

You need to provide some settings to deploy the Web application with MSDeploy, and most of them are given to you by the Administrator of the target server. Table 38.1 summarizes required settings.

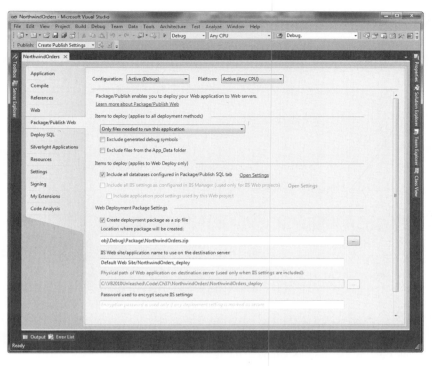

FIGURE 38.3   Setting options for packaging Web applications for deployment.

TABLE 38.1   Required Settings for MSDeploy Publish

Option	Description
Service URL	The URL of the MSDeploy service provided by the host or administrator.
Site/Application	The name of the site and application on the target IIS. Here you can include subfolders.
Mark as IIS application on destination	Will mark the application as a root if you specify a subfolder in the Site/Application option. The target server must support this.
Do not delete extra files on destination	When unchecked, MSDeploy deletes all files from the target folder before publishing new files. The suggestion is keeping it unchecked only at the first publishing.
Allow Untrusted Certificate	Allows host and administrator to use self-signed certificates, according to the administrator instructions.
Username/Password	Credentials required to access the target IIS, provided by the server administrator.

FIGURE 38.4   Setting options for the MSDeploy publish.

When you provide all required settings, simply click **Publish** to get your application deployed to the Web server with MSDeploy, remembering that this tool provides the opportunity to deploy additional requirements such as SQL Server databases and GAC settings.

Summary

In this chapter, we discussed how to deploy ASP.NET Web applications in both the classic fashion and a new one based on the Microsoft Web Deployment tool so that you can now know how to take advantage of the 1-Click publish deployment system for quickly deploying your Web applications directly from Visual Studio 2010.

CHAPTER 39

Building Rich Internet Applications with Silverlight

The evolution of Internet during the years had the consequence of requiring web applications to be even more powerful and interactive, with the addition of multimedia, animations, high-quality graphics, and even business capabilities. Although powerful for its business productivity, ASP.NET has lacked in terms of interactivity and media features. If you think of the Adobe Flash plug-in for a web browser, you can have a good idea of how multimedia and interactivity can improve the success of web applications. A few years ago, Microsoft realized that it should create a plug-in for a web browser with media, interactivity, and business features for the .NET platform integrating the coolest WPF graphic characteristics into web applications produced on the robust ASP.NET. This is where Microsoft Silverlight comes in. In this chapter you learn about building RIA (Rich Internet Applications) with Silverlight and Visual Basic 2010, taking a tour of the most important features of this technology.

> **NOTE**
>
> The requirement of this chapter is that you first read discussions about WPF, starting from Chapter 31, "Creating WPF Applications," until Chapter 35, "Introducing Data-Binding."

Introducing Silverlight

Microsoft Silverlight is a cross-browser, cross-platform, and cross-device plug-in for building rich Internet applications, which offers the best from WPF and ASP.NET. Basically Silverlight is a plug-in for web browsers that needs to be installed on the client side to run new generation web applications, and its size is about 4 megabytes. By installing Silverlight you allow your web browser to run cool applications where data access, multimedia, and rich contents can be linked together. As you see later in this chapter, developing Silverlight applications can be easier to you if you are already familiar with WPF; Silverlight can be considered as a WPF subset for the web, meaning that you can create the user interface with XAML and write Visual Basic code to execute the application tasks. Before continuing to read this chapter, you need to install the Silverlight plug-in and the latest updates of the Visual Studio tools. Basically you need the following components:

▶ Silverlight tools for Visual Studio, which install the Silverlight runtime and enables the IDE to the Silverlight development

▶ Silverlight Toolkit, which contains additional user controls to improve your development experience

Considering the development state of Silverlight, all the discussions and code examples provided in this chapter will be on Silverlight 4; although, it will probably still be a beta version when this book is published. This is because the final version should be available in a reasonable time, and it will provide so many new functionalities that discussing Silverlight 3 would be ineffective at this point. All the required components and tools are available from the official Silverlight website from Microsoft at the following address: http://silverlight.net. After installing the preceding components, you are ready to start your first Silverlight application with Visual Basic 2010. What makes Silverlight so powerful is that you can still write code the way you know, thus taking advantage of you existing .NET Framework and Visual Basic skills without the need to change your mind by writing in different languages and on different technologies.

Creating Silverlight Projects with Visual Basic 2010

One of the greatest benefits of Microsoft Silverlight is that you can create applications with Visual Basic 2010 the same way you create .NET applications. When you select **File**, **New Project**, in the New Project dialog, you have a project templates folder named Silverlight and a number of available project templates, as shown in Figure 39.1.

The project template for general purposes is the Silverlight Application. Ensure this is selected and then follow these steps:

1. Leave the project name unchanged, and then click **OK**

2. You will be asked to specify how the new Silverlight application will be hosted. Basically Silverlight applications are based on user controls that need to be hosted by an ASP.NET web application, such as a website or an MVC application. Also you can host your Silverlight applications inside existing web applications instead of specifying a new one. When the dialog appears, leave unchanged the default selection on a new web application (see Figure 39.2 for details) and then click **OK**. Also notice how

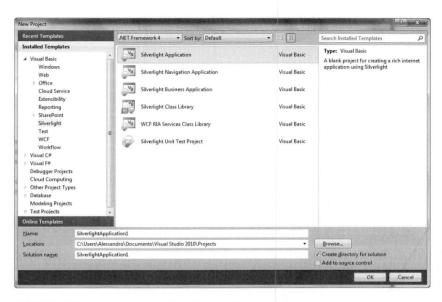

FIGURE 39.1   Selecting a Silverlight project template.

you can select the Silverlight runtime version and how to enable the application for RIA Services, which is introduced later in this chapter.

FIGURE 39.2   Selecting a host project type.

After a few seconds the new project is ready. You notice how Visual Studio looks, which is similar to WPF projects, as demonstrated in Figure 39.3.

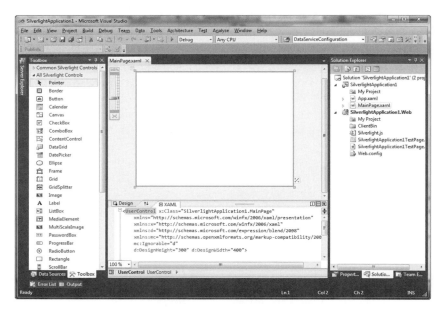

FIGURE 39.3   The IDE is ready on the new Silverlight project.

There are obviously several differences from WPF; first, in the XAML code editor, you can notice how the root element is a `UserControl`. This is because you essentially develop Silverlight controls to be hosted by an ASP.NET application. Next, notice the presence of two projects in Solution Explorer. The first one is the actual Silverlight application, which will be executed on the client side. The structure of the project is similar to WPF projects, thus with XAML files and Visual Basic code behind files.

TIP ON WPF AND SILVERLIGHT

Silverlight applications work within a web context, although the most recent version has more privileges than in the past. Considering web limitations imposed by the Silverlight base class library, you can notice several similarities with the WPF programming model (such as UI elements and user controls); this is the reason why multiple chapters were offered about WPF.

The second project is the web application that hosts the Silverlight user control. Notice the presence of a .js file that contains the JavaScript code that makes the control reachable from the ASP.NET application. Also you can notice the availability of an .aspx web page that shows the Silverlight control and of an HTML page for hosting the Silverlight application for testing. When you have your project, you are ready to add and manage user interface elements.

Adding Controls and Handling Events

Adding controls and UI elements to a Silverlight user control is an easy task and looks like what was already described about WPF. While you go through adding controls, you can also notice how Silverlight properties are in most cases the same as WPF properties. Replace the Background property value in the main Grid from White to SteelBlue. This provides better visibility of the user control in the web browser. Notice that you can still apply brushes as in WPF. Next, add a TextBlock control and place it at the top of the user control. Set its properties so that the foreground color is white and the font size is 24. Finally drag a Button control from the toolbox onto the user control surface. Also notice how Visual Studio also generated the appropriate XAML code for each of the operations accomplished. To handle events, you still write event handlers as you are used to doing in other .NET applications. In this case, double-click the Button and write the following simple handler:

```
Private Sub Button1_Click(ByVal sender As System.Object,
                          ByVal e As System.Windows.RoutedEventArgs) _
                          Handles Button1.Click
    MessageBox.Show("You clicked a Silverlight button!")
End Sub
```

It is important that Silverlight still offers the routed events infrastructure as in WPF, so basically handling events in both technologies is identical. Now press **F5** to start the application with an instance of the Visual Studio debugger attached. Figure 39.4 shows how the application runs inside the web browser.

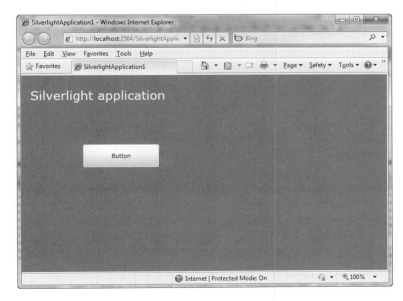

FIGURE 39.4   The Silverlight application running.

39

Now that you have built and run your first rich Internet application, you need to learn how Silverlight applications are packaged and deployed.

How Silverlight Applications Are Packaged

When you create a Silverlight application, in the web host project you can notice the presence of a folder named **ClientBin**. When you compile the project, this folder contains the build output of the Silverlight client project (not the web project). For this you need to know that Silverlight applications are packaged into .xap files, which contain the actual application and its resources. Thus when the build process is complete, the ClientBin folder contains the generated .xap file. When you run the application by pressing **F5**, it will be packaged and deployed on the local file system and will be hosted by the ASP.NET development server so that you can run it in your web browser. Because of all these operations, you can deploy the application with existing web deploying techniques.

Playing Media

As in WPF, Silverlight provides its implementation of the `MediaElement` control that enables media reproduction and streaming from networks. This means that you can interact with the control the same way as in WPF, but you cannot play media files from a local file system for security reasons. Right-click the Silverlight project in Solution Explorer and then select **Add New Item**. (You could also create a new project from scratch but you need to know how to change the default page.) In the dialog select the **Silverlight User Control** item template, as shown in Figure 39.5.

FIGURE 39.5   Adding a new user control.

The goal of the example is implementing a basic media player. When ready, write the XAML code shown in Listing 39.1 and notice how basically the implementation is identical to WPF.

LISTING 39.1   Implementing a Basic Media Player with Silverlight

```xaml
<UserControl x:Class="SilverlightApplication1.MediaPlayerControl"
    xmlns="http://schemas.microsoft.com/winfx/2006/xaml/presentation"
    xmlns:x="http://schemas.microsoft.com/winfx/2006/xaml"
    xmlns:d="http://schemas.microsoft.com/expression/blend/2008"
    xmlns:mc="http://schemas.openxmlformats.org/markup-compatibility/2006"
    mc:Ignorable="d"
    d:DesignHeight="300" d:DesignWidth="400">

    <Grid x:Name="LayoutRoot" Background="White">
        <Grid.RowDefinitions>
            <RowDefinition/>
            <RowDefinition Height="40"/>
        </Grid.RowDefinitions>

        <!-- Set the MediaElement.Source property
        pointing to a video on a web server-->
        <MediaElement Grid.Row="0" Name="Media1"
         Source="http://www.mywebsite.com/MyVideo.wmv"/>
        <StackPanel Grid.Row="1" Orientation="Horizontal">
            <StackPanel.Resources>

                <!—Using a style for buttons—>
                <Style x:Key="ButtonStyle" TargetType="Button">
                    <Setter Property="Width" Value="80"/>
                    <Setter Property="Height" Value="30"/>
                    <Setter Property="Margin" Value="5"/>
                </Style>
            </StackPanel.Resources>

            <Button Name="PlayButton" Style="{StaticResource ButtonStyle}"
                    Content="Play"/>
            <Button Name="PauseButton" Style="{StaticResource ButtonStyle}"
                    Content="Pause"/>
            <Button Name="StopButton" Style="{StaticResource ButtonStyle}"
                    Content="Stop"/>
        </StackPanel>
    </Grid>
</UserControl>
```

39

Just remember to assign the MediaElement.Source property with a valid media content address from a web server. Now switch to the code-behind file and write the Visual Basic code shown in Listing 39.2 that can provide reproduction capabilities.

LISTING 39.2   Enabling the Media Player to Content Reproduction

```vb
Partial Public Class MediaPlayerControl
    Inherits UserControl
    Public Sub New()
        InitializeComponent()
    End Sub

    'If you plan to set the MediaElement.Source property
    'in code, ensure its value is not Nothing
    Private Sub PlayButton_Click(ByVal sender As System.Object,
                        ByVal e As System.Windows.
                        RoutedEventArgs) Handles PlayButton.Click
        Me.Media1.Play()
    End Sub

    Private Sub PauseButton_Click(ByVal sender As System.Object,
                        ByVal e As System.Windows.
                        RoutedEventArgs) Handles PauseButton.Click
        Me.Media1.Pause()
    End Sub

    Private Sub StopButton_Click(ByVal sender As System.Object,
                        ByVal e As System.Windows.
                        RoutedEventArgs) Handles StopButton.Click
        Me.Media1.Stop()
    End Sub

    Private Sub Media1_MediaFailed(ByVal sender As Object,
                        ByVal e As System.Windows.
                        ExceptionRoutedEventArgs) Handles Media1.
                        MediaFailed
        MessageBox.Show(e.ErrorException.Message)
    End Sub
End Class
```

Figure 39.6 shows how the new user control looks after implementing the user interface.

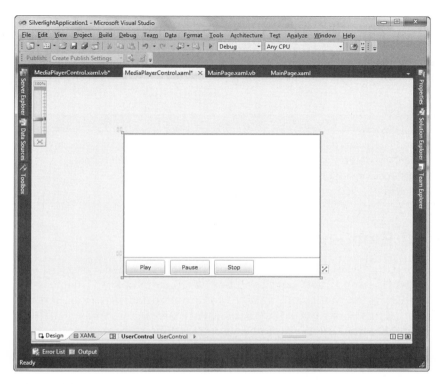

FIGURE 39.6   The new media player control within the Visual Studio Designer.

Before running the application, you need to replace the startup object with the new user control. This is accomplished by replacing the code in the Application.Startup event handler available in the App.xaml.vb code file. The original event handler looks like this:

```vb
Private Sub Application_Startup(ByVal o As Object,
                                ByVal e As StartupEventArgs) _
                                Handles Me.Startup
    Me.RootVisual = New MainPage()
End Sub
```

The RootVisual property (of type UIElement) represents the root element in the user interface and is assigned with an instance of the desired page. According to this, replace the RootVisual assignment as follows:

```vb
Me.RootVisual = New MediaPlayerControl
```

Finally ensure that you have supplied a valid media URL for the MediaElement.Source property and then run the application by pressing **F5** to play/pause/stop the media file.

39

SUPPORTED MEDIA FORMATS

Unlike the WPF `MediaElement`, Silverlight's version cannot play all media directly. It supports only some specific encoding formats, which are described in detail at the following MSDN page: http://msdn.microsoft.com/en-us/library/cc189080(VS.95).aspx.

CAPTURING CAMERA

Silverlight 4 introduces new interesting graphic APIs that enable accessing the webcam installed on your machine and microphone so that you can capture the cam output. Check out the MSDN documentation about the `System.Windows.Media.VideoCaptureDevice` class.

Animating UI Elements

Silverlight enables animating elements in the user interface similarly to what happens in WPF, so this section provides a brief and fast description of animations. Read Chapter 33, "Brushes, Styles, Templates, and Animations in WPF," for further details. There are several kinds of available animations, such as `DoubleAnimation`, `PointAnimation`, and `ColorAnimation`, all coming from the `System.Windows.Media.Animations` namespace. To understand how animations work in Silverlight, look at the code shown in Listing 39.3.

LISTING 39.3   Implementing Double Animations

```
<UserControl x:Class="SilverlightApplication1.AnimatingUIElements"
    xmlns="http://schemas.microsoft.com/winfx/2006/xaml/presentation"
    xmlns:x="http://schemas.microsoft.com/winfx/2006/xaml"
    xmlns:d="http://schemas.microsoft.com/expression/blend/2008"
    xmlns:mc="http://schemas.openxmlformats.org/markup-compatibility/2006"
    mc:Ignorable="d"
    d:DesignHeight="300" d:DesignWidth="400">

    <Grid x:Name="LayoutRoot" Background="White">
        <Grid.ColumnDefinitions>
            <ColumnDefinition/>
            <ColumnDefinition/>
        </Grid.ColumnDefinitions>

        <!-- Replace with a valid image file -->
        <Image Grid.Column="0" Name="Image1"
            Source="/SilverlightApplication1;component/Images/AnImageFile.jpg">

            <Image.RenderTransform>
                <TransformGroup>
                    <SkewTransform x:Name="SkewImage"/>
```

```
                    <ScaleTransform x:Name="ScaleImage"/>
                </TransformGroup>
            </Image.RenderTransform>

        <Image.Triggers>
            <EventTrigger RoutedEvent="Image.Loaded">
                <EventTrigger.Actions>
                    <BeginStoryboard>
                        <Storyboard x:Name="ImageStoryBoard">
                            <DoubleAnimation Storyboard.TargetName="SkewImage"
                                            Storyboard.TargetProperty="AngleY"
                                            From="0" To="15" Duration="0:0:3"
                                            AutoReverse="True"
                                            RepeatBehavior="Forever" />
                            <DoubleAnimation Storyboard.TargetName="ScaleImage"
                                            Storyboard.TargetProperty="ScaleX"
                                            From="1" To="0.3" Duration="0:0:3"
                                            AutoReverse="True"
                                            RepeatBehavior="Forever" />
                            <DoubleAnimation Storyboard.TargetName="ScaleImage"
                                            Storyboard.TargetProperty="ScaleY"
                                            From="1" To="0.3" Duration="0:0:3"
                                            AutoReverse="True"
                                            RepeatBehavior="Forever" />
                        </Storyboard>
                    </BeginStoryboard>
                </EventTrigger.Actions>
            </EventTrigger>

        </Image.Triggers>
    </Image>

<TextBlock Grid.Column="1" Text="Animated Text" FontSize="24"
            FontFamily="Verdana" FontWeight="Bold"
            HorizontalAlignment="Center"
            VerticalAlignment="Center" RenderTransformOrigin="0.5 0.5">

<TextBlock.Foreground>
  <LinearGradientBrush>
    <GradientStop Offset="0" Color="Red" />
    <GradientStop Offset="0.5" Color="Yellow" />
    <GradientStop Offset="1" Color="Orange"/>
  </LinearGradientBrush>
</TextBlock.Foreground>

<TextBlock.RenderTransform>
```

39

```
            <TransformGroup>
                <RotateTransform x:Name="RotateText" />
                <SkewTransform x:Name="SkewText"/>
            </TransformGroup>
        </TextBlock.RenderTransform>

        <TextBlock.Triggers>
          <EventTrigger RoutedEvent="TextBlock.Loaded">
            <BeginStoryboard>
              <Storyboard x:Name="TextAnimation">
                <DoubleAnimation Storyboard.TargetName="RotateText"
                                 Storyboard.TargetProperty="Angle"
                                 From="0" To="360" Duration="0:0:5"
                                 RepeatBehavior="Forever" />

                <DoubleAnimation Storyboard.TargetName="SkewText"
                                 AutoReverse="True"
                                 Storyboard.TargetProperty="AngleX"
                                 From="0" To="45" Duration="0:0:5"
                                 RepeatBehavior="Forever" />

              </Storyboard>
            </BeginStoryboard>
          </EventTrigger>
        </TextBlock.Triggers>
      </TextBlock>
    </Grid>
</UserControl>
```

Basically you can specify some transformations for user interface elements you want to animate, and then you can establish the event that will launch the animation with an EventTrigger element within a Control.Triggers property node. The actual animation is provided by a StoryBoard object that contains one or more DoubleAnimation objects to animate the desired transformations. Figure 39.7 shows the result of the animation running.

Introducing Navigation Applications

If you have experience with Silverlight versions prior to 3.0, you probably know how difficult it was to create multipage applications. Silverlight did not have a "master page" approach like in ASP.NET, and programming for user control complicated things. Fortunately, starting from Silverlight 3.0, a new interesting object named Navigation Framework was introduced. This offers the ability of having a master page and then navigating different pages with different user controls. To create a navigation application, select **File, New Project** and then the **Silverlight Navigation Application** project template in the Silverlight templates folder, as shown in Figure 39.8.

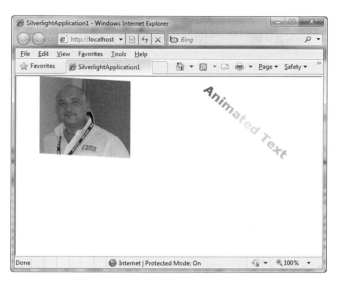

FIGURE 39.7   Animations in action.

FIGURE 39.8   Creating a new navigation application.

When the project is ready, you can notice that the main page offers a page skeleton with borders and buttons. This can be considered as the master page. If you take a look at the XAML code, you notice the presence of the following lines, among others:

```
<navigation:Frame x:Name="ContentFrame"
```

```
                Style="{StaticResource ContentFrameStyle}"
                Source="/Home"
                Navigated="ContentFrame_Navigated"
                NavigationFailed="ContentFrame_NavigationFailed">
    <navigation:Frame.UriMapper>
      <uriMapper:UriMapper>
        <uriMapper:UriMapping Uri="" MappedUri="/Views/Home.xaml"/>
        <uriMapper:UriMapping Uri="/{pageName}"
         MappedUri="/Views/{pageName}.xaml"/>
      </uriMapper:UriMapper>
    </navigation:Frame.UriMapper>
  </navigation:Frame>
```

The `System.Windows.Controls` namespace provides a `Frame` control that has an infrastructure for navigating between pages via a relative `Uri` that basically contains the folder
and filename for the page to be browsed. This is accomplished by setting properties in
the `Frame.UriMapper` property. Among the big number of files in the project, pages are
stored in the Views subfolder. A couple of predefined pages are available, such as
Home.xaml and About.xaml. The goal is now showing how you can add and browse a
new page. Right-click the **Views** subfolder and select **Add New Item**. When the dialog
appears, choose the **Silverlight Page** item template in the Silverlight folder and leave
unchanged the Page1.xaml filename. When the new page is ready, add a simple text
message to the main grid:

```
<Grid x:Name="LayoutRoot">
    <TextBlock Text="This is a secondary page"
               FontSize="32"/>
</Grid>
```

This is just a simple sample, but obviously this is the place where you can provide your
complex user interface. Now go back to the MainPage.xaml file and add the following
button just above the other ones:

```
<HyperlinkButton x:Name="CustomLink" Style="{StaticResource LinkStyle}"
                 NavigateUri="/Page1" TargetName="ContentFrame"
                 Content="page1"/>
```

This can take advantage of an existing style for hyper-linked buttons and launch the new
page specified via the `NavigateUri` property. What happens behind the scenes when you
require browsing a new page is determined by the `ContentFrame_Navigated` event handler
that appears as follows in the code-behind file:

```
Private Sub ContentFrame_Navigated(ByVal sender As Object,
        ByVal e As NavigationEventArgs) Handles ContentFrame.Navigated
    For Each child As UIElement In LinksStackPanel.Children
        Dim hb As HyperlinkButton = TryCast(child, HyperlinkButton)
```

```
            If hb IsNot Nothing AndAlso hb.NavigateUri IsNot Nothing Then
                If hb.NavigateUri = e.Uri Then
                    VisualStateManager.GoToState(hb, "ActiveLink", True)
                Else
                    VisualStateManager.GoToState(hb, "InactiveLink", True)
                End If
            End If
        Next
End Sub
```

The code gets the instance of HyperlinkButton controls and invokes the GoToState method to browse the specified page inside the Frame control. Now run the application by pressing **F5**. When ready, click the page1 hyperlink at the top of the page. This redirects to the new custom page, as shown in Figure 39.9.

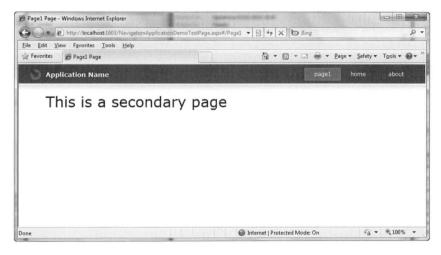

FIGURE 39.9   The custom page being browsed via the navigation framework.

39

Take a look at the Uri in the address bar of your web browser and look how it is formed by the relative path of the loaded page separated by a # symbol. Simply click **Home** or **About** to show predefined pages or go back to Visual Studio for editing your code and adding new custom pages. Finally notice how you can press back and forward buttons in your browser to navigate pages. This is possible thanks to the System.Windows.Navigation.NavigationService object that provides, behind the scenes, support for browsing and loading pages into the Frame and for maintaining the URL history. Another important class in navigation applications is System.Windows.Navigation.NavigationContext, which is responsible for keeping track of the page context such as the URL and parameters passed in query string.

Introducing WCF RIA Services

WCF RIA Services (formerly known as .NET RIA Services) are a recent framework, offered by the System.Windows.Controls.Ria.dll assembly, for exposing data through networks that can then be consumed by Silverlight applications and that typically are implemented as a middle-tier for business applications. In this section you learn how to create a Silverlight business application consuming data from an Entity Data Model exposed through RIA Services.

DATA ACCESS AND SILVERLIGHT

WCF RIA Services provide a well structured and fast way for building a line of business applications, but they are not the only way you can access data from a Silverlight application. Generally speaking, you can implement your logic within a WCF service and expose data that a Silverlight application can consume, such as Entity Data Models or LINQ to SQL models.

To create a business application based on WCF RIA Services, create a new project by selecting the **Silverlight Business Application** project template, as shown in Figure 39.10.

FIGURE 39.10   The WCF RIA Services project template.

Name the new project as **NorthwindBusinessApplication** and click **OK**. When the project is ready, in Solution Explorer you notice a plethora of files and folders. This is because RIA Services projects have an interesting structure based on models and views, other than providing login and authentication infrastructure. Also you can notice when opening the designer that the new project is based on the navigation application template as described in the previous section, so this can help you build complex user interfaces. The first thing is now adding a data source containing data you want to expose through the network.

Adding the Data Source

To add a data source based on the Northwind database (used in several other code examples in this book), follow these steps:

1. Right-click the **NorthwindBusinessApplication.Web** project and select **Add New Item**; in the dialog select the **ADO.NET Entity Data Model** template, name it **Northwind.edmx**, and click **OK**.

2. When the wizard starts, choose to generate the model from an existing database, and next select the Northwind database available on SQL Server as the data source.

3. When the list of database objects is available, select at least the **Orders** table and then click **Finish**.

> **TIP**
>
> The web application project represents the server-side application that exposes data through services. Remember that Silverlight applications act on the client side and will consume data from services, so this is the reason why you just added the data model (and will add domain services) to the server-side application.

At this point you have a data source that you can expose. Remember to build the project, so that it will be updated with references to the new EDM.

Adding the Domain Service Class

To make the data model consumable from clients, you need to implement your business logic. In WCF RIA Services-based applications, this is accomplished by implementing a Domain Service Class. Such kinds of classes inherit from `LinqToEntitiesDomainService(Of T)` and expose queries and methods for performing CRUD (Create/Read/Update/Delete) operations and can contain other custom logic. To add one, right-click the **Services** folder and select **Add New Item**. In the Add New Item dialog, select the **Domain Service Class** template and name it **OrdersDomainService.vb**. The goal is to provide logic for accessing the `Orders` entity set (see Figure 39.11).

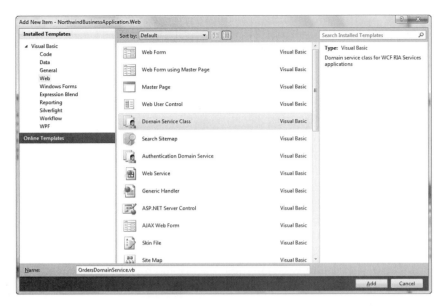

FIGURE 39.11   The item template for adding a domain service class.

At this point Visual Studio requires you to specify entities you want to be mapped into the domain service class and what access level. Figure 39.12 shows the dialog that Visual Studio 2010 shows to provide such specifications.

Ensure that the Enable Client Access check box is flagged so that Silverlight applications can consume data. Select the entity data model from the combo box and then choose one or more entities you want to be exposed by the domain service class. Also check the corresponding Enable Editing check box if you want to provide the ability of data editing. After you click **OK**, Visual Studio generates a domain service class that looks like the code shown in Listing 39.4.

LISTING 39.4   The Domain Service Class

```
Imports System
Imports System.Collections.Generic
Imports System.ComponentModel
Imports System.ComponentModel.DataAnnotations
Imports System.Data
Imports System.Linq
Imports System.Web.DomainServices
Imports System.Web.DomainServices.Providers
Imports System.Web.Ria
Imports System.Web.Ria.Services
```

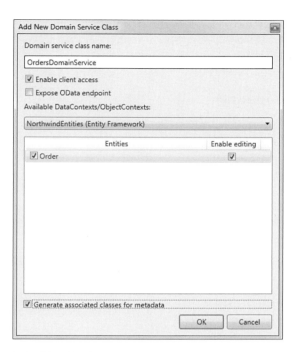

FIGURE 39.12   Specifying settings for the new domain service class.

```
'Implements application logic using the NorthwindEntities context.
' TODO: Add your application logic to these methods or in additional methods.
' TODO: Wire up authentication (Windows/ASP.NET Forms) and uncomment the following
to disable anonymous access
' Also consider adding roles to restrict access as appropriate.
'<RequiresAuthentication> _
<EnableClientAccess()> _
Public Class OrdersDomainService
    Inherits LinqToEntitiesDomainService(Of NorthwindEntities)

    'TODO: Consider
    ' 1. Adding parameters to this method and constraining returned results, and/or
    ' 2. Adding query methods taking different parameters.
    Public Function GetOrders() As IQueryable(Of Order)
        Return Me.ObjectContext.Orders
    End Function

    Public Sub InsertOrder(ByVal order As Order)
        If ((order.EntityState = EntityState.Added) _
                = false) Then
```

```
            If ((order.EntityState = EntityState.Detached)  _
                    = false) Then
                Me.ObjectContext.ObjectStateManager.
                    ChangeObjectState(order, EntityState.Added)
            Else
                Me.ObjectContext.AddToOrders(order)
            End If
        End If
    End Sub

    Public Sub UpdateOrder(ByVal currentOrder As Order)
        If (currentOrder.EntityState = EntityState.Detached) Then
            Me.ObjectContext.AttachAsModified(currentOrder,
                            Me.ChangeSet.GetOriginal(currentOrder))
        End If
    End Sub

    Public Sub DeleteOrder(ByVal order As Order)
        If (order.EntityState = EntityState.Detached) Then
            Me.ObjectContext.Attach(order)
        End If
        Me.ObjectContext.DeleteObject(order)
    End Sub
End Class
```

You can see how Visual Studio 2010 automatically implements logic for querying, adding, updating, and removing orders in the Orders entity set, working against an instance of the ObjectContext class from the Entity Framework. You can eventually add your own logic or edit the default one. For example, replace the GetOrders default method with the following that simply sorts orders by customer ID:

```
Public Function GetOrders() As IQueryable(Of Order)
    Return Me.ObjectContext.Orders.OrderBy(Function(ord) ord.CustomerID)
End Function
```

Then add the following simple method for saving changes, remembering that you can take advantage of your existing Entity Framework skills:

```
Public Sub SaveChanges()
    Me.ObjectContext.SaveChanges()
End Sub
```

Comments added by the IDE give you some suggestions to improve the class logic, for example by providing authentication applying the RequiresAuthentication attribute. When you have the domain service class, which actually returns data, you first need to build again the project; then you are ready to bind such data to appropriate controls in the user interface.

Data-Binding to Controls

Silverlight 4 introduces the drag'n'drop data-binding, which works like the same technique in WPF. This is useful in WCF RIA Services applications, because it enables easily generating data-oriented web pages. At this point you need to add user controls for showing data within the desired page. In the Silverlight project, expand the **Views** folder and double-click the **Home.xaml** page. You could consider adding a dedicated page but for the sake of simplicity, an existing one can do the work the same. When the page is opened inside the Visual Studio designer, build the project and then open the Data Sources window by selecting the **Data, Show Data Sources** command. In the Data Sources window you find some business objects produced by the generation of the RIA Services application, including the Order entity. Drag this onto the DataGrid and when you release the mouse, you notice that Visual Studio 2010 has generated the following XAML code:

```
<riaControls:DomainDataSource AutoLoad="True"
            d:DataContext="{d:DesignInstance my:Order,
            CreateList=true}" Height="0"
            Name="OrderDomainDataSource"
            QueryName="GetOrdersQuery" Width="0">
    <riaControls:DomainDataSource.DomainContext>
        <my:OrdersDomainContext />
    </riaControls:DomainDataSource.DomainContext>
</riaControls:DomainDataSource>
<sdk:DataGrid AutoGenerateColumns="False" Height="200"
            ItemsSource=
            "{Binding ElementName=OrderDomainDataSource,
            Path=Data}" Name="OrderDataGrid"
            RowDetailsVisibilityMode="VisibleWhenSelected"
            Width="400">
    <sdk:DataGrid.Columns>
        <sdk:DataGridTextColumn x:Name="CustomerIDColumn"
            Binding="{Binding Path=CustomerID}"
            Header="Customer ID"
            Width="SizeToHeader" />
        <sdk:DataGridTextColumn x:Name="EmployeeIDColumn"
            Binding="{Binding Path=EmployeeID}"
            Header="Employee ID" Width="SizeToHeader" />
        <sdk:DataGridTextColumn x:Name="FreightColumn"
            Binding="{Binding Path=Freight}"
            Header="Freight" Width="SizeToHeader" />
```

```
<sdk:DataGridTemplateColumn x:Name="OrderDateColumn"
    Header="Order Date" Width="SizeToHeader">
   <sdk:DataGridTemplateColumn.CellTemplate>
       <DataTemplate>
           <sdk:DatePicker
               SelectedDate=
               "{Binding Path=OrderDate,
               Mode=TwoWay,
               NotifyOnValidationError=true,
               TargetNullValue=''}" />
       </DataTemplate>
   </sdk:DataGridTemplateColumn.CellTemplate>
</sdk:DataGridTemplateColumn>
<sdk:DataGridTextColumn x:Name="OrderIDColumn"
    Binding="{Binding Path=OrderID}"
    Header="Order ID" Width="SizeToHeader" />
<sdk:DataGridTemplateColumn
    x:Name="RequiredDateColumn"
    Header="Required Date" Width="SizeToHeader">
   <sdk:DataGridTemplateColumn.CellTemplate>
       <DataTemplate>
           <sdk:DatePicker
               SelectedDate=
               "{Binding Path=RequiredDate,
               Mode=TwoWay,
               NotifyOnValidationError=true,
               TargetNullValue=''}" />
       </DataTemplate>
   </sdk:DataGridTemplateColumn.CellTemplate>
</sdk:DataGridTemplateColumn>
<sdk:DataGridTextColumn x:Name="ShipAddressColumn"
    Binding="{Binding Path=ShipAddress}"
    Header="Ship Address" Width="SizeToHeader" />
<sdk:DataGridTextColumn x:Name="ShipCityColumn"
    Binding="{Binding Path=ShipCity}"
    Header="Ship City" Width="SizeToHeader" />
<sdk:DataGridTextColumn x:Name="ShipCountryColumn"
    Binding="{Binding Path=ShipCountry}"
    Header="Ship Country" Width="SizeToHeader" />
<sdk:DataGridTextColumn x:Name="ShipNameColumn"
    Binding="{Binding Path=ShipName}"
    Header="Ship Name" Width="SizeToHeader" />
<sdk:DataGridTemplateColumn
    x:Name="ShippedDateColumn"
    Header="Shipped Date"
    Width="SizeToHeader">
```

```
          <sdk:DataGridTemplateColumn.CellTemplate>
              <DataTemplate>
                  <sdk:DatePicker
                      SelectedDate=
                      "{Binding Path=ShippedDate,
                      Mode=TwoWay,
                      NotifyOnValidationError=true,
                      TargetNullValue=''}" />
              </DataTemplate>
          </sdk:DataGridTemplateColumn.CellTemplate>
      </sdk:DataGridTemplateColumn>
      <sdk:DataGridTextColumn
          x:Name="ShipPostalCodeColumn"
          Binding="{Binding Path=ShipPostalCode}"
          Header="Ship Postal Code"
          Width="SizeToHeader" />
      <sdk:DataGridTextColumn
          x:Name="ShipRegionColumn"
          Binding="{Binding Path=ShipRegion}"
          Header="Ship Region"
          Width="SizeToHeader" />
      <sdk:DataGridTextColumn
          x:Name="ShipViaColumn"
          Binding="{Binding Path=ShipVia}"
          Header="Ship Via"
          Width="SizeToHeader" />
    </sdk:DataGrid.Columns>
</sdk:DataGrid>
```

The `DataGrid` is now data-bound to a `DomainDataSource` control, which is the design-time representation of the domain service class, whereas the `DomainDataSource.DomainContext` property represents the data context for querying, loading, and submitting data. Notice how, similarly to what happens in Windows Presentation Foundation, the IDE generated `DataGrid` columns specific for the bound data type. At this point build the project. Further considerations on executing the application are discussed in the next subsection.

DATAPAGER CONTROL

Silverlight 4 introduces a `DataPager` control that you can use for paging data from RIA Services. This control is not covered here, so check out the MSDN documentation.

Running the Application

After implementing business logic and providing data-binding for UI data controls, you are ready to run the application, so press **F5**. After a few seconds you can see how the list of orders is correctly shown within the `DataGrid` in the Home page, as demonstrated in Figure 39.13.

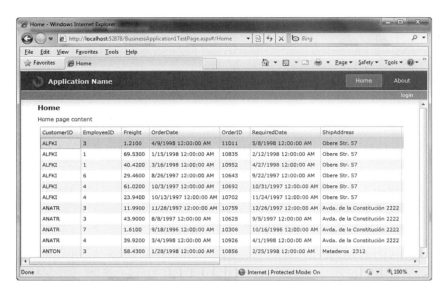

FIGURE 39.13   The application based on WCF RIA Services shows requested data.

You could of course create a different page for showing data and making it reachable via the navigation framework, as described in the dedicated section of this chapter.

"Out of Browser" Applications

Starting from Silverlight 3, you have the possibility of locally installing Silverlight applications so that they can be run in a desktop environment. This kind of application is generally known as "Out of Browser." Typically you use such a feature if you want to have a local copy of the application that does not need to be connected to a network for most of its requirements. To make a Silverlight application to be installable you simply need to enable out-of-browser settings. To demonstrate how this works, create a new Silverlight project with Visual Basic 2010. When the new project is ready, in the main page type the following XAML:

```
<Grid x:Name="LayoutRoot" Background="White">
    <StackPanel>
        <Button Content="Get status" Height="40"
                HorizontalAlignment="Left" Margin="5"
                Name="Button1" VerticalAlignment="Top"
                Width="150" />
        <TextBlock Height="30" HorizontalAlignment="Left"
                Margin="5" Name="TextBlock1"
                VerticalAlignment="Top" Width="340"
                FontSize="16" />
```

```
        </StackPanel>
</Grid>
```

The goal is programmatically understanding if the application is running inside or outside a web browser, so when the user clicks the button, a text message will be shown. Now in the code-behind file, handle the `Button.Click` event as follows:

```
Private Sub Button1_Click(ByVal sender As System.Object, _
                          ByVal e As System.Windows. _
                          RoutedEventArgs) Handles Button1.Click

    Me.TextBlock1.Text = "Running out of browser: " & _
    App.Current.IsRunningOutOfBrowser.ToString
End Sub
```

The `App.Current` property, of type `Application`, provides access to several application-level objects, including some for working with out-of-browser features. The `IsRunningOutOfBrowser` property simply returns `True` or `False` according to the execution context. Before running the demo application, you need to enable specific settings, so click **My Project** in Solution Explorer; ensure the Silverlight tab is selected and check the **Enable Running Application out of the Browser** check box. Then click the **Out-of-Browser Settings** button that launches the same-named dialog where you can customize settings for your offline application, as shown in Figure 39.14.

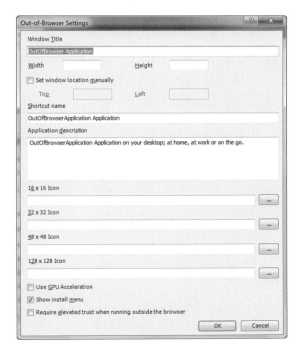

FIGURE 39.14   Customizing settings for out-of-browser applications.

Settings are self-explanatory; particularly notice that if you do not want a default icon to be used, you can supply your own. Also notice how you can provide a shortcut name; this is because you can choose adding a shortcut to the desktop or to the Start menu to the offline application. Now you can run the application. When ready, click the button so that you can verify that the code can determine that the application is running inside the browser, as shown in Figure 39.15. To install the application locally, simply right-click in the browser window and select the **Install ApplicationName onto This Computer** command, as shown in the just-mentioned figure. At this point the Install Application dialog will ask you to specify where you want to place shortcuts for running the application locally, such as the Desktop, the Start menu, or both (see Figure 39.16 for an example).

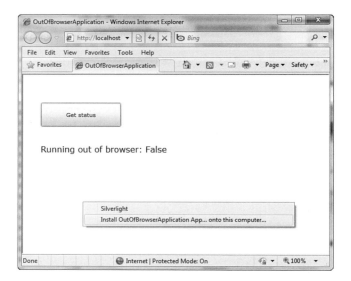

FIGURE 39.15   Running the application and selecting the local installation option.

FIGURE 39.16   Installing the application locally.

After it's installed, the application will be automatically launched out of the browser. Figure 39.17 shows how the demo application looks. Notice that you can uninstall the application by simply right-clicking inside the local window and then choosing the **Remove** command.

FIGURE 39.17   The application running out of the browser, locally.

ELEVATED PERMISSIONS

Silverlight 4 introduces elevated permissions for Out-of-Browser applications. This is interesting because it enables access to local resources such as user-level folders and to the COM model so that you can interact with other applications such as Microsoft Outlook.

Summary

In this chapter you saw that Silverlight is a cross-browser, cross-platform, and cross-device plug-in for building Rich Internet Applications based on the .NET Framework. You saw how many similarities there are between Silverlight and WPF in both creating projects and in writing code (XAML and Visual Basic). You saw how Silverlight programming is based on the concept of user control and how you add user controls to the user interface and handle events. Next you saw some common scenarios, such as playing media contents and animations. You also took a tour inside some new features: navigation applications, which provide a framework for browsing pages as if you had master page and subpages, WCF RIA Services, a new data framework for building business applications, and the Out-of-Browser applications that offer the possibility of locally installing a Silverlight application to desktop environments.

39

CHAPTER 40

Building and Deploying Applications for Windows Azure

Maintaining servers and data centers has costs and requires a company to have people specifically working on maintenance and administration. To reduce costs, a new way of thinking about data and web applications working on data is taking place: *cloud computing*. Basically the idea of cloud computing is that you eliminate physical servers and data centers from your company's location and deploy your web applications to servers that are elsewhere in the world and that are maintained by another company, taking advantage of network connections for accessing your data. Microsoft is working hard on its own cloud computing platform, known as Windows Azure Services Platform. This platform is composed of several services, such as applications hosted on a 64-bit operating system, SQL Server data access, and .NET services. A deep discussion on Azure would probably require an entire book; in this chapter you learn what Windows Azure is and how you can build and deploy Visual Basic Web applications to Azure using Visual Studio 2010, while further discussions on the numerous offered services are available in the MSDN official documentation.

About Windows Azure Platform

The Windows Azure Services Platform is the cloud computing platform from Microsoft. It offers an infrastructure for scaling applications on the Internet where services and applications are hosted on Microsoft data centers. This means that with Windows Azure you do not need physical servers in your company because data and applications will be hosted by Microsoft servers. Windows Azure is instead just a part of the Azure Services Platform and is a 64-bit operating system providing the runtime and the environment for hosting your applications and the platform's services and for managing the applications' lifecycle as well.

One of the biggest benefits in developing for Windows Azure is that you can keep your existing skills in developing ASP.NET and Silverlight Web applications with just slight modifications due to the platform infrastructure, still utilizing Visual Studio 2010 as the development environment. The goal of this chapter is introducing you to developing and deploying your Visual Basic applications to the Azure platform. In-depth discussions are not possible here; although it is important to understand how you use Visual Studio 2010 to build and deploy Visual Basic applications. The Azure Services Platform offers several services, which can be summarized as follows:

▶ **Windows Azure**, which is the previously described operating system, whose development fully integrates with Visual Studio and that is available for several programming languages not only in the .NET family, such as PHP and Python. Windows Azure offers a Service Hosting space that runs applications and a Storage Account service where you place your data.

▶ **Windows Azure AppFabric**, formerly known as .NET Services, which brings identity security and connectivity to applications. The idea of AppFabric is controlling Web applications by integrating with identity and authorization providers, such as the Windows Live ID (service known as *Access Control*) and of providing bridges for easily connecting applications together (service known as *Service Bus*).

▶ **SQL Azure**, which is a Web-based relational database, providing well-known SQL Server features to the cloud development and that can also be reached from SQL Server Management Studio 2008 R2.

With particular regard to Windows Azure, the Storage Account, which is enabled when you create your account, is composed by the following areas:

▶ **Blob Storage**, where you can place files and streams that you can reach via HTTP and HTTPS addresses

▶ **Tables Storage**, where you can organize data within tables

▶ **Queues Storage**, a service for sending and receiving messages on the network

The Blob storage is particularly useful when you need to store some files, which can be of any kind, to use in your applications. The Windows Azure Platform Developer Center contains hundreds of learning resources about all the previously mentioned services. You can find it here: http://msdn.microsoft.com/en-us/azure/default.aspx. This chapter explains what tools are necessary for building and deploying Web applications to Azure; and the last section gives you the basics for activating and managing the Storage account. Before getting your hands dirty on writing code, it is important to mention how you can register to the Windows Azure Services Platform.

> **NOTE ON THE VISUAL STUDIO TOOLS FOR WINDOWS AZURE**
>
> Because of the release timing of Azure, this chapter has been written on Visual Studio 2010 Beta 2 and the November 2009 CTP Windows Azure Services Platform. So, when building your applications for Azure, check for changes introduced in new versions and keep your development environment up to date. The Visual Studio 2010 Tools for Windows Azure has an option (enabled by default) for automatically updating tools.

Registering for the Windows Azure Developer Portal

To deploy hosted applications to Windows Azure, you first need to register and get an account. At the moment of writing this chapter, Windows Azure and related services in the platform are in Community Technology Preview, which means free evaluation. When this book is live, Azure will no longer be in CTP, meaning that you will have to pay to use services because Microsoft will be already charging customers for using Azure. If you are interested in Microsoft cloud computing and in purchasing services, *ensure you read this page about pricing first*: http://www.microsoft.com/windowsazure/pricing/. Only if you decide to pay for cloud computing services, go to the following link: http://www.microsoft.com/windowsazure/account/ and click Get Your Account. At this point you need to log in with a valid Windows Live ID. After you've logged in, follow the instructions shown to get your tokens. You will also receive an email with instructions to follow to activate your token on Windows Azure. Only when you are a registered user can you visit the Windows Azure Developer portal that is located at the following address: http://windows.azure.com. Your new account will give you access to two main features: the Service Hosting, which is where you will publish your applications, and the Storage Account where you will have access to the blog storage, queues, and tables. Later in this chapter you see how to manage applications within the Windows Azure Developer Portal. Before going into that, you need to enable Visual Studio 2010 for cloud development.

Downloading and Installing Tools for Visual Studio

Visual Studio 2010 is the ideal development environment for Windows Azure. To enable the IDE, you need to download and install Windows Azure Tools for Visual Studio 2010. You can find them at the following link: http://www.microsoft.com/windowsazure/. Click the **Get Tools & SDK** button to download the installer. This will install tools for Visual Studio so that you can create and manage projects the usual way, and the Windows Azure SDK. If you have also installed Visual Studio 2008, tools will affect this version, too. The Windows Azure SDK is composed by the Development Fabric, a tool that reproduces locally the hosting services on the cloud and that is required for running your applications locally, the Development Storage, which reproduces locally the environment for publishing blobs, queues and messages, and the documentation. The Windows Azure SDK also contains sample applications with full source code for further studies. Also ensure to periodically check out the official Cloud Computing tools team blog from Microsoft, available here: http://blogs.msdn.com/cloud/.

40

Additional Tools

With the growing diffusion of Windows Azure, lots of tools are coming out. Particularly there is the need for tools for managing the Storage Account, especially when you need to manage files in the blog storage both locally and online. Two tools are free: The first one is an add-on from Microsoft for the Windows Management Console, enabling managing files in the blob storage and queues located in this space on the MSDN Code Gallery: http://code.msdn.microsoft.com/windowsazuremmc. The last section in this chapter shows an example of using this tool for managing files and using them. The second tool was developed by me and published onto CodePlex, named WPF Client for the Windows Azure Blog Storage, an open source WPF application written in Visual Basic located here: http://azureblobclient.codeplex.com/.

Creating a Demo Project

Creating applications for Windows Azure is something that affects a big plethora of scenarios, because you can generally build and deploy any kind of Web applications. This chapter provides an example of a Silverlight Web application to show how different technologies (ASP.NET, Silverlight, and Azure) can coexist in the cloud development. With that said, run Visual Studio 2010 and open the New Project dialog.

VISUAL STUDIO REQUIRES ELEVATED PRIVILEGES

To test your Windows Azure applications locally, Visual Studio needs to be run with elevated privileges (**Run as Administrator**). This is required because Visual Studio needs to launch the Development Fabric, which also needs to be run with elevated privileges.

Click the **Cloud Service** folder and select the **Windows Azure Cloud Service** project template. Name the new project as **AzureBookstore**. See Figure 40.1 for details.

After you click OK, another dialog displays requesting you to specify the application type. In this dialog select the **ASP.NET Web Role** option and press the right arrow so that everything appears as in Figure 40.2.

It is possible to select different kinds of projects, such as ASP.NET MVC 2 or WCF projects. The ASP.NET Web Role is the most common template for classic ASP.NET applications. After this, Visual Studio generates a new solution storing two projects: The first project is the Cloud service that stores information for the Windows Azure hosting service. The second project is the ASP.NET Web application that you actually work on. Before putting hands on the code, an explanation about both projects is required.

Understanding Web Roles and Web Configuration

A key concept in Windows Azure development is the *role*, which is typically a single component running in the Azure environment and built in managed code. Roles can be of two types: web roles and worker roles. A Web role is generally an ASP.NET Web applica-

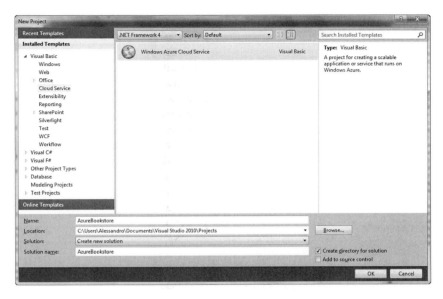

FIGURE 40.1   Creating the new project.

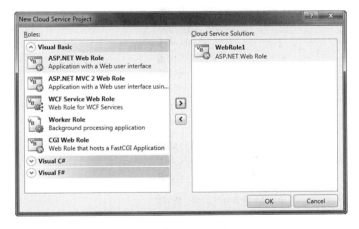

FIGURE 40.2   Selecting the project type.

tion, like the case of our sample scenario. As you may remember from Figure 40.2, additional Web roles are available for WCF and FastCGI applications. You may instead think of worker roles as of services running behind the scenes, like in the case of Windows services, in the cloud. An Azure project can have multiple roles and multiple instances of one role; moreover, you can configure roles as required. When you create new Cloud projects, the new solution will contain a Web role project (simply an ASP.NET Web project) and a service project where you can configure role properties. To access roles configuration, in Solution Explorer right-click the **WebRole1** role and select **Properties**. At this point a special implementation of the **My Project** designer will pop up. Figure 40.3 shows what you will see on the screen.

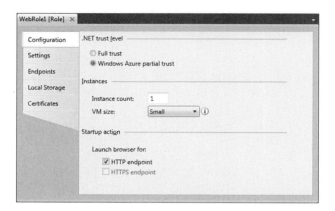

FIGURE 40.3   Accessing role configuration options.

The **Configuration** tab enables first setting the .NET trust level for roles. By default the trust level is **Full Trust**. The Windows Azure partial trust level has instead some limitations and denies your role access to some resources, such as the Registry, isolated storage, printing, and OleDb connections. The full restrictions list is available here: http://msdn. microsoft.com/en-us/library/dd573355.aspx. The **Instance Count** field enables setting how many instances of the role are permitted, whereas **VM Size** enables specifying the size of the virtual machine hosting your service. Small means one CPU core, 1.7 gigabytes of memory, and 250 gigabytes of hard disk space. Medium means two CPU cores, 3.5 gigabytes of memory, and 500 gigabytes of hard disk space. Large means four CPU cores, 7 gigabytes of memory, and 1 terabyte of hard disk space; finally, ExtraLarge means eight CPU cores, 15 gigabytes of memory, and 2 terabytes of hard disk space. The Startup action group enables specifying if debugging should be launched via an HTTP or and HTTPS endpoint (which must be defined in the Endpoints tab). In the Settings tab you can define settings that you can access via the Windows Azure SDK Runtime API. By default each role has a DiagnosticsConnectionString that defines whether you need access to the local storage or the online services. In the Endpoints tab you can define endpoints for your application. Deciding to apply for an HTTPS endpoint also requires a valid SSL certificate. You add certificates to your deployment via the Certificates tab. Finally, the Local Storage tab enables configuring the file system storage resources local for each instance. All the preceding options and settings are reflected into the ServiceConfiguration.cscfg and ServiceDefinition.csdef files that you can see in Solution Explorer and that are basically XML representations of settings.

ADDING MULTIPLE ROLES AND 64-BIT CONSIDERATIONS

You can add multiple web roles and worker roles by right-clicking the Roles folder in Solution Explorer. Another consideration that you need to keep in mind is that Windows Azure is a 64-bit operating system, so take care of this if you plan to invoke unmanaged code that might fail.

The default role for the new project is associated with the ASP.NET project that will actually run the application. You can therefore build your application directly within the Web project or add a Silverlight project, as explained in next section.

Adding a Silverlight 3 Project

A web project can host Silverlight applications, as you may remember from previous discussions about this technology. This also true in Windows Azure scenarios. The goal of this chapter is building a Silverlight application capable of showing and editing a list of books within a `DataGrid` control, also providing the ability of reading and saving data to Xml taking advantage of the isolated storage. At this point right-click the web project name in Solution Explorer and click **Add New Item**. Notice that we are not adding a new project, but simply an item. When the Add New Item dialog appears, click the **Silverlight** folder on the left and select the **Silverlight Application** item template, naming the new item as **BookStore.vbproj** (see Figure 40.4 for details).

FIGURE 40.4   Adding a Silverlight project to the solution.

When you add the new project, a dialog asks for specifying the Silverlight version, the project path, and other information such as enabling debugging. Leave the default settings unchanged, as shown in Figure 40.5, and continue.

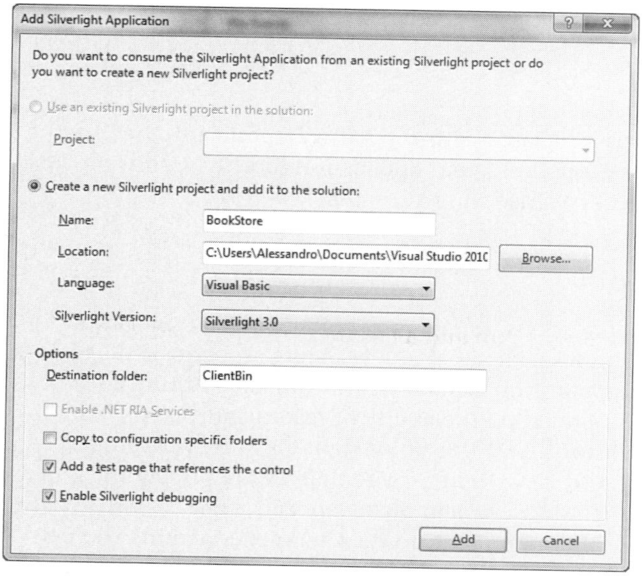

FIGURE 40.5   Setting options for the new Silverlight project.

Because we use LINQ to Xml for listing and saving books, and because this will be accomplished using a DataGrid control, add references to the System.Xml.dll, System.Xml.Linq.dll and System.Windows.Controls.Data.dll assemblies. Now there is the need of implementing a Book class representing one book and a BooksCollection class representing a typed collection of books, so add a new code file to the Silverlight project named Book.vb. Code in Listing 40.1 demonstrates this.

LISTING 40.1   Implementing Classes for Representing Books

```
Imports System.Collections.ObjectModel


Public Class Book

    Public Property Title As String
    Public Property Author As String
    Public Property DatePublished As Date
    Public Property ISBN As String


End Class
```

```
Public Class BooksCollection
    Inherits ObservableCollection(Of Book)

    Public Sub New(ByVal source As IEnumerable(Of Book))
        For Each b As Book In source
            Me.Add(b)
        Next
    End Sub

    Public Sub New()

    End Sub
End Class
```

For the sake of clarity, implement just a `DataGrid` and a `Button` for saving data. The following XAML code must replace the `Grid` definition:

```xml
<Grid x:Name="LayoutRoot" Background="Green">
    <Grid.RowDefinitions>
        <RowDefinition/>
        <RowDefinition Height="50"/>
    </Grid.RowDefinitions>
    <data:DataGrid Name="BooksGrid" Grid.Row="0" ItemsSource="{Binding}"
                AutoGenerateColumns="True" />
    <StackPanel Grid.Row="1" Orientation="Horizontal">
        <Button Width="100" Height="40" Margin="5"
                Content="Save" Name="SaveButton"/>
    </StackPanel>
</Grid>
```

The `DataGrid` is defined within the `System.Windows.Controls.Data` namespace; because of this, you need to add the following Xml namespace declaration at page level to use it:

```
xmlns:data="clr-namespace:System.Windows.Controls;assembly=System.Windows.Con-
trols.Data"
```

Now it is time to write Visual Basic code. Our goal is reading data from an Xml file containing books' definitions and that is stored in the Silverlight's isolated storage. If the file is not found, which is the case of the first run, an empty books collection is defined. Finally the code provides the ability of saving data to the isolated storage. Listing 40.2 shows all these operations (read comments within code for explanations).

LISTING 40.2   Defining Code for Retrieving, Showing, and Saving Books Definitions

```
Imports System.Xml.Linq
Imports System.IO, System.Text
```

```vb
Imports System.IO.IsolatedStorage

Partial Public Class MainPage
    Inherits UserControl

    'Declaring a books collection
    Private MyBooks As BooksCollection

    'Required for understanding if the DataGrid
    'is in edit mode
    Private isEditing As Boolean = False

    Public Sub New()

        InitializeComponent()
    End Sub

    'Used to generate data if the data file is not
    'found
    Private Function CreateData() As BooksCollection
        Dim b As New Book With {.ISBN = "0000000"}

        Dim bc As New BooksCollection
        bc.Add(b)
        Return bc
    End Function


    'Attempts to read the data file from the isolated storage
    'If found, with a LINQ to Xml query a new books collection
    'is returned. If not found, a new empty collection is
    'generated and returned
    Private Function GetBooks() As BooksCollection
        Try
            Dim doc As XDocument

            Using store As IsolatedStorageFile = IsolatedStorageFile.
                                                 GetUserStoreForApplication
                Dim st As IsolatedStorageFileStream = _
                        store.OpenFile("Books.xml", FileMode.Open)
                doc = XDocument.Load(st)
                st.Close()
            End Using

            Dim query = From pbook In doc...<Book>
                        Select New Book With {.Author = pbook.@Author,
                                              .Title = pbook.@Title,
```

```vb
                                                .DatePublished = Date.
                                                Parse(pbook.@DatePublished),
                                                .ISBN = pbook.@ISBN
                    }

        Return New BooksCollection(query)


    Catch ex As Exception
        Return CreateData()
    End Try
End Function



Private Sub MainPage_Loaded(ByVal sender As Object,
                            ByVal e As System.Windows.
                            RoutedEventArgs) Handles Me.Loaded
    'Populates data
    Me.MyBooks = GetBooks()
    'Sets data-binding
    Me.DataContext = Me.MyBooks
End Sub

'Saves data to the isolated storage. The Xml data is generated
'with LINQ to Xml embedded-expressions
Private Sub SaveButton_Click(ByVal sender As System.Object,
                             ByVal e As System.Windows.
                             RoutedEventArgs) Handles SaveButton.Click
    Dim data = <?xml version="1.0" encoding="utf-8"?>
                <Books>
                    <%= From b In MyBooks
                        Select <Book Author=<%= b.Author %>
                                     Title=<%= b.Title %>
                                     ISBN=<%= b.ISBN %>
                                     DatePublished=<%= b.DatePublished.
                                                        ToString %>/>
                    %>
                </Books>

    Using store As IsolatedStorageFile = IsolatedStorageFile.
                                         GetUserStoreForApplication
        Dim st As IsolatedStorageFileStream = _
                store.OpenFile("Books.xml", FileMode.Create)
        data.Save(st)
        st.Close()
    End Using
End Sub
```

```
    Private Sub BooksGrid_BeginningEdit(ByVal sender As Object,
                                ByVal e As System.Windows.Controls.
                                DataGridBeginningEditEventArgs) _
                                Handles BooksGrid.BeginningEdit
        isEditing = True
    End Sub


    'Allows DataGrid editing
    Private Sub BooksGrid_KeyDown(ByVal sender As Object,
                            ByVal e As System.Windows.Input.
                            KeyEventArgs) Handles BooksGrid.KeyDown
        If isEditing = False Then
            'If the user press Delete, removes the selected item
            If e.Key = Key.Delete Then

                If Me.BooksGrid.SelectedItem IsNot Nothing Then
                    Me.MyBooks.Remove(CType(Me.BooksGrid.SelectedItem, Book))
                End If
                'If the user press Insert, adds a new empty item to the collection
            ElseIf e.Key = Key.Insert Then
                Dim b As New Book With {.DatePublished = Today}
                Dim index As Integer = MyBooks.IndexOf(CType(Me.BooksGrid.
                                                        SelectedItem, Book))

                MyBooks.Insert(index + 1, b)
                BooksGrid.SelectedIndex = index
                BooksGrid.BeginEdit()
            End If
        End If
    End Sub


    Private Sub BooksGrid_RowEditEnding(ByVal sender As Object,
                                ByVal e As System.Windows.Controls.
                                DataGridRowEditEndingEventArgs) _
                                Handles BooksGrid.RowEditEnding
        isEditing = False
    End Sub
End Class
```

Now right-click the **BookStoreTestPage.Aspx** file in Solution Explorer and set it as the start page. Our application is now ready to be started. One of the biggest benefits of the Windows Azure SDK tools is that you can test your application locally before you deploy it to the cloud. This is possible because of the Windows Azure Simulation Environment that is a full-featured environment reproducing locally the cloud system.

Testing the Application Locally

When you run an Azure application locally for the first time, the environment needs to be initialized. Fortunately Visual Studio and the Windows Azure SDK will do the work for you. The first thing you notice is that the tools generate a new database on your machine; this is required for storing blobs, tables, and queues. This step also reserves local ports for reaching the previously mentioned contents locally. You can see this when you press **F5**. The Windows Azure Simulation Environment is started, and a dialog shows the progress of the database generation and IPs initialization, as represented in Figure 40.6.

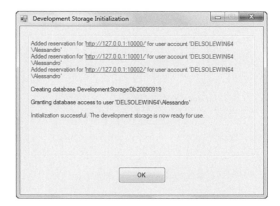

FIGURE 40.6   Completion of the Simulation Environment initialization.

This also creates a local developer account that replicates on your local machine what you can activate on the online services. After you click **OK**, you can see the application correctly running in your web browser. Figure 40.7 demonstrates this.

You can now try to add or delete other books and finally save changes. So we reached our objective locally. The next step should be deploying the application to the cloud, but doing making this, here's some brief information about the Simulation Environment tools. The Simulation Environment is essentially composed of two main tools: the Development Storage, which is used for locally storing blobs, tables, and queues, and the Development Fabric that is useful for monitoring running services. The Simulation Environment provides a tray bar icon that you can right-click to access both tools. Figure 40.8 displays how the Development Fabric gives information about the running application.

It is worth mentioning that the Development Fabric can show information about multiple running Azure services. Figure 40.9 shows instead the Development Storage UI. Notice that here you can just enable or disable endpoints for blobs, tables, and queues, but the suggestion is to leave unchanged the default settings.

Because the application runs correctly, we can now deploy it to the cloud environment of Windows Azure.

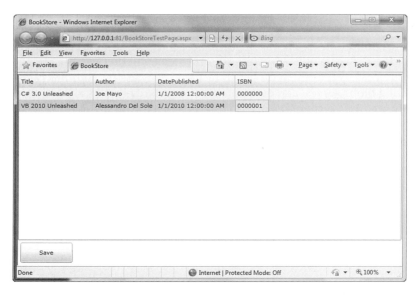

FIGURE 40.7   The application running locally.

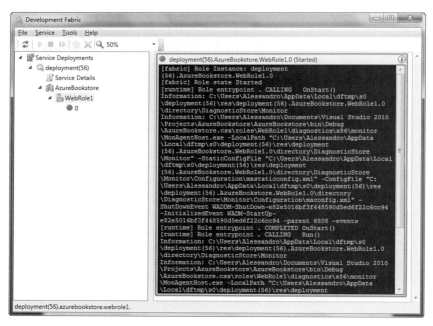

FIGURE 40.8   The Development Fabric shows services information.

FIGURE 40.9   The Development Storage user interface.

Deploying Applications to Windows Azure

Deploying applications to Windows Azure is basically a publishing process similar to the one that involves classic ASP.NET applications, but it differs in the target place (the cloud) and in the application files. Right-click the Azure project in Solution Explorer (in our example it is AzureBookstore) and click **Publish** in the pop-up menu. Visual Studio generates a Publish subfolder under the Bin\Debug or Bin\Release (depending on your output configuration) where required files are stored; moreover, Visual Studio launches Windows Explorer pointing to this new folder so that you can easily understand what files are required. Also, Visual Studio launches your Web browser opening the Windows Azure Developer Portal (http://windows.azure.com) on the Internet, which is the place where you administer deployments. This requires you to log in with your Windows Live ID. Figure 40.10 shows the login page.

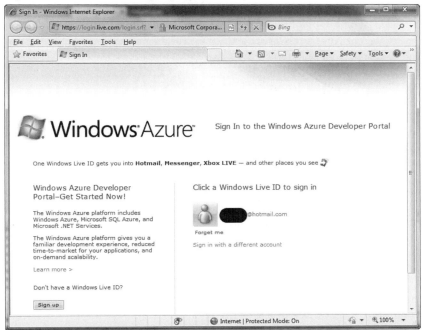

FIGURE 40.10   The login page to the Windows Azure Developer Portal.

When logged in, you can choose what cloud services you want to administer (for example Windows Azure, .NET Services, or SQL Azure) other than seeing available projects, if any. Figure 40.11 shows this Welcome page.

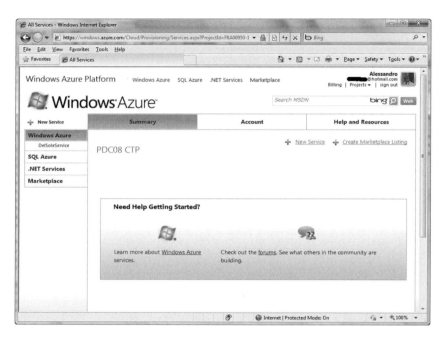

FIGURE 40.11 The Welcome page in the Windows Azure Developer Portal.

Ensure that Windows Azure is selected on the left. Now click the **New Service** link. This opens a new page where you can decide to create a new Hosted Service (that enables deploying a Web application) or a new Storage Account (which enables creating storages for blobs, tables, and queues), as shown in Figure 40.12.

Click Hosted Services to publish the sample application. In next page you need to type a label and a description for the service. See Figure 40.13 for an example.

Click **Next**. The subsequent step is really important because it is the place where you can customize your application's address on the Internet. Windows Azure's domain is http://CustomName.cloudapp.net, where **CustomName** is the name you provide for your application. In this example I'm using my name, so the complete application address will be alessandrodelsole.cloudapp.net. Replace my name with yours and check if the address is available with the **Check Availability** button. You can then choose the data center location, such as northern and southern regions in the United States. By the way, for this example select **Anywhere US**, as shown in Figure 40.14.

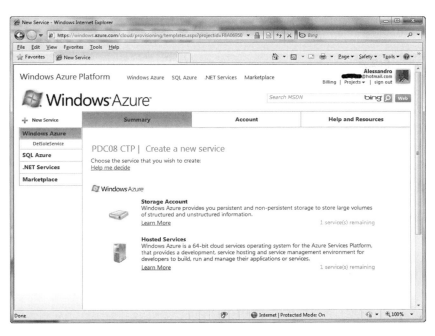

FIGURE 40.12 Choosing between a storage account and a hosted service.

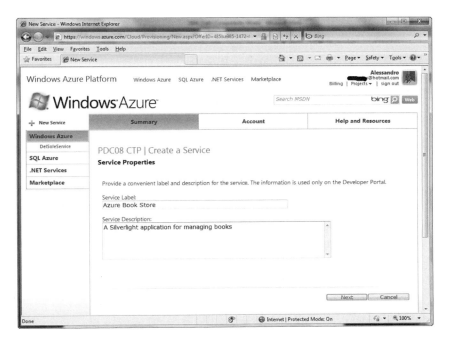

FIGURE 40.13 Providing service label and description.

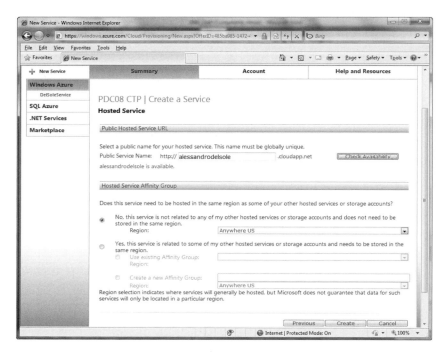

FIGURE 40.14   Specifying the application address.

When you click Create, the new service is created and ready to receive the application deployment. The deployment can be of two types: staging and production, as also represented in Figure 40.15.

The Staging deployment is intended for configuration and testing purposes. After ensuring all works correctly, you can move the application to the Production state. You could also directly deploy your application to the Production state, but this is not always the best choice. Now click the **Deploy** button for the Staging deployment. On the next page you have to specify the Application Package and the Configuration Settings. Both files are stored in the Publish folder previously described. As an alternative you can indicate files from an online Azure storage. The application package is a file with .cspkg extension and contains all the required application files in one package. The configuration file has .cscfg extension and contains information on the web roles involved in your application. Figure 40.16 shows how you indicate both files with regard to the current example.

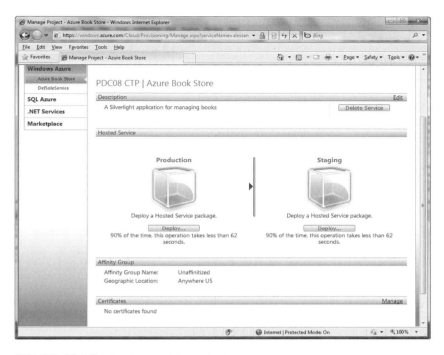

FIGURE 40.15   Deployment types in Azure.

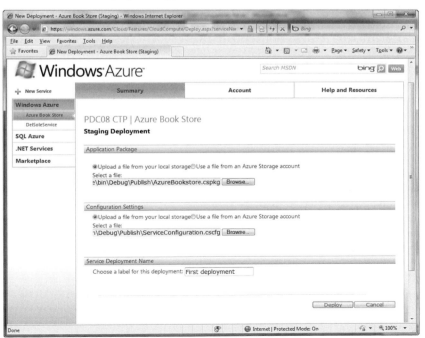

FIGURE 40.16   Providing deployment information.

Also specify a label for the current deployment. This is free text. At this point you can click the **Deploy** button and wait until the deployment process is completed; this process can last several minutes, so be patient. When the process is finished, the application is not running yet. Click **Run** to make your application run in the Staging deployment and wait until the WebRole1 shows a green circle and the Ready word (see Figure 40.17).

There is a new link named Web Site URL. This is a temporary address for your application that you can use for your testing purposes. If you click it, the Web browser will attempt to run the application in its staging state, but in this particular example, you will see nothing. The reason is that, obviously, the Web browser searches for the Default.aspx page that is empty in our example because we created a new page for hosting a Silverlight page. Append /BookStoreTestPage.Aspx to the web address. After a few seconds, the sample application is correctly shown in the Web browser, as demonstrated in Figure 40.18.

REPLACING THE DEFAULT.ASPX PAGE

If you want to make your Silverlight application start automatically, in Solution Explorer remove the Default.aspx page and rename the test page for Silverlight (in our example it is named **BookStoreTestPage.Aspx**) into **Default.Aspx** and set it as the start page.

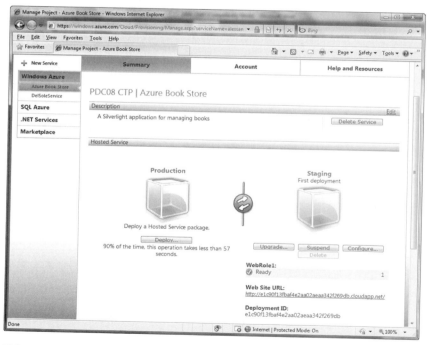

FIGURE 40.17   The staging deployment is completed.

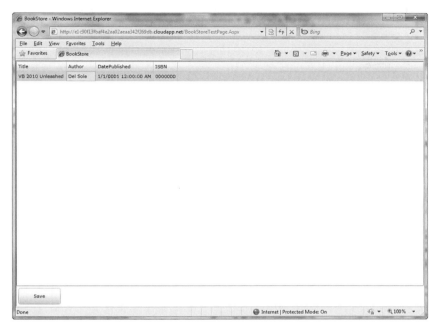

FIGURE 40.18   The sample application running in the staging context.

Close the Web browser to return to the Azure administration page. If you want to edit the application configuration file, click **Configure**. This opens a new page showing the configuration file content within an editable text box. Click **Suspend** if you want to stop running the application keeping it in the cloud; instead click **Upgrade** if you want to upload a new version of the application. At this point, supposing all works correctly, we can move the application to the production state, by simply clicking the rounded button at the center of the page. After a few seconds the application is available on the cloud, and it is reachable on the Internet (see Figure 40.19 for details).

Now you can finally run the application on the cloud. The sample application is, in this case, http://alessandrodelsole.cloudapp.net. To ensure the correct page is shown, the full address is http://alessandrodelsole.cloudapp.net/BookStoreTestPage.Aspx. Figure 40.20 shows the application running from the Windows Azure location.

With a few steps you successfully published a Web application to Windows Azure making it reachable from the Internet. If you plan on building data-centric applications requiring SQL Server database, the suggestion is that you visit the SQL Azure Developer Portal where you can find lots of information about creating and consuming databases on the cloud. You can find the portal here: http://msdn.microsoft.com/en-us/sqlserver/dataservices/default.aspx.

40

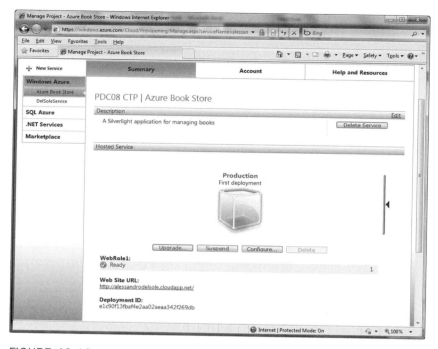

FIGURE 40.19   The application has been moved to the production deployment.

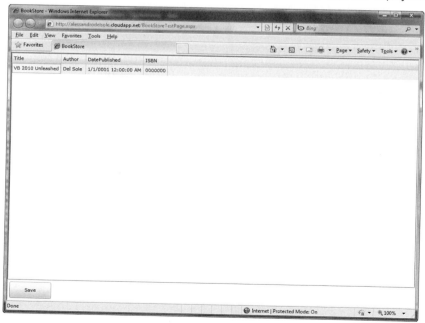

FIGURE 40.20   The application running from Windows Azure in the production deployment.

Activating the Storage Account

The second service available when you register to the Windows Azure Services Platform is the Storage Account. It provides a web space for uploading files (blob storage), for organizing simple data (tables storage), and for sending/receiving simple messages (queue storage). To enable your Storage Account, follow these steps:

1. Log into the Windows Azure Developer Portal and go to the services page shown in Figure 40.11;

2. Click **New Service**; when the Create New Service page is loaded, click **Storage Account**.

3. Provide a label and a description for your account; then click **Next**.

4. Type the public name that will be part of your account's URL and check for its availability, leaving unchanged the location options. Figure 40.21 shows an example.

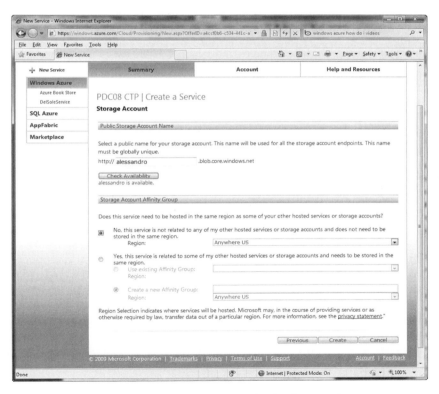

FIGURE 40.21   Specifying the public name for the Storage Account.

Now click **Create** so that the Storage Account creation is finalized. When you create the Storage Account, a Shared Key is also generated. This is a unique identifier that you need for accessing the storage from client applications and that is for login purposes. You can check this out by clicking the new account name on the left of the page, under the Windows Azure title. As mentioned when discussing local tests, a local developer account is also created and replicates locally what you can do with the online services. The local developer account has a built-in storage account with a prefixed user name (devstoreaccount1) and shared key, so for this you need to do nothing. About the online services, the Storage Account has the following endpoints:

▶ http://publicname.blob.core.windows.net for the blob storage

▶ http://publicname.queue.core.windows.net for the queue storage

▶ http://publicname.table.core.windows.net for the table storage

In the preceding bulleted list, publicname stands for the account public name you provided a few steps ago. Such endpoints are the way you access contents in the Storage Account via Http (or Https if available). For the local developer account, the endpoints will be the following (requires the Windows Azure Simulation Environment running):

▶ http://127.0.0.1:10000 for the blob storage

▶ http://127.0.0.1:10001 for the queue storage

▶ http://127.0.0.1:10002 for the tables storage

Because both the online and local services do not offer tools for managing contents on the Storage Account, you need to recur to external client tools or to build your own tool utilizing the Windows Azure SDK API. Fortunately there are several free tools, such as the Windows Azure Management Console Snap-in that is related to blobs and queues.

LEARNING VIDEOS

Microsoft produced several free "How-do-I" videos about learning to manage the Storage Account features. You can find them here: http://msdn.microsoft.com/en-us/azure/dd439432.aspx.

Using the Windows Azure Management Console Snap-In

Often you need to store files for your applications when deployed to Windows Azure. This can be accomplished in two ways, both as an administration task and programmatically. If you need to store files programmatically, look at the additional Windows Azure examples located on MSDN Code Gallery here: http://code.msdn.microsoft.com/windowsazuresamples and search for the **StorageClient** sample application, which implements code taking advantage of the REST APIs for managing the blob storage programmatically. If you instead need to upload files to the Blob storage as a simple repository for your applications, an easy way is installing the Windows Azure Management Console Snap-In. This can be found on Code Gallery and as well here: http://code.msdn.microsoft.com/windowsazuremmc. Download the compressed archive and extract it to a folder. Now run the StartHere.cmd file, which contains scripts for building the application and for installing the snap-in to the Microsoft Management Console in Windows.

IMPORTANT NOTE

The installation process requires the .NET Framework 3.5 SP 1 be installed on your machine. This is because the component is distributed in source code and the setup procedure will build the binary library for you. If you are running Windows 7 you do not need to install the framework.

When you run the utility, it looks like Figure 40.22.

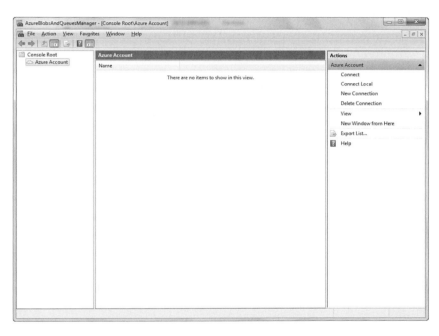

FIGURE 40.22   The Windows Azure MMC running.

The first step is establishing a connection to the local developer account or to the online services. For example, right-click on Azure Account and select the **New Connection** command. Now fill the text boxes in the dialog with your account name and key, as shown in Figure 40.23.

FIGURE 40.23   Adding a new online connection.

You notice that Service URLs will be automatically populated for you when writing the account name. When you click **OK** the connection is established, in this case to the online Storage Account. If you need a connection to the local developer account, simply select the **Local Connection** command. (You will not be prompted for credentials.) When ready, click on the **BLOB Containers** item in the left tree view control. This shows existing containers and enables you to add new containers. Basically a container is just a folder where you can upload files. In the Windows Azure terminology, files are called blobs. Figure 40.24 shows what I have on my Storage Account, which is a container named videos and where there is one file stored, as you can see at the bottom of the application.

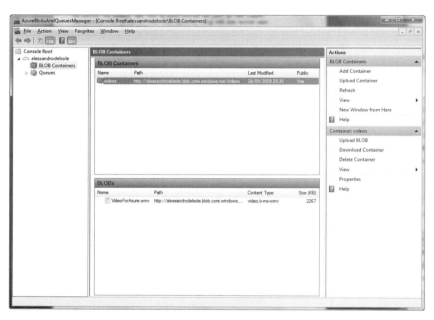

FIGURE 40.24   Showing containers and blobs in the Storage Account.

On the right side of the application, you can find a pane offering common commands. You can add a new container, upload an existing one, remove containers, or just upload and delete blobs. It is worth mentioning that when you create a new container you can make it public or private. If you mark it as private, you need your shared key to access it every time. If your container will store files that must be reached by all users, it will be marked as public. You can check this out by clicking the **Add Container** command from the right pane. Also notice that container names must be lowercase. If you try to type uppercase characters, they will be automatically converted into lowercase. After you have uploaded blobs to the Storage Account, you can access them simply via Http URLs. Continuing the example of my account, represented in Figure 40.24, to access the VideoForAzure.Wmv file, you simply need the following URL: http://alessandrodel-sole.blob.core.windows.net/videos/VideoForAzure.wmv. If it is a media or browsable content, you can type the address in your Web browser address bar or just use the URL in your applications according to your needs. In case your blobs are stored within the local developer account, you simply invoke them with the local URL, keeping in mind that the Windows Azure Simulation Environment must be running: `http://127.0.0.1:10000/VideoForAzure.Wmv`.

Summary

The Windows Azure Services Platform is the new cloud computing platform by Microsoft and includes several services such as Windows Azure, SQL Azure, and Windows Azure AppFabric. Windows Azure is a 64-bit operating system enabling Web applications to be hosted and running in a cloud environment. To develop applications for the cloud, you use Visual Studio 2010 that must be enabled installing the appropriate tools. After you install such tools and register for the Windows Azure services, you can begin developing and deploying applications. Basically you create ASP.NET Web applications or Silverlight applications that can be deployed to Azure. You can test your applications locally before deployment, due to the presence of the Windows Azure Simulation Environment that includes tools for locally running applications with the same environment that is on the cloud. This tooling is installed together with the Azure SDK and tools for Visual Studio. To publish a Web application to the Azure Services Platform you simply use Visual Studio instrumentation that redirects you to the appropriate page in the Windows Azure Developer Portal. When you get an account on Windows Azure, you obtain two services: the hosting service on Windows Azure, which allows publishing applications to the cloud, and the storage account. This is an additional service providing web space for storing online files (blob storage), simple data structures (tables storage), and messages (queue storage). You activate the storage account in the Azure Developer Portal, but you actually manage contents through external tools, such as the Windows Azure Management Console Snap-In that enables publishing blobs to the blob storage both locally and online.

40

Creating and Consuming WCF Services

During the years several technologies were developed for distributed applications that communicate over networks. The idea is that client applications can exchange information with a service via a network protocol such as the Http or TCP, just to mention some. Among these technologies there are SOAP (an Xml-based information exchange system), Microsoft Messaging Queue (a message-based system), the well-known Web services, and the .NET Remoting (which connects applications based on the .NET Framework). Although powerful, all these technologies have one limitation: Two or more applications can connect only if all of them rely on the same technology. Just for clarification, an application based on MSMQ cannot communicate with another one based on SOAP. To avoid this limitation, Microsoft created the Windows Communication Foundation (also known as WCF for brevity) technology that was first introduced with the .NET Framework 3.0 and that is basically a unified programming model for distributed applications. With WCF developers can write code for exchanging data and information between services and clients without worrying about how data is transmitted because this is the job of the .NET Framework. WCF is another big technology and covering every single aspect would require an entire book; therefore, in this chapter you learn about implementing, configuring, hosting, and consuming WCF services with Visual Basic 2010.

Introducing Windows Communication Foundation

WCF is a technology that enables data and information exchange between services and clients through messages. Basically the service exposes information through the network and is nothing but a .NET assembly. Then the client receives that information and can send back other information or data. In this section you learn how data exchange between the service and clients works before creating your first WCF service.

WCF 4

Windows Communication Foundation in .NET Framework 4 is also known as WCF 4, although this is actually the third version. There are some improvements in the new version of WCF, but we focus on them only when required, preferring to illustrate how you implement and consume services to make migration from previous versions easier.

This is important because you need to know some fundamentals about WCF infrastructure before putting your hands on the code. If you ever developed .NET Web Services (.asmx), you notice several similarities with WCF, at least in the implementation, but lots of things more under the hood make WCF more powerful. Moreover, although Web services are obviously still allowed and supported in .NET Framework 4.0, WCF is the main technology for data exchange through networks and is intended to be a replacement of Web services, even because WCF provides fully integrated support with client and Web applications, such as WPF and Silverlight.

Understanding Endpoints

A WCF service is a .NET assembly (in the form of dll) relying on the `System.ServiceModel` namespace and exposing objects and members like any other class library. Thus client applications can invoke members and use objects exposed by services. Behind the scenes this happens through message exchanges. Client and services exchange messages through *endpoints*. An endpoint is the place where client and service meet and is where both applications exchange their information, so it can be considered like a communication port. Each WCF service offers at least one endpoint; multiple endpoints serve as communication ports for different data types (for example .NET objects and messages). But every endpoint needs to be configured with some other information to be a functional place for meeting the needs of service and clients. The configuration is provided by the `Address`, `Binding`, and `Contract` as explained in the next section.

Address, Binding, Contract: The ABC of WCF

When a client application attempts to reach a service, it needs to know some information for finding the service and for data exchange. The service exposes such information via the ABC, which represents the *Address*, *Binding* and *Contract* properties in the service. The *Address* is the physical URI where the service is running. For example, on the local machine the Address could be http://localhost/MyService.svc or http://www.something.com/MyService.svc if the service is running on the Internet. The *Binding* property is a complex object and basically is responsible for

- ▶ Establishing how service and clients communicate (with a `Behavior` object)

- ▶ Establishing what protocol and credentials must be used within the communication

- ▶ Handling data transmission to the target (via a `Channel` object), converting data into an acceptable format, and transmitting data via the specified protocol (such as Http, Https, and so on)

The *Contract* is probably the most significant item in the ABC. It establishes what data can be exchanged and what .NET objects/members are exposed by the service and that the client must accept; this is defined as platform-independent because clients will just accept the contract without worrying about the code that implemented objects on the server side. If you think of classic managed class libraries, when you add a reference to a class library, you just want to use its members, but in most cases you will not worry about the code that implemented those members. With WCF it is basically the same thing. For code, a contract is a .NET interface that defines public members available from the service to clients. Such an interface is then implemented by a class that actually makes members available to the external world. All these concepts will be explained in code. There are different contract types in WCF, but the most important are summarized in Table 41.1.

TABLE 41.1   WCF Contracts

Contract	Description
ServiceContract	Provides the service skeleton and defines methods that will be available to the public
DataContract	Defines classes that will be available to the public as data objects
MessageContract	Used to exchange data with SOAP-based applications and serializes data into SOAP messages.

As you see in the next section, contracts are applied with special .NET attributes. The good news about the ABC is that all information is typically stored inside the configuration file and therefore can be edited with any text editor by system and network administrators too, without the need of recompiling the source code, which make services administration simpler. At this point you are ready to create your first WCF service with Visual Basic 2010.

Implementing WCF Services

Visual Studio 2010 offers some project templates for creating WCF projects. Table 41.2 lists them all.

TABLE 41.2   WCF Project Templates

Template	Description
WCF Service Application	Used for creating a self-hosted WCF service

TABLE 41.2   Continued

Template	Description
WCF Service Library	Used for creating a WCF service to be manually hosted and configured
WCF Workflow Service	Allows creating a WCF service with integration with Workflow Foundation
WCF Syndication Library	Generates a WCF service enabled for RSS syndication
WCF RIA Services Class Library	Only available within Silverlight projects, allows adding a WCF service with Silverlight integration

This book covers the WCF Service Application template that is useful because it provides service self-hosting. Basically a WCF service cannot be run or consumed as a standalone and must be hosted inside a .NET application. Host applications can be of several types: Console applications, Internet Information Services, and ASP.NET Development Server are all valid host applications. The WCF Service Application template provides hosting inside the ASP.NET Development Server that ships with Visual Studio and is appropriate for local testing purposes. Select the **File, New Project** command, and in the New Project dialog select the **WCF Service Application** template, as shown in Figure 41.1. Name the new project as **BookService** and then click **OK**.

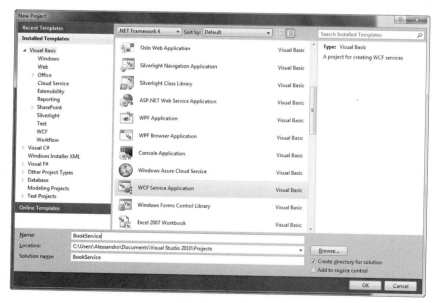

FIGURE 41.1   Creating a new WCF project.

The goal of the example is to offer a way for validating books' information, such as ISBN code, title, and author. The service exposes a Book class representing a single book and a method named `ValidateBook` that provides the validation logic. Before writing custom code, taking a look at the auto-generated code is a good idea for understanding what WCF needs. Visual Studio 2010 generated a Web project visible in Solution Explorer. The new project contains the following files:

- IService1.vb, which defines the contract interface

- Service1.svc.vb (nested into Service1.svc as a code-behind file), which defines the class that implements the contract

- Service1.svc, which is the actual service that exposes data and that is be consumed by clients

- Web.config, which provides definitions for the ABC

NOTE ON THE WEB.CONFIG FILE

With the .NET Framework 4.0 and Visual Studio 2010, the Web.config file does not contain a WCF metadata definition in case you use the default settings because they are considered as implicit. This is important with regard to the current example. If you decide instead to implement custom settings, the Web.config stores the metadata definition. Because configuration files in client applications reflect Web.config files from services, later in this chapter you see the client-side metadata definition mapping the implicit metadata of the current sample service.

Let's take a look at the IService1.vb file, which is reported in Listing 41.1 and that defines a couple of contracts.

LISTING 41.1   Auto-Generated Contracts

```
' NOTE: You can use the "Rename" command on the "Refactor" menu
' to change the interface name "IService1" in both code and
' config file together.
<ServiceContract()>
Public Interface IService1

    <OperationContract()>
    Function GetData(ByVal value As Integer) As String

    <OperationContract()>
    Function GetDataUsingDataContract(ByVal composite As _
                                      CompositeType) As CompositeType


    ' TODO: Add your service operations here

End Interface
```

```
' Use a data contract as illustrated in the sample below
' to add composite types to service operations.
<DataContract()>
Public Class CompositeType

    <DataMember()>
    Public Property BoolValue() As Boolean

    <DataMember()>
    Public Property StringValue() As String
End Class
```

The `IService1` interface is decorated with the `ServiceContract` attribute, meaning that it establishes what members the service defines and makes available to the public. The interface defines two methods, both decorated with the `OperationContract` attribute. Such attribute makes methods visible to the external world and consumable by clients. You need to remember that in WCF marking a method as `Public` is not sufficient to make it available to clients; it needs to be marked as `OperationContract` to be visible. Methods exposed by WCF services are also known as *service operations*, and this definition will be recalled in the next chapter with regard to WCF Data Services. Notice how the `GetDataUsingDataContract` method receives an argument of type `CompositeType`. This type is a custom class declared as `DataContract`, meaning that the WCF service can exchange data of this type. Members from this class also need to be marked as `DataMember` to be visible to the external world. As for service operations, marking a member as `Public` is not sufficient; you need to decorate members with the `DataMember` attribute. The `Service1` class shows an example of implementing the contract and the logic for service operations. Listing 41.2 shows the auto-generated sample code.

LISTING 41.2   Auto-Generated Contracts Implementation

```
' NOTE: You can use the "Rename" command on the "Refactor" menu to
' change the class name "Service1" in code, svc and config file together.
Public Class Service1
    Implements IService1

    Public Sub New()
    End Sub

    Public Function GetData(ByVal value As Integer) As String _
                Implements IService1.GetData
        Return String.Format("You entered: {0}", value)
    End Function

    Public Function GetDataUsingDataContract(ByVal composite As CompositeType) As _
                CompositeType Implements IService1.GetDataUsingDataContract
```

```
        If composite Is Nothing Then
            Throw New ArgumentNullException("composite")
        End If
        If composite.BoolValue Then
            composite.StringValue &= "Suffix"
        End If
        Return composite
    End Function
End Class
```

The class just implements the contract interface and provides logic for service operations working like any other .NET class. The content of the .svc file is discussed later; for now let's make some edits to the code replacing the auto-generated one with custom implementation.

Implementing Custom Logic for the WCF Service

Rename the IService1.vb file to **IBookService.vb** and then switch to the code editor. Right-click the IService1 identifier and select **Rename**; finally provide the new IBookService identifier and click **OK**. Visual Studio will prompt for confirmation and will rename the instances in code as well. This is important to update all references inside the project to the interface, including references inside the .Svc file. Now delete the code for the CompositeType class and replace the entire code with the one shown in Listing 41.3.

LISTING 41.3   Implementing Custom Contracts

```
<ServiceContract()>
Public Interface IBookService

    <OperationContract()>
    Function ValidateBook(ByVal bookToValidate As Book) As String

End Interface

<DataContract()>
Public Class Book

    <DataMember()>
    Public Property Title As String

    <DataMember()>
    Public Property ISBN As String

    <DataMember()>
    Public Property Author As String

    <DataMember()>
```

```
        Public Property DatePublished As Date?
End Class
```

The `IBookService` contract simply defines a `ValidateBook` method that will be invoked for validating a book. A single book is represented by the `Book` class, which exposes four self-explanatory properties. Now switch to the `Service1` class and, following the steps described before, rename the `Service1` identifier into `BookService`. Then replace the auto-generated code with the one shown in Listing 41.4.

LISTING 41.4   Implementing the Service Logic

```vb
Imports System.Text.RegularExpressions
Public Class BookService
    Implements IBookService

    Private Const isbnPattern As String = _
    "ISBN(?:-13)?:?\x20*(?=.{17}$)97(?:8¦9)([ -])\d{1,5}\1\d{1,7}\1\d{1,6}\1\d$"

    Public Function ValidateBook(ByVal bookToValidate As Book) As _
                String Implements IBookService.ValidateBook

        Dim isValidIsbn As Boolean = Regex.IsMatch(String.Concat("ISBN-13: ",
                                                    bookToValidate.ISBN),
                                                    isbnPattern)

        If isValidIsbn = False Then
            Return "Invalid ISBN"
        End If

        Dim isValidAuthor As Boolean = String.IsNullOrEmpty(bookToValidate.Author)
        If isValidAuthor = True Then
            Return "Author not specified"
        End If

        Dim isValidTitle As Boolean = String.IsNullOrEmpty(bookToValidate.Title)
        If isValidTitle = True Then
            Return "Title not specified"
        End If

        If bookToValidate.DatePublished Is Nothing Then
            Return "Book data is valid but date published was not specified"
        End If

        Return "Valid book"
    End Function
End Function
```

```
End Class
```

The code for the `ValidateBook` method is quite simple. It makes use of a regular expression for checking if the ISBN code is valid and then goes ahead checking for valid properties in the `Book` class instance that must be validated.

NOTE ON THE REGULAR EXPRESSION PATTERN

The regular expression pattern for checking ISBNs is from the RegExLibrary website at the following address: http://regexlib.com/REDetails.aspx?regexp_id=1748. There are a lot of patterns for validating ISBNs; the one used in this book is just an example and you can replace it with a different one.

Now right-click the **BookService.svc** file in Solution Explorer; select **View in Browser**. In a few seconds the WCF service will be hosted by the ASP.NET Development Server and will run inside the Web browser, as demonstrated in Figure 41.2.

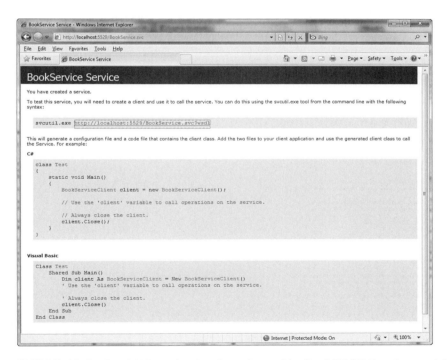

FIGURE 41.2   The WCF service has been hosted by the ASP.NET Development Server and is now running.

This test is required to ensure that the service works correctly. Notice how information is provided on how consuming the service is. The web page shows information explaining that you should invoke the **SvcUtil.exe** command-line tool pointing to the wdsl metadata of the service.

SvcUtil is described in next section; for the moment click the link available near SvcUtil.exe. By doing so you access metadata offered by the WCF service, including contracts and members, as reported in Figure 41.3.

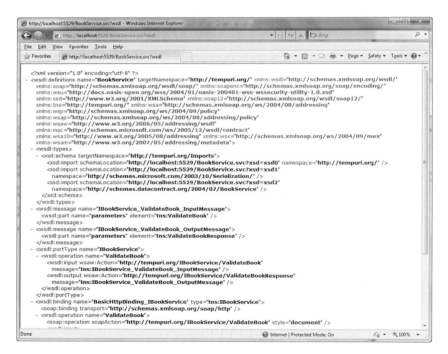

FIGURE 41.3   Exploring the service's metadata.

Basically client applications invoke service members passing through the service metadata. The next section explains how you invoke service members through a proxy class, but before going into that let's take a look at the BookService.svc file.

EXPOSING GENERICS IN WCF

Since WCF services metadata are exposed via WSDL, there are some issues with generics that are not supported by this. I suggest you read this blog post by MVP Jeff Barnes that provides explanations and workarounds: http://bit.ly/4CzGv3. Another suggestion is to investigate how WCF Data Services work for exposing entities (see Chapter 42, "Implementing and Consuming SCF Data Services," for in formation about Data Services).

Right-click this file and select **View Markup**. The XHTML code for this file is the following:

```
<%@ ServiceHost Language="VB" Debug="true"
    Service="BookService.BookService" CodeBehind="BookService.svc.vb" %>
```

This file defines the service entry point. Particularly it states that the BookService class is the service entry point because it defines the real logic that implements the contract. There is some other information such as the programming language used and the code-behind the file, but the Service tag is absolutely the most important. After this overview of the service implementation, it's time to consume the service from a client application.

EXPOSING ENTITY DATA MODELS AND LINQ TO SQL CLASSES

WCF services are also used to expose Entity Data Models and LINQ to SQL classes via serialization. Entities and their members in EDMs are marked by default respectively with the DataContract and DataMember attributes, whereas LINQ to SQL classes have to be enabled for serialization by setting the Serialization Mode property of the DataContext class as Unidirectional and then marking entities with DataContract. In Chapter 42 you learn about WCF Data Services that provide an easy implementation of WCF services by exposing data models without the need of making such customizations manually. Thus you should create custom WCF services for exposing data models only when you need to handle special scenarios that require implementing different business logic than the one offered by Data Services.

Consuming WCF Services

Clients can easily consume WCF services by adding a service reference directly from Visual Studio 2010. In the next example you create a simple Console client application for validating ISBNs by invoking objects from the WCF service implemented in the previous section.

Creating the Client and Adding a Service Reference

Add a new Console project to the current solution and name it **BookClient**. The first step you have to accomplish is adding a service reference to the WCF service. Right-click the new project name in Solution Explorer and select **Add Service Reference**. This brings up the Add Service Reference dialog where you need to enter the full Web address of your service. If the service you want to add a reference to is available in the current solution, as in the current example, simply click **Discover**. The service appears in the dialog, as shown in Figure 41.4.

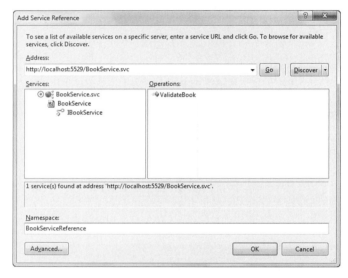

FIGURE 41.4   The Add Service Reference dialog enables adding a reference to a WCF service.

Click the service name on the left to allow the development server to correctly host the service and discover its members. At this point the dialog lists available contracts (IBookService in this case) and their members. Replace the Namespace identifier with BookServiceReference.

Understanding the Proxy Class

The WCF service is exposed through the network via a WSDL. To consume objects and data exposed by the WSDL, the client needs a proxy class that is responsible for translating WSDL information into managed code that you can reuse. This is accomplished via a command-line tool named SvcUtil.exe that is part of the .NET Framework. Fortunately you do not need to run SvcUtil manually because Visual Studio will do the work for you. When you click **OK** from the Add Service Reference dialog, Visual Studio invokes SvcUtil and generates a proxy class. You notice, in Solution Explorer, a new folder named Service references. This folder contains all service references and, for the current example, it stores a new item named BookServiceReference. This new item provides all metadata information required to consume the service and especially the proxy class. Click the **Show All Files** button in Solution Explorer and expand the **Reference.svcmap** file; then double-click the **Reference.vb** file. This code file exposes the BookServiceReference namespace to provide client-side code for accessing members exposed from the service. Particularly this namespace exposed client-side implementations of the Book class and the IBookService interface. The most important class exposed by the namespace is named BookServiceClient and is the actual proxy class, which inherits from System.ServiceModel.ClientBase, and which is responsible for connecting to the service and for closing the connection other than exposing service members such as the ValidateBook that was implemented on the service side. The namespace also exposes the IBookServiceChannel interface that inherits from IClientChannel, which provides members for the request/reply infrastructure required by WCF services. You instantiate the proxy class to establish a connection with the WCF service, and you interact with the proxy class for accessing members from the service, as explained in next section.

Invoking Members from the Service

To invoke service members, you need to create an instance of the proxy class, which in our example is named BookClient.BookServiceReference.BookServiceClient. Creating an instance of the class can establish a connection to the WCF service and give you access to public members. Continuing with the previous example, the client application could have an instance of the Book class and invoking the ValidateBook method for checking if the Book instance is correct according to our needs. Code in Listing 41.5 shows how to accomplish this.

LISTING 41.5   Instantiating the Proxy Class and Invoking Service Members

```
Imports BookClient.BookServiceReference


Module Module1

    Sub Main()
        'Creates an instance of the proxy class
        'and automatically establishes a connection
        'to the service
        Dim client As New BookServiceClient

        'A new book
        'Note that the RegEx pattern requires to write the ISBN in the form
        'provided below, so like: 000-0-0000-0000-0 including the minus
        'character
        Dim myBook As New Book
        With myBook
            .Author = "Alessandro Del Sole"
```

```
        .Title = "VB 2010 Unleashed"
        .ISBN = "978-0-6723-3100-8
"
        .DatePublished = Date.Today
    End With

    'Invokes the ValidateBook method from
    'the service
    Console.WriteLine(client.ValidateBook(myBook))
    Console.WriteLine("Done")
    Console.ReadLine()
    client.Close()

    End Sub
End Module
```

Therefore in the client you can invoke all public members from the service, where public means functions decorated with the `OperationContract` attribute and data classes decorated with the `DataContract` attribute. Running the code in Listing 41.5 produces the result shown in Figure 41.5, but you can try to change the ISBN code to check how the application works with different values.

FIGURE 41.5   The client application validated a book.

Remember to close the connection to the service invoking the `Close` method on the proxy class. This ensures that the service will be shut down.

Understanding the Configuration File

When you add a proxy class to your WCF service, Visual Studio also updates the configuration file to provide information on how to reach and interact with the service. The most important information is stored in the `System.ServiceModel` section of the **app.config** file. Listing 41.6 shows the most interesting excerpt.

LISTING 41.6   Configuration Settings for the Client

```
<system.serviceModel>
    <bindings>
        <basicHttpBinding>
            <binding name="BasicHttpBinding_IBookService"
                closeTimeout="00:01:00"
                openTimeout="00:01:00" receiveTimeout="00:10:00"
                sendTimeout="00:01:00"
                allowCookies="false" bypassProxyOnLocal="false"
                hostNameComparisonMode="StrongWildcard"
                maxBufferSize="65536" maxBufferPoolSize="524288"
                maxReceivedMessageSize="65536"
                messageEncoding="Text" textEncoding="utf-8"
                transferMode="Buffered"
                useDefaultWebProxy="true">
                <readerQuotas maxDepth="32" maxStringContentLength="8192"
                    maxArrayLength="16384"
                    maxBytesPerRead="4096" maxNameTableCharCount="16384" />
                <security mode="None">
                    <transport clientCredentialType="None"
                        proxyCredentialType="None"
                        realm="" />
                    <message clientCredentialType="UserName"
                            algorithmSuite="Default" />
                </security>
            </binding>
        </basicHttpBinding>
    </bindings>
    <client>
        <endpoint address="http://localhost:5529/BookService.svc"
            binding="basicHttpBinding"
            bindingConfiguration="BasicHttpBinding_IBookService"
            contract="BookServiceReference.IBookService"
            name="BasicHttpBinding_IBookService" />
    </client>
</system.serviceModel>
```

Substantially the app.config file maps the related nodes in the Web.config file from the service. This is important to remember in case you want to implement a custom configuration different from the default one. The bindings node defines how data and information are transferred. The basicHttpBinding binding is the simplest way and uses Http protocol and Text or Xml as the encoding format. WCF offers lots of other bindings specific for particular needs, such as secured communications or peer-to-peer applications. Table 41.3 summarizes built-in bindings.

TABLE 41.3   WCF Built-In Bindings

Binding	Description
BasicHttpBinding	Used for ASP.NET-based Web services. It uses the HTTP protocol and text or XML for messages encoding.
WSHttpBinding	Used for secured communications in nonduplex service contracts.
WSDualHttpBinding	Used for secured communications in duplex service contracts including SOAP.
WSFederationHttpBinding	Used for secured communications according to the WS-Federation protocol that provides an easy authentication and authorization system within a federation.
NetTcpBinding	Used for secured communications between WCF applications distributed across multiple machines.
NetNamedPipeBinding	Used for secured communications between WCF applications on a same machine.
NetMsmqBinding	Used for messaging communications between WCF applications.
NetPeerTcpBinding	Used for peer-to-peer applications.
MsmqIntegrationBinding	Used for communications between WCF applications and MSMQ applications across multiple machines.
BasicHttpContextBinding	Similar to BasicHttpBinding but with the capability of enabling cookies.
NetTcpContextBinding	Used for communications between WCF applications that need to use SOAP headers for data exchange across multiple machines.
WebHttpBinding	Used for WCF services exposed via endpoints requiring HTTP requests instead of SOAP endpoints.
WSHttpContextBinding	Similar to WsHttpBinding with the ability of enabling SOAP headers for information exchange.

In addition to built-in bindings, WCF enables defining custom bindings, but this is beyond of the scope of this chapter.

IMPLEMENTING SECURE BINDINGS ON BOTH SERVICE AND CLIENTS

The current code example makes use, on both the service and client side, of the basicHttpBinding, which is the simplest binding available. Using a different binding strictly depends on the particular scenario you need to work on. Because of this, look at the official MSDN documentation related to built-in bindings, which also provides examples and explanations on when each binding should be used. The documentation is located at the following address:

http://msdn.microsoft.com/en-us/library/ms730879(VS.100).aspx.

Notice how you can customize timeouts (`closeTimeout`, `openTimeout`, `sendTimeout`, and `receiveTimeOut`) and other interesting options such as `maxBufferSize` and `maxReceivedMessageSize`. These two are important because you might be required to increase the default size in case your application transfers big amounts of data. Now take a look at the `client` node. This defines the endpoint's ABC, such as the address pointing to the physical URI of the service, the contract interface (`BookServiceReference.IBookService`), and the binding transport protocol. Notice that when moving the service to production, the address URI must be replaced with the Internet/intranet address of your service. This can be accomplished by simply replacing the `address` item in the configuration file without the need of rebuilding the application.

Handling Exceptions in WCF

WCF applications can throw communication exceptions that both services and clients need to handle. Typically the most common exception in the WCF development is the `System.ServiceModel.FaultException` that offers a generic, strongly typed flavor and a nongeneric one. The exception needs to be first handled in the WCF service but the nongeneric implementation is less useful than the generic one because it provides less detailed information. Because of this we now consider how to handle the `FaultException(Of T)`. Replace the `ValidateBook` method definition in the `IBookService` interface as follows:

```
<OperationContract()> <FaultContract(GetType(Book))>
Function ValidateBook(ByVal bookToValidate As Book) As String
```

The `FaultContract` attribute receives the type that may encounter processing errors during the invocation of the service operation. This can allow the `FaultException` to throw detailed SOAP information for that type. To accomplish this, replace the `ValidateBook` method implementation in the `BookService` class with the following:

```
Public Function ValidateBook(ByVal bookToValidate As Book) As _
            String Implements IBookService.ValidateBook

    Try
        Dim isValidIsbn As Boolean = Regex.IsMatch(String.
                            Concat("ISBN-13: ",
                            bookToValidate.ISBN), isbnPattern)

        If isValidIsbn = False Then
            Return "Invalid ISBN"
        End If

        Dim isValidAuthor As Boolean = _
            String.IsNullOrEmpty(bookToValidate.Author)
        If isValidAuthor = True Then
            Return "Author not specified"
```

```
            End If

            Dim isValidTitle As Boolean = _
                String.IsNullOrEmpty(bookToValidate.Title)
            If isValidTitle = True Then
                Return "Title not specified"
            End If

            If bookToValidate.DatePublished Is Nothing Then
                Return _
                "Book data is valid but date published was not specified"
            End If

            Return "Valid book"

        Catch ex As FaultException(Of Book)
            Throw New FaultException(Of Book)(bookToValidate, _
                                        ex.Reason, ex.Code)
        Catch ex As Exception
            Throw
        End Try
End Function
```

The intercepted FaultException is rethrown to the caller specifying the instance of the Book class that caused the error, a Reason property that contains a SOAP description of the problem, and a Code property that returns a machine-readable identifier used for understanding the problem. With these pieces of information, client applications can understand what the problem was during the communication.

Hosting WCF Services in Internet Information Services

Host applications for WCF services can be of different kinds. Other than the ASP.NET Development Server, you can host services inside managed applications, Windows services, and Internet Information Services as well. In most cases the need will be to deploy to IIS so we will cover this scenario. To host your WCF service in IIS on your development machine, follow these steps:

1. Restart Visual Studio 2010 under administrator privileges.
2. Go to the My Project designer for the WCF service project and select the **Web** tab.
3. Check the **Use Local IIS Web Server** option and specify, if required, a different directory; then rerun the WCF service (see Figure 41.6).

Visual Studio will request your permission for creating and configuring a virtual directory on IIS so you just need to accept. When this is done, remember to replace the endpoint

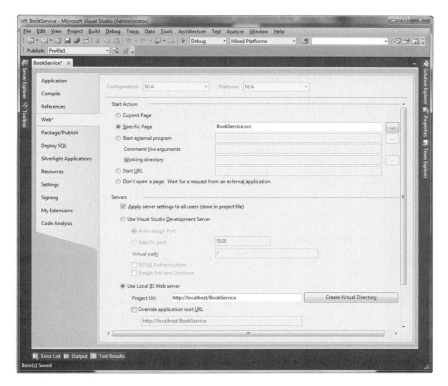

FIGURE 41.6   Setting IIS as the deployment Web server.

address in the client application configuration file with the new service URI. To host a WCF service on a nondevelopment machine, you need to create a directory under the Default Website and link the physical folder to the folder where the .svc file is placed together with the compiled dll service. This is accomplished via the Internet Information Services Manager administrative tools available in the Windows operating system.

Configuring Services with the Configuration Editor

WCF services enable high-level customizations over their configuration. This task can be complex if you consider that there are hundreds of options that you should translate into Xml markup. Fortunately the .NET Framework offers a graphical tool called WCF Service Configuration Editor that you can also launch from the Tools menu in Visual Studio. In this section you see how this tool can be used for enabling tracing for WCF services. Tracing is useful because it enables recording into log file (with .svclog extension) events occurring during the WCF service running time. When launched, open the Web.config file for your service. When ready click the **Diagnostics** folder on the left and then click the **Enable Tracing** command under the Tracing title on the right (see Figure 41.7).

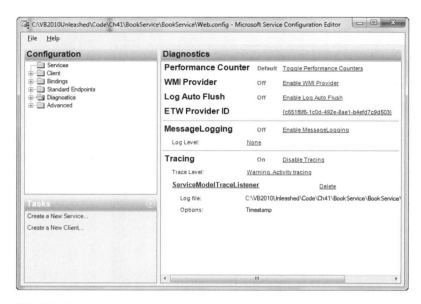

FIGURE 41.7   Enabling tracing for WCF services.

By default tracing records messages classified at least as warnings. To modify this behavior simply click the **Trace Level** link. If you click the **ServiceModelTraceListener** link you can also specify additional information to be tracked, such as the process ID, the call stack, and the Thread ID. To view the log of recorded information you need to run the Service Trace Viewer tool that is available in the shortcuts folder for Visual Studio in the Windows' All Programs menu. When the tool is running, open the .svclog file, which usually resides in the service folder. Figure 41.8 shows an example of log analysis.

The tool provides tons of information about every event occurring at the service level and is helpful if you encounter any problems.

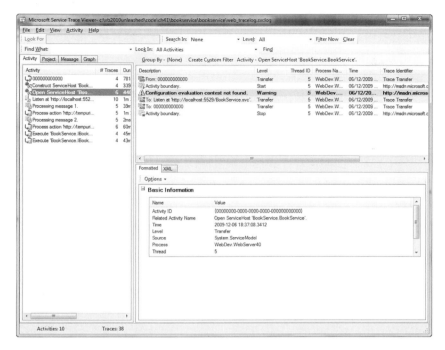

FIGURE 41.8   The Service Trace Viewer tool in action.

Summary

Windows Communication Foundation is a unified programming model for distributed applications that share information across networks. In this chapter you got started with WCF, getting an introductive overview and then learning the basics about metadata. Particularly you learned that WCF services expose endpoints to be accessible from clients and that each endpoint exposes the so-called ABC, which stands for Address-Binding-Contract. The contract is a .NET interface (marked with the ServiceContract attribute) that establishes service operations that can be consumed by clients. Services expose information and data through a class that implements the contract, and that is the main entry point in the service. WCF services can expose also objects marked with the DataContract attribute and that represent data that service and clients can exchange. Next you understood how to consume WCF services from clients by adding service references and creating proxy classes to access service members. The last part of this chapter provided an overview of exceptions handling and particular configurations with specific tools such as the Configuration Editor and the Service Trace Viewer.

CHAPTER 42

Implementing and Consuming WCF Data Services

The growth of networks such as the Internet or local Intranets raised even more the need of implementing infrastructures for data exchange between companies or among users. Windows Communication Foundation introduced an important unified programming model for information exchange over networks, but implementing a custom logic is not always an easy task. For this, Microsoft created an extraordinary platform named WCF Data Services, formerly named WCF Data Services, which takes advantage of the WCF technology for specifically exposing and consuming data over networks with a unified programming model that can propagate different kinds of data sources based on the .NET Framework and that can offer such infrastructure to the most common client applications types. In this chapter you start to build REST-enabled, data-oriented applications with WCF Data Services.

What Are Data Services?

WCF Data Services are one of the latest data access technologies created by Microsoft and was first introduced with .NET Framework 3.5 Service Pack 1, whereas the .NET Framework 4 introduces some new features to the platform. Data Services are also known as Project Astoria, which is the code name for the data platform, and the development team is also known as Astoria Team. WCF Data Services are basically a framework for exposing data through networks such as the Internet or a local intranet and are based on the Windows Communication Foundation technology. At a higher level, Data Services are REST-enabled WCF services in that they support the Representational State Transfer programming model that enables querying data via http requests. WCF Data Services can propagate through networks several kinds of data sources, such as entity data models or in-memory collections that can be consumed by several kinds of client applications, both Windows and Web, such as WPF, Windows Forms, Silverlight, and ASP.NET Ajax. This data access technology is particularly useful when you need an easy and fast way for implementing data exchange between a server and several clients, which can reach the service just with a web reference, through a unified programming model that can simplify your life—especially when you do not need deep customizations on the business logic. Clients can access data in two ways: via Uri, with http requests, or via a specific LINQ provider known as LINQ to WCF Data Services. Clients can perform CRUD operations using LINQ as well. In this chapter you learn to implement WCF Data Services exposing data from entity data models and consuming them from client applications using both Uri and LINQ approaches. As I said before, WCF Data Services can expose several kinds of data sources, but the most common scenario (and the most modern) is exposing data from entity data models based on the Entity Framework, as shown with examples in this chapter.

Querying Data via Http Requests

WCF Data Services can be queried via http requests. This is possible because of the REST approach offered by this particular kind of WCF services and that is basically a special XML serialization format for data exchange; XML is perfect at this point because it allows standardizing how data is exchanged in both directions. Querying a Data Service is substantially performed by writing an Uri (Uniform Resource Identifier) in your web browser addresses bar or in managed code. For example, suppose you have a Data Service exposing data from the Northwind database. When deployed, the service has the following address:

```
http://localhost:4444/Northwind.svc
```

Http requests sent to a Data Service are represented by the http verbs: GET, (read), POST (update), PUT (insert), and DELETE. The following Uri sends a GET request and demonstrates how you can query the Customers collection and get all the Customer objects:

```
http://localhost:4444/Northwind.svc/Customers
```

As you see later when discussing service implementations, this Http request can show the full customers list. You can then filter your query results. For example, you can retrieve all orders from the ANATR customer as follows:

```
http://localhost:4444/Northwind.svc/Customers('ANATR')/Orders
```

Finally you could also perform other operations such as ordering via the query string. For example, the following Uri contains a query string that retrieves the same orders as previously mentioned but is ordered according to the OrderDate property:

```
http://localhost:4444/Northwind.svc/Customers('ANATR')/Orders?orderby=OrderDate
```

For entity data models, an Uri can be summarized as follows:

```
http://website/ServiceName.svc/EntitySetName/NavigationProperty(PrimaryKey)
```

The best way to understand is always by getting your hands on code, so the next section explains how to implement an ADO.NET Data Service, whereas in the second part of the chapter, you see how to consume the service itself.

Implementing WCF Data Services

To implement an ADO.NET Data Service, you first create a Web application, add your data source, and finally add a service to your project. The goal of the next example is to expose data within a master-detail relationship from the Northwind database via an entity data model. Run Visual Studio 2010 and create a new Web application, naming the new project **NorthwindDataService**. Figure 42.1 shows the New project window to explain the selection.

FIGURE 42.1   Creating a new Web application for hosting a Data Service.

When the new project is ready, add a new entity data model to the project pointing to the Northwind database, ensuring that Customers, Orders, and Order_Details tables are selected and correctly mapped into the new EDM. If you need a recap on building EDMs, read Chapter 27, "Introducing the ADO.NET Entity Framework." When ready, in Solution Explorer right-click the project name and select **Add New Item**. In the Add new item dialog, search for the ADO.NET Data Service template and name the new service as NorthwindService.svc, as shown in Figure 42.2.

FIGURE 42.2   Adding a Data Service to the project.

After a few seconds the WCF service is added to the project. If you double-click the NorthwindService.svc file, the code editor lists the auto-generated code expressed in Listing 42.1.

LISTING 42.1   Starting Code for a Data Service

```
Imports System.Data.Services
Imports System.Data.Services.Common
Imports System.Linq
Imports System.ServiceModel.Web

Public Class NorthwindService
    ' TODO: replace [[class name]] with your data class name
    Inherits DataService(Of [[class name]])

    ' This method is called only once to initialize service-wide policies.
    Public Shared Sub InitializeService(ByVal config As DataServiceConfiguration)
        ' TODO: set rules to indicate which entity sets and service operations are
        'visible, updatable, etc.
        ' Examples:

        'config.SetEntitySetAccessRule("MyEntitySet", EntitySetRights.All)
        'config.SetServiceOperationAccessRule("MyServiceOperation",
                                        ServiceOperationRights.AllRead)
        config.DataServiceBehavior.MaxProtocolVersion = _
```

```
        DataServiceProtocolVersion.V2
    End Sub
End Class
```

This is the point where we need to make some considerations. First, WCF Data Services are implemented by both the System.Data.Services.dll and System.Data.Services.Client.dll assemblies. The most important namespaces exposed by such assemblies are System.Data.Services, System.Data.Services.Common, and System.Data.Services.Client. On the server side, they need to work with the System.ServiceModel namespace that provides support for WCF. The entry point of a Data Service is the System.Data.Services.DataService(Of T) class that is the base class for each service. If you take a look at the code, you see that the NorthwindService class inherits from DataService(Of T). Comments suggest replacing the standard [[class name]] identifier with the appropriate one, which is NorthwindEntities in our case. With that said, the inheritance declaration becomes the following:

```
Inherits DataService(Of NorthwindEntities)
```

Notice how the InitializeService method (invoked to start the service) receives a config argument of type DataServiceConfiguration; with this class you can configure the service behavior, for example access authorizations for your data source. The SetEntitySetAccessRule enables establishing access authorizations on entities from the EDM. For example, if you want clients to gain full access on the Customers entity, you write the following line:

```
config.SetEntitySetAccessRule("Customers", EntitySetRights.All)
```

You need to provide an access rule for each entity. As an alternative, you can use an * character for providing the same access level to all entities. This is not the best approach, but it can be useful for demonstration purposes. With that said uncomment the line of code for the previously mentioned method and replace the default line with the following one:

```
'Allows clients performing complete C.R.U.D. operations on all entities
config.SetEntitySetAccessRule("*", EntitySetRights.All)
```

The access rule is set via one of the EntitySetRights enumeration's values, which are summarized in Table 42.1

TABLE 42.1   EntitySetRights Enumeration's Values

Value	Description
All	Provides full access to entities.
AllRead	Provides reading access to both multiple and single entities.
AllWrite	Provides writing access to both multiple and single entities.
None	No authorization offered.

TABLE 42.1 Continued

Value	Description
OverrideEntitySetRights	If entities have explicit access rules, these are overridden with the ones specified here.
ReadMultiple	Provides reading access to multiple entities.
ReadSingle	Provides reading access to a single entity.
WriteAppend	Allows adding new entities.
WriteDelete	Allows deleting entities.
WriteMerge	Allows merging entities with existing data.
WriteReplace	Allows replacing entities.

Just remember that if you want to perform classic insert/update/delete operations, you need to provide All access level. Basically you just completed the most basic steps for getting a Data Service up and running. If you now press **F5** to start the application, your web browser shows the result of the XML serialization of your data, according to the REST model. This result is shown in Figure 42.3.

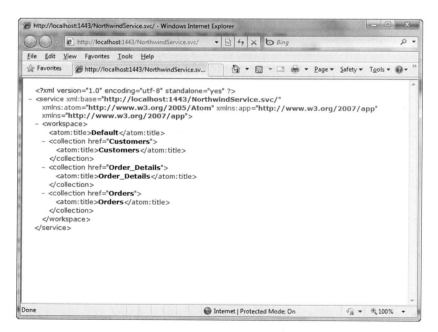

FIGURE 42.3 The Data Service running shows serialized data in the Web browser.

42

TURN OFF RSS READING VIEW

If you do not get the result shown in Figure 42.3 and instead see an RSS feeds reading view, you need to turn off such view in your browser. If you run Internet Explorer, you can select **Tools, Internet Options, Content** and then click the Settings button, finally you unflag the **Turn On Feed Reading View** check box. You will need to restart Internet Explorer for the change to take effect.

Notice how the service tag stores the service address. This is important because you use such an address later when instantiating the service. Also notice how the three entitysets (Customers, Orders, and Order_Details) are serialized. Now type the following Uri in the browser address bar, replacing the port number with the one you see on your machine:

```
http://localhost:1443/NorthwindService.svc/Customers
```

This line fetches the full customers list, as shown in Figure 42.4.

FIGURE 42.4   Fetching the customers list via Uri.

You can simply scroll the page to see how each customer is serialized in the query result. If you look at Figure 42.4, you can easily understand how each customer property is represented. You can also perform some more complex queries. For example, you might want to retrieve master-details data such as all orders from a specific customer, as in the following Uri:

```
http://localhost:1443/NorthwindService.svc/Customers('ANATR')/Orders?orderby=OrderD
ate
```

This Uri will retrieve the result shown in Figure 42.5.

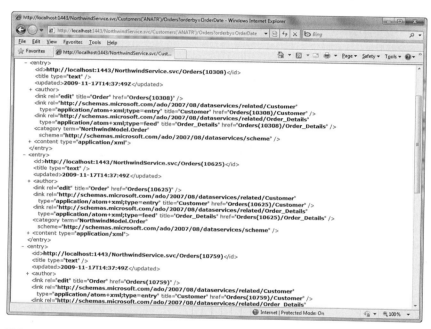

FIGURE 42.5   Retrieving master-details data via Uri.

You can perform complex queries via Uri, and this is one of the allowed modes for querying data from client applications, so you need to understand how query strings are composed. For this, read the following document from the MSDN Library for a full list of supported operators: http://msdn.microsoft.com/en-us/library/cc668784(VS.100).aspx. Generally you cannot query your service this way, whereas you will instead do it from a client application. This is what the next section begins to show. Of course what has been described until now is not all about the server side; other interesting features are described later in this chapter, but first you need to know how to reference a data service from the client side.

Deploying WCF Data Services to Internet Information Services

In real-world applications you will probably host your Data Services on web servers such as Internet Information Services. Because they are WCF services, you will deploy them with related techniques described in this page on the MSDN Library: http://msdn.microsoft.com/en-us/library/ms730158(VS.100).aspx. For demonstration purposes and for a better focusing on services implementation, in this book we simply deploy Data Services to the ASP.NET development server so that we can take advantage of the Visual Studio environment features.

Consuming WCF Data Services

You essentially consume WCF Data Services the same way you consume pure WCF services. Basically you need to add a service reference from the client and then instantiate the proxy class. Such a class will be generated for you by Visual Studio 2010 and will expose members for accessing data on the server. As mentioned at the beginning of this chapter, WCF Data Services can be consumed by different kinds of clients such as Windows (Console, Windows Forms, WPF) and Web (Silverlight, ASP.NET Ajax) applications. The next example shows you how to consume Data Services from a Console client application. Such a project template is useful for focusing on concepts that you can apply to other kinds of applications.

NOTE FOR SILVERLIGHT DEVELOPERS

Basically WCF Data Services can be consumed from Silverlight applications with the same programming techniques described in this chapter, except that they work asynchronously. If you are interested in this kind of development, I suggest you to read this blog post from the Microsoft Visual Studio Data Team Blog: http://blogs.msdn.com/vsdata/archive/2009/10/22/accessing-master-detail-data-through-ado-net-data-service-in-a-silverlight-application-part-1.aspx.

Creating a Client Application

The goal of the next example is to show how you can perform read/insert/update/delete operations against a Data Service from a client. Follow these steps:

1. Add to the current solution a new Console project and name it **NorthwindClient**.
2. Right-click the project name and select **Add Service Reference**. This adds a reference to the Data Service similar to what happens for WCF services. Because in our example the service is available in the current solution, just click **Discover**. In real

applications you will instead type the Uri of your service. Figure 42.6 shows how the **Add Service Reference** dialog appears now.

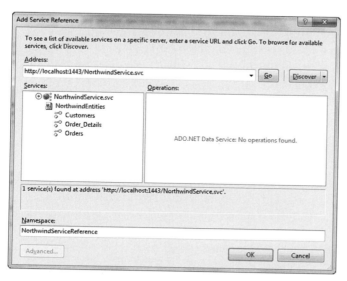

FIGURE 42.6   Adding a reference to the ADO.NET Data Service.

3. Replace the default identifier in the **Namespace** textbox with a more appropriate one, such as **NorthwindServiceReference**; then click **OK**.

TIP

If the Data Service also exposes service operations (see the next section for details), these will be listed in the right side of the dialog.

At this point Visual Studio 2010 generates what in WCF is defined as a proxy class, which is client code. Basically it generates a number of classes: one class that inherits from `System.Data.Services.Client.DataServiceContext` and that can be considered as the Astoria counterpart for the Entity Framework's `ObjectContext` and a series of counterpart classes for entities in the EDM. This means that, for our example, you have `Customer`, `Order`, and `Order_Detail` classes implemented on the client side. All these classes implement the `INotifyPropertyChanged` interface so that they can notify the UI of changes on the original data source. Instead the `DataServiceContext` class also exposes properties of type `System.Data.Services.Client.DataServiceQuery(Of T)` that are collections of the previously mentioned classes and that represent strongly typed queries against entity sets exposed by a Data Service. For example, the `DataServiceContext` class in our example (automatically named `NorthwindEntities` for consistency with the related context in the service) exposes the `Customers`, `Orders`, and `Order_Details` properties, respectively, of type

DataServiceQuery(Of Customer), DataServiceQuery(Of Order), and
DataServiceQuery(Of Order_Detail). Although you should never manually edit auto-
generated code, if you are curious, you can inspect previously mentioned classes by
expanding the NorthwindServiceReference item in Solution Explorer and clicking the
Reference.vb file. This is the place where all the client code is implemented. You notice
lots of similarities with an entity data model implementation, but do not become
confused because WCF Data Services are a different thing. By the way, such similarities can
help you understand how to perform data operations. For example, there are methods for
adding objects (AddToCustomers, AddToOrders) and for removing objects (DeleteObject).
For now, add the following Imports directives that allow shortening lines of code:

```
Imports NorthwindClient.NorthwindServiceReference
Imports System.Data.Services.Client
```

The next step is instantiating the proxy client class. At module level, add the following
declaration:

```
Private northwind As New _
       NorthwindEntities(New _
       Uri("http://localhost:1443/NorthwindService.svc"))
```

Notice how the instance requires you to specify the service Uri. This is the same that is
specified when adding the service reference. The northwind variable represents the
instance of the DataServiceContext class that exposes members for working against entities exposed by the Data Service and that allows performing CRUD operations. The first
operation I am going to explain is insertion. Consider the following function:

```
Private Function AddNewOrder(ByVal relatedCustomer As Customer) As Order


    Dim newOrder As New Order
    With newOrder
        .Customer = relatedCustomer
        .OrderDate = Date.Today
        .ShipCountry = "Italy"
        .ShipCity = "Milan"
        .ShipName = "First"
    End With

    northwind.AddToOrders(newOrder)
    northwind.SetLink(newOrder, "Customer", relatedCustomer)
    northwind.SaveChanges()
    Return newOrder
End Function
```

The code first creates an instance of a new order and populates the desired properties.
Notice how a relationship to the specified customer is also set. This relationship is just set
in-memory, but it needs to be explicitly set when sending changes to the actual database.

The new order is added to the model via the AddToOrders method, whereas SetLink explicitly sets the relationship. The method requires the new object as the first argument, the navigation property in the model as the second argument, and the master object in the master-details relationship. Finally the code saves the new data to the database invoking SaveChanges. Later you see how to send to the data source changes in a batch. Performing an update operation is an easy task. You simply get the instance of the desired object and edit properties. The following snippet demonstrates how to update an existing order:

```
Private Sub UpdateOrder(ByVal OrderID As Integer)
    'Retrieving the one instance of the specified Order with
    'a lambda.
    Dim ord = northwind.Orders.Where(Function(o) o.OrderID = _
            OrderID).First

    ord.ShipName = "Second"
    ord.ShipCity = "Cremona"
    ord.ShipCountry = "Italy"
End Sub
```

The code shows how you simply get the instance of your object and replace properties. If you want to save changes at this point, invoke SaveChanges. We are not doing this now because we will save changes in the batch later.

EXTENSION METHODS

WCF Data Services do not support First and Single extension methods directly on the data source. This is the reason why in the previous code snippet we had to pass through a Where method.

The next step is implementing a deletion method. This is also a simple task, as demonstrated by the following code:

```
Private Sub DeleteOrder(ByVal OrderID As Integer)

    Dim ord = northwind.Orders.Where(Function(o) o.OrderID = _
            OrderID).First
    northwind.DeleteObject(ord)
End Sub
```

Also in this case you simply get the instance of the object you want to remove and then invoke the DeleteObject method. The last step is showing how you can save multiple changes to entities in one shot. The following code demonstrates this:

```
Private Sub SaveAllChanges()
    northwind.SaveChanges(Services.Client.SaveChangesOptions.Batch)
End Sub
```

SaveChanges receives an argument of type `System.Data.Services.Client.` `aveChangesOptions`, which is an enumeration whose most important value is `Batch`, which enables saving all pending changes with a single http request; thus it is efficient with regard to performances. Now we just need to invoke the various methods from within the `Sub Main`. The following code first creates a new order, updates it, and finally deletes it:

```
Sub Main()


    Dim cust = northwind.Customers.Where(Function(c) c.CustomerID = _
            "ALFKI").First

    Try
        Dim anOrder = AddNewOrder(cust)

        Console.WriteLine("Added new order: {0}", anOrder.OrderID)

        UpdateOrder(anOrder.OrderID)
        Console.WriteLine("Updated order {0}. ShipCity now is {1},
                    ShipName now is {2}",
                    anOrder.OrderID, anOrder.ShipCity,
                    anOrder.ShipName)


        'Replace the order ID with a valid one
        DeleteOrder(anOrder.OrderID)
        Console.WriteLine("Order deleted")

        SaveAllChanges()

        Console.ReadLine()
        northwind = Nothing

    Catch ex As DataServiceQueryException
        Console.WriteLine("The server returned the following error:")
        Console.WriteLine(ex.Response.Error.Message)
        Console.ReadLine()
    Catch ex As Exception

    End Try
End Sub
```

The code also is ready for intercepting a `DataServiceQueryException`, a particular object that provides client information from `DataServiceException` objects thrown on the server side. If you now run the application, you get messages informing you about the data operations progress, as shown in Figure 42.7.

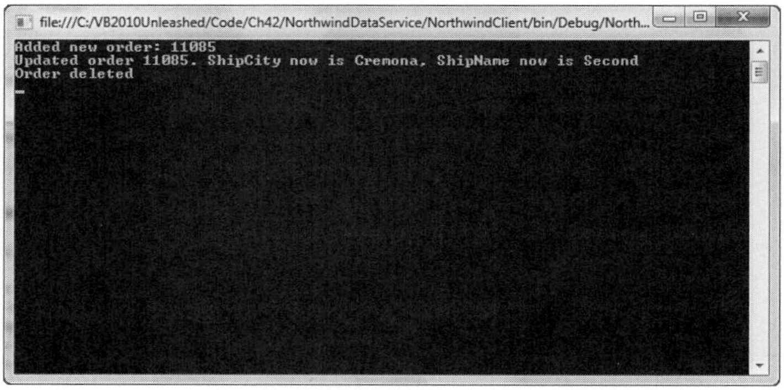

FIGURE 42.7   The sample application performs all operations.

Querying Data

One of the most common requirements of any data framework is the ability to perform queries. WCF Data Services allow two modes on the client side. The first one is utilizing query strings similarly to what it is possible to do with Uris. To accomplish this you invoke the `Execute(Of T)` method from the `DataServiceContext` class, where T is the type you want to retrieve a collection of. For example, the following code returns a collection of orders for the specified customer, sorted by order date:

```
Dim myOrders = Northwind.Execute(Of Order)(New _
             Uri("/Customers('ANATR')/Orders?orderby=OrderDate", _
             UriKind.Relative))
```

This way is efficient but avoids the strongly typed approach provided by LINQ. Fortunately the .NET Framework also enables using a special LINQ provider known as LINQ to Data Services. The following code snippet demonstrates how you can obtain the same result as previously by writing a LINQ query:

```
Dim myOrders = From ord In northwind.Orders
             Where ord.Customer.CustomerID = "ANATR"
             Select ord
```

Of course this is powerful but not necessarily the best choice. For example, you might want to prevent indiscriminate data access from clients, or you might simply want better performances implementing queries on the server side and exposing methods returning query results. This is where *service operations* take place.

Implementing Service Operations

Service operations are .NET methods that can perform data operations on the server side. With service operations developers can preventively establish access rules and customize the business logic, such as data validation or access restrictions. They are basically WCF extensions for Data Services and perform operations via Http requests, meaning that you can execute service operations within a web browser or from a client application. Service operations can return the following types:

▶ IQueryable(Of T) in data-centric scenarios with EDMs or LINQ-to-SQL models

▶ IEnumerable(Of T)

▶ .NET primitive types, because Data Services can also expose in-memory collections

▶ No type (Sub methods)

Service operations can be used for both reading and writing data to the service. In a reading situation, service operations are Function methods marked with the WebGet attribute, whereas in writing situations they are decorated with the WebInvoke attribute. The next example explains how to read order details for the specified order and return fetched data to the client. First, add the following method to the NorthwindService class:

```
<WebGet()> Public Function GetOrderDetails(ByVal OrderID As Integer) _
               As IQueryable(Of Order_Detail)

    If OrderID > 0 Then
        Dim query = From det In Me.CurrentDataSource.Order_Details
                    Where det.OrderID = OrderID
                    Select det

        Return query
    Else
        Throw New DataServiceException(400,
                                "OrderID is not valid")
    End If
End Function
```

The method explanation is quite simple. It performs a simple validation on the OrderID argument; if valid, it executes a LINQ to Data Services query for getting related order details returning an IQueryable(Of Order_Detail) type. Notice the CurrentDataSource object, which represents the instance of the NorthwindEntities class on the server side. If the OrderID is considered invalid, the method throws a DataServiceException, which is specific for throwing errors from the service. You can specify an Http error code and an error message. To make a service operation recognizable and executable, you need to set permissions for it. This is accomplished by invoking the

DataServiceConfiguration.SetServiceOperationAccessRule method; therefore, uncomment the following line of code in the InitializeService method:

```
'config.SetServiceOperationAccessRule _
("MyServiceOperation", ServiceOperationRights.AllRead)
```

Then you need to replace the operation name as follows:

```
config.SetServiceOperationAccessRule("GetOrderDetails",
                        ServiceOperationRights.AllRead)
```

In our scenario we just need to read data from the service, so the AllRead permission is appropriate. If you now run the service, you can type the following line in the browser address bar to invoke the service operation, making sure to type the appropriate port number of the development server on your machine:

```
http://localhost:1443/NorthwindService.svc/GetOrderDetails?OrderID=10250
```

Basically you invoke the operation writing its name after the service address. Notice that operations' names and parameters are case-sensitive. At this point you are ready for calling the service operation from the client application. Return to the NorthwindClient project, and add the following method that invokes the service operations for fetching order details:

```
Private Sub ViewDetails(ByVal OrderID As Integer)
    Console.WriteLine("Showing details for Order ID: " _
                    & OrderID.ToString)

    Dim details = northwind.Execute(Of Order_Detail) _
                    (New Uri("GetOrderDetails?OrderID=" & _
                    OrderID.ToString,
                    UriKind.Relative))

    For Each detail In details
        Console.WriteLine("ID: {0}, Unit price: {1}, Quantity: {2}",
                        detail.OrderID,
                        detail.UnitPrice,
                        detail.Quantity)
    Next
    Console.ReadLine()
End Sub
```

The code is still quite simple. It invokes the service operation building a query string concatenating the supplied order ID. Notice how the Execute(Of Order_Detail) method is invoked because the service operations return a collection of the same type. The method requires you to specify the Uri of the service operation, which in this case is its name followed by the order Id. Before you run the application, you need to update the service reference. This step can be performed later in this case, because you do not invoke a managed method, whereas you invoke a service operation via a query string. To update the service reference, in Solution Explorer, just right-click the **NorthwindServiceReference** item and select **Update Service Reference**. Updating the service reference is something that you must do each time you perform changes on the service after a reference has been already added in the client application. If you now run the application, you get details for the specified order, as shown in Figure 42.8.

FIGURE 42.8   Getting order details via a service operation.

If you want to perform insertions, updates, or deletions, you can implement web invokes on the server side. This is accomplished by decorating methods with the `WebInvoke` attribute. The MSDN documentation provides examples on `WebInvoke` at this address: http://msdn.microsoft.com/en-us/library/system.servicemodel.web.webinvokeattribute(VS.100).aspx.

Implementing Query Interceptors

In the previous section I covered service operations, which act on the server side. But they are not the only server-side feature in Data Services. Another interesting feature is known as query interceptors. Basically interceptors are .NET methods exposed by the service class enabling developers to intercept Http requests and to establish how such requests must be handled, both in reading (*query interceptors*) and in writing (*change interceptors*) operations. This section describes both query interceptors and change interceptors.

Understanding Query Interceptors

Query interceptors are public methods for intercepting HTTP GET requests and allow developers to handle the reading request. Such methods are decorated with the `QueryInterceptor` attribute that simply requires specifying the entity set name. For a better understanding, consider the following interceptor (to be implemented within the `NorthwindService` class) that returns only orders from the specified culture:

```
<QueryInterceptor("Orders")> Public Function OnQueryOrders() As  _
```

```
                               Expression(Of Func(Of Order, Boolean))
        'Determines the caller's culture
        Dim LocalCulture = WebOperationContext.Current.
                             IncomingRequest.Headers("Accept-Language")

        If LocalCulture = "it-IT" Then
            Return Function(ord) ord.ShipCountry = "Italy"
        Else
            Throw New DataServiceException("You are not authorized")
        End If

End Function
```

OnQueryOrders will be invoked on the service each time an HTTP GET requests is sent to the service. The code just returns only orders where the ShipCountry property's value is Italy, if the client culture (the caller) is it-IT. Differently, the code throws a DataServiceException. The most important thing to notice in the code is the returned type, which is an Expression(Of Func(Of T, Boolean)). This is an expression tree generated starting from the lambda expression actually returned. You may remember from Chapter 21, "Advanced Language Features," how the Func object enables generating anonymous methods on-the-fly, receiving two arguments: The first one is the real argument, whereas the second one is the returned type. The lambda expression is the equivalent of the following LINQ query:

```
Dim query = From ord In Me.CurrentDataSource.Orders
            Where ord.ShipCountry = "Italy"
            Select ord
```

The big difference is that this kind of query returns an IQueryable(Of Order), whereas we need to evaluate the result of an expression tree, and this is only possible with lambdas. You can easily test this interceptor by running the service and typing the following Uri in the browser address bar, replacing the port number:

```
http://localhost:1443/NorthwindService.svc/Orders
```

This Uri automatically fetches only orders targeting Italy, if your local culture is it-IT. If it is not, the Visual Studio debugger shows an exception. By the way, it is important to provide sufficient information about exceptions from the server side, because clients need detailed information for understanding what happened. This is a general rule explained here together with a practical example. WCF Data Services provide a simple way for providing descriptive error messages other than throwing exceptions. This requires the following line of code in the InitializeService method:

```
config.UseVerboseErrors = True
```

On the client side, failures from query interceptors are handled by DataServiceQueryException objects. This is the reason why I already implemented such an object in the Try..Catch block in the client application's main window. According to the previous example, if your culture is different from it-IT, when you run the client application, you should get the error message shown in Figure 42.9.

The server returned the following error:<?xml version="1.0" encoding="utf-8" standalone="yes"?>
<error
xmlns="http://schemas.microsoft.com/ado/2007/08/dataservices/metadata">
 <code></code>
 <message xml:lang="it-IT">You are not authorized</message>
 <innererror>
  <message>Exception has been thrown by the target of an invocation.</message>
  <type>System.Reflection.TargetInvocationException</type>
  <stacktrace>   at
System.RuntimeMethodHandle._InvokeMethodFast(IRuntimeMethodInfo
method, Object target, Object[] arguments, SignatureStruct& sig,
MethodAttributes methodAttributes, RuntimeType typeOwner)
   at System.RuntimeMethodHandle.InvokeMethodFast(IRuntimeMethodInfo
method, Object target, Object[] arguments, Signature sig, MethodAttributes
methodAttributes, RuntimeType typeOwner)
   at System.Reflection.RuntimeMethodInfo.Invoke(Object obj, BindingFlags
invokeAttr, Binder binder, Object[] parameters, CultureInfo culture, Boolean
skipVisibilityChecks)
   at System.Reflection.RuntimeMethodInfo.Invoke(Object obj, BindingFlags
invokeAttr, Binder binder, Object[] parameters, CultureInfo culture)
   at
System.Data.Services.DataServiceConfiguration.ComposeQueryInterceptors(IData
Service service, ResourceSetWrapper container)</stacktrace>
  <internalexception>
   <message>You are not authorized</message>
   <type>System.Data.Services.DataServiceException</type>
   <stacktrace>   at NorthwindDataService.NorthwindService.OnQueryOrders() in
C:\VB2010Unleashed\Code\Ch42\NorthwindDataService\NorthwindDataService\
NorthwindService.svc.vb:line 50</stacktrace>
  </internalexception>
 </innererror>
</error>

OK

FIGURE 42.9   The detailed information about the error.

Notice how, other than the error message you provided via the DataServiceException, there is a lot of information that can be useful to understand what happened. You thus could implement a log system for redirecting to you, as a developer, all collected information. Until now we talked about query interceptors, which intercept GET requests. We now cover change interceptors.

Understanding Change Interceptors

Change interceptors are conceptually similar to query interceptors, but they differ in that they can intercept http requests of type POST, PUT, and DELETE (that is, CRUD operations via Uri). They are public methods returning no type; therefore, they are always Sub decorated with the ChangeInterceptor attribute pointing to the entity set name. Each interceptor receives two arguments: the data source (generally a single entity) and the System.Data.Services.UpdateOperations enumeration, which allows understanding what request was sent. Take a look at the following interceptor:

```
<ChangeInterceptor("Orders")> _
Public Sub OnOrdersChange(ByVal DataSource As Order,
                          ByVal Action As UpdateOperations)
```

```
    If Action = UpdateOperations.Add OrElse _
       Action = UpdateOperations.Change Then

        'If data does not satisfy my condition, throws an exception
        If DataSource.OrderDate Is Nothing Then
            Throw New DataServiceException(400,
                    "Order date cannot be null")
        End If

    ElseIf Action = UpdateOperations.Delete Then
        If DataSource.ShippedDate IsNot Nothing Then
            Throw New DataServiceException(500,
            "You are not authorized to delete orders with full info")
        End If

    End If
End Sub
```

You decide how to handle the request depending on the UpdateOperations current value. Add corresponds to an insert operation, Delete to a delete operation, Change to an update operation, and None means that no operations were requested for the data source. The preceding code performs the same actions on both Add and Change operations and throws an exception if the new or existing order has null value in the OrderDate property. A different check is instead performed about Delete requests; in my example the code prevents from deleting an order whenever it has value in the ShippedDate property. No other code is required for handling situations in which supplied data are valid, because the Data Services framework automatically persists valid data to the underlying source. Change interceptors come in when a client application invokes the DataServiceContext.SaveChanges method. On the server side, change interceptors are raised just before sending data to the source and collecting information on the CRUD operation that sent the request.

Understanding Server-Driven Paging

The new version of WCF Data Services introduced by .NET 4.0 presents a new feature known as *server-driven paging*. This feature enables paging data directly on the server and provides developers the ability of specifying how many items a page must return, also offering an Uri for browsing the next page. To enable server-driven paging, you simply invoke the DataServiceConfiguration.SetEntitySetPageSize method that requires specifying the entity set name and the number of items per page. The following code demonstrates this:

```
config.SetEntitySetPageSize("Orders", 4)
```

If you now start the service and try to fetch all orders, you get the result shown in Figure 42.10.

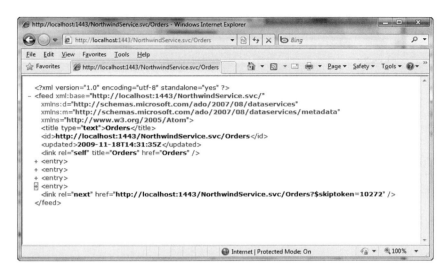

FIGURE 42.10   Server-driven paging demonstration.

For the sake of clarity all `entry` items within the browser window are collapsed, but you can easily see how each of them represents an order. Therefore the page shows exactly four items for how it was specified within the service. Another thing that is worth mentioning is the `link rel` tag that contains the Uri for moving to the next four items as follows:

```
http://localhost:1443/NorthwindService.svc/Orders?$skiptoken=10272
```

Server-driven paging is intended for use within the service; if you instead require to implement paging on client applications, you can still work with client paging that you accomplish specifying `$skip` and `$take` clauses within http requests.

Summary

WCF Data Services are REST-enabled WCF services supporting http requests such as GET, POST, PUT, and DELETE and constitute a data platform for exposing data through networks. In this chapter you got a high-level overview of Data Services; you first learned implementing services seeing how they can be easily created within ASP.NET Web applications, by simply adding the WCF Data Service item. Services running within a Web browser can then be easily queried via http requests (Uri). Next you saw how to consume WCF Data Services from client applications and perform CRUD operations taking advantage of the `DataServiceContext` class that exposes appropriate members for such kinds of operations. After this you saw how to implement service operations and interceptors for best results on the server side. Finally you took a tour into a new feature of Data Services in .NET 4, the server-driven paging for best performances on the server side.

CHAPTER 43

Serialization

Most real-world applications need to store, exchange, and transfer data. Due to its special nature, the .NET Framework stores data into objects and can exchange data via objects. If you need to store data only for your application, you have lots of alternatives. The problem is when you need to exchange and transfer data with other applications. In other words, you need to think of how your objects are represented and decide if you need to convert them into a different format. This is because another application cannot understand objects in their pure state; therefore, how information is persisted needs to be standardized. Serialization enables you to save your object's state to disk and then re-create the object according to the specified format. With serialization you simply store your data and transfer data to other applications that can re-create the information. For example, you have an application that needs to store and transfer data to another application through a network. With the .NET Framework, you serialize your data (that is, save the result of the serialization process to a stream), transfer your data to the target application, and wait for the target application to deserialize (that is, re-creating the object starting from the serialized information) your data and use it. In this chapter you learn to implement serialization in your applications, understanding what decisions you should make if you need to transfer data to non-.NET and non-Windows applications, too. Moreover, you get information on serialization techniques that have been introduced in .NET Framework 3.5 and 4.0.

Objects Serialization

Serializing .NET objects is the easiest serialization mode. In this particular scenario you need a file stream where you have to place data and a formatter establishing the serialization mode. When you have the formatter instance, you simply invoke the `Serialize` method. The `System.Runtime.Serialization.Formatters` namespace provides two sub namespaces, `Binary` and `Soap`, exposing respectively the following formatters: `BinaryFormatter` and `SoapFormatter`. The first one serializes objects in a binary way. It is efficient but you should use it only if you are sure that your objects will be deserialized by .NET applications, because such binary format is not universal. If you instead want to be sure that your objects can be shared across different applications and platforms, you should prefer the `SoapFormatter` that produces an Xml-based result useful when working with Soap web services.

Binary Serialization

The following example shows how you can serialize a typed collection of strings into a file on disk using the `BinaryFormatter` class:

```
Dim stringSeries As New List(Of String) From
                    {"Serialization", "demo",
                     "with VB"}

Dim targetFile As New _
    FileStream("C:\temp\SerializedData.dat",
               FileMode.Create)
Dim formatter As New BinaryFormatter

formatter.Serialize(targetFile, stringSeries)
targetFile.Close()
formatter = Nothing
```

> **NOTE**
>
> The above code example requires `Imports System.IO` and Imports `System.Runtime.Serialization.Formatters.Binary` directives.

The code simply creates a new file named `SerializedData.Dat` and puts the result of the binary serialization in the file. If you examine the content of the file with the Windows Notepad, you can obtain a result similar to what is shown in Figure 43.1.

You don't effectively need to know how your objects are serialized, but it is interesting to understand what kind of information is placed into the target file, such as the serialized type, assembly information, and the actual data. To deserialize a binary file you simply

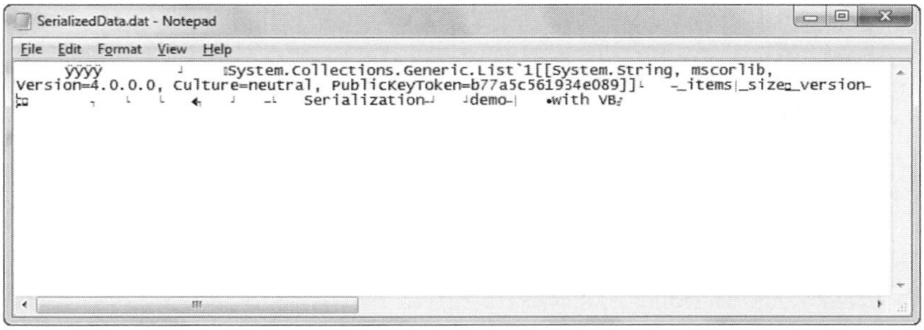

FIGURE 43.1   Examining the result of the serialization process.

invoke the `BinaryFormatter.Deserialize` method, as shown in the following code which you write right after the preceding example:

```
Dim sourceFile As New FileStream("C:\temp\SerializedData.dat",
                                FileMode.Open)

formatter = New BinaryFormatter
Dim data = CType(formatter.Deserialize(sourceFile),
              List(Of String))

sourceFile.Close()
formatter = Nothing

'Iterates the result
For Each item In data
    Console.WriteLine(item)
Next
```

Notice that `Deserialize` returns `Object`; therefore, the result needs to be converted into the appropriate type that you expect. If you run the preceding code you see on your screen how the strings from the collection are correctly listed. This kind of serialization is also straightforward because it enables serializing entire object graphs. Moreover, you can use this technique against user interface controls in Windows Forms and WPF applications to persist the state of your interface objects that can be later re-created.

HANDLING SERIALIZATION EXCEPTIONS

Remember to perform serialization and deserialization operations within a `Try..Catch` block and implement code for handling the `SerializationException` exception that provides information on serialization/deserialization errors.

Creating Objects Deep Copies with Serialization

In Chapter 4, "Data Types and Expressions," I illustrated how to create objects' copies implementing the `ICloneable` interface and how you can clone an object with the

MemberWiseClone method. Such scenarios have a big limitation: They cannot create copies of an entire object graph. Luckily binary serialization can instead serialize entire object graphs and thus can be used to create complete deep copies of objects. The code in Listing 43.1 shows how to accomplish this by implementing a generic method.

LISTING 43.1   Implementing Deep Copy with Serialization

```vb
Imports System.Runtime.Serialization
Imports System.Runtime.Serialization.Formatters.Binary
Imports System.IO

Public Class CreateDeepCopy

    Public Shared Function Clone(Of T)(ByVal objectToClone As T) As T

        'If the source object is null, simply returns the current
        'object (as a default)
        If Object.ReferenceEquals(objectToClone, Nothing) Then
            Return objectToClone
        End If

        'Creates a new formatter whose behavior is for cloning purposes
        Dim formatter As New BinaryFormatter(Nothing,
                                    New StreamingContext(
                                        StreamingContextStates.Clone))
        'Serializes to a memory stream
        Dim ms As New MemoryStream
        Using ms
            formatter.Serialize(ms, objectToClone)

            'Gets back to the first stream byte
            ms.Seek(0, SeekOrigin.Begin)
            'Deserializes the object graph to a new T object
            Return CType(formatter.Deserialize(ms), T)
        End Using
    End Function
End Class
```

Because you are not limited to file streams, taking advantage of a memory stream is good in such a scenario. You invoke the preceding method as follows:

```vb
Dim result As Object = CreateDeepCopy.Clone(objectToClone)
```

You could also implement extension methods for providing deep copy to all types.

Soap Serialization

Soap serialization works similarly to binary serialization. First, you need to add a reference to the `System.Runtime.Serialization.Formatters.Soap.dll` assembly. Then you add an `Imports System.Runtime.Serialization.Formatters.Soap` directive. At this point you can serialize and deserialize your objects. To continue the example of the typed collection shown in the previous section, write the following code to accomplish serialization with the Soap formatter:

```
'Requires an Imports System.Runtime.Serialization.Formatters.Soap directive
Dim stringToSerialize As String = "Serialization demo with VB"

Dim targetFile As New FileStream("C:\temp\SerializedData.xml",
                                 FileMode.Create)

Dim formatter As New SoapFormatter
formatter.Serialize(targetFile, stringToSerialize)
targetFile.Close()
formatter = Nothing
```

Basically there is no difference in the syntax for the Soap formatter if compared to the binary one.

TIP ON GENERIC COLLECTIONS

The `SoapFormatter` class does not allow serializing generic collections. This is the reason why a simpler example against a single string is provided.

You can still examine the result of the serialization process with the Windows Notepad. Figure 43.2 shows how the target file stores information in a XML fashion.

FIGURE 43.2   Examining the result of the Soap serialization process.

Typically the Soap serialization is intended to be used when working with Soap web services. If you want to serialize objects in a pure XML mode, you can take advantage of Xml serialization, which is described in the "XML Serialization" section later in this chapter.

Providing Serialization for Custom Objects

You can make your custom objects serializable so that you can apply the previously described techniques for persisting and re-creating objects' state. To be serializable, a class (or structure) must be decorated with the `Serializable` attribute. This is the most basic scenario and is represented by the following implementation of the `Person` class:

```
Imports System.Runtime.Serialization


<Serializable()>
Public Class Person
    Public Property FirstName As String
    Public Property LastName As String
    Public Property Age As Integer
    Public Property Address As String
End Class
```

If you do not need to get control over the serialization process, this is all you need. By the way, there can be certain situations that you need to handle. For instance, you might want to disable serialization for a member that could result obsolete if too much time is taken between serialization and deserialization. Continuing the `Person` class example, we decide to disable serialization for the `Age` member because between serialization and deserialization the represented person might be older than the moment when serialization occurred. To accomplish this you apply the `NonSerialized` attribute. The big problem here is that this is a field-level attribute; therefore, it cannot be applied to properties. In such situations using auto-implemented properties is not possible; therefore, you must write them the old-fashioned way. The following code shows how you can prevent the Age member from being serialized:

```
<NonSerialized()> Private _age As Integer
Public Property Age As Integer
    Get
        Return _age
    End Get
    Set(ByVal value As Integer)
        _age = value
    End Set
End Property
```

The subsequent problem is that you need a way for assigning a valid value to nonserialized members when deserialization occurs. The most common technique is implementing the `IDeserializationCallBack` interface that exposes an `OnDeserialization` method where you can place your initialization code. The following is the revisited code for the `Person` class according to the last edits:

```
Imports System.Runtime.Serialization


<Serializable()>
Public Class Person
    Implements IDeserializationCallback


    Public Property FirstName As String
    Public Property LastName As String

    <NonSerialized()> Private _age As Integer
    Public Property Age As Integer
        Get
            Return _age
        End Get
        Set(ByVal value As Integer)
            _age = value
        End Set
    End Property

    Public Sub OnDeserialization(ByVal sender As Object) Implements _
            System.Runtime.Serialization.IDeserializationCallback.
            OnDeserialization
        'Specify the new age
        Me.Age = 32
    End Sub
End Class
```

When the deserialization process invokes the `OnDeserialization` method, members that were not serialized can be correctly initialized anyway. Another consideration that you need to take care of is versioning. When you upgrade your application to a new version, you might also want to apply some changes to your classes, for example adding new members. This is fine but can result in problems if the previous version of your application attempts to deserialize an object produced by the new version. To solve this problem, you can mark a member as `OptionalField`. In this way the deserialization process is not affected by new members and both `BinaryFormatter` and `SoapFormatter` will not throw exceptions if they encounter new members during the process. Because the `OptionalField` attribute works at field level, this is another situation in which you cannot take advantage of auto-implemented properties. The following code shows how you can mark the `Address` member in the `Person` class as optional:

```
<OptionalField()> Private _address As String
```

```
Public Property Address As String

    Get
        Return _address
    End Get
    Set(ByVal value As String)
        _address = value
    End Set
End Property
```

The member is still involved in the serialization process, but if a previous version of the application attempts to perform deserialization, it will not throw exceptions when it encounters this new member that was not expected.

NonSerialized events

Visual Basic 2010 introduces a new feature known as *NonSerialized Events*. Basically you can now decorate an event with the NonSerialized attribute in custom serialization. A common scenario for applying this technique is when you work on classes that implement the INotifyPropertyChanged interface because it is more important serializing data and not an event that just notifies the user interface of changes on data. The following code shows an example about NonSerialized events inside a class that implements INotifyPropertyChanged:

```
<Serializable()>
Public Class Customer
    Implements INotifyPropertyChanged

    <NonSerialized()>
    Public Event PropertyChanged(
            ByVal sender As Object,
            ByVal e As System.ComponentModel.PropertyChangedEventArgs) _
            Implements System.ComponentModel.
                    INotifyPropertyChanged.PropertyChanged

    Protected Sub OnPropertyChanged(ByVal strPropertyName As String)
        If Me.PropertyChangedEvent IsNot Nothing Then
            RaiseEvent PropertyChanged(Me,
                    New PropertyChangedEventArgs(strPropertyName))
        End If
    End Sub
```

XML Serialization

> **NOTE**
>
> Code examples shown in this section require `Imports System.IO` and `Imports System.Xml.Serialization` directives.

One of the main goals of serialization is to provide a way for exchanging data with other applications so that such applications can re-create objects' state. If you want to share your objects with non-.NET applications or with applications running on different platforms, a convenient way for serializing objects is provided by the Xml serialization. As you know, Xml is a standard international file format for data exchange. Xml files are basically text files organized according to a hierarchical structure and therefore can be manipulated in whatever platforms and applications. Xml serialization thus provides two great benefits: absolute interoperability and background compatibility. If you upgrade or modify your applications, Xml format remains the same. Opposite to such benefits, Xml serialization has two limitations: It cannot serialize object graphs (therefore single objects) and cannot serialize private members. Xml serialization is performed by taking advantage of objects exposed by the `System.Xml.Serialization` namespace. Particularly you can use the `XmlSerializer` class that requires a `System.IO.Stream` object for outputting serialized data and the data itself. The following code shows how you can serialize a typed collection of strings using Xml serialization:

```
Dim stringSeries As New List(Of String) From
    {"Serialization", "demo",
     "with VB"}

Dim targetFile As New FileStream("C:\temp\SerializedData.xml",
                                 FileMode.Create)
Dim formatter As New XmlSerializer(GetType(List(Of String)))

formatter.Serialize(targetFile, stringSeries)
targetFile.Close()
formatter = Nothing
```

The `XmlSerializer` constructor requires the specification of the data type you are going to serialize, which is accomplished via the `GetType` operator. To serialize data you invoke the `XmlSerializer.Serialize` method. As you can see, there are no big differences with other serialization techniques shown in the previous section. To check how your data was serialized, you can open the SerializedData.xml file. In this case you can accomplish this with an Xml editor or with a web browser instead of Notepad. Figure 43.3 shows the serialization result within Internet Explorer.

Notice how the newly obtained file has a perfect Xml structure and therefore can be shared with other applications having the ability of performing Xml deserialization. To

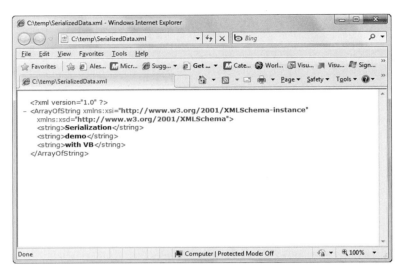

FIGURE 43.3   The Xml serialization result shown in Internet Explorer.

deserialize your data you simply invoke the `XmlSerializer.Deserialize` method, as shown in the following code:

```
Dim sourceFile As New FileStream("C:\temp\SerializedData.xml",
                                 FileMode.Open)

formatter = New XmlSerializer(GetType(List(Of String)))
Dim data = CType(formatter.Deserialize(sourceFile),
                 List(Of String))

sourceFile.Close()
formatter = Nothing

'Iterates the result
For Each item In data
    Console.WriteLine(item)
Next
```

Customizing Xml Serialization

Consider the following implementation of the `Person` class:

```
Public Class Person
    Public Property FirstName As String
    Public Property LastName As String
```

```
    Public Property Age As Integer
End Class
```

When you serialize an instance of that `Person` class, you would obtain an Xml representation similar to the following:

```
<?xml version="1.0" ?>
<Person xmlns:xsi="http://www.w3.org/2001/XMLSchema-instance"
        xmlns:xsd="http://www.w3.org/2001/XMLSchema">
  <FirstName>Alessandro</FirstName>
  <LastName>Del Sole</LastName>
  <Age>32</Age>
</Person>
```

The `System.Xml.Serialization` namespace offers attributes for controlling output of the Xml serialization to affect the target file. For example, see the following code:

```
Imports System.Xml.Serialization


<XmlRoot("Contact")> Public Class Person
    <XmlIgnore()> Public Property FirstName As String
    Public Property LastName As String
    <XmlAttribute()> Public Property Age As Integer
End Class
```

When an instance is serialized, the output looks like the following:

```
<?xml version="1.0" ?>
<Contact xmlns:xsi="http://www.w3.org/2001/XMLSchema-instance"
         xmlns:xsd="http://www.w3.org/2001/XMLSchema"
         Age="32">
  <LastName>Del Sole</LastName>
</Contact>
```

The `XmlRoot` attribute changed the name of the root element from `Person` to `Contact`. The `XmlIgnore` attribute prevented a property from being serialized, whereas the `XmlAttribute` attribute treated the specified member as an Xml attribute instead of an Xml element. You can find the complete attributes list in the dedicated page of the MSDN Library at http://msdn.microsoft.com/en-us/library/ system.xml.serialization.xmlattributes_ members(VS.100).aspx. The reason why you should get a reference on the Internet is that Xml serialization is a settled concept for most developers, whereas .NET Framework 4.0 provides a new, more interesting way for Xml serialization, known as XAML serialization, which is covered later in this chapter and that is more important to learn.

Custom Serialization

In most cases the .NET built-in serialization engine is good enough. But if it does not meet your particular needs, you can override the serialization process with custom serialization. Basically this means implementing the ISerializable interface that requires the implementation of the GetObjectData method. Such a method is important because it is invoked during serialization. Moreover a custom implementation of the class constructor must be provided. Basically you have to first reproduce at least what built-in formatters do during serialization. Code in Listing 43.2 shows how to provide custom serialization for the Person class.

LISTING 43.2   Providing Custom Serialization

```
Imports System.Runtime.Serialization
Imports System.Security.Permissions

<Serializable()>
Public Class Person
    Implements ISerializable

    Public Overridable Property FirstName As String
    Public Overridable Property LastName As String
    Public Overridable Property Age As Integer

    <SecurityPermission(SecurityAction.Demand,
                        SerializationFormatter:=True)>
    Protected Sub GetObjectData(ByVal info As System.Runtime.Serialization.
                                    SerializationInfo,
                      ByVal context As System.Runtime.Serialization.
                                    StreamingContext) _
                  Implements System.Runtime.Serialization.ISerializable.
                                    GetObjectData

        info.AddValue("First name", Me.FirstName)
        info.AddValue("Last name", Me.LastName)
        info.AddValue("Age", Me.Age)
    End Sub

    'At deserialization time
    Protected Sub New(ByVal info As SerializationInfo,
                      ByVal context As StreamingContext)
        MyBase.New()
        Me.FirstName = info.GetString("First name")
        Me.LastName = info.GetString("Last name")
        Me.Age = info.GetInt32("Age")
```

```
      End Sub
End Class
```

The GetObjectData method is basically invoked when you pass an object to the Serialize method of a formatter and require an info argument of type SerializationInfo. This class stores all information needed for serialization. It exposes an AddValue method that stores data and a value utilized for recognizing data. Notice that the information is retrieved by the special constructor implementation that is invoked at deserialization time via GetXXX methods where XXX corresponds to .NET types such as Int32, Boolean, Short, and so on. Also notice how GetObjectData is decorated with the SecurityPermission attribute demanding for permissions about the serialization formatter. This is necessary because the permission is allowed only to full-trusted code, thus intranet and Internet zones are not allowed. Both GetObjectData and the constructor are Protected so that derived classes can still take advantage of them but are prevented from being public. If you are sure that your class will not be inherited, GetObjectData can also be Private.

INHERITANCE TIP

When you create a class that inherits from another class where ISerializable is implemented, if you add new members, you can also provide a new implementation of both GetObjectData and the constructor.

Implementing ISerializable is not the only way for controlling serialization. You can control serialization events, too.

Serialization Events

The serialization process raises four events, which are summarized in Table 43.1.

TABLE 43.1   Serialization Events

Event	Description
OnSerializing	Occurs just before serialization begins
OnSerialized	Occurs just after serialization completes
OnDeserializing	Occurs just before deserialization begins
OnDeserialized	Occurs just after deserialization completes

Serialization events are handled differently than classic events. There is an attribute for each event that you can handle as follows:

```
'Invoke this method before
'serialization begins
```

```
<OnSerializing()>
Private Sub FirstMethod()

End Sub


'Invoke this method after
'serialization completes
<OnSerialized()>
Private Sub SecondMethod()

End Sub


'Invoke this method before
'deserialization begins
<OnDeserializing()>
Private Sub ThirdMethod()

End Sub


'Invoke this method after
'deserialization completes
<OnDeserialized()>
Private Sub FourthMethod()

End Sub
```

The runtime takes care of invoking the specified method according to the moment represented by each attribute. In this way you can provide additional actions based on serialization events.

Serialization with XAML

This book has five chapters dedicated to the Windows Presentation Foundation technology, due to its importance in modern application development. You learned what XAML is and how you use it to define applications' user interface. XAML offers other advantages that can be taken in completely different scenarios; one of these is serialization. The System.Xaml.dll assembly implements the System.Xaml namespace that offers the XamlServices class whose purpose is providing members for reading and writing XAML in serialization scenarios. Because XAML is substantially Xml code that adheres to specific schemas, serialization output will be under Xml format. The good news is that you are not limited in using XAML serialization only in WPF applications. You simply need to add a reference to System.Xaml.dll. To understand how it works, create a new console project with Visual Basic and add the required reference. The goal of the code example is to understand how entire objects' graphs can be serialized with this technique. Consider the following implementation of the Person class:

```
Public Class Person
    Public Property FirstName As String
    Public Property LastName As String
    Public Property Age As Integer
    Public Property Friends As List(Of Person)
End Class
```

Other than the usual properties, it exposes a Friends property of type List(Of Person). This enables creating a simple object graph. Now consider the following code that creates two instances of the Person class that populates the Friends property of the main Person instance that we serialize:

```
Dim oneFriend As New Person With {.LastName = "White",
                                 .FirstName = "Robert", .Age = 35}
Dim anotherFriend As New Person With {.LastName = "Red",
                                      .FirstName = "Stephen", .Age = 42}

Dim p As New Person With {.LastName = "Del Sole", .FirstName = "Alessandro",
                          .Age = 32,
                          .Friends = New List(Of Person) _
                                     From {oneFriend, anotherFriend}}
```

Using objects and collection initializers makes this operation straightforward. To serialize an object graph, you simply invoke the XamlServices.Save shared method that requires an output stream and the object to be serialized. The following code snippet demonstrates this:

```
Imports System.IO, System.Xaml
'...
Using target As New FileStream("C:\Temp\Person.xaml", FileMode.Create)
    XamlServices.Save(target, p)
End Using
```

SERIALIZING GENERIC COLLECTIONS

When you serialize generic collections, especially custom ones, ensure that they implement the IList or IDictionary interfaces or the serialization process might not work correctly.

43

The previously described serialization process produces the following output:

```
<Person Age="32"
    FirstName="Alessandro"
    LastName="Del Sole"
    xmlns="clr-namespace:XamlSerialization;assembly=XamlSerialization"
    xmlns:scg="clr-namespace:System.Collections.Generic;
                 assembly=mscorlib"
    xmlns:x="http://schemas.microsoft.com/winfx/2006/xaml">

  <Person.Friends>
    <scg:List x:TypeArguments="Person" Capacity="4">
      <Person Friends="{x:Null}" Age="35" FirstName="Robert"
              LastName="White" />
      <Person Friends="{x:Null}" Age="42" FirstName="Stephen"
              LastName="Red" />
    </scg:List>
  </Person.Friends>
</Person>
```

This technique is efficient and makes output readable. As usual in Xaml files, the Xaml schema is pointed to via the x namespace. Notice how the scg namespace points to the System.Collections.Generic .NET namespace, required for deserializing the content as a generic collection. Also notice how the Person.Friends element defines subsequent Person elements storing information on child Person classes being part of the Friends property. Finally, notice how the Friends property for nested Person elements is null. (We did not define child elements for the property.) Deserializing such content is also straightforward. To accomplish this you simply invoke the XamlServices.Load shared method converting its result into the appropriate type. The following code shows how deserialization works, iterating the final result for demonstrating that deserialization was correctly performed:

```
Using source As New FileStream("C:\temp\person.xaml", FileMode.Open)
    Dim result As Person = CType(XamlServices.Load(source), Person)

    'Shows:
    'White
    'Green
    For Each p In result.Friends
        Console.WriteLine(p.LastName)
    Next
    Console.ReadLine()
End Using
```

XAML serialization can be used in different situations, such as persisting the state of WPF controls but also serializing entire .NET objects graphs.

Serialization in Windows Communication Foundation

There are situations in which serialization is required for persisting state of objects from WCF services. Starting with .NET Framework 3.0, you can serialize objects exposed by WCF services taking advantage of the `DataContractSerializer` class (which inherits from `XmlObjectSerializer`). The usage of such a class is not so different from other serialization classes. The only need is that you must mark your serializable classes either with the `Serializable` or with the `DataContract` attribute and, in this case, their members with the `DataMember` attribute. To see how this works in code, create a new WCF service project within Visual Studio 2010 (see Chapter 41, "Creating and Consuming WCF Services," for a recap) and name it **WcfPersonService**. Rename the default `IService1` interface to `IPersonService`; then rename the default `Service1` class to `PersonService`. The new service exposes a special implementation of the `Person` class. Listing 43.3 shows the complete code for the WCF sample service.

LISTING 43.3   Exposing Serializable Objects from WCF Services

```
<ServiceContract()>
Public Interface IPersonService

    <OperationContract()>
    Function GetPersonFullName(ByVal onePerson As Person) As String
End Interface

<DataContract()>
Public Class Person

    <DataMember()>
    Public Property FirstName As String

    <DataMember()>
    Public Property LastName As String
End Class
Public Class PersonService
    Implements IPersonService

    Public Function GetPersonFullName(ByVal onePerson As Person) As String _
                Implements IPersonService.GetPersonFullName

        Dim fullName As New Text.StringBuilder
        fullName.Append(onePerson.FirstName)
        fullName.Append(" ")
        fullName.Append(onePerson.LastName)
```

```
            Return fullName.ToString
    End Function
End Class
```

Notice how you simply decorate the Person class and its members respectively with the DataContract and DataMember attributes. Now create a new console project for testing the WCF service and serialization. Name the new project as **TestWcfSerialization**; then add a service reference to the WcfPersonService project (see Chapter 41 for a recap). This adds a reference to the WCF service creating a proxy class in Visual Basic. All you need to do now is to get the instance of the service client and invoke the DataContractSerializer class that requires a stream for putting serialized data to. Code in Listing 43.4 shows both serialization and deserialization processes.

LISTING 43.4   Performing WCF Serialization

```vbnet
Imports TestWcfSerialization.PersonServiceReference
Imports System.IO
Imports System.Runtime.Serialization

Module Module1

    Sub Main()

        Dim client As New PersonServiceClient
        Dim p As New Person With {.FirstName = "Alessandro", .LastName = "Del Sole"}

        Dim target As New FileStream("C:\Temp\WcfSerialized.xml", FileMode.Create)
        Dim serializer As New DataContractSerializer(GetType(Person))
        serializer.WriteObject(target, p)
        target.Close()
        serializer = Nothing

        Console.ReadLine()
        Dim source As New FileStream("C:\Temp\WcfSerialized.xml", FileMode.Open)
        serializer = New DataContractSerializer(GetType(Person))

        Dim result As Person = CType(serializer.ReadObject(source), Person)

        Console.WriteLine(result.LastName)
        Console.ReadLine()
    End Sub
End Module
```

Notice how you invoke the WriteObject instance method for persisting data. The method requires the file stream instance and the data instance as arguments. WriteObject can also serialize an entire object graph, similarly to the binary standard serialization. Also notice that data is serialized to Xml format. To deserialize objects you simply invoke the `ReadObject` instance method converting the result into the appropriate type. Serialization in WCF can cause special exceptions: `InvalidDataContractException`, which is thrown when the data contract on the service side is badly implemented, and `System.ServiceModel.QuotaExceededException` that is thrown when serialization attempts to write a number of objects greater than the allowed number. Such a number is represented by the `DataContractSerializer.MaxItemsInObjectsGraph` property and the default value is `Integer.MaxValue`. The following snippet shows how you catch the previously mentioned exceptions:

```
Try
    serializer.WriteObject(target, p)
Catch ex As InvalidDataContractException
    'Data contract on the service side is wrong
Catch ex As QuotaExceededException
    'Maximum number of serializable object exceeded
Finally
    target.Close()
    serializer = Nothing
End Try
```

If you wonder when you would need WCF serialization, there can be several answers to your question. The most common scenarios are when you have WCF services exposing LINQ to SQL models or Entity Data Models. Data exchange from and to clients is performed via WCF serialization. This requires a little bit of work in LINQ to SQL whereas Entity Data Models are serialization-enabled, which is covered in "Serialization in the ADO.NET Entity Framework" section.

JSON Serialization

Starting from .NET Framework 3.5, managed languages support the JavaScript Object Notation (JSON) serialization, offered by the `System.Runtime.Serialization.Json` namespace, which is particularly useful when you need to serialize objects as javascript-compliant and that you use in WCF and ASP.NET Ajax applications. Conceptually JSON serialization works like the WCF serialization illustrated previously. The only difference is that you use a `DataContractJsonSerializer` class that works as in the following code snippet:

```
Dim target As New FileStream("C:\Temp\WcfSerialized.xml", FileMode.Create)
Dim jsonSerializer As New DataContractJsonSerializer(GetType(Person))
jsonSerializer.WriteObject(target, p)
```

To deserialize objects you invoke the `DataContractJsonSerializer.ReadObject` method converting the result into the appropriate type.

Serialization in the ADO.NET Entity Framework

When you create Entity Data Models, entities are automatically decorated with `Serializable` and `DataContract` attributes and their members as `DataMember` as you can easily check by investigating the code-behind file for EDMs. This enables binary and Xml serialization for entities also in WCF scenarios. To understand how this works, create a new console project and add a new EDM wrapping the Northwind database (see Chapter 27, "Introducing the ADO.NET Entity Framework," for a review), including only the `Customers` and `Orders` tables. Basically you use formatters as you did in the objects serialization with no differences. Code in Listing 43.5 shows how to accomplish this.

LISTING 43.5   Serializing Entities from an Entity Data Model

```
Imports System.Runtime.Serialization.Formatters.Binary
Imports System.IO

Module Module1
    Sub Main()
        Using northwind As New NorthwindEntities
            'Retrieves the first order, as an example
            Dim anOrder As Order = northwind.Orders.Include("Customer").First

            'Same as classic objects serialization
            Dim formatter As New BinaryFormatter
            Using stream As New FileStream("C:\temp\EFSerialization.dat",
                            FileMode.Create)
                formatter.Serialize(stream, anOrder)
            End Using

            Dim newOrder As Order
            Using source As New FileStream("C:\temp\EFSerialization.dat",
                            FileMode.Open)
                newOrder = CType(formatter.Deserialize(source), Order)
            End Using
        End Using

        Console.ReadLine()
    End Sub
End Module
```

If you need to retrieve data via a WCF service, you use a `DataContractSerializer` taking advantage of serialization in WCF scenarios as described before in this chapter. Listing 43.5 shows an example of binary serialization, but you can also take advantage of other techniques described in this chapter as well.

Summary

Serialization is the capability to save objects' state to disk (or memory) and to re-create the state later. The .NET Framework offers several serialization techniques, all provided by the `System.Runtime.Serialization` namespace. You can perform binary serialization via the `BinaryFormatter` class or soap serialization (Xml-based mode for Soap web services) via the `SoapFormatter` class. In both cases you simply need an output stream and then you invoke the `Serialize` method for performing serialization, whereas `Deserialize` is for performing deserialization. Another common technique is the Xml serialization that creates Xml documents starting from your objects and that is useful if you need to exchange your data with non-.NET applications or with non-Windows applications, due to the standard format of this kind of document. If you need deep control over the serialization process, you implement the `ISerializable` interface that requires the implementation of the `GetObjectData`, where you can customize the behavior of the process other than handling serialization events. The .NET Framework 4.0 also retakes techniques first introduced with the .NET 3.5 version, such as WCF serialization, which take advantages of the `DataContractSerializer` class or the XAML serialization that is performed via the `XamlServices` class. Finally, you can serialize entities from an Entity Data Model using all preceding techniques so that you can easily exchange (or save the state of) your data without changing the programming model.

43

Processes and Multithreading

In our everyday life we all do a number of things such as go to work, have appointments, stay with friends or with the family; we are all very busy, of course. Sometimes we can make two things simultaneously, such as speaking on the phone while writing something on a piece of paper, but in most cases we do just one thing at a time: after all, there is only one of us. It would be great if we could share our things to do with other people so that multiple people do the same work concurrently. We would be less tired and we would have more time for resting or staying with our family. In the computers' world, the problem is similar. You can compare a person of the real world to an application. If an application has to complete hard and long work totally alone, it can cause overhead on the system and take more time. Moreover, recent hardware architectures (such as multi-core processors) would remain unexploited. So it would be useful having the ability to split the work of an application among multiple parts that could work concurrently. This is where threading comes in the .NET development. With threading you can create multiple threads of work to perform multiple tasks concurrently so that your applications can take the best of performances and resources. But threading is not the only way you request actions. In many circumstances you need to launch external executables and possibly hold a reference to them in your code, so you also often work with processes. In this chapter you take a look at how the .NET Framework enables managing processes and how you can split operations across multiple threads, both created manually and provided by the .NET thread pool.

Managing Processes

You use the System.Diagnostics.Process class to manage processes on your machine.

This class offers both shared and instance members so that you can launch an external process but also get a reference to one or more processes. The following code shows how to launch an external process via the shared implementation of the Start method:

```
Process.Start("Notepad.exe")
```

Any call to the Process.Start method will return a Process object. You can also specify arguments for the process by specifying the second parameter for the method as follows:

```
Process.Start("Notepad.exe", "C:\aFile.txt")
```

One of the most important features of the Start method is that you can also supply the username, password, and domain for launching a process:

```
Process.Start("Notepad.exe", "C:\aFile.txt",
              "Alessandro", Password, "\\MYDOMAIN")
```

Notice that the password is necessarily an instance of the System.Security.SecureString class, so see the MSDN documentation about this. The Process class also has an instance behavior that enables getting a reference to a process instance. This is useful when you want to programmatically control a process. With regard to this, you first need an instance of the ProcessStartInfo class that can store process execution information. The class exposes lots of properties, but the most important are summarized in the following code snippet:

```
Dim procInfo As New ProcessStartInfo
With procInfo
    .FileName = "Notepad.exe"
    .Arguments = "aFile.txt"
    .WorkingDirectory = "C:\"
    .WindowStyle = ProcessWindowStyle.Maximized
    .ErrorDialog = True
End With
```

Particularly, the ErrorDialog property makes the Process instance show up an error dialog if the process cannot be started regularly. When you have done this, you simply create an instance of the Process class and assign its StartInfo property; finally you invoke Start as demonstrated in the following code:

```
Dim proc As New Process
proc.StartInfo = procInfo
proc.Start()
```

```
'Alternative syntax:
'Dim proc As Process = Process.Start(procInfo)
```

Approaching processes in this fashion is helpful if you need to programmatically control processes. For example, you can wait until a process exits for the specified number of milliseconds as follows:

```
'Waits for two seconds
proc.WaitForExit(2000)
```

To close a process you write the following code:

```
proc.Close()
```

Finally, you can kill unresponsive processes by invoking the Kill method as follows:

```
proc.Kill()
```

The Process class also exposes the EnableRaisingEvents boolean property which allows setting if the runtime should raise the Exited event when the process terminates. Such an event is raised if either the process terminates normally or because of an invocation to the Kill method. Until now you saw how launching processes but the Process class is also useful when you need to get information on running processes as discussed in next subsection.

Querying Existing Processes

You can easily get information on running processes through some methods from the Process class that provide the ability of getting process instances. For example, GetProcesses returns an array of Process objects, each one representing a running process whereas GetProcessById and GetProcessByName return information on the specified process given the identification number or name, whereas GetCurrentProcess returns an instance of the Process class representing the current process. Then the Process class exposes lots of useful properties for retrieving information, each of them self-explanatory such as ProcessName, Id, ExitCode, Handle, or HasExited but also other advanced information properties, such as PageMemorySize or VirtualMemorySize, which respectively return the memory size associated with the process on the page memory or the virtual memory. The Visual Studio's Object Browser and IntelliSense can help you with the rest of available properties. At the moment focus on how you can get information on running processes. The coolest way for getting process information is using LINQ to Objects. The following query, and subsequent For..Each loop, demonstrates how to retrieve a list of names of running processes:

```
Dim processesList = (From p In Process.GetProcesses
                     Select p.ProcessName).AsEnumerable

For Each procName In processesList
    Console.WriteLine(procName)
Next
```

Notice that the query result is converted into `IEnumerable(Of String)` so that you can eventually bind the list to a user interface control supporting the type.

Introducing Multithreading

A thread is a unit of work. The logic of threading-based programming is performing multiple operations concurrently so that a big operation can be split across multiple threads. The .NET Framework 4.0 offers support for multithreading via the `System.Threading` namespace. But .NET 4.0 also introduces a new important library, which is discussed in Chapter 45, "Parallel Programming," which provides support for the parallel computing. For this reason this chapter provides summary information on the multithreading approach so that in next chapter you get more detailed information on the task-based programming.

IMPORTS DIRECTIVES

Code examples shown in this chapter require an `Imports System.Threading` directive.

Creating Threads

You create a new thread for performing an operation with an instance of the `System.Threading.Thread` class. The constructor of this class requires you to also specify an instance of the `System.Threading.ThreadStart` delegate that simply points to a method that can actually do the work. Then you simply invoke the `Thread.Start` instance method. The following code snippet demonstrates how you can create a new thread:

```
Private Sub simpleThread()
    Dim newThread As New Thread(New ThreadStart(AddressOf _
                                                executeSimpleThread))

    newThread.Start()
End Sub


Private Sub executeSimpleThread()
    Console.WriteLine("Running a separate thread")
End Sub
```

To actually start the new thread, you invoke the method that encapsulates the thread instance, which in this case is `simpleThread`.

Creating Threads with Lambda Expressions

You might recall from Chapter 21, "Advanced Language Features," that lambda expressions can be used anywhere there is the need for a delegate. This is also true in threading-based programming. The following code snippet demonstrates how you can take advantage of statement lambdas instead of providing an explicit delegate:

```
Private Sub lambdaThread()
    Dim newThread As New Thread(New _
```

```
                    ThreadStart(Sub()
                                  Console.WriteLine("Thread with lambda")
                              End Sub))
    newThread.Start()
End Sub
```

Now you can simply invoke the lambdaThread method to run a secondary thread, and with one method you reach the same objective of the previous code where two methods were implemented.

Passing Parameters

In many cases you might have the need to pass data to new threads. This can be accomplished by creating an instance of the ParameterizedThreadStart delegate, which requires an argument of type Object that you can use for sharing your data. The following code demonstrates how you create a thread with parameters:

```
Private Sub threadWithParameters(ByVal parameter As Object)
    Dim newThread As New Thread(New _
                              ParameterizedThreadStart(AddressOf _
                              executeThreadWithParameters))
    newThread.Start(parameter)
End Sub
```

Notice how the Thread.Start method has an overload that takes the specified parameter as the data. Because such data is of type Object, you need to convert it into the most appropriate format. The following code demonstrates how to implement a method that the delegate refers to and how to convert the data into a hypothetical string:

```
Private Sub executeThreadWithParameters(ByVal anArgument As Object)
    Dim aString = CType(anArgument, String)
    Console.WriteLine(aString)
End Sub
```

Of course you can take advantage of lambda expressions if you do not want to provide an explicit delegate also in this kind of scenario.

Understanding the .NET Thread Pool

In the previous section you saw how simple it is to create and run a new thread. When you have one or two threads, things are also easy for performance. But if you decide to split a process or an application across lots of concurrent threads, the previous approach can cause performance and resources overhead. So you should manually search for the best configuration to fine-tune system resources consumption with your threads. Your application can run on different configurations in terms of available memory, processors, and general resources, so it is difficult to predict how many threads you can launch concurrently on target machines without affecting performance and causing overhead.

Fortunately the .NET Framework maintains its own set of threads that you can also reuse for your purposes instead of writing code for creating and running new threads, ensuring that only the specified number of threads will be executed concurrently, all controlled by the Framework. The set is named *thread pool* and you access it via the System.Threading.ThreadPool class. This class offers static methods for assigning tasks to threads in the box; because the thread pool has a predefined number of available threads If they are all busy doing something else, the new task is put into a queue and is executed when a thread completes its work. To take advantage of threads in the thread pool, you invoke the System.Threading.ThreadPool.QueueUserWorkItem method, as demonstrated in the following code:

```
Sub QueueWork()


    ThreadPool.QueueUserWorkItem(New WaitCallback(AddressOf FirstWorkItem))
    ThreadPool.QueueUserWorkItem(New WaitCallback(AddressOf SecondWorkItem))
    ThreadPool.QueueUserWorkItem(New WaitCallback(Sub()
                                                      Console.
                                                      WriteLine _
                                                      ("Third work item")
                                                  End Sub))


End Sub

Private Sub FirstWorkItem(ByVal state As Object)
    Console.WriteLine("First work item")
End Sub
Private Sub SecondWorkItem(ByVal state As Object)
    Console.WriteLine("Second work item")
End Sub
```

With QueueUserWorkItem you basically ask the runtime to put the specified task in the execution queue so that it will be executed when a thread in the thread pool is available. The WaitCallBack delegate simply allows passing state information and requires referred methods to have an argument of type Object in their signatures. Notice how you can still use lambdas to supply the desired action.

Getting and Setting Information in the Thread Pool

You can query information on the thread pool by invoking the ThreadPool.GetMaxThreads, ThreadPool.GetMinThreads, and ThreadPool.GetAvailableThreads methods. GetMaxThreads return the maximum number of concurrent threads that are held by the thread pool; GetMinThreads return the number of idle threads that are maintained waiting for the first new task being requested, whereas

GetAvailableThreads return the number of available threads. Whichever you use, they all return two values: the number of worker threads and of completion threads. Worker threads are units of execution, whereas completion threads are asynchronous I/O operations. The following code demonstrates how you get information on available threads:

```
Sub PoolInfo()
    Dim workerThreads As Integer
    Dim completionPortThreads As Integer

    ThreadPool.GetAvailableThreads(workerThreads,
                                   completionPortThreads)
    Console.WriteLine("Available threads: {0}, async I/O: {1}",
                      workerThreads, completionPortThreads)
    Console.ReadLine()
End Sub
```

workerThreads and completionPortThreads arguments are passed by reference; this is the reason why you need variables for storing values. Similarly you can use SetMaxThreads and SetMinThreads to establish the maximum number of requests held by the thread pool and the minimum number of idle threads. The following line is an example:

```
ThreadPool.SetMaxThreads(2000, 1500)
```

CHANGING DEFAULT VALUES

You should take care of editing the default values for the thread pool. You should do it only when you have a deep knowledge of how many resources will be consumed on the machine and of system resources so that edits will not be negative for the target system. Generally default values in the thread pool are high enough, but you can check this out by invoking GetMaxThreads.

Threads Synchronization

Until now you saw how to create and rung new threads of execution to split big operations across multiple threads. This is useful but there is a problem: Imagine you have multiple threads accessing the same data source simultaneously; what happens to the data source and how are threads handled to avoid errors? This is a problem that is solved with the so-called thread synchronization. Basically the idea is that when a thread accesses a resource, this resource is locked until required operations are completed to prevent other threads from accessing that resource. Both Visual Basic and the .NET Framework respectively provide keywords and objects to accomplish threads synchronization, as covered in the next subsections.

The SyncLock..End SyncLock Statement

The Visual Basic language offers the `SyncLock..End SyncLock` statement that is the place where you can grant access to the specified resource to only one thread per time. For example, imagine you have a class where you define a list of customers and a method for adding a new customer to the list, as demonstrated by the following code snippet:

```
Private customers As New List(Of String)


Sub AddCustomer(ByVal customerName As String)

    SyncLock Me
        customers.Add(customerName)
    End SyncLock
End Sub
```

Basically the preceding code locks the entire enclosing class, preventing other threads from accessing the instance until the requested operation completes. By the way, locking an entire class is not always the best idea, because it can be expensive in terms of resources and performances, and other threads cannot also access other members. Unfortunately you cannot directly lock the resource; the MSDN documentation in fact states that you need to declare a *lock object* that you can use as follows:

```
Private customers As New List(Of String)
Private lockObject As New Object()

Sub AddCustomer(ByVal customerName As String)

    SyncLock lockObject
        customers.Add(customerName)
    End SyncLock
End Sub
```

The lock object is typically a `System.Object`. Using an object like this can ensure that the code block executed within `SyncLock..End SyncLock` will not be accessible by other threads. Another approach is using `GetType` instead of the lock object, pointing to the current type where the synchronization lock is defined. The following code demonstrates this:

```
Class Customers
    Inherits List(Of String)

    Public Sub AddCustomer(ByVal customerName As String)
        SyncLock GetType(Customers)
            Me.Add(customerName)
        End SyncLock
    End Sub
End Class
```

The `SyncLock..End SyncLock` statement is typical of Visual Basic language grammar. By the way, the statement is translated behind the scenes into invocations to the `System.Threading.Monitor` class as is described in next section.

Synchronization with the `Monitor` Class

The `System.Threading.Monitor` class is the support object for the `SyncLock..End SyncLock` statement, and the compiler translates `SyncLock` blocks into invocations to the `Monitor` class. You use it as follows:

```
Sub AddCustomer(ByVal customerName As String)
    Dim result As Boolean

    Try
        Monitor.Enter(lockObject, result)
        customers.Add(customerName)
    Catch ex As Exception
    Finally
        Monitor.Exit(lockObject)
    End Try
End Sub
```

> **TIP**
>
> `Monitor.Enter` now has an overload that takes a second argument of type `Boolean`, passed by reference, indicating if the lock was taken. This is new in .NET Framework 4.0.

Basically `Monitor.Enter` locks the object whereas `Monitor.Exit` unlocks it. It is fundamental to place `Monitor.Exit` in the `Finally` part of the `Try..Catch` block so that resources will be unlocked anyway. At this point you might wonder why use `Monitor` instead of `SyncLock..End SyncLock` because they produce the same result. The difference is that `Monitor` also exposes additional members, such as the `TryEnter` method that supports timeout, as demonstrated here:

```
Monitor.TryEnter(lockObject, 3000, result)
```

This code attempts to obtain the lock on the specified object for three seconds before terminating.

Read/Write Locks

A frequent scenario is when you have a shared resource that multiple reader threads need to access. In a scenario like this, you probably want to grant writing permissions just to a single thread to avoid concurrency problems. The .NET Framework provides the

`System.Threading.ReaderWriterLockSlim` class, which provides a lock enabled for multiple threads reading and exclusive access for writing.

READERWRITERLOCK CLASS

The .NET Framework still provides the `ReaderWriterLock` class, as in its previous versions, but it is complex and used to handle particular multithreading scenarios. Instead, as its name implies, the `ReaderWriterLockSlim` class is a light-weight object for reading and writing locks.

Generally an instance of this class is declared as a shared field and is used to invoke both methods for reading and writing. The following code demonstrates how you enable a writer lock:

```
Private Shared rw As New ReaderWriterLockSlim


Sub AddCustomer(ByVal customerName As String)
    Try

        rw.EnterWriteLock()
        customers.Add(customerName)
    Catch ex As Exception
    Finally
        rw.ExitWriteLock()
    End TrThe
End Sub
```

This ensures that only one thread can write to the customers' collection. The next code snippet shows instead how you can enable a reader lock:

```
Sub GetInformation()
    Try
        rw.EnterReadLock()
        Console.WriteLine(customers.Count.ToString)
    Catch ex As Exception
    Finally
        rw.ExitReadLock()
    End Try
End Sub
```

`ReaderWriterLockSlim` is an object you should use if you expect more readers than writers; in other cases you should consider custom synchronization locks implementations.

Summary

This chapter covered processes management and multithreading with Visual Basic 2010. First you saw how to utilize the `System.Diagnostics.Process` class for launching and managing external process from your applications, including programmatic access to processes. Next you got an overview of threads and the `System.Threading.Thread` class, understanding how a thread is a single unit of execution and seeing how you create and run threads both programmatically and inside the .NET's thread pool. In the final part of this chapter you learned about synchronization locks, which are necessary so that multiple threads access the same resources concurrently. For this, remember the `SyncLock..End SyncLock` VB statement and the `Monitor` class.

44

CHAPTER 45

Parallel Programming

Modern computers ship with multi-core architectures, meaning that they have more than one processor. The simplest home computer has at least dual-core architecture, so we're sure you have a machine with multiple processors, too. Generally managed applications do their work using only one processor. This makes things easier, but with this approach you do not unleash all system resources. The reason is that all elaborations rely on a single processor that is overcharged and will take more time. Having instead the possibility of scaling the application execution over all available processors is a technique that would improve how system resources are consumed and would speed up the application execution. The reason is simple: Instead of having only one processor doing the work, you have all available processors doing the work concurrently. Scaling applications across multiple processors is known as *parallel computing*, which is not something new in the programming world, in which the word "parallel" means that multiple tasks are executed concurrently, in parallel. What is actually new is the availability in .NET Framework 4.0 of a new library dedicated to parallel computing for the Microsoft platform. This library is called Task Parallel Library and also includes Parallel LINQ, which is discussed in Chapter 29, "Overview of Parallel LINQ." In this chapter you learn what the library is, how it is structured, and how you can use it for writing parallel code in your applications, starting from basic concepts going through concurrent collections.

Introducing Parallel Computing

The .NET Framework 4.0 provides support for parallel computing through the Task Parallel Library (also referred to as TPL), which is a set of APIs offered by specific extensions of the System.Threading.dll assembly. The reference to this assembly is included by default when creating new projects, so you do not need to add one manually. The TPL is reachable via the System.Threading and System.Threading.Tasks, namespaces that provide objects for scaling work execution over multiple processors. Basically you write small units of work known as tasks. Tasks are scheduled for execution by the TPL's Task Scheduler, which is responsible for executing tasks according to available threads. This is possible because the Task Scheduler is integrated with the .NET Thread Pool. The good news is that the .NET Framework can automatically take advantage of all available processors on the target machines without the need to recompile code.

> **NOTE**
>
> Parallel computing makes it to easier to scale applications over multiple processors, but it remains something complex in terms of concepts. This is because you will face again some threading concepts, such as synchronization locks, deadlocks, and so on. The suggestion is to have at least a basic knowledge of threading issues before writing parallel code. Another important consideration is when should you use parallel computing? The answer is not easy because you are the only one who knows how your applications consume resources. The general rule is that parallel computing gives the best results when you have intensive processing scenarios. In simpler elaborations, parallel computing is not necessarily the best choice and can cause performance loss. Use it when your applications require hard CPU loops.

Most of the parallel API are available through the System.Threading.Tasks.Task and System.Threading.Tasks.Parallel classes. The first one is described in detail later, whereas we now provide coverage of the most important classes for parallelism.

Introducing Parallel Classes

Parallelism in the .NET Framework 4.0 is possible due to a number of classes, some responsible for maintaining the architecture of the TPL and some for performing operations in a concurrent fashion. The following subsection provides a brief coverage of the most important classes, describing their purpose.

The Parallel Class

The System.Threading.Tasks.Parallel class is one of the most important classes in parallel computing, because it provides shared methods for running concurrent tasks and for executing parallel loops. In this chapter you can find several examples of usage of this class; for now you just need to know that it provides the Invoke, For, and ForEach shared methods. The first one enables running multiple tasks concurrently, whereas the other ones enable executing loops in parallel.

The TaskScheduler Class

The System.Threading.Tasks.TaskScheduler class is responsible for the low-level work of sending tasks to the thread queue. This means that when you start a new concurrent task, the task is sent to the scheduler that checks for thread availability in the .NET thread pool. If a thread is available, the task is pushed into the thread and executed. Generally you do not interact with the task scheduler. (The class exposes some members that you can use to understand the tasks state.) The first property is Current, which retrieves the instance of the running task scheduler. This is required to access information. For example, you can understand the concurrency level by reading the MaximumConcurrencyLevel property as follows:

```
Console.WriteLine("The maximum concurrency level is {0}",
                 TaskScheduler.Current.MaximumConcurrencyLevel)
```

There are also some protected methods that can be used to force tasks' execution (such as QueueTask and TryDequeue) but these are accessible if you want to create your custom task scheduler, which is beyond of the scope in this chapter.

The TaskFactory Class

The System.Threading.Tasks.TaskFactory class provides support for generating and running new tasks and is generally exposed as a shared property of the Task class, as explained in the next section about tasks. The most important member is the StartNew method, which enables creating a new task and automatically starting it.

The ParallelOptions Class

The System.Threading.Tasks.ParallelOptions class provides a way for setting options on tasks' creation. Specifically it provides properties for setting tasks' cancellation properties (CancellationToken), the instance of the scheduler (TaskScheduler), and the maximum number of threads that a task is split across (MaxDegreeOfParallelism).

Understanding and Using Tasks

Parallel computing in the .NET Framework development relies on the concept of tasks. This section is therefore about the core of the parallel computing, and you learn to use tasks for scaling unit of works across multiple threads and processors.

What Is a Task?

Chapter 44, "Processes and Multithreading," discusses multithreading and illustrates how a thread is a unit of work that you can use to split a big task across multiple units of work. Different from the pure threading world, in parallel computing the most important concept is the *task*, which is simply the basic unit of work, which can be scaled across all available processors. A task is not a thread; a thread can run multiple tasks, but each task can be also scaled across more than one thread, depending on available resources. The task is therefore the most basic unit of work for operations executed in parallel. In terms of code, a task is nothing but an instance of the System.Threading.Tasks.Task class that holds a reference to a delegate, pointing to a method that does some work. The implementation is similar to what you do with `Thread` objects but with the differences previously discussed. Basically you have two alternatives for executing operations with tasks: The first one is calling the `Parallel.Invoke` method; the second one is manually creating and managing instances of the `Task` class. The following subsections cover both scenarios.

Running Tasks with `Parallel.Invoke`

The first way for running tasks in parallel is calling the `Parallel.Invoke` shared method. This method can receive an array of `System.Action` objects as parameter, so each `Action` is translated by the runtime into a task. If possible, tasks are executed in parallel. The following example demonstrates how to perform three calculations concurrently:

```
'Requires an Imports System.Threading.Tasks directive


Dim angle As Double = 150
Dim sineResult As Double
Dim cosineResult As Double
Dim tangentResult As Double


Parallel.Invoke(Sub()
                    Console.WriteLine(Thread.CurrentThread.
                                ManagedThreadId)
                    Dim radians As Double = angle * Math.PI / 180
                    sineResult = Math.Sin(radians)
                End Sub,
                Sub()
                    Console.WriteLine(Thread.CurrentThread.
                                ManagedThreadId)
                    Dim radians As Double = angle * Math.PI / 180
                    cosineResult = Math.Cos(radians)
                End Sub,
                Sub()
                    Console.WriteLine(Thread.CurrentThread.
                                ManagedThreadId)
                    Dim radians As Double = angle * Math.PI / 180
                    tangentResult = Math.Tan(radians)
                End Sub)
```

In the example the code takes advantage of statement lambdas; each of them is translated into a task by the runtime that is also responsible for creating and scheduling threads and for scaling tasks across all available processors. If you run the code you can see how the tasks run within separate threads, automatically created for you by the TPL. As an alternative you can supply `AddressOf` clauses pointing to methods performing the required operations, instead of using statement lambdas. Although this approach is useful when you need to run tasks in parallel the fastest way, it does not enable you to take control over tasks themselves. This is instead something that requires explicit instances of the `Task` class, as explained in the next section.

Creating, Running, and Managing Tasks: The `Task` Class

The `System.Threading.Tasks.Task` class represents the unit of work in the parallel computing based on the .NET Framework. Differently from calling `Parallel.Invoke`, when you create an instance of the `Task` class, you get deep control over the task itself, such as starting, stopping, waiting for completion, and cancelation. The constructor of the class requires you to supply a delegate or a lambda expression to provide a method containing the code to be executed within the task. The following code demonstrates how you create a new task and then start it:

```
Dim simpleTask As New Task(Sub()
                                'Do your work here...
                           End Sub)


simpleTask.Start()
```

You supply the constructor with a lambda expression or with a delegate and then invoke the `Start` instance method. The `Task` class also exposes a `Factory` property of type `TaskFactory` that offers members for interacting with tasks. For example, you can use this property for creating and starting a new task all in one as follows:

```
Dim factoryTask = Task.Factory.StartNew(Sub()
                                            'Do your work here
                                        End Sub)
```

This has the same result as the first code snippet. The logic is that you can create instances of the `Task` class, each with some code that will be executed in parallel.

GETTING THE THREAD ID

When you launch a new task, the task is executed within a managed thread. If you want to get information on the thread, in the code for the task you can access it via the `System.Threading.Thread.CurrentThread` shared property. For example, the `CurrentThread.ManagedThreadId` property will return the thread id that is hosting the task.

Creating Tasks That Return Values

The Task class also has a generic counterpart that you can use for creating tasks that return a value. For example consider the following code snippet that creates a task returning a value of type Double, which is the result of calculating the tangent of an angle:

```
Dim taskWithResult = Task(Of Double).
    Factory.StartNew(Function()
```

```
                    Dim radians As Double _
                        = 120 * Math.PI / 180
                    Dim tan As Double = _
                        Math.Tan(radians)
                    Return tan
                End Function)
```

```
Console.WriteLine(taskWithResult.Result)
```

Basically you use a Function, which represents a System.Func(Of T) so that you can return a value from your operation. The result is accessed via the Task.Result property. In the preceding example, the Result property contains the result of the tangent calculation. The problem is that the start value on which the calculation is performed is hard-coded. If you want to pass a value as an argument, you need to approach the problem differently. The following code demonstrates how to implement a method that receives an argument that can be reached from within the new task:

```
Private Function CalcTan(ByVal angle As Double) As Double


    Dim t = Task(Of Double).Factory.
        StartNew(Function()
                    Dim radians As Double = angle * Math.PI / 180
                    tangentResult = Math.Tan(radians)
                    Return tangentResult
                End Function)
        Return t.Result
End Function
```

The result of the calculation is returned from the task. This result is wrapped by the Task.Result instance property, which is then returned as the method result.

Waiting for Tasks to Complete

You can explicitly wait for a task to complete by invoking the Task.Wait method. The following code waits until the task completes:

```
Dim simpleTask = Task.Factory.StartNew(Sub()
                                            'Do your work here
                                        End Sub)
simpleTask.Wait()
```

You can alternatively pass a number of milliseconds to the Wait method so that you can also check for a timeout. The following code demonstrates this:

```
simpleTask.Wait(1000)
If simpleTask.IsCompleted Then
    'completed
Else
```

```
    'timeout
End If
```

Notice how the `IsCompleted` property enables checking if the task is marked as completed by the runtime. Generally `Wait` has to be enclosed inside a `Try..Catch` block because the method asks the runtime to complete a task that could raise any exceptions. This is an example:

```
Try
    simpleTask.Wait(1000)
    If simpleTask.IsCompleted Then
        'completed
    Else
        'timeout
    End If

    'parallel exception
Catch ex As AggregateException

End Try
```

Exception Handling

Handling exceptions is a crucial topic in parallel programming. The problem is that multiple tasks that run concurrently could raise more than one exception concurrently, and you need to understand what the actual problem is. The .NET Framework 4.0 offers the `System.AggregateException` class that wraps all exceptions occurred concurrently into one instance. The class then exposes, over classic properties, an `InnerExceptions` collection that you can iterate for checking what exceptions occurred. The following code demonstrates how you catch an `AggregateException` and how you iterate the instance:

```
Dim aTask = Task.Factory.StartNew(Sub() Console.
                                  WriteLine("A demo task"))

Try
    aTask.Wait()
Catch ex As AggregateException
    For Each fault In ex.InnerExceptions
        If TypeOf (fault) Is InvalidOperationException Then
            'Handle the exception here..
        ElseIf TypeOf (fault) Is NullReferenceException Then
            'Handle the exception here..
        End If
    Next
Catch ex As Exception
```

```
End Try
```

Each item in InnerExceptions is an exception that you can verify with TypeOf. Another problem is when you have tasks that run nested tasks that throw exceptions. In this case you can take advantage of the AggregateException.Flatten method, which wraps exceptions thrown by nested tasks into the parent instance. The following code demonstrates how to accomplish this:

```
Dim aTask = Task.Factory.StartNew(Sub() Console.
                                        WriteLine("A demo task"))

Try
    aTask.Wait()
Catch ex As AggregateException
    For Each fault In ex.Flatten.InnerExceptions
        If TypeOf (fault) Is InvalidOperationException Then
            'Handle the exception here..
        ElseIf TypeOf (fault) Is NullReferenceException Then
            'Handle the exception here..
        End If
    Next
Catch ex As Exception

End Try
```

Basically Flatten returns an instance of the AggregateException storing inner exceptions that included errors coming from nested tasks.

Cancelling Tasks

There are situations in which you want to cancel task execution. To programmatically cancel a task, you need to enable tasks for cancellation, which requires some lines of code. You need an instance of the System.Threading.CancellationTokenSource class; this instance tells to a System.Threading.CancellationToken that it should be canceled. The CancellationToken class provides notifications for cancellation. The following lines declare both objects:

```
Dim tokenSource As New CancellationTokenSource()
Dim token As CancellationToken = tokenSource.Token
```

Then you can start a new task using an overload of the TaskFactory.StartNew method that takes the cancellation token as an argument. The following line accomplishes this:

```
Dim aTask = Task.Factory.StartNew(Sub() DoSomething(token), token)
```

You still pass a delegate as an argument; in the preceding example the delegate takes an argument of type CancellationToken that is useful for checking the state of cancellation during the task execution. The following code snippet provides the implementation of the DoSomething method, in a demonstrative way:

```
Sub DoSomething(ByVal cancelToken As CancellationToken)

    'Check if cancellation was requested before
    'the task starts
    If cancelToken.IsCancellationRequested = True Then
        cancelToken.ThrowIfCancellationRequested()
    End If

    For i As Integer = 0 To 1000

        'Simulates some work
        Thread.SpinWait(10000)
        If cancelToken.IsCancellationRequested Then

            'Cancellation was requested
            cancelToken.ThrowIfCancellationRequested()
        End If
    Next

End Sub
```

The IsCancellationRequested property returns True if cancellation over the current task was requested. The ThrowIfCancellationRequested method throws an OperationCanceledException to communicate to the caller that the task was canceled. In the preceding code snippet the Thread.SpinWait method simulates some work inside a loop. Notice how checking for cancellation is performed at each iteration so that an exception can be thrown if the task is actually canceled. The next step is to request cancellation in the main code. This is accomplished by invoking the CancellationTokenSource.Cancel method, as demonstrated in the following code:

```
tokenSource.Cancel()


Try
    aTask.Wait()
Catch ex As AggregateException
    'Handle concurrent exceptions here...
Catch ex As Exception

End Try
```

45

> **NOTE**
>
> The `OperationCanceledException` is correctly thrown if Just My Code is disabled (see Chapter 5, "Debugging Visual Basic 2010 Applications," for details on Just My Code). If it is enabled, the compiler sends a message saying that an `OperationCanceledException` was unhandled by user code. This is benign, so you can simply go on running your code by pressing F5 again.

The Barrier Class

The `System.Threading` namespace in .NET 4.0 introduces a new class named `Barrier`. The goal of this class is bringing a number of tasks that work concurrently to a common point before taking further steps. Tasks work across multiple phases and they signal they arrived at the barrier, waiting for all other tasks to arrive. The constructor of the class offers several overloads but all have in common the number of tasks participating in the concurrent work. You can also specify the action to take once they arrive at the common point (that is, they reach the barrier and complete the current phase). Notice that the same instance of the `Barrier` class can be used multiple times, for representing multiple phases. The following code demonstrates how three tasks reach the barrier after their work, signaling the work completion and waiting for other tasks to finish:

```vb
Sub BarrierDemo()
    ' Create a barrier with three participants
    ' The Sub lambda provides an action that will be taken
    ' at the end of the phase
    Dim myBarrier As New Barrier(3,
                        Sub(b)
                            Console.
                            WriteLine("Barrier has been " & _
                            "reached (phase number: {0})",
                            b.CurrentPhaseNumber)
                        End Sub)

    ' This is the sample work made by all participant tasks
    Dim myaction As Action =
        Sub()
            For i = 1 To 3
                Dim threadId As Integer =
                    Thread.CurrentThread.ManagedThreadId
                Console.WriteLine("Thread {0} before wait.", threadId)

                'Waits for other tasks to arrive at this same point:
                myBarrier.SignalAndWait()
                Console.WriteLine("Thread {0} after wait.", threadId)
            Next
        End Sub
```

```
    ' Starts three tasks, representing the three participants
    Parallel.Invoke(myAction, myAction, myAction)

    ' Once done, disposes the Barrier.
    myBarrier.Dispose()
End Sub
```

Basically the code performs these steps:

1. Creates an instance of the `Barrier` class, adding three participants and specifying the action to take when the barrier is reached.

2. Declares a common job for the three tasks (the `myAction` object) which simply performs an iteration against running threads simulating some work. When each task completes the work, the `Barrier.SignalAndWait` method is invoked. This tells the runtime to wait for other tasks to complete their work before going to the next phase.

3. Launches the three concurrent tasks and disposes the `myBarrier` object at the appropriate time.

The code also reuses the same Barrier instance in order to work across multiple phases. The class also exposes interesting members such as:

▶ `AddParticipant` and `AddParticipants` methods which respectively allow adding one or the specified number of participant tasks to the barrier

▶ `RemoveParticipant` and `RemoveParticipants` methods which respectively allow removing one or the specified number of participant tasks from the barrier

▶ `CurrentPhaseNumber` property of type `Long`, which returns the current phase number

▶ `ParticipantCount` property of type `Integer`, which returns the number of tasks involved in the operation

▶ `ParticipantsRemaining` property of type `Integer`, which returns the number of tasks that have not invoked the `SignalAndWait` method yet

A Barrier represents a single phase in the process while multiple instances of the same Barrier class, like in the preceding code, represent multiple phases.

Parallel Loops

The Task Parallel Library offers the ability of scaling loops such as `For` and `For Each`. This is possible due to the implementation of the shared `Parallel.For` and `Parallel.ForEach` methods. Both methods can take advantage of a multicore architecture for the parallel execution of loops, as explained in next sections. Now create a new Console application with Visual Basic. The goal of the next example is to simulate an intensive processing for demonstrating the advantage of parallel loops and demonstrating how the Task Parallel Library is responsible for managing threads for you. With that said, write the following code:

```
'Requires an Imports System.Threading directive

    Private Sub SimulateProcessing()
        Threading.Thread.SpinWait(80000000)
    End Sub

    Private Function GetThreadId() As String
        Return "Thread ID: " + Thread.CurrentThread.
                        ManagedThreadId.ToString
    End Function
```

TIP

The `Thread.SpinWait` method simply tells a thread that it has to wait for the specified number of iterations to be completed. You might often find this method in the code samples about parallel computing with the .NET Framework.

The `SimulateProcessing` method just simulates an intensive processing against fictitious data whereas `GetThreadId` can help demonstrate the TPL influence on threads management. Now in the `Sub Main` of the main module, write the following code that takes a StopWatch object for measuring elapsed time:

```
Dim sw As New Stopwatch
sw.Start()
'This comment will be replaced by
'the method executing the loop
sw.Stop()
Console.WriteLine("Elapsed: {0}", sw.Elapsed)
Console.ReadLine()
```

This code helps to measure time in both classic and parallel loops as explained soon.

NOTE

For Parallel LINQ, parallel loops give the most out in particular circumstances such as intensive processing. If you simply need to iterate a collection without heavy CPU business, probably parallel loops will not be so helpful, and you will still prefer classic loops. Choose parallel loops only when your processing is intensive enough to require the work of all processors on your machine.

Parallel.For Loop

Writing a parallel For loop is an easy task, although it is important to remember that you can generally take advantage of parallelism against intensive and time-consuming operations. Imagine you want to invoke the code defined at the beginning of this section for a finite number of times to simulate an intensive processing. This is how you would do it with a classic For loop:

```
Sub ClassicForTest()
    For i = 0 To 15
        Console.WriteLine(i.ToString + GetThreadId())
        SimulateProcessing()
    Next
End Sub
```

Nothing new here; the code simply writes the thread identifier at each step and simulates an intensive processing. If you run the code, you get the result shown in Figure 45.1 where you can see how all the work relies on a single thread and how the loop result is ordered.

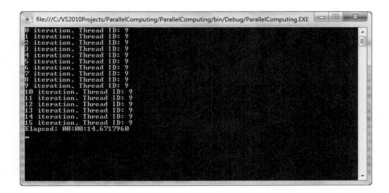

FIGURE 45.1   Running a classic For loop to demonstrate single threading.

The next code snippet is instead how you write a parallel loop that accomplishes the same thing:

```
'Requires an Imports System.Threading.Tasks directive
    Sub ParallelForTest()
        Parallel.For(0, 16, Sub(i)
                                Console.WriteLine(i.ToString + _
                                GetThreadId())
                                SimulateProcessing()
                            End Sub)
    End Sub
```

Basically `Parallel.For` receives three arguments: The first one is the "from" part of the `For` loop, the second one is the "to" part of the `For` loop (and it is exclusive to the loop), and the third one is the action to take at each step. Such action is represented by a `System.Action(Of Integer)` that you write under the form of a statement lambda that takes a variable (`i` in the above example) representing the loop counter. To provide a simpler explanation, the `Sub..End Sub` block in the statement lambda of the parallel loop contains the same code of the `For..Next` block in the classic loop. If you run the code, you can see how things change, as shown in Figure 45.2.

FIGURE 45.2   The parallel loop runs multiple threads and takes less time.

You immediately notice two things: The first one is that `Parallel.For` automatically splits the loop execution across multiple threads, differently from the classic loop in which the execution relied on a single thread. Multiple threads are shared across the multicore architecture of your machine, thus speeding up the loop. The second thing you notice is the speed of execution. Using a parallel loop running the previous example on my machine took about 5 seconds less than the classic loop. Because the loop execution is split across multiple threads, such threads run in parallel. This means that maintaining a sequential execution order is not possible with `Parallel.For` loops. As you can see from Figure 45.2, the iterations are not executed sequentially, and this is appropriate, because it means that multiple operations are executed concurrently, which is the purpose of the TPL. Just be aware of this when architecting your code.

Parallel.ForEach Loop

Similarly to `For` loops, the `Parallel` class offers an implementation of `For..Each` loops for iterating items within a collection in parallel. Still taking advantage of methods shown at the beginning of this section for retrieving thread information, simulate intensive processing and measuring elapsed time; imagine you want to retrieve the list of image files in the user level Pictures folder simulating an intensive processing over each filename. This task can be accomplished via a classic `For..Each` loop as follows:

```
Sub ClassicForEachTest()
```

```
    Dim allFiles = IO.Directory.
        EnumerateFiles("C:\users\alessandro\pictures")

    For Each fileName In allFiles
        Console.WriteLine(fileName + GetThreadId())
        SimulateProcessing()
    Next
End Sub
```

The intensive processing simulation still relies on a single thread and on a single processor, thus it will be expensive in terms of time and system resources. Figure 45.3 shows the result of the loop.

FIGURE 45.3   Iterating items in a collection under intensive processing is expensive with a classic For..Each loop.

Fortunately the Task Parallel Library enables iterating items in a collection concurrently. This is accomplished with the `Parallel.ForEach` method, which is demonstrated in the following code:

```
Sub ParallelForEachTest()


    Dim allFiles = IO.Directory.
                   EnumerateFiles("C:\users\alessandro\pictures")
    Parallel.ForEach(Of String)(allFiles, Sub(fileName)
                                              Console.WriteLine( _
                                              fileName + GetThreadId())
                                              SimulateProcessing()
                                          End Sub)

End Sub
```

`Parallel.ForEach` is generic and therefore requires specifying the type of items in the collection. In this case the collection is an `IEnumerable(Of String)`, so `ForEach` takes (Of

String) as the generic parameter. Talking about arguments, the first one is the collection to iterate, whereas the second one is an Action(Of T), therefore a reference to a delegate or a statement lambda like in the preceding example, representing the action to take over each item in the collection. If you run the code snippet, you get the result shown in Figure 45.4.

FIGURE 45.4   Performing a Parallel.ForEach loop speeds up intensive processing over items in the collection.

The difference is evident. The parallel loop completes processing in almost half the time of the classic loop; this is possible because the parallel loop automatically runs multiple threads for splitting the operation across multiple units of work, but particularly it takes full advantage of the multicore processors architecture of the running machine to take the most from system resources.

The ParallelLoopState Class

The System.Threading.Tasks.ParallelLoopState enables getting information on the state of parallel loops such as Parallel.For and Parallel.ForEach. For example, you can understand if a loop has been stopped via the Boolean property IsStopped or if the loop threw an exception via the IsExceptional property. Moreover you can stop a loop with Break and Stop methods. The first one requests the runtime to stop the loop execution when possible, but including the current iteration while Stop does the same but excluding the current iteration. Basically you need to pass a variable of type ParallelLoopState to the delegate invoked for the loop or let the compiler infer the type as in the following example:

```
'The compiler infers ParallelLoopState
'for the loopState identifier
Parallel.For(0, 16, Sub(i, loopState)
                    Console.WriteLine(i.ToString + _
                            GetThreadId())
                    SimulateProcessing()

                    If loopState.IsExceptional Then
```

```
            'an exception occurred
        End If

        'Breaks the loop at the 10th iteration
        If i = 10 Then
            loopState.Break()
        End If
    End Sub)
```

Debugging Tools For Parallel Tasks

Visual Studio 2010 introduces two useful tool windows that you can use for debugging purposes when working on both parallel tasks and loops. To understand how such tooling works, consider the following code that creates and starts three tasks:

```
Sub CreateSomeTaks()
    Dim taskA = Task.Factory.StartNew(Sub() Console.WriteLine("Task A"))
    Dim taskB = Task.Factory.StartNew(Sub() Console.WriteLine("Task B"))
    Dim taskC = Task.Factory.StartNew(Sub() Console.WriteLine("Task C"))
End Sub
```

Place a breakpoint on the End Sub statement and run the code. Because the tasks work in parallel, some of them maybe running at this point and other maybe not. To understand what is happening, you can open the **Parallel Tasks** tool window (select Debug, Windows, Parallel Tasks if not already visible). The window shows the state of each task, as represented in Figure 45.5.

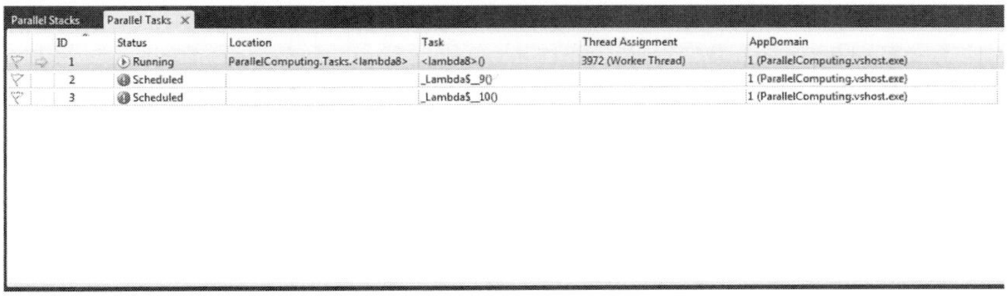

	ID	Status	Location	Task	Thread Assignment	AppDomain
	1	Running	ParallelComputing.Tasks.<lambda8>	<lambda8>()	3972 (Worker Thread)	1 (ParallelComputing.vshost.exe)
	2	Scheduled		_Lambda5__9()		1 (ParallelComputing.vshost.exe)
	3	Scheduled		_Lambda5__10()		1 (ParallelComputing.vshost.exe)

FIGURE 45.5   The Parallel Tasks tool window.

Among the other information, the window shows the task ID, the status (that is, if it is running, scheduled, waiting, dead-locked or completed), the delegate that is making the actual job (in the Task column) and the actual thread that refers to the task. Next you can take advantage of the **Parallel Stacks** tool window (which can be enabled via Debug, Windows, Parallel Stacks) that shows the call stack for threads and their relationships. Figure 45.6 shows an example.

45

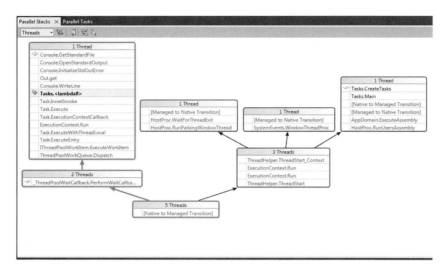

FIGURE 45.6   The Parallel Stacks window.

For each thread the window shows a information that you can investigate by right click-ing on each row.

Concurrent Collections

Parallel computing basically relies on multithreading, although with some particular speci-fications for taking advantage of multicore architectures. The real problem is when you need to work with collections, because in a multithreaded environment, multiple threads could access a collection attempting to make edits that need to be controlled. The .NET Framework 4.0 introduces a number of *thread-safe* concurrent collections, exposed by the System.Collections.Concurrent namespace, which is useful in parallel computing with the .NET Framework because they grant concurrent access to their members from threads.

WHAT DOES THREAD-SAFE MEAN?

A collection is *thread-safe* when access to its members is allowed to only one thread per time (or to a few threads in particular cases).

Table 45.1 summarizes concurrent collections in .NET 4.0.

TABLE 45.1   Available Concurrent Collections

Collection	Description
ConcurrentBag(Of T)	Represents an unordered collection of items
ConcurrentQueue(Of T)	Represents a concurrent FIFO collection
ConcurrentStack(Of T)	Represents a concurrent LIFO collection

TABLE 45.1   Continued

Collection	Description
ConcurrentDictionary(Of TKey, TValue)	Represents a concurrent Dictionary(Of TKey, TValue)
BlockingCollection(Of T)	A thread-safe collection with bounding and blocking capabilities against threads

The first four listed collections are essentially thread-safe implementations of generic collections you already learned in Chapter 16, "Working with Collections," whereas the BlockingCollection is a little bit more complex but interesting.

ConcurrentBag(Of T)

The ConcurrentBag(Of T) is the most basic concurrent collection, in that it is just an unordered collection of items. The following code demonstrates how you use it for adding, iterating, counting, and removing items:

```
'Creating an instance
Dim cb As New ConcurrentBag(Of String)

'Adding some items
cb.Add("String one")
cb.Add("String two")
cb.Add("String three")

'Showing items count
Console.WriteLine(cb.Count)

'Listing items in the collection
For Each item In cb
    Console.WriteLine(item)
Next

'Removing an item
Dim anItem As String = String.Empty
cb.TryTake(anItem)
Console.WriteLine(anItem)
```

You add items to the collection by invoking the Add method. The Count property gets the number of items in the collection, whereas the IsEmpty property tells you if the collection is empty. To remove an item, you invoke TryTake, which takes the first item, assigns it to the result variable (in this case anItem), and then removes it from the collection. It returns True if removing succeeds, otherwise False. Keep in mind that this collection offers no order for items; therefore, iteration results are completely random.

45

ConcurrentQueue(Of T)

The ConcurrentQueue(Of T) collection is just a thread-safe implementation of the Queue(Of T) collection; therefore, it takes the logic of FIFO (First-In, First Out), where the first element in the collection is the first to be removed. The following code shows an example:

```
'Creating an instance
Dim cq As New ConcurrentQueue(Of Integer)

'Adding items
cq.Enqueue(1)
cq.Enqueue(2)

'Removing an item from the queue
Dim item As Integer
cq.TryDequeue(item)
Console.WriteLine(item)

'Returns "1":
Console.WriteLine(cq.Count)
```

The main difference with Queue is how items are removed from the queue. In this concurrent implementation, you invoke TryDequeue, which passes the removed item to a result variable by reference. The method returns True in cases of success, otherwise False. Still the Count property returns the number of items in the queue.

ConcurrentStack(Of T)

ConcurrentStack(Of T) is the thread-safe implementation of the Stack(Of T) generic collection and works according to the LIFO (Last-In, First-Out) logic. The following code shows an example of using this collection:

```
'Creating an instance
Dim cs As New ConcurrentStack(Of Integer)

'Adding an item
cs.Push(1)
'Adding an array
cs.PushRange(New Integer() {10, 5, 10, 20})


Dim items() As Integer = New Integer(3) {}

'Removing an array
cs.TryPopRange(items, 0, 4)

'Iterating the array
```

```
Array.ForEach(Of Integer)(items, Sub(i)
                                     Console.WriteLine(i)
                                 End Sub)
```

```
'Removing an item
Dim anItem As Integer
cs.TryPop(anItem)
Console.WriteLine(anItem)
```

The big difference between this collection and its thread-unsafe counterpart is that you can also add an array of items invoking PushRange, whereas you still invoke Push to add a single item. To remove an array from the stack, you invoke TryPopRange, which takes three arguments: the target array that will store the removed items, the start index, and the number of items to remove. Both PushRange and TryPopRange return a Boolean value indicating if they succeeded. The Array.ForEach loop in the preceding code is just an example for demonstrating how the array was actually removed from the collection. Finally, you invoke TryPop for removing an item from the stack; such an item is then assigned to a result variable, passed by reference.

ConcurrentDictionary(Of TKey, TValue)

The ConcurrentDictionary collection has the same purpose of its thread-unsafe counterpart, but it differs in how methods work. All methods for adding, retrieving, and removing items return a Boolean value indicating success or failure, and their names all start with Try. The following code shows an example:

```
'Where String is for names and Integer for ages
Dim cd As New ConcurrentDictionary(Of String, Integer)

Dim result As Boolean

'Adding some items
result = cd.TryAdd("Alessandro", 32)
result = cd.TryAdd("Nadia", 28)
result = cd.TryAdd("Roberto", 35)

'Removing an item
result = cd.TryRemove("Nadia", 28)

'Getting a value for the specified key
Dim value As Integer
result = cd.TryGetValue("Alessandro", value)

Console.WriteLine(value)
```

The logic of the collection is then the same of Dictionary, so refer to this one for details.

BlockingCollection(Of T)

The BlockingCollection(Of T) is a special concurrent collection. At the highest level the collection has two characteristics. The first is that if a thread attempts to retrieve items from the collection while it is empty, the thread is blocked until some items are added to the collection; the second one is that if a thread attempts to add items to the collection, but this has reached the maximum number of items possible, the thread is blocked until some space is freed in the collection. Another interesting feature is completion; you can mark the collection as complete so that no other items can be added. This is accomplished via the CompleteAdding instance method. After you invoke this method, if a thread attempts to add items, an InvalidOperationException is thrown. The following code shows how to create a BlockingCollection for strings:

```
Dim bc As New BlockingCollection(Of String)


bc.Add("First")
bc.Add("Second")
bc.Add("Third")
bc.Add("Fourth")

'Marks the collection as complete
bc.CompleteAdding()

'Returns an exception
'bc.Add("Fifth")

'Removes an item from the collection (FIFO)
Dim result = bc.Take()
Console.WriteLine(result)
```

You add items by invoking the Add method, and you mark the collection complete with CompleteAdding. To remove an item, you invoke Take. This method removes the first item added to the collection, according to the FIFO approach. This is because the BlockingCollection is not actually a storage collection, whereas it creates a ConcurrentQueue behind the scenes, adding blocking logic to this one. The class also exposes some properties:

- ▶ BoundedCapacity, which returns the bounded capacity for the collection. You can provide the capacity via the constructor. If not, the property returns -1 as the value indicating that it's a growing collection.

- ▶ IsCompleted, which indicates if the collection has been marked with CompleteAdding and it is also empty.

- ▶ IsAddingCompleted, which indicates if the collection has been marked with CompleteAdding.

The class has other interesting characteristics. For example, the beginning of the discussion explained why it is considered as "blocking." By the way, it also offers methods whose names all begin with `Try`, such as `TryAdd` and `TryTake`, which provides overloads that enable doing their respective work without being blocked. The last feature of the `BlockingCollection` is a number of static methods that you can use for adding and removing items to and from multiple `BlockingCollection` instances simultaneously, both blocking and nonblocking. Such methods are `AddToAny`, `TakeFromAny`, `TryAddToAny`, and `TryTakeFromAny`. The following code shows an example of adding a string to multiple instances of the collection:

```
Dim collection1 As New BlockingCollection(Of String)
Dim collection2 As New BlockingCollection(Of String)

Dim colls(1) As BlockingCollection(Of String)
colls(0) = collection1
colls(1) = collection2

BlockingCollection(Of String).AddToAny(colls, "anItem")
```

All mentioned methods take an array of collections; this is the reason for the code implementation as previously illustrated.

Summary

Parallel computing enables taking advantage of multicore architectures for scaling operations execution across all available processors on the machine. In this chapter you learned how parallel computing in .NET Framework 4.0 relies on the concept of tasks; for this you learned how to create and run tasks via the `System.Threading.Tasks.Task` class to generate units of work for running tasks in parallel. You also learned how to handle concurrent exceptions and request tasks' cancellation. Another important topic in parallel computing is loops. Here you learned how the `Parallel.For` and `Parallel.ForEach` loops enable multithreaded iterations that are scaled across all available processors. Finally you took a tour inside the new concurrent collections in .NET Framework 4.0, a new set of thread-safe collections that you can use to share information across tasks.

45

Working with Assemblies

So many times in this book, and of course in many other .NET resources, you find the word *assembly* associating it to managed executable files such as .NET applications and libraries. You need to know some key concepts about assemblies to understand how they actually work, what kind of information they offer, and how you can avoid bad surprises when executing them. In this chapter you first get an overview of assemblies' structure and base concepts; then you pass through advanced concepts that can help you understand their context of execution.

Assembly Overview

Assemblies can be discussed with two points of view: a physical one and a logical one. For the physical point of view, an assembly is an .exe or .dll file containing executable modules and resources. From a logical point of view, an assembly is the smallest unit for deploying .NET applications that also provides version information and enables code reuse. Chapter 47, "Reflection," discusses how, from the physical perspective, an assembly is a container of Intermediate Language code, metadata, and resources. Now we focus the discussion on the logical perspective so that you can understand some other purposes of this unit of work. In some cases details of some of the topics have been previously discussed, but for your convenience they are summarized in this chapter.

Information Stored Within Assemblies

An assembly doesn't necessarily coincide with a standalone application. In many cases assemblies are also compiled class libraries. Independently from what kind of assembly you are working with, it exposes the following information:

- ▶ **Types:** Through the IL code necessary to the application execution, assemblies can expose reusable types that can be consumed by other assemblies. This is the reason why assemblies are considered the smallest unit for code reuse.

- ▶ **Version:** Assemblies contain version information, and all modules within the assembly have the same version; this is important to the CLR that can distinguish between assemblies with the same name but with different version numbers without registration.

- ▶ **Scope:** Assemblies provide the scope of exposed types, establishing whether they can be externally visible. This is accomplished in code by Visual Basic qualifiers such as `Public`, `Friend`, and `Private`.

Assembly Location

To understand where assemblies are located, you must consider that they are generally divided into *private assemblies* and *shared assemblies*. Private assemblies are standalone assemblies or assemblies that reside exclusively in the same folder of the application that holds a reference. This is a common scenario, because it makes the deployment easier because you just need to distribute the content of the application folder (known as *XCopy* mode). Every application holding a reference to a private assembly needs to have a copy of the assembly inside its folder. This means that if you have ten applications referencing the assembly, you will also have ten copies of the assembly. Shared assemblies are instead files with a digital signature that can be installed to a particular location known as the Global Assembly Cache that allows having a single shared copy of the assembly only if this comes from a trusted publisher. The Global Assembly Cache is an important topic that Chapter 53, "Understanding the Global Assembly Cache," addresses, so read it for further details.

BINDING, CODEBASE, PROBING

When one assembly is referenced by another one, the .NET runtime needs to link them. This process is known as *binding* and is performed based on the assembly version, culture information, and strong name if available. When the runtime resolves binding, it searches for the physical assembly. This search process is known as *probing*. Because a signed assembly has also signature information that is kept when you add a reference, search is first performed in the GAC. If the assembly is not found there, the runtime searches for it looping through the application folder and subfolders until it's found. If you plan to place assemblies to locations different from the GAC and the application folder, you can place a `codeBase` suggestion in the application configuration file to tell the runtime where the required assembly will be found.

Signing Assemblies

To mark your assemblies as trusted, you need to add a digital signature known as a *strong name*. This becomes mandatory if you want to install an assembly to the GAC. Chapter 53 also provides a thorough discussion on signing assemblies with a strong name.

Assembly Information and Attributes

As you saw in different parts of the book, assemblies contain information that can make them recognizable from the external world, such as name, version, author, and copyright information. All these items are part of the assembly metadata and are injected to the assembly by adding some attributes declaration to the AssemblyInfo.vb file through instances of the `Assembly` attribute. Such attributes are covered in Chapter 3, "The Anatomy of a Visual Basic Project," particularly in Listing 3.3, which shows how to map properties assigned via the My Project Designer, so have a look. Now that you know more about assemblies' contents and purposes, let's see where the CLR executes these complex units of work.

Understanding Application Domains

An application domain is a unit of isolation for executing managed code. For a better understanding, let's make a comparison with the Win32 world. In Win32 you have processes. Each process is isolated from other processes by the system so that a process cannot interfere with other processes and with resources required by such processes. This prevents process corruption and unexpected crashes. In .NET Framework architecture the idea of isolation is provided by application domains, so an application domain is the place where an assembly runs isolated from other assemblies; when an application is started, the CLR creates one application domain for it. Although a Win32 process can host multiple application domains, when an assembly is executing within an application domain, it cannot interfere with other assemblies within different application domains, although application domains can communicate with each other. One assembly can create multiple application domains (which are handled by the CLR) and run separate assemblies within such domains, as I will explain in next section.

Creating Application Domains and Executing Assemblies

You have basically two ways for executing assemblies inside application domains: getting the instance of the default application domain for the running assembly (that is, your application) and creating a new application domain. The `System.AppDomain` class provides a shared property named `CurrentDomain`, of type `System.AppDomain`, which represents the instance of the current application domain. You get the instance and then execute the assembly as follows:

```
Dim currentDomain As AppDomain = AppDomain.CurrentDomain
currentDomain.ExecuteAssembly("AnotherApp.exe")
```

The `AppDomain` class exposes an instance `ExecuteAssembly` method that enables executing the specified assembly within an application domain. Generally executing an assembly in the current application domain is not a good idea, because you cannot unload the assembly when the execution has completed. Because of this, a better approach is to create a new application domain. For now let's see how you can get information on application domains:

```
'Shows the AppDomain friendly name
Console.WriteLine(currentDomain.FriendlyName)
'Shows the AppDomain id within the process
Console.WriteLine(currentDomain.Id)
'Shows the working directory for the running
'assembly within the AppDomain
Console.WriteLine(currentDomain.BaseDirectory)
'Returns True if the code is classified as
'fully-trusted
Console.WriteLine(currentDomain.IsFullyTrusted)
```

Notice how you can interrogate some properties for retrieving application domain information. The AppDomain class offers a number of other advanced properties that are not covered here. A useful resource for finding information related to AppDomain properties is the MSDN Library: http://msdn.microsoft.com/en-us/library/system.appdomain(VS.100).aspx. Now it's time to understand how it is possible to create new application domains and execute assemblies. Basically you invoke the AppDomain.CreateDomain static method and then you invoke ExecuteAssembly.

> **APPDOMAIN.LOAD**
>
> The AppDomain class exposes a Load method that also enables loading an assembly. According to the official MSDN documentation, usage of this method should be always restricted to COM interoperability scenarios. So always prefer ExecuteAssembly instead.

Also remember to unload the application domain after loaded assemblies have completed their work. The following code provides an example:

```
Dim secondDomain As AppDomain = AppDomain.
    CreateDomain("secondDomain")

Try
    secondDomain.ExecuteAssembly("MyApp.exe")
Catch ex As AppDomainUnloadedException
    Console.WriteLine("The AppDomain was already unloaded")
Catch ex As Exception
Finally
    Try
        AppDomain.Unload(secondDomain)
    Catch ex As CannotUnloadAppDomainException
```

```
            Console.Write("Unable to unload the AppDomain")
        End Try
    End Try
End Try
```

The CLR throws an AppDomainUnloadedException if the code attempts to access an already unloaded application domain. As you can see from the code, you unload an application domain by invoking the AppDomain.Unload shared method that takes the application domain instance as an argument. It is worth mentioning that, if the application domain cannot be unloaded, a CannotUnloadAppDomainException is thrown. The AppDomain.CreateDomain method offers several overloads. One of them allows taking an argument of type AppDomainSetup that is a special object that gives you the opportunity to set some application domain properties. The following code provides an example:

```
Dim domainSetup As New AppDomainSetup
With domainSetup
    'Sets the current directory for the AppDomain
    .ApplicationBase = Environment.CurrentDirectory
    'Sets the application name
    .ApplicationName = "App domain demo"
    'Allows assembly binding redirection
    .DisallowBindingRedirects = False
    'Disallows code download from assemblies
    'via http
    .DisallowCodeDownload = True
    'Assigns a config file to the new app domain,
    'in this case the app.config of the current domain
    .ConfigurationFile = AppDomain.CurrentDomain.
                            SetupInformation.ConfigurationFile
End With

Dim thirdDomain As AppDomain = AppDomain.
    CreateDomain("thirdDomain", Nothing, domainSetup)
```

Notice that the second argument is of type System.Security.Policy.Evidence and is useful if you want to assign specific security policies to the application domain. In this demonstrative code this is not accomplished. For this particular topic, notice that application domains are important for security policies that you apply to your code. In the next section you learn about changes introduced in the .NET Framework 4 to the managed security model.

CREATING AND EXECUTING DYNAMIC CODE AT RUNTIME

In next chapter you learn about Reflection, and you see how you can create assemblies and code at runtime. When you have a dynamically created assembly with custom code, you can execute the assembly within an application domain with the same techniques shown in this section.

Overview of Security Changes in .NET 4.0

> **NOTE**
>
> Because of the topic complexity and of the recent changes introduced by .NET Framework 4.0, this section requires you to have existing knowledge and skills on Code Access Security in the .NET Framework. We focus on some of the most important additions to the security model remembering that this is a complex architecture that would require an entire book for complete coverage;, keep in mind that here we provide an overview of what the MSDN documentation discusses in detail.

Assemblies contain code that is executed when you run the application. As for the operating system and for any development environment, code is executed according to security rules that prevent the code from unauthorized access to system resources. The .NET Framework 4.0 introduces a new security model, highly simplified if compared to the previous Code Access Security platform. The code will still be classified as fully trusted and partially trusted, in which full trust means that the code has elevated permissions for accessing resources, whereas partial trust means that the code is restricted by the permissions it has. The security model provided by the CLR is now easier to understand and to implement, differently from what Code Access Security was in the past.

> **NOTE ON SECURITY CHANGES**
>
> Extensive changes have been introduced to the security model for code access, whereas the role-based security model basically offers the same features as in the past. For this reason in this section we cover changes about the code access security model, whereas for further details on the role-based model, you can check out the MSDN documentation here: http://msdn.microsoft.com/en-us/library/shz8h065(VS.100).aspx.

The following are the major changes in the security model offered by .NET 4.0:

▶ Code Access Security policies and machine-wide security policies are now turned off by default.

The *transparency model* has been enforced and applied to the .NET Framework and managed applications. Basically the transparency model can separate code that runs as part of the application (transparent code) and code that runs as part of the .NET infrastructure (critical code). As a result, critical code can access privileged resources, such as native code, whereas transparent code can only access resources allowed by the specified permissions set and cannot invoke or inherit from critical code; with the transparency model groups of code isolated based on privileges. Such privileges are divided into full-trust and partial-trust in the sandboxed model.

▶ The enforcement of the transparency model is also the reason why the .NET Framework configuration tool is no longer available for setting CAS policies.

▶ The *sandboxed model* allows running code in a restricted environment that grants code the only permissions it actually requires, and the natural place for the model is the application domains described in the previous section.

▶ Desktop applications always run as fully trusted. This is also true for applications started from Windows Explorer, a command prompt, and from a network share.

▶ Permissions are still a central part in security, but some security actions from the System.Security.Permission.SecurityAction class have been deprecated. In detail they are Deny, RequestMinimum, RequestOptional, and RequestRefuse.

▶ You can expose partially trusted assemblies via the AllowPartiallyTrustedCallers attribute.

▶ To enable constraints on types that can be used as evidence objects, .NET Framework 4 introduces the System.Security.Policy.EvidenceBase base class that must be inherited from all objects that want to be candidate as evidence.

TRANSPARENCY MODEL

The transparency model is not new in the .NET Framework; it was first introduced with version 2.0 as a mechanism for validating code efficiency. In .NET 4 it has been revisited (this is the reason why it is also known as Level 2) and provides an enforcement mechanism for code separation.

46

The next sections provide explanations and code examples about new security features in .NET Framework 4 with Visual Basic 2010.

Permissions

With the exceptions described in the previous bulleted list for deprecated security actions, applying permissions in the new security model is similar to the previous versions of the .NET Framework. This means that you can leverage permissions from the System.Security.Permissions namespace, such as FileIOPermission, UIPermission, IsolatedStoragePermission, and EnvironmentPermission. The following code demonstrates how you use the declarative syntax for implementing a class that requires the caller code having the FileIOPermission to execute. Such a class simply implements a method that returns an XDocument from a text file:

```
'The caller code will need the FileIOPermission permission
'with unrestricted access otherwise it will fail
<FileIOPermission(Security.Permissions.SecurityAction.Demand,
                Unrestricted:=True)>
Class XmlParse

    Shared Function String2Xml(ByVal fileName As String) As XDocument
        'Expects an Xml-formatted string
```

```
        Return XDocument.Parse(fileName)
    End Function
End Class
```

You can also use the imperative syntax, which looks like this:

```
Dim fp As New FileIOPermission(PermissionState.Unrestricted)
Try
    fp.Demand()

Catch ex As Security.SecurityException

End Try
```

You create an instance of the required permission and then invoke `Demand` for checking if the application has that level of permissions. If not, a `System.Security.Security Exception` is thrown.

The Transparency Level 2

By default, when you create a new application it relies on security rules provided by the Transparency Level 2 of .NET Framework 4.0. The level name has this form to allow distinction from the old transparency level of previous .NET versions (known as Transparency Level 1). So the Transparency Level 2 security rules are applied implicitly, but a better idea is applying them explicitly by applying the `System.Security.SecurityRules` attribute that can be added at the assembly level as follows:

```
<Assembly: SecurityRules(Security.SecurityRuleSet.Level2)>
```

Applying the attribute explicitly is appropriate for code reading and future maintenance and avoids confusions. This level of enforcement brings into the .NET Framework some new ways of thinking about security policies. Most rely on the concept of *host*, where this means an environment is responsible for executing applications; ClickOnce, ASP.NET, and Internet Explorer are host examples. For code trust, applications that are not hosted, such as programs launched from a command prompt, from Windows Explorer or from a shared network path, now run as full-trust. Instead, hosted or sandboxed applications still run according to host-based policies and run as partial-trust. For hosted and sandboxed applications, it is worth mentioning that they are considered as *transparent* because they run with the limited permissions set granted by the sandbox. This means that you will no longer need to check for permissions when running partially trusted code, because transparent applications run with the permissions set granted by the sandbox, so your only preoccupation should be targeting the sandbox permissions set and to not write code requiring the full-trust policy. Talking about transparency, it is important to mention that its mechanism can separate code that is part of the .NET infrastructure (and that thus requires high privileges such as invoking native code), which is called *critical code*, and code that is part of the application, also known as *transparent code*. The idea behind the scenes is separating groups of code based on privileges. When working with sandboxes, such privileges are of two types: fully trusted, which is the unrestricted level, and the partially trusted, which is the level restricted to the permission set established in the sandbox.

DESKTOP APPLICATIONS

With the Transparency Level 2 enabled, desktop applications run as full-trust.

The `System.Security.SecurityRules` attribute is not the only one that you can apply for establishing permissions rules. There are other attributes available, summarized in Table 46.1.

TABLE 46.1   Security Attributes

Attribute	Description
SecurityTransparent	Specifies that the code is transparent, meaning that it can be accessed by partially trusted code, that it cannot allow access to protected resources, and that it cannot cause an elevation of privileges. All types and members are transparent.
SecurityCritical	Code introduced by types exposed from the assembly is considered as security-critical meaning that it can perform operations that require an elevation of privileges, whereas all other code is transparent. Methods overridden from abstract classes or implemented via an interface must be also explicitly marked with the attribute.
SecuritySafeCritical	Specifies that types expose critical code but allows access from partially trusted assemblies.

If you do not specify any other attribute other than `SecurityRules`, for fully trusted assemblies the runtime considers all code as security-critical, thus callable only from fully trusted code, except where this could cause inheritance violations. If the assembly is instead partially trusted, specifying no attribute other than `SecurityRules` will make the runtime consider types and members as transparent by default but they can be security-critical or security-safe-critical. For further detail on inheritance in the transparency model and on attributes listed in Table 46.1, visit the following page in the MSDN Library: http://msdn.microsoft.com/en-us/library/dd233102(VS.100).aspx. So this is the reason why it is opportune to explicitly provide the most appropriate attribute. The following is an example of applying both the `SecurityRules` and `SecurityTransparent` attributes:

```
<Assembly: SecurityRules(Security.SecurityRuleSet.Level2)>
<Assembly: SecurityTransparent()>
Class Foo
End Class
```

> **TIPS ON** SECURITYTRANSPARENT
>
> Transparency enforcements are handled by the Just-in-Time compiler and not by the CLR infrastructure. This means that if you apply the `SecurityTransparent` attribute to an assembly, the assembly cannot call transparent and security-safe-critical types and members independently from the permissions set (including full-trust). In such a scenario, if the code attempts to access a security-critical type or member, a `MethodAccessException` will be thrown.

Sandboxing

You can execute partially trusted code within a sandbox that runs with the specified permissions set. Code, including assemblies, executed within the sandbox will be also granted to just the specified permissions set. To create and run a sandbox, you need an instance of the `AppDomain` class. The example here creates a sandbox for running an external assembly given the `LocalIntranet` zone's permissions. Before showing the sandbox example, follow these steps:

1. Create a new Console application and name the new project as **ExternalApp**.
2. In the `Main` method simply add a `Console.Writeline` statement for showing whatever text message you like.
3. Build the project; then create a new folder named C:\MyApps and copy the newly generated ExternalApp.exe into C:\MyApps.

Such steps are required to have a simple external assembly to run inside the security sandbox. Now close the ExternalApp project and create a new Console project, naming it **SandBox**. The goal is to create a sandbox with `LocalIntranet` permission and run an external assembly inside the sandbox so that this external application will also be granted the same permissions. When ready, first add the following `Imports` directives:

```
Imports System.Security
Imports System.Security.Policy
Imports System.Reflection
```

Now move inside the `Main` method. The first thing you need is an Evidence object that you assign with the required permissions set, as demonstrated by the following code:

```
Dim ev As New Evidence()
ev.AddHostEvidence(New Zone(SecurityZone.Intranet))
```

When you have the `Evidence` instance, you can get a sandbox with the specified permissions as demonstrated by the following line:

```
Dim permSet As PermissionSet = SecurityManager.GetStandardSandbox(ev)
```

The `SecurityManager.GetStandardSandbox` returns a sandbox limited to the specified permissions. This sandbox will be used later when running the external assembly. As an alternative you can set your own permissions creating your custom permissions set using the `PermissionSet` object as follows:

```
Dim permSet As New PermissionSet(Permissions.PermissionState.None)
permSet.AddPermission( _
        New SecurityPermission(SecurityPermissionFlag.Execution))
permSet.AddPermission(New UIPermission(PermissionState.Unrestricted))
```

At this point we can put our hands on application domains. The first thing to do is create an instance of the `AppDomainSetup` class for specifying the working directory of the external assembly:

```
Dim ads As New AppDomainSetup()
ads.ApplicationBase = "C:\MyApps"
```

At this point we just need to set the host `Evidence` and then create the `AppDomain`, passing the security information, finally invoking `AppDomain.ExecuteAssembly` to run the sandboxed assembly:

```
Dim hostEvidence As New Evidence()
Dim sandbox As AppDomain = AppDomain.
    CreateDomain("Sandboxed Domain", hostEvidence, ads, permSet, Nothing)

sandbox.ExecuteAssemblyByName("ExternalApp")
```

The `AppDomain.CreateDomain` method has an overload that allows creating an application domain with a permissions set. Because the application domain has security permissions, an instance of the `Evidence` class is required to tell the runtime that the assembly will be affected by such permissions. Other arguments are the `AppDomainSetup` instance and the permissions set under which the external assembly is going to be run. The last null argument can be replaced with a reference to the strong name, in case you want to add it to the full trust list. This would first require the current application to be signed with a strong name (covered in Chapter 53) and then by getting a reference to the strong name via the `System.Security.Policy.StrongName` class as shown in the following line:

```
Dim fullTrustAssembly As StrongName = Assembly.
    GetExecutingAssembly.Evidence.GetHostEvidence(Of StrongName)()
```

The `Assembly.Evidence.GetHostEvidence(Of StrongName)` method returns the reference to the strong name. (The `System.Assembly` class is discussed in the next chapter on Reflection). Finally, you pass the strong name reference to `AppDomain.CreateDomain` as follows:

```
Dim sandbox As AppDomain = AppDomain.
    CreateDomain("Sandboxed Domain", hostEvidence, ads,
                permSet, fullTrustAssembly)
```

Listing 46.1 shows the complete code example for your convenience.

LISTING 46.1   Running a Sandboxed Assembly

```vb
Imports System.Security
Imports System.Security.Policy
Imports System.Reflection

Module Module1

    Sub Main()
        Dim ev As New Evidence()
        ev.AddHostEvidence(New Zone(SecurityZone.Intranet))

        Dim permSet As PermissionSet = SecurityManager.GetStandardSandbox(ev)

        Dim ads As New AppDomainSetup()
        ads.ApplicationBase = "C:\MyApps"

        Dim hostEvidence As New Evidence()
        Dim sandbox As AppDomain = AppDomain.
            CreateDomain("Sandboxed Domain", hostEvidence, ads,
                        permSet, Nothing)

        'The assembly runs in a LocalIntranet sandboxed environment
        sandbox.ExecuteAssemblyByName("ExternalApp")
    End Sub
End Module
```

SANDBOXES COMPLEXITY

Working with sandboxes can include complex scenarios. Particularly, you might have the need to execute not-trusted code from an external assembly with customized permissions sets. This also requires advanced application domains concepts. Fortunately the MSDN Library provides an interesting walk-through covering these scenarios, available at http://msdn.microsoft.com/en-us/library/bb763046(VS.100).aspx. This is also useful to get a practical example about implementing the `MarshalByRefObject` for dynamic code execution within application domains.

Conditional APTCA

You can allow an assembly to be called by partially trusted code by applying the `System.Security.AllowPartiallyTrustedCallers` attribute at the assembly level. This can be accomplished as follows:

```
Imports System.Security


<Assembly: AllowPartiallyTrustedCallers()>
```

Without this attribute, only full-trusted code can call the assembly. Different from previous versions, in the .NET Framework 4.0 this attribute no longer requires an assembly to be signed with a strong name, and its presence involves in the security checks all security functions present in the code.

Migrating from Old CAS-Based Code

If you move your existing code to .NET Framework 4 and you made use of Code Access Security policies, you might be advised with a message saying that CAS is obsolete. In these particular situations you can add a specific section to the application configuration file, which allows legacy policies that look like this:

```
<configuration>
  <runtime>
    <NetFx40_LegacySecurityPolicy enabled="true"/>
  </runtime>
</configuration>
```

Of course, you always need to check if legacy policies are appropriate in the particular scenario you are facing. The suggestion is to read the MSDN documentation about CAS migration, available at http://msdn.microsoft.com/en-us/library/ee191568(vs.100).aspx.

Summary

Understanding how assemblies work and how they can be managed is a key topic in .NET development. In this chapter you first got an overview of assemblies, about their structure, their locations, and what kind of information they share, such as code and metadata. Next the discussion focused on Application Domains and the `System.AppDomain` class, which provide units of isolation for executing assemblies. Finally you got an overview of the new security model introduced by .NET Framework 4.0, starting from discussing the transparency level and the sandboxed model until analyzing specific code examples.

46

There are situations in which you need to implement logic for performing some tasks depending on user choices. This kind of a situation is not uncommon. The problem is when you cannot predetermine the code required for executing actions depending on user input. Think of code generators: Such tools know how to generate code but cannot predetermine what code has to be generated until the users specify their requirements. Also think of assemblies external from your application. In some cases you might want to use types from an external assembly; in other cases you might just want to get information on types provided by the assembly; and in other cases you might want to reach members with limited scope visibility that you could not reach by simply adding a reference. Reflection is a key part in the .NET Framework that enables accomplishing all these mentioned scenarios. In this chapter you learn to use Reflection to both inspect assemblies and types and to generate and consume code on-the-fly.

Introducing Reflection

Reflection is an important part of the .NET Framework that provides the ability for interrogating assemblies' metadata and collecting information on types exposed by assemblies. Reflection also enables invoking code from external assemblies and generating code on-the-fly. You can take advantage of Reflection by using objects exposed by the `System.Reflection` namespace. It can be particularly useful when you need to generate code according to some user input or when you are in late bound scenarios where making decisions on what code must be invoked (or generated) is something determined at runtime. Before putting your hands on code, it is necessary to get an overview of how assemblies are structured so that you can have a better understanding of what kind of information you can investigate with the Reflection.

Understanding Assemblies' Metadata

As you know, when you build an executable with Visual Basic, you build a .NET assembly. An assembly is basically a container of metadata and code. Metadata is information that the CLR uses in correctly loading and running the assembly. Figure 47.1 represents how an assembly is structured.

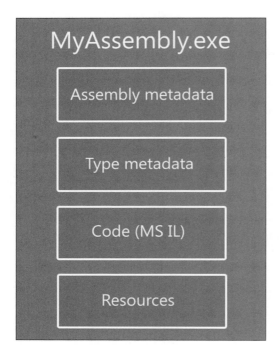

FIGURE 47.1   How an assembly is structured.

The Assembly Metadata, also known as *assembly manifest*, basically provides assembly information such as the name, version, culture, copyright information, and signature. The Type Metadata contains information on types defined within the assembly, such as class names and names of class members, including their parameters. The Code part is the actual Intermediate Language code that will be executed when the assembly is loaded. The Resources block contains all resources required by the assembly, such as images, icons, and strings. Also notice that types within an assembly can be grouped into multiple modules. A module is a container of types whereas an assembly is a container of modules. With Reflection you can inspect metadata and code from an assembly using Visual Basic code, including assembly information.

> **NOTE**
>
> When talking about assemblies, we usually refer to single file executables. Assemblies can be composed of multiple linked files; keep in mind that assembly metadata needs to reside only in the main assembly. This is a special case and cannot be accomplished with Visual Studio (you should use manually MSBuild), but it is something that it is worth mentioning.

Preparing a Sample Assembly

Before showing Reflection capabilities, a good idea is to prepare an appropriate code example. First, create a new class library project and name it **People**. The goal of the library is to expose a special implementation of the Person class, with interfaces and enumerations implementations for a better demonstration on Reflection. When ready, write the code in Listing 47.1, which is quite simple.

LISTING 47.1   Preparing Code for Reflection

```
Imports System.Text


Public Enum Genders
    Male = 0
    Female = 1
End Enum


Public Interface IPerson
    Property FirstName As String
    Property LastName As String
    Property Age As Integer
    Property Gender As Genders
    Event InstanceCreated()
    Function BuildFullName() As String
End Interface


Public Class Person
    Implements IPerson

    Public Property FirstName As String Implements IPerson.FirstName
    Public Property Gender As Genders Implements IPerson.Gender
    Public Property LastName As String Implements IPerson.LastName
    Public Property Age As Integer Implements IPerson.Age
    Public Event InstanceCreated() Implements IPerson.InstanceCreated

    Public Overridable Function BuildFullName() As String _
                Implements IPerson.BuildFullName
```

47

```
        Dim fullName As New StringBuilder
        fullName.Append(LastName)
        fullName.Append(" ")
        fullName.Append(FirstName)
        fullName.Append(", ")
        fullName.Append(Gender.ToString)
        fullName.Append(", of age ")
        fullName.Append(Age.ToString)

        Return fullName.ToString
    End Function
End Class
```

Build the project; then add a new Console project to the current solution. Finally add a reference to the People class library so that, just for demo purposes, you can load the assembly for Reflection without specifying the full path.

Getting Assembly Information

You get assembly metadata information creating an instance of the System.Reflection.Assembly class. This class provides both static and instance members for accessing assembly information. Typically you use one of the methods summarized in Table 47.1 to load an assembly for getting information.

TABLE 47.1   Methods for Loading an Assembly

Method	Description
GetAssembly	Loads an assembly containing the specified type
GetCallingAssembly	Gets the assembly that stores the code that invoked the current method
GetExecutingAssembly	Returns the instance of the current assembly
GetEntryAssembly	Returns the instance of the assembly that ran the current process
Load	Loads the specified assembly into the current application domain
LoadFile	Loads the specified assembly from the specified path
LoadFrom	Loads the specified assembly into the current application domain, given the specified path
ReflectionOnlyLoad	Like Load, but allows only Reflection inspection and not code execution
ReflectionOnlyLoadFrom	Like LoadFrom, but allows only Reflection inspection and not code execution

When you get the instance of the assembly you want to inspect, you can access information via some useful properties. The code in Listing 47.2 shows how to accomplish this. (See comments for explanations.)

LISTING 47.2   Inspecting Assembly Information

```
Imports System.Reflection


Module GettingAsmInfo

    Sub Main()

        'Infers System.Reflection.Assembly
        Dim asm = Assembly.ReflectionOnlyLoadFrom("People.dll")

        With asm
            'Gets the full assembly name with
            'version and culture
            Console.WriteLine("Assembly name:")
            Console.WriteLine(.FullName)
            'Gets whether the assembly is fully trusted
            Console.WriteLine("Is full-trust: {0}", .IsFullyTrusted)
            'Gets the assembly entry point. If empty, the
            'constructor is the entry point
            Console.WriteLine("The entry point method is: {0}", .EntryPoint)
            'Gets the .NET version that the
            'assembly was built upon
            Console.WriteLine("Image runtime version: {0}", .ImageRuntimeVersion)
            'Gets whether the assembly was loaded from
            'the GAC
            Console.WriteLine("Loaded from the GAC: {0}", .GlobalAssemblyCache)
            'Gets the assembly location
            Console.WriteLine("Assembly path: {0}", .Location)

            'Gets an array of modules loaded
            'by the assembly
            Console.WriteLine("Loaded modules: ")
            For Each item As System.Reflection.Module _
                In .GetLoadedModules
                Console.WriteLine("    {0}", item.Name)
            Next
        End With
        Console.ReadLine()
    End Sub
End Module
```

47

Notice how the code uses the `ReflectionOnlyLoadFrom` method to enable only inspection without code execution capabilities. If you run the preceding code, you get the following result:

```
Assembly name:
People, Version=1.0.0.0, Culture=neutral, PublicKeyToken=null
Is full-trust: True
The entry point method is:
Image runtime version: v4.0.21006
Loaded from the GAC: False
Assembly path: C:\Users\Alessandro\documents\visual studio
2010\Projects\Reflection\Reflection\bin\Debug\People.dll
Loaded modules:
    People.dll
```

Notice that the RTM version number of the .NET Framework 4 has a build number different than the previous one. The `Assembly.GetModules` method returns an array of modules loaded by the instance of the assembly. Other interesting methods are `GetExportedTypes`, which return an array of publicly visible types, and `GetFiles`, which returns an array of `FileStream` objects, each representing a file in the assembly's resources. Inspecting assembly information is just the first level of Reflection. The next step is inspecting types.

Reflecting Types

Reflection enables retrieving information on programs, including modules, types, and type members defined within an assembly. For example you might want to enumerate all types and type members defined in the People.dll assembly. Take a look at the following code:

```
Dim asm = Assembly.LoadFrom("People.dll")


Console.WriteLine("Enumerating types:")
For Each t In asm.GetTypes
    Console.WriteLine("Type name: {0}", t.ToString)

    Console.WriteLine(" Constructors:")
    For Each constructor In t.GetConstructors
        Console.WriteLine("      " + constructor.ToString)
    Next

    Console.WriteLine(" Methods:")
    For Each method In t.GetMethods
        Console.WriteLine("      " + method.ToString)
    Next

    Console.WriteLine(" Properties:")
```

```
    For Each [property] In t.GetProperties
        Console.WriteLine("      " + [property].ToString)
    Next

    Console.WriteLine(" Fields:")
    For Each field In t.GetFields
        Console.WriteLine("      " + field.ToString)
    Next

    Console.WriteLine(" Events:")
    For Each [event] In t.GetEvents
        Console.WriteLine("      " + [event].ToString)
    Next
Next
```

You still get the instance of the desired assembly; then you can iterate types (or modules if preferred). The `Assembly.GetTypes` method returns an array of `System.Type` objects defined in the assembly that you can iterate for detailed information. The `System.Type` class exposes several `GetX` methods, in which `X` can stand for `Constructors`, `Properties`, `Methods`, `Fields`, and `Events`. Each of these methods returns a `XInfo` class instance, such as `MethodInfo`, `PropertyInfo`, `FieldInfo`, and so on. Each class exposes interesting properties about the inspected member for further information such as `IsPrivate`, `IsPublic`, or `IsStatic`.

USING TOSTRING

Each `XInfo` class also exposes a `Name` property that returns the name of the member. In this case `ToString` was used instead of the name to return the full member signature.

Also, the `System.Type` class offers some useful properties enabling you to understand what kind of type you are inspecting such as `IsClass`, `IsInterface`, or `IsEnum`. The `Namespace` property enables instead getting the namespace exposing the inspected type. Notice that the preceding code inspects all types defined in the specified assembly, including the ones that are usually part of My Project. Also notice that Reflection considers properties' getters and setters such as methods that thus will be listed within this category. For a better understanding, the following is an excerpt of the output produced by the previously illustrated code:

```
Enumerating types:
Type name: People.My.MyApplication
 Constructors:
     Void .ctor()
 Methods:
     System.String GetEnvironmentVariable(System.String)
     Microsoft.VisualBasic.Logging.Log get_Log()
```

```
    Microsoft.VisualBasic.ApplicationServices.AssemblyInfo get_Info()
    System.Globalization.CultureInfo get_Culture()
    System.Globalization.CultureInfo get_UICulture()
    Void ChangeCulture(System.String)
    Void ChangeUICulture(System.String)
    System.String ToString()
    Boolean Equals(System.Object)
    Int32 GetHashCode()
    System.Type GetType()
  Properties:
    Microsoft.VisualBasic.Logging.Log Log
    Microsoft.VisualBasic.ApplicationServices.AssemblyInfo Info
    System.Globalization.CultureInfo Culture
    System.Globalization.CultureInfo UICulture
  Fields:
  Events:
Type name: People.My.MyComputer
  Constructors:
    Void .ctor()
  Methods:
    Microsoft.VisualBasic.Devices.Audio get_Audio()
    Microsoft.VisualBasic.MyServices.ClipboardProxy get_Clipboard()
    Microsoft.VisualBasic.Devices.Ports get_Ports()
    Microsoft.VisualBasic.Devices.Mouse get_Mouse()
    Microsoft.VisualBasic.Devices.Keyboard get_Keyboard()
    System.Windows.Forms.Screen get_Screen()
    Microsoft.VisualBasic.Devices.Clock get_Clock()
    Microsoft.VisualBasic.MyServices.FileSystemProxy get_FileSystem()
    Microsoft.VisualBasic.Devices.ComputerInfo get_Info()
    Microsoft.VisualBasic.Devices.Network get_Network()
    System.String get_Name()
    Microsoft.VisualBasic.MyServices.RegistryProxy get_Registry()
    System.String ToString()
    Boolean Equals(System.Object)
    Int32 GetHashCode()
    System.Type GetType()
  Properties:
    Microsoft.VisualBasic.Devices.Audio Audio
    Microsoft.VisualBasic.MyServices.ClipboardProxy Clipboard
    Microsoft.VisualBasic.Devices.Ports Ports
    Microsoft.VisualBasic.Devices.Mouse Mouse
    Microsoft.VisualBasic.Devices.Keyboard Keyboard
    System.Windows.Forms.Screen Screen
    Microsoft.VisualBasic.Devices.Clock Clock
    Microsoft.VisualBasic.MyServices.FileSystemProxy FileSystem
    Microsoft.VisualBasic.Devices.ComputerInfo Info
```

```
        Microsoft.VisualBasic.Devices.Network Network
        System.String Name
        Microsoft.VisualBasic.MyServices.RegistryProxy Registry
  Fields:
  Events:
Type name: People.My.MyProject
  Constructors:
  Methods:
        System.String ToString()
        Boolean Equals(System.Object)
        Int32 GetHashCode()
        System.Type GetType()
  Properties:
  Fields:
  Events:
Type name: People.My.MyProject+MyWebServices
  Constructors:
        Void .ctor()
  Methods:
        Boolean Equals(System.Object)
        Int32 GetHashCode()
        System.String ToString()
        System.Type GetType()
  Properties:
  Fields:
  Events:
Type name: People.Genders
  Constructors:
  Methods:
        Boolean Equals(System.Object)
        Int32 GetHashCode()
        System.String ToString()
        System.String ToString(System.String, System.IFormatProvider)
        Int32 CompareTo(System.Object)
        System.String ToString(System.String)
        System.String ToString(System.IFormatProvider)
        Boolean HasFlag(System.Enum)
        System.TypeCode GetTypeCode()
        System.Type GetType()
  Properties:
  Fields:
        Int32 value__
        People.Genders Male
        People.Genders Female
  Events:
Type name: People.IPerson
```

```
Constructors:
Methods:
    System.String get_FirstName()
    Void set_FirstName(System.String)
    System.String get_LastName()
    Void set_LastName(System.String)
    Int32 get_Age()
    Void set_Age(Int32)
    People.Genders get_Gender()
    Void set_Gender(People.Genders)
    System.String BuildFullName()
    Void add_InstanceCreated(InstanceCreatedEventHandler)
    Void remove_InstanceCreated(InstanceCreatedEventHandler)
Properties:
    System.String FirstName
    System.String LastName
    Int32 Age
    People.Genders Gender
Fields:
Events:
    InstanceCreatedEventHandler InstanceCreated
Type name: People.Person
Constructors:
    Void .ctor()
Methods:
    System.String get_FirstName()
    Void set_FirstName(System.String)
    People.Genders get_Gender()
    Void set_Gender(People.Genders)
    System.String get_LastName()
    Void set_LastName(System.String)
    Int32 get_Age()
    Void set_Age(Int32)
    Void add_InstanceCreated(InstanceCreatedEventHandler)
    Void remove_InstanceCreated(InstanceCreatedEventHandler)
    System.String BuildFullName()
    System.String ToString()
    Boolean Equals(System.Object)
    Int32 GetHashCode()
    System.Type GetType()
Properties:
    System.String FirstName
    People.Genders Gender
    System.String LastName
    Int32 Age
```

```
Fields:
Events:
    InstanceCreatedEventHandler InstanceCreated
Type name: People.IPerson+InstanceCreatedEventHandler
Constructors:
    Void .ctor(System.Object, IntPtr)
Methods:
    System.IAsyncResult BeginInvoke(System.AsyncCallback, System.Object)
    Void EndInvoke(System.IAsyncResult)
    Void Invoke()
    Void GetObjectData(System.Runtime.Serialization.SerializationInfo,
        System.Runtime.Serialization.StreamingContext)
    Boolean Equals(System.Object)
    System.Delegate[] GetInvocationList()
    Int32 GetHashCode()
    System.Object DynamicInvoke(System.Object[])
    System.Reflection.MethodInfo get_Method()
    System.Object get_Target()
    System.Object Clone()
    System.String ToString()
    System.Type GetType()
Properties:
    System.Reflection.MethodInfo Method
    System.Object Target
Fields:
Events:
```

Notice how also `EventHandler` types, generated behind the scenes when you implement a simple event, are inspected and illustrated. Also notice how the members' signature recalls the Intermediate Language syntax.

Reflecting a Single Type

Reflecting all types within an assembly can be useful, but probably in most cases you will be interested in reflecting a single type. To accomplish this you need the instance of a `System.Type`; then invoke members described in the previous section. For example, imagine you want to inspect members from the `Person` class. You first get the type instance, and then you can perform reflection as demonstrated by the following code:

```
Dim myType As Type = (New People.Person).GetType


Console.WriteLine(" Methods:")
For Each method In myType.GetMethods
```

```
        Console.WriteLine("      " + method.ToString)
    Next

    Console.WriteLine(" Properties:")
    For Each [property] In myType.GetProperties
        Console.WriteLine("      " + [property].ToString)
    Next

    Console.WriteLine(" Fields:")
    For Each field In myType.GetFields
        Console.WriteLine("      " + field.ToString)
    Next

    Console.WriteLine(" Events:")
    For Each [event] In myType.GetEvents
        Console.WriteLine("      " + [event].ToString)
    Next
```

The preceding code produces the following result:

```
Methods:
    System.String get_FirstName()
    Void set_FirstName(System.String)
    People.Genders get_Gender()
    Void set_Gender(People.Genders)
    System.String get_LastName()
    Void set_LastName(System.String)
    Int32 get_Age()
    Void set_Age(Int32)
    Void add_InstanceCreated(InstanceCreatedEventHandler)
    Void remove_InstanceCreated(InstanceCreatedEventHandler)
    System.String BuildFullName()
    System.String ToString()
    Boolean Equals(System.Object)
    Int32 GetHashCode()
    System.Type GetType()
 Properties:
    System.String FirstName
    People.Genders Gender
    System.String LastName
    Int32 Age
 Fields:
 Events:
    InstanceCreatedEventHandler InstanceCreated
```

For more details, the MSDN documentation on the System.Reflection namespace and the System.Type class are a good source of information on available members.

REFLECTION SECURITY CONSIDERATIONS

Reflection is both a key topic and a powerful tool in the .NET developer toolbox. By the way, you had the opportunity to understand how fragile your code is in security terms because with a few lines of code anyone can see types and members exposed by the assembly. Because preventing Reflection is not possible, if you want to protect your code, you need to use an obfuscation tool such as Dotfuscator (shipped with Visual Studio 2010) that can add a more effective protection.

Invoking Code Dynamically

Reflection also enables executing dynamic code, meaning that you can pick up types defined within an assembly, creating instances and invoking types from Visual Basic code without having a reference to that assembly. For example, imagine you want to load the People.dll assembly and create and populate an instance of the Person class, as shown in Listing 47.3.

LISTING 47.3   Creating and Running Dynamic Code

```
Imports System.Reflection
Module DynamicCode

    Sub DynCode()
        Dim asm = Assembly.LoadFrom("People.dll")

        'Gets the type definition
        Dim personType = asm.GetType("People.Person")

        'Gets the LastName property definition
        Dim lastNameProperty As PropertyInfo = personType.
                                            GetProperty("LastName")
        'Gets a reference to the property setter
        Dim lastNamePropSet As MethodInfo = lastNameProperty.
                                      GetSetMethod

        Dim firstNameProperty As PropertyInfo = personType.
                                            GetProperty("FirstName")
        Dim firstNamePropSet As MethodInfo = firstNameProperty.
                                    GetSetMethod

        Dim ageProperty As PropertyInfo = personType.GetProperty("Age")
        Dim agePropSet As MethodInfo = ageProperty.GetSetMethod

        'Creates an instance of the Person class
        Dim newPerson As Object = _
```

```
        Activator.CreateInstance(personType)

        'Each method is invoked upon the new type instance
        lastNamePropSet.Invoke(newPerson, New Object() {"Del Sole"})
        firstNamePropSet.Invoke(newPerson, New Object() {"Alessandro"})
        agePropSet.Invoke(newPerson, New Object() {32})

        'Gets the BuildFullName method from the Person class
        Dim buildFullNameMethod = personType.GetMethod("BuildFullName")

        'The method returns String but Invoke returns Object, so
        'a conversion is required
        Dim result As String = CStr(buildFullNameMethod.
                                Invoke(newPerson, Nothing))

        Console.WriteLine(result)
        Console.ReadLine()
    End Sub
End Module
```

When you have the type instance, you invoke the GetProperty method to get a reference of the desired property. This returns a PropertyInfo object. To set the property value, you need a reference to the setter method that is obtained via the GetSetMethod and that returns a MethodInfo object. (If you also want the ability to get a property value, you need to invoke instead GetGetMethod the same way.) When you have all properties, you need an instance of the class. This can be obtained by calling the Activator.CreateInstance method, which takes the type instance as the argument. The System.Activator class contains members for creating code locally or retrieving code from a remote location. Having an instance of the class is required before you set properties, because it is against the instance that property setters will be invoked. To actually run the property setter, you call the MethodInfo.Invoke instance method; the first argument is the type instance, whereas the second argument is an array of items of type Object, each to be used as a property value. In our case each property in the Person class accepts just one value, so each array can store just one item. Similarly you can get reference to methods invoking GetMethod on the type instance, as it happens in Listing 47.3, to get a reference to the Person.BuildFullName method. When you call Invoke to run the method, you can pass Nothing as the second argument if the original method does not require parameters. The code simply produces the following result:

```
Del Sole Alessandro, Male of Age: 32
```

After seeing how you can call dynamic code provided by an existing assembly, let's now see how to create code at runtime.

SECURITY NOTE

In many cases you notice that you can also invoke members marked as private or with limited visibility. Although this can seem exciting, take care. If you invoke a private member but you are not completely sure about its purpose, you expose your code to potential uncontrollable dangers.

Generating Code at Runtime with Reflection.Emit

The `System.Reflection.Emit` namespace provides objects for generating assemblies, types, and type members at runtime. Basically you need to perform the following operations sequentially:

1. Create an in-memory assembly within the current application domain with an instance of the `AssemblyBuilder` class.

2. Create a module for containing types via an instance of the `ModuleBuilder` class.

3. Create types with instances of the `TypeBuilder` class.

4. Add members to the `TypeBuilder` via XBuilder objects, such as `MethodBuilder`, `FieldBuilder`, and `PropertyBuilder`.

5. Save the assembly to disk if required.

The code in Listing 47.4 demonstrates how to create dynamically a simple implementation of the `Person` class with one property and one method.

LISTING 47.4   Generating Code at Runtime

```
Imports System.Reflection
Imports System.Reflection.Emit


Module CreatingCode

    Sub CreateAssembly()

        'Creates assembly name and properties
        Dim asmName As New AssemblyName("People")
        asmName.Version = New Version("1.0.0")
        asmName.CultureInfo = New Globalization.CultureInfo("en-US")

        'Gets the current application domain
```

```vb
Dim currentAppDomain As AppDomain = AppDomain.CurrentDomain

'Creates a new in-memory assembly in the current application domain
'providing execution and saving capabilities
Dim asmBuilder As AssemblyBuilder = currentAppDomain. _
                                DefineDynamicAssembly(asmName, _
                                AssemblyBuilderAccess.RunAndSave)

'Creates a module for containing types
Dim modBuilder As ModuleBuilder = _
    asmBuilder.DefineDynamicModule("PersonModule", _
                            "People.dll")

'Creates a type, specifically a Public Class
Dim tyBuilder As TypeBuilder = _
    modBuilder.DefineType("Person", _
                        TypeAttributes.Public _
                        Or TypeAttributes.Class)
'Defines a default empty constructor
Dim ctorBuilder As ConstructorBuilder = _
    tyBuilder.DefineDefaultConstructor(MethodAttributes.Public)

'Defines a field for storing a property value
Dim fldBuilder As FieldBuilder = _
    tyBuilder.DefineField("_lastName", _
                        GetType(String), _
                        FieldAttributes.Private)

'Defines a property of type String
Dim propBuilder As PropertyBuilder = _
    tyBuilder.DefineProperty("LastName", _
                            PropertyAttributes.None, GetType(String), _
                            Type.EmptyTypes)

'Defines a series of attributes for both getter and setter
Dim propMethodAttributes As MethodAttributes = _
    MethodAttributes.Public Or _
    MethodAttributes.SpecialName Or _
    MethodAttributes.HideBySig

'Defines the getter method for the property
Dim propGetMethod As MethodBuilder = _
    tyBuilder.DefineMethod("get_LastName", _
                        propMethodAttributes, _
                        GetType(String), _
                        Type.EmptyTypes)
```

```vb
'Generates IL code for returning the field value
Dim propGetMethodIL As ILGenerator = propGetMethod.GetILGenerator
propGetMethodIL.Emit(OpCodes.Ldarg_0)
propGetMethodIL.Emit(OpCodes.Ldfld, fldBuilder)
propGetMethodIL.Emit(OpCodes.Ret)

'Defines the setter method for the property
Dim propSetMethod As MethodBuilder = _
    tyBuilder.DefineMethod("set_LastName",
                            propMethodAttributes,
                            GetType(String),
                            Type.EmptyTypes)

'Generates the IL code for setting the field value
Dim propSetMethodIL As ILGenerator = propSetMethod.GetILGenerator
propSetMethodIL.Emit(OpCodes.Ldarg_0)
propSetMethodIL.Emit(OpCodes.Ldarg_1)
propSetMethodIL.Emit(OpCodes.Stfld, fldBuilder)
propSetMethodIL.Emit(OpCodes.Ret)

'Assigns getter and setter to the property
propBuilder.SetGetMethod(propGetMethod)
propBuilder.SetSetMethod(propSetMethod)

'Defines a public method that returns String
Dim methBuilder As MethodBuilder = _
    tyBuilder.DefineMethod("BuildFullName",
                            MethodAttributes.Public,
                            GetType(String),
                            Type.EmptyTypes)

'Method body cannot be empty, so just return
Dim methodILGen As ILGenerator = methBuilder.GetILGenerator
methodILGen.EmitWriteLine("Method implementation needed")
methodILGen.Emit(OpCodes.Ret)

'Creates an instance of the type
Dim pers As Type = tyBuilder.CreateType

'Enumerates members for demo purposes
For Each member In pers.GetMembers
    Console.WriteLine("Member name: {0}", member.Name)
Next

'Saves the assembly to disk
```

47

```
        asmBuilder.Save("People.dll")
        Console.ReadLine()
    End Sub
End Module
```

After you create an `AssemblyName` for assigning assembly properties and get the instance of the current application domain, you use the `AppDomain.DefineDynamicAssembly` method to generate an in-memory assembly. The method returns an instance of the `AssemblyBuilder` class and receives the `AssemblyName` instance and a value from the `AssemblyBuilderAccess` enumeration that establishes the access level for Reflection. `RunAndSave` enables executing and saving the assembly, but you can also limit Reflection with the `ReflectionOnly` value. The next step is creating an instance of the `ModuleBuilder` class that can act as a container of types. This is accomplished by invoking the `AssemblyBuilder.DefineDynamicModule` method that requires you to specify the module name and the filename. (This one should be the same as for `AssemblyName` if you want metadata to be merged into a single assembly.) When you have a module, you can put your types into it. For each type you need to create an instance of the `TypeBuilder` class, which you accomplish by invoking the `ModuleBuilder.DefineType` method that receives the type name and qualifiers as arguments. Qualifiers are one or more values from the `TypeAttributes` enumeration; in the current example, `Public` and `Class` values are assigned to the new type to create a new class with public visibility. The `TypeBuilder` class provides lots of methods for adding members, such as constructors, field, properties, and methods. For constructors, the code demonstrates how to add a public, empty, and default constructor invoking the `TypeBuilder.DefineDefaultConstructor`, but you can supply constructor overloads via the `DefineConstructor` method. To implement properties, you first need to supply fields. These are implemented via the `TypeBuilder.DefineField` method that requires three arguments: the field name, the type (retrieved via `GetType`), and qualifiers, determined with values from the `FieldAttributes` enumeration. Similarly you implement properties invoking the `TypeBuilder.DefineProperty` method, but this is not enough because you also need to explicitly generate the getter and setter methods for each property. These are special methods that require providing some properties defined within the `propMethodAttributes` variable that takes values from the `MethodAttributes` enumeration. When you establish method attributes, you create two `MethodBuilder` instances. Such a class generates each kind of method, including special ones. You just supply the method name, attributes, the return type, and an array of type parameters. The actual problem is how you implement method bodies. As a general rule, methods implemented via Reflection cannot have an empty method body, so you must provide some Intermediate Language code to populate the method body. This is accomplished by invoking methods from the `ILGenerator` class that enable injecting IL code to the method. Consider the following snippet, excerpted from Listing 47.4:

```
'Generates IL code for returning the field value
Dim propGetMethodIL As ILGenerator = propGetMethod.GetILGenerator
propGetMethodIL.Emit(OpCodes.Ldarg_0)
propGetMethodIL.Emit(OpCodes.Ldfld, fldBuilder)
```

```
propGetMethodIL.Emit(OpCodes.Ret)
```

The `MethodBuilder.GetILGenerator` method returns an instance of the `ILGenerator` class. Then you invoke the `Emit` method to execute IL code. In the preceding snippet, the IL code simply returns the value of the `fldBuilder` variable and pushes the value onto the stack and then returns. Actions to execute via the IL are taken via shared fields from the `OpCodes` class, each related to an IL instruction.

NOTE ON OPCODES

Reflection is powerful, but because you need to know the MS Intermediate Language in detail before implementing dynamic code, and because this would be beyond of scope in this book, you should look at the appropriate MSDN documentation at http://msdn.microsoft.com/en-us/library/8ffc3x75(VS.100).aspx.

When you provide the method body for getters and setters, you add them to the related properties via the `PropertyBuilder.SetGetMethod` and `PropertyBuilder.SetSetMethod` methods. Similarly you implement any other method, and the sample code demonstrates this by providing a simple method body that invokes `EmitWriteLine`, a method that sends to the assembly the appropriate IL code for writing a message to the Console window. Finally you simply invoke `AssemblyBuilder.Save` to save the assembly to disk. More than running the code, you can ensure if everything works by inspecting the assembly with a Reflection tool such as Microsoft IL Disassembler. Figure 47.2 shows how the assembly looks if opened with ILDasm, demonstrating the correct result of our work.

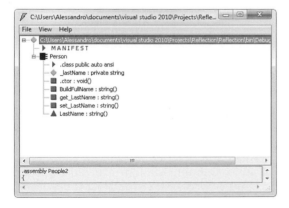

FIGURE 47.2   The assembly created at runtime opened in IL Disassembler.

Typically you will prefer code generators instead of Reflection to generate code on-the-fly because in that case you do not need to know about Intermediate Language. After you define your types on-the-fly, you can then consume them using techniques described in the "Invoking Code Dynamically" section.

Late Binding Concepts

Late binding is a particular programming technique that you use to resolve types at runtime and for types dynamic loading that is accomplished by assigning objects to variable of type Object. For a better understanding, consider its counterpart, the early binding. This happens at compile time where the compiler checks that argument types utilized to invoke methods match their signatures. An example is the background compiler that provides real-time check for types used in code, thanks to early binding. On the contrary, late binding requires you to specify the function signatures; moreover you must ensure that the code uses the correct types. Basically this means that binding requirements, such as binary files to load or methods to invoke, is long delayed, in many cases until before the method is invoked. Reflection greatly uses late binding because in many cases you work with objects of type Object, and this requires late resolution for invoking appropriate members. The following example, although not related to Reflection, demonstrates how to invoke members from objects declared as Object that are instead of different types, but this is determined late at runtime:

```
' This code creates an instance of Microsoft Excel and adds a new WorkBook.
' Requires Option Strict Off
Sub LateBindingDemo()
    Dim xlsApp As Object
    Dim xlsBook As Object
    xlsApp = CreateObject("Excel.Application")
    xlsBook = xlsApp.Workbooks.Add
End Sub
```

OPTION STRICT OFF BEST PRACTICES

Because in lots of situations turning Option Strict to Off can be very dangerous, if you need to work with late-binding you should consider moving the code that requires such a technique to a separate code file and just mark this code file with Option Strict Off, instead of setting it Off at the project level.

As you can see, invoking members from Object in late binding is different because the compiler cannot predetermine if members exist, and you don't have IntelliSense support. But if the actual type defines members that you are attempting to invoke, they will be correctly bound at runtime. Just remember that late binding requires an Option Strict Off directive and that should be used carefully.

Summary

In this chapter we covered one of the most important topics in the .NET development, Reflection. You saw what Reflection is and how assemblies are structured. Talking in code terms, you then saw how to interrogate assembly information and how to reflect types to inspect types and type members exposed by an entire assembly or by a single type. Next dynamically invoking code from an external assembly without the need of having a reference to that assembly was also explained. Finally, you saw how to take advantage of the `System.Reflection.Emit` namespace to create an assembly, types, and members at runtime.

47

CHAPTER 48

Coding Attributes

Executables produced by .NET languages are different from classic (Win32) executables. Other than the Intermediate Language, they store additional information on types defined in the assembly, on members, on data. The information is referred to as metadata. Assemblies' metadata also contains information about attributes, which are basically declarative programming elements that enable annotating types with custom information and that can condition types' behavior according to the information provided. They are pieces of information for types, and therefore they are part of the application metadata. You can find attributes in lots of different scenarios in.NET development. For example, you saw attributes in Chapter 27, "Introducing the ADO.NET Entity Framework," when discussing how the Entity Framework defines entities. Chapter 43, "Serialization," discussed serialization and the `Serializable` attribute. In this chapter you reach two objectives: First you take a tour for applying attributes, which is a specific recap of information that you should already know. The second objective is to learn to create custom attributes and to provide additional information to your applications by taking advantage of metadata.

Applying Attributes

Until now you have gotten a lot of examples about applying attributes, but for the sake of completeness we provide information here. When applying attributes to your own types or members, you enclose the attribute name between angle brackets, as in the following example:

```
<Serializable()>
Public Class Person

End Class
```

In this case the `Serializable` attribute is parameterless (and in this case you can omit round parenthesis).

When you apply an attribute, your object is *decorated* with that attribute. Another common description utilized when applying attributes is that an object is *marked*. Referring to the previous example, you can say that the `Person` class is decorated with the `Serializable` attribute or that it is marked as `Serializable` as well. Attributes can receive arguments. The following example shows how to pass arguments to the `CLSCompliant` attribute:

```
<CLSCompliant(True)>
Public Class Person

End Class
```

Attributes arguments are separated by commas according to the number of arguments required. As explained when discussing custom attributes, optional parameters are also allowed. You apply multiple attributes separating them with commas or writing each attribute after the other one. Both the following modes are perfectly legal:

```
<Serializable()>
<CLSCompliant(True)>
Public Class Person

End Class

<Serializable(), CLSCompliant(True)>
Public Class Person

End Class
```

IMPLICIT-LINE CONTINUATION

In the first code snippet notice how attributes no longer require the underscore character when written on multiple lines. This is one of the allowed scenarios for the implicit-line continuation features in Visual Basic 2010.

Attributes can be applied to the following programming elements:

▶ Classes

▶ Structures

- ► Methods (including constructors)

- ► Fields

- ► Properties

- ► Interfaces

- ► Delegates and events

- ► Parameters and return values

- ► Enumerations

As mentioned at the beginning of this chapter, attributes are information that is stored in the assembly metadata. Figure 48.1 represents how such information is stored within the assembly, including type information and member information.

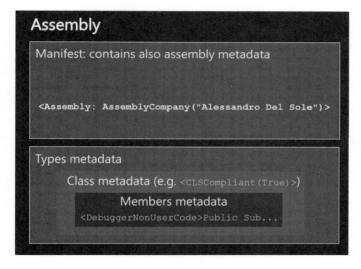

FIGURE 48.1   Attribute information stored in the assembly metadata.

Considering the representation shown in Figure 48.1, you may notice the description about assembly metadata. You can apply attributes at the assembly level, in the `AssemblyInformation.vb` file. Generally assembly level attributes are set at design time with the My Project window's tabs (see Chapters 3, "The Anatomy of a Visual Basic Project," and 20, "The My Namespace," for details). This means that each application property has a related assembly-level attribute. There is just one attribute named Assembly that requires the specification of nested attributes setting particular properties. For example, the following attributes' specifications set the title, description, and company name properties for the application:

```
<Assembly: AssemblyTitle("CodingAttribute")>
<Assembly: AssemblyDescription("Demo for Chapter 48")>
<Assembly: AssemblyCompany("Alessandro Del Sole")>
```

In the preceding code, Assembly is the main attribute, whereas `AssemblyTitle`, `AssemblyDescription`, and `AssemblyCompany` are other attributes that are nested into the `Assembly` declaration. Examining AssemblyInfo.vb you can see available assembly-level attributes, and you discover how each attribute is related to an application property settable in My Project. Until now you saw how to apply existing attributes, but these special objects provide great flexibility over your object development and provide the ability to deeply enhance your types, especially if you create custom attributes, as you will better understand in next section.

Coding Custom Attributes

A custom attribute is a class that inherits, directly or indirectly, from `System.Attribute`. When coding custom attributes, the class name should end with the Attribute word. This is not mandatory but, other than being required by Microsoft's Common Language Specification, it provides a better way for identifying attributes in code. When applying attributes you can shorten the attribute name excluding the Attribute word. For example, imagine you have a `Document` class representing a simple text document. You might want to provide further information on the document, such as the author, reviewer, or last edit date. This information can be provided and stored in the assembly metadata taking advantage of a custom attribute. Code in Listing 48.1 shows the implementation of a custom attribute that exposes document properties that is explained next.

LISTING 48.1   Writing a Custom Attribute

```vb
<AttributeUsage(AttributeTargets.Class Or AttributeTargets.Property)>
Public Class DocumentPropertiesAttribute
    Inherits Attribute

    'Attributes can be inherited
    'therefore private fields are Protected
    Protected _author As String
    Protected _reviewer As String

    Public Overridable ReadOnly Property Author As String
        Get
            Return Me._author
        End Get
    End Property

    Public Overridable ReadOnly Property Reviewer As String
        Get
            Return Me._reviewer
        End Get
    End Property
```

```
      Public Overridable Property LastEdit As String

      Public Sub New(ByVal author As String, ByVal reviewer As String)
          Me._author = author
          Me._reviewer = reviewer
          Me._lastEdit = CStr(Date.Today)
      End Sub
End Class
```

In Visual Basic every custom attribute is a class with `Public` or `Friend` access level and decorated with the `AttributeUsage` attribute that basically allows specifying what programming elements can be targeted by the custom attribute. Programming elements are specified via the `System.AttributeTargets` enumeration; the enumeration exposes a number of elements, each of them self-explanatory about the targeted programming element. For example, `AttributeTargets.Class` allows applying the attribute to reference types, whereas `AttributeTargets.Methods` allows applying the attribute to methods. IntelliSense shows the full list of the enumeration members, which is straightforward. You notice that an available member for each element is described in the previous section for targetable programming elements. `AttributeTargets` members support bitwise operators so that you combine multiple targets using `Or`. Actual metadata is exposed to the external world via properties that can be either read-only or read/write. Attributes can receive arguments, although this is not mandatory. For arguments, it is important to understand how you can ask for required parameters and optional ones. This is not something that you define as you would usually do in other programming elements such as methods. Basically required parameters are specified in the class constructor. Continuing with the example of Listing 48.1, our custom attribute requires the specification of the author and the reviewer of the document, whereas the last edit date is optional and is still available via a specific property. Optional parameters initialization is not required; in the mentioned example a default value for the `LastEdit` property is supplied. As explained in next subsection, optional arguments are invoked with named parameters.

TYPES FOR ATTRIBUTES PARAMETERS

You should have noticed that the `LastEdit` property in the custom attribute is of type `String` instead of type `Date`. There are some limitations in the applicable data types for attributes parameters. For example, `Decimal`, `Object`, and `Date` are not supported (like structured types as well). Supported types are instead numeric types (`Bytes`, `Short`, `Integer`, `Long`, `Single`, and `Double`), string types (`String` and `Char`), enumerations, and the `Boolean` type. Take care of these limitations that may result in exceptions when passing arguments.

There are several other ways for customizing attributes, but before discovering them here's how to apply custom attributes to complete the discussion over parameters.

48

Applying Custom Attributes

The previous subsection discussed the definition of a custom attribute for assigning metadata to a class representing a basic text document. Code in Listing 48.2 implements the related Document class that is decorated with the DocumentPropertiesAttribute.

LISTING 48.2   Applying Custom Attributes

```
<DocumentProperties("Alessandro Del Sole",
                    "Robert White",
                    LastEdit:="10/06/2009")>
Public Class Document

    Public Property Text As String

    Public ReadOnly Property Length As Integer
        Get
            Return Text.Length
        End Get
    End Property

    <DocumentProperties("Alessandro Del Sole",
                        "Stephen Green")>
    Public Property DocumentName As String

    Public Sub SaveDocument(ByVal fileName As String)
        '...
    End Sub

    Public Sub LoadDocument(ByVal filneName As String)
        '...
    End Sub
End Class
```

When you apply an attribute, you can shorten its name by excluding the Attribute word in the identifier. For example, DocumentPropertiesAttribute can be shortened as DocumentProperties. The Visual Basic compiler correctly recognizes the identifier of an attribute. Then you must provide required arguments, respecting the data type. Such arguments are defined in the constructor of the attribute definition (see the previous subsection). If you want to also specify an optional argument, such as the LastEdit one in the previous example, you need to perform it via a named parameter. Named parameters are literals followed by the := symbols and by information of the required type. This is the only way for providing optional arguments. Notice also how the custom attribute is applied at both class and property level; this is allowed by the attribute definition. Attributes are therefore useful for providing additional information that will be stored in the assembly metadata, to custom objects. Attributes are flexible for other reasons that are covered in next sections.

Applying Attributes Multiple Times

According to the particular nature of your custom attributes, you can decide whether multiple instances can be applied to programming elements. This is accomplished by setting the AllowMultiple property as True in the AttributeUsage. The following is an example:

```
<AttributeUsage(AttributeTargets.Class Or AttributeTargets.Property,
                AllowMultiple:=True)>
Public Class DocumentPropertiesAttribute
    Inherits Attribute
```

Notice that AllowMultiple is optional and thus is invoked as a named parameter. The following is an example on how you apply multiple instances of an attribute:

```
<DocumentProperties("Alessandro Del Sole",
                    "Stephen Green")>
<DocumentProperties("Alessandro", "Stephen",
                    LastEdit:="10/07/2009")>
Public Property DocumentName As String
```

In the particular example of the DocumentProperties attribute, multiple instances probably do not make much sense, but this is the way for applying them.

Defining Inheritance

There are situations where you create classes that inherit from other classes that are decorated with attributes. Attribute inheritance is not automatic in that you can establish whether your attributes are inheritable. You establish this behavior by setting the Inherited property at AttributeUsage level. By default, if you do not explicitly set Inherited, it is considered as True. The following example shows how you enable attribute inheritance:

```
'Attribute is also inherited
<AttributeUsage(AttributeTargets.Class Or AttributeTargets.Property,
                Inherited:=True)>
Public Class DocumentPropertiesAttribute
```

The following snippet shows instead how to make an attribute not inheritable:

```
'Attribute is not inherited
<AttributeUsage(AttributeTargets.Class Or AttributeTargets.Property,
                Inherited:=False)>
Public Class DocumentPropertiesAttribute
```

Inheritance is enabled by default because if a base class is decorated with attributes, derived classes probably also need them. Because of this, you should be careful when disabling

48

inheritance. Code in Listing 48.3 shows an example about declaring two attributes with inheritance definitions and how a derived type is influenced by attribute inheritance.

LISTING 48.3   Conditioning Attribute Inheritance

```vb
<AttributeUsage(AttributeTargets.Class Or AttributeTargets.Method,
                Inherited:=False)>
Public Class FirstAttribute
    Inherits Attribute

    'Implement your code here..
End Class

<AttributeUsage(AttributeTargets.Class Or AttributeTargets.Method)>
Public Class SecondAttribute
    Inherits Attribute

    'Implement your code here..
End Class

Public Class Person
    Public Property LastName As String
    Public Property FirstName As String

    'The base class takes both attributes
    <First(), Second()> Public Overridable Function FullName() As String
        Return String.Concat(LastName, " ", FirstName)
    End Function
End Class

Public Class Contact
    Inherits Person

    'This derived class takes only the Second attribute
    'because First is marked as Inherited:=False
    Public Overrides Function FullName() As String
        Return MyBase.FullName()
    End Function
End Class
```

Notice how the FullName method in the Contact class inherits just the Second attribute appliance whereas the First attribute is not applied because of inheritance settings.

Reflecting Attributes

Attributes are about application's metadata. Because of this, you can use Reflection (see Chapter 47, "Reflection," for details) for checking if a type recurs to custom attributes and investigate metadata (that is, application information). To accomplish this you invoke the `System.Reflection.MemberInfo.GetCustomAttributes` and `System.Reflection.Attributes.GetCustomAttributes` shared methods. The first one returns all attributes applied to the specified type whereas the second one returns an array of custom attributes applied to an assembly, a type or its members, and method parameters. The following is the most basic example for retrieving information about attributes applied to members of the `Document` class:

```vb
'Requires an Imports System.Reflection directive


    Public Sub GetMyAttributes()
        'About members in the Document class
        Dim info As System.Reflection.MemberInfo = GetType(Document)
        'Retrieves an array of attributes
        Dim attributesList() As Object = info.GetCustomAttributes(True)

        'Enumerates applied attributes
        For i As Integer = 0 To attributesList.Length - 1
            Console.WriteLine(attributesList(i))
        Next (i)
    End Sub
```

The following example is instead a little bit more complex and shows how you can perform actions on each attribute instance through `Attribute.GetCustomAttributes`:

```vb
Public Sub GetMyAttributesComplex()
    Dim typeToInvestigate As Type = GetType(Document)

    ' Get the type information for the DocumentName property.
    Dim member_Info As PropertyInfo =
        typeToInvestigate.GetProperty("DocumentName")
    If Not (member_Info Is Nothing) Then

        'Iterate through all the attributes of the property.
        Dim attr As Attribute
        For Each attr In Attribute.GetCustomAttributes(member_Info)
            ' Check for the DocumentPropertiesAttribute attribute.
            If attr.GetType().
                Equals(GetType(DocumentPropertiesAttribute)) Then
```

48

```
                Console.WriteLine("Author: {0}", CType(attr,
                            DocumentPropertiesAttribute).Author)

            'Additional ElseIf conditions here for other attributes..
            End If
        Next attr
    End If
End Sub
```

In this particular scenario the code is used to iterate applied attributes.

Summary

Attributes provide great flexibility in .NET development by giving you the ability to decorate your types and members with custom additional information that is stored in the
assembly metadata. All custom attributes are public classes deriving from
System.Attribute and can be applied to different programming elements, such as assemblies, classes, modules, methods, properties, and so on. For this, the Visual Basic language
requires you to decorate your custom attributes with the AttributeUsage attribute that
provides specifications on targeted elements. When defining custom attributes you can
provide both required and optional parameters; the first ones are established in the
constructor. All parameters refer to attribute information that is exposed to the external
world via properties. Remember that you need to provide a named parameter when invoking optional arguments. You can also decide to make your attributes inheritable
(Inherited property) and to make them applicable more than once (AllowMultiple).
Finally, you can investigate assemblies' and types' attributes via Reflection.

CHAPTER 49

Platform Invokes and Interoperability with the COM Architecture

The .NET Framework 4.0 Base Class Libraries offer tons of objects and methods for covering almost everything in modern application development. In most cases objects and methods are managed wrappers of the Windows Application Programming Interface (API) so that you can use them in the managed environment of the CLR. There can be situations where you need to access some operating system functionalities that have not been wrapped yet by the .NET Framework or you have legacy code exposed by COM objects, such as type libraries. Both the .NET Framework and Visual Basic still enable interoperability with the COM architecture, and in this chapter you see how to reach these objectives.

Importing and Using COM Objects

The .NET Framework 4.0, like previous versions, offers support for interoperability with the COM architecture via an engine named *Runtime Callable Wrapper*, which is the infrastructure that provides a communication bridge between .NET and COM. It is also responsible for type marshaling and handling events. Because of this engine, you can import COM objects and use them in your managed applications. Basically you can import two kinds of COM components: type libraries and ActiveX components. Importing COM components is basically accomplished via two command-line tools: **TlbImp.exe**, which is required to import a type library, and **AxImp.exe**, which is instead required for importing ActiveX controls. This chapter does not discuss how to invoke such tools from the command line, whereas you instead see how to import

COM components from within Visual Studio so that the IDE can do the work for you. In the next example you see how to import an ActiveX control into the Visual Studio toolbox and use the control in code.

Importing COM Components into Visual Studio

Create a new Windows Forms project with Visual Basic and, when ready, open the Visual Studio toolbox. When done, right-click the toolbox and select **Choose Items**. This launches the same-named dialog that you already know because of adding .NET controls to the toolbox. Select the **COM** tab and search for the **Windows Media Player** item, as shown in Figure 49.1.

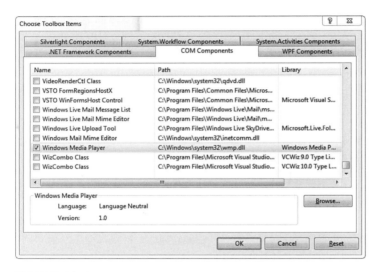

FIGURE 49.1   Choosing a COM component to add to the toolbox.

When you click **OK**, Visual Studio generates two files for you:

▶ **Interop.WMPLib.dll**, which is a CLR wrapper for using COM objects exposed by the Windows Media Player type library in a .NET fashion

▶ **AxInterop.WMPLib.dll**, which is a Windows Forms proxy that provides the infrastructure required for hosting the control in your forms

At this point notice that the Windows Media Player ActiveX control is available inside the toolbox. Now drag the control over the current form and design the media player as you like. At this point Visual Studio generates some code for you to declare the control and enables you to use it. If you expand the Form1.designer.vb file, you find the following initialization code for the ActiveX control:

```
Friend WithEvents AxWindowsMediaPlayer1 As AxWMPLib.AxWindowsMediaPlayer
```

...

```
Me.AxWindowsMediaPlayer1.Enabled = True
Me.AxWindowsMediaPlayer1.Location = New System.Drawing.Point(24, 13)
Me.AxWindowsMediaPlayer1.Name = "AxWindowsMediaPlayer1"
Me.AxWindowsMediaPlayer1.OcxState = _
CType(resources.GetObject("AxWindowsMediaPlayer1.OcxState"),
System.Windows.Forms.AxHost.State)
Me.AxWindowsMediaPlayer1.Size = New System.Drawing.Size(239, 196)
Me.AxWindowsMediaPlayer1.TabIndex = 0
```

AXHOST CLASS

ActiveX controls are wrapped by the System.Windows.Forms.AxHost class that enable treating COM components as you would do with .NET objects.

Now you can work with the ActiveX control in a managed way, as illustrated in next subsection.

Using COM Objects in Code

When you have an instance of the ActiveX control, or of a type library, you can access its members like any other .NET object, thus invoking methods, assigning properties, or handling events. For example the following code assigns the URL property of the media player with a media file to start playing:

```
Private Sub Form1_Load(ByVal sender As Object,
                    ByVal e As System.EventArgs) Handles Me.Load

    AxWindowsMediaPlayer1.URL = "C:\users\alessandro\music\MySong.mp3"

End Sub
```

You can also handle events if available, as demonstrated by the following code snippet:

```
Private Sub AxWindowsMediaPlayer1_MediaError(ByVal sender As Object,
                        ByVal e As AxWMPLib.
                        _WMPOCXEvents_MediaErrorEvent) _
                        Handles AxWindowsMediaPlayer1.
                        MediaError

    MessageBox.Show("An error occurred while opening media")
End Sub
```

In this particular case the MediaError event is raised when an error occurs in playing the media file. At a more general level, notice how wrapping an ActiveX control allows importing different kinds of members, including events.

49

Catching Exceptions

When you implement `Try..Catch..End Try` blocks, you can intercept and handle only CLS-compliant exceptions, that is, exceptions inheriting from `System.Exception`. Exceptions wrapped by the COM import tools are not CLS-compliant, so a classic `Try` block would fail. To intercept exceptions coming from wrapped objects, the .NET Framework offers the `System.Runtime.CompilerServices.RuntimeWrappedException` that can be used for error handling when working with wrappers. The following code shows an example:

```
Try
    AxWindowsMediaPlayer1.URL = "C:\users\alessandro\music\MySong.mp3"

Catch ex As RuntimeWrappedException

Catch ex As Exception

End Try
```

Other than usual exception properties, this class exposes a `WrappedException` property, of type `Object`, which represents the occurred problem.

Releasing COM Objects

You should always explicitly release objects that wrap COM components so that associated resources are also released. You accomplish this by invoking the `System.Runtime.InteropServices.Marshal.ReleaseCOMObject` method. Continuing with the previous example, you release the `AxWindowsMediaPlayer1` object as follows:

```
Private Sub Form1_FormClosing(ByVal sender As Object,
                              ByVal e As System.Windows.Forms.
                              FormClosingEventArgs) Handles _
                              Me.FormClosing
    System.Runtime.InteropServices.Marshal.
    ReleaseComObject(AxWindowsMediaPlayer1)
End Sub
```

This is important because COM objects treat system resources differently from .NET objects; therefore, an explicit release is required.

Exposing .NET Objects to the COM World

Although in modern world applications this practice is less frequent than in the past, you can expose .NET objects to the COM world. For example, a VB 6 application can consume an object like this. To demonstrate how you accomplish this export, create a new class library and rename Class1.vb to Contact.vb. The first thing you need to do to make a class consumable from COM is enable the COM interoperability support. Now open My Project and then select the Compile tab. Flag the **Register for COM Interop** item at the bottom of the page, as shown in Figure 49.2.

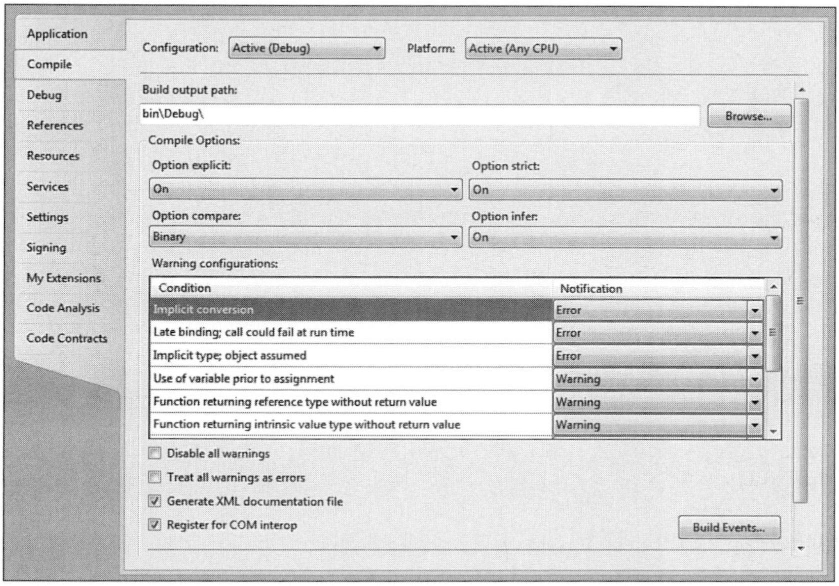

FIGURE 49.2   Registering an assembly for COM Interoperability.

This operation tells Visual Studio that it needs to register the COM component on build and adds the following line of code in AssemblyInfo.vb so that it makes it visible to COM:

```
<Assembly: ComVisible(True)>
```

CLASS REQUIREMENTS FOR COM EXPOSURE

Any class that you want to expose to COM has the following requirements: It must have a public, empty, parameterless constructor, any member, including types, to be exposed must be Public (no other modifiers are allowed), and it cannot include abstract class-es. (This is just because they cannot be consumed.)

The ComVisible attribute establishes the visibility level and granularity not only at assembly level, but also for classes and class members. At the moment implement the Contact class as follows:

```
Public Class COMContact
```

```
    Public Property FirstName As String
    Public Property LastName As String
    Public Property Email As String
    Public Property BirthDay As Date

    Public Sub New()

    End Sub
End Class
```

Now you can decide the visibility level for each member in the class by decorating the class and its members with the System.Runtime.InteropServices.ComVisible attribute. The following code demonstrates how to make COM-visible only some members from the Contact class:

```
Imports System.Runtime.InteropServices


<ComVisible(False)>
Public Class COMContact

    <ComVisible(True)>
    Public Property FirstName As String
    <ComVisible(True)>
    Public Property LastName As String
    <ComVisible(True)>
    Public Property Email As String

    <ComVisible(False)>
    Public Property BirthDay As Date

    Public Sub New()

    End Sub
End Class
```

The class is marked as ComVisible(False) simply because not all its members are COM-visible. Notice that a public, empty constructor is required for COM-visible objects.

The next step should be to register the COM component after the build process. Fortunately, on the development machine Visual Studio 2010 does the work for you. (This requires the IDE to be launched with elevated privileges.) Therefore, simply compile the project to have a class library that is consumable from the COM architecture.

P/Invokes and Unmanaged Code

One of the biggest benefits of the .NET Framework is that the technology is a bridge between you and the Windows operating system and is responsible for managing a lot of system features (such as memory management) highly reducing the risk of bad system resources management that could lead the system to unwanted crashes or problems. This is the reason why (as you may recall from Chapter 1, "Introducing the .NET Framework 4.0") .NET programming is also known as *managed*. The .NET Framework base class library exposes managed wrappers for most of the Windows API system so that you do not need to manually handle system resources, and you can take all advantages from the CLR. By the way, there are situations in which you still need to access the Windows API (for example when there is not a .NET counterpart of an API function), and thus you need to work with *unmanaged code*. Basically unmanaged code is all code not controlled by the .NET Framework and that requires you to manually handle system resources. When you work with unmanaged code, you commonly invoke Windows API functions; such invocations are also known as *Platform Invokes* or, simpler, *P/Invokes*. In this section I cover both situations, starting with P/Invokes.

NOTE ON UNMANAGED CODE

You should always avoid unmanaged code. The .NET Framework 4.0 offers an infinite number of managed objects and methods for performing almost everything, and if something from the Windows API has not been wrapped yet, you can find lots of open-source or free third-party libraries to help you solve your problems without P/Invokes. Using unmanaged code means working directly against the operating system and its resources, and if your code does not perfectly handle resources, it can lead to hard problems. Moreover, when performing unmanaged calls you need to be certain that they work or exist on all versions of the Windows operating system you plan to support for your application. In a few words, always search through the Base Class Library to ensure that a .NET counterpart for the Windows API already exists. It probably does.

Understanding P/Invokes

Calls to Windows API functions are known as Platform Invokes or P/Invokes. The Visual Basic programming language offers two ways for performing platform invokes:

▶ Declare keyword

▶ System.Runtime.InteropServices.DllImport attribute

The Declare keyword has a behavior similar to what happened in Visual Basic 6, and it has been kept for compatibility, but you should always prefer the DllImport attribute because this is the one way recognized by the Common Language Specification. Now we can see how to declare a P/Invoke. The next example considers the PathIsUrl function, from the Shlwapi.dll system library, which checks if the specified is an URL and returns a value according to the result. This is with the Declare keyword:

```
Declare Function PathIsUrl Lib "shlwapi.dll" Alias _
        "PathIsURLA" (ByVal path As String) As Integer
```

MATCHING NUMERIC TYPES

Keep in mind the difference in numeric types between the Windows API system and the .NET common types system, because generally Windows APIs return Long; however when you perform P/Invokes you must use the .NET counterpart that is Integer. The same is for Integer in the Windows API, which is mapped by Short in .NET. Similarly, remember to use the IntPtr structure for declarations that require a handle (or a pointer) of type Integer.

As you can see, the API declaration looks similar to what you used to write in VB 6. The following is instead how you declare the API function via the DllImport attribute:

```
'Requires an
'Imports System.Runtime.InteropServices directive
<DllImport("shlwapi.dll", entrypoint:="PathIsURLA")>
Shared Function PathIsURL(ByVal path As String) As System.Int32
End Function
```

Among its number of options, the most important in DllImport are the library name and the entrypoint parameter that simply indicates the function name. It is important to remember that P/Invokes must be declared as Shared, because they cannot be exposed as instance methods; the only exception to this rule is when you declare a function within a module. When declared, you can consume P/Invokes like any other method (always remembering that you are not passing through the CLR) as demonstrated here:

```
Dim testUrl As String = "http://www.visual-basic.it"
Dim result As Integer = PathIsURL(testUrl)
```

Both Declare and DllImport lead to the same result, but from now we use only DllImport.

Encapsulating P/Invokes

Encapsulating P/Invokes in classes is a programming best practice and makes your code clearer and more meaningful. Continuing the previous example, you could create a new class and declare inside the class the PathIsUrl function, marking it as Shared so that it can be consumed by other objects. By the way, there is another consideration to make. If you plan to wrap Windows API functions in reusable class libraries, the best approach is to provide CLS-compliant libraries and API calls. For this reason we now discuss how you can encapsulate P/Invokes following the rules of the Common Language Specification. The first rule is to create a class that stores only P/Invokes declarations. Such a class must be visible only within the assembly, must implement a private empty constructor, and will expose only shared members. The following is an example related to the `PathIsUri` function:

```
Friend Class NativeMethods
    <DllImport("shlwapi.dll", entrypoint:="PathIsURLA")>
    Shared Function PathIsURL(ByVal path As String) As System.Int32
    End Function

    Private Sub New()

    End Sub
End Class
```

The class is marked with `Friend` to make it visible only within the assembly. Notice that a CLS-compliant class for exposing P/Invokes declarations can have only one of the following names:

▶ `NativeMethods`, which is used on the development machine and indicates that the class has no particular security and permissions requirements

▶ `SafeNativeMethods`, which is used outside the development machine and indicates that the class and methods have no particular security and permissions requirements

▶ `UnsafeNativeMethods`, which is used to explain to other developers that the caller needs to demand permissions to execute the code (demanding permissions for one of the classes exposed by the `System.Security.Permissions` namespace)

To expose P/Invokes to the external call, you need a wrapper class. The following class demonstrates how you can expose the `NativeMethods.PathIsUrl` function in a programmatically correct approach:

```
Public Class UsefulMethods

    Public Shared Function CheckIfPathIsUrl(ByVal path As String) _
        As Integer
        Return NativeMethods.PathIsURL(path)
    End Function

End Class
```

49

Finally, you can consume the preceding code as follows (for example adding a reference to the class library):

```vbnet
Dim testUrl As String = "http://www.visual-basic.it"
Dim result As Integer = UsefulMethods.CheckIfPathIsUrl(testUrl)
```

Working with unmanaged code is not only performing P/Invokes. There are some other important concepts about error handling and type marshaling, as explained in next sections.

Converting Types to Unmanaged

When you work with P/Invokes, you might have the need to pass custom types as function arguments. If such types are .NET types, the most important thing is converting primitives into types that are acceptable by the COM/Win32 architecture. The System.Runtime.InteropServices namespace exposes the MarshalAs attribute that can be applied to fields and method arguments to convert the object into the most appropriate COM counterpart. The following sample implementation of the Person class demonstrates how to apply MarshalAs:

```vbnet
Imports System.Runtime.InteropServices


Public Class Person

    <MarshalAs(UnmanagedType.LPStr)>
    Private _firstName As String
    <MarshalAs(UnmanagedType.SysInt)>
    Private _age As Integer

    Public Property FirstName As String
        Get
            Return _firstName
        End Get
        Set(ByVal value As String)
            _firstName = value
        End Set
    End Property


    Public Property Age As Integer
        Get
            Return _age
        End Get
        Set(ByVal value As Integer)
            _age = value
        End Set
    End Property
```

```
Sub ConvertParameter(<MarshalAs(UnmanagedType.LPStr)> _
                        ByVal name As String)
    End Sub
End Class
```

The attribute receives a value from the `UnmanagedType` enumeration; IntelliSense offers great help about members in this enumeration, showing the full members list and explaining what each member is bound to convert. You can check this out as an exercise.

The `StructLayout` Attribute

An important aspect of unmanaged programming is how you handle types, especially when such types are passed as P/Invoke arguments. Differently from P/Invokes, types representing counterparts from the Windows API pass through the Common Language Runtime and, as a general rule, you should provide the CLR the best way for handling them to keep performance high. Basically when you write a class or a structure, you give members a particular order that should have a meaning for you. In other words, if the `Person` class exposes `FirstName` and `Age` as properties, keeping this order should have a reason, which generally is dictated only by some kind of logic. With the `System.Runtime.InteropServices.StructLayout` attribute, you can tell the CLR how it can handle type members; it enables deciding if it has to respect a particular order or if it can handle type members the best way it can according to performances. The `StructLayout` attribute's constructor offers three alternatives:

- ▶ `StructLayout.Auto`: The CLR handles type members in its preferred order.

- ▶ `StructLayout.Sequential`: The CLR handles type members preserving the order provided by the developer in the type implementation.

- ▶ `StructLayout.Explicit`: The CLR handles type members according to the order established by the developer, using memory offsets.

By default, if `StructLayout` is not specified, the CLR assumes `Auto` for reference types and `Sequential` for structures. For example, consider the `COMRECT` structure from the Windows API, which represents four points. This is how you write it in Visual Basic, making it available to unmanaged code:

```
<StructLayout(LayoutKind.Sequential)>
Public Structure COMRECT

    Public Left As Integer
    Public Top As Integer
    Public Right As Integer
    Public Bottom As Integer

    Shared Sub New()

    End Sub
```

49

```
Public Sub New(ByVal left As Integer,
               ByVal top As Integer,
               ByVal right As Integer,
               ByVal bottom As Integer)

        Me.Left = left
        Me.Top = top
        Me.Right = right
        Me.Bottom = bottom
    End Sub
End Structure
```

TIPS ON DEFAULT OPTIONS

StructLayout must be applied explicitly if your assembly needs to be CLS-compliant. This happens because you have two choices, Sequential and Explicit. Instead, for classes this is not necessary, because they are always considered as Auto. Because of this, in this section we describe only structures.

This is how instead you can apply StructLayout.Explicit, providing memory offsets:

```
<StructLayout(LayoutKind.Explicit)>
Public Structure COMRECT

    <FieldOffset(0)> Public Left As Integer
    <FieldOffset(4)> Public Top As Integer
    <FieldOffset(8)> Public Right As Integer
    <FieldOffset(12)> Public Bottom As Integer

    Shared Sub New()

    End Sub

    Public Sub New(ByVal left As Integer,
                   ByVal top As Integer,
                   ByVal right As Integer,
                   ByVal bottom As Integer)

        Me.Left = left
        Me.Top = top
        Me.Right = right
```

```
        Me.Bottom = bottom
    End Sub
End Structure
```

The `FieldOffset` attribute specifies the memory offset for each field. In this case the structure provides fields of type `Integer`, so each offset is four bytes.

The `VBFixedString` attribute

The `VBFixedString` attribute can be applied to structure members of type `String`, in order to delimit the string length, since by default string length is variable. Such delimitation is established in bytes instead of characters. This attribute is required in some API calls. The following is an example:

```
Public Structure Contact
'Both fields are limited to 10 bytes size
    <VBFixedString(10)> Public LastName As String
    <VBFixedString(10)> Public Email As String
End Structure
```

Notice that the `VBFixedString` can be applied to fields but is not valid for properties.

Handling Exceptions

Functions from Windows API generally return a numeric value as their result (called `HRESULT`), for communicating with the caller if the function succeeded or failed. Prior to .NET 2.0, getting information on functions failures was a difficult task. Starting from .NET 2.0 you can handle exceptions coming from the P/Invokes world with a classic `Try..Catch` block. The real improvement is that the .NET Framework can wrap unmanaged errors that have a .NET counterpart into managed exceptions. For example, if a Windows API invocation causes an out-of-memory error, the .NET Framework maps such error as an `OutOfMemoryException` that you can embrace within a normal `Try..Catch` block. By the way, it is reasonable that not all unmanaged errors can have a managed counterpart, due to differences in COM and .NET architectures. To solve this, .NET provides the `System.Runtime.InteropServices.SEHException`, in which `SEH` stands for *Structured Exception Handling* and that maps all unmanaged exceptions that .NET cannot map. The exception is useful because it exposes an `ErrorCode` property that stores the `HRESULT` sent from P/Invokes. You use it like this:

```
Try
    'Add your P/Invoke here..
Catch ex As SEHException
    Console.WriteLine(ex.ErrorCode.ToString)
```

49

```
Catch ex As Exception

End Try
```

TIP

The SEHException does not provide a good number of exception details, differently from managed exceptions, but it is the most appropriate exception for error handling in a Try..Catch block within unmanaged code.

There is also an alternative, which requires some explanation. P/Invokes raise Win32 errors calling themselves the SetLastError native method that is different from how exceptions are thrown in the Common Language Runtime. In earlier days you could call the GetLastError method to retrieve the error code, but this is not the best choice because it can refer to managed exceptions, other than Win32 exceptions. A better, although not the ultimate, approach can be provided by invoking the System.Runtime.InteropServices.Marshal.GetLastWin32Error method, which can intercept the last error coming from a Win32 call. To make this work, first you need to set the SetLastError property in the DllImport attribute as True; then you can invoke the method. The following code shows an example on the Beep function, which returns a numeric value as the result:

```
<DllImport("kernel32.dll", entrypoint:="Beep", SetLastError:=True)>
Public Shared Function Beep(ByVal frequency As UInteger,
                            ByVal duration As UInteger) As Integer
End Function

    Dim beepResult = NativeMethods.Beep(100, 100)
    If beepResult = 0 Then
        Console.WriteLine(Marshal.GetLastWin32Error())
    End If
```

Here you need to know first what values can return a particular function. Beep returns zero if it does not succeed. So after a check on the result value, the Marshal.GetLastWin32Error method is invoked to understand the error code.

References to the Win32 API calls

Developers can reference the MSDN documentation or the Windows SDK to get detailed information on the Windows API functions and their signatures. The following are resources available on the Internet for your reference:

► MSDN reference: http://msdn.microsoft.com/en-us/library/aa383749(VS.85).aspx

► Windows SDK:
http://www.microsoft.com/downloads/details.aspx?FamilyID=c17ba869-9671-4330-a63e-1fd44e0e2505&displaylang=en

► PInvoke.net website: http://www.pinvoke.net

Summary

In this chapter you learned some concepts on how the .NET technology can interoperate with the COM legacy architecture and components. In the first part of the chapter you learned how to import COM components into managed applications, understanding how Visual Studio generates .NET wrappers to interact with COM. Next you learned how to create and expose .NET libraries to COM, utilizing the Visual Studio instrumentation and applying the `ComVisible` attribute to classes and class members to grant visibility granularity. In the last part of the chapter, you saw how to call and run unmanaged code, with particular regard to Platform Invokes and types conversions for working directly against the Windows operating system.

49

Documenting the Source Code

One of the most common programming rules states that documenting the source code is fundamental. This is of course the truth but you have to think about the way source code is commented. Classical comments are useful to explain what code does so that you can easily remember how your code works if you need to retake it after a long time, or they can help other developers to understand your code. But this is not the only way of documenting code in .NET development. A sophisticated environment such as Visual Studio offers the IntelliSense technology that not only speeds up the way you write code but is also shows instructions on how you use objects and members. This is possible because of special kinds of comments that you can add to your code, known as XML comments. Such comments allow writing the source code documentation, explaining objects' and members' behavior, and also providing descriptions and examples that can be shown up by IntelliSense. But that is not all. Documenting code with XML comments is particularly important if you develop reusable compiled libraries and allow automating the process of building compiled documentation files (such as .chm files) in a similar way to the MSDN documentation. In this chapter you learn to use XML comments to provide simple and complex source code documentation, also learning how to build compiled documentation.

Understanding XML Documents

XML documents are not new in Visual Basic 2010; they were first natively introduced with Visual Basic 2005. (In versions prior to 2005, XML comments were possible only via third-party add-ins.) To understand why XML documents are an essential topic, let's take a look at a method invocation within the code editor. Figure 50.1 shows how IntelliSense appears on an uncommented method.

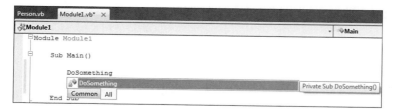

FIGURE 50.1 Uncommented members make IntelliSense unable to display useful information.

As you can see from Figure 50.1, IntelliSense will correctly show up, but it will just show the method name in a tooltip, without providing information on the method usage. This is because the method was not commented with XML comments. Now take a look at Figure 50.2 that shows how IntelliSense can provide information if the method was commented with XML comments.

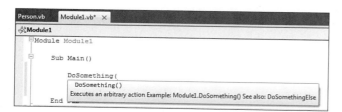

FIGURE 50.2 Commented members are well described when IntelliSense shows up in the code editor.

The difference is evident. Objects and members decorated with XML comments can provide full explanation on their usage. This works in the code editor when IntelliSense shows up with both source files and with compiled executables. As mentioned at the beginning of this chapter, providing XML comments is not only useful for IntelliSense but also when you investigate objects in the Object Browser or for automating the process of building compiled documentation for your libraries. Because of this, adding XML comments to your code is something necessary in most cases, especially if you develop reusable assemblies. In the next sections you learn practical techniques for commenting the source code and getting the most out of XML comments with Visual Basic.

Enabling XML Comments

When Visual Studio builds the project output, it also creates an XML document storing all XML comments. The XML document constitutes the actual code documentation. In Visual Studio 2010 XML comments are enabled by default. Before reading this chapter, ensure that XML comments are effectively enabled in your project. To accomplish this, open **My Project**; select the **Compile** tab and, if it's not checked, check the **Generate XML Documentation** file box. See Figure 50.3 for details.

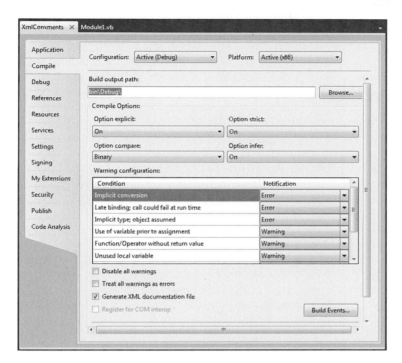

FIGURE 50.3   Enabling Xml comments.

Behind the scenes this requires the Visual Basic compiler to be launched by Visual Studio with the /doc option, which makes the compiler also generate the XML documentation. At this point you are ready to implement XML comments in your Visual Basic code.

Implementing XML Comments

XML comments have a double purpose. The first one is enabling additional help within IntelliSense when you write code. The second one is generating an XML file storing information that can be built into a compiled documentation file, such as the .Chm format that also allows navigation between documented items. In this section you learn to implement XML comments understanding the various tags and why they are important; although in some cases it might not seem to be. Before implementing comments, create a new Console application and implement a `Person` class as follows:

```
Public Class Person
```

```
    Public Overridable Property FirstName As String
    Public Overridable Property LastName As String
    Public Overridable Property Age As Integer

    Public Overridable Function GetFullName() As String
        Dim fn As New Text.StringBuilder
        fn.Append(Me.FirstName)
        fn.Append(" ")
        fn.Append(Me.LastName)
        Return fn.ToString
    End Function
End Class
```

The Person class will be the base for our experiments. You implement an XML comment by typing three apostrophes. The Visual Studio code editor adds a comment skeleton to your code that first looks like the following example:

```
''' <summary>
'''
''' </summary>
''' <returns></returns>
''' <remarks></remarks>
Public Overridable Function GetFullName() As String
    Dim fn As New Text.StringBuilder
    fn.Append(Me.FirstName)
    fn.Append(" ")
    fn.Append(Me.LastName)
    Return fn.ToString
End Function
```

As you can see, these comments have typical XML structure according to the <tag> </tag> syntax. The summary XML tag enables describing what an object (or member) does. The description will be also available within IntelliSense. The remarks tag enables providing additional information on what you already specified in the summary, and the information will also be displayed within the Object Browser (but not within IntelliSense). The returns tag specifies the type returned by the member (being a method or a property); in case the member is a method that does not return a value, Visual Studio will not add the returns tag. For a better understanding, populate comments as follows:

```
''' <summary>
''' Gets the complete person's name
''' </summary>
''' <returns>String</returns>
''' <remarks>This method returns the complete person's name</remarks>
Public Overridable Function GetFullName() As String
    Dim fn As New Text.StringBuilder
```

```
        fn.Append(Me.FirstName)
        fn.Append(" ")
        fn.Append(Me.LastName)
        Return fn.ToString
End Function
```

Now go to the Main method in your Console application, and write the following code that instantiates and populates the Person class:

```
Dim p As New Person With {.FirstName = "Alessandro", .LastName = "Del Sole",
                          .Age = 32}


Dim fullName As String = p.GetFullName
```

When typing code, you notice how IntelliSense provides information on the GetFullName method according to the XML comment's content. This is represented in Figure 50.4.

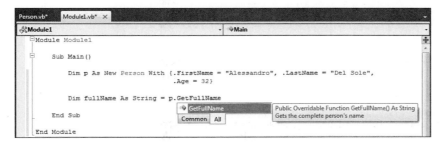

FIGURE 50.4   IntelliSense shows the information provided by the XML comments.

As you can see, IntelliSense basically shows the content of the summary tag whereas it does not show the content of the returns and remarks tags. This makes sense in that IntelliSense's tooltips are the fastest way for getting help. If you instead open the Object Browser on the Person class, you get a result that looks similar to Figure 50.5.

You obtain the same detailed information if you build a compiled documentation file, as described later in this chapter. The one shown before is the most basic implementation of XML comments. By the way, this great Visual Basic feature allows defining complex documentation over your code, which can be particularly useful also due to the integration with the Visual Studio environment.

SCOPE

XML comments can be applied to both public and private objects and members.

50

Defining Complex Code Documentation

The MSDN documentation says that the Visual Basic compiler can parse any valid XML tag. The MSDN also recommends a series of tags that are specific to the code documentation. Table 50.1 summarizes recommended tags.

FIGURE 50.5   The Object Browser shows information provided by XML comments.

CASE-SENSITIVENESS

Tags within XML comments are case-sensitive and lowercase. Take care of this to ensure that the Visual Basic compiler correctly recognizes tags.

NOTE ON COMPLEX DOCUMENTATION

You can generally appreciate complex documentation generated with XML comments only when building compiled help files. This is because within IntelliSense or in the Object Browser only a few tags' contents will be shown. For example, XML comments allow building bulleted lists or specifying links to other documentation regarding different code; all this cannot be shown in IntelliSense but makes a lot of sense in a help file or a help system built on html pages. If you are interested only in building documentation for Visual Studio internal usage, you can theoretically limit XML comments to the basic implementations.

Let's go back to the Person class and provide an XML comment for the FirstName property. The XML comment must look like this:

```
''' <summary>
''' Contains the person's first name
```

TABLE 50.1   Recommended Tags for XML Comments

Tag	Description
c	Identifies a code element
cref	Creates a cross reference to another documented object
code	Provides a code snippet about the code usage
example	Provides a description about how code can be used
exception	Allows specifying the exception that your member could throw
include	Points to an external XML file containing documentation for the code
list	Allows generating a bulleted, numbered, or tabled list
para	Allows formatting its content as a paragraph
param	Defines a parameter that can be referenced by paramref
paramref	Allows formatting a word as a parameter defined via param
permission	Specifies the Code Access Security permission required by the commented member
remarks	Provides additional notes on your code
returns	Specifies the .NET type returned by your member
see	Provides a link to another member
seealso	Adds a member in the See Also section of the compiled documentation
summary	Provides a description about a member; also shown within IntelliSense
typeparam	Provides type parameter name and description when declaring generic types
value	Describes the value of a member (for example, a property)

```
'''   </summary>
'''   <value>Person's first name</value>
'''   <returns>String</returns>
'''   <remarks></remarks>
Public Overridable Property FirstName As String
```

Here there is a new tag, value. The summary tag describes a property whereas value describes the property's value. Do the same thing on the LastName property specifying the appropriate description, similarly to FirstName. Other tags can be added in a straightforward way, thanks to the always present IntelliSense. Figure 50.6 shows how IntelliSense provides available XML tags, according to the particular context where they have to be added.

50

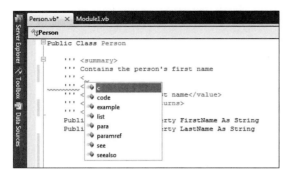

FIGURE 50.6   IntelliSense helps you select XML tags according to the particular context.

Referring to Code Elements

XML comments enable references to other code elements with specific tags. The first one is c that identifies the element within angle bracket as code. To show an example, rewrite XML comments for the GetFullName method as follows:

```
''' <summary>
''' Gets the complete person's name
''' </summary>
''' <returns>String</returns>
''' <remarks>This method concatenates <c>LastName</c> and
''' <c>FirstName</c> properties</remarks>
Public Overridable Function GetFullName() As String
    Dim fn As New Text.StringBuilder
    fn.Append(Me.FirstName)
    fn.Append(" ")
    fn.Append(Me.LastName)
    Return fn.ToString
End Function
```

Notice how the c tag embraces both LastName and FirstName properties, communicating to the compiler that both tags represent a code element. Also notice how it is enclosed and nested within a remarks tag (IntelliSense can be helpful in choosing the allowed tags.) This is not the only way for referring to code; you can provide an entire code example that will be included in your documentation. To accomplish this you first declare an example tag, which contains the example description and then a code tag that contains a code snippet demonstrating the member purpose. With that said, edit the preceding XML comment as follows:

```
''' <summary>
''' Gets the complete person's name
''' </summary>
''' <returns>String</returns>
''' <remarks>This method concatenates <c>LastName</c> and
```

```
''' <c>FirstName</c> properties
''' <example>This example shows how you can invoke
''' the <c>GetFullName</c> method
''' <code>
''' Dim result As String = Person1.GetFullName()
''' </code>
''' </example>
''' </remarks>
Public Overridable Function GetFullName() As String
```

This is useful because your documentation also shows examples on your libraries.

WHY DON'T I SEE THEM?

Code, c and example tags provide documentation that is not available within IntelliSense whereas it is available within the generated XML file; thus you can appreciate them when building an html-based or compiled documentation or within the Object Browser.

XML comments easily allow referring to and documenting members' arguments. For a better understanding, write the following overload of the GetFullName method that accepts a Title argument:

```
Public Overridable Function GetFullName(ByVal Title As String) As String

    If String.IsNullOrEmpty(Title) = True Then Throw New _
                                        ArgumentNullException

    Dim fn As New Text.StringBuilder
    fn.Append(Title)
    fn.Append(" ")
    fn.Append(Me.FirstName)
    fn.Append(" ")
    fn.Append(Me.LastName)
    Return fn.ToString
End Function
```

Now add an XML comment. It look likes this:

```
''' <summary>
''' Gets the complete person's name
''' </summary>
''' <param name="Title"></param>
''' <returns>String</returns>
''' <remarks></remarks>
```

```
Public Overridable Function GetFullName(ByVal Title As String) As String
```

The param tag allows referring to a member's argument, specified by the name attribute. If you try to type name on your own, you notice how IntelliSense helps you choose the argument. XML comments also allow specifying an exception that your member could encounter, according to the actions it takes. For example, the GetFullName method could throw a NullReferenceException if the Title argument is an empty or null string. For this, you use an exception tag to specify the exception. The tag is used with cref. This one is straightforward in that it allows pointing a reference to a .NET object taking advantage of IntelliSense. For example, the following tag (which must be added before the method definition) specifies what exception can be thrown:

```
''' <exception cref="ArgumentNullException">
''' The exception that is thrown when <paramref name="Title"/> is Nothing
''' </exception>
''' <returns>String</returns>
''' <remarks></remarks>
Public Overridable Function GetFullName(ByVal Title As String) As String
```

When typing cref, you notice the IntelliSense window showing all available objects. You simply pick the exception you are interested in. This speeds up the way you write your comment, also ensuring that you type a valid object name. You can also specify the description for the exception. The good news about cref is that it creates a cross-reference to the documentation related to the pointed object. For example, when you create a compiled documentation file based on the XML comments, cref allows redirecting to another page showing information on the pointed object. Also notice how you can refer to the argument by specifying the paramref tag within a descriptive text, which requires a name attribute pointing to the argument. paramref also takes advantages of IntelliSense.

Referring to an External Documentation File

The Visual Basic compiler can link documentation to your code from an external XML document. To accomplish this, you use the include tag. The tag requires a file attribute that points to the external document and a path attribute that points to the position in the document providing documentation for the given member. The following code sets external documentation for the Age property:

```
''' <include file="ExternalDoc.xml" path="Help/Property[@name='Age']"/>
Public Overridable Property Age As Integer
```

To understand how the path tag works, here is the XML representation of the external document:

```
<?xml version="1.0" encoding="utf-8" ?>
<Help>
  <Property name="Age">
    <summary>Returns how old a person is</summary>
    <returns>Integer</returns>
```

```
    </Property>
    <!-- Other properties...-->
    <Property>

    </Property>
</Help>
```

Creating Lists

Documentation often requires bulleted and numbered lists or tables, as in any other kind of document. Luckily XML comments allow easily building lists. This is accomplished with the `list` tag that requires a `type` attribute specifying if the list is a bulleted or numbered list or a two-column table. The following example shows how to build a numbered list on the `Person` class documentation:

```
'''  <summary>
'''  Represents a human being
'''  </summary>
'''  <remarks>
'''  <list type="number">
'''  <item><description>Instantiate the class</description></item>
'''  <item><description>Populate its properties</description></item>
'''  <item><description>Eventually retrieve the full
'''  name</description></item>
'''  </list>
'''  </remarks>
Public Class Person
....
End Class
```

The `type` attribute can have one of the following values: `bullet` (bulleted list), `number` (numbered list), and `table` (two-column table). Notice how each item in the list is represented by an `item` tag that requires a nested `description` tag providing the actual description. In case you want to provide a table, each item must contain a `term` tag and a `description` tag as in the following example:

```
'''  <item><term>Action one</term></item>
'''  <item><description>Instantiate the class</description></item>
```

The items content will be also shown in IntelliSense and the Object Browser but it will be actually formatted as a list only in the compiled documentation.

Documenting Permissions Requirements

There are situations where your objects expose members that require special permissions to access system resources. You can provide documentation about required permissions by adding a permission tag with cref, pointing to the desired .NET permission. The following example shows how to comment the GetFullName method with the UIPermission requirement:

```
''' <permission cref="System.Security.Permissions.UIPermission"/>
Public Overridable Function GetFullName() As String
```

Of course, you can specify multiple permissions by adding multiple permission tags.

Specifying Links to Other Resources

When documenting the code, it is not unusual to provide links to other members. XML comments allow this by specifying see and seealso tags. The see tag allows specifying a link to another member's documentation from within the description text. The seealso tag does the same, but it differs in that the link to the other member appears in the *See Also* section of the compiled page. The following example demonstrates this on the FirstName property providing a link to LastName:

```
''' <remarks>Use the <see cref="LastName"/>
''' property for the person's last name</remarks>
Public Overridable Property FirstName As String
```

If you want the link to be shown in the *See Also* section, simply replace see with seealso.

Xml Comments and Generics

When you define your custom generics, you can take advantage of XML comments to describe the type parameter. This is accomplished via the typeparam tag, as shown in the following code snippet:

```
''' <summary>
''' A test class
''' </summary>
''' <typeparam name="T">
''' A type parameter that must implement IEnumerable
''' </typeparam>
''' <remarks></remarks>
Public Class TestGenerics(Of T As IEnumerable)

End Class
```

The Visual Basic compiler automatically recognizes the generic implementation and thus adds for you the typeparam tag when adding the XML comment.

Generating Compiled Help Files

When you document your source code with XML comments, you might want to generate compiled help files that you can distribute together with your libraries. Generally compiled help files are .chm files that can be easily opened with the Windows integrated Help Viewer. The .chm file format is the most appropriate in such situations because it is a standalone and does not require additional applications. There are several tools that can generate .chm files starting from XML documents, but probably the most common is Microsoft SandCastle, an open source tool from Microsoft that is also used to build documentation. SandCastle is a great tool with one limitation: It works from the command line only, and command lines are often complex. To make things easier, several developers have built their own GUIs for SandCastle so that you can build your documentation with a few mouse clicks.

NOTE

SandCastle is still available in the Beta 1 of Visual Studio 2010. This is the reason why the application is not covered in detail. Maybe when you are reading this book, an updated version of SandCastle will be released or, if not, you can download the source code and simply build it inside Visual Studio 2010.

With that said, follow these steps:

1. Download the SandCastle installer from the CodePlex community at http://www. codeplex.com/sandcastle. When downloaded, install the application.

2. Download the SandCastle Help File Builder graphical tool from CodePlex at http://www.codeplex.com/shfb. This open source application allows creating projects and invokes SandCastle with the appropriate command lines for you.

3. Run the Help File Builder, specify an XML document and settings, and build your documentation.

Pages on CodePlex for both tools provide advanced documentation that let you understand how easy you can build compiled .chm files for your source code.

Summary

This chapter covered how to use XML comments instead of classic comments. With XML comments you specify tags that identify an element in the code as a special formatted element in the generated documentation file. Such a file is an XML document that enables IntelliSense documentation for your own code and constitutes the source for automating building compiled help files that accompany your libraries as the documentation. To automate this process you were informed about the existence of Microsoft SandCastle, a free tool from Microsoft that is available on CodePlex as an open-source application.

CHAPTER 51

Advanced Compilations with MSBuild

In your developer life you have probably worked at least once with mixed solutions, composed by both Visual Basic and Visual C# projects because this is not an uncommon situation in .NET development, or simply with solutions made of application projects and deployment projects. But while you know how the Visual Basic and C# compilers work, did you ever wonder how Visual Studio builds executables from mixed solutions? The answer is the MSBuild.exe, the build engine from Microsoft that this chapter discusses.

Introducing MSBuild

MSBuild.exe is a command-line tool that has been included in the .NET Framework since the 2.0 version and that can perform advanced and complex compilations. The Visual Basic compiler (the Vbc.exe tool) enables building an executable from multiple code files, but if you invoke it from the command line manually, you need to specify every single code file that must be compiled to produce the assembly; moreover, you are required to specify references, imports, and so on. The most important thing is that the VB compiler cannot build assemblies starting from neither project files nor from solution files. MSBuild goes beyond such limitations, providing the ability to build solutions (.sln files), including solutions composed by mixed projects, project files produced by Visual Studio (such as Visual Basic .vbproj files) and custom project files in one command line. For example, the following command line can build a solution without the need to invoke the compiler and specify all other requirements:

```
MSBuild MsBuildTest.sln
```

COMMAND PROMPT

To run MSBuild without specifying the .NET Framework path in the command line, start the Visual Studio command prompt available in the Visual Studio's shortcuts folder in the Windows Start menu.

Figure 51.1 shows the build output in the Console window, where you can get details on the build process.

FIGURE 51.1   Building a project with MsBuild from the command line.

MSBuild is based on Xml files known as *projects*. Project files are easy to create, understand, and extend; projects are actually nothing new to you, because when you create projects with Visual Basic, these are compliant with the MSBuild Xml schema (http://schemas.microsoft.com/developer/msbuild/2003). This is the reason why you can build your projects with MSBuild. Basically a project contains all information required to build the final executables including code files, configuration properties, target options, and so on. Let's see how a project is structured.

Introducing Projects

The best way for understanding how projects are structured is opening and analyzing an existing one. Create a new Console application with Visual Basic 2010, save it, and close it. Then open the project folder in Windows Explorer and open the ConsoleApplication1.vbproj file with the Windows Notepad. Listing 51.1 shows the content of the project file.

LISTING 51.1   A Basic Project File

```
<?xml version="1.0" encoding="utf-8"?>
<Project ToolsVersion="4.0" DefaultTargets="Build"
xmlns="http://schemas.microsoft.com/developer/msbuild/2003">
  <PropertyGroup>
    <Configuration Condition=" '$(Configuration)' == '' ">Debug</Configuration>
    <Platform Condition=" '$(Platform)' == '' ">x86</Platform>
    <ProductVersion>
    </ProductVersion>
    <SchemaVersion>
    </SchemaVersion>
    <ProjectGuid>{A30BC355-A5C8-4C56-97F0-C1A4F0A58222}</ProjectGuid>
    <OutputType>Exe</OutputType>
    <StartupObject>ConsoleApplication1.Module1</StartupObject>
    <RootNamespace>ConsoleApplication1</RootNamespace>
    <AssemblyName>ConsoleApplication1</AssemblyName>
    <FileAlignment>512</FileAlignment>
    <MyType>Console</MyType>
    <TargetFrameworkVersion>v4.0</TargetFrameworkVersion>
    <TargetFrameworkProfile>Client</TargetFrameworkProfile>
  </PropertyGroup>
  <PropertyGroup Condition=" '$(Configuration)|$(Platform)' == 'Debug|x86' ">
    <PlatformTarget>x86</PlatformTarget>
    <DebugSymbols>true</DebugSymbols>
    <DebugType>full</DebugType>
    <DefineDebug>true</DefineDebug>
    <DefineTrace>true</DefineTrace>
    <OutputPath>bin\Debug\</OutputPath>
    <DocumentationFile>ConsoleApplication1.xml</DocumentationFile>
    <NoWarn>42016,41999,42017,42018,42019,42032,42036,42020,42021,42022</NoWarn>
  </PropertyGroup>
  <PropertyGroup Condition=" '$(Configuration)|$(Platform)' == 'Release|x86' ">
    <PlatformTarget>x86</PlatformTarget>
```

```
  <DebugType>pdbonly</DebugType>
  <DefineDebug>false</DefineDebug>
  <DefineTrace>true</DefineTrace>
  <Optimize>true</Optimize>
  <OutputPath>bin\Release\</OutputPath>
  <DocumentationFile>ConsoleApplication1.xml</DocumentationFile>
  <NoWarn>42016,41999,42017,42018,42019,42032,42036,42020,42021,42022</NoWarn>
</PropertyGroup>
<PropertyGroup>
  <OptionExplicit>On</OptionExplicit>
</PropertyGroup>
<PropertyGroup>
  <OptionCompare>Binary</OptionCompare>
</PropertyGroup>
<PropertyGroup>
  <OptionStrict>Off</OptionStrict>
</PropertyGroup>
<PropertyGroup>
  <OptionInfer>On</OptionInfer>
</PropertyGroup>
<ItemGroup>
  <Reference Include="System" />
  <Reference Include="System.Data" />
  <Reference Include="System.Deployment" />
  <Reference Include="System.Xml" />
  <Reference Include="System.Core" />
  <Reference Include="System.Xml.Linq" />
  <Reference Include="System.Data.DataSetExtensions" />
</ItemGroup>
<ItemGroup>
  <Import Include="Microsoft.VisualBasic" />
  <Import Include="System" />
  <Import Include="System.Collections" />
  <Import Include="System.Collections.Generic" />
  <Import Include="System.Data" />
  <Import Include="System.Diagnostics" />
  <Import Include="System.Linq" />
  <Import Include="System.Xml.Linq" />
</ItemGroup>
<ItemGroup>
  <Compile Include="Module1.vb" />
  <Compile Include="My Project\AssemblyInfo.vb" />
  <Compile Include="My Project\Application.Designer.vb">
    <AutoGen>True</AutoGen>
    <DependentUpon>Application.myapp</DependentUpon>
  </Compile>
```

```
      <Compile Include="My Project\Resources.Designer.vb">
        <AutoGen>True</AutoGen>
        <DesignTime>True</DesignTime>
        <DependentUpon>Resources.resx</DependentUpon>
      </Compile>
      <Compile Include="My Project\Settings.Designer.vb">
        <AutoGen>True</AutoGen>
        <DependentUpon>Settings.settings</DependentUpon>
        <DesignTimeSharedInput>True</DesignTimeSharedInput>
      </Compile>
    </ItemGroup>
    <ItemGroup>
      <EmbeddedResource Include="My Project\Resources.resx">
        <Generator>VbMyResourcesResXFileCodeGenerator</Generator>
        <LastGenOutput>Resources.Designer.vb</LastGenOutput>
        <CustomToolNamespace>My.Resources</CustomToolNamespace>
        <SubType>Designer</SubType>
      </EmbeddedResource>
    </ItemGroup>
    <ItemGroup>
      <None Include="My Project\Application.myapp">
        <Generator>MyApplicationCodeGenerator</Generator>
        <LastGenOutput>Application.Designer.vb</LastGenOutput>
      </None>
      <None Include="My Project\Settings.settings">
        <Generator>SettingsSingleFileGenerator</Generator>
        <CustomToolNamespace>My</CustomToolNamespace>
        <LastGenOutput>Settings.Designer.vb</LastGenOutput>
      </None>
    </ItemGroup>
    <Import Project="$(MSBuildToolsPath)\Microsoft.VisualBasic.targets" />
</Project>
```

TIPS FOR CREATING PROJECTS FILES FROM SCRATCH

When working with MSBuild, you often manually create project files. Visual Studio 2010
IDE offers a powerful Xml editor that is optimal for this purpose. To take advantage of
the Xml editor and IntelliSense feature, create a new Xml file from Visual Studio and
add a Project node like the one shown in Listing 51.1, ensuring that the Xml schema
for MSBuild is referred. This enables IntelliSense and you can better understand all
available members for each particular section and subsection in the project file.

Project files are composed of different Xml sections. The first you encounter are ItemGroup
and PropertyGroup, discussed in next sections.

Understanding `ItemGroup` Sections

You include files and contents in the build process within `ItemGroup` sections, each representing a particular action. For example, the following snippet shows how to include a code file in the build process specifying that it must be compiled via the `Compile` element:

```
<ItemGroup>
  <Compile Include="Module1.vb" />
</ItemGroup>
```

The next snippet shows how to add a reference to an external assembly:

```
<ItemGroup>
  <Reference Include="System.Core" />
</ItemGroup>
```

The following snippet instead shows how to specify an `Imports` directive against the specified namespace:

```
<ItemGroup>
  <Import Include="Microsoft.VisualBasic" />
</ItemGroup>
```

Notice how you can also embed resource files, specifying the .resx file, the associated code-behind file, and namespace:

```
<ItemGroup>
  <EmbeddedResource Include="My Project\Resources.resx">
    <Generator>VbMyResourcesResXFileCodeGenerator</Generator>
    <LastGenOutput>Resources.Designer.vb</LastGenOutput>
    <CustomToolNamespace>My.Resources</CustomToolNamespace>
    <SubType>Designer</SubType>
  </EmbeddedResource>
</ItemGroup>
```

Then you can also add files to the project without assigning build actions, using the `None` element as follows:

```
<ItemGroup>
  <None Include="My Project\Application.myapp">
    <Generator>MyApplicationCodeGenerator</Generator>
    <LastGenOutput>Application.Designer.vb</LastGenOutput>
  </None>
</ItemGroup>
```

Understanding `PropertyGroup` Sections

When MSBuild builds project, it needs some properties such as the output configuration, output type, target assembly name, and so on. All such properties are stored within

PropertyGroup nodes inside the project file and are basically key/value pairs. If you take a look at these elements in Listing 51.1, you notice how they are self-explanatory. For example, the following excerpt specifies properties for the output assembly:

```
<PropertyGroup>
  <Configuration Condition=" '$(Configuration)' == '' ">Debug</Configuration>
  <Platform Condition=" '$(Platform)' == '' ">x86</Platform>
  <ProductVersion>
  </ProductVersion>
  <SchemaVersion>
  </SchemaVersion>
  <ProjectGuid>{A30BC355-A5C8-4C56-97F0-C1A4F0A58222}</ProjectGuid>
  <OutputType>Exe</OutputType>
  <StartupObject>ConsoleApplication1.Module1</StartupObject>
  <RootNamespace>ConsoleApplication1</RootNamespace>
  <AssemblyName>ConsoleApplication1</AssemblyName>
  <FileAlignment>512</FileAlignment>
  <MyType>Console</MyType>
  <TargetFrameworkVersion>v4.0</TargetFrameworkVersion>
  <TargetFrameworkProfile>Client</TargetFrameworkProfile>
</PropertyGroup>
```

Also look at Listing 51.1 to understand how properties map application options that generally you set in Visual Studio via My Project, for example the VB Defaults (Option Strict, Option Explicit, and so on). Thus properties are fundamental items required to tell MSBuild how it must build the executable. You can also provide custom properties. For example, the following section defines an Xml element named DataFolder that declares a property named MyDataDirectory, which is used later for demonstrating MSBuild targets but that is an example of how you store custom information inside property groups:

```
<PropertyGroup>
  <DataFolder>MyDataDirectory</DataFolder>
</PropertyGroup>
```

No matter where you place this PropertyGroup node in the Xml project file, just take care to write it as a child node of Project.

Understanding Tasks and Creating Targets

MSBuild has the concept of a task, which is simply a unit of work that can be executed during the build process. You can add both predefined and custom tasks to the build process inside the project file. (Most built-in tasks are self-explanatory, and if you use Visual Studio to create the project file, IntelliSense can be helpful as usual.) Tasks are specified within Target elements. A target is basically a container for tasks, and you can execute tasks by referring the enclosing `Target` element. For example, the following task sends a message to the specified output log (which is the Console window by default):

```
<Target Name="SendMessage">
  <Message Importance="high"
           Text="This is a custom message to demonstrate tasks"/>
</Target>
```

The important thing is assigning the `Name` property so that you can later refer to target. To execute a task in the build process, you need to run MSBuild by supplying a `/target:` switch (or simply `/t:`) and passing the target name as in the following example:

```
MsBuild MsBuildTest.vbproj /target:SendMessage
```

Figure 51.2 shows how the message appears in the log.

FIGURE 51.2   Executing a message task.

You can also execute multiple targets in a single command line by separating their names with a semicolon. With tasks you can execute also external applications that can influence the build process. The following code demonstrates how to accomplish this:

```
<Target Name="ExecuteMyCustomTool">
  <Exec Command="MyExternalFile.exe" ContinueOnError="false"
        WorkingDirectory="C:\MyAppsFolder"/>
</Target>
```

The `Exec` built-in task enables running the external application to be executed specified with the `Command` property and that resides in the `WorkingDirectory` path. You can also set if the build process must break in case the external application returns an error code (`ContinueOnError`).

INTERACTING WITH MSBUILD IN CODE

MSBuild is a managed application taking advantage of Microsoft.Build.Framework.dll assembly and of the `Microsoft.Build.Framework` namespace. They also expose types for writing code against MSBuild, such as the `ILogger` and `ITask` interfaces.

FINDING AND USING THE FULL LIST OF BUILT-IN TASKS

In this chapter it is not possible to summarize all built-in tasks for MsBuild. The full list is available in the MSDN documentation at http://msdn.microsoft.com/en-us/library/7z253716(VS.100).aspx. Another interesting way for taking advantage of built-in tasks is editing the project file within Visual Studio 2010 so that IntelliSense pops up all available tasks within the `Target` element. Also notice that you can build your custom tasks by writing types that implement the `ITask` interface.

Inside target definitions you can also refer to properties defined inside `PropertyGroup` nodes. The following code demonstrates how you can create a directory during the build process by assigning to the new directory the name of a folder previously defined within properties:

```
<Target Name="CreateDataDir">
  <MakeDir Directories="$(MyDataDirectory)"/>
</Target>
```

To add a reference to a property value, you use the $ symbol followed by the name of the property enclosed within parentheses. Now consider the following sample project that invokes the Visual Basic compiler to build multiple code files into one executable:

```
<?xml version="1.0" encoding="utf-8"?>
<Project ToolsVersion="4.0" DefaultTargets="Compile"
        xmlns="http://schemas.microsoft.com/developer/msbuild/2003">

  <!-- Defines a series of custom items
       pointing to VB code files -->
  <ItemGroup>
    <VBFile Include="File1.vb"/>
    <VBFile Include="File2.vb"/>
  </ItemGroup>

  <!-- Defines a property storing the
  output exe name-->
  <PropertyGroup>
```

```
      <AssemblyName>MyApp.exe</AssemblyName>
  </PropertyGroup>

  <!-- Creates a new target-->
  <Target Name = "Compile">
    <Vbc
        Sources = "@(VBFile)"
        OutputAssembly = "$(AssemblyName)">
      <Output
          TaskParameter = "OutputAssembly"
          ItemName = "EXEFile" />
    </Vbc>
  </Target>
</Project>
```

Vbc is a predefined tag that tells MSBuild to run the Visual Basic command-line compiler against the specified set of files. By mixing the preceding code with concepts previously discussed, it should be clearer how you could run an external tool instead of a .NET compiler, such as a documentation compiler, against a set of desired files and to let MSBuild pass all information to the external tool and build the final file.

Advanced MSBuild Features

MSBuild offers some advanced techniques that you can use to enhance building your projects. At a higher level, such techniques enable performing operations over items and establishing how to collect build information. The following sections discuss advanced MSBuild techniques.

Batching

The batching feature in MSBuild simply enables you to perform a kind of For..Each loop over items within an ItemGroup section. Imagine you have two collections of items within an ItemGroup section, where for each item a value is specified. For a better understanding, create a new Xml file named MSBuildDemo.proj and type the following code:

```
<?xml version="1.0" encoding="utf-8"?>
<Project ToolsVersion="4.0" DefaultTargets="Build"
        xmlns="http://schemas.microsoft.com/developer/msbuild/2003">
  <ItemGroup>
    <SampleCollection Include="Item1">
      <Number>1</Number>
    </SampleCollection>
    <SampleCollection Include="Item2">
      <Number>2</Number>
    </SampleCollection>
    <SampleCollection Include="Item3">
```

```
    <Number>3</Number>
  </SampleCollection>

  <SampleCollection2 Include="Item4">
    <Number>1</Number>
  </SampleCollection2>
  <SampleCollection2 Include="Item5">
    <Number>2</Number>
  </SampleCollection2>
  <SampleCollection2 Include="Item6">
    <Number>3</Number>
  </SampleCollection2>
</ItemGroup>

<Target Name="ShowIterations">
  <Message
      Text = "Number: %(Number) -- Items in SampleCollection:
      @(SampleCollection) SampleCollection2: @(SampleCollection2)"/>
</Target>
</Project>
```

The goal of the new target is iterating all items in both collections and associating each number to the appropriate item; in other words, the goal is to display what items in both collections the number 1 is associated to and so on for other numbers. Now type the following command line:

```
MSBuild MsBuildDemo.proj /t:ShowIterations
```

As you can see, MSBuild correctly shows the list of numbers and collections they belong to, as represented in Figure 51.3.

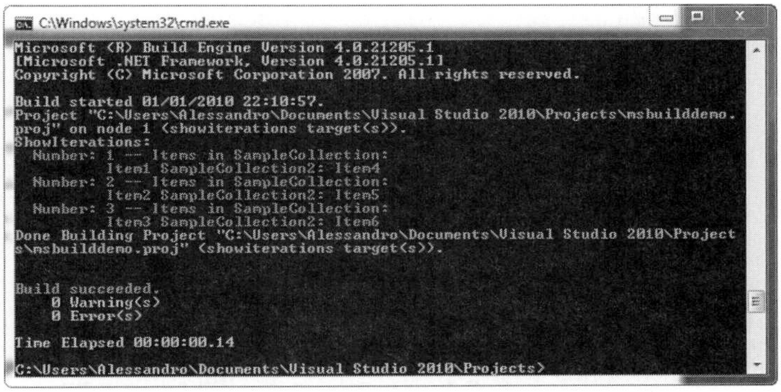

FIGURE 51.3   Demonstrating batching technique with MSBuild.

Thus with batching you can run the same target over all items within a group in a simple way.

Logging

When you run MSBuild, the tool displays events and output information to the Console window as the default log. You can choose different output targets and detail level for logging by utilizing some specific command-line switches. For example, imagine you want to redirect log information to a text file instead of showing messages in the Console window, providing a high-level of verbosity about events details. This can be accomplished with the following command line:

```
MSBuild ConsoleApplication1.sln
/logger:FileLogger,Microsoft.Build.Engine;logfile=ExternalLog.log;append=tru
e;verbosity=detailed;encoding=utf-8 /noconsolelogger
```

The /noconsolelogger switch tells MSBuild to not send any message to the Console window. The /logger switch enables specifying where the log needs to be sent; several logs are available, such as XmlLogger or FileLogger that requires the output target file (logfile property), the verbosity level (to choose among quiet, minimal, normal, detailed, and diagnostics), the specification of appending the log if the output file already exists (append property), and eventually the encoding format.

CUSTOM LOGGERS AND REFERENCE

You can build your custom loggers by creating a type that implements the ILogger interface and then building the type into a dll class library. The MSDN reference about logging and custom loggers is available at the following address:
http://msdn.microsoft.com/en-us/library/ms171470(VS.100).aspx.

Transformations

Transformations apply to a list of items and enable changing a piece of information for each item in the list into a different format. Consider the following items group, which refers to all text files within a directory:

```
<ItemGroup>
    <MyFiles Include="C:\MyDocs\*.Txt"/>
</ItemGroup>
```

Then imagine you want to send the list of files to the logger. This is accomplished with the following line, to be added into the item group:

```
<Message Text="@(MyFiles)"/>
```

THE @ CHARACTER

The @ character is used for referring to a list of items, differently from $ that is used for referring to a property value.

51

Now imagine you want to construct the list of items only with the filename and extension without the full path. Transformations enable accomplishing this with a syntax that takes the form of @(itemgroup->'%(itemmetadata)') and where itemmetadata is the piece of information we want to retrieve from the original item and that must be one of the forms recognized by MSBuild, also known as well-known item metadata. So the transformation can be written as follows:

```
<Message Text="@(MyFiles->'%(FileName)%(Extension)')"/>
```

FileName and Extension are two of the available well-known item metadata and are information that MSBuild can distinguish within a list of items. The full list item metadata is available at http://msdn.microsoft.com/en-us/library/ms164313.aspx. Suppose you have the following pathnames:

```
C:\MyDocs\Doc1.txt
C:\MyDocs\Doc2.txt

C:\MyDocs\Doc3.txt
```

When you run MSBuild with the preceding specified transformation, the logger displays the following output:

```
Doc1.txt
Doc2.txt

Doc3.txt
```

This is possible because of the well-known item metadata information.

Summary

This chapter covered the usage of MSBuild, the build engine for Microsoft platforms that can perform simple and complex compilations from the command line. You first saw how this tool is important because it can work even when Visual Studio is not installed; then you saw the tool in action with some demonstrative command lines. Finally, you got information on advanced features such as tasking, logging, and transformations.

CHAPTER 52

Building Customizations for Microsoft Office

The Microsoft Office suite is with no doubt one of the most popular software packages for office automation inside companies. Applications such as Word, Excel, Outlook, and PowerPoint help people make their work productive, and they can be considered part of daily life. In many cases Microsoft Office is also used at home. For example, this book was written with Word 2007. The entire software suite provides features that generally satisfy most people's needs, but there are situations in which you would need a particular feature that is not natively available. Fortunately the Office applications are extensible and can be customized with add-ins that can be developed with Visual Studio 2010 to provide additional capabilities. This opens important business scenarios; you can increase your business by producing Office add-ins by taking advantage of your existing .NET and VB skills, just using nothing but Visual Studio 2010. You can enhance Microsoft Word with a custom task pane enabled for speech recognition; imagine how this scenario can help people with disabilities. Writing customizations for Microsoft Office is an important development area and is another demonstration of how you can use Visual Studio 2010 to develop almost everything. In this chapter you learn how to build customizations for Microsoft Word and Excel and to understand what components are required to accomplish this.

> **NOTE**
>
> At the time of this writing, the most-recent official version is Microsoft Office 2007. Although a beta version of Office 2010 is available, for the sake of stability this chapter provides code examples for Office 2007. By the way, when Office 2010 is available in RTM, you will use most techniques shown here for the new version, too.

Introducing the Visual Studio Tools for Office

Building custom add-ins for Microsoft Office is possible due to the Visual Studio Tools for Office components (also called VSTO for brevity). VSTO are a set of tools integrated into Visual Studio 2010 that provide project templates, assemblies, and instruments related to the Office development. In Visual Studio 2010, VSTO provides support for building customizations for the most recent versions of Microsoft Office, such as 2003, 2007, and 2010 (see note at the beginning of this chapter). VSTO relies on a special redistributable runtime known as VSTO Runtime that is required to run your add-ins on target machines. Later in this chapter you see how to include such runtime in distributions. VSTO are helpful because they provide full integration between Visual Studio and Office applications, also offering the opportunity of adding Windows Forms controls to your solutions so that you can deeply customize add-ins implementing interactive features.

> **USING WPF AGAINST VSTO**
>
> VSTO and Office applications natively support only Windows Forms user controls. If you want to include a WPF control, you need to add an `ElementHost` Windows Forms control that can host the WPF user control.

An important concept that you need to remember in the Office development is about host applications. When you build an Office add-in, the application that runs the add-in is also called a host application. Basically a host application is an instance of the Office application that hosts your add-ins. After a general overview of VSTO, it is time to consider Visual Studio projects.

Understanding Application-Level Solutions and Document-Level Solutions

With the VSTO you can build essentially two types of solutions:

- ▶ **Document-level** solutions, where an add-in is loaded only in the context of a specific document or workbook

- ▶ **Dpplication-level** solutions, where an add-in is loaded each time the host application is loaded that can affect both the application and every document or workbook

Visual Studio 2010 provides project templates for creating both types of solutions, and in this chapter you get examples for both scenarios.

What Are Office Business Applications?

When talking about developing for Office, you often hear about Office Business Applications (also known as OBAs). An OBA is basically a custom add-in for Microsoft Outlook or Microsoft Excel that enables adding form regions or components to the host application where you can add business features. (For example, you might want to add functionalities for scheduling appointments with your customers or features strictly related to your type of job.) Office Business Applications are beyond of the scope of this chapter; you can visit the dedicated MSDN website at http://msdn.microsoft.com/en-us/office/aa905528.aspx.

Creating an Application-Level Add-In for Microsoft Word

In this section you learn how to build an application-level add-in for Microsoft Office, which includes an example that targets Microsoft Word, but the idea behind the code structure is almost the same for Excel and PowerPoint. The goal of the sample add-in is to provide a custom task pane where you place user controls for retrieving revisions and comments from the active Word document and saving information into an Xml file. The first step is creating a new project. In the New Project dialog, select the **Visual Basic, Office, 2007** folder. Select the Word 2007 add-in template and then name the new project as **WordSummaryAddin**. Figure 52.1 shows details about this.

FIGURE 52.1   Creating a new application-level add-in project for Word.

When you click **OK** the new project is generated. You notice the presence of a file called ThisAddIn.vb. This code file defines a class called ThisAddIn that represents the running instance of the add-in and that is useful for interacting with the add-in at runtime. This class exposes two events: Startup and ShutDown. The first event is raised when the add-in is loaded, whereas the second one is raised when the add-in is shutting down; an add-in is shut down when you disable it from the host application or when you shut down the host application itself. Before writing code for the add-in, there is the need of a new user control representing the custom task pane. Add a new User Control item to the project (Windows Forms) and name it **SummaryTaskPane**, as shown in Figure 52.2.

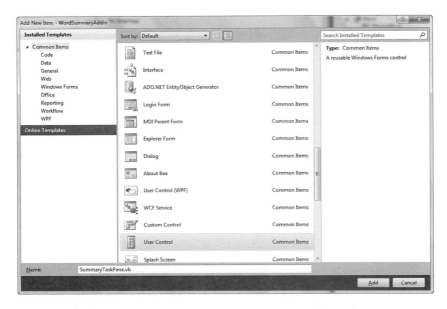

FIGURE 52.2   Adding a new WinForms user control to the project.

On the user control's surface add the following items:

▶ A Label whose Text property is Select items

▶ A CheckBox named CommentsCheckBox and whose Text property is Comments

▶ A CheckBox named RevisionsCheckBox and whose Text property is Revisions

▶ A Button named CreateSummaryButton and whose Text property is Create summary

At the end of these tasks, your user control must look like the one shown in Figure 52.3.

Now switch to the code editor to write Visual Basic code that gives life to the just-drawn controls. The first consideration is that Visual Studio automatically added to the project some assemblies for the Microsoft Office programmability. You can take a look by activating the All Files view and then expanding References in Solution Explorer. The assemblies

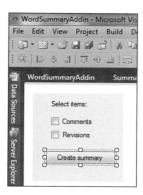

FIGURE 52.3   The customizations added to the new user control.

expose several namespaces for working with Office, but the most important are
`Microsoft.Office`, `Microsoft.Office.Tools`, and `Microsoft.Office.Interop`. This last
one provides wrappers for interoperating between the COM Office architecture and the
managed .NET architecture. For example, it exposes a `Word.Document` object representing a
document in Word or other objects such as `Word.Revision` or `Word.Comments` that respectively represent a single revision and a single comment in the active document. The code
takes advantage of LINQ for querying comments and revisions collection in the active
document and then saves the query results into an Xml document. Listing 52.1 shows the
complete code for that (see Chapter 28, "Manipulating Xml Documents with LINQ and
Xml Literals," for information on LINQ to Xml).

LISTING 52.1   Implementing a Custom Task Pane

```
Imports Microsoft.Office.Interop.Word
Imports System.Windows.Forms

Public Class SummaryTaskPane

    Private Function GetRevisions() As XElement

        'Queries for available revisions
        'The ActiveDocument properties represents the active
        'document in Word and the Revisions property is a
        'collection of Word revisions
        Dim revisions = <Revisions>
                            <%= From rev In Globals.
                                ThisAddIn.Application.ActiveDocument.Revisions.
                                OfType(Of Revision)() _
                                Select _
```

```vb
                              <Revision Text=<%= rev.Range.Text %>
                                   Author=<%= rev.Author %>
                                   Timestamp=<%= rev.Date.ToString %>/> %>

                     </Revisions>

     Return revisions
End Function

Private Function GetComments() As XElement

     'Same as the previous method, but with regard
     'to comments
     Dim comments = <Comments>
                         <%= From comm In Globals.ThisAddIn.
                             Application.ActiveDocument.Comments.
                             OfType(Of Comment)
                             Select <Comment
                                         Text=<%= comm.Range.Text %>
                                         Author=<%= comm.Author %>
                                         Date=<%= comm.Date.ToString %>
                                     />
                         %>
                     </Comments>
     Return comments
End Function

'Creates a new Xml document adding the content
'of the XElement objects returned by the
'above methods
Private Sub CreateSummary(ByVal fileName As String, ByVal comments As Boolean,
                         ByVal revisions As Boolean)

     If comments = False And revisions = False Then
         Throw New ArgumentException
     End If

     Dim doc As New XDocument
     doc.Declaration = New XDeclaration("1.0", "utf-8", "yes")

     Dim rootElement As New XElement("Summary")


     If comments Then rootElement.Add(GetComments)
```

```vb
        If revisions Then rootElement.Add(GetRevisions)

        doc.Add(rootElement)
        Try
            doc.Save(fileName)
            doc = Nothing
        Catch ex As Exception
            Throw
        End Try
    End Sub

    Private Sub CreateSummaryButton_Click(ByVal sender As System.Object,
                                ByVal e As System.EventArgs) _
                                Handles CreateSummaryButton.Click
        Dim saveFile As New SaveFileDialog
        With saveFile
            .Title = "Select the target"
            .Filter = "Xml files¦*.xml¦All files¦*.*"

            If .ShowDialog = DialogResult.OK Then
                Try
                    Me.CreateSummary(.FileName, CommentsCheckBox.Checked,
                                RevisionsCheckBox.Checked)

                Catch ex As Exception
                    MessageBox.Show(ex.Message)
                End Try
            End If
        End With
    End Sub
End Class
```

Now it's time for some considerations. The ThisAddIn class offers an Application property that represents the instance of the host application, Word in this particular example. The property provides an ActiveDocument property that is a reference to the current document opened inside Word. The GetRevisions and GetComments method query the active document for desired properties and build XML elements that are returned under the form of XElement objects to the calling CreateSummary method, which adds the two XElement instances to a new XDocument object that is actually the final Xml document. Now go to the ThisAddIn.vb code file, where you need to create an instance of the custom task pane and add it to the Word's task panes collection. Listing 52.2 demonstrates this.

LISTING 52.2   Adding the New Task Pane to Microsoft Word

```vb
Imports Microsoft.Office.Tools

Public Class ThisAddIn
    Private summaryPane As CustomTaskPane

    Private Sub ThisAddIn_Startup() Handles Me.Startup
        summaryPane = Me.CustomTaskPanes.Add(New SummaryTaskPane,
                         "Summary task pane")
        summaryPane.Visible = True

    End Sub

    Private Sub ThisAddIn_Shutdown() Handles Me.Shutdown

    End Sub
End Class
```

The `CustomTaskPanes.Add` method requires the instance of the new task pane and some descriptive text. At this point you can simply press **F5** to test your custom component. Visual Studio 2010 launches Microsoft Word 2007 attaching an instance of its debugger enabling you with the usual debugging techniques. When Word is running, type some text into the new document and then add some comments and revisions. Figure 52.4 shows an example of both the sample document and the new task pane.

When ready, simply apply the flag on both the `Comments` and `Revisions` check boxes; then click the `Create Summary` button. At this point a new Xml document storing the desired information will be created, as illustrated in Figure 52.5, which shows the document opened with Internet Explorer.

Remember that running your code is considered as the first add-in deployment on the development machine. The last section of this chapter provides an overview of add-ins deployment that clarifies the sentence.

Creating a Document-Level Add-In for Microsoft Excel

In the previous section you saw how you can create an application-level solution for Office. In this section you learn how to build document-level solutions, which is the other solution type available. In next example you create a document-level add-in for customizing a specific workbook in Microsoft Excel. Create a new Office project with Visual Basic, ensuring that the **Excel 2007 Workbook** template is selected (see Figure 52.6 for details). Name the new project **CustomExcelWorkbook** and then click **OK**.

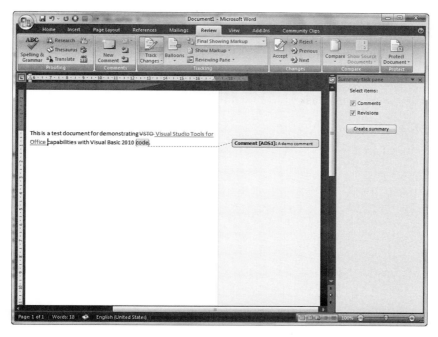

FIGURE 52.4   The new custom task pane for Word in action.

FIGURE 52.5   The resulting Xml document is formed correctly and stores the desired information.

FIGURE 52.6   Creating a document-level solution for Excel 2007.

This launches the Visual Studio Tools for Office Project Wizard. First you need to specify the document you want to extend with your add-in. You can select an existing document or a new one. Figure 52.7 shows how the selection dialog appears.

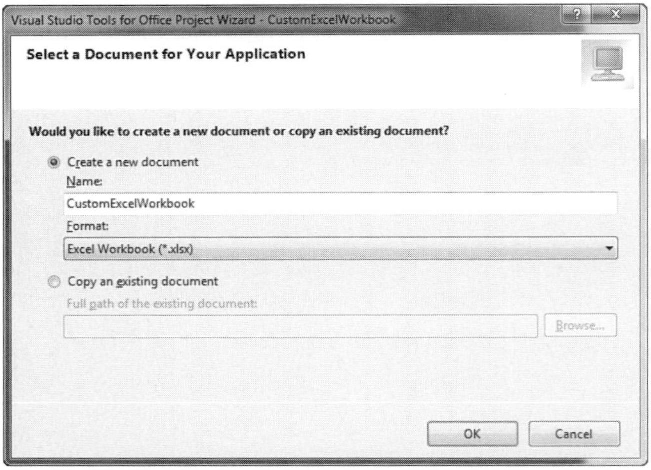

FIGURE 52.7   Choosing the document to customize.

Leave unchanged the default selection about creating a new document and click **OK**. Because in document-level solutions VSTO needs access to the VBA object model, the first time you create one you will be asked to grant permissions for this particular task. Figure 52.8 shows the question you will receive.

FIGURE 52.8   Granting access to the VBA object model.

After a few seconds, the new Office project is ready within Visual Studio; notice the presence of a code file called ThisWorkbook.vb that implements a `ThisWorkbook` class representing the instance of the current workbook. Also you notice three more files, each representing a spreadsheet in the workbook. By default a new Excel workbook contains three sheets, so when you create a new document-level project you have three code files. We can now start customizing the user interface for the new document.

Designing the Add-In

You notice how the IDE embeds a fully functional instance of Microsoft Excel in the designer. This is useful because you can drag and drop Windows Forms controls from the toolbox onto the document's surface. The goal of the example is to provide controls for filtering a list of orders. So in the first row add the following columns titles: Order ID, Ship Country, and Shipped Date. Next, add the fictitious orders information listed in Table 52.1 according to the column titles.

TABLE 52.1   Populating Orders Information

Order ID	Ship Country	Shipped Date
10001	USA	11/25/09
10002	Italy	11/25/09
10003	United Kingdom	11/26/09
10004	Brazil	11/27/09

Now select the cell range from A2 to C5 and name the range as Orders. The next step is to add a TextBox named FilterTextBox whose Text property is Type your filter here; the last step is to add a Button named FilterButton and whose Text property is Go Filter!. The result of the previous listed steps is shown in Figure 52.9.

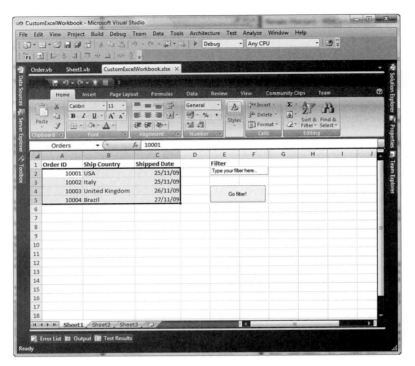

FIGURE 52.9   Design-time customizations onto the Excel document within Visual Studio.

When controls are available over the document's surface, it's time to start writing some Visual Basic code to make it alive.

Interacting with Documents via Visual Basic 2010 Code

Imagine you want to provide your users the ability of filtering orders by the ship Country name. The users can type the filter criteria in the `TextBox`, and then a LINQ query will be executed when they click the `Go Filter` button. Basically the LINQ query filters a list of orders, so you first need a class for handling each order. The class can be easily implemented as follows:

```
Public Class Order


    Public Property ShippedDate As Object
    Public Property ShipCountry As Object
    Public Property OrderID As Object
End Class
```

Then you need to write code that performs the query and then returns all the orders that match the specified criteria. Code in Listing 52.3 shows how to accomplish this and must be written in the Sheet1.vb code file.

LISTING 52.3   Implementing LINQ Filtering in the Document-Level Excel Solution

```
Public Class Sheet1

    Private Sub Sheet1_Startup() Handles Me.Startup

    End Sub

    Private Sub Sheet1_Shutdown() Handles Me.Shutdown

    End Sub

    Private Function GetOrders(ByVal criteria As String) As String

        'Creates a collection of Order objects
        Dim result As New List(Of Order)

        'Declares a Range object, which represents
        'a set of Excel cells
        Dim cellRange As Excel.Range

        Dim oneOrder As Order

        'Gets the content of the specified cells range
        'resizing the array
        cellRange = CustomExcelWorkbook.Globals.Sheet1.Range("Orders").Resize(1, 1)

        'Loops until a null value is found
        Do Until IsNothing(cellRange.Value)
            'creates a new Order...
            oneOrder = New Order With {.OrderID = cellRange.Value.ToString, _
                        .ShipCountry = cellRange.Offset(0, 1).Value.ToString, _
                        .ShippedDate = CDate(cellRange.Offset(0, 2).Value)}

            '...adding it to the collection..
            result.Add(oneOrder)
            '...then moves to the next row
            cellRange = cellRange.Offset(1, 0)
        Loop

        'Queries for orders matching the specified criteria
        Dim query = From ord As Order In result
                    Where ord.ShipCountry.ToString.StartsWith(criteria)
                    Select ord
```

52

```
        Dim ordersList As New Text.StringBuilder

        For Each item In query
            ordersList.Append(item.OrderID.ToString)
            ordersList.AppendLine()
        Next

        Return ordersList.ToString

    End Function

    Private Sub GoButton_Click(ByVal sender As System.Object, _
                            ByVal e As System.EventArgs) Handles GoButton.Click

        MessageBox.Show("The following orders match your search criteria: " & _
                    Environment.NewLine & GetOrders(Me.FilterTextBox.Text))
    End Sub
End Class
```

When you complete this step, you are ready to run and test the customization.

Running the Customized Document

To see the document-level add-in in action, you simply press **F5**. Visual Studio launches an instance of Microsoft Excel opening the specified document, attaching an instance of the debugger to the host application. You notice that the document shows required customizations. Also notice that, for Excel workbooks, customizations affect only the selected sheet. To check if everything works correctly, type U in the text box and then press Go Filter!. Figure 52.10 shows the result of this filter.

Same as for application-level add-ins, running the customization on the development machine is considered as the first deployment. The next section provides some information on deploying VSTO add-ins using ClickOnce.

Deploying VSTO Add-Ins

You can deploy VSTO add-ins to customers in several ways including Windows Installer and ClickOnce (See Chapter 54, "Setup & Deployment Projects for Windows Installer," and Chapter 55, "Deployingt Applications with ClickOnce"). The consideration you have to do is that VSTO add-ins require the full trust level. Because of this, deploying via Windows Installer can be a little bit more difficult than using ClickOnce because you have to set manually different settings. ClickOnce is instead more appropriate for at least three reasons:

> ▶ It is easy to configure and takes care of security settings for you; this is also the reason why Visual Studio automatically adds a test certificate to your solution when

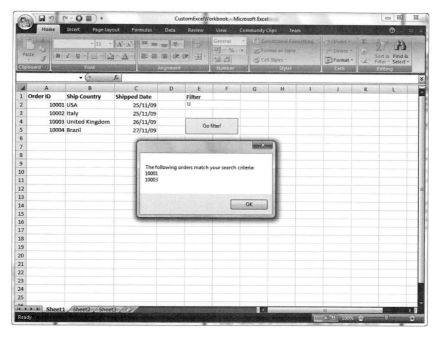

FIGURE 52.10   The document-level add-in correctly filters orders.

you first run it. Replacing the test certificate with a valid one contributes to granting full trust security settings.

▶ It provides a simple way for releasing updates.

▶ Starting from .NET 3.5 Service Pack 1, it sends installation error messages to the Windows Application log so that you can analyze the reason for eventual errors during the setup process.

UNDERSTANDING CLICKONCE

If you have never deployed applications via ClickOnce before, I suggest you read Chapter 55 first. In this particular situation we just mention the steps required to perform a ClickOnce publish but focus on more ClickOnce details in Chapter 55.

To deploy a VSTO add-in, select the **Build, Publish** command and then specify the target location, where Visual Studio generates the Setup.exe bootstrapper and a .Vsto file that installs your add-in on the target machine. It also generates an Application Files subfolder where the IDE places required files.

VISUAL STUDIO REQUIRES ADMINISTRATIVE PRIVILEGES

Differently from Visual Studio 2008, Visual Studio 2010 requires elevated administrative privileges to publish Office customizations via ClickOnce.

When you double-click the .Vsto file (or run Setup.exe), the ClickOnce installer guides you through the installation process. Figure 52.11 shows the step where ClickOnce asks for your confirmation before installing the customization.

FIGURE 52.11   ClickOnce confirmation request.

If there are any failures during the installation process, errors are sent to the Windows Application log reachable from the Windows Event Viewer (**All Programs, Administrative Tools, Event Viewer**). Figure 52.12 shows a sample message related to an error that occurred during the installation of an add-in.

Logs are useful because you can check what happened in detail and focus on solving errors.

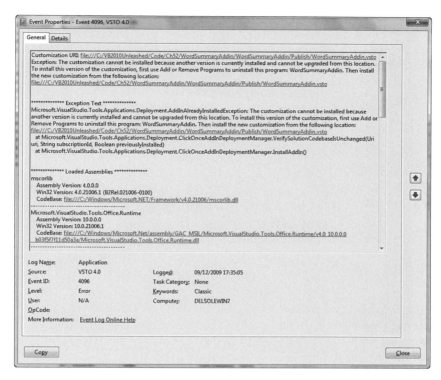

FIGURE 52.12   The Windows Application log stores error messages from VSTO installations.

Summary

This chapter explained how to take advantage of the Visual Studio 2010 development environment to create .NET-based additional components for the Microsoft Office System. You saw how to distinguish between application-level solutions and document-level solutions; then you saw how it is simple to create add-ins for Microsoft Word, with a sample custom task pane, and Microsoft Excel writing Visual Basic 2010 code for the .NET Framework. Finally you got some information on deploying your add-ins using ClickOnce.

CHAPTER 53

Understanding the Global Assembly Cache

The Visual Studio IDE is a great place for creating applications, but in most cases you need to deploy them to your customers. The .NET Framework offers a nice infrastructure for accomplishing this, but you need to know some concepts about the infrastructure before effectively deploying applications. Often you can also create libraries and reference those libraries, or third-party libraries, other than the .NET Framework base libraries in your projects. Such libraries need to be deployed together with your application, but the .NET deployment model for assemblies works differently from the COM model. The goal of this chapter is to illustrate how .NET base libraries are organized, why you can be sure to find them on a target machine, and how you deploy your own libraries or third-party libraries that your applications work with. This information is important if you consider that deploying an application is not only deploying the executable, but also all libraries required by the application. This is the reason why you need to read this chapter before discovering the deploying modes offered by the .NET Framework and Visual Studio 2010.

The Dll Hell Problem

One of the biggest problems of the COM programming model is the *Dll hell*. Basically COM components (such as ActiveX controls or type libraries) need to be registered so that the system knows where to find them even if they are not available in the application directory. The problem is when you have different versions of the component installed on the same machine. Registration can be painful, and there are often a lot of problems in making an application recognize the correct version of the component. In many cases an application will not work correctly. This is the reason why the situation is called Dll hell. The .NET Framework, since version 1.0, provides a brilliant way to solve this big problem by introducing assemblies and the *Global Assembly Cache* (GAC). Before discussing the GAC, it is important to understand how assemblies can be deployed and recognized by applications and why they solve the Dll hell problem. To accomplish this, we need to discuss the most basic mode for deploying assemblies, which is the XCopy deployment.

XCopy Deployment

If you have been an MS-DOS person, you will surely remember the XCopy command. It allowed copying entire directory trees, including files and subdirectories, from one location to another. In honor of this command, the most basic deployment technique in the .NET Framework is XCopy deployment. The reason for this name is that a .NET application can work when the executable and the assemblies referenced by such executable all reside in the same folder. According to this, you can deploy an application by simply copying its folder. This approach has a huge implication: Because an application folder contains a copy of required assemblies, these are isolated from one another and do not require registration anymore. Because they are no longer required to be registered, multiple versions of an assembly can reside on the same machine avoiding the big problem of the Dll hell.

BASE CLASS LIBRARY ASSEMBLIES

Of course the preceding discussion is not valid when talking about the Base Class Library assemblies, being part of the .NET Framework, and that thus cannot be included in the application folder. They instead stay in the GAC as covered in next section.

When you compile your project, Visual Studio generates a Bin subfolder within the project folder. Bin contains Debug and Release subfolders (referring to default build configurations). Both folders contain the executable and referenced assemblies. Basically you can perform an XCopy deployment simply by distributing the content of the Release folder, and your application will work. XCopy deployment is something that you have to know to understand how things work, but obviously in a business environment, you will deploy your applications with professional installers, such as Windows Installer and ClickOnce that are discussed in the next two chapters. Another consideration about XCopy deployment is that in this way every application keeps its own copy of referenced assemblies. This means that if you have ten applications referring to the same assembly, you will have ten copies of the assembly. This is good in that assemblies will not interfere with each other, especially in the case of different versions. But if you have ten copies of the same version of your assembly, this can be annoying. A solution to this issue is provided by the Global Assembly Cache that also solves other problems, which is the subject of next section.

The Global Assembly Cache

The .NET Framework consists of hundreds of libraries and tools. Most libraries implement the Base Class Library and BCL's assemblies are located in GAC. This is the reason why you can be sure that a .NET application requiring only base assemblies can correctly work on a target machine having the .NET Framework installed. The GAC can be considered as a repository of shared assemblies; shared means that an application can simply have a reference to an assembly available in the GAC instead of bringing its own copy of the assembly as happens in the XCopy deployment. The GAC is basically a folder in the system and is generally located at C:\Windows\Assembly. Because of the particular nature of this folder, its representation within Windows Explorer is a little bit different than other folders. Figure 53.1 shows how the GAC is represented in Windows Explorer.

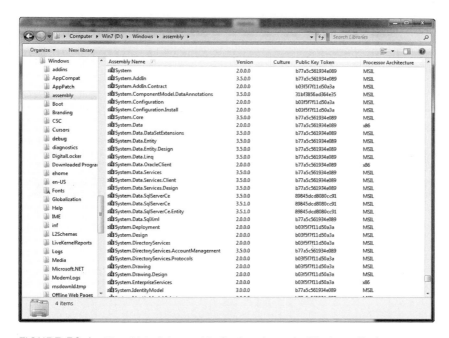

FIGURE 53.1   The Global Assembly Cache shown in Windows Explorer.

You may notice from Figure 53.1 how the GAC lists installed assemblies, their version number, the public key token, and the target processor architecture. The public key token is a unique identifier that identifies the assembly within the .NET infrastructure. If the assembly targets a specific culture, this information is also shown. You can easily notice how different versions of the same assembly can be available in the GAC. (For example, check the System.Data.SqlServerCe.dll assembly.) This is important because it means that the GAC is responsible for handling different versions of the same assembly, solving the versioning problem (and the registration one).

Installing and Uninstalling Assemblies

A common way for referring to assemblies available in the GAC is saying that they are installed into the GAC. By the way, installing an assembly to the GAC simply means making the assembly recognizable by the GAC and by the .NET Framework while the physical file stays in its original location. Suppose you have an assembly named C:\MyAssemblies\MyLibrary.dll and you want to install this assembly into the GAC. The installation procedure simply adds to the GAC metadata information for the assembly but does not copy the file to the GAC; instead, MyLibrary.Dll remains in C:\MyAssemblies. Installing and uninstalling assemblies to and from the GAC is a step that you have to divide in two parts: development time and real deployment time. At development time, you have two opportunities for installing assemblies to the GAC. The first way is invoking the **GacUtil.exe** command-line tool passing the /i option and the assembly name. The following is a command-line example for installing an assembly:

```
GacUtil.exe /i C:\MyAssemblies\MyLibrary.dll
```

You uninstall an assembly from the GAC by simply passing the /u option to GacUtil, as in the following command line:

```
GacUtil.exe /u C:\MyAssemblies\MyLibrary.dll
```

The second way for installing assemblies is dragging them to Windows Explorer opened to the GAC folder. To uninstall one or more assemblies, simply right-click the assembly name and choose **Uninstall**.

INSTALLING AND UNINSTALLING REQUIRE ELEVATED PRIVILEGES

The Global Assembly Cache folder can be protected by administrators using an Access Control List. If this is your scenario, remember that installing assemblies to the GAC and uninstalling as well require elevated privileges. Moreover, if you are a Windows Vista or a Windows 7 user, you will be required to run the command prompt or Windows Explorer with administrator privileges before attempting to install or uninstall assemblies.

Both ways can be useful at development time, but they cannot be absolutely indicated at deployment time for several reasons. The most important of them is that both ways have no reference counting but, as you can easily understand, it is not appropriate to require your user to manually manipulate the GAC with Windows Explorer. Because of this, you should always choose professional installation systems, such as Windows Installer, that implement features for correctly installing and uninstalling assemblies without troubles. The next chapter discusses setup and deployment projects for Windows Installer, covering GAC situations. ClickOnce has instead some limitations from this point of view, because it does not allow installing assemblies to the GAC; thus you must be aware of this when deciding the deployment strategy. By the way, installing assemblies to the Global Assembly Cache has a huge requirement: you can only install assemblies signed with a strong name.

Signing Assemblies with Strong Names

A strong name is basically a signature that is added to assemblies to provide uniqueness and represents the assembly's identity. It is composed by the assembly name, version, and culture plus a public key and a digital signature. The public key is generated starting from the related private key, which is stored in the assembly manifest.

SECURITY ISSUES

To avoid security issues, strong-named assemblies can only use type from other strong-named assemblies (such as the Base Class Library assemblies).

You have two modes for signing an assembly with a strong name; the first is invoking command-line tools such as Sn.exe and Al.exe. But because most of your developer life is spent within Visual Studio, the second mode is offered by the IDE. To add a strong name to your assembly, you first open **My Project** and then select the **Signing** tab where you flag the **Sign the Assembly** check box as shown in Figure 53.2.

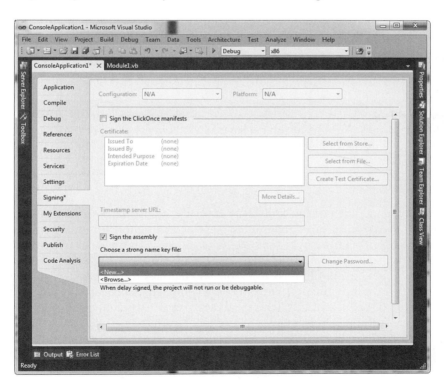

FIGURE 53.2   Adding a strong name to the project.

You can either add a new strong name or import an existing one. To add a new strong name, click the <**New...**> item in the combo box (see Figure 53.2). You will be prompted for specifying the filename and a password. This generates a .pfx file that is added to the project and that is visible in Solution Explorer. For example, in the Create Strong Name Key dialog, type **MyStrongName** as the filename and **MyStrongName** as the password. Figure 53.3 shows how to accomplish this.

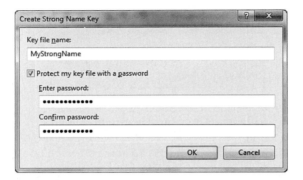

FIGURE 53.3   Providing name and password for the new strong name.

Specifying a password is not mandatory. If you do not provide a password, Visual Studio generates an .snk file instead of a .pfx one. By the way, I strongly recommend you provide a password.

KEEP YOUR PASSWORD

Take note of the password you assign to strong names. It will be required every time you open the project from another computer different from the one where you first added the strong name.

Remember that strong names are not the equivalent of certificates (such as Authenticode) that instead provide security trust, other than uniqueness, according to .NET security requirements. Finally, strong names can be applied to assemblies with the delay signing technique (see the Delay sign option in the MyProject Signing tab). In a few words, this technique writes only the public key in the executable and requires the private key to be passed at a later stage, preventing the project from being compiled, debugged and run from within Visual Studio. Because of this, when you delay sign an assembly, you need to skip the signature verification (e.g. running the Sn.exe tool passing the -Vr option). It is also worth noting that you can disable signing enforcement on a machine even at the specific assembly signature level, in the event you actually need to delay sign but still want to debug. This topic is not covered because of its particular nature; you can get further information in the official MSDN documentation at http://msdn.microsoft.com/en-us/library/t07a3dye(VS.100).aspx.

CLS-COMPLIANT ASSEMBLIES

Signing assemblies with strong names is mandatory in case you want them to be CLS-compliant.

Top Reasons for Installing (or Not) Assemblies to the GAC

As a general rule, installing assemblies to the GAC is something that should be restricted only to particular scenarios. There are obviously situations when you instead want to take advantage of the GAC that can be summarized as follows:

▶ **Multiple applications referencing the same assemblies:** In this case it can be convenient to have a single copy of assemblies in the GAC instead of providing several copies in the application folder.

▶ **Versioning:** The GAC can maintain different versions of the same assembly. This problem is solved also by the XCopy deployment, but your company can have a deployment strategy that prefers the GAC.

▶ **Security:** The GAC can be managed by system administrators for controlling permissions using the Access Control List. If you need such granularity of control, installing assemblies to the GAC is a good choice.

In all other cases you should refrain from installing assemblies to the GAC. Remember that this procedure affects the .NET Framework and any mistake can be fatal.

Adding References from Visual Studio to Your Own Assemblies

By default, when you install your own assemblies to the GAC, they will not be visible in the Add Reference dialog in Visual Studio. If you need to add a reference to a custom assembly that was installed to the GAC, follow these steps:

1. Open the Windows Registry Editor (RegEdit.exe).

2. Locate the HKEY_LOCAL_MACHINE\SOFTWARE\Microsoft\.NETFramework\AssemblyFolders key.

3. Add a subkey to the key from Step 2, specifying a descriptive name representing the folder where your assemblies reside and a value pointing to that folder. This is an example: HKEY_LOCAL_MACHINE\SOFTWARE\Microsoft\.NETFramework\AssemblyFolders\ *MyAssemblies="C:\\MyAssemblies"*.

Now you can find your assemblies in the Add Reference dialog.

Summary

By reading this chapter you can understand important concepts that you need to know before deploying .NET applications. You saw how the .NET Framework brilliantly solves the Dll Hell problem by avoiding the need of component registration and allowing the XCopy deployment. Then you saw what the Global Assembly Cache is and how you can manage it for sharing assemblies among multiple applications. You got information on strong names and on how to apply them to your assemblies so that these can be installed to the GAC. Finally, you understood how to configure Windows Registry for making custom assemblies in the GAC visible from the Add Reference dialog in Visual Studio. All this information is important to understand how you deploy libraries, controls, and more generally, assemblies together with your executables. Now that you know this, you are ready to deploy your applications with Visual Studio tools.

CHAPTER 54

Setup & Deployment Projects for Windows Installer

When you deliver your application to your customers, you do not tell them that it supports the XCopy deployment; neither do you provide technical explanations on how .NET applications work. This is because modern applications require a convenient setup procedure that can install them in a professional fashion, putting files in the appropriate places, creating shortcuts in the Windows user interface, checking for system requirements, and performing components registration. The users are generally just required to select the target folder and what options in your applications they want to be installed on their machine. Creating a user-friendly setup procedure is something that increases professionalism and gives customers the first good impression of your work. The .NET-based applications, such as the ones you create with Visual Basic 2010, can be deployed in several modes. One of these is taking advantage of the Windows Installer engine that provides great flexibility over installation requirements and takes the maximum from integration with the operating system. In this chapter you learn how to create a setup project for Windows Installer with Visual Studio 2010 so that you can deploy your Visual Basic applications the most professional way possible.

Windows Installer Overview

Windows Installer is the Microsoft technology for deploying applications. This technology has been part of the Windows operating system for many years and can be considered as an engine for installing .Msi packages. An .Msi package, or installer package, contains all files to be installed with your application and other important information such as shortcuts, icons, license agreements, other redistributable packages, and key/values to be written to the Windows Registry.

Windows Installer is the most powerful technology for deploying .NET applications with Visual Studio 2010. This is because Windows Installer has few limitations, whereas it brings lots of benefits. Windows Installer makes it difficult to provide updates, so if you plan to release frequent updates for your applications, you should consider ClickOnce, which is discussed in next chapter. You should choose Windows Installer as the deployment system for your application if you meet one or more of the following requirements:

▶ Adding values to the Windows Registry

▶ Customizing installation folders

▶ Installing assemblies to the Global Assembly Cache or installing and registering COM components

▶ Installing Windows services and peripheral drivers

▶ Executing custom actions and specifying launch conditions

▶ Managing ODBC components

▶ Creating custom shortcuts in the Windows user interface

▶ Elevated permissions and deeper interaction with the user

In scenarios different from the ones listed, you might instead consider ClickOnce. Visual Studio 2010 is the perfect environment for creating projects that can build Windows Installer packages that install your applications on target machines the most appropriate way. In next section you see how to accomplish this.

Creating a Setup Project

The goal of this chapter is to exemplify how you create a setup project for a Windows client application. First, create a new WPF project with Visual Basic and name it **DeploymentDemo**. This project just serves as the demo application to be deployed. When the new project is ready, right-click the solution name in Solution Explorer and then select **Add, New Project**. In the New Project dialog select the **Other Project Types, Setup and Deployment, Visual Studio Installer** templates subfolder and then choose the **Setup Wizard** project template, as shown in Figure 54.1. Name the new project **SetupExample** and then click **OK**.

The Setup Wizard is the most common project template for generating setup procedures for Windows Installer because it simplifies the process of packaging the output of other projects in the current solution through a number of guided steps.

Choose Add To Solution.
Not create new solution

FIGURE 54.1   Adding a new setup project to the solution.

NOTE

The Setup Project and the CAB Project templates enable, respectively, creating an empty project for creating a Windows Installer package and creating an empty project for packaging the application into CAB archives. The Merge Module Project is used to create a merge module that is basically an additional component for Windows Installer packages and that contains redistributable packages generally storing libraries and components. Finally the Web Setup Project is useful for deploying web applications.

When you click **OK**, the Setup Wizard will be launched. The first dialog is just a welcome one so click **Next**. The second dialog requires you to specify the project type. Leave unchanged the default selection for a Windows application, as shown in Figure 54.2, and then click **Next**.

The third dialog is important because it enables selecting the content of your package. Although you can perform this later, this is the best place for adding contents. You must select the **Primary Output** option, as demonstrated in Figure 54.3, to include the application's executable and its dependencies.

When you click **Next** you go ahead to the fourth dialog that enables specifying additional files to be packaged. Because this is not our case, click **Next** again. The fifth and last dialog contains a summary report for the new project, as shown in Figure 54.4.

If you missed something you can step back to the previous dialogs. Now click **Finish** so that Visual Studio generates the setup project for you. The new project is now available in

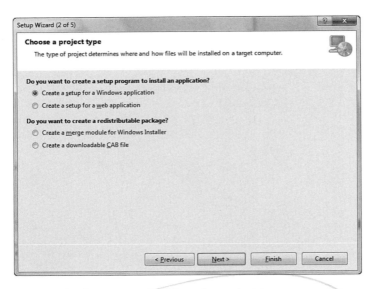

FIGURE 54.2   Choosing the installer project type.

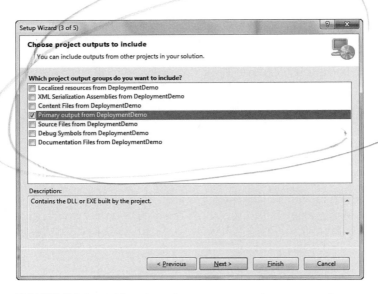

FIGURE 54.3   Adding the primary output to the setup project.

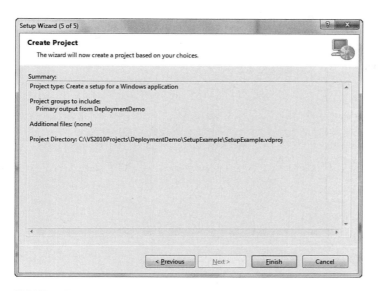

FIGURE 54.4   The summary report provided before the project generation.

Solution Explorer and is almost ready to be built for deployment. To make the deployment the most accurate possible, you can perform some customizations, which are discussed in next section.

Configuring the Setup Project

There are different ways for configuring your Windows Installer package through the setup project. The first way is setting the package's properties, which you accomplish by first clicking on the project name in Solution Explorer and then switching to the Properties window. All the available properties affect layout, messages, and target folders when launching the installer. Figure 54.5 shows an example of how you can set properties.

Properties are self-explanatory, but you can click on each of them to get a description at the bottom of the window. Focus on the `Manufacturer` property that determines the destination folder for the application on the target machine, although the installer lets you modify the destination.

SOLUTION EXPLORER TOOLBAR

When you create setup projects, Solution Explorer shows an extended toolbar that now provides buttons for accessing editors for specific package properties, such as the Registry editor and the file types' editor. In the next sections we often refer to these buttons, so take a look at Solution Explorer to locate them.

54

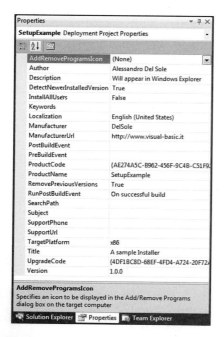

FIGURE 54.5   Setting project properties that affect the installer package.

Editing the File System

You can manage files to be installed with your package in the File System editor, which can be enabled with the appropriate button from Solution Explorer. Figure 54.6 shows how it looks when the new project is created.

You can select a folder to add other files in the right side of the window or add shortcuts to your executable as well. For example, you can add shortcuts for the user's desktop and Programs menu by selecting the appropriate folders in the left side of the window and then right-clicking the right side of the window; then choose **Create New Shortcut**. Finally you will be required to specify the executable to be linked via a dialog window. You can specify additional folders and Windows special folders; for this, it is worth mentioning that you can add assemblies to the Global Assembly Cache. This is one of the reasons why you should choose Windows Installer for deploying your applications. To specify assemblies that must be installed to the GAC, right-click **File System on Target Machine**; then select **Add Special Folder, Global Assembly Cache Folder**. This creates a reference to the GAC in the file system editor. Now right-click the **Global Assembly Cache Folder** item and select **Add, Assembly**. Figure 54.7 shows an example, adding to the project the WCF service library that we created in Chapter 41, "Creating and Consuming WCF Services."

You can select one or more assemblies via a dialog window. Notice that Visual Studio can determine all assemblies' dependencies and can automatically add related assemblies to the project.

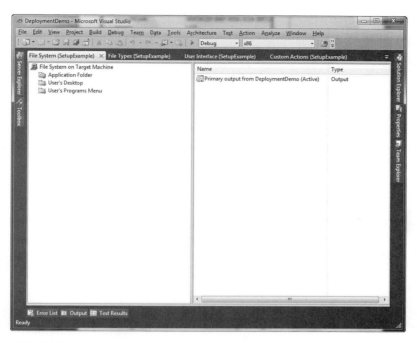

FIGURE 54.6   The file system editor.

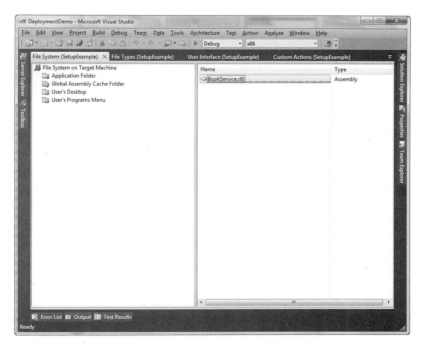

FIGURE 54.7   Specifying assemblies to be installed to the GAC.

Editing Registry Values

One of the biggest benefits in deploying applications with Windows Installer is that you can add keys and values to the Windows Registry on the target machine. You create keys, subkeys, and values by selecting the **Registry Editor** in Solution Explorer and then right-clicking the desired root key; finally add the required key or value. Figure 54.8 shows how to accomplish this.

Values are then visible on the right side of the editor. You have complete control over the Registry and that Visual Studio prepares a Registry key for your own application under HKEY_LOCAL_MACHINE\Software.

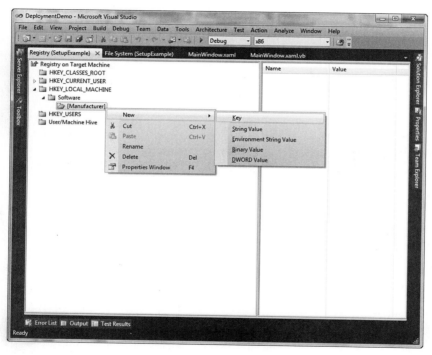

FIGURE 54.8   Adding a new key in the Registry editor.

Customizing Dialogs

Windows Installer dialogs are customizable, meaning that you can replace default text messages and title bitmaps, but you can also add your own dialogs. To edit dialogs, select the **Dialog Editor** in Solution Explorer and then select the desired dialog. Changes are performed via the Properties window. Figure 54.9 shows an example.

Each dialog offers a BannerBitmap property that you can replace with your own bitmap image. Other properties depend exclusively on the specific dialog. For example the

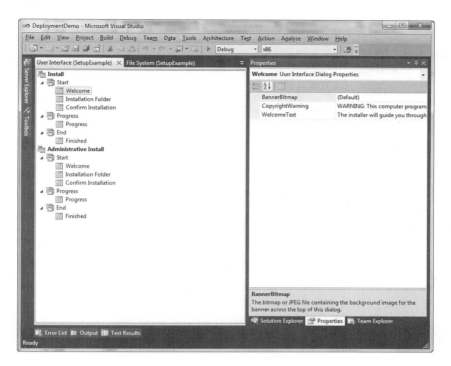

FIGURE 54.9   Customizing the installer dialogs.

Welcome dialog has `CopyrightWarning` and `WelcomeText` properties that contain text that you can replace with your own.

Creating File Types

There are situations in which you need to associate a custom file extension to your executable. Visual Studio enables putting this information into Windows Installer packages in a convenient way. You provide custom extensions to be associated to the executable and actions to be executed over the extension via the File Types editor. You add an extension by right-clicking the **File Types on Target Machine** item and then selecting **Add File Type**. When the new file type is added to the editor, you customize its properties via the Properties window. Figure 54.10 shows an example of this kind of customization.

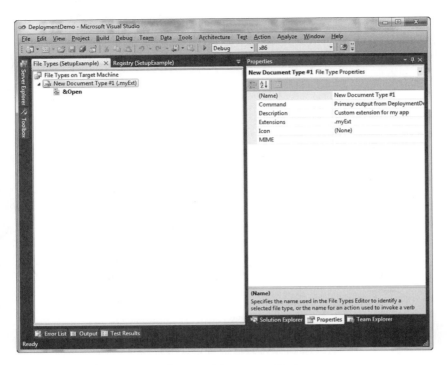

FIGURE 54.10   Adding and customizing a new file type.

Providing Custom Actions

A custom action enables specifying that an external file or that an instance of the
`Installer` class must be executed at the specified installation time. A typical example is
when you need to include in your installation package the redistributables of a particular
runtime or components (for example the MDAC components) used by your application
that need to be installed before the application itself. To add a custom action, select the
Custom Actions editor from Solution Explorer; then right-click the installation phase that
is appropriate for you and select **Add Custom Action**, as shown in Figure 54.11.

At this point you will be asked to specify the executable to be run at the established
moment, via a dialog window. You can pick up the executable from the list of files available
in the current package; if the required executable is not part of the file system yet,
add it to the package, and then re-add the custom action.

MANAGED CUSTOM ACTIONS

It is worth mentioning that you could create a class library with Visual Basic and implement
it as a custom action during the installation. This provides great granularity on custom
functionalities, such as asking for a product key or downloading updates and so on.

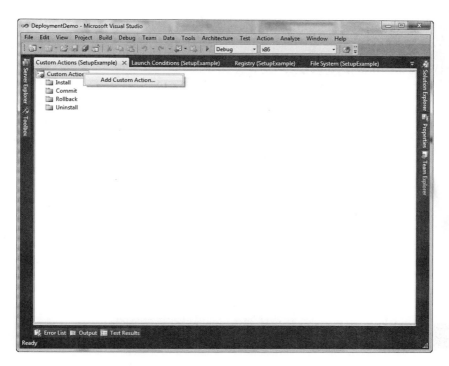

FIGURE 54.11   Adding a custom action.

Specifying Launch Conditions

Launch conditions enable specifying minimum system requirements needed for continuing the installations. You add launch conditions via the Launch Conditions editor that you can start with the appropriate button in Solution Explorer. There are two launch conditions types; the first type enables searching for the specified file or component on the target system, whereas the second type enables specifying custom conditions such as hardware requirements. When the editor is ready, simply right-click the desired condition type and then click **Add Launch Condition**. Figure 54.12 shows a sample launch condition that checks for the machine's physical memory.

The Condition property contains the condition that must be True for the installation to begin. The Message property contains a localizable text that will be shown whether the condition is evaluated as False. The full list of available conditions can be found in the MSDN Library at http://msdn.microsoft.com/en-us/library/cz6k1z02(VS.100).aspx.

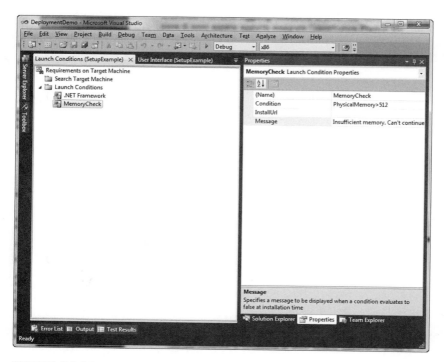

FIGURE 54.12   Adding a custom launch condition.

Package Configuration and Prerequisites

You can configure additional properties for your setup package by right-clicking the project name and selecting **Properties**. This shows the project Property Page represented in Figure 54.13, where you can specify the output name, how the installer will be packaged (for example, Msi or Cab format), or the compression type.

Notice that by clicking the **Configuration Manager** button you can edit existing configurations (that is, Debug and Release) or add new ones to affect your output packages. This is also the place where you can set up your package to target 64-bit machines. Another important task is setting up prerequisites. Click the **Prerequisites** button to launch the dialog shown in Figure 54.14.

Prerequisites are those packages or runtime components that must be installed together with the application so that it can work correctly. After you set up all properties shown in this section, you can build and distribute your package.

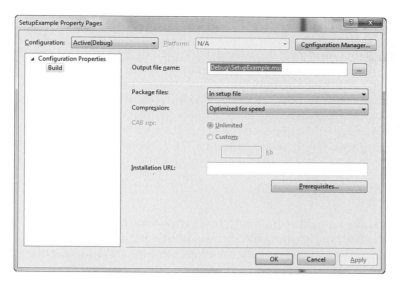

FIGURE 54.13   The project's property page.

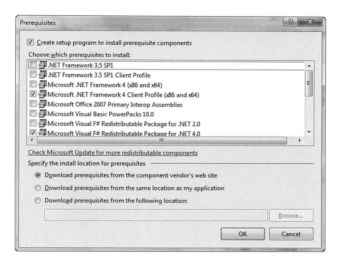

FIGURE 54.14   Checking and selecting prerequisites.

Building and Deploying the Windows Installer Package

To create your Windows Installer distributable package, right-click the setup project name in Solution Explorer and select **Build**. As an alternative, you can choose the appropriate **Build** command from the Build menu. This generates a bootstrapper named Setup.exe and the Windows Installer package with an .Msi extension, which in our case is named SetupExample.Msi. The output will be available in the project subfolder related to the current configuration (Bin\Debug or Bin\Release). These are the files that you need to distribute to your customers for installing your application. They simply run the Setup.exe bootstrapper that correctly starts the Windows Installer package.

Summary

In this chapter we covered how to create setup projects for Windows Installer in Visual Studio 2010. First you read about the reasons why you should choose such a technique; then you saw how to generate a setup project with the Project Wizard. Next the discussion focused on configuring and customizing your project with special integrated editors. Finally, you saw how to build and deploy your Windows Installer package.

CHAPTER 55

Deploying Applications with ClickOnce

Sometimes customers want simple installations for applications they purchase. They do not want to step through complex guided procedures with several dialogs and lots of options. They simply want to make just two or three mouse clicks and nothing more. To accomplish this particular scenario, Microsoft created ClickOnce: the one-click deployment technology for .NET Framework. ClickOnce is useful for installations that are just a few steps but it is also the easiest way for bringing automatic updating capabilities to your applications. In this chapter you learn about deploying client applications with ClickOnce and discover some new features.

Introducing ClickOnce

ClickOnce is the deployment technology offered by all Visual Studio editions, including the Express versions, which enables creating distribution procedures for Windows client applications in a simple way, according to *one-click deployment* logic. The idea behind ClickOnce is that the final user will have the ability to install an application with a minimum number of mouse clicks and interactions. This technology was first introduced with .NET Framework 2.0 and Visual Studio 2005 and has been improved during the years. Now in .NET 4.0 and Visual Studio 2010, ClickOnce offers additional deployment options that are explained in this chapter. ClickOnce enables publishing the deployment package to file system folders, FTP servers, and Http servers and can make applications available online, offline, or both.

Before illustrating how you publish deployment packages with ClickOnce, it is important to understand how it works and when you should use it.

How ClickOnce Handles Applications

Different from Windows Installer, which is integrated in the operating system, ClickOnce is integrated with the .NET Framework. Applications deployed via ClickOnce run in a security sandbox that is fully managed by the .NET Framework. This provides great flexibility, because the .NET Framework can apply managed trust rules to ClickOnce-deployed applications and provide the infrastructure for automating application updates. For example, thanks to the .NET integration, developers can write code to programmatically check for updates or to access the deployment system. By the way, ClickOnce has some limitations for Windows Installer. The next section explains limitations and provides information on when you should use ClickOnce for your deployments.

When Should I Use ClickOnce?

ClickOnce is a powerful technology and is useful when you need to deploy applications that require a minimum amount of interaction from the user. ClickOnce is appropriate in the following scenarios:

► You want to provide your application with the capability of being frequently updated without writing a single line of code.

► Your application makes use of third-party components that are not required to be installed into the Global Assembly Cache.

► You want your application to be installed by nonadministrative users.

► You want to simply deploy add-ins for Microsoft Office.

► Your installation process does not require you to customize the target system other than creating shortcuts.

Opposite to the preceding listed advantages, ClickOnce has limitations that you must consider when choosing the most appropriate development system for you:

► You cannot install assemblies to the Global Assembly Cache.

► ClickOnce does not enable writing values to the Windows Registry.

► It does not enable deep installation customization.

► It does not enable choosing the target folder for the application on the target machine. This is because, as ClickOnce is integrated with the .NET Framework, applications run inside a security sandbox managed by .NET which has its own folders.

If you need to perform just one of these customizations, ClickOnce is not appropriate, and you need to recur to Windows Installer. At this point we take a look to the practical ClickOnce deployment.

> **NOTE ON CLIENT APPLICATIONS**
>
> With the growth of WPF applications, ClickOnce has been erroneously considered as a technology for deploying such kind of applications. This is true in part, meaning that ClickOnce is not limited to WPF applications, whereas it can generally deploy all kinds of Windows client applications, including Windows Forms and Console applications.

Deploying Applications with ClickOnce

To deploy an application with ClickOnce, you have three options: the Publish command in the Build menu, right-clicking the project in Solution Explorer, and selecting Publish or the Publish Now button in the ClickOnce configuration page within My Project. For now we focus on the first option, whereas the second option is covered in the next section. Now create a new WPF project with Visual Basic and name it **ClickOnceDemo**. There is no need to write code for the application because we need only a base for our example. In order to deploy an application with ClickOnce, follow these steps:

1. Click **Build, Publish,** Visual Studio launches the Publish Wizard. Figure 55.1 shows the first dialog of the wizard, in which you need to specify the location where the application will be published. Notice how the dialog also explains available possibilities, such as disk path, network shared path, ftp server, or website. You can change the target type and location by clicking **Browse.** In this case let's publish the application to the local Internet Information Services website, which requires Visual Studio to be running with administrator privileges.

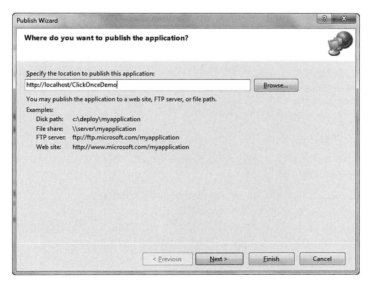

FIGURE 55.1   Choosing the target location for the ClickOnce deployment.

PUBLISHING TO FILE SYSTEM

Publish the application to a local folder on the file system if you want to deploy the application on media supports such as CD-ROM or zipped archives. This option can make the application available only offline.

2. Click **Next**. The second dialog of the wizard enables specifying if the application will be available offline. In this case the .NET Framework creates a shortcut in the Start menu for launching the application and another one in the Add/Remove Programs tool for enabling uninstalling the application. Figure 55.2 shows how you set this option. Basically, this is all the information that Visual Studio needs to create a ClickOnce deployment.

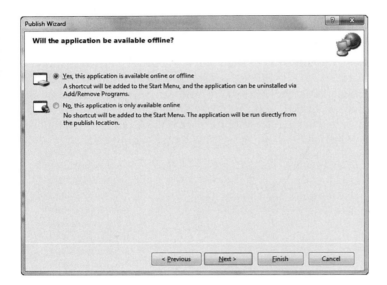

FIGURE 55.2   Specifying how the application will be available.

3. Click **Next**. You will see the last dialog of the wizard showing the deployment information summary (see Figure 55.3).

4. Click **Finish**, Visual Studio generates all the required files and folders. Because the deployment is currently done for a web server, Visual Studio also generates a Publish.htm web page that is the place from which users can install the application. Figure 55.4 shows the page created for this sample application.

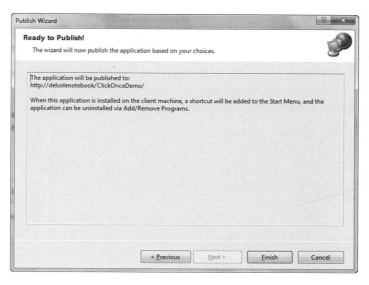

FIGURE 55.3   Collecting summary information for the ClickOnce deployment.

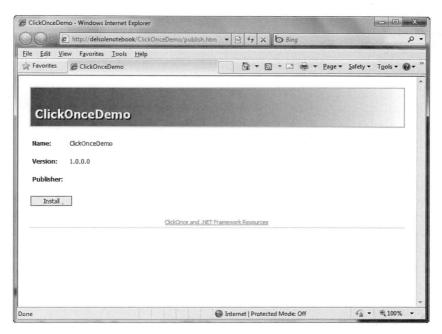

FIGURE 55.4   The Web page from which the application will be downloaded.

TIPS ON THE PUBLISH.HTM WEB PAGE

Being a simple Html page, the default Publish.htm can be edited to accomplish your particular needs or just to provide a different appearance. In this case the web page address points to the local IIS, but if you publish the application onto a real server, you probably do this via an FTP account, whereas the web page address, where users install the application from, is something like this: http://www.something.com/ClickOnceDemo/publish.htm.

Now click **Install**. At this point a security warning informs you that the application is downloading from a website with other information about the publisher, as shown in Figure 55.5.

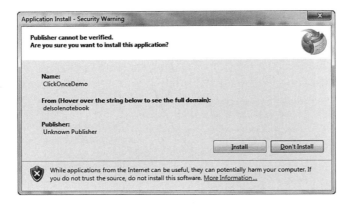

FIGURE 55.5   ClickOnce shows a security warning asking confirmation before installing the application and providing information on the application's publisher and source.

Because you are the publisher and you trust yourself, click **Install**. This installs the application on your system, and a shortcut will be added to the Start menu. To remove the application simply open the **Control Panel**, **Programs and Features** tool, and then select the application from the list.

Structure of a ClickOnce Deployment

The publish process, whatever target you select, generates a subfolder containing the following elements:

- ▶ A bootstrapper file named Setup.exe, which launches the installation.

- ▶ The application manifest, which contains information on how the application has to be run in the ClickOnce context.

- ▶ The Publish.htm file (only if the application has been published to a Web or FTP space).

▶ A subfolder containing the actual application and related files. This subfolder has a version number that is recognized by the .NET Framework when the application finds updates.

If you publish the application to the file system for deploying to media supports such as a CD-ROM, you just need to copy to the media the content of the publish folder.

TIP

Unless you specify a publish folder, the deployment package is published to Bin\Debug\Publish or Bin\Release\Publish depending on the selected configuration.

Configuring ClickOnce

You can customize your ClickOnce deployment by setting its property page in My Project. Click the **Publish** tab to activate the ClickOnce options designer represented in Figure 55.6.

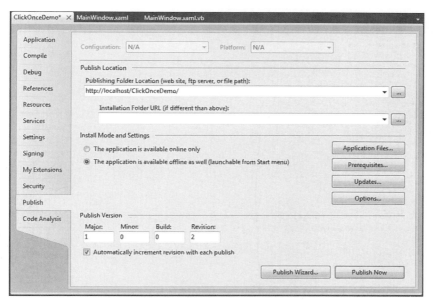

FIGURE 55.6   The ClickOnce properties designer enables customizing the deployment.

Notice that the upper part of the designer shows properties that you already set with the Publish Wizard. The Publish Version group enables specifying the deployment version that is important for allowing automatic updates. Automatically incrementing the revision number is a convenient way for allowing installed applications to check for updates. Just remember that the publish version is just a ClickOnce-related version and does not affect the application version. Now let's take a look at the other available options.

Application Files

By clicking the **Application Files** button, you can view or specify files that need to be included in the deployment package. If you want some required files included in the deployment package (such as documents or databases), you need to set their Build Action property as **Content**. Generally Visual Studio can automatically classify files according to their role in the project, so this is something that you rarely need to perform manually.

Prerequisites

Prerequisites are those files that the application needs to work correctly, for example runtime components such as the .NET Framework or third-party controls, which the installer installs on the target machine before the application is installed. Generally Visual Studio can detect the appropriate prerequisites and select them for you, but there are situations in which you need to perform this manually, for example when you need to install third-party components. Figure 55.7 shows the Prerequisites dialog.

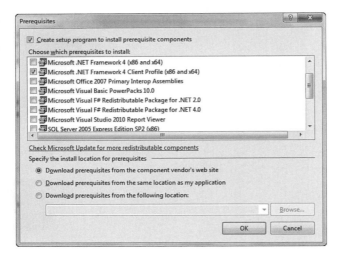

FIGURE 55.7 Selecting prerequisites for your applications.

If you use third-party components, ensure that the producer made available a redistributable package that you can include in the deployment prerequisites. The .NET Framework will always be included as a prerequisite, because ClickOnce cannot predict if on the target machine the .NET Framework is already available.

Custom Prerequisites

Visual Studio 2010 does not provide a built-in functionality for packaging custom prerequisites. To accomplish this particular need, follow the instructions described in this page of the MSDN Library: http://msdn.microsoft.com/en-us/library/ms165429(VS.100).aspx. An alternative is using a free tool called Boostrapper Manifest Generator, which is available on the MSDN Code Gallery. At the time of this writing, the tool is only available for Visual Studio 2008, so periodically check its workspace for updates at http://code.msdn. microsoft.com/bmg.

Updates

One of the most important features in ClickOnce (and one of the reasons why you should use it) is the capability of updating applications without writing code to accomplish this. The idea is that you publish a new version of the application and when you run the old version, this checks for updates and automatically upgrades to the new version. Notice that automatic updates are not available for applications published to the file system. To enable automatic updates, click the **Updates** button and then in the Application Updates dialog, check **The Application Should Check for Updates** check box, as shown in Figure 55.8.

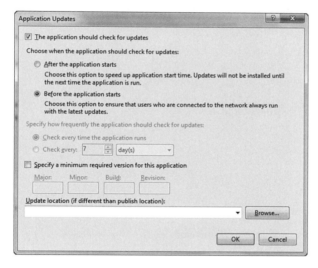

FIGURE 55.8   Enabling automatic updates.

For example, you can decide if the application will be updated before it starts (default option) so that users always run the latest updates or if it will be updated after it starts, but in this case changes will be applied only at the next start. You can also specify how frequently the application has to check for updates. The default setting is that the application checks for updates each time it runs; otherwise, you can specify a time interval expressed in days or hours or minutes. (This option is available only if you decide to update the application after it starts.)

TESTING UPDATES

When you enable updates, if you want to ensure that this feature works correctly, perform any kind of modification to the application (for example, add a button); then publish it again. Finally run the application and check that the new version is actually downloaded and installed.

Options

Additions introduced to ClickOnce by the .NET Framework 3.5 SP 1 have been reprised in .NET Framework 4.0 to provide better installation customization. When you click the **Options** button, you have access to additional features. For example, you can edit the Description part in the deployment manifest so that you can set a full description for your installation. Figure 55.9 shows an example of how you can specify information.

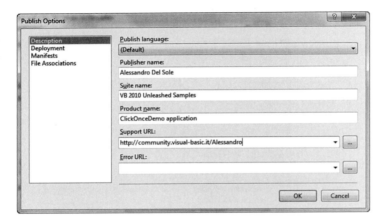

FIGURE 55.9   Setting description options for the deployment package.

Consider that the Publisher name will be utilized to create a root shortcuts folder in the Start menu, whereas the Suite name value will be utilized to create a shortcuts subfolder for the current application. The Deployment option enables setting some aspects of the publish process. Figure 55.10 shows an example for setting such options.

For example, you can decide if the Publish.htm web page has to be created and shown, if the wizard generates an Autorun.inf file for automatic CD start, or if the deployment will use the .deploy extension. Pay attention to this particular option. Unless you uncheck this check box, the application files will be deployed with the addition of the .deploy extension, which may cause errors if your application attempts to access external files. If this is your case, disable the extension and deploy the application again. The Manifest option enables establishing how application URLs must be treated, but more particularly it enables setting if a desktop shortcut needs to be created for your application (see Figure 55.11).

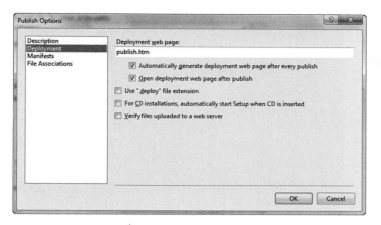

FIGURE 55.10   Setting deployment options.

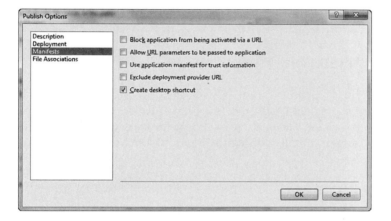

FIGURE 55.11   Setting manifest options.

Another useful option is the File Associations that is basically the only Registry customization allowed to ClickOnce and that enables assigning a file extension to your executable.

Security Considerations

Depending on how an application is deployed or what system resources it needs to have access to, it will be considered under the Full Trust or the Partial Trust rules of .NET Framework Code Access Security. For example, an application that needs to access the Registry or other system resources needs to be full-trusted, but this is not a good idea if your application will be deployed via the Internet, which should instead be partial-trusted. You set the trust level for your ClickOnce deployments in the My Project, Security tab (see Figure 55.12).

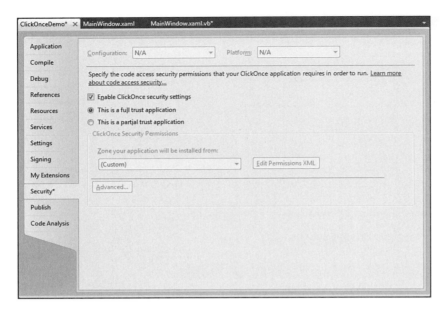

FIGURE 55.12   Specifying security settings for the ClickOnce deployment.

The ClickOnce manifest can be signed with Full Trust or Partial Trust. This second option is divided into the Internet and intranet zones. You can choose the most appropriate for you or even create a custom configuration by editing the application manifest file (Edit Permissions XML button).

Providing Certificates

To make ClickOnce deployments the most trustable possible, you should use a certificate. If you take a look at Solution Explorer after you publish the application, you notice that Visual Studio has signed the assembly with a .pfx strong name. This is good in local test scenarios, but the most convenient way (although not mandatory) for providing security information to customers is adding an Authenticode certificate, especially if your application is deployed via the Internet. Visual Studio adds a test certificate, as demonstrated in Figure 55.13, which shows the Signing tab in My Project.

The test certificate is intended for local testing purposes only and should never be used in real-life deployment, in which you will instead prefer an Authenticode certificate that you can purchase from the specific authorities. After you add a valid certificate, to sign the ClickOnce manifest, full and trusted information will be shown to your customers when they download and install the application.

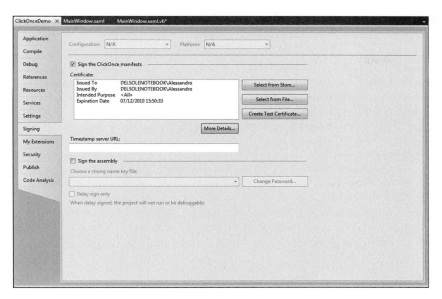

FIGURE 55.13   Signing the ClickOnce manifest.

Programmatically Accessing ClickOnce

As pointed out at the beginning of this chapter, ClickOnce is handled by the .NET Framework, but more precisely it is part of the .NET Framework. This means that it can be accessed via managed code. The .NET Framework exposes the `System.Deployment` namespace that offers a managed way for interacting with ClickOnce; particularly the subnamespace `System.Deployment.Application` and the `System.Deployment.Application.ApplicationDeployment` class are the most useful items because they offer objects that enable developers to programmatically access ClickOnce information from an application. The `ApplicationDeployment` class exposes a shared `CurrentDeployment` property that enables access to interesting information on the current application deployment. The following code demonstrates how you can use the property to retrieve information on the current deployment:

```
Private Sub GetClickOnceInformation()
    'Checks if the application has been deployed with ClickOnce
    If ApplicationDeployment.IsNetworkDeployed = True Then

        'Retrieves the data folder for this application
        Dim dataFolder As String = ApplicationDeployment.
                                    CurrentDeployment.DataDirectory
        'Retrieves the path where updates will be
```

```
            'downloaded from
            Dim updatesPath As Uri = ApplicationDeployment.
                            CurrentDeployment.UpdateLocation
            'Gets the version number for updates
            Dim updateVersion = ApplicationDeployment.
                            CurrentDeployment.UpdatedVersion
            'Determines the last time that updates where checked for
            Dim lastUpdate As Date = ApplicationDeployment.
                            CurrentDeployment.TimeOfLastUpdateCheck

        End If
    End Sub
```

You can also programmatically check and download updates; this can be useful if you do not want the application to be automatically updated but you still want to provide the user the ability of updating the application manually. The following code demonstrates this:

```
Private Sub ApplicationUpdate()

    Dim isUpdateAvailable As Boolean = _
        ApplicationDeployment.CurrentDeployment.CheckForUpdate

    If isUpdateAvailable = True Then
        ApplicationDeployment.CurrentDeployment.Update()
    End If
End Sub
```

Both methods offer an asynchronous counterpart (CheckForUpdateAsync and UpdateAsync) that can be used as well.

Registration-Free COM

One of the biggest benefits from ClickOnce is that users that do not have administrator permissions can install applications. By the way, there are situations in which an application is deployed together with some COM libraries but this can be a problem because such libraries need to be registered and a non-administrator user does not have the appropriate permissions for this. Fortunately with ClickOnce you can take advantage of a technique known as Registration-Free COM which basically makes a reference to a COM library visible to the application only, without the need of registration. You simply need to right-click the library name in Solution Explorer, References and then select Properties. Finally set the Isolated property as True (see Figure 55.14).

When you build the project, Visual Studio also generates a manifest file that provides the actual state of isolation of the library. Listing 55.1 shows a sample manifest file.

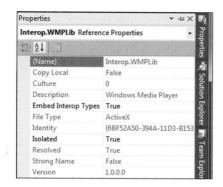

FIGURE 55.14   Isolating the library for Registration-Free COM.

LISTING 55.1   Sample Manifest for Registration-Free COM

```xml
<?xml version="1.0" encoding="utf-8"?>
<assembly xsi:schemaLocation="urn:schemas-microsoft-com:asm.v1 assem-
bly.adaptive.xsd"
          manifestVersion="1.0" xmlns:asmv1="urn:schemas-microsoft-com:asm.v1"
          xmlns:asmv2="urn:schemas-microsoft-com:asm.v2"
          xmlns:asmv3="urn:schemas-microsoft-com:asm.v3"
          xmlns:dsig="http://www.w3.org/2000/09/xmldsig#"
          xmlns:co.v1="urn:schemas-microsoft-com:clickonce.v1"
          xmlns:co.v2="urn:schemas-microsoft-com:clickonce.v2"
          xmlns="urn:schemas-microsoft-com:asm.v1"
          xmlns:xsi="http://www.w3.org/2001/XMLSchema-instance">
  <assemblyIdentity name="Native.MyCOMLibrary" version="1.0.0.0" type="win32" />
  <file name="wmp.dll" asmv2:size="11406336">
    <hash xmlns="urn:schemas-microsoft-com:asm.v2">
      <dsig:Transforms>
        <dsig:Transform
        Algorithm="urn:schemas-microsoft-com:HashTransforms.Identity" />
      </dsig:Transforms>
      <dsig:DigestMethod Algorithm="http://www.w3.org/2000/09/xmldsig#sha1" />
      <dsig:DigestValue>cCyT3Cw0dm68HkliYf3ncYjoCKU=</dsig:DigestValue>
    </hash>
    <typelib tlbid="{6bf52a50-394a-11d3-b153-00c04f79faa6}"
         version="1.0" helpdir="" resourceid="0" flags="HASDISKIMAGE" />
    <comClass clsid="{6bf52a52-394a-11d3-b153-00c04f79faa6}"
            threadingModel="Apartment"
            tlbid="{6bf52a50-394a-11d3-b153-00c04f79faa6}"
            progid="WMPlayer.OCX.7"
```

55

```
                 description="Windows Media Player ActiveX Control" />
  </file>
</assembly>
```

The manifest file is part of the setup process, so you need to include it in your ClickOnce deployment (Visual Studio takes care for you). If you are interested in understanding how the Registration-Free COM technique actually works, you can read a specific article in the MSDN Magazine available at this address: http://msdn.microsoft.com/en-us/magazine/cc188708.aspx.

Summary

This chapter described how to build deployment packages with ClickOnce, the one-click deployment technology included in the .NET Framework. You saw how to use the Publish Wizard to create a setup procedure in a few steps; then you saw how you can configure the deployment options with the Visual Studio designer, including allowing automatic updates and adding publisher information. You then stepped through security considerations required so that you can understand what happens on the target machines. Finally the discussion focused on how to programmatically interact with ClickOnce by writing Visual Basic code taking advantage of the `System.Deployment.Application.ApplicationDeployment` class.

Installing Visual Studio 2010

Installing Visual Studio 2010 and required components is a key step in your development experience. In this appendix you can find useful information to get the most out of the Visual Studio installation and first run.

Installing Visual Studio 2010

When you insert the installation media in your DVD-Rom drive, the Setup.exe application starts. In the Setup dialog, as shown in Figure A.1, click the **Install Microsoft Visual Studio 2010** link. After a few seconds, the installer loads required components. After loading setup components, you will be asked to read and accept the license agreement and review user information. At this point click **Next** so that you can choose what feature you want to install. As you can see in Figure A.2, the installer shows a list of available features. For this book, the only features that are not strictly required are Visual C#, Visual F#, Visual C++, the Graphics Library, and SharePoint Development Tools. Also notice that if you want to install Visual C++, you have the ability to specify the components, such as compilers and libraries for the managed and the unmanaged environment. When you decide on your favorite features, click **Install**. At this point you need to wait for the installation process to complete. A dialog continuously informs you of the process state telling you what component is being currently installed, as shown in Figure A.3. If you have experience with previous Visual Studio versions, you notice that the Setup dialog windows don't show anymore pictures and animated content to provide better performance. After installing the Microsoft .NET Framework 4.0, the setup

FIGURE A.1   The startup dialog of the Visual Studio installation.

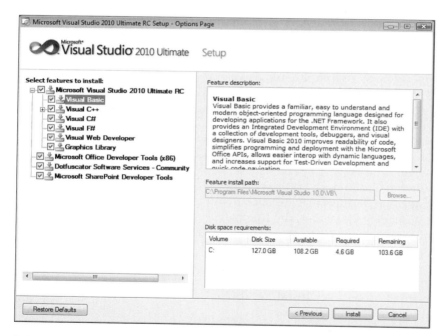

FIGURE A.2   Choosing features to install.

reboots your machine. When rebooted, the installation continues from the point it was interrupted. After a number of minutes the Visual Studio setup finishes. In the final dialog you have an opportunity to choose to close the setup process or to install the offline documentation (see Figure A.4).

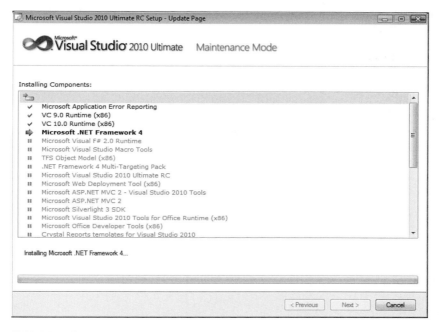

FIGURE A.3   Getting information on the setup process state.

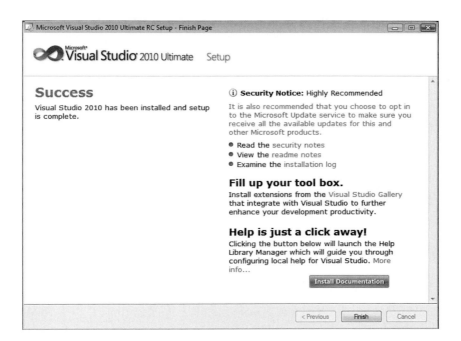

FIGURE A.4   Setup completes, so now it's time to install the documentation.

Installing the offline documentation is useful if you want to have a local copy of the MSDN library, as described in the next section.

Installing the Offline Documentation

When the installation finishes, click the **Install Documentation** button. This launches the new Help Library Manager. The first thing you are asked to specify is the target directory for the offline help, as shown in Figure A.5. Leave the default setting unchanged and then click **OK**.

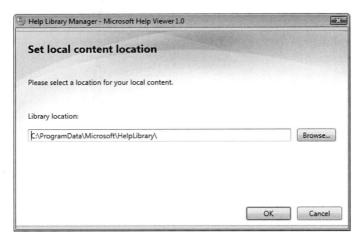

FIGURE A.5   Setting the target folder for the MSDN Library.

At this point the Library Manager shows you a series of options; click **Find Contents on Disk**. This lists available components that you can install to your local machine from the installation media (see Figure A.6 for details). Ensure you add at least the **VS Documentation** element and then click **Update**.

After a few minutes the offline documentation will be available on your computer. At this point you can return to the final Setup dialog, as shown in Figure A.4, where you just click **Finish** to return to the operating system.

Finding Additional Contents Online

Because including the entire MSDN Library in one installation media is not possible, you have the ability of installing additional documentation from the Internet. This is something that can be accomplished after you run Visual Studio for the first time. On the Help menu, click the **Manage Help Settings** command. This launches again the Help Library Manager. In the list of available options, select **Find Content Online**. At this point the Help Manager lists available contents, as shown in Figure A.7.

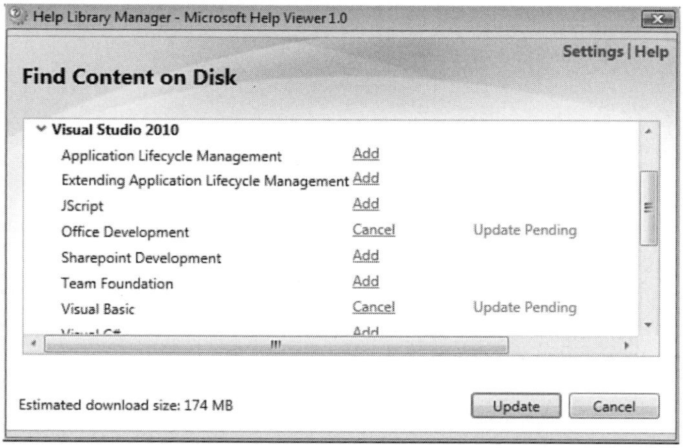

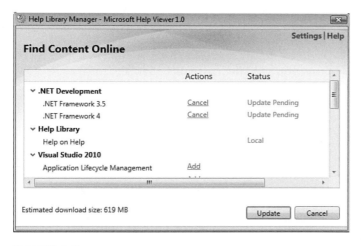

FIGURE A.6   Selecting documentation contents.

FIGURE A.7   Selecting additional help contents available on the Internet.

When ready, click **Update** and wait for the documentation to be installed.

Running Visual Studio 2010 for the First Time

When you run Visual Studio 2010 for the first time, the IDE needs to be configured. It first requires you to specify one of the default environment settings, as shown in Figure A.8.

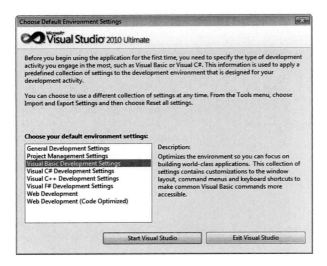

FIGURE A.8   Selecting a default environment setting.

Choosing one of the development settings configures menus, buttons, and icons to provide the appropriate shortcuts according to the selected profile. A popular choice is the **General Development Settings** so that you can later customize the IDE according to your particular needs, but you can also consider the **Visual Basic Development Settings** that configures the IDE with the most-common shortcuts for Visual Basic, especially if you come from the Visual Basic 6 experience. You can revert changes later from the Tools menu, as described in Chapter 56, "Advanced IDE Features."

APPENDIX B

Useful Resources and Tools for Visual Basic

The Visual Basic 2010 language is the most powerful version ever and enables you to access every feature and technology exposed by .NET Framework 4. But the Framework is a large technology, and the language has so many features that remembering everything is almost impossible. So, instead of remembering everything, it is important for you to know where to search for information, resources, and learning material. Moreover, Visual Studio 2010 is a powerful development environment that includes a plethora of tools to make your development experience great. There are some situations in which the IDE does not include particular features that are instead provided by third-party tools. This appendix gives you a number of Visual Basic resources inside the MSDN documentation and websites for you to bookmark in your Favorites. Also, this appendix provides a list of useful tools for you as a Visual Basic developer. They are all free tools, so you can enjoy their functionalities.

Visual Basic Resources in MSDN

Following are learning resources for Visual Basic 2010 inside the MSDN Library and websites:

The Visual Basic Developer Center: The principal website from Microsoft dedicated to Visual Basic: http://msdn.com/vbasic.

Visual Basic "How Do I" videos: A portal where you can find a lot of videos illustrating programming techniques and usage of Microsoft technologies with Visual Basic: http://msdn.microsoft.com/en-us/vbasic/bb466226.aspx.

Visual Basic Code Samples: A portal where you can find an updated list of open source projects and applications from the MSDN Code Gallery and the CodePlex community targeting Visual Basic: http://msdn.microsoft.com/en-us/vbasic/ms789074.aspx.

Visual Basic Tutorials, a portal where you can find a list of tutorials covering a great number of Microsoft technologies with VB: http://msdn.microsoft.com/en-us/vbasic/ms789086.aspx.

Visual Basic Community Content, a web page offering news about contents produced by community members such as Microsoft Visual Basic MVPs: http://msdn.microsoft.com/en-us/vbasic/ms789066.aspx.

Visual Basic MSDN Library, probably the most important reference for every Visual Basic developer, where you can find documentation, language reference, walkthroughs and examples: http://msdn.microsoft.com/en-us/library/2x7h1hfk.aspx.

.NET Framework Developer Center, the principal website for information on all .NET-based Microsoft technologies: http://msdn.microsoft.com/en-us/netframework/default.aspx.

Also don't forget to use search engines, which in most cases will be your best friends. Typically they will return the most accurate results if your search is performed by writing English strings.

Useful Developer Tools for Visual Basic

This section provides a list of free useful tools that will enrich your developer toolbox.

Coding Tools

In this section you can find a list of tools to improve your productivity in writing better code.

CodeRush Xpress from DevExpress is a free Visual Studio add-in that enhances the Visual Studio code editor by providing refactoring tools to write better, more-readable, and more-efficient code. If you used Refactor! Express in the past, CodeRush is its more powerful successor. You can find it at http://www.devexpress.com/Products/Visual_Studio_Add-in/CodeRushX/.

Code Snippet Editor is an open source tool written in Visual Basic for creating and exporting reusable code snippets with advanced functionalities in VB, C#, and Xml languages via a comfortable graphical user interface. It is available at http://www.codeplex.com/SnippetEditor.

Vsi Builder 2008 is a free tool from the author of this book that enables creating .Vsi packages for deploying code snippets, add-ins, and additional contents for Visual Studio. You can download it from http://code.msdn.microsoft.com/VsiBuilder.

P/Invoke Interop Assistant is an open source tool that lets you write P/Invokes in the better way: http://clrinterop.codeplex.com/.

Networking

One of the most famous tools in networking is **Fiddler**, which is a free Web debugging proxy that can log all http and https traffic between the computer and the Internet. Other than inspecting http traffic, Fiddler can set breakpoints and walk through incoming or outgoing data. You can find it at http://www.fiddler2.com/fiddler2/. Fiddler is particularly useful in debugging WCF services and WCF Data Services, other than requests coming from Web browsers such as Internet Explorer and Firefox.

Data Access

For data access tools, you can find **LINQPad** very useful. This is a free tool that provides advanced instrumentation for querying data sources and that can generate the necessary code using LINQ. Visual Basic is one of the supported languages. You can find it at http://www.linqpad.net. Although LINQPad requires .NET Framework 3.5 to be executed, the generated queries can be reused in the current Visual Basic version.

Diagnostics and Performance

This section lists a number of tools for Visual Studio diagnostics and applications performance.

Visual Studio 2010 Diagnostic Tool enables collecting traces, dumps, and performance information about Visual Studio 2010. Such information can be useful if you are interested in sending your feedback to Microsoft about problems occurring during the Visual Studio 2010 lifetime. It is available from the Visual Studio Gallery at http://visualstudiogallery. msdn.microsoft.com/en-us/e8649e35-26b1-4e73-b427-c2886a0705f4.

Windows Performance Toolkit is capable of analyzing performances of WPF applications through different kinds of analysis methods. You can obtain the toolkit in two ways: The first way is downloading and installing the previously described VS 2010 Diagnostic Tool, whereas the second one is downloading and installing the Microsoft Windows SDK for Windows 7 and Windows Server 2008 R2 available from at http://www.microsoft.com/downloads/details.aspx?FamilyID=c17ba869-9671-4330-a63e-1fd44e0e2505&displaylang=en.

Miscellaneous

In this section you can find a list of tools not strictly related to a single technology or that cannot be classified in other sections.

.NET Reflector is a free tool capable of exploring .NET assemblies via Reflection. The tool can show the Intermediate Language or offer decompilation results in both Visual Basic and Visual C# of the specified executable. Reflector is not only useful for reflecting or decompiling assemblies, but is also particularly useful for inspecting .NET Framework Base Class Libraries and understanding how many things are implemented behind the scenes. You can find it at http://www.red-gate.com/products/reflector/.

XAML PowerToys is a free add-in for Visual Studio 2010 that integrates the WPF and Silverlight designers with tools for generating business forms and objects enabled for the Model-View-ViewModel pattern and adds design-time functionalities for rearranging UI elements. You can find at http://karlshifflett.wordpress.com/xaml-power-toys/.

Windows Azure Management Tool is an open source snap-in for Windows Management Console that provides client-side access to Windows Azure's blob storage and queues, where you can easily upload your contents. It is available at http://code.msdn.microsoft.com/windowsazuremmc.

Where Do I Find Additional Tools?

If you are interested in enhancing your toolbox with third-party tools, often check out the Visual Studio Gallery (http://visualstudiogallery.com) that contains hundreds of useful tools divided into categories. Also visit both the MSDN Code Gallery (http://code.msdn.microsoft.com) and the CodePlex community (http://www.codeplex.com) where you can find hundreds of useful tools, which are free in most cases.

Index

SYMBOLS

A

I

ICloneable interface, **248**
    implementation, 117
IComparable interface, **107, 351-352**
IComparer interface, **352-353**
icons, My Project, **33**
IConvertible interface, **353-356**
IDE (Integrated Development Environment)
    navigation, 9-11
identifiers
    naming conventions, 67-68
    reserved keywords, applying, 69
IDisposable interface, **345**
IDocument interface, **346**
IEnumerable interface, **348-351**
If operators, ternary, **507-509**
IFormattable interface, **356-358**
IIS (Internet Information Services), **867**
    applications, publishing, 1161
    WCF services, 944-945
IList interface, **345**
ILogger interface, **1113**
ImageBrush, **746**
ImageButton control, **846**
Image control, **726, 783, 846**
ImageMap control, **846**
images
    assignment, 473
    viewing, 781-783
imperative mode, **690-692**
implementation
    auto-generated contracts, 932
    Calendar controls, 719
    CheckBox controls, 719
    custom extension methods, 495
    custom task panes, 1123
    derived classes, Class Designer, 413-416
    double animation, 880
    events, raising, 378
    Expander controls, 724
    flow documents, 787
    generics, methods, 363
    Icloneable interface, 117
    IComparable interface, 351
    IConvertible interface, 353
    IDisposable interface, 271-272
    IEnumerable interface, 349

IEnumerator interface, 349
IFormattable interface, 356
interfaces, 107, 303, 343-345
IValueConverter interface, 825-828
LINQ, providers, 527
menus, 731
PasswordBox control, 732
Silverlight media players, 877
spell check, 796
strings, formatters, 822-828
submenus, 731
TabControl controls, 738
ToolBar controls, 740
TreeView controls, 741
values, converters, 822-828
WCF Data Services, 929-937, 951-957, 963-965
Xml comments, 1093
Implements keyword, **303, 343**
implicit conversions, **110-111**
    conditions, 42
implicit-line continuation, **65-67, 1066**
    LINQ, 526, 533-539
implicit type condition, **43**
importing
    COM objects, 1075-1078
    configurations, 40
    Xml namespaces, 292-294, 652
Imports directive, **17, 64**
    namespaces, 284, 291-292
Imports keyword, **652**
Imports System.Threading directive, **996**
incremental architecture, **3.** *See also* .NET Framework
indexers, **234**
inequality(<>) operator, **125**
inferences
    local type, 485-488
    multidimensional arrays, 490
    types, lambda expressions, 503-504
    Xml schemas, 649-654
information messages, **29**
infrastructure
    layers, LINQ, 528
.NET Framework. *See* .NET Framework
inheritance, **61-62, 107, 316-318**
    applying, 318-321
    chains, avoiding, 340

UNLEASHED

Unleashed takes you beyond the basics, providing an exhaustive, technically sophisticated reference for professionals who need to exploit a technology to its fullest potential. It's the best resource for practical advice from the experts, and the most in-depth coverage of the latest technologies.

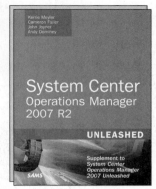

System Center Operations Manager (OpsMgr) 2007 R2 Unleashed
ISBN-13: 9780672331176

OTHER UNLEASHED TITLES

Microsoft Dynamics CRM 4 Integration Unleashed
ISBN-13: 9780672330544

Microsoft Exchange Server 2010 Unleashed
ISBN-13: 9780672330469

WPF Control Development Unleashed
ISBN-13: 9780672330339

Microsoft SQL Server 2008 Reporting Services Unleashed
ISBN-13: 9780672330261

ASP.NET MVC Framework Unleashed
ISBN-13: 9780672329982

SAP Implementation Unleashed
ISBN-13: 9780672330049

Microsoft XNA Game Studio 3.0 Unleashed
ISBN-13: 9780672330223

Microsoft SQL Server 2008 Integration Services Unleashed
ISBN-13: 9780672330322

IronRuby Unleashed
ISBN-13: 9780672330780

Microsoft SQL Server 2008 Integration Services Unleashed
ISBN-13: 9780672330322

Microsoft SQL Server 2008 Analysis Services Unleashed
ISBN-13: 9780672330018

ASP.NET 3.5 AJAX Unleashed
ISBN-13: 9780672329739

Windows PowerShell Unleashed
ISBN-13: 9780672329883

Windows Small Business Server 2008 Unleashed
ISBN-13: 9780672329579

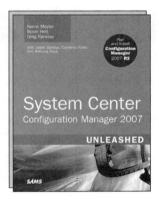

System Center Configuration Manager 2007 Unleashed
ISBN-13: 9780672330230

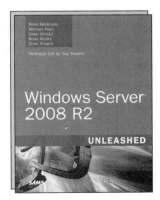

Windows Server 2008 R2 Unleashed
ISBN-13: 9780672330926

SAMS

informit.com/sams

FREE Online Edition

Your purchase of **Visual Basic 2010 Unleashed** includes access to a free online edition for 45 days through the Safari Books Online subscription service. Nearly every Sams book is available online through Safari Books Online, along with more than 5,000 other technical books and videos from publishers such as Addison-Wesley Professional, Cisco Press, Exam Cram, IBM Press, O'Reilly, Prentice Hall, and Que.

SAFARI BOOKS ONLINE allows you to search for a specific answer, cut and paste code, download chapters, and stay current with emerging technologies.

Activate your FREE Online Edition at www.informit.com/safarifree

> **STEP 1:** Enter the coupon code: ZOBNJFH.

> **STEP 2:** New Safari users, complete the brief registration form.
> Safari subscribers, just log in.

If you have difficulty registering on Safari or accessing the online edition, please e-mail customer-service@safaribooksonline.com